British banking

British banking

A guide to historical records

JOHN ORBELL
Head of Record Services, ING Barings

ALISON TURTON
Head of Archives, The Royal Bank of Scotland Group

LONDON AND NEW YORK

First published 2001 by Ashgate Publishing

Published 2017 by Routledge
2 Park Square, Milton Park, Abingdon, Oxon OX14 4RN
711 Third Avenue, New York, NY 10017, USA

Routledge is an imprint of the Taylor & Francis Group, an informa business

Copyright © John Orbell and Alison Turton, 2001

John Orbell and Alison Turton have asserted their moral right under the Copyright, Designs and Patents Act, 1988, to be identified as the authors of this work.

All rights reserved. No part of this book may be reprinted or reproduced or utilised in any form or by any electronic, mechanical, or other means, now known or hereafter invented, including photocopying and recording, or in any information storage or retrieval system, without permission in writing from the publishers.

Notice:
Product or corporate names may be trademarks or registered trademarks, and are used only for identification and explanation without intent to infringe.

British Library Cataloguing in Publication Data
British Banking: A Guide to Historical Records. –
   (Studies in British Business Archives)
   1. Banks and banking—Great Britain—Archival resources.
   I. Orbell, John 1950–. II. Turton, Alison.
   332.1'0941

US Library of Congress Cataloging in Publication Data
The Library of Congress Control Number was pre-assigned as:
   00–135280

ISBN 13: 978-0-7546-0295-8 (hbk)

Contents

Foreword by Professor L S Pressnell — *vii*

Acknowledgements — *ix*

The historical structure and functions of British banking — *1*

Banking archives — *13*

Select bibliography — *26*

User's guide — *38*

Abbreviations — *44*

Lists of records of banks — *45*

Lists of records of associations of banks and bankers — *562*

Guide to minor collections — *573*

Index of names — *581*

Index of places — *626*

Index of types of bank and association — *658*

Index of archive repositories — *660*

Foreword

This substantially expanded Guide to historical records of British banking is testimony to the fulfilment of the purposes of the original publication. That has not only proved useful to a wide range of historians, but has also stimulated identification of many additional banking records. Those indeed were the hopes of the Business Archives Council when initiating the project some thirty years ago, and of the many financial institutions and other holders of banking records whose assistance was sought and generously given.

Over 700 archive collections in local record offices, university and local libraries and, of course, the banks themselves are represented. This wide coverage has brought, as the editors acknowledge in their introductory comments, unstinted help from many people concerned with the preservation of records.

Notable aspects of the *Guide* include expanded coverage of the records of major domestic banks, British overseas banks, merchant banks and discount houses. Of distinctive interest are additions, often small in themselves but particularly valuable in the light of existing scant documentation, to listings of records of long defunct banks. A feature likely to earn wide and warm appreciation is the provision, for most entries, of brief histories which ease the often bewildering path through numerous name changes, especially of local banks, before their complete disappearance or amalgamation. Along with that aid are, in many cases, references to existing studies of particular banks or groups of banks.

Another welcome feature is a new section describing the functions and records of collective banking activities: the committees and associations of clearing banks, merchant banks and discount houses; the English and Scottish Institutes of Bankers; and associations of bank employees.

Wider knowledge and understanding of financial history as a whole is facilitated by the *Guide*. Whilst it would be invidious to focus on any particular aspect, it indicates the ample scope for fruitful study whether at local, regional, national or international levels. Moreover, as non-banking historians have demonstrated, bank records concern not just banks but also the infinitely varied activities they financed. Yet that is not all. If historical study provides an indispensable link with our past, acquaintance with original records offers not only authenticity, but the indefinable satisfaction, indeed the excitement known to all historians, of direct contact with it. In this very thorough scholarly *Guide*, the editors and all who assisted in its production have made a notable contribution to historical study and, there need be no reticence in saying it, to its enjoyment.

L S Pressnell
April, 2000

Acknowledgements

The preparation of this *Guide* would not have been possible without the generous co-operation of the London and Edinburgh banking communities; with considerable openness and public spiritedness, they have freely provided us with a very great deal of information about their accumulations of historical records. We are extremely grateful both to them and to their archivists on to whom a great deal of work was loaded. Without their enthusiastic help, the compilation of this book would not have been possible.

In particular we are grateful to Henry Gillett and John Keyworth of the Bank of England; Alan Cameron and Seonaid McDonald of Bank of Scotland; Peter Emmerson and Jessie Campbell of Barclays Bank plc; Barbara Peters and Tracey Earle of Coutts and Co; Dr John Booker of Lloyds TSB Group plc; Edwin Green and Sara Kinsey of HSBC Holdings plc; Fiona MacColl and Susan Snell of National Westminster Bank plc; Vic Gray and Melanie Aspey of N M Rothschild and Sons Ltd; and our colleagues Jane Waller of ING Barings and Philip Winterbottom and Vicki Wilkinson of The Royal Bank of Scotland. Kit Farrow of the London Investment Banking Association gave us access to the archives of the Accepting Houses Committee and the Issuing Houses Association. Richard Vardy gave help with the archives of the London Discount Market Association and Dr Charles Munn did likewise with the archives of the Chartered Institute of Bankers in Scotland. We also received much help from the staffs of the British Bankers Association and the Chartered Institute of Bankers.

Archivists and librarians working in a very large number of record offices and other institutions have responded to our questions with their usual sense of courtesy and thoroughness; they devoted much time to supplying us with copies of lists and in checking questions of fact and we are very grateful to them. In particular Cynthia Short, Lesley Richmond and Nick Mayes kindly undertook surveys of the archives of Yorkshire Bank plc, Clydesdale Bank plc and the British Bankers Association on our behalf. Adrian Allan also undertook valuable investigative work.

In writing the history of individual banks we have drawn heavily on the published work of many historians. We are mindful of the debt that we owe to them and in particular to Harold Preston for his work on East Anglian banks, to Jack Parker for his study of Hertfordshire banks and to John Andrews ['John Ryton'] for his work on banks in Exeter. We are similarly thankful to the anonymous compilers of the list of defunct banks which appears annually in the *Banker's Almanac*; the accuracy and usefulness of their work certainly does not diminish with the passage of time. We have found G L Grant's *The Standard Catalogue of Provincial Banks and Banknotes*, published as long ago as 1977, and Fred Wellings's and Alistair Gibbs' more recent *Bibliography of Banking History*, published between 1995 and 1997, to be of enormous help.

Professor Leslie Pressnell played a key role in originating the first edition of this book. We are grateful for the foundations which he laid down and for his

x   ***Acknowledgements***

continuing support and enthusiasm for its successor edition. Sam Twining, President of the Business Archives Council, and Edwin Green, the Council's former Chairman, have been especially generous in their support.

It is hard to think that a book of this length and mass of detail does not contain a fair number of inaccuracies. For them we take responsibility, but we have done our very best to eradicate as many as possible.

John Orbell
Alison Turton
April, 2000

The historical structure and functions of British banking

JOHN ORBELL

An understanding of the nature and significance of bank archives is greatly helped by knowledge of the changing structure and functions of banking. Historically, there are four well-defined categories of banks in Britain: clearing banks, merchant banks, discount houses and British-owned and - registered overseas banks. At their head is the Bank of England.

The original function and structure of these banks was largely determined by their customers' need for safe methods of savings and payments. The bill of exchange, in particular, was at the heart of banking and closely associated in different ways with each category of bank until well into the twentieth century. A bill, in effect, represents an undertaking to make a payment at a future date – usually three or six months – in respect of goods received in the present. It provides, say, a merchant with credit for the period between purchasing and selling goods. However, while this assisted management of the merchant's cash flow, it did nothing to assist the manufacturer from whom the goods were purchased; he or she might need funds immediately in order to purchase raw materials or to pay wages. The manufacturer, however, could raise funds by discounting the bill he or she received. This was achieved by finding a third party with surplus funds to purchase the bill for an amount slightly less than its face value; the difference represented a commission and charge for interest. When the bill fell due for payment, or in other words matured, it was presented to the merchant or his bank or agent for payment.

This explains the bill-discounting mechanism in its simplest form. In practice it was a good deal more elaborate and two features are worthy of more lengthy explanation. One is the mechanism for finding parties to discount bills and the other is the provision of guarantees – or acceptances – to facilitate the discounting process.

In the eighteenth and nineteenth centuries a mechanism developed in London for discounting bills originating in regions that were relatively short of capital. In these regions, country banks discounted bills for their customers but might not have sufficient resources – derived from deposits and partners' capital – in order to discount all the bills coming forward. Thus they sent at least some bills to the London money market for re-discount. They sent these bills either to the London bank that acted as their

2 *British banking – a guide to historical records*

agent or – increasingly from the period of the European Wars, 1793 to 1815 – to London bill brokers who put those wishing to dispose of bills in touch with others who had surplus funds for purchasing bills. Later these bill brokers evolved into discount houses, which borrowed money in order to acquire bills on their own account.

The ability to discount bills – especially foreign bills – in the London money market was much facilitated by the provision of a guarantee that a bill would be honoured when it fell due for payment. Such guarantees were especially vital when the standing of the drawer of the bill was unknown in the market. The guarantee, which was otherwise known as an 'acceptance', was provided by the bank or merchant bank on which the bill was drawn. It 'accepted' the bill or otherwise promised that the bill would be paid when it matured and in return for this was paid a commission.

THE BANK OF ENGLAND

Since its formation in 1694, the Bank of England has been at the centre of British banking. It functions quite separately from the rest of the sector, undertaking activities different from those of other British banks. From its beginnings, it carried on some central banking functions and, by the very late-nineteenth century and especially in the inter-war period, developed as a modern central bank participating in the management of the national economy and influencing and regulating the activities of the banking sector.

Formed by merchants and financiers, the Bank of England soon obtained a monopoly in England of joint stock banking; it was Britain's first joint stock bank although its establishment was followed quickly by the formation of the Bank of Scotland in 1695. From the outset it was the government's banker, for example making interest free loans in return for renewal of its statutes. It also held government balances, handled its foreign payments, received subscriptions from investors for government securities, purchased gold and silver for the Royal Mint, and so on. From its earliest days, the Bank also acted as a commercial bank, although in recent years this function formed only a minor part of its activities. Originally it held the accounts of London-based chartered companies, merchants and, later, large manufacturing companies; it discounted their bills of exchange, made short term loans to them and provided them with other general banking services.

An increasingly important role carried on alongside those of central and retail banking was the issue of bank notes that originally passed into circulation through loans made to the British government and through credit extended in the money market. These notes were literally promises to pay and thus were backed by substantial bullion reserves. By 1770 the

Structure and functions of British banking 3

bank had a virtual monopoly of note issue in London, its notes having displaced those of London's private bankers. The 1844 Bank Charter Act was designed to ensure ultimate concentration of note issue in England and Wales in the Bank's hands by restricting private issue, within prescribed limits, to those banks already issuing their own notes at the time of the passing of the Act. The issue of Bank of England notes in the provinces was stimulated by the opening of Bank branches in major regional cities, beginning in the 1820s with those in Manchester and Liverpool and followed shortly afterwards with others at Birmingham, Leeds, Newcastle and elsewhere.

Confidence in the stability of the Bank, reflected by confidence in its note issue, led to it playing a major role in the money market and to its emergence as lender of last resort. Merchants who could not find accommodation from their private banks, especially at times of market turbulence and contraction of liquidity, sought credit from the Bank. Eventually the Bank came to act in a similar way for private banks that had run short of cash at times of panic and heavy withdrawal of deposits by customers. London private banks, and later country and joint stock banks, began to hold some of their reserves as deposits at the Bank. In the 1820s, the Bank also emerged as lender of last resort to the emerging discount houses, providing the vital mechanism of allowing the immediate repayment of short term loans made to them by private and joint stock banks.

In the twentieth century the Bank maintained its roles of government banker, private banker, note issuer and lender of last resort. Along the way, it accumulated a number of other responsibilities as its role of central bank matured. These included management of the Exchange Equalisation Account, supervision of the money market and intervention in the currency markets to influence sterling exchange rates. Maintenance of an industrial policy of rationalisation, reconstruction and renewal in the inter-war period, especially when bank stability and the national economic interest were at stake, was also important. Added to these were regulation of the banking community to preserve good order and, most importantly, general control of the money markets through influence upon interest rates.

CLEARING BANKS

The origins of the clearing banks in England lie largely in two distinct yet ultimately closely linked groups of banks, London private banks and country private banks. Each group derived capital from partnerships, limited initially to six individuals, although the principle of multi-partnered banks was well established in Scotland in the eighteenth century.

The oldest London private banks were established about a century before the formation of the Bank of England. Their origins can be traced

4   *British banking – a guide to historical records*

to the early-seventeenth century activities of two separate groups – money scriveners and goldsmiths. Scriveners or scribes were commonly employed to copy financial and legal documents. Most of them specialised in conveyancing and ultimately became notaries but a few, in managing clients' estates and trusts, developed money-broking functions. In this role they served the landed gentry as financial intermediaries, although their fortunes declined from the 1660s as the volume of land transactions diminished. Goldsmiths, by contrast, were a respected and tightly controlled group of craftsmen by the sixteenth century, when their position was entrenched by the sudden increase in gold supplies consequent upon the dissolution of the monasteries and distribution of their assets.

Many goldsmiths developed strong connections with the Crown, fashioning precious ornaments for the royal family and serving in senior positions in the Mint. From the 1640s most not only dealt in plate and jewellery but also served as custodians of valuables deposited for safekeeping due to civil disturbance and the royal seizure of private gold deposited in the Tower of London. Thereafter they developed banking activities by accepting money deposits in trust, returnable on demand. They made short term advances, discounted bills of exchange, dealt in bullion and foreign exchange, and held customers' funds in current and deposit accounts. By 1677 there were forty-four goldsmith bankers in London, known as 'keepers of running cashes'.

By the eighteenth century London private banks, for the most part highly respected and conservative institutions, fell into two groups. The West End banks, which included famous names such as Coutts, Childs, Drummonds and Hoares, catered for the needs of the aristocracy, gentry and wealthy gentlemen. They made transfers and collected payments, made advances which often turned into long term commitments secured by mortgage on landed property, invested customers' surplus funds in government and similar stocks, and provided other services.

The second group was based in the City of London and had merchants, manufacturers and country banks as their customers. Their main business was the discount of bills of exchange of their customers and the rediscount of bills sent from the country by country banks. Like the West End banks, they maintained current and deposit accounts; made collections, payments and transfers; invested funds; made short term loans especially to brokers; but generally did not make long term loans. An important and lucrative activity was agency work for country banks. This work included the provision of clearing facilities for notes issued by other banks, transfer and payment facilities for customers and a mechanism for the purchase of gold, silver and, later, Bank of England notes. It also included provision of overdrafts in times of difficulty, the investment of their own and customer funds in securities and bills, and the rediscount of bills.

Structure and functions of British banking 5

In extending their business beyond London, private banks were severely restricted by inadequate communications and capital as well as by legal constraints on the size of firms. On the other hand, as economic activity quickened in provincial England in the eighteenth century, demand for banking services increased. Therefore local banks funded by local capital were established; they came to be known as country banks. In order to establish London representation, the partners of these banks sometimes established their own London bank. Conversely, the partners of London banks were sometimes admitted as partners of country banks.

By the mid-eighteenth century about a dozen country banks existed and by 1784 numbers rose to about 120. Expansion was then especially rapid with the number of firms growing to about 290 by 1797, 370 by 1800 and 650 by 1810. Local merchants, manufacturers such as brewers, malsters and millers, and professional men such as solicitors and surgeons formed most of these banks. In their earliest form they might only consist of a general office equipped with a counter and some secure storage for notes and bullion. Initially their range of activities was restricted to issuing their own bank notes, receiving deposits, providing remittance facilities, maintaining current accounts, discounting bills of exchange and making short term loans. Most country banks were restricted to a single office, but a few had branches in neighbouring towns and villages. Others established a wider presence through the participation of their partners in the partnerships of other local banks.

Concern about the stability of the country's financial structure in the deflationary period after the European Wars combined with the experience of banking during the financial crisis of 1825 led to measures to protect the currency and to strengthen the banking system. On the one hand, this resulted in the formal establishment of the gold standard in 1816, the restriction of private note issues to denominations of £5 and above and to the establishment of Bank of England branches in major provincial cities. On the other hand, it resulted in legislation that in 1826 enabled the formation of joint stock banks.

Joint stock banks had multi-shareholders and were led by a board of directors who appointed professional bankers to manage the business. Because no restriction was placed on the number of shareholders they had ready access to capital. The first English joint stock bank opened in 1826; by 1833 there were almost fifty in England and Wales and this number doubled within three years. They were empowered to issue their own bank notes outside a radius of sixty-five miles of London. This restriction, so far as London was concerned, resulted in a delay in opening joint stock banks in the capital where the first one did not appear until 1833. Other restrictions on their activities, including a prohibition on handling bills of exchange with a due date of less than six months, severely curtailed their

6 *British banking – a guide to historical records*

numbers; by 1844 only five London-based joint stock banks had been formed.

Notwithstanding some unsatisfactory formations, most joint stock banks were successful both in London and in the provinces. Their wide capital base gave customers greater confidence in their standing, provided additional strength at times of financial panic and enabled more extensive facilities and services to be provided to customers, especially those in the emerging manufacturing sector. Soon joint stock banks overhauled the private banks with their more slender resources. Faced with such competition, some private banks were converted into joint stock banks with the partners assuming the management of the new concern in the form of general manager, senior director and principal shareholder. More frequently private banks were sold to joint stock banks and were converted into branches. It was often through such acquisitions that joint stock banks established a regional presence.

Between 1825–26 and 1841–42 the number of country banks fell from 554 to 311; by the latter date 118 joint stock banks existed. But the impact of joint stock banks was more profound than these statistics suggest. This was because joint stock banks often had numerous branches and many more customers, drawn from groups that had not formerly banked, than private banks. This said, many private banks survived until the end of the nineteenth century with some confronting competition head on through the establishment of branch networks albeit, for the most part, on a relatively modest scale.

A combination of the low interest rates that characterised the 1890s and a greater preference for banking with banks with large capital resources following the 1890 Baring Crisis sounded the death knell for private banking. By the 1920s only a handful of private London and country banks survived. Most had either been acquired by joint stock banks or had closed in the face of overwhelming competition. Some, however, merged together and either immediately or subsequently acquired limited liability. The most notable example was Barclays and Co Ltd (later renamed Barclays Bank Ltd) which was formed in 1896 through the merger of, for the most part, long-established and powerful private banks. They were spread across the country and many were owned by Quakers.

The number of joint stock banks did not rise in tandem with the fall in numbers of private banks. In the last decades of the century, the number of newly formed joint stock banks was counteracted by the merger of small joint stock banks to form larger and more widely spread units. However, most remained district or regional banks until the 1880s and 1890s when the large clearing banks with national branch networks began to appear in England and Wales on the one hand and in Scotland on the other.

A characteristic of such formations was the establishment of large London, Edinburgh or Glasgow head offices. So far as London was

Structure and functions of British banking

concerned, this was often achieved by the acquisition of a London-based bank that had membership of the important London Clearing House. Here member banks settled payments due by one to another but for a long time its membership was the preserve of private banks which aimed to exclude their more powerful joint stock bank competitors. Thus Lloyds Bank in 1884 and Midland Bank in 1891 acquired London banks and subsequently both shifted their head offices from Birmingham to the City.

By 1918 the so-called 'Big-Five' English clearing banks – Barclays, Lloyds, Midland, National Provincial and Westminster – were clearly recognisable; they controlled two thirds of the country's banking resources. More gradual consolidation followed, especially in the late-1920s and early-1930s when some banks, damaged by industrial recession, merged with stronger competitors. Major consolidation resumed in the 1960s, on relaxation of longstanding official constraints, with the merger of National Provincial Bank, Westminster Bank and District Bank to form National Westminster Bank and of Barclays Bank with Martins Bank.

From the 1970s the government's schemes of monetary control encouraged the commercial banks to compete more actively with one another and with other financial institutions. As a result of this and also of the introduction of new technology, many began to provide additional services, such as credit cards, savings schemes, property and travel insurance, automated teller machines and house purchase loans. They also established offshore representation. Diversification has gathered pace in recent years using the new technologies to deliver services such as 'telephone' and 'Internet' banking and international payments. A significant feature of the 1990s has been the linking of traditional banks with retail businesses, such as food retail companies, in order to provide retail banking services in a convenient and competitive way.

Further major consolidation occurred during and since the 1990s when Lloyds Bank acquired TSB to form Lloyds TSB Group, Hongkong and Shanghai Banking Corporation acquired Midland Bank, subsequently renamed HSBC, and The Royal Bank of Scotland acquired National Westminster Bank.

MERCHANT BANKS

Merchant banks – now generally referred to as investment banks – often have diverse origins but have evolved through specialisation in at least one of three functions – trading as merchants in commodities, financing international trade through accepting bills of exchange and providing long term finance through the issuance of securities. Important characteristics of many include an internationally spread business, relatively small capi-

8 British banking – a guide to historical records

tal resources and prolonged private ownership by founding families who came originally from overseas.

Trading internationally in commodities as merchants – or merchanting – was often the original activity of merchant banks. This involved the purchase of goods in one international market for sale in another, sometimes for sole account although, more often than not, for joint account with other merchants. This led to merchants of recognised proficiency acting as agents for merchants based in other markets and receiving in return a commission income for the services they provided. These services might include buying and selling goods; arranging shipping, insurance and warehousing; making and collecting payments; dealing in foreign exchange; and holding balances or investing surplus funds. Some of these were banking functions and in due course gave rise to the term merchant banking.

To an extent, merchant banks financed their customers' trade through advances secured on the underlying commodities. However, because they had relatively modest capital, especially from the late-nineteenth century, and because they were not significant deposit-takers, merchant banks had limited resources from which to make loans. So most of their finance of international trade was provided by means of guarantees. On the basis of their reputation, they guaranteed payment of – or 'accepted' – their merchant customers' bills of exchange when they fell due for payment. Thus the bills they accepted were easily traded in the bill market. This device – the so-called bill on London – enabled the banks, on the basis of reputation alone, to finance a large share of international trade regardless of whether that trade touched Britain's shores.

As well as providing merchants with 'commercial credits' for financing international trade, merchant banks also provided 'financial credits', based also on the bill of exchange, to customers such as governments, central banks and other businesses in need of short-term finance. The importance of such business increased in the twentieth century, especially for British-based industrial companies, as the traditional business of financing merchants declined due to fundamental changes in the structure and organisation of world trade.

The third historic function of merchant banks – the issuance of securities – began in the early-nineteenth century when London overtook Amsterdam as the leading international capital market. Given the international connections of merchant banks, they were well positioned to access this market in order to raise long-term finance for foreign borrowers mostly through the issue of bonds. Initially the banks' customers were European and North American governments; they were joined in the 1820s by Latin American governments and in the second half of the century by the governments, city councils and major businesses of most countries.

Structure and functions of British banking

Thus merchant banks developed powerful international connections, raising finance for balancing government budgets, waging war and construction of infrastructure including in particular railways, canals, ports and water supply and drainage facilities needed for the development of cities. A development of this business was the issuance of securities for British companies. On the one hand this involved the issue of securities to fund infrastructure projects, especially transport developments. On the other, it involved providing companies with general financial advice often linked to a stock market transaction, for example the conversion of a private partnership into a public company via the issue of shares on the London Stock Exchange. In the 1920s and 1930s this work developed into complex transactions such as mergers and acquisitions, the rescue of companies in difficulty and the rationalisation of whole industries. The provision of corporate finance advice became a highly important function of merchant banks after 1945 when British industry experienced a wave of mergers and takeovers.

Merchant banks developed other activities. One was private banking for individuals associated with its merchant, corporate and sovereign clients. In the late-nineteenth century these services extended beyond maintaining current accounts and making advances to managing securities, collecting dividends, providing trustee and executor services, providing travel facilities and ultimately giving investment management advice. Similarly merchant banks provided a wide range of other services to sovereign and institutional clients such as paying interest due to their bondholders, operating sinking funds for the repayment of bonds, making and collecting payments for their account, operating bank accounts and acting as purchasing agents.

London's merchant banks were invariably formed as partnerships by overseas merchants who wanted to establish a presence in London. In due course their London business came to dominate the family's other houses and won international prestige for its financial power and for the quality of its business. It was not until well into the twentieth century that most converted from partnerships into private companies and later, as family control declined, into public companies. Numbers gradually declined so that in the early-1980s around fifteen houses survived. In the 1990s several were acquired by European and other overseas banks anxious to diversify into investment banking.

DISCOUNT HOUSES

These institutions are unique to the London money market, although most have now either disappeared or become almost unrecognisable following fundamental changes in the 1980s and 1990s in the way the markets

10 British banking – a guide to historical records

operated. In their final form, they carried on business as principals, purchasing and selling short-term assets such as bills of exchange and certificates of deposit, deriving their profit from narrow margins between selling and buying prices. Their portfolios were financed by borrowing very short term, largely from banks and a range of financial intermediaries. They provided the vital mechanism in the London money market whereby banks and other financial institutions regulated their financial position on a daily basis.

Discount houses were formed in the nineteenth century either as partnerships or, in the latter half of the century, also as joint stock companies. They trace their origins to the bill brokers who were at work in the closing decades of the eighteenth century. By the end of the European Wars, 1793 to 1815, possibly twenty existed; their numbers subsequently increased slightly, but there were also failures. They supplemented the work of London private banks, acting as the agents of country banks, in providing the mechanism whereby country banks with surplus deposits were able to invest in bills of exchange while other country banks with limited deposits found opportunities to rediscount bills of exchange. Through such a role, the bill broker facilitated the movement of bills from industrialising areas, where capital was in relatively short supply, to agricultural areas where it was relatively plentiful.

Bill brokers converted to bill dealers after the European Wars when a general fall in interest rates led London private banks to put out at least part of their liquid reserves at rates below the yield achieved from investment in bills of exchange. This transformation was facilitated by the Bank of England's willingness, from the late-1820s, to provide dealers with rediscount facilities in time of need. The effect of this was to enable bill brokers to borrow funds in order to finance a portfolio of bills but also to retain high liquidity through the Bank of England's rediscount facilities. Without this change in function, the business of the bill brokers might otherwise have declined with the advent of joint stock banks with branch networks spread across the country.

In the second half of the nineteenth century the importance of discounting inland bills began to decline as other forms of finance and money transfer – for example the overdraft and the cheque – developed. At the same time the importance of foreign bills increased in step with the rapid increase in international trade. Thus the discount houses developed large businesses through discounting bills accepted by London merchant banks thereby making the 'bill on London' the principal instrument for international trade finance. Bills were discounted predominantly in connection with trade finance but at the end of the century a growing volume of finance bills were being drawn in connection with the international movement of short-term funds.

Structure and functions of British banking

The outbreak of war in 1914 much reduced the volume of foreign trade and therefore the discount of foreign bills; the volume of this business was never to recover. However, the war caused a massive increase in the expenditure of the British and allied governments. This led to a substantial increase in the volume of short term government debt, much of it represented by treasury bills. Thus discount houses began to hold a large proportion of their assets in these instruments. In the 1930s, with a reduction of the supply of treasury bills to the market, the houses increasingly turned to bond dealing and particularly dealing in gilted edged securities.

OVERSEAS BANKS

The presence of many 'overseas' banks, owned by British shareholders and with their headquarters in the City of London yet with their principal banking activities located overseas, was a longstanding feature of British banking. The establishment of many of these publicly owned joint stock banks, from the second quarter of the nineteenth century, reflected in particular the close link between the economic and financial systems of Britain and its Empire.

These banks were concerned predominantly with banking in a given territory, country or region, although some were formed with the aim of serving whole continents. A few banks operated outside the Empire, such as in Latin America, where sterling was the principal currency used in overseas trade and London their major source of external long-term capital. A distinctive group comprised the 'exchange banks' which specialised in the provision of short-term finance for overseas trade, most notably by providing bill finance and overseas currencies. From the late nineteenth century foreign – especially European – owned joint stock banks established branches in Britain, particularly in the City of London, although this study is not concerned with such formations.

The functions of these overseas banks were similar to those of British domestic banks. They provided banking services to local individuals, businesses, institutions and governments and to do so they established branch networks. While in some cases there were local boards, a remarkable feature of many of these banks was the leadership and control exercised from London. Several carried on the functions of central banks – especially with regard to note issue – until superceded by locally-owned banks.

In the twentieth century steady consolidation characterised this sector of banking as many banks merged together or were taken over, especially by London-based clearing banks. This trend was influenced by, *inter alia*, recession in world trade in the 1920s and 1930s, the constraints on international trade and payments during the Second World War, decolonisation

12 *British banking – a guide to historical records*

and associated local ownership and banking controls, and by the disappearance of the Sterling Area by the early-1970s.

In contrast to this dramatic decline in numbers was a rise in the range and scale of services offered. Many banks became international as opposed to empire-based. Another dimension of this change was the integration of the international activities of Britain's clearing banks with their domestic activities leading to disappearance of many overseas banks as separate entities. While such growth, diversification and integration was influenced by external pressures, they owed much more to the opportunities that the euro-currency markets offered from the mid-1960s for short-term and long-term international financing on a scale and of a complexity hitherto unknown. In the 1990s Hongkong and Shanghai Banking Corporation (HSBC) and Standard Chartered Bank are the only significant survivors in this sector, although the former now has very important UK domestic operations having acquired Midland Bank. All the remaining banks have either closed or been fully integrated into either non-British banks or the major British commercial banks.

Banking Archives

JOHN ORBELL and ALISON TURTON

The archives of British banks break down into three broad groups, the first relating to a bank's internal affairs, the second covering the activities of its customers and the third relating to the involvement and interests of its directors or proprietors outside the bank. This chapter seeks to describe the purpose, format and research value of the chief series of historical records commonly found in bank archives.

It is, however, important to appreciate that information available in bank archives extends well beyond the boundaries of banking and monetary history to cover details of the people, property and events underlying or initiating banking transactions. Customer ledgers, for example, are helpful to users such as art and architecture historians, owners of historic buildings, museum curators and auction house staff in ascertaining the patrons of eighteenth and nineteenth century artists, the makers of specific pieces of furniture and other works of art, or the architects, craftsmen and gardeners who worked on particular country houses. The personal records of bank directors or customers may throw unexpected light on their business involvements, lifestyles, philanthropy and families and on the institutions with which they were concerned.

Many records are similar for all banks and these are described below. Discount houses and merchant banks created some distinctive series of records largely relating to the services that they provided to their customers and these are covered in separate sections.

PARTNERSHIP RECORDS

The most notable group of ownership records of private banks is partnership agreements that provide names, addresses and perhaps the other occupations of partners, their capital contributions and their shares of profits. They record the constitution of partnerships and the terms under which they were formed or could be dissolved. Partnership or private ledgers may contain balance sheets and profit and loss accounts, and perhaps other general accounts of the bank but they will almost certainly contain capital contribution and profit distribution accounts. Minutes of partners' meetings were seldom kept, doubtless because the close working

14   *British banking – a guide to historical records*

environment of the 'partners' room' made a formal record of decision-taking unnecessary. Partnership records will also include papers and accounts relating to partners' private investments, to other work undertaken and to public offices held.

CORPORATE RECORDS

Joint stock banks have more diverse and much more voluminous ownership records than partnerships. The most bulky may be share registers recording names of shareholders, perhaps their addresses and occupations, the size of their holding and the dates of acquisition and sale of shares. Dividend books and sheets record profit allocation to shareholders. The 'constitution' of early joint stock banks was embodied in a deed of settlement, otherwise known as a deed of constitution or deed of co-partnership or co-partnery. It laid down the conditions under which the bank operated and was signed by all shareholders, an important undertaking in early joint stock banks that did not benefit from limited liability. After the 1856 Joint Stock Companies Act this document was succeeded by the memorandum and articles of association.

Annual and extraordinary meetings of shareholders were minuted and recorded in annual general meeting or shareholders' minute books. Sometimes proceedings were recorded verbatim. The names of shareholders attending annual general meetings were either recorded with the minutes or noted in attendance books. Matters considered at annual general meetings largely concerned ownership, such as changes in share or loan capital or election or dismissal of directors, and performance. The minutes may also provide useful reviews of the local economy and of local events in the previous year. Annual general meetings of early banks formed the sole means by which directors advised shareholders of performance in the previous year. Eventually printed annual reports were issued to shareholders for approval at general meetings. In their earliest form, they seldom extended beyond a profit and loss account, the interpretation of which is always in some doubt in view of a desire to indicate favourable performance and to avert a loss of confidence by shareholders and customers. Latterly, the reports listed the branch banks and often also the names of local agents or managers.

A most useful group of records concerns amalgamations of banks. Sometimes these amalgamation papers do not extend beyond an amalgamation agreement between two banks, but frequently supporting papers have survived. These record the performance of the bank over, perhaps, the previous decade. They provide key financial information on the bank being acquired: profit and loss accounts and balance sheets of previous years, lists of current clients with balances, lists of bad and doubtful debts,

Banking archives

details of staff and pension fund commitments, valuations of buildings, and so on. Often such records include correspondence between partners or directors regarding the takeover negotiations.

The day-to-day affairs of a bank were under the supervision of a board of directors responsible for monitoring performance and making key decisions. The proceedings of boards were summarised in board or directors' meeting minutes, and this was often done in great detail. Rough minutes, recording duplicate information, may also have survived and help to explain the process of decision making. Minutes include details of decisions covering a wide range of subjects – performance of the business and events likely to effect this; expansion of the business through, say, the acquisition of other banks or the establishment of more branches; changes in the type of business undertaken; the expansion of share capital; changes in the distribution of a bank's assets; the establishment of links with corresponding banks; the rebuilding of premises; the appointment of senior staff; and so on. They also contain much useful information about customers, as board sanctions were required for particularly large customer loans and overdrafts, and about discussion of particularly large bad debts. Reports on the performance of the bank and other significant issues discussed might be summarised in the minutes or kept separately as 'board papers'.

As banks grew in size so committees subordinated to the board were formed, each dealing with a different area of the business and each keeping its own minutes and other records. In some cases 'regional' committees were formed to handle various aspects of the bank's business on a geographical basis.

INTERNAL ACCOUNTING RECORDS

Banks internal financial records include the usual range of account books kept by any business organisation – day books, cash books or waste books giving details of daily transactions, journals which summarise these, and general ledgers to which information in the journals was posted. The general ledgers, otherwise known as 'impersonal' or 'nominal' ledgers, are the most useful source of providing the basic income and expenditure accounts of the bank which, after analysis, will provide a basic measure of the bank's performance. Sometimes summary books containing the balances of general accounts were kept.

Income accounts include, for example, interest received from funds placed at call with discount houses; commission received from discounting; charges received from customers for the provision of services such as the operation of accounts and the sale or purchase of securities; commissions received from accepting, underwriting or issuing; and profits made

16 British banking – a guide to historical records

through transactions in securities. Expenditure accounts will cover office expenses, salaries, pension contributions, premises costs, and so on, as well as other 'cost' accounts such as bad debts written off. These accounts go to form the general profit and loss account which is kept in general or private ledgers, or in special profit and loss account books.

General ledgers also contain the information underlying the bank's balance sheet, which shows the composition of its assets and liabilities at a particular time, especially at the end of its financial year. On the one side are the bank's liabilities including shareholders' funds, reserves and customers' deposits; the asset side includes money at call, bills discounted, investments, advances and buildings. The striking of a balance of total customer deposits and other funds in the bank was a time-consuming exercise and special books recording the balance of each customer's account, whether struck quarterly, half-yearly or annually, were sometimes kept. In the absence of customer account ledgers these balance books provide useful lists of customers and indication of the relative size of their accounts, albeit at a single point in time.

Other accounting records include head office ledgers, in the case of banks with branches. These show transactions between branch and head office and perhaps between branches. They are important in showing the relative importance of each branch, especially through their running costs and contribution to turnover. Branches themselves often also maintained account books showing the total number of accounts, the number of accounts opened and closed and the balance of cash held in the accounts on a weekly or monthly basis.

STAFF RECORDS

Staff registers and salary books are the most common of the surviving classes of staff records and are particularly useful in identifying individual staff and showing total numbers employed, promotion prospects, lengths of service, different salary grades, and so on. Other records include pension fund contribution ledgers and papers such as minutes and accounts concerning pension fund administration. Similar records relate to the administration of widows' and orphans' funds. There are various other records of differing degrees of usefulness: appearance (i.e. attendance) books, clerk apprenticeship agreements, papers concerning social clubs, rules for the guidance of managers and clerks, and so on.

Other types of record more particular to banks include staff fidelity bonds and declarations of secrecy. From the eighteenth century employers such as banks required those appointed to positions of trust to provide personal sureties, fidelity bonds, to make good any loss arising from the conduct of the person guaranteed. Early bonds may take the form of

Banking archives **17**

handwritten personal undertakings, but later specialised insurance companies, such as the Bankers' Guarantee and Trust Fund, were established producing printed forms that were completed for each staff member. These have often survived in large quantities with associated registers of bonds issued.

New bank staff were, and still are, required to sign an undertaking not to reveal the confidential affairs of the bank or its customers to a third party. These declarations of secrecy, which latterly assumed a standard printed form, may be pasted into guardbooks.

PREMISES RECORDS

As premises became larger and more elaborate, so premises records became more important. They include architectural plans and drawings, photographs and perhaps correspondence with architects and minutes of committees supervising particularly large building schemes such as the construction of new head offices. Deeds are the most frequently surviving records, but they are often held outside the bank's historical archive by the company's property department or legal advisers. Property records relating to active branches are generally unavailable for research to avoid compromising the security of the premises.

BANK AND BRANCH ADMINISTRATION RECORDS

The survival rate of letters sent to a bank, or of copies of those dispatched, is generally low, and especially so if they are not bound into letterbooks or kept in organised bundles. The volume of correspondence sent and received will tend to vary with the distance of a bank from its customers or agents. Thus a local country bank probably corresponded with customers relatively infrequently, with business being conducted at intervals and with decisions and notes being recorded in memorandum or interview books. For banks based in the country, the most frequently surviving correspondence is with their London agent and for banks based in the capital it is correspondence with their country customers.

Given the distance of merchant and overseas banks from their customers, correspondents or branches, extensive correspondence with these parties was created and, relatively speaking, much has survived. It covers a much wider range of topics than those dealt with in the correspondence of domestic banks. Whereas correspondence with customers has fairly narrow terms of reference, that with correspondents or agents covers not only the affairs of customers but deals with a wide range of matters, such as the local business community, local projects seeking finance, the political climate, the state of crops, output of raw materials and prices current.

18 *British banking – a guide to historical records*

With the increasing volume of correspondence conducted by the business community towards the end of the nineteenth century, more organised methods of letter-keeping began to emerge. Subject files organised into registry systems replaced general letterbooks and bundles. Certainly, from the First World War many banks had such systems in operation and much of this material has survived.

From the late nineteenth century the growth of large London- and Edinburgh-based banks with *extensive* provincial branch networks created a need for quick communication to local branch managers of information regarding changing services, agencies and procedures. This was done initially through the production of stencil-duplicated sheets called circulars which were sent by head office to branch officials notifying procedural changes, branch openings, staff appointments or new official signatories, and requesting returns relating to account numbers or staffing. Part of the function of circulars was latterly superseded by instruction books.

Instruction books, or procedural manuals, appear from the late nineteenth century as a more comprehensive version of the early rules for clerks and subsequent instructional circulars pasted into guardbooks. Latterly they take the form of updateable loose-leaf files containing precise procedures regarding the conduct of different kinds of accounts and services, such as the signatories required, the interest to be applied, and so on. These books were generally issued to every branch and are often annotated with updated information provided in circulars. They are a vital record of the procedures and regulations of banking business.

CUSTOMER RECORDS

These form the most bulky, diverse and, in many ways, most useful bank archives for the general historian. However, their large volume has meant that survival of a comprehensive series of records is unlikely.

This is especially so of customer account ledgers which record daily transactions of customers. From the seventeenth century until the introduction of account mechanisation, between the 1930s and 1960s, customer account transactions were recorded in large single or double entry ledgers showing payments in and out of each customer's account. Arrangement of the ledgers depended on the size of the business and the bank's own practice. The ledgers may be organised alphabetically, chronologically or entirely haphazardly and may or may not be accompanied by name indices.

Customer accounts identify the bank's customers by name and perhaps give details of their addresses. Transaction details include date, amount, whether a debit or credit, and a narrative indicating the purpose of the transaction so as to identify one transaction from another. A customer's account will also show bank charges made and interest credited by the

Banking archives 19

bank. However, the narrative written against each transaction is not always easy to interpret. In the eighteenth and early nineteenth centuries, customers were often required to visit their bank periodically to examine the ledgers and sign off each page as a true record. On account of their considerable volume, often just one or two ledgers from an entire series survived, but this is not so of many of the old London private banks such as Hoares, Coutts and Drummonds and of merchant banks such as Barings, Brandts, Kleinworts and Rothschilds, where large series have been retained.

In the early days of banking, especially in the country, often no clear distinction between current and deposit accounts was made, although by the mid-nineteenth century it was common for the latter to be kept in separate deposit ledgers or registers. Since then most banks have created new ledger series for other types of account – such as savings accounts (sometimes known as 'home safe' accounts from the mid-1920s) and dormant accounts. Deposit receipt registers are a type of ledger particularly, but not exclusively, associated with Scottish banks relating to money lodged in temporary interest-bearing accounts for which deposit receipts were issued. Deposit receipt registers may give the customer's name, the sum deposited, interest due and the number of the deposit certificate given out.

Should a customer not wish to keep his or her surplus capital in an interest-bearing deposit account, he or she might invest it in securities. Certainly banks held securities for clients, mostly as collateral for loans but sometimes for the efficient collection of dividends or for safe custody at a time when securities were often in the form of bearer stock. Customer securities were generally recorded in a security register; it shows the identity of customers, the nature of their investments, the periods for which these investments were held, and so on. Securities held for safe custody were recorded, often along with other types of customer property, in a safe custody register.

From the mid-eighteenth century customers were issued with a passbook for each of their accounts which was completed when they visited their bank as a personal record of transactions. Passbooks, headed up with the name of the bank and customer, usually give only transaction dates and amounts. They are more commonly found amongst the papers of customers than those of banks and are often deposited in local record offices in estate collections and other personal papers. They continued to be used by most banks until account processing was mechanised, usually by the 1960s, whence they were superseded by printed customer statements. Passbooks are still used by many building societies.

Signature books were compiled from the eighteenth century to provide samples of customer signatures against which signed cheques and other

20   British banking – a guide to historical records

authorities could be validated. They provide a record of those authorised to sign against particular accounts and may give the name, address and occupation, as well as the signature, of each customer. They may also show how the customer was introduced to the bank and latterly what type of account he or she opened. Sometimes separate books were maintained for company accounts; these give corporate details as well as lists of all authorised cheque signatories. Authorities or mandate guardbooks, sometimes also known as periodic payments registers, were registers of customer instructions to the bank regarding signatories on particular accounts, changes of customer names, arrangements for standing orders or receipt of dividends, company resolutions, and so on. Such instructions were often advised on printed forms or as letters to the bank and pasted into large guardbooks.

Account opened books, commonly kept from the early nineteenth century, are registers of accounts opened giving the name and address, and sometimes occupation and signature, of each customer. They might also provide the date on which the account was opened, the account number allocated and related information such as the identity of the person who introduced the customer.

Most banks provided facilities for the safe custody of valuable items in strongrooms, occasionally fitted out with purpose-built individual strongboxes. Safe custody registers or safe deposit registers were a record of when and by whom a safe custody item was deposited. The item was invariably described solely in physical terms as, for example, a sealed brown envelope or a tin chest, as the contents remained confidential. The books may be annotated with details of when and by whom the property was withdrawn and include the signature of the withdrawer. Sometimes a receipt was issued to the depositor, the details of which were recorded in a receipt register. Box books also relate to safe custody activities but sometimes record only the visits of customers to view their safe custody items.

In assessing lending risk, banks needed an understanding of the character and resources of their customers. This might be achieved through knowledge of the customer over many years or it might be acquired through referral for references to third parties. In addition, many businesses regarded banks as a source of reliable information on the standing and worth of individuals and businesses and referred to banks for references and opinions. Such information about customers and opinions received and given was often recorded in character or opinion books. Their contents vary in format and detail but may give the name of the customer and the institution to which the opinion was supplied or from which it was sought, details of the reference and possibly the security provided by referees as guarantors, endorsers or acceptors.

Until relatively recent years branch managers bore much of the responsibility for granting all but the largest loans or other facilities to customers

Banking archives

and kept a daily record of decisions, instructions, interviews or correspondence regarding the conduct of particular accounts or advances in customer interview books or daily remembrancers. The format and content of these books varies and they may include such material as presscuttings and staff lists and may be used almost like a diary or an *aide-memoire*.

Probate books or registers were kept to record particulars of all probates or letters of administration exhibited to a banker regarding a deceased customer. The books are usually arranged chronologically and give the name and address of the deceased, the name of the executors or administrators, the sworn value of the estate, the registration office, the dates of death and probate and why it was exhibited. Probate book entries may be cross-referenced in the customer account ledgers.

CUSTOMER FINANCIAL INSTRUMENTS

The nature, purpose and key role of the bill of exchange in the development of British banking has already been discussed in the preceding chapter. This was only one of a range of financial instruments offered by banks.

Post bills were introduced in 1724 as a means of transmitting money by mail without the risk of loss to highwaymen. They were payable at three, and later seven, days after 'sight'. In 1836 sixty-day bills were introduced to allow money to be sent abroad. After the establishment of international cable transfers, they became less popular and they were officially withdrawn in 1906. The bank post bill, although obsolete, survived until 1934.

The predecessors of bank notes were receipts issued by seventeenth century goldsmiths. Given in exchange for money accepted for safe custody, these receipts, which were often discharges contained in correspondence, represented a promise to pay on demand and their face value was reduced upon part payment. Gradually these receipts became assignable and formal printed bank notes evolved. Essentially a promissory note drawn by a banker and payable on demand, until the mid-nineteenth century the word 'banknote' in law meant only Bank of England notes, but the 1844 Bank Charter Act referred to provincial issues as bank notes. Most country banks, with the notable exception of those in Lancashire, issued notes as it was not only profitable, but also essential if a bank's business was to be extended in and beyond its locality.

From 1782 stamp duty, a tax requiring documents to be impressed with a stamp, was imposed on bills of exchange and bank notes. When the Stamp Acts were restructured in 1808, the banker's licence was introduced as a licence to issue re-issuable bank notes. The licences, which could be acquired by simple registration and at a modest cost, were required for

22 British banking – a guide to historical records

each note issuing branch or agency of a bank that issued notes when the act came into force. Banker's licences did not form a licence to bank and implied no authority or stature as a banking organisation. They carry the following information: the names of all the partners; the town where notes were issued; the name of the bank and the style of partnership names employed. Licences had to be reissued if the details changed in any respect and penalties for misuse were heavy.

Note registers provide a record of bank notes issued or destroyed and are of limited research use. Early registers are often arranged by denomination and may give the number of the note, the date of issue and by whom it was signed. During the course of circulation, some notes became dirty or defaced and these were gradually withdrawn and cancelled prior to destruction. Later registers took the form of journals stating the value and serial numbers of notes issued or destroyed. Sometimes they show the balance of notes in circulation.

A cheque is a dated order drawn on a bank by the drawer in order to pay a named person or bearer a certain sum of money on demand at the bank or branch on which the cheque is drawn. The earliest cheques, dating from the mid-seventeenth century, were used by the customers of goldsmith bankers. They were known as 'drawn notes' and were entirely handwritten. By the 1750s, however, some bankers had developed printed forms with a set position on the paper for the cheque number and amount for ease of administration. When left blank, these are described as cheque forms, not cheques. Indeed the word cheque, originally 'check', probably derives from the security border, usually a scroll design, between the cheque and counterfoil in early cheque books or from the practice of 'checking' that the numbered instructions and counterfoils matched. From the 1850s payment of stamp duty, having been simplified and reduced to one penny in 1853, would be indicated on cheques by an adhesive or embosed stamp or printed medallion. Later in the century, the printing of personalised cheques emblazoned with corporate names was introduced. From the 1960s mechanical handling of cheques through the clearing house prompted the introduction of encoded characters and the format of some cheque forms was subsequently altered by the issue of illustrated cheques.

From the mid-eighteenth century banks provided services to customers abroad. The earliest instruments of foreign credit available to travellers were the bill of exchange, essentially a commercial instrument, and the circular letter of credit, which remained available to tourists until the 1950s. The circular letter of credit was endorsed with details of withdrawals to the stated sum and could be used at banks in different towns as the traveller moved on. However, they were large in format, accumulated commission and charges and could not be used to settle accounts with traders but simply to acquire foreign currency.

Banking archives

The circular note, forerunner of the traveller's cheque, was introduced as the exchange note by Robert Herries, a London banker, in the 1770s. These notes were the first form of credit provided specifically for travellers and were bought by customers from their banker before their journey and cashed at the places of business of the bank's correspondents without charge or deduction. The profit lay in the bank's use of the money from the time of purchase of the notes until they came back for payment. In the twentieth century the circular note was superseded by the traveller's cheque, a name derived from an initiative of the American Express Company in 1891.

The records deriving from the issue of traveller's money include blank and completed letters of credit and circular notes, registers of issue (detailing the customer's name, the number, date and validity of the note, and where and by whom it was paid), letters of introduction and printed lists of each bank's foreign correspondents. Bankers might also be asked to procure passports for customers and correspondence relating to such activities may survive.

CUSTOMER RECORDS PARTICULAR TO MERCHANT BANKS

Many of the archives created by merchant banks differ only slightly from those of country banks and joint stock banks, although in volume terms merchant bank archives are considerably less bulky than those of joint stock banks. However customer records are a major exception to this rule. Particular series of archives were created in connection with the three principal specialisations which historically characterise merchant banks, namely merchanting and agency work, finance of international trade and the issuance of securities.

Records relating to merchanting comprise accounts giving details of trading in commodities either for sole account or for joint account with other merchants; memorandum books describing trade procedures and the characteristics of different commodities and commodity markets; circulars and other intelligence about international markets and commodity output and prices; correspondence between merchants relating to transactions; papers relating to legal disputes; and papers relating to ship management, insurance, warehousing and so on.

Trade finance records include accounts relating to the operation of individual customer credits; agreements relating to the granting of credits; character reports relating to the customer; correspondence relating to the operation of the credit; and papers relating to the internal administration of the merchant bank's trade finance business and to the financial markets generally.

Records relating to security issuance are perhaps of the greatest interest, especially where the customer was a government, municipality or

24   *British banking – a guide to historical records*

important business. Records cover the negotiation of the issue and often include correspondence with finance ministers, senior civil servants, diplomats, senior directors and other banks involved in the transaction. This correspondence provides details of the customer, of the international capital markets, of the political background to the issue and of the project being financed. Where this project involved the construction of infrastructure – for example railways, ports, telephone systems and water supply and sewerage facilities – there might be detailed surveys, accounts and plans. Other records deal with the issue process and include prospectuses, certificates and registers giving details of underwriting syndicates and of subscribers.

Other record series relate to less important areas of business such as private banking and include current account ledgers, signature books, probate registers and correspondence. Security registers giving details of customer portfolios – name of investment and dates of purchase and sale – were created as a result of the management of client securities. Sinking fund and other accounts relate to paying agency work in London for overseas borrowers.

An especially important series is the correspondence exchanged with correspondent and agent banks in important overseas financial markets such as Amsterdam, Paris, Berlin, New York, Boston, St Petersburg, Vienna and so on. This correspondence was not transaction-related but involved the exchange of general intelligence about market conditions and political events.

RECORDS PARTICULAR TO DISCOUNT HOUSES

Discount houses created comparatively few record series relating to the execution of their business. These largely consist of ledgers and registers showing funds placed with them by other institutions and of their holdings of short-term assets such as bills. Diaries and memorandum books show the daily position of the firm and provide details of the money markets, especially interest rates.

PARTNERS', DIRECTORS' AND SENIOR MANAGERS' PRIVATE PAPERS

Partners and senior managers tended to keep their own private records relating to key business matters; where these survive they can be of the greatest value. Such records include diaries, journals, memorandum books and correspondence relating to the bank's business. Their papers may also cover private and public appointments, such as their membership of government or Bank of England committees, their directorships of industrial companies, their trusteeships and their connections with charitable organisations. Other papers relate to their private property, perhaps including country estates, and to family matters.

BIBLIOGRAPHY

John Armstrong and Stephanie Jones, *Business Documents: Their Origins, Sources and Uses in Historical Research* (London, 1987)

The Bankers' Almanac: Register of Bank Name Changes and Liquidations (East Grinstead, 1992)

John Booker, *Travellers' Money* (Stroud, 1994)

G L Grant, *The Standard Catalogue of Provincial Banks and Banknotes* (London, 1977)

Edwin Green, 'Bank Archives for the Historian', *Business Archives,* 49 (1983)

V H Hewitt and John Keyworth, *As Good as Gold: 300 Years of British Banknote Design* (London, 1987)

John Orbell, *A Guide to Tracing the History of a Business* (Aldershot, 1987)

George Rae, *The Country Banker. His Clients, Cares and Work* (London, 1885)

H P Sheldon, *The Practice and Law of Banking* (London, 1st edition,1920, 9th edition, 1962)

William Thomson, *Dictionary of Banking. A Concise Encyclopaedia of Banking Law and Practice*, 7th edition (London, 1930)

Alison Turton (ed.), *Managing Business Archives* (Oxford, 1991)

Select bibliography

BANKING HISTORY BIBLIOGRAPHIES

Fred Wellings and Alistair Gibb, *Bibliography of Banking Histories*, 2 vols (Kirkcaldy, 1995–97)

INDIVIDUAL BANK HISTORIES

G T Amphlett, *History of the Standard Bank of South Africa Ltd 1862–1913* (Glasgow, 1914)

James L Anderson, *The Story of the Commercial Bank of Scotland Ltd During its Hundred Years from 1810 to 1910* (Edinburgh, 1910)

A Andréades, *History of the Bank of England* (London, 1909, reprinted 1966)

Anon, *The Arms Granted to the Union Bank of Scotland Ltd* (c.1947)

Anon, *Arthur Heywood, Sons and Co 1773–1883* (Liverpool, 1949)

Anon, *A Bank in Battledress Being the Story of Barclays Bank (Dominion, Colonial and Overseas) during the Second World War 1939–1945* (priv. pub., 1948)

Anon, *The Bank of London and South America. A Short History 1862–1970* (priv. pub., 1970)

Anon, *A Banking Centenary. Barclays Bank (Dominion, Colonial and Overseas) 1836–1936* (priv. pub., 1938)

Anon, 'Barclay and Co', *Journal of the Institute of Bankers*, 17 (1896)

Anon, *Bolton Branch of The Royal Bank of Scotland. The Story of Bolton's First Commercial Bank* [Hardcastle, Cross and Co] (priv. pub., 1993)

Anon, *Cater Ryder, Discount Bankers, 1816–1966* (priv. pub., 1966)

Anon, 'Consolidation and Expansion. Troubled Times. New Beginnings' [National Bank of Scotland], *Three Banks Review*, 94–96 (1972)

Anon, *Cox and King's. The Evolution of a Military Tradition* (priv. pub., 1990)

Anon, 'Curries and Co. The Early Years', *Three Banks Review*, 61–62 (1964)

Anon, *Cox's 1758–1923. The Story of an Army Agent* (priv. pub., n.d.)

Anon, *Drummonds Bankers. A History* (priv. pub., 1993)

Select bibliography

Anon, 'From Redcoat to Battledress. The Story of Holt's Agency 1809–1959', *Three Banks Review*, 45 (1959)

Anon, *George Peabody and Co, J S Morgan and Co, Morgan Grenfell and Co, Morgan Grenfell and Co Ltd 1838–1958* (priv. pub., 1958)

Anon, *Gosling's Branch 1650–1982* (priv. pub., 1982)

Anon, *Hambros Bank Ltd 1839–1939* (priv. pub., 1939)

Anon, *C Hoare and Co, Bankers. A History* (priv. pub., c.1994)

Anon, *How to Mismanage a Bank. A Review of the Western Bank of Scotland* (Edinburgh, 1859)

Anon, *The National Commercial Bank of Scotland. A Short History of the Bank* (priv. pub., 1947)

Anon, *The National Bank of Scotland Centenary* (priv. pub., 1925)

Anon, 'The New Oriental Bank Corporation. A Lesson in Bad Banking', *Bankers' Magazine*, 57 (1894)

Anon, *Our Bank. The Story of the Commercial Bank of Scotland* (Edinburgh, 1941)

Anon, *Over Two Centuries of Banking in Manchester* [Manchester and Salford Bank, Heywood Brothers] (priv. pub., 1994)

Anon, *Prescott's Bank 1766–1966* (priv. pub., c.1966)

Anon, 'Prescott's Bank', *National Provincial Bank Review* (1966–68)

Anon, *The Royal Bank of Scotland. A History* (priv. pub., 1997)

Anon, *The Samuel Family of Liverpool and London* (London, 1958)

Anon, *Sheffield and Rotherham Bank. A Banking Bicentenary 1792–1992* (priv. pub., 1992)

Anon, *A Sketch of the History of the Pontefract Bank* (Pontefract, 1879)

Anon, *Standard Chartered Bank. A Story Brought Up To Date* (London, 1980, revised 1983)

Anon, *Williams Deacon's 1771–1970* (Manchester, 1971)

Jacques Attali, *A Man of Influence. Sir Siegmund Warburg 1902–1982* (London, 1986)

Jules Ayer, *A Century of Finance 1804–1904. The London House of Rothschild* (priv. pub., 1905)

Paul Bareau, *Ionian Bank Ltd. A History* (priv. pub., 1953)

J Bennett Miller, 'The Paisley Union Bank Robbery', *Miscellany*, 1 (1971)

A G B Bethell, *The National Provincial Bank* (London, 1939)

W H Bidwell, *Annals of an East Anglian Bank* [Gurney and Co] (Norwich, 1900)

C W Boase, *A Century of Banking in Dundee; Being the Annual Balance Sheets of the Dundee Banking Company from 1764 to 1864* (Edinburgh, 1867)

H Bolitho and D Peel, *The Drummonds of Charing Cross* (London, 1967)

Andrew Boyle, *Montagu Norman. A Biography* [Bank of England] (London, 1967)

28 British banking – a guide to historical records

L F Bradburn, *The Old Bank Oxford* [Parsons, Thomson and Parsons] (Oxford, 1977)

Bo Bramsen and Kathleen Wain, *The Hambros 1779–1979* (London, 1979)

L J Broomhead, *The Great Oak. A Story of the Yorkshire Bank* (Leeds, 1981)

J C Brown, *A Hundred Years of Merchant Banking. A History of Brown Brothers and Co, Brown Shipley and Co and the Allied Firms* (New York, 1909)

Maureen Brown and June Masters, *The Bassetts. Leighton Buzzard's First Family* (Leighton Buzzard, 1989)

Kathleen Burk, *Morgan Grenfell 1838–1988. The Biography of a Merchant Bank* (Oxford, 1989)

S J Butlin, *Australia and New Zealand Bank. The Bank of Australasia and the Union Bank of Australia Limited 1828–1951* (London, 1961)

Alan Cameron, *Bank of Scotland 1695–1995. A Very Singular Institution* (Edinburgh, 1995)

R Cameron, *Banking in the Early Stages of Industrialisation* (Oxford, 1967)

R H Campbell, 'Edinburgh Bankers and the Western Bank of Scotland', *Scottish Journal of Political Economy* (1955)

John Cassey, 'The Frauds of John Sadleir', *The Banker*, 112 (1962)

George Chandler, *Four Centuries of Banking as Illustrated by the Banks, Customers and Staff Associated with the Constituent Banks of Martins Bank Ltd*, 2 vols (London, 1964–68)

Stanley Chapman, 'The Foundation of the English Rothschilds. N M Rothschild as a Textile Merchant 1799–1811', *Textile History*, 8 (1977)

Stanley Chapman, *N M Rothschild 1777–1836* (priv. pub., 1977)

C Chappell, *The Dumbell Affair* (Prescot, 1981)

N M Chappell, *New Zealand Banker's Hundred. A History of the Bank of New Zealand 1861–1961* (Wellington, 1961)

Ron Chernow, *The Warburgs. A Family Saga* (London, 1993)

John Clapham, *The Bank of England. A History 1694–1914*, 2 vols (Cambridge, 1944, reprinted 1944, 1970)

P Clarke, *The First House in the City. An Excursion into the History of Child and Co to Mark its 300th Year of Banking at the Same Address* (London, 1973)

Henry Clay, *Lord Norman* [Bank of England] (London, 1957)

George and Pamela Cleaver, *The Union Discount. A Centenary Album* (priv. pub., 1985)

Ernest H Coleridge, *The Life of Thomas Coutts, Banker*, 2 vols (London, 1920)

M Collis, *Wayfoong. The Hongkong and Shanghai Banking Corporation* (London, 1965)

Select bibliography

Count E C Corti, *The Rise of the House of Rothschild* and *The Reign of the House of Rothschild*, 2 vols (London, 1928)

P L Cottrell, 'London Financiers and Austria 1863–1875. The Anglo-Austrian Bank', *Business History*, 11 (1969)

W S Cowin, 'An Old Castletown Banking House' [George Quayle and Co], *Proceedings of the Isle of Man Natural History and Antiquarian Society* (1948)

W F Crick and J E Wadsworth, *A Hundred Years of Joint Stock Banking* [Midland Bank Ltd] (London, 1936, reprinted 1958)

Julian Crossley and John Blandford, *The D C O Story. A History of Banking in Many Countries 1925–1971* [Barclays Bank Dominion, Colonial and Overseas] (priv. pub., 1975)

C L Currie, *Bertram Wodehouse Currie 1827–96. Recollections, Letters and Journals* (priv. pub., 1901)

T G Davies, *A Brief History of the C W S Bank* (Manchester, 1930)

Richard Davis, *The English Rothschilds* (London, 1983)

Baron E B d'Erlanger, *My English Souvenir* (1978)

H G De Fraine, *Servant of this House. Life in the Old Bank of England* (London, 1960)

Laurie Dennett, *The Charterhouse Group 1925–1979. A History* (London, 1979)

K F Dixon, *The Story of Alexanders Discount Co Ltd 1810–1960* (priv. pub., c.1960)

H T Easton, *The History of a Banking House. Smith, Payne and Smiths* (London, 1903)

Aytoun Ellis, *Bold Adventure* [National Provincial Bank Ltd] (priv. pub., c.1953)

Aytoun Ellis, *Heir of Adventure. The Story of Brown Shipley and Co, Merchant Bankers, 1810–1960* (priv. pub., c.1960)

J Eunson, 'The Western Bank of Scotland 1832 to 9th November 1857', *Scottish Bankers' Magazine*, 75 (1983)

Niall Ferguson, *The World's Banker: The History of the House of Rothschild* (London, 1998)

John Fforde, *The Bank of England and Public Policy 1941–1958* (Cambridge, 1992)

Jane Fiske (ed.), *The Oakes Diaries. Business, Politics and the Family in Bury St Edmunds*, 2 vols (Woodbridge, 1990–91)

R M Fitzmaurice, 'A Chapter in Cornish Banking History. The Crisis of 1879 and the Failure of Tweedy, Williams and Co', *Journal of the Royal Institution of Cornwall* (1991)

William Forbes, *Memoirs of a Banking House* [Sir William Forbes, James Hunter and Co] (London and Edinburgh, 1860)

30   *British banking – a guide to historical records*

Hubert Fox, *Quaker Homespun. The Life of Thomas Fox of Wellington, Sergemaker and Banker 1747–1821* (London, 1958)

W Lionel Fraser, *All to the Good* [Helbert Wagg] (London, 1963)

C F Freebairn, 'An Old Banking Institution. The Paisley Union Bank', *Scottish Bankers' Magazine*, 16 (1924)

Richard Fry, *Bankers in West Africa. The Story of the Bank of British West Africa Limited* (London, 1976)

Roger Fulford, *Glyn's 1753–1953. Six Generations in Lombard Street* (London, 1953)

John A Gibbs, *The History of Antony and Dorothea Gibbs* (priv. pub., 1922)

John Giuseppi, *The Bank of England. A History from its Foundation in 1694* (London, 1966)

J S Gladstone, *The History of Gillanders, Arbuthnot and Co and Ogilvy, Gillanders and Co* (1910)

Eric Gore Brown, *Glyn Mills and Co* (priv. pub., 1933)

Victor Gray and Melanie Aspey (eds.), *The Life and Times of N M Rothschild 1777–1836* (priv. pub., 1998)

Edwin Green, *The Making of a Modern Banking Group. A History of the Midland Bank Since 1900* (priv. pub., 1979)

Edwin Green, *Debtors to Their Profession. A History of The Institute of Bankers 1879 to 1979* (London, 1979)

Edwin Green and Sara Kinsey, *The Paradise Bank. The Mercantile Bank of India 1893–1984* (Aldershot, 1999)

T E Gregory, *The Westminster Bank Ltd Through a Century*, 2 vols (London, 1936)

Percival Griffiths, *A History of the Inchcape Group* (priv. pub., 1977)

John Hargrave, *Professor Skinner Alias Montagu Norman* [Bank of England] (London, c.1940)

Edna Healey, *Coutts and Co 1692–1992. The Portrait of a Private Bank* (London, 1992)

Elizabeth Hennessy, *A Domestic History of the Bank of England 1930–1960* (Cambridge, 1992)

J A Henry and H A Siepmann, *The First Hundred Years of the Standard Bank* (London, 1963)

Ralph W Hidy, *The House of Baring in American Trade and Finance. English Merchant Bankers at Work 1763–1861* (Harvard, 1949, reprinted 1970)

F G Hilton Price, *The Marygold by Temple Bar being a History of the Site Now Occupied by ... the Banking House of Child and Co* (London, 1902)

F G Hilton Price, 'Some Account of the Business of Alderman Edward

Select bibliography

Backwell, Goldsmith and Banker in the 17th Century', *London and Middlesex Archaeological Society Transactions,* 6 (1890)

H P R Hoare, *Hoare's Bank. A Record 1673–1932* (London, 1932)

H P R Hoare, *Hoare's Bank. A Record 1672–1955* (London, 1955)

R A Hodgson, 'Gunners Bank', *Portsmouth Archives Review,* 2–4 (1977–80)

A R Holmes and Edwin Green, *Midland. 150 Years of Banking Business* (London, 1986)

William Howarth, *A Short History of the London and South Western Bank Ltd* (London, 1913)

William Howarth, *Barclay and Company Limited being a History of the Old Firm of Barclay and Company and also of the Various Institutions* (London, 1901)

William Howarth, *Somme Olde Curiosities by a Knyghte offe ye Quille* (London, 1890)

Wallis Hunt, *Heirs of Great Adventure. The History of Balfour, Williamson and Co Ltd 1851–1951* (priv. pub., 1951)

Horace G Hutchinson, *The Life of Sir John Lubbock, Lord Avebury,* 2 vols (London, 1914)

A W Isaac, *The Worcester Old Bank* (priv. pub., 1908)

Samey Japhet, *Recollections From My Business Life* (priv. pub., 1931)

Peter R Jenkins, *A History of Banking in Sussex* (1984)

Geoffrey Jones, *Banking and Empire in Iran. The History of the British Bank of the Middle East* and *Banking and Oil,* 2 vols (Cambridge, 1986–87)

Ivy Frances Jones, *The Rise of a Merchant Bank. A Short History of Guinness Mahon* (Dublin, 1974)

Stephanie Jones, *Two Centuries of Trading. The Origins and Growth of the Inchcape Group* (London, 1986)

K R Jones, *The Cox's of Craig's Court* (priv. pub., 1953)

D M Joslin, *A Century of Banking in Latin America to Commemorate the Centenary in 1962 of The Bank of London and South America Ltd* (Oxford, 1963)

Alexander Keith, *The North of Scotland Bank Limited 1836–1936* (Aberdeen, 1936)

I M Kennedy, 'Charles William Boase' [Dundee Banking Co], *Scottish Bankers' Magazine,* 47 (1956)

Marion Kent, 'Agent of Empire. The National Bank of Turkey and British Foreign Policy', *Historical Journal,* 18 (1975)

Frank H H King, *The History of the Hongkong and Shanghai Banking Corporation,* 4 vols (Cambridge, 1987–91)

Frank H H King, *Eastern Banking. Essays in the History of the Hongkong and Shanghai Banking Corporation* (1983)

32 British banking – a guide to historical records

M W Kirby, *Men of Business and Politics. The Rise and Fall of the Quaker Pease Dynasty of North East England 1700–1943* (1984)

Grace Lawless, *The Story of the Bosanquets* (Canterbury, 1966)

R E Leader, *The Sheffield Banking Company Limited. An Historical Sketch 1831–1916* (Sheffield, 1916)

J A S L Leighton-Boyce, *Smiths the Bankers 1658–1958* (London, 1958)

J O Leslie, 'Robert Carrick' [Ship Bank], *Scottish Bankers' Magazine*, 44 (1956)

H Lloyd, *The Quaker Lloyds in the Industrial Revolution* (London, 1975)

S Lloyd, *The Lloyds of Birmingham* (Birmingham, 1907)

Fiona Maccoll, *The Key to Our Success. A Brief History of the NatWest Group* (London, 1996)

Simone Mace, 'The Archives of the London Merchant Bank of N M Rothschild and Sons', *Business Archives*, 64 (1992)

A MacKenzie, 'Sir William Forbes Bt. of Pitsligo' [Sir William Forbes, James Hunter and Co], *Scottish Bankers' Magazine*, 44 (1953)

Compton Mackenzie, *Realms of Silver. One Hundred Years of Banking in the East* [Chartered Bank of India, Australia and China] (London, 1954)

I C Macsween, 'The Western Bank of Scotland 1832–1857', *Scottish Bankers' Magazine,* 49 (1949)

J M McBurnie, *The Story of the Lancashire and Yorkshire Bank Ltd 1872–1922* (Manchester, 1922)

Charles A Malcolm, *The History of the British Linen Bank* (Edinburgh,1950)

Charles A Malcolm, *The Bank of Scotland 1695–1945* (Edinburgh, c.1948)

S Marriner, *Rathbones of Liverpool 1845–73* (Liverpool, 1961)

W Marston Acres, *The Bank of England From Within 1694–1900*, 2 vols (London, 1931)

J B Martin, *The Grasshopper in Lombard Street* [Martin and Co] (London, 1892)

E Mathew, 'James Dennistoun of Golfhill' [Glasgow Bank], *Scottish Bankers' Magazine*, 49 (1958)

P W Matthews and Anthony W Tuke, *History of Barclays Bank Ltd* (London, 1926)

Wilfred Maude, *Antony Gibbs and Sons Limited. Merchants and Bankers 1808–1958* (London, 1958)

Frank T Melton, *Sir Robert Clayton and the Origins of English Deposit Banking 1658–1685* (Cambridge, 1986)

Frank T Melton, 'Robert and Sir Francis Gosling, Eighteenth Century Bankers and Stationers' in Robin Myers and Michael Harris (eds.), *Economics of the British Book Trade 1605–1939* (London, 1985)

D T Merrett, *A N Z Bank. A History of the Australia and New Zealand Banking Group Limited and its Constituents* (Sydney, 1985)

Select bibliography

D M Mitchell, 'Mr Fowle Pray Pay the Washwoman. The Trade of a London Goldsmith Banker, 1660–1692', *Business and Economic History*, 23 (1994)

David J Moss, 'The Bank of England and the Country Banks. Birmingham 1827–33', *Economic History Review*, 34 (1981)

Michael Moss and Iain Russell, *An Invaluable Treasure. A History of the TSB* (London, 1994)

R H Mottram, *The Westminster Bank 1836–1936* (London, 1936)

F S Moxon, *A Brief History of Pedders and Co, Preston Old Bank, 1776–1861* (c.1930s)

Stuart Muirhead, *Crisis Banking in the East. The History of the Chartered Mercantile Bank of India, London and China 1853–93* (Aldershot, 1996)

Charles W Munn, *Clydesdale Bank. The First One Hundred and Fifty Years* (Glasgow, 1988)

Charles W Munn, 'Dundee Banking Co', *Three Banks Review*, 127 (1980)

Neil Munro, *The Royal Bank of Scotland 1727–1927* (priv. pub., 1928)

A J Murray, *Home from the Hill. A Biography of Frederick Huth, Napoleon of the City* (London, 1970)

S Neave, *The Western Bank Failure and the Scottish Banking System* (Glasgow, 1858)

John Orbell, *Baring Brothers and Co Limited. A History to 1939* (priv. pub., 1985)

John Orbell, *A Guide to the Baring Archive at I N G Barings* (priv. pub., 1998)

Augustus Prevost, *History of Morris, Prevost and Co* (priv. pub., 1904)

Muriel Lloyd Prichard, 'The Alexander Family's Discount House', *Journal of the Friends' Historical Society*, 49 (1959–60)

Robert S Rait, *The History of the Union Bank of Scotland* (Glasgow, 1930)

W Rathbone, *William Rathbone. A Memoir* [Rathbone Brothers] (priv. pub., 1905)

Richard Reed, *National Westminster Bank. A Short History* (London, 1983, reprinted 1989)

J M Reid, *The History of the Clydesdale Bank 1836–1938* (Glasgow, 1938)

R D Richards, *The Early History of Banking in England* (London, 1929)

Ralph Richardson, *Coutts and Co. Bankers. Edinburgh and London* (London, 1900)

Berry Ritchie, *The Abbey National Story. A Key to the Door* (London, 1989)

Richard Roberts, *Schroders. Merchants and Bankers* (London, 1992)

Richard Roberts and David Kynaston (eds.), *The Bank of England. Money, Power and Influence 1694–1994* (Oxford, 1995)

34 *British banking – a guide to historical records*

R O Roberts, 'The Operations of The Brecon Old Bank, Wilkins and Co 1778–1890', *Business History*, 1 (1958)

C H Robertson, 'The Arbroath Banking Co', *Three Banks Review*, 131 (1981)

R M Robinson, *Coutts Bank* (London, 1929)

C Roth, *The Sassoon Dynasty* (London, 1941)

Philip T Saunders, *Stuckey's Bank* (Taunton, 1928)

Richard Saville, *Bank of Scotland. A History 1695–1995* (Edinburgh, 1996)

R S Sayers, *The Bank of England 1891–1944*, 3 vols (Cambridge, 1976)

R S Sayers, *Lloyds Bank in the History of English Banking* (Oxford, 1957)

R S Sayers, *Gilletts in the London Money Market 1867–1967* (Oxford, 1968)

Matthew Slattery, 'The National Bank 1835–1970', *Three Banks Review,* 93–96 (1972)

P E Smart, 'A Victorian Polymath. Sir John Lubbock' [Robarts, Lubbock and Co], *Journal of the Institute of Bankers*, 100 (1979)

Andrew St George, *JOH* [Jocelyn O Hambro, Hambros Bank] (priv. pub., 1992)

M Veronica Stokes, *A Bank in Four Centuries. Coutts and Co* (priv. pub., 1972)

Norio Tamaki, *The Life Cycle of the Union Bank of Scotland 1830–1954* (Aberdeen, 1983)

Audrey M Taylor, *Gilletts. Bankers at Banbury and Oxford* (Oxford, 1964)

John Thomson, *Arthur B Gillett 1875–1954. Memoirs from Some of His Friends* (Gloucester, 1954)

M F Tighe, 'Gunner and Company of Bishop's Waltham', *Southampton University Archaeological Group Journal,* 2 (1993)

Anthony W Tuke and R J H Tilman, *Barclays Bank Limited 1926–1969. Some Recollections* (London, 1972)

B B Turner, *Chronicles of the Bank of England* (London, 1897)

Stephen H Twining, *The House of Twining 1706–1956* (priv. pub., 1956)

G Tyson, *100 Years of Banking in Asia and Africa 1863–1963* [National and Grindlays Bank Ltd] (London, 1963)

J E Wadsworth, *Counter Defensive. The Story of a Bank in Battle* [Midland Bank Ltd] (London, 1946)

David Wainwright, *Henderson. A History of the Life of Alexander Henderson, First Lord Faringdon, and of Henderson Administration* (London, 1985)

Jehanne Wake, *Kleinwort Benson. The History of Two Families in Banking* (Oxford, 1997)

Rodney Wilson, 'Financial Development of the Arab Gulf. The Eastern Experience 1917–50' [Eastern Bank Ltd], *Business History* 29 (1987)

J R Winton, *Lloyds Bank 1918–1969* (Oxford, 1982)

Select bibliography

Hartley Withers, *National Provincial Bank 1833 to 1933* (London, 1933)
Philip Ziegler, *The Sixth Great Power. Barings 1762–1929* (London, 1988)

GENERAL, REGIONAL OR SECTORAL BANKING HISTORIES

A S J Baster, *The Imperial Banks* (London, 1929, reprinted 1977)
A S J Baster, *The International Banks* (London, 1929, reprinted 1977)
S J Butlin, *Foundations of the Australian Monetary System 1788–1851* (Melbourne, 1953, reprinted 1968)
Youssef Cassis, *La Cité de Londres 1870–1914* (Paris, 1987)
Youssef Cassis, *City Bankers 1890–1914* (Cambridge, 1994)
Charles H Cave, *A History of Banking in Bristol from 1750 to 1899* (Bristol, 1899)
Stanley Chapman, *The Rise of Merchant Banking* (London, 1984)
Stanley Chapman, *Merchant Enterprise in Britain* (Cambridge, 1992)
S G Checkland, *Scottish Banking. A History 1695–1973* (Glasgow, 1975)
Michael Collins, *Money and Banking in the UK. A History* (Cambridge, 1988)
Charles Northcote Cooke, *The Rise, Progress and Present Condition of Banking in India* (Calcutta, 1863)
P L Cottrell and B L Anderson, *Money and Banking in England. The Development of the Banking System 1694–1914* (Newton Abbot, 1974)
P L Cottrell, *Industrial Finance 1830–1914. The Finance and Organisation of English Manufacturing Industry* (London, 1979)
A S Davies, *The Early Banks of Mid-Wales* (Welshpool, 1935)
P G M Dickson, *The Financial Revolution in England 1688–1756* (London, 1967)
E Edwards, *Personal Recollections of Birmingham and Birmingham Men* (Birmingham, 1877)
A E Feavearyear, *The Pound Sterling* (Oxford, 1931, revised 1963)
G A Fletcher, *The Discount Houses in London* (London, 1976)
H R Fox-Bourne, *English Merchants. Memoirs in Illustration of Progress of British Commerce*, 2 vols (London, 1866)
J C Gibson, *The Old Private Banks of Stirling* (Stirling, 1930)
C A E Goodhart, *The Business of Banking 1891–1914* (London, 1972)
Edwin Green, *Banking. An Illustrated History* (Oxford, 1989)
Francis Green, 'Early Banks in West Wales', *Transactions of the Historical Society of West Wales*, 6 (1916)
T E Gregory (ed.), *Select Statutes. Documents and Reports Relating to British Banking* (Oxford, 1929, reprinted 1964)
L H Grindon, *Manchester Banks and Bankers* (Manchester, 1877)
W C E Hartley, *Banking in Yorkshire* (Clapham, 1975)

36 British banking – a guide to historical records

C E Hicks, 'The Cornish Banking Crisis of 1879', *Bankers' Magazine* (1952)

F G Hilton Price, *A Handbook of London Bankers* (London, 1876, reprinted 1970)

William Howarth, *Our Leading Banks* (London, 1894)

William Howarth, *The Banks in the Clearing House* (London, 1905)

John Hughes, *Liverpool Banks and Bankers 1760–1837* (Liverpool, 1906)

A G E Jones, 'The Banks of Bath', *Notes and Queries*, 203 (1958)

A G E Jones, 'Early Banking in Suffolk', *Notes and Queries*, 199–200 (1954–55)

A G E Jones, 'Early Banking in Ipswich' *Notes and Queries*, 196 (1951)

Geoffrey Jones, *British Multinational Banking 1830–1990* (Oxford, 1993)

Geoffrey Jones, 'Lombard Street on the Riviera. The British Clearing Banks and Europe 1900–1960', *Business History*, 24 (1982)

Reg C Jones, *Arian. The Story of Money and Banking in Wales* (Swansea, 1978)

D M Joslin, 'London Private Bankers 1720–1785', *Economic History Review*, 2 (1954)

A W Kerr, *History of Banking in Scotland* (Glasgow, 1884)

W T C King, *History of the London Discount Market* (London, 1936, reprinted 1972)

Sara Kinsey and Lucy Newton, *International Banking in an Age of Transition* (Aldershot, 1998)

David Kynaston, *The City of London*, 3 vols (London, 1994–99)

R E Leader, 'The Early Sheffield Banks', *Journal of the Institute of Bankers*, 38 (1917)

David J Moss, 'The Private Banks of Birmingham 1800–1827', *Business History*, 24 (1982)

R H Mottram, *Miniature Banking Histories* (London, 1930)

Charles W Munn, *The Scottish Provincial Banking Companies 1747–1864* (Glasgow, 1981)

Philip Ollerenshaw, *Banking in Nineteenth Century Ireland. The Belfast Banks 1825–1914* (Manchester, 1987)

Jack Parker, *Nothing for Nothing for Nobody. A History of Hertfordshire Banks and Banking* (Stevenage, 1986)

H Pemberton, 'Two Hundred Years of Banking in Leeds', *The Thoresby Miscellany*, 13 (1963)

M Perkins, *Dudley Tradesmen's Tokens of the Seventeenth, Eighteenth and Nineteenth Centuries and History of Dudley Banks, Bankers and Banknotes from the Earliest to the Present Times* (Dudley, 1905)

Maberly Phillips, *Banks, Bankers and Banking in Northumberland, Durham and North Yorkshire* (London, 1894)

Select bibliography

Manfred Pohl and Sabine Freitag, *Handbook on the History of European Banks* (Aldershot, 1994)

L S Pressnell, *Country Banking in the Industrial Revolution* (Oxford, 1956)

Harold Preston, *Early East Anglian Banks and Bankers* (Thetford, 1994)

Ernest Quarmby, *Banknotes and Banking in the Isle of Man: A Guide for Historians and Collectors*, 2nd edition (London, 1994)

H Ling Roth, *The Genesis of Banking in Halifax with Sidelights on Country Banking* (Halifax, 1914)

John Ryton, *Banks and Banknotes of Exeter 1769–1906* (Exeter, 1984)

R S Sayers, *Central Banking after Bagehot* (Oxford, 1957)

T J Smith, *Banks and Bankers of Leek* (Leek, 1891)

Mark Solly, *Banks in the Isle of Man* (Isle of Man, 1995)

R Somers, *The Scotch Banks and the System of Issue* (Edinburgh, 1873)

S E Thomas, *The Rise and Growth of Joint Stock Banking in Britain to 1860* (London, 1934)

J E Wadsworth, *The Banks and the Monetary System in the UK 1959–71* (London, 1973)

Joseph Wechsberg, *The Merchant Bankers* (London, 1967)

C R Whittlesey and J S G Wilson (eds.), *Essays in Money and Banking in Honour of R S Sayers* (Oxford, 1968)

User's guide:
Function and arrangement of the book

The principal function of this *Guide* is to describe the surviving historical records of banks in England, Scotland, Wales, the Channel Islands and the Isle of Man. It includes goldsmith banks, country and London private banks, joint stock banks, present day clearing banks, merchant banks, British-owned overseas banks where the bank's records remain within Britain, and discount houses. Also included are institutions that represent the collective business interests of banks and the professional and employment interests of bankers.

However, a parallel function is to provide histories of the banks to which these records relate in order to extend the value of the book to a wider range of users and to provide the records with a context and sense of relative historical significance. It means that a few important banks for which no historical records survive are excluded although, in order to redress this anomaly, brief histories have been included of present day long-established banks of importance.

BANK RECORD ENTRIES

Entries have been arranged alphabetically with records described according to the bank to which they relate. Each entry comprises the name of the bank; the town or city and county or country where it was or still is located; a brief history of the bank; a list of relevant bibliographical references used in the writing of the history section; and details of surviving records and the locations at which they are kept.

Bank name

The name of the bank at the beginning of each entry is, in virtually all cases, the final name under which the bank operated. All previous names are usually referred to in the history section and are also included in the extensive name index at the end of the book.

Bank location

The bank location is the last known city, town or village at which the bank operated or, in the case of companies which still trade, it is the bank's present address. For multi-site banks, it is the location of the head office. For overseas banks, the continent(s) where the bank operated is (are) also given.

History

A brief history of each bank is provided; for the most part, it approximates in length to the historical importance and size of the bank. These histories are not definitive but focus on name changes; functions; capital (usually paid-up capital); area of operation; number and, where feasible, location of branches; acquisitions of other banks; and cause of disappearance or, if still active, current status. These histories are not the result of primary research, but are based on published information. Where accuracy is in question, the most recently published information is given.

Much basic information has been taken from G L Grant, *The Standard Catalogue of Provincial Banks and Banknotes* (London, 1977) and from the list of defunct banks published annually in *The Banker's Almanac*. In adding to the broad facts provided by these two publications, the compilers have drawn extensively upon information in the official histories of many banks and, in particular, upon the work of chroniclers of local banks in specific areas. Most notable amongst these is the work of Harold Preston on East Anglian banks, *Early East Anglian Banks and Bankers* (Thetford, 1994), and of Jack Parker on Hertfordshire banks, *Nothing for Nothing for Nobody* (Stevenage, 1986). More dated publications which have also been of great assistance include those of F G Hilton Price *A Handbook of London Bankers* (London, 1876); Maberly Phillips, *A History of Banks, Bankers and Banking in Northumberland, Durham and North Yorkshire* (London, 1894); and Charles H Cave, *A History of Banking in Bristol* (Bristol, 1899).

Bibliography

The publications section lists monographs, leaflets and periodical articles which contain substantive information relating to the bank. Often these publications were privately published and distributed and may not be found in copyright or public libraries. Many are, however, held in the Business Archives Council's library which may be visted by appointment (see address below). This section does not offer exhaustive bibliographies of the bank concerned and users may wish to refer to published bibliographies. By far the most notable is that compiled by Fred Wellings and Alistair Gibb, *Bibliography of Banking Histories* (2 vols, Kirkcaldy, 1995–

40   British banking – a guide to historical records

97). The publications cited in the text are included within a bibliography that also lists some important general works.

Records

The records section for each entry is headed by an address for the location of the records in 2000, whether they are held by a company or institution, or are in private ownership or are deposited in a public repository. As far as possible, the Business Archives Council will keep a record of subsequent changes in the location of records. Changes in the address of many publicly funded record offices can be discovered through reference to the Royal Commission on Historical Manuscripts [HMC]'s *Record Repositories in Great Britain* (HMSO), Janet Foster and Julia Shepherd, *British Archives* (London) and HMC's website – http://www.hmc.gov.uk. In many entries, as a result of the division of a bank's records, they are shown at two or more locations. These locations are numbered Records 1, Records 2, and so on. Branch records of banks are listed separately after the central administrative records and are arranged alphabetically by branch name. Complete consistency has not proved possible in describing branch records as information has not been made available in a standard format. Researchers are advised to contact the clearing bank archivists to enquire about the records of surviving branches.

Records are described by series and are listed chronologically by the opening date of each series rather than functionally. The diversity of lists received from record offices, both in format and terminology, has made it difficult to standardise the record summaries or arrange them consistently in any other way. An indication of extent is sometimes provided through the inclusion, in brackets, of the number of volumes in the series. The records which have been included are those about which banks have been prepared to release information. This has varied from bank to bank but for the most part records dated after 1960 have been excluded. Also largely excluded are details of single or small groups of items of minor importance such as deeds, bank notes, passbooks and cheques, particularly where these have been deposited in a public repository. Where banks have been taken over by other banks, central administrative and branch records may be continued under the entry for the successor bank.

TRADE, PROFESSIONAL AND EMPLOYMENT ORGANISATION ENTRIES

For trade organisations, entries have been arranged in a similar way to those of banks. Only large institutions and those for which substantive archives survive have been included.

User's guide **41**

APPENDIX

An appendix carries details of small archive collections, held in record offices, which cannot be linked to specific banks because details of provenance are not available. Other collections are of a more general nature and relate to banking issues rather than to the business of specific banks.

ACCESS TO RECORDS

Users of the *Guide* should be aware that the co-operation of banks and record offices in providing details of records does not imply that access to records will be granted. Access to privately held records is at the discretion of the bank holding or owning the records and can be given only when it does not compromise the bank's duties of confidentiality and when facilities exist for assistance to be given to the researcher. Banks have particular obligations of confidentiality to their customers and it is rarely the case that access to customer records will be given unless those records are more than 100 years old. Some banks stipulate longer periods while others may be prepared to provide access to more recent records provided that the consent of the customer or his or her successors is forthcoming.

It is therefore vital that researchers wishing access to records should in the first instance apply in writing to the bank. Where banks have archivists, application should be made to the Archivist. These banks include Bank of Scotland, Barclays, Coutts, HSBC, Hoares, ING Barings, Lloyds TSB, Rothschilds and The Royal Bank of Scotland (see addresses below). In making application, it is sensible for researchers to explain their research interests in full and bear in mind that specific queries will be easier to answer than general ones. Instant access to archives may well not be possible and particular conditions of access may exist. These may include the provision of a letter of introduction and a request for the bank to be able to review research based on information taken from archives prior to publication.

Where records have been publicly deposited, researchers should write to the chief archivist of the repository named in the relevant records section. Some records in public repositories are governed by conditions of access – such as particular closure periods for certain series of records – applied at the request of the depositing bank or institution. Researchers should contact the appropriate repository well before making a research expedition.

42 *British banking – a guide to historical records*

USEFUL ADDRESSES

General

Business Archives Council, 101 Whitechapel High Street, London E1 7RE
tel: 0207 247 0024; fax: 0207 422 0026

National Register of Archives, Royal Commission on Historical Manuscripts, Quality House, Quality Court, Chancery Lane, London WC2A 1HP
tel: 0207 242 1198; fax 0207 831 3550; e-mail: nra@hmc.gov.uk; http:// www.hmc.gov.uk

National Register of Archives (Scotland), National Archives of Scotland, H M General Register House, Edinburgh EH1 3YY
tel: 0131 535 1314; fax: 0131 557 9569; e-mail: research@nas.gov.uk

Bank archives

Mr H Gillett, Archivist, Bank of England, Threadneedle Street, London ECR 8AH
tel: 0207 601 5096/4889; fax: 0207 601 4837; e-mail: archive@bankof england.co.uk

Ms H Redmond-Cooper, Deputy Archivist, Bank of Scotland, 12 Bankhead Crossway South, Sighthill, Edinburgh EH11 4EN
tel: 0131 529 1288/1305; fax: 0131 529 1307; e-mail: archives@ bankofscotland.co.uk

Mrs J Campbell, Senior Archivist, Barclays Bank plc, Dallimore Road, Wythenshawe, Manchester M23 9JA
tel: 0161 946 3035; fax: 0161 946 0226; e-mail: jessie.campbell@ barclays.co.uk

Ms T Earl, Archivist, Coutts and Co, 440 Strand, London WC2R 0QS
tel: 0207 753 1000; fax and e-mail unavailable

Jane Waller, Archivist, ING Barings, 60 London Wall, London EC2M 5TQ
tel: 0207 767 1401/1944; fax: 0207 767 7131; e-mail: jane.waller@ing-barings.com

Dr J Booker, Archivist, Lloyds TSB Group plc, Archives, Head Office, 71 Lombard Street, London EC3P 3BS
tel: 0207 356 1032; fax: 0207 356 1038; e-mail: sampsok@lloydstsb.co.uk

Mr E Green, Archivist, HSBC Holdings plc, 10 Lower Thames Street, London EC3R 6AE
tel: 0207 260 7956; fax: 0207 260 7977; e-mail: group.archives@ hsbcgroup.com

Ms M Aspey, Archivist, N M Rothschild and Sons Ltd, New Court, St Swithins Lane, London EC4P 4DU
tel: 0207 430 2616; fax: 0207 430 2791; e-mail: melanie.aspey@ rothschild.co.uk

Ms A Turton, Archivist, The Royal Bank of Scotland plc, Regents House, 42 Islington High Street, London N1 8XL
tel: 0207 615 6127; fax: 0207 837 7560; e-mail: archives@rbos.co.uk

Abbreviations

c.	circa
cent.	century
Co	company
d.	died
est.	established
inc.	incorporated – i.e. registered
Ltd	limited
(m)	microfilm copy
n.d.	no date
(p)	photocopy
plc	public limited company
re	relating to
[w]	wanting – i.e. the record series is incomplete

Lists of records of banks

ABERDEEN BANKING CO
Aberdeen, Grampian

History: This co-partnery was established in 1767 with a paid-up capital of about £21,500, mostly provided by landowners and merchants; it was the tenth provincial banking company to be formed in Scotland and the second in Aberdeen. Its establishment was partly a response to the problem of the proliferation of small bank notes of doubtful value in circulation in Scotland during the 1760s. The bank struggled to survive during its first eighteen months, a result of aggressive competition from the Glasgow-based Thistle Bank and the British Linen Co; it was not until 1771 that a substantial profit was made. By 1769 eight agencies had been formed in the counties of Aberdeen, Banff and Kincardine. Between 1778 and 1806 the bank was so successful that paid-up capital was raised to £80,000 through transfer of retained profits. The bank appeared to continue to operate successfully, but there were underlying problems; by 1828 very large sums had been advanced to businesses in which the directors of the bank were interested and it was only on the appointment of a new cashier in 1839 that these were identified as bad debts. This resulted in a reconstruction in 1842–43, but by 1849 paid-up capital had been reduced to £7,000 as a result of the failure of the firms to which the large advances had been made. Some retiring partners attempted to bring lawsuits against the directors, which do not seem to have been resolved. The business was acquired by the Union Bank of Scotland (est. 1830) in 1849.

Robert S Rait, *The History of the Union Bank of Scotland* (Glasgow, 1930); Norio Tamaki, *The Life Cycle of the Union Bank of Scotland 1830–1954* (Aberdeen, 1983)

Records: Bank of Scotland Archive, Operational Services Division, 12 Bankhead Terrace, Sighthill, Edinburgh EH11 4DY

Copy letterbook 1767–69; ledger 1770–71; register of deposit receipts 1839–46; ledger 1844–47.

46   *British banking – a guide to historical records*

Aberdeen: balance sheets 1768–87; **Portsoy:** teller's cash book 1842–47; **Tarland:** cash books 1837–45; deposit receipts register 1845–49.

ABERDEEN COMMERCIAL BANKING CO
Aberdeen, Grampian

History: Aberdeen Commercial Banking Co, also known as Commercial Banking Co of Aberdeen, was established in 1778 in Castle Street, Aberdeen, as a co-partnership of sixteen local merchants and manufacturers. It issued its own notes and briefly opened a branch in Arbroath (by 1793). In 1833 the co-partnership was dissolved and the business and premises were taken over by National Bank of Scotland (est. 1825). It became National Bank's Aberdeen branch.

Records: The Royal Bank of Scotland plc, Archive Section, 36 St Andrew Square, Edinburgh EH2 2YB

Bank notes and proofs c.1800; directors' sederunt book 1814–39; historical notes 1887.

ABERGAVENNY FINANCIAL CO LTD
Abergavenny, Gwent

History: This joint stock company was formed in 1885. It was liquidated in 1890 when its business was acquired by the Birmingham District & Counties Banking Co Ltd (est. 1836).

Records: Barclays Bank plc, Group Archives, Dallimore Road, Wythenshawe, Manchester M23 9JA

Share certificates 1885–91; directors' report 1890.

SAMUEL ADAMS & CO
Hertford and Ware, Hertfordshire

History: Samuel and Thomas Adams established this private bank at Ware probably in 1813; it was also known as the Ware Bank. Both partners were maltsters, barge owners and coal merchants; by 1845 Samuel Adams was described as the most important maltster in the country. In 1814 the business of the failed Hertford bank of Christie & Cathrow (est. 1807) was acquired and thereafter the bank became known as the Hertford & Ware Bank. Although damaged by the failure of its London agents, Pole, Thornton & Co, in 1825, the bank survived after a public statement of support by its leading customers. It failed in 1856.

Jack Parker, *Nothing for Nothing for Nobody* (Stevenage, 1986)

Records of banks **47**

Records: County Record Office, County Hall, Hertford SG13 8DE

Liquidation papers 1843–60; agreements for clerks' services 1849–51. [Ref: D/EL B338–355]

ADELPHI BANK LTD
Liverpool, Merseyside

History: This joint stock bank was formed in 1862 and had two notable features; it was the first bank to establish an effective presence in both Liverpool and Manchester and many of its directors and customers were Wesleyans. By 1871 its balance sheet totalled £353,000, paid-up capital was £130,000 and deposits stood at £106,000. By 1888 the balance sheet totalled £580,000, rising to £892,000 by 1892. By then eight Manchester branches existed plus others at Bootle, Macclesfield and Southport. Further branches were soon opened at Ancoats, Cadishead and Hyde. In 1899, when paid-up capital was £200,000, the bank encountered difficulties and sought amalgamation with the Lancashire & Yorkshire Bank Ltd (est. 1872). The consideration was £130,000 in cash and shares.

George Chandler, *Four Centuries of Banking* (London, 1964–68)

Records: Barclays Bank plc, Group Archives, Dallimore Road, Wythenshawe, Manchester M23 9JA

Memorandum and articles of association 1861; balance sheets 1871–92; declaration of trust re transfer of shares to Lancashire & Yorkshire Bank 1899.

AFRICAN BANKING CORPORATION LTD
London and Africa

History: This British-owned overseas bank was formed in 1890 to do business in southern Africa where it competed with the longer established Standard Bank. Initially it acquired the staff, premises and business of the Cape of Good Hope Bank, which had failed in 1890, and absorbed the Western Province Bank (est. 1847), the Kaffrarian Colonial Bank (est. 1862) and the Worcester Commercial Bank (est. 1850) in 1891 and 1892. These acquisitions provided an immediate extensive presence in southern Africa. In 1891 branches were opened at Lagos and Tangier, but were disposed of to the Bank of British West Africa Ltd in 1894. A New York branch was opened shortly after 1900. By 1913 assets totalled £6.6 million, market capitalisation was £500,000 and there were forty-five branches. However, while well run, the bank lacked the size and capital to compete effectively and was acquired by Standard Bank of South Africa Ltd (est. 1862) in 1920.

48   British banking – a guide to historical records

Records 1: Guildhall Library, Aldermanbury, London EC2P 2EJ

Prospectus 1890; memorandum and articles of association 1890–1963; shareholder circulars 1890–1920; 'foreign staff books' (2) 1891–1903; supplementary journals (2) 1891–1906; power of attorney registers (3) 1891–1907 [w]; customer account ledgers (21) 1891–1916 [w]; seal registers (3) 1891–1930; weekly abstracts (monthly from 1916) of general ledger balances (4) 1892–1921; bank notes issued register 1893–1914; general ledgers (14) 1894–1922; general ledger balances (11) 1895–1908; profit and loss accounts: investments (2) 1895–1904, commissions (3) 1895–1906, charges (3) 1895–1908, exchange (2) 1899–1906; half-yearly (1895–1911) and annual (1911–20) reports and accounts 1895–1920; investment registers (2) 1898–1921; legal opinions and related papers 1898–1930, 1949; 'branch analysis' book 1901–18; agreements re staff 'guarantee and savings fund' 1901, 1919; 'branch drafts payable' books (16) 1901–25 [w]; 'bills accepted' 1909–12; New York agency accounts (3) 1909–18; 'balances with bankers' (4) 1909–21; office expenditure ledgers (2) 1910–21; journals (16) 1910–24 [w]; 'paid register of Australian bills purchased' 1911–14; register of customer accounts opened and closed 1911–28; 'bills lodged for collection: paid register' 1911–15; head office accounts (2) 1916–18; registers of bills purchased by branches (7) 1917–20 [w]; quarterly statements of assets and liabilities 1918–20; correspondence registers (4) 1918–21; amalgamation agreement and related papers 1920; liquidation papers 1921–45. [Ref: MS 24824–24861]

Records 2: Standard Chartered Bank plc, Head Office, 1 Aldermanbury Square, London EC2V 7SB

Directors' meeting minute books (10) 1890–1915; registers of shareholders c.1891–1906.

AGRA BANK LTD
London and Asia

History: This overseas bank originated as Agra & United Services Bank, a private bank formed in India in 1833 and headquartered in Calcutta. Initially banking services were provided to British residents. By 1857 agencies existed at Bombay, Madras, Agra, Lahore and Canton. In 1857, when the bank was incorporated as a limited liability company with a paid-up capital of £1 million, the head office was relocated to London. In the early 1860s branches were opened at Sydney and Melbourne and in 1864 the business merged with the London private bank of Masterman, Peters, Mildred, Birkbeck & Co (est. 1778); the new bank was called Agra & Masterman's Bank Ltd. It failed in 1866 when it was the second largest exchange bank in the East after the Oriental Bank Corporation. It resumed

Records of banks **49**

as Agra Bank Ltd and was placed in voluntary liquidation in 1900 following over exposure to the Indian tea industry. In 1890 it had eight branches and assets of about £7 million.

Charles Northcote Cooke, *The Rise, Progress and Present Condition of Banking in India* (Calcutta, 1863)

Records: The Baring Archive, ING Baring Holdings Ltd, 60 London Wall, London EC2M 5TQ

Annual report and accounts with list of shareholders 1855; report of committee of enquiry 1857. [Ref: HC 2.441,446,480]

ALEXANDERS & COLLETT
Woodbridge, Suffolk

History: This private bank was established in 1797 as Brooke, Riches & Collett; it was also known as the Woodbridge Bank. Between 1801 and 1805 the bank was styled Riches, Collett & Co and, following its combination with the Woodbridge branch (est. 1804) of Alexanders & Co of Ipswich, it became known as Alexanders, Riches, Collett & Co in 1805. Between 1810 and 1826 its title was Alexanders & Collett and thereafter it was part of Alexanders & Co of Ipswich.

Harold Preston, *Early East Anglian Banks and Bankers* (Thetford, 1994)

Records: Barclays Bank plc, Group Archives, Dallimore Road, Wythenshawe, Manchester M23 9JA

Probate of will 1789–90; bank notes 1803–26, 1882; cheques 1808–14; correspondence with London agent 1809.

ALEXANDERS DISCOUNT PLC
London

History: This City of London discount house was formed in 1810 by the Quaker William Alexander. William, formerly a senior bank clerk with Smith, Wright & Gray and latterly with Robarts, Curtis & Co, joined John Rickman as a partner in a bill broking business in 1806. In 1810 he established his own business which had a capital of £5,000; by 1811 its bill discount turnover was about £1 million, yielding a commission income of £1,200. Loans were also made out of the short-term deposits placed with him by banks. After William's death in 1819, his widow ran the business until joined by her son, George, when the title changed to Anne & G W Alexander. Under George's leadership for 50 years, it became one of London's largest discount houses being renamed A & G W Alexander & Co in 1831. Deposits rose to £2 million in 1847 and to £4

50   *British banking – a guide to historical records*

million 10 years later. In 1864 the firm amalgamated with Roger Cunliffe & Son and was renamed Alexanders, Cunliffe & Co. The Cunliffes withdrew to join the new National Discount Co Ltd (est. 1869) in 1877, when the business was renamed Alexanders & Co. From then it was the second largest London house after the National and the third largest following the formation of Union Discount Co of London Ltd in 1885; it remained so until recent times. In 1891 the business was transferred to a limited company, Alexanders & Co Ltd, with a paid-up capital of £500,000. In 1911 the business became publicly-owned and from 1919 was known as Alexanders Discount Co Ltd. In 1984 it was acquired by Mercantile House Holdings plc which in the same year acquired Jessel, Toynbee & Gillett plc and merged their assets and business into Alexanders. In 1987 Credit Lyonnais SA (est. 1863) acquired the business and the name was changed to C L Alexanders Discount plc but reverted to Alexanders Discount plc in 1989.

K F Dixon, *Alexanders Discount Company Limited 1810–1960* (priv. pub., c.1960); Muriel F Lloyd Prichard, 'The Alexander Family's Discount House', *Journal of the Friends' Historical Society*, 49 (1959–60)

Records: Alexanders Discount plc, Broadwalk House, 5 Appold Street, London EC2A 2DA

Ledger 1810–16; will and other papers re G W Alexander c.1836–90; 'enquiries credits' c.1849–57, 1860s–1870s, 1892–95, 1911–38; papers re shares c.1840s–1860s; papers re Helen C Alexander c.1858–97; profit and loss accounts 1864–88; customer ledger 1865–1870s; day books re bill transactions (2) 1874–c.1912, 1929–32; 'bankruptcies and bad debts' 1875–80; stock records 1884–85, 1888–94; will of William D Alexander 1887; salary book 1890–1971; balance sheets re London discount houses c.1890–1961; directors' and general meeting minutes (15) 1891 on; ledgers (3) 1891–1923; valuation and balance sheets 1891–1906, 1919–46; papers re pension fund including rules 1899–1960s; private memorandum book c.1890s; papers re R H Alexander c.1903–1930s; 'bills due/bought' book 1910–14; agreements and other papers re premises c.1915–38; seal books (4) 1929–35, 1945–57; share registers 1930 on; staff register 1933–c.1940; presscuttings 1935–56; papers re capital reorganisation 1954.

ALLIANCE BANK
Manchester, Greater Manchester

History: This joint stock bank was formed in 1836 out of the failed business of the Northern & Central Bank of England (est. 1834). In 1842 it was acquired by the Bank of Manchester (est. 1829), apparently in order to acquire the services of its capable manager.

Records of banks 51

Leo H Grindon, *Manchester Banks and Bankers. Historical, Biographical and Anecdotal* (Manchester, 1877)

Records 1: The Royal Bank of Scotland plc, Archive Section, Regent's House, 42 Islington High Street, London N1 8XL

Deeds of settlement 1839; lists of shareholders 1841.

Records 2: Centre for Kentish Studies, County Hall, Maidstone ME14 1XQ

Annual report 1841. [Ref: U1287 C32]

ALLIANCE BANK LTD
Liverpool and London

History: This joint stock bank was established in 1862 as Alliance Bank of London & Liverpool Ltd with a paid-up capital of £250,000. It had offices and directors in both London and Liverpool; two Liverpool directors were provided by the merchant bank of Frederick Huth & Co. Early on, branches were opened at Southwark (1863), Birkenhead (1863) and Manchester (1864). In 1864, when customer deposits totalled £6 million, the bank's title was altered to Alliance Bank Ltd to reflect its geographical spread. During the following years it experienced large losses and, during the financial panic of 1866, a run on all its branches. Continuing poor results led to the separation of the Liverpool and London businesses. In 1870 the Southwark branch was sold to London Joint Stock Bank (est. 1836) and in 1871 the bank was reconstructed. The Liverpool business was sold to the National Bank of Liverpool Ltd (est. 1836), while the remaining business was transferred to a new company also known as Alliance Bank Ltd that had a paid-up capital of £777,000. In 1872 the Manchester branch was sold to Lancashire & Yorkshire Bank Ltd (est. 1872). However, Alliance Bank expanded rapidly in London and in 1892 had twelve branches there. In 1892 it amalgamated with Parr's Banking Co Ltd (est. 1865) to form Parr's Banking Co & Alliance Bank Ltd.

T E Gregory, *The Westminster Bank Through A Century* (London, 1936)

Records 1: The Royal Bank of Scotland plc, Archive Section, Regent's House, 42 Islington High Street, London N1 8XL

Merchant customers' letterbooks 1859–65; prospectus 1862; articles of association 1862; security register 1862–65; list of shareholders 1863; annual reports 1863–78; sub-committee minutes 1865–86; miscellaneous notices and instructions 1866–92; papers re reconstruction 1868–71; London committee minutes 1869–78; directors' meeting minute books (3) 1871–92; annual general meeting minutes 1871–92; seal register 1882–

52 British banking – a guide to historical records

95; branch committee minutes (2) 1886–92; register of members 1890; agreement re transfer of securities to Parr's Banking Co Ltd 1892; amalgamation papers 1892.

London, Battersea: architectural drawings 1887; **London, Streatham Broadway:** architectural drawings 1887; **Macclesfield:** letterbook 1841–42.

Records 2: HSBC Holdings plc, Group Archives, 10 Lower Thames Street, London EC3R 6AE

London, Southwark: signature books 1864–1928.

ANGLO ARGENTINE BANK LTD
London and Latin America

History: This overseas bank was founded in the City of London in 1889 as the London & Argentine Bank Ltd, but changed its name almost immediately to the Anglo Argentine Bank Ltd. Its prestigious board of directors included Sampson S Lloyd, chairman of Lloyds Banking Co Ltd, and Edward Bunge of Bunge, Born & Co, the international trading house. Branches were opened at Buenos Aires, Argentina, and Montevideo, Uruguay. By 1890 its assets totalled almost £1 million and its market capitalisation was £200,000. It remained a small bank and in 1900 was acquired by the Bank of Tarapaca & London Ltd (est. 1888) which was then renamed the Bank of Tarapaca & Argentina Ltd, later known as Anglo-South American Bank Ltd.

David Joslin, *A Century of Banking in Latin America. The Bank of London & South America Ltd 1862–1962* (Oxford, 1963)

Records: Lloyds TSB Group plc, Archives, Head Office, 71 Lombard Street, London EC3P 3BS

Staff record book 1889–1901.

ANGLO-AUSTRIAN BANK LTD
London and Europe

History: This bank was incorporated in Austria as the Anglo-Austrian Bank in 1863 by a group of British financiers led by George Glyn of Glyn, Mills & Co, who had already sponsored the Ottoman Bank (est. 1856). The bank aimed to be both a government bank and a commercial bank with a branch network. Management committees existed in both London and Vienna and finance was provided to the Austrian government and to railway companies, either by short-term advances or by issuance of bonds. The bank worked closely with the International Financial Society and the

Records of banks **53**

Ottoman Bank and by the late 1860s did business outside Austria, for example arranging finance for the Portuguese and Romanian governments. In 1914 it encountered difficulties and was supported by the Bank of England; in 1922 it was wound up and its business transferred to the newly formed Anglo-Austrian Bank Ltd in which the Bank of England was a large shareholder. The bank continued to operate an extensive branch network in Austria, Czechoslovakia and neighbouring countries. The Czechoslovakian business was transferred to the Anglo-Czecho-Slovakian Bank and in 1926 the Austrian branches were sold to the Credit Anstalt of Vienna. In the same year it amalgamated with the British Trade Corporation (est. 1916) to form the Anglo-International Bank Ltd. The Anglo-Austrian Bank Ltd was voluntarily liquidated in 1927.

P L Cottrell, 'London Financiers and Austria 1863–1875. The Anglo Austrian Bank', *Business History*, XI (1969) and reprinted in RTP Davenport-Hines (ed.), *Capital, Entrepreneurs and Profits* (London, 1990)

Records 1: Public Record Office, Ruskin Avenue, Kew, Richmond, Surrey TW9 4DU

Papers re reconstruction 1921–26. [Ref: T160/3277/1–3]

Records 2: The Baring Archive, ING Baring Holdings Ltd, 60 London Wall, London EC2M 5TQ

Memorandum re bank 1863; papers re bank's negotiation for the issue of an Austrian government loan 1863–65. [Ref: HC9.25–65]

ANGLO-BRAZILIAN COMMERCIAL & AGENCY CO LTD
London and Latin America

History: This overseas bank was founded jointly in 1918 by the London & Brazilian Bank Ltd (est. 1862) and the British Trade Corporation Ltd (est. 1916) in order to win business in Brazil, formerly the preserve of German merchants. It encountered strong competition, especially from the London & River Plate Bank Ltd, and was wound up in 1929.

Records: Lloyds TSB Group plc, Archives, Head Office, 71 Lombard Street, London EC3P 3BS

Directors' meeting minute book 1918–29.

ANGLO-EGYPTIAN BANK LTD
London and Africa

History: This overseas bank was formed in London in 1864 as the Anglo-Egyptian Bank Ltd with a paid-up capital of £500,000, much of which was

54 British banking – a guide to historical records

contributed by French investors. Directors were drawn from Agra & Masterman's Bank Ltd and General Credit & Finance Co of London. In 1866, following heavy losses, paid-up capital was increased to £800,000 and in 1867 the bank was reconstructed under the title of the Anglo-Egyptian Banking Co Ltd. Its first branch was opened at Alexandria, the centre of Egypt's burgeoning cotton trade, followed in 1878 by other branches at Cairo and in Cyprus (closed shortly afterwards) as well as an agency in Paris. Much of the bank's first business involved financing the Egyptian government, but in the 1880s general banking services and trade finance, especially for cotton, became important. In 1881 a branch opened at Malta, where the leading customer was the British government, especially the Admiralty, and another branch followed at Gibraltar. The business of the Commercial Bank of Alexandria Ltd (est. 1872) was acquired in 1884. In 1887 the original name was revived following a further reconstruction which resulted in stability and prosperity. In 1890 total assets were £2.5 million, market capitalisation was £400,000 and there were five branches. By 1913 the bank had total assets of £5.5 million and eleven branches. During the First World War it grew rapidly and benefited greatly from British army accounts; by 1919 deposits stood at over £17 million. In the post-war years, expansion into Palestine through the opening of a branch in Jerusalem in 1918 took place. Subsequently the bank was appointed bankers to the Palestine Civil Administration and through this provided mortgage loans to farmers. In 1920 Barclays Bank Ltd (est. 1896) acquired a controlling interest and in 1925 the bank merged with the Colonial Bank (est. 1836) and the National Bank of South Africa (est. 1891) to form Barclays Bank (Dominion, Colonial & Overseas).

Anon, *A Banking Centenary. Barclays Bank (Dominion, Colonial and Overseas) 1836–1936* (priv. pub., 1938)

Records: Barclays Bank plc, Group Archives, Dallimore Road, Wythenshawe, Manchester M23 9JA

Directors' meeting minute books (15) 1864–1925; general meeting minutes 1865–1924; memorandum and articles of association 1887; bad debts books (3) 1889–1926; branch statistics 1897–1935; secretary's out-letterbooks (12) 1900–27 [w]; chairman's out-letterbooks (6) 1901–26; staff provident fund ledgers (7) 1906–42; staff provident fund supplement to trust deed 1907; general manager's out-letterbook 1922–26; head office expenses analysis 1922–27; half-yearly balance sheets and profit and loss accounts etc 1923–26; list of foreign shareholders 1925; secretary's out-letterbook re liquidation of accounts 1926.

Records of banks

ANGLO-INTERNATIONAL BANK LTD
London and Europe

History: This bank was formed in London in 1926, the result of an amalgamation of the Anglo-Austrian Bank Ltd (est. 1863) and the British Trade Corporation Ltd (est. 1916). Both banks were in difficulties and their amalgamation was sponsored by the Bank of England which became the majority shareholder. Paid-up capital was £2 million. The Bank of England viewed the new bank as a vehicle for assisting in the reconstruction of Germany and central Europe. In 1927 the Anglo-Russian Bank was acquired and an interest in the Anglo-Czecho-Slovakian Bank was sold, while in 1932 Romanian branches were disposed of. In the early 1930s, the financial collapse of Germany and eastern Europe seriously damaged the bank leaving 80 per cent of its assets frozen. In 1933 the Bank of England, which had to support the bank for the rest of the decade, advised that it be placed in 'private orderly liquidation' and its business was secretly run down. In 1940 the British Overseas Bank Ltd (est. 1919) was appointed the bank's managers and in 1944 the banking business was transferred to Glyn Mills & Co (est. 1757). The bank, then reduced solely to a holder of frozen assets in Europe, was placed under management of Continental Assets Realisation Trust Ltd. By 1951 its liquidation was well underway, but not finally completed until 1962.

Records: The Royal Bank of Scotland plc, Archive Section, Regent's House, 42 Islington High Street, London N1 8XL

Security ledgers (7) 1928–44; 'correspondence files' being papers exchanged with correspondent banks, etc 1941–42, 1944.

ANGLO-SOUTH AMERICAN BANK LTD
London and Latin America

History: This overseas bank was established in 1888 as the Bank of Tarapaca & London Ltd to provide banking services in Chile. The promoter was John North, a British businessman with large interests in the Chilean nitrate industry and its associated infrastructure. In 1890 total assets were £1.2 million and market capitalisation stood at £550,000. Initial paid-up capital was £500,000. The main branch was at Valparaiso with others in the nitrate area at Iquique and Pisagua. Initially the bank was closely associated with North's businesses but after his death, in 1896, it became more broadly based. From the late 1890s, the bank spread throughout Chile opening branches at Santiago and in the pastoral and copper producing regions. Expansion outside Chile began in 1900 with the acquisition of the small Anglo Argentine Bank Ltd (est. 1889), which resulted in a name change to the Bank of Tarapaca & Argentina Ltd and

56 British banking – a guide to historical records

then to the Anglo-South American Bank Ltd in 1907. Branches opened at Hamburg in 1905 and at New York in 1907, and in 1912 the London Bank of Mexico & South America Ltd (est. 1864) was acquired. In 1918 the bank acquired control of the Commercial Bank of Spanish America Ltd (est. 1904) and during the First World War expanded into Spain. In 1920 the British Bank of South America Ltd (est. 1863), which had a large presence in Brazil, was acquired thereby making the Anglo-South American Bank the largest British bank in Latin America. Also in 1920 Banco A Edwards y Cia was acquired to give a stronger presence in Chilean domestic banking. In 1923 the Paris branch was converted into the Banque Anglo Sud Americaine and the New York branch became the Anglo American Trust Co Ltd. In 1928 there were thirty-nine branches, total assets were £76 million and capitalisation was £6.8 million; it was the largest British overseas bank. However, by then retrenchment was underway, caused by generally poor management and, in particular, by over commitment to the Chilean nitrate industry. In 1931 the Bank of England rescued the bank from near collapse and in 1936, when still greatly weakened, it was acquired by Bank of London & South America Ltd (est. 1862).

David Joslin, *A Century of Banking in Latin America. The Bank of London & South America Ltd 1862–1962* (Oxford, 1963)

Records 1: Bloomsbury Science Library, University College London, Gower Street, London WC1E 6BT

Letterbooks and files, Iquique to/from Valparaiso and elsewhere 1888–89 1922–29; letterbooks, Santiago to/from London (7) 1895–1907; letterbooks, Punta Arenas to London and branches (10) 1904–34; letterbooks, Valparaiso to/from London and branches (37) 1906–36; letterbooks, Santiago to/from London and branches (39) 1907–37; letterbooks, Coquimbo to/from branches (5) 1911–12, 1923–29, 1932–33; letterbooks, Montevideo to/from various (2) 1912–13, 1931–32; letterbooks, Barranquilla to/from various (3) 1921–22, 1927–28, 1933–34; letterbooks, Buenos Aires to/from London, Santiago and branches (3) 1924–25, 1929–33; letterbooks, Cartagena to Bogota and branches (3) 1925–34; letterbooks, Bogota to London and branches (23) 1926–36; letterbooks, Santa Maria to London and branches (2) 1927–28, 1932–34. [Ref: BOLSA]

Records 2: Lloyds TSB Group plc, Archives, Head Office, 71 Lombard Street, London EC3P 3BS

Staff ledger 1889–1907; annual reports 1889–1935; staff register c.1920; 'left service' ledger 1924–44; amalgamation papers 1936–49.

Records of banks 57

ARBROATH BANKING CO
Arbroath, Tayside

History: This bank was founded in 1825 as a co-partnership by William Kidd, merchant, and James Marnie, manufacturer, both former town provosts, to provide credit to local businessmen. The bank had an authorised capital of £100,000, of which £40,000 was initially paid-up. It attracted 113 shareholders, primarily local merchants, manufacturers and farmers. The bank issued its own notes and opened a branch in Forfar in 1825. During the mid 1830s it played a prominent role in financing the Arbroath & Forfar Railway. However, by 1844, when note circulation was £13,787 and deposits totalled £137,279, the bank became illiquid with large amounts of capital tied up in property. In 1844 it was acquired by Commercial Bank of Scotland (est. 1810) which paid £10,500 for the business and its Arbroath and Forfar property.

C H Robertson, 'The Arbroath Banking Co', *Three Banks Review,* 131 (1981)

Records: The Royal Bank of Scotland plc, Archive Section, 36 St Andrew Square, Edinburgh EH2 2YB

Partnership agreement 1825; merger agreement with Commercial Bank of Scotland 1844.

ARKWRIGHT & CO
Wirksworth, Derbyshire

History: This private bank was established in 1780 as John Toplis. In 1804 it was known as Arkwright, Toplis & Co and later, in 1829, as Arkwright & Co. It was otherwise known as the Wirksworth Bank and the Derbyshire Bank. In 1875 the business was acquired by Moore & Robinson's Nottinghamshire Banking Co Ltd (est. 1802).

Records: Lloyds TSB Group plc, Archives, Head Office, 71 Lombard Street, London EC3P 3BS

Customer ledgers (6) 1804–67 [w]; security books (2) 1857–1900; probate register 1869–1924; profit and loss ledger 1870–1901; amalgamation papers 1875.

THOMAS ASHBY & CO
Staines, Surrey

History: This private bank was established in 1796 as Thomas Ashby & Co. It traded as Thomas Ashby Senr. & Sons from 1811 and subsequently as Thomas Ashby & Co; it was also known as the Staines Bank. In 1877 it

58   *British banking – a guide to historical records*

acquired La Coste & Co (est. 1807) of Chertsey and, following this, at least eleven branches were opened. In 1904 the bank was acquired by Barclay & Co Ltd (est. 1896).

P W Matthews & Anthony W Tuke, *History of Barclays Bank Ltd* (London, 1926)

Records: Barclays Bank plc, Group Archives, Dallimore Road, Wythenshawe, Manchester M23 9JA

Cheque forms 1809–95; passbook 1879–81; charge forms 1886–92; cheque book 1900; staff photograph c.1910.

ASHTON, STALYBRIDGE, HYDE & GLOSSOP BANK LTD
Ashton-under-Lyne, Greater Manchester

History: This joint stock bank was established in 1836 with a paid-up capital of £20,000. It acquired limited liability in 1884. In 1900, when paid-up capital was £50,000, it was acquired by Parr's Bank Ltd (est. 1865).

T E Gregory, *The Westminster Bank Through a Century* (London, 1936)

Records: The Royal Bank of Scotland plc, Archive Section, Regent's House, 42 Islington High Street, London N1 8XL

Deeds of settlement 1836–82; stock register 1836–1900; staff secrecy pledges 1836–1900; directors' minute books (4) 1836–1902; manager's memorandum book 1875–80; half-yearly general balance books 1880–1900; lists of shareholders 1895–99; articles of association 1898; amalgamation agreement 1900.

ATHERLEY & DARWIN
Southampton, Hampshire

History: This private bank was formed in 1770 as Sadleir, Hilgrove, Lowder & Durell. It was styled Atherley, Fall & Atherley from 1821, Atherley & Darwin from 1862 and latterly Atherley, Fall & Co. In 1869 the business merged with Maddison & Co (est. 1785), also of Southampton, to form Maddison, Atherley, Hankinson & Darwin.

Records: Lloyds TSB Group plc, Archives, Head Office, 71 Lombard Street, London EC3P 3BS

General ledgers (2) 1797–1803, 1827–30.

ATKINSON, CRAIG & CO
Penrith, Cumbria

Records of banks   **59**

History: This private bank was formed in 1815 and failed in 1840.

Records: Department of Manuscripts and University Archives, Cambridge University Library, West Road, Cambridge CB3 9DR

Estate, personal and business papers of M Atkinson c.1796–1833. [Ref: Add. MS 7923]

ATTWOOD, SPOONER & CO
Birmingham, West Midlands

History: Isaac Spooner, James Matthias, Aaron Attwood and Thomas Aynsworth formed this private bank in 1791. It became the largest private bank in Birmingham and traditionally held farmers' as well as manufacturers' accounts. In March 1865 the business failed, allegedly due to large withdrawals by the Attwood family. At this time the bank had provisionally agreed to merge with the Birmingham Joint Stock Bank (est. 1861) which, following the collapse, acquired just Attwoods' premises in New Street, Birmingham.

E Edwards, *Personal Recollections of Birmingham and Birmingham Men* (Birmingham, 1877); D J Moss, 'Private Banks of Birmingham', *Business History*, 24 (1982); D J Moss, 'The Bank of England and the Country Banks: Birmingham 1827–33', *Economic History Review*, 34 (1981)

Records: Lloyds TSB Group plc, Archives, Head Office, 71 Lombard Street, London EC3N 4AE

Cash book 1813–45; private ledgers (2) 1854–76 [w].

JOHN AYLWARD
London

History: John Aylward (died 1705) was a general merchant and banker. From at least 1672 he was based at Malaga, Spain. He moved to St Malo, France, in 1687 and subsequently, in 1698, to London where he remained until his death. His trade was chiefly with Spain, Italy, the Low Countries, France and England. His banking activities undoubtedly developed out of his merchanting business and were, presumably, subsidiary to it.

F W Steer, *The Arundel Castle Archives* (1968–80)

Records: The Duke of Norfolk's Archives, Arundel Castle, Arundel BN18 9AB

Letters 1672–76, 1683–1705; miscellaneous business and legal papers 1676–1705; accounts, bills and receipts 1682–1702; papers of his wife 1682–1713; personal correspondence 1683–96; letterbook 1686–87.

60 *British banking – a guide to historical records*

JONATHAN BACKHOUSE & CO
Darlington, County Durham

History: This important private bank was formed in 1774 by James Backhouse (died 1798) and his son Jonathan (died 1826), linen and worsted manufacturers. From 1774 the firm was styled James & Jonathan Backhouse; from 1778 James & Jonathan Backhouse & Co; and from 1798 Jonathan Backhouse & Co; it was otherwise known as the Darlington Bank. In 1815 a branch was opened at Durham after the failure there of Mowbray, Hollingsworth & Co (est. c.1790) and another was opened in 1816 at Sunderland when John & Thos. Cooke & Co (est. 1803) failed. In 1825 other branches were opened at Newcastle and South Shields and another, at about this time, at Stockton-on-Tees. Afterwards agencies were opened at Bishops Auckland, Staindrop, Barnard Castle, Reeth, Richmond, Northallerton, Thirsk, Ayton and Yarm. In 1836 the Newcastle business, followed shortly afterwards by those at Sunderland and South Shields, was sold to the newly formed Northumberland & Durham District Banking Co of which Jonathan Backhouse became manager and Thomas Backhouse a director. Throughout its history the Backhouse family provided the firm's partners and it also established strong links with other powerful private banks through marriage to the Pease family in 1774 and to the Gurney family of Norwich in 1811. In 1893 the balance sheet totalled £3.44 million, capital and reserves were £250,000 and deposits were £2.99 million. In 1896 the business merged with other important private banks to form Barclay & Co Ltd of London.

William Howarth, *Barclay & Co Limited, Being a History of the Old Banking Firm of Barclay & Co* (London, 1901); P W Matthews & Anthony W Tuke, *History of Barclays Bank Ltd* (London, 1926); Maberly Phillips, *Banks, Bankers and Banking in Northumberland, Durham and North Yorkshire* (London, 1894); 'Barclay & Co', *Journal of the Institute of Bankers*, 17 (1896)

Records 1: Durham Record Office, County Hall, Durham DH1 5UL

Banker's licence 1814; letter and bank note proofs 1845. [Ref: D/XD/16/23, D/Wa/1/3/13–14]

Records 2: Durham University Library, Archives and Special Collections, 5 The College, Durham DH1 3EQ

Backhouse family papers nineteenth cent. [Unlisted]

EDWARD BACKWELL
London

Records of banks **61**

History: Edward Backwell (c.1618–83) was apprenticed to London goldsmith Thomas Vyner between 1635 and 1651. He traded as a goldsmith banker in the City of London at Cheapside from 1653 and at the sign of the Unicorn, Lombard Street, from 1654. Elected Alderman of the City of London, he was by the 1650s an active and full-time banker serving an extensive clientele, including government departments and the Protectorate. Along with Sir Thomas Vyner, he produced bullion for Cromwell's coinage. During the 1660s he provided financial services to the Crown. There were runs on his bank in 1665 and 1667, but he continued to thrive and by 1671 over one-fifth of the money in the Exchequer was on loan from Backwell. He kept running cashes and substantial clearing accounts for fellow bankers, carried on an extensive bullion and bills of exchange business with the continent, acted for Charles II as paymaster to overseas garrisons and as agent for the Queen's dowry and was active in various syndicates of tax farmers. His deposits were largely reinvested in the King and government departments. He lost £256,000 with the 'stop' on the Exchequer in 1672 and was insolvent by 1682.

F G Hilton Price, 'Some Account of the Business of Alderman Edward Backwell, Goldsmith and Banker in the Seventeenth Century', *London and Middlesex Archaeological Society Transactions*, 6 (1890); Stephen Quinn, 'Banking Before the Bank: London's Unregulated Goldsmith-Bankers, 1660–1694' (unpub. mss., University of Illinois, 1994); Stephen Quinn, 'Balances and Goldsmith-Bankers: the Co-ordination and Control of Debt Clearing in Seventeenth-Century London', in D M Mitchell (ed.), *Goldsmiths, Silversmiths and Bankers* (London, 1995); Stephen Quinn, 'Goldsmith-Banking: Mutual Acceptance and Interbanker Clearing in Restoration London', *Explorations in Economic History*, 34 (1997); H G Roseveare, 'The Advancement of the King's Credit, 1660–1672' (unpub. mss., Cambridge University, 1962)

Records: The Royal Bank of Scotland plc, Archive Section, Regent's House, 42 Islington High Street, London N1 8XL

Customer ledgers (9) 1663–72; 'Dunkirk' ledger 1656–77; list of tallies 1668; payment instruction 1671.

BACON, COBBOLD & CO
Ipswich, Suffolk

History: This private bank was formed in 1786 as Crickitt, Truelove & Kerridge. The original partners were C A Crickitt MP, who also founded the Colchester Bank, J Kerridge and William Truelove. From 1807 the bank was styled Crickitt, Bacon & Co; from 1826 Bacon, Cobbold, Rodwell, Dunningham, Cobbold & Co (following the entry of the Cobbold family

62   *British banking – a guide to historical records*

of brewers who strengthened the bank after the 1825 banking crisis); Bacon, Cobbold & Co from 1877; Bacon, Cobbold, Tollemache & Co from 1885; and again Bacon, Cobbold & Co from 1899. In 1893 the business merged with Cox, Cobbold & Co of Harwich with which common partners had been shared since about the 1830s. Branches were acquired or opened at Debenham (1839), Woodbridge (1846), Felixstowe (1892), Derby Road, Ipswich (1900) and Dovercourt (1901). The Capital & Counties Bank Ltd (est. 1877) acquired the bank in 1905.

Harold Preston, *Early East Anglian Banks and Bankers* (priv. pub., 1994); A G E Jones, 'Early Banking in Ipswich', *Notes and Queries*, 196 (1951)

Records: Lloyds TSB Group plc, Archives, Head Office, 71 Lombard Street, London EC3P 3BS

Security register 1868–78; day book 1882–88; memorandum book 1886–93; private ledger 1892–1908; balance sheets 1893–1904; amalgamation papers 1904–06.

Ipswich: security registers (3) 1876–1904 [w], signature books (2) 1879–1908.

M & R BADCOCK
Taunton, Somerset

History: This private bank was established by John and Isaac Badcock, woollen drapers, during the late 1790s as an adjunct to their drapery business which had been formed in 1777; it was otherwise known as the Taunton Bank. Isaac died in 1816 and the firm was carried on by John and his son, John, and Daniel Badcock. Branches were opened at Dunstone and Bampton in 1846; later there was at least one additional branch at Williton. The business was later known as H, H J & D Badcock and as M & R Badcock. It was acquired by Stuckey's Banking Co (est. 1826) in 1872.

Philip T Saunders, *Stuckey's Bank* (Taunton, 1928)

Records 1: The Royal Bank of Scotland plc, Archive Section, Regent's House, 42 Islington High Street, London N1 8XL

Partnership agreements (5) 1844–72; letters of advice from customers 1858; private ledger 1868–78; amalgamation papers 1872–74; suspense account 1872–93; private papers of H J Badcock 1877–1926.

Records 2: Somerset Record Office, Obridge Road, Taunton TA2 7PU

Correspondence 1801–31. [Ref: DD/X/HRG4]

Records of banks

63

BALA BANKING CO LTD
Bala, Gwynedd

History: This joint stock bank was formed in 1864 with a paid-up capital of £9,000. Its deposits eventually grew to about £100,000 and it had offices at Bala, Corwen and Dolgellau. The business failed in 1876, having suffered a heavy loss through the failure of a Liverpool corn merchant, and in 1877 was taken over by the North & South Wales Bank (est. 1836) which paid depositors in full.

Records: HSBC Holdings plc, Group Archives, 10 Lower Thames Street, London EC3R 6AE

Liquidation papers 1877.

BALFOUR WILLIAMSON & CO LTD
London and Latin America

History: Scottish traders at Liverpool formed this firm of merchants and merchant bankers in 1851. The firm was associated initially with the Chilean trade, later extending to California. It was a pioneer in the large-scale trade in fruit and Pacific grain. The Bank of London & South America Ltd (est. 1862) acquired the business in 1960, when it acted as a subsidiary specialising in overseas financial and trading operations. It was sold to Lonrho Ltd in 1975.

Wallis Hunter, *Heirs of Great Adventure. The History of Balfour, Williamson & Co Ltd* (priv. pub., 1951–60)

Records: Lloyds TSB Group plc, Archives, Head Office, 71 Lombard Street, London EC3P 3BS

Copy letterbook with financial statements 1852–70; directors' meeting minutes 1960–68.

BANK OF AFRICA LTD
London and Africa

History: This overseas bank was incorporated in 1879 to provide banking services in southern Africa, especially in the colonies of Cape of Good Hope and Natal. The local business of the Oriental Bank Corporation (est. 1851), along with sixteen branches, was acquired to form the nucleus of the new bank. The initial nominal capital was £1 million in 40,000 shares, 10 per cent of which were reserved for subscription in southern Africa. The first head office was at Port Elizabeth but this transferred to Cape Town in 1892. In 1890 total assets equalled £3.37 million and there were nineteen branches. By 1903 nominal capital was £3 million of which

64   *British banking – a guide to historical records*

£1 million was paid-up. In 1912 the bank was acquired by the National Bank of South Africa Ltd (est. 1891) for £1.25 million. It then had over sixty branches, about two-thirds of which were in the Orange Free State and Natal and a few in Rhodesia and Portuguese East Africa.

Anon, *A Banking Centenary. Barclays Bank (Dominion, Colonial & Overseas) 1836–1936* (priv. pub., 1938)

Records: Barclays Bank plc, Group Archives, Dallimore Road, Wythenshawe, Manchester M23 9JA

Directors' meeting minute books (5) 1879–1912; secretary's letterbook 1880–85; credit information on firms in difficulties 1889–1912; agenda book 1905–07; committee book reports 1905–09; house magazine 1906–08.

BANK OF ASIA
Unknown location

History: In the mid-1830s an application was made for a charter for a bank to be called the Bank of Asia. However, it appears that no such bank was established.

Records: Public Record Office, Ruskin Avenue, Kew, Richmond, Surrey TW9 4DU

Prospectus and other papers re application for a charter 1833–36. [Ref: T1/3471]

BANK OF BIRMINGHAM
Birmingham, West Midlands

History: This joint stock bank, formed in 1832, was the second of its kind to be established in Birmingham. However it soon encountered strong competition as in 1833 branches were opened in Birmingham by three banks based outside the city. It also suffered because of the unpopularity of its manager, who had formerly been a partner in Moilliet & Sons. In 1836 the bank was weakened by a major bad debt and was acquired by the Birmingham Banking Co (est. 1829) in 1838.

E Edwards, *Personal Recollections of Birmingham and Birmingham Men* (Birmingham, 1877)

Records 1: HSBC Holdings plc, Group Archives, 10 Lower Thames Street, London EC3R 6AE

Deed of settlement 1832.

Records of banks 65

Records 2: Birmingham City Archives, Chamberlain Square, Birmingham B3 3HQ

Deed of settlement 1832; directors' report with list of shareholders 1833.

BANK OF BOLTON LTD
Bolton, Greater Manchester

History: This joint stock bank was established in 1836. It was incorporated as a limited company, Bank of Bolton Ltd, in 1880 and was acquired by Manchester & County Bank Ltd (est. 1862) in 1896.

Records: The Royal Bank of Scotland plc, Archive Section, Regent's House, 42 Islington High Street, London N1 8XL

Deed of settlement 1836; prospectus 1836; directors' meeting minutes 1836–97; customer ledgers (2) 1839–43, 1893–95; probate register 1839–1900; tender letters, new building 1868; certificate of incorporation 1873; shareholder registers 1873–77, 1879–95; directors' attendance book 1879–97; annual reports 1880–96; board agenda books (3) 1888–97; manager's letterbook 1888–1900; loan minute books (2) 1890–98; customer reference book 1891–1912.

Farnworth: private memorandum books (3) 1864–1903; **Tyldesley:** private memorandum book 1886–97; salary book 1892–1935.

BANK OF ENGLAND
London

History: The Bank of England was formed in 1694 by act of parliament in return for undertaking to make loans to the government to fund the war against France. Its initial subscribed capital, provided by almost 1,300 investors, was £1.2 million, which matched the sum lent to the government by January 1695. By further acts of parliament in 1696 and 1708, the Bank received what amounted to a monopoly of joint stock banking (except in Scotland) which was retained until 1826, meaning that all other banks had to be partnerships of not more than six people. When in 1709 the Bank's charter was renewed, the authorised capital was increased to almost £4.5 million and was soon paid-up. Meanwhile the first services were provided for the government, for example the circulation of Exchequer Bills from 1696 and the receiving agency for the 1707 Lottery. Alongside this, a more broadly-based banking business developed, running accounts for non-government customers, discounting bills and dealing in exchange and bullion. Almost immediately, the Bank issued its own notes but had no monopoly in this. As a testament to its stability, the Bank withstood without difficulty the South Sea Bubble of 1720. In 1734 it

66 British banking – a guide to historical records

moved to its Threadneedle Street site. In the 1740s, with the resumption of war with France coupled with a Jacobite rebellion at home, £1 million was advanced to the government and the Bank's capital was increased to about £11 million. More government funds were raised through the issue of annuities at a time when, between 1727 and 1763, the national debt increased sixfold to £140 million, and then to £250 million by 1783; this represented a huge increase in the Bank's activities. By the early 1780s, it charged the government £550 per £1 million of capital managed. During the European Wars (1793–1815) the Bank's central importance in national affairs was underlined through its successful management of the currency during the prolonged suspension of cash payments. The Bank, with unimpaired credit, thus carried on its business through the issue of bank notes that were inconvertible into gold. The Bank also facilitated government expenditure through the expansion of the National Debt to an unprecedented level. Larger premises were required for this increased workload; in about 1800 the acquisition of the Bank's entire Threadneedle Street site was completed and Sir John Soane was commissioned to modify and extend the existing structures behind his famous perimeter screen wall. Following the financial crisis of 1825, the Bank was permitted to open branches that facilitated both its commercial banking business and its management of the national currency. Branches opened at Newcastle, Gloucester, Manchester, Swansea, Birmingham, Liverpool, Bristol, Leeds and Exeter before 1828 and shortly afterwards at Hull, Norwich, Plymouth, Portsmouth and Leicester. This, together with a growing perception of the Bank's stability, led to the number of accounts increasing from 850 to 4,000 between 1823 and 1833. Thus the Bank's role as a commercial bank continued; it was only at the end of the century that an increasing responsibility for the country's financial system dictated that it was no longer appropriate to compete for ordinary banking business. In 1834 the government's Exchequer was swept away and the Bank now acted in its place, confirming its role as the government's banker. Meanwhile the Bank's responsibility for note issue increased. In 1833, when joint stock banks were first permitted within London, they were not allowed to issue their own notes and then in 1844 no new partnerships or new joint stock banks outside Scotland were permitted to issue notes. In the second half of the nineteenth century the Bank's history, while for the most part unremarkable, was dominated by a growing control over the monetary system through the use of Bank Rate. In 1855 the Western Branch (sold to Royal Bank of Scotland in 1930) was opened in London's West End, to accommodate merchants who had moved their homes from the City. The Law Courts Branch (closed 1980s) opened in 1868 to provide an enhanced service to the courts and legal profession in such matters as estates in Chancery, funds paid into court and trust administration. In 1890 the

Records of banks 67

Bank's role as guardian of financial good order was underlined through the launch of its first 'lifeboat' to rescue a bank in danger of collapse, namely Baring Brothers, in what became known as the Baring Crisis. During the First World War the Bank managed a huge increase in government debt and, with varying success, exercised an unprecedented control over the banking and monetary system including the establishment of a moratorium at the beginning of the 1914–18 war. In these years many overseas governments opened accounts at the Bank for the first time. Between the wars the Bank was dominated by its greatest leader, Montagu Norman, and under him its metamorphosis into a fully-fledged central bank was virtually completed. In the 1920s the overwhelming economic need was perceived to be a return to the gold standard which was achieved (but without a gold circulation) in 1925 and maintained until 1931. In achieving this, the Bank's role was of central importance, especially in obtaining sources of overseas finance during the 1931 crisis. Less visible was its work in connection with German reparations, the repayment arrangements for British government overseas war debt, the establishment of central banks in the Dominions and India and the encouragement of central banking in Europe as a means to monetary stability and settlement of inter-allied war debts. Following the departure from gold, the Exchange Equalisation Account, now required to smooth variations in sterling exchange, was established and managed. At home the Bank confirmed its intention of withdrawing from commercial banking which, *inter alia*, had already entailed the closure of the Western Branch, and it promoted the rationalisation and reconstruction of old industries through its involvement in Bankers' Industrial Trust Development Co Ltd and Securities Management Ltd. In the 1930s it handled the conversion of War Loan to 3.5 per cent as a step to cheaper money. Added to this was the supervision of an increasing range of controls over the markets required to protect the economy from forces emanating from abroad. All of this activity took place during the wholesale rebuilding of the Bank's premises, to the designs of Sir Herbert Baker, but which retained Soane's perimeter walls. Controls were greatly added to during the Second World War to ensure economic stability at home and to conduct economic warfare abroad. In particular the Bank administered Exchange Control regulations, introduced in 1939, until their abolition in 1979. The Bank was involved in the establishment in 1946 of the International Monetary Fund and The International Bank for Reconstruction and Development, both born at the 1944 meetings at Bretton Woods. In 1946 the Bank was nationalised although it maintained a degree of autonomy from government. In the post-war world it developed its main functions of acting as the government's bank and as the banker's bank. Its supervision of the financial markets and of banks and other financial institutions was much extended in the 1980s. In 1997,

68   *British banking – a guide to historical records*

however, those supervisory functions were hived off to an entirely separate new body. In its operational role, the Bank also lost its traditional management of the National Debt to a new government agency, but gained independence in setting Base Rate through a new Monetary Policy Committee.

Anon, *Bank of England Guide to the Archives* (priv. pub., 1998); W Marston Acres, *The Bank of England From Within* (Oxford, 1931); John H Clapham, *The Bank of England. A History* (Cambridge, 1944); John Fforde, *The Bank of England and Public Policy 1941–1958* (Cambridge, 1992); John Giuseppi, *The Bank of England. A History from its Foundation in 1694* (London, 1966); Elizabeth Hennessy, *A Domestic History of the Bank of England 1930–1960* (Cambridge, 1992); R S Sayers, *The Bank of England 1891–1944* (Cambridge, 1976)

Records 1: Bank of England, Threadneedle Street, London EC2R 8AH

Governors and Secretaries (1694–1986): records of the Bank's Court of Directors and Committee of Treasury, and files of successive governors and secretaries, including a large proportion of the Bank's oldest records which were used extensively by Sir John Clapham in the preparation of his official history of the Bank, published in 1944; more recent material including the personal files of directors and senior officials.

Establishment Department (1695–1989): staff and accommodation records including recruitment, work assessment, reclassification schemes, pensions, building plans 1934–79, staff lists, and the quarterly staff magazine; minutes and accounts of the Bank of England Club (founded in 1883 to provide clerks with canteen facilities); material re the Bank's now discontinued picquet which was provided by detachments of British troops from 1895.

Administration Department (1695–1989): records concerning major facilitative functions of the Bank, including the Governor's 'Empire Letters' to governors and central banks abroad, 1928–74; Banking Department general ledger (the Bank's main book of account including details of all income and expenditure 1695–1983); the Bank's 'red book' containing half-yearly balances 1806–1970; papers of twentieth-century officials and advisers including Sir Maurice Parsons, L P Thompson-McCausland, Professor Henry Clay, H A Siepmann and Lord Cobbold.

Cashier's Department (1694–1989): returns of notes issued 1844–1988; customers' correspondence and summaries of transactions on their behalf 1794–1918; papers re the purchase and sale of bullion 1758–1918; ledgers 1694–1945; ledgers and letterbooks from the Bank's branches 1826–1986.

Records of banks 69

Accountant's (later Registrar's) Department (1694–1987): records arising from registration of government stock issues, including the history and management of stocks, legal opinions and court cases 1694–1978, dividend payments 1790–1967, and the issue of loans 1870–1985.

Economic Intelligence Department (1758–1993): records dealing primarily with the department's preparation of British balance of payments estimates, but also including papers re a wide range of domestic economic statistics and information. The latter include home finance reports, aggregated from a large number of statistical returns made by banks and discount houses, and information on industrial output, investment and prices, etc, compiled by the Industrial Finance Unit. (In the 1980s the Central Statistical Office assumed some of the Department's functions).

Overseas Department (1800–1985): records dealing with overseas financial and economic intelligence and many aspects of relations with other central banks and the League of Nations from 1931, post-war reconstruction 1941–64, and international monetary reform 1958–64; papers of Sir Otto Niemeyer 1922–65, which cover almost every foreign country.

Exchange Control Department (1932–82): records mainly re the working of Defence (Finance) Regulations 1939, and thereafter the Exchange Control Act 1947.

Printing Works (1837–1989): accounts and other papers re the design and printing of bank notes and experiments with watermarks; *The Britannia Quarterly*, founded in 1919 as a sporting and social diary of the Bank's printing works at St Luke's, Old Street, London; papers re German forgeries during the Second World War.

Audit Department (1894–1973): records, including reports, letters and replies, re audits at head office, the printing works and branches.

Securities Management Trust Ltd (1900–77): records of a wholly-owned subsidiary of the Bank which was set up in 1929 to investigate and advise on financial, industrial and economic questions and to aid the formulation and execution of schemes of arrangement for the financing, development, amalgamation or reconstruction of companies; papers of Sir Charles Bruce-Gardner, Frank Hodges and other directors.

Bankers' Industrial Development Trust Co Ltd (1930–44): records of a company established in 1930 by the Bank and other financial institutions to receive and consider schemes submitted by industries which sought rationalisation, either on an industrial or regional basis.

Freshfields (1695–1931): records concerning the work of the Bank's solicitors including the prosecution of forgers 1696–1905, most notably

70 British banking – a guide to historical records

the Warren Case of 1873; letters written from prison by forgers and debtors seeking clemency or financial help 1782–1844; legal opinion on the security of loans to government, local authorities, commercial undertakings and private individuals; documents re the failure of business customers; and civil court actions (usually stock management cases) including the South Sea Bubble 1720–23.

Museum printed and manuscript collections (1681–1987): material from a variety of sources illustrating the Bank's history, including title deeds, maps and plans; examples of bonds, stock receipts, mortgages, etc; papers on events such as the defence of the bank against the Chartists 1844; papers of Humphrey Morice (died 1731), a former governor.

Records 2: Department of Western Manuscripts, Bodleian Library, Broad Street, Oxford OX1 3BG

Charter of incorporation 1694; rules and order for Bank 1694; list of staff with salaries c.1710. [Ref: Ms Eng.hist b 1 fol 36,57; Ms Rawlinson D 1126 fol 61]

Records 3: The Royal Bank of Scotland plc, Archive Section, Regent's House, 42 Islington High Street, London N1 8XL

London, Western: customer memorandum book 1855–62; agents' letterbooks (4) 1858–77, 1885–98; deposition of witnesses re forgery 1873; remembrancers (2) 1875–82; opinion book 1881–88; memoranda re share transactions 1897–98; circular re take-over by Royal Bank of Scotland 1930.

Records 4: Public Record Office, Ruskin Avenue, Kew, Richmond TW9 4DU

Records of Royal Mint 1657–1951; correspondence with National Debt Office 1808–1942; papers re regulation of Bank's affairs 1808–1946; bankruptcy books 1832–51; ledgers, journals and cash books re daily transactions on Exchequer account (59)1854–1946; registers of transactions on Exchequer account re supply services (63)1854–1955; registers of daily receipts into Exchequer account (34) 1855–1954; Finance Division out-letters 1886–1913; Treasury out-letters 1915–19. [Ref: MINT18; NDO7; T241; AO18; T257–258; T256; T239; T97; T111]

BANK OF INDIA
London and Asia

History: The formation of this bank was proposed in 1836, but it appears never to have commenced business.

Records of banks 71

Records 1: The Baring Archive, ING Baring Holdings Ltd, 60 London Wall, London EC2M 5TQ

Note of a meeting of the directors 1836. [Ref: HC1.48b]

Records 2: University of London Library, Senate House, Malet Street, London WC1E 7HU

Papers re establishment 1833–36. [Ref: ULL MS 172]

Records 3: Public Record Office, Ruskin Avenue, Kew, Richmond, Surrey TW9 4DU

Prospectus and papers re establishment 1833–36. [Ref: T1/3471]

BANK OF LEEDS LTD
Leeds, West Yorkshire

History: This joint stock bank was established in 1864 and was acquired by National Provincial Bank of England (est. 1833) in 1878.

Records: The Royal Bank of Scotland plc, Archive Section, Regent's House, 42 Islington High Street, London N1 8XL

Information book (customers, salaries interest rates etc) 1865–80.

BANK OF LONDON
London

History: This joint stock bank was established in Threadneedle Street, City of London, in 1855 with a paid-up capital of £300,000. At the end of its first year, deposits stood at £1.36 million and by 1864 they had grown to £4.89 million. A branch was opened in Charing Cross. In 1866 the bank experienced serious difficulties, in part caused by default on a £500,000 loan made to the Atlantic & Great Western Railway. Attempts were made to reach agreement with the Consolidated Bank for the transfer to it of the Bank of London's business, but the agreement was soon rescinded. The company was placed in the care of a committee to manage its liquidation and shareholders subsequently received substantial payments.

T E Gregory, *The Westminster Bank Through A Century* (London, 1936)

Records: The Royal Bank of Scotland plc, Archive Section, Regent's House, 42 Islington High Street, London N1 8XL

Engraving, Threadneedle Street office 1855; staff rules book 1865; amalgamation agreement 1866; creditors' agreement 1867.

72 *British banking – a guide to historical records*

BANK OF LONDON & SOUTH AMERICA LTD
London and Latin America

History: This bank was incorporated in London in 1862 as the London, Buenos Aires & River Plate Bank Ltd, its promoters being City bankers and River Plate merchants. Paid-up share capital was initially £200,000, rising to £600,000 by 1867. In 1863 the first branch opened at Buenos Aires and benefited from the services of a local director, Noberto de la Riestra, a former Argentine finance minister. It provided local banking services, issued notes and financed Argentina's trade with Britain. A branch at Montevideo, Uruguay, also opened in 1863, and other Argentine branches quickly followed at Rosario and Cordoba, although the latter had agency status until 1869. The bank was renamed the London & River Plate Bank Ltd in 1865. The Buenos Aires private bank, Banco Carabassa, was acquired in 1891 and, later in the 1890s, the branch network was extended to Paysandu, Mendoza, Bahia Blanca and Tucuman. In the early 1890s the bank withstood a series of banking crises in both Argentina and Uruguay which confirmed it as one of the largest and most successful banks in the region. In 1891, as a result of the growing trade between Brazil and Argentina, the bank extended its operations to Brazil through the acquisition of the Brazilian business of the English Bank of Rio de Janeiro Ltd (est. 1863). Before 1914 Brazilian branches were opened at Pernambuco, Para, Santos, Sao Paulo, Vitoria, Bahia, Curitiba and Manaos. In 1891 a New York branch was opened, followed by one in Paris in 1895. In 1906 the first Chilean branch opened at Valparaiso but a second, at Santiago, did not follow until 1917. By the First World War the bank was the largest and most successful British overseas bank in terms of assets and in 1918 was acquired by Lloyds Bank Ltd for £5.9 million. Expansion followed, with branches opening in Paraguay and, in much larger numbers, in Colombia, where the local banking business of Frank A Koppel was acquired. In 1923 the bank merged with the London & Brazilian Bank Ltd (est. 1862) and changed its name to the Bank of London & South America Ltd. Lloyds remained the controlling shareholder with a 57 per cent interest, and duplicated branches and other facilities were closed. The depression of the early 1930s created severe difficulties for the bank but it remained fundamentally strong. As a direct result of this, in 1936 the Anglo-South American Bank Ltd (est. 1888), then in serious difficulties, was acquired at the behest of the Bank of England. The number of countries in which the bank had branches was doubled; it was now the sole British overseas bank operating in the continent. After 1945 the business prospered and in the late 1950s and 1960s, under the leadership of Sir George Bolton, it was transformed into a truly international bank rather than one focused on Latin America. In 1958 a joint venture with the Bank of Montreal, known

Records of banks 73

as the Bank of London & Montreal Ltd, was formed to acquire the bank's branches in Central America and in the north eastern countries of South America. A further eighteen branches were soon opened in the Caribbean and on the mainland and in 1970 the business was reorganised. In 1960 the old established merchant house of Balfour Williamson & Co Ltd (est. 1851) was acquired and a year later the Compania Financiera de Londres was formed at Buenos Aires to assist in financing industrial development. In 1965, in order to support increasing activity in the eurobond and eurodollar markets, Mellon Bank & Trust Co of the USA acquired a 15 per cent interest in the bank. In 1971 the bank, along with Lloyds Bank Europe, was transferred to a new public company in which Lloyds Bank had a 55 per cent interest, Lloyds & Bolsa International Bank Ltd, and in 1973 Lloyds acquired all the shares it did not own. The bank was renamed Lloyds Bank International Ltd in 1974. Ownership was transferred to Lloyds Bank plc in 1985. In 1988 the bank was renamed Lloyds Bank (BLSA) Ltd.

David Joslin, *A Century of Banking in Latin America. The Bank of London & South America Ltd 1862–1962* (Oxford, 1973)

Records 1: Lloyds TSB Bank plc, Archives, Head Office, 71 Lombard Street, London EC3P 3BS

Annual reports 1921–71; general meeting minutes 1923–61; head office and branch accounts with profit and loss accounts 1924–33; board minutes (14) 1925–74; summary balance sheets 1936–41, 1948–63; summary profit and loss ledgers (45) 1936–64; register of staff leavers 1944–52; register of staff entering bank 1944–58; executive committee minutes (8) 1948–55, 1964–71; chairman's committee minutes (6) 1959–64.

Records 2: Bloomsbury Science Library, University College London, Gower Street, London WC1E 6BT

Secretary's letterbooks (2) 1863–1923; letter packets, branches to Montevideo 1865–67, 1870–73; letterbooks, London to Buenos Aires (33) 1865–1923; letterbooks, Montevideo to London, Paris, Buenos Aires and branches (28) 1869–1922; letterbooks, Buenos Aires to London, Paris and branches (35) 1869–1925; letterbooks, branches to Buenos Aires (11) 1870–1931; letterbooks, London to Montevideo (10) 1872–1920; letterbooks, Rosario to Buenos Aires and London (6) 1872–86, 1890–1921; letterbooks and packets, Rio de Janeiro to/from London and branches (59) 1891–1930; letterbooks, Paysandu to various (4) 1892–1919; letterbooks, Paris to Buenos Aires (4) 1893–1908; letterbooks, Para to various (2) 1894–1901; letterbooks, Mendoza to Buenos Aires (7) 1896–1922; letterbooks, Bahia to Buenos Aires (4) 1898–1922; let-

74   *British banking – a guide to historical records*

ters, Santos to Rio, 1899–1901; letterbooks, Sao Paulo to various (3) 1899–1900, 1914–23; letters, Pernambuco to/from Rio and branches 1901–02, 1923; letterbooks, Salto to various (2) 1905–17, 1913–50; letterbooks, Valparaiso to London, Buenos Aires and Santiago (16) 1906–31; letterbooks, Bahia to London (2) 1913–21; letterbooks, Santiago to London, Buenos Aires and Valparaiso (21) 1913–31, 1937–38; letterbooks, Santiago to London, Valparaiso and Buenos Aires (11) 1914–23; letterbook, Rosario to various 1918–23; letters, Brazilian branches to/from London 1919–22; letterbook, Montevideo 1919–24; letterbooks, Sao Paulo to Rio, London and branches (3) 1919–30; letterbooks, Para to London, Rio and branches (66) 1919–37; letterbooks, Bogota to London and elsewhere (2) 1920–30; letterbook, London to Valparaiso 1921–26; letterbooks, Antofagasta to London and branches (15) 1921–31; letterbooks, Rio to London and elsewhere (15) 1922–33; letters from Paysandu 1922–37; letterbooks, Buenos Aires to/from London and branches (9) 1922–37; letterbook, Rio Grande to London 1923–30; letterbook, Porto Alegre to Rio 1923–30; letterbooks, Brazilian branches to/from London (11) 1923–33; letterbook, Bogota to various 1924–30; letterbooks, Valparaiso to/from London, Buenos Aires and branches (21) 1924–32, 1937–39; letterbooks, Barranquilla to London and branches (2) 1925–30; letterbooks, Chilean branches to/from London 1926–27, 1932–34; letterbooks, Bahia to Rio and London (3) 1926–35; letterbooks, Asuncion to Buenos Aires (2) 1928–30, 1933–34; reports, Pelotas to London 1929; letters, Vitoria to London 1931–33. [Ref: BOLSA]

BANK OF MANCHESTER LTD
Manchester, Greater Manchester

History: This joint stock bank was established in 1829 with a nominal capital of £2 million. It appeared to trade successfully and in 1842 acquired the Alliance Bank (of Manchester) (est. 1836) which had been formed to salvage part of the business of the defunct Northern & Central Bank of England (est. 1834). In 1842 the bank collapsed with losses of £800,000. It took ten years to wind up the bank's business which in 1852 was reformed with a new board and deed of settlement. In 1858 it acquired limited liability and in 1863, when its paid-up capital was £227,000, it amalgamated with Heywood, Kennard & Co (est. 1800) of London to form Consolidated Bank Ltd.

T E Gregory, *The Westminster Bank Through A Century* (London, 1936); Leo H Grindon, *Manchester Banks and Bankers* (Manchester, 1877)

Records: The Royal Bank of Scotland plc, Archive Section, Regent's House, 42 Islington High Street, London N1 8XL

Records of banks 75

Presscuttings 1828–29, 1852–63, 1923; papers re Edmund Burdekin, general manager 1829–42; deeds of settlement 1829, 1836, 1858; share certificate: 1830; forms n.d.; salaries book 1830–1916; bank notes 1833–40; manager's letterbook 1833–67; shareholder list 1836; advances: securities 1837–62, correspondence 1862; share transfer: forms 1841, register 1845–65; annual report 1842; booklet re acquisition of Alliance Bank 1842; directors' meeting minutes 1844–65; indenture re assets realisation 1849; daily minutes 1856–63; certificate of incorporation 1859; resolutions re customer accounts 1861; papers re bills of exchange 1861–62; papers re merger with Heywood Kennard & Co 1863.

BANK OF MAURITIUS LTD
London and Africa

History: This British-owned overseas bank was formed in London in 1894 to take over the Mauritius business of the New Oriental Bank Corporation (est. as Oriental Bank Corporation in 1851); its paid-up capital was £125,550. The bank's only Mauritius branch was at Port Louis and much of its business derived from the finance of the island's sugar industry. Lord Stanmore, former Governor of Mauritius, was a prime mover in the bank's formation and its first chairman. The bank made steady but cautious progress, but was always vulnerable to fluctuating world sugar prices and was hampered by an inability to employ profitably all of its resources. In 1911 a branch was opened in the Seychelles and in 1913 assets totalled £600,000. By 1916, when its reserve fund was £100,000 and its assets were £800,000, the Mercantile Bank of India Ltd (est. 1853) acquired its business and the bank was placed in voluntary liquidation.

Records: HSBC Holdings plc, Group Archives, 10 Lower Thames Street, London EC3R 6AE

Memorandum and articles of association 1894–1911; seal book 1894–1916; annual reports and balance sheets 1895–1915; share registers (3) 1895–1916; directors' meeting minutes 1912–16; staff report 1916; amalgamation papers 1916.

BANK OF NIGERIA LTD
London and Africa

History: This British-owned overseas bank was formed in 1899 as the Anglo-African Bank Ltd to do business in British colonies in West Africa. It was promoted by a syndicate of traders, including the Royal Niger Co and the African Association, as a direct competitor to the Bank of British West Africa Ltd whose local monopoly power the syndicate's members resented. The Anglo-African Bank's branches were mostly in the Niger

76 *British banking – a guide to historical records*

region of Nigeria and on the Ivory Coast. In 1905 it was renamed the Bank of Nigeria Ltd. By 1912 its paid-up capital was just over £60,000 and it had ten branches. In the same year it merged with the Bank of British West Africa Ltd (est. 1894), the two by then having endured many years of intense competition, and was placed in voluntary liquidation.

Richard Fry, *Bankers in West Africa. The Story of the British Bank of West Africa Ltd* (London, 1976)

Records: Guildhall Library, Aldermanbury, London EC2P 2EJ

Directors' and general meeting agenda book 1913–40; signature book 1907–19; amalgamation papers, 1911–13. [Ref: MS 24523–24524]

BANK OF PRESTON
Preston, Lancashire

History: This joint stock bank was promoted in 1836 but not formed.

Records: Lancashire Record Office, Bow Lane, Preston PR1 2RE

Papers re promotion 1836. [Ref: DDTs Box 33]

BANK OF SCOTLAND
Edinburgh, Lothian

History: The Governor and Company of the Bank of Scotland was created by an act of the parliament of Scotland in 1695. Its nominal capital was £1.2 million Scots, it was granted a monopoly of banking in Scotland for twenty-one years and its proprietors were given limited liability. The bank began trading in 1696, 136 proprietors in Scotland and thirty-six in London subscribing a paid-up capital of £120,000. Unlike the Bank of England, the company was formed primarily as a trading bank, designed to help develop Scotland's North Sea trade and economic development, and possessed very limited responsibility for handling government revenues in Scotland. After the Act of Union of 1707, the bank oversaw the Scottish Mint and supervised the re-minting of the Scottish coinage into sterling. The issue of paper currency, either as transferable bills of exchange or promissory notes, was an important part of the bank's daily business, and the right of note issue has been maintained to the present day. Early attempts at providing a branch network failed and the bank's activities were confined to Edinburgh and the east coast of Scotland. In 1727 the Royal Bank of Scotland was founded and there followed a period of intense competition as the banks tried to drive each other out of business. After 1750, with the shift of economic focus in Scotland to Glasgow and the west, Edinburgh's banks faced energetic new competitors more

Records of banks 77

attuned to the needs of developing commerce. From the 1770s the bank began to develop a branch system in Scotland, extending to eighteen branches in 1793, fifty-four in 1853 and 111 by 1900. During the nineteenth century Scotland created more capital than could be re-invested locally and there developed a need to place funds either in government bonds or in overseas investment. Until the opening of a London branch in 1865, this was undertaken by Smiths, Payne & Smith, Coutts & Co and the Bank of England. Plans were developed for an English branch network but opposition from English banks and an 1875 agreement between English and Scottish banks whereby they agreed not to open branches in each other's country, prevented this. In 1955 The Bank of Scotland (1951) Act permitted the bank to raise capital on the open market rather than by private act of parliament as had previously been the case. In 1955 it acquired the Glasgow-based Union Bank of Scotland Ltd (est. 1830) and in 1958 bought a consumer credit company, now known as NWS Bank plc, which has continued to specialise in short term credit operations, leasing and consumer lending. In 1971 the bank also acquired British Linen Bank (est. 1746) which in 1977 was revived as the bank's merchant banking subsidiary. The 1970s and 1980s saw a rapid expansion of the bank's activities. Financing of North Sea oil led to the establishment of branches in the USA and Russia and to the formation of an international division. A credit and processing centre was established in 1985 and the bank attempted to expand within the UK market by using electronic technology rather than the creation of a branch network. In the 1990s the Bank of Wales plc was established as a regional bank and more recent ventures have included Countrywide Bank Ltd, New Zealand, and Bank West of Perth, Australia.

Alan Cameron, *Bank of Scotland 1695–1995. A Very Singular Institution* (Edinburgh, 1995); Charles A Malcolm, *The Bank of Scotland 1695–1945* (Edinburgh, 1945); Manfred Pohl & Sabine Freitag, *Handbook on the History of European Banks* (Aldershot, 1994); Richard Saville, *Bank of Scotland. A History 1695–1995* (Edinburgh, 1996)

Records 1: Bank of Scotland Archive, Operational Services Division, 12 Bankhead Terrace, Sighthill, Edinburgh EH11 4DY

Teller's book 1696–1701; cash books 1696–1737; general journals 1696–1809; directors' and general meeting minutes 1696–1936; ledgers, journals, allotment records, transfer ledgers re bank stock and investment 1696–twentieth cent; bank note registers 1696–twentieth cent; minutes of proprietors in England 1697–1702; list of proprietors 1697–1861; ledgers, lists, receipts etc re dividends paid 1698–twentieth cent; general ledgers 1703–1964; 'adventurers' journals' 1706–69; committee of directors min-

78　　　*British banking – a guide to historical records*

utes 1711–1805; salary lists 1730–1823; 'adventurers' ledgers' 1731–49; letterbooks to British correspondent banks 1751–1923; promissory notes 1764–1809; 'directors' daily sheets or order books 1793–1803; letters to 'private parties' 1801–twentieth cent; ledgers (3) 1803–22; private and secret letterbooks 1803–1970; directors' standing order book 1809–23; directors' duty rosters 1809–64; correspondent department in-letters from private parties 1809–1968; register and other papers re bad debts c.1809– twentieth cent; deposit receipt registers 1810–twentieth cent; cash, deposit, consignment, parish savings bank accounts balance books 1819–32; customer signature books 1820–1935; investment ledgers 1828–71; customer credit opinions 1830–84; deposits, loans, investments and circulation statements 1832–twentieth cent; law department records c.1833–twentieth cent; circular letters 1834–94; accounts with British correspondents 1834–98; London office abstracts and balances 1834–1959; proprietors' meetings minutes 1834–1971; customer report books (3) 1837–54; directors' administrative order book 1837–57; government account ledger 1837–63; government account cash books 1838–75; register of annuities falling due 1840–94; bond books (3) 1844–1903; safe custody registers 1846–twentieth cent; branch profit statements 1846–62; manager's cash account proposals 1852–94; closing entry book 1853–55; books of annual reports of Scottish banks (3) 1853–1917; bills of exchange books 1854–1938; customer credits books 1854–1942; salary books 1855–1945; minute books (2) 1855–64; fidelity books 1857–twentieth cent; balance sheets and profit and loss accounts 1856–1946; arrangements, accounts, letters re foreign correspondents 1860–70; casual proposals and order book 1860–80; manager's private letterbooks (5) 1862–71, 1877–78, 1893; private letterbooks (27) 1862–1900, 1927; correspondents' commission on accounts etc 1864– 67; half-yearly balance books 1865–1960; official letterbooks (6) 1867–73; business statistics books (2) 1868–1913; security registers 1870–twentieth cent; bank property reports c.1870–1935; opinion books (2) 1873–75; special Edinburgh and London office in-letterbooks (17) 1874–98; security registers for bills overdrafts etc (7) 1874–1936; failure book 1875–1907; bank surveyor's letterbooks 1875–1929; 'progressive view of overdrafts and deposits' 1879–88; procedure books (3) 1879–98; benefit/pension fund accounts 1880–n.d.; clerk of work's letterbooks 1882–1931; cash credit proposals book 1883–94; specifications for work at bank premises 1884–1935; review of current accounts 1885–1902; ledger balances 1886– 1961; discount account proposals book 1887–1903; letters from Edinburgh office 1888–96; analysis of expenditure book' 1896–97; accountants' office circular letters 1903–24; security letterbook 1904.

Aberdeen, George Street: 1878–1943; **Aberdeen, 40 Union Street:** 1780– 1923; **Aberdeen, 355 Union Street:** 1932–58; **Aberfeldy:** 1857–1924;

Records of banks 79

Aberfoyle: 1923–61; Airdrie: 1836–56; Alexandria: 1906–34; Alloa: 1832–1956; Alva: 1955–58; Alyth: 1864–89; Annan: 1864–1928; Arbroath: 1855–1927; Ardgay: 1906–07; Ardrossan: 1839–1905; Auchterarder: 1834–1946; Auchtermuchty: 1833–1957; Avoch: 1895–1953; Ayr: 1776–1934; Ayr, Burns Statue Square: 1922–51; Ballater: c.1883–1912; Banff and Macduff: 1878–1951; Barrhead: 1857–1942; Bathgate: 1848–84; Bearsden: 1891–1925; Beauly: 1864–1910; Bellshill: 1874–1928; Blackwaterfoot: 1924–30; Blackford: 1868–1951; Blairgowrie, High Street: 1839–1943; Blairgowrie, Wellmeadows: 1865–1934; Bonar Bridge: 1857–61; Bo'ness: 1898–c.1961; Bonnyrigg and Lasswade: 1874–1950; Bothwell: 1923–32; Braemar: 1873–1957; Brechin: 1872–1959; Broadford: 1911–59; Brodick: 1922–28; Buckie: 1876–1934; Buchlyvie: 1876–78; Burghead: 1866–1904; Callander: 1842–58; Camelon: 1924–52; Campbeltown: 1884–1930; Carnoustie: 1874–1936; Castle Douglas: 1840–64; Coatbridge: 1900–21; Coldstream: 1855–1930; Coupar Angus: 1853–1956; Crieff: 1818–1971; Cromarty: 1839–46; Cullen & Portknockie: 1837–1955; Cupar: 1955–58; Denny: 1874–78; Dingwall: 1839–1959; Dornoch: 1839–1938; Doune: 1840–1956; Dumbarton: 1879–1958; Dunblane: 1843–1958; Dundee: 1872–1954; Dunfermline: 1783–1939; Dunkeld: 1834–1903; Dunning: 1856–1967; Dysart: 1854–1928; Edinburgh (twenty-nine branches): c.1854–1969; Edzell: 1945–55; Elgin: 1839–1930; Eskbank: 1896–1953; Falkirk: 1826–69; Fochabers: 1804–44; Forfar: 1865–1933; Forres: 1839–1938; Fort Augustus: 1883–1944; Fortrose: 1864–1926; Fort William: 1874–51; Fraserburgh: 1835–1958; Galashiels: 1857–1953; Garmouth: 1841–1968; Gatehouse of Fleet: 1856–1924; Glasgow (twelve branches): c.1855–1938; Glenlivet: 1875–79; Glenrothes: 1854–55; Glenurquhart: 1877–84; Gorebridge: c.1925–50; Grahamston: 1922–25; Grangemouth: 1874–1927; Grantown-on-Spey: 1839–1940; Greenock (two branches): 1836–1926; Gullane: c.1922–42; Haddington: c.1783–1947; Halkirk: 1883–1940; Hamilton: 1857–81; Hawick: 1904–31; Helensburgh: 1869–1949; Hillfoot: 1933–38; Hopeman: c.1907–52; Huntly: c.1887–1951; Inverleithen: 1863–1956; Inverness: 1775–1937; Inverurie: 1834–1958; Jedburgh: 1864–1928; Kelso: 1774–1859; Killin: 1853–1957; Kilmarnock: 1838–1929; Kincardine: 1832–1907; Kinghorn: 1932–69; Kingussie: 1846–1925; Kirkcaldy: 1785–1959; Kirkcudbright: 1790–1957; Kirkwall: 1878–80; Kirriemuir: 1876–1968; Kyle of Lochalsh: c.1906–26; Lairg: 1865–1958; Lamlash: 1879–1913; Lauder: 1839–1947; Leith: 1829–1910; Lerwick: 1838–1958; Leslie: 1865–1957; Lochgelly: 1856–1955; Lochmaddy: 1875–84; Lockerbie: 1877–1939; Lossiemouth: 1865–1954; Macduff: 1875–1955; Mallaig: 1835–1950; Milngavie: 1886–1926; Moffat: 1857–1946; Montrose: 1835–1930; Motherwell: 1865–1926; Nairn: 1842–1958; New Cumnock:

80   *British banking – a guide to historical records*

1838–1933; **New Pitsligo:** 1852–58; **Oban:** 1865–1927; **Paisley:** 1836–1938; **Peebles:** 1857–1930; **Perth:** 1784–1930; **Pitlochry:** 1835–1958; **Polmont:** c.1914–70; **Port Glasgow:** 1883–1925; **Portsoy:** 1846–1949; **Partick:** 1911–51; **Rothes:** 1855–1928; **Rothesay:** 1879–1928; **St Andrews:** 1792–1935; **Saltcoats:**1878–1925; **Sandyford:** 1894–95; **Scone:** 1930–68; **Shawlands:** 1908–11; **Slamannan:** 1878–81; **Stevenston:** 1912–17; **Stirling:** 1788–1927; **Stonehaven:** 1825–1953; **Stornoway:** 1874–1907; **Strathaven:** 1837–74; **Tain:** 1879–1960; **Tarbert:** 1947–53; **Tarland:** 1857–1965; **Thurso:** 1840–1942; **Tillicoultry:** c.1854–1957; **Troon:** 1937–44; **Turriff:** 1881–1957; **Uddingston:** 1868–72; **Ullapool:** 1865–74; **Walkerburn:** 1937–42; **West Linton:** 1857–1960; **Wick:** 1878–1958; **Wishaw:** 1921–25.

Records 2: National Library of Scotland, Department of Manuscripts, George IV Bridge, Edinburgh EH1 1EW

Miscellaneous papers 1700, 1864; papers re bank stock 1727–31; bonds in favour of bank 1739–1834; list of adventurers 1753; memorials 1754, 1763; deeds re directors 1756–81; discharges 1773–81; correspondence: to secretary 1776, 1785, Henry and Robert Dundas 1792–1817, Wilsons of Bannockburn re transactions 1811–32, Edward Ellice 1828, Foreign Mission Committees of Scottish Churches 1875–1924; letters and accounts 1777–1827, 1836–65; assignation 1788; receipts 1824–74; bills 1825; bank statements 1842–53; legal opinions 1853–57; passbooks 1873–79. [Ref: Numerous, refer to repository]

Records 3: Business Records Centre, Archive Department, University of Glasgow, Glasgow G12 8QQ

Directors' meeting minutes extracts 1696–1918; copy memoranda and correspondence re proposed merger 1845–50; balance sheets and related papers 1866–1973. [Ref: Scottish Banking Collection]

Records 4: Local Studies Library, Angus District Council, County Buildings, Forfar DD8 3LG

Deposit notes 1857–68. [Ref: X/103]

Records 5: National Archives of Scotland, HM General Register House, Princes Street, Edinburgh EH1 3YY

Bond and assignations 1714–34, 1757–58; correspondence of David Drummond, treasurer, 1750–90; sederunt book of James, Smith & Sons, agents, Brechin, 1830–31; Seaforth Trust loan papers 1833. [Ref: GD190/3/250; GD64/356; GD190/3/277–8; CS96/1259; GD48/194]

Records of banks

BANK OF STOCKPORT
Stockport, Greater Manchester

History: This joint stock bank was established in 1836 and was acquired by Manchester & County Bank Ltd (est. 1862) in 1872.

Records: The Royal Bank of Scotland plc, Archive Section, Regent's House, 42 Islington High Street, London N1 8XL

Deed of settlement 1836; directors' meeting minute books 1836–68; fortnightly balances 1836–71; directors' and managers' register 1836–83; declarations of secrecy 1836–98; half-yearly report 1850; letters re customers' accounts 1858–81; managers' notebook 1858–84; commission register 1864–85; list of shareholders eligible for directorships 1865–72; annual general meeting minutes 1869–71.

BANK OF WALES LTD
Swansea, West Glamorgan

History: This joint stock bank was established with limited liability in 1863 with a paid-up capital of £40,000. In the same year branches were opened at Hay, through the acquisition of the Herefordshire Banking Co's branch; at Hereford, through the acquisition of the business of Matthews & Co (est. c.1800); Neath; Newport; Pembroke Dock; Bridgend; Briton Ferry; and Cowbridge. In 1864 it acquired Lock, Hulme & Co (est. 1833) of Pembroke and Tenby, and, in the same year, James McLean & Co of Pembroke Dock. In 1864 other branches were opened at Cardiff, Haverford West and Usk. The bank amalgamated with Provincial Banking Corporation Ltd (est. 1864) in 1865.

Reg Chambers Jones, *Arian. The Story of Money and Banking in Wales* (Swansea, 1963)

Records: Barclays Bank plc, Group Archives, Dallimore Road, Wythenshawe, Manchester M23 9JA

Directors' meeting minute books (2) 1862–63; lease, Bridgend House 1864; cheque 1864; impersonal ledger 1864–70.

BANK OF WALSALL & SOUTH STAFFORDSHIRE
Walsall, West Midlands

History: This joint stock bank was formed in 1835. It failed in 1840.

Records: Walsall Local History Centre, Essex Street, Walsall WS2 7AS

Deed of settlement 1836; correspondence from H Duignan & Son, Walsall bankers c.1837–40. [Ref: 48/1/61]

82   *British banking – a guide to historical records*

BANK OF WEST AFRICA LTD
London and Africa

History: The establishment of this bank was proposed in about 1879, but no evidence exists to show that it was formed. It may have been linked with another bank of the same name for which a prospectus was submitted to the Stock Exchange in 1881.

Records: Guildhall Library, Aldermanbury, London EC2P 2EJ

Draft prospectus c.1879. [Ref: MS 28528]

BANK OF WESTMORLAND LTD
Kendal, Cumbria

History: This joint stock bank was formed in 1833. Its first directors were two solicitors, a newspaper publisher and a mill owner, all of whom worked in Kendal, and its customers largely comprised private individuals. Branches were opened at Kirkby Stephen (1867), Sedbergh (1880), Bowness and Ambleside (1883) and Orton (1891). In 1888 the bank adopted limited liability. In 1893, when deposits stood at £300,000 and paid-up capital was £26,000, the business was acquired by London & Midland Bank Ltd (est. 1836) for £102,000 cash.

W F Crick & J E Wadsworth, *A Hundred Years of Joint Stock Banking* (London, 1936)

Records 1: HSBC Holdings plc, Group Archives, 10 Lower Thames Street, London EC3R 6AE

List of shareholders 1833; architectural drawings, head office 1833; out-letterbook 1833–34; share ledger 1834–90; general meeting minutes 1834–93; directors' meeting minute books (4) 1857–93; auditors' reports 1878, 1884; balance sheets 1878–92; valuation of investments 1888–90; annual reports 1888–93; amalgamation papers 1893.

Records 2: Cumbria Record Office, County Offices, Kendal, Cumbria LA9 4RQ

Deed of settlement 1834; manager's personal letterbook 1849–72; liquidation papers c.1890–95. [Ref: WDX/64; WD/MM 155–156; WDB/54]

BANK OF WHITEHAVEN LTD
Whitehaven, Cumbria

History: This joint stock bank was established in 1837, the year in which it acquired the private bank of Hartley & Co (est. 1793) of Whitehaven. From the outset it issued its own notes. It was subsequently incorporated

Records of banks **83**

as a limited liability company and was acquired by Manchester & Liverpool District Banking Co Ltd (est. 1829) in 1916.

Records: The Royal Bank of Scotland plc, Archive Section, Regent's House, 42 Islington High Street, London N1 8XL

Directors' meeting minute books (7) 1838–1916; deed of settlement 1859; security registers (3) 1861–1916; note registers 1864–1918; salary book 1865–1917; share transfer register 1866–1913; shareholders' registers 1866–1903, 1906–16; annual general meeting minutes 1867–1916; dividend registers (6) 1870–1915; monthly balance sheets (5) 1871–1915; loans ledger, railway securities 1872–1911; managers' diaries (33) 1873–1916; half-yearly returns on unstamped notes and bills in circulation 1873–1919; branch statistics book 1875–82; summary of shareholder books (2) 1883–97; general ledger 1884–94; deposit receipt ledger 1884–1935; security register 1886–1916; half-yearly summaries of notes and bills 1893–1916; head office ledger of branch deposits 1896–1943; half-yearly reports 1899–1911; directors' register 1901–08; deposit ledger 1902–47; banker's licence 1911; London drafts book 1915–16 amalgamation papers 1916.

Aspatria: deposit ledger 1884–1913; deposit receipt ledger 1884–1935; security book 1887–1916; **Workington:** letterbooks (9) 1865–1916; customer accounts ledger 1900–03.

BARCLAY, BEVAN, TRITTON, RANSOM, BOUVERIE & CO
London

History: This important private bank was established by John Freame, a Quaker goldsmith banker, who traded in Lombard Street, City of London, from 1690; by 1698 his business was known as Freame & Gould. James Barclay, John Freame's son-in-law, entered the partnership in 1736, replacing J Gould, when the firm was renamed Freame & Barclay. In 1766 the bank was restyled Freame, Smith & Bening, the latter partner having formerly been a clerk in the firm. In 1767 the first member of the Bevan family joined the partnership and in 1770, on the death of Joseph Freame, the Freame family withdrew. In 1770 the bank became known as Smith, Bevan & Bening and as Barclay, Bevan & Bening in 1776. In 1783 J H Tritton became a partner and from about 1785 the bank was styled Barclays, Tritton, Bevan & Co. In 1791, on the withdrawal of Silvanus Bevan, who then joined the brewing business of Barclay, Perkins & Co, the business was restyled Barclay & Tritton resuming its previous name in 1797. From 1834 the business was known as Barclays, Bevan, Tritton & Co. In 1865 Spooner, Attwood, Twells & Co (est. 1801), of the City of London, was acquired when the bank was restyled Barclays, Bevan, Tritton, Twells & Co. In 1880 the Twells name was dropped from the title and in 1888 the

84   *British banking – a guide to historical records*

bank amalgamated with Ransom, Bouverie & Co (est. c.1782) of Pall Mall, London, when it became known as Barclay, Bevan, Tritton, Ransom, Bouverie & Co. The Pall Mall premises became the firm's first branch. In 1894 Hall, Bevan, West & Bevans (est. 1805) of Brighton was acquired. The firm acted as London agent to a number of country banks. In 1896 it was the lead bank, along with Gurney, Birkbeck, Barclay & Buxton of Norwich and Jonathan Backhouse & Co of Darlington, in the amalgamation of twenty banks to form the joint stock bank of Barclay & Co Ltd. At that time it had a balance sheet total of almost £30 million and paid-up capital of £2 million. Its senior partner, Francis Augustus Bevan, was the new bank's first chairman.

F G Hilton Price, *A Handbook of London Bankers* (London, 1876); William Howarth, *The Banks in the Clearing House* (London, 1905); William Howarth, *Barclay & Co Limited* (London, 1901); P W Matthews & Anthony W Tuke, *History of Barclays Bank Ltd* (London, 1926); Manfred Pohl & Sabine Freitag, *Handbook on the History of European Banks* (Aldershot, 1994)

Records: Barclays Bank plc, Group Archives, Dallimore Road, Wythenshawe, Manchester M23 9JA

Partners' and Barclay family's personal and business papers 1661–1932; customer and other papers 1728–72; discounts ledger, Freame & Gould 1729–33; shop debit and credit ledgers (14) 1733–47; deeds and other papers re London property 1736–1889; extracts from settlement book of David Barclay & Sons 1749–59; cash books, Freame, Barclay & Freame account (7) 1760–64; discount ledgers 1768–1875; partnership agreements 1780–1896; receipts 1784–87; first of exchange 1784–1825; promissory notes 1787–96; private accounts ledgers (73) 1787–1896; customer correspondence 1792; bills of exchange 1794–1828; cheques 1794–1898; ledger, sundries written off 1798–1923; safe custody registers (3) 1798–1925; drafts 1804–11; cash book 1807–14; cheque books 1808–93; letterbook 1812–16; customer reference book 1814–44; current account abstracts 1817, 1857; loans list 1818–29; bills of exchange 1823; interest due list 1823–26; in-letters, Joseph Gurney Barclay 1823–90; staff register 1826–1902; loan ledgers 1830–94; signature books 1830–1909; bank note n.d.; balance sheet, discount ledger and exchequer bills 1830–50; cheque book 1834–88; in-letters, country and Scottish bank agencies 1836–98; coupons and dividends register 1837–52; property ledger 1837–96; private accounts ledger 1838–73; partnership papers 1838–89; current account ledgers 1840–51; staff appointments 1851, 1888–89; applications for employment 1855–1903; press cutting 1864; papers re Overend, Gurney & Co 1865–70; ledger extracts 1865–96; salary lists 1867–79, 1890–92; employee

Records of banks **85**

indemnity 1871; securities for advances 1879–83; clerks' guarantee fund rules 1880–91; private accounts ledgers (15) 1887–1904; papers re amalgamation with Ransom, Bouverie & Co 1888; ledger, stock and dividends n.d.; salaries list 1891; statements of assets and liabilities 1891–93; balance sheet 1891–95; draft 1892; employment agreements 1894; papers re merger with Brighton Union Bank 1894; in-letters, foreign firms 1894–96; passbook, clerks' provident fund 1894–1913; papers re creation of Barclay & Co Ltd 1896; loan statements 1896–97; letterbooks, re interest and dividends 1897–1916.

BARCLAYS BANK (CANADA)
London and North America

History: This British overseas bank was established at Montreal, Canada, in 1929 by charter of the Canadian Parliament. It was owned by an investment company, Barclays Canada Ltd, set up in 1927 as a joint venture of Barclays Bank Ltd (est.1896) and Barclays Bank (Dominion, Colonial & Overseas) (est. 1925). It planned to open branches throughout Canada and initially it financed Canadian trade with Britain and the British Empire. Like other chartered banks, until 1949 it was empowered to issue its own notes. In the 1930s branches opened at Vancouver and Toronto and in 1936 Barclays Trust Co of Canada, an independent company, was established to provide trustee services. By 1938 total assets stood at £2.6 million. After the Second World War, other branches were opened and numbered seven by 1955. However, the bank was not entirely successful as exchange controls impeded expansion financed from Britain. In 1956 the bank was sold to Imperial Bank of Canada, Barclays Bank Ltd receiving 10 per cent of Imperial Bank's equity as consideration. The trust company was sold in the same year to the Royal Trust Co.

Anthony W Tuke & R J H Gillman, *Barclays Bank Ltd 1926–1969* (priv. pub., 1972)

Records: Barclays Bank plc, Group Archives, Dallimore Road, Wythenshawe, Manchester M23 9JA

London committee papers 1925–56; London committee minutes (3) 1928–56; profit and loss account papers 1930–55; shareholder committee minutes 1931–56; Barclays Trust Co of Canada Ltd papers 1931–53; Montreal and Toronto branches statistics 1931–44; balance sheets and auditors' reports 1934–53; pension fund papers 1941–52; pension fund accounts 1941–53; by-laws and related papers 1941–70; annual general meeting minutes (2) 1956–72; manuscript history of bank 1958; balance sheets and related papers 1962–71.

86 British banking – a guide to historical records

Montreal, Uptown: premises papers 1943–48; **Toronto:** premises papers 1929–52; **Vancouver:** premises papers 1934–51.

BARCLAYS BANK (FRANCE) LTD
London and Europe

History: This overseas bank traced its origins to the Paris branch of Cox & Co (est. 1758), army agents, which was established in 1914 on the outbreak of war. In 1915 it was incorporated as Cox & Co (France) Ltd when the London & South Western Bank Ltd (est. 1862) joined the venture adding substantially to the paid-up capital of £100,000. New branches were quickly established at Rouen, Le Havre and Marseilles, followed by others at Amiens, Bordeaux and Lyons. In January 1918 London & South Western Bank Ltd amalgamated with London & Provincial Bank Ltd (est. 1864), to form London, Provincial & South Western Bank Ltd. This bank amalgamated with Barclays Bank Ltd in October 1918 so that Barclays Bank became a shareholder in Cox & Co (France) Ltd for the first time. In 1919 a further branch opened at Cologne, to serve the British Army of the Rhine; it closed in 1925. Two north African branches were established in 1919 and 1920. In the 1920s other branches opened in the south of France and at Monte Carlo to serve British tourists. In 1922 Barclays bought out the other shareholders when the business was transferred to Barclays Bank (Overseas) Ltd with a paid-up capital of £250,000; it was known as Barclays Bank (France) Ltd from 1926. In 1928 total assets were £9 million, falling to £7 million in 1938 and rising to £15 million by 1955 when there were twelve branches. In the late 1960s the north African branches were closed and in 1967 a London office was opened. This was Barclays Bank's vehicle for dealing in sterling and euro currency deposits and its inclusion within Barclays Bank (France) was for technical and procedural reasons only. Shortly afterwards, the French business was transferred to a French registered company, Barclays Bank SA, while Barclays Bank (France) Ltd, the activities of which were now largely those of its London office, was renamed Barclays Bank (London & International) Ltd. In 1976 the business was renamed Barclays Merchant Bank Ltd and then Barclays de Zoete Wedd Ltd in 1986.

Anthony W Tuke & R J H Gillman, *Barclays Bank Limited 1926–1969* (priv. pub., 1972)

Records: Barclays Bank plc, Group Archives, Dallimore Road, Wythenshawe, Manchester M23 9JA

Seal book 1920–84; director, share, etc, register 1922–68; accounting papers 1922–68; memorandum and articles of association 1922–76; advances limits books (2) 1929–34.

Records of banks

BARCLAYS BANK INTERNATIONAL LTD
London

History: This British-owned overseas bank traced its origins to the Colonial Bank (est. 1836) in which Barclays Bank Ltd (est. 1896) acquired a major interest from the late 1910s. In 1925 Barclays reorganised its overseas banking interests by reconstructing Colonial Bank under the title Barclays Bank (Dominion, Colonial & Overseas) and including within it the Anglo-Egyptian Bank Ltd (est. 1864) and the National Bank of South Africa (est. 1890). The new bank represented a determined attempt by Barclays to extend its business overseas. By 1928 the bank was the third largest British-owned overseas bank with a balance sheet total of £71.68 million and 455 branches. Ten years later it was the largest such bank when its balance sheet totalled £113 million. This position was retained in 1955 when assets totalled £574.4 million and branches numbered 997. A year earlier the bank was renamed Barclays Bank (DCO). In 1971 its South African business was hived off and renamed Barclays National Bank and the remaining part of the business was absorbed into the Barclays Group. Including the parent's International Division, it did business under the title Barclays Bank International Ltd. In the 1970s, many branches were hived off into country-wide banks in which local investors, including governments, took substantial interests. In 1984 the bank was completely merged with the domestic banking business of Barclays Bank plc.

Anon, *A Bank in Battledress Being the Story of Barclays Bank (Dominion, Colonial and Overseas) During the Second World War 1939–45* (priv. pub., 1948). Anon, *A Banking Centenary. (Dominion, Colonial and Overseas)* (priv. pub., 1938); Julian Crossley & John Blandford, *The D C O Story. A History of Banking in Many Countries 1925–71* (priv. pub., 1971)

Records: Barclays Bank plc, Group Archives, Dallimore Road, Wythenshawe, Manchester M23 9JA

Premises photographs c.1900s–80s; staff provident fund ledgers (8) 1906–42; seal registers (25) 1923–84; committee mintues 1925–46; bank ledgers 1925–52; head office general ledgers (32) 1925–54; branch ledgers (6) 1925–54; furniture and fittings ledgers 1925–60; reports of overseas visits 1925–66; inspection reports 1925–80; director's meeting minutes (19) 1925–84; general managers' files 1925–85; annual report and accounts 1925–85; investment ledgers 1926–34; balance sheets 1926–41; investment ledgers (10) 1926–54; share registers (22) 1926–56; daily report books (93) 1926–68; reports of ordinary general meetings 1926–69; directors' files 1926–80; board papers 1926–84; London committee minutes (8) 1929–61; advances registers 1932–44; essay competition entries 1943–46; diaries of Julian Crossley, chairman (9) 1943–65.

BARCLAYS BANK SAI LTD
London and Europe

History: Barclays Bank Ltd established this small overseas bank in Rome in 1925; its capital was £100,000 and it provided banking services to British customers. A branch was established at Genoa in 1926, but was closed in 1937. Initially the Rome branch prospered but, with the decline of British visitors after the Second World War, the business was sold to Banca Commerciale Italiana in 1950.

Anthony W Tuke & R J H Gillman, *Barclays Bank Ltd 1926–1969* (priv. pub., 1972)

Records: Barclays Bank plc, Group Archives, Dallimore Road, Wythenshawe, Manchester M23 9JA

Staff files 1919–57; general manager's papers 1924–51; directors' meeting minute books (4) 1925–35; advances limits books (3) 1925–50; balance sheets 1925–50; annual general meeting minute books (2) 1925–50; management committee minute books (2) 1925–50; chairman's notes on directors' meetings 1925–50; inspection reports, Rome and Genoa branches 1926–39; general ledger 1929–31; salary and bonus papers, Rome and Genoa branches 1930–38; staff record cards 1934; particulars of staff file 1935–40; share register n.d.; directors' and committee meeting minute books (3) 1937–50.

BARCLAYS PLC
London

History: This joint stock company was established in Lombard Street, City of London, in 1896 as Barclay & Co Ltd; it had a balance sheet total of almost £30 million, paid-up capital of £2 million and 182 branches. It was the result of an amalgamation of twenty, mostly private, banks led by Barclay, Bevan, Tritton, Ransom, Bouverie & Co (est. 1690) of London; Jonathan Backhouse & Co (est. 1774) of Darlington, Durham and Stockton-on-Tees; and Gurneys, Birkbecks, Barclay & Buxton (est. 1775) of Norwich. Their co-operation was facilitated by family links which had developed between the Gurney, Backhouse and Barclay families through intermarriage and by their mutual interests as Quakers. The other constituents were Gurneys, Birkbeck, Barclay, Buxton & Cresswell (est. 1782) of King's Lynn; Gurneys, Birkbecks, Barclay & Buxton (est. 1792) of Fakenham; Gurneys, Birkbeck, Barclay, Buxtons & Orde (est. 1782) of Halesworth; Gurneys, Birkbeck, Barclay, Buxtons & Orde (est. 1781) of Great Yarmouth; Gurney, Birkbeck, Barclay & Buxton (est. 1774) of Wisbech; Gurneys, Alexanders, Birkbeck, Barclay, Buxton & Kerrison (est. 1744)

Records of banks

of Ipswich; Gurneys, Round, Green, Hoare & Co (est. 1774) of Colchester; Goslings & Sharpe (est. 1650) of London; Sparrow, Tufnell & Co (est. 1805) of Chelmsford and Braintree; Bassett, Son & Harris (est. 1812) of Leighton Buzzard; Sharples, Tuke, Lucas & Seebohm (est. 1820) of Hitchin; Gibson, Tuke & Gibson (est. 1824) of Saffron Walden; Fordham, Gibson & Co (est. 1808) of Royston; John Mortlock & Co Ltd (est. c.1780) of Cambridge; Veasey, Desborough & Co (est. 1804) of Huntingdon; Molineux & Co (est. 1789) of Lewes; and Woodall Hebden & Co (est. 1788) of Scarborough. All the original shareholders were partners in these founding banks and shares were not sold on the stock market until 1902. The bank grew rapidly by amalgamation with and acquisition of other banks, viz.: Woods & Co (est. 1859) of Newcastle upon Tyne in 1897; Swaledale & Wensleydale Banking Co Ltd (est. 1836) in 1899; Parsons, Thomson, Parsons & Co (est. 1771) of Oxford in 1900; Milbanke, Woodbridge & Co (est. 1809) of Chichester in 1900; Woodbridge, Lacy, Hartland, Hibbert & Co (est. 1791) of Uxbridge in 1900; York Union Banking Co Ltd (est. 1833) of York in 1902; Priestman, Roper & Co (est. 1792) of Richmond in 1902; Marten, Part & Co (est. 1858) of St Albans in 1902; J & J W Pease (est. 1820) of Darlington in 1902; Thomas Ashby & Co (est. 1796) of Staines in 1904; Bolitho, Williams, Foster, Coode, Grylls & Co Ltd (Consolidated Bank of Cornwall) of Penzance in 1905; Hammond & Co (est. 1770) of Newmarket in 1905; Leatham, Tew & Co (est. 1801) of Pontefract and Wakefield in 1906; Wooten, Tubb & Co (est. 1805) of Oxford in 1909; Stamford, Spalding & Boston Banking Co Ltd (est. 1831) in 1911; J A Baty (est. 1880) of Newcastle upon Tyne in 1911; Simonds, Simonds & Co (est. 1814) of Reading in 1913; Nevile, Reid & Co (est. 1780) of Windsor in 1914; United Counties Bank Ltd (est. 1907) in 1916; London, Provincial & South Western Bank Ltd (est. 1862) in 1918; Gillett & Co (est. 1784) of Banbury in 1919; Henry Tubb & Co of Bicester (est. 1793) in 1920; Union Bank of Manchester Ltd (est. 1836) in 1940; and Gunner & Sons (est. 1809) of Bishop's Waltham in 1953. The company was known as Barclays Bank Ltd from 1917. By 1926 Barclays had 1,837 branches, sub-branches and agencies. By far the largest merger was that with Martins Bank Ltd (est. 1831 as the Bank of Liverpool) in 1969 which added 700 branches to Barclays' network. Barclays Export & Finance Co Ltd was established in 1964 followed the next year by Barclays Life Assurance Co Ltd. At about the same time diversification into insurance broking, leasing and factoring took place. A credit card business, Barclaycard, was launched in 1966. A foreign department was established in 1911 and foreign business later developed through interests in Cox & Co (est. 1758), acquired via amalgamation with London, Provincial & South Western Bank Ltd in 1918, in Colonial Bank (est. 1836), in National Bank of South Africa (est. 1890) and in Anglo-Egyptian Bank Ltd (est.

90 *British banking – a guide to historical records*

1864). The last three named came under the ownership of Barclays Bank (Dominion, Colonial & Overseas) in 1925. In 1976 a merchant bank, County Bank Ltd, was established which was significantly developed in the mid 1980s into Barclays de Zoete Wedd Ltd through the acquisition of the stockbrokers, de Zoete & Bevan, and the stockjobbers, Wedd, Durlacher, Mordaunt & Co. In 1984 a major reorganisation resulted in the domestic and foreign retail banking businesses being merged under a holding company, Barclays plc; this had 2,900 British branches and 2,400 branches overseas. Many investment banking activities were given up in 1998.

P W Matthews & Anthony W Tuke, *History of Barclays Bank Ltd* (London, 1926); Anthony W Tuke & R J H Gillman, *Barclays Bank Ltd 1926–1969* (Oxford, 1972); Manfred Pohl & Sabine Freitag, *Handbook on the History of European Banks* (Aldershot, 1994)

Records 1: Barclays Bank plc, Group Archives, Dallimore Road, Wythenshawe, Manchester M23 9JA

Directors' meeting minutes 1896–1980s; committee minutes 1896–1980s; departmental records 1896–1990s; regional office records 1896–1990s; circulars 1896–1990s; branch photographs 1900s–90s.

Accrington: signature books 1873–1938; manager's diary 1902–09; customer balances 1959–61; **Addiscombe:** manager's minute book 1881–1909; **Alford:** customer account ledger 1861–63; **Alnwick:** staff salary lists 1897–1933; **Ambleside:** home safe ledgers 1926–71; **Astley:** signature book 1907–14; **Atherton:** signature books 1921–43; reference book 1935–64; **Attleborough:** reference book 1900–13; **Aylsham:** deposit receipt ledgers 1856–1907; customer account ledgers 1877–93; **Banbury:** customer account ledger 1819–23; **Banstead:** signature book 1905–26; **Barnsley:** staff register 1896–1981; **Bexleyheath, Market Place:** signature book 1886–99; **Bicester:** customer account ledger 1916–19; **Bilston:** monthly balances 1856–76; customer account ledger 1866–71; **Birkenhead:** staff register 1909–29; **Bishop's Stortford:** customer account ledgers 1791–1810; **Bishops Waltham:** customer account ledger 1935–44; **Bootle:** customer account ledger 1880–1926; **Bradford:** signature book 1886–1901; **Brentford:** signature book 1888–1907; **Brierfield:** signature book 1899–1930; **Brighton, North Street:** customer account ledgers 1805–58; signature books 1869–1906; letterbooks 1805–12,1864–88; **Builth Wells:** letterbooks 1885–98; **Bungay:** customer account ledger 1858–59; **Burnley:** signature books 1893–1935; **Burnley, Colne Road:** signature book 1899–1935; **Burnley, Harle Syke:** signature book 1919–34; **Bury:** manager's diary 1888–91; **Bury, Broad Street:** signature book 1880–89; **Bury, Silver Street:** signature books 1869–93; signature book re friendly societies 1863–91; reference book 1885–88; **Bush Hill Park:** signature book 1905–

Records of banks 91

27; **Cambridge Benet Street:** customer account ledgers 1798–1807; **Cardiff Bay:** customer account ledgers 1868–1944; signature books 1889–1926; **Cardiff, Canton:** signature book 1919–25; **Carlisle, English Street:** signature books 1886–1935; **Caversham:** customer account ledger 1928–34; **Chelmsford:** customer account ledgers 1896–1919; **Chichester:** manager's diary 1849–57; bankers' account ledgers 1894–1900; customer account ledgers 1809–96; balances 1827–65; signature book 1914–18; **Colchester:** customer account ledgers 1806–51; **Cowbridge:** customer account ledgers 1864–73; **Cranbrook:** letterbook 1934–48; **Crewe:** letterbook 1904–19; **Didsbury:** signature book 1891–1926; **Dudley:** customer account ledger 1834–39; balances, profit and loss 1869–74; **East Grinstead:** customer account ledgers 1838–60; signature book 1897–1915; **Erith:** signature book 1895–1926; **Esher:** signature book 1905–39; **Grangetown:** signature book 1913–42; **Grasmere:** signature book 1910–38; **Grays:** signature book 1877–99; inspections and staff reports 1888–1932; letterbook 1924–26; **Guernsey:** closed account ledgers 1940–45; customer account ledgers 1940–48; **Halesworth:** letterbook 1872–96; signature book 1897–1903; **Hampton:** signature books 1890–1904; **Hanley:** letterbook 1897–1907; **Haverfordwest:** customer account ledgers 1838–78; **Hawkshead:** signature book 1916–38; **Hanwell:** staff book 1899–1937; **Haywards Heath:** signature book 1901–13; **Henley:** customer account ledgers 1896–98; **Hersham:** signature book 1900–28; **High Wycombe:** customer account ledger 1913; **Holsworthy:** staff register 1921–39; **Holt:** customer account ledgers 1812–30; bills discounted book 1822–25; **Horbury:** manager's minute book 1904–06; **Hoylake:** signature book 1897–1938; **Hull, Story Street:** staff registers 1906–62; **Hull, Trinity House Lane:** signature book 1858–1929; salary lists and reports 1929–44; manager's diaries 1932–64; reference book 1933–47; **Huntingdon:** salary list 1846–1945; **Hyde:** reference book 1922–42; **Ipswich:** customer account ledgers 1783–1881; petition for shorter working hours 1876; signature book 1895–1903; loan ledger 1945–55; manager's diaries 1881–83; signature book 1885–95; **Ipswich:** manager's diary 1972–76; **Irlam:** signature books 1931–69; **Jersey:** customer account ledgers 1940–49; **Kendal:** reference book 1875–83; signature books 1891–1930s; **Kingsland:** signature books 1865–81; **Leeds, Albion Street:** signature book 1863–82; **Leicester, Gallowtree Gate:** customer account ledger 1872; **Leigh:** signature books 1874–1935; **Leighton Buzzard:** signature book 1893–1907; **Letchworth:** salary lists 1930–43; **Lewes:** guarantee agreements 1891–96; signature books 1894–1913; **Liverpool, Castle Street:** letterbook 1904–09; **Liverpool, Clubmoor:** signature book 1930–38; **Liverpool, Great Crosby:** signature books 1901–38; **Liverpool, Heywoods:** customer account ledgers 1788–1810; signature book 1836–1938; staff registers 1836–1977; manager's minute book 1883–1924;

92   British banking – a guide to historical records

Liverpool, Victoria Street: staff registers 1881–1939; signature book 1881–1940; manager's diary 1943–54; **Liverpool, Water Street:** customer account ledgers 1831–40; customer reference books 1845–1933; staff register 1926; **London, Aldersgate Street:** staff register 1926–62; **London, Balham:** signature books 1881–1940; **London, Battersea Park:** manager's minute book 1865–1912; signature books 1887–1926; salary book 1899–1911; **London, Bermondsey:** staff reports 1930s–1960s; **London, Bermondsey, Tower Bridge:** signature books 1880–1933; **London, Bishopsgate:** signature book 1890–1908; **London, Bloomsbury:** signature book 1888–1909; **London, Bond Street:** signature book 1905–16; **London, Bow:** signature books 1864–1911; letterbook 1891–93; **London, Camberwell:** staff reports 1899–1925; **London, Cannon Street:** signature books 1907–27; **London, Cavendish Square:** customer account ledger 1895–96; **London, Chelsea:** signature books 1887–1929; **London, City Office:** branch statistics 1918–59; **London, Earls Court:** signature book 1896–1902; **London, East Sheen:** staff register 1899–1932; **London, Eltham High Street:** letterbook 1907–46; signature book 1910–20; salary list 1946–56; customer account ledgers 1949–60; loan ledger 1958–60; **London, Fenchurch Street:** signature books 1876–1937; ledger, produce security 1940–65; **London, 109 Fenchurch Street:** letterbook 1919–35; **London, 114 Fenchurch Street:** signature books 1929–70; **London, 168 Fenchurch Street:** signature books 1866–1913; **London, Finsbury:** signature book 1868–1978; **London, Finsbury Pavement:** signature book 1888–1902; **London, Fleet Street:** drafts 1896–99; cash account re liquidation of partnership accounts 1896–1914; list of loans and overdrafts 1897–98; salary book 1897–1927; circular re move to temporary premises 1898; diary 1898–1919; policy book 1898–1948; bank rate cards 1898–1957; unclaimed balances ledger 1900–68; opinion 1902; valuation of securities 1902; passbook 1902–51; safe registers (4) 1906–36; photographs, including property and staff 1900s–60s; security ledgers (4) 1910–72; holiday register 1913–32; indemnity ledger 1913–51; letters from customers and others 1913, 1956–58; testimonials re appointment of porter 1914; loans paid off ledgers (2) 1914–37; account of Land Law Co Ltd 1923–67; bond registers (10) 1923–72; pensions rules 1924; cheque books 1920s; loan account ledgers (3) 1932–53; coupons ledgers (5) 1936–62; stocks and shares books (12) 1938–67; transfer ledgers (2) 1940–49; investment ledger 1940–42; ledgers, impersonal balance summary (2) 1944–65; deposit ledger 1947–52; inoperative wills ledger 1948–50; transfer ledger 1949–63; historical booklets 1950; paper on mechanisation of bookkeeping 1951–62; stock ledger 1951–72; shares books (2) 1952–54; cheques 1958–60; guarantee register 1959–64; share ledgers, marking names (2) 1959–71; staff rules 1962; lists of current account balances 1970–71; architectural plans: strongroom n.d., 19 Fleet Street n.d.; **London, Fulham,**

Records of banks 93

Munster Park: signature book 1900–26; **London, Hackney, Mare Street:** manager's diary 1948–50; signature book 1913–26; **London, Hackney, Amhurst Road:** signature book 1887–1913; **London, Hackney, Triangle:** signature book 1883–1902; **London, Hampstead:** signature books 1864–1922; staff reports 1899–1933; **London, Hampstead, England's Lane:** signature books 1897–1926; **London, Kennington:** letterbook 1917–28; **London, Kew Green:** signature book 1909–27; **London, King's Road:** manager's minute books 1887–1919; **London, Kingston Hill:** staff book 1900–42; **London, Kilburn:** signature books 1864–1919; **London, Leytonstone:** signature books 1886–1927; **London, Leytonstone Road:** manager's minute book 1908–52; **London, 54 Lombard Street:** customer account ledgers 1768–1875; staff registers 1826–1945; signature book 1852–1909; salary lists 1867, 1890–92, 1937; managers' diaries 1882–1922; letterbooks 1897–1916; reference books 1814–44; **London, 68 Lombard Street:** customer account ledgers 1770–1930; signature books 1811–1913; **London, Lower Tottenham:** managers' minute book 1907–39; **London, Ludgate Circus:** customer account ledgers 1906–49; signature books 1880–1940; **London, Merton:** signature book 1898–1929; staff reports 1898–1941; letterbook 1935–47; **London, Pall Mall:** customer account ledgers 1802–88; signature books 1800–79; **London, Palmers Green:** signature book 1914–17; staff register 1914–62; **London, Poplar:** signature books 1883–1927; staff register 1899–1938; **London, Spitalfields:** signature books 1898–1924; **London, Stock Exchange:** staff registers 1919–38; **London, Streatham Common:** staff register 1899–1960; **London, Tooting:** staff reports 1898–1941; manager's meeting minutes 1898–1928; **London, Tulse Hill:** manager's meeting minutes 1892–1934; **London, Wanstead:** staff register 1899–1956; **London, West Streatham:** manager's minute book 1908–50; **London, Whitehall:** customer account ledgers 1759–1831; signature book 1805–1936; account ledgers, Duchy of Cornwall and Duchy of Lancaster 1826–41; account ledgers, Prince of Wales 1863–1910; **London, Wimbledon Park:** signature book 1910–26; **Loughborough:** signature book 1890–1917; **Luton:** signature book 1856–79; **Lymm:** signature book 1906–31; **Manchester, King Street:** manager's diary 1870; **Manchester, Norfolk Street:** signature book 1852–72; **Manchester, Old Trafford:** signature book 1928–35; **Manchester, York Street:** reference book 1836–50; customer account ledger 1836–43; signature book 1917–25; **Middlesborough:** staff registers 1947–50; **Miles Platting:** signature books 1925–35; **Millom:** reference book 1896–1939; letterbook 1929–52; **Morecambe:** staff register: 1883–1971; **Needham Market:** customer account ledgers 1802–72; **New Barnet:** signature books 1885–1921; **New Brighton:** signature book 1897–1926; **Newcastle:** letterbooks 1860–91; **Newmarket:** signature book 1902–11; **Newport Pagnall:** customer account ledgers 1820–29; **Northampton:**

94   *British banking – a guide to historical records*

signature book 1880s; **Northwich:** manager's diary 1922–40; **Norwich, 28 London Street:** signature book 1892–1912; **Norwich, 30 London Street:** signature book 1885–1902; **Norwich, Bank Plain:** customer account ledgers 1775–1818; reference books 1841–1943; signature books 1853–1905; **Ossett:** manager's minute books 1888–1907; **Otley:** signature books 1876–1969; reference books 1915–67; **Oxford:** customer account ledgers 1790–1919; subscriptions ledgers 1849–1903; **Penarth:** reference book 1918–35; **Penzance:** signature book 1911–26; customer account ledgers 1934–45; **Pewsey:** reference book 1928–40; customer account ledger 1934–41; **Portsmouth:** letterbook 1905–19; **Preston:** letterbook 1894–1903; **Reading:** customer account ledgers 1858–1959; signature books 1867–1907; loans register 1949–62; **Richmond, 39 George Street:** signature books 1873–1918; **Richmond, 61 George Street:** signature book 1898–1913; **Richmond-upon-Thames:** letterbook 1907–09; **Saffron Walden:** customer account ledgers 1825–38; staff register 1955–57; **Seaham:** signature book 1896–1923; **Settle:** customer account ledgers 1791–1836; manager's diary 1866–89; **Shipley:** signature book 1877–93; **Sidcup:** customer account ledgers 1927–30; **Smethwick:** signature book 1877–1906; **Smithdown:** reference book 1886–1923; signature book 1923–38; **South Ealing:** letterbook 1912–14; **Southend:** signature book 1906; **Southend-on-Sea:** signature books 1900–24; **Southport:** signature book 1891–1914; **Sowerby Bridge:** signature book 1873–1902; **St Ives:** customer account ledgers 1862–73; salary lists 1896–1941; **Stockport, Bridge Street:** salary lists 1904–53; **Stockport, Great Underbank:** signature book 1906–11; **Sudbury:** customer account ledgers 1859–70; **Sunbury-on-Thames:** reference book 1908–09; **Swansea:** signature books 1863–69; customer account ledger 1868–71; **Thetford:** customer account ledger 1915–20; **Treherbert:** signature book 1895–1923; **Tunbridge Wells:** customer account ledgers 1848–73; **Tyldesley:** reference book 1871–1954; **Ulverston:** customer account ledgers 1834–68; signature book 1850s–1860s; **Uppingham:** customer account ledgers 1847–68; **Wallingford:** customer account ledgers 1927–38; **Walsall:** reference book 1949; **Walton-on-Thames:** signature book 1876–1919; **Watford:** staff register 1899–1946; **Wavertree:** signature book 1886–1930; **West Bromwich:** customer account ledger 1805–1936; **Weymouth:** manager's meeting minutes 1927–36; **Winchmore Hill:** signature books 1902–17; **Wisbech:** customer account ledgers 1792–1803; **Woking:** salary list 1904–29; **Wokingham:** customer account ledgers 1914; **Woodbridge:** customer account ledgers 1805–71; **Ynysybwl:** signature book 1895–1928; **York:** signature books 1904–19.

Records 2: Modern Records Centre, University Library, University of Warwick, Coventry CV4 7AL

Records of Barclays Bank Staff Association 1940s on. [Ref: MS 396]

BARINGS, SHORT & COLLYNS
Exeter, Devon

History: This private bank was established in 1770 as Barings, Lee, Sellon & Green and also traded under the name of the Devonshire Bank. The senior partner was John Baring, an MP for Exeter, who was also a partner in the London merchant house of John & Francis Baring & Co (later Baring Brothers) and a founder of the Plymouth Bank of Baring, Lee, Sellon & Tingcombe (est. c.1782). The Baring family were leading merchants in Exeter and had been so almost since John Baring's father, also called John, had set up in business there in 1717. The banking business traded under several names: Baring (sic), Jackson, Short & Co (1774); Barings, Short & Hogg (1783); and Barings, Short & Collyns (1789). Baring Brothers & Co in London acted as a London agent, making and collecting payments. The bank closed in 1810.

John Ryton, *Banks and Bank Notes of Exeter 1769–1906* (priv. pub., 1983)

Records 1: Devon Record Office, Castle Street, Exeter EX4 3PU

Partnership agreements and other papers 1782–1834. [Ref: 1926 B/B/B 7–16]

Records 2: The Baring Archive, ING Baring Holdings Ltd, 60 London Wall, London EC2M 5TQ

Partnership agreement 1800. [Ref: LEG41.1]

THOMAS BARNARD & CO
Bedford, Bedfordshire

History: This private bank was established in 1799 by the Barnard family alongside its coal merchanting business; its partnership capital in 1799 was about £10,000 rising to £30,000 in 1813. By 1850 the coal business had been given up. In 1915, when deposits were about £250,000 and partners' capital and reserves were £80,000, the bank was acquired by Parr's Bank Ltd (est. 1865).

T E Gregory, *The Westminster Bank Through A Century* (London, 1936); L S Pressnell, 'Joseph Barnard. Westminster's Predecessor in Bedford', *Westminster Bank Review* (Feb. 1962)

Records 1: The Royal Bank of Scotland plc, Archive Section, Regent's House, 42 Islington High Street, London N1 8XL

Photograph, Thomas Barnard and wife 1909; balance sheets 1909–15.

96 *British banking – a guide to historical records*

Records 2: Bedfordshire and Luton Archives and Record Service, The Record Office, County Hall, Cauldwell Street, Bedford MK42 9AP

Accounts 1801–90; partnership agreements and related papers 1801–1912; balance sheets 1801–1914; T Barnard's passbook and accounts 1806–53; correspondence: swindle 1809–15, run on bank 1809–10, note issue dispute 1798–1833, indemnifications for lost bank notes 1813–81; papers re staff including fidelity bonds 1823–1910; security register 1841–83; papers: public appointments of T Barnard 1863–1901, partners' income tax 1859–1916, sale of business 1902–15; cash book, account with London agents 1866–76; safe custody registers 1869–83; partners' ledgers (2) 1872–95; profit and loss statements 1872–1915; papers re securities 1884–1904. [Ref: BD]

BARNETT, HOARE & CO
London

History: This bank traced its origins to about 1728 when John Bland (died 1764) traded as a goldsmith at the sign of the Black Horse, Lombard Street in the City of London, although goldsmith bankers – in particular Humphrey Stokes – had operated at this address since at least 1665. The business was known as John Bland & Son by 1740 and was styled Bland, Barnett & Co by 1761; Bland, Barnett & Bland by 1763; Bland & Barnett by 1766; Bland, Barnett & Hoare by 1772, following the admission of Samuel Hoare, who had formerly been with Gurneys of Norwich; Barnett, Hoare, Hill & Barnett by 1790; Hoare, Hill & Barnett by 1800; Hoare, Barnett, Hoare & Co by 1808; and Barnett, Hoare & Co by 1826. In 1864 the bank merged with another Lombard Street bank, Hanbury & Lloyd (est. 1771), to form Barnetts, Hoares, Hanbury & Lloyd in which the Barnett partners were initially the dominant force.

F G Hilton Price, *A Handbook of London Bankers* (London, 1876); R S Sayers, *Lloyds Bank in the History of English Banking* (Oxford, 1957)

Records: Lloyds TSB Group plc, Archives, Head Office, 71 Lombard Street, London EC3P 3BS

Waste books (3) 1768–69; personal and business account books (3) 1770–74; bills registers (2) 1774–75; general ledgers (32) 1778–91, 1794, 1802–33; 'stock books' with customer balances, balance sheets, etc (67) 1798–1864; partnership agreement 1806; sundry accounts book 1809–62; customer ledger 1817–60; stock ledger 1821–52; signature book 1825–39; private letterbook 1840–71; private ledger 1849–59; monthly summaries of bank and customer accounts 1853–60; general ledger 1859–64; amalgamation papers 1864.

Records of banks   **97**

BARNETTS, HOARES, HANBURY & LLOYD
London

History: This private bank, based in the City of London, was formed in 1864 by the amalgamation of two long-established and important Lombard Street businesses, Barnett, Hoare & Co (est. 1728) and Hanbury & Lloyd (est. 1771). The Lloyd partners belonged to the Birmingham-based Lloyd family, founders of Lloyds Banking Co Ltd; the London bank acted as the Birmingham bank's agents. In 1884 the business, then one of London's leading private banks but weakened by fraud, merged with Bosanquet, Salt & Co (est. 1780) of London and Lloyds Banking Co Ltd (est. 1765) to form Lloyds, Barnetts & Bosanquets Bank Ltd.

F G Hilton Price, *A Handbook of London Bankers* (London, 1876); Howard Lloyd, *Notes and Reminiscences of Lloyds Bank 1862 to 1892* (unpub. mss., 1917); R S Sayers, *Lloyds Bank in the History of English Banking* (Oxford, 1957)

Records: Lloyds TSB Group plc, Archives, Head Office, 71 Lombard Street, London EC3P 3BS

Clerk book 1863–84; private ledgers (3) 1864–82; stock books (2) 1865–83; private letterbooks (2) 1870–84; widows' fund papers 1874–84; partners' letterbooks (3) 1881–86; amalgamation papers 1882–84; head office diary 1884.

BARNSLEY BANKING CO LTD
Barnsley, South Yorkshire

History: This joint stock bank was incorporated in 1832 with a paid-up capital of £25,000. Its first directors comprised four landowners, a wine merchant, a chemist and a linen manufacturer. In particular the bank served the local linen and coal mining industries and by the 1850s had emerged as Barnsley's leading bank. Initially no branches were opened and in 1879, when the company assumed limited liability, only one existed. By 1890 paid-up capital had risen to £60,000 and deposits stood at £550,000. In 1897 the bank amalgamated with the County Bank (est. 1830).

Records: HSBC Holdings plc, Group Archives, 10 Lower Thames Street, London EC3R 6AE

Prospectus 1831; directors' meeting minute books (2) 1831–96; share registers (3) 1831–96; deed of settlement 1832; fidelity bonds 1832; analysis of balance sheets 1832–58; share certificates and transfers 1832–96; annual reports 1833–96; 'books of credit', memoranda re bills and advances

98 British banking – a guide to historical records

(2) 1841–60; estimates for building head office 1857–60; securities rental accounts 1882–95; security book 1882–97; security valuations 1883–93; balance sheet and profit and loss account 1896.

BARTLETT, NELSON & PARROTT
Buckingham, Buckinghamshire

History: Philip Box, a mercer and draper, formed this private bank in 1783. In 1811 it was sold to Bartlett & Nelson and in 1830 acquired G Parrott & Co (est. 1795), also of Buckingham, and became known as Bartlett, Parrott & Co. Branches were opened at Brackley (1841), Stony Stratford (1843) and Winslow (1844). In 1853 the business along with T R Cobb & Son (est. 1783) of Banbury and Cobb, Bartlett & Co (est 1795) of Aylesbury were acquired by the Bucks & Oxon Union Bank which was formed for the purpose.

Records 1: Lloyds TSB Group plc, Archives, Head Office, 71 Lombard Street, London EC3P 3BS

Partnership agreement 1853.

Records 2: Buckinghamshire Record Office, County Hall, Aylesbury HP20 1UA

Letters, notebooks and papers of M D Mansell agent at Newport Pagnell 1798–1822. [Ref: D/U/9]

BASSETT, SON & HARRIS
Leighton Buzzard, Bedfordshire

History: This private bank was established in 1812 as Bassett & Grant and was otherwise known as the Bedfordshire Bank; one of its partners had formerly been the local agent for Rickford & Son (est. 1795) of Aylesbury. Branches were opened at Ampthill (1813), Dunstable (1814), Hitchin (1820) and Newport (1820). In 1820 three of its partners established Sharples, Bassett & Co at Hitchin and in 1827 completely severed their connection with the Bedfordshire Bank. In 1854 the business became known as Bassett, Son & Harris and in 1896 merged with other mostly private banks to form Barclay & Co Ltd. By then it had branches at Fenny Stratford, Newport Pagnell, Olney, Toddington, Woburn, Woburn Sands and Wolverton.

Maureen Brown & June Masters, *The Bassetts. Leighton Buzzard's First Family* (Leighton Buzzard, 1989); P W Matthews & Anthony W Tuke, *History of Barclays Bank Ltd* (London, 1926)

Records of banks 99

Records 1: Barclays Bank plc, Group Archives, Dallimore Road, Wythenshawe, Manchester M23 9JA

Ledgers, private 1812–96; ledgers, impersonal 1812–1912; partnership agreements: 1820–42, related correspondence 1835–42; partners' meeting minutes 1823–26; bad debt accounts 1827; correspondence 1855–1910; circular re new Woburn branch 1863; papers re charitable subscriptions 1870; papers of executors and trustees of Francis Bassett 1875–1910; ledgers, general balances 1876–96; ledgers, J D Bassett's account n.d.; balance sheets 1889–95; papers re amalgamation 1896; cheques, dividends and debits 1899–1909; bank note printing plates n.d.

Dunstable: cheque n.d.; **Leighton Buzzard:** current account ledgers 1819–50; cheque and cheque forms 1819–91; general balance ledgers 1839–67; probate register 1861–96; accounts and letters re building 1866–96; drawing of bank n.d.; **Newport Pagnell:** bank notes 1815–82; cheques and deposit receipts 1819–91; deposit account ledger 1821–57; account book 1866–96; **Stratford:** signature books 1859–60.

Records 2: Bedfordshire and Luton Archives and Record Service, The Records Office, Cauldwell Street, Bedford MK42 9AP

Partnership agreements 1842–53; family and estate records n.d. [Ref: X636, Z455, Z694]

BATE & ROBINS
Stourbridge, West Midland

History: This private bank was formed in 1762 and traced its origins to a local mercer and draper, William Collis, who subsequently took into partnership his relative William Robins. By 1770 the business was styled Bate & Robins and was otherwise known as Stourbridge Old Bank. It served the local ironfounding, nailmaking and glassmaking industries and latterly two major customers were Eagle Iron & Coal Co and Rounds Green Colliery. Between 1810 and 1851, the bank may also have been known as Hill, Waldron & Co and Hill, Bate & Robins. Thomas Bate died in 1847 and in 1851 his sole surviving partner, William Robins, sold the business to Birmingham & Midland Banking Co (est. 1836), later renamed Midland Bank Ltd, for £18,000. Its deposits were then £250,000, almost equal to those of Birmingham & Midland. It became Midland Bank's first branch.

Records 1: HSBC Holdings plc, Group Archives, 10 Lower Thames Street, London EC3R 6AE

Comparative statement of properties at Blaenavon, Plymouth and Rhymney 1836; memorandum of agreement with schedule of accounts 1851.

100   *British banking – a guide to historical records*

Records 2: Hereford and Worcester Record Office, St Helen's Branch, Fish Street, Worcester WR1 2HN

Report re merger 1851–52. [Ref: b705:260]

BECK & CO
Shrewsbury, Shropshire

History: This private bank was established in 1800 and opened a branch at Welshpool in 1816, following the failure of the Montgomeryshire Old Bank. It was otherwise known as Shrewsbury & Welshpool Old Bank. In 1880 Lloyds Banking Co Ltd (est. 1765) acquired the bank's business.

Records: Lloyds TSB Group plc, Archives, Head Office, 71 Lombard Street, London EC3P 3BS

Letter and memorandum book 1836–42; private ledger 1840–50; letterbook 1852–57; amalgamation papers 1880–84.

BECKETT & CO (LEEDS BANK)
Leeds, West Yorkshire

History: This important private bank was established by John Beckett in 1774 as Wilson, Beckett, Calverley & Lodge; it was also known as the Leeds Bank. The Beckett family had developed a banking business alongside their merchanting of woollen goods in the Portuguese market during the eighteenth century. It was known as Beckett, Calverley & Co from 1797, as Beckett, Blaydes & Co from 1820 and later as Beckett & Co. In 1868 it acquired Cooke, Vernon, Walker, Jackson & Milner (est. 1750) of Doncaster and, in 1875, Bower, Hall & Co (est. 1790) of Beverley, Hull and Malton. The Beverley, Hull and Malton business, known also as Beckett & Co, acted independently from the Leeds business. The Leeds business was also associated with Beckett, Birks & Co (est. 1796) of Barnsley which had been established by John's brother, Joseph. In 1921 Becketts amalgamated with London, County, Westminster & Parr's Bank Ltd (est. 1909), the combined businesses then having thirty-seven branches, £10.7 million deposits and partnership capital of £600,000.

T E Gregory, *The Westminster Bank Through A Century* (London, 1936); W C E Hartley, *Banking in Yorkshire* (Clapham, 1975)

Records: The Royal Bank of Scotland plc, Archive Section, Regent's House, 42 Islington High Street, London N1 8XL

Partnership deeds 1776–1920; statistics and balance books (2) 1782–1892; signature books (3) 1785–1840; ledger balance books (4) 1797–1822; customer account ledgers (10) 1813–25; list of foreign bills credited to

Records of banks 101

accounts 1815–16; security register 1820s; correspondence with Bank of England 1832–88; miscellaneous partners' private letters 1840–69; memorandum books (2) 1840–92; staff registers (4) 1840–1920; security receipt books (2) 1841–79; bad and doubtful debt registers (3) 1847–91; private ledgers (5) 1857–1920; sundry attendance book 1859–1911; customer interview books (4) 1864–70; outstanding balances 1872–1920; customer balance sheets 1877–91; balance sheets and consolidated accounts 1891–1920; letters to East Riding Bank 1895–1906; branch earnings and expenses 1896–1920; premises register 19th cent; partners' meeting minutes 1902–23; bill register 1904–14; information book 1910–20; investment ledgers (3) 1910–20; branch balance sheets 1912–13; balance sheet working papers 1915–17; staff list 1920; amalgamation papers 1920–21.

Bradford: signature book 1875–1921; list of accounts 1918; business diary 1919–20; **Doncaster:** customer average balance book 1889–90; business diary 1919–20; **Hunslett:** business diary 1919–20; **Harrogate:** business diary 1919–20; **Retford:** customer average balance book 1886–94; information book 1886–94; business diary 1919–20; **Worksop:** customer average balance book 1888–90; business diary 1919–20.

BECKETT & CO (YORK & EAST RIDING BANK)
York, North Yorkshire

History: This important private bank was formed in 1875 through the purchase by Beckett & Co (of Leeds) of the three firms of Bower Hall & Co (est. 1790) located at Beverley, Malton and Hull. It was also styled the East Riding Bank and acted independently from Becketts' Leeds Bank. In 1879 it acquired the failed bank of Swann, Clough & Co (est. 1771) of York and became known as the York & East Riding Bank; it then had branches at Beverley, Driffield, Helmsley, Malton, Pickering, Pocklington and York. In 1884 its head office was moved to York. In 1921 both Beckett banks were taken over by London, County, Westminster & Parr's Bank Ltd (est. 1909), the combined businesses then having thirty-seven branches, partnership capital of £600,000 and deposits of over £10.7 million.

T E Gregory, *The Westminster Bank Through A Century* (London, 1936); W C E Hartley, *Banking in Yorkshire* (Clapham, 1975)

Records: The Royal Bank of Scotland plc, Archive Section, Regent's House, 42 Islington High Street, London N1 8XL

Branch balance sheets 1875–84; private ledgers (4) 1875–1920; branch statistics book 1876–86; monthly balance sheets 1877–79; partners' meeting minutes 1904–15.

Beverley: customer papers 1864–84; securities for advances 1866–90; information books 1880; business diary 1919–20; **Bridlington:** business diary 1919–20; **Driffield:** information book 1883–92; customer average balance book 1888–90; business diary 1919–20; **Goole:** business diary 1919–20; **Malton:** customer balances book 1886–90; **Ripon:** business diary 1919–20; **Scarborough:** balance sheets 1904–20; business diary 1919–20; **Scunthorpe:** business diary 1919–20; **Tadcaster:** business diary 1919–20; **York:** information book 1886–89; customer balance book 1889–90.

BECKETT, BIRKS & CO
Barnsley, South Yorkshire

History: This private bank was established by Joseph Beckett, a leading local businessman, in 1796 as Beckett, Clarke & Co; it was otherwise known as the Barnsley Bank. Joseph's brother, John, was responsible for founding the leading Leeds bank of Beckett & Co in 1774. The Barnsley firm was subsequently styled Beckett, Birks & Co and in 1840 was acquired by the Wakefield Banking Co (est. 1832) which was then renamed Wakefield & Barnsley Union Banking Co.

W C E Hartley, *Banking in Yorkshire* (Clapham, 1975)

Records: Barclays Bank plc, Group Archives, Dallimore Road, Wythenshawe, Manchester M23 9JA

Partnership agreement 1796–1833; cheque and receipt 1827–38; out-letter to John Birks 1835.

BEECHING & CO
Tonbridge, Kent

History: This private bank was formed at Tonbridge by Thomas Beeching, a draper. He had opened a shop in about 1789 and conducted some banking business from this date. By 1815 Beeching had begun to issue bank notes. Branches were opened at Tunbridge Wells (1826), Hastings (1859), Southborough (1874) and Bexhill-on-Sea (1885). The bank, seriously weakened by the speculation of a partner, was acquired by Lloyds Bank Ltd (est. 1765) in 1890.

Howard Lloyd, *Notes and Reminiscences of Lloyds Bank 1862 to 1892* (unpub. mss., 1917)

Records 1: Lloyds TSB Group plc, Archives, Head Office, 71 Lombard Street, London EC3P 3BS

Amalgamation papers 1890–98.

Records of banks 103

Records 2: Centre for Kentish Studies, County Hall, Maidstone ME14 1XQ

Loan agreements 1789–1808. [Ref: U642 T38]

A W BELLAIRS & SON
Stamford, Lincolnshire

History: This private bank was established in about 1783 as A W Bellairs & Son; it was also known as the Stamford Bank. It was associated with a bank of the same name at Derby (est. c.1783 and known as the Derby Bank) and with Geo. Bellairs of Leicester (est. c.1783 and known as the Leicester Bank). All three banks failed in 1814.

Records: Department of Manuscripts and Special Collections, Hallward Library, University of Nottingham, University Park, Nottingham NG7 2RD

Papers re failure 1808–14. [Ref: Dr E 89–92]

ROBERT BENSON, LONSDALE & CO LTD
London

History: This City of London merchant bank dates back to the 1780s when the Benson family, originally from the Lake District, became established at Liverpool as textile merchants. The business moved to London in 1852 and gradually emerged as a merchant bank with interests in the finance of international trade and security issuance. In particular the firm was closely connected with the supply of capital to United States railroads in the late nineteenth century. In 1947 Robert Benson & Co Ltd, as it was then known, merged with Lonsdale Investment Trust Ltd to form Robert Benson Lonsdale & Co Ltd. In 1961 it merged with Kleinwort, Sons & Co Ltd (est. 1792) to form Kleinwort Benson Ltd.

Jehanne Wake, *Kleinwort Benson Ltd. The History of Two Families in Banking* (Oxford, 1997)

Records: Guildhall Library, Aldermanbury, London EC2P 2EJ

Balance sheets, profit and loss and other general accounts 1890s–1960s; security books (3) 1898–1933; papers re Mexican cotton estates c.1900–1960s; papers re Manila Railway (1906) Ltd 1916–54; register of members and directors (2) 1926–66; papers re New York agents 1930–39; 'monthly letter' to clients 1931–39; fees and profits estimates 1946–55; seal books 1948–62; new issue files 1956–63; papers re merger with Kleinworts 1950s–1960s.

104   *British banking – a guide to historical records*

Note: The above summary is subject to amendment and extension as the records were being organised at the time of publication.

BENTLEY & BUXTON
Leicester, Leicestershire

History: This private bank, established in about 1781, was the first to be formed at Leicester; it was also known as the Leicester Bank. William Bentley was a leading draper who had discounted bills for many years before establishing a bank. The business failed in 1803.

Records: Leicestershire Record Office, Long Street, Wigston Magna, Leicester LE8 2AH

Notices re payment of interest on liabilities 1807. [Ref: 8D39/9611 a & b]

BERWICK, LECHMERE & CO
Worcester, Hereford & Worcester

History: This private bank traced its origins to Berwick & Co, established in 1772 by Joseph Berwick, Receiver General of Taxes for Worcestershire; it was otherwise known as Worcester Old Bank. Much of his capital was derived from his collected taxes, which could be held for six months before remittance to London. In 1781 Samuel Wall, a Hereford haberdasher, and Elias Isaac, formerly a partner in the bankers Isaac Baldwin & Shapland (est. c.1785) of Marshfield, were admitted as partners. By 1785 the firm's capital was £20,000, half of which Berwick contributed. From 1791 until his death in 1798, he held a 20 per cent interest in the City of London bankers, Robarts, Curtis & Co (est. 1791). For a while he also had an interest in Wakeman, Farley & Turner (est. c.1793) of Kidderminster. In about 1800 (Sir) Anthony Lechmere married Joseph Berwick's daughter and became a partner; he had been a partner in the Tewkesbury bank of Lechmere & Co (est. 1792) since 1792. This marriage facilitated the merger of the two banks in 1831 to form Berwick, Lechmere & Co, sometime known as Berwick, Lechmere & Isaac. The bank, which had branches at Bromyard (1879), Malvern (1847), Malvern Link (1892), Tenbury Wells (1887), Upton upon Severn (1792) and West Malvern, was acquired by the Capital & Counties Bank Ltd (est. 1877) in 1906.

A W Isaac, *Worcester Old Bank* (priv. pub., 1908)

Records: Lloyds TSB Group plc, Archives, Head Office, 71 Lombard Street, London EC3P 3BS

Partnership agreements 1766–1905; general ledgers (6) 1781–1835 [w]; balance sheets 1798, 1891, 1903; private ledgers (11) 1803–96; discounted

Records of banks 105

bills ledgers (27) 1803–36 [w]; petty ledgers (2) 1825–41; debts memorandum books (3) c.1828–33; deposit ledgers (5) 1835–1905 [w]; dormant petty cash book 1858–1905; security register 1860–70; investment ledger 1863–86; security ledger 1886–97; amalgamation papers 1905–28.

Malvern: memorandum book 1904–08; profit and loss accounts 1885–86; **Tewkesbury:** memorandum books (3) 1859–1915 [w]; **Worcester:** memorandum books (2) 1878–1922.

WILLIAM & JOHN BIGGERSTAFFE
London

History: This private bank traced its origins to William Biggerstaffe who in 1790 was agent to the cattle market at West Smithfield, London. This involved keeping traders' books and dealing with drovers' banks. It was a short step from this to provide banking services to those connected with the market; by 1838 the firm was referred to as a banking agent. In the mid-nineteenth century William and John Biggerstaffe formed a partnership and were succeeded as proprietors by Thomas Milloy, Thomas Lloyd and Assheton Leaver. In 1918, upon the death of Assheton Leaver, the bank was sold to National Provincial & Union Bank of England Ltd (est. 1833).

Records: The Royal Bank of Scotland plc, Archive Section, Regent's House, 42 Islington High Street, London N1 8XL

Title deeds 1807–1934; amalgamation papers 1918; character book with account details, largely re meat traders 1918–25.

BIRKBECK BANK
London

History: This bank traced its origins to the Birkbeck Building Society, formed in 1851. It developed a large deposit taking business which quickly developed into banking; cheque books were issued from 1858. By about 1872 its banking business traded under the title of Birkbeck Bank. In 1910, when its balance sheet totalled £12.3 million, the bank experienced a run and was supported by the Bank of England. In 1911 it suspended payments when its business and Chancery Lane premises were purchased by London, County & Westminster Bank Ltd (est. 1909).

T E Gregory, *The Westminster Bank Through a Century* (London, 1936)

Records 1: The Royal Bank of Scotland plc, Archive Section, Regent's House, 42 Islington High Street, London N1 8XL

Liquidator's statement 1915; drawing, Chancery Lane n.d.

106   *British banking – a guide to historical records*

Records 2: Bodleian Library Department of Western Manuscripts, Broad Street, Oxford OX1 3BG

Letters to Asquith re bank failure 1911. [Ref: MS.Asquith 24, fols.21–32]

BIRMINGHAM JOINT STOCK BANK LTD
Birmingham, West Midlands

History: This joint stock bank was established in 1861 and opened for business at the beginning of 1862. Under the direction of Joseph Beattie, the bank quickly emerged as a leading Birmingham bank and strong local rival to Lloyds Banking Co Ltd. Three branches were established in Birmingham at Temple Row (1861), New Street (1865) and Great Hampton Street (1874). The New Street branch was formerly the premises of Attwood, Spooner & Co (est. 1791), the leading private bank which the Birmingham bank negotiated to purchase at the time of its failure in 1865. In 1889, when paid-up capital was £300,000, the business was acquired by Lloyds, Barnetts & Bosanquets Bank Ltd (est. 1765), formerly Lloyds Banking Co Ltd.

Howard Lloyd, *Notes and Reminiscences of Lloyds Bank 1862–1892* (unpub. mss., 1917); R S Sayers, *Lloyds Bank in the History of English Banking* (Oxford, 1958)

Records: Lloyds TSB Group plc, Archives, Head Office, 71 Lombard Street, London EC3P 3BS

Prospectus 1861; directors' meeting minute books (3) 1861–67, 1875–89; rough minute books (2) 1862–89; salary report 1864; books with details of debts of Attwoods, Spooner & Co (2) 1865; amalgamation papers 1889.

Birmingham, New Street: signature book 1871–91; customer status reports 1876–90; memorandum book 1886–89; **Birmingham, Temple Row:** signature books (2) 1862–81; memorandum book 1865–86.

BLACKBURN BANK LTD
Blackburn, Lancashire

History: This small bank was formed in about 1881. It opened no branches and in 1906 was absorbed by the Union Bank of Manchester Ltd (est. 1836).

Records: Barclays Bank plc, Group Archives, Dallimore Road, Wythenshawe, Manchester M23 9JA

Minutes 1881–92, 1901–07.

Records of banks 107

BODENHAM, GARRETT & SON
Hereford, Hereford & Worcester

History: This private bank was formed in 1800 and was otherwise known as the Hereford City & County Bank. It failed in 1826.

Records: Public Record Office, Ruskin Avenue, Kew, Richmond TW9 4DU

Correspondence c.1822–25. [Ref: C 110/96–98]

BOLDERO, LUSHINGTON, BOLDERO & LUSHINGTON
London

History: This City of London private bank was formed in the early eighteenth century by Thomas Minors, probably a goldsmith banker. In 1754 the firm was known as Minors & Boldero and in 1763 as Boldero, Carter & Co. In 1770 some partners may have withdrawn to form Boldero, Carter, Barnston, Snaith & Carter while the original business continued in Lombard Street as Boldero, Kendell, Adey & Co. The latter firm moved to 30 Cornhill in 1787 and in 1801 was renamed Boldero, Lushington, Boldero & Lushington. The business was discontinued in 1812.

F G Hilton Price, *A Handbook of London Bankers* (London, 1876)

Records: Guildhall Library, Aldermanbury, London EC2P 2EJ

Sale particulars of 30 Cornhill premises 1812. [Ref: MS69 ff186–7]

BOLITHO, WILLIAMS, FOSTER, COODE, GRYLLS & CO LTD
Penzance, Cornwall

History: This private bank was established by the Bolitho family, tin smelters and merchants, in 1795 as Bolitho & Co. In 1835 a branch opened at St Ives. It was known as Bolitho, Sons & Co from 1838 and was otherwise known as the Mounts Bay Bank. It acquired Ricketts, Enthoven & Co of Penzance, then in difficulties, in 1847 and Vivian, Grylls, Kendall & Co (est. 1788) of Helston in 1879. In 1863 branches were opened at St Just and Hayle and in 1876 at Helston. In 1889 Bolitho, Sons & Co joined with Robins, Foster, Coode & Bolitho (est. 1807) of Liskeard under the title of Bolitho, Foster, Coode & Co Ltd. The new bank acquired Hodge & Co (est. 1804) of Plymouth Dock in 1889; Williams, Williams & Grylls (est. 1866) of Falmouth in 1890; Willyams, Treffry & Co (est. 1864) of St Austell in 1890; Willyams, Willyams & Co (est. 1759) of Truro in 1890; Bain, Field, Hitchins & Co (est. 1879) of Redruth in 1891; and Batten, Carne & Carne's Banking Co Ltd (est. 1890) of Penzance in 1896. In 1890 the bank was renamed Bolitho, Williams, Foster, Coode, Grylls & Co Ltd

108   *British banking – a guide to historical records*

and was otherwise known as the Consolidated Bank of Cornwall. The bank was acquired by Barclay & Co Ltd (est. 1896) in 1905.

P W Matthews & Anthony W Tuke, *History of Barclays Bank Ltd* (London, 1926)

Records 1: Barclays Bank plc, Group Archives, Dallimore Road, Wythenshawe, Manchester M23 9JA

Bolitho, Sons & Co: cheques and bank notes 1800s–1866; customer ledgers 1829–83; private ledgers 1836–61, 1887–89; banker's ledger 1872–86; correspondence re Helston premises 1877–91.

Robins, Foster, Coode & Bolitho: cheques and cheque forms 1836–71; letters 1839–82; private ledgers 1873–91.

Bolitho, Williams, Foster, Coode, Grylls & Co Ltd: articles of association and balance sheet 1889; securities 1889–91; branch statistics 1889–1900; general meeting minutes 1889–1905; cheque, cheque form and cheque book order form 1889–1921; shareholder register 1890–1904; half-yearly balances 1890–1905; directors' meeting minutes 1891–93; private ledgers 1891–1902; press cuttings 1891–1903; investments 1891–1905; list of directors and committees n.d.; loan applications 1903–14.

Devonport: private ledgers 1889–1913; **St Austell:** cheque form 1889.

Records 2: Cornwall Record Office, County Hall, Truro TR1 3AY

Letterbooks 1837. [Ref: X679/2–4]

BOROUGH OF ST MARYLEBONE BANKING CO
London

History: This joint stock bank was established in 1837 and had premises in Cavendish Square in the West End of London and, briefly, in the City of London. It failed in 1841 when false accounting and fraud were uncovered; its liabilities totalled £85,000.

Records 1: City of Westminster Archives Centre, 10 St Ann's Street, London SW1P 2XR

Papers including letterbook with minutes re public enquiry into failure 1841–45. [Ref: Acc581; D:Misc142]

Records 2: Public Record Office, Ruskin Avenue, Kew, Richmond TW9 4DU

Papers re director's resignation 1838. [Ref: J90/821]

Records of banks 109

BOROUGH OF TYNEMOUTH TRADING BANK
North Shields, Tyne & Wear

History: This small bank was registered under the Friendly Societies Act in 1885. It was acquired by York City & County Bank Ltd (est. 1830) for £1,800 in 1896.

Records: HSBC Holdings plc, Group Archives, 10 Lower Thames Street, London EC3R 6AE

Customer account ledgers (2) 1888–97; deposit account ledger 1888–1910; general ledger 1892–98.

BOSANQUET, SALT & CO
London

History: This bank was established in 1867 through the merger (effective from 1871) of two long-established Lombard Street banks, Bosanquet, Whatman, Harman & Bosanquet and Stevenson, Salt & Sons. Bosanquets traced its origins to Bowles, Beachcroft & Reeves (est. 1780) which by 1796 changed its name to Bowles, Beachcroft, Brown, Reeves, Collins & Co and did business at Exchange Alley, off Cornhill in the City of London. In about 1796 Beachcroft and Reeves left this firm and with Samuel Bosanquet, formerly with the bankers Foster, Lubbock & Co, formed the firm of Bosanquet, Beachcroft & Reeves; it was located in Lombard Street. Further name changes followed: Bosanquet, Beachcroft, Pitt & Anderdon in 1809; Bosanquet, Pitt, Anderdon & Franks in 1816; and Bosanquet, Whatman, Harman & Bosanquet from 1854. Stevenson, Salt traced its origins to the bank of William Stevenson, established in Queen Street, City of London, in 1787. Stevenson, the son of John Stevenson, a mercer and banker at Stafford, had been a partner in the Stafford bank of Stevenson, Salt & Co (est. 1737) from 1777, for which his London bank acted as agents. In 1799 it moved to Lombard Street, in 1801 became known as Stevenson & Salt and was renamed Stevenson, Salt & Sons in 1838. The merged firm had close links with Lloyds Banking Co Ltd (est. 1765) of Birmingham, acting as London agent for many of its branches, the connection having been established through Lloyds' acquisition of Stevenson, Salt & Co of Stafford in 1866. In 1884 Lloyds Banking Co Ltd acquired Bosanquet, Salt & Co and another London private bank, Barnetts, Hoares, Hanbury & Lloyd, to form Lloyds, Barnetts & Bosanquets Bank Ltd, later known as Lloyds Bank Ltd. The merger provided Lloyds with access to the London Clearing House for the first time.

F G Hilton Price, *A Handbook of London Bankers* (London, 1876); Grace Lawless, *The Story of the Bosanquets* (Canterbury, 1966)

110   *British banking – a guide to historical records*

Records: Lloyds TSB Group plc, Archives, Head Office, 71 Lombard Street, London EC3P 3BS

Partnership agreements 1867–71; private ledger 1882–84; amalgamation papers 1884.

BOURNE, RHODES & CO
Alford, Lincolnshire

History: This private bank was established as Bourne, Rhodes & Co in 1844 and was taken over by Stamford, Spalding & Boston Banking Co (est. 1831) in 1861.

Records: Barclays Bank plc, Group Archives, Dallimore Road, Wythenshawe, Manchester M23 9JA

Balance book 1861.

BOUVERIE, MURDOCH & CO
London

History: This private bank was established as Bouverie & Co in 1813. It was known as Bouverie & Lefevre from 1827, as Bouverie, Norman & Murdoch from about 1831, as Bouverie, Murdoch & Bouverie from 1851 and as Bouverie, Murdoch, Bouverie & James from 1853. The bank was based in London's West End, originally in Craven Street, Strand, and from 1830 in Haymarket. The bank amalgamated with Ransom & Co (est. 1782) to form Ransom, Bouverie & Co in 1856.

F G Hilton Price, *A Handbook of London Bankers* (London, 1876); P W Matthews & Anthony W Tuke, *History of Barclays Bank Ltd* (London, 1926)

Records: Barclays Bank plc, Group Archives, Dallimore Road, Wythenshawe, Manchester M23 9JA

Customer account ledgers (4) 1800–12; signature book 1835–56.

BOWER HALL & CO
Beverley, Humberside

History: This private bank was established in Beverley, Malton and Hull in 1790 as Sir Christopher Sykes & Co. It was subsequently known as Sykes, Creyke & Co; R C Broadley, Sykes & Co from 1801; Robert Raikes & Co from 1805; Raikes, Currie & Co from 1808; Bower, Dewsbury & Co from 1811; Bower, Hutton & Hall from 1840; and Bower, Hall & Co from 1850. It was otherwise known as the East Riding Bank from 1840

Records of banks 111

and was acquired by Beckett & Co (est. 1774) of Leeds in 1875. Thereafter it was known as Beckett & Co, but operated independently of the Leeds business.

W C E Hartley, *Banking in Yorkshire* (Clapham, 1975)

Records 1: The Royal Bank of Scotland plc, Archive Section, Regent's House, 42 Islington High Street, London N1 8XL

Balance books 1808–13; note register 1824–68; papers re securities 1831–80; customer papers 1838, 1873–77; partnership deeds 1849–62; property purchase agreements 1861–62; private ledger 1867–75; papers re admission of partner 1870–81; balance sheet 1874; papers re financial position 1874; amalgamation agreement 1875; premises valuation 1875.

Records 2: Brynmor Jones Library, University of Hull, Hull HU6 7RX

'Hull account' 1793; valuation of securities 1794–98; stock accounts 1794–99; balances of accounts 1795–99; 'list of our friends at Hull' n.d. [Ref: DDSY/79/3]

BOWES, HODGSON, FALCON, KEY & CO
Workington, Cumbria

History: This private bank was formed in about 1801 and failed in 1811; it was also known as the Workington Bank.

Records: Cumbria Record Office, The Castle, Carlisle CA3 8UR

Till books 1800–13. [Ref: Allison MSS]

BOWLES, OGDEN, WYNDHAM & BARROW
Salisbury, Wiltshire

History: This private bank was established in about 1790 as Bowles, Ogden & Wyndham; it was otherwise known as the Salisbury & Shaftesbury Bank and was connected with the City of London bank of Bowles, Beachcroft & Reeves (est. 1780). It issued its own notes at both Salisbury and Shaftesbury. It was styled Bowles, Ogden, Wyndham & Barrow from 1810, in which year it failed.

L S Pressnell, *Country Banking in the Industrial Revolution* (Oxford, 1956)

Records: Wiltshire and Swindon Record Office, County Hall, Trowbridge BA14 8JG

Ledger 1799–1804; deeds re bankruptcy of partners 1810. [Ref: 1972/1; 776]

112   British banking – a guide to historical records

BRADFORD BANKING CO LTD
Bradford, West Yorkshire

History: This bank was established in 1827 with a paid-up capital of about £20,000; it was Bradford's first joint stock bank. Its leading promoter, and first manager, was Samuel Laycock who had formerly been manager of the Bradford office of Wentworth, Chaloner & Co (est. 1812) of Yorkshire and London which had failed in 1825. The new bank had strong links with the local worsted industry and with ironmasters and wool merchants, but no branches were opened and so the bank lost ground to more aggressive competitors. By 1879 paid-up capital was £408,000 and deposits totalled £2.286 million. Increasing competition meant that deposits fell from £2.3 million in 1899 to £1.7 million in 1909. A year later, when paid-up capital was still £408,000, the business was acquired for £793,000 by London, City & Midland Bank Ltd (est. 1836).

W F Crick & J E Wadsworth, *A Hundred Years of Joint Stock Banking* (London, 1936); W C E Hartley, *Banking in Yorkshire* (Clapham, 1975)

Records 1: HSBC Holdings plc, Group Archives, 10 Lower Thames Street, London EC3R 6AE

Formation papers 1825–27; deed of constitution 1827; private ledger 1827–30; security registers (7) 1827–1909; directors' meeting minute books (16) with rough copy minute books (8) 1827–1910; profit and loss statement 1828; general meeting minute books (3) 1828–1910; abstracts of shareholders' wills (2) 1845–97; safe custody register 1855–82; annual reports 1864–96; balance sheets 1868–1908; income tax returns 1870–1909; salary book 1871–1910; list of shareholders 1875; staff register c.1890; amalgamation papers 1909–10.

Records 2: West Yorkshire Archive Service, Bradford District Archives, 15 Canal Road, Bradford BD1 4AT

Deed of constitution 1827; papers of John Wood: share certificates 1827–31, share receipts 1827–28, passbook 1845–50; memorandum and articles of association 1862; report and balance sheet 1873. [Ref: B942 PAM; 10D76/3/box 152; DB39 C42/3, 5, 6; 28D78/21]

BRADFORD COMMERCIAL JOINT STOCK BANKING CO LTD
Bradford, West Yorkshire

History: This joint stock bank was established in 1833 and assumed limited liability in 1880. It was acquired by Bradford District Bank Ltd (est. 1862) in 1904, when its paid-up capital was £325,000.

Records 1: The Royal Bank of Scotland plc, Archive Section, Regent's House, 42 Islington High Street, London N1 8XL

Note register 1833–34; weekly returns 1833–64, 1860–1906; annual general meeting minutes 1834–77; deed of covenant and certificates of incorporation 1875, 1880; directors' meeting minute books 1885–1904; stockbroker's report 1896; annual report 1904; amalgamation agreement 1904.

Records 2: West Yorkshire Archive Service, Bradford District Archives, 15 Canal Road, Bradford BD1 4AT

Deed of covenant 1833; legal papers c.1833–1906; certificate of incorporation 1880. [Ref: 10D76/3/box 152]

BRADFORD DISTRICT BANK LTD
Bradford, West Yorkshire

History: This joint stock bank was established with limited liability in 1862 by leaders in the local woollen industry. A branch opened in Keighley in 1867. The property and business of London & Northern Bank Ltd (est. 1898) were acquired in 1899 and the Bradford Commercial Joint Stock Banking Co Ltd (est. 1833) was acquired in 1904. Immediately prior to this, paid-up capital was £344,000. Between 1897 and 1911 branches were established at Huddersfield, Clayton, Wibsey, Bingley, Dewsbury, Shipley, Silsden, Halifax and Cross Hills. The bank was taken over by National Provincial & Union Bank of England Ltd (est. 1833) in 1918.

Records: The Royal Bank of Scotland plc, Archive Section, Regent's House, 42 Islington High Street, London N1 8XL

Declaration of secrecy register 1862–1912; directors' meeting minute books (12) 1862–1919; half-yearly reports 1863–1917; salary books 1870–1918; subscriber contract 1875; annual reports 1891–1917; signature book 1899–1914; register of directors 1901–17; private minutes 1910–19; balance sheets 1910–19; comparative statistics of branches 1910–20; interview books 1910–30; private ledgers 1913–19; photographs, war service staff 1914–18; shareholders' register 1916–18; cheque forms n.d.; amalgamation papers 1918–26.

BRADFORD OLD BANK LTD
Bradford, West Yorkshire

History: This private bank was established in 1804 by Edmund Peckover and by his nephew, Charles Harris, as Peckover, Harris & Co. The Peckovers were wool staplers who had engaged in quasi-banking activities since at

114 *British banking – a guide to historical records*

least the 1790s; they were related to the eponymous banking family at Fakenham and Wisbech, to the Gurneys of Norwich and to partners in the Craven Bank at Settle. Initially the bank was located in Bank Street and moved to Kirkgate in 1813. From the outset it issued its own notes. It was styled Peckover, Harris & Harris from c.1817; Charles, Henry & Alfred Harris from 1823; H A & W M Harris from 1840; and Harris & Co from 1850. It survived a run during the 1825 financial panic due to the support of leading Bradford firms. In 1864 the business was reorganised as a joint stock bank with limited liability under the title of Bradford Old Bank Ltd; its paid-up capital was about £146,700, its deposits were £893,500 and its balance sheet total was £1.09 million. In 1875 it acquired Harrison & Co (est. 1785) of Ripon, Knaresborough, Harrogate, Pateley Bridge and Tadcaster. By 1906 it had nineteen branches and four sub-branches, paid-up capital of £500,000, deposits of £1.3 million and a balance sheet total of £3.48 million. In 1907 it amalgamated with Birmingham District & Counties Banking Co Ltd (est. 1836) to form United Counties Bank Ltd.

P W Matthews & Anthony W Tuke, *History of Barclays Bank Limited* (London, 1926)

Records 1: Barclays Bank plc, Group Archives, Dallimore Road, Wythenshawe, Manchester M23 9JA

Customer account correspondence 1777–1863; statements of account and letter, Leeds & Liverpool Canal Co 1784–1845; bill of exchange register 1785; cash book, Edmund Peckover 1792–93; estate papers 1802–1900; trustee accounts 1803–68; partnership agreements 1804–10; bill of exchange 1806; notebook, valuation of bankrupt Robert Chamberlain 1807–08; draft forms 1807–24; probate of will, Edmund and May Peckover 1809, 1827; bank notes c.1800s–22; private ledgers (8) 1810–99; private papers, Henry Harris 1820–1900; circulars 1838, 1852; executors' ledger, Thomas Lister 1846–68; notice re opening hours 1850; customer signature book 1850–68; cheque book 1863; private letterbooks (2) 1863–72; certificate of incorporation 1864; memorandum and articles of association 1864–75; half-yearly accounts 1864–1907; declarations of secrecy 1865–1900; cheque form 1866; petty expenses ledgers 1870–72; superannuation fund subscription book 1872–1906; dividend statements and warrants 1884–1907; directors' meeting minute books (2) 1893–1903; general meeting minute books 1893–1907; share certificates 1898–1906; centenary booklet 1903; report and accounts 1903–07; share transfer notices 1904–07; merger papers Bradford Old Bank Ltd and Birmingham District & Counties Banking Co Ltd 1907.

Records 2: West Yorkshire Archive Service, Bradford District Archives, 15 Canal Road, Bradford BD1 4AT

Memorandum and articles of association 1864; centenary souvenir 1903.
[Ref: 10D76/3/box 152; DB17 C32/5]

BRETT & CO
Stone, Staffordshire

History: This private bank was established in Stone in 1801 and may also have been known as Brett & Gilbert. It failed in 1826.

Records: William Salt Library, Eastgate Street, Stafford ST16 2LZ

Counsel's opinion on liabilities of executors of deceased partners 1825. [Ref: 93/24/41]

M & J BRICKDALE
Taunton, Somerset

History: This private bank was formed in about 1783 as Matthew & John Brickdale; it was otherwise known as the Taunton Bank and, from 1814, as Taunton Old Bank. It failed in 1819.

Records: Somerset Record Office, Obridge Road, Taunton TA2 7PU

Papers re business and failure 1775–1853, including letterbook of Robert Beadon, solicitor 1819–28; partnership agreements 1776–85; papers re debts 1816. [Ref: DD/DP 6/4–7/20; DD/DP 10/9; DD/WY/ Bx 151]

BRIDGES & CO
Hadleigh, Essex

History: This private bank was formed in about 1799 by a Harwich banker who also had banking interests at Manningtree. The bank was otherwise known as the Hadleigh Bank. Subsequently it may have been acquired by the Mills family of Colchester, owners of a Hadleigh bank.

Harold Preston, *Early East Anglian Banks and Bankers* (Thetford, 1994)

Records: Essex Record Office, Stanwell House, Stanwell Street, Colchester CO2 7DL

Draft partnership agreements 1799–1816. [Ref: D/DHW B10]

BRIDGES, MARRATT & BRIDGES
Manningtree, Essex

History: This private bank was established in about 1790 by a Harwich banker who subsequently had banking interests at Hadleigh; it also traded as the Manningtree & Mistley Bank. By 1815 Bridges was bankrupt when

116   *British banking – a guide to historical records*

the Hadleigh business may have been acquired by the Mills family of Colchester and that at Manningtree by Alexanders & Co (est. 1744) of Ipswich.

Harold Preston, *Early East Anglian Banks and Bankers* (Thetford, 1994)

Records: Essex Record Office, Stanwell House, Stanwell Street, Colchester CO2 7DL

Draft partnership agreements 1799–1816. [Ref: D/DHW B10]

BRIGHTWEN & CO
London

History: This discount house was formed in the City of London in 1860 by George Brightwen, formerly a partner in the Gurney family's East Anglian banks, who in 1856 had resigned to become 'joint manager' of the London Discount Co. On this company's winding up, in about 1859, Brightwen established himself as a bill dealer. William Gillett soon joined him as partner and their firm was styled Brightwen, Gillett & Co. Gillett left in 1867 to form Gillett Brothers & Co. C E Tritton, later Sir Ernest Tritton, also of East Anglian banking stock, joined as partner and his family led the business in the twentieth century. In 1939 Brightwen was absorbed by Cater & Co Ltd to form Cater, Brightwen & Co Ltd.

Anon, *Cater Ryder 1816–1966* (priv. pub., c.1971)

Records: Guildhall Library, Aldermanbury, London EC2P 2EJ

Receipts for quarterly salaries 1861–82; general ledgers (3) 1867–91; deed re retirement of William Gillett 1867; partnership agreements 1869–98; annual analysis of profit and loss account 1876–1916. [Ref: MS 18520–18523, 24696]

BRISTOL & WEST OF ENGLAND BANK LTD
Bristol, Avon

History: This joint stock bank was formed in 1879 out of the business of some branches of the West of England & South Wales District Bank Ltd (est. 1834) which had failed in 1878. Its paid-up capital was £112,000. In 1892, when it had twenty-two branches, it was acquired by Lloyds Bank Ltd (est. 1765).

Charles H Cave, *A History of Banking in Bristol from 1750 to 1899* (Bristol, 1899)

Records: Lloyds TSB Group plc, Archives, Head Office, 71 Lombard Street, London EC3P 3BS

Amalgamation papers 1892–1909.

Bristol, Corn Street: signature book 1879–95; **Bristol, Kingswood:** signature book 1885–1932; **Bristol, Temple Gate:** signature book 1881–1932.

BRITISH BANK OF NORTHERN COMMERCE LTD
London and Europe

History: This overseas bank was formed in 1912 largely by Scandinavian interests that included Knut Wallenberg, the leader of the Stockholms Enskilda Bank. It specialised in financing Anglo-Scandinavian trade and quickly gained a high reputation. Its balance sheet total grew to £22 million by 1920. During the First World War it joined with the merchant bankers, C J Hambro & Son (est. 1839), to arrange loans to the British government from Scandinavian sources. In 1920, in order to identify more clearly with Britain and thereby expand its business, it merged with Hambros to form Hambros Bank of Northern Commerce Ltd. At the time, the balance sheet totals of the two banks were of similar size.

Bo Bramsen & Kathleen Wain, *The Hambros 1779–1979* (London, 1979)

Records: Guildhall Library, Aldermanbury, London EC2P 2EJ

Memorandum and articles of association 1912; general ledgers (5) 1912–27; annual reports and balance sheets 1913–22; amalgamation papers 1920. [Ref: MS 19040, 19044, 19182]

BRITISH BANK OF SOUTH AMERICA LTD
London and Latin America

History: This British-owned overseas bank was established in 1863 as the Brazilian & Portuguese Bank Ltd, its promoters being London and Oporto merchants and bankers associated with Brazil. Paid-up capital was £500,000 and almost a third of the shares were marketed in Brazil and Portugal. In its early years, the bank had only one Brazilian branch, at Rio de Janeiro, and an agency at Oporto which was unsuccessful and was closed in 1866 prompting a name change to the English Bank of Rio de Janeiro Ltd. In 1867 further branches opened, at Pernambuco and Santos, and in these years the bank outstripped its main rival, the Bank of London & Brazil Ltd. From 1878 security issues were made for Brazilian-based businesses, beginning with the Companhia Paulista. In the 1880s more branches were opened, at Para (1883) and Sao Paulo (1886), and later at Buenos Aires and Montevideo (1888) in order to finance Brazilian trade with Argentina and Uruguay. In 1891 the Brazilian business and assets were sold for £875,000 to the local Banco de Credito Universal and the bank was renamed the British Bank of South America Ltd. However, later that year

118   British banking – a guide to historical records

a concession to operate in Brazil was repurchased and in 1892 the bank reopened its Brazilian branches. Initially progress was slow and the Para and Santos branches were closed, but in the decade before 1914 the bank prospered both in Argentina and Brazil and by 1912 paid-up capital reached £1 million. In 1920 the Anglo-South American Bank Ltd (est. 1888), which had no Brazilian branches, acquired control of the bank, but the British Bank continued to trade as a separate entity. However, the branch network was rationalised by merging the Argentine branches with those of the Anglo-South American Bank and, initially, the Anglo's Uruguayan branches with those of the British Bank. The British Bank's London and Manchester offices were combined with those of the Anglo-South American Bank in 1931. In 1936 the bank's business was merged into that of the British Bank of London & South America Ltd following the latter's acquisition of the Anglo-South American Bank Ltd. The British bank was then placed in voluntary liquidation and finally wound up in 1961.

David Joslin, *A Century of Banking in Latin America. The Bank of London & South America Ltd 1862–1962* (Oxford, 1963)

Records 1: Lloyds TSB Group plc, Archives, Head Office, 71 Lombard Street, London EC3P 3BS

Annual reports 1863–1936; staff registers (6) 1868–1936; 'left service' ledgers 1920–36.

Records 2: Bloomsbury Science Library, University College London, Gower Street, London WC1E 6BT

Letterbooks, Sao Paulo to London, Rio and branches (14) 1886–1927; letters, London and branches to Sao Paulo 1892–1913; letterbooks, London to Montevideo (5) 1912–13. [Ref: BOLSA]

BRITISH BANK OF THE MIDDLE EAST LTD
London and Asia

History: This British-owned overseas bank was established as the Imperial Bank of Persia in 1889. Its legal framework rested on a concession granted by the Shah of Persia to Baron Julius de Reuter entitling him to form a state bank with a head office in Tehran and an exclusive right to issue notes. However the bank was also granted a Royal Charter in Britain, which provided for a London board of directors. The initial paid-up capital of £1 million was fifteen times oversubscribed. During its early years, the bank was not overly profitable. Despite buying the Persian business of the New Oriental Bank Corporation (est. 1851) in 1890 and establishing branches throughout Persia, the bank was badly effected by the depreciation of silver which resulted in a capital write down to £650,000

Records of banks 119

in 1895. A slow recovery followed. The First World War was a profitable period, due largely to the financing of the British government's operations in Persia. The bank continued to grow and profit in the 1920s. The number of Persian branches reached a peak of twenty-five by 1929 but a shifting political climate forced change. In 1929 the nationalist government established its own state bank which in 1930 received sole right to issue notes. In 1935 Persia was renamed Iran resulting in a name change to The Imperial Bank of Iran. In 1949 banks were required to transfer 55 per cent of their deposits to the state bank and in 1951 the bank's foreign exchange permit was withdrawn. From the late 1940s less profitable branches were closed and in 1952 no new business was transacted in Iran. To compensate for this loss in activity, new branches were opened elsewhere, in the 1940s in the Gulf States and Fertile Crescent including Kuwait (1942), Bahrain (1944) and Dubai (1946). Here the bank pioneered modern banking and often operated initially with no competition. This changing geographical spread resulted in a name-change in 1949 to The British Bank of Iran & the Middle East. Following withdrawal from Iran in 1952, a new charter was acquired together with a new name, The British Bank of the Middle East. Nationalisation of banking operations and political conflicts caused withdrawal from certain countries in the 1960s and 1970s, but oil industry development in the Gulf States led to continued and profitable growth. In 1959 the Hongkong & Shanghai Banking Corporation Ltd (est. 1865) acquired the bank but it continued as a separate entity. In 1980 the head office was transferred to Hong Kong and thence to Jersey in 1994.

Geoffrey Jones, *The History of the British Bank of the Middle East* (Cambridge, 1986–87)

Records 1: HSBC Holdings plc, Group Archives, 10 Lower Thames Street, London EC3R 6AE

Prospectus 1889; deed of settlement 1889; concession agreement 1889; directors' meeting minutes 1889 on; annual reports 1889 on; share allotment book 1889; investment ledger c.1889–1913; special staff and semi-official letters from Tehran c.1889–1917; share ledgers (3) 1889–1945; general ledgers (32) 1889–1946; founders' share ledgers (3) 1889–1952; staff report books (14) 1889 on; reports on office in Persia c.1890–1906; powers of attorney books (4) c.1890–1911; deposit account ledgers (53) 1890–1929; note registers (5) c.1890–1933; special letters to chief office and branches in Persia c.1890–1937; chairman's addresses to shareholders 1890–1950; balance sheets 1890–1977; special staff and semi-official letters to Tehran 1891–1917; letters to staff officers in Persia 1891–1921; progress reports 1893–1936; private ledgers (3) 1893–1977; security registers (11) 1898–1943; dividend lists 1899–1950; charges ledgers

120 *British banking – a guide to historical records*

(18) 1899–1962; letters to Persian minister and Foreign Office c.1900–08; letters re branches and inspections (5) 1900–15; premises photograph albums (7) c.1900 on; press cuttings books (3) c.1900 on; interest and commission account ledgers (8) 1902–27; papers re officers' provident fund 1905–44; premises account book 1908–65; premises memorandum book 1909–14; confidential in-letterbooks (73) 1917–53; staff out-letterbooks (15) 1919–35; bad debt register 1919–39; telegram copy books (31) 1920–50; registers of loans granted 1922–40; branch statistics 1924–56; confidential out-letterbooks (29) 1925–53; branch balance sheets (6) 1928–50; current account ledgers (16) 1929–58.

Persian Bank Mining Rights Corp: various papers and correspondence 1889–1921; prospectus 1890; agreement 1890; applications for shares 1890.

Records 2: Centre for Middle East Studies, St Antony's College, Oxford OX2 6JF

Press cuttings books (3) 1890–1906; letters from Tehran to London 1917–24.

BRITISH GUIANA BANK
London and Latin America

History: This overseas bank, which applied for a royal charter in the late 1830s, appears not to have been formed. It may have been associated in some way with the Colonial Bank that was formed in 1836 under charter to provide banking services in the West Indies and British Guiana.

Records: Public Record Office, Ruskin Avenue, Kew, Richmond TW9 4DU

Papers re establishment 1836–40. [Ref: T1/3474]

BRITISH LINEN BANK
Edinburgh, Lothian

History: British Linen Co was established in 1746 by Royal Charter to acquire the business of the Edinburgh Linen Co-partnery (est. c.1727). The new company was empowered to 'carry on the Linen Manufactory in all its branches' and was granted limited liability. The name 'British' in its title (as opposed to 'Scottish') reflected suspicion of Scottish institutions after the Jacobite Rising of 1745. The key figures in the company's establishment were the 3rd Duke of Argyll, Lord Milton, the Earl of Panmure and George Middleton, a London banker. Its initial nominal capital of £100,000 was not increased until 1806, when it was raised to £200,000.

Records of banks

From the late 1760s the company gradually moved towards banking, began issuing notes and was recognised as a bank by the Royal Bank of Scotland in 1765 and by the Bank of Scotland in 1771. Its great strength was its spread of agents throughout the country, a network developed through its linen trade business. Many of these agencies became branches, of which there were nine by 1780. Capital was raised in 1813 to £600,000, despite the objections of the Bank of Scotland and the Royal Bank of Scotland which argued that the company was overstepping its original aim of promoting the linen industry. In 1808 the company acquired 38 St Andrew Square as a new head office; 39 and 40 were purchased in 1835. The depression of 1837 brought a temporary halt to prosperity, but the company did not suffer as much as other banks; it had been careful in granting advances and had recognised the precarious financial state of many of England's business houses. Indeed, the company even managed to acquire the Paisley Banking Co (est. 1783) in that year which had surplus assets of £20,000 and branches in Glasgow, Irvine and Stranraer. Growth continued and by 1845 the company was entitled to circulate notes, without cover, to the value of £438,000. Apart from a temporary paralysis in trade caused by the collapse of the Western Bank of Scotland (est. 1832) in 1857 and the suspension of the City of Glasgow Bank (est. 1839) in 1878, the British Linen Co survived periods of economic stagnation relatively unscathed; it emerged as a major Scottish bank with a large branch network. In 1906 its name was changed to British Linen Bank. In 1919 the bank became a wholly-owned subsidiary of Barclays Bank Ltd (est. 1896), a parent which provided improved foreign connections and increased its total assets from £29 million in 1918 to £36 million in 1920. It retained a board of directors in Edinburgh, its separate structure and its note issue. In 1969 the Bank of Scotland and the British Linen Bank merged. The full amalgamation occurred in 1971 when a thirty-five per cent equity stake in the Bank of Scotland was issued to Barclays Bank Ltd (est. 1896). The terms allowed for the continuation of the British Linen Bank as a separate Scottish institution. In 1977 permission was granted for the resumption of British Linen Bank as the merchant banking arm of the Bank of Scotland.

Charles A Malcolm, *The History of the British Linen Bank* (Edinburgh, 1950)

Records 1: Bank of Scotland Archive, Operational Services Division, 12 Bankhead Terrace, Sighthill, Edinburgh EH11 4DY

Journals of the daily transactions 1746–69; cash books 1746–1844; charters 1746–1955; proprietors' meetings minutes 1746–1955; directors' meetings minutes 1746–1965; stock ledgers 1746–1971; dividend books

122   British banking – a guide to historical records

1747–1810; English and foreign letterbooks 1748–63; ledgers of accounts current 1748–99; letterbooks (main series) 1748–1800; stock transfers 1748–1972; Scotch letterbooks 1749–61; ledgers of the daily transactions 1750–1800; ledgers 1751–73; letters to William Tod and Messrs Tod and Anderson, London 1758–63; letterbooks 1760–64; register of demand and optional notes 1761–65; register of cash credits 1765–97; register of confirmations 1766–85; report by Archibald Trotter on the dispute between the British Linen Co and Ebenezer McCulloch 1772; interest ledgers 1784–1801; directors' letterbooks 1785–1848; letterbooks 1789–1900; branch letterbooks 1790–1808; inspectors' department widows' fund register 1800–1910; note circulation in England 1812–33; stock (investment) ledgers 1819–1920; law department miscellaneous papers 1821–1940; papers re meetings of creditors of Fife Bank 1825–26; branch cash accounts 1837–67; memorandum re fluctuations in banking profits 1840; list of branch officers 1845–1946; register of lodgements for safekeeping 1847–1950; miscellaneous papers including: papers re application for supplementary charter 1848–1906; salary books 1849–1970; reports, general balances and balance sheets 1860–1911; general and particular register of sasines 1863–65; papers re proposed changes in Bank Acts 1864–81; papers on proposed Scottish bank in London and on London business 1866–1900; general manager's private letters and papers 1866–1919; Edinburgh cash accounts 1869–1934; officers' guarantee fund minutes 1877–1955; secretary's letterbooks 1880–1971; bank notes printed 1899–1961; statements of the bank's investments 1907–19; papers re staff 1914–18; papers re amalgamation with Barclays Bank 1919–20; seal registers 1930–71; head office (outstanding) ledgers 1947–65; general ledgers 1953–69.

Aberdeen (three branches): 1833–1970; **Airdrie:** 1882–1969; **Alexandria:** 1886–1968; **Annan:** 1826–1966; **Arbroath:** 1825–1970; **Aviemore:** 1966–69; **Ayr (two branches):** 1874–1970; **Balfron:** 1836–1969; **Bathgate:** 1963–70; **Bearsden:** 1931–69; **Bishopton:** 1938–70; **Bo'ness:** 1923–42; **Brechin:** 1836–1971; **Broxburn:** 1879–1968; **Burnside:** 1925–69; **Carluke:** 1837–1969; **Castle Douglas:** 1821–1970; **Clarkston:** 1913–69; **Clydebank:** 1882–1970; **Coatbridge:** 1898–1969; **Coldstream:** 1823–1968; **Crieff:** 1879–1970; **Cumbernauld:** 1964–70; **Cupar:** 1792–1970; **Dalmuir:** 1905–69; **Dalry:** 1872–1971; **Dumbarton:** 1884–1970; **Dumfries:** 1771–1970; **Dunbar:** 1790–1970; **Dundee (four branches):** 1811–1970; **Dunfermline:** 1831–1970; **Dunoon:** 1883–1971; **Duns:** 1784–1968; **East Kilbride:** 1963–71; **Edinburgh (twenty-four branches):** 1746–1971; **Elgin:** 1808–1969; **Falkirk (two branches):** 1897–1970; **Falkland:** 1878–1970; **Forfar:** 1872–1969; **Forres:** 1770–1969; **Fort William:** 1791–1970; **Galashiels:** 1873–1969;

Records of banks   123

Galston: 1876–1971; Girvan: 1874–1970; Glasgow (forty-five branches): 1791–1970; Glenrothes: 1960–70; Golspie: 1838–1971; Gourock (two branches): 1911–68; Greenock (two branches): 1784–1971; Haddington: 1822–1971; Hamilton: 1821–1968; Hawick: 1783–1970; Helensburgh: 1962–70; Helmsdale: 1875–1969; Huntly: 1926–70; Innerleithen: 1923–70; Inverness: 1769–1969; Irvine: 1837–1970; Jedburgh: 1791–1970; Johnstone: 1924–70; Kelso: 1833–1969; Killearn: 1932–67; Kilmarnock: 1864–1970; Kinghorn: 1876–1970; Kingussie: 1835–1969; Kinross: 1828–1970; Kirkcaldy: 1871–1970; Kirkconnel: 1925–70; Kirkwall: 1953–70; Kirriemuir: 1825–1969; Lanark: 1879–1970; Langholm: 1783–1970; Largs: 1885–1970; Lesmahagow: 1878–1970; Leven: 1889–1970; Linlithgow: 1874–1970; Loanhead: 1875–1970; London (two branches): 1878–1970; Melrose: 1833–1969; Methil: 1922–71; Moffat: 1855–1970; Montrose: 1791–1970; Motherwell: 1885–1971; Musselburgh: 1931–70; Nairn: 1836–1970; Newcastleton: 1893–1969; Newtonmore: 1879–1970; Newton Stewart: 1804–1970; Newtown St Boswells: 1903–70; North Berwick: 1857–1970; Oban: 1910–70; Paisley: 1837–1971; Peebles: 1825–1970; Perth (three branches):1807–1968; Polmont: c.1914–70; Port Glasgow: 1911–19; Port William: 1878–1971; Prestwick: 1947–69; Renfrew: 1897–1970; Roslin: 1936–70; Rothesay: 1924–71; Rutherglen: 1930–42; Sanquhar: 1830–1970; Selkirk: 1825–1969; Shotts: 1957–67; Stevenston: 1922–70; Stewarton: 1924–68; Stirling: 1874–1970; Stornoway: 1878–1969 Stranraer: 1837–1970; Tain: 1811–1969; Thornhill: 1852–1970; Thurso: 1875–1970; Tillicoultry: 1922–41; Troon: 1874–1969; Turriff: 1925–70; Uddingston: 1887–1970; Uphall: 1921–70; Wick: 1872–1969; Wigtown: 1825–1971; Wishaw: 1882–1970; Wooler: 1878–1970.

Records 2: Business Records Centre, Archive Department, University of Glasgow, Glasgow G12 8QQ

Directors' meeting minutes extracts 1746–1920; accounts and balance sheets 1865–1971 [w]. [Ref: Scottish Banking Collection]

Records 3: National Library of Scotland, Department of Manuscripts, George IV Bridge, Edinburgh EH1 1EW

Notes and accounts re bank 1739–60; correspondence and papers re establishment of bank, particularly accounts with Lord Milton 1744–65; accounts re transactions of Lord Milton 1746–62; papers re bank 1753–57. [Ref: MSS 17594–600; Ch.14879–83]

Records 4: Dumfries and Galloway Archives, 33 Burns Street, Dumfries DG1 2PS

124   *British banking – a guide to historical records*

Accounts between Hugh Corrie, writer, and British Linen Bank 1778–91; architectural drawings of Annan branch by Walter Newall (1780–1836) n.d., c.1840. [Ref: GGD 37/7/7; GGD 131/B1/16B, 17]

Records 5: National Archives of Scotland, HM General Register House, Princes Street, Edinburgh EH1 3YY

Miscellaneous titles and records 1767–1881. [Ref: GD190/3/46]

BRITISH MUTUAL BANK LTD
London

History: This bank, based in the City of London, traced its origins to the British Mutual Investment, Loan & Discount Co which was formed in 1857 'to continue and develop for traders what had formerly been non-trading co-partnerships consisting of lenders and borrowers who had equally shared profit and loss'. The business was renamed British Mutual Investment Co Ltd in 1869, British Mutual Banking Co Ltd in 1882 and British Mutual Bank Ltd in 1945. In 1950 its first branch was opened in London's St James's Street; it also established the first bank on a cross-Channel ferry service. By 1951 deposits stood at £2.24 million. In that year, the business was acquired by Martins Bank Ltd (est. 1831).

George Chandler, *Four Centuries of Banking* (London, 1964–68)

Records: Barclays Bank plc, Group Archives, Dallimore Road, Wythenshawe, Manchester M23 9JA

Prospectus 1857; press cuttings, annual reports and shareholder notices 1857–1940; certificates of incorporation/change of name/alteration of objects 1857–1945; agreements, transfer of property and assets 1869–76; memorandum and articles of association 1875–1951; signature books (7) 1880–1942; share registers (2) 1883–1951; impersonal ledgers (2) 1896–1950; cheques 1912; accounting papers 1915–50; directors' meeting minute books (5) 1923–62; directors' committees rota 1923; dividend warrants 1930–51; manager's letter of resignation 1939; general balance ledgers (3) 1940–51; papers re amalgamation with Martins Bank, staff issues 1941–52; papers re services of executor and trustee department 1944; new issues book 1945–47; share transfer registers 1947–51; register of directors and secretaries 1948–49.

British Mutual Bank Nominees Ltd: directors' meeting minute book 1938–45; resolutions 1940–51.

BRITISH OVERSEAS BANK LTD
London and Europe

Records of banks 125

History: This bank was established in 1919 by Prudential Assurance Co and eight British banks as 'a protective alliance, firstly for the promotion of mutual interests and secondly for the development of business in fresh fields'. The bank was formed to 'facilitate the foreign trade of the British Isles and the Empire by specialising in all matters of exchange, payments and receipts abroad and the handling of foreign collections, documents and securities'. Acceptance finance was especially important, in particular for trade with Eastern Europe and Spain. In 1920 it established the Anglo-Polish Bank, after taking over a Warsaw private bank, and subsequently it acquired control of an Estonian bank. In 1923 the London & Liverpool Bank of Commerce Ltd (est. 1879) was purchased, but shortly afterwards it was placed in voluntary liquidation. In 1924 Williams Deacon's Bank, Union Bank of Scotland and Prudential Assurance Co acquired the voting shares of the other participating banks. In 1930 the foreign business of H S Lefevre & Co (est. 1790) was acquired, followed by that of Frederick Huth & Co (est. 1809) in 1936. Large bad debts incurred in Germany and eastern Europe in the late 1930s meant that the business was wound down just before and during the Second World War. In 1940 it took over management of the Anglo-International Bank Ltd (est. 1926) which was itself being run down. The bank's banking business was sold to Glyn, Mills & Co (est. 1753) in 1944 and at the same time its produce business, acquired from Huths, was disposed of to Matheson & Co. The remainder of its assets was placed under management of Continental Assets Realisation Trust Ltd. In 1954 it was placed in liquidation and was finally wound up in 1962.

Bickham Sweet-Escott, *Gallant Failure. The British Overseas Bank 1919– 1939. A History* (unpub. mss., 1977)

Records 1: The Royal Bank of Scotland plc, Archive Section, Regent's House, 42 Islington High Street, London N1 8XL

Prospectus 1919; shareholder list 1919; reports on countries files 1919– 26; papers re British companies' foreign trade, letters of credit and bank structure 1919–26; memorandum and articles of association and related papers 1919–c.1930; correspondence with Williams Deacon's Bank 1919– 26; annual reports 1920, 1929–26, 1939; marketing booklet c.1924; annual general meeting resolutions 1929, 1939; staff papers 1930; customer details book 1936–38; share register, British Overseas Bank Nominees Ltd 1944–48; liquidation agreement 1954.

Records 2: Public Record Office, Ruskin Avenue, Kew, Richmond TW9 4DU

Papers re constitution, capital issue and formation 1919. [Ref: T1/12342/ 26605/19]

126 British banking – a guide to historical records

BROMAGE & CO
Monmouth, Gwent

History: This private bank was founded in 1819 as Bromage, Snead & Co and was later known as Bromage & Co; it was otherwise styled the Monmouth Bank. It was connected with Bromage, Snead & Snead (est. 1827) of Chepstow which failed in 1866. In 1894 it was acquired by Lloyds Bank Ltd (est. 1765).

Records: Lloyds TSB Group plc, Archives, Head Office, 71 Lombard Street, London EC3P 3BS

Partnership agreement 1821; amalgamation papers 1861–66.

JOSEPH BROOKS
Woodstock, Oxfordshire

History: This private bank failed in 1807. It had also been known as the Woodstock Bank.

Records: Berkshire Record Office, Shire Hall, Shinfield Park, Reading RG2 9XD

Private papers of Joseph Brooks, some re banking 1785–1836. [Ref: D/ESV(M) B6–22]

BROOKS & CO
London

History: Accounts of the history of this private bank vary. It appears to trace its origins to Cunliffe, Brooks & Co of Lombard Street, City of London, which was formed in about 1815 as the London agent of Cunliffe, Brooks & Co (est. 1792) of Blackburn, Lancashire. In 1864 the business, then virtually a discount house and known as Roger Cunliffe & Co, was acquired by the London discount house of A & G W Alexander & Co. At this time the London banking business was reconstituted in a new firm, Brooks & Co, which worked closely with the Blackburn bank and was acquired by Lloyds Bank Ltd (est. 1765) in 1900.

Records: Lloyds TSB Group plc, Archives, Head Office, 71 Lombard Street, London EC3P 3BS

Salary books (2) 1873–1900; amalgamation papers 1900.

BROOKSBY & CO
Newark, Nottinghamshire

History: Unknown

Records of banks 127

Records: Nottinghamshire Archives, County House, Castle Meadow Road, Nottingham NG2 1AG

Partnership agreement 1785. [Ref: DDT 126/4]

BROTHERS SWAINE & CO
Halifax, West Yorkshire

History: This private bank was formed in 1779 as Hainsworth, Holden, Swaine & Pollard and was known as Hainsworth, Swaine & Pollard from 1780 and as Brothers Swaine & Co from 1802; it otherwise traded as the Halifax Commercial Bank. Also in 1802 its partners established a firm to act as its London agents. The Swaine family, who provided the most important partners, was long established at Halifax, latterly working as textile merchants and manufacturers. In 1807 the bank suspended payment and in 1808 the partners were declared bankrupt. The firm of John Rawson, William Rawson, John Rhodes & Rawdon Briggs was then established and took over much of Swaines' business.

Records: Barclays Bank plc, Group Archives, Dallimore Road, Wythenshawe, Manchester M23 9JA

Papers re securities 1802–07; papers re failure 1807.

BROWN & COOMBS
Windsor, Berkshire

History: This private bank was established in 1801 as James Coombs; its partners had interests in the ironmongery trade. It had representation at Eton and was also known as the Windsor & Eton Bank. The bank was subsequently styled Coombs, Brown, Coombs & Co and as Brown & Coombs. It failed in 1816.

L S Pressnell, *Country Banking in the Industrial Revolution* (Oxford, 1956)

Records: Barclays Bank plc, Group Archives, Dallimore Road, Wythenshawe, Manchester M23 9JA

Bank notes 1800s; bank note forms 1800s.

BROWN, JANSON & CO
London

History: This private bank was established in Threadneedle Street, City of London, in 1813 as Nicholson, Janson & Co. Its partners were Leeds woollen merchants who established simultaneously a bank in Leeds under

128   *British banking – a guide to historical records*

the title of Nicholson, Brown & Co, later Williams Brown, Janson, Barr & Co, which was acquired by Lloyds Bank Ltd in 1900. The London business moved to Abchurch Lane in 1815 and was renamed Brown, Janson & Co in 1823. Lloyds Bank Ltd (est. 1765) acquired the bank in 1900. W S Draper, a partner, was joint general manager of Lloyds from 1918 to 1929.

Records: Lloyds TSB Group plc, Archives, Head Office, 71 Lombard Street, London EC3P 3BS

Partnership agreements 1814, 1891; private ledgers (2) 1844–56, 1890–1900; salary books (2) 1873–98; amalgamation papers 1900.

BROWN SHIPLEY & CO LTD
London and Liverpool, Merseyside

History: This merchant bank traced its origins to Alexander Brown, an Irish linen merchant who settled at Baltimore, USA, in about 1800. He soon emerged as a leading merchant, leaving an estate of US$2 million when he died in 1834. His business was known initially as Alexander Brown and later as Alexander Brown & Sons. Subsequently branch houses, in the form of interlocking partnerships, were established at New York, Philadelphia and Liverpool and branch offices in the southern USA. The Liverpool house, known initially as William Brown & Co, was formed in 1810 by Alexander's son William (later Sir William). Initially it acted as agent for the Baltimore house, but increasingly developed its own business as merchants and shippers and later as financiers of trade. It specialised in cotton and became one of the leading 'American' houses in Liverpool. In 1824 the house was renamed Wm & Jas Brown & Co. The American William Shipley became a partner in 1825 and in 1837 the house was renamed Brown Shipley & Co. Sir William Brown died in 1864, by which time he was a leading figure in Liverpool's economic and public life as well as being a major benefactor to the city. Merchanting was given up in the wake of the American Civil War and in 1863 an office in the City of London was opened; the Liverpool branch closed in 1888. By the end of the nineteenth century, Brown Shipley's main activity was the provision of acceptance credits, mostly to American businesses, to finance their international trade. It also participated in security issues made by Brown Brothers, continued to do foreign exchange business and did some deposit banking. From the early nineteenth century, circular letters of credit were issued to private individuals travelling abroad and, by 1900, this became particularly important business along with associated activities such as mail handling for clients. A West End office was established in 1900 (closed 1955) to undertake this work. From 1900 until 1915 Montagu Norman, grandson of a senior partner and later Governor of the Bank of

Records of banks 129

England, was a partner. In 1918 the interlocking partnership with Brown Brothers ended; the American firm in 1931 merged with Harrimans to form Brown Brothers Harriman. Between the wars a prominent position was secured in the foreign exchange market and a more broadly-based business was built in financing the wool, timber and fur trades. Exposure to central European business at the time of the 1930s credit crisis was small. Limited liability was adopted in 1946, when the name changed to Brown Shipley & Co Ltd. In the 1950s, drawing on past specialisations, the firm figured prominently in the new business of supplying foreign bank notes to other banks and to travel agents. Fund management and corporate finance activity also began and in the 1970s and 1980s Brown Shipley functioned as a rounded London merchant bank. It had been a member of the Accepting Houses Committee for many years. In 1993 the merchant banking business was sold to Guinness Mahon of London when Brown Shipley continued as an investment management business.

John Crosby Brown, *A Hundred Years of Merchant Banking. A History of Brown, Brothers & Co, Brown Shipley & Co and their Allied Firms* (priv. pub., 1909); Aytoun Ellis, *Heir of Adventure. The Story of Brown Shipley & Co, Merchant Bankers, 1810–1960* (priv. pub., 1960)

Records 1: Guildhall Library, Aldermanbury, London EC2P 2EJ

Ledger with miscellaneous general and US business accounts 1860–66; private out-letterbook, mostly to Liverpool house 1864–65; 'travellers ledger', US customers 1864–65; customer ledger 1864–67; 'finance' out-letterbooks, mainly to New York house (12) 1864, 1866, 1868–77; private out-letterbooks, mostly to New York house (16) 1864–1914 [w]; private out-letterbooks to USA houses (4) 1864–1900, 1910–20; miscellaneous private in-letters from Liverpool and USA houses 1868–88 [w]; current account ledgers, businesses (2) 1871–75, 1887; private in letterbook, from Liverpool 1877–88; weekly and monthly returns of Liverpool house 1883–88; minute book 1884–86; new account records 1889–1901; papers re New York exchange business for Standard Bank of South Africa 1895–1921; current account ledgers, individuals and businesses 1895–1934 [w]; 'partners' files inwards', confidential letters from US houses (10) 1895, 1912–37; applications for current accounts (15) 1896–1928; letters of introduction sent by London house 1896–1901; partnership agreements and related papers 1900–16; private in-letters from US houses (2) 1901–04; current account ledgers, individuals (5) 1902–35 [w]; bookkeeper's memorandum book 1903–43; plans of London office 1903–65; bad debts balance book 1904–16; private out-letterbooks (10) 1908–12, 1921–30; investment ledger 1909–12; monthly statements of capital and deposits 1911–12; deposit accounts receipt advices with letters 1911–12; annual

130   *British banking – a guide to historical records*

reports of bills payable department 1911–27; 'private and confidential memoranda' (3) 1911–68; quarterly analysis of some general accounts of US houses 1912; profit and loss accounts analysis for US houses 1912–17 [w]; weekly asset and liability balances of US houses 1912–17; short loans to discount houses ledger 1912–26; 'American accounts' being general accounts analysis and summaries 1913–17; partnership matters correspondence 1914–15; register of sundry coupons payable 1914–23; weekly debit and credit balances of customer accounts 1915–17; solicitors' letters re split between US and London houses 1917; copies of 'hegira' cables between London and US houses 1919–24; commercial credit applications (10) 1920–30, 1934–38; 'partners' files outwards letters to New York house (2) 1921–39; letters between US and London partners 1926–32; correspondence with German clients 1926–39; commercial customers' cash accounts (3) 1928–35 [w]; London dollar exchange ledger 1934–36; foreign exchange ledger 1935–36.

Pall Mall: current account ledger 1902–03; current account applications (24) 1904–38; current account ledgers (3). 1919–26 [w]. [Ref: MS 20101–20154]

Records 2: Record Office and Local History Department, Liverpool Libraries and Information Services, William Brown Street, Liverpool L3 8EW

Liverpool: memoirs and diaries of G A Brown 1803–61; customer ledgers (2) 1836–45; apprenticeship indenture 1842; letterbook 1851–59.

BUCKLE, CRAWSHAW JUNR. & PROCTOR
Chepstow, Gwent

History: This private bank was established in 1804 as George Buckle, William Crawshaw Junr. & James Proctor; it otherwise traded as the Chepstow Bank. It ceased business in 1829.

Records: Gwent Record Office, County Hall, Cwmbran NP44 2XH

Partnership agreements 1791–1820; account book 1811–17. [Ref: D25.0378, 0730, 1022–3, 1032, 1145]

BUCKLEY, SHAW & CO
Saddleworth, Greater Manchester

History: This private bank was established as Buckley, Roberts & Co in about 1806, the partnership comprising James Buckley, John Roberts, John Platt, John Wrigley and Robert Shaw. It survived a run on local banks in 1825. It was restyled Buckley, Shaw & Co before 1830 and in

Records of banks 131

1833 its business was reconstructed as a joint stock bank called the Saddleworth Banking Co.

Records: The Royal Bank of Scotland plc, Archive Section, Regent's House, 42 Islington High Street, London N1 8XL

Ashton-under-Lyne: deposit account ledger 1825–31; **Dobcross:** current account ledgers (12) 1806–34; deposit ledger 1824–59; stock book 1831–32; deposit lodgement ledgers (5) 1831–67.

BUCKS & OXON UNION BANK LTD
Buckingham, Buckinghamshire

History: This joint stock bank was formed in 1853 to acquire three private banks, T R Cobb & Son (est. 1783) of Banbury; Bartlett, Parrott & Co (est. 1783) of Buckingham; and Cobb, Bartlett & Co (est. 1795) of Aylesbury and Thame. The initial capital was £10,000. Limited liability was acquired in 1866 when paid-up capital, which by then was £55,000, was increased to £80,000. Branches were opened at Watford (1856), Hemel Hempstead (1856), Watlington (1885), Chesham (1889), Wolverton (1892), Wealdstone (1895) Great Missenden (1895) and St Albans Road, Watford (1898). In the 1890s the bank was damaged by the depreciation of its gilt portfolio, prompting its acquisition by Lloyds Bank Ltd (est. 1765) in 1902.

R S Sayers, *Lloyds Bank in the History of English Banking* (Oxford, 1957)

Records: Lloyds TSB Group plc, Archives, Head Office, 71 Lombard Street, London EC3P 3BS

Agreement for establishment 1852; directors' attendance book 1853–59; general meeting minute book 1853–64; monthly balance sheets 1853–74; directors' meeting minute books (5) 1853–1902; draft minute books (2) 1853–1902; branch returns 1857–66; articles of association c.1866; annual reports 1866–77; balance sheets and profit and loss accounts 1876–1902; investment ledger 1878–1902; superannuation fund minutes and ledger (2) 1887–1902; private ledger 1893–96; staff book 1902; amalgamation papers 1902–04.

BULPETT & HALL
Winchester, Hampshire

History: This private bank was established in 1786 at Alresford as Knapp, Son & Co. In 1789 it established a presence at Winchester which became the main office. In 1835 a branch was opened at Alton and also at Alresford. From 1838 it was known as Bulpett & Hall; it was otherwise styled the Winchester Bank and later the Winchester, Alresford & Alton Bank. It

132   *British banking – a guide to historical records*

amalgamated with Prescott, Dimsdale, Cave, Tugwell & Co Ltd (est. 1766) in 1892.

Anon, *'Prescott's Bank', National Provincial Bank Review* (1966–68)

Records: The Royal Bank of Scotland plc, Archive Section, Regent's House, 42 Islington High Street, London N1 8XL

Amalgamation papers 1892.

BURDON, FORSTER, BURRELL, RANKIN & KENT
Newcastle upon Tyne, Tyne & Wear

History: This private bank was established in 1784 by Francis Foster, Robert Rankin and Joseph Harris of Newcastle and Palfrey Burrell of Alnwick. Harris was the managing partner until 1785 when the business became known as Foster, Burrell, Rankin & Anderson. It was known as Burdon, Forster, Burrell, Rankin & Kent from 1786 and was otherwise styled the Commercial Bank. A branch was established at Alnwick. In 1793 the bank suspended payment during a general financial panic but all its liabilities were met in full. Its business was taken over by Surtees, Burdon & Co (est. 1768) of Newcastle upon Tyne.

Maberly Phillips, *Banks, Bankers and Banking in Northumberland, Durham and North Yorkshire* (London, 1894)

Records: Northumberland Record Office, Melton Park, North Gosforth, Newcastle upon Tyne NE3 5QX

Partnership agreement 1791; prospectus 1793. [Ref: ZCK 10]

JOHN & ANDREW BURT
East Grinstead, West Sussex

History: This private bank was formed in 1807 and failed in 1816.

Records: West Sussex Record Office, County Hall, Chichester, West Sussex PO19 1RN

Partnership agreement 1806; papers re liabilities 1806–07; inventory of fixtures 1818.

FREDERICK BURT & CO
London

History: This private bank was established in 1872 and was located in Cornhill, City of London. It was acquired by London & County Banking Co Ltd (est. 1836) in 1907.

Records of banks 133

Records: The Royal Bank of Scotland plc, Archive Section, Regent's House, 42 Islington High Street, London N1 8XL

Status reports on firms 1887–1902.

BURTON, LLOYD, LLOYD & SALT
Shrewsbury, Shropshire

History: This private bank was formed in 1812 as Scott, Burton, Pemberton, Lloyd & Coupland and was subsequently known as Burton, Lloyd, Lloyd & Salt. It also traded as the Salop Bank. In 1884 it merged with Rocke, Eyton, Campbell & Bayley (est. 1792), also of Shrewsbury, to form Eyton, Burton & Co.

Records: Lloyds TSB Group plc, Archives, Head Office, 71 Lombard Street, London EC3P 3BS

Papers of George Butler Lloyd 1867–91.

BURTON UNION BANK LTD
Burton upon Trent, Staffordshire

History: This joint stock bank was formed in 1839 through the merger of two Burton upon Trent private banks, Blurton, Webb & Peel (est. 1806, known as Meek, Mousley & Co until 1812) and Henry Clay & Co (est. 1790, known as Wilson, Dalrymple & Co until 1811). The new bank was known initially as the Burton, Uttoxeter & Staffordshire Union Bank, from 1843 as the Burton, Uttoxeter & Ashbourne (sic) Union Bank and from 1893 as the Burton Union Bank Ltd. Branches were located at Burton upon Trent, Uttoxeter (1839), Ashbourne (1843), Swadlincote (1890), Borough Road, Burton (1890), Coalville (1891), Derby (1898) and Tutbury (1898). In 1899 Lloyds Bank Ltd (est. 1765) acquired the business.

Records: Lloyds TSB Group plc, Archives, Head Office, 71 Lombard Street, London EC3P 3BS

Deed of settlement 1839; profit and loss book 1839–84; annual reports 1840–67; letterbook 1841–44; balance sheets 1841–99; amalgamation papers 1899.

Burton upon Trent: profit and loss book 1876–1900; **Uttoxeter:** deed book c.1853–99.

BURY BANKING CO LTD
Bury, Greater Manchester

134 British banking – a guide to historical records

History: This joint stock bank was formed in 1836 out of the business of the private bank of Grundys & Wood (est. 1798) whose partners became important shareholders and managers in the new concern. Nominal capital was £200,000 rising to £400,000 in 1879 and to £1 million a year later when limited liability was obtained. In 1887 deposits stood at £900,000 and at least five branches existed – Heywood, Radcliffe, Ramsbottam, Tottington and Whitefield. In 1888, when the business experienced difficulties resulting in the write off of £100,000 bad debts, the bank was acquired by the Lancashire & Yorkshire Bank Ltd (est. 1872) for £400,000.

George Chandler, *Four Centuries of Banking* (London, 1964–68)

Records: Barclays Bank plc, Group Archives, Dallimore Road, Wythenshawe, Manchester M23 9JA

Deed of settlement 1836; income tax returns 1880–87.

THOMAS BUTCHER & SONS
Tring, Hertfordshire

History: This private bank was established in 1836 by Thomas Butcher, a grocer, tea dealer and tallow chandler, and his son, Thomas; it was otherwise known as the Tring, Aylesbury & Chesham Bank. The partnership was later extended to include Butcher's younger sons and was restyled Thomas Butcher & Sons. Branches or agencies were opened at Aylesbury (1837), Chesham (c.1840) and Great Berkhamsted and in 1890 its balance sheet totalled £272,000. The bank was acquired by Prescott, Dimsdale, Cave, Tugwell & Co Ltd (est. 1766) in 1900 for £42,200.

Anon, 'Prescott's Bank: Amalgamation and Expansion', *National Provincial Bank Review* (1966–68); Jack Parker, *Nothing for Nothing for Nobody* (Stevenage, 1986)

Records: The Royal Bank of Scotland plc, Archive Section, Regent's House, 42 Islington High Street, London N1 8XL

Note registers (3) 1836–99; balance sheet 1890; amalgamation papers 1900.

Chesham: note register 1840–58.

A BUTLIN & SON
Rugby, Warwickshire

History: This private bank traced its origins to Samuel Clay's bank which was purchased in about 1790 by Mrs Anne Butlin, a local draper, and

Records of banks   **135**

renamed A Butlin & Son. In 1868 Lloyds Banking Co Ltd (est. 1765) acquired the bank for £15,000.

Howard Lloyd, *Notes and Reminiscences of Lloyds Bank 1862 to 1892* (unpub. mss., 1917)

Records: Lloyds TSB Group plc, Archives, Head Office, 71 Lombard Street, London EC3P 3BS

Amalgamation papers 1869.

CAITHNESS BANKING CO
Wick, Highland

History: This private bank was established in Wick as Caithness Banking Co in 1812 by John MacLeay and his father, William, and brothers, Kenneth and Alexander, to provide banking facilities for local businessmen. It issued its own bank notes, but remained on a modest scale. Its resources were diminished by the death of MacLeay family members and by the banking crisis of 1825. In 1826 it was acquired by the Commercial Bank of Scotland (est. 1810).

Records: The Royal Bank of Scotland plc, Archive Section, 36 St Andrew Square, Edinburgh EH2 2YB

Deposit receipts 1823–25; deposit accounts schedule 1825.

CALEDONIAN BANKING CO
Inverness, Highland

History: This joint stock bank was established in 1838 with a paid-up capital of about £31,000. Between 1838 and 1845 it established twenty branches in the Moray Firth, Caithness and Wester Ross districts of the Highlands and raised its paid-up capital to £75,000. Its expansion eastwards caused friction with the Aberdeen-based North of Scotland Bank (est. 1836). The bank's main customers were farmers, Highland gentry, fishermen, whisky distillers and grain factors as well as summer visitors. The bank enjoyed steady growth and fended off attempts at acquisition by the Union Bank of Scotland (est. 1830) in 1851 and 1856. Then its branch network extended to thirty-four branches, reaching as far as Portree and Stornoway. The collapse of the City of Glasgow Bank in 1878, in which the bank held stock without limitation of liability, was a severe blow and forced the bank to suspend payments temporarily. Support was received from the Bank of Scotland (est. 1695) which enabled the bank to reopen in 1879. In 1882 limited liability was acquired. The bank, however, remained crippled and in decline; capital and reserves for 1896, for example,

136 British banking – a guide to historical records

amounted to £222,000 and by 1907 were £195,000. The causes of the bank's downfall were lax lending and investment controls and the failure of the Scottish India Coffee Co of Madras which in 1902 owed the bank £300,000. In 1907 the Bank of Scotland acquired several of the bank's branches, namely Ardgay, Avoch, Bonar Bridge, Broadford on Skye, Buckie, Burghead, Cromarty, Dingwall (Tulloch Street), Dornoch, Drumnadrochit, Elgin (164 High Street), Fort Augustus, Fortrose, Fort William, Gairloch, Garmouth, Grantown-on-Spey, Halkirk, Hopeman, Inverness High Street (head office), Kingussie, Kyle of Lochalsh, Lairg, Lochcarron, Lochmaddy, Mallaig, Muir of Ord, Nairn, Portree and Stornoway. The bank was placed in liquidation in 1907.

Alan Cameron, *Bank of Scotland 1695–1995. A Very Singular Institution* (Edinburgh, 1995); S G Checkland, *Scottish Banking A History 1695–1973* (Glasgow, 1975); Richard Saville, *Bank of Scotland. A History 1695–1995* (Edinburgh, 1996)

Records: Bank of Scotland Archive, Operational Services Division, 12 Bankhead Terrace, Sighthill, Edinburgh EH11 4DY

Directors' meeting minute books 1838–1907; branch records 1838–1907; papers: miscellaneous 1838–1907, bank's affairs during crisis 1878–79, Northern Infirmary, Inverness c.1900–07, railway amalgamations 1905–07; record of notes issued and retired 1839–1907; general meeting minutes 1840–79; bad debts book 1840–1907; manager's letterbooks 1851–69; general ledger 1879–80; annual balances 1880–1900; weekly view of overdrafts 1901–06; general letterbooks 1905–07; letterbook re amalgamation 1907–09; letterbooks re liquidation 1907–08; general ledger balances 1907; liquidation ledger 1907–10; deposit receipts, bills etc 1907–11.

Avoch: 1895–1907; **Bonar Bridge:** 1857–61; **Buckie:** 1876–1907; **Burghead:** 1866–1904; **Cromarty:** 1839–46; **Dingwall:** 1839–46; **Dornoch:** 1839–1906; **Elgin:** 1839–46; **Forres:** 1839–1907; **Fort Augustus:** 1883–96; **Fortrose:** 1864–98; **Garmouth:** 1841–1907; **Glenlivet:** 1875–79; **Glenurquhart, Drumnadrochit:** 1877–84; **Grantown-on-Spey:** 1839–1907; **Halkirk:** 1883–1907; **Kingussie:** 1846–65; **Lairg:** 1865–1907; **Lochmaddy:** 1875–84; **Mallaig:** 1835–1904; **Nairn:** 1842–1907; **Rothes:** 1855–1907; **Stornoway:** 1874–1907; **Thurso:** 1840–55; **Tomintoul:** 1840–42; **Ullapool:** 1865–74.

CALL, MARTEN & CO
London

History: This private bank was founded in 1773 as Pybus, Hyde, Dorset & Cockell with premises in New Bond Street in London's West End. It did

Records of banks *137*

business under several different names including Pybus, Call, Marten & Hale in 1810 and Sir W P Call (Bart.), Arnold & Marten in 1827. From 1830 it was known as Call, Marten & Co. In 1865, when the bank's offices were in Old Bond Street, it was absorbed by Herries, Farquhar & Co (est. c.1770).

F G Hilton Price, *A Handbook of London Bankers* (London, 1876)

Records: Lloyds TSB Group plc, Archives, Head Office, 71 Lombard Street, London EC3P 3BS

Signature books 1810–94.

CAPITAL & COUNTIES BANK LTD
Southampton, Hampshire, and later London

History: This joint stock bank was formed in 1877 as the Hampshire & North Wilts Banking Co through the merger of the Hampshire Banking Co (est. 1834) and the North Wilts Banking Co (est. 1835). Initially the business had fifty-six branches and paid-up capital was £300,000; its head office was at Southampton. It was renamed the Capital & Counties Bank in 1878 and subsequently it emerged as one of the first banks with a nation-wide branch network. It acquired limited liability in 1880 and was admitted to the London Clearing House in 1882, following its acquisition in 1878 of the failed Lombard Street bank of Willis, Percival & Co (est. 1670). Thereafter its head office was in the City of London. Its paid-up capital was £400,000 in 1883 and £932,000 in 1892. Under the leadership of E B Merriman, the bank grew by acquisition and by opening new branches so that by 1894 it had 117 branches and sixty-one agencies; by 1918 it had 473 branches, mostly located in the West Country, central and southern England, East Anglia and London (twenty-two branches). Prompted by the need to secure a more widely spread branch network and an overseas business, it merged with Lloyds Bank Ltd (est. 1765) in 1918. It then had deposits of £60 million and 330,000 accounts whereas Lloyds had £174 million deposits and 660,000 accounts. Banks acquired through acquisition were: Willis, Percival & Co of London in 1878; Locke, Tugwell & Meek (est. 1775) of Devizes in 1883; Haydon, Smallpiece & Co (est. 1765) of Guildford in 1883; the Gloucestershire Banking Co (est. 1831) in 1886; Knight, Jenner & Co (est. 1806) of Farnham in 1886; the Northamptonshire Banking Co Ltd (est. 1831) and the Western Counties Bank Ltd (est. 1885) in 1890; Garfit, Claypon & Co (est. 1754) of Boston and Watts & Co (est. 1840) of Teignmouth in 1891; Mellersh & Co (est. 1808) of Godalming and Wells, Hogge & Lindsell (est. 1830) of Biggleswade in 1893; Slocock, Matthews, Southby & Slocock (est. 1791) of Newbury in 1895; St Barbe, Daniell & Co of Lymington, Henty & Co (est. c.1790) of

138 British banking – a guide to historical records

Worthing and Thomas Wheeler & Co (est. 1812) of High Wycombe in 1896; Eliot, Pearce & Co (est. 1791) of Weymouth in 1897; the Glamorganshire Banking Co Ltd (est. 1836) and I & I C Wright & Co (est. 1759) of Nottingham in 1898; Oakes, Bevan, Tollemache & Co (est. 1830) of Bury St Edmunds in 1900; Lacons, Youell & Kemp (est. 1791) of Great Yarmouth and Moore & Robinson's Nottinghamshire Banking Co Ltd (est. 1836) in 1901; Cornish Bank Ltd (est. 1879) in 1902; Hammond & Co (est. 1788) of Canterbury in 1903; Foster & Co (est. 1804) of Cambridge in 1904; Bacon Cobbold & Co (est. 1786) of Ipswich in 1905; Berwick, Lechmere & Co (est. 1772) of Worcester in 1906; and Eyton, Burton & Co (est. 1884) of Shrewsbury in 1907.

William Howarth, *Our Leading Banks* (London, 1894); R S Sayers, *Lloyds Bank in the History of English Banking* (Oxford, 1957)

Records 1 : Lloyds TSB Group plc, Archives, Head Office, 71 Lombard Street, London EC3P 3BS

Private minute books (2) 1876–1924; deed of settlement 1877; head office circular books (5) 1877–1917; annual reports 1877–1918; general memorandum book 1878–1918; premises ledgers (2) 1880–1902; chairman's agenda book 1889–1917; private letterbooks (5) 1891–1918; register of directors 1900–18; memorandum and instruction book 1905; articles of association 1908–18; bad and doubtful debts book 1916–17.

Alford: security registers (2) 1891–1920; signature book 1891–1924; **Alresford:** security registers (2) 1876–1920; **Andover:** security register c.1881–85; signature book c.1891–1909; **Basingstoke, Winchester Street:** signature book c.1864–1900; **Biggleswade:** signature book 1894–1916; **Bishop's Stortford:** security register 1904–c.1914; **Boston:** security registers (3) 1891–1921; **Brighton:** signature books (5) c.1875–1919; security register c.1917–20; **Bury St Edmunds:** letterbook 1909–15; **Chichester:** signature book c.1873–1908; **Chippenham:** signature books (4) 1863–1927; **Christchurch:** memorandum books (2) 1912–18; **Cirencester:** customer books (2) 1886–91, 1908–14; **Cromer:** memorandum book 1897–1903; **Daventry:** letterbook 1916–46; **Dovercourt:** security register c.1905–23; **Ely:** quarterly totals 1850–1922; security registers (2)1904–20; **Fareham:** memorandum book 1900–14; **Great Yarmouth:** security registers (4) 1901–21; memorandum books (5) 1907–18; **Guernsey:** memorandum book 1903–08; **Guildford:** signature book c.1885–1905; **Harwich:** security register c.1905–21; **Hereford:** signature book 1887–1916; letterbook 1884–93; **High Wycombe:** letterbook 1909–28; **Ipswich:** signature book 1909–16; **Kettering:** security registers (3) 1890–1918; **King's Lynn:** security register c.1901–19; **Leatherhead:** signature book 1896–1920; **London, Covent Garden:** signature books (2) 1887–1931; security

Records of banks 139

register 1881–1923; **London, King's Cross:** signature book 1904–21; **London, Ludgate Hill:** signature book 1878–81; profit and loss ledger 1891–1917; **London, Oxford Street:** signature book 1883–1906; **London, Piccadilly:** letterbooks (5) 1890–1916; **London, Woolwich:** signature book 1880–97; **Malmesbury:** signature books (2) 1897–1925; **Malvern:** memorandum book 1904–08; **Marlow:** security register c.1910–16; **Melksham:** security register 1903–13; **Newbury:** memorandum book 1915–20; **Northampton:** memorandum book 1890–93; **Nottingham:** memorandum books (2) 1900–25; **Portswood:** security register c.1912–21; **Ramsgate:** memorandum book 1898–1912; **Redditch:** signature book 1887–1925; security registers (2) 1888–1922; **Redhill:** memorandum book 1903–11; **Salisbury:** signature book 1889–1919; security register c.1879–1920; letterbooks (2) 1905–15; **Sheringham:** letterbook 1912–19; **Southampton:** signature books (3)1876–99; **Spilsby:** security register c.1891–94; status enquiry book 1901–07; **Stamford:** security register 1891–1908; signature book 1890–1932; **Sudbury:** signature book c.1905–27; **Tewkesbury:** memorandum book c.1904–15; status enquiry book c.1913–22; **Wellingborough:** security register c.1891–1906; memorandum book 1912–19; **Weymouth:** diary 1898; **Winchester:** signature books (2) c.1880–1904; memorandum book 1906–09; **Wirksworth:** memorandum books (2) 1903–17; **Woking:** signature book 1888–1902; memorandum books (4) 1907–20; **Woodbridge:** memorandum books (3) 1905–19; **Worcester:** letterbooks (2) 1906–20.

Records 2: Bedfordshire and Luton Archives and Record Service, The Records Office, Cauldwell Street, Bedford MK42 9AP

Luton: heating plans 1898; **Sandy/Potton:** passbook 1893–97. [Ref: X 597/12; CD 873]

Records 3: West Sussex Record Office, County Hall, Chichester PO19 1RN

Cheque books nineteenth cent. [Add. Ms. 2784]

CARLISLE & CUMBERLAND BANKING CO LTD
Carlisle, Cumbria

History: This was the first joint stock bank to be formed at Carlisle. It was established in 1836 and won a reputation for sound management. Early branches included Wigton (1836), Appleby (1837), Penrith (1861), Keswick (1865), Alston (1869), Longtown (1876), Cockermouth (c.1897), St Nicholas Carlisle (1898) and Haydon Bridge (1892, closed 1893). In 1876 the balance sheet totalled £850,000 and in 1878 paid-up capital was increased from £75,000 to £100,000. Limited liability was obtained in 1880

140   *British banking – a guide to historical records*

and in 1882 the business of Mackie, Davidson & Gladstone (est. 1860) of Carlisle was acquired. In 1903 the balance sheet totalled £1.13 million. The Bank of Liverpool Ltd (est. 1831) acquired the bank in 1911.

George Chandler, *Four Centuries of Banking* (London, 1964–68)

Records: Barclays Bank plc, Group Archives, Dallimore Road, Wythenshawe, Manchester M23 9JA

Minute books (6) 1836–1911; registers of shareholders (5) 1836–1911; bank note registers (2) 1836–79; registers of deposited documents (2) 1836–82; deeds of settlement 1837–1911; report and accounts 1837–1911 [w]; cheques and deposit receipts 1838–48; letters from customers 1841–49; circular to John Crosby 1842; probate register 1882–1900; reserves and investments account 1887–1910; bank notes n.d.; amalgamation papers 1903–11.

CARLISLE CITY & DISTRICT BANKING CO LTD
Carlisle, Cumbria

History: This joint stock bank was formed in 1836 following the failure of several local private banks and opened for business in 1837; its paid-up capital was £125,000. The new bank was based upon the business of the Carlisle branch of Wakefield & Co (est. 1840) of Kendal, which was purchased for £20,000, and upon that of the Carlisle branch of the Leith Banking Co (est. 1792). The latter's manager joined the new bank but later absconded owing funds to the bank. In 1837, the Borough Bank, a newly-promoted Carlisle joint stock bank, was absorbed along with the business of Joseph Sanderson (est. 1829) of Cockermouth. Branches were later opened at Workington and Maryport and were added to in 1872 when Carrick & Lee (est. 1830) of Brampton and Haltwhistle was acquired. The business was reconstructed in 1878, when limited liability was acquired, and recovered its former prosperity. The private bank of Joseph Dickinson (est. 1847) of Alston was acquired in 1890. In 1896, when the bank had eight branches, deposits of almost £750,000 and paid-up capital of £100,000, it was acquired by London & Midland Bank Ltd (est. 1836).

W F Crick & J E Wadsworth, *A Hundred Years of Joint Stock Banking* (London, 1936)

Records: HSBC Holdings plc, Group Archives, 10 Lower Thames Street, London EC3R 6AE

Prospectus 1837; deed of settlement 1837; balance sheets 1837–80, 1896; fidelity bonds and guarantees 1837–81; directors' meeting minute book

Records of banks 141

1879–80; shareholders' minutes 1880; articles of association 1881; board agenda books (2) 1885–96; amalgamation papers 1896.

CASSONS & CO
Porthmadog, Gwynedd

History: This private bank was formed in 1847 to acquire the Porthmadog, Pwllheli and Ffestiniog branches of the North & South Wales Bank (est. 1836) which disposed of them following the financial crisis of that year. Branches were added at Blaenavon and Harlech. In 1875, when deposits totalled £242,000, the North & South Wales Bank reacquired the business for £12,000.

Records: HSBC Holdings plc, Group Archives, 10 Lower Thames Street, London EC3R 6AE

Private ledgers (2) 1848–74; general ledger 1847–72; purchase agreement papers 1875.

CATER ALLEN LTD
London

History: This City of London discount house was formed in 1888 as Vaile & Carew. It was known as Vaile & Co from 1892, as Vaile, Allen & Co from 1893, as Allen Hellings & Co from 1904, and as Allen, Harvey & Ross from 1905. At some stage it acquired Clarke & Harvey. In 1934 the business was reorganised as a private unlimited company and became a private limited company in 1943. In 1946 it became a public company and in 1981 merged with Cater Ryder plc to form Cater Allen plc. A year later it was renamed Cater Allen Ltd and by 1998 was owned by Cater Allen Holdings plc.

Records: Cater Allen Ltd, 20 Birchin Lane, London EC3V 9DJ

General ledgers (17) 1892–1945; investment ledgers (4) 1909–46; private ledgers (4) 1920–46; partnership accounts (2) 1934–46.

Note: These records were originally listed in the late 1970s; it has not proved possible to establish the current status of the records.

CATTLE TRADE BANK LTD
Liverpool, Merseyside

History: This joint stock bank was established in 1920 through the purchase of the Birkenhead branch (est. 1912) of the cattle bank of E Reed & Sons (est. 1863). Its paid-up capital was £32,000. In 1923 the Bank of Liverpool & Martins Ltd (est. 1831) acquired the bank for £53,000.

142   *British banking – a guide to historical records*

Records: Barclays Bank plc, Group Archives, Dallimore Road, Wythenshawe, Manchester M23 9JA

Memorandum and articles of association 1920; certificate of incorporation 1920; certificate to commence business 1920; annual report 1923; amalgamation papers 1923.

CENTRAL BANK OF LONDON LTD
London

History: This joint stock bank was formed in 1863 as the East London Bank with offices in Cornhill in the City of London. Branches were soon opened at Southwark and then at Shoreditch and Whitechapel, the bank's early business being firmly rooted in the East End trades. Deposits reached £495,000 by 1865. The business was renamed the Central Bank of London Ltd in 1870 and by the middle of the 1870s other branches had been opened at Mile End, Blackfriars, Newgate Street, Tottenham Court Road and Clerkenwell. Deposits reached £1 million in 1877 and more branches opened in the early 1880s at Shaftesbury Avenue and Bethnal Green. In 1889 the business of the failed Bethnal Green Bank was acquired. However, the bank remained of moderate size relative to its London joint stock bank competitors and in 1891 was acquired for £469,000 by the Birmingham & Midland Bank Ltd (est. 1836), which was three times its size and which sought a London base. By then the Central Bank's deposits had reached £1.6 million, paid-up capital was £156,000 and it had ten branches. The enlarged bank, renamed the London & Midland Bank Ltd, occupied the Central Bank's old head office in Cornhill.

Records: HSBC Holdings plc, Group Archives, 10 Lower Thames Street, London EC3R 6AE

Articles of association 1863; directions for branch managers 1863; directors' meeting minute books (6) 1863–91; committee minute books (5) 1863–91; resolutions and orders 1863–91; annual reports 1864–91; general meeting minute books (2) 1864–91; balance sheets 1864–88; balance books (2) 1864–94; general ledgers (4) 1868–89; security registers (3) 1868–1904; records of proceedings in bankruptcies 1872–93; branch ledgers (9) 1873–89; branch balance sheets (2) 1878–91; salary registers (2) 1880–91.

London, Tooley Street: security register 1876–91.

CENTRAL BANK OF SCOTLAND
Perth, Tayside

Records of banks 143

History: This joint stock bank was established in 1834 and was the first of its kind in Perth. Its initial capital was £79,000. It was financially crippled by 1864 and the Bank of Scotland (est. 1695), which had provided support for several years, assumed control of seven of its nine branches, at Auchterarder, Blackford, Coupar-Angus, Crieff, Dunkeld, Killin and Pitlochry. In 1868 the bank acquired the remaining business, although some shareholders declined to sell their interest and consequently the bank retained a nominal independence until 1880, when the Bank of Scotland finally bought them out.

Records 1: Bank of Scotland Archive, Operational Services Division, 12 Bankhead Terrace, Sighthill, Edinburgh EH11 4DY

Ledgers 1834–43; directors' meeting minutes 1834–68; contract of co-partnery and related papers 1834–68; staff bonds of security 1834–68; miscellaneous legal and other papers 1834–68; stock journal and subscriptions 1834–72; annual and monthly balance books 1837–55; deposit books 1843–68; balance ledger 1855–68; accounts of notes issued 1858–68; papers re bank's holdings of railway and other securities 1860–67; register of members 1862–69; signature book 1865–67; reports by directors of Central Bank 1866; minutes of agreement between Bank of Scotland and Central Bank of Scotland 1868; miscellaneous account books 1870–96.

Auchterarder: 1834–68; **Coupar Angus:** 1853–68; **Crieff:** 1835–68; **Dunkeld:** 1834–51; **Killin:** 1853–68; **Pitlochry:** 1835–47.

Records 2: Perth & Kinross Council Archive, A K Bell Library, 2–8 York Place, Perth PH2 8EP

Prospectus 1833; contract of co-partnership 1834; circular 1834; cash credit account bond 1838; articles of roup re shares 1855. [Ref: B59/37/14/10–13, 19]

Records 3: Business Records Centre, Archive Department, University of Glasgow, Glasgow G12 8QQ

Balance sheets 1865–68. [Ref: Scottish Banking Collection]

CHANNEL ISLANDS BANK LTD
Jersey, Channel Islands

History: This joint stock bank originated as the private bank of Horman, Anthoine, Ahier, Le Gros & Co (est. 1858), otherwise known as the Channel Islands Bank. A local banking crisis in 1873 prompted its reorganisation as a joint stock company in 1874, but many of the characteristics of a private bank were retained. In 1876 paid-up capital was £12,000 and deposits were £75,000. In 1887, when it acquired limited liability, it had

144 British banking – a guide to historical records

eleven shareholders, most of whom were directors. The private bank of Charles Godfray (est. 1797), known also as Jersey Old Bank, was purchased for £5,000 in 1891. In 1897, when deposits had grown to £311,000 and paid-up capital stood at £20,000, London & Midland Bank Ltd (est 1836) acquired the business for the equivalent of £60,000.

Records: HSBC Holdings plc, Group Archives, 10 Lower Thames Street, London EC3R 6AE

Directors' meeting and committee minute books (4) 1874–1907; auditors' reports 1879–97; articles of association 1887; act of registration 1887; balance sheets 1887–96; security lists with valuations 1887–96; acquisition agreement with liquidator 1897.

CHARTERED BANK
London, Asia and Australia

History: This British-owned overseas bank was formed in 1853 by Royal Charter to undertake a general banking business and to finance the local and international trade of India, China and Australia. It was known as The Chartered Bank of India, Australia & China although initially operations in Australia were prohibited. The bank was formed to take advantage of the retreat of the East India Co and its initial paid-up capital was £500,000. Delays in obtaining a banking certificate meant that the first branches, at Calcutta, Bombay and Shanghai, did not open until 1858, followed by Hong Kong in 1859, Singapore in 1861, Karachi in 1863 (closed 1868) and Penang in 1875. Agencies, which were managed by the bank and not by nominated merchant houses, followed at Batavia (1859), Rangoon (1861), Hankow (1863, closed 1875), Colombo (1877) and Yokohama (1880). Each branch and agency was allocated capital to be employed locally to the best ability of the local manager or agent. In the 1870s, the bank was empowered to make long-term loans (initially prohibited) on security of land, crops, etc. By the 1890s it was the leading bank in India, and in Hong Kong and Shanghai was rivalled only by the Hongkong & Shanghai Banking Corporation (est. 1865). By 1890 total assets were £16 million, growing to £27 million by 1913. In 1894 the first independent agency was opened at Bangkok, followed by similar agencies at Kobe (1895), Tientsin (1895), Karachi (1895), Madras (1900) and Saigon (1903). The first agencies outside Asia opened at New York (1902) and Hamburg (1904). In the last years of the nineteenth century, the bank lead-managed its first bond issues, for the Chinese and Japanese governments. In 1927 a major interest was taken in the P&O Banking Corporation (est. 1920), majority owner of the Allahabad Bank, which in 1938 became wholly owned. In the same year the first British branch opened in Manchester;

Records of banks   145

another opened at Liverpool ten years later. Chartered Bank's business was greatly damaged by the Second World War, civil war in China and nationalisation in India. In 1949 only one branch was permitted in China, at Shanghai. In order to expand into new areas, the Eastern Bank Ltd (est. 1909), which had branches in the Middle East as well as in India, was acquired in 1957. The Cyprus branches of the Ionian Bank (est. 1838) were also purchased in 1957; a year earlier the bank's name had been changed to The Chartered Bank. In 1959 it joined local investors in setting up the Irano British Bank, which had twenty-four branches when it was nationalised in 1979. In 1969 its majority interest in the Allahabad Bank was nationalised. In 1970, in order to increase in size and compete more effectively in international banking, The Chartered Bank merged with Standard Bank Ltd, to form Standard Chartered Banking Group Ltd, known subsequently as Standard Chartered plc.

Anon, *A Story Brought Up To Date* (priv. pub., 1983); Compton Mackenzie, *Realms of Silver. One Hundred Years of Banking in the East* (London, 1955)

Records 1: Guildhall Library, Aldermanbury, London EC2P 2EJ

Note: At the time of publication the very extensive archives of Chartered Bank were being catalogued.

Records 2: Standard Chartered Bank plc, Aldermanbury Square, London EC2V 7SB

Directors' meeting minutes 1852 on.

Records 3: County Record Office, County Hall, Hertford SG13 8DE

Correspondence between 1st Earl of Lytton and Chartered Mercantile Bank of India, London & China 1880. [Ref: D/EK F62]

CHARTERHOUSE BANK LTD
London

History: This merchant bank traced its origins to the business of S Japhet formed by Saemy Japhet (1856–1954) at Frankfurt in 1880. This broking firm moved its head office to Berlin in 1891 and opened a branch (capital £15,000) in the City of London in 1896. By 1901 the London capital was £200,000, much of which was contributed by the Berlin firm of Robert Warschauer & Co. In 1900 Saemy Japhet moved to London which then became the firm's head office. The firm concentrated on security broking, largely arbitrage and commission business, with its clients mostly based in Europe and the USA. In 1910 Sir Ernest Cassel became a sleeping partner, doubling the capital to £400,000, and a close connection also existed with

146 *British banking – a guide to historical records*

the armaments dealer, Sir Basil Zaharoff. The firm was greatly disrupted during the First World War, when its business was largely restricted to security transactions connected with the USA, Sweden and Spain. In 1919 a foreign exchange department was established and shortly afterwards acceptance finance was provided. Membership of the prestigious Accepting Houses Committee was taken up in 1921. In this year the bank converted to a private limited company and in the 1920s expanded rapidly before its activities were curtailed by the financial crisis in Central Europe in the early 1930s. After 1945 the most profitable activity was bullion exporting. In 1954, following Saemy Japhet's death, the business, which had been converted to a public company in 1953, was acquired by Charterhouse Industrial Development Co Ltd. Under its new owner, the bank expanded rapidly, entering new areas such as insurance broking, export finance, fund management and corporate finance. It traded under the name of Charterhouse Japhet Ltd from 1964. From 1980 the bank was known as Charterhouse Japhet plc and in 1981 acquired the London merchant bank of Keyser Ullmann Ltd (est. 1966). In 1986 the bank was acquired by The Royal Bank of Scotland plc (est. 1727), re-registered as a private company and changed its name to Charterhouse Bank Ltd. In 1993 Royal Bank of Scotland sold most of its interest to Credit Commerce de France and Berliner Handels-und Frankfurter Bank. Acquired by HSBC in 2000.

Laurie Dennett, *The Charterhouse Group 1925–1979. A History* (London, 1979); Saemy Japhet, *Recollections of My Business Life* (priv. pub., 1931)

Note: Apply to HSBC Holdings for archive details.

CHASEMORE, ROBINSON & SONS
Croydon, London

History: This private bank was established in 1838 as Cane, Chasemore, Robinson & Sons; it was also known as the Union Bank of Croydon. It was acquired by Union Bank of London Ltd (est. 1839) in 1891.

Records: The Royal Bank of Scotland plc, Archive Section, Regent's House, 42 Islington High Street, London N1 8XL

Partnership agreements (2) 1863, 1873.

CHESTERFIELD & NORTH DERBYSHIRE BANKING CO
Chesterfield, Derbyshire

History: This joint stock bank was established in 1833 with a paid-up capital of £23,280. By 1878 capital had increased to £35,000 and there was a branch at Clay Cross. The bank failed in 1878 and was acquired by Crompton & Evans' Union Bank Ltd (est. 1877).

Records of banks
147

Records: The Royal Bank of Scotland plc, Archive Section, Regent's House, 42 Islington High Street, London N1 8XL

Annual report 1859; directors' meeting minutes 1876–78; liquidator's report and accounts 1879–85.

CHILD & CO
London

History: During the mid-seventeenth century William Wheeler and Robert Blanchard operated old-established goldsmith shops in Strand, London. After the death of Wheeler in 1661, his widow married Blanchard and the two businesses were merged. Later in the 1660s Blanchard, trading at the sign of the Marygold, was joined in partnership by Francis Child. By 1673, when Blanchard & Child moved to 1 Fleet Street, then adjoining Temple Bar, the firm's banking activities were more important than the business of goldsmith. In 1681 Francis Child, who had married Blanchard's step-daughter, inherited the entire business. He was knighted in 1689 and later served as Lord Mayor of London and as an MP. Supported by the patronage of the Earl of Dorset, Lord Chamberlain, he regularly made advances to the Treasury and in 1698 was appointed 'jeweller in ordinary' to King William III; his jewellery business was one of the largest in London. Child died in 1713 and his three surviving sons ran the business in succession until the 1750s. In 1729 Child & Co issued its first printed bank note and in 1762 its first printed cheque. During the eighteenth and nineteenth centurjes, in addition to the bank's large aristocratic customer base, it attracted many customers from the legal profession due to its proximity to the Inns of Court. It also developed links with many Oxford colleges. Francis Child's grandson, Robert, had no male issue and the business was inherited by his granddaughter, Sarah Sophia Fane, who married the 5th Earl of Jersey. Sarah was senior partner of Child & Co from 1806 to 1867. In 1874 Temple Bar was dismantled and Child & Co took advantage of this opportunity entirely to rebuild the bank premises to the design of architect John Gibson. The new bank opened in 1880. In 1923 the 8th Earl of Jersey sold the firm to Glyn, Mills & Co (est. 1753), although Child & Co continued to trade independently. A branch was briefly opened in Oxford during the 1930s. In 1939 Glyn, Mills & Co was itself acquired by The Royal Bank of Scotland (est. 1727). In 1991 the branch was relaunched as a private banking arm of The Royal Bank of Scotland plc.

Anon, *Child & Co. The First House in the City* (priv. pub., 1992); Philip Clarke, *The First House in the City* (London, 1973); Eric Gore Brown, *Glyn Mills & Co* (London, 1933); F G Hilton Price, *The Marygold by*

148   *British banking – a guide to historical records*

Temple Bar (London, 1902); William Howarth, *Somme Olde Curiosities by a Knight offe ye Quille* (London, 1890)

Records 1: The Royal Bank of Scotland plc, Archive Section, Regent's House, 42 Islington High Street, London N1 8XL

Title deeds 1625–c.1955; customer ledgers 1663–1755; scrapbooks 1671–1932; Francis Child: ledger 1682–1726, journal 1700–13; balance books 1685–1926; journal re creditors and debtors 1691–1836; customer correspondence and other papers 1692–1900; drawn notes 1699–1753; private journals 1700–24; profit and loss ledgers 1717–62; loans details 1717–56; private ledger 1717–67; details of cash received and paid 1726–28; Christmas box books 1726–1984; signature books 1731–1909; bank notes 1740–52; account books, Earl of Jersey 1751–99; engravings of Fleet Street 1753–1878; daily journal entries 1753–54; papers re partnership matters 1755–1935; partnership agreements 1757–1924; executorship papers 1759–1900; private letterbook 1762–1835; box books 1763–1900; cheques and cheque forms c.1763–1900; foreign payments journal 1769–1854; record of Bank of England customer stockholdings c.1775; legal papers re partnership 1783–1952; passbooks: 1786–1945, Bank of England 1783–1806, 1878–1924, Royal Bank of Scotland 1906–24, The National Bank 1906–24, Glyn, Mills & Co 1924–33; expenses journals 1785–1935; parcel books 1786–1900; annual balances notebook 1789–1938; staff caricatures book 1791–1935; customer will probates 1792–1880; promissory note forms 1793, 1805; notes re Child's Place tenants c.1793–98; customer stock transactions 1794–1900; case and opinion re property insurance 1795; pocket account book 1800–14; papers re property rents and leases c.1805–40; list of land tax assessments c.1805; powers of attorney re forces pay and treasury pensions 1807–1914; commission books 1812–79; male servant tax assessments 1812; lists of interest outstanding 1812–13; papers re trusts 1819–51; alterations plan, Brick Court, 1824; partnership correspondence 1833–49; balance papers 1835–1933; fire insurance policies 1836–1934; partnership dispute letterbooks 1839–49; papers re clerk fraud 1841; bonds of indemnity 1840–45; solicitors' bills of charges 1857–1928; notes re income tax payable 1859–62; details of bills of exchange 1866–1939; papers re property taxes and rates 1867–1905; coin and notebooks 1870–1940; jewel closet books 1844–1900; letters from foreign correspondent banks 1858–75; papers re sinking fund creation 1871; press cuttings re new premises 1874–80; papers re bank rebuilding 1877–82; *Ye Marygold*, history of Child & Co 1875; liquidation papers, Willis, Percival & Co 1878; bank day books 1878–1936 [w]; photographs of premises 1870s; architectural drawings c.1870s, 1920s–1966; security memorandum book 1879–86; Christmas fund book 1880–1927; rules for clerks 1878, 1881; clerks' holiday cards 1881–1901;

Records of banks 149

plate glass insurance policies 1881–1927; correspondence re pensions 1882–83; rates assessment returns c.1885; loans book 1889–1900; foreign correspondent details 1890–1902; balance sheets 1891–1923, 1926–29; papers re balance sheet audits 1891–1900, 1930–34; papers re telephone installation 1892–99; valuations of plate 1894, 1907; stockbroker expense accounts 1898–1910; circular notes 1899–c.1915; staff magazine 1902; powers of attorney 1905–18; press cuttings 1909–58; land tax return papers 1910; papers re purchase of 3 Fleet Street 1911–12; letters from Lord Mayor and Corporation thanking for hospitality 1911–25; papers re bombing precautions 1915; inventory, furniture and fittings 1915, 1924; customer shareholding record cards c.1914–55; salary cash books 1916–24; papers re tax liability 1916–20; letter re forged cheques 1916; foreign stock details 1919–39; coupon account commission book 1919–36; list of clerks awaiting appointment 1919–27; papers re staff killed or wounded in war 1920; papers re acquisition by Glyn, Mills & Co 1922–24; correspondence from Glyn, Mills & Co 1924–38; account with Glyn, Mills & Co ledger 1924–34; rifle club papers 1937–39; cash book 1939; papers re acquisition by Royal Bank of Scotland 1939.

Oxford: premises papers 1930–34; photographs 1933, c.1977.

Records 2: West Yorkshire Archive Service, Yorkshire Archaeological Society, Claremont, 23 Clarendon Road, Leeds LS2 9NZ

Correspondence with a Yorkshire customer 1781–1820; accounts, statements, cheque books etc c.1800–30. [Ref: DD56 M10; DD56/P]

CITY BANK LTD
London

History: This joint stock bank was formed by charter in 1855 and became a leading London bank. Its chief promoter was Sir Robert Carden, a stockbroker and influential City figure, and its head office was in Threadneedle Street, City of London. The initial paid-up capital was £150,000 and by 1863 deposits had grown to £3.5 million. An important foreign business was built up, with the bank acting as London correspondent for forty overseas banks and providing bill finance for international trade. Branches grew from five in 1873 to fourteen in 1894; they were located throughout London and subsequently in the suburbs including Croydon and Bromley. Limited liability was acquired in 1880. In 1883 paid-up capital was increased to £1 million and deposits stood at over £5 million by 1887. During the 1890s, City Bank competed with difficulty with its larger London competitors and in 1898 London & Midland Bank Ltd (est. 1836) acquired the business for the equivalent of £2.556 million. The City Bank then had £9 million deposits, twenty-one branches and paid-up capital of £1 million. The enlarged

150   *British banking – a guide to historical records*

bank, called the London, City & Midland Bank Ltd, was Britain's fourth largest with deposits amounting to £32 million. This amalgamation was an important advancement for Midland Bank, providing it with a substantial foreign business for the first time and a spacious head office in Threadneedle Street. The Vanner family became important in City Bank's affairs; James Vanner, a leading silk manufacturer and insurance underwriter, led the amalgamation negotiations.

William Howarth, *Our Leading Banks* (London, 1894); W F Crick & J E Wadsworth, *A Hundred Years of Joint Stock Banking* (London, 1936)

Records: HSBC Holdings plc, Group Archives, 10 Lower Thames Street, London EC3R 6AE

Papers of Vanner family 1839–1906; directors' meeting minute books (6) 1854–98; staff appointment list 1855–58; weekly balance book 1855–79; deeds of settlement 1855–81; balance sheet books (3) 1855–98; staff registers 1855–99; charter of incorporation 1856; annual reports (4) 1856–98; general meeting minute books (2) 1856–98; committee minute books (3) 1856–98; foreign banks arrangement book 1862–98; correspondent banks arrangement book 1862–1904; profit and loss ledgers 1867–98; rules for branch managers 1874; rules of accountant's office 1883; accountant's reports 1884–91; security book 1888–1901; premises reference book 1890–98; amalgamation papers 1898; regulations n.d.

London, Aldgate: cash book re building expenses 1876–82; letterbook 1879–99; **London, Cambridge Circus:** security ledger 1890–98; signature book 1890–98; **London, Holborn:** security registers (4) 1879–99; **London, Old Bond Street:** signature books 1865–98; **London, Old Street:** deposit receipt book 1894–98; **London, Paddington:** journal, cash book and letterbook 1873–1903; **London, Tottenham Court Road:** signature books 1880–97.

CITY OF BIRMINGHAM BANK LTD
Birmingham, West Midlands

History: This joint stock bank was established in 1897 as a reaction to the disappearance of locally-controlled banks through their amalgamation with banks based in London. Its paid-up capital was £100,000 and it soon attracted deposits of £245,000. However, the strength of competition resulted in immediate heavy losses and, without having opened branches, it was acquired by London, City & Midland Bank Ltd (est. 1836) in 1899 for £120,000.

Records: HSBC Holdings plc, Group Archives, 10 Lower Thames Street, London EC3R 6AE

Records of banks 151

Articles of association 1897; investment list 1897; share registers (2) 1897–98; share transfer registers (2) 1897–98; annual returns and summary book 1897–98; directors' meeting minute books (2) 1897–99.

CITY OF GLASGOW BANK
Glasgow, Strathclyde

History: This co-partnery was formed in 1839 with a paid-up capital of £650,000 provided by 779 partners; it was Glasgow's second largest bank. It stopped briefly during the 1857 financial panic, but overall experienced steady expansion. It placed emphasis on a large branch network and by the middle of the 1870s had 133 offices. By that time deposits totalled £8 million, but an unduly high percentage of assets were in the form of customer loans. In addition 50 per cent of lending was to just three customers, while other monies had been placed in unlikely investments such as United States railroad stock and New Zealand land, especially via the New Zealand & Australian Loan Co. In the late 1870s the bank was in serious difficulties but these were concealed by the publication of misleading balance sheets and by the bank's purchase of its own shares in order to support market price. The bank's failure in 1878 represented a major banking collapse and scandal. Partners lost all of their £1 million paid-up capital and had to provide an additional £4.4 million to cover outstanding liabilities; only 254 shareholders remained solvent. Several directors and managers were jailed for fraud.

S G Checkland, *Scottish Banking. A History 1695–1973* (Glasgow, 1975)

Records 1: Clydesdale Bank plc, Head Office, 30 St Vincent Place, Glasgow G1 2HL

Contract of co-partnership 1839; list of partners 1844; instructions to agents and accountants 1873; customer's passbook 1877; press cuttings 1878; claims lodged through North of Scotland Bank 1878; report on trial 1879.

Records 2: Glasgow University Archives and Business Records Centre, 13 Thurso Street, Glasgow G11 6PE

Balance sheets 1857–78; list of branches and partners 1874; extracts of private ledgers and other accounts 1876–78; list of shareholders 1878; papers re liquidation 1878–85. [Ref: Scottish Banking Collection; UGD 108]

Records 3: Glasgow City Archives, Mitchell Library, North Street, Glasgow G3 7DN

Papers re collapse and liquidation of bank 1871–88. [Ref: T-BK 162/54, 179/4; T-HB23, 126–7; T-HL148]

152 *British banking – a guide to historical records*

CLARKE, MITCHELL, PHILLIPS & SMITH
Leicester, Leicestershire

History: This private bank was established in 1819 as John Clarke & Josh. Phillips. It was subsequently known as Clarke, Mitchell, Phillips & Smith and otherwise traded as the Leicester & Leicestershire Bank. Branches were established at Melton Mowbray, Oakham and Uppingham. In 1831 the partners acquired Goodacre & Buzzard (est. 1803) of Lutterworth which then traded under the same partnership name as the Leicester Bank. Both banks failed in 1843.

Records: Leicestershire Record Office, Long Street, Wigston Magna, Leicester LE8 2AH

Commissions of bankruptcy against customers 1830–40; bank note c.1842; statement of distribution of assets received under bankruptcy of bank c.1843. [Ref: 109'30/13; Misc 1328]

SIR ROBERT CLAYTON
London

History: This scrivener bank was established by Robert Abbott at the sign of The Flying Horse, Cornhill, City of London, in 1638. Abbott developed banking activities alongside his work as a scrivener. When he died in 1658 his business passed to two of his scribes, Robert Clayton and John Morris, trading variously as Robert Clayton & Partner, John Morris & Partner and Morris, Clayton & Co. The scriveners' shop burned down in the Great Fire of 1666, prompting a move to Austin Friars and subsequently, in 1672, to Old Jewry. The firm flourished, specialising in deposit banking and mortgage loans and, after 1661, developed an important business outside London. Country mortgages were offered on the basis of land assessment by the firm's own agents and estates mortgaged to the firm were often also managed by it. Morris died in 1682 leaving the business to Robert Clayton who had been knighted in 1671 and served as Lord Mayor of London from 1679 to 1680. He was subsequently appointed Commissioner of the Customs, from 1689 to 1697, and governor of the Bank of England, from 1702 to 1707. He also held other civic positions. However after Morris's death the banking business dwindled due to Clayton's age, ill-health and loss of key advisers. Clayton died in 1707 and the firm passed to his son, William Clayton, and was wound up by 1730.

Frank T Melton, *Sir Robert Clayton and the Origins of English Deposit Banking 1658–1685* (Cambridge, 1986)

Records 1: Surrey Record Office, Guildford Muniment Room, Castle Arch, Guildford GU1 3SX

Records of banks 153

Business ledgers 1653–56, 1658–63, 1682–86; Peter Clayton's miscellaneous business accounts n.d. [Ref: 84/1/1, 84/1/2–4, 84/2/1]

Records 2: Guildhall Library, Aldermanbury, London EC2P 2EJ

Current account ledgers (5) 1645–52, 1669–80; business papers 1639–58. [Ref: MS2931, MS6428, MS2931a]

Records 3: Buckinghamshire Record Office, County Hall, Aylesbury HP20 1UA

Bond abstracts, etc 1632–77; personal vouchers 1653–84; partners' correspondence 1659–79; petty cash accounts 1634–36, 1680–82. [Ref: D135/A1/1–6]

Records 4: John Rylands University Library, University of Manchester, Deansgate, Manchester M3 3EH

Business correspondence 1656–1707; receipts and business papers 1659–97. [Ref: Eng.MSS 906, 943, 959, 986; Rylands Chs. 3682, 3698, 3776]

Records 5: Archives Department, British Library of Political and Economic Science, London School of Economics, 10 Portugal Street, London WC2A 2HD

Receipts, bills, bonds, promissory notes, petitions, wills, affidavits n.d. [Ref: Clayton papers]

CLEMENT ROYDS & CO
Rochdale, Greater Manchester

History: This private bank traced its origins to the Rochdale branch, established in 1819, of John, William & Christopher Rawson (est. 1811) of Halifax; it was otherwise known as Rochdale Old Bank. The firm had previously offered banking facilities in Yorkshire Street but only on the weekly market day. The bank, managed locally by Thomas Rawson, issued its own notes. In 1827 a local woollen manufacturer and merchant, Clement Royds, purchased the Rochdale business which traded as Royds, Smith & Co and, by 1828, as Clement Royds & Co. Clement Royds was succeeded as senior partner by his son, William Edward Royds, in 1854 and then by his grandson, Clement Molyneux Royds, in 1871. In 1881 the bank was acquired by Manchester & Salford Bank Ltd (est. 1836).

Records: The Royal Bank of Scotland plc, Archive Section, Regent's House, 42 Islington High Street, London N1 8XL

Customer ledgers 1824–29; rent ledger 1830–55; customer correspondence 1842; press cutting book 1869–81; signature book 1877–81; copper

154 *British banking – a guide to historical records*

printing plates for forms of acknowledgement and instructions c.1870s; photograph, Albert Hudson Royds c.1880s; drawing, Clement Molyneux Royds c.1880s.

CLYDESDALE BANK PLC
Glasgow, Strathclyde

History: This bank was formed in 1838 by a group of middle-ranking Glasgow businessmen from liberal-radical backgrounds who were much involved in the government and philanthropy of Scotland. Their leader was James Lumsden. There was, however, considerable support for the bank from Edinburgh where 40 per cent of shareholders were based. The number of shareholders was 776 on formation and paid-up capital was £375,000, rising shortly afterwards to £500,000. By late 1840 nine branches existed, that in Edinburgh being based in the premises of the recently closed bank of Ramsays, Bonars & Co (est. 1738). In 1844 Greenock Union Bank (est. 1840) was acquired, followed by Edinburgh & Glasgow Joint Stock Bank (est. 1838) in 1858 and Eastern Bank of Scotland (est. 1838) of Dundee in 1863. By 1874 paid-up capital was £1 million and in 1877 a branch was established in London, although the idea had first been mooted in 1865 when Clydesdale acted as a member of a consortium of Scottish banks in planning a joint London presence. In 1874 three branches were established in North West England, at Carlisle, Whitehaven and Workington. These were the first branches to be established by any Scottish bank in the English regions and generated great protest from English banks. In 1919, when Clydesdale Bank was the third largest Scottish bank, it was acquired by London Joint, City & Midland Bank Ltd (est. 1836), but continued to function independently. Midland merged it in 1950 with another of its Scottish subsidiaries, North of Scotland Bank Ltd (est. 1836), under the title Clydesdale & North of Scotland Bank Ltd. This title was shortened in 1963 to Clydesdale Bank Ltd. In 1987 National Australia Bank Ltd acquired the bank.

Charles W Munn, *Clydesdale Bank. The First One Hundred & Fifty Years* (Glasgow, 1988); J M Reid, *The History of the Clydesdale Bank 1838–1938* (Glasgow, 1938)

Records 1: Clydesdale Bank plc, Head Office, 30 St Vincent Place, Glasgow G1 2HL

Contract of co-partnership 1838; directors' meeting minute books (18) 1838 on; annual general meeting press cuttings 1838–1949; branch letterbook 1851–61; instructions to agents 1859, 1890; correspondence 1864–67; general manager's office papers 1864–91; notes on banking practice 1873; general manager's office memorandum books (5) 1877–1910; statement of

Records of banks 155

debt books (12) 1878–86, 1896–1968; list of shareholders 1881–1919; directors' meetings general manager's books (52) 1909–47, 1952–58; general manager's letterbooks (9) 1911–38; accountant's memorandum book, 1911 on; list of correspondents 1922; instruction book 1927.

Carnoustie: letterbook 1878; **Portobello:** charges account: 1873–99.

Records 2: Glasgow University Archives and Business Records Centre, 13 Thurso Street, Glasgow G11 6PE

Directors' meeting minute extracts 1838–1917; balance sheets and profit and loss accounts 1865–1971; annual reports 1890–1926. [Ref: Scottish Banking Collection]

Records 3: Archives, Argyll and Bute District Council, Kilmory, Lochgilphead, Argyll PA31 8RT

Campbeltown: branch trial balance 1852. [Ref: DR4/3/47]

COBB & CO
Margate, Kent

History: This private bank, which developed out of the Cobb family's brewing business, was formed in about 1785 and was sometimes known as Francis Cobb & Son; it was otherwise styled the Margate Bank and the Isle of Thanet Bank. Branches were opened at Westgate on Sea (1877), Birchington on Sea (1884) and Broadstairs (1887). Lloyds Bank Ltd (est. 1765) acquired the business in 1891.

Keith Lampard, 'Cobb & Son, Bankers at Margate 1783–1840' (PhD thesis, University of Kent)

Records 1: Lloyds TSB Group plc, Archives, 71 Lombard Street, London EC3P 3BS

Day book 1782–89; customer ledgers (11) 1793–1887 [w]; petty cash book 1811; agency account book 1821–33; partners' cash book 1841–48; partnership ledgers (3) 1841–1901; security register 1865–89; cash book 1872–83; standing order list 1874–91; security list 1878–91.

Records 2: Centre for Kentish Studies, County Hall, Maidstone ME14 1XQ

Papers re brewing and shipping c.1761–1962; paid cheques 1775–1876; customer correspondence 1771–1881; account books 1781–1834; note registers 1789–1871; correspondence with other banks 1794–1869; waste books 1800–61; cash books c.1803–80; ledgers 1808–55; partnership agreements 1842–92; amalgamation papers 1891–93.

156   *British banking – a guide to historical records*

COCKS, BIDDULPH & CO
London

History: This important private bank was formed in 1757 and was based in St Paul's Churchyard, City of London, before moving to Whitehall in London's West End in 1759. Its founder was Francis Biddulph of Ledbury, Hereford and Worcester, who was joined in partnership by two sons of his neighbour, Sir Charles Cocks. The bank traded under a number of titles largely comprising a combination of the Cocks and Biddulph surnames but including Biddulph, Cocks, Eliot & Praed (1776–82) and Biddulph, Cocks & Ridge (1792–1820); from 1865 it was known continuously as Cocks, Biddulph & Co. A particularly close connection existed with the Cornish Bank (est. 1771) of Truro owned by the Eliot and Praed families who provided partners for the London firm in the late eighteenth century. The bank won a reputation for exclusiveness, providing banking services to the aristocracy and middle class; its eighteenth century customers included the Dukes of Gloucester and Northumberland, Lords Dudley, Leicester and Sefton, the Bishop of London and Thomas Chippendale. In the late nineteenth century an important customer was the Prince of Wales. The bank also acted as London agents for many country banks. In 1886 Codd & Co (est. 1802) of Westminster was acquired and in 1893 140 new accounts were brought to Cocks by the chief clerk of Hallett & Co, navy agents, which had recently failed. In 1892 capital (including reserves and property) was increased from £78,000 to £200,000. In 1919, when deposit and current accounts totalled £1.125 million, the Bank of Liverpool & Martins Ltd (est.1831) acquired the bank.

George Chandler, *Four Centuries of Banking* (London, 1964–68)

Records 1: Barclays Bank plc, Group Archives, Dallimore Road, Wythenshawe, Manchester M23 9JA

Customer ledgers 1759–1831; private ledger 1765–68; country bank account ledgers (8) 1775–1801; customer balance books 1786–98; cheques 1792–1900s; letter of attorney 1801; signature books 1805–1937; customer stock books 1808–17; general manager's letterbooks (3) 1817–1918; dormant account books 1817–1926; customer accounts: Duchy of Lancaster 1826–41; ledger, exchequer bills, stocks and bonds 1836–64; securities 1846–1907; loan books 1852–1933; half-yearly balances 1875–1919; discounted bills 1880–93; cash books (3) 1882–1919; cheque book 1886–87; press cuttings 1887, 1919; balance sheets 1892–1915, 1919; private ledgers (2) 1892–1920; staff book 1899–1928; photographs of partners 1890s–1920s; cheque books 1908–10; business name registration certificate 1917.

Records of banks   157

Records 2: Hereford Record Office, The Old Barracks, Harold Street, Hereford HR1 2QX

Private papers of J Biddulph 1812–40. [Ref: G2]

COGGAN, MORRIS & CO
Staines, Surrey

History: This private bank was formed in 1810 and failed in 1813.

Records: London Metropolitan Archive, 40 Northampton Road, London EC1R 0HB

Draft partnership agreement 1810. [Ref: Acc 27/6]

COLE, HOLROYD & CO
Exeter, Devon

History: This private bank was established in 1807 as Russell, Brooke, Green, Cole, Perring & Co; it was otherwise known as Devon County Bank. Its founding partners were Robert Russell, a local carrier, John Cole, from a local merchanting family, and Joseph Green, Philip Perring and Charles Brooke who lived in London. The bank was known as Russell, Brooke & Co from 1810. George Holroyd, agent of the Exeter branch of Bank of England, joined as a partner in around 1833 at about the time of that branch's closure. In 1842 the business was sold to the National Provincial Bank of England (est. 1833) for £13,000.

John Ryton, *Banks and Bank Notes of Exeter 1769–1906* (priv. pub., 1984)

Records: The Royal Bank of Scotland plc, Archive Section, Regent's House, 42 Islington High Street, London N1 8XL

Partnership agreements (3) 1807–33; private ledgers (2) 1808–64; licences to issue notes 1810–41; information book 1817–41; balance sheet books (2) 1817–42; monthly balances of private ledger (3) 1817–64; private journals (2) 1817–64; stock balance books (2) 1818–42; statements of transactions in treasury bills 1826–35; papers re partnership matters 1834–42; list of customers 1842; amalgamation papers 1842.

COLONIAL BANK
London and North America

History: Formed in 1836 by Royal Charter, the Colonial Bank provided the first banking services in the West Indies and British Guiana. The Committee of West Indian Merchants played a significant role in its formation. Business began in 1837 with the head office based in London and

158   British banking – a guide to historical records

the major local office at Kingston, Jamaica. Initial paid-up capital was £500,000, of which a quarter was raised in the West Indies, and by the end of 1837 thirteen branches or agencies had been established throughout the West Indies. The bank financed trade and provided local banking services such as advances and exchange and issued bank notes; its business was closely linked with local commodity production, especially sugar. Following a difficult decade in the 1840s, the bank achieved prosperity, culminating in 1871 when £100,000 reserves were capitalised to increase paid-up capital to £600,000. In 1890 a New York agency was established. In that year total assets equalled £2.36 million and there were fourteen branches. In the late nineteenth and early twentieth centuries the bank's business, which remained tied to the local sugar industry, declined. In 1914 William Aitken, later 1st Lord Beaverbrook, acquired a major interest and instituted a policy of diversification, which restored the bank's business; its staff rose from 114 in 1914 to 404 in 1920. In 1913 total assets were £3.58 million and there were twenty branches. In 1916 a London branch was opened and in 1917 the bank expanded beyond the West Indies to British West Africa where, by 1918, twelve branches existed, mostly in Nigeria, the Gold Coast and Sierra Leone. In 1917 capital was increased by £1 million to £3 million, much of it being taken up by Barclays Bank Ltd (est. 1896). In 1925 Colonial Bank was reorganised and became the chief vehicle for the expansion of Barclays' overseas banking business, also embracing the Anglo-Egyptian Bank Ltd (est. 1864) and the National Bank of South Africa Ltd (est. 1890), under the name of Barclays Bank (Dominion, Colonial and Overseas).

Anon, *A Banking Centenary (Barclays Dominion, Colonial & Overseas) 1836–1936* (priv. pub., 1938)

Records 1: Barclays Bank plc, Group Archives, Dallimore Road, Wythenshawe, Manchester M23 9JA

Charter 1836; directors' meeting minute books (24) 1836–1925; committees meeting minute books (8) 1836–1925; press cuttings re opening 1837; profit and loss accounts 1837–1916; treasury committee minutes (3) 1837–1921; annual reports 1838–1925 [w]; head office procedure instructions (8) 1837–1914; general ledgers (19) 1845–1926; branch superintendent's statements (2) 1846–66; unclaimed dividend book 1847–1935; list of bank officers 1860; branch ledgers (13) 1863–1926 [w]; 'journal' of branch manager 1877; branch premises expenditure book 1879–1925; branch committee meetings agenda books (4) 1879–1925; court and committees attendance book 1888–1922; investment and loan account ledgers (4) 1894–1915; head office circulars (3) 1897, 1918–27; general manager's notes on banking policy and practices (2) 1898–1913; share transfer regis-

Records of banks **159**

ters (3) 1898–1925; bad debts by branch books (5) 1899–1913; investment register 1899–1918; unpaid and unaccepted remittance books (2) 1899–1918; balance sheets 1899–1925; current account ledgers (9) 1899–1926 [w]; bill purchase ledger 1905–12; standing orders 1907–20; shareholder registers (6) 1908–25; dividend register 1908–15; court meetings agenda books (3) 1913–26; establishment committee minutes 1915–18, 1925; investment ledger 1916–21; finance committee agenda books (4) 1918–25; pension fund rules 1919; bad debt provision book 1920–25; branch charges of business returns to head office (4) 1920–27; assets and liabilities of branches (3) 1921–27; head office charges of business book 1922–27; British Empire Exhibition visitors' books (2) 1924–25.

Antigua: note registers 1837–1953; general ledger 1837–39; letterbooks 1837–82; **Berbice:** general ledger 1840; letterbooks 1837–51; **Dakar:** ledger 1919–22; **Demerara:** letterbooks 1837–76; **Dominica:** inspection report 1887; **Durban:** letterbook 1854–57; **Jamaica:** staff attendance book 1893–1907; **Nablus:** customer account ledgers 1929–57; ledger, dormant accounts 1953–57; general ledgers 1929–57; impersonal ledgers 1929–57; ledger, register of claims against Israeli accounts 1953–55; staff register 1954–57; **St Kitts:** fixed deposit ledger 1878–1912; branch inspection papers 1887–1924; **St Lucia:** letterbooks 1837–49.

Records 2: Public Record Office, Ruskin Avenue, Kew, Richmond, Surrey TW9 1DU

Papers re application for charter 1837; petition against bank 1839; papers re note issue 1920. [Ref: T1/3473; T1/12592/23410/20]

COLONIAL BANK OF NEW ZEALAND
London and Australasia

History: This bank was incorporated in New Zealand in 1874 and aimed to be New Zealand's first home-grown banking institution to serve the whole of the country. Paid-up capital was initially £300,000 and rose to £400,000. There was a London board but the head office was based in Dunedin; branches were subsequently opened. In 1896 the business was sold to the Bank of New Zealand for £450,000.

Records: Southampton City Archives Office, Civic Centre, Southampton SO9 4XR

Prospectus 1874; papers re foundation and liquidation 1874, 1896. [Ref: D/MW Boxes 45–46]

COMMERCIAL BANK OF LONDON
London

160   *British banking – a guide to historical records*

History: This bank was established in Lothbury, City of London, in 1840. By 1850 its paid-up capital was £134,780 and its deposits were £613,000. Deposits peaked at £1.5 million in 1856 but then declined as the bank encountered difficulties. It had one branch. In 1861 £67,000 was lost as a result of fraud by a bookkeeper which caused the bank to seek the assistance of the London & Westminster Bank (est. 1834) in order to prevent a run. The business was transferred to the London & Westminster Bank and the bank was wound up.

T E Gregory, *The Westminster Bank through a Century* (London, 1936)

Records: The Royal Bank of Scotland plc, Archive Section, Regent's House, 42 Islington High Street, London N1 8XL

List of customers 1861.

COMMERCIAL BANK OF MANCHESTER
Manchester, Greater Manchester

History: This joint stock bank was proposed in 1827 as Manchester's first joint stock bank. However, it appears not to have been formed. It may have been an early attempt to form the Bank of Manchester (est. 1829).

Leo H Grindon, *Manchester Banks and Bankers* (Manchester, 1877)

Records: Leicestershire Record Office, Long Street, Wigston Magna, Leicester LE8 2AH

Prospectus 1827. [Ref: 3D42/3/13–24]

COMMERCIAL BANK OF SCOTLAND LTD
Edinburgh, Lothian

History: This co-partnery was founded in Edinburgh in 1810 to provide banking facilities to commercial, industrial and agricultural businesses of modest means. With an initial authorised capital of £3 million, of which £450,000 was paid-up, it presented a considerable challenge to existing banks. From the outset it issued its own notes and began to establish branches over a wide geographical area. By 1815 it had fourteen branches. It acquired the Caithness Banking Co (est. 1812) of Wick in 1826 and secured a Royal Charter in 1831. By 1840 there were forty-five branches and in 1844 the Arbroath Banking Co (est. 1825) was taken over. By 1850 it had fifty-four branches, the second largest network of any Scottish bank. In 1882 it adopted limited liability and in 1883 a London office was opened. The bank thrived during the early twentieth century, increasing its branches from 138 in 1900 to 240 in 1920. During the inter-war period it became the second largest bank in Scotland in terms of liabilities, deposits

Records of banks 161

and advances and in 1928 pioneered a scheme to attract small savers by offering favourable interest rates on small deposits. Despite its success and large number of branches, the Commercial Bank's capital resources were modest and its interests were undiversified. In 1954 the bank purchased Scottish Midland Guarantee Trust Ltd, the hire purchase subsidiary of Scottish Motor Traction Ltd, and thereby became the first British bank to take a direct financial interest in a hire purchase business. Later, in 1958, a merger agreement was reached with National Bank of Scotland Ltd (est. 1825), its owners, Lloyds Bank Ltd (est. 1765), surrendering control for a major stake in the new bank which was styled National Commercial Bank of Scotland Ltd.

Anon, *Our Bank. The Story of the Commercial Bank of Scotland Ltd 1810–1941* (Edinburgh, 1941); James L Anderson, *The Story of the Commercial Bank of Scotland Limited During Its Hundred Years from 1810 to 1910* (Edinburgh, 1910)

Records 1: The Royal Bank of Scotland plc, Archive Section, 36 St Andrew Square, Edinburgh EH2 2YB

Draft articles of co-partnership 1810; directors' meeting minutes 1810–1959; stock ledgers 1810–1922; staff books 1810–1957; staff biography notebooks 1810–65; bank note forgeries 1810; staff silhouette portraits c.1810–37; profit records 1811–56; deposit receipts book 1811–1900; correspondence re staff salaries 1811–57; annual salaries list 1811–56; property transactions record 1814–1959; branch statement book 1815–1900; agents' instructions book 1822; cash book 1823–34; salary book, cashiers and accountants 1823–27; papers re note circulation and forgeries c.1823–1909; private branch letterbooks 1824–35; staff duty lists 1820s; salary notebook 1830–35; customer references c.1830–60; branch inspection reports 1830–69; branch committee reports 1831–82; royal charter warrant 1831; monthly agency balance books 1832–1959; remarks on agencies and agents c.1833–36; branch profit and loss statement c.1835; salary registers, head office 1836–42; Glasgow premises papers c.1840, 1854–55; correspondence re reserve fund 1840; tellers' accounts 1842–48; salaries schedule 1843–83; bank notes 1843–1956; architectural plans and drawings: head office 1844–51, branches 1872–1959; engravings of directors c.1850; salary committee report 1854; annual reports 1855, 1878–1958; bond of fidelity 1856; staff photographs 1858–60, 1883–1915, 1940; branch committee meeting notebook 1859–62; Glasgow committee report 1861; stock issue book 1864; correspondence from apprenticeship applicants 1864–72; salary register 1866–86; lists of branches 1868–69; bank secretary retiral testament 1881; papers re bank officers' guarantee fund 1882–1900; London agency report and letter 1883–84; report on directors'

162 *British banking – a guide to historical records*

remuneration 1883; Glasgow branch abstract of charges 1884; list of agents and correspondents 1886; pension fund rules 1886; heritable property ledger 1887–1959; note circulation and coin reserves statistics book 1889–1927; notice re secrecy rules 1890; branch photographs 1890–1958; annual general meeting reports 1893–1951; agency houses register 1898–1948; branch inspectors' notebooks 1899–1929; London agency establishment correspondence 1917–18; correspondence re Scottish banks in London 1919; Christmas cards 1926–58; trustees account ledger 1929–41; monthly balances 1933–59; annual balance book 1934–48; branch expenditure: ledger 1935–59, register 1935–55; accountant's private cash book 1937–59; correspondence re Scottish banks' committee 1942–53; staff magazine, *The Griffin* 1944–59; staff association dinner menus 1948–54; foreign bills discounted 1948–59; branch weekly statements 1948–59; bank offices valuation 1958; petitions and extraordinary general meeting report re merger 1958–59.

Aberdeen: agency correspondence 1812–45; ledger 1814–18; **Annan:** photographs of agents 1812–1980; **Crail:** premises photographs 1920s; **Cupar:** current account ledger 1891–98; **Dalkeith:** cash book 1811–13; **Dundee, Commercial Street:** deposit receipt books 1872–1900; **Edinburgh, Leith:** report 1856; charges account book 1881–1900; **Glasgow, Great Western Road:** premises photographs 1963–c.1970; **Hawick:** notebook detailing bonds 1829–1900; charges book 1883–1900; **Lerwick:** scroll cash book 1866–68; **London Lombard Street:** accounts opened books 1884–1900; bad debts book 1892–1900; premises photographs c.1897; **Peebles:** premises photographs 1880–1991; **Uphall:** premises photographs 1898–1913.

Records 2: Business Records Centre, Archive Department, University of Glasgow, Glasgow G12 8QQ

Directors' meeting minutes and letterbooks extracts 1810–1922; annual reports 1878–1926. [Ref: Scottish Banking Collection]

COMMERCIAL BANK OF SPANISH AMERICA LTD
London and Latin America

History: This British overseas bank originated in 1881 when two Colombians resident in London established Enrique Cortes & Co, a confirming house which received and sold Colombian coffee and exported textiles. In 1884 the firm acquired limited liability when its paid-up capital was £32,000. It prospered and soon moved into trade finance. In 1904 a merger was effected with the largely exhausted London Bank of Central America Ltd (est. 1893, but tracing its origins to Banco de Nicaragua est. 1888) when the new firm of Cortes Commercial & Banking Co Ltd was formed

Records of banks   *163*

with a paid-up capital of £141,400. Rapid expansion followed and in 1907 branches or agencies existed in Colombia, Nicaragua, San Salvador, Ecuador and Peru which financed coffee, cocoa, rubber and bullion exports. In 1910 the Anglo-South American Bank Ltd (est. 1888) acquired a minority interest and in 1911 the name was changed to the Commercial Bank of Spanish America Ltd. Agencies were opened in New York and Paris in about 1912. By 1913 the bank had total assets of £400,000 and nine branches. The business was greatly damaged by the First World War and in 1917 the Anglo-South American Bank acquired full control. Post-war expansion followed including the establishment of branches in Mexico, Guatemala and at San Francisco. In 1926 all branches, other than the one at Iquitos (closed 1931), Peru, were merged into the Anglo-South American Bank Ltd. The bank was wound up in 1934.

David Joslin, *A Century of Banking in Latin America. The Bank of London & South America Ltd 1862–1962* (Oxford, 1963)

Records: Bloomsbury Science Library, University College London, Gower Street, London WC1E 6BT

Letterbooks, Caracas to/from London and New York (4) 1912–16 [w]; letterbook, Puerto Cabello 1920–22; letterbooks, Bogota to/from London, New York and elsewhere (6) 1920–27; letters, Federation of British Industries to Bogota, 1924–27. [Ref: BOLSA]

CONSOLIDATED BANK LTD
Manchester and London

History: This bank was formed with limited liability in 1863 by the amalgamation of Bank of Manchester Ltd (est. 1829) and Heywood, Kennard & Co (est. 1800) of Lombard Street, City of London. In August 1863 it acquired Hankeys & Co (est. 1685) of Fenchurch Street, London, and transferred to its premises in 1864. A branch opened in Norwich in 1864. In 1866 it acquired the business of Bank of London (est. 1855) of Threadneedle Street but then encountered difficulties. Unprepared to cover the Bank of London's acceptances, it stopped payment a few days later; it reopened after six weeks. The bank recovered during the 1870s and by 1877 its paid-up capital was £800,000 and its reserves were £145,000; it then had three branches in Salford, Manchester and Charing Cross, London. From the late 1880s it adopted a vigorous policy of branch expansion, opening offices in Patricroft, Pendleton and Longsight (all 1887), Leigh and Tyldesley (both 1888), Radcliffe (1892), Deansgate, Manchester (1893) and Salford Cattle Market (1894). It amalgamated with Parr's Banking Co & Alliance Bank Ltd in 1896 when the latter changed its name to Parr's Bank Ltd.

164   *British banking – a guide to historical records*

T E Gregory, *The Westminster Bank Through A Century* (London, 1936); William Howarth, *Our Leading Banks* (London, 1894); Leo H Grindon, *Manchester Banks and Bankers* (Manchester, 1877)

Records: The Royal Bank of Scotland plc, Archive Section, Regent's House, 42 Islington High Street, London N1 8XL

Deeds of settlement 1858, 1863; directors' meeting minute books (2) 1863–96; daily minutes 1863–96; half-yearly balance sheets, profit and loss accounts and branch accounts 1863–96; circulars and notices 1863–99; correspondence with London office 1863–95; salary books 1864–93; amalgamation papers, Bank of London 1866; doubtful debt papers 1867–95; manager's letterbooks (2) 1867–97; board agenda books (6) 1873–96; directors' reports 1874–93; list of shareholders 1880; comparative statistics with other banks' performances 1885, 1890, 1893; bank and trade daily interest rates book 1891–1907; amalgamation papers 1892–96; papers re Baring Brothers & Co guarantee fund 1893; branch staff reports 1894–96; auditor's securities report 1895; staff list 1896.

COOKE, FOLJAMBE, PARKER & WALKER
Retford, Nottinghamshire

History: This private bank was established at Retford, possibly in about 1808, by the proprietors of Cooke & Co (est. 1750) of Doncaster; it was sometimes known as Sir W B Cooke, Childers & Co and also as Foljambe's Bank. It opened a branch in Worksop in about 1817 and was acquired by Beckett & Co of Leeds (est. 1774) in 1868.

Records: The Royal Bank of Scotland plc, Archive Section, Regent's House, 42 Islington High Street, London N1 8XL

General ledger 1841–67.

COOKE, VERNON, WALKER, JACKSON & MILNER
Doncaster, South Yorkshire

History: This private bank was established at Doncaster in 1750 as Ellison, Cooke, Childers & Swan. Subsequently it was styled Cooke, Ellison & Co; Cooke, Yarborough & Co; Yarborough & Co by 1810; and Cooke, Vernon, Walker, Jackson & Milner by 1858. In about 1808 H S Foljambe of Retford joined the partnership and a bank was subsequently established at Retford, Nottinghamshire. In 1847 the Doncaster firm absorbed Leatham, Tew & Co (est. 1801), also of Doncaster. A branch opened at Ollerton in 1864. The bank was acquired by Beckett & Co (est. 1774) of Leeds in 1868.

Records: The Royal Bank of Scotland plc, Archive Section, Regent's House, 42 Islington High Street, London N1 8XL

Partnership agreements 1785–1813, 1848–62; papers re Cooke family 1737–1854; balance sheets 1802–05; letter with London agents 1807–19; private ledgers (2) 1807–67; general statement books 1809–48; customer accounts: R Littlewood 1824, W S Clarke 1831–38; sundry balances 1826–66; papers re partnership matters 1838–65; premises valuations 1842–67; papers re increase in capital 1846–66; papers re applications for employment 1852–66; premises plan n.d.; amalgamation papers 1866–76.

CO-OPERATIVE BANK PLC
Manchester, Greater Manchester

History: This bank was formed in 1872 as the Loan and Deposit Department of the Co-operative Wholesale Society (CWS). The CWS had been formed in 1863 to supply, and if need be to produce, goods and services for local retail societies. The CWS Bank, as the department soon became generally known, was seen as a means of channelling the funds of members of the co-operative movement into activities associated with the movement thereby giving it financial independence. Early clients included retail societies and other businesses operating on co-operative principles. Total assets grew from almost £200,000 in 1873 to £11 million in 1919 and to £43.5 million in 1929; the number of current accounts expanded from sixty to 5,300 and then to 26,000 respectively. The increase largely comprised individual account holders who had been able to open deposit accounts since 1910. From 1912 trades union also became increasingly important customers. One early area of business involved lending to retail societies which lent-on to members to enable their purchase of homes. In the early 1920s the first branches of the bank opened at London, Newcastle, Bristol and Salford, although previously CWS offices in these cities (and elsewhere) had provided basic banking services. The department, by now known as the Banking Department, expanded rapidly after 1945 and in 1970 its business was transferred to the newly established Co-operative Bank Ltd which commenced business in 1971. In 1973 the banking department of the Scottish Co-operative Wholesale Society was absorbed. Rapid expansion followed and in 1975 clearing bank status was acquired. The bank was known as The Co-operative Bank plc in 1993 and its ultimate owner was the Co-operative Wholesale Society Ltd.

T G Davies, *A Brief History of the CWS Bank and Some Account of its Present Activities* (priv. pub., 1930)

Records: The Co-operative Bank plc, 1 Balloon Street, Manchester M60 4EP

166 *British banking – a guide to historical records*

Impersonal ledgers (5) 1873–1971; published quarterly accounts 1878–93; cash book 1902–14; customer ledger 1905; summaries of investments (6) 1913–25; staff records from 1914 on; investment register 1915–26; deposit note registers (50) 1919–47; development bond registers (2) 1920–25; customer investment register 1925–66; cash in transit registers (4) 1929–47; daily cash summaries (2) 1932–40; daily balance books (10) 1932–49; sundry day books (19) 1932–65; current account weekly summaries (4) 1933–47.

Note: These records were originally listed in the early 1980s; it has not proved possible to establish the current status of the records.

COOPER, PURTON & SONS
Bridgnorth, Shropshire

History: This private bank was established in 1817 and had offices at both Bridgnorth and Wenlock. It was acquired by Birmingham Banking Co Ltd (est. 1829) in 1889.

Records: HSBC Holdings plc, Group Archives, 10 Lower Thames Street, London EC3R 6AE

Cash and discount ledger 1819–20.

GEORGE & THOMAS COPEMAN
Aylsham, Norfolk

History: This private bank was formed in 1809 as Robert & Edward Copeman; its partners were attorneys. It was known as Robert & George Copeman from 1840 to 1847 and thereafter as George & Thomas Copeman; it was otherwise called the Aylsham Bank. In 1855 it was acquired by Gurneys, Birkbecks & Co (est. 1775) of Norwich.

Harold Preston, *Early East Anglian Banks and Bankers* (Thetford, 1994)

Records: Barclays Bank plc, Group Archives, Dallimore Road, Wythenshawe, Manchester M23 9JA

Banker's licence 1823; bank notes 1847–55; partnership agreement 1855; photographs, Aylsham Bank n.d.; agreement for sale of bank 1855.

CORGAN, PAGET & MATHEWS
Chipping Norton, Oxfordshire

History: This private bank was formed in about 1790 and was otherwise known as Chipping Norton Bank. It failed in 1816.

Records: Oxfordshire Archives, County Hall, New Road, Oxford OX1 1ND

Papers re failure c.1816–34. [Ref: Stockton Sons & Fortescue Collection Boxes 1–2]

CORNISH BANK LTD
Truro, Cornwall

History: This joint stock bank traced its origins to the private bank of Sir John Molesworth & Son formed in 1771 and styled Praed & Co in 1800 and Tweedy, Williams & Co in 1830. Its early partners, including Sir John Molesworth Bt., Sir Francis Bassett (later Lord De Dunstanville) and David Jenkins, were closely associated with the Cornish copper industry which the bank, *inter alia*, financed. Matthew Boulton, of the early steam engine builders, Boulton & Watt, was a customer. By 1777 the bank's London agents were Biddulph, Cocks & Co (est. 1775) in which the Cornish Bank provided some of the partners until 1792. In 1802 a connected bank was formed in London called Praeds & Co (merged with Lloyds Bank Ltd 1891). Subsequently the Truro bank operated branches at Falmouth, Redruth and Penryn. In 1879 the bank failed, following the collapse of the City of Glasgow Bank and of the West of England & South Wales District Bank Ltd. It was reconstituted in 1879 as a joint stock bank known as The Cornish Bank Ltd which by 1902 had thirty branches and a paid-up capital of £150,000. In that year it was acquired by the Capital & Counties Bank Ltd (est. 1877).

R M Fitzmaurice, 'A Chapter in Cornish Banking History. The Crisis of 1879 and the Failure of Tweedy, Williams & Co, The Cornish Bank', *Journal of the Royal Institution of Cornwall* (1991); C E Hicks, 'The Cornish Banking Crisis of 1879', *Bankers' Magazine* (1952)

Records: Lloyds TSB Group plc, Archives, Head Office, 71 Lombard Street, London EC3P 3BS

Minute book 1774–1830; annual reports 1879–1901; directors' meeting minute books (10) 1879–1906; rough minute books (5) 1888–1905; letterbooks (4) 1889–1905; audit books and papers 1894–97, 1900–01; amalgamation papers 1902, 1920.

COUNTY BANK LTD
Manchester, Greater Manchester

History: This joint stock bank was established in 1862 in York Street, Manchester, as the Manchester & County Bank Ltd; it embraced another Manchester joint stock bank proposed at this time, namely the Northern Counties Bank. Its initial paid-up capital was almost £224,000 and the first branches were soon opened at Preston, Bacup and Blackburn. It

168 *British banking – a guide to historical records*

moved to King Street in 1879 and acquired the Saddleworth Banking Co (est. 1833) in 1866, the Bank of Stockport (est. 1836) in 1872 and the Bank of Bolton Ltd (est. 1836) in 1896. By 1877 paid-up capital was £660,000, reserves totalled £405,000 and there were nineteen branches (including Ashton-under-Lyne, Bolton, Burnley, Darwen and Oldham) and twelve sub-branches. The bank was restyled County Bank Ltd in 1934 and merged with the District Bank Ltd (est. 1829) in 1935; it then had 190 branches. The name of County Bank Ltd was revived in 1965 as the merchant banking subsidiary of the National Provincial Bank Ltd (which then owned the District Bank) and, subsequently, of National Westminster Bank Ltd.

Leo H Grindon, *Manchester Banks and Bankers* (Manchester, 1877); Richard Reed, *National Westminster Bank. A Short History* (London, 1989)

Records: The Royal Bank of Scotland plc, Archive Section, Regent's House, 42 Islington High Street, London N1 8XL

Prospectus 1862; articles of association 1862, 1912; general minutes 1862–1935; half-yearly account books 1862–86, 1893–1935; directors' minute books 1865–71, 1931–35; branch statistics 1877–1923; list of shareholders 1885; circulars 1887–1935; half-yearly reports 1895–1920; general memorandum book 1897–1914; book of instructions to staff 1899; annual reports 1914–34; superannuation fund rules 1928; widows' and orphans' fund rules 1929; private agenda book 1934–35; private minute book 1934–35; procedural instructions re amalgamation 1935.

Accrington: minute book 1891–1918; **Bacup:** manager's private letterbooks (2) 1864–1924; **Blackburn:** minute book 1891–1910; **Bolton:** out-letterbooks (9) 1897–1930; staff applications 1897–1915; manager's reference book 1897–1902; minute books (5) 1898–1931; manager's information book 1906–08; **Brierfield:** character books 1890s–1934; **Buxton:** salary and expenses book 1873–1900; **Chadderton:** premises lease and accounts 1898–1939; salary increase notice 1919; **Chorley:** minute book 1903–36; **Colne:** minute book 1872–1909; **Delph:** customer signature books (3) 1862–1929; list of expenses 1868; opinion book 1886–1942; customer information book 1901–41; customer papers 1908–32; letterbooks (2) 1922–38; **Dobcross:** deposit account ledgers (5) 1831–67; title deeds schedule 1868; list of expenses 1883; **Farnworth:** minute book 1891–1937; **Hayfield:** safe custody register 1901; circulars 1934–35; customer stock register 1935–49; teller's cash book 1937–62; **Hollingworth:** circulars re account transfers 1935; **Hollinwood:** minute book 1891–1931; **Marple:** photograph 1914; **Oldham:** opinion books (2) 1878–1937; register of cotton securities 1887–1934; **Oldham, Mumps:** manager's minute book 1906–30; **Stockport:** weekly balance

Records of banks   169

book 1872–94; manager's memorandum book 1883–89; manager's reference book 1891–1920; staff register 1894–1948; out-letters 1910–30; **Tyldesley:** manager's memorandum book 1896–1923; staff record book 1896–1938; **Uppermill:** cash balance book 1886–87; **Walkden:** minute book 1898–1938; **West Houghton:** manager's letterbook 1923–36; **West Loughton:** sanction letters 1902–38; **Wigan:** out-letterbooks (2) 1868–89.

COUNTY OF GLOUCESTER BANK LTD
Cheltenham, Gloucestershire

History: This joint stock bank was formed out of the business of the Gloucester County & City Bank (est. 1834) in 1836 as the County of Gloucester Banking Co. Its early growth was largely by acquisition of private banks, viz: Pitt, Bowley, Croome & Wood (est. 1790) of Cirencester, Wood, Pitt & Co (est. 1792) of Tetbury and Vizard & Co of Dursley, all in 1836; Watts, Wyatt & Co (est. 1830) of Stroud in 1838; T & R Strange (est. 1807) of Swindon in 1842; and Cheltenham & Gloucestershire Banking Co (est. 1836), its chief competitor, in 1856. In 1889 limited liability was acquired under the title of County of Gloucester Bank Ltd. By 1897 the bank was one of the largest in South West England and operated branches in Gloucestershire, Wiltshire, Oxfordshire, Berkshire, Glamorganshire and Gwent (Monmouthshire) which included branches and sub-branches at Cirencester, Tetbury, Dursley, Swindon, Stow, Faringdon, Burford, Stroud, Cheltenham, Wotton (1863), New Swindon (1872), Bourton on the Water (1888), Cardiff (1888), Winchcombe (1888), Cardiff Docks (1889), Fairford (1889), Lechlade (1889), Newport (1889), Barry Docks (1890), Roath (1894), Cricklade and Highworth. Lloyds Bank Ltd (est. 1765) acquired the bank in 1897.

R S Sayers, *Lloyds Bank in the History of English Banking* (Oxford, 1957)

Records 1: Lloyds TSB Group plc, Archives, Head Office, 71 Lombard Street, London EC3P 3BS

Deed of settlement 1836; private ledger 1836–53; minute books (7) 1836–95; general meeting minute books (2) 1836–1901; local directors' meeting minute books (2) 1860–79; amalgamation papers 1897.

Cheltenham: signature book 1863–99; **Cirencester:** security book 1879–90; **Dursley:** memorandum book 1889–97; **Gloucester:** signature book c.1838–90.

Records 2: Gloucester Library, Local Studies Dept, Brunswick Road, Gloucester GL1 1HT

170　　　*British banking – a guide to historical records*

Deed of settlement 1836; letter from William Pitt 1836; notices, rules, etc, 1838–97; annual reports 1866–97. [Ref: 6142; JQ 13.13; (H)F7.6(20); JV13.2; JR13.4–7; JF13.4,7; (H)E13.23]

Records 3: Gloucestershire Record Office, Clarence Row, Alvin Street, Gloucester GL1 3DW

Miscellaneous papers 1809–46. [Ref: D025]

COUNTY OF STAFFORD BANK LTD
Bilston and later Wolverhampton, West Midlands

History: This joint stock bank was established at Bilston in 1836 and was known as the Bilston District Banking Co. It moved to Wolverhampton in 1843 and issued its own notes until 1881. It acquired limited liability and was restyled County of Stafford Bank Ltd in 1873. In 1899 its business was sold to the National Provincial Bank of England Ltd (est. 1833).

Records: The Royal Bank of Scotland plc, Archive Section, Regent's House, 42 Islington High Street, London N1 8XL

Deed of settlement 1836; balance sheets book and bad debt accounts 1836–98; directors' meeting minute books (3) 1836–1900; annual general meeting minutes 1838–73; customer papers 1840–48, 1873–97; bills of exchange 1846–53; licence to issue notes with list of shareholders 1856; deed of assent to increase capital 1864; security ledger c.1880–99.

COUTTS & CO
London

History: This private bank traces its origins to John Campbell, a Scottish goldsmith who began business at the sign of the Three Crowns, Strand, in London's West End in 1692. He quickly attracted distinguished customers including his kinsman the Earl, later 1st Duke, of Argyll, and was commissioned by Queen Anne to make the collars and badges for the Scottish Order of the Thistle. A fellow Scot, George Middleton, was taken into partnership in 1708, and in 1712 married Campbell's daughter, Mary. Middleton was forced to stop payment temporarily during the 1720 financial crisis and his recovery took three years. His brother-in-law, George Campbell, entered the partnership in 1727 and was joined by Middleton's nephew David Bruce in 1744. Middleton died in 1747 when the goldsmith business was discontinued. In 1755 the business became known as Campbell & Coutts following the entry into the partnership of James Coutts, the husband of John Campbell's granddaughter. James's brother, Thomas Coutts, joined in 1761 and their partnership continued until 1775 when James retired and the business adopted the title of Thomas Coutts & Co. Thomas soon took in partners, the best

Records of banks   *171*

known of whom were Edmund Antrobus, Edward Marjoribanks and Coutts Trotter. By 1800 the bank, which had been based at 59 Strand since 1739, had a customer list that was both distinguished and wide-ranging, including royalty and the cow keeper of Covent Garden. In 1816 the business of Davison, Noel, Templer, Middleton & Wedgwood (est. 1793) was acquired. On Thomas Coutts's death in 1822, the bank was renamed Coutts & Co and his half-share in it passed to his second wife, the former actress Harriot Mellon. On her death, in 1837, her fortune was left to Thomas's youngest grandchild, Angela Burdett (later Baroness Burdett-Coutts who died in 1906), which included her interest in Coutts which was held in trust (from which Angela received the income). In 1840 the accounts and assets of Hammersley, Greenwood & Brooksbank (est. 1795) were taken over. The bank was by now unquestionably one of the leading private banks in London. In the following years, younger members of the Marjoribanks, Antrobus and Coulthurst families entered the partnership and were joined by new blood in the form of Lord Archibald Campbell, R R Pym, W R Malcolm and members of the Ryder family. In 1892, following a series of crises in the financial community, the bank converted from a partnership to an unlimited liability company. In 1904 it moved across Strand to its present day site at No 440. Ten years later, the well-known private bankers, Robarts, Lubbock & Co (est. 1772), were acquired when Coutts gained its first branch, at Robarts's premises in Lombard Street, and a seat in the London Clearing House. In 1920 Coutts merged with the National Provincial & Union Bank of England Ltd (est. 1833), subsequently a constituent of National Westminster Bank plc, but retained its separate identity as a prestigious private bank. More branches were established, the first in London's West End in 1921, and in 1961 the first branch outside London opened at Eton. In the middle of the 1970s, the bank's premises were reconstructed behind most of the original 1831 Nash facade. In 1990 HandelsBank NatWest of Zurich and NatWest International Trust Holdings Ltd were transferred to form an enlarged Coutts Group, within National Westminster Bank, specialising in providing retail banking services to high income private customers.

E H Coleridge, *The Life of Thomas Coutts, Banker* (London, 1920); Edna Healey, *Coutts & Co 1692–1992. The Portrait of a Private Bank* (Sevenoaks, 1992); Ralph Richardson, *Coutts & Co Bankers* (London, 1900); Ralph M Robinson, *Coutts. The History of a Banking House* (London, 1929)

Records: Coutts & Co, 440 Strand, London WC2R 0QS

Papers of John Campbell c.1692–1712; out-letterbooks c.1700–50; customer wills and probates c.1700–1920; customer account ledgers (c.4,000) 1712 on; partners' wills and related papers 1712–76; private ledgers 1716–

172   British banking – a guide to historical records

19, 1734 on; waste books (3) 1719–26; customer oubliette material 1720–1914; private and business papers of certain partners 1760–1900; annual balance books (c.160) 1761–1920; in-letters (c.4,000) 1770 on; partners' letterbooks 1777 on; partnership agreements 1777–1827; probate registers 1786–1961; safe custody books 1790–1960; signature books (22) 1794–1917; leases, plans, elevations re premises eighteenth cent; customer mandates 1802–1900; clerk books 1810–1928; money lent books 1817–1946; salary books 1818 on; registers of new accounts 1824–1971; strongroom diaries (c.80) 1854–1972; customer address books (18) 1856–1912; staff address books 1857–1912; managing directors' minutes 1892 on; general meeting minutes 1892 on; sealing committee minutes 1914 on; papers re redevelopment of 440 Strand site 1973–78.

COVENTRY & WARWICKSHIRE BANKING CO
Coventry, West Midlands

History: This joint stock bank was formed in 1835 and acquired the local private bank of Beck & Prime (est. 1790), supposedly in order to obtain the services of James Beck as general manager. In 1839 the Coventry private bank of Goodall, Gulson & Co (est. 1810) was also acquired. The bank's operations were always entirely Coventry based and in 1879 Lloyds Banking Co Ltd (est. 1765) acquired the business.

Howard Lloyd, *Notes and Reminiscences of Lloyds Bank 1862–1892* (unpub. mss., 1917); R S Sayers, *Lloyds Bank in the History of English Banking* (Oxford, 1957)

Records 1: Lloyds TSB Group plc, Archives, Head Office, 71 Lombard Street, London EC3P 3BS

Deed of settlement 1835; directors' meeting minute books (12) 1835–77; general meeting minutes 1837–68; amalgamation papers 1879–97.

Coventry: security ledgers (2) c.1860s–1870s.

Records 2: Warwickshire Record Office, Priory Park, Cape Road, Warwick CV34 4JS

Sale of shares 1858. [Ref: CR1300/28]

COVENTRY UNION BANKING CO LTD
Coventry, Warwickshire

History: This joint stock bank was formed in 1836 and was largely based upon the business of the local private bank of Bunney, Bunney & Pepper (est. 1800) which it acquired for £5,000; two Bunney partners became directors along with a ribbon manufacturer, a maltster, a wine merchant

Records of banks 173

and a London doctor. Also in 1836, a branch was opened at Coleshill and another was established at Atherstone through the acquisition of the private bank of Chapman & Co (est. c.1790) for £4,250. The bank encountered severe difficulties in 1841 resulting in reorganisation and the sale in 1845 of the Atherstone branch to the Leicestershire Banking Co (est. 1829) for £6,000. No further branches were opened and by the 1880s the Coventry Union Banking Co was the only surviving purely local bank at Coventry. Deposits grew from £130,000 in 1840 to £420,000 in 1889 when paid-up capital was £56,000. In this year the Birmingham & Midland Bank Ltd (est. 1836) acquired the business for the equivalent of £125,000.

W F Crick & J E Wadsworth, *A Hundred Years of Joint Stock Banking* (London, 1936)

Records 1: HSBC Holdings plc, Group Archives, 10 Lower Thames Street, London EC3R 6AE

Deed of settlement 1836; trustees' declaration and conveyances 1836–73; directors' meeting minute books (4) 1836–80; note registers (3) 1836–85; signature book 1836–86; securities 1836–94; 'board memorandums' (3) 1852–89; annual reports 1877–88; amalgamation papers 1888–89.

Coleshill: note register 1837–83; security book and safe custody register 1869–89; reference book 1889.

Records 2: Warwickshire Record Office, Priory Park, Cape Road, Warwick CV34 4JS

Prospectus 1836; title deeds 1841, 1851; legal papers re security 1877; passbook nineteenth cent. [Ref: CR1020/159; CR619/48; CR1709/171, 182, 183]

COX & CO
London

History: This private bank, located in London's West End, traced its origins to 1758 when Richard Cox (1718–1803) was appointed regimental agent to the First Foot Guards. This role extended beyond the payment of officers and men to the provision of supplies and the marketing of commissions; inevitably Cox & Co became involved in providing banking services to army officers. By 1815 the firm was the largest army agent, acting for the entire Household Brigade, most cavalry and infantry regiments, the Royal Artillery and the Royal Wagon Train. The partnership was variously known as Cox & Drummond (1765); Cox & Mair (1772); Cox, Mair & Cox (1779); Cox, Cox & Greenwood (1783); Cox & Greenwood (1791); Cox, Greenwood & Cox (1801); Greenwood & Cox (1803);

174   *British banking – a guide to historical records*

Greenwood, Cox & Co (1806); Cox, Hammersley & Co (1833); and Cox & Co (1834). Between 1905 and 1911, branches were opened in India at Rawalpindi (1907), Srinagar (1907), Bombay (1908), Karachi (1908) and Calcutta (1911); sub-branches operated at Muree and Gulmarg. Further branches opened at Alexandria (1919), Cairo (1920) and Rangoon (1921). Henry S King & Co (est. 1868) was absorbed in 1922. By 1923 deposits stood at £11 million in London, £2.8 million in India and £1 million in Egypt. In 1915 Coxs established Cox & Co (France) Ltd in which the London & South Western Bank Ltd (est. 1862) took a joint interest. The firm, whose business diminished after the war, was damaged through diversification into cotton finance. The French joint venture passed into the ownership of Barclays Bank Ltd (est. 1896) in 1922 and was eventually called Barclays Bank (France). In 1923, at the behest of the Bank of England, Lloyds Bank Ltd (est. 1765) acquired the business. The Egyptian branches were sold to the National Bank of Egypt in 1926 but the Indian business, administered by Lloyds' new Eastern Department, continued until 1960. The London office became Lloyds' Pall Mall branch, providing banking services to the armed forces.

Anon, *Cox's & King's. The Evolution of a Military Tradition* (priv. pub., 1990); Anon, *1758–1923. The Story of an Army Agent* (priv. pub., n.d.); K R Jones, *The Cox's of Craig's Court* (priv. pub., 1953)

Records: Lloyds TSB Group plc, Archives, Head Office, 71 Lombard Street, London EC3P 3BS

Cox family papers 1718–1865; non-military business papers 1743–1848; regimental account ledgers (177) 1758–1836; partnership papers 1766–1892; cash book 1767–68; profit and loss accounts (24) 1772–1899; army agency papers 1773–1920; Hammersley papers 1795–1840; partnership agreements 1805–1905; dormant account balance books (2) 1819, 1822; 'old corps' letterbook 1821; outstanding account ledger 1824; out-letterbook 1835–53; public office letterbook 1866; balance sheets 1892–1922; memorandum re average figures for Indian branches 1908–14; report on foreign department 1918; report on United States army branch 1919; report on Indian business 1922.

COX, COBBOLD & CO
Harwich, Essex

History: This private bank was formed in the 1770s by Charles Cox, packet boat agent. The business was known as Bridges, Cox & Godfrey from 1812, as Cox & Nunn from 1815, as Cox & Knocker from 1823, as Cox & Cox from 1835 and as Cox, Cobbold & Co from 1839; it was otherwise known as the Harwich Bank. From 1812 a link existed with

Bridges & Co (est. c.1810) of Hadleigh and Manningtree while for many years the bank shared partners with Bacon, Cobbold & Co (est. 1786) of Ipswich. The latter firm acquired the business in 1893.

Harold Preston, *Early East Anglian Banks and Bankers* (Thetford, 1994)

Records: Lloyds TSB Group plc, Archives, Head Office, 71 Lombard Street, London EC3P 3BS

Note registers (3) 1811–91; partnership agreement 1812; general ledgers (2) 1815–18, 1838–42; stock book 1822–80; balance book 1839–44; security registers (2) 1855–1908.

CRAVEN BANK LTD
Settle and later Skipton, North Yorkshire

History: This joint stock bank traced its origins to the leading private bank, established at Settle in 1791, of William & John Birkbeck, Wm. Alcock, John Peart, Jos. Smith & Wm. Lawson, all of whom were leading businessmen in Skipton, Settle, Grassington and Giggleswick. It subsequently traded under several names and was otherwise styled the Craven Bank. The Birkbecks were especially important, not just in business but as Quakers who in 1780 became connected through marriage to the Gurney family, bankers in Norfolk. In 1782 John Birkbeck became a partner in the Gurneys' King's Lynn bank. A connection through marriage also existed with the Crewdson family of Kendal, leading Quaker bankers. In the 1790s an agency was established at Skipton and in 1826 representation there was extended through the acquisition of Chippendale, Netherwood & Carr (est. 1807). Branches were established at Clitheroe (1838) and Keighley (1840). In 1880 the business, by then an important district bank, was converted into a joint stock bank under the title of the Craven Bank Ltd with its head office at Skipton. Its nominal capital was £1.2 million and, on formation, it had branches at Settle, Keighley, Ilkley, Burnley, Clitheroe and Colne and sub-branches at Barnoldswick, Gisburn, Bradford, Cross Hills, Haworth, Denholm, Skilsden, Nelson and Padiham. New branch openings followed at Otley (1882) and Bingley (1883). In 1891 paid-up capital was increased from £175,000 to £210,000. In 1906 the Bank of Liverpool Ltd (est. 1831) acquired the bank when it had paid-up capital of £210,000, reserves of £90,000 and fourteen branches and twenty-six sub-branches.

George Chandler, *Four Centuries of Banking* (London, 1964–68); W C E Hartley, *Banking in Yorkshire* (Clapham, 1975)

Records 1: Barclays Bank plc, Group Archives, Dallimore Road, Wythenshawe, Manchester M23 9JA

176   *British banking – a guide to historical records*

Declarations of trust 1757–73; diary, William Birkbeck IV 1777; promissory note 1779; customer ledgers 1791–1803, 1827–36; in-letters 1794–97, 1868; customer stock ledger 1804–40; bank notes 1809–91; profit and loss sheets 1811–44; private ledgers (2) 1825–87; minutes of Settle Mechanics' Institute 1831–87; legal case correspondence 1842–46; banker's licences 1843, 1905–06; partnership agreements 1844–68; impersonal ledger 1845–1911; memorandum and articles of association 1862–80; manager's diary 1866–72, 1889; prospectus 1880; registers of shareholders (4) 1880–90; minute books (4) 1880–1906; report and accounts 1880–1905; lists of shareholders 1881–92, 1906; bills of exchange 1880s; papers re merger with Bank of Liverpool 1892–1906; head office instructions 1901; staff contract 1916.

Records 2: West Yorkshire Archive Service, Leeds District Archives, Chapeltown Road, Sheepscar, Leeds LS7 3AP

Business papers of William Birkbeck and other papers re bank 1773–1823. [Ref: Birkbeck MSS]

Records 3: West Yorkshire Archive Service, Yorkshire Archaeological Society, Claremont, 23 Clarendon Road, Leeds LS2 9NZ

Cheque book stubs and passbooks 1862–93. [Ref: DD81/TLE 28/ VI]

CREDIT FONCIER OF ENGLAND LTD
London

History: This finance house, which specialised in company promotions, was formed in 1864 by Albert Grant as the Credit Foncier. Shortly afterwards, he promoted a twin company, the Credit Mobilier, and later in 1864 merged both into the Credit Foncier & Mobilier of England Ltd. Between 1864 and 1866, eleven major company promotions were arranged, but most were unsuccessful and led to the lock up of funds. In 1866 the business was reconstituted as Credit Foncier of England Ltd with Grant remaining as manager until he resigned in 1868. An investigation then uncovered fraud and in the 1870s the business was preoccupied with recovering its funds. It was wound up in the 1880s.

P L Cottrell, 'Albert Grant', *Dictionary of Business Biography* (London, 1984)

Records: Devon Record Office, Castle Street, Exeter EX4 3PU

Correspondence, reports, share certificates and papers 1866–86. [Ref: 1137 M/B 2/8]

W D CREWDSON & CO
Kendal, Cumbria

History: This private bank was formed in 1788 as Maude, Wilson & Crewdson. It subsequently traded under several titles including Wilson, Crewdson & Co (1812–15), Wilson, Crewdsons, Bateman & Co (from 1815) and W D Crewdson & Co (1830–40); it was otherwise known as the Kendal Bank. Its founding partners were Quakers who came from long-established and successful business families at Kendal. The most important founding partner was Joseph Maude who was also connected with Maude, Wilson & Smith (est. c.1793), bankers at Otley, Yorkshire. In 1840 the bank merged with its longstanding Kendal rival, John Wakefield & Sons (est. 1788), to form Wakefield, Crewdson & Co.

George Chandler, *Four Centuries of Banking* (London, 1964–68)

Records: Barclays Bank plc, Group Archives, Dallimore Road, Wythenshawe, Manchester M23 9JA

Letters to Deborah Braithwaite 1789–1838; diaries of W D Crewdson I & II 1794–97, 1823–29; banker's licence 1810; bank notes 1815–24; private ledgers (2) 1820–40; letters to partners 1828–40; daily balance states 1833.

CROMPTON & EVANS' UNION BANK LTD
Derby, Derbyshire

History: This joint stock bank was formed with limited liability in 1877 with a paid-up capital of £160,000 to acquire the private banks of Crompton, Newton & Co (est. c.1685) of Derby; Crompton, Newton, Walker & Co (est. 1808) of Chesterfield; and W & S Evans & Co (est. 1771) of Derby. Branches were opened at Wirksworth and Mansfield in the first year of operation. The bank acquired the failed Chesterfield & North Derbyshire Banking Co (est. 1834) in 1878; Wilson & Sons (est. 1853) of Alfreton in 1879; and J Taylor & Sons (est. 1846) of Bakewell in 1879. By 1890, thirteen branches existed, the number rising to nineteen branches and twenty-seven sub-branches by 1914. Deposits grew from £1.187 million in 1878, to £3 million in 1894 and to £5.61 million in 1913, while paid-up capital was increased to £250,000 in 1897 and remained at this level until 1914. In this year Parr's Bank Ltd (est. 1865) acquired the bank.

T E Gregory, *The Westminster Bank Through a Century* (London, 1936)

Records: The Royal Bank of Scotland plc, Archive Section, Regent's House, 42 Islington High Street, London N1 8XL

178 *British banking – a guide to historical records*

Prospectus 1877; articles of association 1877; share allotment books (3) 1877–96; annual general meeting minutes 1877–1913; list of overdrawn accounts taken over from Chesterfield & North Derbyshire Bank 1878; head office instructions to branches 1879–1914; annual reports 1882–1914; staff instructions 1883; deposit receipt specimen n.d.; general manager's letterbook 1884–1917; balance sheets 1888–89; clerk application registers 1891–1913; committee minutes 1895–1914; registers of members (3) 1896–1913; chairmen's agenda books (7) 1896–1918; salary books (3) 1897–1913; select committee minutes 1905–13; directors' meeting minute books (2) 1905–13; seal register 1905–17; memoranda re investments and advances 1906–13; rough minute book 1908–13; directors' correspondence 1911–14; amalgamation papers 1913–14.

Bakewell: half-yearly returns 1879–1913; **Chesterfield:** profit and loss account book 1877–84; list of overdrawn accounts 1882; weekly advances memorandum book 1886–90; general ledger balances (5) 1896–1913; **Derby:** security ledgers (8) 1870s–1920; advances statistics 1901–13; seal register 1905–17; **Hathersage:** half-yearly returns 1892–93.

CROMPTON, EWBANK & CO
York, North Yorkshire

History: This private bank was established in York in 1784 as Crompton, Mortimer & Co. It was subsequently styled Crompton, Gray & Eaton and, from 1790, as Crompton, Ewbank & Co. It may have been connected with the Derby bank of Crompton, Newton & Co (est. c.1685). It ceased business in 1798.

Records: The Royal Bank of Scotland plc, Archive Section, Regent's House, 42 Islington High Street, London N1 8XL

Notice of opening 1771.

CROMPTON, NEWTON & CO
Derby, Derbyshire

History: The year of formation of this private bank is uncertain, different sources stating either 1685 or the 1710s; it was otherwise known as Derby Old Bank. There may have been a connection with Crompton, Ewbank & Co (est. 1784, ceased 1798) of York. In 1808 the partners formed Crompton, Newton, Walker & Co at Chesterfield; it was otherwise known as Scarsdale & High Peak Bank. In 1877 both banks joined with W & S Evans & Co (est. 1771) of Derby to form the important joint stock bank of Crompton & Evans' Union Bank Ltd.

T E Gregory, *The Westminster Bank Through a Century* (London, 1936)

Records: The Royal Bank of Scotland plc, Archive Section, Regent's House, 42 Islington High Street, London N1 8XL

Memorandum and cash books (3) 1707–79; Samuel Crompton: private account book and papers 1739–68, investment and loan ledger 1755–1877; accounts with London agent 1761–66, 1777–85; drafts drawn on London banks 1775; Gilbert Crompton: personal cash book 1806–30, receipted bills 1811–43, private account books (4) 1821–42, correspondence 1840–43; partnership agreements 1808; cash balance books (3) 1808–29; balance sheet 1877.

Chesterfield: deposit ledger 1808–15; customer ledger 1808–24; note registers 1821–25; papers re Alton colliery 1858–73; **Derby:** customer account ledger 1834–36.

CROXON, JONES & CO (OLD BANK) LTD
Oswestry, Shropshire

History: This joint stock bank traced its origins to the private bank of Croxon, Jones & Co established in 1792 by Edward Croxon and John Sheppard; the Croxons were an old-established family of Welsh flannel merchants. By 1811, John Gibbons and Thomas Lovatt had joined the partnership; by 1828 it was known as Croxon, Longueville, Croxon, Jones & Co and by 1835 as Croxon, Jones & Co. It also traded as Oswestry Old Bank. In 1893 the business was converted into a joint stock bank, Croxon, Jones & Co (Old Bank) Ltd, with a paid-up capital of £35,000. In 1894, Parr's Banking Co & Alliance Bank Ltd (est. 1865) acquired the bank.

A Stanley Davis, *The Early Banks of Mid Wales* (Welshpool, 1935); T E Gregory, *The Westminster Bank Through A Century* (London, 1936)

Records 1: The Royal Bank of Scotland plc, Archive Section, Regent's House, 42 Islington High Street, London N1 8XL

Balance sheet 1893; notice of amalgamation 1894.

Records 2: Shropshire Records and Research Centre, Castle Gates, Shrewsbury SY1 2AQ

Partnership agreements 1812–47. [Ref: 800/Box 69D]

CULL & CO LTD
London

History: This small merchant bank was established in the City of London in 1921 and, *inter alia*, was an early specialist in corporate finance advisory work. By the 1940s its clients included major businesses such as the

180   *British banking – a guide to historical records*

Chester Beatty Group and British Celanese Ltd. In 1922 it became a private unlimited company and in 1935 a private limited company. In 1944, when the elderly owners wished to retire, Morgan Grenfell acquired its business and the firm was placed in liquidation.

Records: Guildhall Library, Aldermanbury, London EC2P 2EJ

Memorandum and articles of association 1935; directors' meeting minute books (2) 1935–43; share register 1935–43; private ledgers (5) 1935–43; cash books (4) 1935–43; seal register 1935–44; office ledgers (4) 1935–44; amalgamation papers 1943–44. [MS 28186, 28334–28340]

CUMBERLAND UNION BANKING CO LTD
Workington and later Carlisle, Cumbria

History: This joint stock bank was formed at Workington in 1829 as the Cumberland Union Banking Co with a paid-up capital of £20,000. In its first year branches were opened at Cockermouth, Carlisle, Wigton and Maryport followed, soon afterwards, by a branch at Penrith based upon the business of William James's private bank. The Carlisle branch was closed in 1837 but was re-established in 1861. The large private bank of Joseph Monkhouse, Head & Co (est. 1804) of Carlisle, with branches at Whitehaven, Workington and Brampton, was acquired in 1865 when the head office was transferred to Carlisle. The unrelated business of Charles Head & Co (est. 1830) of Hexham was acquired at about the same time. These acquisitions made the bank the largest in Cumberland. Limited liability was acquired at this time and more branches were soon established at Harrington, Kirkoswald, Holborn Hill, Egremont, Cleator Moor and, in 1871, at Barrow in Furness. This growth was fuelled by the rapidly growing coal, iron and steel, and engineering industries but in the 1880s the bank suffered from overlending to a narrow local industrial base. In this weakened position, York City & County Bank Ltd acquired the business in 1901. It then had paid-up capital of £250,000, deposits of £2.13 million and nineteen branches and eight sub-branches.

W F Crick & J E Wadsworth, *A Hundred Years of Joint Stock Banking* (London, 1936)

Records: HSBC Holdings plc, Group Archives, 10 Lower Thames Street, London EC3R 6AE

Current account ledger 1829–30; deeds of settlement 1829–65; general meeting minute book 1829–1901; directors' meeting minute books (9) 1829–1905; manager's memorandum book 1849–78; general ledgers (4) 1851–75; note register 1851–97; balance books (6) 1851–1901; head office letters 1851–1905; declarations of secrecy (2) 1852–1901; customer

Records of banks 181

balance sheet book 1865–66; share register 1865–67; annual reports 1865–96; board agenda books (6) 1865–1905; current account ledger 1866–1902; committee minute book 1867–68; bill register 1867–1870s; security books (7) 1868–1901; salary registers (2) 1871–89; branch letterbooks (8) 1876–91; branch inspection reports 1876–1901; manager's interview books (2) 1879–98; directors' attendance books (4) 1880–1905; enquiry book 1883–87; half-yearly balance sheets 1884–1900; register of overdrafts 1885–88; amalgamation papers 1901–02.

Brampton: deposit account ledgers (4) 1856–1906; general ledger 1877–89; **Carlisle:** general ledgers (2) 1861–78; signature book 1861–1908.

CUNLIFFE, BROOKS & CO
Blackburn, Lancashire and Manchester, Greater Manchester

History: This private bank was founded in 1792 by two calico manufacturers and merchants, Roger Cunliffe and William Brooks. A London firm was established in about 1815 under the title of Roger Cunliffe & Son which acted as London agent. In 1864 the London firm, then largely a bill broker, merged with A & G W Alexander & Co, later known as Alexanders Discount Co Ltd. Soon afterwards another London business was opened in Lombard Street under the name of Brooks & Co. The Blackburn firm opened a Manchester branch in 1819 which, by the 1840s, had become the main focus of the bank's business. Other branches opened at Altrincham (1856) and Sale (1881), both in Cheshire, and at Darwen (1889), Lancashire. Lloyds Bank Ltd (est. 1765) acquired Cunliffe, Brooks & Co and Brooks & Co of London in 1900.

Leo H Grindon, *Manchester Banks and Bankers* (Manchester, 1877)

Records: Lloyds TSB Group plc, Archives, Head Office, 71 Lombard Street, London EC3P 3BS

Profit and loss accounts 1823–1900; staff appearance books 1847–98; list of partners 1851–1900; salary books 1862–1900; bad debt book 1867–97; enquiry reply book 1870s; minute books 1884–1900; amalgamation papers 1893.

Altrincham: signature book 1856–1905; profit and loss ledger 1857–98; **Blackburn:** salary books (2) 1860–1917.

ROGER CUNLIFFE SONS & CO LTD
London

History: This discount house traced its origins to the firm of Roger Cunliffe & Son, private bankers, which was formed in the City of London

182 **British banking – a guide to historical records**

in about 1815 by Cunliffe, Brooks & Co (est. 1792), bankers at Blackburn, Lancashire. Roger Cunliffe, who led the London business, was a partner in the Blackburn bank. The title changed to Cunliffes, Brooks, Cunliffe & Co in about 1826. In about 1835 the firm was reorganised when Roger Cunliffe broke away to do business on his own account. In 1851 the title of his firm was Roger Cunliffe Sons & Co and it continued under that name until 1939 when it was converted into a private limited company, Roger Cunliffe Sons & Co Ltd. In 1941 this firm was acquired by the discount house, Cater, Brightwen & Co Ltd.

Anon, *Cater Ryder Discount Bankers 1816–1966* (priv. pub., 1971)

Records: Guildhall Library, Aldermanbury, London EC2P 2EJ

Partnership agreements 1835–83; will of Roger Cunliffe 1864. [Ref: MS 18524–18526]

CURRIES & CO
London

History: This private bank traced its origins to Mason, Currie, James & Yallowley, which began trading as bankers from offices at Cornhill, City of London, in 1773. The firm had a capital of £30,000, largely provided by John Mason, a director of the Sun Fire Office, and William Currie, a malt distiller. Its main business lay in discounting bills of exchange and dealing in government securities; its customers were largely merchants, linen and woollen drapers, distillers and brewers. It acted as London agent for only four country banks. The Currie family dominated the partnership from the outset and from 1826 the firm was known simply as Curries & Co. Between 1781 and 1843 the bank's annual profit increased from £5,000 to £17,000. In 1842 Curries & Co acquired the business of Dorrien, Magens, Mello & Co (est. 1794). In 1864 Glyn, Mills & Co (est. 1753) acquired Curries & Co and closed the Cornhill premises, thereafter adopting the style Glyn, Mills, Currie & Co.

Anon, 'Curries & Co. The Early Years', *Three Banks Review*, 61–62 (1964); Eric Gore Brown, *Glyn Mills and Co* (priv. pub., 1933); Roger Fulford, *Glyn's 1753–1953. Six Generations in Lombard Street* (London, 1953)

Records: The Royal Bank of Scotland plc, Archive Section, Regent's House, 42 Islington High Street, London N1 8XL

Partnership agreements 1757–1859; customer account ledgers 1773–91; assignment of stock in trade 1774; profit and loss accounts 1774–80, 1813–14, 1854–63; staff salary and Christmas money books 1774–1864;

Records of banks 183

bills of exchange 1778–93, 1833–61; papers re partnership shares 1780, 1830, 1856; banker's cash notes 1782–1818; customer balances papers 1786–89, 1815–64; partners' balance sheets 1786–89; correspondence with customers 1795–1864; customer consol, scrip, bill and stock transaction papers 1798–1812, 1842–47; customer loan papers 1799–1801, 1826–36, 1856–63; cheques 1799–1862; promissory note 1816; passbook 1836–39; property lease agreements: Cornhill 1851–52, Change Alley 1831–42; clerks' fidelity bonds 1842–63; half-yearly accounts 1845–48; cash book 1846–62; general ledger 1847–64; annual balance sheets 1854–63; papers re acquisition of Dorrien, Magens, Mello & Co 1841–47; tax assessment certificates and receipts 1860–64; correspondence re merger with Glyn, Mills & Co 1864.

CURTEIS, POMFRET & CO
Rye, East Sussex

History: This private bank was established in 1790 as E J Curteis, Wm. Curteis, Woollet & Dawes. In 1866 it was renamed R Curteis, Pomfret & Co and was also styled the Rye Bank. A branch was opened at Tenterden, Kent, in 1832. Lloyds Bank Ltd (est. 1765) acquired the business in 1893.

Records: Lloyds TSB Group plc, Archives, Head Office, 71 Lombard Street, London EC3P 3BS

Audited customers' balance sheets 1815–47; amalgamation agreement 1893.

Rye: signature book 1881–93; manager's diaries 1887–92.

DALE, YOUNG & CO
South Shields and later Newcastle upon Tyne, Tyne & Wear

History: This private bank was formed in 1858 by John B Dale, former manager of the South Shields branch of the Northumberland & Durham District Bank (est. 1836) who, following its failure in 1857, became a partner in the newly-formed Newcastle private bank of Hawks, Grey, Priestman & Co. On its dissolution in 1858, he established Dale, Miller & Co, known as Dale, Young & Co from 1866 and as Dale, Young, Nelson & Co from 1882. In 1866 a branch was opened at Jarrow and from 1883 the bank's chief office was located at Newcastle. In 1891 the title reverted to Dale, Young & Co. In that year the balance sheet totalled £500,000, deposits stood at £390,000 and partners' capital and reserves were £100,000. In 1892 the business amalgamated with the North Eastern Banking Co Ltd (est. 1872).

Maberly Phillips, *Banks, Bankers and Banking in Northumberland, Durham and North Yorkshire* (London, 1894)

184   *British banking – a guide to historical records*

Records 1: Barclays Bank plc, Group Archives, Dallimore Road, Wythenshawe, Manchester M23 9JA

Correspondence re merger 1892–94.

Records 2: Durham County Record Office, County Hall, Durham DH1 5UL

Partnership agreements 1858–80; merger agreement 1892. [Ref: D/X 344/1–5]

ROBERT DAVIES & CO
London

History: This private bank was established in 1841 in Shoreditch in the East End of London. It failed in 1860 when its business was acquired by London & County Joint Stock Banking Co (est. 1836).

Records: The Royal Bank of Scotland plc, Archive Section, Regent's House, 42 Islington High Street, London N1 8XL

Manager's information book 1853–67; notice of take-over 1860.

DAVIES, BANKS & CO
Kington, Hereford & Worcester & Knighton, Powys

History: This private bank was formed in 1789 as Greenly, Harris, Thomas, Meredith & Co. It was known as Meredith & Co from 1792, as Edmund Cheese, James Davies & James Crummer from 1808, and later as Harris, Cheese, Davies & Crummer and as Davies, Crummer, Cheese & Oliver. It was otherwise styled the Kington & Radnorshire Bank. In 1838 a branch was established at Knighton which in 1856 was acquired by the North & South Wales Bank (est. 1836) for £1,000; the branch's deposits then stood at £12,000. The remaining business, subsequently styled Davies, Banks & Co, was acquired in 1910 by the Metropolitan Bank (of England & Wales) Ltd (est. 1829) for £29,500.

Records: HSBC Holdings plc, Group Archives, 10 Lower Thames Street, London EC3R 6AE

Bill books (3) 1808–1924; partnership agreements 1812, 1857; general ledgers (2) 1863–93; 'valuation book' (balance sheets) 1867–99; current account ledger 1868–79; deposit account ledgers (3) 1880–1901; 'manager's book', deposit account journal 1881–83; balance sheets 1893–1910; security register 1898–1910; partners' private ledger 1901–08; drib ledgers (2) 1908–18; agreement with Metropolitan Bank 1910.

Penybont: general ledger 1891–99; **Rhayader:** general ledgers (4) 1873–1904; deposit ledger 1897–1900; security register 1901.

Records of banks

DAVISON, NOEL, TEMPLER, MIDDLETON & WEDGWOOD
London

History: This private bank was established in 1792 at Stratford Place, Oxford Street, in London's West End, under the title of Edwards, Smith, Templer, Middleton, Johnson & Wedgwood, and was otherwise known as the London & Middlesex Bank. George Templer had amassed a fortune in India; John Wedgwood was son of the potter, Josiah Wedgwood; and the senior partner, Gerard Noel Edwards of Exton Park, Rutland, was a connection of the Earls of Gainsborough and later changed his surname to Noel. In 1794 Smith's name disappeared from the title. The firm encountered difficulties in 1803 and was rescued by a £100,000 advance from Alexander Davison, a British government 'contractor'. In 1804 the business, then generally known as Davison, Noel, Templer, Middleton, Johnson & Wedgwood, moved to Pall Mall and in 1806 was known as Davison, Noel, Templer, Middleton & Wedgwood. Its financial difficulties persisted, despite capital injections by Lord Barham and Josiah Wedgwood, and in 1816 the business was wound up, customers being recommended to transfer their accounts to Thomas Coutts & Co (est. 1692) of London.

F G Hilton Price, *A Handbook of London Bankers* (London, 1876)

Records 1: Coutts & Co, 440 Strand, London WC2R 0QS

Papers re partners 1794–1816; customer list 1816; customer ledger 1816; John Wedgwood oubliette (i.e. papers of the London & Middlesex Bank, Newton Abbot Office) 1801–16.

Records 2: City of Westminster Archives Centre, 10 St Ann's Street, London SW1P 2XR

Personal letterbooks of Hastings Nathaniel Middleton (3) 1816–21. [Ref: Acc 796]

Records 3: Leicestershire Record Office, Long Street, Wigston Magna, Leicester LE18 2AH

Country ledger 1792–1803; miscellaneous ledgers and journals 1803–16; papers re business of clients, including Joseph Shaw, Receiver General of Surrey n.d.; cheques and promissory notes n.d.; lists of debtors, creditors and assets n.d.; correspondence re winding up n.d. [Ref: Exton MSS]

DAWES, TOMES & RUSSELL
Warwick, Warwickshire

186   *British banking – a guide to historical records*

History: This private bank, which was also known as the Warwick Old Bank, was established in 1791. The Warwick & Leamington Banking Co (est. 1834) acquired the business in 1834.

Records: Lloyds TSB Group plc, Archives, Head Office, 71 Lombard Street, London EC3P 3BS

Cash book 1826–27.

DAY, DAY & DAY
Swaffham, Norfolk

History: This private bank was established by 1790 by Starling Day, a Norwich wool factor and general merchant. Originally the business was known as Starling Day & Co and later as Starling Day, Starling Day jun., Thomas S Day and Henry Day and then as Thomas Starling Day, Henry Day & William Day. An office was opened in Norwich in 1806 when the business became known also as the Norwich & Swaffham Bank. The business failed during the 1825 financial crisis.

Harold Preston, *Early East Anglian Banks and Bankers* (Thetford, 1994)

Records: Barclays Bank plc, Group Archives, Dallimore Road, Wythenshawe, Manchester M23 9JA

Bank notes 1818–31.

DAY, NICHOLSON & STONE
Rochester, Kent

History: This private bank was established in 1782 as Day, Hulkes & Co; it was otherwise known as the Rochester, Chatham & Stroud Bank. Subsequently it was styled Day, Nicholson & Stone. It was acquired, along with the East of England Bank (est. 1836), by the newly-formed Provincial Banking Corporation Ltd in 1864.

Records: Barclays Bank plc, Group Archives, Dallimore Road, Wythenshawe, Manchester M23 9JA

Private journal 1781–1843; cheques and deposit receipts 1820–63; passbook 1846–1934; security register 1856–92.

DEANE & CO
Winchester, Hampshire

History: This private bank was established in Winchester in 1787 as Wallers & Co. It was styled Deane & Co from 1820 and issued its own

Records of banks **187**

notes. The bank was acquired by Prescott, Dimsdale, Cave, Tugwell & Co Ltd (est. 1766) in 1891.

Records: The Royal Bank of Scotland plc, Archive Section, Regent's House, 42 Islington High Street, London N1 8XL

Press cuttings 1819; balance sheet 1890; amalgamation agreement 1891.

DERBY & DERBYSHIRE BANKING CO LTD
Derby, Derbyshire

History: This joint stock bank was established in 1833 and opened for business in 1834. By 1837 paid-up capital was £41,000 and a branch had been opened at Belper. In 1880 it acquired limited liability. In 1898, when it was acquired by Parr's Bank Ltd (est. 1865), it had eight branches, viz.: Belper, Crick, Driffield, Litchurch, Long Eaton, Matlock Bath, Matlock Bridge and Melbourne. By then paid-up capital was £78,000 and deposits were £750,000.

T E Gregory, *The Westminster Bank Through a Century* (London, 1936)

Records: The Royal Bank of Scotland plc, Archive Section, Regent's House, 42 Islington High Street, London N1 8XL

Minutes of provisional committee 1833; deed of settlement 1833; customer ledger 1835; amalgamation papers 1898.

DERBY COMMERCIAL BANK LTD
Derby, Derbyshire

History: This joint stock bank was established in 1868 with a paid-up capital of £18,000. It was intended to serve small tradesmen and industrialists, but early on encountered heavy losses that checked its progress. From its formation it had limited liability. By 1885 paid-up capital was £50,000 and deposits were £300,000. No branches were opened. In the late 1880s the bank's business declined; its deposits had fallen to £236,000 in 1888. In 1890 it was acquired by the Birmingham & Midland Bank Ltd (est. 1836) for the equivalent of £125,000.

W F Crick & J E Wadsworth, *A Hundred Years of Joint Stock Banking* (London, 1936)

Records: HSBC Holdings plc, Group Archives, 10 Lower Thames Street, London EC3R 6AE

Prospectus 1868; articles of association 1868; directors' meeting minute books (4) 1868–86; half-yearly balance sheets 1868–89; circulars re amalgamation 1889.

188 *British banking – a guide to historical records*

DEVON & CORNWALL BANKING CO LTD
Plymouth, Devon

History: This joint stock bank was formed in 1832 as the Plymouth & Devonport Banking Co to acquire the business of the private bank of Hingston & Prideaux (est. 1809). The bank expanded rapidly throughout Devon, Cornwall and Dorset where it became a major regional bank; in 1833 it was renamed the Devon & Cornwall Banking Co. This expansion was achieved partly by acquisition of other banks which included Nicholson & Co (est. 1829) and George Fox & Co (est. 1832), both of Kingsbridge, in 1832; Prideaux & Bentall (est. 1809) of Totnes in 1833; Prout & Stapleton (est. 1832) of Dartmouth in 1834; Hurley & Co (est. 1810) of Cullompton in 1836; Sparkes & Co (est. 1818) of Exeter in 1836; Western District Banking Co (est. 1836) of Truro in 1844; Green & Vittery (est. 1839) of Brixham in 1875; and the Three Towns Banking Co Ltd (est. 1856) of Plymouth in 1890. Elsewhere branches were established as entirely new entities. As early as 1836, branches existed at Plymouth, Devonport, Exeter, Kingsbridge, Totnes, St Austell, Ashburton, Tavistock, Cullompton, Newton Abbot, Dartmouth, Bodmin and Liskeard. Twenty-six branches existed by 1880 and fifty-five by 1906 when Lloyds Bank Ltd (est. 1765) acquired the business.

John Ryton, *Banks and Bank Notes of Exeter 1769–1906* (priv. pub., 1984); R S Sayers, *Lloyds Bank in the History of English Banking* (Oxford, 1957)

Records: Lloyds TSB Group plc, Archives, Head Office, 71 Lombard Street, London EC3P 3BS

Directors' meeting minute book 1831–41; annual reports 1851, 1855, 1862–1906; articles of association 1899; amalgamation papers 1906.

Exeter: security registers (2) 1862–1906; memorandum book 1893–1905; **Redruth:** security register 1879–94; signature books 1886–1914; **Torquay:** inspection report book 1855–67.

DICKINSON & GREEN
Ware, Hertfordshire

History: This private bank, which was also known as the Ware Bank, was established in 1808 by John Baron Dickinson, a wealthy brewer, maltster and barge owner, by John and Thomas Green, attorneys and later maltsters, and by Edward Green of Thundridge. Its initial capital was £8,000, rising to £10,000 in 1810. The bank's partners and many of its major customers were closely connected with the malting trade and the bank failed when this industry encountered difficulties in 1813.

Jack Parker, *Nothing for Nothing for Nobody* (Stevenage, 1986)

Records: County Record Office, County Hall, Hertford SG13 8DE

Private ledger 1809–14. [Ref: 79951X]

DICKSON & WOODS
Alnwick, Northumberland

History: This private bank was formed in 1857 after the collapse of the Northumberland & Durham District Banking Co (est. 1836) when the closure of its Alnwick branch provided an excellent opportunity to establish a new bank. It was also known as the Alnwick & County Bank. Its partners were William Dickson, a local solicitor, and William Woods, a Newcastle banker. Woods was in the process of attempting to rescue the Newcastle, Shields & Sunderland Union Joint Stock Bank (est. 1836) and went on to form the important Newcastle private bank of Woods & Co in 1859. The Northumberland & Durham District Banking Co's local manager became manager of the new bank. When Woods died in 1864, Dickson became sole partner and on his death, in 1875, his trustees sold the business to the North Eastern Banking Co Ltd (est. 1872).

Maberly Phillips, *Banks, Bankers and Banking in Northumberland, Durham and North Yorkshire* (London, 1894)

Records: Barclays Bank plc, Group Archives, Dallimore Road, Wythenshawe, Manchester M23 9JA

Circular re merger with North Eastern Banking Co Ltd 1875.

Bellingham: bills discounted book 1872–1918.

DILWORTH, ARTHINGTON & BIRKETT
Lancaster, Lancashire

History: This private bank was formed in about 1793 and was also known as Dilworth, Hargreaves & Co. The business was connected through marriage to John Wakefield & Sons, bankers at Kendal. It failed in 1826.

Records 1: Durham County Record Office, County Hall, Durham DH1 5UL

Letter re stop 1826. [Ref: D/Pe 2/7]

Records 2: Lancaster District Library, Local History Department, Market Square, Lancaster LA1 1HY

Discharge of partner from bankruptcy with list of creditors 1826. [Ref: MS 7339]

190   *British banking – a guide to historical records*

DIMSDALE, FOWLER, BARNARD & DIMSDALES
London

History: This important private bank, located in Cornhill, City of London, traced its origins to 1759 and the creation of a partnership of Sir George Amyand Bart., Roger Staples and George Mercer trading as Amyand, Staples & Mercer. By about 1761 the business was known as Dimsdale, Archer & Byde and in 1774 two partners broke away to form Staples, Baron, Dimsdale, Son & Co. There were several further changes in name. By 1796 the bank had assets totalling £215,000 rising to £374,000 in 1824. In 1850 the bank, then known as Barnard, Barnard & Dimsdale, merged with the London private bank of Drewett & Fowler (est. 1797) to form Dimsdale, Drewett, Fowler's & Barnard. Thereafter several name changes occurred which included: Dimsdale, Drewett, Fowler & Barnard (1853); Dimsdale, Fowler & Barnard (1865); and Dimsdale, Fowler, Barnard & Dimsdales (1872). Profits averaged £12,000 annually between 1872 and 1875 and rose to an annual average of £23,400 between 1886 and 1890. In 1891 the bank merged with Prescott, Cave, Buxton, Loder & Co (est. 1766) of London, Miles, Cave, Baillie & Co (est. 1750) of Bristol and Tugwell, Brymer, Clutterbuck & Co (est. c.1760s) of Bath to form Prescott, Dimsdale, Cave, Tugwell & Co Ltd.

Anon, *'Prescott's Bank', National Provincial Bank Review* (1966–68); F G Hilton Price, *A Handbook of London's Bankers* (London, 1876)

Records: The Royal Bank of Scotland plc, Archive Section, Regent's House, 42 Islington High Street, London N1 8XL

Partnership agreement 1774; current account ledger 1774–75; balance sheets 1777–91; unpaid bills and drafts 1778–1893; balances of current, bankers and discount accounts 1795–1800; security ledgers (2) 1862–1906; partnership ledgers 1872–90.

DINGLEY, PETHYBRIDGE & CO and DINGLEY, PEARSE & CO
Launceston, Cornwall and Okehampton, Devon

History: These private banks were established in 1855 and 1856 respectively. Both were acquired by National Provincial & Union Bank of England Ltd (est. 1833) in 1922.

Records: The Royal Bank of Scotland plc, Archive Section, Regent's House, 42 Islington High Street, London N1 8XL

Details of staff, premises etc. (2) 1871–1922; amalgamation papers 1922.

Stratton: cash journal 1855–57; day books (4) 1907–17.

DISTRICT BANK LTD
Manchester, Greater Manchester

History: This joint stock bank was promoted in 1829 by Joseph Macardy, a Manchester stockbroker, as the District Union Banking Co. Prior to commencing business in December 1829, it was restyled the Manchester & Liverpool District Banking Co. In 1836 it acquired the Stockport private bank of Christy, Lloyd & Co (est. 1825). The Manchester office, initially in Norfolk Street, was moved to Spring Gardens in 1834. Branches were opened in Oldham, Liverpool and Hanley in 1830 and by late 1833 seventeen branches existed. The Nantwich & South Cheshire Joint Stock Bank (est. 1839) was acquired upon its failure in 1844, followed by Lloyd, Entwisle & Co (est. 1771) of Manchester in 1863 and J O & G Alcock (est. 1830) of Burslem in 1865. In 1880, when limited liability was acquired, the bank had fifty-four branches and sub-branches in Lancashire, Cheshire, Derbyshire, Shropshire, Staffordshire and Yorkshire. In 1881 the Southport & West Lancashire Banking Co Ltd (est. 1881) was acquired. The bank opened an office in London in 1885 and in 1891 acquired Wm., John & Thos. Brocklehurst & Co (est. 1816) of Macclesfield. Branches continued to be opened in the north-west and Wales and the Lancaster Banking Co Ltd (est. 1826) and the Bank of Whitehaven Ltd (est. 1837) were acquired in 1907 and 1916 respectively. The bank was restyled District Bank Ltd in 1924. A second office was opened in London in 1925. In 1935 the business amalgamated with County Bank Ltd (est. 1862) of Manchester, with a network of 190 branches, which increased paid-up capital to £3 million. By the late 1930s branches had been opened east of the Pennines, in the Midlands, southern England and Wales and this expansion of the network resumed after the Second World War. The bank was acquired by National Provincial Bank Ltd (est. 1833) in 1962, but continued to operate independently until 1969 when it had 570 branches.

Fiona Maccoll, *The Key to Our Success. A Short History of the NatWest Group* (London, 1996); Richard Reed, *National Westminster Bank. A Short History* (London, 1989); R H Mottram, *Miniature Banking Histories* (London, 1930)

Records: The Royal Bank of Scotland plc, Archive Section, Regent's House, 42 Islington High Street, London N1 8XL

General ledger 1829; share ledger 1829–38; list of managers 1829–1916; directors' meeting minute books (17) 1829–1968; appeal to Stockport shareholders 1830; Liverpool shareholders' minutes 1830; bills of exchange 1830–64; past due bills register 1830–96; instructions for directors and officers 1831; deeds of settlement 1831, 1843; procedural instruction books 1831–1968; guardbook of minutes, inspection reports and accounts

192   *British banking – a guide to historical records*

1832–43; general meeting: report 1832, shareholder signatures 1837, proceedings 1837, 1915; share certificates 1833–38; power of attorney 1834; shareholder lists 1834–82; share register 1837–57, 1915–29; monthly balance sheets 1838–42; annual reports 1838–1969 [w]; promissory note 1839; agenda book 1839–40; declarations of secrecy 1839–70; branch weekly returns register 1842–46; memorandum books, London agent 1842–1909; staff register 1846–66; investments memorandum book 1849–56; list of securities held against advances 1849–73; staff rules 1850; dividends memorandum book 1851–97; circulars 1857–1969 [w]; branch architectural drawings c.1862–1960s; bills for acceptance registers (4) 1864–1900; memorandum book re directors 1865–99; partnership information book 1865–1900; registers of bankruptcies and liquidations (2) 1865–1915; draft minute book 1866–67; board committee meeting minute books 1866–67, 1959–69; correspondence book, London agent 1868–74; papers re incorporation of company 1870–71, 1880; grant of arms 1871; seal book 1871–88; lists of bills 1871–73, 1912; head office day book sheets 1872; list of shareholders 1873; statistics: branches 1877–1923, 1946–67, reserves and dividends 1911–33; bank rate memorandum book 1880–93; agreements with correspondents 1888–1917; foreign department: correspondence 1888–1969, manuals 1918–37; pension fund rules 1889–1964; pension fund minutes 1889–1970; transactions rates book 1880s; stationery/forms 1880s–1969; correspondence re overseas business 1892–1941; bank note indemnities 1893–1922; memorandum and articles of association 1895–1951; directors' committee minute books (10) 1896–1959; head office staff register 1897–1914; daily administrative committee minutes: head office 1897, Lancaster area 1907–16; head office minute books (27) 1897–1923; bank notes nineteenth cent; statement re Dumbells Banking Co 1900; press cuttings re proposal to merge with Lloyds Bank 1903; list of directors 1903–69; lists of branches 1905–08, 1937–69; papers re merger: Lancaster Banking Co 1906–07, Bank of Whitehaven 1915, County Bank 1935; staff dinner menus 1907–39; pension fund: trust deeds 1908–22, pension register 1919–70, annual reports 1925–48, papers 1925–70; salary registers (7) 1909–41; photographs: premises 1900s, 1960s, staff 1937–39; staff sports club papers 1911–69; balance sheets 1914–69; balance sheets and profit and loss accounts 1914–n.d.; silver coin returns 1915; staff appointment papers 1915, 1924–26; foreign department minutes 1917–59; staff register 1918–20; accountant's statistics book 1920–68; marketing booklets 1920–60s; coins held books 1924–25; circular notes 1924–69; staff record cards n.d.; analysis of advances 1928–38; press advertising guard book 1929–34; joint general manager's file 1920s–1930s; London foreign manager's minutes 1931–69; authorised signature lists 1932–35, 1964–68; passbooks 1934–69; telegraph code book 1935; general manager's minutes and papers 1935–69; staff gazette 1937–40; staff

Records of banks 193

articles of service 1938; advertising poster, home safes c.1930s; staff instructions 1944–69; book of remembrance c.1945; *District Bank Review* 1946–68; London directors' meeting minute books 1947–69; investment committee minutes 1949–61; property valuation books 1949; staff club magazine 1952–68; capital reorganisation papers 1957; valuation of investments 1958–69; mechanisation correspondence 1959–70; staff training/ recruitment literature 1950s–68; correspondence with National Provincial Bank 1962–69; annual returns 1962–71; economics department minutes 1963–68; papers re merger 1968.

Adlington: papers re premises 1908–30; **Alderley Edge:** branch minutes 1896–97; memorandum book 1896–1935; **Ashton:** customer ledger 1831–34; local board minutes 1831–95; expenses book 1833–41; signature book 1862–89; declarations of secrecy 1865–79; manager's opinion book 1867–75; branch minute books (2) 1886–98; notice re holiday closure c.1960s; **Bacup:** staff attendance book 1936–49; branch minutes 1937–43; **Banbury:** branch minutes 1939–55; **Barrow:** advances registers (2) 1898–1927; manager's letterbooks (2) 1899–1911; branch minutes 1910–25; **Bowness:** branch minutes 1924–62; **Brierfield:** minute book, customer interviews 1954–69; **Burslem:** head office letter 1865; **Bury:** list of securities 1849–73; branch returns 1867–76; local board minutes 1875–95; **Cannock:** information book 1883–1908; **Chadderton:** premises papers 1898–1939; **Cheadle:** manager's opinion book c.1877–1927; information book 1886–1908; branch minute books (3) 1886–1924; **Chelford:** signature book 1904–30; register of letters received 1920–21; clearing register 1923; cash book 1929; **Chester:** branch minutes 1908–38; **Chorley:** information book 1907–44; premises papers 1911–14; branch minutes 1911–60; bullion railway permits 1928; photograph, trade exhibition stand 1934; **Coventry:** branch minutes 1940–64; **Crewe:** branch minutes 1886–1963; profit and loss book 1873–1907; **Delph:** opinion book 1886–1942; customer information books 1901–69; letterbooks 1922–38; **Dukinfield:** manager's minutes 1898–1909; **Eskdale:** lease 1920; **Fallowfield:** information book 1889–1908; manager's minute books (4) 1889–1947; **Fenton:** out-letterbooks (3) 1874–1923; expenses book 1875–99; information book 1883–1908; branch minute books (2) 1885–1939; property conveyance 1925; **Grange over Sands:** manager's diary 1909; rent receipt books 1939–59; **Hanley:** bad debts register 1839–86; securities for advances register 1879–1924; manager's minute books (5) 1885–1945 [w]; half-yearly returns 1888–1957; staff photograph 1897; abstract of customers' balances 1907–50; letterbooks (2) 1911–20; letterbooks re staff 1919–29; salary book 1927–58; staff salary and pension sheets 1938–39; **Haslingden:** branch minutes 1885–1906; **Hayfield:** safe custody register 1901–70; stock book 1935–49; letterbooks 1935–50; teller's cash book 1937–62; **Keswick:** head office letterbook 1920–29; customer orders book

194 *British banking – a guide to historical records*

1921–54; branch minutes 1924–67; **Kirkbride:** premises lease 1921; **Kirby Lonsdale:** manager's information book 1888–1902; head office letterbooks (3) 1890–1931; applications for overdrafts book 1898–1931; general ledgers (2) 1899–1908; expenses books (4) 1908–69; branch minute books (3) 1913–69; abstracts of customer balances 1925–69; **Knutsford:** branch minutes 1909–40; **Lancaster:** loan sanctions register 1921–31; **Levenshulme:** branch minutes 1898–1959; **Littleborough:** premises lease 1889; **Liverpool, Water Street:** premises papers 1830–1960s; bankruptcies register 1834–38; opinion book 1835–42; manager's letterbooks (63) 1836–1932; bad debt ledger abstract 1839; minute books (59) 1844–1970; signature book 1845–71; local board minute books (2) 1845–95; analysis book 1880–1908; information book 1891–1908; **London, City Office:** probate register 1885–1919; analysis of transactions book 1885–1908; information book 1886–1908; manager's minute books (20) 1888–1959; passbooks 1899–1906; deposit receipts register 1938–41; savings account ledger 1962–68; general ledgers 1964–66; loans ledger 1967–68; **London, Piccadilly:** customer information book 1866–68; **London, Cornhill:** branch minutes 1886–1928; **Manchester Head Office:** share ledger 1829–38; register of bills 1830–96; local board minute books (2) 1831–76; signature books 1832–1939; expenses book (2) 1833–74; security registers 1835–97; papers re securities 1841–47, 1868; customer mandates book 1848–1903; safe custody registers (3) 1848–95; advances registers 1861–78; manager's memorandum book 1873–95; manager's letterbook 1874–77; bank notebook 1880–93; staff photographs 1881, 1890; bearer bonds register 1895–1910; staff register 1897–1914; papers re new building 1959–69; **Manchester, Cheetham Hill:** branch minutes 1945–58; **Manchester, King Street:** passbook 1865–81; staff photograph albums c.1900–71; papers re premises rebuilding 1961–66; architectural drawings n.d.; **Manchester, Portland Street:** customer mandate books 1897–1921; **Market Drayton:** papers re premises rebuilding 1867–70; shareholder minute book 1872–95; letterbook 1887–1915; **Maryport:** manager's opinion book 1919–27; **Nantwich:** copy deed of settlement 1843; routine business correspondence 1870s–1880s; receipts 1902–14; **Oldham:** papers re establishment 1831–33; **Padiham:** manager's minute books (3) 1938–69; **Preston, Fishergate:** passbooks 1835–36, 1917–34; correspondence from Lancaster branch 1909; customer correspondence 1910; staff files 1912–29; sub-branches results book 1914–55; **Ramsbottom:** current account ledger 1900–50; branch minutes 1908–39; guarantee 1921; **Rochdale:** expenses book 1833–46; manager's out-letterbook 1839–72; **Rugeley:** building work bill of charges 1833–35; manager's minutes 1924–63; **Ruislip:** branch minutes 1939–67; **Settle:** staff file 1957–68; **Sevenoaks:** branch minutes 1939–54; **Shrewsbury:** branch minutes 1934–51; **Southampton:** branch minutes 1960–65; **Stafford:** declarations of secrecy 1832, 1863–74; balance sheets 1833–41; customer papers 1834–59;

Records of banks

expenses book 1839–69; bill of exchange 1841; passbook 1843–50; local board minutes 1843–64; premises receipts 1844–46, 1865–68; salary books (3) 1855–1906, 1949–50; weekly abstract book 1874–1931; letterbooks (7) 1875–1923; information book (3) 1878–1908; architectural drawings 1880, 1957; manager's diary 1883–85; minute books (2) 1886–88, 1906–15; half-yearly returns abstracts 1936–65; **Stalybridge:** declarations of secrecy book 1834–91; passbook 1835; **Stockport:** branch minute books (4) 1829–93; committee of management minutes 1829–30; record book 1829–42; safe custody book 1830–72; directors' declaration of secrecy book 1830–39; copy deed of settlement 1843; opinion book 1867–1900; manager's information book 1883–1921; expenses book 1883–90; abstracts of accounts 1874–81; list of proprietors 1884–95; salary book 1888–1929; **Stockport, Heaviley:** branch minute books (4) 1913–69; **Stoke-on-Trent:** customer ledger 1875–92; papers re new premises 1877–80; information book 1883–1908; **Stone:** expenses book 1857–1968; letters from head office 1870, 1904; annual debit balances statement 1872–78; building works bills 1873–1900; **Tunstall:** probate register 1878–1929; staff photograph 1918; **Ulverston:** manager's out-letterbooks (2) 1907–16; branch minutes (2) 1910–33; receipt 1912; **Wakefield:** branch minutes 1960–69; **Walton Le Dale:** cheque book register 1920–51; **Warrington:** instructions re bad debts 1839; declarations of secrecy 1839–69; passbook 1866–90; list of local proprietors n.d.; **Whitehaven:** deposit account ledger 1896–1943; deposit receipts book 1916–59; manager's diaries (4) 1917–20; opinion book 1920–31; **Wigan:** passbooks 1833–55, 1864–68; local directors' minute book 1836–58; staff register 1870–1921; information books (2) 1883–1908; **Wilmslow:** memorandum book 1898–1914; **Windermere:** out-letterbooks (4) 1907–28; applications for overdrafts 1926–31.

DIXON & CO
Chester, Cheshire

History: This private bank was established in 1808 as Rowton, Rordkin & Marshall; it was also known as the Chester Bank. It appears to have failed during the panic of 1810 and was reformed immediately as Dixon & Chilton. In 1827 it acquired the Chester banking business of D Wardell (est. 1813) when its name was changed to Dixon & Wardell; subsequently the bank was styled Dixon & Co. It was acquired by Parr's Banking Co Ltd (est. 1865) in 1878.

T E Gregory, *The Westminster Bank Through A Century* (London, 1936)

Records: The Royal Bank of Scotland plc, Archive Section, Regent's House, 42 Islington High Street, London N1 8XL

Cash balance book 1849–69; amalgamation agreement 1878.

196 British banking – a guide to historical records

DIXON, DALTON & AMPHLETT
Dudley, West Midlands

History: This private bank is believed to trace its origins to Edward Dixon (1741–1807) who may have been in partnership with John Finch. In 1803 the bank was known as Edward Dixon & Son and its subsequent titles included Edward Dixon, Son & Co (1805–07), Dixon, Dalton & Co (1809–11) and Edward Dixon, George Dalton & Co (1828–35). In 1844, when known as Dixon, Dalton & Amphlett, it failed and its business was taken over by the Birmingham Banking Co (est. 1829).

M Perkins, *Dudley Tradesman's Tokens of the Seventeenth, Eighteenth and Nineteenth Centuries and History of Dudley Bankers and Bank Notes from the Earliest to the Present Time* (Dudley, 1905)

Records 1: Archives & Local History Service, Mount Pleasant Street, Coseley, Dudley WV14 9JR

List of creditors and debts of E Dalton c.1844.

Records 2: Staffordshire Record Office, Eastgate Street, Stafford ST16 2LZ

Partnership agreement 1844. [Ref: D695/4/20/5/4]

Records 3: Lloyds TSB Group plc, Archives, Head Office, 71 Lombard Street, London EC3P 3BS

Deed of apprenticeship 1800.

DORRIEN, MAGENS, MELLO & CO
London

History: This private bank was formed as Dorrien, Rucker & Carleton in Finch Lane, City of London, in 1770. The firm was styled Dorrien, Rucker, Dorrien & Martin from 1776, Dorrien, Mello & Martin from 1779, Dorrien, Magens, Dorrien, Mello & Co from 1814 and Dorrien, Magens, Mello & Co from 1828. In 1842 the business of the bank, along with two of its partners, John Dorrien Magens and John Arnold Mello, was transferred to Curries & Co (est. 1773).

F G Hilton Price, *A Handbook of London Bankers* (London, 1876)

Records: The Royal Bank of Scotland plc, Archive Section, Regent's House, 42 Islington High Street, London, N1 8XL

Correspondence from customers 1785, 1819–25; private account books (4) 1806–42; unpaid bills of exchange 1810–41; customer bonds 1811, 1827; partnership agreements 1814–28; agreement re assignment of bills

Records of banks   *197*

of exchange 1815; household account books 1818–22; staff salaries and Christmas money papers 1820–27; discount and note account books, including balance sheets (5) 1820, 1824–27; customer standing order instructions 1823–40; post book 1824–29; bill book 1840–41; customer correspondence re merger with Curries & Co 1841–42.

DRUMMOND & CO
London

History: This private bank was founded in about 1712 by Scotsman Andrew Drummond who had been apprenticed as a goldsmith in Edinburgh. He traded as a goldsmith at the sign of the Golden Eagle on the east side of Charing Cross, a residential area favoured by the Scottish gentry in London's West End. By 1717 Drummond had developed a banking business which soon overshadowed his goldsmithing activities. Scots and army agents predominated amongst his early customers. By 1744 he had over 400 customers including English as well as Scottish aristocrats, men of the arts, hospitals and religious and charitable institutions. In 1760 the firm moved to the west side of Charing Cross. Andrew Drummond died in 1769 and a series of subsequent partnership agreements divided the business among three branches of the Drummond family. The bank proved highly successful during the eighteenth century and by 1795 Drummonds had over 2,850 accounts. In addition, two of the partners were involved in substantial Treasury contracts for the payment of British troops in Canada and America before and during the War of American Independence. Despite the repeated commercial crises of the early nineteenth century, the business thrived owing to its large and aristocratic connections and the meticulous rules concerning the succession of shares in the business and the distribution of profits and loans to partners. In 1824 customer deposits exceeded £2 million. Between 1877 and 1881 new premises were constructed on the existing site and were extended to the south in 1921. In 1924 Drummonds was acquired by The Royal Bank of Scotland Ltd (est. 1727) for £958,400, although it continued to trade independently.

Anon, *Messrs Drummonds Bankers. A History* (priv. pub., 1993); H Bolitho & D Peel, *The Drummonds of Charing Cross* (London, 1967); Neil Munro, *The History of the Royal Bank of Scotland* (Edinburgh, 1928)

Records 1: The Royal Bank of Scotland plc, Archive Section, Regent's House, 42 Islington High Street, London N1 8XL

Customer ledgers 1716–45; note drawn on Andrew Drummond 1723; bills of exchange, receipts, cheques, customer instructions 1727–1822; powers of attorney 1734–1835; notice re payment of creditors 1746; executorship and trusteeship papers 1750–1859, 1885–1900; title deeds re bank prop-

198   *British banking – a guide to historical records*

erty 1768, 1878–92; exchequer bill papers 1771–1841; partnership agreements 1772–1892; partners' papers 1774–1950; customer balance sheets 1775–1844; staff salary papers 1777–1900; customer correspondence 1784–1900; papers re staff working conditions and procedures 1788–1956; balance statements 1788–1884; papers re constitution and division of the partnership 1788–1892; inventory of George Drummond's property 1789; papers re bank house 1789–1871; passbooks c.1780s–1900; cheque books c.1780s–1960s; partners' accounts 1790–1841; staff lists 1792–1900; signature and address books 1793–1900; correspondence re overdrafts and loans 1795–97, 1872; staff recruitment papers 1799–1900; property rebuilding and alteration papers 1810–1963; statements of assets 1816–41; papers re forgeries 1819–1910; architectural plans 1823–1968; plate waste books 1830–79; papers re stock and annuity transactions 1833–87; balance books 1841–89; profit and loss statements 1843–89; legal papers 1839–1941; staff cartoons c.1848–1890s; pension papers 1856–1900; letter of introduction re circular notes 1860s; correspondence re purchase and sale of stock 1870–83; photographs and drawings of bank 1877–1982; record of large advances 1880–87; accounts opened books 1880–1900; property valuations 1880–1914; surveyor's reports on property 1880–1923; plate receipt books 1881–89; list of foreign government bonds 1891; letters of credit books 1893–1900; resolutions 1895; partners' and directors' meeting minute books 1897–1970; draft share transfer forms c.1890s; papers re bill brokers 1903–07; circular note register 1909–47; authorised signatories correspondence 1918–20; memorandum and articles of association 1923; papers re acquisition by Royal Bank of Scotland 1924; annual profit and loss calculations 1924–25, 1930–31; board correspondence 1939, 1963–70; local board papers 1955–70; branch inspection reports 1958–62; papers re drive-in bank 1961–68; staff training papers 1962–63; anniversary exhibition papers 1968; branch statistics 1969–70.

Records 2: Hampshire Record Office, Sussex Street, Winchester SO23 5TH

Partnership agreements (8) 1780–1892; correspondence of Drummond family re banking and partnership matters 1811–91; deed of settlement 1894; papers re Drummond family eighteenth to nineteenth cents. [Ref: 3M60]

Records 3: Guildhall Library, Aldermanbury, London EC2P 2EJ

Correspondence with John Knight, Shropshire 1812–21. [Ref: 5863A boxes 6–7]

DUDLEY & WEST BROMWICH BANKING CO
Dudley, West Midlands

History: This joint stock bank was formed in 1833 out of the private bank of Hornden, Molineux & Co (est. 1806) which was also connected with Hornden & Molineux of Wolverhampton. C H Hornden became manager. In 1874 the bank amalgamated with the Birmingham Town & District Banking Co (est. 1836) to form the Birmingham, Dudley & District Banking Co.

M Perkins, *Dudley Tradesman's Tokens of the Seventeenth, Eighteenth and Nineteenth Centuries and History of Dudley Bankers and Bank Notes from the Earliest to the Present Times* (Dudley, 1905)

Records: Barclays Bank plc, Group Archives, Dallimore Road, Wythenshawe, Manchester M23 9JA

Deeds of settlement: 1831–33, 1860; share allotment letter 1833; directors' meeting minute books (8) 1833–89; impersonal ledgers 1834–48; share certificates 1834–74; share transfers 1835; branch information books (6) 1835–81; certificate of incorporation and related papers 1857–87; cheques, cheque books and deposit receipts 1850s–73; bank notes 1868–87; rules for clerks 1869; balance sheet 1877; circular: merger with Birmingham Town & District Banking Co 1880, Birmingham, Dudley and District Banking Co 1889; directors' report and accounts 1887–88; dividend warrants 1889; list of shareholders 1889.

H DUIGNAN & SON
Walsall, West Midlands

History: This private bank was established in about 1840 by Henry and William Henry Duignan who expanded their business as solicitors to embrace banking. In 1864 the recently established Staffordshire Joint Stock Bank acquired the bank for £2,250.

Records 1: HSBC Holdings plc, Group Archives, 10 Lower Thames Street, London EC3R 6AE

Agreement with Staffordshire Joint Stock Bank 1864.

Records 2: Walsall Local History Centre, Essex Street, Walsall WS2 7AS

Correspondence sent to Bank of Walsall & South Staffordshire re banking business c.1837–40. [Ref: 48/1/61]

DUMBELL'S BANKING CO LTD
Douglas, Isle of Man

History: This joint stock bank was formed in 1874 to acquire the business of the private bank of Dumbell, Son & Howard (est. 1853) of Douglas,

200   *British banking – a guide to historical records*

Isle of Man, which had opened branches in Castletown and Ramsey in 1855. Its paid-up capital was £60,000. In 1899 its balance sheet totalled £1.3 million but the bank was in difficulties due to a high level of bad debts caused by ill-advised lending for speculative ventures. In 1900 the bank suspended payments and its premises and goodwill were acquired by Parr's Bank Ltd (est. 1865) for £40,300. The bank's managers were later jailed in connection with the bank's failure.

C Chappell, *The Dumbell Affair* (Prescot, 1981); T E Gregory, *The Westminster Bank through a Century* (London, 1936); Ernest Quarmby, *Bank Notes and Banking in the Isle of Man* (London, 1994); Mark Solly, *Banks in the Isle of Man* (Isle of Man, 1995)

Records 1: The Royal Bank of Scotland plc, Archive Section, Regent's House, 42 Islington High Street, London N1 8XL

Articles of association 1874; circular re dispute with Bank of Mona 1876; half-yearly general meeting reports and accounts 1879–98; papers re failure and takeover 1900–10.

Records 2: The Manx Museum and National Trust, Douglas, Isle of Man IM1 3LY

Correspondence of George Dumbell re establishment of bank 1853–61; miscellaneous personal and business papers of Dumbell family n.d.; balance sheets 1885–99. [Ref: Bridge House Papers MS 4126 C; MD 229; MD 15006]

DUNDEE BANKING CO
Dundee, Tayside

History: This extended co-partnery, with unlimited liability, was established in Dundee in 1763 by George Dempster of Dunnichen, MP, to provide banking facilities for local merchants and manufacturers. Styled George Dempster & Co, it was also known as Dundee Banking Co and had thirty-six partners, largely local merchants, and a nominal capital of £12,000 of which 10 per cent was paid-up. The bank issued notes, lent money and discounted bills and in 1764 the co-partnery was extended to include twenty-four new members. For many years it was Dundee's only bank and survived the financial crisis of 1772 despite the collapse of its Edinburgh and London agents. Its note issue (£32,000 by 1768 and £61,000 by 1800) was successful and to extend the circulation the bank opened branches in Brechin, Arbroath, Forfar and Kirkcaldy by 1793 (those in Brechin and Kirkcaldy were later closed) and also began to accept deposits in 1792. Its balance sheet total grew from £31,900 in 1764, to £176,000 in 1795, to £600,000 in 1815 and to £740,000 in 1850. In 1838 it acquired

Records of banks 201

Dundee New Bank (est. 1802) and the services of its able manager, C W Boase, who subsequently stabilised Dundee Banking Co's operations by building large balances of call money in Edinburgh and London. In 1857 branches were opened in Lochee, Alyth and Broughty Ferry. A takeover attempt by Dundee Union Bank (est.1809) in 1857 failed due to inadequate support from the partners. In 1864, however, the bank was acquired by The Royal Bank of Scotland (est. 1727). At that time it had capital of £100,000, deposits of £722,000, note circulation of £53,943 and four branches.

C W Boase, *A Century of Banking in Dundee; Being the Annual Balance Sheets of the Dundee Banking Company from 1764 to 1864* (Edinburgh, 1867); C W Munn, 'Dundee Banking Co', *Three Banks Review* 127 (1980); I M Kennedy, 'Charles William Boase', *Scottish Bankers' Magazine* 47 (1956); S G Checkland, *Scottish Banking. A History 1695–1973* (Glasgow, 1975)

Records 1: The Royal Bank of Scotland plc, Archive Section, 36 St Andrews Square, Edinburgh EH2 2YB

Directors' sederunt book 1763–67; bank notes issued at branches book 1805–36; passbooks 1825–41, 1861–62; board private book 1838–57; petty cash book 1838–41.

Dundee, Lochee: cash books 1857–63; tellers' cash books 1857–64; current account ledgers 1857–64; deposit receipt ledger 1857–64; draft book 1857–64; letterbook 1857–64; savings account book 1857–64; savings account cash paid books 1857–1900; savings account cash received book 1857–75.

Records 2: Dundee Central Library Local Studies Department, The Wellgate, Dundee DD1 1DB

Contract of co-partnery and list of partners 1826–58. [Ref: Lamb Collection].

DUNDEE NEW BANK
Dundee, Tayside

History: This private bank traced its origins to the Dundee Commercial Banking Co which was formed in 1792. It was reconstructed in 1802 as the Dundee New Bank with a paid-up capital of £5,800; it was otherwise known as Ransom, Morland & Co. Some of its partners were partners in the London private bank of Ransom, Morland & Co (est. 1782). Three branches were opened in Brechin (1802), Forfar (by 1803) and Arbroath (by 1810). In 1809 the London-based partners, along with Glasgow mer-

202 British banking – a guide to historical records

chants, established the Glasgow Bank. Dundee New Bank was acquired by Dundee Banking Co (est. 1763) in 1838.

C W Boase, *A Century of Banking in Dundee; Being the Annual Balance Sheets of the Dundee Banking Company from 1764 to 1864* (Edinburgh, 1867)

Records 1: The Royal Bank of Scotland plc, Archive Section, 36 St Andrews Square, Edinburgh EH2 2YB

Partnership agreements 1791, 1806; deed of declaration 1802; private directors' meeting minutes 1802–38; balance books 1806–36; papers re legal action c.1807; petty cash book 1827–38.

Records 2: Perth & Kinross Council Archive, A K Bell Library, 2–8 York Place, Perth PH2 8EP

Correspondence, accounts and partnership agreements, papers of Lord Kinnaird 1801–38. [Ref: MS100]

Records 3: Buckinghamshire Record Office, County Hall, Aylesbury HP20 1UA

Miscellaneous correspondence of Spencer Bernard, director 1780–1832. [Ref: D/SB PFE/1/1/786 -796]

Records 4: Business Records Centre, Archive Department, University of Glasgow, Glasgow G12 8QQ

Partners' meeting minutes extracts 1802–03; private letterbook 1802–04. [Ref: Scottish Banking Collection]

DUNDEE UNION BANK
Dundee, Tayside

History: This co-partnery was formed in 1809; by 1812 its paid-up capital was £56,200 and deposits were £113,000. In 1844 the bank was absorbed by the Western Bank of Scotland.

Records: Business Records Centre, Archive Department, University of Glasgow, Glasgow G12 8QQ

Deed of accession to the contract of co-partnery 1832. [Ref: UGD/85]

DUNSFORD & CO
Tiverton, Devon

History: This private bank was established in 1788 and in its early years appears to have been known as Dickinson, Lewis, Besley & Son, as

Records of banks 203

Dunsford & Barne and as Dickinson, Dunsford, Barne & Boase; it was otherwise known as the Tiverton Bank and, later, as the Tiverton & Devonshire Bank. It was styled Dunsford, Dunsford & Taylor from 1858 and was subsequently styled Dunsford & Co. The bank was acquired by Stuckey's Banking Co Ltd (est. 1826) in 1883.

Philip T Saunders, *Stuckey's Bank* (Taunton, 1928)

Records: The Royal Bank of Scotland plc, Archive Section, Regent's House, 42 Islington High Street, London N1 8XL

Deposit receipt 1877; customer letter re overdraft 1880; cheques n.d.; amalgamation papers 1883.

EASTERN BANK LTD
London and Asia

History: This British-owned overseas bank was formed at the comparatively late date of 1909. It had a paid-up capital of £400,000 and did business in India; it may be regarded as a latter day eastern exchange bank. It had powerful institutional shareholders, especially E D Sassoon & Co, the eastern trading company which also had extensive interests in the Hongkong & Shanghai Banking Corporation (est. 1865) and the Imperial Bank of Persia (est. 1889). The Eastern Bank always remained comparatively small; its balance sheet total on formation was £2.2 million. This grew to £3.3 million by 1913, when there were three branches; by 1928 these figures were £11.5 million and twelve respectively. By 1938 branch numbers remained unchanged but then grew to twenty-three by 1955. The bank's late date of formation meant that it experienced difficulty in winning business from its established competitors which induced it to expand outside India. In 1920, for example, it was the first British bank to open a branch on the western side of the Persian Gulf, at Bahrain, and consequently it benefited from the development of the local oil industry in the 1930s. Barclays Bank Ltd (est. 1896) began to acquire a substantial shareholding from the 1920s and with Sassoons owned 67 per cent of the shares by 1957. In that year the Chartered Bank (est. 1853) acquired this interest which provided a platform for the acquisition of all remaining shares. Eastern Bank continued to trade as a separate entity until 1971.

Rodney Wilson, 'Financial Development of the Arab Gulf. The Eastern Experience 1917–50', *Business History*, 29 (1987)

Records 1: Guildhall Library, Aldermanbury, London EC2P 2EJ

Preliminary expenses ledger 1909–10; papers re tax assessments 1909–63; memorandum and articles of association 1909–64; salary and wage regis-

204 *British banking – a guide to historical records*

ter 1910–12; staff terms of service agreements 1910–19; staff registers (2) 1910–46; staff powers of attorney 1910–55; half-yearly profit and loss accounts head offices and branches 1910–59; analysis of profit and loss and general charges for income tax (2) 1910–59; seal registers (6) 1910–70; half-yearly and annual balance sheets and profit and loss accounts 1910–71; general ledgers (102) 1910–71; register of bad and doubtful debts 1911–63; unpaid accounts (3) 1911–65; powers of attorney 1912–68; finance committee reports (9) 1918–43; general manager's private/official letters to branches (2) 1918–23; staff photographs 1919–65; comparative statements of charges re head office and branches 1920–60; land and house property ledger 1920–64; inspector's circulars 1921–22; working papers re half-year and annual accounts 1923–71; general manager's miscellaneous correspondence 1924–71; guarantee books (2) 1929–70; inspector's miscellaneous papers 1920s–1940s; inspector's reports on branches 1920s–1950s; plans and elevations of head office and branches 1920s–1960s; guarantee papers 1931–70; general ledger statements (49) 1935–60; general manager's loans correspondence re branches 1930s–1960s; miscellaneous correspondence with branches 1930s–1960s; papers re exchange rates and sterling positions 1943–67; general manager's confidential telegrams (2) 1944–62; half-yearly reports of branches to head office 1946–71; sites for business papers c.1955–71; papers re Chartered Bank acquisition 1957; branch photographs 1950s–1970s; branch premises files 1950s–1960s; 'limit applications' being applications for credits, c.1960–70; papers re insurance 1962–71; papers re senior managers' overseas tours 1963–67; private office papers of general manager 1964–67; miscellaneous financial returns of branches to head office 1966–71; premises subject papers 1960s; papers re integration with Chartered Bank 1970–71.

Records 2: Standard Chartered Bank plc, Head Office, 1 Aldermanbury Square, London EC2V 7SB

Directors' meeting minute books (5) 1909–71.

EASTERN BANK OF SCOTLAND
Dundee, Tayside

History: This joint stock bank, formed in 1838, was the successor to the Dundee Commercial Bank (est. 1825) which had run into difficulties and sustained large losses. Before its parlous condition became widely known, it was reconstructed as the Eastern Bank of Scotland with a paid-up capital of £112,500. It had head offices at both Dundee and Edinburgh and five branches were soon opened. In 1844 the bank divided into two entities, the Edinburgh section being hived off to form the North British Bank

Records of banks

which was soon wound up; its business was acquired by the City of Glasgow Bank (est. 1839) and formed its Edinburgh branch. The remaining business continued under the title of Eastern Bank of Scotland. In 1857 it first discussed amalgamation with Clydesdale Bank (est. 1838) and the two finally merged in 1863.

W F Crick & J E Wadsworth, *A Hundred Years of Joint Stock Banking* (London, 1936)

Records 1: Clydesdale Bank plc, Head Office, 30 St Vincent Place, Glasgow G1 2HL

List of partners 1838; banker's licences 1838–61; statements of affairs 1840–44; annual reports 1849–61; amalgamation agreement 1862; statements of assets and liabilities 1863.

Records 2: Perth & Kinross Council Archive, A K Bell Library, 2–8 York Place, Perth PH2 8EP

Prospectus 1838; list of partners 1840–41. [Ref: B59/37/14/14–16]

EAST MORLEY & BRADFORD DISTRICT DEPOSIT BANK LTD
Bradford, West Yorkshire

History: This joint stock bank was established in 1870 and acquired limited liability in 1901 with a capital of £50,000. It had two branches in Bradford and one in Saltaire. It was acquired by Union Bank of Manchester Ltd (est. 1836) in 1918.

Records: Barclays Bank plc, Group Archives, Dallimore Road, Wythenshawe, Manchester M23 9JA

Agreement for sale, memorandum and articles of association, reports and accounts, list of shareholders and circulars re amalgamation 1901–22.

EAST OF ENGLAND BANK

Norwich, Norfolk

History: This joint stock bank was established in 1836 out of the business of the Norfolk & Norwich Joint Stock Banking Co (est. 1826). It expanded rapidly and opened thirty-three branches, mostly in Norfolk and Suffolk, by 1864. In this year the bank experienced difficulties and was reconstructed as the Provincial Banking Corporation Ltd.

Harold Preston, *Early East Anglian Banks and Bankers* (Thetford, 1994)

Records: Barclays Bank plc, Group Archives, Dallimore Road, Wythenshawe, Manchester M23 9JA

206   *British banking – a guide to historical records*

Powers of attorney re deed of settlement 1836; share payment receipt 1836; partners' return 1847; cheques 1849; lease 1853; balance sheet 1864; report re reconstruction as Provincial Banking Corporation 1864.

EATON, CAYLEY & CO
Stamford, Lincolnshire

History: This private bank was established in Stamford in 1800 by William Jackson and William Johnson as Jackson & Johnson; it was otherwise known as the Stamford & Rutland Bank. Following Jackson's death, Stephen Eaton, banker at Thrapston, joined the partnership which was known as William Johnson & Stephen Eaton from 1810. It was subsequently known as Eaton & Cayley from 1819; as Eaton, Cayley & Michelson from 1837; as Eaton & Michelson from 1844; as Eaton, Cayley, Eaton & Michelson from 1859; as Eaton, Cayley, Michelson & Cayley from 1861; as Eaton, Cayley & Michelson from 1868; and as Eaton, Cayley & Co from 1879. Branches were opened at Oakham, Peterborough and Uppingham and there was a connection with Hammond & Co (est. 1770) of Newmarket and with Johnson, Eaton & Eland (est. 1810) of Thrapston. Upon George Cayley's death in 1891, the Stamford, Spalding & Boston Banking Co Ltd (est. 1831) absorbed the bank.

P W Matthews & Anthony W Tuke, *History of Barclays Bank Ltd* (London, 1926)

Records 1: Barclays Bank plc, Group Archives, Dallimore Road, Wythenshawe, Manchester M23 9JA

Bank notes 1819–34; in-letters 1825; cheques 1827–51; partnership investment correspondence including lists of accounts 1834–35; partners' deeds of indemnity and papers re Thrapston Bank 1834–62; deed of covenant and release of partners' executors 1837; notebook re settlement between Eaton, Cayley & Co and new partners 1837–59.

Uppingham: security registers (3) 1844–96; manager's letterbooks (2) 1846–73; ledgers general balances 1873–91.

Records 2: Northamptonshire Record Office, Woolton Hall Park, Northampton NN4 9BQ

Oat, bean, barley and malt accounts 1818–23; corn speculation accounts 1818–23; account books (4) 1819–34; Mr Cayley's duplicate private ledgers 1819–34; profit and loss books (2) 1819–36; mutilated bank notes and related guarantees c.1819–36; investment ledgers: 1821–59, Mrs Eaton 1836–57; papers re foreign stock 1824–34; notes 'brought down' accounts 1825–33; note registers 1825–37; account books with Eaton, Cayley &

Records of banks

Michelson: executors of Stephen Eaton 1834–47, Stephen Eaton and Edward Cayley 1836–47, Mrs Eaton (4) 1834–59; customer papers 1836–1906; contingent account book 1837. [Ref: E&C 1–339]

EDINBURGH & GLASGOW JOINT STOCK BANK
Glasgow, Strathclyde

History: This bank was formed in 1844 by merger of the Glasgow Joint Stock Bank (est. 1840) and the Edinburgh & Leith Bank (est. 1838) which in 1842 had acquired the Southern Bank of Scotland (est. 1838). The new bank had a paid-up capital of £1 million and 1,600 shareholders. However, it's performance suffered as a result of differences between its Edinburgh and Glasgow boards and in 1847 heavy losses resulted from loans secured on railway securities when the bank had to be supported by the Bank of England. In 1850 a merger with Clydesdale Bank (est. 1838) and the City of Glasgow Bank (est. 1839), which would have created Scotland's largest bank, was proposed but negotiations broke down. In 1849 further heavy losses were sustained through advances to the Royal Bank of Australia (est. 1842) and, in this weakened condition, the bank almost collapsed at the time of the Western Bank of Scotland's (est. 1832) failure in 1857. A year later, when there were eighteen branches, the business was acquired by Clydesdale Bank. Its winding up showed a deficit of £26,000 so, in effect, its shareholders lost their entire capital.

Records: Clydesdale Bank plc, Head Office, 30 St Vincent Place, Glasgow G1 2HL

General meeting notebook 1840–58; agreement with Glasgow Joint Stock Bank 1844; directors' Glasgow committee minutes (2) 1851–58; trustee committee minutes 1858–60.

ELAND & ELAND
Thrapston, Northamptonshire

History: This private bank was established in 1810 by Stephen Eaton who soon took into partnership George Eland, a draper. Eaton moved to Stamford in about 1812 where he joined the bank of William Johnson & Stephen Eaton (est. 1800). The Thrapston was subsequently styled Eaton & Eland, Eland & Yorke, Eland & Elands and Eland & Eland; it was otherwise known as the Thrapston & Kettering Bank. The firm failed in 1888, when its balance sheet totalled £84,000, and was taken over by the Stamford, Spalding & Boston Banking Co Ltd (est. 1831).

P W Matthews & Anthony W Tuke, *History of Barclays Bank Ltd* (London, 1926)

208   *British banking – a guide to historical records*

Records: Barclays Bank plc, Group Archives, Dallimore Road, Wythenshawe, Manchester M23 9JA

Receipts 1852–76; cheques 1876–83; balance sheet 1888.

SIR WM. ELFORD, TINGECOMBE & CO
Plymouth, Devon

History: This private bank was established in about 1782 as Culme, Fox & Tingecombe; it was otherwise known as the Plymouth Bank. It was renamed Sir Wm. Elford, Tingecombe & Co in 1804 and failed in 1825.

Records: The Royal Bank of Scotland plc, Archive Section, Regent's House, 42 Islington High Street, London N1 8XL

Papers re failure 1823–63.

ELIOT, PEARCE & CO
Weymouth, Dorset

History: This bank was formed in 1791 as Bower & Bower and was later known, *inter alia*, as William Eliot & Edward Pearce and as Eliot, Pearce & Eliot; it was also styled Weymouth Old Bank. Branches were established at Dorchester and Portland in Dorset and at Bournemouth and Boscombe in Hampshire. The bank encountered financial difficulties in the 1890s, which were exacerbated by involvement in unsuccessful land speculation at Dorchester. It failed in 1897 when Capital & Counties Bank Ltd (est. 1877) acquired its business.

Records: Lloyds TSB Group plc, Archives, Head Office, 71 Lombard Street, London EC3P 3BS

Amalgamation papers 1897.

EQUITABLE BANK LTD
Halifax, West Yorkshire

History: This joint stock bank was formed as the Halifax Equitable Bank Ltd in 1899 by the Halifax Equitable Building Society (est. 1871) as a means of attracting deposits; only members could be shareholders. Assets rose from £43,000 in 1905, to £148,000 in 1910, to £339,000 in 1915 and to £1.176 million in 1920. In 1927 paid-up capital reached £100,000 and there were sixteen branches and eight sub-branches, mostly in Lancashire and Yorkshire. This wider regional presence resulted in a name change to the Equitable Bank Ltd in 1913. In 1927 the business was acquired by Bank of Liverpool & Martins Ltd (est. 1712).

George Chandler, *Four Centuries of Banking* (London, 1964–68)

Records: Barclays Bank plc, Group Archives, Dallimore Road, Wythenshawe, Manchester M23 9JA

Shareholder registers (3) 1900–26; press cuttings, new branches 1924–31; balance sheet booklet 1925; report and accounts 1926; papers re merger with Bank of Liverpool & Martins Ltd 1925–27.

ERLANGERS LTD
London

History: This merchant bank traced its origins to the Erlanger family, bankers at Frankfurt. In 1859 Emile Erlanger established his own private banking house of Emile Erlanger & Cie of Paris which worked closely with the Frankfurt firm and also with J Henry Schroder & Co (est. 1818) of London, especially in the issue of bonds for sovereign clients. In 1870, when the Paris market was paralysed by the Franco-Prussian War, Erlanger established Emile Erlanger & Co in the City of London. It eventually outgrew the Paris firm in importance as an issuing house for sovereign, municipal and corporate borrowers and also developed as an accepting house. The business was known as Erlangers from 1917 and as Erlangers Ltd from 1928. In the 1930s its provision of corporate finance advice to British industry became a major activity. The London business was converted into a private limited company in 1928 and in 1959, when still led by the Erlanger family, it merged with Philip Hill, Higginson & Co Ltd (est. 1907) to form Philip Hill, Higginson, Erlangers Ltd which from 1965 was known as Hill Samuel & Co Ltd.

Baron E B d'Erlanger, *My English Souvenir* (1978)

Records: Lloyds TSB Group plc, Archives, Head Office, 71 Lombard Street, London EC3P 3BS

General meeting minutes n.d.; balance sheets 1928–59; directors' meeting minute books (7) n.d.; routine ledgers 1940–59; private ledgers 1949–59; committee minutes 1953.

SIR JAMES ESDAILE, ESDAILE, GRENFELL, THOMAS & CO
London

History: This private bank was established in 1781 in Birchin Lane, City of London, as Esdaile, Hammet & Esdaile. It moved shortly afterwards to Lombard Street. In 1792 it merged with Smith, Wright & Co (est. 1759), also of Lombard Street, to form Sir James Esdaile, Esdaile, Smith, Wright, Hammett & Co. In 1798 it was known as Sir James

210   *British banking – a guide to historical records*

Esdaile, Esdaile, Hammett, Esdaile & Hammett and later as Sir James Esdaile, Esdaile, Grenfell, Thomas & Co. The firm failed in 1837 but was supported by a loan from City of London bankers which was repaid in 1873.

F G Hilton Price, *A Handbook of London Bankers* (London, 1876); Anon, 'The Esdaile Crisis', *Three Banks Review*, 70 (1966)

Records: The Royal Bank of Scotland plc, Archive Section, Regent's House, 42 Islington High Street, London N1 8XL

Cheques 1794–1824; customer ledgers: Birmingham Bank 1819–20, town 1819–20, country banks 1822; papers re failure 1836–37.

SIR STEPHEN EVANS (EVANCE)
London

History: Stephen Evans was apprenticed to the London goldsmith Henry Nelthorpe between 1669 and 1676. By 1677 and until after 1697, he traded as a goldsmith-banker at the sign of the Black Boy, Lombard Street, City of London, in partnership with Peter Percival. By 1702 he was in partnership with William Hales, his own former apprentice. He was knighted in about 1694. He kept running cashes and traded in gold, silver and plate. He was a Commissioner of Excise and, from 1697, was jeweller to the King. In partnership with Joseph Herne, he became an important financier to the Crown. Evans stopped payment in 1721.

Records: Public Record Office, Ruskin Avenue, Kew, Richmond TW9 4DU

Bullion book 1688–90; commission of bankruptcy, Sir Stephen Evans and William Hales 1711. [Ref: PRO C114/179; C104/171]

EVERARDS & CO
King's Lynn, Norfolk

History: This private bank was established in 1764 as Audley & Fydell, its partners being wine merchants; it was also known as the Lynn Bank. In 1807 its title was changed to Bagge & Bacon, Bagge being an importer, brewer and shipowner. From 1826 the Everard family of brewers acquired an interest when the bank became known as Everards & Blencowe and, from 1854, as Everards & Co. The bank was acquired by Gurneys, Birkbeck & Cresswell (est. 1782) of King's Lynn in 1861.

Harold Preston, *Early East Anglian Banks and Bankers* (Thetford, 1994)

Records of banks

Records 1: Barclays Bank plc, Group Archives, Dallimore Road, Wythenshawe, Manchester M23 9JA

Agreement, John Everard re provision of annuities for family 1755.

Records 2: Norfolk Record Office, Gildengate House, Anglia Square, Norwich NR3 1EB

Partnership agreements eighteenth to nineteenth cents; account with London correspondent 1769–78; customer passbooks (3) 1809–26; letterbooks (5) 1826–58; customer accounts not taken over by Gurneys 1861–85; Everard family papers and accounts 1761–1845. [Ref: Bradfer-Lawrence records]

EXCHANGE & DISCOUNT BANK LTD
Leeds, West Yorkshire

History: This joint stock bank was formed in 1866 out of the business of the private bank of Cousins, Allen & Co (est. 1860) of Leeds whose business was largely that of bill discounting. Branches were opened at Bradford and Hull. By 1870 paid-up capital was £50,000 and deposits were £51,000; 10 years later paid-up capital was £100,000 and deposits totalled £168,000. The business enjoyed almost unbroken prosperity but, having encountered stiff competition in the late-1880s, was acquired by the Birmingham & Midland Bank Ltd (est. 1836) in 1890 for the equivalent of £225,000. Its paid-up capital and deposits were then £100,000 and £422,000 respectively.

Records: HSBC Holdings plc, Group Archives, 10 Lower Thames Street, London EC3R 6AE

Partnership agreement 1863; directors' meeting minutes 1865–71; annual reports 1874, 1889; security book 1883–89; amalgamation papers 1890–99.

EYTON, BURTON & CO
Shrewsbury, Shropshire

History: This private bank, which was also known as Salop Old Bank, was formed in 1884 through the merger of two Shrewsbury private banks, Rocke, Eyton, Campbell & Bayley (est. 1792) and Burton, Lloyd, Lloyd & Salt (est. 1812). In 1907 it was acquired by Capital & Counties Bank Ltd (est. 1877).

Records 1: Lloyds TSB Group plc, Archives, Head Office, 71 Lombard Street, London EC3P 3BS

Amalgamation papers 1907–10.

212   *British banking – a guide to historical records*

Records 2: Shropshire Records and Research Centre, Castle Gates, Shrewsbury SY1 2AQ

Partnership agreements 1792–1866. [Ref: 665/477; 665/339; 1135/1]

FARLEY, LAVENDER & CO
Worcester, Hereford and Worcester

History: This private bank was formed in 1794; it was also known as the Worcester Bank. It was associated with the firm of Farley, Turner & Jones (est. c.1793) of Kidderminster and it failed in 1857.

Records: Hereford and Worcester Record Office, St Helen's Branch, Fish Street, Worcester WR1 2HN

Partnership agreement 1821; papers: salaries 1829–36, law suits 1820–40, failure 1857. [Ref: 705:380 BA 2309/1]

FARROW'S BANK LTD
London

History: This joint stock bank was formed in 1907 to acquire the business of a friendly society of the same name established in 1904. It suspended payment in 1920.

R Woodruff, 'Farrow's Bank Ltd', *Counterfoil*, 30 (1994)

Records 1: Public Record Office, Ruskin Avenue, Kew, Richmond TW9 4DU

Papers re failure 1921–25. [Ref: T172/1209; T160/284/13669]

Records 2: Leicestershire Record Office, Long Street, Wigston Magna, Leicester LE18 2AH

Leicester: account book 1917–21. [Ref: Misc 1015]

FINCHAM & SIMPSON
Diss, Norfolk

History: This private bank was established in 1802 as Oakes, Fincham & Co; it was also known as the Diss Bank. It worked closely with Oakes & Co (est. 1795) of Bury St Edmunds. In 1854 its title was Oakes, Fincham, Bevan, Moor & Simpson and from 1856 it was known as Fincham & Simpson, indicating the discontinuation of the Bury bank's interest. A branch operated at East Harling from 1844 and a connection appears to have existed with Fincham, French & Simpson (est. c.1864) of Eye. In 1871 the bank was acquired by the London & Provincial Bank Ltd (est. 1864).

Harold Preston, *Early East Anglian Banks and Bankers* (Thetford, 1994)

Records: Barclays Bank plc, Group Archives, Dallimore Road, Wythenshawe, Manchester M23 9JA

Papers re suspension of business 1871.

THOMAS FIRTH & SON
Northwich, Cheshire

History: This private bank was established in 1828 by Thomas Firth, a rock salt merchant, alongside his other trading activities. A branch was opened at Winsford. The firm was acquired by Parr's Banking Co Ltd (est. 1865) in 1865.

Records: The Royal Bank of Scotland plc, Archive Section, Regent's House, 42 Islington High Street, London N1 8XL

Amalgamation agreement 1864.

FLOOD & LOTT
Honiton, Devon

History: This private bank was formed in 1786 as How, Lott & Lathy and was subsequently known as Flood, Lott & Lott; Flood, Flood & Lott; and Flood & Lott. It also traded as the Honiton Bank. It failed in 1847.

Records: Devon Record Office, Castle Street, Exeter EX4 3PU

Partnership agreements 1786, 1830; notice to creditors 1848. [Ref: 337 B/ (75/1), (90/12), (27/29)]

SIR WILLIAM FORBES, JAMES HUNTER & CO
Edinburgh, Lothian

History: This private bank was established by John Coutts, an Edinburgh merchant who by 1723 acted as a banker. On his death in 1750, his four sons carried on his businesses and a London house called Coutts, Stephen, Coutts & Co was formed. In 1754 his son, James, moved to London where he married the niece of George Campbell, London goldsmith and banker, and subsequently joined with Campbell to form Campbell & Coutts, later known as Coutts & Co. The Edinburgh firm recruited Sir William Forbes as an apprentice in 1754; he became a partner in 1761. Soon the management of the Edinburgh and London businesses was in the hands of Forbes and James Hunter (later Sir James Hunter-Blair, died 1787); from 1762 they concentrated solely on banking. In 1763 the Edinburgh firm was reconstituted as John Coutts & Co, its partners being Forbes, Hunter, Robert

214 British banking – a guide to historical records

Herries and John Stephen. In 1773 the firm was renamed Sir William Forbes, James Hunter & Co. Its balance sheet total rose steadily, from £39,800 in 1754, to £58,350 in 1764 and to £84,600 in 1772. From 1782 the firm issued notes. Following the death of Forbes in 1806, his son William succeeded him as senior partner; he died in 1828. In 1838 the firm formed an alliance with the Glasgow Union Banking Co (est. 1830); they merged in 1843 when the Glasgow Union Bank changed its name to the Union Bank of Scotland. The Edinburgh business was carried on by a new Edinburgh head office.

William Forbes, *Memoirs of a Banking House* (London & Edinburgh, 1860); A MacKenzie, 'Sir William Forbes Bt. of Pitsligo', *Scottish Bankers' Magazine*, 43 (1953)

Records: Bank of Scotland Archive, Operational Services Division, 12 Bankhead Terrace, Sighthill, Edinburgh EH11 4DY

Miscellaneous legal and business papers 1778–1840; agreements with Bank of Scotland 1790–1805; papers re affairs of Logan of Castlemains and others 1792–1837; balance sheets etc 1793–96; papers re several English companies and sequestrations 1798–1817; papers re exchanges 1805; papers on death of Sir William Forbes 1806; papers re property tax 1807–14; notebooks re bank note paper 1807–08; papers re revenue remittances 1809–19; miscellaneous states and balances 1811–19; government stock dividend receipts and notebook 1813–17; states of bank notes 1814–45; bond of caution by King Charles X of France and related papers 1832; balance sheet 1838.

FORDHAM, GIBSON & CO
Royston, Hertfordshire

History: This private bank was established in Royston in 1808 as Fordham, Flower & Fordham; it was also known as the Royston Bank. Its founders were brewers and woolstaplers. It was styled John Fordham & Co from 1825 and Fordham, Gibson & Co from 1883. Sub-branches were opened at Cambridge (1880) and Buntingford (1890). In 1896, when its balance sheet totalled over £663,000, it joined with other banks to form Barclay & Co Ltd.

P W Matthews & Anthony W Tuke, *History of Barclays Bank Ltd* (London, 1926); Jack Parker, *Nothing for Nothing for Nobody* (Stevenage, 1986)

Records: Barclays Bank plc, Group Archives, Dallimore Road, Wythenshawe, Manchester M23 9JA

Records of banks **215**

Share receipts, local gas and railway companies 1848–66; cheques 1868, 1895; cheque form 1860s; private account ledgers (4) 1878–96; partnership agreements 1879–83; solicitor's bill of charges 1883; security returns 1883–91; balance sheets 1883–96; banker's licence 1887; amalgamation papers re Barclay & Co Ltd 1896–1902.

FOSTER & CO
Cambridge, Cambridgeshire

History: This private bank was formed in 1804 by the Foster family of corn millers (whose milling business continued until 1915). Its first name was Foster & Foster and it was called Foster & Co from 1904; it was also known as the Cambridge & Cambridgeshire Bank. Many customers were drawn from the local agricultural industry. By 1904 branches existed at St Ives (1830), St Neots (1830), Royston (1834), Ely (1835), Newmarket (1844), Bishop's Stortford (1874), Littleport (1889), Saffron Walden (1901) and Wisbech; a sub-branch was at Royston. The Capital & Counties Bank Ltd (est. 1877) acquired the bank in 1904.

Harold Preston, *Early East Anglian Banks and Bankers* (Thetford, 1994)

Records: Lloyds TSB Group plc, Archives, Head Office, 71 Lombard Street, London EC3P 3BS

Customer ledger 1813–22; amalgamation papers 1903–05.

Bishop's Stortford: security register c.1886–1903; **Cambridge:** signature books (3) 1860–99; **Ely:** letterbooks (2) 1841–74.

THOMAS FOWLE
London

History: Thomas Fowle (1637–92) was apprenticed to London goldsmith James Pewte (Pute) from 1652 to 1660. By 1664 he traded as a goldsmith-banker at the sign of the Black Lion, Fleet Street, City of London, selling jewellery and plate and offering a range of financial services including clearing and drawing accounts and the provision of loans on the security of notes, bonds, mortgages and pawns. His banking activities grew significantly during the 1670s and by 1689 he received over £3,000 in loan interest annually. He was knighted in 1686 and was Prime Warden of the Goldsmiths' Company in 1687. After Fowle's death in 1692, his business was continued as a partnership between his nephew, Robert Fowle, and a former apprentice, Thomas Wotton.

D M Mitchell, 'Mr Fowle Pray Pay the Washwoman. The Trade of a London Goldsmith-Banker, 1660–1692', *Business and Economic History*, 23 (1994)

216 **British banking – a guide to historical records**

Records: Public Record Office, Ruskin Avenue, Kew, Richmond TW9 4DU

Partnership agreement 1692; day book 1664–67; personal notebook including customer balances 1674–92; goldsmith notes, letters, bonds and legal documents, 1660–c.1710. [Ref: PRO C104/108; C114/179; C104/120; C104/107–8; C104/112; C104/115; C104/117–125]

FOX, FOWLER & CO
Wellington, Somerset

History: This important private bank traced its origins to Thomas Fox who in 1772 was a partner in the Wellington woollen firm of Were & Sons. In 1782 he married the daughter of a partner in the London bankers, Smith, Wright & Gray, and in 1787 established the firm of Fox & Co, bankers and woollen merchants; the two functions were not entirely separated until the 1870s. In 1879 the business was renamed Fox Bros, Fowler & Co and was later known as Fox, Fowler & Co. From the 1870s the business expanded rapidly with branches being opened in Somerset and Devon, especially from 1878 following the failure of the West of England & South Wales District Bank Ltd (est. 1834). Full branches included those at Wellington (1787); Tavistock (1791); Launceston (1832); Holsworthy (1875); Bridgwater (1878); Weston super Mare (1878); Torrington (1879); Taunton (1879); South Molton (1879); Ilfracombe (1879); Bideford (1879); Barnstaple (1880); Crediton (1881); Minehead (1884); Exeter (1885); Tiverton (1890); Lynton (1890); Okehampton (1908); Langport (1913); Honiton (1919) and Dulverton. Two private banks were acquired, Marshall, Harding & Hiern (est. 1791) of Barnstaple in 1888 and Gill, Morshead & Co (est. 1791) of Tavistock in 1889. Howard Lloyd, a senior director of Lloyds Bank, whose sister had married into the Fox family, advised on the late-nineteenth century expansion. In 1921, when the bank had deposits of £3.5 million and fifty-five branches or sub-branches, it was acquired by Lloyds Bank Ltd (est. 1765). It was the last private country bank to issue notes.

Hubert Fox, *Quaker Homespun. The Life of Thomas Fox of Wellington, Sergemaker and Banker 1747–1821* (London, 1958); R S Sayers, *Lloyds Bank in the History of English Banking* (Oxford, 1957)

Records: Lloyds TSB Group plc, Archives, Head Office, 71 Lombard Street, London EC3P 3BS

Note register 1824–1921; balance sheets 1920, 1922; branch balance sheets 1921; amalgamation papers 1921–25.

Records of banks 217

Bridgewater: memorandum books (3) 1905–21; **Taunton:** memorandum book 1886–1906; **Tavistock:** security books (3) 1889–1922; signature book c.1889–1925; memorandum book c.1908–24.

R & W F FRYER
Wolverhampton, West Midlands

History: This private bank was formed in 1807 by Richard Fryer, an innkeeper. An anecdotal account of its foundation relates how Fryer discovered a chest of gold coins that had been hidden at his inn during the 1745 Jacobite Rising, which provided the capital of his bank. The bank had major interests in iron and coal businesses at Hatherton near Cannock Chase. It was small, yet sound and profitable, and was acquired by Lloyds Banking Co Ltd (est. 1765) for £20,000 in 1872.

Howard Lloyd, *Notes and Reminiscences of Lloyds Bank 1862 to 1892* (unpub. mss., 1917)

Records: Lloyds TSB Group plc, Archives, Head Office, 71 Lombard Street, London EC3P 3BS

Amalgamation papers 1865–72.

FRYER, ANDREWS & CO
Wimborne, Dorset

History: This private bank was established in about 1790 as William Fryer, Edwin Andrews, John Fryer & W R Fryer; it was also known as the Wimborne, Poole & Blandford Bank. It was subsequently styled Fryer, Andrews & Co and also the Dorset Bank. It was connected with banks of the same name at Poole (est. by 1820) and Ringwood (est. by 1820); there may also have been representation at Blandford. It was acquired by National Provincial Bank of England (est. 1833) in 1840.

Records 1: The Royal Bank of Scotland plc, Archive Section, Regent's House, 42 Islington High Street, London N1 8XL

Extracts from W Fryer's letterbook 1811–28; circulars re take over 1841.

Records 2: Dorset Record Office, Bridport Road, Dorchester DT1 1RP

Agreement re assignment of business to National Provincial Bank with list of customers 1841. [Ref: D1/JT1]

FULLER, BANBURY, NIX & CO
London

218   *British banking – a guide to historical records*

History: This private bank was established in 1737 as Atkins, Honeywood & Fuller of Lombard Street, City of London. It was known as Honeywood & Fuller in 1746; as Honeywood, Fuller & Cope in 1754; as Fuller & Cope in about 1761; as Fuller, Blake & Halford in about 1770; as Fuller, Halford & Vaughan in 1774; as Fuller, Son, Halford & Vaughan in 1778; as Richard Fuller, Sons & Vaughan in 1781; as Richard Fuller, George Fuller & Co in 1805; and as Fullers & Co in about 1827. In 1859 the firm merged with Sapte, Muspratt, Banbury & Co (est. 1787) of Lombard Street to form Fuller, Banbury, Nix & Mathieson. In 1881 the firm's title changed to Fuller, Banbury, Nix & Co. In 1891 it was acquired by Parr's Banking Co Ltd (est. 1865) which thereby obtained membership of the London Clearing House.

F G Hilton Price, *A Handbook of London Bankers* (London, 1876); William Howarth, *Somme Olde Curiosities by a Knight offe ye Quille* (London, 1890)

Records: The Royal Bank of Scotland plc, Archive Section, Regent's House, 42 Islington High Street, London N1 8XL

Papers re loans 1806–57; papers re securities for loans 1834–91; papers re investments 1861–93; papers re G Banbury's account 1862–77; amalgamation agreement 1883; winding-up account book 1895.

GARFIT, CLAYPON & CO
Boston, Lincolnshire

History: This private bank traced its origins to a corn merchant business formed in 1754. Branches included those at Louth (1754), Horncastle (1819), Spalding (1822), Spilsby (1859), Skegness (1881), Alford (1887), Wainfleet (1889) and Lincoln (1890). Capital & Counties Bank Ltd (est. 1877) acquired the business in 1891.

Records 1: Lloyds TSB Group plc, Archives, Head Office, 71 Lombard Street, London EC3P 3BS

Private cash books (2) 1791–92; cash book 1791–98; general ledgers (2) 1808–14 [w]; partnership agreement 1814; amalgamation papers 1891–92.

Alford: security register c.1883–93; **Boston:** security register 1877–91; **Louth:** signature books (2) c.1863–91; **Spilsby:** security book 1878–83.

Records 2: Spalding Gentlemen's Society, The Museum, Broad Street, Spalding PE11 1TB

Notebook of Spalding agent c.1791–93.

Records of banks

GENERAL CREDIT & DISCOUNT CO OF LONDON LTD
London

History: This discount house traced its origins to the General Credit & Finance Co of London Ltd, established in the City of London in 1863 with a paid-up capital of £1 million; its business was very substantial. It had many French shareholders and a board of directors was located in Paris as well as in London. The business acted, *inter alia*, as an issuing house specialising in bond issues for overseas governments, in which it worked closely with the Société Générale, and it also financed railway construction. Following the 1866 Overend Gurney crisis, it was placed in voluntary liquidation, as many of its funds were locked up in railways. The business was acquired by the newly-established General Credit & Discount Co of London Ltd whose directors included leading financiers such as Sir Edward Blount and Sir Henry Wolff. The company specialised in bill business, but it diversified into railway finance which created difficulties in the late 1870s, leading to merger in 1885 with the United Discount Corporation Ltd (est. 1867) to form the Union Discount Co of London Ltd.

George and Pamela Cleaver, *The Union Discount. A Centenary Album* (priv. pub., 1985)

Records: Union plc, 39 Cornhill, London EC3V 3NU

Directors' meeting minutes 1866–80; annual reports 1867–84.

GERRARD & KING LTD
London

History: This discount house was established in the City of London in 1870 as Gerrard & Middleton, under the leadership of W D Gerrard. It was renamed Gerrard & Co in 1874 and Gerrard & Reid in 1892, following the admission to the partnership of Sandeman Reid, son of a Northumberland engineer. The business operated on a small scale but it expanded following its merger with Tallack & Co (est. 1932) in 1934. In 1946 a partner left to form Clive Discount Co Ltd. Prior to the Second World War, Gerrards was a bill broker but thereafter it became a fully-fledged discount house. It acquired limited liability in 1948 and in 1958 Minster Trust Ltd acquired a substantial interest when capital was increased to £500,000. Minster soon withdrew and the business expanded under K H Whitaker's management. Capital was increased to over £1 million in 1959 and discount facilities were made available at the Bank of England for the first time. The business was converted to a public company in 1962, in 1969 it acquired the City's second largest discount house, National Discount Co Ltd (est. 1856), and in 1970 it was renamed Gerrard

220 *British banking – a guide to historical records*

& National Discount Co Ltd. The business was later known as Gerrard & National Ltd and in 1997 merged with King & Shaxson Ltd (est. 1886) to form Gerrard & King Ltd.

Records: Gerrard & National Holdings plc, 32 Lombard Street, London EC3V 9BE

General ledgers (2) 1874–c.1930; office tenancy agreements 1875–1954; partnership agreements 1882–1937; brokerage account book 1909–32; 'jobbing' account book 1938–45; day book showing general payments and receipts 1940–45; audited accounts 1948–55; register of members 1948–59; seal register 1948–c.1960; daily balance books (2) 1955–70; papers re Minster Trust 1957–58; dividend account books 1957–80; day book re stock purchases 1960–66.

ANTONY GIBBS & SONS LTD
London, Liverpool, Latin America and Australia

History: This merchant bank, based in the City of London, traced its origins to Antony Gibbs (died 1815), merchant of Exeter and London. Gibbs set up a business in 1778 that failed in 1789. He then went to Madrid to act as agent for British manufacturers and exported Spanish goods. He moved to Lisbon in 1797 and to Cadiz in 1802 and then established Antony Gibbs & Son in London in 1808, initially acting as a 'commissioner for dealing with Portuguese property sent to England in the war'; the name changed to Antony Gibbs & Sons in 1813. Also in 1808, a sister house, Anthony (sic) Gibbs Son & Branscombe, was established at Cadiz, and Gibbs, Casson & Co of Gibraltar followed in 1818 but closed in 1833. The business was largely focused on Latin America, and further branches opened at Lima in 1822 and Valparaiso in 1826, followed by several others. In Peru, Bolivia and especially Chile, Gibbs became leaders in the production and marketing of nitrate and nitrate of soda, working closely with local governments, and this became Gibbs' major activity. Its business expanded in other directions in the closing years of the century to embrace issues of fixed interest debt for sovereign and business clients from 1887; private banking, especially for Spanish and Latin American clients, including the King of Spain; and acceptance finance, especially for Latin American clients. In the late nineteenth century further houses were opened, *inter alia*, in Australia and at Liverpool and Bristol. Much of this expansion took place under the leadership of Henry Gibbs, later 1st Lord Aldenham. The collapse in the nitrate trade after 1918 injured Gibbs and its nitrate interests were hived off into a separate entity, which was subsequently nationalised. The firm fell back on its other businesses and diversified them from Latin America. They now included insurance broking

Records of banks

and a significant business trading in timber, especially that produced in Australia. Shortly after the Second World War, the different partnerships in London, North and South America and Australia were reorganised and transferred to limited liability companies, the London company being known as Antony Gibbs & Sons Ltd. In 1972, when Gibbs was still controlled by its founding family, the Hongkong & Shanghai Banking Corporation (est. 1865) acquired a 20 per cent interest in the firm. In 1980 this bank acquired full ownership but the profitability of Gibbs was disappointing. In 1982 its activities were merged with those of other parts of the Hongkong & Shanghai Banking Corporation and the name of Antony Gibbs & Sons ceased to be widely used.

J A Gibbs, *The History of Antony & Dorothea Gibbs* (priv. pub., 1922); Wilfred Maude, *Antony Gibbs & Sons Ltd, Merchants and Bankers 1808–1958* (priv. pub., 1958)

Records: Guildhall Library, Aldermanbury, London EC2P 2EJ

Gibbs family papers 1744–1905; London ledgers (3) 1809–14; register of bills payable and receivable 1809–14; London journals (2) 1813–19; general ledgers (61) 1815–1918 [w]; extracts from letters re Guano business 1840–56; out-letterbooks of H H Gibbs (5) 1845–88; Guano ledgers (5) 1850–66, 1882–83; papers re partnership matters 1852–75; in-letterbook of W Gibbs 1854–55; information books re clients etc (3) 1859–1905; out-letterbooks of G L M Gibbs (5) 1863–81; papers re Gibbs' Ceylon estates 1865–96; South American manager's letters re nitrate 1872–99; out-letterbook of A G H Gibbs 1874–1936; papers re Guano cargoes 1879–80; scrapbook of deposit letters 1880–1910; papers re iodine industry c.1880–1954; special out-letterbooks (2) 1881–1922; West India ledgers (2) 1882–1909; balance books (2) 1882–1925; private letters to partners books (5) 1884–1919; out-letterbooks of F A Keating (5) 1884–1911; general private out-letterbooks re Greek loans (4) 1888–1901; London private accounts of West Coast partners and managers 1889–1910; private journal 1891–1929; scrapbook re issues and company reports 1891–1904; deposit account register 1895–1908; correspondence of J I Smail 1896–97; public loans accounts ledger 1896–1914; scrapbook of deposit agreements 1896–1918; papers re American copper mines 1897–1905; copy out-letterbooks to South America (3) 1897–1936; papers re sale of warships to Japan and UK 1903–05; commission ledgers (4) 1904–18; dividend department out-letterbook 1907–17; general out-letterbooks (6) 1907–34; general private-out-letterbooks to South America (4) 1910–19; South American branches powers of attorney 1910–25; general out-letterbook re Australian branches 1911–30; out-letterbook of G H B Gibbs 1911–34; general private out-letterbooks re North American business (2) 1912–31; chartering

222 British banking – a guide to historical records

ledgers (2) 1913–30; general private out-letterbook re Mexican loans 1914–28; letters from Australian partners 1918–20; papers re Chilean nitrate of soda sales 1918–28; commission ledger, South America 1919–23; partners' and special West Coast letters to/from London 1921–54; consignment ledger 1927–36; 'small trading account ledger' 1928–30; registers of bills receivable and payable (2) 1936–41; directors' meeting minutes 1946–63.

Arequipa: accounts 1819–72; private letters to London 1873–79; **Australian branches:** letters from V Gibbs to London 1873; private letterbooks (12) 1910–13; annual accounts 1881–1924; general private out-letterbook 1911–30; **Bristol:** sales day book 1775–1875; partnership agreements and papers 1839–72; partnership accounts 1844–80; annual accounts 1881–1909; **Concepcion:** accounts 1938–39; **Guayaquil:** accounts 1819–39; **Iquique:** private letters to London re fire insurance 1873, 1877; private letters to London books (4) 1878–81; annual accounts 1882–1909; **Lima:** annual accounts 1819–72; private ledgers and journals (2) 1843–75; private letters to Valparaiso 1873–79; letterbooks (3) 1912–20; **Liverpool:** papers re Jamaican plantations 1828–54; rough cash book 1827–28; private ledgers (3) 1833–1903; partnership agreements and papers 1839–72; papers re ships 1839–63; current account ledger re North American customers 1839–41; commodity information book 1853–90; private journal 1871–82; clerks' book 1881–1909; reports on standing of merchants 1884–1908; papers re closure of Liverpool house 1908–09; **Melbourne:** papers re sheep farming 1883–87; letterbook 1897–98; papers re New Zealand Exploration Co 1897–98; **New York:** journal 1913–20; ledger 1913–20; annual accounts 1913–28; **Santiago:** private ledger and journal (2) 1911–39; letters to London 1941–69; **South American branches:** annual accounts 1910–24; **Tacna:** annual accounts 1847–71; **Tarapaca:** private letters to Lima 1873–79; **Valparaiso:** annual accounts 1819–72, 1882–1909, 1938–39; private ledger and journal 1847–66; private letterbooks London to Valparaiso (83) 1852–66 1875–1913; private letters to Lima 1873–79; private letters to Tarapaca 1873–79; private letters to London books (31) 1876–1933; private letters to/from London, 1919–52. [Ref: MS11021–96, 11107–400, 11467–74, 16869–904, 19862–89]

GIBSON & WILSON
Kirkby Lonsdale, Cumbria

History: This private bank was established in about 1810 as Joseph Gibson, William Gibson, Warwick Pearson & Edward Wilson; it was also known as the Lonsdale Bank. It was later known as Gibson & Wilson and in about 1843 it was acquired by the Lancaster Banking Co (est. 1826).

Records of banks 223

Records: The Royal Bank of Scotland plc, Archive Section, Regent's House, 42 Islington High Street, London N1 8XL

Declaration of confidence 1825; stock order contract notes 1825–42; amalgamation notice 1843.

Kirkby Lonsdale: John Allen's cash book 1809–24.

GILES & CO
Rochford, Essex

History: This private bank was established in 1828 by James Giles, formerly manager of William Jackson's bank at Rochford, under the title of Giles & Co. It was acquired by Sparrow, Tufnell & Co (est. 1801) of Chelmsford in 1853.

P W Matthews & Anthony W Tuke, *History of Barclays Bank Ltd* (London, 1926)

Records: Barclays Bank plc, Group Archives, Dallimore Road, Wythenshawe, Manchester M23 9JA

Current account ledgers 1847–49; general transactions journal 1848–49.

GILLETT & CO
Banbury & Oxford, Oxfordshire

History: This private bank was established in 1784 as Bignell, Heydon & Watt and was also known as Banbury New Bank. It was styled Heydon & Watt from 1797 and subsequently as Heydon, Watt & Heydon. The Heydon family were mercers and the Bignell family were solicitors. In 1819 the bank was acquired by Richard and Charles Tawney trading as R & C Tawney and, from 1825, as Gillett & Tawney or otherwise as the Banbury Bank. The bank was forced to close briefly during the panic of 1825, but it reopened with the support of a number of influential customers. It was subsequently styled Gillett, Tawney & Gillett; J C & A Gillett & Co; and, from 1894, as Gillett & Co. By 1876 a branch at Woodstock, a sub-branch at Brackley and market day agencies at Heyford, Witney and Steeple Aston operated. In 1877 two members of the Gillett family opened a connected firm in Oxford and also joined the partnership of J W Clinch & Sons (est. 1807) of Witney, which was later renamed Gilletts & Clinch. There was also a connection with the London discount house, later known as Gillett Brothers Discount Co Ltd (est. 1867). In 1919 Barclays Bank Ltd (est. 1896) acquired the bank. It then had principal offices in Banbury and Oxford; branches at Abingdon, Brackley, Chipping Norton, East Oxford, Summertown, Witney and Woodstock; an agency at Charlbury; and

224   *British banking – a guide to historical records*

sub-branches at Bamford, Byfield, Deddington, Didcot, Eynsham and Woodford.

P W Matthews & Anthony W Tuke, *History of Barclays Bank Ltd* (London, 1926); R S Sayers, *Gillets in the London Money Market 1867–1967* (Oxford, 1968); Audrey M Taylor, *Gilletts, Bankers at Banbury and Oxford* (Oxford, 1964); John Thomson, *Arthur B Gillett 1875–1954. Memories from Some of his Friends* (Gloucester, 1954)

Records 1: Barclays Bank plc, Group Archives, Dallimore Road, Wythenshawe, Manchester M23 9JA

Accounts and other papers of R C Tawney 1804–37; correspondence and other papers 1815–1928; cheques, drafts, orders and receipts 1818–c.1910; in-letters 1819–22; bank note ledger 1819–24; general ledgers (2) 1819–27; current account ledgers (4) 1819–27, 1838–46; private ledgers (3) 1819–27, 1858–94; remittance notes, London agent 1820–23; cheques and bank notes 1820–1921; partners' papers 1821–1910; letterbooks (2) 1821–27, 1914–19; safe book 1822–25; notice re reopening of Banbury Bank 1823; unidentified account 1823; passbook 1824–34; account of crisis 1825; out-letter 1826; prospectuses, banker's licences, circulars, articles of agreement and other papers 1828–1902; day book, Joseph Gillett 1834–45; ledger, Banbury Bank 1838–46; customer account cards, list and balances schedule 1840; interest ledger 1840–86; will probate, Henry Tawney 1845; balance book 1846–55; papers of A R Tawney 1847–51; papers of Charles Gillett 1848–78; Inland Revenue residuary account, J A Gillett 1853; customer balances 1853; ledgers, Charles Gillett (4) 1855–95; staff record cards 1855–1919; cash book, Martha Gillett 1857–82; papers re establishment of country bankers' clearing house 1858–90; partnership agreements 1867–1904; salary receipt books 1869–1909; partners' ledger 1895–1932; unclaimed balances schedules 1900–28; notes on bank history 1900–59; ledgers, J A Gillett (2) 1904–17; papers re merger with Barclay & Co 1904–47; banker's licences 1911; balance sheets 1911–18; papers re securities for an advance 1911–30.

Records 2: Oxfordshire Archives, County Hall, New Road, Oxford OX1 1ND

Gillett family papers: 1846–93, estate 1795–1945, debts 1819–96, treasurership of local authority 1838–1921, securities for loans 1847–88. [Ref: Gil]

GILLETT BROTHERS DISCOUNT CO LTD
London

History: This City of London discount house was formed as a partnership in 1867 by members of the Gillett family, bankers at Banbury, Oxfordshire. Known as Gillett Brothers & Co, bill brokers and money dealers, its first partners were George and Alfred Gillett who benefited from the connections and capital of their younger brother William who earlier had been in partnership in the successful London-based bill discounting business of Brightwen, Gillett & Co. The initial capital was £50,000, much of which was lent by William. In 1873 an abortive attempt was made to transfer the business to a publicly-owned joint stock company, The Bankers' Discount Association Ltd, but it reverted quickly to partnership status. The firm expanded and its assets in the 1880s totalled about £2 million. In 1894 the business passed to a new generation of partners and in 1919 converted to a private limited company, Gillett Brothers Discount Co Ltd, with a capital of £100,000. During the First World War, treasury bills became the most important instruments in which the firm dealt and between the wars bonds also became significant. In 1942 Hohler & Co (est. 1820) was acquired, increasing the balance sheet total from £14 million to £24 million, and in 1946 the business converted to a public company. In 1983 Gilletts merged with the discount house of Jessel Toynbee plc (est. 1922) to form Jessel, Toynbee & Gillett plc.

R S Sayers, *Gilletts in the London Money Market 1867–1967* (Oxford, 1968)

Records 1: Guildhall Library, Aldermanbury, London EC2P 2EJ

Circulars re establishment and re Brightwen Gillett & Co 1864,1867; premises papers 1867–1964; papers re Bankers' Discount Association Ltd 1873, 1894, c.1965; calculations and statistics re business 1873–1965; weekly account balances 1875–1929; private ledgers (9) 1887–1923; 'tenders and bank returns' with details of bids at auction re government bills etc 1889–99; analysis etc of bill portfolio 1892–1917; partnership agreement 1894; papers re staff including analysis 1898–c.1965; papers re partnership and corporate matters 1902–58, 1965; private cash book 1904–17; balance sheets 1909–46; essays/articles/lectures re discount banking 1917, 1949–61; account of City financial arrangements in 1914 c.1920; calculations re profitability 1904–20; crisis expenses and income tax account book 1919–21; papers of Sir George Gillett re Gilletts' history 1936; account of history of London money market by Sir George Gillett 1938; papers re Gillett family etc 1939–40; papers re acquisition of Hohler & Co c.1942; memorandum and articles of association 1946; report on interview with Margaret Gillett and related papers 1957; papers re Alfred Gillett's will (died 1894) c.1965. [Ref: MS 24679–24704]

226   *British banking – a guide to historical records*

Records 2: Alexanders Discount plc, Broadwalk House, 5 Appold Street, London EC2A 2DA

Agreements 1919–25; share registers (3) 1919–c.1933; directors' meeting minute books (4) 1919–77; balance sheets and related papers 1920–32; memorandum and articles of association 1927; pension fund papers 1928 on; private ledger c.1946–54; board meeting agenda 1948–63; papers re writing of official history 1957–1960s.

GILLETTS & CLINCH
Witney, Oxfordshire

History: This private bank was established in 1807 as John Clinch & Co; it was also known as the Witney Bank. It was subsequently styled Jno. Wms. Clinch, Jas. Clinch junr. & Wm.Clinch and, from about 1877, as Gilletts & Clinch when two members of this family of Banbury bankers joined the partnership. It was acquired by Gillett & Co (est. 1784) of Banbury in 1891.

P W Matthews & Anthony W Tuke, *History of Barclays Bank Ltd* (London, 1926); Audrey M Taylor, *Gilletts. Bankers at Banbury and* Oxford (Oxford, 1964)

Records: Barclays Bank plc, Group Archives, Dallimore Road, Wythenshawe, Manchester M23 9JA

Ledger, accounts of John Clinch and Henry Salmon 1803–25; cheques and cheque forms 1819–50, 1890s.

GILL, MORSHEAD & CO
Tavistock, Devon

History: This private bank was formed at Tavistock in 1791 as Gill & Rundle, the Gill family being operators of woollen mills and an iron foundry. From 1817 it was known as Gill, Rundle & Co and as Gill, Morshead & Co from 1875; it was otherwise known as the Tavistock Bank. Branches were opened at Launceston (1832) and later at Morwellham while there were agencies at Calstock (1879) and at Gunnislake and Holsworthy (1885). Fox Bros, Fowler & Co (est. 1787) acquired the business in 1889.

Records: Lloyds TSB Group plc, Archives, Head Office, 71 Lombard Street, London EC3P 3BS

Customer ledger 1822–24.

Records of banks

GLAMORGANSHIRE BANKING CO LTD
Swansea, West Glamorgan

History: This joint stock bank was formed in 1836 to acquire the private banks of Williams & Rowland (est. 1821) of Neath and Eaton & Co (est. 1809) of Swansea. In 1841 it acquired Walters, Voss & Walters (est. 1821) of Swansea. Branches were established at Aberavon (1861); Morriston, Swansea (1873); Pontardawe (1873); Pontarddulais (1877); Briton Ferry (1889); Clydach, Swansea (1889); Pontypridd (1890); Ammanford (1891); and Llanelli (1893). The business acquired limited liability in 1882 and was acquired by Capital & Counties Bank Ltd (est. 1877) in 1898.

R S Sayers, *Lloyds Bank in the History of English Banking* (Oxford, 1957)

Records: Lloyds TSB Group plc, Archives, Head Office, 71 Lombard Street, London EC3P 3BS

Deed of settlement with supplements 1836–77; directors' meeting minute books (7) 1836–84; private letterbook 1871–75; monthly balance books (3) 1877–85; rough minute books (2) 1878–84; managing director's diaries (3) 1880–83; monthly balance sheets 1886; amalgamation papers 1898, 1920.

GLASGOW & SHIP BANK
Glasgow, Strathclyde

History: This bank was formed in 1836 through merger of the Ship Bank (est. 1749) and the Glasgow Bank Co (est. 1809). The four remaining partners of the Ship Bank and all except three of the twenty-seven partners of the Glasgow Bank Co became partners in the new co-partnery. In 1843, when the bank was in decline, the result of fraud and lock up of its resources, it was acquired by Glasgow Union Banking Co (est. 1830).

Records 1: Bank of Scotland Archive, Operational Services Division, 12 Bankhead Terrace, Sighthill, Edinburgh EH11 4DY

Private ledger 1836–50; ledgers 1837–44; deposit receipt registers 1838–43.

Glasgow, Trongate: ledger 1839–43.

Records 2: Business Records Centre, Archive Department, University of Glasgow, Glasgow G12 8QQ

Bill of exchange books 1809–45; miscellaneous papers re routine transactions 1834–44. [Ref: UGD 94]

228 British banking – a guide to historical records

GLASGOW ARMS BANK
Glasgow, Strathclyde

History: This co-partnery was formed in 1749 and was also known as Cochran, Murdoch & Co and, from 1763, as Spiers, Murdoch & Co; its rivals were the Ship Bank (est. 1749) and the Thistle Bank (est. 1761). Initially its partners comprised about thirty Glasgow merchants but the number declined to ten by 1772. The bank failed in 1793.

Records: Glasgow City Archives, Mitchell Library, North Street, Glasgow G3 7DN

Cashier's corroboration bond 1750; appointment of accountant 1751. [Ref: B10/15/6106; B10/15/6511]

GLASGOW BANK CO
Glasgow, Strathclyde

History: This private bank was established in 1809 by sixteen partners; it was the last of the private-partnership banks formed in Glasgow. The original partners had formed Dundee New Bank (est. 1802) with such success that the partners repeated the exercise through establishing Glasgow Bank Co. The principal partner was James Dennistoun and the cashier was William B Cabbell, formerly with Ransom, Morland & Co (est. 1782) of London. The capital was £200,000 in forty shares. A branch was established at Kirkcaldy. In 1818 a further seven partners joined the company in order to strengthen local connections with Glasgow in the face of strong competition from the new Glasgow agencies of The Royal Bank of Scotland and British Linen Bank. In 1837 the bank merged with the Ship Bank (est. 1749) to form the Glasgow & Ship Bank.

E Mathew, 'James Dennistoun of Golfhill', *Scottish Bankers' Magazine,* 49 (1958); Robert S Rait, *The History of the Union Bank of Scotland* (Glasgow, 1930)

Records 1: Bank of Scotland Archive, Operational Services Division, 12 Bankhead Terrace, Sighthill, Edinburgh EH11 4DY

Ledgers 1809–37; claim book 1829–43; protested bills register 1830–32; private ledger 1835–36.

Records 2: Business Records Centre, Archive Department, University of Glasgow, Glasgow G12 8QQ

Correspondence re routine transactions 1834–37. [Ref: UGD 108]

Records 3: National Archives of Scotland, HM General Register House, Princes Street, Edinburgh EH1 3YY

Records of banks

Statement of Earl of Rosslyn accounts and papers 1815–17 [Ref: GD164/1162]

GLASGOW JOINT STOCK BANK
Glasgow, Strathclyde

History: This bank, promoted by Andrew Tennent, the Scottish bank promoter, was formed in 1843 with a paid-up capital of £562,000. A year later it merged with the Edinburgh & Leith Bank (est. 1838) to form the Edinburgh & Glasgow Bank.

Records: Clydesdale Bank plc, Head Office, 30 St Vincent Place, Glasgow G1 2HL

Directors' meeting minutes 1840–44.

GLOUCESTER COUNTY & CITY BANK
Gloucester, Gloucestershire

History: This joint stock bank was formed in 1834 and was reorganised to form the County of Gloucester Banking Co in 1836.

Records 1: Gloucester Library, Local Studies Dept, Brunswick Road, Gloucester GL1 1HT

Deed of settlement 1834; analysis of deed of settlement 1835. [Ref: JV 13.6; JF 13.51]

Records 2: Lloyds TSB Group plc, Archives, Head Office, 71 Lombard Street, London EC3P 3BS

Deed of settlement 1835.

GLOUCESTERSHIRE BANKING CO LTD
Gloucester, Gloucestershire

History: This joint stock bank was formed in 1831. In the same year it acquired the private bank of Hartland & Co (est. 1809) of Tewkesbury which also had offices at Cheltenham and Evesham and an agency at Stroud. The senior partner of this bank, Nathaniel Hartland, was a leading manager in the Gloucestershire Banking Co and another important figure was Samuel Baker, a Bristol shipowner and merchant. Russell & Skey (est. 1809) of Gloucester was acquired in 1832; James Wood (est. 1716) of Gloucester in 1836; Cripps & Co (est. 1796) of Cirencester, with a branch at Stow, in 1842; J W R Hall (est. 1836) of Ross in 1858; and Webb & Co (est. 1790) of Ledbury in 1883. Later branches existed at Ledbury, Cirencester, Tewkesbury, Evesham, Stow, Cheltenham, Newnham, Stroud,

230   British banking – a guide to historical records

Ross, Lydney, Moreton in the Marsh, Coleford, Hereford, Newent, Monmouth, Redditch, Evesham and Abergavenny. Limited liability was acquired in 1873. In 1885 subscribed capital stood at £2 million. The bank merged with the Capital & Counties Bank Ltd (est. 1877) in 1886.

R S Sayers, *Lloyds Bank in the History of English Banking* (Oxford, 1957)

Records 1: Lloyds TSB Group plc, Archives, Head Office, 71 Lombard Street, London EC3P 3BS

Deed of settlement and supplements 1831–63; branch manager's rules 1831–86; directors' meeting minute books (6) 1836–86; weekly committee minute books (3) 1843–86 [w]; annual reports 1868–85; private ledger 1870–85; amalgamation papers 1883–86.

Gloucester: customer ledgers (2) 1845–52; comment book c.1846–69; notebooks re customers (6) 1848–56; profit and loss ledger 1878–80; **Redditch:** security register c.1878–1904; **Stroud:** security register c.1836–46.

Records 2: Gloucester Library, Local Studies Dept, Brunswick Road, Gloucester GL1 1HT

Draft deed of settlement 1831; annual reports 1836, 1851, 1884. [Ref: J13.1; JR13.1 (1–7)]

Records 3: Hereford & Worcester Record Office, St Helen's Branch, Fish Street, Worcester WR1 2HN

Receipts, accounts and vouchers c.1850s. [Ref: 705:66]

GLYN, MILLS & CO
London

History: Vere, Glyn & Hallifax was established in 1753 by Joseph Vere, Richard Glyn and Thomas Hallifax, and was based at 70 Lombard Street in the City of London. Its name changed to Glyn & Hallifax in 1766. Richard Glyn was Lord Mayor of London in 1758. The connection with the Mills family was forged in 1772 when support from William Mills allowed the bank to survive a severe financial crisis; its name was then changed to Hallifax, Mills, Glyn & Mitton. Thereafter it had several titles including Hallifax, Mills, Glyn, Mills & Mitton (1776), Hallifax, Glyn, Mills & Mitton (1782), Glyn, Mills & Mitton (1789), Glyn, Mills, Hallifax & Co (1796), Glyn, Mills, Hallifax, Glyn & Co (1808), Glyn, Hallifax, Mills & Co (1826) and Glyn, Mills & Co (1851). By 1800 the bank had moved to Birchin Lane. It prospered, developing a large business as Lon-

Records of banks 231

don agent for many of the growing number of provincial banks, providing banking facilities for more than 200 railway companies and, with Barings, handling the important Canadian financial agency. In 1841 Glyn's acquired Ladbroke & Co (est. 1736) and in 1864 also took over the substantial business of Curries & Co (est. 1773) when it became known as Glyn, Mills, Currie & Co. In 1885 the firm was the first private bank to publish a half-yearly balance sheet and then registered as a joint stock company under the title of Glyn, Mills, Currie & Co with paid-up capital and reserves totalling about £1.5 million. By 1890 the bank had established many international links and handled share issues for major companies at home and abroad. Glyns acquired Holt & Co (est. 1809) in 1923 when its name changed to Glyn, Mills, Currie, Holt & Co. Child & Co (est. c.1580s) was acquired in 1924 when the firm reverted to the name of Glyn, Mills & Co. A new head office building at 67 Lombard Street was completed in 1933. In 1939 Glyn's was acquired by The Royal Bank of Scotland (est. 1727), but thereafter continued to trade separately. During the war the bank evacuated to Osterley Park, home of the family of Lord Jersey. Although Glyns had been a founder member of the London Clearing House and provided private banking services, it had always offered some services more normally undertaken by merchant banks, for example issuing securities and operating investment and registrar departments. In 1962 a branch was opened in Millbank, London. In 1965 Glyn, Mills Finance Co was established to accept large, long-term deposits at competitive rates of interest. In 1970 The Royal Bank of Scotland rationalised its subsidiaries merging Glyn, Mills & Co and Williams Deacon's Bank to form Williams & Glyn Bank Ltd.

Roger Fulford, *Glyn's 1753–1953. Six Generations in Lombard Street* (London, 1953); Eric Gore Brown, *Glyn, Mills & Co* (priv. pub., 1933); William Howarth, *The Banks in the Clearing House* (London, 1905)

Records 1: The Royal Bank of Scotland plc, Archive Section, Regent's House, 42 Islington High Street, London N1 8XL

Solicitors' bills of charges 1754–1918; clerks' fidelity bonds 1754–99; bonds and share certificates 1771–1900; Christmas money books/lists 1772–1900; bills of exchange 1783–1886; papers of Glyn family trusts 1785–1900; inventory, Birchin Lane premises 1788; customer correspondence 1788–1900; correspondence with country banks 1794–1914; partnership agreements 1796–1879; bad debts book 1796–1821; fire insurance policies 1801–04; property papers, Change Alley 1803–36; salary receipt books 1810–46; clerks' salary books 1810–48; papers re railway and canal company shares 1819–1900; periodical return book 1819–1935; exchequer bills bought book 1819–61; box books c.1810s–1820s, 1890–

232 British banking – a guide to historical records

1900; town balance book 1822; cheques 1823–1860s; discount books 1824–27; clerk registers 1829–1900; cartoon portraits, staff and partners 1831–1940; correspondence re underwriting and registrarship 1833–1900; correspondence re Esdaile, Esdaile, Grenfell, Thomas & Co 1836–73; authorised signatures list 1838; applications for clerkships, lists and letters 1843–1850s; Bank of England returns 1844–1940; guarantee books 1846–1906; papers re Canadian customers and debentures 1847–73; letters of hypothecation 1850–1900; opinion book 1852–60; customer notebook and letterbook, B W Currie 1853–93; loans book 1854–55; railway company account details 1856–71; corresponding banks book 1859–1909; letterbooks: 1870–1941, P C Glyn 1862–69, G G Glyn 1863–66, discount office 1869–84, B W Currie 1870–93; papers re merger with Curries & Co 1864–67; collateral security book 1864–91; balances books: 1894–1925, weekly 1864–1941, annual 1868–1938, town office 1881–1941, country office 1929–37; staff admissions register and regulations 1865–1900; papers re Overend Gurney crisis 1866–67; expenses ledgers 1866–1934; investment ledgers 1867–1934; solicitors' charges book 1867–1945; plans, Lombard Street site c.1867–1930s; loans and discounts summary books 1868–1900; general information book 1870–1902; papers re alterations, Lombard Street 1872–79, 1890–95; foreign exchanges book 1873–1901; passbooks 1873–76; unpaid bills book 1876–1938; housekeeping books 1878–1914; dividend orders register 1879–1930; probate book 1880–1908; correspondence and specimens re bank note printing 1880–1930; cheques issued register 1881–1900; country banks results books 1881–1937; solicitors' correspondence 1884–1920; memorandum and articles of association 1885–1926, 1939; stock ledger 1885–94; general arrangements book 1886–1924; customer information book 1887–1900; title deeds, Lampton Hall 1887–1950; terms with customers books 1887–1900; *Glyn's Gleanings*, scrapbook 1888–1958; staff seniority lists c.1889–1900; annual reports, railway and transfer offices 1890–1936; premises photographs 1893–1950s; partners' dividend receipts 1895–1930; Gold Standard Defence Association papers 1895–1901; brokers' books, money at call 1895–1935; staff photographs c.1869–1960s; investment summary ledgers 1897–1943; accounts of ladies and titled persons books 1899; dividend orders books 1900–29; profit and loss books 1901–34; investment ledger 1901–04; interest in suspense books 1904–26; correspondence, A H Mills 1904–14; brokers' outstanding bills book 1909–39; interest rate book 1910–32; letters to bank from staff on active service 1915–18; discounts book 1918–27; statistics books 1919–36, 1950–67; circular notes, unused c.1920; papers re special cheques 1920–46; monthly statements of assets and liabilities 1921–41; monthly averages book 1921–42; board statistical reports 1923–35; certificates of incorporation and change of name 1923–63; papers re income tax 1924–34; papers re disposal of interest in British

Records of banks
233

Overseas Bank 1924; private ledger 1924–48; dividend notices book 1925–39; coin with cashiers book 1925–39; brokers' loans book 1928–40; papers re mechanisation 1932–1950s; papers re registrars 1934–52; general ledger 1935–38; transfers journal 1935–56; plate valuation 1937; papers re wartime staff employment 1938–40; papers re wartime procedures 1938–40; house club papers 1938–68; papers re acquisition by Royal Bank of Scotland 1939; papers re evacuation of Central Clearing House 1939–41; registers of directors 1938–69; agreements re Osterley Park 1939, 1951; printed reports and accounts 1939–64; inter-director correspondence 1940; staff association papers 1940–78; file re Holts branch Army and RAF agency 1942–43; papers re absorption of British Overseas Bank and Anglo International Bank 1944–45; staff assurance scheme minute book 1947–55; staff training papers 1948–70; press cuttings re bank 1948–64; chairman's daily conference summaries 1950–65; staff statistics 1950–67; staff newsletters 1954–70; advertising: album 1956–61, correspondence 1966–68; files re Glyn's future 1959–70; superannuation fund trust deed 1962; salaries committee minutes 1963–64; general management committee minutes 1964–69.

Records 2: Northumberland Record Office, Melton Park, North Gosforth, Newcastle upon Tyne NE3 5QX

Papers re financial difficulties 1772. [Ref: 2DE/36/2/1–88]

Records 3: National Archives of Canada, Ottawa 4, Ontario, Canada

Correspondence and papers re business with Canada 1837–93.

GODFREY & RIDDELL
Newark, Nottinghamshire

History: This private bank was established in 1801 as Welby, Godfrey & Lawrence. By 1811 its capital was £20,000. It was styled Godfrey & Hutton from 1815, Godfrey, Hutton & Godfrey from about 1826 and later Godfrey & Riddell. In 1880 it was acquired by Samuel Smith & Co (est. c.1663) of Nottingham.

Records: Nottinghamshire Archives, County House, Castle Meadow Road, Nottingham NG2 1AG

Papers re partnership dispute 1802–08. [Ref: CP5/6133–222]

GODWIN, MINCHIN & CO
Portsmouth, Hampshire

History: This private bank was formed in about 1797 as Griffiths, Chaldecott, Drew & Godwin. It was known as Godwin, Minchin, Carter &

234 *British banking – a guide to historical records*

Goldson from 1806 and as Godwin, Minchin & Carter from 1817; it also traded as the Portsmouth, Portsea & Hampshire Bank. It was connected with Griffiths, Chaldecott & Drew (est. 1783) of Chichester. It failed in 1819.

Records: Portsmouth City Record Office, 3 Museum Road, Portsmouth PO1 2LE

Counsel's opinion on liability of estate of deceased partner 1819. [Ref: 16A/19]

GOSCHENS & CUNLIFFE
London

History: This merchant bank traced its origins to German partners who set up in business in the City of London in 1814 as commission agents exporting colonial produce and cotton to Germany. Quickly it emerged as a major London house, although in the mid-nineteenth century it had a modest capital of £40,000. By 1849 it played a major role in financing Cuba's sugar trade, and in 1863 it was a founder member of the International Financial Society, formed to issue and invest in foreign securities. Subsequently Goschens were important in sponsoring and issuing securities of UK-based companies. In 1914 its founding membership of the Accepting Houses Committee confirmed the firm's prestigious status. In 1920 it amalgamated with Cunliffe Brothers (est. 1820) to form Goschens & Cunliffe. The business, which was badly weakened by default of German customers in the early 1930s, ceased to trade in 1940 when its business was transferred to Guinness Mahon (est. 1836).

Records: Guildhall Library, Aldermanbury, London EC2P 2ES

Out-letterbooks to agents, Eitzen & Co of Hamburg (2) 1903–08; out-letterbooks, chiefly to government re enemy debts (7) 1915–29; out-letterbook, to Clearing Office re enemy debts 1921–23; confidential out-letterbook 1926–36; register of open policies 1928–40; out-telegram books (2) 1938–41. [Ref: MS 11046, 11052–52D]

GOSLINGS AND SHARPE
London

History: This leading private bank was established in Fleet Street, City of London, by goldsmith banker Henry Pinckney who was at work in about 1650, trading at the sign of the Three Squirrels. It appears that the Chambers family then led the business and in the early-eighteenth century the Gosling family, in the form of Sir Francis Gosling, became connected; by 1750 the business was styled Gosling & Bennett. Thereafter the Gosling

Records of banks **235**

name predominated. In 1754 the firm was known as Gosling, Bennett & Gosling followed by Sir Francis Gosling, Gosling & Clive in 1763, Gosling & Clive in 1768, Gosling, Clive & Gosling in 1772, Robert & Francis Gosling in 1778, Robert, Francis & William Gosling in 1786 and then Goslings & Sharpe from 1794. The bank had a distinguished customer list including the aristocracy, clergy and leading figures such as Lord Clive, Warren Hastings, Alexander Pope and Sir Edwin Landseer. Customers also included Christian societies, newspapers and insurance companies. In 1896 the firm joined with a number of mostly private banks to form Barclay & Co Ltd.

F G Hilton Price, *A Handbook of London Bankers* (London, 1876); William Howarth, *Somme Olde Curiosities by a Knight offe ye Quille* (London, 1890); P W Matthews & Anthony W Tuke, *History of Barclays Bank Ltd* (London, 1926); Frank Melton, 'Robert and Sir Francis Gosling, Eighteenth Century Bankers and Stationers' in Robin Myers & Michael Harris (eds.) *Economics of the British Book Trade 1605–1939* (London, 1985)

Records: Barclays Bank plc, Group Archives, Dallimore Road, Wythenshawe, Manchester M23 9JA

Legal opinions 1702–1853; cheques 1714–1841; current account ledgers (712) 1717–1896, 1909–59; partnership agreements 1719–1896; letters from customers and others 1719–1896; profit and loss account ledger 1727–1845; bonds 1731,1777; letters to S Bennet, partner 1741–69; cash balance books 1742–1896; annuity 1755; insurances 1769–1867; property valuation, Fleet Street 1785; country bank account ledgers 1787–1834; promissory notes 1794–1859; passbooks 1795–1951; staff lists 1801–97; signature books 1806–96; inventory of fixtures 1830; property repair bill 1831; annuity ledger 1843–56; receipts for extra watching of premises by police 1854–1932; subscriptions to charities 1858–61; lawsuit papers 1874–79; clerk salary records 1874–96; papers re merger with Barclay & Co 1896–97; ledger re loans not taken over by Barclay & Co 1896–1910.

JOHN C GOTCH & SONS
Kettering, Northamptonshire

History: This private bank was formed in 1792 as Keep & Co. It failed in 1825 and resumed as John Cooper Gotch & Sons. It failed in 1857.

Records: Northamptonshire Record Office, Wootton Hall Park, Northampton NN4 8BC

Papers re Gotch family 1795–1865; banker's licences 1808–24; customer papers 1810–24; papers re proposed Bank Act 1815–18; partnership agree-

236   *British banking – a guide to historical records*

ment 1822; papers re bank's indebtedness 1825–57; historical notes n.d.
[Ref: GK691–928, 2001–2366]

GRAHAMSTOUN BANKING CO
History: Unknown.

Records: Glasgow City Archives, Mitchell Library, North Street, Glasgow G3 7DN

Legal papers 1806. [Ref: T-TH 7/15]

GRANT & MADDISON'S UNION BANKING CO LTD
Southampton, Hampshire

History: This joint stock bank was formed in 1888 through the amalgamation of Maddison, Atherley & Co (est. 1869) of Southampton and Grant, Gillman & Long (est. 1787) of Portsmouth. Initially branches operated at Southampton, Portsmouth High Street and Gosport; others were subsequently established at Commercial Road, Portsmouth (1888); Lyndhurst (1893); North End, Portsmouth (1897); and Avenue, Southampton (1900). In 1903 Lloyds Bank Ltd (est. 1765) acquired the business.

Records: Lloyds TSB Group plc, Archives, Head Office, 71 Lombard Street, London EC3P 3BS

Shareholders' register 1889–95; profit and loss accounts 1897–1903; amalgamation papers 1902–03.

Southampton: private ledger 1887–1903.

GRAY DAWES BANK LTD
London

History: Gray Dawes was established as a shipping and insurance agency in the City of London in 1865 and latterly became a merchant bank. Its fortunes were initially wedded to an interlocking network of international trading and shipping partnerships in which Sir William Mackinnon, of the powerful Indian and Far Eastern merchants, Mackinnon, Mackenzie & Co, and later the Inchcape family, were leaders; in 1958 the surviving businesses merged to form Inchcape & Co Ltd. Gray Dawes was the London 'end' of Mackinnon Mackenzie and of the other interlocking partnerships. Before 1900 Gray Dawes also acted as a confirming house which inevitably meant that banking services were provided to the businesses it represented. Its bills were accepted as bank bills and in 1915 it obtained recognition as a merchant bank for the purpose of sharing brokers' commissions and commission on new issues. When it converted to

Records of banks *237*

limited liability, in 1951, the Inchcape family was the sole owner. From 1958 it was fully owned by Inchcape & Co Ltd and in the late 1960s concentrated on banking. In 1971 the Bank of England granted it authorised bank status when it became a fully-fledged merchant bank. In 1980 it was renamed Gray Dawes Bank Ltd and in 1983 the Inchcape Group sold the business to Banque Arab & Internationale d'Investissement.

Percival Griffiths, *A History of the Inchcape Group* (priv. pub., 1977); Stephanie Jones, *Two Centuries of Trading. The Origins and Growth of the Inchcape Group* (London, 1986)

Records: Guildhall Library, Aldermanbury, London EC2P 2EJ

Family papers of A Gray 1854–1910; application letters re overseas postings 1868–84; cash journal 1869–77; mortgages, letters, etc, re advances 1872–90; partners' private ledgers (4) 1874–1952; powers of attorney 1874–95; papers re client trusteeships 1879–94; correspondence re Florida Land & Colonisation Co 1883–97; partnership agreements 1885–1939; letters re dispute of T M Russell's will 1891–98; letterbook 1892–1914; investment papers 1892–1965; out-letterbook re J B Gray's financial affairs 1894–1905; balance sheets and profit and loss accounts 1909–50; correspondence re advances made in East Africa 1916–38; papers re indebtedness of Smith Mackenzie to Gray Dawes 1918–41; partners' private memorandum file 1919–23; sports club minutes 1920–35; papers re Mesopotamia Persia Corporation 1920–37; private journals (2) 1920–52; investment schedules and correspondence 1921–56; papers re agency for British India Steam Navigation Co 1924–57; general ledgers (8) 1924–59 [w]; department profit and loss accounts 1927–30; papers re inward freight department 1920s–1930s; insurance department records 1920s–1950s; residue cash book 1935–43; papers re impact of Second World War 1938–45; journals (3) 1940–59; cash books (6) 1946–59 [w]; revenue and expenditure ledger 1951–55; memorandum and articles of association 1952, 1958; currency and record accounts ledger 1953–61; deposit and loan account ledger 1958–59; sundry accounts ledger 1958–73. [Ref: MS 27600–687]

GREENOCK BANKING CO
Greenock, Strathclyde

History: This bank was established in 1785 and was Greenock's first bank. It was never very successful and failed in 1842 when its business was acquired by the Western Bank of Scotland (est. 1832) of Glasgow.

Records: The Royal Bank of Scotland plc, Archive Section, 36 St Andrews Square, Edinburgh EH2 2YB

238 British banking – a guide to historical records

Journal 1786; state books, containing monthly financial abstracts (2) 1813–28.

GREENWAY, SMITH & GREENWAYS
Warwick, Warwickshire

History: This private bank was formed in 1791 as Whitehead, Weston & Co and served the farming industry. The Greenway family later owned the business when it was known as Kelynge, Greenway & Co and, from about 1869, as Greenway, Smith & Greenways; it was also styled the Warwick & Warwickshire Bank. It had links with Whitehead, Greenway, Lowe & Gillett of Shipston and of Stratford on Avon. A branch opened at Leamington in 1863. In 1887, when deposits were about £250,000, it failed following speculation and fraud by its partners. Its business was then acquired by Staffordshire Joint Stock Bank (est. 1864).

W F Crick & J E Wadsworth, *A Hundred Years of Joint Stock Banking* (London, 1936)

Records 1: HSBC Holdings plc, Group Archives, 10 Lower Thames Street, London EC3R 6AE

Agreement with Staffordshire Joint Stock Bank 1887.

Records 2: Warwickshire Record Office, Priory Park, Cape Road, Warwick CV34 4JS

Miscellaneous records 1743–1918; papers re liquidation 1887–89; *History of a Bank Smash* by J Lloyd Evans 1888. [Ref: CR556/1, 2, 896–965; CR1500/16/325; CR935/12]

Records 3: Leamington Spa Library, Avenue Road, Leamington Spa CV31 3PP

Programme of public demonstration n.d.; 'History of a Bank Smash' by J Lloyd Evans 1888.

GREGSON, PARKE & CLAY
Liverpool, Merseyside

History: This private bank was formed in the 1780s as William Gregson, Sons, Parke & Morland, William Gregson and Thomas Parke being long-established and leading Liverpool merchants and businessmen. The bank was also known as the Liverpool Bank and it held the accounts of Liverpool Corporation. The business was damaged by the financial difficulties of 1793 and, after a public expression of support, was reformed as William Gregson, Sons, Parke & Clay. This partnership continued until 1805 after

Records of banks 239

which the bank was continued by John Gregson and James Gregson, both sons of William (died 1800), and by Henry Clay under the title Gregson, Parke & Clay. John Gregson committed suicide in 1807 when the bank immediately ceased business. It subsequently met its liabilities in full.

John Hughes, *Liverpool Banks and Bankers 1760–1837* (Liverpool, 1906)

Records: Lancashire Record Office, Bow Lane, Preston PR1 8ND

Papers re winding up 1807–38. [Ref: DDCm/7/23–40 *inter alia*]

GRINDLAY BRANDTS LTD
London

History: This merchant bank traced its origins to Wilhelm Brandt (died 1832), an important Hamburg merchant who was based for most of his working life at Archangel, Russia, where he imported sugar and, *inter alia*, owned a sugar refinery and ships. In 1805 his brother, Emanuel Heinrich (died 1852), became London agent for the Archangel business and thereby established the Brandt family's London business. E H Brandt became London representative for other Archangel houses and in 1827 also for his brother's newly formed St Petersburg house. The London business was renamed Emanuel Henry Brandt's Son & Co from 1840 on E H Brandt's retirement. In 1841 a house was opened at Riga and in 1849 the family's Russian businesses were formed into two separate entities with the Archangel and Riga houses breaking away from the house at St Petersburg which in 1849 opened a branch at Hamburg. However the City of London business continued to serve both entities and was controlled by them. The London business was renamed E H Brandt's Son & Co in 1857 and Wm Brandt's Sons & Co in 1858 and at about this time, under the distinguished leadership of Augustus Brandt (died 1904), it became entirely independent of the family's Russian houses. It now expanded rapidly to become one of London's leading merchant banks, extending its accepting and agency services to, *inter alia*, Argentina, Germany and North America. In 1886 the Calcutta house of C Scholvin & Co was acquired but was closed in 1892. After 1918 the firm diversified into foreign exchange business and resumed its involvement in timber trading but was damaged by the German financial crisis of 1931. The business remained owned by a family partnership until 1952 when it was converted into a limited company, Wm Brandt's Sons & Co Ltd. In 1974 it became known as Brandts Ltd and in 1976 was acquired by Grindlays Bank Ltd and renamed Grindlay Brandts Ltd. Following the acquisition of Grindlays Bank plc by the Australia & New Zealand Banking Group in 1984, the business was renamed ANZ Merchant Bank Ltd in 1986. From 1989 it was known as ANZ McCaughan Merchant Bank Ltd.

240 *British banking – a guide to historical records*

C Amburger, *William Brandt and the Story of his Enterprise* (unpub mss., n.d.)

Records 1: Department of Manuscripts & Special Collections, Hallward Library, University of Nottingham, University Park, Nottingham NG7 2RD

Letters, shipping lists, bills, contracts 1810–18; trade circular books (45) 1829–1934; miscellaneous correspondence (business and family) 1833– c.1880; Russian letterbooks (4) 1914–16, 1922; Petrograd letterbooks (5) 1914–23; inland letterbooks (17) 1915–19.

Records 2: Archives Department, British Library of Political and Economic Science, London School of Economics, 10 Portugal Street, London WC2A 2HD

General ledgers (14) 1871–1903 [w]; Russian current account ledgers (48) 1876–1947; Eastern and inland current account ledgers (61) 1878–1947; continental inland current account ledgers (2) 1883–87; day books (2) 1901–16; private and trust account ledgers (22) 1905–26; H H Brandt and A P Brandt accounts (10) 1906–26; North American current account ledgers (26) 1912–47; South American current account ledgers (18) 1913–47; German current account ledgers (39) 1914–26; registers of bills accepted before due date 1914; general continental current account ledgers (17) 1914–47; Dutch current account ledgers (14) 1915–27; cash books (20) 1916–17; bills payable journals (2) 1919–24; nostro ledgers (19) 1921–47; foreign exchange inland current account ledgers (5) 1922–26; foreign exchange sterling account ledgers (8) 1922–47; timber account ledgers (2) 1923–26; Scandinavian current account ledgers (2) 1925–26; bills payable and receivable registers (47) twentieth cent; foreign exchange journals (6) twentieth cent; bills receivable and payable journals (7) twentieth cent; insurance journals (6) twentieth cent; investment journals (2) twentieth cent; dividend journals (5) twentieth cent; cash receivable and payable journals (29) twentieth cent; American, German, Eastern and Inland journals (27) twentieth cent; historical typescript by C Amburger, 'William Brandt and the Story of his Enterprise' n.d.

GRINDLAYS BANK PLC
London and Asia

History: This overseas bank traces its origins to Leslie & Grindlay, agents and bankers to the British army and business community in India, which was formed in 1828. It was known as Grindlay, Christian & Matthews in 1839 and as Grindlay & Co from 1843. Branch firms were opened at Calcutta in 1854 and at Bombay in 1865. From 1908 these

Records of banks 241

firms became branches and were thereafter administered directly from London. Additional branches were opened at Simla (1912), Delhi (1923), Lahore (1924) and Peshawar (1926). The bank was acquired by National Provincial Bank Ltd (est. 1833) in 1924 but continued to operate as a separate entity under the title of Grindlay & Co Ltd. In 1928 its balance sheet totalled almost £3 million. It was renamed Grindlays Bank Ltd in 1947. The National Provincial Bank's interest was sold to the National Bank of India Ltd (est. 1863, as Calcutta City Banking Corporation) in 1948. The head office of this bank had been transferred from Calcutta to London in 1865. After the 1948 acquisition the two banks operated separately until they merged under the title of National Overseas & Grindlays Bank Ltd, which was renamed National & Grindlays Bank Ltd in 1959, Grindlays Bank Ltd in 1975 and Grindlays Bank plc in 1982. The bank was acquired by the Australia & New Zealand Banking Group in 1984.

Geoffrey Tyson, *100 Years of Banking in Asia and Africa 1886–1963* (London, 1963)

Records 1: The Royal Bank of Scotland plc, Archive Section, Regent's House, 42 Islington High Street, London N1 8XL

Ledger balances 1923; amalgamation agreements 1923–24; papers re purchase 1923–31; memorandum and articles of association 1924; correspondence with National Provincial Bank head office 1931–50; balance sheet, detailing customer services 1936; annual reports 1936–48; correspondence re pension scheme 1943–44; papers re disposal to National Bank of India 1945–48.

Records 2: Australian & New Zealand Banking Group Ltd, Group Archives, 90 Bourke Street, Melbourne, Vic 3000, Australia

Unspecified records.

GRUNDYS & WOOD
Bury, Greater Manchester

History: This private bank was formed in 1798, probably by John Grundy and Abraham Wood, woollen merchants. Their sons, John Grundy, Edward Grundy and Abraham Wood, later assumed management of the business and in 1836 converted it into a joint stock bank, Bury Banking Co, in which they were important managers and shareholders.

George Chandler, *Four Centuries of Banking* (London, 1964–68)

Records: Barclays Bank plc, Group Archives, Dallimore Road, Wythenshawe, Manchester M23 9JA

242 *British banking – a guide to historical records*

Deed of settlement 1836; bank notes 1830s; profit and loss ledger, income tax returns 1880–87.

GUERNSEY BANKING CO LTD
Guernsey, Channel Islands

History: This joint stock bank was established in 1847 as Priaulx Le Marchant & Co. It was reconstructed as a joint stock bank under the title of Guernsey Banking Co in 1847 and subsequently acquired limited liability. The bank was acquired by National Provincial Bank Ltd in 1924.

Records: The Royal Bank of Scotland plc, Archive Section, Regent's House, 42 Islington High Street, London N1 8XL

Customer ledgers (5) 1827–1924; waste books (2) 1827–28; journals with balance sheets 1827–34; letterbooks (2) 1827–38; minute books (3) 1827–1938; notes issued register c.1835–50; partnership agreement 1846; notice registers (2) 1847–1906; bills discounted register 1871–1948; deed of incorporation 1873; advances ledger 1892–1924; memorandum and articles of association 1898; share register 1898–1924; committee minute book 1898–1927; list of shareholders 1911–24; amalgamation papers 1924.

GUERNSEY COMMERCIAL BANKING CO LTD
Guernsey, Channel Islands

History: This joint stock bank was established in 1835. It acquired limited liability in 1912 when its paid-up capital was £42,000, reserves were £25,000 and deposits were £335,000. The bank was purchased by Westminster Bank Ltd (est. 1909) in 1924.

T E Gregory, *The Westminster Bank Through A Century* (London, 1936)

Records: The Royal Bank of Scotland plc, Archive Section, Regent's House, 42 Islington High Street, London N1 8XL

Deed of incorporation 1835; directors' meeting minute books (5) 1835–1924; rough minute books (2) 1835–1924; amalgamation papers 1924.

GUINNESS, MAHON & CO LTD
London

History: This merchant bank was established in Dublin in 1836 as land agents (discontinued in 1953) under the title of Guinness & Mahon. The founder was Robert R Guinness, a great nephew of Arthur, head of the eponymous brewery; he became one of Ireland's leading business figures. A banking function quickly developed and soon became the chief activity. The business was renamed Guinness, Mahon & Co in 1851 and in 1873 a

Records of banks 243

London agency was opened under the leadership of Richard Guinness. By the 1890s, Guinness Mahon was one of only two surviving banking partnerships in Ireland and the London agency assumed a much greater importance, its banking business becoming increasingly international. This diminished during the First World War, partly because partnership capital fell from almost £750,000 in 1914 to £170,000 in 1920 following the withdrawal of partners. However the London business flourished between the wars to become the firm's principal focus of activity, although the Dublin business also successfully converted to merchant banking. In 1939 certain banking business of London Merchant Bank Ltd (est. 1873) was acquired followed by the current business of Goschens & Cunliffe (est. 1814) in 1941. The firm registered in Eire as a private unlimited company in 1942, reverting to its original name of Guinness & Mahon, and in 1966 became Guinness, & Mahon Ltd. Meanwhile the London business of Guinness Mahon & Co became a limited company in 1961 with a balance sheet total of £25.5 million. By then it was a fully-fledged merchant bank with membership of the Accepting Houses Committee. In 1973 the London business, then owned by Guinness Mahon Holdings Ltd, was acquired from the Guinness family by the international merchanting company, Lewis & Peat Ltd, the new group company being called Guinness Peat Group Ltd. However the merchant bank continued business under its previous name and in 1982 the commodity interests of the Group were sold back to the founder of Lewis & Peat, Lord Kissin. In 1985–86 the brokers Henderson Crosthwaite were acquired and in 1988 Guinness Mahon demerged from Guinness Peat Group to form Guinness Mahon Holdings plc. In 1989 the Bank of Yokohama became a major shareholder and by 1991 acquired full ownership. In 1994 the Irish business of Guinness & Mahon Ltd was sold to the Irish Permanent Building Society and renamed Guinness & Mahon (Ireland) Ltd. In 1998 the Bank of Yokohama sold Guinness Mahon Holdings to Investec, a financial services group based in South Africa.

Manfred Pohl & Sabine Freitag (eds.), *Handbook on the History of European Banks* (Aldershot, 1994); Ivy Frances Jones, *The Rise of a Merchant Bank. A Short History of Guinness Mahon* (priv. pub., 1974)

Records: Guinness Mahon & Co Ltd, PO Box 442, 32 St Mary at Hill, London EC3P 3AJ

Papers re Guinness family 1753–1887; partnership agreements 1831–1947; balance sheets, profit and loss accounts, etc, 1840–46, 1883–1956; papers re partnership matters 1848–1950s; papers re general business 1853–1954.

244 *British banking – a guide to historical records*

GUNDRY & CO
Bridport, Dorset

History: This private bank was formed in 1790 and failed in 1847.

Records: Dorset Record Office, Bridport Road, Dorchester DT1 1RP

Partnership agreement and other papers 1797.

Lyme Regis: plan of buildings 1825. [Ref: D/BGL: ASS, D1/LJ 21, D1/LJ 21]

GUNNER & CO
Bishop's Waltham, Hampshire

History: This private bank was established in 1809 as Fox, Steele, Seymour & Gunner; it was also known as Bishop's Waltham & Hampshire Bank. It was renamed Seymour & Gunner from 1834 and Gunner & Sons from 1840. When acquired by Barclays Bank Ltd (est. 1896) in 1953, it was the last surviving private country bank.

R A Hodgson, 'Gunners Bank', *Portsmouth Archives Review*, 2–4 (1977–80); M F Tighe, 'Gunner & Company of Bishop's Waltham', *Southampton University Archaeological Group Journal*, 2 (1993)

Records 1: Barclays Bank plc, Group Archives, Dallimore Road, Wythenshawe, Manchester M23 9JA

Cash balances ledger 1809–15; private accounts ledger 1809–36; general balance ledgers (4) 1809–86; banker's licence 1810; current account ledgers (51) 1820–1953; security receipt book 1842–88; cheque forms and cheque books 1840s–1951; trial balances 1853–1940; Barclays & Co ledgers 1859–78, 1900–15, 1952–53; loan papers 1869–1904; letterbook 1873–78; bills register 1876–1905; securities as bankers 1923; guarantee 1940; day book 1941–50; cash books (4) 1945–53; waste books (2) 1950–53; paying-in book 1950s.

Records 2: Hampshire Record Office, Sussex Street, Winchester SO23 8TH

Waste book 1809–10; balance book 1813–33; bill register 1815–1939; profit and loss accounts 1854–82; security registers twentieth cent. [Ref: 44M73]

GURNEYS, ALEXANDERS, BIRKBECK, BARCLAY, BUXTON & KERRISON
Ipswich, Suffolk

History: This private bank traces its origins to the Needham Market Bank established in 1744 by Samuel Alexander. The business came to provide banking facilities on market days at nearby Ipswich and in 1767 established a branch there; in 1804 this became the chief office. Other branches opened at Hadleigh (1822), Manningtree (1822), Woodbridge (1826), Sudbury (1830), Lavenham (1830), Debenham (1874), Clare (1891), Felixstowe (1891), Long Melford (1891) and Wickham Market (1891). The names under which the business traded included: Alexanders, Cornwell & Spooner (1767–95); Alexanders & Spooner (1795–1809); Alexanders & Co (1818–65); Alexanders & Maw (1865–78); Alexanders, Birkbeck, Barclays & Buxton (1878–82); Gurneys, Alexanders, Birkbeck, Barclay & Buxton (1882–87) which reflected the first interest in the bank of the Gurneys of Norwich; and Gurneys, Alexanders, Birkbeck, Barclay, Buxton & Kerrison until 1896. In this year the bank was one of several leading banks which merged to form Barclay & Co Ltd.

Harold Preston, *Early East Anglian Banks and Bankers* (Thetford, 1994)

Records: Barclays Bank plc, Group Archives, Dallimore Road, Wythenshawe, Manchester M23 9JA

Will probates 1739–1865; release, Needham Market property 1761; cheques 1761, 1814–95; current account ledgers 1776–1881; bank notes 1783–1896; indemnities 1784–1877; rent ledger 1789–98; historical essay and papers 1818–75; promissory notes 1820, 1864–1919; correspondence, Thomas Maw trustee and executorship 1820–88; ledgers, impersonal 1820–29, 1854–1903; legal opinions 1822–59; passbooks 1823–37; deposit ledger 1824–41; bill forms 1833; in-letters 1837–1905; ledgers, general balances 1840–42; circulars of other organisations 1840–93; loan and stock account ledgers 1842–50; deposited assurance policies 1857; cheque 1860; plan, Ipswich property 1864; mortgages 1864, 1881; papers re failure Overend, Gurney & Co 1865–67; balance sheets 1869–96; photographs of partners c.1860s; partnership agreement 1878; deed of covenant 1878; credit arrangements register 1878–98; forms 1883–95; letters re London agent's balance 1884; surety bonds 1880s; memorandum re bookkeeping practice 1894; banker's licence 1895; cheque ledgers 1895–1902; overdrawn accounts report 1896; account balance schedules 1896.

Needham Market: current account ledgers 1802–76; ledgers, Ipswich Bank's weekly accounts 1802–12, 1836–40, 1866–90; customer accounts balance book 1807–74; letterbook 1842–64; passbook 1879–80; **Norwich:** promissory note 1807; **Sudbury:** securities for advances 1824–70; current accounts ledgers 1859–86; assignment and mortgage 1867–69; **Woodbridge:** security register 1788–1832; bill registers 1805–36 current

246   *British banking – a guide to historical records*

account ledgers 1805–20, 1845–71; in-letters and other papers 1856–1920.

GURNEYS, BIRKBECKS, BARCLAY & BUXTON
Norwich, Norfolk

History: This important private bank was established in 1775 by John and Henry Gurney, merchants, whose family had carried on banking functions for many decades. The family were leading Quakers which was an important determinant of the principles upon which they based their business and upon the links which they developed with other banks and families of bankers. Their bank was to become the most important in East Anglia, its influence extending throughout the region either by the establishment of local private banks in which the Gurney family was an important participant or through marriage to other local banking families. Thus the bank became closely allied through interlocking partnerships to banks at Fakenham (est. 1792), Great Yarmouth (est. 1781), Halesworth (est. 1782), Ipswich (est. 1744), King's Lynn (est. 1782) and Wisbech (est. 1754), all of which came to carry the Gurney name. The Norwich bank traded under several titles but as Gurneys, Birkbeck & Martin from 1826 following the entry of Henry Birkbeck and Simon Martin; as Gurneys & Birkbeck (1839–1840s); as Gurneys & Birkbecks (1850s–66); and as Gurneys, Birkbecks, Barclay & Buxton (1866–96). Their business was otherwise known as the Norwich & Norfolk Bank. Alliances were also made through marriage with the Pease and Backhouse banking families in North East England and a family interest also existed with important London banks including the discount bankers, Overend Gurney & Co. The failure of the latter in 1866 badly damaged the Gurney family's wealth and standing; confidence in their bank was only restored following the entry into it of H F Barclay, S G Buxton and T F Buxton, already related to the Gurneys and leading London bankers. In 1855 the business of Copeman & Co (est. 1809) of Aylsham was acquired followed, more importantly, in 1870 by many of the branches of the failed Norwich bankers, Harveys & Hudsons (est. 1792). Ten branches were acquired – Botesdale, Brandon, Bury St Edmunds, Diss, East Harling, Higham, Newmarket, Thetford, Wotton and Wymondham. Branches already existed at Attleburgh (1826), Aylsham (1855), Dereham (by 1830), Holt (1838) and North Walsham (by 1830) and after 1870 were to be formed at Cromer (by 1879), Hunstanton (by 1883), Loddon (by 1883) and Methwold (by 1883). In 1878 Huddeston & Co (est. 1776) of Bury St Edmunds was also acquired. In 1896 the Gurneys were a major participant in the merger of leading banks, mostly located in London, East Anglia and the North East, to form Barclay & Co Ltd of London.

Records of banks 247

W H Bidwell, *Annals of an East Anglian Bank* (Norwich, 1900); Harold Preston, *Early East Anglian Banks and Bankers* (Thetford, 1994)

Records: Barclays Bank plc, Group Archives, Dallimore Road, Wythenshawe, Manchester M23 9JA

Property papers 1581–1898; in-letters re Overend, Gurney & Co, advances, branches, investments, property, staff, lawsuit, etc 1745–1929; customer account ledgers 1763–69, 1781–85, 1863–77; corporate customer papers 1771–1894; securities for advances 1772–1896; miscellaneous private papers 1777–1893; drafts 1779–1824; bills of lading 1770s; ship insurance letterbook 1780–83; terms of partnership 1780–1800; partnership agreement 1780, 1855–95; bill of exchange 1781, 1785; general balances ledger 1784–91; partners' ledgers 1787–1829; executor and trusteeship papers 1798–1911; cheques and cheque forms 1803–95; register of reports, letters, clerks errors, rates etc 1808–1910; personal papers of Richard H Gurney 1810–35; partnership papers 1811–1909; letters re Overend, Gurney & Co 1812–19, 1866–72; customer authorities 1813–60; out-letters, Joseph John Gurney 1817–32; securities and advances papers 1818–98; settlement book 1826–74; circular re interest 1827; balance sheets and audit papers 1829, 1860–1919; passbooks 1830–31, 1865–1906; bills of exchange 1831–37; clerks' guarantee book 1833–1910; press cuttings: 1857–96, scrapbook 1835–44; account balances ledger 1838–42; interest ledger 1839; notebook of signatories, bill stamps and notes 1839–44; estimate ledgers 1839–75; account summaries 1841–96; supplementary ledgers (3) 1842–66; note registers (9) 1844–1904; insurance receipts 1846–60; accounting papers and annual returns 1848–95; ledgers, Barclay & Co account (2) 1850–81; private accounts ledgers (4) 1853–79; final accounts ledgers 1854–65; journal and balance sheets 1854–73; papers re Gurney & Co, Yarmouth, account 1856; unclaimed balances register 1856–96; H T Barclay: transfer ledger 1864–1911, servants' account ledgers 1882–96, estate account ledger 1891–92; estimate book 1866–75; new fund: ledger c.1866–1901, journals (4) 1866–96; bankruptcy papers 1866–97; solicitors: accounts 1867–96, letterbook 1902–12; branch statistics 1868–96; settlements journal 1870–96; income tax returns 1870–97; account statements book 1870–1915; overs notebook 1872–77; inspection report book 1872–85; brokers' accounts 1873–95; notes on advances 1873–1902; manager's in-letters 1874–75; jotting book, Barclay & Co adjustment 1874–82; loan account ledgers 1874–1901; branch annual returns 1875–79; discount diary 1875–80; merger papers: Alexander & Co 1877–97, Colchester Bank 1891–95, Barclay & Co 1891–96; notebook re advance requests c.1879; staff appointment letters 1880–1931; ledger, Norwich Bank account 1882–90; interest book 1883–1905; private accounts books (2) 1890–1900; capital reorganisation papers

248   *British banking – a guide to historical records*

1891; H F Barclay, estate account ledger 1891–92; customer balance sheets and other papers 1891–1903; account balances ledgers 1892–1926; annual returns 1895; liabilities and assets statistics 1896–1901; merger papers 1896–1906; bill books 1896–1908; private cash book 1899–1911.

GURNEYS, BIRKBECKS, BARCLAY & BUXTON
Fakenham, Norfolk

History: This private bank was formed in 1792 as Gurneys, Birkbeck, Taylor & Peckover and it was influenced by Quaker principles. Three of the founding partners were also in the Gurney bank at King's Lynn, then known as Gurney, Birkbeck & Taylor. There was also a connection with the Wisbech Bank of Gurneys, Birkbeck, Taylor & Peckover. In 1816 Joseph Peckover withdrew and was replaced by Charles Buxton, who in turn was replaced in 1817 by Abraham Rawlinson. The bank was subsequently known as Gurneys & Birkbeck (1829–late 1840s); Gurneys & Birkbecks (late 1840s–66); and Gurneys, Birkbecks, Barclay & Buxton (1866–96); it was also known as the Fakenham Bank. In 1896 the bank merged with other banks to form Barclay & Co Ltd.

Harold Preston, *Early East Anglian Banks and Bankers* (Thetford, 1994)

Records: Barclays Bank plc, Group Archives, Dallimore Road, Wythenshawe, Manchester M23 9JA

Drafts 1786, 1804–07; private account ledgers 1793–1839; cheques 1795, 1816, 1849–94; bills of exchange 1805, 1816; ledgers, trustee accounts 1807–30; bank note register 1846–95; interest calculations and valuation of investments 1851–62; correspondence, terms of service 1854; overdrawn accounts at Fakenham and Holt 1896.

GURNEYS, BIRKBECK, BARCLAY & BUXTON
Wisbech, Cambridgeshire

History: This private bank was established in 1754 by Jonathan Peckover, merchant. In 1782 he joined in partnership with the Gurneys of King's Lynn who in that year had established the local bank of Gurneys, Birkbeck & Taylor. The bank was renamed Gurneys, Birkbeck, Taylor & Peckover; it was also known as the Wisbech & Lincolnshire Bank. Prior to 1800 branches were established at Holbeach and Chatteris and subsequently were opened at March, Whittlesey, Long Sutton and Sutton Bridge. Like other Gurney banks, it was much influenced by the Quaker principles and connections of its partners. In 1896, when the bank was known as Gurneys, Birkbeck, Barclay & Buxton, it merged with leading banks to form Barclay & Co Ltd.

Harold Preston, *Early East Anglian Banks and Bankers* (Thetford, 1994)

Records: Barclays Bank plc, Group Archives, Dallimore Road, Wythenshawe, Manchester M23 9JA

Draft partnership agreement 1792; partnership correspondence 1792–95; post bills 1793–94; receipt form 1794; drafts 1794; cheque 1802; bank note register 1809–1909; abstract of advances 1837; papers re merger with Barclay & Co 1896.

Holbeach: bills of exchange 1800–92; **Smithfield:** paying-in slips 1802; **Wisbech:** drafts 1789–1830; cheque n.d.; bank note 1809; bills of exchange 1813–14, 1827.

GURNEYS, BIRKBECK, BARCLAY, BUXTON & CRESSWELL
King's Lynn, Norfolk

History: This private bank was formed as Gurneys, Birkbeck & Taylor in 1782 by members of the Gurney family, bankers at Norwich. In the same year they formed Gurneys, Birkbeck, Taylor & Peckover of Wisbech. The business was also known as the Lynn Regis & Lincolnshire Bank. It was much influenced by the Quaker principles and connections of its partners. In 1861 Everards & Co (est. 1764) of King's Lynn was acquired followed in 1888 by Jarvis & Jarvis (est. 1808), also of King's Lynn. Branches were opened at Swaffham (1807) and Downham Market (c.1810). In 1896 the bank, which had been known as Gurneys, Birkbeck, Barclay, Buxton & Cresswell since 1866, merged with other leading private banks to form Barclay & Co Ltd.

Harold Preston, *Early East Anglian Banks and Bankers* (Thetford, 1994)

Records: Barclays Bank plc, Group Archives, Dallimore Road, Wythenshawe, Manchester M23 9JA

Drafts 1782–1809; cheques c.1780s–1893; bill of exchange 1811; bank note 1825; bill of exchange 1825; note registers 1829–97; partnership agreements 1866; letters re partnership affairs 1869; balance sheet 1896.

Downham Market: bill of exchange 1825; cheques 1894–1906.

GURNEYS, BIRKBECK, BARCLAY, BUXTON & ORDE
Halesworth, Suffolk

History: This private bank was established in 1782 by the partners of Gurneys & Turner, bankers of Great Yarmouth, who had established their business a year earlier; throughout its history it remained under

250   British banking – a guide to historical records

control of the Yarmouth bank. The business operated under several titles including Gurneys, Turner & Brightwen (1815–20); Gurneys, Turner, Brightwen & Lloyds (1820–39); Gurneys, Birkbeck, Brightwen & Orde (1864–69); and Gurneys, Birkbeck, Barclay, Orde & Buxtons (1870–1880s); it was also known as the Halesworth & Suffolk Bank. Branches were opened at Bungay (1808), Harleston (1808), Southwold (1829), Eye (by 1808), Framlingham (by 1808), Yoxford (by 1808), Woodbridge (by 1808), Aldeburgh (by 1808) and Saxmundham (by 1808). The bank was much influenced by the Quaker principles and connections of its partners. In 1896 the business, then known as Gurneys, Birkbeck, Barclay, Buxton & Orde, merged with other leading banks to form Barclay & Co Ltd.

W H Bidwell, *Annals of an East Anglian Bank* (Norwich, 1900); Harold Preston, *Early East Anglian Banks and Bankers* (Thetford, 1994)

Records: Barclays Bank plc, Group Archives, Dallimore Road, Wythenshawe, Manchester M23 9JA

Drafts 1785–1811; bank notes 1797–99; bill of exchange 1809; cheques 1809–94; accounts of settlement 1840–75; pass book 1864–76; balance sheet summaries 1876–96; papers re merger with Barclay & Co 1896.

Saxmundham: accounts re building and furnishings 1871–73.

GURNEYS, BIRKBECK, BARCLAY, BUXTONS & ORDE
Great Yarmouth, Norfolk

History: This private bank was formed in 1781 as Gurneys & Turner, the former partners belonging to the Norwich banking family and James Turner being a local merchant. In 1782 the partners also established another bank by the same name at Halesworth. The business traded under several titles including Gurneys, Turner & Brightwen (1816–1850s); Gurneys, Birkbeck, Brightwen & Orde (1864–66); and Gurneys, Birkbeck, Barclay, Buxtons & Orde (1880s–96); it was otherwise known as the Yarmouth & Suffolk Bank. Branches existed at Bungay (1790–1803), Lowestoft (1820s) and Beecles (c.1823). The firm was much influenced by the Quaker principles and connections of its partners. In 1896 the bank, then known as Gurneys, Birkbeck, Barclay, Buxtons & Orde, merged with other leading banks to form Barclay & Co Ltd of London.

W H Bidwell, *Annals of an East Anglian Bank* (Norwich, 1900); Harold Preston, *Early East Anglian Banks and Bankers* (Thetford, 1994)

Records: Barclays Bank plc, Group Archives, Dallimore Road, Wythenshawe, Manchester M23 9JA

Records of banks 251

Drafts 1780–99, 1811; cheques and bills 1783–1919; bonds 1783–1840; bills of exchange 1789–1820; bank note indemnities 1790–1866; partnership agreement 1793; overs and shorts 1801–04; guarantees and authorities 1804–16; bank notes 1805–37; partnership in-letters 1818–19; papers re embezzlement 1818–19; Orde family papers 1829–1930; private ledgers: 1840–1906, J H Orde 1861–75; settlement accounts 1853–75; bank note register 1854–96; cash book 1856–62; customer information book 1859–62; powers of attorney registers 1865–90; correspondence re failure of Overend Gurney & Co 1866–72; bank estate and share ledgers (5) 1871–1936; correspondence 1874–76; balance sheet summaries 1875–96; amalgamation papers, Barclay & Co 1896–1920.

GURNEYS, ROUND, GREEN, HOARE & CO
Colchester, Essex

History: This private bank was established as Crickitt & Co in 1774. The Crickitt family were also connected with Crickitt, Round & Green (est. 1774) of Chelmsford; Crickitt, Truelove & Kerridge (est. 1786) of Ipswich; and Crickitt, Wood & Co (est. 1817) of Woodbridge. The bank was subsequently known as Crickitt, Round & Green; Crickitt & Round; and between 1823 and 1825 as Crickitt, Round & Crickitt. The business failed during the 1825 financial crisis, but was reformed as Round, Green, Green & Pattison (until 1826) and was known as Round, Green & Co from 1827 to 1883. Further difficulties were encountered in 1883, when John Gurney Hoare became a partner and the title changed to include his name. In 1891 the Gurneys also became major partners when the bank was known as Gurneys, Round, Green, Hoare & Co. In 1896 the bank was one of twenty leading banks which merged to form Barclay & Co Ltd.

Harold Preston, *Early East Anglian Banks and Bankers* (Thetford, 1994)

Records 1: Barclays Bank plc, Group Archives, Dallimore Road, Wythenshawe, Manchester M23 9JA

Private account ledgers of Crickitt & Co, mainly customer accounts (2) 1787–89, 1798–99; partnership agreements 1856–82; drawing of bank 1879; papers re amalgamation 1896.

Records 2: Essex Record Office, PO Box 11, County Hall, Chelmsford CM1 1LX

Papers re failure 1825–26. [Ref: D/DOp B123/1–2, 1065–69]

JAMES GUTHRIE
Newark, Nottinghamshire

252   *British banking – a guide to historical records*

History: This private bank was established by James Guthrie and was also known as Newark upon Trent Bank. It failed in 1793.

Records: Nottinghamshire Archives, County House, Castle Meadow Road, Nottingham NG2 1AG

Grant of commission of bankruptcy 1793. [Ref: DDT 126/5]

HALIFAX & DISTRICT PERMANENT BANKING CO LTD
Halifax, West Yorkshire

History: This joint stock bank was established in 1909. It was acquired by Union Bank of Manchester Ltd (est. 1836) in 1917 when it had branches at Bradford, Halifax, Huddersfield and Sheffield.

Records: Barclays Bank plc, Group Archives, Dallimore Road, Wythenshawe, Manchester M23 9JA

Memorandum and articles of association 1909; list of shareholders 1916; agreement for sale/merger with Union Bank of Manchester 1916–17.

HALIFAX & HUDDERSFIELD UNION BANKING CO LTD
Halifax, West Yorkshire

History: This joint stock bank was formed in 1836 out of the private banks of John Rawson, William Rawson & Christopher Rawson (est. 1811) of Halifax and John Rawson, William Rawson, Charles Rawson & Co (est. 1811) of Huddersfield. The first chairman was Christopher Rawson and the Rawson family provided four of the bank's subsequent chairmen. Paid-up capital on formation was £83,000, rising to £200,000 in 1862 and to £300,000 in 1888. Limited liability was acquired in 1882. Between 1886 and 1903, at least seven branches were opened including offices at Sowerby Bridge (1886), Elland (1886), Brighouse (1894), Bradford (1895) and Leeds (1903). In 1910 the bank merged with its rival, the Halifax Joint Stock Banking Co Ltd (est. 1829) which in 1911 was renamed the West Yorkshire Bank Ltd.

H Ling Roth, *The Genesis of Banking in Halifax with Side Lights on Country Banking* (Halifax, 1914)

Records 1: Lloyds TSB Group plc, Archives, Head Office, 71 Lombard Street, London EC3P 3BS

Deed of settlement 1836; general meeting minute book 1837–1910; amalgamation papers 1910–12.

Records 2: Calderdale District Archives, Calderdale Central Library, Northgate House, Northgate, Halifax HX1 1UN

Records of banks 253

Title deeds, accounts, correspondence etc c.1836–1908. [Ref: FW:108]

HALIFAX COMMERCIAL BANKING CO LTD
Halifax, West Yorkshire

History: This bank traced its origins to John Rawson, William Rawson, John Rhodes and Rawdon Briggs who formed their business in 1807, out of that of the recently collapsed bank of Brothers Swaine & Co (est. 1779). Rhodes and Briggs had already been partners as merchants. The bank, which was also known as Halifax New Bank, was wound up in 1811 when two competing businesses emerged from it, viz: John, William & Christopher Rawson & Co (which in 1836 formed the Halifax & Huddersfield Union Banking Co) and Rhodes, Briggs & Garlick which was also known as the Halifax Bank. In 1819 the partners of this latter bank opened a branch in Rochdale, which was sold to a local woollen merchant, Clement Royds, in 1827. In 1818 their bank was renamed Rawdon Briggs, Rawdon Briggs jun. & William Briggs and in 1836, when it was known as Rawdon Briggs & Sons, it was converted into a joint stock bank, Halifax Commercial Banking Co. On formation its paid-up capital was £50,000, provided by 172 shareholders, and the former senior partners of Rawdon Briggs & Sons became chairman and deputy chairman. Other directors were drawn from the local textile industry. Paid-up capital rose to £100,000 in 1864 and to £200,000 by 1900. In 1864 limited liability was acquired. Between 1863 and 1911, seventeen branches and sub-branches were opened including offices at Bradford (1875), Leeds (1898), Hull (1899), Pontefract (1901), Dewsbury (1903) and Sowerby Bridge (1910). By 1919 paid-up capital was £200,000 and deposits exceeded £4 million. The business was then a prominent regional bank and its acquisition in 1920 by the Bank of Liverpool & Martins Bank Ltd (est. 1831) was for a consideration of £540,000.

George Chandler, *Four Centuries of Banking* (London, 1964–68); H Ling Roth, *The Genesis of Banking in Halifax with Side Lights on Country Banking* (Halifax, 1914)

Records: Barclays Bank plc, Group Archives, Dallimore Road, Wythenshawe, Manchester M23 9JA

Promissory notes 1763–1802; bank notes 1806–19; papers re customer bankruptcies 1806–49; partnership agreement 1818; cash book 1820–21; manager's diary 1826–31; deed of settlement 1836; annual reports 1836–55, 1893–1919; directors' meeting minutes 1836–55, 1912–22; list of shareholders n.d.; banking account returns 1840–48; income tax returns 1845–63; memorandum re Hull agent 1847; list of closed accounts 1855; press cuttings 1894–1961; branch insurance policies 1905–20; staff in-

254 British banking – a guide to historical records

structures book n.d.; share transfer certificates 1911–18; shareholder registers (2) 1918–20.

HALL & JENKINS
Daventry, Northamptonshire

History: This private bank was established 1809 as Hall, Oakden & Co. It was known as Hall & Morgan from 1822 and subsequently as Hall & Jenkins. It ceased trading in about 1837 when it appears to have been acquired by Northamptonshire Union Bank (est. 1836).

Records: The Royal Bank of Scotland plc, Archive Section, Regent's House, 42 Islington High Street, London N1 8XL

Cash books (2) 1824–38.

HALL, BEVAN, WEST & BEVANS
Brighton, East Sussex

History: This private bank was established in North Street, Brighton, in 1805 by William Golding, James Browne, Nathaniel Hall, Richard Lashmar and Thomas West; it was also known as Brighton Union Bank and its initial partnership capital was £1,800. It operated under several names including Browne, Hall, Lashmar & West (1809), Browne, Hall & West (1818), Hall & West (1820), Hall, West & Borrer (1823), Hall, West & Co (1855), Hall, Lloyd & Bevan (1860), Hall, Bevan, West & Hall (1878) and Hall, Bevan, West & Bevans (1891). Branches were opened at Cuckfield (by 1866), Hove (1871), Burgess Hill (1877), Haywards Heath (1878), Preston (1880) and subsequently Shoreham. The bank was acquired in 1894 by Barclay, Bevan, Tritton, Ransom, Bouverie & Co (est. 1694) of London, which in 1896 joined with other banks to form Barclay & Co Ltd.

P W Matthews & Anthony W Tuke, *History of Barclays Bank Ltd* (London, 1926)

Records: Barclays Bank plc, Group Archives, Dallimore Road, Wythenshawe, Manchester M23 9JA

Bank notes 1807–93; notice re bank note theft 1812; cheques, receipts and drafts 1825–97; cheque book 1880; balance sheets 1891–92; papers re amalgamation 1896.

HAMBROS PLC
London

History: This leading merchant bank traced its origins to Calmer Joachim Levy who set up in business as a merchant at Copenhagen, Denmark, in

Records of banks 255

1779, at the same time changing his name to Hambro. His son, Joseph, who made his mark by becoming banker to the King of Denmark, and his grandson, Carl Joachim, later known as Baron Hambro, established C J Hambro & Son in the City of London in 1839. The house traded as merchants and as financiers of trade, focusing on Scandinavian trade with Britain. In the 1840s it became independent of the Copenhagen business and established its reputation as a major London house by bringing out bond issues for the government of Denmark at the time of Denmark's war with Prussia over Schleswig and Holstein. Shortly afterwards, Hambros' strong links with Italy were established when a bond issue was made for Sardinia, ostensibly to finance railway development, but in reality to restore the country's finances and facilitate the first steps to Italian reunification. In these years, links with Greek finance were also developed. On the death of Baron Hambro in 1877, the house's capital amounted to £650,000, mostly provided by its new leader Everard Hambro. He built links with North America, financing North Atlantic trade and making bond issues, especially for United States railroad companies. However, the most important transaction of this decade was the issue, with Barings, of the Italian Stabilisation Loan in 1881–82. In 1920 Hambros merged with the British Bank of Northern Commerce Ltd (est. 1912) to form Hambros Bank of Northern Commerce Ltd which, a year later, was renamed Hambros Bank Ltd. The paid-up capital of the new bank was £1 million and the volume of Scandinavian business, in particular acceptance finance (especially for Finnish customers), increased substantially. By the late 1920s the Hambro family had increased their ownership, thereby re-establishing control of the bank. In the 1920s the geographical spread of business expanded to Hungary and Romania, especially with regard to bond issues, but business in Scandinavia and Greece remained strong. With embargoes placed by the British authorities on sterling bond issues for foreign customers, in the 1930s the issuing business and associated corporate finance advisory work was largely confined to UK companies such as John Brown & Co Ltd and the Consett Iron Co Ltd. In the post-war years, the bank developed along lines similar to other London merchant banks, especially in corporate finance, foreign exchange dealing and bond issues denominated in eurodollars. Less typically, it became heavily involved in diamond broking and bullion trading. In 1970 the business adopted a new holding company structure at the head of which was Hambros Ltd and, later, Hambros plc. In the mid 1980s, its insurance business, Hambro Life, was sold and an estate agencies business, to be known as Hambro Countrywide, was acquired. In 1998 much of Hambros' business was acquired by Société Générale.

Anon, *Hambros Bank Ltd, London, 1839–1939* (priv. pub., 1939); Bo Bramsen & Kathleen Wain, *The Hambros 1779–1979* (London, 1979);

256   British banking – a guide to historical records

Manfred Pohl & Sabine Freitag (eds.), *Handbook on the History of European Banks* (Aldershot, 1994)

Records: Guildhall Library, Aldermanbury, London EC2P 2EJ

'Correspondence' re general banking activities including: Danish government bond issue 1836–37, Sardinian government finance 1851–61, Russian compensation payments to Denmark 1857–58, copper and tin speculation 1889–92, 1936–25, House of Savoy accounts 1910–25; 'loans papers' re bond issues and connected matters, including business not taken up, for overseas borrowers, mostly sovereign entities and railway companies, with many based in Italy, Greece, Scandinavia and Latin America, but also some UK companies c.1840s–1918; 'general business papers' re miscellaneous transactions, eg protest of bills, securities, often of a legal nature 1840s–1920s; staff salary, bonus, etc lists 1856–1924; 'private letters' of partners re business and family matters 1861–92; annual balances of accounts 1863–66; premises papers 1864–66; annual balances of accounts re partnership capital account 1864–1906; 'synopsis of journal' 1867–1916; Hambro family trust accounts ledger 1881–1918; annual balances of securities 1887–1920; E Hambro private out-letterbook re foreign loans 1889–90; stockholder ledger 1889–1924; press cutting re bond issues, redemptions, etc (2) 1889–1927; general out- letterbook re foreign loans and general business 1901; half-yearly lists of house securities 1905–10; general ledgers (19) 1912, 1922–60; special advance account ledger 1913–22; amalgamation papers 1920s; journal 1921–38; annual reports 1922–59; Hambro family papers including genealogy, reminiscences, photographs, etc twentieth cent. [Ref: MS 19031–19223]

HAMMERSLEY, GREENWOOD & BROOKSBANK
London

History: This private bank traced its origins to Ransom, Morland & Hammersley established at 57 Pall Mall, in London's West End, in the mid 1780s. By 1787 it was banker to the Prince of Wales, and in 1792 the Prince's debts to Hammersleys, totalling over £46,000, were discharged by the banker, Thomas Coutts. By 1796 Thomas Hammersley was in partnership with Montolieu, Brooksbank, Greenwood & Drewe at 76 Pall Mall. The business was of considerable size, employing sixteen clerks in 1801. Montolieu withdrew in 1804 and Drewe withdrew by 1820; in 1823 the bank was styled Hammersley, Greenwood & Brooksbank and was based at 69 Pall Mall. In 1838 a merger with Coutts was proposed but did not proceed. However in 1840, following the death of the senior partner, Hugh Hammersley, Coutts & Co (est. 1692) acquired the bank's assets when its business was discontinued.

Records of banks **257**

Edna Healey, *Coutts & Co 1692–92. The Portrait of a Private Bank* (London, 1992); F G Hilton Price, *A Handbook of London Bankers* (London, 1876)

Records 1: Coutts & Co, 440 Strand, London WC2R 0QS

Signature book 1795–1840; papers re merger 1840.

Records 2: London Metropolitan Archive, 40 Northampton Road, London EC1R 0HB

List of bank drafts in account book of B Latrobe, architect 1792–95. [Ref: Acc 931/1]

Records 3: Buckinghamshire Record Office, County Hall, Aylesbury HP20 1UA

Papers of Sir Scrope Bernard Morland, director, including correspondence with clients and other banks 1780–1832. [Ref: D/SB/PFD/2–10]

HAMMOND & CO
Newmarket, Suffolk

History: This private bank was established in 1770 by the Hammond family, grocers of Newmarket. In 1837 Richard Eaton, a local landowner, was taken into partnership when the bank's style changed to Eaton, Hammond & Co, reverting again to Hammond & Co in 1861. The business was also known as the Newmarket Bank. From 1888 a branch existed at Soham. In 1905 the bank amalgamated with Barclay & Co Ltd (est. 1896).

P W Tuke & Anthony W Tuke, *History of Barclays Bank Ltd* (London, 1926); Harold Preston, *Early East Anglian Banks and Bankers* (Thetford, 1994)

Records: Barclays Bank plc, Group Archives, Dallimore Road, Wythenshawe, Manchester M23 9JA

Bill of exchange registers 1788–1895; ledgers, private accounts 1790–1846; ledgers, London agents (Biddulph, Cocks & Ridges) 1800–46 [w], 1884–89, 1903–19; ledger, current account including profit and loss 1804–13; cheque form 1864; bank notes 1887–1900; note for collection and payment at Cocks, Biddulph & Co 1902.

HAMMOND & CO
Canterbury, Kent

History: This private bank was formed in 1788 as Gipps, Simmons & Gipps. Of the three partners, James Simmons was a stationer, printer,

258   *British banking – a guide to historical records*

publisher and mill owner; George Gipps MP was a hop dealer and apothecary; and his nephew, Henry Gipps, was a woollen draper. The business was known as Hammond, Plumptre, Furley, Hilton & McMaster from 1816; as Hammond, Plumptre, Furley, Hilton & Furley from 1839; as Hammond, Plumptre, Hilton & Furley from 1860; as Hammond, Plumptre, Furley, Hilton & Furley from 1865; and as Hammond, Plumptre, Furley, Hilton & McMaster from 1879. However, the bank was generally known as Hammond & Co, or as the Canterbury Bank, and was one of the largest and best-managed private banks in Kent. Its balance sheet total was £173,000 in 1815 and £300,000 in 1840. Branches were opened at Whitstable (1863) and Ramsgate (1866). In 1903, when styled Hammond, Plumptre, Hilton, McMaster & Furley, the business was acquired by Capital & Counties Bank Ltd (est. 1877) for almost £200,000 plus the value of premises.

Records: Lloyds TSB Group plc, Archives, Head Office, 71 Lombard Street, London EC3P 3BS

Day book 1782–1803; notice of establishment 1788; customer and general accounts balance books (2) 1788–1802; summary of general accounts 1789–1901; salary and agreements book 1815 on; general ledger 1885–1905; amalgamation papers 1897–1904; partnership agreement 1898.

Ramsgate: memorandum book 1898–1912; **Whitstable:** signature books (2) 1893–1903.

HAMPSHIRE BANKING CO
Southampton, Hampshire

History: This joint stock bank was established in 1834. It expanded by acquisition of other banks or of parts of them, beginning in 1840 with most branches of the failed Southern District Banking Co (est. 1836). Subsequent acquisitions were largely of private banks: Wickham & Co (est. 1807) of Winchester in 1854; Heath & Co (est. 1790) of Andover in 1861; Atkins & Sons (est. 1818) of Portsmouth in 1863; Raggett, Seymour & Co (est. 1806) of Basingstoke and Odiham in 1864; Le Neveu, Sorel & Co (est. 1862), otherwise known as the English & Jersey Union Bank, in 1873 when it was in difficulties; and de Carteret & Co (est. 1846), otherwise styled the Jersey Joint Stock Bank, also in 1873. In 1876 paid-up capital was £200,000. A year later there were forty-four branches located throughout Hampshire, Sussex, Surrey, the Isle of Wight and the Channel Islands and one office in London. In 1877 the Hampshire Banking Co merged with the North Wilts Banking Co (est. 1835), which was of equal size, to form the Hampshire & North Wilts Banking Co which was renamed the Capital & Counties Bank in 1878.

Records of banks 259

R S Sayers, *Lloyds Bank in the History of English Banking* (Oxford, 1957)

Records: Lloyds TSB Group plc, Archives, Head Office, 71 Lombard Street, London EC3P 3BS

Deed of settlement with supplements 1834–63; general memorandum book 1834–76; branch inspection report book 1834–77; shareholders' register 1835–84; annual reports 1836–76; amalgamation papers 1876; private minute book 1876–93.

Brighton: signature books (2) 1862–85; **Chichester:** signature book c.1873–1908; **Jersey:** letterbooks (2) 1873–75; **Southampton:** signature book c.1834–c.1876; security register 1865–70.

HAMPSON, AUSTIN & GRIFFITHS
Luton, Bedfordshire

History: This private bank was established in 1806 and was also known as the Luton Bank. It failed in 1824.

Records: Bedfordshire and Luton Archives and Record Service, The Records Office, Cauldwell Street, Bedford MK42 9AP

Hampson family papers including business records 1823–36. [Ref: X 808/3–15]

HANBURY & LLOYD
London

History: This private bank was established in Lombard Street, City of London, in 1771 as Hanbury, Taylor, Lloyd & Bowman. The Hanbury and Lloyd partners were members of the families which had formed Taylor & Lloyds of Birmingham in 1765, the firm from which Lloyds Bank Ltd was to evolve. Hanbury was a tobacco merchant and Bowman was the bank's manager who had formerly been cashier with Smith & Payne (est. 1758), leading London bankers. The London bank was renamed Taylor, Lloyd & Bowman in 1784; Taylor, Lloyd, Hanbury & Co in 1791; Taylor, Lloyd, Hanbury & Bowman in 1801; Hanbury, Taylor & Lloyd in 1815; and Hanbury & Lloyd from 1858. Despite the dilution of the family connection from the early nineteenth century, the bank continued to act as London agents for Lloyds in Birmingham. The business merged with Barnett, Hoare & Co (est. c.1728) in 1864 to form Barnetts, Hoares, Hanbury & Lloyd.

F G Hilton Price, *A Handbook of London Bankers* (London, 1876); R S Sayers *Lloyds Bank in the History of English Banking* (Oxford, 1957)

260   *British banking – a guide to historical records*

Records: Lloyds TSB Group plc, Archives, Head Office, 71 Lombard Street, London EC3P 3BS

Partnership agreement 1790; private ledger 1834–49; letterbook of James Taylor 1844–63; account ledger 1861–63.

HANKEYS & CO
London

History: This private bank was established by 1685 when Samuel Hankey was trading at the sign of the Ring in Fenchurch Street, City of London, probably as a goldsmith banker and pawnbroker. The firm was known as Sir Henry Hankey & Sons from about 1735 and by the 1760s was trading at the sign of the Three Golden Balls in Fenchurch Street. Between 1739 and 1768 the firm was known as Sir Joseph Hankey & Co. It was styled Hankey, Hall, Hankey & Alers from 1804 and Hankeys & Co from 1810. It was acquired by Consolidated Bank Ltd (est. 1863) in 1865.

F G Hilton Price, *A Handbook of London Bankers* (London, 1876)

Records 1: The Royal Bank of Scotland plc, Archive Section, Regent's House, 42 Islington High Street, London N1 8XL

Waste book 1697–1705; signature book c.1790s; cash book 1831.

Records 2: West Sussex Record Office, County Hall, Chichester PO19 1RN

Cheque books 1798–1835. [Mitford MSS. 1192–1204]

HARDCASTLE, CROSS & CO
Bolton, Greater Manchester

History: This private bank was established in 1818 by five local cotton spinners and solicitors as Hardcastle, Cross, Ormrod, Barlow & Rushton, initially trading from Barlow's property in Water Street alongside an insurance agency and wine and spirits business. Its initial partnership capital was about £6,000. The bank was also known as the Bolton Commercial Bank. By 1822, when the firm moved to Market Street, it had deposits of £44,250. It was known as Hardcastle, Cross & Co from 1825. In 1868 it moved into temporary premises in Corporation Street whilst a new banking house, completed in 1875, was constructed in Deansgate. The bank was acquired by the Manchester & Salford Bank (est.1836) in 1878.

Anon, 'A Bolton Banking Partnership', *Three Banks Review*, 25 (1955); Anon, *Bolton Branch of The Royal Bank of Scotland. The Story of Bolton's First Commercial Bank* (priv. pub., 1993)

Records of banks

261

Records: The Royal Bank of Scotland plc, Archive Section, Regent's House, 42 Islington High Street, London N1 8XL

Customer account ledgers 1818–21, 1858–78; balance books 1818–58; ledger re customer investment in gilts 1822–63; press cutting re bank robbery 1825; cheque 1826; partnership agreements 1827, 1877; private ledger 1830–60; papers re proposed mergers: Bank of Bolton 1836–79, Parr's Banking Co 1875–78; correspondence of Robert Sharpe Barlow re joint stock status 1836; press cuttings books 1836–78; opinions received book 1838–70; case and opinion re partnership capital 1839; rent account book 1839–41; unused bank notes c.1830s; managing partner's notebook 1842–79; tax papers 1845–81; staff salary lists 1845–75 [w]; half-yearly balance books 1848–62; signing authorities books 1848–78; letterbooks 1849–78; balance statements and lists of bills 1850–78; executorship account ledgers 1856–78; list of additions to capital and reserves 1858–73; partners' balance book 1858–77; yearly-balance book 1859–77; biannual balances 1859–77; commissions notebook 1859–69; signature books 1860–78; ledger re transfer of stock held as security 1860–75; cheque books: 1862–63, T L Rushton 1872–73; customer correspondence 1860–78; letter re transfer of London agency 1864; petty cash book 1864–70; architectural drawings of proposed new bank 1868–69; staff correspondence 1869–71; fire assurance registers 1873–78; papers re sale of bank to Manchester & Salford Bank 1873–89; correspondence re local authority bonds in safe custody 1875–76; balance sheets 1875–78; loan agreement 1876; papers re release of security items 1876–78; passbook, Manchester & Liverpool District Banking Co 1878–79.

HARDING & CO
Bridlington, Humberside

History: This private bank was formed in 1802 as Harding, Smith, Faber & Foster. It was later known as Harding, Smith & Stansfeld and afterwards as Harding, Mortlock & Co. Early on, it established an office at Driffield and was otherwise styled the Burlington [sic.] & Driffield Bank. A third office was later opened at Bridlington Quay. York City & County Banking Co (est. 1830) acquired the business for £21,500 in 1878.

W F Crick & J E Wadsworth, *A Hundred Years of Joint Stock Banking* (London, 1936)

Records: HSBC Holdings plc, Group Archives, 10 Lower Thames Street, London EC3R 6AE

Driffield: journals (2) 1825–29, 1845–48; petty cash book 1835–50.

262 British banking – a guide to historical records

HARDY & CO
Grantham, Lincolnshire

History: This private bank was formed in 1819 as Turner, Hardy & Newcome with a capital of £16,000; it became one of Lincolnshire's most important banks. Its subsequent titles included Hardy, Newcome & Walkington and Hardy, Walkington & Hardy. The most important partner throughout its history was John Hardy, a large farmer and innkeeper, while Frank Newcome, a founding partner, had formerly worked with another local bank, Holt, King & Newcome (est. 1812). By 1859 the bank's capital stood at £40,000 and rose to £70,000 by 1895 when deposits were reckoned to be between £300,000 and £400,000. In this year the bank, now known as Hardy & Co, was acquired by the Leicestershire Banking Co Ltd (est. 1829) for £145,000.

W F Crick & J E Wadsworth, *A Hundred Years of Joint Stock Banking* (London, 1936)

Records: HSBC Holdings plc, Group Archives, 10 Lower Thames Street, London EC3R 6AE

Customer ledger 1819–21; receipt registers (3) 1819–40; partnership agreements 1819, 1859; profit and loss books (5) 1837–1900; analysis of income tax payments 1839–43; general balance book 1845–57; payments re new premises 1848–50; security register 1857–84; half-yearly comparative statements 1859–71; balance books (3) 1860–94; analysis of accounts 1872–75; safe custody book 1881–97; loan register 1883–99; amalgamation papers 1895.

HARRIS, BULTEEL & CO
Plymouth, Devon

History: This private bank was formed in 1774 and was also known as The Naval Bank. It had branches or sub-branches at Dartmouth, Newton Abbot, Totnes, Ivybridge, Modbury, Paignton, Saltash, Stonehouse, Mutley, Devonport, Kingsbridge, Yealmpton, and South Brent. In its last years it performed badly and in 1914 ceased to trade, being the only British bank to close as a result of the financial difficulties associated with the outbreak of war. The business and some branches were then acquired by Lloyds Bank Ltd (est. 1765) for £4,000. The purchase was not completed until 1917.

Records: Lloyds TSB Group plc, Archives, Head Office, 71 Lombard Street, London EC3P 3BS

Amalgamation papers 1914–23.

Records of banks

HART, FELLOWS & CO
Nottingham, Nottinghamshire

History: This private bank was formed in 1808 as Fellows & Hart and was located at Bridlesmith Gate, Nottingham; it was otherwise known as the Nottingham & Notts Bank. Its partners were John Fellows, Francis Hart and a Mr Mellor. From about 1824 the business was styled Hart, Fellows & Co and in 1866 was acquired by the English Joint Stock Bank Ltd (est. 1866) which failed in May 1866. The joint stock bank's Nottingham business was then reconstructed as a private partnership, Hart, Fellows & Co, which was acquired in 1891 by Lloyds Bank Ltd (est. 1765).

Records: Lloyds TSB Group plc, Archives, Head Office, 71 Lombard Street, London EC3 3BS

Amalgamation papers 1891–94.

HARTLAND, PRIOR, PROCTOR & EASTHORPE
Tewkesbury, Gloucestershire

History: This private bank was formed at Tewkesbury in 1809 by a family of tanners and was also known as the Gloucestershire Bank. It stopped payment during the 1825 financial crisis but resumed as Hartland, Prior, Proctor & Easthorpe. In 1831 it merged into the newly formed Gloucestershire Banking Co and its three offices at Tewkesbury, Evesham (1813) and Cheltenham (1825) formed that bank's first branches. Nathaniel Hartland joined the Gloucestershire Bank and became a senior manager.

R S Sayers, *Lloyds Bank in the History of English Banking* (Oxford, 1957)

Records: Lloyds TSB Group plc, Archives, Head Office, 71 Lombard Street, London EC3P 3BS

Amalgamation papers 1834.

HARTLEY & CO
Whitehaven, Cumbria

History: This private bank was formed in 1793 as Moore, Harrison & Co and was later known as Hartley & Co. In 1837 it was reconstructed as the Bank of Whitehaven, a joint stock bank.

Records: Cumbria Record Office, The Castle, Carlisle CA3 8UR

Note register 1803–13. [Ref: Allison MSS]

HARTSINCK, HUTCHINSON & PLAYFAIR
London

264 *British banking – a guide to historical records*

History: This private bank operated in Cornhill, City of London, in the 1790s and early nineteenth century.

Records: Guildhall Library, Aldermanbury, London EC2 2EJ

Letters and other papers of William Playfair re the bank 1796–1809. [Ref: MS403]

HART SON & CO LTD
London

History: This merchant bank was formed in the City of London in 1917; its antecedents lay in the stockbrokers, Hart Son & Ichenhausen formed in 1910. It was registered as a public company, Hart Son & Co (London) Ltd, in 1947 and in 1954 re-registered as Hart Son & Co Ltd. At about this time, the solicitor, Michael Richards, with a group of colleagues, acquired the business and built it into a specialist corporate finance advisory house, focusing particularly on mergers and acquisitions, on new issues and on flotations. In the late 1950s paid-up capital was increased from £50,000 to £250,000. In 1960 the merchant bankers, Samuel Montagu & Co Ltd (est. 1853) acquired the business.

Records: HSBC Holdings plc, Group Archives, 10 Lower Thames Street, London EC3R 6AE

Annual returns and papers re sale of business 1947–60; investment records 1956–59.

HARVEYS & HUDSONS
Norwich, Norfolk

History: This important private bank was formed in 1792 by Robert Harvey and James Hudson, the latter having formerly been a partner in the Norwich bank of Hudson & Hatfield (est. 1783). The partnership was known as Harvey & Hudsons from 1807 and as Harveys & Hudsons from 1820. It also traded as the Norwich Crown Bank and later as the Norwich Crown and Suffolk & Norfolk Bank. The latter name change reflected the large network of thirty branch offices established between the early 1820s and 1870. In 1851 Taylor & Dyson (est. 1810), bankers at Diss and Botesdale, was acquired. In 1870, following speculation by a senior partner, Sir Robert Harvey, the bank failed and its business was acquired by the Norwich bankers, Gurneys, Birkbecks, Barclay & Buxton (est. 1775).

Harold Preston, *Early East Anglian Banks and Bankers* (Thetford, 1994)

Records: Barclays Bank plc, Group Archives, Dallimore Road, Wythenshawe, Manchester M23 9JA

Records of banks 265

Cheques 1824, 1856–72; letter re forged note 1848; sketches of staff 1852–57; papers re failure 1859–94; poem re clerk 1850s; postcard of bank 1850s; bank notes 1862–69; dividend registers (3) 1869–84; creditor balance ledgers (4) 1870.

HARWOOD & CO
Thornbury, Avon

History: This private bank was established in 1808 as Ralph, Yates & Parslaw; it was otherwise known as Thornbury Old Bank. The firm was styled Harwood & Co from 1857. It was acquired by Prescott, Dimsdale, Cave, Tugwell & Co Ltd (est. 1891) for £9,000 in 1891.

Anon, 'Prescott's Bank', *National Provincial Bank Review* (1966–68)

Records: The Royal Bank of Scotland plc, Archive Section, Regent's House, 42 Islington High Street, London N1 8XL

Cash balance book 1858; signature book late nineteenth cent.; amalgamation papers 1891.

HAYDON, SMALLPIECE & CO
Guildford, Surrey

History: This private bank was established in 1765 by William Haydon, a draper. It was styled Messrs Haydon's until about 1860 when William Haydon Smallpiece became a partner. In 1883, when it held customer balances of about £140,000, it was acquired by Capital & Counties Bank Ltd (est. 1877).

Records: Lloyds TSB Group plc, Archives, Head Office, 71 Lombard Street, London EC3P 3BS

Amalgamation papers 1883–90.

HEAD & CO
East Grinstead, West Sussex

History: This private bank was established in about 1846 by George Head. It had branches at Edenbridge (1878), Horley (1886) and Oxted (1888). The business failed in 1892 with unsecured liabilities of £150,000 and was acquired by Lloyds Bank Ltd (est. 1765).

Records 1: Lloyds TSB Group plc, Archives, Head Office, 71 Lombard Street, London EC3P 3BS

Amalgamation papers 1892–94.

266 *British banking – a guide to historical records*

Records 2: West Sussex Record Office, County Hall, Chichester PO19 1RN

Papers [Ref: Add. MSS. 27, 632–27, 649]

J M HEAD & CO
Carlisle, Cumbria

History: This private bank was established in 1804 as Joseph Monkhouse Head & Co and was otherwise known as Carlisle Old Bank. It was the only Carlisle bank to survive the 1836 financial crisis and therefore captured much of its competitors' business. Many of its customers were drawn from county and landowning families while the emerging local joint stock banks tended to provide services for rapidly expanding local industry. Branches were established at Whitehaven, Workington and Brampton. In 1865, when still recognised as Carlisle's leading bank, it was acquired by Cumberland Union Banking Co Ltd (est. 1829). This joint stock bank moved its head office from Workington to J M Head & Co's offices in Carlisle and Heads' senior partner became the bank's chairman.

W F Crick & J E Wadsworth, *A Hundred Years of Joint Stock Banking* (London, 1936)

Records: HSBC Holdings plc, Group Archives, 10 Lower Thames Street, London EC3R 6AE

Deposit account balance book 1854–64; security book 1854–65; discount ledger 1857–64; current account balance books (3) 1859–64; banker's references 1864.

HEATH & CO
Andover, Hampshire

History: This private bank was formed in 1790 as Gilbert & Co and was styled Heath & Co from 1809; it was also known as the Andover Bank. The bank was acquired by Hampshire Banking Co (est. 1834) in 1861.

Records: Lloyds TSB Group plc, Archives, Head Office, 71 Lombard Street, London EC3P 3BS

Customer account ledger 1838–45.

HECTOR, LACY & CO
Petersfield, Hampshire

History: This private bank was established in 1808 as Patrick Eyles & Co; it was otherwise known as the Petersfield & Hampshire Bank. It was

Records of banks **267**

styled Hector, Lacy & Co from 1821 and was acquired by the London & County Joint Stock Banking Co (est. 1836) in 1841.

Records: The Royal Bank of Scotland plc, Archive Section, Regent's House, 42 Islington High Street, London N1 8XL

Partnership agreement 1826.

HEDGES, WELLS & CO
Wallingford, Oxfordshire

History: This private bank was formed in 1797. It was then known as Wells, Allnatt, Wells & Wells and was otherwise styled the Wallingford Bank. In 1858 the business was renamed Hedges, Wells & Co and was acquired by Lloyds Bank Ltd (est. 1765) in 1905.

Records 1: Lloyds TSB Group plc, Archives, Head Office, 71 Lombard Street, London EC3P 3BS

Amalgamation papers 1905.

Records 2: Berkshire Record Office, Shire Hall, Shinfield Park, Reading RG2 9XD

Partnership papers, including partners' agreements and correspondence 1828–93; statement of confidence 1847; papers re premises alterations 1877; amalgamation papers 1891–92. [Ref: D/EH B29–33; W/Z 10/15]

HELBERT, WAGG & CO LTD
London

History: This London merchant bank was established as a firm of stock-brokers in 1848, its founders tracing their origins to a German Jewish family. A major client was N M Rothschild & Sons for whom the firm acted as principal broker. The business was known as Helbert, Wagg & Campbell from 1877 and as Helbert, Wagg & Russell from 1899 before reverting to Helbert, Wagg & Co in 1912. One of its first issues was undertaken for the Australian & Eastern Navigation Co in 1864 and by the 1890s issues for businesses such as Liptons and Furness Withey were being lead-managed. In 1913 the business changed from a brokerage house to concentrate on security issues and underwriting, the firm's first bond issue being for the City of Ottawa. During the First World War an acceptance finance business was begun while also the firm began to deal in gilts and treasury bills (until 1919). In 1919 it converted to a private limited company and the acquisition of Bonn & Co in 1921 strengthened its foreign exchange operations. However security issues remained its most important activity. In this, and often working closely with the British

268 British banking – a guide to historical records

Overseas Bank Ltd (est. 1919), it now emerged as a major house and in the 1920s specialised in issues for continental sovereign and municipal clients and for UK and German businesses. In 1926 investment management began with the establishment and management of an investment trust. In the 1930s issues were handled largely for UK businesses, including household names such as Marks & Spencer. This provided a solid foundation for the firm's development in the 1950s into one of the City's first broadly-based corporate finance houses. Investment management also grew quickly. In 1960 Schroders Ltd acquired 70 per cent of Helbert, Wagg Holdings Ltd, owners of the merchant bank of Helbert, Wagg & Co Ltd; the remaining 30 per cent was acquired in 1962. Schroders' merchant banking subsidiary of J Henry Schroder & Co Ltd (est. 1818) was then renamed J Henry Schroder Wagg & Co Ltd.

W Lionel Fraser, *All to the Good* (London, 1963); Richard Roberts, *Schroders. Merchants and Bankers* (London, 1992)

Records: J Henry Schroder & Co Ltd, 120 Cheapside, London EC2V 6DS

No records survive covering the early years when Waggs were stockbrokers. Financial accounts survive from 1915, directors' meeting minutes from 1919 and files covering particular transactions from the 1920s. These formed the basis of that part of Richard Robert's *Schroders. Merchants and Bankers* (1992) devoted to Helbert Wagg. In 1996 a computer-based database giving details of the archives was being established at Schroders' head office. The archives themselves are housed elsewhere and are not readily available and access is limited. Inquiries should be addressed to the Company Secretary.

HELSTON BANKING CO
Helston, Cornwall

History: This joint stock bank was formed in 1836 and failed in 1878.

Records: Cornwall Record Office, County Hall, Truro TR1 3AY

Liquidation agreement 1877. [Ref: X 393/135]

HENLEY, CLARKE, WHEADON & HALLETT
Chard, Somerset

History: This private bank was formed in 1790 and ceased business in around 1800.

Records: Somerset Record Office, Obridge Road, Taunton TA2 7PU

Bill, waste, balance and money books 1791–95; Wheadon family papers re banking 1791–1866. [Ref: DD/SAS C/909]

Records of banks

HENTY & CO
Worthing, West Sussex

History: This bank was founded in about 1808 as Margesson, Henty, Henty & Hopkins and subsequently traded as Henty, Hopkins & Henty and, from about 1829, as Henty, Upperton & Olliver; it was otherwise styled the Worthing & Sussex Bank. Branches were established at Arundel (1808), Steyning (1827), Horsham (1839), Littlehampton (1859) and Crawley (1885). The business was acquired by Capital & Counties Bank Ltd (est. 1877) in 1896.

Records: Lloyds TSB Group plc, Archives, Head Office, 71 Lombard Street, London EC3P 3BS

General and customer account balance book 1827–36.

Horsham: letterbook 1836–42; signature books (3) c.1836–96; 'monthly book' (giving statistics of bills, promissory notes, etc) 1868–73.

HEREFORDSHIRE BANKING CO
Hereford, Hereford & Worcester

History: This joint stock bank was formed at Hereford in 1836 and it acquired Jones & Co of Hereford in 1844. It failed in 1863 when its business was acquired by Midland Banking Co Ltd (est. 1863).

Records 1: Lloyds TSB Group plc, Archives, Head Office, 71 Lombard Street, London EC3P 3BS

Agreement for employment 1837; annual general meeting report 1838; list of shareholders 1843.

Records 2: Barclays Bank plc, Group Archives, Dallimore Road, Wythenshawe, Manchester M23 9JA

Bank notes 1842; circular 1863.

HERRIES, FARQUHAR & CO
London

History: This bank was formed in London's West End in about 1770 by Robert Herries as the London Exchange Banking Co. As a child, Herries lived in Dumfriesshire and later moved to Rotterdam where he worked for a merchant. Afterwards he joined the famous Amsterdam bankers, Hope & Co. Aged 23, he set up in business in Barcelona and in 1762 the Coutts family recruited him to lead their City of London commission and exchange business which was reorganised as Herries, Cochrane & Co. He developed the idea of the traveller's cheque and set up the London Ex-

270   *British banking – a guide to historical records*

change Banking Co in St James's to exploit it. A niche business was soon carved out and extended through the addition of a general banking business. In 1775 the business was renamed Sir Robert Herries & Co and was styled Herries, Farquhar & Co in 1797. Early partners included Thomas Hammersley, who was later to join Cox & Co (est. 1758) where he established a similar business. During and after the Napoleonic Wars, the firm marketed British government securities. In 1865 Call, Marten & Co (est. 1773) of Old Bond Street, London, was acquired. In mid-nineteenth century London, the firm was reckoned to be one of the leading bankers to the aristocracy and gentry. It was acquired in 1893 by Lloyds Bank Ltd (est. 1765).

John Booker, *Travellers' Money* (Bath, 1994); F G Hilton Price, *A Handbook of London Bankers* (London, 1876); R S Sayers, *Lloyds Bank in the History of English Banking* (Oxford, 1957)

Records: Lloyds TSB Group plc, Archives, Head Office, 71 Lombard Street, London EC3P 3BS

General ledgers (2) 1773–1813 [w]; bad debt book 1789–1816; customer ledger 1794–1836; closed accounts register 1795–1840; clerks' salary book 1796–1807; partnership agreements 1797–1807; signature books (3) late eighteenth cent 1821–60; correspondence re overdrafts 1808–15; note registers (3) 1814–64; security ledger 1835–60; standing order book 1840s; London Royal Militia ledger 1855; salary book 1862–95; amalgamation papers 1887–1912; private ledger of A Farquhar 1890–1919.

HEYWOOD BROTHERS & CO
Manchester, Greater Manchester

History: This private bank was established in 1788 by Benjamin Heywood, and his two sons, Benjamin Arthur and Nathaniel, in Exchange Street, Manchester; it traded as Benjamin Heywood, Sons & Co. Benjamin was brother of Arthur Heywood who had established the Liverpool private bank of Arthur Heywood, Sons & Co in 1773. The bank flourished, moving in 1795 to a site in St Ann Street. In 1795 Benjamin Heywood died and the firm became known as Heywood Brothers & Co. In 1814 Benjamin Heywood, eldest son of Nathaniel, was admitted as a partner and in the following year Nathaniel died. His other sons, Thomas and Richard, became partners in 1818 and 1820 respectively. Shortly afterwards the bank opened its first and only branch in Stockport, but it was soon closed. Benjamin Arthur, the senior partner, died in 1828 and in the following year both Thomas and Richard retired, having inherited their uncle's large fortune. With Benjamin Heywood remaining as sole partner, the firm's name was changed to Benjamin Heywood & Co in 1832 and

Records of banks 271

Benjamin Heywood Bart. & Co in 1838. Heywood relied greatly on his head clerk, William Langton, although all of his four sons, Oliver, Arthur, Edward and Charles, joined the partnership. In 1848 new bank premises were built in St Ann Street. Heywood retired in 1860 and the bank again became known as Heywood Brothers & Co. In April 1874 it was acquired by the Manchester & Salford Bank (est. 1836).

Anon, *Over Two Centuries of Banking in Manchester* (priv. pub., 1994); Anon, *Williams Deacon's 1771–1970* (Manchester, 1971); Leo H Grindon, *Manchester Banks and Bankers* (Manchester, 1877)

Records: The Royal Bank of Scotland plc, Archive Section, Regent's House, 42 Islington High Street, London N1 8XL

Letter re forgery, including notes and cheques 1782; drafts and acceptances journal 1788–90; commission and interest book 1788–1840; bad debt register 1788–1836; customer account ledgers 1791–1800; banker's draft forms 1790s; accounts closed book c.1800–47; papers re bad debts 1802–68; customer directories 1815–74; papers re silver coinage receivership 1817; partnership agreements 1828–29, 1861; papers re partner retirements 1828–76; annual summary balances 1828–58; decennial statements book 1828–73; cheques c.1820s–74; bank notes c.1820s; general ledgers 1830–74; signature books 1834–60; authority books 1837–74; profit and loss book 1841–64; unpaid bills 1841–65; letter of guarantee 1847; architectural drawings of new bank c.1840s; credit balances 1851–71; safe custody item inventory c.1852–74; bills of exchange 1853–57; Oliver Heywood's notebook: 1854–64, re Overend Gurney crisis 1866; staff book 1855–74; charges account book 1856–74; stock book c.1858–74; register of customers 1860–62; probate registers 1862–74; memoir of Sir Benjamin Heywood c.1867; summary of business books 1871–74; amalgamation papers 1874–76; manager's character book c.1870s; photographs of partners c.1870s–1880s; memorial volume re statue of Oliver Heywood c.1894.

HEYWOOD, KENNARD & CO
London

History: This private bank was established in St Mary Axe, City of London, in about 1800 as Joseph Denison & Co. It subsequently moved to Fenchurch Street. The firm was known as Denison, Heywood, Kennard & Co from 1836, when it traded in Lombard Street, and as Heywood, Kennard & Co from 1850. It amalgamated with the Bank of Manchester Ltd (est. 1829) to form the Consolidated Bank Ltd in 1863.

F G Hilton Price, *A Handbook of London Bankers* (London, 1876)

272 *British banking – a guide to historical records*

Records 1: The Royal Bank of Scotland plc, Archive Section, Regent's House, 42 Islington High Street, London N1 8XL

Private ledger 1850–59.

Records 2: Brynmor Jones Library, University of Hull, Hull HU6 7RX

Correspondence with Sykes family re banking and financial matters nineteenth cent. [Ref: DDSY/101/50, 55]

ARTHUR HEYWOOD, SONS & CO
Liverpool, Merseyside

History: This private bank, the first to be formed in Liverpool, was established in 1773 by Arthur Heywood; it appears to have traded as Arthur Heywood, Sons & Co for all of its existence, the Heywood family providing most of its senior partners. Arthur Heywood was an international merchant and initially he provided banking services as part of his merchanting business. In 1784 a branch was opened at Manchester but it soon closed. In 1788 Arthur's brother, Benjamin, settled in Manchester and with his two sons opened a bank, Benjamin Heywood & Co. Arthur Heywood's bank was one of the most important in Liverpool, holding the accounts of Liverpool Corporation, of the Docks, of leading merchants such as William Brown and of manufacturers. In 1883 the business was acquired by the Bank of Liverpool Ltd (est. 1831) for £400,000 which represented average annual profits of £50,000 for each of the previous seven years plus £50,000. The bank then had deposits of £2.6 million, 2,749 accounts and two branches, both in Liverpool.

George Chandler, *Four Centuries of Banking*, (London, 1964–68); John Hughes, *Liverpool Banks and Bankers* (Liverpool, 1906)

Records: Barclays Bank plc, Group Archives, Dallimore Road, Wythenshawe, Manchester M23 9JA

Funeral expenses, Benjamin Heywood 1725; private ledgers (3) 1763–1832; bills of exchange 1770–1807; partnership agreements 1774–76; annual expenses, Arthur Heywood 1779–1836; signature books 1770s–1938; letter to Arthur Heywood re Heywood family 1783; inventory and account of partnership 1786; private ledger including account balances 1787–1832; customer ledger 1788–97; apprenticeship agreements 1797–1824; diary of London visit 1808; probate papers, Heywood family c.1816–62; letter to J P Heywood re new bank premises 1833; account of personal estate, Arthur Heywood 1835–37; staff records 1836–1928; balance sheets 1845–82; cheque book 1874–77.

Records of banks **273**

HILL & SON
London

History: This private bank, which was closely connected with the cattle and meat trades, was established near Smithfield meat market in the City of London in 1825. Its founder was Charles Hill, who had earlier been a manager of Sharpe & Sons (est. 1810), bankers at 8 West Smithfield that had failed in 1825. Shortly afterwards, Charles Hill was joined in partnership by his sons, George and John, and in turn they were succeeded by Charles's grandson, John. Branches were opened at Romford (1882), Liverpool and Birkenhead and sub-branches were located at Islington and Deptford. Increasingly the bank had difficulties in lending the more substantial sums needed by larger customers and in 1911 it was acquired by Lloyds Bank Ltd (est. 1765).

F G Hilton Price, *A Handbook of London Bankers* (London, 1876)

Records: Lloyds TSB Group plc, Archives, Head Office, 71 Lombard Street, London EC3P 3BS

Amalgamation papers 1911–27.

Romford: signature book 1882–1916.

PHILIP HILL, HIGGINSON & CO LTD
London

History: This merchant bank was formed in the City of London in 1907 as the London house of Lee, Higginson & Co, investment bankers at Boston, United States. By the 1920s it was an important lead-manager of sterling bond issues for overseas borrowers, especially in conjunction with J Henry Schroder & Co. The business benefited from the leadership of Sir Guy Granet (1867–1943) who emerged in the 1920s as a leading City merchant banker. In 1927 the firm was converted into a private unlimited company. In 1932 it was damaged through the collapse of a major customer, Ivar Kreuger, the Swedish match millionaire, although its sister house in the United States was worse affected. From the 1930s, and following the closure of the London market to bond issues by foreign borrowers, Higginsons focused on providing services to British industry. In 1951 the business was acquired by the industrialist Philip Hill to form Philip Hill, Higginson & Co Ltd that in 1959 merged with Erlangers Ltd (est. 1870) to form Philip Hill, Higginson, Erlangers Ltd. In 1965 this latter business merged with M Samuel & Co Ltd (est. 1831) to form the merchant bank of Hill Samuel & Co Ltd.

Records: Lloyds TSB Group plc, Group Archives, 71 Lombard Street, London EC3P 3BS

274   *British banking – a guide to historical records*

Partnership agreements and files 1907–46; directors' meeting minutes 1927–59; accounts 1939–63.

HILTON, RIGDEN & RIGDEN
Faversham, Kent

History: This private bank was established in 1796 as Bax, Jones & Co; it was otherwise known as the Faversham Commercial Bank. It was styled Jones, Wright & Co from 1806, Wright & Hilton from 1812 and Hilton, Rigden & Rigden from 1840. In 1892 the bank was acquired for about £22,000 by Prescott, Dimsdale, Cave, Tugwell & Co Ltd (est. 1891) of London.

Anon, 'Prescott's Bank. Amalgamation and Expansion', *National Provincial Bank Review* (1966–68)

Records: The Royal Bank of Scotland plc, Archive Section, Regent's House, 42 Islington High Street, London N1 8XL

Customer signature book 1850s–90s; papers re partners 1863–68; amalgamation agreement 1902.

C HOARE & CO
London

History: This private bank is the longest-surviving private bank in Britain, tracing its origins to Richard (later Sir Richard) Hoare (1648–1718) who in 1672 was allowed to keep ledgers as a goldsmith. In 1673 he inherited the goldsmith business of his master, Robert Tempest, at the sign of the Golden Bottle in Cheapside, City of London. In 1686 deposits totalled £19,000 and grew to £113,000 in 1702. In this year, Richard's son, Henry, was taken into partnership when the business was that of a banker and goldsmith. In 1690 Hoares transferred to their present site in Fleet Street, their existing premises dating from 1829. From the outset, their business attracted distinguished customers including Samuel Pepys, Sir Geoffrey Kneller and Dr Hans Sloane. This continued into the nineteenth century when, during the early years, customers included Queen Charlotte, Eton College and Oxford and Cambridge colleges. On Sir Richard's death in 1718, the business was carried on by his sons Henry and Benjamin and subsequently by other members of the Hoare family in whose leadership the bank remains in 2001. Its title changed with the generations: Richard Hoare (1672–98); Richard Hoare & Partners (1698–1718); Henry & Benjamin Hoare (1725–50); Sir Richard Hoare & Partners (1785–87); Henry Hoare & Co (1787–1828); Henry Hugh Hoare & Co (1828–41); Charles Hoare & Co (1841–1928); and C Hoare & Co (from 1928). Since

Records of banks **275**

its earliest days, the bank administered the securities of its customers, an income tax department was established shortly before the First World War and, in the 1920s, a company was established to administer trusts. In the 1930s the first branch was opened in Park Lane, London, and moved to Waterloo Place in 1975 and to Lowndes Street in 1985.

Anon, *C Hoare & Co, Bankers. A History* (priv. pub., c.1990s); H P R Hoare, *Hoare's Bank. A Record 1672–1955. The Story of a Private Bank* (London, 1955)

Records: C Hoare & Co, 37 Fleet Street, London EC4P 4DQ

Customer current account ledgers 1673 on; notes on staff 1674–1906; loan ledgers and accounts 1677–85, 1696 on; analysis of bank's early business 1678–1740; daily cash books 1677–85; goldsmith's debt book 1684–1702; goldsmith's workbook 1684–87; bill book 1688–94; Sir W Benson's private ledgers 1690–1713; daily cash book 1692–95; goldsmith's engravers book 1693–98; Hoare family correspondence 1695 on; customers' addresses 1685–87, 1800–83; goldsmith's plate book 1697–1736; goldsmith's day book 1700–44; copy-letters to customers 1701–06; daily cash book 1701–02; annual signed balance sheets 1702 on; annual division of profit accounts 1702 on; partnership agreements 1702–1928; daily balance books (39) 1707–1848; letters to customers 1708–1869; Queen Anne's privy purse accounts 1710–14; accounts and papers re South Sea Co 1712–25; Hoare family wills 1718–1884; annual shop expenses 1718–1891; private ledgers 1719–1891; mortgage deeds and receipt book 1734–77; private accounts of Henry Hoare 1749–84; miscellaneous letterbooks (5) 1758–59; private accounts of clerk to House of Commons 1760–1820; daily cash book 1762–63; general orders 1766–1807; Michaelmas working papers 1770 on; letters from overseas agents 1767–78; private account of chief clerk 1788–1826; partners' memorandum books 1793 on; applications for employment 1795–1863; signature books 1796–1893; brokerage books (6) 1800s; Lord Chamberlain's Department accounts 1807–11; business diaries of H Hoare 1828–31; papers re building of premises 1829–31; household accounts 1912–21.

HODGE & CO
Devonport, Devon

History: This private bank was established in Plymouth Dock (Devonport) in 1804 as Glencross, Hodge & Norman; it was otherwise known as the Naval & Commercial Bank. The bank became known in 1824 as Hodge & Co and otherwise as the Devonport Bank. A branch was opened in Plymouth in 1876. The bank was acquired by Bolitho, Foster, Coode & Co Ltd (est. 1889) in 1889.

276 British banking – a guide to historical records

P W Matthews & Anthony W Tuke, *History of Barclays Bank Ltd* (London, 1926)

Records: Barclays Bank plc, Group Archives, Dallimore Road, Wythenshawe, Manchester M23 9JA

Customer account ledgers 1809–20; balance sheets 1889.

HODGKIN, BARNETT, PEASE, SPENCE & CO
Newcastle upon Tyne, Tyne & Wear

History: This private bank was established in 1859, following the collapse of the last surviving Newcastle joint stock bank in 1857. The poor trading record of joint stock banks created local enthusiasm for private banks which was fast disappearing elsewhere. The founding partners included Robert Spence, formerly manager of the failed Newcastle, Shields & Sunderland Union Joint Stock Bank (est. 1836); Robert Gurney Hoare, son of a partner of Barnett, Hoare & Co (est. c.1728) of London; and John W Pease. Under Spence's leadership, the bank rapidly expanded by opening branches throughout the North East; by 1903 it operated about thirty which made it a leading bank in the Newcastle area. In 1903 it was acquired by Lloyds Bank Ltd (est. 1765). Its partner, J W Beaumont Pease, later Lord Wardington, was to be Lloyds' chairman from 1922 to 1945.

Maberly Phillips, *A History of Banks, Bankers and Banking in Northumberland, Durham and North Yorkshire* (London, 1894); R S Sayers, *Lloyds Bank in the History of English Banking* (Oxford, 1957)

Records: Lloyds TSB Group plc, Archives, Head Office, 71 Lombard Street, London EC3P 3BS

Customer ledger 1860s; safe custody register 1863 on; security registers 1865 on; investment and liquidation book 1885–1902; private memorandum books 1890s; amalgamation papers 1903.

Alnwick: statistics register 1867–1907; memorandum book c.1888–1920; **Bellingham:** memorandum book 1896–1917; **Blaydon-on-Tyne:** memorandum book 1900–21; **Hexham:** security register 1869–1908; memorandum book 1898–1909; **Morpeth:** memorandum book 1897–1903; **Newcastle, Collingwood Street:** signature books (2) 1883–1902; **Newcastle, Westgate Road:** signature books (2) 1893–1906; memorandum book 1901–06; **North Shields:** signature book 1859–88; security register 1859–1902; **Rothbury:** memorandum book 1890–1910; **Shotley Bridge:** memorandum books (2) 1886–1911; **South Shields:** security registers (2) 1888–1902; memorandum book 1891–1920; **Sunderland:** memorandum book 1901–07.

Records of banks

HOLT & CO
London

History: This private bank was established as an army agent by William Kirkland in St James's, London, in about 1809. Army agents kept the accounts of army regiments, distributing pay and subsistence, dealing in supplies of clothing, claims for pensions and injury, and providing a general banking business for soldiers and their families. Initially agent to the First Regiment of Foot, Kirkland was quickly appointed to other units holding seventeen agencies by 1847. Following army reforms in 1872, competition for agency work grew and Holt & Co amalgamated with another army agent, Lawrie & Son (est. 1794). From 1892 profits had to be made entirely from the banking services offered to officers and their families. Business volume grew significantly during the First World War when Holt & Co dealt with the pay of over 50,000 Army officers; the staff of forty increased to 850. Links were forged with the Royal Navy in 1915 through the acquisition of Woodhead & Co (est. c.1804), naval agents, which continued to trade separately as Woodhead's Branch until 1919. Additionally, in 1918, when the Royal Air Force was formed, the Air Ministry offered part of the official pay agency to Holt & Co. In 1923, upon the death of Vesey Holt, the business was acquired by Glyn, Mills & Co (est. 1753) and in 1930 Holts moved from Whitehall Place to Kirkland House. In 1939 Glyn, Mills & Co was acquired by The Royal Bank of Scotland (est. 1727), although Holts continued to trade as a separate business until the 1960s. During the Second World War the banking and pay departments were evacuated to Osterley Park. The pay agency accounts increased from 2,600 in 1930, to 9,900 in 1939 and to 42,600 by 1945. After the war, the pay and ledger departments were removed to new offices at Lampton, near Osterley, and a pioneering experimental closed-circuit television link set up between Whitehall and Osterley. In 1970, following the introduction of the military salary, the Army and RAF pay agencies were not renewed and the pay department was closed. Holts continued to operate many army-linked accounts and in 1976 opened a branch in Farnborough to serve army customers. In 1992 the business of Holts Branch merged with that of Drummonds in Charing Cross.

Anon, 'From Redcoat to Battledress. The Story of Holt's Agency 1809–1959', *Three Banks Review*, 45 (1959); Eric Gore Browne, *Glyn, Mills & Co* (priv. pub., 1933)

Records: The Royal Bank of Scotland plc, Archive Section, Regent's House, 42 Islington High Street, London N1 8XL

Premises papers, Whitehall Place 1844–81; cheque samples book c.1870–1927; private ledgers 1871–1941; regimental funds ledger 1871–78; cheque

278 British banking – a guide to historical records

books 1874–1900; army pay agency correspondence 1878–1953; private balance books 1881–1922; tax returns 1881–1919; signature books 1882–1939; joint account order books 1883–1900; appointment circulars 1886–91; list of correspondents 1886–1915; power of attorney register 1886–1900; letterbook 1887–88; solicitors' accounts 1888; cheque registers 1890–1946; investment ledgers 1891–1920; articles on deposit book 1893–1900; monthly balances analysis books 1899–1932; tax liability ledger 1899–1915; photographs: staff c.1910–37, partners c.1900–1930s, property 1930s–1960s; balances book 1907–13; subject files 1909–60; passbook, Bank of England securities 1914–22; acquisition papers, Woodhead & Co 1914–15; RAF pay agency correspondence 1917–41; papers re United Services Trustee 1918–46; annual branch accounts 1923–24; press cuttings re amalgamation with Glyn Mills & Co 1923–24; architectural drawings: Kirkland House 1920s–1950s, Osterley House c.1940, Lampton Hall 1950–53; staff dinner menus 1928–33; booklet re opening of Kirkland House c.1930; customer correspondence re mobilisation 1931–40; notes on mechanisation of book-keeping 1933; report on branch departments 1934; papers re wartime premises: Kirkland House 1937–49, Osterley Park 1949–54; agendas and minutes of Holts Central Committee 1939–45; pay agency statistics 1939–48; report on pay agency 1939–41; inventory and valuation 1940; marketing literature 1940–1960s; press cuttings 1943–65; papers re RAF pay agency 1945, 1949; statistics sheets 1949–64; valuation of Holts agency 1954–55; correspondence from Ministry of Defence re end of agency 1969; papers re opening of Farnborough branch 1974–77.

HONGKONG & SHANGHAI BANKING CORPORATION LTD
London and Asia

History: This overseas bank was established in 1865 to provide banking services for customers on the China coast. It was incorporated under a special Hong Kong ordinance allowing it to have a local head office, as opposed to one based in London, issue its own notes and hold government funds. The initial capital of HK$5 million was subscribed by the local European, Indian and American communities and the bank's headquarters were at 1 Queen's Road Central, Hong Kong. By the end of 1866 branch and agencies had been opened in London, China, Japan, India, North America and throughout south east Asia. The expansion of the branch network continued throughout the nineteenth century following the dictates of trade. By 1890, twenty-two branches existed and by 1913 there were thirty-two. Assets then totalled £39 million and this made the bank the second largest of any UK overseas bank. Over-commitment to certain local industries led to setbacks in the 1870s, but under the management of Sir Thomas Jackson (1876–1902) the bank emerged as the foremost finan-

Records of banks 279

cial institution in the East. Much of its prestige derived from its involvement in government finance and loans; in 1874 it handled China's first public bond issue and was thereafter a prime mover in other issues. In the twentieth century this led to the bank's involvement in the China Consortium for multi-national lending to China. The bank also played an important part in the attempt in the 1930s to stabilise China's currency. In 1938 it had forty branches while its total assets were almost £80 million, meaning that it ranked in size just below Barclays (Dominion Colonial & Overseas) and the Standard Bank of South Africa. During the Second World War most of the foreign staff were interned and control of the bank passed to London. Plans were then laid for restarting the business and restoring local economies. The bank had to adjust its business to the scaling down of its operations in China in 1955 and the nationalisation of its interests in other countries. Hong Kong, however, boomed and the bank backed the colony's evolution from trading port to manufacturing centre by vastly expanding its branch network. The bank diversified away from banking in the East after the war; the purchase of the British Bank of the Middle East Ltd (est. 1889) and of the Mercantile Bank Ltd (est. 1892) in 1959 emphasised its entry into new markets. A United States subsidiary was established as early as 1955 and was extended through the acquisition of Marine Midland, a New York State-based bank in 1980, while the Hongkong Bank of Canada was founded in 1981. The geographical spread of the bank was extended to all continents when, in July 1992, Midland Bank plc of London became a wholly-owned member of the bank. The holding company, HSBC Holdings plc, based in London, was created in 1991 to support the increasing diversity of the group.

M Collis, *Wayfoong. The Hongkong & Shanghai Banking Corporation* (London, 1965); Frank H H King, *The History of the Hongkong & Shanghai Banking Corporation* (Cambridge, 1987–91); Frank H H King, *Eastern Banking. Essays in the History of the Hongkong & Shanghai Banking Corporation* (1983)

Records 1: HSBC Holdings plc, Group Archives, 10 Lower Thames Street, London EC3R 6AE

Hong Kong Head Office: annual reports and accounts 1865–1994; deeds of settlement and ordinances 1867–1974; David McLean papers as inspector 1872–74; inspector's reports on branches 1870s–1920s; staff lists 1890–1980s; records re various government and railway loans 1897–1960s; correspondence with European branches (10) 1906–1930s; chief manager's telegram books (88) 1913–69; chief manager's private letters 1921–26, 1928–29; chief manager's local letters 1926–35; market letters from London 1929–35; correspondence with United States branches 1920s–1930s; correspondence with Indian branches (11) 1920s–1930s; correspondence

280 *British banking – a guide to historical records*

with Chinese branches (150) 1920s–1930s; correspondence with London (110) 1920s–1930s; correspondence with Asian branches (80) 1920s–1930s; correspondence with Japanese branches (20) 1920s–1930s; letters from British & Chinese Corporation 1932–1970s; papers of Grayburn, chief manager 1935–41; head office telegram books (25) 1936–51; half-yearly reports from branches 1939–1960s; property records 1940s–1970s; reports on wartime damage to property and staff interned 1940s–1950s; papers of Morse, chief manager 1941–46; balance sheets 1947–72; correspondence re China's foreign trade 1948–73; branch statistics 1965–75; **London Office:** London share registers (6) 1866–1934; registers of London shareholders (17) 1870–1948; standing order books (6) 1880–1958; papers re bond issues etc for China government and railways including papers re British & Chinese Corporation and Chinese Bondholders Committee 1898–1950s; records re Japanese loans 1904–12; records re Siamese loans 1905–22; register of candidates for bank service (4) 1911–18; consultative committee minutes (16) 1912–69; correspondence with branches (350) 1913–40s; reports on juniors going East (5) 1914–1950s; consultative committee agenda books (15) 1916–67; Sir Newton Stabb's papers 1921–30; details of passages for staff going East (2) 1921–52; report on work and procedure of London departments 1922–23; consultative committee agenda books (7) 1926–61; London manager's papers 1933–48; branch reconstruction files 1945–1950s; **Amoy, China:** fixed deposit register 1913–29; loan account register 1916–41; general correspondence with other branches 1931–56; bill records 1935–49; records of drafts issued (2) 1938–51; monthly returns (3) 1940–50; day books (3) 1940–49; other branches accounts (3) 1940–50; charges account ledger 1941–49; current account ledger 1941–42; general ledgers (2) 1941–48; general ledger balance books (2) 1941–50; **Chefoo, China:** charges account ledgers (4) 1938–41; overdrawn current account ledgers (3) 1938–41; **Chungking, China:** telegram books (6) 1943–49; general correspondence with branches 1945–50; **Foochow, China:** signature book 1868–1921; current account records (2) 1873–1918, 1939–42; safe custody register 1888–1949; loan ledger 1900–49; security register 1906–41; bill records (15) 1907–49; charges account ledgers (5) 1914–47; telegram books (22) 1919–50; exchange rates registers (10) 1926–41; general ledgers (3) 1930–49; other branches accounts 1930–37; general ledger balance books (3) 1935–45; records of drafts issued (2) 1935–51; external correspondence 1939–49; general correspondence with other branches (28) 1941–50; managerial correspondence (2) 1942–49; monthly returns 1945–49; **Hankow, China:** external correspondence 1911–50; statistics 1922–35; managerial correspondence 1925–51; security ledger 1926–50; fixed deposit ledger 1933–41; loans register 1933–50; monthly returns 1936–47; overdrawn current account books (3) 1938–41; general ledger balance book 1938–47; telegraphic

Records of banks 281

transfer records 1938–50; records of account with Shanghai branch 1938–50; general correspondence with other branches 1938–50; records of drafts issued 1938–51; charges accounts (3) 1939–41; current account ledger 1939–49; **Harbin, China:** loan ledger 1917–36; correspondence with branches 1920–35; charges account ledgers (10) 1920–47; profit and loss accounts (2) 1929–47; records of accounts with other branches (2) 1929–47; telegram books (2) 1929–54; telegraphic transfer records (4) 1930–41; security registers (2) 1931–38; general ledger balance books (5) 1931–47; bill records (2) 1932–37; exchange account ledgers (10) 1932–41; general ledgers (2) 1933–41; records of drafts issued 1938–51; current account ledger 1941–47; **Hong Kong:** note register 1865–1937; loans and overdraft register 1919–40; general ledgers (10) 1937–50; general ledger balance books (10) 1937–50; standing instructions 1939–45; market research reports 1980s; **Lyons, France:** general correspondence with other branches 1892–1947; telegram book 1923–39; general ledgers (11) 1930s–1940s; general ledger balance book 1940–46; current account ledgers (7) 1940s; **Moukden, China:** managerial correspondence (3) 1929–49; bankers' opinions 1930–39; fixed deposit ledger 1930–33; bill records (4) 1932–49; loan ledger 1933–40; general ledgers (6) 1934–46; records of drafts issued (3) 1935–51; other branches accounts (2) 1935–47; general correspondence with branches (26) 1937–53; external correspondence 1938–41; general ledger balance books (3) 1938–48; **Nanking, China:** general correspondence with branches 1945–49; telegraphic transfer records (2) 1947–48; **Peking, China:** security register 1892–1952; loans registers (2) 1908–51; notes issued registers (2) 1908–24; external correspondence (50) 1911–41; bill records 1918–51; telegram books (20) 1919–55; loans ledger 1922–39; exchange account records (3) 1924–41; general ledgers (9) 1925–51; managerial correspondence (15) 1925–55; general ledger balance books (4) 1928–54; profit and loss accounts (2) 1929–33; bankers' opinions 1929–41; telegraphic transfer records (2) 1929–52; records of other branches accounts (11) 1930–54; general correspondence with branches (25) 1934–54; returns 1935–49; records of drafts issued (5) 1935–51; cash balance books (7) 1935–54; current account ledger 1936–55; fixed deposit register 1937–52; charges account ledgers (6) 1938–54; current account balances (11) 1938–52; current account journals (25) 1947–51; **Shanghai, China:** current account records (7) 1865–67, 1932–1950s; general ledgers (10) 1865–71, 1936–51; Shanghai share register records 1866–1950; deposit at call register 1868–1900; fixed deposit registers (7) 1868–72, 1934–52; general ledger balance books (15) 1873–81, 1934–52; circulars from Hong Kong (2) 1885–1951; gold account records (16) 1888–93, 1931–51; charges ledgers (10) 1898–1950s; general correspondence with other branches (50) 1898–1955; Chinese signature books (2) 1912–41; customs administration papers 1913–41; Chinese government

282   British banking – a guide to historical records

and railway loan records 1913–1950s; managerial correspondence with Hong Kong (10) 1914–37; profit and loss accounts (10) 1918–48; bill schedules and records (40) 1918–48; note register 1923–52; exchange account ledgers (11) 1923–51; correspondence with Hong Kong (6) 1925–55; external correspondence (17) 1928–47; branch accounts records (18) 1929–53; telegrams received and dispatched 1933–58; monthly returns (20) 1933–54; exchange rate records (5) 1937–53; Stabilization Board records 1930s–1950s; bankers' opinions 1930s–1940s; telegram books (6) 1930s–40s; **Tientsin, China:** general ledgers (9) 1881–1911; security registers (6) 1885–1952; safe custody registers (11) 1885–1951; accounts of other branches (12) 1887–1951; note registers (3) 1887–1927; signature books (3) 1888–1905; general ledger balance books (18) 1889–1954; accountant's memorandum book 1890–1929; telegrams received and dispatched (200) 1891–1954; Savings Bank registers (6) 1894–1945; managerial correspondence with Europe and USA (2) 1896–1936; charges account ledgers (8) 1901–51; half-yearly returns (6) 1910–14, 1934–47; managerial correspondence with Asia (3) 1913–39; managerial correspondence with Shanghai (11) 1916–36; managerial correspondence with Hong Kong (5) 1916–35; general correspondence with Chinese branches (24) 1924–54; exchange rate records (4) 1926–41; external correspondence (26) 1928–54; exchange contracts books (5) 1930–49; profit and loss accounts (2) 1933–51; monthly returns (20) 1934–54; sundries account ledgers (6) 1934–51; gold dollar ledger 1934–51; dollar accounts daily balance books (6) 1938–52; bill schedules (7) 1938–47; **Tsingtao, China:** external correspondence 1911–50; safe custody and security register 1912–50; managerial correspondence (5) 1915–51; general correspondence with other branches (50) 1916–55; statistics 1922–35; bill records (9) 1932–51; monthly returns (2) 1935–49; current account ledgers (4) 1940–51; general ledgers (3) 1940–51; telegraphic transfer records 1948–51; general ledger balance book 1950–51; **Vladivostock, Russia:** charges account ledger 1918–24; current account ledgers (2) 1919–25; security register 1919–24; gold purchase register 1920–25; bill records (2) 1923–24; telegraphic transfer records 1924–25; general ledger balance book 1924–25.

Records 2: The Library, School of Oriental & African Studies, Thornhaugh Street, Russell Sq, London WC1H OXG

Letterbooks of David McLean, manager in Shanghai and London (13) 1862–99; diaries, correspondence, other papers and photographs of Sir Charles Addis, London manager and director and central banker 1881–1945. [Ref: MS 380401; PP MS 14]

Records 3: Public Record Office, Ruskin Avenue, Kew, Richmond TW9 4DU

Records of banks **283**

Papers re extension of note issue powers etc 1921–28. [Ref: T160/79/2866]

HUDDERSFIELD BANKING CO LTD
Huddersfield, West Yorkshire

History: This joint stock bank was formed in 1827 as the Huddersfield Banking Co; it was the first of its kind to be established in Yorkshire and became a model for other new formations. Its establishment, in the wake of the failure of five local private banks in 1825, resulted from a loss of confidence in this traditional banking structure. The bank emerged as one of Yorkshire's largest and best-managed banks despite deliberately restricting branch development. Early branches were opened at Wakefield and Saddleworth, but were sold to newly-formed local competitors in the early 1830s. Thereafter no branches were opened until Dewsbury branch was established in 1841; two other branches were opened at Batley and Heckmondwike in 1863. By 1879 paid-up capital was £415,000, deposits totalled £1.96 million and four branches existed. After 1880 a policy of opening sub-branches was pursued and eleven were established, but all relatively close to head office. Limited liability was acquired in 1882. Many of the bank's customers were drawn from the local textile industry and small account holders predominated. The bank's managers included (Sir) Charles Sikes, from 1868 to 1882, the founding father of the Post Office Savings Bank. The bank was acquired by London & Midland Bank Ltd (est. 1836) in 1897 for £1.1 million. It was then one of the largest provincial joint stock banks, with £3.3 million deposits, paid-up capital of £411,000 and fifteen branches.

W F Crick & J E Wadsworth, *A Hundred Years of Joint Stock Banking* (London, 1936); W C E Hartley, *Banking in Yorkshire* (Clapham, 1975)

Records 1: HSBC Holdings plc, Group Archives, 10 Lower Thames Street, London EC3R 6AE

Prospectus 1827; deeds of settlement 1827–41; directors' meeting minute books (8) 1827–98; share register 1827–97; share transfer journal 1827–96; general meeting minute books (2) 1828–97; security registers (4) 1830–97; bad debt ledger 1840–81; safe custody register 1855–97; annual reports 1870–96; branch balance abstract books (2) 1871–97; salary book 1873–93; summary of loan limits and securities 1877; statement of original constitution and present status 1880; half-yearly balance sheets 1880–96; interview book 1882–83; letterbooks (2) 1883–89; general ledgers (5) 1885–97; board agenda 1890–97; amalgamation papers 1897.

284   *British banking – a guide to historical records*

Batley: credit book 1875–84; security registers (4) 1853–90; **Cleckheaton:** discount ledger 1879–89; **Dewsbury:** security registers (6) 1864–98; register of deeds 1880–89; **Heckmondwike:** security register 1885–97.

Records 2: West Yorkshire Archive Service, Bradford District Archives, 15 Canal Road, Bradford BD1 4AT

Deed of settlement 1827; supplementary deed and list of shareholders 1833. [Ref: 10D76/3/box 152]

HUDDLESTON & CO
Bury St Edmunds, Suffolk

History: This private bank was opened in 1776 by William Dalton, wine merchant. In 1794 it was acquired by Edmund Squire and, on his death in 1835, it was taken over by Charles Le Blanc who took into partnership John Worlledge in about 1839. In that year a branch was opened at Mildenhall. The bank traded as J Worlledge & Co from 1845, as Worlledge & Cooper from 1855, as Worlledge, Huddleston & Cooper from 1862, as Huddleston, Cooper, Greene & Co from 1866 and as Huddleston, Greene & Co from 1873. In 1880 the business was acquired by Gurneys, Birkbecks, Barclay & Buxton (est. 1775) of Norwich.

Harold Preston, *Early East Anglian Banks and Bankers* (Thetford, 1994)

Records: Barclays Bank plc, Group Archives, Dallimore Road, Wythenshawe, Manchester M23 9JA

Cheque form 1866; papers re acquisition by Gurneys 1879–82.

HULL BANKING CO LTD
Hull, Humberside

History: This joint stock bank was first promoted as the Hull, East Riding & North Lincolnshire Banking Co, but was eventually formed in 1833 as Hull Banking Co. It embarked upon a rapid branch-opening programme in both East Yorkshire and North Lincolnshire. In 1834 branches were opened at Beverley, Brigg, Goole, Gainsborough, Grimsby and Louth as well as agencies at Howden, Retford and Market Rasen. Other branches followed at Lincoln, South Cave and Market Weighton in 1835. In 1839 a £40,000 bad debt was incurred which wiped out paid-up capital and led to a run on the bank. With depleted resources, but with new capital raised from shareholders, the bank recovered but it meant the closure of ten of its thirteen branches, only those at Barton, Beverley and Grimsby surviving. By 1879 paid-up capital was £121,000, deposits totalled £760,000 and there were

Records of banks   **285**

three branches. Limited liability was acquired in 1880. In 1894 the business was acquired by the County Banking Ltd (est. 1830) when paid-up capital was £160,000, deposits were £1.3 million and there were four branches.

W F Crick & J E Wadsworth, *A Hundred Years of Joint Stock Banking* (London, 1936)

Records: HSBC Holdings plc, Group Archives, 10 Lower Thames Street, London EC3R 6AE

Prospectus 1833; directors' meeting minute books (18) 1833–94; general meeting minute books (2) 1833–94; deed of settlement 1834; balance books (2) 1834–35; share ledgers (3) 1835–79.

Barton: general ledger 1844–50; deposit ledger 1846–60; **Grimsby:** general ledgers (8) 1836–69; **Lincoln:** deposit ledger 1835–45.

HUNTERS & CO
Ayr and Kilmarnock, Strathclyde

History: This private bank was established in Ayr in 1773 as Hunters & Co with a capital of £5,000; its most prominent partners were James Hunter, who had been cashier of Douglas, Heron & Co which failed in 1772, and James Hunter, a partner in the bankers William Forbes, James Hunter & Co of Edinburgh. In 1775 an agent was employed in Kilmarnock and afterwards at Irvine (1786) and Maybole. By 1777 note circulation reached £42,000. The partners by 1790 were Colonel William Hunter of Brownhill, Robert Hunter of Thurston, John Ballantine, merchant, and Hugh Hamilton of Pinmore. In 1821 the Kilmarnock Banking Co (est. 1802) was acquired. In 1841 the number of partners increased to ten but the firm declined as a result of competition from joint stock banks; its deposits fell from £667,700 in 1829 to £428,400 in 1833 and remained at about this level. However, substantial profits were made, viz £5,000 in 1838, £3,600 in 1841and £2,600 in 1842. The business was acquired by Union Bank of Scotland (est. 1830) for £25,000 in 1843, by which time the bank had £500,000 deposits and seven branches, all in Ayrshire.

Robert S Rait, *The History of the Union Bank of Scotland* (Glasgow, 1930)

Records 1: Bank of Scotland Archive, Operational Services Division, 12 Bankhead Terrace, Sighthill Edinburgh EH11 4DY

Inventory of writs and title deeds of properties 1657–1835; letter re subscription money raised by the people of Ayr for street improvements c.1799; contracts of copartnery and minutes of agreement between the partners 1807–43; partners' meeting minutes 1812–43; papers re disputes

286   *British banking – a guide to historical records*

between the partners 1813–29; agreement authorising spending on gifts to former servants n.d.

Girvan: 1830–33.

Records 2: National Archives of Scotland, HM General Register House, Princes Street, Edinburgh EH1 3YY

Bonds, assignations and discharges 1660–1798; letter to A Montgomery 1773; report on affairs 1776; bond of relief 1788. [Ref: GD1/22/32; GD3/5/1095; GD135/2900; GD219/229]

FREDERICK HUTH & CO
London

History: This merchant bank was founded in 1809 by a German merchant, Frederick Huth. He was born in Lower Saxony in 1777 and became apprenticed to a merchant in Hamburg in 1791. In 1797 he was sent to Corunna to work in his employer's Spanish house, doing business with Germany and South America. In 1805, after marriage to the daughter of a leading nobleman, he established his own business and in 1809 evacuated to London at the time of the French occupation of Corunna. He set up as a merchant speculating on his own account and acting as agent for other merchants. The business grew rapidly, specialising in trade with Germany, Spain and South America, and soon provided credits and advances to other merchants. By the mid 1830s the capital of £22,000 had risen to £123,000; in addition £47,000 was employed in an associated house at Lima. In 1839 a Liverpool house was established and by 1850 capital was almost £500,000 when Huth was one of London's leading merchant banks. In the 1830s its most prestigious clients were the Queen of Spain; the Spanish government which remained a client until the 1920s and for which payments were made around the world; and the Bank of the United States. In the late 1830s and in the 1840s a securities business commenced, in particular marketing bonds of United States states to British investors. However, the connection with South America remained particularly strong and by the mid-nineteenth century several branch houses had been opened there. Huths was managed by Daniel Meinertzhagen following Frederick Huth's retirement in the 1850s. In 1917 Huth & Co was founded in New York to undertake foreign exchange business. In 1921 Huths encountered severe difficulties as a result of war losses on its continental acceptance business and the Bank of England took control of its affairs. A merger with Konig Brothers was arranged in 1922 and a new partnership was established, aided by a £2 million Bank of England loan. Associated businesses in Manchester and Valparaiso were hived off and the London merchanting department was closed. In 1930 two subsidiary produce businesses were

Records of banks **287**

set up, Huth Coffee Sales Ltd and Huth Produce Sales Ltd. Huths, however, never fully recovered from its wartime losses. Its surviving banking business was transferred to the British Overseas Bank Ltd (est. 1919) in 1936 and the firm was wound up.

J R Freedman, 'A London Merchant Banker in Anglo-American Trade and Finance 1835–1850' (PhD thesis, University College London, 1969); A J Murray, *Home from the Hill. A Biography of Frederick Huth, Napoleon of the City* (London, 1970)

Records 1: Bloomsbury Science Library, University College London, Gower Street, London WC1E 6BT

Spanish letterbooks (29) 1812–52 [w]; cash books, Glyn Mills account books (13) 1814–49; in-letters 1814–50; insurance ledgers (6) 1819–51 [w]; bills payable and receivable ledgers (40) 1820–51; general ledgers 1821–40; Spanish customer ledgers (2) 1822–41; journals (12) 1822–50 [w]; German letterbooks (84) 1822–55; European customer ledgers (2) 1823–32; English letterbooks (69) 1827–51; sales and returns books (3) 1835–61; personal letterbook 1839; German customer ledgers (2) 1839–43; English customer ledgers (2) 1841–46; memorandum books (2) 1867–1904.

Liverpool: customer ledgers (2) 1839–55.

Records 2: Guildhall Library, Aldermanbury, London EC2P 2EJ

Letters from Spanish merchants 1812–48; miscellaneous papers including security certificates, probates, powers of attorney, bills of lading, etc c.1820–1945; ledger detailing remittances of Valparaiso and Lima houses and monthly stock accounts 1849–1902; partnership agreements and relating papers re South American houses 1853–83; private ledgers re South American houses (2) 1854–1933; agreement re London premises construction 1872; balance sheets and profit and loss accounts of South American houses 1872–85; letters and papers re Lima agents 1875–78; papers re law suits re Huth interest in a Peruvian business 1875–1956; letters re general business from Lima house 1876; papers re liquidation of Liverpool house 1878–79; survey and papers re London premises 1900. [Ref: MS 10700–10706, 22305, 25049–50]

IMPERIAL BANK LTD
London

History: This joint stock bank was formed with limited liability in 1862, its chief promoter being the merchant Sir Andrew Lusk. It acquired the premises of the failed Commercial Bank of London (est. 1840), but not its

288   *British banking – a guide to historical records*

business which passed to the London & Westminster Bank (est. 1834). In 1864 it strengthened its board through the appointment of leading City merchants and financiers such as H L Bischoffsheim, D Stern and A A and P C Ralli. Paid-up capital in 1862 was £100,000 and by year end deposits totalled £500,000. By 1865 these figures were £450,000 and £1 million respectively. In 1866 the first branch was opened in Westminster. Deposits rose to £1.43 million by 1870 and to £3.05 million by 1890, but thereafter they declined. In 1893 the business was acquired by the London Joint Stock Bank Ltd (est. 1836) for £1.03 million in cash. It then had eleven branches, deposits of over £2 million and paid-up capital of £675,000. While in terms of size, it never reached the front rank of London banks, it was reckoned to be well managed and profitable.

W F Crick & J E Wadsworth, *A Hundred Years of Joint Stock Banking* (London, 1936)

Records: HSBC Holdings plc, Group Archives, 10 Lower Thames Street, London EC3R 6AE

Signature books (6) 1862–99; counter order books 1864–74; security book 1866–74; country office counter orders (4) 1869–98; safe custody books (4) 1874–93; annual reports 1881–90; directors' meeting minute book 1882–89; directors' attendance book 1887–1919; amalgamation agreement 1893.

Waltham Abbey and Cheshunt: signature books (2) 1869–93; **Westminster:** security book 1866–73; counter orders 1867–1917.

ING BARING HOLDINGS LTD
London and Liverpool, Merseyside

History: This merchant bank, which initially traded as John & Francis Baring & Co, was established in London in 1762 by the Baring family of Exeter. It acted as agents for the family's Exeter business but soon undertook speculative trading in commodities on its own account. This was added to and in the nineteenth century was replaced by agency work for overseas merchants and, more importantly, by financing the international trade of merchants through the acceptance of bills of exchange and by the provision of advances. Less important activities included the ownership and management of merchant ships. In 1801 the business was renamed Sir Francis Baring & Co after its senior partner who was reckoned to be London's most powerful financier. During the War of American Independence, Barings participated in the marketing of British government securities for the first time. During the Napoleonic Wars, when government borrowing reached record levels, Barings was a major loans contractor. At the

Records of banks 289

same time, the firm emerged as a financier of overseas governments, for example the Portuguese government shortly after 1800. In 1803–04, in an operation on joint account with Hope & Co of Amsterdam, US$11.25 million bonds were issued for the United States government to finance its purchase of Louisiana from France. From 1807 the business was known as Baring Brothers & Co. As the London capital market grew and as foreign borrowers increasingly sought access to it, so Barings vied with Rothschilds for leadership in bond issues for overseas governments and businesses such as railway companies. Barings specialised geographically in the finance of the USA, Canada, Argentina and Russia, and held financial agencies in London for their governments. The proceeds of these issues financed railway construction and urban development, the cornerstones of an industrialising economy, and balanced government budgets. But issues were also arranged for other governments such as France, Austria, Spain, Chile, Japan, China, Belgium and Mexico. Alongside this business, private banking was also undertaken, largely for individuals associated with Barings' sovereign and business clients, such as James Monroe, Napoleon III, Prince de Talleyrand, Achille Fould and the King of the Belgians. Clients also included literary figures such as Nathaniel Hawthorne. In 1890 Barings suffered a liquidity crisis and, in what was known as the 'Baring Crisis', was rescued by a Bank of England loan guaranteed by the British banking community. The business was reconstructed as Baring Brothers & Co Ltd, still under the control of the Baring family, and by 1900 had re-emerged as one of London's leading merchant banks. In 1886 Barings' first issue of securities was made for a domestic business when the brewers Arthur Guinness Son & Co Ltd were floated. This heralded the beginning of corporate finance advisory work which was consolidated in the 1920s and 1930s when complex schemes of company rescue, reorganisation and rationalisation were carried out, including the reorganisation of the armaments manufacturers, Armstrong Whitworth, and the creation of the Lancashire Cotton Corporation through the merger of over one hundred textile companies. New industries such as motor car manufacture, urban transport systems and electricity supply were also financed. At the same time, bond issues for overseas governments declined on account of embargoes established to support sterling. From the 1950s to the 1970s the business comprised corporate finance, banking and fund management largely for British-based entities as the London capital market was effectively closed to foreign borrowers. In the 1980s the business once more became internationally spread and comprised three major parts – Baring Brothers & Co Ltd (merchant banking), Baring Asset Management Ltd (fund management) and Baring Securities Ltd (security broking) – owned by a holding company called Barings plc. The latter company was wholly owned by The Baring Foundation, an entity with charitable status. In 1995

290 British banking – a guide to historical records

Barings suffered an insolvency crisis as a result of unauthorised dealings by an employee. The business was placed in administration and its assets were shortly afterwards acquired by ING Group of the Netherlands.

Ralph W Hidy, *The House of Baring in American Trade and Finance. English Merchant Bankers at Work 1763–1861* (Cambridge, Massachusetts, 1949); John Orbell, *A History of Baring Brothers to 1939* (priv. pub., 1985); John Orbell, *A Guide to The Baring Archive at ING Barings* (priv. pub., 1998); Philip Ziegler, *The Sixth Great Power. Barings 1762–1929* (London, 1988)

Records 1: The Baring Archive, ING Baring Holdings Ltd, 60 London Wall, London EC2M 5TQ

Eighteenth and nineteenth century correspondence archive, viz: private and business papers of Sir Francis Baring 1762–1810; legal papers 1804–1903; miscellaneous accounts 1811–1905; reports on business houses 1816–1903; partners' English correspondence 1817–1905; Scandinavia and Baltic correspondence 1818–89; statistics and commercial intelligence (10) 1820–1905; France correspondence 1820–1905; Portugal correspondence 1820–1905; New Granada correspondence 1821–1903; partners' general correspondence 1821–1905; Netherlands correspondence 1822–1903; Germany and Austria correspondence 1823–1905; Spain correspondence 1824–69; Brazil correspondence 1824–89; Peru correspondence 1824–1904; staff correspondence 1824–1905; Argentina correspondence 1824–1905; USA correspondence 1824–1905; Belgium correspondence 1825–1901; Italy correspondence 1825–1903; Russia correspondence 1825–1906; India correspondence 1830–73; correspondence with Liverpool house 1833–1905; Mexico correspondence 1826–1904; Cuba correspondence 1828–1904; Far East correspondence 1828–1905; proposals for business 1830–1904; Canada correspondence 1835–1901; Australasia correspondence 1838–78; Turkey correspondence 1840–1905; Chile correspondence 1846–91; Spanish Central America correspondence 1851–1903; estate papers 1853–1905; papers of Ship Department and of ships managed 1863–79; Uruguay correspondence 1866–99.

Journals (204) 1766–1911; general ledgers (123) 1766 on; American client ledgers (302) 1800 on; Dutch client ledgers (3) 1813–34; French client ledgers (199) 1814 on; English client ledgers (457) 1814 on; security certificates (c600) 1818 on; security deposited registers (6) 1819–93; Stock Office memorandum and advice books (8) 1823 on; Spanish client ledgers (112) 1831 on; annual accounts books (193) 1832 on; salaries and wages books and files (49) 1832 on; Baring Brothers Liverpool account ledgers (22) 1833 on; security registers re client portfolios (8) 1834–1902; loans and stocks books (21) 1836–1925; personnel record books (16) 1840 on;

Records of banks 291

maps and plans (8) 1845–1913; prospectuses for Baring issues (309) 1850–1966; architectural plans and drawings 1867 on; Far East client ledgers (12) 1868–1907; produce business accounts (8) 1871–1938; subscription and allotment registers re Baring issues (42) 1876 on; American stock transfer registers (5) 1877 on; foreign exchange trading ledgers (169) 1878 on; securities and scrip allotment books (12) 1881 on; specimen issue papers (98) 1882 on; security registers re registered securities (16) 1885 on; charitable donation registers (6) 1887 on; security registers re inscribed English stocks (4) 1888 on; Stock Office files (17) 1889 on; directors' and general minute books (7) 1890 on; share registers and ledgers (7) 1890 on; annual reports and accounts (105) 1890 on; bullion accounts and statistics (15) 1890 on; security registers re client portfolios (170) 1891 on; correspondent registers (4) 1893–1933; Atchison, Topeka Railroad reorganisation registers (9) 1894 on; bail registers (6) 1894 on; partners' files (c.3,000) 1895 on; securities held abroad registers (15) 1897 on; Credit Department files (c.300) 1900 on; pension fund records (20) 1900 on; periodical payment instructions (8) 1900 on; security transfer registers (5) 1901–20; stock broker account ledgers (32) 1903 on; credit memorandum books (19) 1905 on; credit ledgers (24) 1906 on; sinking fund record books (5) 1907 on; United States dividend books (5) 1908 on; seal registers (33) 1910 on; Bank of England cash books (6) 1910 on; foreign bills collected registers (7) 1910–28; securities against loans registers (8) 1910 on; general accounts analysis (20) 1911 on; sports club records (11) 1911 on; signature books (4) 1912 on; stock order books (16) 1913 on; credit registers (26) 1914 on; personnel administration files 1916 on; insurance registers (7) 1917 on; money at call books (14) 1919 on; correspondent address books (4) 1922 on; staff bank account ledgers (76) 1923 on; expenses registers (23) 1926 on; drafts registers (8) 1927 on; trust account ledgers (18) 1929 on; cheque book registers (5) 1930 on; issue papers 'bibles' (60) 1934 on; annual accounts working papers (39) 1935 on; Economic Adviser's papers (5) 1969–76; brochures and other publications (55) 1970–97; Foreign Exchange Adviser's papers (8) 1975–82.

Liverpool: general ledgers (28) 1832 on; journals (9) 1858 on; reports on businesses (12) 1876 on; cash books (17) 1912 on; correspondence (92) 1923 on; security registers (2) 1960 on.

Records 2: Lewisham Local Studies & Archives, Lewisham Library, 199/201 Lewisham High Street, London SE13 6LG

Papers re Sir Francis Baring's estates and household including deeds 1767–1865, financial papers 1797–1837, plans 1809–43; correspondence 1806–37. [Ref: A62/6]

292   *British banking – a guide to historical records*

Records 3: Berkshire Record Office, Shire Hall, Shinfield Park, Reading RG2 9XD

Correspondence of M Van de Weyer with Baring Brothers 1864–68. [Ref: D/EB 1089 Vdw F5/1–5]

Records 4: National Library of Scotland, Department of Manuscripts, George IV Bridge, Edinburgh EH1 1EW

Papers of Alexander Baring, First Lord Ashburton c.1790s-c.1840s.

Records 5: National Archives of Canada, Ottawa 4, Ontario, Canada

Correspondence and papers re business with Canada, USA and Latin America dealing with trade and trade finance and with issuing bonds for entities such as governments, municipalites banks and railroad companies 1820s–70.

FRANCIS & WILLIAM INGRAM & CO
Wakefield, West Yorkshire

History: This private bank was established in 1785 as Ingram, Kennet & Ingram; it was otherwise styled the Wakefield Bank. It was renamed Francis & William Ingram & Co in about 1804 and was connected with a bank of the same name at Halifax (est. 1785). It failed in 1816.

Records: Barclays Bank plc, Group Archives, Dallimore Road, Wythenshawe, Manchester M23 9JA

Draft 1805.

INTERNATIONAL BANK OF LONDON LTD
London

History: This joint stock bank was registered in 1879 to acquire the International Bank of Hamburg & London Ltd (est. 1872). By 1903 its paid-up capital was £300,000. It was placed in voluntary liquidation in 1905.

Records: The Royal Bank of Scotland plc, Archive Section, Regent's House, 42 Islington High Street, London N1 8XL

Papers re liquidation 1904–09.

INTERNATIONAL FINANCIAL SOCIETY
London and Europe

History: This merchant bank was formed in the City of London in 1863 by a consortium of seven leading London merchant banks, viz: Robert

Records of banks **293**

Benson & Co; Samuel Dobree & Sons; Fruhling & Goschen; Frederick Huth & Co; Heath & Co; George Peabody & Co; and Stern Brothers. Through combining, these houses believed that they could compete more effectively with larger houses such as Barings, Rothschilds and the Crédit Mobilier in winning mandates to make bond issues for European governments and for European and UK infrastructure projects. The Society had a chequered career, but was the most successful of a number of similar businesses founded at this time. By the 1890s it had adopted the characteristics of an investment trust and in 1969 was acquired by Second Consolidated Trust Ltd.

P L Cottrell, *Investment Banking in England 1856–1881. A Case Study of the International Financial Society* (1985)

Records: Brynmor Jones Library, University of Hull, Hull HU6 7RX

Directors' meeting minute books (11) 1863–81, 1886–1912; draft minute book 1863–68; balance books (4) 1863–78; committee meeting minute books (4) 1863–1882; capital journal (3) 1864–86; cash books (11) 1867–1911; bill registers (2) 1865–1908 [w].

INTERNATIONAL WESTMINSTER BANK LTD
London and Europe

History: This overseas bank was formed in 1913 as the London, County & Westminster Bank (Paris) Ltd, a subsidiary of London, County & Westminster Bank Ltd (est. 1836). A branch was opened in Paris in 1913, acquiring the Place Vendôme premises and part of the business of the liquidated Banque Franco Américaine. Branches were established in Bordeaux (1917), Madrid (1917), Barcelona (1917), Lyons (1918), Marseilles (1918), Nantes (1919), Antwerp (1919), Brussels (1919), Bilbao (1919) and Valencia (1920). The bank was renamed London, County, Westminster and Parr's Foreign Bank Ltd in 1918 and Westminster Foreign Bank Ltd in 1923. All the Spanish branches were closed in 1923 and 1924 due to deteriorating economic conditions. In 1961 the bank was licensed to deal in deposits and commenced eurodollar operations on its own account. In 1963 it was given authorised bank status allowing the establishment of a London branch. A branch was opened in Nice in 1970. The bank was restyled International Westminster Bank Ltd in 1973 and National Westminster Bank SA in 1988. It ceased to trade in 1989 when its business was transferred to National Westminster Bank plc.

Records: The Royal Bank of Scotland plc, Archive Section, Regent's House, 42 Islington High Street, London N1 8XL

294   *British banking – a guide to historical records*

Articles of association 1913, 1923, 1982; directors' meeting minutes 1913–17; board committee meeting minutes 1913–64; foreign business committee minutes (20) 1913–39; authorised signature specimens and books 1913–29; share certificate counterfoils 1913–18; staff application forms and record sheets 1913–15; staff committee minutes (4) 1914–39; accounts: 1914–19, for publication 1928–39, 1945–58; certificates of incorporation 1914–23; war bond posters c. 1914–20; premises committee minutes 1915–38; branch reports and correspondence 1915–50; Spanish branches: photographs 1917–23, constitution papers 1917–20, closure papers 1922, bad and doubtful debt ledgers 1922; staff salary files 1917–18; papers re share capital increase 1917–20; staff magazine c.1920–57 [w]; security registers 1920–22; papers re registration in Spain 1920; premises title deed details c.1922; change of name certificate 1923; brochures: services in France and Belgium 1926, Nice office opening 1970, bank services 1970–73; football club photograph 1929; staff lists 1920s–1970s; sanction books (2) 1936–40; war procedure books (3) 1939; annual reports 1941–69; report on bank during war 1945; papers re bank history 1946–72; telegraphic code book 1953; directors' branch visit briefing notes 1950s; annual general meeting minutes 1959–91; reports to board, including accounts 1962–75; review of French provincial branches 1968; specimen cheques, France and Belgium n.d.

Antwerp: branch photographs 1919–72; **Barcelona:** papers 1919–28; **Bilbao:** savings account register 1919–22; passbooks 1921; **Bordeaux:** cheque forms 1913–20; **Brussels:** passbooks 1920, 1940s–50s; staff lists 1928–40; correspondence re German administration of the branch 1940–44; letters to manager from Banque Centrale Vienne 1943–48; book detailing help given to prisoners of war by staff 1944; branch photographs 1945, 1960, 1972–90; **Madrid:** cheque book 1917–24; press cutting 1923; closure notice 1923; **Paris:** cheque books 1913, 1920; branch photographs c.1913–19; **Valencia:** branch photograph 1920.

IONIAN BANK LTD
London and Europe

History: This British overseas bank traced its origins to 1838 when John Wright, of the London bank of John Wright & Co (est. 1813), convened meetings to promote the formation of a bank to do business in the Ionian Islands. The resident agent in London for the Ionian States together with the British government, which then held suzerainty over the states, encouraged the formation. In 1839 the Ionian State Bank, soon renamed the Ionian Bank, was formed with a subscribed capital of £100,000. Initially it functioned under the laws of the Ionian States until it received a Royal Charter in Britain in 1844. In 1840 the first branches were opened at Corfu, Zante and

Records of banks 295

Cephalonia where the bank's staple business was to finance the growing trade, especially in currants and olive oil, between the islands and Britain; the bank provided the first channel for making credit remittances to and from the islands. By 1840 the Ionian government was already a customer and received loans to finance land drainage. As well as being a deposit bank, the bank also had sole right of note issue for twenty years. In 1845 agencies were opened at Athens and Patras and at Venice and Trieste shortly afterwards. In 1860 the privilege of note issue was renewed for a further twenty years. Greece was handed suzerainty of the islands in 1864 when the Athens agency was converted to a branch and then to a local head office in 1873. This transfer marked the gradual move of the business to mainland Greece, where a branch network was established and where the bank emerged as a major commercial bank. In 1880 most of the privileges, including note issue, were renewed for a further twenty-five years, although the monopoly of banking in the islands was given up. In 1883 the bank gave up its Royal Charter and registered in Britain as a limited liability company. The right to issue notes was renewed again from 1905, but the expectation that this concession would end in 1920 meant that other lines of business were established, such as financing trade in the eastern Mediterranean generally. The bank's paid-up share capital, which stood at £316,000 in 1905, was increased to £486,000 in 1910. In 1907 a branch was opened at Alexandria, Egypt, to finance cotton cultivation and trade. By 1909 seven other Egyptian branches or agencies were open and in the 1920s the bank was perhaps the major financier of Egyptian cotton exports. During the two world wars local banking services were provided to allied governments and to their forces in the eastern Mediterranean and the Balkans, for example in Salonika. In 1922 a branch was established at Constantinople but was closed in 1929. More successful diversification to Cyprus occurred in 1926. In the late 1930s a two-thirds interest in the rival Banque Populaire was acquired and in 1939 an insurance company was formed. In the mid 1950s Behrens Trust acquired a substantial interest in the bank which resulted in the disposal of its assets. The bank retreated from the eastern Mediterranean in 1957, selling its Greek branches to the Commercial Bank of Greece and its Cyprus branches to The Chartered Bank. Also, in 1957 its Egyptian business was sequestrated by the Egyptian government. Thereafter it functioned as a UK-based merchant bank. In the late 1970s the banking business was discontinued but remaining activities were continued under the name of Ionian Securities Ltd.

Paul Bareau, *Ionian Bank Ltd. A History* (priv.pub., 1953)

Records: Archives Department, British Library of Political and Economic Science, London School of Economics, 10 Portugal Street, London WC2A 2HD

296 British banking – a guide to historical records

Cases for legal opinion 1836–1907; prospectuses, acts of parliament, deeds of settlement, charters and other papers re constitution (22) 1837–1923; ledger 1839–48; papers re Corfu branch 1839–50; 'establishment of the Ionian Bank' being staff books (3) 1839–1900s; court minute books (22) 1839–53, 1884–1969; annual reports and accounts (3) 1839–1974; share registers (5) 1839–95, 1927–79; general meeting minute books (2) 1842–1977; press notices re accounts and meetings 1877–1939; accountant's report on branches 1879; share transfer register 1879–1919; papers re purchases and sales of bank's shares 1879–1926; bookkeeping instructions, printed, 1880; correspondence with lawyers 1883–1923; committees minute book 1886–99; papers re stamp duty on shares 1887, 1898; instructions for preparing half-yearly accounts 1882; papers re note issue 1885–1908; memorandum re agrarian loans c.1890; reports on Crete 1898–99; papers re Athens branch and Greek branches generally 1903–04, 1922–49; report on Egypt 1905; amalgamated profit and loss accounts drafts 1907–29, 1957; balance sheets 1907–29, 1957; papers re Greek bonds lodged at Bank of England, 1908–09; general meetings proceedings (2) 1909–40; comparative statement of profits and reserves 1910–15; correspondence between London general manager and branches, mostly Alexandria 1921–48; papers re acquisition and closure of Constantinople branch 1922–30; head office ledgers (9) 1924–57; investments ledger 1925–51; Greek correspondents details 1925–38; correspondence between London and New York 1926, 1928; key register 1927–67; correspondence etc between general manager and Nicosia manager 1927–33; inspector's reports on branches 1930, 1940, 1942; papers re fraud 1932; papers re Cyprus business 1933–57; register of shareholders' probates 1939–51; papers re bank's history 1930s–1950s; cable test books 1930s; accounts showing liquidity position 1945–48; branch managers' half-yearly reports 1945–55 [w]; seal book 1949–64; circulars to Alexandria branch 1950–55; yearly accounts head office and branches 1951–57; Egypt economic reports 1951–56; papers re sale of branches and business 1953–58; exchange position papers re Alexandria branch 1953–55; luncheon guest records (6) 1960s–1970s; wine cellar book 1962–75; administrative committee minute book 1973–75.

ISLE OF MAN JOINT STOCK BANKING CO
Douglas, Isle of Man

History: This joint stock bank was formed in 1836 out of the private bank of Wulff, Forbes & Co (est. 1826) with a capital of £47,500. Financial difficulties caused by an increasing overdraft with its London agents, Williams Deacon's Bank, forced the closure of the bank in 1843.

Ernest Quarmby, *Bank Notes and Banking in the Isle of Man* (London, 1994)

Records 1: Cumbria Record Office, County Offices, Kendal, Cumbria LA9 4RQ

Papers re winding up 1839–1950s. [Ref: WD/MM 94]

Records 2: Manx National Heritage Library, Douglas, Isle of Man IMI 3LY

Correspondence re failure 1843. [Ref: Bridge House MSS 2534, 2543C]

ISLE OF WIGHT JOINT STOCK BANKING CO
Newport, Isle of Wight

History: This joint stock bank was established in 1842 out of the private bank of Bassett & Co (est. c.1790) to restore public confidence following the failure of James Kirkpatrick (est. c.1793) of Newport. It was acquired by National Provincial Bank of England (est. 1833) in 1844.

Records: The Royal Bank of Scotland plc, Archive Section, Regent's House, 42 Islington High Street, London N1 8XL

Amalgamation papers 1844.

JACKSON, JACKSON, GOODCHILD, JACKSON & JONES
Sunderland, Tyne & Wear

History: This private bank was formed in 1800 as Goodchild, Jackson, Goodchild Junr. & Heurtley and from its outset was closely connected with the City of London bank of Jackson, Goodchild & Co (closed c.1819) of Upper Thames Street. In 1803 it was badly damaged by a general financial crisis, but continued following a statement of public support. With other local banks, it experienced severe difficulties in 1815 but this time did not receive public support and failed. Its partners were later declared bankrupt. In about 1810 it was known as Goodchild, Jackson, Goodchild Junr., Jackson & Jones and later as Jackson, Jackson, Goodchild, Jackson & Jones.

Maberly Phillips, *A History of Banks, Bankers and Banking in Northumberland, Durham and North Yorkshire* (London, 1894)

Records: Durham University Library, Archives and Special Collections, 5 The College, Durham DH1 3EQ

Papers re failure c.1815–19. [Ref: Fenwick Collection 32]

JARVIS & JARVIS
King's Lynn, Norfolk

298   *British banking – a guide to historical records*

History: This private bank was established in 1808 as Massey & Jarvis and from 1847 was known as Jarvis & Jarvis. There may have been an earlier connection with Gales, Dixon & Massey, bankers at King's Lynn in the late eighteenth century. The bank also traded as the Lynn Regis & Norfolk Bank. In 1888, when it was in difficulties following the death of Sir Lewis Jarvis, the bank was acquired by Gurneys, Birkbeck, Barclay, Buxton & Cresswell, also of King's Lynn.

Harold Preston, *Early East Anglian Banks and Bankers* (Thetford, 1994)

Records: Barclays Bank plc, Group Archives, Dallimore Road, Wythenshawe, Manchester M23 9JA

Authorisation to receiver to pay sums due to creditors c.1888.

JENNER & CO
Sandgate, Kent

History: This bank was formed in 1872 and was one of the last private country banks to be established in Britain. It also traded as the Sandgate & Shorncliffe Bank. The business was acquired by Lloyds Bank Ltd (est. 1765) in 1898.

Records: Lloyds TSB Group plc, Archives, Head Office, 71 Lombard Street, London EC3P 3BS

Amalgamation papers 1897–98.

F W JENNINGS
Leek, Staffordshire

History: This private bank was established in 1855 by Francis Jennings; it was also known as the Leek Bank. It was acquired by Parr's Banking Co Ltd (est. 1865) in 1878.

T J Smith, *Banks and Bankers of Leek 1818–91* (Leek, 1891)

Records: The Royal Bank of Scotland plc, Archive Section, Regent's House, 42 Islington High Street, London N1 8XL

Amalgamation agreement and circulars 1877.

JESSEL, TOYNBEE & GILLETT PLC
London

History: This City of London discount house was established in 1922 as Jessel, Toynbee & Co. It acquired limited liability and converted to a

Records of banks   *299*

public company in 1943. In 1983 it merged with Gillett Brothers Discount Co Ltd to form Jessel, Toynbee & Gillett plc.

Records: Alexanders Discount plc, Broadwalk House, 5 Appold Street, London EC2A 2DA

Partnership papers 1922; balance sheets 1922–24, 1935–77 [w]; memorandum and articles of association 1943; list of shareholders 1943; annual returns 1948–1960s.

JONES & BLEWITT
Chepstow, Newport and Pontypool, Gwent

History: This private bank had offices in Chepstow, Newport and Pontypool. In 1844 it was acquired by the Monmouthshire & Glamorganshire Banking Co (est. 1836). Its date of establishment is unknown.

Records: Public Record Office, Ruskin Avenue, Kew, Richmond TW9 4DU

Partnership agreement 1833. [Ref: J90/1826]

DAVID JONES & CO
Llandovery, Dyfed

History: This private bank was formed in 1799 as W & D Jones & Co and was otherwise known as the Banc Yr Eidion Ddu and as the Llandovery & Llandeilo Bank. Its principal partner was David Jones, the son of a Carmarthenshire farmer, and his customers were largely drawn from the local farming and cattle droving community. In 1839 David Jones merged with Jones, Evans & Co (est. 1831) of Lampeter. By 1909, when it was acquired by Lloyds Bank Ltd (est. 1765), it was the largest bank in Carmarthenshire with branches at Lampeter (1831), Llandeilo (1842), Ammanford (1902) and Tregaron (1903) and with sub-branches at Brynamman, Cwmgorse, Llanebrie and Llanbyther.

Francis Green, 'Early Banks of West Wales', *Transactions of the Historical Society of West Wales,* 6 (1916)

Records: Lloyds TSB Group plc, Archives, Head Office, 71 Lombard Street, London EC3P 3BS

Customer ledger 1803–27; private memorandum book 1874–77; amalgamation papers 1909.

300 *British banking – a guide to historical records*

JONES & DAVIS
Monmouth, Gwent

History: This private bank was established in 1813 as Jones & Davis and in 1836 was reconstructed as the Monmouthshire & Glamorganshire Banking Co.

Records 1: Gwent Record Office, County Hall, Cwmbran NP44 2XH

Partnership agreements 1812, 1829; notices of dissolution 1814, 1837. [Ref: D1110.256–8, 260]

Records 2: Public Record Office, Ruskin Avenue, Kew, Richmond TW9 4DU

Securities for loans with related papers c.1823–26; partnership agreement 1833. [Ref: J90/1826]

WILLIAM JONES & SON
Bilston, West Midlands

History: This private bank was formed in 1824 as Jones, Son & Foster and was otherwise known as the Bilston & Staffordshire Bank. In 1845 the business was divided into two independent entities, William Jones & Son and Foster & Baldwin, with William Jones paying £5,085 for Foster's share in Jones, Son & Foster. Jones later took William Hatton, an iron merchant, into partnership. In 1864 the business was acquired for £9,000 by the newly-formed Staffordshire Joint Stock Bank Ltd and formed the basis of its initial business.

W F Crick & J E Wadsworth, *A Hundred Years of Joint Stock Banking* (London, 1936)

Records: HSBC Holdings plc, Group Archives, 10 Lower Thames Street, London EC3R 6AE

Partnership agreement 1845; amalgamation agreement 1863.

JONES, LOYD & CO
London

History: This important private bank was established in the City of London by Joseph Jones in about 1784, when the London operation of the Manchester bank of John Jones & Co (est. 1771) became independent. The firm, initially known as Joseph Jones & Co, was styled Joseph & Daniel Jones & Co from 1791, Daniel Jones, Barker, Loyd & Co from 1794, Jones, Loyd, Hulme & Co from 1798 and Jones, Loyd & Co from 1808. In the mid-nineteenth century the senior partner was Samuel Jones

Records of banks 301

Loyd, later Lord Overstone. Close links with the Manchester house were severed in 1848 when it was acquired by new partners. Jones Loyd & Co was acquired by London & Westminster Bank (est. 1834) in 1864, at which time it was reckoned to be the largest private bank in the City.

T E Gregory, *The Westminster Bank Through a Century* (London, 1936); Leo H Grindon, *Manchester Banks and Bankers* (Manchester, 1877); F G Hilton Price, *A Handbook of London Bankers* (London, 1876)

Records 1: The Royal Bank of Scotland plc, Archive Section, Regent's House, 42 Islington High Street, London N1 8XL

Securities as banker 1803–39; customer estate papers 1806; passbooks 1807–13; bills and drafts on London 1808–56; architectural plans, 43 Lothbury 1808–09,1856; promissory notes 1810–18; partnership agreements 1809–51; trustee deed 1810; papers re bankruptcy and unpaid bills 1816–58; *London Gazette* notice re retirement of William Fox 1817; correspondence from S J Loyd 1820–26, 1855–56; letters from Manchester house 1825–56; Edward Loyd: Cheetham Hall property papers 1829–59, papers re sister's children 1852, executors' debits 1864–74, estate papers n.d.; correspondence with other banks: Arthur Heywood Sons & Co 1833, Parker Shore & Co 1837, Bath Old Bank 1841; papers re partner retiral 1836–51; correspondence re failure of T Wiggin & Co 1836–51; papers re advances to particular firm 1837–43; power of attorney 1845; banker's receipt 1845; prospectus, West Midlands Railway 1845; stock books 1845–64; legal opinions 1848; application for clerkship 1850; country deposit ledger 1861–64; cheque n.d.; balance of accounts 1863; papers re disposal of business to Manchester & Liverpool District Bank 1863; deed and other papers re merger with London & Westminster Banking Co 1864; letter from night-watchman 1864; invoice for sherry 1864; staff lists n.d.; indemnity 1869; annuities purchase receipt 1870; correspondence re staff pensions 1880–82; photograph, Lothbury, London nineteenth cent.

Records 2: Archives Department, British Library of Political and Economic Science, London School of Economics, 10 Portugal Street, London WC2A 2HD

Journals 1829–34; day books 1830–48; ledgers 1832–38; bills receivable books 1833–38. [Ref: Coll misc 4 953]

KELLOW & PRITCHARD
Southampton, Hampshire

History: This private bank was formed in 1801 as Hunt, Trim & Co. By 1809 it was styled Trim & Toomer and was restyled Kellow & Pritchard in 1823. It failed in 1825.

302   *British banking – a guide to historical records*

Records: Southampton City Archives Office, Civic Centre, Southampton SO9 4XR

Partnership agreement 1800. [Ref: D/Z51]

KENSINGTONS, STYAN & ADAMS
London

History: This private bank was formed in Lombard Street, City of London, in 1775 as Wickenden, Moffatt, Kensington & Boler. The firm was styled Moffatt, Kensington & Boler in 1786, Moffatt, Kensingtons & Styan in 1791, Kensingtons & Co in 1807 and Kensingtons, Styan & Adams in 1812. The bank failed in 1812.

F G Hilton Price, *A Handbook of London Bankers* (London, 1876)

Records: Nottinghamshire Archives, County House, Castle Meadow Road, Nottingham NG2 1AG

Papers re failure c.1803–12. [Ref: CP 5/8/85–135]

KERRISON & SONS
Norwich, Norfolk

History: This private bank was formed in 1768 as Allday & Co and was known subsequently as Allday & Kerrison by 1776, as Kerrison & Kerrison by 1804 and later as Kerrison & Sons. It also traded as the Norwich Bank. It failed in 1808 on the death of Sir Roger Kerrison, apparently with debts of £460,000. The business was then taken over by Harvey & Hudsons (est. 1792) of Norwich.

Harold Preston, *Early East Anglian Banks and Bankers* (Thetford, 1994)

Records: Barclays Bank plc, Group Archives, Dallimore Road, Wythenshawe, Manchester M23 9JA

Title deeds, Norwich property 1790–1809; bill of exchange 1806.

KEWNEY & KING
Grantham, Lincolnshire

History: This private bank was established in Grantham in 1812 as Holt, King & Co and was also known as Grantham Bank. It issued its own notes. The firm was styled Kewney & King from 1835 and failed in 1848.

Records: Nottinghamshire Archives, County House, Castle Meadow Road, Nottingham NG2 1AG

Partnership agreement 1824; balance sheet and accounts 1824–25. [Ref: DDFM 49/3–4]

KILMARNOCK BANKING CO
Kilmarnock, Strathclyde

History: This private bank was established in 1802. In 1821 it was acquired by Hunters & Co (est. 1773) of Ayr.

Robert S Rait, *The History of the Union Bank of Scotland* (Glasgow, 1930)

Records: Bank of Scotland Archive, Operational Services Division, 12 Bankhead Terrace, Sighthill, Edinburgh EH11 4DY

Ayr: cash account ledger 1802–05.

HENRY S KING & CO
London

History: This bank traced its origins to Smith Elder & Co established at 65 Cornhill, City of London, in 1816. Initially its business was wide-ranging and included banking, book selling and shipping and acting as stationers and East India agents. In 1857 Henry King joined the business and in 1868 he took over the banking and agency activities under the title of Henry S King & Co. By 1922 the firm was located in Pall Mall, in London's West End, and had branches in the City of London, at Bombay, Calcutta, Delhi and Simla in India and at Port Said in Egypt. A lack of family succession resulted in Kings being absorbed by Cox & Co (est. 1758) in 1923.

Records: Lloyds TSB Group plc, Archives, Head Office, 71 Lombard Street, London EC3P 3BS

Amalgamation papers 1922–23.

KINNERSLEY & SONS
Newcastle-under-Lyme, Staffordshire

History: This private bank was established in Newcastle-under-Lyme in about 1780 as T Kinnersley; it was otherwise known as the Newcastle & Staffs Bank and as the Old Bank. It was styled Thomas Kinnersley & Sons by 1825 and was acquired by the National Provincial Bank of England (est. 1833) in 1855.

Records 1: The Royal Bank of Scotland plc, Archive Section, Regent's House, 42 Islington High Street, London N1 8XL

Accounts with London agent 1799–1805.

304   *British banking – a guide to historical records*

Records 2: Staffordshire Record Office, County Buildings, Eastgate Street, Stafford ST16 2LZ

Amalgamation papers 1855. [Ref: D593/T/1/14]

KLEINWORT BENSON LTD
London

History: This City of London merchant bank traced its origins to Alexander Kleinwort, a Hamburg shipping clerk who emigrated to Cuba in 1838 and joined the merchant house of James Drake. He relocated to London in 1855 and quickly emerged as senior partner. By 1883 he and his sons were in sole control of the business which was renamed Kleinwort Sons & Co. The business was quickly established as a major financier of international trade through the provision of acceptance credits to merchants and it also became involved in the issuance of securities. The business was badly affected by the First World War as it provided banking facilities to continental, largely German, clients. In the 1920s, like other London merchant banks, it re-focused on providing financial services to British business and, in particular, it developed issuing and corporate finance services for corporate clients. The business was once again damaged by the German financial collapse of 1931. In 1961 it merged with the merchant bank of Robert Benson, Lonsdale Ltd to form Kleinwort Benson Ltd, Bensons bringing strength in corporate finance and Kleinworts strength in banking. In the 1970s a strong investment management business – including unit and investment trust management – also developed along with a wide-range of other activities including insurance broking, commodity dealing and bullion broking and dealing. In 1986 the insurance business of Transinternational Life was acquired followed by the brokers Grieveson Grant as part of Kleinworts' adjustment to deregulation of the securities market. In 1995 Kleinworts was acquired by Dresdner Bank and was renamed Dresdner Kleinwort Benson.

Stefanie Diaper, 'The Story of Kleinwort, Sons & Co in Merchant Banking 1855–1966' (Ph D thesis, University of Nottingham, 1983); Jehanne Wake, *Kleinwort Benson.The History of Two Families in Banking* (Oxford, 1997)

Records 1: Guildhall Library, Aldermanbury, London EC2P 2EJ

Customer account ledgers, arranged by geographical location (c.450) 1863–1929; monthly balances of accounts (11) 1865–1924; partners' account ledgers (with stock accounts 1866–89) (8) 1866–89; information books arranged by geographical location (42) 1875–1926; telegraphic keys and code books (5) 1875–1932 [w]; client security registers (4)

Records of banks 305

1877–1915; sundry debtors and creditors ledgers (16) 1878–1932; register of enquiries received re businesses 1880–99; 'stock depot' being tabulated registers of client securities (3) 1881–1928; 'commission balances' re commission paid to agents (3) 1889–1944 [w]; stock account ledgers (2) 1890–1918; 'statistics' being comparative statements re bills, commissions and other accounts (2) 1891–1938; advance accounts ledgers (15) 1892–1931; 'stock depot securities' being registers of client and partners' securities (2) 1892–1929; 'conti nostri' accounts ledgers (34) 1901–27; joint exchange, travellers, commercial, letters of credit, etc, accounts with Goldman Sachs, New York (38) 1899–1931; 'statistics' being monthly totals of bills, etc, (6) 1900–23; 'syndicate and underwriting accounts etc' (7) 1902–55; stock ledgers recording securities and dividends paid (3) 1903–36; exchange joint account ledgers (18) 1904–32; private ledger balances (21) 1905–61; partners' super tax returns 1909–19; client security ledgers re Goldman Sach issues 1911–12; bearer stock number books (6) 1912–36; agents commission accounts (6) 1912–65; 'exchange and sundry notes accounts and gold shipments (nostri)' 1912–25; registered stock numbers books (5) 1913–39; Bank of England moratorium accounts ledger 1914–22; private journal 1915–37; cash books (3) 1915–18, 1956–65; partners' private ledgers (8) 1918–29; forward exchange accounts ledgers (4) 1920–24; 'joint stocks accounts' re issues partially underwritten by Kleinworts 1920–32; partners' security register 1920–27; private ledger 1920–44; 'trust companies accounts' (2) 1920–43; minutes and accounts of Second Guardian Trust Ltd (6) 1920s–60s; partners' joint investment account no 2 1922–24; 'returns of industrial securities' being notes, memos, etc, re company financial performance 1923–32; 'registers of collateral securities held overseas 1923–40; 'freehold and leasehold property accounts' re office premises 1923–32; partners' trust accounts 1924–48; summary of monthly turnover (2) 1924–27; 'monthly bill balances' re bills payable and receivable 1924–28; forward exchange ledger 1924–27; 'balance sheets' being summaries of monthly balances of accounts 1924–29; annual profit and loss accounts re foreign exchange operations (2) 1926–38; stock books re commodities shipped and sold (3) 1926–45; partners' accounts (ie of individual partners) ledgers (28) 1926–63; 'forward exchange book' 1927–30; 'collateral securities' being security registers (2) 1927–48; accounts of Foreign Holdings Ltd (8) 1927–55; Exchange Department journal 1929–30; Exchange Department term account journal 1929–30; rents book 1931–46; income tax accounts ledger 1932–55; monthly balances being statements of debit and credit balances (4) 1934–51; 'sales journal' re commodity transactions 1935–64; 'investment companies accounts' 1936–45; quarterly valuations of securities 1943–55; 'particulars of charges account' being cash books re staff and office payments (3)

306 *British banking – a guide to historical records*

1950–61; 'charges account books' re miscellaneous house payments 1953–65; private journal re 'special nominal accounts' 1961–64; 'special nominal accounts' ledgers (2) 1951–61; general ledger, journal and cash book of Kleinwort Ltd (3) 1955–61; day books (4) 1956–65; 'purchase journal' re commodity transactions 1957–64. [Ref: MS 22001–22155]

Records 2: Guildhall Library, Aldermanbury, London EC2P 2EJ

Statistics book 1858–90; protested bills of exchange 1860s–1990s; letters re J Kleinwort of Hamburg 1870s–1900s; bad and doubtful debts records 1870s–1950s; partners' correspondence books 1880s–1910s; country correspondence logbooks 1892–1934; papers re: Winter & Smillie of USA 1880s–1910s, Goldman Sachs & Co of USA 1890s–1910s, Kansas City Southern Railway 1899–1905, Pacific Mills Ltd of British Columbia 1910–74, Stern Brothers 1910–11, Ocean Falls Syndicate 1910s, Cuban Ports 1911–19, Studebaker Corp 1911–12, Henri Hoechstaedte & Cie 1911–28, Sperling & Co 1911–13, Société Foncière Belgo Canadienne 1911–49, Sumitomo Bank 1912–39, Gerhard & Hey of Moscow 1912–17, Brown Shoe Co 1912–13, City of Edmonton 1913–14, State of Bahia 1913–15, National Cloak & Suit Co 1914–15, Debenhams Ltd 1920s–30s, Dunlop Rubber Co Ltd 1920s–1930s, Northumberland Shipbuilding Co Ltd 1920s, Allatini Mines Ltd 1920s–1950s, Automatic Machine Corp Ltd 1920s–1950s, Kraehnholm Manufacturing Co of Tallinn 1923–54, Kux Bloch & Co 1930s–1940s; client information log books 1905–11; business proposals 1907–12; staff papers 1910 on; correspondence with: German banks and clients 1913–58, East European clients 1913–32, Dutch banks and clients 1914–74, Russian clients 1914–20, Scandinavian clients 1914–30, British clients 1918–58, French clients 1930–37; partnership accounts 1920s; profit and loss accounts 1920s–1950s; annual accounts' 1920s on; papers re Fenchurch Street premises 1920s on; records of subsidiary companies 1920s on; seal registers 1948–62; general meeting minute book 1948–53; papers re British Committee for German Affairs 1952–58; annual reports 1960s on.

Note: Records summarised in section 2 are in the process of being catalogued. The papers are extensive and the summary is approximate.

HENRY KNAPP & JOHN TOMKINS
Abingdon, Oxfordshire

History: This private bank was established in 1801; it was otherwise known as the Abingdon & Wantage Bank. It failed in 1847.

Records: Berkshire Record Office, Shire Hall, Shinfield Park, Reading RG2 9XD

Records of banks **307**

Partnership agreement 1846; balance sheet 1847. [Ref: D/EM B16; D/EBr B3]

KNARESBOROUGH & CLARO BANKING CO LTD
Knaresborough, North Yorkshire

History: This joint stock bank was established in 1831 as Knaresborough & Claro Banking Co. It adopted limited liability in 1881 as Knaresborough & Claro Banking Co Ltd and amalgamated with the National Provincial Bank of England Ltd (est. 1833) in 1903.

Records: The Royal Bank of Scotland plc, Archive Section, Regent's House, 42 Islington High Street, London N1 8XL

Deed of settlement 1831; registers of notes issued and burnt (4) 1831–1918; banker's licences 1851–87; amalgamation papers 1903.

JAMES KNIGHT & SONS
Farnham, Surrey

History: This private bank was formed by James Stevens, a hop grower and wool stapler, as Stevens & Co, in 1806. The bank was acquired by the Knight family of wealthy brewers who renamed it Knight, Jenner & Co in 1828. In 1886, when known as James Knight & Sons, the business was acquired by the Capital & Counties Bank Ltd (est. 1877). It then had deposits of £27,000 and was acquired for £9,000.

Records: Lloyds TSB Group plc, Archives, Head Office, 71 Lombard Street, London EC3P 3BS

Amalgamation papers 1886.

LACONS, YOUELL & KEMP
Great Yarmouth, Norfolk

History: This important private bank was formed as Lacons, Fisher & Co in 1791, the original partners being Edmund Lacon, a brewer, and James Fisher, a merchant. The business traded under several titles including Lacons, Youell & Co and Lacons, Youell & Kemp but was otherwise styled the Yarmouth, Norfolk & Suffolk Bank. When Harveys & Hudsons (est. 1791) of Norwich failed in 1870, Lacons acquired some of its offices. A large branch network was established with offices in Suffolk at Lowestoft (1819), Beccles (1824), Halesworth (1870), Southwold (1870), Newmarket (1893) and Saxmundham (1893) and in Norfolk at North Walsham (1811), Norwich (1870), East Dereham (1881), King's Lynn (1889), Cromer (1889), Fakenham (1894), Acle (1898), Gorleston-on-Sea

308   *British banking – a guide to historical records*

(1894), Swaffham (1893), Sheringham (1894), Holt (1893) and Foulsham (1894). A Cambridgeshire branch also existed at Wisbech (1894). The bank was one of the largest in East Anglia and was acquired by the Capital & Counties Bank Ltd (est. 1877) in 1901.

Harold Preston, *Early East Anglian Banks and Bankers* (Thetford, 1994)

Records: Lloyds TSB Group plc, Archives, Head Office, 71 Lombard Street, London EC3P 3BS

Customer ledger 1791–95; amalgamation papers 1901.

Cromer: memorandum book 1897–1903; **Norwich:** signature book 1886–1900.

LACY, HARTLAND, WOODBRIDGE & CO
London

History: This private bank was established as Pocklington & Lacy in 1809 by Joseph Pocklington, formerly a meat salesman, and Benjamin W Lacy. From 1849 it was known as Pocklington, Lacy & Son, as Lacy & Son from 1851 and as Lacy, Son & Hartland from 1875. It specialised in providing services to the London meat trade and was based in London's Smithfield meat market. When the Metropolitan Meat Market opened in Islington in 1855, a branch was established there followed by another at the Foreign Cattle Market at Deptford in about 1872. Subsequently three other branches were opened, at Bermondsey, Brentford and Southall. In 1880 H W Woodbridge, a partner in the Uxbridge private bank of Woodbridge, Lacy, Hartland, Hibbert & Co (est. 1791) was admitted as a partner when the business was renamed Lacy, Hartland, Woodbridge & Co. The Brentford and Southall branches were subsequently transferred to the Uxbridge bank. In 1891, when capital and deposits were £20,000 and £170,000 respectively, the bank was acquired by London & Midland Bank Ltd (est. 1836) for £30,000.

W F Crick & J E Wadsworth, *A Hundred Years of Joint Stock Banking* (London, 1936)

Records 1: HSBC Holdings plc, Group Archives, 10 Lower Thames Street, London EC3R 6AE

Balance sheet 1873; amalgamation papers 1891.

Records 2: Barclays Bank plc, Group Archives, Dallimore Road, Wythenshawe, Manchester M23 9JA

Bills of exchange, receipt and claim for dividend 1886–99; photographs of partners c.1880s–1920s.

Records of banks

LADBROKE & CO
London

History: Sir Robert Ladbroke, Son, Rawlinson & Porker were trading as bankers at 10 Lombard Street, City of London, by 1771; the firm had probably been at work as goldsmiths as early as 1736. Sir Robert Ladbroke was Lord Mayor, Alderman and a Member of Parliament for the City of London and colonel of the City militia. By 1774 the firm had moved to Cornhill. In 1827 its style, which had previously changed to Ladbrokes & Gillman, became Ladbroke, Kingscote & Gillman. In July 1841 the firm was wound up upon the retirement of Felix Ladbroke and its business, comprising about 290 accounts having a total balance of £236,000, was largely transferred to Glyn, Mills & Co (est. 1753).

F G Hilton Price, *A Handbook of London Bankers* (London, 1876)

Records 1: The Royal Bank of Scotland plc, Archive Section, Regent's House, 42 Islington High Street, London N1 8XL

Customer balance books 1841–45.

Records 2: Surrey Record Office, County Hall, Penrhyn Road, Kingston upon Thames KT1 2DN

Sir Robert Ladbroke: notebook containing will 1773, probate of will 1773, administration 1776; miscellaneous bonds and papers re bankers c.1792–1827; agreements with clerks 1799–1841. [Ref: 6632]

LAMBTON & CO
Newcastle upon Tyne, Tyne & Wear

History: This important private bank was formed in 1788 as Bland, Randell, Chambers, G Hoar, Smoult & Ashworth; it was otherwise known as the Bank in Newcastle and informally as The Bank of the Coal Trade on account of its substantial connection with coal mining. It was one of the great private banks of Newcastle where it was rivalled only by Hodgkin & Co (est. 1859) and where joint stock banks were shunned following the failure of most local ones by the mid 1850s. In 1790 Thomas Davison Bland retired when Ralph John Lambton, uncle of the 1st Earl of Durham who was a major local land and colliery owner, was admitted as a partner; the style of the firm then became Lambton, Williamson, Randell, Chambers & Smoult. Thereafter the business operated under a number of titles but the Lambtons remained senior partners and from 1844 the bank was known as just Lambton & Co. The Fenwick family was also important after its entry in 1795. The bank considered converting to joint stock status in 1836, and issued a prospectus as the Lambton Banking Co, but

310   *British banking – a guide to historical records*

apparently was dissuaded from doing so by a major customer. In 1840 its note issue was given up. Branches were opened throughout North East England. In 1893 its published balance sheet totalled £3.8 million while deposits were £3 million and partners' capital and reserves were £700,000. In 1908 the business was acquired by Lloyds Bank Ltd (est. 1765).

Maberly Phillips, *A History of Banks, Bankers & Banking in Northumberland, Durham and North Yorkshire* (London, 1894); L S Pressnell, *Country Banking in the Industrial Revolution* (Oxford, 1956); R S Sayers, *Lloyds Bank in the History of English Banking* (Oxford, 1957)

Records: Lloyds TSB Group plc, Archives, Head Office, 71 Lombard Street, London EC3 3BS

Customer ledgers (4) 1788–91, 1800–01, 1815–16; bills discounted registers (2) 1788–1861[w]; partnership agreements 1797–1892; securities for loans registers from 1797; salary book 1818–1908; list of clerks 1818–1908; profit and loss accounts 1822–40 [w]; balance books 1839–57; note register 1841–55; letterbooks (6) 1846–1909; safe custody receipt book 1850–1908; interest rate book from 1854; general ledgers (4) 1856–1920; waste book 1857; inventory of securities and deeds 1858–90; status enquiry reply book 1860–67; standing order books (25) 1868–1908; deposit account ledger 1870s; signature books 1870–1908; probate register 1877–1908; security ledger 1886–1908; partnership papers 1889–1900; safe custody register 1889–1903; partners' ledger monthly balance book 1892–1901; papers re proposed amalgamation 1902; amalgamation papers 1907–08.

Newcastle, Elswick Road: security register 1899–1916; **Newcastle, Quayside:** signature book 1866–1908; memorandum book 1904–09; **North Shields:** security register 1858–1900; status enquiry book 1859–88; memorandum book 1887–1911; **Sunderland:** letterbooks (2) 1892–1925.

LANCASHIRE AND YORKSHIRE BANK LTD
Manchester, Greater Manchester

History: This joint stock bank traced its origins to the Manchester branch of the Alliance Bank of London & Liverpool Ltd (est. 1862) which opened in 1864. During its early years, performance was unremarkable and led to the sale of its Liverpool branch to the National Bank of Liverpool Ltd (est. 1863) in 1871 and the disposal of its Manchester branch in 1872 to the Lancashire & Yorkshire Bank Ltd which was formed for this purpose. John Mills, who had managed the branch since its inception, was the chief architect of this operation and of the bank's subsequent successful expansion. On formation, nominal capital was £1 million of which £250,000

Records of banks 311

was paid-up. The first branches were opened at Waterfoot in 1872; at Pendleton, Shudehill and Sowerby Bridge in 1873; at Burnley and Warrington in 1874; at Bacup, Rochdale and Todmorden in 1875; at Blackburn and Nelson in 1876; at Lymm in 1877; at Bury, Haslingden and Dewsbury in 1881; at New Cross in Manchester and at Swinton in 1881; and at Elland and Bowdon in 1883. Deposits grew from £770,000 in 1875 to £1.25 million in 1883, to £1.5 million in 1887 and to £2.7 million in 1889. In 1888 the Bury Banking Co Ltd (est. 1836) was acquired, followed in 1894 by Preston Union Bank Ltd (est. 1869); by Adelphi Bank Ltd (est. 1862) of Liverpool in 1899; by the West Riding Union Bank Ltd (est. 1832) in 1902; and by the Mercantile Bank of Lancashire Ltd (est. 1890), the bank's last acquisition, in 1904. By 1896 the number of branches had grown to thirty-six when deposits stood at £4 million; by 1916 these were 128 and £16 million respectively. Paid-up capital subsequently rose to £1 million in 1919. In 1927 the bank was acquired by the Bank of Liverpool & Martins Ltd (est. 1831). By then it was of major regional importance but had not been able to transform itself into a national bank through acquisition of a London-based bank.

George Chandler, *Four Centuries of Banking* (London, 1964–68); J M McBurnie, *The Story of the Lancashire and Yorkshire Bank Ltd 1872–1922* (Manchester, 1922); Mrs John Mills, *Threads from the Life of John Mills, Banker* (Manchester,1899)

Records: Barclays Bank plc, Group Archives, Dallimore Road, Wythenshawe, Manchester M23 9JA

Minute books (13) 1864–1924; certificates of incorporation 1872–1926; register of drafts 1875–1970; private minutes 1886–1927; diary, J H S Crompton 1889; agreement re merger with Bury Banking Co 1880–89; list of shareholders 1880s; circulars 1891–1927; memorandum and articles of association 1892–1926; out-letterbooks (3) 1898–1907; architectural plans, Radcliffe branch 1897; staff photographs 1900–10; balance sheets 1900–27; branch architectural drawings 1901–23; annual general meeting minutes 1904–28; cartoon re proposed merger with Parr's Bank 1910; registers of shareholders (9) 1911–27; branch bookkeeping manual 1916; cheques 1919; combined register 1920–23; widows' and orphans' fund minute books 1922–25; Chancery Court case papers 1923–25; papers re merger with Bank of Liverpool 1927–28.

LANCASTER BANKING CO LTD
Lancaster, Lancashire

History: This joint stock bank was established in Penny Street, Lancaster, in 1826 in the premises of the failed private bank of Dilworth, Arthington

312   *British banking – a guide to historical records*

& Birkett (est. c.1780). Branches were opened at Chorley, Kirkham, Preston and Ulverston but the former two had closed by 1837. In 1844 the private bank of Gibson & Wilson (est. c.1810) of Kirkby Lonsdale was acquired and additional branches were opened in Fishergate, Preston and Barrow-in-Furness. The Lancaster head office moved to the former premises of Thomas Worswick Sons & Co (est. c.1780) in Church Street in 1837 and a new office was built on the site in 1870. Limited liability was acquired in 1896. In 1907 the bank merged with Manchester & Liverpool District Banking Co Ltd (est. 1829).

Records 1: The Royal Bank of Scotland plc, Archive Section, Regent's House, 42 Islington High Street, London N1 8XL

Partnership agreement 1826; customer ledger 1826–29; directors' resolution and order books (9) 1826–1909; investment ledger 1827–57; annual general meeting report books (2) 1828–1907; note circulation statistics 1833–39; investment journal 1835–76; investment and profit and loss ledger 1836–94; lists of directors and proprietors 1838–94; papers re share capital 1841; deeds of settlement 1852, 1882; dividend and salaries register 1863–1918; management committee minutes 1862–66; profit and loss and expenses ledger 1842–58; half-yearly balance sheets 1873–94; half-yearly balance book 1886–1900; annual reports 1889, 1903–06; branch overdraft registers (9) 1885–96; branch profit statistics 1899–1902; register of managers and directors 1901–07, 1921–31; amalgamation papers 1906–07; applications for advances 1906–11.

Barrow in Furness: bad debts suspense account book 1876–97; proprietors' ledger 1896–1908; manager's letterbooks (4) 1880–1911; overdrafts registers 1885–1919; **Blackpool:** overdrafts register 1885–96; **Chorley:** profit and loss ledgers (2) 1867–1907; general ledger 1879–80; **Fleetwood:** general ledger 1875–92; overdrafts register 1885–91; **Kirkby Lonsdale:** overdrafts register 1885–88; manager's information book 1888–1912; letterbooks 1890–1931; general ledgers 1899–1908; **Lancaster:** general ledger 1830–31; manager's memorandum books (4) 1831–1908; manager's letterbooks (6) 1832–1908; manager's information book 1862–65; manager's diaries (12) 1877–1908; **Lytham:** overdrafts register 1885–92; **Preston:** security book c.1855–76; letterbooks (5) 1862–78, 1907–08; deposit register 1869–1880s; advances register c.1880; information book 1885–94; overdrafts register 1885–94; customer mandates 1887–91; head office letters 1906–08; **Ulverston:** manager's letterbooks (5) 1883–1907; overdrafts register 1885–95; half-yearly balance sheets 1897–1907; manager's diaries 1904–09; **Windermere:** general letters 1883–1913; overdrafts register 1885; register of drafts 1886–1911.

Records of banks *313*

Records 2: Lancaster District Library, Local History Department, Market Square, Lancaster LA1 1HY

Deeds of settlement 1826–96; extracts from annual reports 1869–1907; directors' reports 1892–1900; list of directors, branches, agents 1832–85.

Records 3: Cumbria Record Office, 140 Duke Street, Barrow-in-Furness LA14 1XW

Ulverston: ledger c.1835–46; bank note 1907. [Ref: BDB 39, Z 1924]

J & J LARGE
Wootton Bassett, Wiltshire

History: This private bank was established in 1807. It also had a presence at Bath. The bank failed in 1822.

Records: Gloucestershire Record Office, Clarence Row, Alvin Street, Gloucester GL1 3DW

Assignment and sale of estates of Joseph Large [1808–16] 1822. [Ref: D182/V/21]

LAZARD BROTHERS & CO LTD
London

History: This merchant bank traces its origins to Alexandre, Lazare and Simon Lazard, three brothers who left Lorraine, France, in 1847/48 to establish a small merchant business at New Orleans, United States. They moved on to San Francisco to participate in the boom resulting from the gold rush, prospered and in 1856 opened a Paris house called Lazard Freres. The Franco-Prussian War paralysed this business and resulted in the formation, in 1870, of Lazard Brothers & Co in London. During 1876 and 1877, the Lazard houses were converted into a general banking business based in San Francisco, Paris, London and New York, the latter house being established in 1877. In 1884 the San Francisco business was sold and subsequently formed the Anglo & London-Paris National Bank. In the 1890s the London business emerged as an important merchant bank and flourished under leadership of Robert Kindersley, later 1st Lord Kindersley, who was admitted a partner in 1906. In late 1919 Lazards was converted into a private limited company and at this time W D Pearson, later 1st Lord Cowdray, of the eponymous international contracting business, acquired a 50 per cent interest in the business. By the 1920s Lazards had become a major London issuing house, marketing sterling bonds for overseas borrowers, and in the 1930s refocused its business on providing corporate finance advice to British-based companies. By 1927 branches

314   *British banking – a guide to historical records*

existed at Antwerp and Brussels and there was a Madrid-based affiliate. In 1931 Lazards encountered difficulties as a result of the activities of its Brussels office and was supported by the Bank of England. In 1941 a large holding in AW Bain & Sons Ltd, insurance brokers, was acquired and in 1949 a major interest was taken in the Australian issuing house, Anglo-Australian Corporation. In the 1950s and 1960s corporate finance advisory work and asset management developed rapidly and in 1960 Lazards merged with the smaller corporate finance house of Edward de Stein & Co. By the late 1960s the business was almost fully-owned by Pearsons and in the 1990s their interest continued to be substantial. Strong links remained with Lazard firms in New York and Paris.

Note: It is not known if any records of historical interest survive.

LEACH, POLLARD & HARDCASTLE
Bradford, West Yorkshire

History: This private bank was established as Leach, Pollard & Hardcastle prior to 1777 and failed in 1781. It was also known as the Bradford Bank and was associated with Hainsworth, Holden, Swaine & Pollard (est. 1779) which failed in 1807, when known as Brothers Swaine & Co.

Records: Barclays Bank plc, Group Archives, Dallimore Road, Wythenshawe, Manchester M23 9JA

Partnership agreement 1777; bankruptcy petition 1781.

LEAMINGTON BANK
Leamington Spa, Warwickshire

History: This joint stock bank was established in 1835 with a paid-up capital of £38,650 and failed in 1837 when it was heavily in debt to its London agents, the London & Westminster Bank (est. 1833).

T E Gregory, *The Westminster Bank Through a Century* (London, 1936)

Records 1: Leamington Spa Library, Avenue Road, Leamington Spa CV31 3PP

Deed of settlement 1835.

Records 2: Warwickshire Record Office, Priory Park, Cape Road, Warwick CV34 4JS

Abstract of agreements re debt to London & Westminster Bank 1837–39. [Ref: CR611/288]

Records of banks 315

LEAMINGTON PRIORS & WARWICKSHIRE BANKING CO LTD
Leamington, Warwickshire

History: This joint stock bank was formed in 1835 with a paid-up capital of £22,000. Two joint stock banks had already been formed at Leamington and intense local competition encouraged the quick establishment of branches at Warwick, Banbury, Southam and Kenilworth. Early on, the bank experienced difficulties and the 1847 financial crisis resulted in the closure of the Warwick (reinstated 1887) and Banbury branches. The bank's customers were dominated by landowners and farmers, agricultural merchants and other businesses in the agricultural sector. In 1880, when limited liability was acquired, paid-up capital was £32,000 and deposits were £212,000. By the 1880s the bank was the last surviving native joint stock bank at Leamington and in 1889 it was acquired by the Birmingham & Midland Bank Ltd (est. 1836) for the equivalent of £102,000. It then had a paid-up capital of £40,000 and deposits of £204,000.

W F Crick & J E Wadsworth, *A Hundred Years of Joint Stock Banking* (London, 1936)

Records 1: HSBC Holdings plc, Group Archives, 10 Lower Thames Street, London EC3R 6AE

Deed of settlement 1835; directors' meeting minute books (4) 1835–89; reports of shareholders' meetings 1837–64; general meetings minute book 1845–71; weekly balance sheets (14) 1845–89; general ledgers (6) 1854–89; security register 1864–83; annual reports 1886–88; amalgamation papers 1889–90.

Records 2: Leamington Spa Library, Avenue Road, Leamington Spa CV31 3PP

Deed of settlement 1835.

Records 3: Warwickshire Record Office, Priory Park, Cape Road, Warwick CV34 4JS

Share transfer 1839; passbook 1867–90. [Ref: CR807; CR1709/488]

LEATHAM, TEW & CO (EAST RIDING BANK)
Doncaster, South Yorkshire

History: This private bank was established in Doncaster in 1801 by John Leatham, James Jackson, Thomas William Tew and Edward Trueman and traded as Leatham, Jackson & Co; the bank was otherwise known as the Doncaster Bank. It was renamed Leatham, Tew, Trueman & Co in 1824 when it was also known as the East Riding Bank. From 1834 it was known

316 **British banking – a guide to historical records**

as Leatham, Tew & Co. The partners also owned banks by the same name at Pontefract and Wakefield and there was also an association with Hayes, Leatham & Co (est. 1792) of Malton and Lister, Moorson & Co (est. 1792) of Scarborough. The Doncaster firm was sold to Cooke & Co (est. 1750) of Doncaster in 1847.

Records 1: The Royal Bank of Scotland plc, Archive Section, Regent's House, 42 Islington High Street, London N1 8XL

Papers re purchase 1843–47.

Records 2: Barclays Bank plc, Group Archives, Dallimore Road, Wythenshawe, Manchester M23 9JA

Letters re dissolution of Doncaster partnership 1846–47.

LEATHAM TEW & CO (PONTEFRACT BANK AND WEST RIDING BANK)
Pontefract and Wakefield, West Yorkshire

History: This private bank was established in Pontefract in 1801 by John Leatham, James Jackson, Thomas William Tew and Edward Trueman and traded as Leatham, Jackson & Co. At the same time connected banks were also established at Doncaster and Wakefield. The bank was styled Leatham, Tew, Trueman & Co from 1824 and Leatham, Tew & Co from 1834. The Pontefract firm was also known as the Pontefract Bank while the Wakefield firm was also known as the West Riding Bank. There was also an association with Hayes, Leatham & Co (est. 1792) of Malton and with Lister, Moorson & Co (est. 1792) of Scarborough. In 1906, when the business was acquired by Barclay & Co Ltd (est. 1896), it had branches in Goole, Castleford and Pontefract.

Anon, *A Sketch of the History of the Pontefract Bank* (Pontefract, 1879); P W Matthews & Anthony W Tuke, *History of Barclays Bank Ltd* (London, 1926)

Records: Barclays Bank plc, Group Archives, Dallimore Road, Wythenshawe, Manchester M23 9JA

Impersonal ledgers, including profit and loss account (14) 1800–1906; partnership agreements 1801–1905; cheques and receipts 1804–1904; partnership papers 1806–1901; articles of apprenticeship 1807; ledger, petty expenses 1809–43; bank note, draft form, cheque and deposit receipt proofs c.1800s; correspondence: customer accounts 1816–1906, miscellaneous 1833–91, failure of Overend Gurney 1866–68, profit and loss 1871–1906, property 1877–88, forged notes 1880–82, will of P Tew 1921–22; bank notes 1810s; bank note registers (3) 1822–99; cancelled bank

Records of banks 317

notes 1822–99; general balance ledgers (4) 1822–1906; trustee account ledger 1822–23; customer account ledgers 1829–40; general balances of deposits 1829; partners' agreements 1830–1912; staff appointment agreements 1831–89; partnership letterbook 1832–35; notebook, stock purchase procedures and list of customers c.1830s; income tax returns 1842–1912; customer information book 1844–65; monthly abstracts, liabilities and assets 1844–1906; railway company letters, certificates, circulars 1845–88; dividends received list 1851–63; property papers: Pontefract 1879–80, Castleford 1880, 1890, 1909, Snaith 1882, Goole 1884–86, Normanton 1889–99; agreement re chief cashier annuity 1881; rent ledger 1888–1910; rent accounts 1869–1911; rent book 1898–1909; papers re Barclay & Co merger, including balance sheets 1894–1906; bank note register 1908–88.

Goole: partnership meeting agendas 1895–1900; **Pontefract:** title deeds 1659–1834; blank drafts 1800; memorandum book 1800–26; receipts, cheques and bills 1803–1905; private letterbook 1805–28; draft 1806; correspondence: partnership 1808–1907, property 1858–95; cheques 1858–61; customer ledger 1822–74; customer information book 1826, 1931–33; passbook 1871–74; manager's letterbooks 1874–1906; partners' minutes 1891–1906; bank note 1905; **Wakefield:** cash book 1809–11; letters, customer opinions 1809–89; memorandum book, including partnership minutes 1809–98; banker's licences 1809–1906; private letterbook, W Leatham 1826–37; partnership meeting agendas 1833–1902; notebook re customer accounts/interviews 1835–37; cheques 1842, 1858; passbooks 1873–1907; ledger, West Riding Police pension fund 1873–1907; information book 1877–1900; manager's letterbooks (2) 1882–97.

LECHMERE, ISAAC, MARTIN & CHERRY
Tewkesbury, Gloucestershire

History: This private bank was formed in 1792 and was otherwise known as Tewkesbury Old Bank. In about 1800 Anthony Lechmere married the daughter of Joseph Berwick of Berwick & Co (est. 1772), bankers at Worcester. This eventually led to a merger of Lechmeres and Berwicks in 1831 to form Berwick, Lechmere & Co.

Records: Hereford & Worcester Record Office, St Helen's Branch, Fish Street, Worcester WR1 2HN

Partnership agreements 1797–1805. [Ref: 705:134 BA 1531/93 (ii)]

LEDGARD & SONS
Ringwood, Hampshire

318   *British banking – a guide to historical records*

History: This private bank was formed in 1821 and was also known as the Ringwood & Poole Bank or the Town & County of Poole Bank; it was closely associated with Geo. Welch Ledgard & Sons (est. 1821) of Poole. The business failed in 1861 and was acquired by the Wilts & Dorset Banking Co (est. 1835).

Records: Lloyds TSB Group plc, Archives, Head Office, 71 Lombard Street, London EC3P 3BS

Partnership agreement 1821; amalgamation papers 1861–66.

LEEDS & COUNTY BANK LTD
Leeds, West Yorkshire

History: This joint stock bank was formed in 1862 out of the business of the Joint Stock Banking Co of Pontefract, Wakefield and Goole (est. 1861). By 1879 five branches had been established, paid-up capital was £230,000 and deposits were £863,000. The bank was acquired by the Birmingham & Midland Bank Ltd (est. 1836) for the equivalent of £187,000 in 1890. By then its deposits had grown to £1.08 million, paid-up capital was £137,000 and there were twelve branches.

W F Crick & J E Wadsworth, *A Hundred Years of Joint Stock Banking* (London, 1936)

Records: HSBC Holdings plc, Group Archives, 10 Lower Thames Street, London EC3R 6AE

Notices to shareholders 1862–90; annual list and summaries of shareholdings (3) 1863–85; declarations of secrecy 1863–90; directors' meeting minute books (7) 1863–90; seal books (4) 1863–91; general minutes 1863–92; index of securities 1864–90; amalgamation papers 1890.

Wakefield: general ledgers (3) 1863–79.

LEEDS & WEST RIDING JOINT STOCK BANKING CO
Leeds, West Yorkshire

History: This joint stock bank was formed in 1835 based on the business of the private bank of George Smith & Son (est. 1831). It failed in 1846 as a result of its involvement in railway company securities.

Records: West Yorkshire Archive Service, Leeds District Archives, Chapeltown Road, Sheepscar, Leeds LS7 3AP

Letters, bill etc 1839–45; list of shareholders 1842. [Ref: Acc 2205]

Records of banks **319**

H S LEFEVRE & CO
London

History: H S Lefevre & Co was established as a City of London private bank in about 1790. By the mid-nineteenth century it had assumed the characteristics of a merchant bank and undertook a securities and acceptance business. In 1914 it was one of the founding members of the Accepting Houses Committee and remained a member until the late 1940s. Its most active partner at the end of the nineteenth and in the early twentieth century was Gaspard Farrer, a senior partner of Baring Brothers. By the 1920s and 1930s problems of management succession resulted in the sole surviving partner winding up the firm in 1949.

Records: The Baring Archive, ING Baring Holdings Ltd, 60 London Wall, London EC2M 5TQ

Private ledgers (3) 1880–1904; private journals (2) 1880–1949; balance sheet and profit and loss account book 1893–1902; profit and loss realised on security transactions etc 1901–49; general and client account balances (4) 1902–49.

LEICESTER & WARWICKSHIRE BANKING CO
Hinckley, Leicestershire

History: This joint stock bank was established in 1840 and failed in the same year.

Records: Public Record Office, Ruskin Avenue, Kew, Richmond TW9 4DU

Agreement re winding up of bank 1842. [Ref: J90/711]

LEICESTERSHIRE BANKING CO LTD
Leicester, Leicestershire

History: This joint stock bank was formed as the Leicestershire Banking Co in 1829 with paid-up capital of £14,000. It expanded quickly and by 1835 its paid-up capital was £36,000, its deposits exceeded £118,000 and it had branches at Hinckley (1830), Market Harborough (1834) and Ashby de la Zouche (1835). The latter branch had been formed out of the business of the failed private bank of Fishers, Simmonds & Mammatt (est. 1780) which had been acquired for £3,500 in 1835. Also in 1835, the private bank of Miller & Co (est. 1776) of Leicester was acquired followed in 1838 by the Market Harborough branch of the Northamptonshire Banking Co (est. 1836). In 1845 the Atherstone branch of Coventry Union Banking Co (est. 1836) was purchased for £6,000. Deposits stood at

320   *British banking – a guide to historical records*

£550,000 by 1851 and customers comprised numerous firms in the local footwear and hosiery industries as well as many others drawn from agriculture. In 1872 paid-up capital was £225,000 and deposits were £1 million. In 1878 Middleton & Co (est. 1790) of Loughborough was acquired and in 1880 the bank registered for limited liability when it increased its paid-up capital to £400,000. By 1900 twenty-eight branches, all in Leicestershire or Northamptonshire, had been established including offices at Melton Mowbray (1836), Atherstone (1840), Market Bosworth (1841), Kettering (1856), Oakham (1872), Uppingham (1872), Nuneaton (1874), Bedworth (1875), Swadlincote (1877) and Coalville (1877) and later at Peterborough, Grantham, Northampton, Wellingborough and Burton. In 1895 the private bank of Hardy & Co (est. 1819) of Grantham was acquired. The Leicestershire Banking Co Ltd was now one of the largest banks in provincial England and had deposits of £3.3 million, a paid-up capital of £490,000 and a reputation for sound management. In 1900 the bank was acquired by London, City & Midland Bank Ltd (est. 1836) for the equivalent of £1.335 million.

W F Crick & J E Wadsworth, *A Hundred Years of Joint Stock Banking* (London, 1936)

Records 1: HSBC Holdings plc, Group Archives, 10 Lower Thames Street, London EC3R 6AE

Deed of settlement 1829; declarations of secrecy 1829–96; directors' meeting minute books (21) 1829–1900; profit and loss ledgers (6) 1829–1900; deeds of covenant 1836–73; general ledgers (13) 1842–1901; general minute books (2) 1845–72, 1897–98; staff list 1871–99; premises ledger 1872–1900; security books (22) 1873–90; general managers' memoranda 1874–79; general manager's letterbook 1876–1900; bills of exchange diaries (6) 1877–99; note circulation ledger 1878–1900; customers' bills discounted (11) 1878–1900; returned-bills book 1879–85; bad debt ledger 1879–98; loan register 1883–99; bill balance book 1885–96; country bills for collection books (8) 1888–1900; weekly balance sheets 1890–94; abstract of balance sheets 1894–99; discount ledger 1895–1901; bill register 1895–1901; branch receipts and expenditure 1896–1905; foreign bills for collection 1897–1908; amalgamation papers 1900.

Ashby: directors' meeting minutes 1837–57; **Grantham:** general ledger 1883–96; **Hinckley:** private ledger 1848–53; **Kettering:** manager's diary 1877–88.

Records 2: Leicestershire Record Office, Long Street, Wigston Magna, Leicester LE18 2AH

Records of banks 321

Prospectus and papers re formation 1829; shareholders' resolutions with deeds of settlement and names of shareholders 1829–80; shareholders' meeting minutes re merger 1900.

Leicester: architectural plans 1872–74. [Ref: 3D42/3; 109'30/14; Misc 613]

WILLIAM LEWIS AND THOMAS SALT
Birmingham, West Midlands

History: Unknown

Records: William Salt Library, Eastgate Street, Stafford ST16 2LZ

Partnership agreement 1760. [Ref: D1716 bdl 7/22]

LEWIS'S BANK LTD
Liverpool, Merseyside

History: This bank was established in 1928 as a department of Lewis's Ltd, a leading department store company established in about 1850 and based in Liverpool. In 1934 the banking business was transferred to a private limited company called Lewis's Bank Ltd. Branches were opened in Lewis's stores at, *inter alia*, Liverpool, Manchester, Glasgow, Leeds, Hanley, Leicester, Bristol and in Selfridges in London. In 1958 the bank was acquired by Martins Bank Ltd (est. 1831) with which it had been closely connected for several years. The bank was sold on to Lloyds Bank Ltd (est. 1765) in 1967.

Records 1: Lloyds TSB Group plc, Archives, Head Office, 71 Lombard Street, London EC3P 3BS

Directors' meeting minutes 1934–41.

Records 2: Barclays Bank plc, Group Archives, Dallimore Road, Wythenshawe, Manchester M23 9JA

Cheques 1950s.

LEY & CO
Bideford, Devon

History: This private bank was established in about 1790 as Cutcliffe, Ley, Glubb & Willcock; it was otherwise known as the Bideford Bank. It was styled Ley & Co from 1810 and was acquired by the National Provincial Bank of England (est. 1833) in 1843.

Records: The Royal Bank of Scotland plc, Archive Section, Regent's House, 42 Islington High Street, London N1 8XL

322   British banking – a guide to historical records

Notice of amalgamation 1844.

LEYLAND & BULLINS
Liverpool, Merseyside

History: This important private bank was formed in 1807 as Leyland & Bullin by Thomas Leyland (died 1827) and his nephew, Christopher Bullin. Leyland had made his fortune as a shipowner and merchant and in 1802 joined the Liverpool private bank of Clarkes & Roscoe (est. 1774) as senior partner. However he withdrew in 1806, immediately prior to establishing his own bank. Another nephew, Christopher Bullin, joined in 1815 prompting a name change to Leyland & Bullins. The business emerged as one of the most substantial and reputable private banks in England. By 1901 deposits reached £1.38 million and partners' capital was £287,000. In this year Leylands was acquired by the North & South Wales Bank Ltd (est. 1836); it paid £210,000 for the business's goodwill.

W F Crick & J E Wadsworth, *A Hundred Years of Joint Stock Banking* (London, 1936); John Hughes, *Liverpool Banks and Bankers 1760–1837* (Liverpool, 1906)

Records: HSBC Holdings plc, Group Archives, 10 Lower Thames Street, London EC3R 6AE

Balance books (2) 1807–32; passbooks 1807–36; profit and loss ledgers (4) 1807–60, 1865–78; bills sent for acceptance books (7) 1807–24; cash books (15) 1811–31, 1887–94; cash balance book 1815–19; commission ledger 1818–22; profit and loss settlements (2) 1819–78; private ledger 1826–90; cash book, Masterman & Co, 1833–39; passbooks, Bank of England (2) 1836–39; investment ledger 1850–62; loan ledger 1878–88; general ledgers (7) 1879–1901; advances ledgers (2) 1885–94; private ledgers (5) 1889–93; rough office diaries (5) 1889–93; private ledgers holding accounts with other banks (2) 1890–93; suspense account ledgers (2) 1890–96; weekly balances, private deposit accounts 1899–1901; agreement with North & South Wales Bank 1901.

LINCOLN & LINDSEY BANKING CO LTD
Lincoln, Lincolnshire

History: This joint stock bank was formed in 1833 with a paid-up capital of £20,000; it was the first such bank to be established in North Lincolnshire and South Humberside. The new company's chairman was a local surgeon and the directors included a grazier and a merchant. Branches were opened at Louth, Gainsborough and Horncastle in 1833 and at Brigg in 1834, while agencies were formed at Alford, Market Rasen and Sleaford

Records of banks 323

by 1836. In 1839 deposits reached £200,000 as the bank expanded into south Humberside following the withdrawal from this area of the Hull Banking Co (est. 1833). By 1860 customer account balances totalled £300,000 and advances stood at £380,000. The bank's customers were drawn from the farming and, later, also from the agricultural support industry, in particular agricultural machinery manufacturers. In 1874 the business of the Boston private bankers, Gee, Wise & Gee (est. 1788), was purchased followed in 1878 by the acquisition for £1,250 of the Gainsborough business of the Nottingham & Nottinghamshire Banking Co (est. 1834). In 1880 the bank acquired limited liability and in 1892 a branch was opened in the rapidly expanding fishing port of Grimsby. By 1912 the bank was one of the strongest provincial joint stock banks when it had a capital of £163,000, total deposits of £1.8 million and thirty branches and agencies. In the following year it was acquired by London, City & Midland Bank Ltd (est. 1836) for the equivalent of £570,000.

W F Crick & J E Wadsworth, *A Hundred Years of Joint Stock Banking* (London, 1936)

Records: HSBC Holdings plc, Group Archives, 10 Lower Thames Street, London EC3R 6AE

Deed of settlement 1833; general minute books (2) 1833–1913; directors' meeting minute books (15) 1833–1914; registers of deeds (2) 1834–84; balance sheets 1834–1912; half-yearly balances 1877–1907; agreement to purchase the Gainsborough business of the Nottingham & Nottinghamshire Bank 1878; memorandum and articles of association 1902; amalgamation papers 1913.

Barton: general ledger 1835–43; **Brigg:** security ledgers 1853–97; signature book 1894–1913; **Louth:** board minute book 1833–78; **Spilsby:** profit and loss book 1869–1900.

LIVERPOOL BOROUGH BANK
Liverpool, Merseyside

History: This joint stock bank was formed in 1836 out of the private bank of Samuel Hope & Co whose partners were appointed managers. It failed in 1857 with debts of £940,000.

John Hughes, *Liverpool Banks and Bankers 1760–1837* (Liverpool, 1906)

Records 1: Barclays Bank plc, Group Archives, Dallimore Road, Wythenshawe, Manchester M23 9JA

Share certificates 1847; liquidation report 1859.

324 *British banking – a guide to historical records*

Records 2: The Baring Archive, ING Baring Holdings Ltd, 60 London Wall, London EC2M 5TQ

Annual report 1857; minutes of creditors' meeting 1857. [Ref: HC3.90]

LIVERPOOL COMMERCIAL BANKING CO LTD
Liverpool, Merseyside

History: This joint stock bank was formed in 1832 and opened for business in 1833. Its chief promoter, and future chairman, was Christopher Rawson, a member of the eponymous Halifax banking family that promoted the Halifax & Huddersfield Union Banking Co (est. 1836) which was closely associated with the Liverpool Commercial Bank. In 1869 the bank's balance sheet totalled £1.3 million and paid-up capital was £350,000. In 1860 limited liability was acquired and in 1889 the bank amalgamated with the Bank of Liverpool Ltd.

George Chandler, *Four Centuries of Banking* (London, 1964–68)

Records 1: Barclays Bank plc, Group Archives, Dallimore Road, Wythenshawe, Manchester M23 9JA

Prospectus 1832; directors' meeting minute books (4) 1832–94 [w]; general minutes synopses register 1832–86; deeds of settlement 1833; declarations of secrecy 1833–90; general meeting reports and resolutions 1833–84; deed of covenant with N Bold 1851; papers re annual reports 1853–59; certificate of incorporation 1860; statement of assets and liabilities 1860; legal opinion re shares 1860; deeds, Liverpool Banking Corporation 1860–70; reports and accounts 1860–62, 1870; papers re foreign office 1865; customer account books: N Bold 1865, Cowie McIver & Co 1867–76; letterbook 1866–70; manager's diary 1871–96; current account statement, Williams Deacon's Bank 1874; papers re merger with Bank of Liverpool 1883–89; report on customers with advances 1889–90; provident fund agreement 1894.

Records 2: The Baring Archive, ING Baring Holdings Ltd, 60 London Wall, London EC2M 5TQ

Annual reports 1885–87. [Ref: 102137–102138]

LIVERPOOL UNION BANK LTD
Liverpool, Merseyside

History: This joint stock bank was formed in 1835 but did not open its first branch until 1877; it had deliberately focused its early business on the trade of Liverpool. Between 1884 and 1899 fourteen branches were opened, but by 1900 this number was reduced to twelve comprising six branches in

Liverpool, three in Birkenhead and others at Chester and at Heswall and Douglas, Isle of Man. The bank was influential and well-managed. Its customers were predominantly merchants and brokers associated with the port of Liverpool. Limited liability was acquired in 1882. Paid-up capital was £600,000 when the business was acquired by Lloyds Bank Ltd (est. 1765) in 1900. Henry Bell, one of the Union Bank's senior managers, became Lloyds Bank's general manager from 1912.

R S Sayers, *Lloyds Bank in the History of English Banking* (Oxford, 1957)

Records 1: Lloyds TSB Group plc, Archives, Head Office, 71 Lombard Street, London EC3P 3BS

Deed of settlement 1835; directors' meeting minute books (3) 1835–66, 1887–1903; signature books (3) 1830s–1912; shareholders' register 1888–96; amalgamation papers 1899–1904.

Records 2: The Baring Archive, ING Baring Holdings Ltd, 60 London Wall, London EC2M 5TQ

Annual reports 1881–95 [w]; list of shareholders 1894. [Ref: 102137–102139]

LIVERPOOL UNITED TRADES BANK
Liverpool, Merseyside

History: This joint stock bank was formed in 1836 and ceased business in 1838.

Records: Lancashire Record Office, Bow Lane, Preston PR1 8ND

Notice re application for shares c.1836. [Ref: DDTs Box 33]

LLOYDS BANK (EUROPE)
London and Europe

History: This overseas bank traced its origins to 1911 when Armstrong & Co of Paris and Le Havre, agents for several British banks, was acquired for £40,000 by Lloyds Bank Ltd. It was renamed Lloyds Bank (France) Ltd and in 1917 became known as Lloyds Bank (France) & National Provincial Bank (France) Ltd when the National Provincial Bank Ltd took a 50 per cent interest. The aim was to create a 'British bank conducted on British lines' for British customers. The business was restyled Lloyds & National Provincial (Foreign) Bank Ltd in 1919. By 1919 there were eleven branches in France, Belgium, Germany and Switzerland; in 1929 there were ten branches and by 1938 fourteen branches. By 1930 deposits totalled £10 million and rose to £12 million by 1938. However, like

326   *British banking – a guide to historical records*

similar British-owned banks established in Europe at this time, the venture was not especially profitable. This induced National Provincial Bank to withdraw in 1955 when the bank was renamed Lloyds Bank (Foreign). It was not until the creation of the eurodollar market in the 1960s, which radically changed the bank's activities, that the business became consistently profitable and was no longer dependent on its parent for periodic support. By the mid 1960s, branches were located at London, Paris, Biarritz, Bordeaux, Le Havre, Lille, Nice, Roubaix, St Jean de Luz, Cannes, Brussels, Antwerp, Geneva, Zurich and Monte Carlo. By 1970 there were nineteen branches when deposits stood at £561 million. The bank was renamed Lloyds Bank (Europe) in 1964 and in 1971 merged with the Bank of London & South America Ltd (est. 1862) to form Lloyds & Bolsa International, known simply as Lloyds Bank International from 1974.

Geoffrey Jones, 'Lombard Street on the Riviera. British Clearing Banks and Europe 1900–1960', *Business History*, 24 (1982); J R Winton, *Lloyds Bank 1918–69* (Oxford, 1982)

Records 1: Lloyds TSB Group plc, Archives, Head Office, 71 Lombard Street, London EC3P 3BS

Certificate of incorporation 1911; agreement with Armstrong & Co 1911; letterbook 1911–14; profit and loss ledgers (2) 1911–38; shareholders' minute book 1911–62; directors' meeting minute books (43) 1911–68; share register 1911–71; register of directors 1911–73; agreement with National Provincial Bank 1917; audited balance sheets 1917–55; profit and loss comparative statements 1919–38; branch balance sheets, profit and loss accounts and liability statements for branches: England 1919–45, France 1919–47, Belgium 1923–46, Germany 1919–25, Switzerland 1919–45; head office general ledgers (5) 1922–40; agenda books (29) 1926–65; sale agreement with National Provincial Bank 1954; private minute book 1956–69; agenda papers 1964–71.

Antwerp: credit balances 1937; half-yearly report 1938; **Biarritz:** half-yearly report 1938; **Brussels:** credit balances 1937; half-yearly report 1938; **Cannes:** half-yearly report 1938; **Geneva:** half-yearly report 1938; **London, City Office:** profit and loss accounts 1918–70; **London, Haymarket:** profit and loss accounts 1920–63; **Le Havre:** half-yearly report 1938; **Le Touquet:** credit balances 1937; half-yearly report 1938; **Lille:** credit balances 1937; half-yearly report 1938; **Monte Carlo:** half-yearly report 1938; **Nice:** half-yearly report 1938; **Paris:** credit balances 1937; half-yearly reports 1937–38; **Pau:** credit balances 1937; half-yearly report 1938; **Roubaix:** credit balances 1937; half-yearly report 1938.

Records of banks **327**

Records 2: The Royal Bank of Scotland plc, Archive Section, Regent's House, 42 Islington High Street, London N1 8XL

Correspondence and agreement between National Provincial Bank and Lloyds Bank (France) Ltd re establishment of joint ancillary bank 1916–18; balance sheets and statistics 1931–54; chairman's correspondence 1932–55; general correspondence 1934–54; papers re legal case 1935–38; papers re cash and currency position 1936–37; investigation report 1938; correspondence and reports re Belgian subsidiary 1952–54; press cutting, sale of holding to Lloyds Bank 1954.

City Office: inspection papers 1937–39; **Paris:** special report 1935; inspection papers 1938.

LLOYDS BANK INTERNATIONAL
London, Latin America and elsewhere

History: This bank was formed in 1971 as Lloyds & Bolsa International through the merger of Lloyds Bank Europe (est. 1911) and the Bank of London & South America Ltd (est. 1862); it became known as Lloyds Bank International in 1974. Lloyds Bank Ltd acquired all the shares it did not own in 1973 and through the bank offered a wide range of financial services internationally. It operated throughout Europe, in South and Central America and in the Middle and Far East. From 1969 Lloyds Bank Ltd pursued a 'group bank' concept which led to the eventual amalgamation of Lloyds Bank and Lloyds Bank International by Act of Parliament in 1986. Amalgamation drew together the commercial banking operations into an International Banking Division, with the merchant and investment banking services forming a separate unit.

J R Winton, *Lloyds Bank 1918–1969* (Oxford, 1982)

Records: Lloyds TSB Group plc, Archives, Head Office, 71 Lombard Street, London EC3P 3BS

Memorandum and articles of association 1971, 1974; chairman's committee minute books (3) 1971–79; annual reports and accounts 1971–84; executive committee minute books 1973–81.

LLOYDS BANK PLC
Birmingham, West Midlands, and later London

History: This clearing bank traces its origins to the private bank of Taylor & Lloyds founded at Dale End, Birmingham, in 1765. This was the first bank to open in Birmingham and was otherwise known as Birmingham Old Bank. The original partners were John Taylor (1711–75), his son John

328   *British banking – a guide to historical records*

Taylor (1738–1814), Sampson Lloyd (1699–1779) and his son Sampson Lloyd (1728–1807); the Taylors were Unitarian button manufacturers and the Lloyds were Quaker ironmongers. The initial capital was £8,000. The business grew steadily and by 1775 had 277 customers, largely traders and small manufacturers. The Taylors withdrew in 1852 when the bank was renamed Lloyds & Co. The failure in 1865 of Lloyds' greatest rival in Birmingham, Attwood, Spooner & Co, prompted the conversion of the bank into a joint stock company with limited liability. Known as Lloyds Banking Co Ltd, its nominal capital was £2 million. Prior to this, only one branch had existed, at Oldbury (est. 1864), but by the end of 1865 there were fourteen offices and fifty staff. By 1884 subscribed capital was £4.7 million and thirty-five branches were located throughout Warwickshire, Shropshire, Staffordshire and Worcestershire. Between 1884 and 1889 the business was styled Lloyds, Barnetts & Bosanquets Bank Ltd following merger with the leading London private banks of Barnetts, Hoares, Hanbury & Lloyd (est. 1864) and Bosanquet, Salt & Co (est. 1867); this name was abbreviated to Lloyds Bank Ltd in 1889. Thereafter the bank expanded rapidly and by 1918 was one of the 'big five' with a national branch network. Expansion was achieved, in part, through the acquisition of other banks. These were J L Moilliet & Sons (est. 1766) of Birmingham and P & H Williams of Wednesbury in 1865; Stevenson, Salt & Co (est. c.1737) of Stafford and the Warwick & Leamington Banking Co (est. 1834) in 1866; A Butlin & Son of Rugby in 1868; R & W F Fryer (est. 1807) of Wolverhampton in 1872; Shropshire Banking Co (est. 1836) in 1874; Coventry & Warwickshire Banking Co (est. 1835) in 1879; Beck & Co (est. 1800) of Shrewsbury in 1880; the Whitchurch & Ellesmere Banking Co (est. 1840) in 1881; Barnetts, Hoares, Hanbury & Lloyd and Bosanquet, Salt & Co, both of London, in 1884; Pritchard, Gordon & Co (est. 1799) of Bridgnorth in 1888; the Birmingham Joint Stock Bank (est. 1861) and the Worcester City & County Banking Co (est. 1840) in 1889; Wilkins & Co (est. 1778) of Brecon and Beeching & Co (est. c.1789) of Tonbridge in 1890; Praeds & Co (est. 1802) of London, Cobb & Co (est. c.1785) of Margate and Hart, Fellows & Co (est. 1808) of Nottingham in 1891; Twining & Co (est. c.1824) of London and the Bristol & West of England Bank (est. 1879) in 1892; Herries, Farquhar & Co (est. c.1770) of London and Curteis, Pomfret & Co (est. 1790) of Rye in 1893; Bromage & Co (est. 1819) of Monmouth in 1894; Pagets & Co (est. 1825) of Leicester in 1895; the County of Gloucester Banking Co (est. 1836) and Williams & Co (est. 1792) of Chester in 1897; Jenner & Co (est. 1872) of Sandgate in 1898; the Burton Union Bank (est. 1839) and Stephens, Blandy & Co (est. 1791) of Reading in 1899; Vivian, Kitson & Co (est. 1833) of Torquay, the Liverpool Union Bank (est. 1835), Cunliffe, Brooks & Co (est. 1792) of Blackburn, Brooks & Co (est. c.1815) of Lombard Street, London, William

Records of banks   329

Williams Brown & Co (est. 1813) of Leeds and Brown, Janson & Co (est. 1813) of London in 1900; the Bucks & Oxon Union Bank (est. 1853) and Pomfret, Burra & Co (est. 1791) of Ashford in 1902; Hodgkin, Barnett, Pease, Spence & Co (est. 1859) of Newcastle and Grant & Maddison's Union Banking Co (est. 1888) of Southampton in 1903; Hedges, Wells & Co (est. 1797) of Wallingford in 1905; the Devon & Cornwall Banking Co (est. 1832) in 1906; Lambton & Co (est. 1788) of Newcastle in 1908; David Jones & Co (est. 1799) of Lampeter in 1909; Hill & Son (est. 1825) of London in 1911; Peacock, Willson & Co (est. 1792) of Sleaford in 1912; the Wilts & Dorset Banking Co Ltd (est. 1835) in 1914; the Capital & Counties Bank Ltd (est. 1877) in 1918; the West Yorkshire Bank Ltd (est. 1829) in 1919; Fox, Fowler & Co (est. 1772) of Wellington in 1921; and Cox & Co (est. 1758) of London in 1923. Between 1910 and 1912 the head office moved to London from Birmingham and by 1923 the number of branches totalled 1,626 with 203 opening in 1919 alone. There were 1,851 branches in 1959 and 2,037 by 1969. From 1918 a decentralised regional structure was created which, by 1939, had developed into six local committees at Liverpool, Salisbury, London, Yorkshire, Birmingham and Newcastle. Each comprised five or six members chosen on account of their local standing; the chairmen were members of Lloyds Bank Ltd's main board. Local committees were known as district committees between 1961 to 1968 and as regional boards from 1968 to 1991. By 1969 the whole branch network in England and Wales, apart from some London branches, was organised into sixteen regions under fifteen regional boards. In 1898 the Colonial & Foreign Department (known as the Overseas Department in 1951) was established to deal with all foreign transactions at branch level: foreign exchange, import and export finance, foreign securities and correspondent work for overseas banks. The Executor and Trustee Department was formed in 1910, opening its first branch in 1933. By 1958, thirty-two executor and trustee branches existed and administered about 20,000 estates and trusts. Overseas banking began in 1911 when Lloyds Bank (France), later known as Lloyds Bank (Europe) was established out of the business of Armstrong & Co of Paris. However, Lloyds Bank Ltd's major overseas interest was the London & River Plate Bank Ltd (est. 1862), in which a shareholding was acquired in 1918. In 1923 this bank merged with the London & Brazilian Bank Ltd (est. 1862) to form the Bank of London & South America Ltd, one of the largest British-owned overseas banks. The Eastern Department of Lloyds, established in 1924, acted as 'head office' for a network of Indian and Egyptian branches acquired through the acquisition of Cox & Co and Henry S King & Co.The Egyptian branches were sold to the National Bank of Egypt in 1926 and the Indian branches were disposed of to National & Grindlays Bank in 1961. Other interests in foreign banks included the National Bank

330   *British banking – a guide to historical records*

of New Zealand in which a shareholding was acquired in 1919; it became wholly owned in 1966. In 1918 an interest, disposed of in the late 1960s, was also acquired in the Bank of British West Africa Ltd. American First Western Bank & Trust Co was purchased in 1973 and renamed Lloyds Bank California. In the UK, in 1967 Lewis's Bank Ltd (est. 1928), which operated ten branches in Lewis's department stores, was purchased from Martins Bank Ltd (est. 1831). A full merger between Lloyds Bank and Martins Bank was considered throughout the 1960s and in 1968 a proposed merger of Lloyds, Martins and Barclays was disallowed by the Monopolies and Mergers Commission; Barclays and Martins alone subsequently merged. Lloyds then pursued a 'group bank' concept, namely a structure based upon a strong domestic base with branches abroad and able to withstand growing international competition. In pursuance of this, Lloyds acquired full control of the Bank of London & South America Ltd and during 1971and 1973 merged it with Lloyds Bank Europe to form Lloyds Bank International. By 1974 Lloyds Bank Group had been created and consisted of the UK retail bank (Lloyds Bank Ltd), Lloyds Bank International, Lloyds Bank California and the National Bank of New Zealand. A separate board was established to control the domestic business and its subsidiaries, leaving the main Lloyds board to direct group strategy. In 1982 Lloyds Bank Ltd was renamed Lloyds Bank plc and in 1986 Lloyds Bank International merged with Lloyds Bank plc forming a unified domestic and international entity and signalling the abandonment of the group bank structure. In 1990, as part of a general re-structuring process, the retail banking operations moved to new headquarters in Bristol. In the 1990s the bank embarked upon a major extension of its UK retail banking operations through the acquisition in 1995 of both Cheltenham & Gloucester Building Society and TSB Group. The acquisition of TSB resulted in the group being renamed Lloyds TSB Group plc.

Manfred Pohl & Sabine Freitag (eds.), *Handbook on the History of European Banks* (Aldershot, 1994); R S Sayers, *Lloyds Bank in the History of English Banking* (Oxford, 1957); J R Winton, *Lloyds Bank 1918–1969* (Oxford, 1982)

Records 1: Lloyds TSB Group plc, Archives, Head Office, 71 Lombard Street, London EC3P 3BS

Private ledger 1765–1865; daily balances of receipts and payments 1835–64; bad debts and disposal of securities files 1840–1914; note registers (2) 1842–65; customer ledger 1863–65; share allotment book 1865; directors' meeting minutes 1865 on; articles of association 1865 on; annual general meeting minutes 1865 on; annual reports from 1865; share applications register 1865–67; balance sheets 1865–85; premises ledger 1865–71; pri-

Records of banks 331

vate letterbooks (2) 1865–77; widows' fund ledgers (2) 1865–1915; share registers 1866 on; board agenda books and papers 1866–1902, 1944 on; chairman's agenda books (14) 1866–1902; 'reference' (later 'county') committee minute and agenda books (27) 1867–1901; profit and loss account books (7) 1866–1903; shareholders' cash book 1866; letterbooks (2) and other correspondence of Howard Lloyd 1868–1902; secretary's private memorandum book 1868–71; rules for branch managers 1870s, 1890s; staff register 1870s–c.1950; special committee minute book 1871–1900; senior staff salary book 1876–1918; bill committee memorandum book 1878–84; seal register 1883–95; Birmingham committee minute and agenda books (5) 1884–92; properties and investments ledger 1884–99; London (later 'weekly') committee minute books (5) 1884–1901; building committee minutes 1886–87; daily committee minute books (10) 1886–1901; private minute book 1889–1923; premises committee minute books (31) 1890–1937; properties committee minute books 1891–1902; investment committee minute books (14) 1891–1947; 'county' committee minutes 1892–93; widows' fund subscription book 1900–16; investment ledgers (5) 1900–22, 1932–60; staff rules and instructions 1902–14; South Wales inspector letterbook 1902–15; weekly liabilities and assets ledgers (9) 1906–27; overseas department profit and loss ledgers (2) 1908–71; staff committee minute books (47) 1909–64; general manager's staff letters (7) 1919–22; West Yorkshire committee minute books (2) 1920–30; West Yorkshire committee chairman's minute books (5) 1921–30; overseas department private memorandum book 1922–48; secretary's department procedure book 1924–61; general manager's committee minute books (3) 1925–38; chief general manager's files 1927–45; minutes and correspondence re 'managers' meetings' 1930–54; Eastern committee minute books (3) 1934–44, 1957–60; overseas department half-yearly statistics 1937–62; wartime staff department files 1939–48; overseas department annual reports 1944–80; reports on information technology introduction 1966–93; 'Lugano Affair' files 1974–78; Lloyds Bank Group committee minute books (3) 1974–85.

Aberdare: profit and loss ledgers (2) 1890–1956; memorandum books (2) 1901–26; **Aldershot:** profit and loss ledger 1917–66; **Alford:** memorandum book 1919–39; security register 1919–c.1944; **Alnwick:** profit and loss ledgers (3) 1903–67; memorandum books (2) c.1888–1938; **Alton:** memorandum books (2) 1921–47; **Altrincham:** memorandum books (4) 1900–47; **Altrincham, Broadheath:** memorandum book 1903–50; **Amersham:** profit and loss ledger 1918–36; memorandum books (2) 1918–47; **Ammanford:** profit and loss ledgers (3) 1910–66; **Andover:** memorandum books (2) 1914–46; profit and loss ledgers (2) 1914–49; **Alresford:** security register 1898–1920; **Arundel:** profit and loss ledgers

332 British banking – a guide to historical records

(2) 1918–65; memorandum book 1919–36; **Ashburton:** memorandum book 1907–35; **Ashby-de-la- Zouch:** memorandum book 1900–34; profit and loss ledgers (3) 1900–67; **Ashford:** profit and loss ledgers (2) 1902–30; memorandum books (3)1902–31; **Ashington:** memorandum books (2) 1924–32, 1941–48; profit and loss ledger 1936–64; **Atherstone:** memorandum books (2) 1889–1947; **Axminster:** profit and loss ledgers (3) 1906–65; memorandum books (2) 1908–39; **Baldock:** profit and loss ledger 1937–67; memorandum books (2) 1919–52; **Banbury:** memorandum book 1902–35; **Bargoed:** profit and loss ledgers (3)1904–67; **Basingstoke, Winchester Street:** profit and loss ledger 1949–67; **Beaconsfield:** profit and loss ledger 1918–45; **Bedford:** memorandum book 1919–39; **Beecles:** memorandum books (2) 1919–52; **Bellingham:** profit and loss ledgers (2) 1903–66; memorandum books (3) 1896–1942; **Biggleswade:** profit and loss ledgers (2) 1918–67; memorandum books (3) 1919–31; **Birkenhead, Charing Cross:** memorandum books (2) 1900–34; profit and loss ledgers (2) 1930–66; **Birmingham, Aston:** memorandum books (6) 1874–1941; **Birmingham, Bourneville:** memorandum book 1909–34; **Birmingham, Bristol Street:** memorandum books (2) 1925–33; liabilities and assets book 1944–58; **Birmingham, Coleshill:** memorandum book 1903–30; profit and loss ledger 1903–32; **Birmingham, Colmore Row:** manager's diaries (27) 1876–1903; profit and loss ledgers (5) 1884–1966; **Birmingham, Corporation Street:** memorandum books (2) 1919–39; **Birmingham, Cradleigh Heath:** memorandum books (2) 1913–41; **Birmingham, Deritend:** memorandum books (4) 1878–1935; **Birmingham, Edgbaston:** profit and loss ledgers (2) 1874–1928; memorandum books (4) 1874–1930; **Birmingham, Erdington:** memorandum book 1895–1935; **Birmingham, Gravelly Hill:** memorandum book 1913–34; **Birmingham, Great Hampton Street:** memorandum books (5) 1873–1925; head office instructions 1874–83; profit and loss ledgers (2) 1929–75; **Birmingham, Halesowen:** profit and loss ledger 1900–29; **Birmingham, Handsworth:** memorandum book 1925–33; **Birmingham, Harborne:** memorandum books (3) 1884–1939; profit and loss ledgers (2) 1918–67; **Birmingham, Highgate:** profit and loss ledgers (3) 1900–67; **Birmingham, Holyhead Road:** memorandum book 1904–44; profit and loss ledgers (2) 1932–67; **Birmingham, King's Heath:** memorandum books (3) 1913–36; profit and loss ledgers (2) 1913–65; **Birmingham, King's Norton:** memorandum books (2) 1890–42; **Birmingham, Ladywood:** memorandum books (3) 1894–1927; profit and loss ledgers (2) 1897–1927; **Birmingham, Long Acre:** memorandum books (2) 1888–1945 [w]; profit and loss ledger 1933–57; **Birmingham, Moseley:** profit and loss ledgers (3) 1894–1967; memorandum books (3) 1898–1939; **Birmingham, New Street:** memorandum books (11) 1880–1913; profit and loss ledgers (2) 1923–66; **Birmingham, Oldbury:** profit and loss

Records of banks **333**

ledgers (3) 1866–1930; memorandum books (2) 1885–1935; letterbook 1886–1925; **Birmingham, Old Square:** memorandum book 1922–39; **Birmingham, Selly Oak:** memorandum books (2) 1895–1934; **Birmingham, Shirley:** memorandum book 1908–36; **Birmingham, Smallbrook Queensway:** memorandum books (5) 1887–1937; profit and loss ledgers (4) 1888–1965; **Birmingham, Small Heath:** letterbook 1914–31; **Birmingham, Smethwick:** memorandum books (3) 1876–1935; profit and loss ledgers (2) 1931–66; **Birmingham, Solihull:** memorandum book 1877–1927; profit and loss ledgers (4) 1894–1966; **Birmingham, Sparkbrook:** profit and loss ledger 1954–67; **Birmingham, Sparkhill:** profit and loss ledgers (2) 1907–22, 1952–67; **Birmingham, Stirchley:** memorandum book 1901–33; profit and loss ledgers (2) 1901–67; **Birmingham, Summerfield:** memorandum books (3) 1894–1934; profit and loss ledger 1897–1925; **Birmingham, Temple Row:** memorandum books (6) 1890–1925; salary book 1894–1927; **Birtley:** memorandum book 1905–39; **Blaenavon:** memorandum book 1910–34; **Blackburn:** salary book 1860–1917; profit and loss ledgers (3) 1900–66; **Blackhill:** memorandum books (2) 1897–1942; **Blandford:** memorandum book 1924–34; **Blaydon on Tyne:** memorandum book: 1900–21; **Bloxwich:** profit and loss ledgers (3) 1902–67; memorandum book 1903–45; **Blyth:** memorandum books (2) 1909–60; **Boston:** memorandum books (3) 1924–40; **Bournemouth:** memorandum book 1895–1917; profit and loss ledgers (2) 1918–20, 1941–65; **Bournemouth, Boscombe:** memorandum book 1909–34; profit and loss ledgers (2) 1909–57; **Bournemouth, Malmesbury Park:** letterbook 1908–32; **Bournemouth, West Southbourne:** memorandum book 1923–31; **Bournemouth, Westbourne:** memorandum books (2) 1909–36; profit and loss ledgers (4) 1909–66; **Brackley:** memorandum book c.1902–49; **Brecon:** memorandum book 1898–1934; profit and loss ledger 1949–66; **Bridgend:** memorandum book 1888–1903; profit and loss ledgers (5) 1888–1967; **Bridgewater:** memorandum books (4) 1905–32; profit and loss ledgers (2) 1921–67; **Brigg:** profit and loss ledger 1920–49; memorandum books (2) c.1926–38; **Brighton:** signature book 1896–1907; profit and loss ledgers (4) 1896–1967; security register 1925–30; **Bristol, Cheltenham Road:** memorandum book 1904–39; profit and loss ledgers (3) 1919–67; **Bristol, Clare Street:** profit and loss ledger 1918–42; **Bristol, Corn Street:** profit and loss ledgers (3) 1892–1967; manager's diaries (12) 1925–35; **Bristol, Clifton:** profit and loss ledgers (4) 1892–1967; **Bristol, Kingswood:** memorandum book 1892–1924; **Bristol, Merchant Street:** profit and loss ledger 1957–67; **Bristol, Redland:** profit and loss ledgers (4) 1904–65; memorandum book 1916–26; **Bristol, St George:** profit and loss ledgers (2) 1892–1926, 1943–59; **Bristol, Temple Gate:** profit and loss ledgers (3) 1892–1949; memorandum books (2) 1895–1949; **Bristol, Whiteladies:** profit and loss ledgers (2) 1918–41;

334   British banking – a guide to historical records

memorandum book 1920–42; **Broadstairs:** memorandum book 1898–1936; **Bromley:** memorandum book 1914–31; **Bromsgrove:** profit and loss ledger 1889–1940; letterbook 1894–1921; memorandum book 1916–34; **Broseley:** reference book: 1883–1905; **Buckingham:** memorandum book 1902–26; profit and loss ledger 1902–32; **Buckley:** memorandum book 1907–56; profit and loss ledger 1941–66; **Budleigh Salterton:** profit and loss ledgers (3) 1906–67; memorandum book 1911–35; **Builth Wells:** memorandum book 1919–35; **Burslem:** memorandum book 1919–35; **Burton on Trent:** memorandum books (4) 1876–1927; profit and loss ledgers (2) 1876–1930; **Caerphilly:** memorandum book 1909–41; **Callington:** profit and loss ledgers (2) 1930–62; **Camborne:** profit and loss ledgers (2) 1906–31; memorandum books (2) 1906–47; **Cambridge:** memorandum books (30) 1905–45; **Cannock:** memorandum books (2) 1881–1932; profit and loss ledgers (4) 1881–1965; **Cardiff:** memorandum book 1892–98; **Cardiff, St Mary Street:** memorandum book 1909–16; **Carlisle:** memorandum book 1919–39; profit and loss ledgers (3) 1919–66; **Carmarthen:** memorandum books (2) 1890–1949; profit and loss ledgers (2) 1890–1965; **Caterham Valley:** profit and loss ledgers (2) 1886–1925; **Caversham:** memorandum book 1928–51; profit and loss ledgers (2) 1928–65; **Cheltenham:** memorandum books (3) 1889–1926; **Cheltenham, Montpellier:** memorandum book 1918–45; **Chesterfield:** profit and loss ledgers (2) 1921–67; potential business memorandum book 1932–42; **Chester le Street:** profit and loss ledger 1903–18; memorandum books (3) 1904–47; **Chichester:** memorandum book: 1920–37; **Cirencester:** memorandum book 1897–1933; **Consett:** memorandum book 1905–c.1935; **Cotteridge:** memorandum book 1922–38; **Coventry:** memorandum books (19) 1874–1915; profit and loss ledgers (2) 1874–1927; **Cranbrook:** profit and loss ledgers (3) 1913–60; **Crawley:** memorandum book 1919–31; **Crewkerne:** profit and loss ledgers (2) 1914–67; **Cullompton:** memorandum book 1906–56; profit and loss ledgers (2) 1906–64; **Cromer:** profit and loss ledgers (2) 1934–67; **Darlaston:** memorandum book 1886–96; **Darlington:** memorandum books (3) 1910–39; **Dartford:** memorandum book 1928–34; **Darwen:** profit and loss ledgers (3) 1900–66; memorandum book 1901–45; **Daventry:** profit and loss ledgers (3) 1918–67; memorandum book 1920–37; **Deal:** profit and loss ledgers (2) 1924–67; memorandum books (3)1896–1936; **Derby:** profit and loss ledgers (4) 1899–1967; memorandum books (2) 1899–1930; **Doncaster:** profit and loss ledgers (2) 1911–62; memorandum book 1912–45; **Dorchester:** memorandum book 1906–34; **Dover:** profit and loss ledgers (4) 1895–1956; memorandum book 1920–45; **Dovercourt:** memorandum book 1919–34; **Dowlais:** memorandum book 1893–1937; **Droitwich:** profit and loss ledger 1889–1913; memorandum book 1889–1940; **Dudley:** memorandum books (2) 1879–1937; profit and loss ledgers (3) 1916–68; **Dudley, Netherton:** profit and

Records of banks   335

loss ledgers (2) 1902–65; **Dunstable:** memorandum book 1923–33; profit and loss ledgers (2) 1923–67; **Durham:** memorandum books (2) 1912–23; **Eastbourne:** memorandum books (2) 1902–21; **Ebbw Vale:** memorandum book 1908–37; **Edenbridge:** memorandum books (2) 1892–1942; profit and loss ledgers (3) 1892–1967; **Ellesmere:** memorandum book 1883–1909; **Ely:** profit and loss ledger 1918–48; memorandum book 1924–38; **Epsom:** memorandum book 1919–36; profit and loss ledgers (3) 1934–67; **Evesham:** memorandum books (3) 1889–1929; profit and loss ledgers (4) 1889–1960; **Faringdon:** profit and loss ledgers (2) 1897–1966; **Faversham:** profit and loss ledger 1918–33; memorandum book 1921–35; **Felling:** memorandum book 1923–57; **Fenton:** memorandum books (2) 1896–1949; profit and loss ledgers (3) 1896–1967; **Ferndown:** memorandum book 1930–52; profit and loss ledgers (2) 1930–67; **Foleshill:** profit and loss ledgers (4) 1900–67; memorandum book 1904–26; **Folkestone:** profit and loss ledgers (6) 1891–67; memorandum books (7) 1905–34; **Fowey:** memorandum book 1906–23; profit and loss ledgers (2) 1906–45; **Frome:** profit and loss ledgers (2) 1914–66; **Gateshead:** memorandum books (2) 1905–18; **Gillingham (Dorset):** memorandum book 1925–47; **Glastonbury:** memorandum book 1914–39; profit and loss ledger 1947–66; **Gloucester:** memorandum book 1918–35; **Gosport:** profit and loss ledgers (2) 1918–67; **Grantham:** memorandum book 1919–37; profit and loss ledgers (2) 1919–66; **Gravesend:** profit and loss ledger 1918–48; memorandum book 1921–34; **Great Bridge:** security register c.1885–92; profit and loss ledgers (2) 1902–64; memorandum book 1926–40; **Great Yarmouth:** memorandum book 1919–38; **Grimsby:** memorandum book 1914–36; **Guernsey:** profit and loss ledgers (2) 1918–54; memorandum book 1919–35; wartime occupation files 1940–43; **Guildford:** memorandum book 1913–24; **Hadleigh:** profit and loss ledgers 1919–31, 1944–65; **Hanley:** memorandum books (5) 1877–1942; profit and loss ledgers (6) 1877–1967; **Harwich:** memorandum book 1919–32; **Haslemere:** profit and loss ledgers (3) 1918–65; memorandum book 1919–38; **Hastings:** memorandum books (3) 1892–1937; **Havant:** memorandum book 1935–50; **Hawarden:** memorandum books (2) 1902–54; profit and loss ledger 1931–62; **Haywards Heath:** profit and loss ledger 1918–48; **Hebburn:** memorandum book 1907–47; profit and loss ledgers (2) 1936–67; **Hednesford:** memorandum book 1897–1951; **Hemel Hempstead:** profit and loss ledgers (2) 1902–32; **Heswall:** memorandum book 1900–48; profit and loss ledgers (2) 1900–67; **Hexham:** memorandum books (4) 1898–1951; **Highbridge:** salary book 1905–72; profit and loss ledger 1914–43; memorandum books (2) 1920–47; **High Wycombe:** profit and loss ledger 1918–33; memorandum books (2) 1920–37; **Holbeach:** memorandum book c.1926–48; **Holsworthy:** memorandum books (2) 1899–1943; **Horley:** memorandum books (2) 1917–43; profit and loss ledger 1928–

336   *British banking – a guide to historical records*

58; **Hull:** memorandum book 1911–24; **Hungerford:** profit and loss ledgers (2) 1918–66; **Huntingdon:** memorandum book 1930–51; **Ipswich:** memorandum books (6) 1919–32; **Ironbridge:** memorandum books (3)1874–1932; letterbooks (2) c.1894–1927; profit and loss ledgers (2) 1900–60; **Jarrow:** profit and loss ledgers (3) 1903–65; memorandum books (2) 1905–42; **Kendal:** memorandum books (2) 1920–49; **Kettering:** memorandum book 1920–37; **Kidderminster:** memorandum books (4) 1889–1931; **Kingsbridge:** profit and loss ledger 1892–1927; memorandum books (2) 1893–1936; **King's Lynn:** letterbook 1912–34; profit and loss ledgers (3) 1918–67; memorandum books (2) 1919–35; **Knighton:** profit and loss ledger 1919–35; memorandum book 1919–40; **Lampeter:** memorandum books (3) 1910–49; signature book 1911–c.1939; **Langley:** profit and loss ledger 1957–65; **Leamington Spa:** profit and loss ledgers (6) 1866–1966; memorandum books (3)1883–1921; **Leatherhead:** memorandum book 1924–36; **Leeds:** memorandum books (12) 1900–40; salary book 1901–30; manager's diaries (4) 1909–30; letterbooks (4) 1909–30; **Leicester, Granby Street:** profit and loss ledgers (3) 1918–67; **Leominster:** memorandum books (3) 1880–1917; manager's diaries (3) 1887–89; profit and loss ledger 1889–1913; **Lichfield:** profit and loss ledgers (6) 1866–1966; memorandum book 1893–1918; **Liskeard:** memorandum book 1907–23; **Littlehampton:** profit and loss ledgers (2) 1918–67; **Littleport:** profit and loss ledger 1918–48; memorandum book 1939–52; **Liverpool:** memorandum book 1924–31; **Liverpool, Church Street:** profit and loss ledger 1931–41; **Liverpool, Victoria Street:** profit and loss ledgers (2) 1921–66; **Llandridod Wells:** memorandum book 1914–39; **Llanelli:** staff book 1922–48; **London, Balham:** memorandum book 1926–39; **London, Belgrave Road:** profit and loss ledgers (2) 1926–66; **London: Blackheath:** memorandum book 1928–34; profit and loss ledgers (2) 1928–65; **London, Butler Place:** profit and loss ledgers (2) 1918–67; **London, Camberwell:** memorandum book 1926–47; **London, Camden Town:** memorandum books (2) 1926–33, 1937–40; profit and loss ledger 1957–67; **London, Covent Garden:** memorandum book 1919–36; **London, Cricklewood:** memorandum book 1923–36; profit and loss ledger 1923–65; **London, Deptford:** memorandum book 1927–35; **London, East Dulwich:** profit and loss ledger 1930–67; **London, Edgware:** profit and loss ledgers (2) 1923–63; **London, Edgware Road:** memorandum books (9) 1898–1931; profit and loss ledgers (3) 1898–1966; **London, Enfield:** memorandum books (3) 1896–1956; **London, Fenchurch Street:** memorandum book 1910–21; **London, Finchley Road:** memorandum book 1985–1931; **London, Finsbury Circus:** memorandum book 1930–32; **London, Finsbury Park:** memorandum books (2) 1927–34; profit and loss ledgers (2) 1927–67; **London, Golders Green:** profit and loss ledger 1914–38; memorandum books (2) 1924–36; **London, Great Portland**

Records of banks **337**

Street: memorandum book 1922–33; **London, Greenwich:** memorandum book 1927–39; **London, Hampstead:** signature book 1885–93; memorandum books (5) 1885–1932; **London, Harringay:** memorandum book 1926–36; profit and loss ledger 1926–43; **London, Hendon:** profit and loss ledgers (2) 1924–67; **London, Hendon Central:** memorandum book 1927–31; profit and loss ledgers (2) 1927–72; **London, Herne Hill:** memorandum book 1926–38; profit and loss ledger 1958–67; **London, Islington:** memorandum book 1921–35; **London, Kensington High Street:** memorandum books (2) c.1920–39; **London, King's Cross:** memorandum book 1922–24; **London, Kingsway:** memorandum book 1914–37; **London, Knightsbridge:** signature book 1911–24; memorandum books (4) 1911–36; profit and loss ledger 1942–67; **London, Leicester Square:** profit and loss ledgers (2) 1920–41; **London, Lewisham:** memorandum book 1927–38; **London, Ludgate Hill:** profit and loss ledger 1918–46; staff register c.1920–47; memorandum book c.1925–43; **London, Mile End:** memorandum books (3) 1925–40; **London, Mincing Lane:** memorandum books (2) 1928–41; **London, Moorgate:** profit and loss ledgers (2) 1931–67; **London, Newington Causeway:** profit and loss ledgers (2) 1918–67; **London, New Oxford Street:** profit and loss ledger 1923–38; memorandum book 1938–41; **London, Old Bond Street:** memorandum book 1920–24; **London, Old Street:** profit and loss ledger 1920–39; **London, Paddington:** profit and loss ledgers (2) 1918–67; **London, Park Lane:** profit and loss ledgers (3) 1928–68; **London, Peckham:** memorandum book 1922–33; profit and loss ledgers (2) 1922–67; **London, Peckham Rye:** memorandum book 1926–32; **London, Piccadilly:** profit and loss ledger 1906–36; **London, St James's Street:** profit and loss ledgers (6) 1884–1971; manager's diaries (23) 1905–29; memorandum book 1921–24; **London, Shoreditch:** profit and loss ledgers (3) 1918–67; memorandum books (3) 1920–46; **London, Spitalfields:** memorandum books (2) 1924–37; **London, Stratford:** memorandum book 1924–47; **London, Streatham:** profit and loss ledgers (2) 1921–56; **London, Swiss Cottage:** profit and loss ledger 1938–41; **London, Tooting Broadway:** memorandum book 1927–41; **London, Tottenham:** memorandum book 1929–46; **London, Tottenham Court Road:** memorandum book 1913–29; profit and loss ledgers (2) 1913–66; **London, Upper Tooting:** memorandum book 1926–36; **London, West Dulwich:** profit and loss ledger 1952–65; **London, West Kensington:** memorandum books (8) 1897–1946; profit and loss ledger 1944–66; **London, Westminster House:** memorandum book 1925–32; **London, West Smithfield:** memorandum books (4) 1911–33; **London, Whitechapel:** memorandum books (31) 1914–48; **London, Wood Green:** memorandum book 1927–36; profit and loss ledger 1927–67; **London, Woolwich:** memorandum books (2) 1919–37; **Longfleet:** memorandum book 1930–48; profit and loss ledger 1930–67; **Longton:** profit and loss

338   *British banking – a guide to historical records*

ledgers (4) 1867–1966; memorandum books (4) 1871–1947; **Ludlow:** memorandum book 1919–32; **Luton:** memorandum books (3) 1919–33; profit and loss ledger 1954–67; **Lydney:** memorandum books (2) 1908–45; profit and loss ledgers (3) 1908–66; **Lymington:** profit and loss ledgers (2) 1914–35, 1967; memorandum book 1920–31; **Lynton:** profit and loss ledgers (3) 1906–67; memorandum book 1908–36; **Maidstone:** profit and loss ledgers (4) 1894–1967; **Malvern:** profit and loss ledgers (2) 1889–1929; memorandum book 1919–28; **Malvern Link:** memorandum book 1914–30; profit and loss ledger 1918–39; **Manchester:** manager's diaries (22) 1900–21; profit and loss ledger 1900–30; liabilities and assets books (3) 1914–34; memorandum books (17) 1922–38; **Manchester, Market Place:** profit and loss ledgers (3) 1909–66; **Mansfield:** memorandum book 1919–42; **Margate:** profit and loss ledger 1891–1915; memorandum books (4) 1891–1936; **Market Harborough:** memorandum book 1909–39; **Melksham:** profit and loss ledger 1914–51; memorandum book 1916–39; **Melton Mowbray:** memorandum book 1907–37; **Mere:** memorandum book 1923–40; **Middlesborough:** profit and loss ledger 1910–40; **Midsomer Norton:** memorandum books (2) 1903–33; **Mildenhall:** profit and loss ledger 1918–68; **Milnsbridge:** memorandum book 1911–49; profit and loss ledger 1947–65; **Modbury:** memorandum book 1906–47; profit and loss ledgers (2) 1906–67; **Monkwearmouth:** profit and loss ledger 1941–42; **Monmouth:** profit and loss ledgers (2) 1894–1922; letterbook 1910–29; **Morley:** memorandum book 1902–49; **Morpeth:** profit and loss ledgers (3) 1903–67; memorandum books (3) 1909–33; **Nailsworth:** memorandum book 1919–33; **Netherfield:** memorandum books (4) 1896–1932; **Newark:** memorandum book 1912–37; profit and loss ledger 1912–43; **Newbiggin by the Sea:** profit and loss ledger 1903; memorandum book 1903–22; **Newbury:** memorandum books (2) 1915–27; **Newcastle, Staffordshire:** memorandum books (2) 1890–1929; **Newcastle upon Tyne, Byker and Heaton:** memorandum books (4) 1924–49; **Newcastle upon Tyne, Elswick Road:** memorandum book 1908–41; **Newcastle upon Tyne, Grey Street:** memorandum books (2) 1921–48; **Newcastle upon Tyne, Osbourne:** memorandum book 1909–25; **Newcastle upon Tyne, Quayside:** memorandum book 1904–09; profit and loss ledgers (2) 1904–67; **Newcastle upon Tyne, Wallsend:** memorandum book 1904–31; **Newcastle upon Tyne, Westgate Road:** memorandum books (4) 1901–36; **Newmarket:** profit and loss ledgers (2) 1918–69; memorandum book 1922–39; **Newnham:** memorandum book c.1922–73; **Newport, Gwent:** memorandum books (2) 1890–1931; **Newport, Shropshire:** profit and loss ledger 1899–1927; memorandum book 1929–38; **North Shields:** profit and loss ledgers (4) 1903–66; memorandum books (2) 1908–62; **Nottingham, Alfreton Road:** memorandum books (6) 1891–1938; profit and loss ledgers (3) 1916–65; **Nuneaton:** letterbook 1902–24;

Records of banks 339

memorandum books (2) 1902–48; **Oakengates:** memorandum book 1913–52; profit and loss ledgers (3) 1913–68; **Oldham:** profit and loss ledgers (2) 1930–67; **Old Hill:** memorandum book 1906–30; profit and loss ledger 1909–39; **Oxford:** memorandum book 1914–32; **Oxted:** profit and loss ledger 1892–1932; **Penrith:** memorandum book 1920–50; **Peterborough:** memorandum book 1919–34; letterbook 1920–23; profit and loss ledgers (2) 1934–67; **Pewsey:** memorandum book 1919–49; **Plymouth:** profit and loss ledger 1906–36; **Plymouth, Stonehouse:** memorandum book 1906–54; **Ponteland:** memorandum book 1908–39; **Pontypool:** memorandum book 1890–1941; profit and loss ledgers (3) 1890–71; **Poole:** salary book 1885–1938; profit and loss ledgers (2) 1914–53; memorandum book c.1923–30; **Poole, Parkstone:** salary book 1895–1951; **Port Talbot:** memorandum books (2) 1898–1936; profit and loss ledgers (3) 1898–1966; **Portland:** profit and loss ledger 1914–46; **Portsmouth, High Street:** memorandum book 1903–38; **Portsmouth, North End:** letterbook 1903–25; **Presteigne:** memorandum books (2) 1889–1935; profit and loss ledgers (2) 1889–1947; **Pwllheli:** profit and loss ledgers (2) 1916–66; memorandum book 1925–37; **Ramsgate:** memorandum book 1898–1914; **Reading:** memorandum book 1911–21; **Redditch:** memorandum book 1892–1915; profit and loss ledgers (3) 1892–1967; **Redruth:** memorandum book 1906–34; **Rhymney:** memorandum book 1906–35; profit and loss ledger 1910–40; **Richmond:** memorandum books (2) 1922–32; **Rickmansworth:** memorandum book 1929–47; profit and loss ledger 1960–67; **Romford:** profit and loss ledger 1911–40; **Rothbury:** memorandum book 1909–37; **Royston:** memorandum book 1932–48; **Rugby:** memorandum books (5) 1878–1945; profit and loss ledgers (2) 1893–1942; **Rugeley:** profit and loss ledgers (2) 1876–1901, 1932–47; **Rushden:** memorandum book 1921–48; **Rye:** memorandum books (2) 1893–1936; **Sacriston:** memorandum books (2) 1921–53; **St Clears:** memorandum book 1921–36; **St Ives:** memorandum book 1907–38; **St Leonards on Sea:** memorandum books (3)1893–1931; profit and loss ledgers (2) 1929–69; **St Neots:** memorandum book 1921–34; **Salcombe:** memorandum book 1906–50; **Sale:** profit and loss ledgers (3) 1900–67; memorandum books (7) 1901–36; **Sandgate:** memorandum books (2) 1898–1940; **Sandwich:** profit and loss ledgers (2) 1918–67; memorandum books (2) 1919–47; **Scunthorpe:** profit and loss ledgers (2) 1918–67; memorandum book c.1926–41; **Sheffield:** profit and loss ledgers (3) 1913–65; **Shepton Mallet:** profit and loss ledger 1948–67; **Shifnal:** profit and loss ledgers (4) 1874–1966; memorandum book 1878–1934; **Shipston on Stour:** memorandum book 1889–1948; profit and loss ledgers (3) 1913–65; **Shotley Bridge:** profit and loss ledgers (2) 1903–67; memorandum books (2) 1915–30; **Shotton:** memorandum book 1903–40; **Shrewsbury:** memorandum books (4) 1877–1930; profit and loss ledgers (2) 1931–70;

340   *British banking – a guide to historical records*

Sleaford: staff record book 1911–51; profit and loss ledgers (2) 1912–67; **Slough Trading Estate:** profit and loss ledgers (2) 1934–66; **South Shields:** memorandum book 1891–1920; letterbooks (3) 1903–12; **Southam:** profit and loss ledgers (3) 1903–62; **Southampton:** memorandum books (5) 1906–45; **Southampton, Avenue:** profit and loss ledger 1918–55; **Southampton, Portswood:** memorandum book c.1920–38; **Southsea, Albert Road:** memorandum books (2) 1910–45; **Southsea, Elm Grove:** profit and loss ledger 1918; **Spalding:** memorandum book 1919–51; **Spennymoor:** profit and loss ledgers (2) 1907–67; **Stafford:** profit and loss ledgers (4) 1866–1943; memorandum books (3) 1891–1933; **Stamford:** memorandum book 1919–38; **Stanley:** memorandum books (4) 1906–56; profit and loss ledgers (2) 1934–66; **Stockton on Tees:** memorandum books (4) 1910–32; **Stoke on Trent:** memorandum book 1922–34; **Stone:** profit and loss ledger 1920–36; memorandum book 1920–47; **Stony Stratford:** memorandum book 1902–39; **Storrington:** memorandum books (2) 1927–47; profit and loss ledger 1927–53; **Stourport on Severn:** memorandum book 1920–37; **Stratford upon Avon:** memorandum book 1895–1922; **Stroud:** memorandum books (2) c.1882–97, 1915–28; profit and loss ledgers (2) 1892–1930; **Sunderland:** memorandum books (2) 1907–17; profit and loss ledger 1939–66; **Sutton Coldfield:** memorandum books (3) 1885–1939; letterbook 1888–1927; profit and loss ledgers (2) 1929–65; **Swadlincote:** profit and loss ledger 1899–1927; memorandum books (2) 1904–36; salary book 1919–52; **Tamworth:** memorandum books (3) 1868–1922, 1935–44; status enquiry book 1879–1906; **Tavistock:** memorandum books (3) 1906–41; **Tenbury Wells:** memorandum books (2) 1889–1927; profit and loss ledgers (3) 1889–1938; **Tenterden:** memorandum books (2) 1902–39; profit and loss ledgers (3) 1902–67; . **Tewkesbury:** memorandum books (3) 1906–45; **Thame:** memorandum book 1902–52; profit and loss ledgers (2) 1902–63; **Thetford:** profit and loss ledger 1918–34; memorandum book 1920–50; **Thirsk:** memorandum book 1919–42; profit and loss ledgers (2) 1919–67; **Thornaby on Tees:** memorandum books (2) 1920–27; **Tiverton:** profit and loss ledgers (2) 1921–68; **Todmorden:** manager's diary 1911–35; memorandum book 1946–49; **Torquay:** profit and loss ledger 1892–1901; memorandum book 1900–32; **Tredegar:** profit and loss ledger 1921–35; **Trowbridge:** salary book 1885–1934; memorandum book 1927–30; **Tunbridge Wells:** profit and loss ledgers (2) 1891–1935; **Tutbury:** memorandum book 1930–44; **Twickenham:** profit and loss ledgers (2) 1929–32, 1951–66; **Uttoxeter:** memorandum book 1916–33; **Uxbridge:** profit and loss ledger 1951–71; **Walsall:** profit and loss ledgers (2) 1866–1925; memorandum books (2) 1876–1935; **Wareham:** profit and loss ledgers (2) 1914–67; **Warwick:** memorandum books (2) 1877–1935; **Washington:** memorandum book 1933–50; **Watford:** profit and loss ledger 1902–29; memorandum book

Records of banks 341

1920–31; **Watford Junction:** profit and loss ledger 1919–49; **Wednesbury:** memorandum books (3) 1896–1938; profit and loss ledgers (3) 1914–65; **Wellington :** memorandum book 1890–1920; **Welshpool:** profit and loss ledgers (3) 1880–1967; memorandum books (2) 1881–1932; **West Bromwich:** memorandum book 1883–1908; **West Cliff:** memorandum book 1922–44; **West Worthing:** memorandum book 1919–39; **Westbury:** profit and loss ledgers (2) 1914–67; **Westcliff on Sea:** profit and loss ledger 1918–48; **Westgate on Sea:** memorandum book 1892–1933; profit and loss ledgers (2) 1929–66; **Weston super Mare:** memorandum book 1915–33; **Weymouth:** memorandum books (2) 1907–35; **Whitehaven:** memorandum book 1919–32; **Whitstable:** memorandum books (2) 1919–40; **Wigton:** profit and loss ledger 1920–35; memorandum book 1920–35; **Willenhall:** memorandum books (3) 1887–1922; **Winchester:** memorandum book 1920–38; **Wisbech:** profit and loss ledgers (2) 1918–67; memorandum book 1919–34; **Woking:** memorandum book 1919–20; **Wolverhampton:** memorandum books (5) 1876–1927; letterbooks (3) 1886–1916; office diary and memorandum book c.1930–50; **Woodbridge:** memorandum book 1918–19; **Worcester:** memorandum books (12) 1920–34; salary book 1921–46; **Workington:** profit and loss ledgers (2) 1924–41; memorandum books (2) 1924–41; **Worthing:** memorandum books (5) 1900–32; **Wrexham:** profit and loss ledgers (3) 1897–1967; memorandum book 1899–1913; **Yeovil:** memorandum books (3) 1919–40.

Records 2: Central Library, Chamberlain Square, Birmingham B3 3HQ

Birmingham: Plans nineteenth–twentieth cents. cheques c.1782–1854. [Ref: MS 891, 459235 (IIR 24)]

Records 3: States of Guernsey Island Archives Service, 29 Victoria Road, St Peter Port, Guernsey, Channel Islands

Papers and accounts re Lloyds Bank during German Occupation 1940–45; references to banking during Occupation in files and minute books of States' Controlling Committee 1940–45.

LOCKE, TUGWELL & MEEK
Devizes, Wiltshire

History: This private bank was formed in 1775 as Sutton, Leech, Bevan & Read. The original partners were James Sutton, John Bevan and Richard Read. The business was later known as Hughes, Locke, Oliver & Co and from 1803 as Locke, Tugwell & Meek; it was also styled the Devizes & Wiltshire Bank. The bank was acquired by the Capital & Counties Bank Ltd (est. 1877) in 1883.

342   *British banking – a guide to historical records*

Records: Lloyds TSB Group plc, Archives, Head Office, 71 Lombard Street, London EC3P 3BS

Amalgamation papers 1883.

LOCKHARTS, MAXTONE, WALLIS & PATERSON
London

History: This private bank was formed in 1787 as Lockhart, James & James and had premises in Pall Mall in London's West End. It was known as Lockharts & Maxtone in 1793 and as Lockharts, Maxtone, Wallis & Paterson in 1797, the year that it closed.

F G Hilton Price, *A Handbook of London Bankers* (London, 1876)

Records: Barclays Bank plc, Group Archives, Dallimore Road, Wythenshawe, Manchester M23 9JA

Cheques and deposit receipt 1793.

LONDON & BRAZILIAN BANK LTD
London and Latin America

History: This British overseas bank was established in the City of London in 1862 as the London & Brazilian Bank Ltd with a paid-up capital of £250,000. It was the first foreign bank to establish a presence in Brazil and its promoters included J W Carter of Robert Benson & Co and members of the Glyn family who were partners in Glyn Mills & Co (est. 1753). To strengthen its position in finance of Brazilian-Portuguese trade, the Anglo-Portuguese Bank (est. 1862) was acquired in 1863. Business commenced in Brazil in 1863 with the opening of the Rio branch, followed shortly afterwards by branches at Recife do Pernambuco (1863), Rio Grande do Sul (1863) and Bahia (1864) to finance sugar, hide and cereal exports. Following a financial crisis in London and political difficulties in Brazil, the bank made slow progress and was reconstructed in 1872 as the New London & Brazilian Bank Ltd. In 1878 it expanded outside Brazil by opening a branch at Montevideo. In the ensuing years it became the largest, most conservative and most highly regarded bank in Brazil. By 1880 it had eight branches, including two in Portugal. Further branches were opened including ones in Argentina at Buenos Aires (1890) and Rosario (1897). The bank reverted to its original title in 1886. Total assets stood at £12 million in 1890 and increased to £22.3 million in 1913; in the same period branch numbers grew from fourteen to sixteen. In 1918 the bank joined the British Trade Corporation to form the Anglo-Brazilian Commercial & Agency Co Ltd. As a result of increased competition and damage inflicted by depreciation of Latin American currencies, in 1923

Records of banks 343

the bank merged with the largest British bank in South America, The London & River Plate Bank Ltd (est. 1862), then in the ownership of Lloyds Bank Ltd, to form the Bank of London & South America Ltd.

David Joslin, *A Century of Banking in Latin America. The Bank of London & South America Ltd 1862–1962* (Oxford, 1963)

Records 1: Bloomsbury Science Library, University College London, Gower Street, London WC1E 6BT

Secretary's reports 1866–1920; letterbooks, Rio de Janiero to London and elsewhere (39) 1868–1924; letters, London to Rio (13) 1873–79, 1892–1912, 1917–18, 1920–24; letterbooks, Pernambuco to London and elsewhere (11) 1876–80, 1897–1924; letterbooks, various (3) 1878–80, 1920–24; cable books, Rio (5) 1879–1924; letterbooks, Sao Paulo to various (24) 1887–1927; letterbooks, Buenos Aires to London and elsewhere (16) 1890–1925; letterbooks, Rosario to London and elsewhere (10) 1897–1927; letters, London to Para and elsewhere 1902–24; letters, London to Buenos Aires and elsewhere (5) 1906–28. [Ref: BOLSA]

Records 2: Lloyds TSB Bank plc, Archives, 71 Lombard Street, London EC3P 3BS

Staff registers (9) 1862–1923; general ledger 1863–66; annual reports 1872–1923; amalgamation agreement 1923.

Filial Porto Allegre, Brazil: journals (3) 1872–89 [w]; **Pelotas, Brazil:** journal 1869–72; **Rio Grande, Brazil:** journals (3) 1867–81 [w].

LONDON & COUNTY BANKING CO LTD
London

History: This joint stock bank was established in Southwark in 1836 as the Surrey, Kent & Sussex Banking Co. Branches were almost immediately opened at Brighton, Canterbury, Croydon, Lewes, Maidstone, Sevenoaks, Tonbridge, Tunbridge Wells and Woolwich. The head office was moved to Lombard Street, City of London, in 1837 and in 1838 the bank was renamed the London & County Banking Co. In 1839 Jeffreys & Hill (est. 1811) of Chatham was acquired followed by Hopkins, Drewett & Co (est. 1827) of Arundel in 1841; Hector, Lacy & Co (est. 1808) of Petersfield in 1841; Ridge & Co (est. c.1783) of Chichester in 1841; Halford, Baldock & Co (est. c.1790) of Canterbury in 1841; Emmerson, Hodgson & Emmerson (est. c.1800) of Sandwich in 1841; Davenport, Walker & Co (est. 1838) of Oxford in 1842; Wilmshurst & Co (est. 1822) of Cranbrook in 1843; T & T S Chapman (est. 1837) of Aylesbury in 1844; and J Stoveld & Co (est. 1806) of Petworth in 1845. By 1845 the bank had

344 *British banking – a guide to historical records*

over forty branches. Other acquisitions quickly followed, viz.: Trapp, Halfhead & Co (est. 1829) of Bedford in 1849; the Berkshire Union Banking Co (est. 1841) in 1851; the business of the Western Bank of London (est. 1856) in 1859; the business of Robert Davies & Co (est. 1841) of Shoreditch, London, which failed in 1860; Nunn & Co (est. 1810) of Manningtree in 1870; Vallance & Payne (est. 1800) of Sittingbourne in 1888; and Hove Banking Co Ltd (est. 1876) in 1891. By 1875 the bank had 150 branches, more than any other British bank. Deposits grew from £84,700 in 1837 to £21.25 million in 1872 to £46.16 million in 1904, while paid-up capital expanded from £23,700 in 1837 to £500,000 in 1857 to £2 million in 1883. Limited liability was acquired in 1866 and by 1904 there were 200 branches. Frederick Burt & Co (est. 1872) of Cornhill, foreign bankers, was acquired in 1907. In 1909 the bank merged with the London & Westminster Bank (est. 1834) to form London, County & Westminster Bank Ltd.

T E Gregory, *The Westminster Bank Through a Century* (London, 1936); William Howarth, *The Banks in the Clearing House* (London, 1905)

Records 1: The Royal Bank of Scotland plc, Archive Section, Regent's House, 42 Islington High Street, London N1 8XL

General ledgers 1836–38; rough directors' meeting minutes 1836–39; press cuttings 1836–39; deed of settlement 1836–83; rent ledgers 1836–1904; list of directors 1836–1905; directors' meeting minute books (23) 1836–1909; salary registers 1836–1915; annual reports 1836–1932; deposit receipt book 1837; committee minutes 1838–39; share register 1838–39; book of business for referral to audit, discount etc committees 1838–39; letters from general manager 1838–40; dividend warrants 1838–58; annual general meeting minute books (3) 1838–1905; bad debts register 1838–1931; share transfer deeds 1839; notice of change of name 1839; general purpose committee minutes 1839–41; board agenda books 1839–43; branch committee minute books (7) 1839–48; instructions to managers 1839–1911; address to shareholders, Thomas Joplin 1840; notes on half-yearly meetings (2) 1840–59; general meeting report books (9) 1840–1908; branch inspector's letterbook 1841–44; register of board instructions to general manager 1841–62; miscellaneous staff papers 1841, 1864–84; board standing order books (2) 1841–93; special committee minutes 1842–49; chairman's personal papers 1842–62; passbook 1843–48; daily committee minute books (60) 1848–1909; securities for advances 1850–91; declarations of secrecy 1853; rules for staff 1853–1908; general memorandum book 1856–62; interest rate instruction 1859; papers re bank treasurerships 1859–62, 1874; register of mortgaged property 1850s; library minutes 1862–66; branch property expenditure books (2) 1862–1905; circulars

Records of banks 345

1862–1920; special committee rough minutes 1863; directors' attendance and fee register 1863–75; manager guarantee policies 1863–76; Lombard Street committee minutes 1864–69, 1907–10; branch statistics 1864–1923; memorandum book 1865; general managers' information books (3) 1865–85; general statistics books 1865–1911; authorised signatories book 1867–80; signature books 1867–1880s; general meeting agenda book 1867–1954; staff registers 1868–97; property conveyances, bank trustees 1872; share certificate 1872; abstract of deeds re security transfers 1872–74; staff records 1873–1942; building committee minute books 1874–1905; unclaimed dividends register 1874–1912; staff letterbook 1877–1919; papers re conversion to limited company 1879–80; credit slips 1870s–1890s; customer security forms 1880; specimen deeds of charge 1880–1900; premises register n.d.; bank officer authorities 1880–1939; pension appeal papers 1885; clerk appointment leaflet 1886; list of shareholders 1887; shareholder list 1887; branch architectural drawings 1887–1908; sterling drafts 1888; premises fixture book c.1890; forms 1895–1908; bank solicitor's correspondence 1896–97; head office committee rough minutes 1896–1904; head office committee minute book 1896–1914; pay award papers, A P G Archer 1897–1925; charitable donation records cards 1897–1932; deeds of appointment power of attorney 1897–1969; memorandum and articles of association 1898–1923; premises ledger n.d.; guide to adjustment of daily balance 1900; premises photographs c.1900–09; inspector of branches guardbook of branch postcards 1900–25; premises subcommittee re Lombard Street papers 1901–03; register of directors 1902–09; daily committee agenda book 1904–05; provident fund subcommittee minutes 1905; sports club reports 1905–10; board reports re advances 1906–09; London branch opening report 1906; daily head office returns 1908–09; amalgamation papers 1909.

Abingdon: insolvent customer papers 1858–75; **Aldershot:** customer general balance guarantee 1895; **Arundel:** passbook 1879–1905; manager's notebook c.1900–05; **Ashford:** branch minute books (2) 1847–58; **Aylesbury:** information book 1878–1932; minute books (3) 1881–91, 1900–13; **Birmingham:** profit and loss statement 1913–37; **Brentford:** information books (2) 1885–1936; **Brentwood:** letterbook 1902; **Brighton:** correspondence book 1847–52; minute books (18) 1852–1926; security for advance 1857; interest warrant 1881; customer information books 1886–1932; **Cambridge:** minute books (5) 1845–90; **Canterbury:** passbooks 1906; **Chatham:** artist's impression of new branch c.1902; **Chelmsford:** quarterly return 1843; **Chichester:** architectural drawing photographs c.1899; notice of branch removal 1900; **Croydon:** minute book 1878–n.d.; **Dartford:** architectural drawings 1888; **Deptford:** deposit receipt 1903; **Dorking:** property sale notice 1847; lost cheque indemnity 1850;

346   *British banking – a guide to historical records*

Farnham: dishonoured drafts book 1880; **Gillingham:** quarterly returns 1899–1916; letterbook 1903–29; **Godalming:** customer papers 1846–54; quarterly returns 1877; notice from manager 1908; **Guildford:** advances guarantees 1877–84; **Halstead:** report on overdrafts 1872; quarterly returns 1874, 1907; **Harrow:** manager's letterbook 1899–1925; **Hastings:** quarterly returns 1848; securities for advances 1856; **Herne Bay:** building construction contract and specifications 1903–04; **Hertford:** safe custody register 1859–76; managers' letterbook 1879–1930; **Hitchin:** status reports 1883–98; **Hythe:** manager's letterbooks 1901–33; **Ilford:** quarterly and half-yearly returns 1905–54; **Leighton Buzzard:** quarterly returns 1856–1909; **London, Aldersgate:** staff duty and salary information 1873–1942; staff letterbooks 1877–1919; **London, Barnet:** premises photograph 1892; **London, Borough:** signature book 1892–1900; **London, Elephant and Castle:** security register 1870; **London, Greenwich:** deposit account ledger 1838–52; quarterly returns from 1842–n.d.; minute books 1845–75; security registers 1859–69; safe custody book 1860–75; passbooks 1867–77; **London, Hackney:** salary claim forms 1878–1903; **London, Hammersmith:** passbook 1884–89; minute book 1901–08; **London, Hanover Square:** correspondence with head office 1868–72; **London, Holborn:** register of correspondence re advances 1876–1914; **London, Kensington:** quarterly returns 1861–1918; **London, Limehouse:** profit and loss statements 1910–30; **London, Lombard Street:** architectural drawings 1883–1960s; **London, New Oxford Street:** manager's letterbook 1877–1909; branch information book 1878–1926; **London, South Kensington:** information book (2) 1876–88; **London, Marylebone:** minute book 1904–14; **London, Minories:** quarterly and half-yearly returns 1900–11; **London, St Mary Axe:** quarterly and half-yearly returns 1900–11; minute book 1906–16; account/loan/staff statistics 1908–56; **London, Shoreditch:** quarterly returns 1862–63; circular re run on branch 1863; **Maidstone:** architectural drawings 1863–93; **Maldon:** papers re bad debts and advances 1866–72; **Manningtree:** property purchase correspondence 1889; **Newbury:** quarterly returns 1852–1909; **Oxford:** correspondence 1848, 1858, 1883; **Petworth:** copy title deeds 1900; **Richmond:** title deeds 1875–1909; **St Albans:** letterbooks 1848–56; security register 1848–60; **St Leonards:** passbook 1905–08; **Sandwich:** letterbook 1853–69; **Teddington:** minute book 1905–30; impersonal ledger 1905–15; **Tunbridge Wells:** quarterly returns 1871–1910; **Uxbridge:** title deeds 1839–1903; securities for advances register 1870–98; safe custody papers 1875–91; **Wallingford:** quarterly returns 1897–1909; **Watford:** gun licence for clerk attending sub-branches 1870; **Weybridge:** title deeds and correspondence re Oaklands Park 1905–20; **Windsor:** head office correspondence 1852–80; premises correspondence 1853–89; branch alteration specifications 1853–58; staff correspondence 1858–1900; stationery and forms samples

Records of banks **347**

c.1860–80; mandates book c.1860s; opinion letters 1867–75; memorandum book 1889–1908; **Wrotham:** debit slip 1849.

Records 2: Bedfordshire and Luton Archives and Record Service, The Records Office, Cauldwell Street, Bedford MK42 9AP

Dunstable: architectural plans 1886; **Luton:** architectural plans 1898 [Ref: BOR DP71; X843/1/30a]

Records 3: London Metropolitan Archive, 40 Northampton Road, London EC1R 0HB

Extracts from deed of settlement c.1852. [Ref: E/SL/170]

LONDON & DUBLIN BANK
London and Europe

History: This joint stock bank was formed in 1843 as a non-note issuing institution. Its aim was to compete with the Bank of Ireland in the Dublin area, where that bank held a note issuing monopoly. The monopoly was lifted however, with the passing of the Bankers (Ireland) Act 1845, and shortly afterwards, in 1848, the London & Dublin Bank was absorbed by The National Bank (est. 1835). The bank had branches at Carrick-on-Shannon, Dublin, Dundalk, Kells, Mullingar, Parsontown and Wicklow. Three of its directors joined the board of The National Bank.

Records: The Royal Bank of Scotland plc, Archive Section, Regent's House, 42 Islington High Street, London N1 8XL

Directors' meeting minute books 1841–51; attendance book 1841–44; agenda book 1845–55.

LONDON & NORTHERN BANK LTD
London

History: This joint stock bank was established in 1898 out of the business of the Leeds Joint Stock Bank Ltd (est. 1891). It ceased business in 1899 when its Leeds office was purchased by Bradford District Bank Ltd (est. 1862).

Records: The Royal Bank of Scotland plc, Archive Section, Regent's House, 42 Islington High Street, London N1 8XL

Prospectus 1898.

LONDON & PROVINCIAL BANK LTD
London

348   *British banking – a guide to historical records*

History: This joint stock bank was formed in 1864 with a head office in Poultry, City of London, as the Provincial Banking Corporation Ltd. Its paid-up capital was £150,000. It was formed to acquire the private bank of Day, Nicholson & Stone (est. 1782) of Rochester and Chatham and the East of England Bank (est. 1836), a joint stock bank based at Norwich. The South Hants Joint Stock Bank appears to have been acquired in 1864. The bank expanded into Wales through acquisition of the Bank of Wales Ltd (est. 1863) in 1865. As a result of losses incurred in Wales, the bank was reconstructed in 1870 when paid-up capital was increased to £157,500; it was retitled London & Provincial Bank Ltd. Deposits then totalled £482,500 and there were two London branches, in Edgware Road and Kingsland Road. The head office was moved to Lothbury at this time. In 1871 branches were opened in Lewisham and Sutton and Fincham & Simpson (est. 1802) of Diss and Eye was acquired. In 1872 a branch was opened at Twickenham and J & W Walters (est. 1827) of Haverfordwest was purchased. In 1873 branches opened in Woolwich, Eastbourne, Carmarthen, Richmond and Stoke Newington. In 1878 paid-up capital stood at £200,000 when deposits were £1.85 million and branches numbered fifty-eight. The North Kent Bank Ltd (est. 1864) was acquired in 1878 and during the late 1870s and 1880s branches continued to be opened in London suburbs, South Wales, East Anglia and the South East. The first branches to be opened in major commercial centres were those in Bristol (1891), Liverpool (1909) and Birmingham (1913). In 1914 Lothbury, which had previously been only an administrative office, became a branch and the bank was admitted to the London Clearing House. Paid-up capital reached £1 million in 1913 when deposits totalled £20.24 million and there were 225 branches. In 1917 the bank amalgamated with the London & South Western Bank Ltd (est. 1862) to form the London, Provincial & South Western Bank Ltd.

William Howarth, *The Banks in the Clearing House* (London, 1905); William Howarth, *Our Leading Banks* (London, 1894); P W Matthews & Anthony W Tuke, *History of Barclays Bank Ltd* (London, 1926)

Records: Barclays Bank plc, Group Archives, Dallimore Road, Wythenshawe, Manchester M23 9JA

Premises register 1857–87; property title deeds and other papers 1860–1917, 1940s–1983; registers of shareholders (76) 1863–1918; half-yearly accounts 1864–1917; memorandum and articles of association 1864–1918; directors' meeting minute books (26) 1864–1918; rota committee minute books (8) 1868–82; cheques, cheque forms and cheque books 1869–1919; agenda books (5) 1871–73, 1901, 1916–17; general meeting minute books 1871–1914; correspondence re premises 1875–99; circulars 1876–1918;

Records of banks **349**

auditor's papers 1879–99; staff reports 1879–1917; staff registers (4) 1884–1919; applications for employment 1897–1906; report re banquet 1900; papers re mergers 1904–18; staff appointment letters 1905–06; share certificate 1906; impersonal ledgers (3) 1910–19; rule books 1914–15; branch profit and loss accounts 1914–17; premises in-letters 1918; specimen agreement re staff guarantee 1918.

LONDON & SOUTH AFRICAN BANK
London and Africa

History: This overseas bank was established by Royal charter in 1860 when its balance sheet totalled £200,000. It operated in the Cape of Good Hope and Natal until 1864 when it received an amended charter which permitted it to operate in all British colonies south of the 22° of latitude. In the late 1860s branches existed at Cape Town, Port Elizabeth, Grahamstown and Durban. In 1877 it was acquired for £320,000 by the Standard Bank of British South Africa Ltd (est. 1862).

George T Amphlett, *History of the Standard Bank of South Africa Ltd 1862–1913* (Glasgow, 1914)

Records: Guildhall Library, Aldermanbury, London EC2 2EJ

Charters (3) 1860–64; general ledgers (2) 1869–77. [Ref: MS24525–8]

LONDON & SOUTH WESTERN BANK LTD
London

History: This joint stock bank was established as the London & South Western Bank Ltd in 1862 to provide banking facilities for small traders in the principal towns in south west England. It commenced business at 27 Regent Street in London's West End in 1863 with a paid-up capital of £58,125. Soon it opened a branch at Camden Town, London, followed by twelve provincial branches at Bristol, Honiton, Ottery St Mary, Sidmouth, Bath, Chard, Crewkerne, Helston, Penzance, Plymouth, Redruth and Southampton. The bank made little progress in the first ten years reducing its capital and closing eight of its provincial branches. The head office moved to Lombard Street, City of London, in 1865 and to Fenchurch Street in 1871. By 1877 paid-up capital stood at £200,000 when deposits totalled over £1 million; by 1904 these figures were £975,000 and £14 million respectively. In 1887 the London Commercial Bank (est. 1866) was acquired but otherwise, as an exception to the rule, the bank did not expand by acquisition of other banks. The bank was a pioneer of suburban banking; in 1903 it had 119 branches in London and the suburbs and twenty-five branches in the provinces. The bank also established a substantial foreign

350   *British banking – a guide to historical records*

connection. In 1917 it merged with the London & Provincial Bank Ltd (est. 1864) to form the London, Provincial & South Western Bank Ltd.

William Howarth, *The Banks in the Clearing House* (London, 1905); William Howarth, *A Short History of the London & South Western Bank Ltd 1862–1912* (London, 1913); P W Matthews & Anthony W Tuke, *History of Barclays Bank Ltd* (London, 1926)

Records 1: Barclays Bank plc, Group Archives, Dallimore Road, Wythenshawe, Manchester M23 9JA

Formation notice 1862; minute book summaries: board 1862–64, house committee 1862–64, general meetings 1866–72; house committee minute books (5) 1862–1905; historical scrapbook 1862–1915; memorandum and articles of association 1862, 1906–18; directors' meeting minute books (10) 1862–1918; general meeting minute book 1862–1918; shareholder registers (16) 1862–1918; general manager's committee minute books (4) 1863–1922; seal books (6) 1863–1903, 1920–75; dividend book 1864; directors' reports 1864–1918; private ledgers (8) 1864–1918; loans ledger 1867–78; letterbook 1868–80; paying-in forms 1860s–1910s; cheques and cheque forms 1860s–1910; staff registers 1872–99; notices to shareholders and resolutions 1874–1917; trustee loans ledger 1877–1900; letters of credit registers 1879–92; in-letters re premises 1879–97; bank note register 1879–98; draft registers 1879–1910; inspection report and general manager's minute book 1881–1913; papers re staff funds 1881–1918; share certificates 1883; share ledgers (2) 1883–1911; premises ledgers (3) 1884–1919; photographs, premises and staff 1888–1890s; head office circulars 1890–1919; shareholder registers (4) 1894–1909; land certificate abstracts 1900–19; property agreements 1903, 1910; balance sheet 1907; bills issued registers 1907–15; instruction book 1909; foreign branch advances 1909–15; foreign bank account ledgers (5) 1909–26; circular letter of credit 1900s; general meeting reports 1910–18; branch profit and loss summaries 1911–17; impersonal ledgers (13) 1911–18; jubilee dinner invitation 1912; loans ledger 1912; Foreign Department warrants registers 1913–15; list of branches and offices 1914; general meeting proceedings 1914–17; passbooks 1914–22; papers re merger with London & Provincial Bank Ltd 1917–18; assignments of property to Barclays Bank Ltd 1920–21.

Records 2: Bristol Record Office, 'B' Bond Warehouse, Smeaton Road, Bristol BS1 6XN

Correspondence of Sir George White re the bank 1906–07. [Ref: 35810/GW/9]

Records of banks 351

LONDON & WESTMINSTER BANK LTD
London

History: This joint stock bank, the first in London, was promoted in 1833 as the Royal Bank of London & Westminster but opened in 1834 under the title of the London & Westminster Bank. Its head office was initially at Throgmorton Street, City of London, but was moved to Lothbury in 1838. The bank's first branch opened in 1834 in Pall Mall in London's West End; it moved to St James's Square in 1844. In 1836 further branches were opened in Holborn, Whitechapel, Southwark and Marylebone. No more branches were established until 1855, when one was opened at Temple Bar. In 1861 the Commercial Bank of London (est. 1840) was acquired, followed by the London & Middlesex Bank (est. 1862) of Lambeth in 1863 and by the important private bankers, Jones, Loyd & Co (est. 1771) of Lothbury in 1864. In the 1880s and 1890s branches were opened at Brompton Square (1881), Westminster (1884), Westbourne Grove (1886), Islington (1886), Holborn Circus (1887), Tottenham Court Road (1887), Hampstead (1890), Oxford Street (1890) and High Street, Kensington (1891). By 1905 there were thirty-five branches, mostly in Central London but some were in the suburbs. Paid-up capital grew from £597,000 in 1836 to £800,000 in 1842, to £1 million in 1849, to £2 million in 1869 and to £2.8 million in 1881. The balance sheet totalled £366,000 in 1834 and £32 million in 1904. Limited liability was acquired in 1880. In 1909 the bank amalgamated with the London & County Banking Co Ltd (est. 1836) to form the London, County & Westminster Bank Ltd. It then had thirty-seven branches and its balance sheet totalled over £33.5 million.

T E Gregory, *The Westminster Bank Through a Century* (London, 1936); William Howarth, *The Banks in the Clearing House* (London, 1905); R H Mottram, *The Westminster Bank 1836–1936* (London, 1936); Manfred Pohl & Sabine Freitag, *Handbook on the History of European Banks* (Aldershot, 1994); Richard Reed, *National Westminster Bank. A Short History* (London, 1989)

Records: The Royal Bank of Scotland plc, Archive Section, Regent's House, 42 Islington High Street, London N1 8XL

Prospectus 1833; account with Coutts & Co 1833–34; correspondence of provisional committee with prospective general manager 1833; letterbook 1833–36; directors' meeting minute books 1833–1909; deed of settlement 1834; sundry board letters 1834–39; head office circulars 1834–60; balance sheets 1834–82; staff record books (2) 1834–1920 including staff appointments book 1834–55; correspondence re proposed association with Agricultural & Commercial Bank of Ireland 1835–36; agreements with country banks 1835–39; officers appointment registers (2) 1835–81; gen-

352 British banking – a guide to historical records

eral meeting minute book 1835–1909; annual reports 1835–1909; staff list 1836; undertakings books 1836–37; papers re increase in capital 1836–80; private minutes 1836–90; circulars to branches 1836–1909; register of officers 1836–1909; list of past due bills 1837; book of weekly statements 1837–40; list of properties 1838; signature book 1841–61; statements of net profits 1840–48; statements of bills discounted and number of accounts as per branch 1845–48; stock book 1845–48; declarations of secrecy 1846–85; daily committee minute books (7) 1846–1907; register of country securities 1859; State of Victoria loan letterbooks (2) 1859–79; register of country and overseas accounts 1860; solicitors' report books (6) 1860–86; secretary's memorandum book 1861–1911; statistics re current accounts 1871–1909; establishment committee minute books (20) 1875–1909; memorandum and articles of association 1897; salary comparison 1909.

London, Bloomsbury: officers' register 1836–1909; **London, Lothbury:** customer ledger 1834; loan ledger 1834–57; general ledgers 1834–1909; deposit ledger 1842–46; **London, Marylebone:** letters to customers 1836–59; **London, Southwark:** customer ledger 1836; general ledger 1836–42; branch diary 1839; general balance book 1844–48; **London, Temple Bar:** customers' order book 1855–73; cashier's order book 1862–75; security register 1875–1909; **London, Westminster:** day book 1834; customer ledger (2) 1834–35; minute book 1834–45; general order book 1871–75.

LONDON & YORKSHIRE BANK LTD
London

History: This joint stock bank was established in 1872. In 1903, when its paid-up capital was £325,000, it was acquired by Union of London & Smiths Bank Ltd (est. 1839).

Records: The Royal Bank of Scotland plc, Archive Section, Regent's House, 42 Islington High Street, London N1 8XL

Staff register 1872–1947; list of shareholders 1897; amalgamation papers 1903.

LONDON, COMMERCIAL & CRIPPLEGATE BANK LTD
London

History: This joint stock bank traced its origins to the Cripplegate Savings Bank which was formed in 1819. It registered as a joint stock bank in 1879 when known as Cripplegate Bank Ltd. It was renamed London, Commercial & Cripplegate Bank Ltd in 1900 and later that year was acquired by Union Bank of London Ltd (est. 1839).

Records of banks

Records: The Royal Bank of Scotland plc, Archive Section, Regent's House, 42 Islington High Street, London N1 8XL

Articles of association 1879; minute books (2) 1896–1906.

LONDON JOINT STOCK BANK LTD
London

History: This bank was formed in 1836, one of the first joint stock banks to be established in the capital; its intention was to provide banking services both in London and the 'metropolitan districts'. Paid-up capital was £217,000. The first premises were in Coleman Street, City of London, but in 1837 the bank moved to nearby Princes' Street. Buttressed by the high standing of its City promoters, who included Joshua Scholefield and the distiller Sir Felix Booth, its deposit base expanded rapidly from £600,000 in 1837 to £2.25 million by 1845. In 1840, a 'Western Branch' was formed through the acquisition of the private bank of Wright & Co (est. 1699) of Covent Garden, London, the business of which soon moved to premises in Pall Mall. No further branches were opened until 1866, when one was established in Chancery Lane. In 1870 a Southwark branch was formed through the purchase of a branch of Alliance Bank Ltd (est. 1862) and in 1872 another branch, at Paddington, was opened. A year before, branches at Smithfield and Islington Cattle Market were acquired via the acquisition of the Albion Bank Ltd (est. 1864). By 1893, eleven London branches existed. A distinctive feature of the bank was its emphasis on international business. Soon after formation, it acted as London correspondent for overseas banks, especially those in the United States, Canada, Australia and India, and supervised this business via a 'foreign committee' established in 1837. By 1870 a strong connection existed with Germany and in 1870–71 the bank made bond issues for Bismarck's North German Confederation. In 1893 the bank merged with The Imperial Bank Ltd (est. 1862) and in 1900 had paid-up capital of £1.8 million, deposits of £17.165 million and thirty-five branches. In 1909 the bank acquired York City & County Bank Ltd (est. 1830) and in 1914 acquired the Portsmouth branch of the Bank of England. By December 1917 it had emerged as Britain's ninth largest bank with 310 branches, deposits of £58.5 million and a paid-up capital of almost £3 million. In 1918, when valued at £6.334 million, it was acquired by London, City & Midland Bank Ltd (est. 1836), the enlarged business being called the London Joint, City & Midland Bank Ltd. The amalgamation created Britain's largest bank, prompting a government review into the efficacy of further concentration in the banking industry.

W F Crick & J E Wadsworth, *A Hundred Years of Joint Stock Banking* (London, 1936); A R Holmes & Edwin Green, *Midland. 150 Years of*

354   *British banking – a guide to historical records*

Banking Business (London, 1986); William Howarth, *Our Leading Banks* (London, 1894)

Records 1: HSBC Holdings plc, Group Archives, 10 Lower Thames Street, London EC3R 6AE

Directors' meeting minute books (10) 1835–1917; profit and loss account ledger 1836–41; daily balances (8) 1836–55; deeds of settlement 1836–68; signature books (10) 1836–71; staff registers 1836–1918; general minute books (4) 1837–1918; annual reports 1837–1918; country office standing orders (14) 1840–98; counter order books (22) 1842–73; private ledgers (45) 1842–1924; monthly balances (2) 1848–65; weekly balance book 1855–79; deposit account signature index books (5) 1859–81; house committee minutes indexes (3) 1871–1918; departments' committee minutes indexes (3) 1871–1918; register of leases and agreements re premises 1872–97; cricket club minute book 1872–1900; staff regulations 1890–1918; half-yearly balance sheets 1897–1918; department committee minute books (2) 1899–1905; general ledgers (2) 1908–16; house committee minute books (2) 1909–18; analysis of accounts 1909–19; weekly balance books (3) 1913–18; amalgamation and liquidation papers 1918–66.

Hull: security and signature books 1909–14; **Knaresborough:** manager's reports 1910–20; **London, Chancery Lane:** signature books 1866–1918; **London, Kingsway:** manager's letterbook and weekly report figures 1908–18; **London, Lambeth:** directors' attendance book 1911–19; **London, Leadenhall Street:** salaries register 1889–1920; **London, Limehouse:** counter order book 1898–1912; signature books 1898–1918; security register 1909–18; **London, Lothbury:** counter orders (51) 1893–1918; **London, Lower Edmonton:** inspectors' attendance book 1901–18; **London, Old Kent Road:** inspectors' attendance book 1909–18; **London, Pall Mall:** general ledger 1840–50; mandate book 1841–48; letterbooks (8) 1859–1918; abstract of branch balance sheets 1864–1918; manager's list of accounts 1875–97; salary book 1903–20; **London, Princes Street:** counter orders (50) 1878–1918; **London, St Mary Axe:** letterbook 1901–12; **Sheffield, Market Place:** staff register and salary book 1909–18; **Workington:** manager's memorandum book 1909–18.

Records 2: Durham County Record Office, County Hall, Durham DH1 5UL

Circular disclaiming connection with a second bank 1841. [Ref: D/Sa/E 997]

LONDON MERCHANT BANK LTD
London and Europe

Records of banks **355**

History: This overseas bank was established in 1873 as the London & Hanseatic Bank Ltd. It was severely damaged at the beginning of the First World War through exposure to clients in Germany, Poland, Latvia, Austria and Russia. It was reorganised in 1916 as London Merchant Bank Ltd and on the outbreak of the Second World War its banking business was transferred to the merchant bankers, Guinness, Mahon & Co. It was then renamed London Merchant Securities Ltd and developed the characteristics of an investment trust. It was subsequently acquired by the property financier, Lord Rayne, and developed a wide range of property and industrial interests.

Records: London Merchant Securities plc, 33 Robert Adam Street, London W1M 5AH

Directors' and general meeting minutes 1873 on; nominal and cash ledgers 1873 on; annual reports 1948 on.

LONDON, PROVINCIAL & SOUTH WESTERN BANK LTD
London

History: This joint stock bank was formed in 1917 by amalgamation of the London & Provincial Bank Ltd (est. 1864) and London & South Western Bank Ltd (est. 1862). It amalgamated with Barclays Bank Ltd (est. 1896) in 1918. It was Barclays' most significant expansion since its formation in 1896, providing a large London presence and a footing in Wales.

Records: Barclays Bank plc, Group Archives, Dallimore Road, Wythenshawe, Manchester M23 9JA

Papers re formation of London, Provincial & South Western Bank and merger with Barclay & Co Ltd 1917–18; directors' meeting minute book 1918; share certificate receipt books (2) 1918; nominee share issue register 1918; list of branches and officers 1918; cheque 1918; agreement re general manager's appointment 1918; shareholder registers (12) 1918.

SIR CHARLES LORAINE BT., BAKER, PEARSON, MAUDE, LORAINE & CO
Newcastle upon Tyne, Tyne & Wear

History: This private bank was formed in 1777 as Baker, Shafto, Ormston, Cuthbert & Lamb and traded as The Tyne Bank. John Baker, coal fitter and senior partner, died in 1784 and by 1788 the business was known as Baker, Hedley & Co. By the mid 1790s the Loraine family, which had long-established links with the Newcastle area, had acquired an interest. Thereafter the bank became known as Sir Wm. Loraine Bt., Baker, Pearson,

356 *British banking – a guide to historical records*

Maude & Co. By 1811 its title was Sir C Loraine, Baker, Pearson, Maude, Loraine & Co and from 1814 Sir Charles Loraine Bt., Baker, Pearson, Maude, Loraine & Co. In 1816 it ceased business but met all its liabilities.

Maberly Phillips, *A History of Banks, Bankers and Banking in Northumberland, Durham and North Yorkshire* (London, 1894)

Records 1: Durham University Library, Archives and Special Collections, 5 The College, Durham DH1 3EQ

Partner's notebook 1783–94; papers re closure 1816–33. [Ref: Baker Baker Papers]

Records 2: Northumberland Record Office, Melton Park, North Gosforth, Newcastle upon Tyne NE3 5QX

Cash book 1777–90; letters re closure 1816. [Ref: NRO 2659/51; ZALC9]

LOVEBAND & CO
Torrington, Devon

History: This private bank was established in 1808 as Cooke & Co; it was otherwise known as the Torrington Bank. It was styled Loveband & Co from 1821 and in 1843 amalgamated with National Provincial Bank of England (est. 1833).

Records: The Royal Bank of Scotland plc, Archive Section, Regent's House, 42 Islington High Street, London N1 8XL

Letter re amalgamation 1893.

LOYD, ENTWISLE & CO
Manchester, Greater Manchester

History: This private bank was established by 1771 in Manchester by John Jones, tea merchant. By 1772 the firm was described as John Jones & Co, 'tea dealers and bankers'. In around 1784 the bank's Manchester and London operations were split and the London bank of Joseph Jones & Co was formed by John Jones's son. The two houses remained closely linked until 1848. The firm was known as Jones, Barkers, Jones & Co from 1792, Jones, Fox & Co from 1797, Samuel and William Jones, Loyds & Co from 1816 and later as Jones, Loyd & Co. In 1848 the link with the London house, also Jones, Loyd & Co, was severed and a new partnership traded as Loyd, Entwisle & Co. The bank was acquired by the Manchester & Liverpool District Banking Co Ltd (est. 1829) in 1863.

Leo H Grindon, *Manchester Banks and Bankers* (Manchester, 1877); F G Hilton Price, *A Handbook of London Bankers* (London, 1876)

Records of banks 357

Records: The Royal Bank of Scotland plc, Archive Section, Regent's House, 42 Islington High Street, London N1 8XL

Draft 1792; notice on meeting re problems with London agent 1793; passbooks 1802–1860s; receipt 1808; government stock receipts issued to Edward Loyd 1824–30; letters from customers 1827–34; William Entwisle: business papers 1841, letters re raising of Company of Rifles, Rusholme, 1859–60; letter re bank note payment 1843; account ledger, trustees of Edward Hobson 1844–59; separation of London and Manchester houses: notice 1848–49, advices listing customer names and balances 1848–49; private ledger 1848–63; weekly balances books 1848–51; architectural drawings 1853; income tax assessments 1854–59; Henry Bury: passbook 1855, letter 1864; solicitor's account 1855–56; character book 1856–61; notice and press cutting re acquisition by Manchester & Liverpool District Banking Co 1863; letter from Manchester & Liverpool District Banking Co 1864.

SIR JOHN WILLIAM LUBBOCK, FORSTER & CO
London

History: This bank was established in the City of London in 1772 as Sir William Lemon, Buller, Furley, Lubbock & Co. The founders were already partners, along with James Willyams, in the Miners' Bank (est. 1759) at Truro, Cornwall. In 1776 John Buller retired when the bank's name changed to Sir William Lemon, Furley, Lubbock & Co. In 1781 J A Clarke joined as a partner and in 1785 Lemon retired, Samuel Bosanquet joined and Edward Forster came in as senior partner in succession to Furley. Thus in 1785 the business was known as Furley, Lubbock, Bosanquet & Co and later as Forster, Lubbock, Bosanquet & Co. In 1800 Bosanquet withdrew to establish the firm of Bosanquet, Beachcroft & Reeves while J W Lubbock and E Forster junior joined, the new firm being known as Forster, Lubbocks, Forster & Clarke. On the death of E Forster senior in 1812, the title changed to Sir John Lubbock, Lubbock, Forster & Clarke. In 1820 it was known as Sir John William Lubbock, Forster, Clarke & Co and in 1835 as Sir John William Lubbock, Forster & Co. The business merged with Robarts, Curtis & Co (est. 1791) of Lombard Street, London, in 1860 to form Robarts, Lubbock & Co.

F G Hilton Price, *A Handbook of London Bankers* (London, 1876)

Records 1: Coutts & Co, 440 Strand, London WC2R 0QS

Miscellaneous cheques and incidental papers eighteenth cent; signature books 1841–60.

Records 2: Centre for Kentish Studies, County Hall, Maidstone ME14 1XQ

358 *British banking – a guide to historical records*

Partnership agreements 1763–1841; Sir J Lubbock business account books 1765–1805; letterbook 1771–73; partnership papers 1772–1841; correspondence 1773–1802; miscellaneous papers including cheques, receipts etc 1777–1842. [Ref: U697 T37; U1979 B1–12]

LUDLOW & TENBURY BANKING CO
Ludlow, Shropshire

History: This joint stock bank was formed at Broad Street, Ludlow, in 1840 and amalgamated with the Worcester City & County Banking Co (est. 1840) in 1864.

Records: Lloyds TSB Group plc, Archives, Head Office, 71 Lombard Street, London EC3P 3BS

Annual reports 1840–59; half-yearly profit and loss sheets 1841–42.

MACHELL, PEASES & HOARE
Beverley, Humberside

History: This private bank was established in 1797 as Appleton, Machell & Co; it was otherwise known as the Beverley Bank. From about 1858 it was styled Machell, Peases & Hoare and was acquired by York Union Banking Co Ltd (est. 1833) in 1894. It was closely connected with Pease, Hoare & Pease (est. 1754) of Hull.

P W Matthews & Anthony W Tuke, *History of Barclays Bank Ltd* (London, 1926)

Records: Barclays Bank plc, Group Archives, Dallimore Road, Wythenshawe, Manchester M23 9JA

Receipts and indemnity 1798; bank notes 1850; cheque forms 1870s.

MADDISON, ATHERLEY & CO
Southampton, Hampshire

History: This private bank was formed in 1869 through the amalgamation of Atherley, Fall & Atherley (est. 1770) and Maddison & Pearce (est. 1785), both of Southampton. In 1888 the firm joined with Grant & Gillman (est. 1787) of Portsmouth to convert their businesses into a joint stock bank known as Grant & Maddison's Union Banking Co Ltd.

Records: Lloyds TSB Group plc, Archives, Head Office, 71 Lombard Street, London EC3P 3BS

Partnership agreement 1875; asset valuation book 1888.

Records of banks 359

MANCHESTER JOINT STOCK BANK LTD
Manchester, Greater Manchester

History: This joint stock bank was formed in 1873 out of the business of the private Manchester bank of Robertson, Fraser & Co (est. 1863). William Fraser, who was a partner in Robertsons and who had worked formerly for the National Bank of Scotland (est. 1825) and then for Sewell & Nephew (est. 1841), was the managing director. The initial paid-up capital was £50,000, rising to £102,000 within two years; deposits reached £100,000 after the first year. The bank enjoyed modest prosperity in the 1880s, although increased competition meant that it made slow progress by the 1890s. In 1892 the business was acquired by London & Midland Bank Ltd (est. 1836) for the equivalent of £229,000. It then had eleven branches, deposits of £520,000 and a paid-up capital of £103,000.

W F Crick & J E Wadsworth, *A Hundred Years of Joint Stock Banking* (London, 1936); Leo H Grindon, *Manchester Banks and Bankers* (Manchester, 1877)

Records: HSBC Holdings plc, Group Archives, 10 Lower Thames Street, London EC3R 6AE

Salaries ledger 1873–85; allotment of shares book 1873–91; directors' meeting minute books (7) 1873–92; general meeting minute book 1873–92; shareholders' register 1873–92; share transfer register 1873–92; share application ledgers (2) 1873–92; general ledger 1873–92; half-yearly balance sheets 1873–93; private letterbook 1873–94; correspondence with Robarts, Lubbock & Co 1878; committee minute book 1882–92; list of shareholders 1890–92; proxy register 1892; amalgamation papers 1892.

Manchester, Deansgate: security register 1885–92.

MANX BANK LTD
Douglas, Isle of Man

History: This joint stock bank was established in 1882 with a paid-up capital of £25,000. Branches were soon opened at Castletown, Peel, Port Erin and Ramsey. By 1900 deposits stood at £224,000. In that year the bank was damaged by a financial crisis which swept the Isle of Man and in a weakened condition it was acquired for £25,000 by the Mercantile Bank of Lancashire Ltd (est. 1890).

George Chandler, *Four Centuries of Banking* (London, 1964–68); Ernest Quarmby, *Bank Notes and Banking in the Isle of Man* (London, 1994)

Records: Barclays Bank plc, Group Archives, Dallimore Road, Wythenshawe, Manchester M23 9JA

360 *British banking – a guide to historical records*

Bank notes c. nineteenth cent-1957

MARSH, STRACEY, FAUNTLEROY & GRAHAM
London

History: This private bank was formed in about 1792 and was sometimes known as Marsh, Sibbald, Stracey & Fauntleroy and as De Vismes, Cuthbert, Marsh, Creed & Co. By 1824 it was known as Marsh, Stracey, Fauntleroy & Graham. When Henry Fauntleroy senior died in 1807, he was succeeded as partner by his son Henry who committed a major fraud on his own bank and on the Bank of England, apparently amounting to £360,000, which in 1824 resulted in the bank's failure and in Fauntleroy's subsequent execution.

F G Hilton Price, *A Handbook of London Bankers* (London, 1876)

Records: University of London Library, Senate House, Malet Street, London WC1E 7HU

Papers, some re a former partner and embezzler 1811–25. [Ref: ULL MS676]

MARTEN, PART & CO
St Albans, Hertfordshire

History: This private bank was established in 1858 as Call, Marten & Co which took over the St Albans business of the failed joint stock bank, Unity Joint Stock Bank. It was formed by partners of the London private bank of Call, Marten & Co (est. 1773) which merged with Herries, Farquhar & Co (est. c.1770) in 1865. It was known as E C Smith, Marten & Co from 1865 and as Marten, Part & Co from 1898. Sub-branches were opened at Harpenden (1887), Radlett (1898) and Elstree (1898). It was acquired by Barclay & Co Ltd (est. 1896) in 1902.

P W Matthews & Anthony W Tuke, *History of Barclays Bank Ltd* (London, 1926); Jack Parker, *Nothing for Nothing for Nobody* (Stevenage, 1986)

Records: Barclays Bank plc, Group Archives, Dallimore Road, Wythenshawe, Manchester M23 9JA

Premises agreement 1784; grant of annuity 1790; power of attorney 1799; private account ledgers (4) 1804–56, 1898–1901; partnership agreements 1805–10; cheques 1835–44; clerk guarantee 1849; signature book 1857–98; current account ledgers (3) 1857–65, 1901–02; general balance ledgers 1866–1901; cheque form 1870s; customer letters and mandates 1887–1904; merger papers Barclay & Co 1892–1904.

MARTINS BANK LTD
Liverpool, Merseyside, and London

History: This important joint stock bank was formed in 1831 as the Bank of Liverpool by leading Liverpool businessmen who included Tories and Reformers; their common interest was to establish a Liverpool-based bank to serve Liverpool. Its nominal capital was £2.5 million which was increased to £3 million in 1835. The eminent North Atlantic merchant, William Brown, was the first chairman underlining the bank's commitment to the finance of trade with North America. Its early customers included, for example, the Bank of Charleston, the Bank of Montreal and the Bank of the State of New York. Annual profits grew from £50,000 at the end of the 1830s to £66,000 in 1845 and to over £100,000 in 1877. Its influence was such that during the 1837 financial crisis, it was instrumental in persuading the Bank of England to rescue Liverpool's leading merchants from ruin. In 1881 the first branch opened and in 1882 limited liability was acquired. Major expansion by acquisition began in 1883 when Liverpool's leading private bankers, Arthur Heywood, Sons & Co (est. 1773), were purchased. Following this, branches were opened at Bootle (1884), Walton (1885), Moss Street (1885), Church Street (1885) and at Smithdown Road, Wavertree, Birkenhead, Toxteth and Woolton (all between 1886 and 1888). In 1888 the Liverpool banking business of Brown Shipley & Co (est. 1810) was acquired following that firm's transfer to London. Profits in the early 1890s fell from £180,000 to £153,000, which induced the bank to expand outside Liverpool. This began with the acquisition in 1893 of Wakefield, Crewdson & Co (est. 1840) of Kendal. By 1899, seventy-five branches, sub-branches and agencies existed, customers numbered 33,000 and deposits totalled £11 million. In 1906 the Craven Bank Ltd (est. 1791) of Skipton was acquired along with fifteen branches; for the first time the bank had more branches outside Liverpool than within it. At the same time paid-up capital was increased to £1.2 million. The Carlisle & Cumberland Banking Co Ltd (est. 1836) was acquired in 1911 and expansion across Yorkshire to the North East coast followed in 1914 through amalgamation with the important North Eastern Banking Co Ltd (est. 1872) which had ninety-nine branches. Paid-up capital reached £1.7 million. Although it was now a major northern bank, national importance through the establishment of a London base and membership of the London Clearing House was only achieved in 1919 when Martin's Bank Ltd (est. 1712) of London was acquired along with fourteen branches in the South East and in London; the bank's name changed to the Bank of Liverpool & Martins Ltd. This London presence was consolidated, also in 1919, through the acquisition of the private bankers, Cocks, Biddulph & Co (est. 1757). A Manchester base was obtained, also in 1919, through amalgamation with the Palatine Bank Ltd (est. 1899) and in 1920 the Halifax

362   British banking – a guide to historical records

Commercial Banking Co Ltd (est. 1836) was acquired followed in 1923 by the much smaller Cattle Trade Bank Ltd (est. 1920). These acquisitions were followed by those of the Equitable Bank Ltd (est. 1899) of Halifax in 1927 and of the important Lancashire & Yorkshire Bank Ltd (est. 1872) in 1928, the balance sheet of the latter being a third the size of that of the Bank of Liverpool. At the same time the bank's name was shortened to Martins Bank Ltd to reflect the much greater national spread of business although the head office remained in Liverpool. Organic expansion now followed; between 1927 and 1935, for example, fifty-six new branches were opened. In 1951 the British Mutual Bank Ltd (est. 1857) was acquired followed by Lewis's Bank Ltd (est. 1928) later that year. Diversification also occurred at this time through the purchase of a 20 per cent interest in the finance house, Mercantile Credit Co Ltd. In 1968 the bank merged with Barclays Bank Ltd (est. 1896).

George Chandler, *Four Centuries of Banking* (London, 1964–68)

Records 1: Barclays Bank plc, Group Archives, Dallimore Road, Wythenshawe, Manchester M23 9JA

Registers of shareholders (40) 1831, 1883–1926, 1968; directors' meeting resolution books (8) 1830–1916; lists of shareholders 1830, 1860–1908; prospectus 1831; share certificates 1831; promissory notes 1831–33; letters from London and Manchester agents 1831–38; share transfers 1831–33, 1837–39; cash book, Adam Hodgson 1831–42; petty cash book 1831–59; deeds of settlement 1831–82; account book, half-yearly statements 1831–84; directors' meeting memorandum minute book 1831–1903; registers of shareholders (38) 1831–1917; directors' meeting minute books (11) 1831–1918; annual reports 1831–82, 1905–18; press cuttings: 1831–1924, re formation 1831–32; directors' record of service 1831–1968; solicitor's bill of charges 1832–33; analysis of annual reports 1832–1901; bill of exchange 1833; security register 1833–41; private minute books (20) 1834–86; deeds of accession, new shareholders 1835–36; reference books (6) 1835–1919; staff notice 1838; opinion book, businesses 1839–42; correspondence and other papers re directors' appointments, premises etc 1839–57; bills of exchange, Bank of Charleston 1842–1945; correspondence re clerks pay 1844, 1853; commission statistics 1862–73; staff fidelity bonds 1862–1911; salary lists 1864–1904; reference books (2) 1866–1919; liquidator's report, Liverpool Borough Bank 1867; photographs, directors and staff c.1877–1918; draft balance sheet 1878; directors' share list 1879; bad debts and recoveries list 1880; notice re acquisition of Heywoods Bank 1882; memorandum and articles of association 1882–1969; analysis of securities 1883–85; prospectus and annual reports 1883–1968; manager's minute book 1885–97; shareholder circulars 1885–1929; seal books (9)

Records of banks 363

1886–1919; staff scrapbooks including cartoons, correspondence, press cuttings (7) 1888–1918; premises statistics 1889; real estate committee minutes 1889–1905; letter to board 1890; private letters 1890–1907; press cuttings re cotton frauds 1892; papers re merger with Wakefield Crewdson & Co 1893; general manager's branches meeting minutes 1898–1904; list of branches 1899–1901; registers of directors 1901–48; shareholder circular re fraud 1902; premises register 1903–08; papers re bank amalgamations 1903–28; analysis of shareholders 1904; branch statistics 1904–05; scrapbooks (3) 1905–60; committee minutes: real estate 1905–40, head office building 1926–33, standing 1933–69; share allotment and application forms 1906; papers re merger with Craven Bank 1906–07; notes on customer accounts 1906–09; papers re merger with Carlisle & Cumberland Banking Co Ltd 1910–12; shareholder circulars 1912–13; papers re mergers 1913–57; papers re merger with North Eastern Banking Co 1914–15; local board minute book, north east 1914–26; directors' resolution book 1916–27; staff instruction book 1917; war loan register 1917–22; staff bonus circular 1918; papers re merger with Martin's Bank 1918; directors' meeting minute books (17) 1918–69; register of directors 1918–80; seal books (53) 1919–69; general ledger 1920; loan security ledgers (3) 1922–30; widows' and orphans' fund rules 1922; telegraphic code books 1924–41; staff accounts ledgers (4) 1925–29, 1938–67; declarations of secrecy 1926–67; papers re grant of arms 1928–55; general meeting proceedings 1930–68; indemnities 1932–75; report on working conditions 1933; share transfer journal 1939–46; circulars 1940–41, 1953–69 [w]; stocks register 1943–46; accounts opened and closed books, Liverpool (3) 1950–69; staff instruction manuals 1952, 1963; copy letters: chief general manager 1954–60, joint general manager 1954–59; forms 1954–69; marketing/recruitment leaflets 1958–59; papers re 400th anniversary dinner 1963; register of directors' shareholdings 1967–68.

Records 2: Centre for Kentish Studies, County Hall, Maidstone ME14 1XY

Papers re share and stock transactions and sub-manager's appointment 1835–51. [Ref: U1287/C 10, 18, 28, 29, 36–9, 73]

Records 3: Public Record Office, Ruskin Avenue, Kew, Richmond TW9 4DU

Papers re mergers with Equitable Bank and Lancashire & Yorkshire Bank 1927–28. [T160/263/10541]

Records 4: Modern Records Centre, University Library, University of Warwick, Coventry CV4 7AL

Records of Martins Bank Staff Association c.1940s on. [Ref: MSS.396]

MARTIN'S BANK LTD
London

History: This joint stock bank traced its origins to the prestigious private bank based at the sign of the Grasshopper, Lombard Street, City of London. In turn, this traced its origins to a long line of powerful goldsmith bankers who occupied the site; thus the bank claimed to have been formed in 1563 despite the linkage of one generation to another being sometimes tenuous. The lineage included Sir Thomas Gresham (died 1579), the so-called 'Father of English Banking'; William Cocknedge; Richard Martin (died c.1616), son of Sir Richard Martin (died 1617), Warden of the Mint, but probably no relative of the later Martins; William Cocknedge; Clement Pung (died 1665); Edward Backwell (bankrupt 1682); Charles Duncombe (died 1711) who in 1677 took into partnership Richard Kent (died 1688); Richard Smith (died 1699); and Elmes Spinks. Smith took Andrew Stone (died 1711) into partnership followed in 1703 by Thomas Martin (died 1765). The business became known as Stone & Co and on Stone's death his partnership share was purchased by Martin for £9,000. However, the Stone family's participation continued for many years and they were to inter-marry with the Martins. Nevertheless the Martin family became progressively more important in the partnership and the bank came to carry their name. By 1731 deposits totalled £100,000 and rose to £250,000 in 1744, reflecting the bank's considerable size. Apart from providing regular banking services to the aristocracy and upper classes, by the mid-eighteenth century the sale of lottery tickets and the distribution of exchequer bills had grown to be of considerable importance. By the 1760s the bank lent heavily to ship's captains and merchants on respondentia bonds, while the partners also participated in the finance of turnpikes. However, deposit banking, including advances, overdrafts and general banking services to private clients, remained its core business; there was little participation in the finance of international trade, railways or manufacturing and agencies for country banks were not taken up. Deposits rose to £518,000 in 1807. Leadership by the Martin family was briefly interrupted between 1831 and 1843, when George Stone was senior partner but during mid-Victorian times John Martin dominated the bank, succeeding as senior in 1844 and retiring in 1875. Richard Biddulph Martin, who had married into the Biddulph family of Cox Biddulph, the important London private bankers, was senior from 1878. By 1886 branches existed at Chistlehurst and Sidcup and agencies were at St Mary Cray, Eltham and Bexleyheath. In 1891, in the wake of the Baring Crisis when the bank had been placed at great risk, it converted to a limited liability company as Martin's Bank Ltd, with a paid-up share capital of £500,000 held by family and close friends. Deposits rose from £1.56 million in 1891, to

Records of banks   365

£3.15 million in 1914 and to £5.32 million in 1918. By then branches existed at Kingsway, Bexleyheath, Bromley, Chislehurst, Dartford, Eltham, Sidcup, Sittingbourne, Bexley, Crayford, Mottingham, Orpington, St Mary Cray and Swanley. The balance sheet total rose from £2.26 million to 1891 to £6.35 million in 1918. In 1919 the Bank of Liverpool Ltd (est. 1831), anxious to acquire national status through a seat in the London Clearing House, amalgamated with Martin's Bank, the new business being known as the Bank of Liverpool & Martins Ltd.

George Chandler, *Four Centuries of Banking* (London, 1964–68); William Howarth, *The Banks in the Clearing House* (London, 1905); John Biddulph Martin, *The Grasshopper in Lombard Street* (1892)

Records 1: Barclays Bank plc, Group Archives, Dallimore Road, Wythenshawe, Manchester M23 9JA

Title deeds and related papers: Lombard Street, London 1700–1982, other 1870–1918; partnership agreements 1714–82; out-letterbooks (18) 1714–1916; notes photographs and other papers collected by John Biddulph Martin for writing bank histories 1718–1903; Martin family personal papers: Joseph Martin 1728–1800, John Biddulph Martin 1770–1897, John Martin 1803–49, James Martin 1819–39, Richard Biddulph Martin 1874–1913; cash balance books (10) 1729–1859; annual balances 1731–1842; bill register 1731–35; will probates 1739–1901; wills 1748–1890; cash books (14) 1754–1873, 1891–93; correspondence: debts 1762, 1887–98, trusteeship 1766–84, 1873–1913, solicitors 1785–1816, 1895–1909, advances 1825–1915, bankruptcies 1858–90, customer 1876–1906, executorships 1878–1912, corporate customers 1878–1913, stock purchase 1889–95, share subscriptions 1910–11; cheques 1770–1876; old debts registers (4) 1773–1912; passbooks 1776–94, 1810–32; clerks' bonds of indemnity 1777–1895; administrations of effects 1778–1903; property bills, receipts, correspondence, etc 1792–1918; clerks' board and salary receipts 1799–1870; legal papers 1800–23; cheque books 1816–70; appointment as Stock Exchange bankers 1825; salary lists 1832–71; customer weekly balances 1847–71; bad and doubtful debts list c.1852; income tax form 1873; loan form 1870s; partnership correspondence 1880–83; staff registers 1882–1925; agreements and press cutting re formation of limited company 1891; memorandum and articles of association 1891; agenda books: directors meetings 1891–94, general meetings 1891–1918; balance sheets 1891–1918; annual returns 1891–1918; directors' meeting minute books (4) 1891–1918; general meeting minute books 1891–1918; stock ledger 1891–1904; general meeting proceedings 1892–1918; loan security ledger 1896–1905; legal case papers 1899–1903; notice re extraordinary general meeting 1906; cheques and dividend warrants, F H Norman, 1909–

366   *British banking – a guide to historical records*

14; bills discounted book 1911–14; foreign exchange ledgers (6) 1911–17; circular re merger with Bank of Liverpool 1918.

Records 2: Hereford & Worcester Record Office, St Helen's Branch, Fish Street, Worcester WR1 2HN

Papers re the Martin and Stone families and their estates, especially in Worcestershire and Gloucestershire, 1349–1940, including accounts, letters, receipts, cases and opinions and other papers re Martin's Bank and its customers c.1770–early nineteenth cent. [Ref: 705:139]

MAURITIUS COMMERCIAL BANK LTD
London and Africa

History: This bank was established in 1838 by Royal Charter. From 1884 Barnett, Hoare & Co and, later, Lloyds Bank Ltd acted as its agents in London. The firm was incorporated with limited liability in 1955. In 1948 Lloyds took an equity interest in the bank; this equalled 16 per cent of equity by the 1970s and 10 per cent by the mid 1990s.

Records: Lloyds TSB Group plc, Archives, Head Office, 71 Lombard Street, London EC3P 3BS

Draft letters patent 1839. [Ref: A12/1d/81]

MAY, WYBORN, WHITE & MERCER
Deal, Kent

History: This private bank was formed in 1802 and failed in 1825.

Records: Department of Manuscripts and University Archives, Cambridge University Library, West Road, Cambridge CB3 9DR

Letterbooks (3) 1771–77, 1794–1801, 1824–29; list of debts on failure 1825. [Ref: Add. MS 7924]

SIR CHARLES E McGRIGOR, BART. & CO
London

History: This private bank was formed in 1840 and suspended payment in 1922.

Records: Public Record Office, Ruskin Avenue, Kew, Richmond TW9 4DU

Government correspondence with creditors re army agency accounts 1922. [Ref: T172/1258]

Records of banks

MEDITERRANEAN BANK

History: Application was made to the Treasury in 1836 for a charter under which a bank to be known as the Mediterranean Bank would be formed. However, it seems that no such bank was ever established.

Records: Public Record Office, Ruskin Avenue, Kew, Richmond TW9 4DU

Papers re application for a charter 1836. [Ref: T1/3472]

MEDLEY, SON & CO
Aylesbury, Buckinghamshire

History: This private bank was formed in 1833; it was otherwise known as the Aylesbury, Uxbridge & Windsor Union Bank which suggests that it had representation at Uxbridge and Windsor. It failed in 1837.

Records: Buckinghamshire Record Office, County Hall, Aylesbury HP20 1UA

Register of debtors and creditors 1837. [Ref: D/X 1/42]

MELLERSH & CO
Godalming, Surrey

History: This private bank was established as Mellersh, Moline & Weale in 1808 by John Mellersh, solicitor, Robert Moline, grocer and corn dealer, and James Weale, mercer and linen draper. It was otherwise known as the Godalming Bank. From 1822 all partners were drawn from the Mellersh family. The Capital & Counties Bank Ltd (est. 1877) acquired the business in 1893.

Records: Lloyds TSB Group plc, Archives, Head Office, 71 Lombard Street, London EC3P 3BS

Amalgamation papers 1893.

MERCANTILE BANK LTD
London and Asia

History: This overseas bank traced its origins to 1853 and the formation of the Mercantile Bank of Bombay which was renamed almost immediately the Mercantile Bank of India, London and China. In the next two years, branches were opened in London, in other major Indian cities and in Singapore, Hong Kong and Shanghai. It then sought a merger with the Chartered Bank of India, Australia & China (est. 1853) so as to benefit from that bank's Royal Charter, but when this proved abortive it applied

368 *British banking – a guide to historical records*

for its own charter, which was granted in 1857. The new bank was called The Chartered Mercantile Bank of India, London & China and had a paid-up capital of £500,000 by 1859. By 1860 there were ten branches and total assets of almost £4.5 million, making it the third largest British overseas bank. After 1865, Indian trade slumped and this, coupled with falling silver prices, made the following decades difficult. By 1890 the bank's total assets reached £10.5 million and branches numbered thirteen, but in 1892, following a run, payments were suspended. The business was then reconstructed as The Mercantile Bank of India Ltd, when its balance sheet totalled over £3 million. Expansion followed in the early twentieth century and included the acquisition of the Bank of Calcutta (est. 1895) in 1906 and of the Bank of Mauritius Ltd (est. 1894) in 1916. Branches were also opened in South East Asia. This expanding geographical coverage resulted in a name change to Mercantile Bank Ltd in 1957, when the balance sheet total exceeded £70 million. In this year the Hongkong & Shanghai Banking Corporation acquired a 20 per cent shareholding and, after protracted negotiations in 1959, purchased the remaining shares not in its ownership. Initially the bank retained independence, operating in those areas where it had expertise, but in 1966 its head office was transferred to Hong Kong. By 1984, with the exception of offices in Bangkok, most of its operations had been integrated with those of the Hongkong & Shanghai Banking Corporation. In that year the bank was sold to Citibank.

Edwin Green & Sara Kinsey, *The Paradise Bank. The Mercantile Bank of India 1893–1984* (Aldershot, 1999); Stuart Muirhead, *Crisis Banking in the East. The History of the Chartered Mercantile Bank of India, London & China 1853–93* (Aldershot, 1996)

Records: HSBC Holdings plc, Group Archives, 10 Lower Thames Street, London EC3R 6AE

Deeds of settlement and charters 1853–88; capital structure summary 1853–1959; bank note registers 1858–1978; branch general balances 1858–1900, 1927–57; balance sheets and profit and loss accounts 1858–1983; annual reports 1858–1983; staff record books 1861–1921, 1960s–1970s; declarations of secrecy 1861–1967; officers register 1864–1967; papers re certain customers 1860s–1890s; bad debts ledger 1873–1915; staff agreement books 1874–1960s; directors' meeting minutes 1885–1977; liabilities of certain customers 1890–92; correspondence between chief manager and inspector 1891–1913; share allotment, call, transfer registers 1892–1914; papers re reconstruction 1892–93, 1957; directors' register 1892–1958; private letters to/from London head office 1892–1964; proceedings of shareholders' meetings 1892–1918, 1938–66; managers' private letters 1892–66; Eastern staff careers summary

Records of banks

book 1892–1966; staff movements 1893–1970; shareholder lists 1894, 1900; note issue papers 1898–1910; general advices from London head office 1899–1962; agreement re Bank of Calcutta acquisition 1906; accountant's letters 1908–59; inspector's letterbooks 1914–23; chairman's statements 1915–59; staff reports 1915–1960s; papers re Bank of Mauritius acquisition 1916; correspondence with auditors 1917–61; branch half-yearly returns 1927–62; Bank of England account 1929–61; staff files 1920s–1950s; branch profit and tax papers 1930s–1960s; note issue statements 1930–49; branch profit and loss accounts 1932–45, 1961–64; letters re local staff 1936–59; head office assessments and general statistics 1937–66; papers re capital alteration 1938–53; correspondence with Bank of England 1939–50; directors' correspondence 1939–52; correspondence with bank's solicitors 1939–60; files re certain corporate customers 1940s–1960s; inspector's letterbooks re S E Asia 1950–54; tea finance questionnaires 1952–59; papers re acquisition by Hongkong & Shanghai Banking Corporation and subsequent integration 1958–70; overseas direct investment returns 1960–75; private ledger 1962–73; head office general ledger 1963–66; semi-official and general letters to/from London office n.d.

Bombay: letterbooks 1920–24, 1931–39; half-yearly reports 1922–47; private letterbooks 1932–62; **Calcutta:** staff registers 1930–45; **Kula Trengganu:** commission account 1929–41; general ledger 1939–56; salary book 1945–63; profit and loss account 1946–64; interest account 1946–59; charges account 1946–67; special letters to/from Malaysian, Singapore and other branches 1947–62; fixed deposit register 1947–64; special letters from London 1957–62; **Shanghai:** general ledger 1925–59; securities records 1929–53; deposit account balances 1934–59; foreign currency sales register 1935–41; general ledger balance book 1937–54; daily business report 1951–56; papers re closure 1954–59.

MERCANTILE BANK OF LANCASHIRE LTD
Manchester, Greater Manchester

History: This joint stock bank was formed in 1890 with a nominal capital of £1 million of which £115,000 was paid-up by 1891. In 1894 and 1896 the Southport branches of the London & Lancashire Bank Ltd (est. 1885) and of the Adelphi Bank Ltd (est. 1862) respectively were acquired. In 1899 the cattle bank of Wm Brown & Sons (est. 1830) of Salford, with four cattle market branches, was acquired followed in 1900 by the Manx Bank Ltd (est. 1882) for £25,000. By 1904, forty-one branches existed – nine in Manchester, six in the Isle of Man, four in northern cattle markets and twenty-two elsewhere, largely in Lancashire. In 1902 deposits began to decline while poorly judged investments led to a write down in assets.

370 *British banking – a guide to historical records*

In a weakened condition, the bank was acquired in 1904 by the Lancashire & Yorkshire Bank Ltd (est. 1872).

George Chandler, *Four Centuries of Banking* (London, 1964–68)

Records: Barclays Bank plc, Group Archives, Dallimore Road, Wythenshawe, Manchester M23 9JA

Memorandum and articles of association 1890; directors' meeting minutes 1890–1904; general meeting minutes 1890–1904; agenda book, overdraft committee 1893–96; security for advance 1894; circular re share applications 1896; instruction book 1900; balance sheet 1904; bank note 1900s.

METROPOLITAN BANK
London

History: This joint stock bank was established in 1839 in Pall Mall, West End of London. In 1841 it failed when its premises were acquired by the Union Bank of London (est. 1839) which declined to purchase the firm's business.

Records: The Royal Bank of Scotland plc, Archive Section, Regent's House, 42 Islington High Street, London N1 8XL

Deed of settlement 1839; notices of opening and amalgamation 1839–41.

METROPOLITAN BANK (OF ENGLAND & WALES) LTD
Birmingham, West Midlands, and later London

History: This joint stock bank was established in 1829 as the Birmingham Banking Co and was based upon the business of the Birmingham private bankers, Gibbins & Lovell (est. 1825). Joseph Gibbins was a founding director along with Paul James who had formerly managed the Birmingham private bankers Galton & James (est. 1804). The new bank progressed well and in 1838 absorbed its rival, the Bank of Birmingham (est. 1832). By the mid 1830s it was Birmingham's strongest bank with a paid-up capital of £100,000; this was doubled to £200,000 in 1837. The first branch opened at Dudley in 1844, through the acquisition of Dixon, Dalton & Amphlett (est. 1791), and the second, at Walsall, was formed in 1848 out of the local private bank of Charles Forster & Sons (est. c.1793). In 1865 the private bank of Little & Woodcock (est. 1762) of Coventry was acquired. During the financial panic of 1866 the bank suffered severe liquidity problems, due to longstanding poor management, and suspended payment with liabilities of £1.8 million. It was soon reconstructed and reopened the following month with a newly subscribed capital of £83,000 and with a new and influential board. By

Records of banks 371

the early 1870s, deposits had recovered to exceed £1 million. In 1880, when deposits equalled £2.5 million, the Stourbridge & Kidderminster Banking Co (est. 1834) was acquired followed in 1889 by the acquisition of Cooper, Purton & Sons (est. 1817) of Bridgnorth, the Staffordshire Joint Stock Bank Ltd (est. 1864) and the Royal Exchange Bank Ltd (est. 1861) of London. The latter transaction was important strategically, resulting in the bank's renaming as the Metropolitan & Birmingham Bank Ltd and in the relocation of its head office to London. In 1892 the South Wales Union Bank Ltd (est. 1873) was acquired when the bank was briefly renamed the Metropolitan, Birmingham & South Wales Bank Ltd. The purchase of the National Bank of Wales (est. 1879) followed a year later. On investigation, it emerged that this bank was insolvent, due largely to a concealed fraud, and losses of £350,000 were incurred. This held back progress for a decade; in this period only one firm, Davies, Banks & Co (est. 1789) of Kington was acquired, in 1910. The bank was renamed the Metropolitan Bank (of England & Wales) Ltd in 1893 when paid-up capital was £470,000. By now deposits had reached £6 million and there were 115 branches. In 1900 132 branches existed rising to 150 in 1910 while in the same period paid-up capital and deposits rose from £500,000 to £550,000 and from £7.9 million to £11 million respectively. In 1914 the bank was acquired by London, City & Midland Bank Ltd (est. 1836) for the equivalent of £1.685 million. Most of the Metropolitan Bank's business was located in the Midlands and Wales; its presence in London remained relatively small.

W F Crick & J E Wadsworth, *A Hundred Years of Joint Stock Banking* (London, 1936); A R Holmes & Edwin Green, *Midland.150 Years of Banking Business* (London, 1986)

Records 1: HSBC Holdings plc, Group Archives, 10 Lower Thames Street, London EC3R 6AE

General ledgers (2) 1829–49, 1884–87; deed of settlement 1830; staff registers 1850–1914; annual reports 1866–69, 1885–1914; directors' meeting minute books (9) 1866–68, 1888–1914; statement of affairs 1870; private minute book re staff 1876–1914; weekly balance sheet returns (8) 1878–1914; signature books (3) 1889–1914; security books (4) 1889–1914; letterbooks (3) 1892–97; analysis of branch profits and losses 1893–1914; press cuttings (2) 1894–1914; quarterly balance sheets 1897–1914; general minute book 1900–14; premises insurance register c.1900–14; share ledgers (10) 1911–14; analysis of balance sheet (3) 1913–14; amalgamation papers 1914.

Chipping Norton: signature books 1880–1914; security register 1898–1914; **Leamington:** authorisations and banker's notices 1900–14; **Neath:**

372   **British banking – a guide to historical records**

letterbooks (3) 1892–97; **Willenhall:** signature books 1889–1914; security register 1890–1914.

Records 2: Birmingham City Archives, Chamberlain Square, Birmingham B3 3HQ

Deeds of settlement 1830–37; press cuttings 1866–69; prospectuses 1866–80; investigation committee report 1868; directors' report 1873.

MIDDLETON, CRADOCK & CO
Loughborough, Leicestershire

History: This private bank was formed in 1790 and was otherwise known as the Loughborough Bank. By 1850 partnership capital was only £5,000 when liabilities were well over £100,000; these amounted to £1,120 and £170,000 respectively in 1873. In 1878 the bank suspended payments despite its assets of £223,000 exceeding liabilities by £6,000. The Leicestershire Banking Co (est. 1829) purchased the bank's goodwill and premises for £6,000.

W F Crick & J E Wadsworth, *A Hundred Years of Joint Stock Banking* (London, 1936)

Records: HSBC Holdings plc, Group Archives, 10 Lower Thames Street, London EC3R 6AE

Draft prospectus n.d.; annual reports 1850–77; bankruptcy papers re partner 1878; list of creditors 1878.

MIDLAND BANKING CO LTD
Birmingham, West Midlands

History: This joint stock bank was established with limited liability in 1863. In this year it acquired the private bank of Goodricke & Holyoake (est. 1816) of Wolverhampton followed in 1864 by the London & Northern Joint Stock Bank Ltd (est. 1862) and in 1872 by the private bank of Saxton Brothers of Market Drayton. Its branch network was well scattered and included branches as distant as Belper, Leeds, Lincoln, Otley, Peterborough and Stamford. In 1881, when its paid-up capital was £300,000 and its deposits totalled £1.52 million, it amalgamated with the Birmingham, Dudley & District Banking Co (est. 1836).

P W Matthews & Anthony W Tuke, *History of Barclays Bank Ltd* (London, 1926)

Records: Barclays Bank plc, Group Archives, Dallimore Road, Wythenshawe, Manchester M23 9JA

Records of banks

Branch credits register 1863–81; general purposes committee minute books (8) 1863–81; weekly returns register 1863–81; directors' meeting minute books (5) 1863–82; general meetings attendance book 1864–80; impersonal ledger 1865–71; branch managers' instructions 1867; cheques 1869–80; directors' meeting agenda books (3) 1871–81; premises ledgers 1877–81; branch correspondence and returns 1877–81; letters and invoices re premises 1877–79; circulars 1879–81; report and accounts 1879–81; branch profit and loss statements 1880; seal book 1880–81; papers re merger with Birmingham, Dudley & District Banking Co 1881.

MIDLAND BANK PLC
Birmingham, West Midlands, later London

History: This joint stock bank was formed in 1836 as the Birmingham & Midland Banking Co. Initially it was a local concern; by 1875 only two branches had been opened, both of which were in the Birmingham area. In 1851 the Stourbridge private bankers, Hill, Bates & Robins (est. 1762), were acquired, followed by the acquisition of Nicholls, Baker & Crane (est. 1782) of Bewdley in 1862. In 1877 the first entirely new branch was opened, at Wednesbury. Deposits grew steadily reaching £112,000 in 1850 and £2 million in 1880. In the latter year limited liability was acquired and the bank was renamed Birmingham & Midland Bank Ltd. In 1883–84 four additional branches were opened, all in the Birmingham area. Others followed quickly and forty-five were in operation by 1890. Many were acquired through the acquisition of other banks. These banks included Union Bank of Birmingham (est. 1878) in 1883; Coventry Union Banking Co (est. 1836) in 1889; Leamington Priors & Warwickshire Banking Co Ltd (est. 1835) and Derby Commercial Bank Ltd (est. 1868), both in 1890; and Exchange & Discount Bank Ltd (est. 1866) of Leeds and Leeds & County Bank Ltd (est. 1862) also in 1890. From the early 1890s the bank, under the able leadership of Edward Holden, masterminded thirteen major amalgamations which resulted in deposits growing from £5.6 million in 1890 to £37.8 million in 1900 and branch numbers rising from forty-five to 280 in the same period. By 1900 the bank had become the fourth largest joint stock bank in England and Wales. A cornerstone of this expansion was the acquisition of a London base. Therefore in 1891 the Central Bank of London Ltd (est. 1863) was acquired, along with its seat in the London Clearing House. At the same time, the bank moved its head office to London and changed its title to London & Midland Bank Ltd. The balance between capital and country was made more equal in 1898 through amalgamation with the City Bank Ltd (est. 1855) which resulted in another name change to London, City & Midland Bank Ltd. Otherwise policy focused upon the acquisition of well-established provincial joint stock

374   British banking – a guide to historical records

banks which resulted in the following being acquired: Manchester Joint Stock Bank Ltd (est. 1873), Bank of Westmorland Ltd (est. 1833), Preston Banking Co Ltd (est. 1844), Carlisle City & District Banking Co Ltd (est. 1837), Channel Islands Bank Ltd (est. 1858), Huddersfield Banking Co Ltd (est. 1827), North Western Bank Ltd (est. 1864), Oldham Joint Stock Bank Ltd (est. 1880) and City of Birmingham Bank Ltd (est. 1897). In the 1890s only one private bank was acquired, Lacy, Hartland, Woodbridge & Co (est. 1809) of London. From 1900 the accent was on filling gaps to establish a truly national branch network. Well-managed banks with large branch networks were acquired: Leicestershire Banking Co Ltd (est. 1829); Sheffield Union Banking Co Ltd (est. 1843); Yorkshire Banking Co Ltd (est. 1843); Nottingham Joint Stock Bank Ltd (est. 1865); North & South Wales Bank Ltd (est. 1836); Bradford Banking Co Ltd (est. 1827); Sheffield & Hallamshire Banking Co Ltd (est. 1836); and Lincoln & Lindsey Banking Co Ltd (est. 1833). Midland's London base was massively strengthened through amalgamation with the Metropolitan Bank (of England & Wales) Ltd (est. 1829) in 1914 and, more particularly, with the London Joint Stock Bank Ltd (est. 1836) in 1918, which resulted in another name change, to London Joint, City & Midland Bank Ltd. In 1923 the title was abbreviated to Midland Bank Ltd. Where expansion by amalgamation was not possible – mostly in East Anglia, the South West and the South East – 400 new branches were opened between 1900 and 1919. Expansion into Scotland and Ireland followed with the major acquisitions of the Belfast Banking Co Ltd (est. 1827) in 1917, the Clydesdale Bank Ltd (est. 1838) in 1919 and the North of Scotland Bank Ltd (est. 1836) in 1924 (the last two merging in 1950). Unlike previous acquisitions, each retained local independence and identity. The range of Midland's services was also broadened, notably through the establishment of an executorship and trusteeship company in 1909. Overseas activities of the Foreign Banks Department (est. 1902) and Foreign Exchange Department (est. 1905), which were significantly bolstered by London Joint Stock Bank's international business, were transferred to the newly-formed Overseas Branch in 1918. These activities were based on correspondent bank relationships and for many years the bank's only direct representation overseas was through a shortlived Petrograd branch, established in 1917. The UK business expanded steadily between the wars, aided by schemes to encourage small depositors and by a net increase of almost 900 branches, including representation at special locations such as factories, universities and passenger liners. The trend continued after the war, one notable development from 1967 being the establishment of twenty-four regional head offices. In the same year, Midland Bank Finance Corporation was established to take charge, *inter alia*, of London money market operations and some corporate services. From the 1960s significant shareholdings were taken in international consortium banks and in the early 1970s overseas offices were established in large numbers. Overseas Branch was reconstructed as International Division in 1974 and from 1975 an interest, which never exceeded 16 per cent, was taken in Standard Chartered Bank Ltd. The 1960s and 1970s were also marked by a series of major outright acquisitions. Northern Bank Ltd (est. 1824), at Belfast, was acquired in 1965 and merged with the Belfast Bank in 1974. Also in 1974 the merchant bank, Samuel Montagu & Co Ltd (est. 1853) became fully-owned. Soon afterwards the fund management and corporate finance company, Drayton Trust, was acquired, prompting a reorganisation of the activities of Montagu, Drayton and Midland Bank Finance Corporation. In 1972 the Thomas Cook Group was also acquired. In the 1980s overseas expansion continued, in particular through the acquisition of Trinkaus & Burkhardt (in 1980) in Germany and Crocker Bank (in 1981) in the United States. Crocker failed to meet expectations and its business was disposed of in 1986. In the late 1980s and early 1990s the bank also sold its interests in Clydesdale and Northern (1987) and Thomas Cook (1992). As well as returning to its original core business as a UK clearing bank, Midland expanded its personal financial services and, in 1989, launched First Direct, the pioneer of telephone banking. In 1992 the bank became a wholly-owned member of HSBC Holdings plc, of which the Hongkong & Shanghai Banking Corporation Ltd was a founder member. Midland continued to do business as one of the major UK clearing banks and as the HSBC Group's principal bank in the UK and Europe. In 1999 the use of the Midland Bank name for retail banking was discontinued and replaced by HSBC.

W F Crick & J E Wadsworth, *A Hundred Years of Joint Stock Banking* (London, 1936); Edwin Green, *The Making of a Modern Banking Group. A History of the Midland Bank Since 1900* (London, 1979); A R Holmes & Edwin Green, *Midland.150 Years of Banking Business* (London, 1986); Manfred Pohl & Sabine Freitag, *Handbook on the History of European Banks* (Aldershot, 1994)

Records 1: HSBC Holdings plc, Group Archives, 10 Lower Thames Street, London EC3R 6AE

Prospectus 1836; deed of settlement 1836; deposit and current account ledgers (3) 1836; cash book 1836; general meeting minute books (4) 1836–1957; directors' meeting minute books (48) 1836–1976; annual reports from 1837; balance sheets 1847–72, 1898, 1901–08; staff registers 1860–1945; overseas arrangements books 1862–1928; secretary's notebooks (2) 1871–98; security register 1876–91; press cuttings re annual general meetings 1879–99; finance committee rough minute book 1885–

376   *British banking – a guide to historical records*

88; overdraft committee minute book 1887–91; branch office abstract of accounts (5) 1888–1900; head office abstract of accounts (5) 1888–1900; branch managers' instruction book 1890; London branches premises reference book 1890–1900; general manager's reference books 1890–1947; staff entry papers, male surnames S only, 1890–1926; branch balance sheet ledgers (95) 1890–1904, 1912–39; papers re branches designed by Woolfall & Eccles c.1890–1950; Birmingham committee minute book 1891; board agenda books (2) 1891–98; expenses and general charges ledgers 1891–1907; summaries of doubtful debts (6) 1891–1911; finance committee minute books (4) 1891–1901, 1905–19, 1929–46; investment registers (2) 1892–96, 1899; staff agreements 1894–1905; bill risks book 1895; projected amalgamations working papers 1896–1924; managing director's diaries 1896–1917; summary of liabilities and assets 1897–1919; managing director's letterbooks 1898–1909; arrangements books, overseas business (4) 1898–1914; general manager's diaries 1899–1953; case papers re various corporate customers 1899–1909; general ledgers (24) 1900–45, 1954–73; premises reference book 1900; head office circulars 1900 on; discount ledger 1900; managing director's reference books 1905–16; chief accountant's weekly comparison between branches book 1905–17; shareholders' meetings verbatim minute books (4) 1906–53; overseas business letterbooks(7) 1906–09, c.1920; summary of shipping department business 1906–27; Russian bond issues papers 1907–13; analysis of interest rates 1907–15; Liverpool committee minutes and papers 1908–54; foreign branch letterbooks 1910–18; managing director's various papers 1911–17; staff refreshment club register 1911–19; staff guarantee fund accounts working papers 1911–19; register of drafts advised to correspondent banks 1911–23; balance sheet working papers 1912–45; reports and correspondence re Russian economic and political situation 1913–18; reports on overseas banking conditions 1913–37; gold ledgers 1913–55; staff war service records 1914–17; monies held abroad books (10) 1915–19; balance sheet abstracts 1916–72; papers re Petrograd office 1917; Russian drib ledgers 1917–24; returns of dormant accounts 1918–61; analysis books re new capital issues 1918–73; chairmen's papers 1919 on; staff department private files, surnames R–W, 1919–36; advertising diaries 1919–49; analysis sheets, half-yearly statement of profits 1919–54; staff association and other clubs papers 1919–61; house magazine and newspapers 1920 on; monthly analysis of balance sheets of London clearing banks 1921–74; Midland Division staff records 1921–79; general manager's letterbooks 1923–32; northern division's diaries 1923–44; Birmingham committee papers 1923–54; papers re head office premises 1923–55; staff loans ledgers 1926–37; chief inspector's diaries 1927–45; management committee minutes 1928 on; bad debts records 1929 on; statement sheets 1929–81; records of marketing including advertisements, films and videos

Records of banks 377

1929 on; overseas branch manager's files 1920s–1960s; report on overseas branch 1930; investment analysis books 1930–75; agreements re German accounts 1931–39; summary of investment sales 1931–77; abstracts of acceptances 1932–70; classification of advances 1933–39; chief accountant's office staff register 1933–65; chief accountant's reference books 1933–66; home counties division diaries 1936–43; report re overseas branch system 1938–41; staff mutual provident fund reports and balance sheets 1938–43; circulars and memoranda re emergency measures 1938–45; general manager's correspondence 1938–47; post-war planning committee minutes and papers 1942–45; summary of investment purchases 1943–69; overseas branch reference book 1945–71; Economic Advisor's files 1945–77; Economics Department staff record book 1946–58; investment ledgers 1946–67; reports and notes re organisation, mechanisation and computerisation 1952–78; analysis of branch profits in North Wales 1955–79; Radcliffe Committee papers 1957–58; analysis book re overseas business 1961–73; European Advisory Committee papers 1964–68; records re launch of Access 1965–78; records of event sponsorship from 1968; staff transfer registers 1968–84; Wilson Committee papers 1977–78.

Barnsley, Market Hill: staff register 1915–22; reference books (3) 1920–32; **Barnsley, Peel Square:** reference books (3) 1897–1932; **Bewdley:** general ledgers (2) 1862; **Birkenhead, Laird Street:** reference book and safe custody register 1909–45; **Birkenhead, North End:** ledgers 1918–21; produce summary and analysis 1928–30; **Birmingham, Handsworth:** reference books 1892–1954; **Birmingham, New Street:** reference books 1886–1932; **Birmingham, Small Heath:** reference books 1886–1945; **Birmingham, Temple Row:** reference books 1896–1951; **Birmingham, Waterloo Street:** reference books 1886–1903; **Boscombe:** salary book 1910–59; **Bournemouth, Old Christchurch Road:** reference books 1893–1934; **Bradford, Overseas Branch:** reference book 1912–37; salary books 1912–59; notebook re cable arrangements 1913–65; bill register 1936–56; **Bradford, St James Market:** signature book 1901–30; **Bristol, Baldwin Street:** security register 1899–1910; salary book 1899–1941; **Bromley:** reference book 1898–1924; **Cardiff Docks:** reference books 1893–1933; **Carlisle:** security and safe custody receipt books 1896–1910; **Chatham:** salary, security and letterbook 1921–45; **Coleshill:** reference books 1889–1930; security books 1889–1950; **Coventry:** reference books 1889–1938; letterbook 1918–30; **Cunard Liners:** correspondence and balance sheets 1920–27; **Dalton in Furness:** private ledgers (13) 1918–44; cash books (4) 1922–44; **Darlaston Green:** reference sheets 1965–75; **Dawlish:** half-yearly returns and analysis 1933–70; **Devizes:** reference book 1912–33; **Dewsbury:** reference book 1928–31; **Egremont, High Street:** reference book 1897–1915; **Erdington:** reference book 1886–1916; securities re-

378   *British banking – a guide to historical records*

ceipts 1912–19; safe custody register 1914–43; **Eye:** salary book 1921–45; **Ffestiniog:** character book 1908–24; **Howden:** reference book 1907–29; **Huddersfield:** salary book 1900–37; **Hull, Whitefriargate:** profit and loss book and salary register 1901–36; **Irthlingborough:** salary book 1913–44; **Jersey:** reference books, signature books and security books 1862–1941; **Keswick:** letterbook 1918–26; **Leeds, City Square:** customer record sheets 1905–23; **Leeds, Park Row:** letterbooks (8) 1890–1911; salary book 1890–1911; **Leicester, Granby Street:** reference books, salary books and manager's diary 1908–53; **Liverpool, Castle Street:** reference book 1930–37; **Liverpool, Cotton Exchange:** salaries book 1897–1953; reference books 1899–1952; **Liverpool, Market Branch:** security register 1908–33; safe custody registers 1908–1938; **Liverpool, North Docks:** safe custody and securities receipt books 1884–1915; **Liverpool, Old Hall Street:** salary books 1908–44; **Liverpool, South:** signature books and security registers 1908–50; **Liverpool, Walton:** general ledger 1909–17; **Llangollen:** security register 1863–1909; **Llanrwst:** letterbooks 1908–20; **London, Aldersgate:** reference books 1909–68; **London, Angel Court:** reference book 1912–31; **London, Barbican:** reference books 1921–60; **London, Bermondsey:** salary book 1891–1922; **London, Cambridge Circus:** signature books 1890–1950; reference books 1901–28; **London, 6 Chancery Lane:** signature books, salary books and reference books 1913–33; **London, 123 Chancery Lane:** signature books 1866–1950; salary book 1925–44; **London, Chiswick:** general charges analysis 1899–1951; **London, Cornhill:** reference and signature books 1891–1910; salary books (2) 1891–1932; security register 1892–1908; profit and loss account book 1892–1969; letterbook 1905–13; **London, Covent Garden:** reference book, salary book and letterbook 1899–1943; **London, Ealing Broadway:** security receipt book 1898–1917; signature books 1898–1927; reference books 1898–1945; **London, Edgware Road:** reference book 1923–34; **London, Electra House:** reference book 1933–72; **London, Fenchurch Street:** reference book 1921–37; **London, Fore Street:** security books 1904–24; **London, Golden Square:** reference book 1927–65; **London, Goswell Road:** reference book 1933–66; **London, Gracechurch Street:** reference books and salary books 1914–38; **London, Holborn Circus:** reference book 1918–36; **London, Holborn Viaduct:** half-yearly returns 1898–1972; staff register 1904–16; **London, Lambeth:** salary books (2) 1922–53; **London, Limehouse:** signature books 1898–1934; **London, Mayfair:** salary book 1900–46; **London, Mincing Lane:** reference books 1914–67; **London, Moorgate:** security books 1919–29; **London, New Bond Street:** security book 1898–1928; **London, Notting Hill:** reference book 1904–14; **London, Old Bond Street:** signature books 1898–1914; security registers 1921–35; reference books 1924–61; **London, Old Kent Road:** letterbook 1920–50; **London,**

Records of banks 379

Pall Mall: manager's interviews diaries 1928–69; analysis of branch profits 1934–40; **London, Peckham High Street:** reference books 1939–64; **London, Regent Street:** signature book and security register 1899–1927; **London, Southall:** reference book 1914–47; **London, Tottenham, Lordship Lane:** security book 1930–37; **London, West Ealing:** reference and signature books 1923–50; **London, Westbourne Grove:** salary books 1904–45; signature books 1904–50; reference books 1920–70; **London, Wimbledon, Southfields:** salary book 1908–59; **London, Willesden Green:** reference book 1904–33; **London, Wood Green:** reference book 1920–41; **Loughborough Junction:** reference books 1914–65; **Louth:** reference books 1921–31; **Machynlleth:** profit and loss forms 1913–79; **Lye:** private ledgers (2) 1890; **Manchester, Chester Road:** salary book 1884–1944; **Manchester, Deansgate:** security register 1892–1920; **Manchester, King Street:** premises working drawings by Lutyens n.d.; **Morley:** security register 1891–1902; **Pontefract:** staff register 1912–34; **Poole:** reference books 1929–59; **Rhyl:** letterbook 1908–25; **Rugby:** reference books 1907–47; **Ruthin:** reference books 1920–37; **Scunthorpe:** reference books 1913–24; **Sheffield, Market Place:** staff registers 1904–29; salary book 1918–45; staff duty rota book 1932–49; **Southport, Queen's Road:** signature book 1911–50; **Stourbridge:** general ledger 1882; **Trawsfynydd:** reference book 1923–49; **Tredegar:** salary book 1914–69; **Wednesbury:** security register 1877–84; open and closed book 1877–1905; **Wellingborough:** manager's letterbook 1920–40; **Welshpool:** signature books 1908–25; reference books 1913–29; **Willenhall:** reference books 1914–30; **Workington:** manager's memorandum book 1918–45; **York, Nessgate:** reference books, security books and signature books 1902–27.

Records 2: Brynmor Jones Library, University of Hull, Hull HU6 7RX

Intelligence Department files containing annual reports, press cuttings, brochures, circulars, etc, re UK and foreign banks, European countries, British business sectors, commodities, post-war planning, etc 1912–55. [Ref: DBM]

MIDLAND COUNTIES DISTRICT BANK LTD
Nottingham, Nottinghamshire

History: This small joint stock bank was established in 1889 as the Nottingham & District Bank Ltd and changed its name in 1899 to the Midland Counties District Bank Ltd. In 1904 it was acquired by Birmingham District & Counties Banking Co Ltd (est. 1836).

Records: Barclays Bank plc, Group Archives, Dallimore Road, Wythenshawe, Manchester M23 9JA

380   *British banking – a guide to historical records*

Certificate of incorporation and change of name 1889–99; memorandum and articles of association 1889; directors' meeting minute book 1890–1904; dividend warrants 1896–1903; directors' report and accounts 1897–1903; shareholder dividend registers 1903–04; current account returns 1904; papers re merger with Birmingham District & Counties Banking Co Ltd 1904–05; high court order re appointment of new liquidator 1922.

MILBANKE, WOODBRIDGE, GRUGGEN & GAUNTLETT
Chichester, West Sussex

History: This private bank was established in East Street, Chichester, in 1809 as Hack, Dendy & Co; its founders were James Hack and Charles Dendy and it was otherwise known as the Chichester Bank. It traded under several names including Dendy, Comper, Gruggen, Dendy, Gruggen & Comper from 1827; Dendy, Comper, Gruggen & Comper from 1843; Gruggen & Comper from 1858; Gruggen, Dendy, Halstead & Gruggen from 1865; Dendy, Halstead & Gruggen from 1867; Halstead, Woodbridge, Gruggen & Gauntlett from 1888; and Milbanke, Woodbridge, Gruggen & Gauntlett from 1891. It did not open branches. In 1900 it amalgamated with Barclay & Co Ltd (est. 1896).

P W Matthews & Anthony W Tuke, *History of Barclays Bank Ltd* (London, 1926)

Records: Barclays Bank plc, Group Archives, Dallimore Road, Wythenshawe, Manchester M23 9JA

Current account ledgers (121) 1809–96; articles of agreement 1810; private ledgers (2) 1813–32, 1859–66; drafts issued ledger 1824–66; general balances ledgers (5) 1827–72; partnership agreements 1827–92; clerks' bonds 1835–62; stock books (5) 1838–1905; cheques 1840–85; bond and certificate registers (3) 1842–1903; safe custody registers (3) 1842–1905; bank note registers (2) 1861–95; bankers' accounts ledgers (2) 1866–1900; stocks bought 1874–86; balance sheets 1875–94; cashier's till book 1883; letters re clerks' misdemeanours 1883–85; partners' photographs 1880s; dividends ledger 1898–1900; report on advances 1900; premises valuation 1900; papers re amalgamation 1900.

MILES, CAVE, BAILLIE & CO
Bristol, Avon

History: This private bank was established in Bristol in 1750, by Siphorus Tyndall, Harford Lloyd, Isaac Elton, William Miller, Thomas Knox and Matthew Hale; it was known as Tyndall, Lloyd, Elton, Miller, Knox & Hale and otherwise as Bristol Bank and, from 1752, as Bristol Old Bank

Records of banks 381

following the opening of a second bank in the city. The bank had strong mercantile connections and was closely involved in financing the West Indies trade. It subsequently traded under many partnership names including Lloyd, Elton, Miller, Tyndall, Knox & Hale (1757); Miller, Tyndall, Elton, Gillam & Edye (1776); Tyndall, Elton, Gillam & Edye (1781); Elton, Edye, Edwards & Skinner (1794); Tyndall, Elton, Edye, Edwards, Edye & Skinner (1795); Elton, Edwards, Baillie, Tyndall & Skinner (1809); Elton, Baillie, Ames, Baillie, Cave, Tyndall, Palmer & Edwards following the acquisition of Cave, Ames & Cave (est. 1786) in 1826; and Baillie, Ames, Baillie, Cave, Tyndall, Palmer & Edwards (1837). In 1877 the bank merged with Miles, Miles, Harford, Miles & Miles (est. 1752), otherwise known as Bristol Bank, to form Miles, Cave, Baillie & Co. In 1891 the bank merged with Dimsdale, Fowler, Barnard & Dimsdales (est. 1759) of London, Prescott, Cave, Buxton, Loder & Co (est. 1766) of London and Tugwell, Brymer & Co (est. c.1760s) of Bath to form Prescott, Dimsdale, Cave, Tugwell & Co Ltd.

Anon, 'Prescott's Bank', *National Provincial Bank Review* (1966–68); Charles H Cave, *A History of Banking in Bristol from 1750 to 1899* (Bristol, 1899)

Records 1: The Royal Bank of Scotland plc, Archive Section, Regent's House, 42 Islington High Street, London N1 8XL

General ledgers (4) 1772–1820; draft partnership agreements 1820–24.

Records 2: Bristol Record Office, 'B' Bond Warehouse, Smeaton Road, Bristol BS1 6XN

Committee minute book 1832–55; epitome of partnership agreement 1851. [Ref: 28048/T P83/17–18]

Records 3: Gloucestershire Record Office, Clarence Row, Alvin Street, Gloucester GL1 3DW

Correspondence 1763–96. [Ref: D1086]

MILFORD, SNOW & CO
Exeter, Devon

History: This private bank was established in 1786 as Milford & Clarke, the partners being Samuel Milford and Richard Hall Clarke; it was also known as Exeter City Bank. Milford was from a leading family of serge and woollen merchants and he and his partner contributed £15,000 each to the partnership's capital. In 1800 a new partnership of John Milford (Samuel's nephew), John Hogg and William Nation was formed which was styled Milford, Hogg, Nation & Co and subsequently Milford, Snow &

382 British banking – a guide to historical records

Co. Milford remained senior partner until 1829 and his family led the bank until the 1890s when the Snow family, which had provided a partner since at least 1833, assumed leadership. In 1901 the bank merged with Sanders & Co (est. 1769) to form Sanders, Snow & Co.

John Ryton, *Banks and Bank Notes of Exeter 1769–1906* (priv. pub., 1984)

Records 1: The Royal Bank of Scotland plc, Archive Section, Regent's House, 42 Islington High Street, London N1 8XL

Correspondence with London agent 1800–02; general ledgers (5) 1816–28, 1846–83; partnership agreements 1820–89; papers re chief clerk 1827–43; private letterbook 1843–87; premises valuation 1884; profit and loss accounts 1895–99; amalgamation papers 1901.

Records 2: Devon Record Office, Castle Street, Exeter EX4 3PU

Partnership agreement and papers 1786, 1800. [Ref: DD 4429]

MILLION BANK
London

History: The Million Bank was formed in 1695 by London bankers who lent money to King William through 'King William's Million Lottery'. The bank's official name was 'The Company of the Million Bank' and it was administered by a board of twenty-four directors. The business soon gave up banking and assumed the nature of an investment trust, investing in government securities. As such it survived until the end of the eighteenth century.

Records 1: Public Record Office, Ruskin Avenue, Kew, Richmond TW9 4DU

General meeting orders 1695–96; lists of subscribers 1695–1700; cash ledgers (8) 1696–1720; 1727–78; dividend books (11) 1701–96; ledgers 1709–16; general expenses books 1709–96; cash books (3) 1725–98; sub-committee minute books (12) 1718–98; 'annuities remaining' 1732; 'names of proprietors' 1732–34; stock transferred account books (2) 1734–96; secretary's cash book 1748–96; receipt book 1748–96; rough journal 1786–98; journal 1796–98; miscellaneous papers including specimen dividend warrants, directors' affidavits, etc, n.d. [Ref: C114/9–23, 153.]

Records 2: Hertfordshire County Record Office, County Hall, Hertford SG13 8DE

Orders of directors and correspondence 1696–1712; act for dissolution of partnership 1796. [Ref: D/ELW.B10; 40112–14]

Records of banks

383

Records 3: Barclays Bank plc, Group Archives, Dallimore Road, Wythenshawe, Manchester M23 9JA

Papers 1695–1793.

MILLS, BAWTREE, DAWNAY, CURZON & CO
Colchester, Essex

History: This private bank traced its origins to John Mills, a tea dealer originally from London who settled in Colchester in 1766 and later married the daughter of Thomas Twining, founder of the eponymous tea merchants. He set up in banking by 1774 and in 1787 took into partnership two Twining cousins when the title of his business was changed to Twining & Mills. From 1797 to 1800 the bank was known as J R & J Mills and in 1799 an office was opened at Hadleigh. From 1800 the business traded as Mills, Bawtree & Co and subsequently traded under several names including Mills, Nunn, Bawtree & Nunn by 1832; Mills, Bawtree, Errington, Bawtree & Grimwade by 1844; and Mills, Bawtree, Dawnay, Curzon & Co in 1883. Additional branches were opened at Witham (1839), Clacton (1880), Kelvedon (1883) and Walton on the Naze (1889). The bank failed in 1891 when different constituents of the Gurney group of East Anglian banks acquired the business of different branches. The Colchester business became known as Gurneys, Round, Green, Hoare & Co.

Harold Preston, *Early East Anglian Banks and Bankers* (Thetford, 1994)

Records 1: Barclays Bank plc, Group Archives, Dallimore Road, Wythenshawe, Manchester M23 9JA

Bank note 1884; passbook 1885–91; cheque and cheque book 1889–91; press cuttings re failure 1891–92.

Records 2: Essex Record Office, Stanwell House, Stanwell Street, Colchester CO2 7DL

assignment of John Mills's partnership share 1821; deed of indemnity re note issue 1884; deed of security re partnership 1890. [Ref: D/DE1 F47, B36; D/DHt B10]

MINET, FECTOR & CO
Dover, Kent

History: This private bank was established in 1700 as Fector & Minet; it was otherwise known as Dover Old Bank. It was acquired by the National Provincial Bank of England (est. 1833) in 1841.

L A M Sencicle, *Banking in Dover* (priv. pub., 1993)

384   *British banking – a guide to historical records*

Records 1: The Royal Bank of Scotland plc, Archive Section, Regent's House, 42 Islington High Street, London N1 8XL

Extracts from I Minet's letterbook 1737–38; balances of notes issued 1777–79; balance sheet 1821; amalgamation papers 1842.

Records 2: Lincolnshire Archives, St Rumbold Street, Lincoln LN2 5AB

Partner's will 1806; papers re partnership matters 1814–42; partner's private diary 1821–27. [Ref: Jarvis V/E passim; Jarvis V/B 7, 9–10; Jarvis V/AS, 11.1–10]

MOGER, SON & JONES
Bath, Avon

History: This private bank was established in 1815 as Dore, Smith, Moger & Evans; it was otherwise known as Bath City Bank. It was styled Smith, Moger & Evans from 1822, Moger & Sons from 1834 and subsequently Moger, Sons & Jones. The bank amalgamated with Prescott, Dimsdale, Cave, Tugwell & Co Ltd (est. 1766) of London in 1891.

Anon, 'Prescott's Bank', *National Provincial Bank Review* (1966–68)

Records: The Royal Bank of Scotland plc, Archive Section, Regent's House, 42 Islington High Street, London N1 8XL

Amalgamation agreement 1891.

J L MOILLIET & SONS
Birmingham, West Midlands

History: This private bank was formed in 1766 by Robert Coales, merchant and sword cutler, at Bartholomew Road, Birmingham; it was Birmingham's second bank. In 1815 Jean Louis Moilliet, a Swiss merchant, was admitted as a partner and at some stage the business became known as Moilliet, Smith, Pearson & Moilliet. From 1840 it was known as J L Moilliet & Sons and was otherwise styled the Birmingham & Warwickshire Bank. In 1865 Moilliets merged with Lloyds & Co (est. 1765), their combined business being converted into a joint stock company with limited liability under the title of Lloyds Banking Co Ltd (est. 1765). When acquired, Moilliets was one-quarter the size of Lloyds which paid £25,000 for the bank's goodwill.

Records: Lloyds TSB Group plc, Archives, Head Office, 71 Lombard Street, London EC3P 3BS

Birmingham, Colmore Row: signature book 1858–65.

MOLINEUX & CO
Lewes, East Sussex

History: This private bank was formed in 1789 as Whitfield, Comber, Molineux & King; it was otherwise known as Lewes New Bank until the failure of Thomas Harben's Lewes Bank in 1793 when it was renamed Lewes Old Bank. The partners were Francis Whitfield, grocer and general provisions dealer, Joseph Molineux, ironmonger, Richard King, tallow chandler and soap maker, and Benjamin Comber, gentleman; they may have advanced funds to wool dealers and farmers for many years before establishing their bank. The bank traded as Whitfield & Molineux from 1806, as Molineux, Hurley, Whitfield & Dicker from 1819, as Hurley, Molineux, Whitfield & Dicker from 1823, as Molineux, Whitfield, Dicker & Molineux from 1842, as Molineux, Whitfield, Dicker & Co from 1853, as Molineux, Whitfield & Co from 1855, as Whitfield, Molineux & Whitfield from 1860, as Whitfield, Molineux, Whitfield & Molineux from 1871, as Molineux, Whitfield & Whitfield from 1886 and as Molineux & Co from 1892. The bank opened branches in Tunbridge Wells (1822), Eastbourne (1854), Battle (1857), Uckfield (1870) and East Grinstead (1887). By 1891 it had capital of £100,000 and deposits of almost £1 million. During the 1890s branches were opened in Newhaven, Brighton, Hailsham, Seaford and Heathfield. In 1896 it was one of twenty banks that merged to form Barclay & Co Ltd.

P W Matthews & Anthony W Tuke, *History of Barclays Bank Ltd* (London, 1926)

Records: Barclays Bank plc, Group Archives, Dallimore Road, Wythenshawe, Manchester M23 9JA

Cash book 1745–1820; general balances ledgers (2) 1781–95, 1875–91; waste book 1788–92; partnership agreement 1789–1883; private accounts ledgers (9) 1789–1924; passbooks 1789–1801; partner's undertaking 1790; bank note registers (5) 1811–86; petty accounts ledgers (9) 1813–73; bank notes 1814–84; cheques, cheque forms and drafts 1820–1901; cash book ledger 1821–26; declaration of confidence 1825–26; partnership papers 1832–96; interest ledgers 1836–81; bills of exchange 1845–71; dividend ledgers 1858–75; powers of attorney registers (2) 1861–95; agency ledger 1865–69; discounts book 1866–75; partnership property papers 1878–96; security ledgers (2) 1888–91; balance sheets 1891–95; signature books 1891–94; disbursement ledgers 1891–95; private journal 1891–94; ledger, Barclay & Co account 1894–98; amalgamation papers, Barclay & Co 1896–97.

386 British banking – a guide to historical records

MONMOUTHSHIRE & GLAMORGANSHIRE BANKING CO
Newport, Gwent

History: This joint stock bank was formed in 1836 out of the business of the private bankers, Jones & Davis (est. 1813) of Monmouth. It subsequently acquired the private banks of Towgood & Co (est. 1819) of Cardiff in 1836, Hills, Osborne & Co (est. c.1800) of Abergavenny in 1837 and Jones & Blewitt of Chepstow in 1844. In 1843 the Towgood business reverted to a private bank. The joint stock bank failed in 1851.

Records: Gwent Record Office, County Hall, Cwmbran NP44 2XH

Passbook 1840–47; legal papers 1842, 1850; overdraft security 1848; letters re staff salary 1849–50; directors' report 1851; agreement for payment of creditors 1851; legal opinion re debts of Coalbrookdale Iron Co 1856. [Ref: D43.545, 6396,7346; D454.507; D982.70–1, 123; D396.148, 154]

MOORE & ROBINSON'S NOTTINGHAMSHIRE BANKING CO LTD
Nottingham, Nottinghamshire

History: This joint stock bank traced its origins to the private bank of Moore, Maltby, Evans & Middlemore, established in 1802. In 1815 it was reconstituted as Moore, Maltby & Robinson and in 1836 was converted into a joint stock bank, Moore & Robinson's Nottinghamshire Banking Co under the management of Thomas Moore and Frederick Robinson. Limited liability was acquired in 1866. In 1895 the private bank of Arkwright & Co (est. 1780) of Wirksworth was acquired. The bank was acquired by the Capital & Counties Bank Ltd (est. 1877) in 1901; it then had two branches.

Records: Lloyds TSB Group plc, Archives, Head Office, 71 Lombard Street, London EC3P 3BS

Deed of settlement 1836; general meeting minute books (3) 1837–1901; committee minute book 1878–79; directors' meeting minute book 1892–1901; amalgamation papers 1901, 1920.

Nottingham: memorandum books (4) 1891–1903; **Wirksworth:** security registers (2) 1889–1901.

MORGAN GRENFELL GROUP
London

History: This merchant bank traced its origins to 1838 when the United States merchant, George Peabody, set up in business in London. He was a

Records of banks 387

partner in the United States merchant house of Peabody, Riggs & Co of Baltimore and in London he undertook a general merchanting business. In about 1845 he severed his connection with Peabody Riggs and in 1851 set up George Peabody & Co, whose functions were to deal in United States securities, to provide acceptance finance and to act as merchants. Most of its business was connected with North America. In 1854 Junius S Morgan became a partner and had full control by 1859. Peabody, who by now was reckoned the leading American merchant in London, withdrew in 1864. He became well known for his philanthropy, notably the building of model homes for London's poor. Morgan, whose London house was now known as J S Morgan & Co, strengthened his United States connections when his son, J Pierpont Morgan, established a New York house. In 1873 this house became linked with the leading New York, Philadelphia and Paris houses of Drexel & Co. In 1866 the London house brought out its first bond issue, for Chile, and its marketing of a bond issue for France at the time of the Franco-Prussian War underlined its status as a major London house. In the 1870s and 1880s a strong position in finance of the United States and Argentine governments was also developed, but most issuing work was for overseas businesses, especially railways. In 1890 Junius Morgan died and Anthony Drexel's death followed in 1893. The Morgan houses now came under the unchallenged leadership of Pierpont [J P] Morgan and the New York house, known as Morgan, Drexel & Co, was renamed J P Morgan & Co. In 1910 the London business was re-named Morgan Grenfell & Co following the admission of Edward Grenfell in 1904. From the 1890s the New York house was clearly the most power-ful and this was underlined during the First World War. Now the New York house played a vital role in financing Britain's war effort and in acting as New York financial and purchasing agents of the British govern-ment; the London house fulfilled an important liaison role. In 1917 the businesses of Andrew Yule & Co Ltd of India and George Yule & Co of London, Indian merchants and bankers, were acquired and in the same year Morgan Grenfell was registered as a private unlimited company. Between the wars Morgans rebuilt its acceptance finance business and, given the difficulties of making sterling bond issues for overseas borrow-ers, issued securities for British businesses for the first time. The first transactions, undertaken in 1927, were for Debenhams Ltd and Anglo-American Oil Co Ltd. General corporate finance work was also undertaken, much relating to industrial rationalisation and for United States companies wishing to expand in Europe, for example for General Motors in its acqui-sition of Vauxhall Motors. In the 1920s both the New York and London businesses were active in bond issues to finance monetary and physical reconstruction in Europe and during the 1931 sterling crisis they played a vital role in financing British government needs. In 1934 the business was

388 *British banking – a guide to historical records*

reorganised as a limited liability company with the formation of Morgan Grenfell & Co Ltd. Now it was legally separated from New York, but the business links remained strong. The private finance house of Cull & Co (est. 1921) was acquired in 1944. In the 1950s the bank was particularly involved in steel industry denationalisation. From the 1960s it developed around the core functions of corporate finance, banking and investment management. Morgan Grenfell Holdings Ltd was formed in 1971 to act as the holding company for the Morgan Grenfell Group. In the 1970s international expansion was renewed and by the early 1980s Morgans was well established in Europe, in the Near and Far East, and in North and South America. In 1981 J P Morgan & Co of New York disposed of its large shareholding which finally severed the London-New York connection, although by then Morgan Grenfell had acted independently for many years. As part of the bank's adjustment to reorganisation of the London securities markets in the mid 1980s, the jobbers Pinchin & Denny and the brokers Pember & Boyle were acquired. The bank converted to a public company, Morgan Grenfell Group plc, in 1986. In 1989 it was acquired by Deutsche Bank which had been a significant shareholder since the early 1980s. Many of its businesses thereafter functioned under the Deutsche Morgan Grenfell title and later the name was largely given up.

Anon, *George Peabody & Co, J S Morgan & Co, Morgan Grenfell & Co, Morgan Grenfell & Co Ltd 1838–1958* (priv. pub., 1958); Kathleen Burk, *Morgan Grenfell 1838–1988.The Biography of a Merchant Bank* (Oxford, 1989); Vincent P Carosso, *The Morgans. Private International Bankers 1854–1913* (Cambridge, Mass., 1987); Manfred Pohl & Sabine Freitag (eds.), *Handbook on the History of European Banks* (Aldershot, 1994);Jean Strouse, *Morgan. American Financier* (New York and London, 1999)

Records: Guildhall Library, Aldermanbury, London EC2P 2EJ

House correspondence: partnership, family, etc, matters 1836 on, North America 1853 on, England 1853 on, China, Japan, etc 1856 on, company statements, prospectuses, etc 1856 on, reports on business houses 1857 on, Latin America 1864 on, Europe c.1869 on, India 1883 on; legal documents including wills, powers of attorney, etc 1840–1900; general ledgers (7) 1854–68; miscellaneous accounts 1854–83; journals (2) 1855–56; private ledgers (2) 1857–77; overseas bond ledger 1862–65; cash book 1863–77; private ledgers (13) 1864–1923; general ledgers (54) 1864–1909; cash book 1864–66; 'domestic' out-letterbook 1864–65; stock ledgers (8) 1864–1909; current account ledgers (3) 1864–67; 'American securities' registers (9) 1864–1903; income tax commissioners account books (5) 1865–1909; prospectuses issued (3) 1865–1914; travellers' credit books (46) 1866–1908; private out-letterbooks (16) 1867–1910; general credit

Records of banks 389

ledgers (23) 1866–1912; 'prospectus books', being prospectuses issued by other houses (8) 1866–1937; 'credit ledgers' being registers of credits granted (22) 1868–1903, 1910–23; iron accounts journal 1868–73; iron contracts books (2) 1868–73; 'joint iron accounts' with J S Morgan 1868–70; 'banking credit ledgers' being registers of credits granted (2) 1869–88; out-letterbooks (8) 1870–71; 'joint exchange accounts' with Drexel Morgan, later J P Morgan, New York (20) 1871–97, 1910–21; 'joint exchange accounts' with Drexel & Co, Philadelphia (31) 1872–1919; 'sundry accounts' with Drexel Morgan, New York (9) 1873–96; private telegram books (13) 1873–1909; 'sterling loans' registers (2) 1873–99 [w]; 'old balances' ledger 1874–1908; 'advertisements of dividends etc' 1874–94; 'extracts of credits' being a summary of the business 1875–77; sundry accounts ledgers (16) 1875–1911; insurance policies 1881–82; customer security registers (5) 1875–1909; signature books (4) 1879–1923; specimen forms and notices (4) 1884–1948; lists of 1886, 1900 and 1910 investments (7) 1886–1923; Argentine government loans ledger 1891–1909; exchange accounts with J C Rogers, Boston (4) 1892–1900; 'sundry accounts' with J P Morgan, New York (7) 1895–1909; 'joint exchange accounts' with J P Morgan, New York (4) 1897–1903; papers re security transactions of individual partners 1885–1931; in-letters to J P Morgan 1898–1900; specimen bond and scrip certificates (3) 1891–1937; 'continental telegrams' sent to Europe 1900–01; E C Grenfell's 'extracts of correspondence' book 1900–36; C Dawkins's out-letterbooks (3) 1900–05; summary balance sheets 1900–16; out-letterbook of J P Morgan 1901; Sovereign Bank of Canada amalgamated interest account books (2) 1902–08; taxation, including excess profit duty, papers 1903–42; travelling credit ledgers containing accounts with Morgan US houses (4) 1909–17; 'current account ledger, sundry accounts' (2) 1909, 1911 [w]; papers re change in corporate status 1910–58; balance sheets and profit and loss accounts 1910–41; accounts of London house sent to New York house 1909–41; monthly summary balance sheets (3) 1910–39; private ledgers (9) 1910–36; general ledgers (9) 1910–18; 'stocks ledger' 1910–11; 'Argentine ledger' 1910–11; credits issued by Morgan London and USA houses book 1910–46; 'banking accounts' being accounts with other banks (2) 1910–11; accounts with Morgan, Harjes & Co (5) 1911–20; 'special exchange accounts' (2) 1911–17; joint sola bill account with Drexel & Co (3) 1911–20; 'commercial credits' books (2) 1912–20; 'general account ledgers, deposit accounts' (2) 1912–22; stock valuation sheets listing investments 1913–27; 'sundry statements re advance accounts' 1913–24; press cuttings book 1914–43; papers re contracts, procedures, financing, etc in connection with work as North American purchasing agents of British government 1914–19; 'supply cables' being cables exchanged between London and New York houses re munition purchases (78) 1915–18; 'general account

390 British banking – a guide to historical records

ledger, advance accounts' 1916–22; 'sundry client accounts' (4) 1916–20; memorandum and articles of association 1917; directors' meeting minute book 1918–34; papers re profit and loss and other general accounts 1923–41; private journal 1924–39; papers, including agenda, minutes, working papers, pamphlets, etc, re work of Transfer Committee formed to facilitate German reparations 1928–30; draft monthly balances of general accounts 1929–41; current and investment accounts of individuals including investors (5) 1933–43; papers re acquisition of Cull & Co 1943–44. [Ref: MS 21760–21803, 28174–28306]

MORRIS PREVOST & CO
London

History: This private bank traced its origins to 1765 and the formation of Zachary, Long & Haldimand, merchants dealing in Italian silks. It was renamed Long & Haldimand in 1766 and was discontinued in 1769. A F Haldimand then worked on his own account until 1806 when he was joined by his sons in A F Haldimand & Sons. Notable transactions at this time included bond issues for Spain and financing development of London's Belgravia. Haldimand's daughters married into the Morris and Prevost families and soon these provided partners. A L Prevost had established his merchant business in London in about 1808; in 1816 it was known as Prevost, Morris & Co and in 1818 as Morris, Prevost & Co. In 1827 A F Haldimand & Sons was liquidated and its business transferred to Morris Prevost. In the same year the Prevost family took an interest in the Liverpool house of Melly & Co, which became known as Melly, Prevost & Co, and from 1829 until 1834 a connection with the Manchester business of Martin & Hartwright also existed. The Liverpool connection diminished in the 1840s. Members of Morris Prevost exercised considerable influence in the City, with several partners being directors (one a Governor) of the Bank of England and of railway companies. Its partners also maintained close links with Switzerland; several had Swiss nationality. At least towards the end of its existence, the firm's business was focused upon the custody of securities for private clients and private banks, many of them based in continental Europe. In 1900 income from commissions and deposits totalled £5,000 and grew steadily to almost £8,000 by 1912. In 1914 the business was purchased by Baring Brothers (est. 1762). Following this, one of its partners entered the partnership of G Pictet & Co of Geneva, private bankers.

Augustus Prevost, *History of Morris Prevost & Co* (priv. pub.,1904)

Records: The Baring Archive, ING Baring Holdings Ltd, 60 London Wall, London EC2M 5TQ

Records of banks **391**

Customer ledgers (6) 1906–14; Barings' acquisition papers, including an accountant's report, 1912. [Ref: 101128–101133; PF 313]

JOHN MORTLOCK & CO LTD
Cambridge, Cambridgeshire

History: This private bank was established by John Mortlock, a cloth merchant, in 1754; his family was to become one of the most powerful in Cambridge. The bank was known as John Mortlock & Sons until 1889 and it also traded as the Cambridge Bank. Branches were opened at Bishop's Stortford (1814 to 1839), Littleport (1816), Royston (1823 to 1827), Saffron Walden (1823) and Ely (1830). In 1868 it acquired Fisher & Son (est. c.1790) of Cambridge. In 1889 limited liability was acquired when the name was changed to John Mortlock & Co Ltd. The bank was of major local importance and it was one of twenty leading banks which merged in 1896 to form Barclay & Co Ltd.

P W Matthews & Anthony W Tuke, *History of Barclays Bank Ltd* (London, 1926); Harold Preston, *Early East Anglian Banks and Bankers* (Thetford, 1994)

Records 1: Barclays Bank plc, Group Archives, Dallimore Road, Wythenshawe, Manchester M23 9JA

Property deeds 1784; bank notes 1791, 1878–82, 1840; credit advice 1839; passbook 1846–58; private account ledgers (3) 1855–1901; cheques 1864–65; cheque form 1869; cheque book 1886–87; directors' meeting agenda books 1889–95; directors' meeting minute books 1889–1901; share certificates 1889–96; share and share transfer ledgers 1889–96; seal book 1892–94; draft form 1896; papers re merger with Barclay & Co, including accounts and deeds schedule 1896–97.

Bishop's Stortford: current account ledgers 1791–1810; **Ely:** customer status journal 1849–53; security registers 1856–71.

Records 2: County Record Office, Shire Hall, Cambridge CB3 0AP

Partners' ledgers 1820–56; balance books 1821, 1842–58, 1866–67; profit and loss ledgers 1791–1828; balance sheets 1793–97; cash books 1776–1819; partnership papers 1805–88; title deeds 1805–77; Cambridge balance sheets 1807–15; bank notes 1807–15; Cambridge and Ely note register 1812–55; letterbooks 1816–20; in-letters 1816–89; weekly account books 1826–28, 1834–38; letters from Ely 1852–57; banker's licences 1859–84; receipts for investments in Cambridge Savings Bank 1863–74; miscellaneous papers and correspondence 1799–1885; Mortlock family and estate papers eighteenth to twentieth cents.

392 *British banking – a guide to historical records*

Bishop's Stortford: balance sheets 1813–26; **Ely:** balance sheets 1810–26; **Royston:** ledger 1825; **Saffron Walden:** balance sheets 1819–25.

NATAL BANK LTD
Africa

History: This bank was formed as Natal Bank in 1854 at Pietermaritzburg, Natal, in southern Africa, and was locally incorporated in 1859. The initial subscribed capital was £20,000. Soon after formation, a branch was opened at Durban but no others followed until 1880. The major customer was the government of Natal. The bank issued its own notes. The business was reconstructed in 1888 when its name was changed to The Natal Bank Ltd. Rapid growth ensued with subscribed capital rising from £163,500 in 1888 to almost £1.74 million in 1902. In 1914 the bank was acquired by the National Bank of South Africa Ltd (est. 1890). It then had thirty-eight branches and agencies, all but one of which was in Natal or the Transvaal.

Anon, *A Banking Centenary. Barclays Bank (Dominion, Colonial & Overseas) 1836–1936* (priv. pub., 1938)

Records: Barclays Bank plc, Group Archives, Dallimore Road, Wythenshawe, Manchester M23 9JA

London committee minute books (4) 1890–1914; sale of business agreement 1914.

NATIONAL BANK LTD
London and Europe

History: This joint stock bank was established in 1835 as the National Bank of Ireland by a group of Members of Parliament and other gentlemen frustrated by the exclusivity of the Bank of Ireland and English orientation of the Provincial Bank of Ireland, the principal existing banks. The founders aimed to form a bank to provide capital for Irish economic development and to serve the needs of small traders and tenant farmers, as well as those of the gentry. The bank's head office was located, at 39 Old Broad Street, London, and although the majority of backers were English, the banking business was initially carried on entirely in Ireland. Lamie Murray, manager of the bank, modelled the organisation on the Provincial Bank of Ireland – a joint stock bank with branches operating as subsidiary companies, the shares being held partly by the parent bank and partly by local people. By late 1835, the bank had opened eleven branches and eighteen sub-branches, issued its own notes and made an unsuccessful attempt to establish a subsidiary company in Belfast under the title of the Belfast National Bank of Ireland. In 1837, owing to administrative prob-

Records of banks 393

lems, the principle of the semi-autonomous branch was abandoned and the capital consolidated. In 1845 the Irish Banking Act ended the Bank of Ireland's monopoly in and around Dublin and a chief office of the National Bank in Ireland was immediately opened at 34–35 College Green. In 1847 National Bank of Ireland absorbed the London & Dublin Bank (est. 1843), regaining a number of branches which it had established in 1837 and had to dispose of because of their proximity to Dublin. In 1854 the bank opened its first branch in England at 13 Old Broad Street, London. In 1856, the bank's name was changed from National Bank of Ireland to The National Bank and, in 1859, it was invited to join the London Clearing House. The expansion of the London business continued and by 1888 the bank was the eighth largest British bank in terms of authorised and issued capital; only four other banks had more branches in London. This growth was sustained with over sixty further branches being opened between 1888 and 1922. After the First World War the board, preoccupied with warding off take-over bids and coping with problems caused by the political and economic situation in Ireland, began to consolidate. In 1922, when a parliament was re-established in Dublin, the bank formed an Irish board to manage the larger Irish side of the business. The bank's problems were compounded by the general economic recession of the 1920s and 1930s and by the effects of the Second World War. During the 1950s and 1960s, the expansion of the Irish economy provided much business for the bank but by the mid 1960s it was apparent that it was no longer appropriate for such an important Irish bank to be controlled from London and operate as a member of the London Clearing. In 1966 the bank's business in Ireland was transferred to a new company, National Bank of Ireland, and sold to Bank of Ireland, whilst the English and Welsh branches passed to National Commercial Bank of Scotland Ltd (est. 1959), although they continued to operate independently as The National Bank Ltd until 1970.

Matthew Slattery, *The National Bank 1835–1970* (priv. pub., 1972); William Howarth, *The Banks in the Clearing House* (London, 1905)

Records: The Royal Bank of Scotland plc, Archive Section, Regent's House, Islington High Street, London N1 8XL

Property papers, Old Broad Street 1807–1934; share ledgers 1834–41, 1920–23; agenda books 1834–36; rough board minute books 1834–37; allotment letters 1834–35; share certificates 1834–67; deeds of settlement 1835–1917; court minute books 1835–1958; dividend warrants 1835–67; balance sheets and profit and loss accounts 1835–1969; papers of Thomas Lamie Murray 1835–53; annual and special general meeting minute books 1836–81, 1916–39; agenda books 1836–84, 1921–66; shareholder lists

394 *British banking – a guide to historical records*

1836, 1910–20; customer opinion book 1836–50; register of correspondence 1836–42; directors' annual reports 1836–69; inspector's reports 1837–41, 1850–57; staff register c.1837–1900; press cuttings 1838–39, 1870–1911; general orders and instruction books 1840, 1857–1941; property insurance policies 1840, 1907–53; special committee minute book 1841–44; London and Dublin committee rough minute book 1843–56; papers re construction of premises, College Green, Dublin 1843; head office general ledgers 1845–1970; general committee agenda book 1846–48; papers re acquisition of London & Dublin Bank 1847; branch weekly balance ledger 1850–60; correspondence with bank solicitor 1851–53; legal papers 1853–77; signature book 1854–1900; declarations of trust 1854–56; property title deed, Pimlico 1858–64; papers re Joseph Neale McKenna 1859–77; bank premises ledgers 1859–1970; biannual reports and accounts 1859–1956; fidelity bond registers 1860–1900; memorandum book c.1860–71; shareholder circulars 1860–69, 1881, 1894, 1961–65; lists of branches 1862–1904; papers re National Bank of Liverpool 1863–71; staff character books c.1863–1900; bank note register 1864–66; cheques 1864–71; chief accountant's files 1869–1966; share transfer deeds c.1860s; biannual ledger balances sheets 1872–1928; customer indemnities 1874, 1883–98; proprietors' meetings proceedings 1877–1965; officer address books 1876–1900; instructions for note issue department 1876, 1885; procedural instructions 1876–1970; bank note specimens and forgeries 1877, 1919–1930s; share transfer instructions 1881–1925; cancelled note register 1882–1929; attendance book, country office clerks 1881–82; register of officials c.1887–1900; London office manager's letterbook 1887–1935; stock purchase journal 1888–1946; staff salary ledger 1892–99; banker's licences 1896–1965; annual general meeting attendance books 1900–66; registers of directors 1901–50; registrar's letterbook 1909–17; branch inspector's instructions 1914, 1919; directors' fees book 1917–41; Dublin court minute books 1917–66; Dublin daily committee minutes 1917–18, 1950–68; branch photographs c.1910s–70; secretary's correspondence re sub-offices 1921–44; papers re possible purchase of Cattle Trade Bank 1922–23; memorandum and articles of association c.1923–68; note issue department account books 1925–40; seal books 1927–70; correspondence re scheme to advertise on wage packets 1929–32; departmental correspondence registers 1929–70; papers re coat-of arms 1929–71; note issue department accounts 1929–67; shareholders' registers c.1920s–60; half-yearly branch reports 1933–62; manager's room statistics books 1939–56; London firewatch registers 1942–45; secretary's correspondence register 1943–70; circulation books, Bank of England 1944–60; certificates of incorporation 1946, 1965; balance sheet analysis books 1947–67; register of directors' interests 1948–66; seal register 1948–70; papers re bank history 1950–75; attendance books 1954–70; papers of Lord Pakenham

Records of banks **395**

1956–60; press cuttings book re customers 1959–58; advertising booklets c.1950s; profit and loss ledger 1960–64, note circulation book 1960–67; review committee minutes 1962–69; papers re sale of part of bank to National Bank of Ireland 1965–66; annual and extraordinary general meeting minute book 1966–70; branch returns re late opening 1969–70.

Clonmell: rough general meeting minute book 1835–53; **London, Baker Street:** correspondence re branch opening 1898–1901; **London, Bayswater:** signature book 1862–66; **London, Camden Town:** staff salaries ledger 1872–75; **London, Grosvenor Gardens:** signature books 1864–1900; general order books 1926–61; press cuttings book 1960; **London, Islington:** security books 1894–1900; **London, Kings Cross:** papers re stock purchases for customers 1857–66, 1874–82; papers re properties mortgaged to the bank 1859, 1873–81; signature book 1868–80; managers' drafts book 1868–1900; bad debts book 1869; security books 1870–97; bank dividend warrants 1875; manager's correspondence 1876–90; papers re customer bankruptcies 1877–79, 1872–89; manager's letterbook 1877–1928; customer indemnities to the bank 1878–94; **London, Notting Hill Gate:** signature books 1868–1900; head office correspondence 1881–1900; general orders book 1924–60; circulars 1963–68; **London, Strand:** signature book 1897–1900; head office special letterbooks 1897–1900; general orders guardbook 1955–61.

NATIONAL BANK OF LIVERPOOL LTD
Liverpool, Merseyside

History: This bank was established with limited liability in 1863 with a nominal capital of £1 million divided into 10,000 shares of £100 each, largely subscribed by shareholders resident in Ireland. It opened for business in 1863 and performed strongly from the outset; by late 1863 deposits totalled £480,000. The company's capital was increased to £3 million in 1864, but the bank's growth was checked by the financial panic of 1866 and losses in subsequent years. It opened at least four branches – at Birkenhead, Bootle, Liverpool and Waterloo. Paid-up capital in 1870 was £449,000. The bank was acquired by Parr's Banking Co Ltd (est. 1865) in 1883.

T E Gregory, *The Westminster Bank Through A Century* (London, 1936)

Records: The Royal Bank of Scotland plc, Archive Section, Regent's House, 42 Islington High Street, London N1 8XL

Minutes of promoters' meetings 1863–66; articles of association 1863–69; daily committee minutes 1864–65; annual report 1870; amalgamation papers 1883–84.

NATIONAL BANK OF SCOTLAND LTD
Edinburgh, Lothian

History: This bank was established in 1825 with an authorised capital of £5 million and, at the time, attracted more shareholders than any other bank in Britain. It opened thirteen branches in its first year, began to circulate notes through the offices of its provincial shareholders and acquired head office premises in St Andrew Square, Edinburgh. In 1831 a Royal Charter was received and expansion continued through acquisition of the Aberdeen Commercial Banking Co (est. 1778) in 1833 and the Perth Union Banking Co (est. 1810) in 1836. In 1843 a bid to take over the Glasgow & Ship Bank (est. 1836) failed leading the bank to open its own Glasgow office later that year. In 1844 it acquired the Bank of Glasgow (est. 1843). In 1864 the bank was the first in Scotland to open a London office where it issued notes, accepted deposits by offering attractive rates of interest and offered foreign services. In 1882 limited liability was acquired and from 1881until the outbreak of the First World War, in terms of liabilities, deposits and advances, National Bank was in Scotland ranked second to the Bank of Scotland. In 1918 National Bank was acquired by Lloyds Bank Ltd (est. 1765), building on an existing foreign exchange connection. Both banks continued to trade as separate entities. A new head office building, commissioned in 1936, was opened in St Andrew Square in 1947. In 1946 the bank pioneered mobile banking services in Britain on the Isle of Lewis. In 1959 Lloyds Bank encouraged the merger of Commercial Bank of Scotland Ltd (est. 1810) with National Bank, accepting in return a major interest in the new bank which was named National Commercial Bank of Scotland Ltd.

Anon, *The National Bank of Scotland. A Short History of the Bank* (priv. pub., 1947); Anon, *The National Bank of Scotland Centenary* (priv. pub., 1925); 'Consolidation and Expansion. Troubled Times. New Beginnings', *Three Banks Review*, 94–96 (1972)

Records 1: The Royal Bank of Scotland plc, Archive Section, 36 St Andrew Square, Edinburgh EH2 2YB

Directors' meeting minutes 1825–1959; stock journals 1825–46; stock ledgers 1825–1918; agencies register 1825–1959; heritable property ledgers 1825–1959; general ledgers 1825–1959; general ledger journals 1825–1959; lists of head office officials 1825–1900; agencies register 1825–1959; bank note registers 1825–57; bank notes 1825–1957; annual reports 1826–40, 1946, 1957; statement of losses books 1826–1904; debt ledgers 1827–49, 1892–1900; balance statements 1828–58; signature book 1831–45; premises register 1833–1950; salary registers 1843–65; Glasgow office drawings 1849; consignation receipt books 1850–1900; widows'

Records of banks
397

and orphans' fund letterbook 1850–82; annuity fund: fees book 1851–96, cash book 1851–1931, ledgers 1851–99, list of contributors 1851–1900, account books 1875–96, leavers book 1896–1931, membership books 1898–1941; branch inspection reports 1857–64; architectural drawings 1863–1959; branch photographs 1864–1959; staff photographs 1866, 1905–50s; officers' guarantee fund: letterbook 1871–94, rules and accounts abstract 1919–38; balance papers: annual 1874–1957, half-yearly 1937–50; income tax account books 1878–1940; circulars 1883–1945; bank note specimen album 1883–95; reports on London and Glasgow offices 1885–1900; Glasgow officers meeting papers 1888–1951; correspondence re Perth site 1893; memorandum re bank investment 1895; statement of interest books 1900–40; head office charges book 1903–31; foreign credits book 1906–44; press cuttings book 1908–51; statement of losses 1911–56; agency houses and furniture books 1914–64; board agenda books 1918–55; chief accountant's letterbooks 1923–38, 1946–47; staff magazine, *The Teller* 1929–59; foreign bank agency files 1933–47; correspondence re mechanisation 1931–59; branch profit and loss sheets 1934–59; property day book 1938–50; cash book sheets 1938–40; committee register 1938–59; rent accounts statement 1939–47; committee book 1941; progressive ledger 1941–46; expenditure accounts book 1946–59; property expenditure ledger 1955–59; branch statements 1956–58; valuation and rating book 1957–59; mobile bank advisory video 1957; rent book 1957; property valuations 1958.

Airdrie: deposit receipt book 1835–1900; **Castle Douglas:** abstract of transactions 1826–28; staff photographs 1915–32; **Dundee, Reform Street:** staff book 1893–1900; salary books 1898–1900; **Edinburgh, Leith:** progressive deposit account ledger 1825–27; progressive cash account ledger 1830–31; customer reference book 1876–1900; manager's notebook re customers and staff 1891–1900; **Edinburgh, Palmerston Place:** inventories and correspondence re fixtures and fittings c.1936–64; **Lerwick:** scroll cash book 1866–68; **London, Nicholas Lane:** deposit ledger 1889–87; rates of interest books 1862–1900; **Pittenweem:** branch ledgers 1899–1900.

Records 2: Lloyds TSB Group plc, Archives, Head Office, 71 Lombard Street, London EC3P 3BS

Papers re amalgamation 1912–19.

Records 3: Business Records Centre, Archive Department, University of Glasgow, Glasgow G12 8QQ

Directors' meeting minutes and annual report extracts 1825–1920; balance sheets 1865–1958; secret letterbook extracts 1825–26. [Ref: Scottish Banking Collection]

398 *British banking – a guide to historical records*

Records 4: National Archives of Scotland, HM General Register House, Princes Street, Edinburgh EH1 3YY

Dingwall: statements and vouchers 1835–37. [Ref: GD46/1/625]

NATIONAL BANK OF SOUTH AFRICA LTD
Africa

History: This bank was established in 1890 as De Nationale Bank der Zuid Afrikaansche Republic Beperkt under the terms of a concession granted to Dutch and German interests by the Transvaal government. Certain privileges were granted to the bank, for example the right to issue notes, and in return the bank acted as the national bank, constructing and operating a mint and undertaking to advance to the government to the limit of 25 per cent of its paid-up capital. Initially paid-up capital was £500,000 (of which the government provided £100,000) and rose to £1 million in 1897. The bank opened for business in 1891 and by 1898 there were thirty-seven branches; much of their business involved the finance of gold and, later, diamond mining. Operations were damaged during the Boer War, as most of the bank's activities were based in the Transvaal which was the centre of hostilities. After the war, in 1902, many privileges were given up and links with the government loosened. The bank's title was then changed to the National Bank of South Africa Ltd. In 1910 the National Bank of the Orange River Colony Ltd (forty-three branches) was acquired, followed by the Bank of Africa Ltd (est. 1879) (sixty-four branches) in 1912 and the Natal Bank Ltd (est. 1854) (thirty-eight branches) in 1914. By late 1914, the National Bank had over 200 branches, mostly in South Africa, but a few were in Rhodesia and Portuguese East Africa. During the First World War the bank extended into the former German colonies in South West and East Africa and in 1918 acquired the banking business in Nyasaland, Northern Rhodesia and Portuguese East Africa of the African Lakes Corp. In all, fifty new branches were established during the war period but in 1919 almost 100 new branches opened including one branch each in Mauritius, India, St Helena and Belgium. In 1922 the issue of notes was discontinued. In the early 1920s the bank performed poorly and in 1925 it was acquired by Barclays Bank Ltd (est. 1896) and merged with the Colonial Bank (est. 1836) and the Anglo-Egyptian Bank Ltd (est. 1864) to form Barclays Bank (Dominion, Colonial and Overseas).

Anon, *A Banking Centenary. Barclays Bank (Dominion,Colonial & Overseas) 1836–1936* (priv. pub., 1938)

Records: Barclays Bank plc, Group Archives, Dallimore Road, Wythenshawe, Manchester M23 9JA

Records of banks 399

London committee agenda books (5) 1891–1930; London committee minutes (5) 1891–1913, 1922–34; memorandum and articles of association 1903; amalgamation papers, Bank of Africa 1910–12; London manager out-letterbook 1910–11; annual reports 1910–25; correspondence re diamond shipments 1916–17; South African shareholder lists 1916; London Office Nominees directors' meeting minutes 1922–30; lists of drawers and acceptors of bills, by branch 1924; returns of overdrawn accounts, bills discounted, etc, by branch, 1924; bad and doubtful debts papers, by branch, 1924; amalgamation papers 1924–26; chairman's letters 1925; head office instructions 1925; balance sheet: 1925, branch 1925–26; widows' and orphans' fund journals and ledgers (6) 1928–49.

NATIONAL BANK OF TURKEY
London and Europe

History: This largely British-owned bank, promoted by a small group of London financiers led by Sir Ernest Cassel, was formed at Istanbul by Imperial Ottoman degree in 1909. Its role was to assist in the modernisation of Turkey and was seen by the British government as a means of countering powerful German and French economic influence in the Ottoman Empire. Its paid-up capital was £250,000 and it had a London committee of directors. In the event, it received lukewarm British government support and found competition with the Imperial Ottoman Bank difficult. In 1919 it was acquired by the British Trade Corporation (est. 1917) and was wound up in 1931.

Marion Kent, 'Agent of Empire. The National Bank of Turkey and British Foreign Policy', *Historical Journal,* 18 (1975); David Wainwright, *Henderson. A History of the Life of Alexander Henderson, 1st Lord Faringdon, and of Henderson Administration* (London, 1985)

Records 1: The Baring Archive, ING Baring Holdings Ltd, 60 London Wall, London EC2M 5TQ

Papers re formation, administration and early business 1909–13. [Ref: PF252–4]

Records 2: Guildhall Library, Aldermanbury, London EC2P 2EJ

Papers re formation and connection with Imperial Ottoman Bank 1910–14. [Ref: MS 24013–24017]

NATIONAL BANK OF WALES LTD
Manchester, Greater Manchester, later Aberdare and later Cardiff, Mid Glamorgan

400   *British banking – a guide to historical records*

History: This joint stock bank was formed at Manchester in 1879 by Manchester-based promoters but in 1880 moved its head office to Aberdare and then to Cardiff in 1882, when its board was locally recruited. Within a year, six branches were opened followed by another five branches and eleven agencies by 1883. In 1879 paid-up capital was £50,000 and deposits reached £33,000; by 1890 these figures were £225,000 and £1.27 million respectively. In 1890, Pugh, Jones & Co (est. 1848), private bankers of Pwllheli and elsewhere in North Wales, was acquired. In 1893 the bank, by now one of the leading financial institutions in Wales, was acquired by the Metropolitan, Birmingham & South Wales Bank Ltd (est. 1829). Shortly afterwards, accumulated losses of £500,000 were uncovered. It transpired that the bank had been insolvent for many years, caused by mismanagement and fraud, and this resulted in a loss to the Metropolitan Bank of £350,000. Lengthy litigation ensued resulting in the imprisonment of the National Bank's general manager and some directors. The transaction crippled the Metropolitan Bank for over a decade.

W F Crick & J E Wadsworth, *A Hundred Years of Joint Stock Banking* (London, 1936)

Records: HSBC Holdings plc, Group Archives, 10 Lower Thames Street, London EC3R 6AE

Articles of association 1879; balance sheet 1883; annual reports 1891–92; liquidator's agreement and accounts 1893.

NATIONAL COMMERCIAL BANK OF SCOTLAND LTD
Edinburgh, Lothian

History: This bank was formed in 1959 by the merger of Commercial Bank of Scotland Ltd (est. 1810) and National Bank of Scotland Ltd (est. 1825), two large banks headquartered in Edinburgh. The new company, National Commercial Bank of Scotland Ltd, occupied a dominant position in Scottish banking with assets of some £300 million and over 400 branches. It was the first Scottish bank to use electronics for centralised banking and pioneered investment management services in Scottish banking. It introduced a new 'Boat Bank' to serve the Orkney Islands in 1962 and a Ladies Branch, staffed by ladies for ladies, in Edinburgh in 1964. Also in 1964, in response to the growth of competition from the secondary banking sector, National Commercial Bank and J Henry Schroder Wagg & Co Ltd joined forces to provide a modern merchant banking service in Scotland, under the style of National Commercial and Schroders Ltd. In 1966, thirty-six English and Welsh branches of The National Bank Ltd of London and Dublin were acquired. In 1969 the bank merged with The Royal Bank of Scotland (est. 1727).

Records of banks 401

'The National Commercial Bank of Scotland', *Three Banks Review*, 82 (1969); 'Consolidation and Expansion. Troubled Times. New Beginnings', *Three Banks Review*, 94–96 (1972)

Records: The Royal Bank of Scotland plc, Archive Section, 36 St Andrew Square, Edinburgh EH2 2YB

Annual balance books 1958–68; constitution 1959; directors' meeting minutes 1959–69; chairman's committee minutes 1959–67; annual reports 1959–68; general ledgers 1959–69; branch profit and loss 1959–63; traveller's cheques instructions book 1959; list of branches 1959–69; circulars 1959–69; premises register 1959–69; branch expenditure book 1959–69; expenditure ledger 1959–69; valuation book 1959–63; architectural drawings 1959–69; branch photographs 1959–69; bank notes, proofs and specimens 1959–69; merger press kit 1959; half-yearly balance books 1960–69; staff magazine, *The Talisman* 1960–68; promotional literature 1960–66; branch manuals 1963–64; memorandum and articles of association 1968; staff association minute book 1968.

NATIONAL DISCOUNT CO LTD
London

History: This City of London discount house was formed in 1856 with a subscribed capital of £200,000. It was the first joint stock company (other than the short-lived Overend Gurney & Co Ltd) to operate in a sector dominated by private partnerships. It avoided the worst effects of the 1866 Overend Gurney Crisis, which claimed many of its competitors, and expanded rapidly in the late 1860s and 1870s when it was London's largest house. Following the formation of the Union Discount Co of London Ltd (est. 1885), it became the second largest house and held this position until recent times. Cunliffe & Fowler was acquired in 1877. In 1969 Gerrard & Reid Ltd (est. 1870) acquired the business which ceased to trade in 1970. The Gerrard business was then renamed Gerrard & National Discount Co Ltd.

W T C King, *History of the London Discount Market* (London, 1936)

Records 1: Guildhall Library, Aldermanbury, London EC2P 2EJ

Deeds of settlement 1856; subscription contract re additional share issue 1856; general meeting minute books (3) 1856–1972; directors' meeting minute books (19) 1856–1971; board minute extracts by subject 1856–1963; building committee minute books 1856–60; general purposes committee minutes, 1856, with weekly reports of supervision committee 1857–63; half-yearly reports and balance sheets 1856–1913; general ledgers (20) 1856–1968; journals 1856–88, 1937–67; manager's cash book 1856–

402 *British banking – a guide to historical records*

57; miscellaneous correspondence 1856–57; sale particulars re office building disposal 1857; depositors' special meeting minutes 1859; shareholder register 1864; audited balance sheets 1866–1947; profit and loss statements 1866–1947; general meeting proceedings reports 1886–1969; stamp duty composition file 1887–1969; letters of guarantee and indemnity, powers of attorney 1895–1942; Bank of England weekly returns (2) 1899–1970; telegraphic codes and test keys twentieth cent; papers re trial of employee 1900; directors' and secretaries' registers (2) 1901–70; scrapbook re 50th anniversary 1906; foreign exchange cash book 1908–26; annual reports and balance sheets 1913–68; general papers re premises 1916–69; investment ledgers 1919–28, 1936–53, 1963–68; customer memorandum books (4) 1920–69; pension fund minutes, balance sheets, trust deeds and general correspondence (from 1954) 1922–1960s; depositors memorandum book 1928–69; treasury bill record book 1928–56; deposit finance books (9) 1936–62; investment finance books (3) 1936–50; deposit advices account book 1937–65; papers re Trading with Enemy Act 1939–50; amortisation of premiums and investment registers (3) 1941–56; Company Registrar returns 1943–71; press cuttings 1945–55; office tenancies papers 1946–69; audited balance sheets and profit and loss accounts 1948–63; safe custody register 1948–70; staff secrecy declarations 1950–69; income and profit taxes papers 1952–66; office repairs and maintenance papers 1954–66; non-security deposit ledgers (5) 1955–69; loan ledgers (3) 1959–68; sundry deposit ledgers (11) 1960–68; analysis of bills held book 1960–65; loans average books (3) 1960–69; analysis of English discounts 1960–63; balance sheet working papers 1961–67; Bowring deposit ledgers (3) 1961–67; rediscount ledgers (2) 1961–69; discount books (4) 1962–69 [w]; clearing bank deposit ledgers (2) 1961–67; valuations of net assets and monthly profit statements 1962–69; security deposit cash books (2) 1962–68; non-security deposit cash books (2) 1962–68; analysis of foreign accounts (2) 1962–64; bill balance books (3) 1962–69 [w]; rediscount books (6) 1963–69; investment books (2) 1963–67; investment sales ledgers (2) 1964–68; investment product book 1965–67; account of fluctuations of bills 1965–69; daily record of bills 'out of security' 1965–69; papers re visits to overseas banks 1965–67; dollar account general ledger 1968–69; acceptance books (2) 1968–69; discount bill book 1968–69; calendar of certificates of deposit (2) 1968–69; certificates of deposit ledger 1968–69; certificates of deposit average book 1968–69; letters of confirmation of loans and deposits 1969. [Ref: MS 18118–18213]

Records 2: Gerrard Group plc, Cannon Bridge, 25 Dowgate Hill, London EC4R 2GM

Prospectus 1866; deed of settlement with supplement 1856, 1866; share registers and indexes (40) 1850s–c.1950s; secrecy declarations book 1856–

Records of banks 403

1950; contracts for erection of new offices 1857–58; property leases 1859–85; bank rate book 'showing the various rates allowed for call and notice money' 1865–1969; transcript of court case re fraud by clerk 1900; contingency account book with related papers 1901–59; anniversary dinner programme 1906; analysis of bills discounted 1938–68.

Records 3: The Baring Archive, ING Baring Holdings Ltd, 60 London Wall, London EC2M 5TQ

Statement of rates for money 1856. [Ref: HC2.469]

NATIONAL PROVINCIAL BANK LTD
London

History: This joint stock bank was promoted by Thomas Joplin from 1828, initially as the Royal Bank and subsequently as the National Provincial Bank of England. It was formed in 1833, with a purely administrative head office in the City of London, and from 1834 opened its first branches in Gloucester, Brecon, Walsall, Birmingham, Wotton under Edge, Boston and Wisbech. By May 1835 twenty branches and sub-branches had been opened but the principle of the semi-autonomous branch with its own local shareholders proved unworkable and was abandoned. Paid-up capital in 1834 was £101,500. By 1865 the bank had 122 branches many of which were established through the acquisition of small private country banks including: Rotton & Co (est. 1806) of Birmingham in 1834; Bloxsome & Player (est. 1813) of Durham in 1835; Pyke, Law & Co (est. 1807) of Barnstaple in 1836; Vye & Harris (est. 1807) of Ilfracombe in 1836; William Skinner & Co (est. c.1815) of Stockton in 1836; Husband & Co (est. 1810) of Devonport in 1839; Harris & Co (est. 1806) of Dartmouth in 1840; Hulke & Son (est. 1808) of Deal in 1840; Fryer, Andrews & Co (est. c.1790) of Wimborne in 1840; Fector & Minet (est. 1700) of Dover in 1841; Cole, Holroyd & Co (est. 1822) of Exeter in 1842; Peter Pew & Co (est. c.1750) of Sherbourne in 1843; Loveband & Co (est. 1808) of Torrington in 1843; Ley & Co (est. c.1790) of Bideford in 1843; Thomas Kinnersley & Sons (est. c.1780) of Newcastle-under-Lyne in 1855; William Moore (est. 1800) of Stone in 1858; Crawshay, Bailey & Co (est. 1837) of Abergavenny in 1868; Bailey & Co (est. 1837) of Newport in 1868; and David Morris & Sons (est. c.1790) of Carmarthen in 1871. The Lichfield, Rugeley & Tamworth Banking Co (est. 1835) was acquired in 1837 followed by the Isle of Wight Joint Stock Banking Co (est. 1842) in 1844 and the Stockton & Durham County Bank (est. 1838) in 1846. In 1866 a new head office was opened in Bishopsgate, where the first London branch was also established which thereby obliged the bank to give up its note issue. The Bank of Leeds (est. 1864) was acquired in 1878 followed by the

404   *British banking – a guide to historical records*

County of Stafford Bank Ltd (est. 1836) in 1899 and the Knaresborough & Claro Banking Co Ltd (est. 1831) in 1903. Limited liability was acquired in 1880. Paid-up capital grew from £450,000 in 1853, to £1.08 million in 1866, to £1.68 million in 1878 and to £3 million in 1905. A half share in Lloyds Bank (France) was acquired in 1918. The bank merged with the important Union of London & Smiths Bank Ltd (est. 1839), which had over 230 branches, in 1918 when it was restyled the National Provincial & Union Bank of England Ltd. It extended its geographical spread through the acquisition of the Sheffield Banking Co Ltd (est. 1831) in 1919; the Bradford District Bank Ltd (est. 1862) in 1918; the Northamptonshire Union Bank Ltd (est. 1836) in 1920; Richards & Co (est. 1854) of Llangollen in 1920; Shilson, Coode & Co (est. 1793) of St Austell in 1920; Dingley & Co (est. 1855) of Launceston in 1922; Dingley, Pearse & Co (est. 1856) of Okehampton in 1922; and the Guernsey Banking Co Ltd (est. 1847) in 1924. The important London private bank of Coutts & Co (est. 1692) was acquired in 1920. The bank's name was shortened to the National Provincial Bank Ltd in 1924. It continued to expand its branch network between the wars and after 1945. It acquired the North Central Wagon & Finance Co Ltd, a leasing and hire purchase company, in 1958 and the Isle of Man Bank Ltd (est. 1865) in 1961. The District Bank Ltd (est. 1829), an important regional bank, was acquired in 1962. In 1965 a merchant banking subsidiary, County Bank Ltd, was formed and in 1968 the bank merged with the Westminster Bank Ltd to form the National Westminster Bank Ltd.

William Howarth, *Our Leading Banks* (London, 1894); William Howarth, *Banks in the Clearing House* (London, 1905); Fiona Maccoll, *The Key to Our Success. A Brief History of the NatWest Group* (London, 1996); Manfred Pohl & Sabine Freitag, *Handbook on the History of European Banks* (Aldershot, 1994); Richard Reed, *National Westminster Bank. A Short History* (London, 1989); Hartley Withers, *National Provincial Bank 1833–1933* (London, 1933)

Records 1: The Royal Bank of Scotland plc, Archive Section, Regent's House, 42 Islington High Street, London N1 8XL

Prospectus and papers re proposed formation 1830; correspondence of Thomas Joplin re proposed bank 1827–34, 1842; directors' meeting minute books (162) 1828–1969; prospectuses 1829–36; powers of attorney 1830–92; deed of settlement 1833, 1882; share registers (5) 1833–64, 1889–93; rotation committee minute books (55) 1833–78; note registers (5) 1833–97; annual reports 1833–1968; acquisition/merger papers, various banks 1833–1969; press notices re share issue 1833; letter of allotment 1833; share certificates 1833–70, 1956–68; share transfer papers 1833–85; gen-

Records of banks 405

eral meeting minute books (6) 1834–1969; extraordinary general meeting minutes 1834–99; annual general meeting proceedings 1834–1958; Gloucester shareholders' resolution 1834; information books re branches 1834; banker's licences 1835–56; deeds of covenant, increase in capital 1836–74; list of managers 1836; papers re general manager 1836–43; private general minute books (10) 1837–1962; bank note ledger 1837–92; bad debts ledger 1837–1936; circulars: London agent 1837, head office and agents' circular books (50) 1838–1936; assignments re bad debts 1839–53; staff record cards 1830s–1969; bank notes 1830s; instructions to local directors and branch managers 1840; bank note registers (3) 1841–86; branch committee minute books (2) 1843–45, 1889–1916; cancelled bank note register 1844–1955; letter re lost bank notes 1844; bank note indemnity books (2) 1845–79; general ledgers (8) 1845–1934; manuscript history of bank c.1850; balance sheet and profit and loss books 1856–81; legal opinions re shareholders 1859–85; circulars 1859–1969; incidental charges book 1859–68; property deed registers (3) 1850s–1920s; branch balance sheets 1860–77; staff payment scales 1860–68, 1919–20; staff lists c.1960–1910; salaries committee minutes 1862–1918, 1948–69; joint stock bank balance sheet details 1862–1924; leaflet re cessation of note issue 1865; candidates for apprenticeship books (3) 1867–1918; character books 1860s–1920s; premises photographs 1860s–1969; law books (3) 1870–1954; general meeting attendance lists 1870–89; chairman's daily books: deposits (3) 1871–73, advances 1872–73; committees reports books, particularly re staff 1872–1919; chairman's books (11) 1873–78; property leases ledgers (2) 1873–1928; pensions register 1874–1925; senior staff salary books 1877–1966; correspondence department minutes 1878–1966; finance committee minute books (3) 1879–1915; annual returns: 1879–83, certificates 1942–46; shareholder circulars 1879–1968; weekly abstracts of accounts 1880–1953; weekly statements of assets and liabilities 1883–1909; staff salary scales 1885–1969; staff agreement books (2) 1886–1916; share register 1889–93; branch committee minute book 1889–1916; register of outstanding notes 1897; widows' and orphans' fund: actuarial report and correspondence 1898–1960s, report and accounts 1944–58; guarantee and benevolent fund accounts 1898–1919; private letterbooks (2) 1899–1918; memorandum and articles of association 1899–1968; registers of directors (2) 1901–23; pension superannuation ledger 1902–19; private court minutes 1904–20; branch premises history ledger 1905–20; pensions record cards 1910–49; loans committee minutes 1912–21; Bank of England returns 1916–30; customer authorities 1917–24; papers re opening of branches 1918; change of name certificate 1918; staff statistics papers 1919–69; general meetings: speech press cuttings 1919–41, question papers 1924–34, chairman's briefing notes 1952–65; papers re local directors 1919–55; local directors' minute books, Bradford (3) 1919–39; staff rules

406   *British banking – a guide to historical records*

1919–68; court minute 1921; merger papers 1918; court agendas 1923–62; branch profit and loss figures 1923–33; general purposes committee minute books 1924–65; memoranda re charity appeals 1926–52; subject files: chief general manager 1927–69, chairman 1957–68; widows' and orphans' fund: minute books 1928–69, rule books 1928–68, report and accounts 1944–66; regulations for admission of staff probationers 1929; sickness fund rule books 1929, 1967; annual reports summary c.1920s; Smith family club rules 1920s; staff advisory committee papers 1920s–69; letter of credit and list of correspondents 1920s; directors' attendance book 1931–34; correspondence re Anglo South American Bank 1931–33; friendly help fund account book 1935–61; Christmas cards 1937–64; distressed areas staff fund papers 1937–45; war book 1938; papers re capital reorganisations 1938, 1957; chief accountant's papers 1938–69; staff appointment papers 1930s–69; air raid damage register 1940; Bankers Health Society correspondence 1946–50; *National Provincial Bank Review* 1948–68; general manager's committee agenda 1953–55; training course file 1958; pensions trust fund rules 1961–63; pensioners' association newsletter 1963–96; officers' pensions minute books (3) 1964–69; comparative bank profit and loss figures 1965; annual and half-yearly results 1966–69; papers re establishment of Channel Islands subsidiary 1968–69; branch computerisation schedules 1964–68; accountant's reports 1968; staff department review papers 1968; branch staff policy notes 1968; staff magazine papers 1968; papers re establishment of National Provincial and Rothschild 1968–70; papers re shares in acquired banks allotted c.1960s.

Bangor: manager's letterbook 1861–93; **Bath:** premises papers 1925–27; weekly balances abstract 1840s; produce register 1931–35; **Beaumaris:** character book 1878–1906; **Birmingham:** character books (6) 1888–1926; produce security register 1925–41; branch account statistics 1946–66; **Bradford:** character book 1912–23; book of wool credits 1930–31; interview book 1913–30; bad debt book 1919–39; security register 1938–58; staff books 1938–76; **Bridgend:** bill registers (3) 1835–57; character books 1898–1929; **Bristol:** character books (8) 1876–1921; interview books (3) 1892–1908; letterbook 1902–03; loan book 1911–24; analysis of advances and discounted bills 1936–48; **Bristol, Corn Street:** plans of premises 1889–90; **Bristol, Redland:** plans of premises 1889–1927; **Bromley:** character books (2) 1920s–40s; **Chumleigh:** office furniture inventory 1866–70; **Chorleywood:** character books (2) 1921–52; **Conway:** character book 1878–1929; **Dartmouth:** correspondence with head office 1850–66; drafts issued book 1876–1966; **Dolgellau:** details of daily payments into branch 1842–63; manager's drafts 1846–52; cash in hand book 1855–59; general ledger and cash book 1861–62; **Gainsborough:** salary register 1919–28; **Hull:** manager's information book 1903–40; manager's memorandum book

Records of banks 407

1903–25; half-yearly returns book 1926–68; **Ilkeston:** minute books (4) 1928–54; **Ipswich:** manager's minute book 1927–32, 1965–69; **Ledbury:** customer ledger 1835–43; deposit ledger 1835–80; **Leeds:** character book 1878–84; signature book 1899–1914; interview book 1911–21; **Lichfield:** security register 1834–72; character books (3) 1877–1908; **Liverpool:** character books 1900s–20s; **Llandudno:** character books (2) 1876–1900; **London, City Office:** memorandum file 1930–60; **London, Finchley Road:** manager's letterbook 1905–21; character books (2) 1913–48; **London, Islington:** character book c.1907–22; **London, Kensington:** branch returns 1897–1964; **London, Hackney:** manager's letter 1904–24; **London, Lombard Street:** information book 1908–48; christmas money sheets 1902–18; **London, Paddington:** profit and loss account book 1904–37; **London, Piccadilly:** character books 1866–1920s; manager's letterbooks 1892–1918; head office letterbooks 1907–18; **London, Prescott's Office:** charity subscriptions list 1904–22; branch letterbook 1908–24; **London, Princes Street:** head office correspondence 1929–45; comparison of accounts 1930–32; staff inspection report 1936; **London, Regent Street:** profit and loss book 1921–62; **London, St Mary Axe:** deposit account ledger 1929–39; security register 1929–51; **London, Tottenham Court Road:** branch returns 1922–70; **London, West Smithfield:** title deeds 1889–1934; character book 1918–25; security registers (10) 1920–39; **Ludlow:** character books (2) 1919–1960s; **Manchester:** security register 1862–71, manager's letterbook 1895–1901; head office letterbook 1913–14; **March:** character books (6) 1875–1952; interview books (3) 1913–26; **Mold:** interview book 1868–70; **Norwich:** staff letterbook 1893–1919; **Nottingham:** manager's letterbook 1906–19; correspondence re Boots 1916–51; customer record book 1936–44; **Penrith:** estimate for new premises 1924–26; **Rugby:** bond register 1841–68; **Saltley:** character book 1928–43; **Scarborough:** manager's letters 1902–26; **Sheffield:** salary ledger 1914–22; **Sherborne:** monthly returns and inspector's observations book 1844–73; letterbooks (2) 1862–1929; character books (4) 1874–1929; interview book 1930–35; **Southampton:** salary book 1868–80; **Stalbridge:** private letterbook 1849–55; **Sutton Coldfield:** character book 1923–30s; **Swansea:** branch statistics 1935–71; **Swinton:** character books (2) 1919–50; manager's memorandum book 1903–34; **Tamworth:** mortgage agreement, Sir Robert Peel 1862–64; **Tavistock:** character books (3) 1922–c.1955; **Tenby:** manager's letterbook 1909–15; **Totnes:** information book 1843–68; manager's correspondence 1847–48; **Whitehaven:** bill of quantities 1926; **Wolverhampton:** information book 1899–1918; branch statistics 1899–1926; **Woodbridge:** weekly balance sheet 1838; **Wotton-under-Edge:** branch minutes 1834–74; **Wrexham:** security register 1849–68; letterbook 1888–1923.

408   *British banking – a guide to historical records*

Records 2: Record Office and Local History Department, Liverpool Libraries and Information Services, William Brown Street, Liverpool L3 8EW

Llangefni: manager's personal papers 1850–86. [Ref: 920 MD]

Records 3: City Record Office, 3 Museum Road, Portsmouth PO1 2LE

Portsmouth: branch architectural plans by A E Cogswell 1914–32. [Ref: 114A/3/1]

Records 4: Glamorgan Record Office, Glamorgan Building, King Edward VII Avenue, Cathays Park, Cardiff CF1 3NE

Caerphilly: waste books 1839–41, 1875–76; current account ledger 1864–70; deposit ledger 1865–74. [Ref: D/D Xhs 4/1–4]

NEVILE, REID & CO
Windsor, Berkshire

History: This private bank was established in 1780 as Ramsbottom & Baverstock; it was otherwise known as the Windsor Bank. It traded as Nevile, Reid & Co from 1838 and was then owned by the partners in the London bank of Williams, Deacon & Co (est. 1771) who also owned a brewery in Windsor trading under the same name. These partners included Lord Kirkaldie and John and W S Deacon and Sykes Thornton. A branch was opened in Datchet. The bank was acquired by Barclay & Co Ltd (est. 1896) in 1914.

P W Matthews & Anthony W Tuke, *History of Barclays Bank Ltd* (London, 1926)

Records 1: Barclays Bank plc, Group Archives, Dallimore Road, Wythenshawe, Manchester M23 9JA

Security registers 1905–14; cheques, Datchet 1909–12.

Records 2: The Royal Bank of Scotland plc, Archive Section, Regent's House, 42 Islington High Street, London N1 8XL

Accounts, correspondence and notes 1870–88.

Records 3: Berkshire Record Office, Shire Hall, Shinfield Park, Reading RG2 9XD

Ledger, account with Williams, Deacon & Co 1838–41; journal 1844–64; private ledgers 1844–62. [Ref: D/ECg B1, 8, 9]

Records 4: London Metropolitan Archive, 40 Northampton Road, London EC1R 0HB

Book of cancelled bank notes n.d. [Ref: Acc 2058/18/3]

NEWCASTLE COMMERCIAL JOINT STOCK BANK
Newcastle upon Tyne, Tyne & Wear

History: This joint stock bank was established in 1836 with a paid-up capital of £75,000. Its business was always small and in 1845 a third of its share capital was returned to shareholders as it could not be profitably employed. By 1855 significant shareholdings in the bank were acquired by London financiers, led by John Sadleir, who then fraudulently used the bank's resources to support the failing Tipperary Bank. This led to the Commercial Bank's failure in 1856 with liabilities of £24,000.

John Casey, 'The Frauds of John Sadleir', *The Banker*, 112 (Oct 1962); Maberly Phillips, *Banks, Bankers and Banking in Northumberland, Durham and North Yorkshire* (London, 1894)

Records: Northumberland Record Office, Melton Park, North Gosforth, Newcastle upon Tyne NE3 5QX

Deed of settlement 1837; mortgage as security for a customer's account 1847. [Ref: NRO530.20/296; ZMD 32/3]

NEWCASTLE, SHIELDS & SUNDERLAND UNION JOINT STOCK BANK
Newcastle upon Tyne, Tyne & Wear

History: This joint stock bank was formed in 1836 out of the business of the private bankers, Chapman & Co (est. 1823) of Newcastle, North Shields and South Shields. The Sunderland business of Sir Wm. Chaytor, Bart., Frankland Wilkinson, Chaytor & Co (est. 1829) was also acquired in 1836. During the financial crisis of 1847 the bank suspended payment. William Woods, a merchant and major shareholder, then led a committee to investigate the bank's affairs and he resuscitated the business. The North and South Shields branches reopened almost immediately, the Berwick branch reopened in late 1847 followed, in 1849, by the branches at Newcastle and Sunderland. In 1853, when the bank was still recovering, shareholder dissent resulted in its management by a committee of major shareholders led by Woods. Abortive attempts were then made to reconstruct the business and in 1859 it was acquired by a private partnership led by Woods and known as Woods, Parker & Co.

P W Matthews & Anthony W Tuke, *History of Barclays Bank Ltd* (London, 1926); Maberly Phillips, *Banks, Bankers and Banking in Northumberland, Durham and North Yorkshire* (London, 1894)

410   *British banking – a guide to historical records*

Records 1: Barclays Bank plc, Group Archives, Dallimore Road, Wythenshawe, Manchester M23 9JA

Deed of settlement 1836; banker's licences 1836–40; securities for advances 1837–55; receipts, cheques and bills 1838–73; bank notes 1839–46; paying-in slip 1846; shareholder and branch returns 1847; manager's accounts 1853–74; affadavits 1853–64; cheque book 1860; passbook 1860–75.

Newcastle: Signature books 1841–60; cheque form 1859.

Records 2: Durham County Record Office, County Hall, Durham DH1 5UL

Report and minutes 1838; list of shareholders 1849. [Ref: NCBI/JB/1860; NCBI/TH/54]

NEW ORIENTAL BANK CORPORATION LTD
London, Asia, Australia and Africa

History: This important British-owned overseas bank traced its origins to the Bank of Western India formed at Bombay in 1842. In 1845 the bank's head office was relocated to London and the business was renamed the Oriental Bank. In 1849 the Bank of Ceylon (est. 1840) was acquired and with it the advantages of formation by charter. A revised charter was received in 1851 when the bank was renamed the Oriental Bank Corporation. Expansion was rapid with branches soon being established outside India, for example at Mauritius, South Africa, Hong Kong, Singapore, Japan and especially China. In 1860 it was the largest British overseas bank by a significant margin; its assets then exceeded £12.6 million and it had fourteen branches. It was in decline by 1880 and the Bank of Africa Ltd (est. 1879) acquired the southern Africa business in 1879. In 1884 the bank failed, largely due to misjudgement of silver price movements and the lock up of funds in Ceylonese coffee plantations and Mauritian sugar estates. The business was reconstituted as the New Oriental Bank Corporation Ltd but failed in 1892.

Anon, 'The New Oriental Bank Corporation. A Lesson in Bad Banking', *Bankers' Magazine*, 57 (1894)

Records 1: Public Record Office, Ruskin Avenue, Kew, Richmond TW9 4DU

Customers' securities for loans 1831–84. [Ref: J90/1770–1774]

Records 2: The Baring Archive, ING Baring Holdings Ltd, 60 London Wall, London EC2M 5TQ

Annual reports 1878–83; shareholder circulars 1884. [Ref: 102137, 102138]

Records of banks

NICHOLS, BAKER & CRANE
Bewdley, Hereford & Worcester

History: This private bank was established in about 1782 as Roberts, Skey & Kendrick. The partners included a solicitor, a merchant and drysalter, and a relative of the founder of the hardware firm of Kendricks. In about 1790 William Skey left to form the rival bank of Samuel Skey, Son & Co. In 1823 the business, then known as Roberts, Baker & Crane and with a capital of £21,000, merged with another local private bank, Pardoe & Nichols. In 1828, Pardoe, a solicitor, withdrew. In 1862 it was acquired for £5,000 by the Birmingham & Midland Banking Co (est. 1836).

W F Crick & J E Wadsworth, *A Hundred Years of Joint Stock Banking* (London, 1936)

Records: HSBC Holdings plc, Group Archives, 10 Lower Thames Street, London EC3R 6AE

London remittance books, Forster & Co (2) 1798–1803, 1810–13; receipt books, bills payable (2) 1812, 1818; general ledger 1812–13; circulars 1813–30; private ledgers, Hoare Barnett & Co (2) 1818–21; bills discounted book 1821–34; cash books (2) 1838–42; acceptance books (2) 1852–55.

WILLIAM & GEORGE NIGHTINGALE
London

History: This bank traces its origins to the goldsmith's business of Glegg &Vere, formed in Lombard Street, City of London, in about 1730. In about 1740 the firm was renamed Vere & Asgill and in 1765 it was known as Sir Charles Asgill, Nightingale & Wickenden. Wickenden left in 1775 to form Wickenden, Moffat, Kensington & Boler. The title changed to Asgill, Nightingale & Nightingale and changed again in 1789 to John, William & George Nightingale. Another name change followed in 1791 to William & George Nightingale and in 1796 the bank suspended payment.

F G Hilton Price, *A Handbook of London Bankers* (London, 1876)

Records: The Royal Bank of Scotland plc, Archive Section, Regent's House, 42 Islington High Street, London N1 8XL

Journal 1740–41.

NORFOLK & NORWICH JOINT STOCK BANKING CO
Norfolk, Norwich

History: This joint stock bank was established in 1826; it was known also as the Stable Bank. Nine branches were opened including ones at Dereham,

412 *British banking – a guide to historical records*

Fakenham, King's Lynn, Bungay and Framlingham. In 1836 the business was formed into the East of England Bank.

Harold Preston, *Early East Anglian Banks and Bankers* (Thetford, 1994)

Records: Barclays Bank plc, Group Archives, Dallimore Road, Wythenshawe, Manchester M23 9JA

Prospectus 1827; press cutting 1827; deed of covenant, transfer to East of England Bank 1836; bank notes 1830s.

NORTH & SOUTH WALES BANK LTD
Liverpool, Merseyside

History: This important joint stock bank was formed in 1836 at Liverpool, then regarded as the economic centre of North Wales. Its provisional committee largely comprised Liverpool merchants and manufacturers but the bank quickly identified with Wales in order to attract shareholders and customers. Its declared policy from the outset was to open branches throughout Wales and to achieve this it began by acquiring private banks. In 1836 R Sankey & Co (est. c.1790) of Holywell and Denbigh was acquired, followed in the same year by Benson & Co (est. 1762) of Aberystwyth for £3,000. Shortly afterwards, eight North Wales branches were acquired from the Central Bank of Liverpool (est. 1836, ceased trading 1839) and at the end of the first year of business the total network comprised thirteen branches and ten sub-branches. Paid-up capital was then £159,000 and deposits were £140,000; the latter rose to £221,000 by 1840. However the bank proceeded too boldly for safety and poor management resulted in losses of £54,000 by 1840. Retrenchment followed, which included the closure of three branches and the fall in deposits to £179,000 by 1841. But other branches were established, most notably at this time through the acquisition of the business of Douglas, Smalley & Co (est. c.1822) of Holywell and Mold on its failure in 1839. In 1845 the bank came under the leadership of George Rae, an outstandingly able joint stock banker who introduced pioneering best-practice techniques. However, during the 1847 financial crisis, he could not quell erroneous rumours that the bank was in difficulties which resulted in a run and suspension of payments. The bank only resumed after determined lobbying persuaded shareholders to subscribe additional capital and depositors to maintain their deposits. Certain branches were discontinued, those at Porthmadog, Pwllheli and Ffestiniog being transferred to Cassons & Co (est. 1847) and that at Cardigan being disposed of to another private bank. By 1850 paid-up capital was £161,000 and deposits had recovered to £454,000. In 1856 the Knighton business of Davies & Co (est. 1789) of Kington was taken over for £1,000 and, as part of a plan to increase deposits, a savings scheme

Records of banks   413

was instituted for dockers at Birkenhead and was soon extended to Rhyl. In 1863 the Liverpool business, which had hitherto been modest, expanded through the establishment of three 'town' branches. By 1868 deposits stood at £1.78 million and paid-up capital was £300,000. In the last quarter of the century rapid expansion transformed the modestly-sized provincial bank into one of the largest and most influential banks in Britain. Much of this expansion was located in Liverpool where branches grew in numbers and were extended into the Wirral. The acquisition of surviving private banks continued with that of Williams & Son (est. 1803) of Dolgellau in 1873 and of Cassons & Co of Portmadog, with five offices, in 1875. The business of the three branches of the collapsed Bala Banking Co Ltd (est. 1864) was taken over in 1877. The bank was incorporated as a limited liability company in 1880 and in 1901 the important Liverpool private bankers of Leyland & Bullins (est. 1807) were acquired. Thereby the size of the business was greatly extended. In 1908 the 'Wales Bank', as it was generally known, was acquired by London, City & Midland Bank Ltd (est. 1836) for the equivalent of £2.625 million. It then had 84 branches, twenty-four sub-branches, paid-up capital of £750,000 and deposits of over £11 million.

W F Crick & J E Wadsworth, *A Hundred Years of Joint Stock Banking* (London, 1936); A R Holmes & Edwin Green, *Midland. 150 Years of Banking Business* (London, 1986)

Records: HSBC Holdings plc, Group Archives, 10 Lower Thames Street, London EC3R 6AE

Prospectus 1836; deed of settlement 1836; directors' meeting minute books (25) 1836–1908; shareholders' minute books (3) 1836–1908; share registers (10) 1836–1905; share ledgers (2) 1836–46; share transfer register 1836–41; share transfer order books 1836–58; security books (3) 1836–70; general ledgers (27) 1836–1907; tellers' cash book 1836; bad debt books (2) 1837–42; bill diary 1838–1909; annual reports 1839–1907 [w]; abstract of balance sheets (21) 1843–1909; staff registers 1845–1909; committee minute books (7) 1846–57; branch inspection reports 1848–64; instructions for officers (7) 1849–1900; rent book 1849–73; memorandum book re banking practice 1851–1907; progressive balance books by branches 1853–1907; head office circulars to branches 1857–1908; register of securities 1860–75; 'own notes issuable' (3) 1861–1908; note registers (7) 1863–1907; loan books (10) 1868–1904; Liverpool manager's letterbook 1869–93; correspondence re proposed amalgamations 1872–1907; customer memorandum book 1874–96; shareholders' registers (3) 1874–89; correspondence re limited liability 1876–79; half-yearly balance working papers 1879–1908; chairman's private letterbook 1880–96; general man-

414 *British banking – a guide to historical records*

ager's memoranda 1891–1901; business reports including reports on foreign and domestic banks 1891–1901; press cuttings book 1894–1908; classification of advances 1907; amalgamation papers 1908–10.

Aberystwyth: general ledgers (9) 1836–80; letterbook 1836–44; deposit receipt ledgers (4) 1836–79; security books (2) 1836–61; private ledgers (6) 1840–76 [w]; general ledger balance books (5) 1846–78; bill of exchange register 1869–73; security register 1878–1909; **Barmouth:** general ledger balance book 1874–82; **Caernarvon:** general ledgers (9) 1836–77; deposit receipt ledger 1836–56; **Dolgellau:** general ledgers (8) 1873–1909; manager's memorandum book 1873–98; **Ffestiniog:** private ledger 1837–39; character book 1875–1909; **Knighton:** general ledger balance books (4) 1856–1909; **Liverpool, Castle Street:** bank note ledger 1836–98; bad debt ledger 1849–75; **Liverpool, Markets:** deposit receipts 1882–1905; security register 1899–1909; correspondence register 1904–09; **Liverpool, North:** general ledgers (4) 1863–78; **Liverpool, North Docks:** security receipt book 1902–09; **Liverpool, South:** signature books (4) 1863–1916; security register 1865–1909; **Llanfyllin:** security register, list debts and overdraft limits and premises details 1870–1909; accounts opened books (2) 1888–1909; **Llangollen:** security registers (2) 1863–1909; signature books (2) 1863–1909; **Llanidloes:** security book 1875–1909; **Llanrwst:** letterbook 1905–09; **Mold:** deposit receipt ledger 1834–74; private ledgers (3) 1838–44; **Oswestry:** general ledgers (10) 1836–81; letterbooks (4) 1862–1902; reference book 1874–92; **Portmadoc:** deposit receipt ledger 1839–42; **Portmadog and Criccieth:** analysis of accounts 1883–89; **Pwllheli:** deposit receipt ledger 1836–48; **Ruthin:** deposit receipt ledger 1838–62; **Rhyl:** letterbook 1898–1909; **Wallasey:** correspondence register 1897–1909; **Welshpool:** general ledger 1836–39; security register 1836–74; signature books 1868–1909; **Wrexham:** general ledger 1836–40; security books (5) 1836–1902; balance books (12) 1837–1909; character book 1873–85; general ledgers (3) 1903–12.

NORTHAMPTONSHIRE BANKING CO LTD
Daventry, Northamptonshire

History: This joint stock bank was formed as the Northamptonshire Central Banking Co in 1836 out of the business of the private bank of Watkins & Co (est. 1783) of Daventry and Northampton. It was renamed Northamptonshire Banking Co in 1838. Branches were opened or acquired at Daventry, Northampton, Stamford and Wellingborough in 1836 and at Kettering in 1876. The business was acquired by Capital & Counties Bank Ltd (est. 1877) in 1890.

Records of banks

Records: Lloyds TSB Group plc, Archives, Head Office, 71 Lombard Street, London EC3P 3BS

Deed of settlement 1836; note journal 1854–76; balance sheets 1881–86; directors' meeting minute book 1888–90; amalgamation papers 1889–93. **Daventry:** general ledger 1836; **Kettering:** security register 1877–90; **Stamford:** security registers (2) 1850–91; **Wellingborough:** signature book 1878–91.

NORTHAMPTONSHIRE UNION BANK LTD
Northampton, Northamptonshire

History: This joint stock bank traced its origins to the private bank of J Percival & Son (est. c.1800). In 1836 John and Samuel Percival converted their bank into the Northamptonshire Union Bank which in 1880 acquired limited liability. In 1887 the private bank of Moxon & Percival (est. 1815) of Towcester was acquired. In 1920 the bank was purchased by the National Provincial & Union Bank of England Ltd (est. 1833).

Records 1: The Royal Bank of Scotland plc, Archive Section, Regent's House, 42 Islington High Street, London N1 8XL

Customer account ledger 1814–17; papers re infringement of Bank of England's monopoly 1836; prospectus 1836; deeds of settlement 1836–99; half-yearly accounts books (3) 1836–1920; annual general meeting minute books (2) 1837–1920; directors' minute books (8) 1849–1921; committee minute books (2) 1856–81; statistics book 1866–1920; half-yearly reports 1888–1919; manager's information book 1890–1905; security registers 1891–96; manager's letterbook 1891–95; salary book 1895–1920; amalgamation papers 1914–20; general ledger 1919–20.

Daventry: waste book 1837; **Wellingborough:** note register 1836–c.1886; customer ledger 1836–39.

Records 2: Bedfordshire and Luton Archives and Record Service, The Records Office, Cauldwell Street, Bedford MK42 9AP

Bedford: signature books c.1890–1920; passbooks n.d. [Ref: Z 419/1–2]

Records 3: Northamptonshire Record Office, Wootton Hall Park, Northampton NN4 9BQ

Title deeds, 41 The Drapery c.1836–60. [Ref: ZB 514]

NORTH EASTERN BANKING CO LTD
Newcastle upon Tyne, Tyne & Wear

416   *British banking – a guide to historical records*

History: This joint stock bank was formed in 1872 and represented the first serious attempt to reintroduce joint stock banking in the north east after a series of disastrous collapses culminating in that of the Northumberland & Durham District Banking Co (est. 1836) in 1857. The bank's manager was recruited from the Clydesdale Bank (est. 1838). Its first offices were opened in Newcastle and Middlesborough and by 1873 branches also existed at West Hartlepool, Consett, Jarrow, Gateshead and Barrow in Furness, Cumbria, as well as at Newcastle's Cattle Market and Quayside. By early 1874 other branches were open at Amble, Chester-le-Street, Houghton-le-Spring and Spennymoor. In 1875 the Alnwick & County Bank (est. 1858) was acquired after which paid-up capital stood at £260,000 and branches numbered about twenty-five. This was followed by the acquisition of Dale, Young & Co (est. 1858) of South Shields and Newcastle in 1892. By 1894, forty branches existed. In 1914 this important regional bank amalgamated with the Bank of Liverpool Ltd (est. 1831).

George Chandler, *Four Centuries of Banking* (London, 1964–68); Maberly Phillips, *Banks, Bankers and Banking in Northumberland, Durham and North Yorkshire* (London, 1894)

Records: Barclays Bank plc, Group Archives, Dallimore Road, Wythenshawe, Manchester M23 9JA

Property papers: Pilgrim Street and Grey Street 1730–1951, Kendal 1740–1870; prospectus 1872; memorandum and articles of association 1872–93, 1911; report and accounts 1872–1914; registers of shareholders (5) 1872–1914; application for share allotment 1872; statistics re shares sold 1872–1910; letterbooks (49) 1872–1915; branch statistics 1872–1913; instruction book 1873–1915; circular re merger with Alnwick & County Bank 1875; correspondence registers (2) 1876–86; in-letters: Benjamin Noble 1882–1903, Brodick Dale 1910–13; legal opinion 1876–77; charges account ledger 1876–84; banker's licences 1878–79; loan security register 1883–91; report re proposed Sunderland branch 1884; staff terms of appointment 1886–93; prospectuses, balance sheets, letters etc of various corporate customers 1892–1902; amalgamation correspondence 1892–94, 1904–05; cheques 1897–1911; staff cartoons n.d.; notice of branch work system c.1900s; plans of branches n.d.; notes on special overdrafts 1912–15; papers re merger with Bank of Liverpool 1914.

NORTHERN & CENTRAL BANK OF ENGLAND
Manchester, Greater Manchester

History: This joint stock bank was established in 1834 with a paid-up capital of £500,000. It absorbed Joseph Haythorne & George Wright (est.

Records of banks 417

1794) of Bristol in 1834; Mare & Eaton (est. 1808) of Nantwich in 1834; and Charles Evans (est. 1810) of Manchester in 1837. Forty branches were opened at places as distant as Clitheroe and Evesham, Grantham and Bangor. Its business expanded rapidly but was poorly managed and soon the bank was in difficulties. It failed in 1836 and was liquidated in 1839.

Leo H Grindon, *Manchester Banks and Bankers* (Manchester, 1877)

Records: The Royal Bank of Scotland plc, Archive Section, Regent's House, 42 Islington High Street, London N1 8XL

Prospectus 1833; deed of settlement 1834; supplementary deed of settlement 1836; agreement for transfer of Bristol branch to National Provincial Bank of England 1836; deed of indemnity re share dividend 1840.

NORTH KENT BANK LTD
London

History: This joint stock bank was established at Greenwich with limited liability in 1864. It was acquired by the London & Provincial Bank Ltd (est. 1833) in 1878.

Records: Barclays Bank plc, Group Archives, Dallimore Road, Wythenshawe, Manchester M23 9JA

Directors' report and accounts including lists of shareholders 1867–69.

NORTH OF ENGLAND UNION & JOINT STOCK BANKING CO
Newcastle upon Tyne, Tyne & Wear

History: This joint stock bank was established in 1832 and was the first such bank at Newcastle. Branches were soon opened at Sunderland, North and South Shields, Durham, Berwick, Morpeth, Blyth, Hexham, Alnwick and Wooler. In 1847 paid-up capital was £340,000. In this year the bank failed with liabilities exceeding assets to the extent of about £500,000. Its failure caused great distress to its 420 shareholders.

Maberly Phillips, *Banks, Bankers and Banking in Northumberland, Durham and North Yorkshire* (London, 1894)

Records: Public Record Office, Ruskin Avenue, Kew, Richmond TW9 4DU

Customer securities for loans 1725–1877. [Ref: J90/1544–1563]

NORTH OF SCOTLAND BANK LTD
Aberdeen, Grampian

418 *British banking – a guide to historical records*

History: This joint stock bank was formed in 1836 with a paid-up capital of £200,000 provided by 1,563 shareholders. The driving force behind its establishment was Arthur Anderson, a leading Aberdeen entrepreneur. It became the most dynamic Scottish bank outside Edinburgh and Glasgow and embarked upon an ambitious programme to open branches. In 1848 it was close to collapse when paid-up capital was reduced from £380,000 to £115,500. In 1888 it again encountered serious difficulties when the local herring fishing industry collapsed. In 1908 it merged with its chief Aberdeen-based competitor, Town & County Bank Ltd (est. 1825), to form North of Scotland & Town & County Bank Ltd. Midland Bank Ltd (est. 1836) acquired the business in 1923, but it continued as an independent entity under the title of North of Scotland Bank Ltd. In 1950 it merged with Midlands' other major Scottish subsidiary, Clydesdale Bank Ltd (est. 1838), to form Clydesdale & North of Scotland Bank Ltd, the title of which was shortened to Clydesdale Bank Ltd in 1963.

W F Crick & J E Wadswoth, *A Hundred Years of Joint Stock Banking* (London, 1936); Alexander Keith, *The North of Scotland Bank Ltd 1836–1936* (Aberdeen, 1936); Charles W Munn, *Clydesdale Bank. The First One Hundred and Fifty Years* (London & Glasgow, 1988)

Records 1: Clydesdale Bank plc, Head Office, 30 St Vincent Place, Glasgow G1 2HL

Instructions to agents and accountants 1848, 1856; declarations of trust 1849–54; circular books (52) 1864–1950; annual reports with press cuttings 1869–1921; descriptions of books in use at branch offices 1872–1909; list of shareholders 1879–1909; contract of co-partnery 1882; note circulation returns books (2) 1882–1918; directors' minute books (3) 1908–22; list of branches and correspondents 1914, 1924; instructions for branch offices 1929.

Records 2: The Royal Bank of Scotland plc, Archive Section, Regent's House, 42 Islington High Street, London N1 8XL

Annual reports 1908–18.

Records 3: Glasgow University Archives and Business Records Centre, 13 Thurso Street, Glasgow G11 6PE

Balance sheets 1865–1910; annual reports 1897–1926. [Ref: Scottish Banking Collection]

NORTHUMBERLAND & DURHAM DISTRICT BANKING CO
Newcastle upon Tyne, Tyne & Wear

Records of banks 419

History: This joint stock bank was formed in 1836 as the Newcastle, Sunderland, Durham, & North & South Shields District Banking Co, but almost immediately abbreviated its name to the Northumberland & Durham District Banking Co. Soon after formation it acquired the Newcastle premises and business of Jonathan Backhouse & Co (est. 1825), private bankers of Darlington. It soon opened branches at Sunderland and at South and North Shields. In 1837 paid-up capital was £140,000. In 1839 Ridley, Bigge & Co (est. 1755) of Newcastle was acquired; its partners became directors and major shareholders. By 1847 branches also functioned in Durham and Alnwick. Following the failure of the North of England Union & Joint Stock Banking Co (est. 1832) in 1847 and of the Newcastle, Shields & Sunderland Union Joint Stock Bank (est. 1836) in 1853, the bank perceived opportunity for expansion and increased its paid-up capital to £600,000. By 1856 its balance sheet totalled £4.2 million which reflected its major importance. In 1857 the bank failed causing great distress to its shareholders who were obliged to meet a call of £35 per share, although they later recovered part of this amount.

Maberly Phillips, *Banks, Bankers and Banking in Northumberland, Durham and North Yorkshire* (London, 1894)

Records 1: Barclays Bank plc, Group Archives, Dallimore Road, Wythenshawe, Manchester M23 9JA

Annual reports 1839–42.

Records 2: Northumberland Record Office, Melton Park, North Gosforth, Newcastle upon Tyne NE3 5QX

Deed of settlement 1836; liquidator's report 1862; liquidation papers 1862–68. [Ref: NE3 5QX Ref: ZR1 34 1; NRO 530.20/272; NRO 997/2/14; NRO 606]

NORTH WESTERN BANK LTD
Liverpool, Merseyside

History: This joint stock bank traced its origins to the private bank of Moss, Dales & Rogers which was established at Liverpool in 1807. The Moss family of shipowners and merchants dominated the partnership which provided services for local shipping and trading businesses, the latter including cotton, tobacco and corn merchants and brokers. In 1864, at the time of the Cotton Famine when additional capital was required, the business was converted into a joint stock bank, North Western Bank Ltd. Its paid-up capital was £270,000 and, at the end of its first year, deposits stood at £722,000. Soon afterwards they reached £1 million, but thereafter contracted significantly; by 1890 they totalled only £1.073 million. In

420	*British banking – a guide to historical records*

1885 expansion through the opening of branches began and eight branches in Liverpool's suburbs existed by 1893. In 1897 the business was acquired by London & Midland Bank Ltd (est. 1836) for the equivalent of £580,000. Deposits then stood at £1.5 million, paid-up capital was £405,000 and there were eight branches.

W F Crick & J E Wadsworth, *A Hundred Years of Joint Stock Banking* (London, 1936)

Records: HSBC Holdings plc, Group Archives, 10 Lower Thames Street, London EC3R 6AE

Current account ledgers (5) 1838–64 [w]; share registers (3) 1864–97; prospectus 1864; annual reports (2) 1864–90; bad debt books (2) 1865–94; directors' meeting minute books (2) 1866–97; general meeting minute books 1866–97; general ledger 1882–85; legal papers re customer 1892–95.

Liverpool, Dale Street: signature books 1864–97; **Liverpool, Cotton Exchange:** salaries book 1891–97.

NORTH WILTS BANKING CO
Melksham, Wiltshire

History: This joint stock bank was formed in 1835 out of the business of the private bank of Moule & Co (est. 1792) of Melksham. The private banks of Everett, Ravenhill & Co (est. 1777) of Warminster and Ward, Brown & Co of Marlborough (est. 1803) were acquired in 1860 and 1866 respectively. By 1877 twelve branches had been established at Melksham, Salisbury, Devizes, Calne, Trowbridge, Swindon, Marlborough, Bradford on Avon, Wotton Bassett, Corsham, Pewsey and New Swindon. In this year the bank amalgamated with its equal, the Hampshire Banking Co (est. 1834), to form the North Wilts & Hampshire Banking Co which was renamed Capital & Counties Bank Ltd in 1878.

R S Sayers, *Lloyds Bank in the History of English Banking* (London, 1957)

Records: Lloyds TSB Group plc, Archives, Head Office, 71 Lombard Street, London EC3P 3BS

Deed of settlement 1835; directors' meeting minute books 1835–77; prospectus 1836; general meeting minute book 1865–76.

NOTTINGHAM & NOTTINGHAMSHIRE BANKING CO LTD
Nottingham, Nottinghamshire

Records of banks 421

History: This joint stock bank was promoted in 1833 as the Nottingham & Nottinghamshire Joint Stock Bank with a nominal capital of £500,000. It was later known as the Nottingham & Nottinghamshire Banking Co. It opened for business in Pelham Street, Nottingham, in 1834. Fear of competition from the Northern & Central Bank of England (est. 1834) prompted the opening of branches at Mansfield (1834), Newark (1835), Worksop (1836) and Retford (1836) and a discount and exchange agency at Loughborough (1834). No further branches were opened until that at Southwell in 1874. Limited liability was acquired in 1884. In 1885 paid-up capital was £300,000 and deposits were £1.34 million rising to £360,000 and £3.8 million respectively in 1917. In 1919, when it amalgamated with London, County, Westminster & Parr's Bank Ltd (est. 1909), it had twenty branches and eighteen sub-branches.

T E Gregory, *The Westminster Bank Through A Century* (London, 1936)

Records: The Royal Bank of Scotland plc, Archive Section, Regent's House, 42 Islington High Street, London N1 8XL

Deeds of settlement 1834, 1873; directors' minute books (15) 1834–1918; bank note register 1834–1918; customer ledger 1834–35; general manager's letterbook 1844–61; investment and property ledgers (2) 1858–80; clerks' salary minute book 1872–1901; officers' engagement agreement book 1873–92; summary of share capital 1880; property register c.1880–96; staff rules book 1893; manager's letterbook 1897–1909; salary book 1901–18; balance sheets 1907–18; allotment register re share exchange 1919; amalgamation papers 1917–18; premises photographs c.1919.

Shepshed: head office letters 1905–18.

NOTTINGHAM JOINT STOCK BANK LTD
Nottingham, Nottinghamshire

History: This joint stock bank was formed in 1865 and was promoted by local lace merchants and manufacturers assisted by Birmingham joint stock bankers. By the end of 1865, deposits had grown to £150,000 and paid-up capital was £69,000. By 1882 its ten branches and sub-branches included those at Eastwood, Ilkeston, Long Eaton and Ripley. Deposits then stood at £731,000, exceeded £1 million by 1892 and then doubled by 1902. Similarly, paid-up capital was increased from £150,000 in 1887 to £200,000 by 1896. In order to encourage deposits, further branches were opened and by 1905 there were twenty-eight (seven in Nottingham) along with a special Savings Bank Department formed to attract small depositors. In 1905, when paid-up capital was £200,000 and deposits exceeded

422   British banking – a guide to historical records

£2 million, the business was acquired by London, City & Midland Bank Ltd (est. 1836) for the equivalent of £560,000.

W F Crick & J E Wadsworth, *A Hundred Years of Joint Stock Banking* (London, 1936)

Records: HSBC Holdings plc, Group Archives, 10 Lower Thames Street, London EC3R 6AE

Provisional committee minutes 1865; prospectus 1865; directors' meeting minute books (4) 1865–1905; annual reports and balance sheets 1865–1904; share transfer register 1865–1900; security registers (3) 1865–80; general ledgers (11) 1865–1905; list of shareholders 1869,1882; general ledger balance book 1873–1903; general manager's letterbook 1879–1903; directors' meeting agenda and rough minutes (2) 1881–99; customer memorandum book 1891–94; salary books 1866–1905; staff expenses book 1879–92.

Hucknall: general ledger 1885–95; **Mansfield:** security ledger 1894–1905.

NUNN & WEBBER
Manningtree, Essex

History: This private bank was established in 1811 as Mills, Nunn & Co. It was known as Cox & Mills in 1815, as Nunn, Mills & Co in 1823, as Nunn, Nunn & Nunn in 1826 and as Nunn & Webber by 1869. It was otherwise known as the Manningtree & Colchester Bank. It was acquired by the London & County Banking Co Ltd (est. 1836) in 1870.

Harold Preston, *Early East Anglian Banks and Bankers* (Thetford, 1994)

Records: The Royal Bank of Scotland plc, Archive Section, Regent's House, 42 Islington High Street, London N1 8XL

Amalgamation papers 1870–74.

OAKES, BEVAN, TOLLEMACHE & CO
Bury St Edmunds, Suffolk

History: This private bank traced its origins to James Oakes & Son (est. 1795) which was also connected with a bank of the same name at Stowmarket formed in 1804. In 1830 the bank merged with Brown, Bevan, Moor & Hanbury (est. 1801) of Bury to form Oakes, Bevan & Hanbury. The firm was subsequently known as Oakes, Bevan, Moor & Hanbury (1830), Oakes, Bevan & Co (1830), Oakes, Bevan, Moor & Bevan (1840), Oakes, Bevan & Co (1854) and Oakes, Bevan, Tollemache & Co (1895);

Records of banks 423

the firm was otherwise known as the Bury & Suffolk Bank. Branches were at Thetford (1798), Sudbury (1805), Haverhill (1810), Mildenhall (1827), Clare (1829), Brandon (1830), Debenham (1839), Soham (1839), Lakenheath (1898), Feltwell (1898) and Eye. The bank was acquired by the Capital & Counties Bank Ltd (est. 1877) in 1900.

Jane Fiske (ed.), *The Oakes Diaries. Business, Politics and the Family in Bury St Edmunds 1778–1827* (Woodbridge, 1990–91); Harold Preston, *Early East Anglian Banks and Bankers* (Thetford, 1994)

Records 1: Lloyds TSB Group plc, Archives, Head Office, 71 Lombard Street, London EC3P 3BS

Partnership agreements 1827–99; cash book 1856–88; merger papers 1899–1903.

Mildenhall: merger papers 1899–1900; **Stowmarket:** agent appointment agreement 1830; **Sudbury:** security register 1878–82; cashier's book 1883–85.

Records 2: Suffolk Record Office, 77 Raingate Street, Bury St Edmunds IP33 2AR

Business correspondence 1786–1836; business memorandum book of James Oakes 1786–1837; papers re audit, securities, assets and liabilities, profits, etc c.1800–1916; bank notes 1816–28; partnership agreements 1829–30, 1861; profit and loss account book 1830–55; bank note register 1837; customer quarterly balance books 1839–43; rough cash books 1848–53; customer overdraft ledger 1894; balance sheet 1899; abstract of balances transferred 1900; list of bad debts n.d.; payments and receipts ledger n.d.; Bevan and Oakes family papers eighteenth–nineteenth cents.

Stowmarket: list of balances 1863; debtors ledger 1892–93; overdraft sheets 1894; **Sudbury:** overdraft balances 1892–93. [Ref: HA 535/3/2–8]

OLDHAM JOINT STOCK BANK LTD
Oldham, Greater Manchester

History: This joint stock bank was formed in 1880 as Oldham's first joint stock bank. It was established by local industrialists, especially drawn from the cotton spinning industry, who were dissatisfied with the support received from the Oldham-based branches of joint stock banks with head-quarters located elsewhere. Initial paid-up capital was £46,000 and by 1882 deposits had climbed to £400,000. In 1882 the bank acquired the Rochdale, Castleton and Wardle branches of Rochdale Joint Stock Bank (est. 1861) for £35,500. From the late-1880s a determined attempt was made to increase deposits through the opening of branches and by 1888

424   *British banking – a guide to historical records*

seven branches and three sub-branches had been established. By 1890 paid-up capital was £117,000 and deposits stood at £1.4 million. In 1898 the bank was acquired by London, City & Midland Bank Ltd (est. 1836) for the equivalent of £600,000. It then had ten branches, £1.41 million deposits and paid-up capital of £200,000.

W F Crick & J E Wadsworth, *A Hundred Years of Joint Stock Banking* (London, 1936)

Records: HSBC Holdings plc, Group Archives, 10 Lower Thames Street, London EC3R 6AE

Prospectus 1880; investment register 1880–86; directors' meeting minute books (4) 1880–98; board agenda 1880–98; reports and balance sheets 1880–98; share registers 1880–98; security registers (3) 1881–98; general ledger 1882–92; investment ledger 1883–98; building society account ledger 1883–98; summary of capital and shareholders 1898.

OVEREND, GURNEY & CO LTD
London

History: This firm of City of London bill brokers was established in 1802 by Thomas Richardson. He was already well known to the Gurney bankers of Norwich and he obtained much business from them. In 1805 he was joined by John Overend when their business was called Richardson, Overend & Co. In 1807 John and Samuel Gurney joined as partners and in 1827 the business became known as Overend, Gurney & Co on the death of Thomas Richardson. By the 1820s, Overends was the largest bill broker in London and the business was probably larger than those of its three greatest rivals combined. It specialised in country bank business, but was important in all areas of bill broking and dealing. It was a giant in the City with a reputation second to none; by 1859 its profits were almost £500,000. In 1865 the firm's balance sheet total exceeded £15 million. In this year the business was reorganised when the partnership was acquired for a consideration of £5 million by Overend, Gurney & Co Ltd, a newly-formed joint stock company with limited liability. In 1866 this new company collapsed, the result of mismanagement by a new generation of leaders who diversified the business into 'almost every kind of speculative and lock up business', especially New Zealand real estate. A massive financial crisis followed, known in the annals of the City of London as the Overend Gurney Crisis. The collapsed business remained in receivership for thirty years.

Anon, *Report of the Committee of the Defence Association (of the Shareholders of Overend Gurney & Co Ltd)* (priv.pub., 1866); W T C King, *History of the London Discount Market* (London, 1936)

Records of banks 425

Records 1: Durham County Record Office, County Hall, Durham DH1 5UL

Papers re failure 1866–93. [Ref: D/HO/F65]

Records 2: The Royal Bank of Scotland plc, Archive Section, Regent's House, 42 Islington High Street, London N1 8XL

Circular re interest rates 1838; prospectus 1865; circular to creditors 1866; report of provisional official liquidators 1866; auction particulars of Lombard Street, London, property 1867.

Records 3: Leicestershire County Record Office, Long Street, Wigston Magna, Leicester LE8 2AH

Papers re liquidation 1866–68. [Ref: 18D67/121–7, 152, 155]

P&O BANKING CORPORATION LTD
London and Asia

History: This overseas bank was established in 1920 by the shipping company, P&O Steam Navigation Co, together with Lloyds Bank Ltd, National Provincial Bank Ltd and Westminster Bank Ltd. Soon afterwards it acquired a majority holding in the Allahabad Bank Ltd (est. 1865), then the oldest bank in India. By 1927 the P&O Bank operated nine branches (exclusive of the Allahabad branches) in India, Ceylon, the Straits Settlements and China. In 1927 the Chartered Bank (est. 1853) acquired a controlling interest and by 1939 had obtained full ownership. The bank was wound up in 1939.

Records: Location unknown

PAGETS & KIRBY
Leicester, Leicestershire

History: This private bank traced its origins to Thomas Paget, a wealthy stockbreeder with important family connections with the lace and hosiery trade. In 1814 he succeeded his father as a partner in Pares & Heygate (est. 1800) of Leicester but withdrew in 1825 to join William Paget, Joseph Paget and Samuel Kirby, the former chief cashier of Pares, in forming Pagets & Kirby. Branches were opened at Melton Mowbray (1835) and at Loughborough (1855). The lack of family succession led to the sale of the business to Lloyds Bank Ltd (est. 1765) in 1895.

L S Pressnell, *Country Banking in the Industrial Revolution* (Oxford, 1956)

Records: Lloyds TSB Group plc, Archives, Head Office, 71 Lombard Street, London EC3P 3BS

426 British banking – a guide to historical records

Partnership agreements 1838–92; private memorandum book 1888–1900; amalgamation papers 1895.

PAISLEY BANKING CO
Paisley, Strathclyde

History: This bank was established in 1783 by nine merchants, mostly located in the Paisley and Glasgow areas but it was soon challenged by the Paisley Union Banking Co (est. 1788). It enjoyed limited expansion, establishing branches in Glasgow, Dundee (2), Stranraer, Irvine and Alloa (4) and was a long-term creditor of The Royal Bank of Scotland which provided credits and held balances for the bank. It was acquired by the British Linen Co (est. 1746) in 1837 which paid £70,000 for its goodwill.

Records: Bank of Scotland Archive, Operational Services Division, 12 Bankhead Terrace, Sighthill, Edinburgh EH11 4DY

Bank note register 1783–1838.

PAISLEY UNION BANK CO
Paisley, Strathclyde

History: This bank was established with nine partners in 1788. Branches were opened as far apart as Brechin, Oban, Newton Stewart, Kirkcudbright and Berwick while other branches were based in England at Carlisle, Penrith and Wigton but were closed by 1810. Subscribed capital was £10,000 and after ten months note circulation was £60,000 and advances and discounts were £30,000. The Glasgow branch was especially successful but was damaged by a £20,000 robbery in 1811. From 1820 the bank's business declined; the balance sheet total fell from £650,000 in 1820 to £544,000 in 1836. Financial crisis in the 1830s caused the three remaining partners to sell their bank to Glasgow Union Banking Co (est. 1830) in 1838 for £20,000. Deposits were then £327,000 and note circulation was £46,000.

J Bennett Miller, 'The Paisley Union Bank Robbery', *Miscellany*, 1 (1971); C F Freebairn, 'An Old Banking Institution. The Paisley Union Bank', *Scottish Bankers' Magazine*, 16 (1924); Robert S Rait, *The History of the Union Bank of Scotland* (Glasgow, 1930)

Records: Bank of Scotland Archive, Operational Services Division, 12 Bankhead Terrace, Sighthill, Edinburgh EH11 4DY

Journal 1795–96; ledger 1836–39; list of debts owing to the bank 1838.

Records of banks

PALATINE BANK LTD
Manchester, Greater Manchester

History: This joint stock bank was formed in 1899 by leading Manchester businessmen as a means of counteracting the increasing tendency to bank mergers and consequent migration of their control to London. The initial paid-up capital was £62,000. Early on, branches were opened at Oldham, Shaw and Rochdale and at four locations in Manchester; by 1919 twelve branches existed. In 1919, when deposits totalled £1 million, the bank merged with the Bank of Liverpool & Martins Ltd (est. 1831).

George Chandler, *Four Centuries of Banking* (London, 1964–68)

Records: Barclays Bank plc, Group Archives, Dallimore Road, Wythenshawe, Manchester M23 9JA

Provisional committee and directors' meeting minutes 1899–1921; memorandum and articles of association 1899, 1907; registers of shareholders (5) 1899–1920; list of shareholders n.d.; press cutting book 1899–1919; conditions of service 1900; instructions to managers 1901–19; agenda book 1914–23; report and accounts 1919; papers re amalgamation with Bank of Liverpool/Martin's Bank 1919.

PALMER & GREENE
Lichfield, Staffordshire

History: This private bank was established in 1765 as Barker & Co. It was styled J B Scott from 1803 and as Palmer & Greene from 1827. The bank failed in 1855.

Records: Staffordshire Record Office, County Buildings, Eastgate Street, Stafford ST16 2LZ

Partnership agreements 1814–46; papers re failure 1855. [Ref: D[w]1851/8/57(a)]

PARES' LEICESTERSHIRE BANKING CO LTD
Leicester, Leicestershire

History: This bank traced its origins to the private bank of Pares & Heygate, established in St Martin's, Leicester, in 1800 by Thomas Pares, Thomas Paget, John Pares and James Heygate. The Pares and Heygate families were already linked through involvement in a Leicester hosiery business. The London office of this latter business acted as agents of the bank until 1830. Thomas Pares and Thomas Paget left the partnership in 1824, James Heygate died in 1833 while William Heygate, son of James, and Isaac Hodgson joined in 1813 and 1825 respectively. In 1836 the bank

428 *British banking – a guide to historical records*

converted into a joint stock company as Pares' Leicestershire Banking Co; its paid-up capital was £16,350 which was doubled in 1837. Initially no permanent branches were established but market day representation was arranged at Melton Mowbray, Hinckley and Loughborough. Limited liability was acquired in 1880 and by 1902 branches existed at Ashby de la Zouche, Hinckley, Loughborough and Lutterworth while nine sub-branches existed outside Leicester. In 1881 paid-up capital was increased to £350,000 and remained at that level. In 1902, when deposits were £2 million, the bank was acquired by Parr's Bank Ltd (est. 1865).

T E Gregory, *The Westminster Bank Through A Century* (London, 1936)

Records 1: The Royal Bank of Scotland plc, Archive Section, Regent's House, 42 Islington High Street, London N1 8XL

Customer ledger 1800–06; deed of settlement 1836; shareholders' journal 1836; directors' minute books (5) 1836–1902; annual reports 1836–1902; private ledgers (9) 1836–1902; annual general meeting minutes 1837–1902; monthly balance book 1844–1902; stock register 1860–83; share register 1880; private cash books (2) 1880–1902; share transfer notice book 1889–1902; rough board minutes 1890–1902; balance sheets 1894–1901; accounts with other banks 1898–99; schedule of bad and doubtful debts 1902; amalgamation papers 1902.

Hinckley: customer ledger 1826–27.

Records 2: Derby Local Studies Library, 25B Irongate, Derby DE1 3GL

Correspondence of Thomas Pares, banker, c.1760–1840s. [Ref: Pares collection]

Records 3: Leicestershire County Record Office, Long Street, Wigston Magna, Leicester LE8 2AH

Receipts 1839; passbook 1844–50; pamphlet re legal case nineteenth cent; memorandum re foundation and development 1864; architectural drawings 1872–74, 1901. [Ref: 2D51/1–2; 10D72/701; DE 2793/21; Misc 59, 613; DG47]

PARKER, SHORE & CO
Sheffield, South Yorkshire

History: This private bank was formed in 1774 by John Shore, the son of a local factor or middleman in the cutlery trade. In 1778 it acquired the business of the failed bank of Benjamin Roebuck (est. 1770). It was known variously as John Shore and Parker, Shore & Blakelock but latterly was known as Parker, Shore & Co; it was also styled Sheffield Bank and

Records of banks 429

Sheffield Old Bank. It grew to be one of Sheffield's most respected banks but in 1843 suspended payment with £500,000 liabilities. In the aftermath of its failure, the Sheffield Union Banking Co was formed which acquired Parker, Shore's premises and much of its business.

E Hartley, *Banking in Yorkshire* (Clapham, 1975); R E Leader, 'The Early Sheffield Banks', *Journal of the Institute of Bankers*, 38 (1917)

Records: HSBC Holdings plc, Group Archives, 10 Lower Thames Street, London EC3R 6AE

Balance sheets and list of profits 1835–43; list of customers' deposits and credit and debit balances 1843; papers re the estates of partners c.1840–60.

PARR'S BANK LTD
Warrington, Cheshire, and London

History: This private bank was established in about 1782 as Parr & Co by Joseph Parr, Thomas Lyon, sugar refiner, and Walter Kerfoot, attorney; it was otherwise known as the Warrington Bank. It was styled Parr, Lyon & Greenall from 1825 and Parr, Lyon & Co from 1851. Branches were opened in St Helens (1839) and Runcorn (1853). Under the leadership of John Dun, in 1865 the bank was reconstructed as a joint stock bank with limited liability. It was called Parr's Banking Co Ltd and the partners in the old business were paid £100,000. The paid-up capital of the new bank was also £100,000 rising to £1.7 million in 1904. The bank expanded by means of acquisition of smaller banks including the private banks of Thomas Firth & Son (est. 1828) of Northwich in 1865; Thomas Woodcock, Sons & Eckersley (est. 1792) of Wigan in 1874; Dixon & Co (est. 1808) of Chester in 1878; F W Jennings (est. 1855) of Leek in 1878; Shrubsole & Co (est. 1792) of Kingston-upon-Thames in 1894; and T Barnard & Co (est. 1799) of Bedford in 1915. More important, it acquired leading London private banks and joint stock banks, viz: National Bank of Liverpool Ltd (est. 1863) in 1883; Fuller, Banbury, Nix & Co (est. 1737) of London in 1891 which provided a seat in the London Clearing House; Alliance Bank Ltd (est. 1862) in 1892 after which the bank became known as Parr's Banking Co & Alliance Bank Ltd; Croxon, Jones & Co (Old Bank) Ltd (est. 1893) of Oswestry in 1894; Sir Samuel Scott Bart. & Co (est. 1824) of London in 1894; the Consolidated Bank Ltd (est. 1829) in 1896; Derby & Derbyshire Banking Co Ltd (est. 1833) in 1898; Ashton, Stalybridge, Hyde & Glossop Bank Ltd (est. 1836) in 1900; Dumbell's Banking Co Ltd (est. 1874) in 1900; Pares' Leicestershire Banking Co Ltd (est. 1836) in 1902; Whitehaven Joint Stock Bank Ltd (est. 1829) in 1908; Robin Brothers (est. 1879) of Jersey in 1908; Stuckey's Banking Co Ltd

430   *British banking – a guide to historical records*

(est. 1826) in 1909; and Crompton & Evans' Union Bank Ltd (est. 1877) of Derby in 1914. By 1890 it had forty-three branches and sub-branches, rising to 136 in 1900 and to 320 branches nationwide by 1914. In 1896 its name was abbreviated to Parr's Bank Ltd. In 1918 it amalgamated with London, County & Westminster Bank Ltd (est. 1834) to form London, County, Westminster & Parr's Bank Ltd.

T E Gregory, *The Westminster Bank Through A Century* (London, 1936); William Howarth, *The Banks in the Clearing House* (London, 1905); William Howarth, *Our Leading Banks* (London, 1894)

Records 1: The Royal Bank of Scotland plc, Archive Section, Regent's House, 42 Islington High Street, London N1 8XL

Customer ledger 1788–95; partnership agreements (6) 1804–57; correspondence with customers 1823–26; salary books (3) 1856–63; counsel's opinion re distribution of profits 1860; papers re Parr family nineteenth century; prospectus 1865; provisional committee list 1865; circular re formation 1865; certificate of incorporation 1865; share ledger 1865–90; annual reports 1865–1917; directors' minute books (7) 1865–1918; weekly balance sheets 1865; select committee minutes 1865–66; counsel's opinion on share deposits 1865, 1883; acquisition agreements/papers: Thomas Firth & Co 1865–66, Metropolitan Bank re Macclesfield business 1867, Woodcock Sons & Eckersley 1874, Dixon & Co 1878, National Bank of Liverpool 1883, Fuller Banbury Nix & Co 1891–92, Croxon Jones & Co 1894, Sir Samuel Scott 1894, Alliance Bank 1896, Thomas Barnard & Co 1915, London, County & Westminster Bank 1918; annual general meeting minutes 1866–1918; deed of mutual release with schedule of assets guaranteed by partners to Parr's Bank 1867; register of staff life assurance policies 1870s–1920; registration certificates 1878–98; dividend register 1885; letters re securities 1891–1909; notebook of J Rae 1890–1905; circulars re Association of English Country Bankers 1888–1910; weekly committee minutes 1892–95; certificates of change of name 1892–96; booklet of agreements with other firms 1892; record of dividends 1892–1918; list of shareholders 1897; general manager's reports 1897–1901; loan papers: Serbian government 1897, Japanese government 1899–1910, South Manchurian railway 1907–11, Yokohama 1909, Osaka 1907, Tokyo 1912; branch and premises committee minutes 1898–1918; directors' correspondence 1897; lists of officers books (8) 1897–1922; papers re projected amalgamation with Union Bank of Manchester 1900; Dumbell's Banking Co: papers re bank note issue and acquisition 1900–10, legal documents re Isle of Man properties 1900–29; register of directors 1901–16; correspondence re bad debts 1902; branch status reports 1903; staff instruction book 1903; statistics of branches and staff 1904; general purposes com-

Records of banks 431

mittee minutes 1908–29; salary book 1908–31; articles of association 1873–1909; daily committee minutes 1909–13; 'A', 'B' and 'C' committee minutes 1910–23; papers re agricultural credit societies 1911–13; agreements with Hongkong & Shanghai Bank 1912, 1916; papers of J W Johnson 1912, 1943; branch results 1913; scheme of charges 1912; dividend counterfoils 1913; widows' and orphans' fund: committee minute 1914, report and valuation 1917; memorandum book re comparative performances with other banks and papers re projected amalgamations 1917; amalgamation papers 1917–18.

Bedford: branch return 1915; **Castletown:** character book 1900–18; **Chard:** character book 1912–53; **Chester:** salary book 1914–54; **Chiswick:** branch return 1908; **Coventry:** salary book 1905–38; memorandum books 1906–26; **Derby:** security ledgers 1870s–1920; **Kingston-upon-Thames:** head office correspondence 1902–05; **Leicester:** list of overdrawn accounts 1904; **London, Bartholomew Lane:** memorandum book 1904–22; **London, Charing Cross:** comparative statements and analysis of profits 1896–1903; **London, Lombard Street:** securities papers 1891–1909; **Manchester:** profits statistics 1896–1908; **Northwich:** letters from general manager 1882–85; branch minute books (3) 1888–1901; **Port St Mary:** character book 1900–18; **Ramsey:** character book 1900–18; **Sherborne:** branch minute book 1916–31; **Somerton:** inspection book 1911–34; **Teddington:** deposit ledger 1899–1917; general ledgers (3) 1899–1918; returns book 1899–1918; branch minute book 1900–18; loan ledgers 1901–18; **Wrexham:** branch signature book 1890–1910; **Yeovil:** head office letterbooks (8) 1910–30.

Records 2: Warrington Local Studies Library, Museum Street, Warrington, Cheshire, WA1 1JB

Papers, deeds and accounts: Lyon family estates 1566–1860, Parr family estates 1600–1900; memorandum and articles of association 1865.

PARSONS, THOMSON & CO
Oxford, Oxfordshire

History: This private bank was established in 1771 as Fletcher & Parsons; its founding partners were William Fletcher and Herbert Parsons, men's mercers. It was otherwise known as Oxford Old Bank. Fletcher died in 1827 and was succeeded by his nephew, Thomas Robinson, after which the business was known as Robinson, Parsons & Co. After Robinson's death in 1848 it was known as Parsons, Thomson, Parsons & Co and from 1877 as Parsons, Thomson & Co. The bank was acquired by Barclay & Co Ltd (est. 1896) in 1900.

432   *British banking – a guide to historical records*

L F Bradburn, *The Old Bank Oxford* (Oxford, 1977); P W Matthews & Anthony W Tuke, *History of Barclays Bank Ltd* (London, 1926)

Records: Barclays Bank plc, Group Archives, Dallimore Road, Wythenshawe, Manchester M23 9JA

Customer ledgers (190) 1802–1901; bank notes 1812–17; notebooks 1814–1900; ledger, creditors and debtors 1819–1925; draft 1820; cheque 1845; ledger, current accounts and profit and loss 1847–89; bank note indemnity in-letters 1847–1901; subscriptions 1849–1903; passport, Herbert Parsons 1855; register, unclaimed balances 1855–71; cash book 1868–80; legal opinion 1868; circular 1882; Oxford Savings Bank bond 1883–84; fraud legal papers 1885–91; impersonal ledgers 1889–1900; balance sheets 1892–1900; valuations, lists of accounts and balance sheet papers 1892–1900; banker's licence 1898; merger papers Barclay & Co Ltd 1900–04.

PAYNE & CO
Crewkerne, Somerset

History: This private bank was established in 1810 as Perham, Phelps & Co. In 1819 it acquired Hoskins & Co (est. 1801), also of Crewkerne, and was styled Payne & Co from 1826. The bank was acquired by Stuckey's Banking Co (est. 1826) in 1829.

Records: The Royal Bank of Scotland plc, Archive Section, Regent's House, 42 Islington High Street, London N1 8XL

Customer ledgers (2) 1810 on.

PAYNE, HOPE & CO
Wells, Somerset

History: This private bank was formed in 1800 and failed in 1831.

Records: Somerset Record Office, Obridge Road, Taunton TA2 7PU

Partnership agreement and papers re failure 1809–31. [Ref: DD/WM 435, 438–441]

PEACOCK, WILLSON & CO
Sleaford, Lincolnshire

History: This private bank was formed in 1792 as Peacock, Handley & Kirton. It was known as Handley, Peacock & Handley from 1827, as Handley, Peacock, Handley & Peacock from 1841, as Peacock, Handley & Co from 1858 and as Peacock, Willson & Co from 1861. Otherwise it was known as the Sleaford Bank and as the Newark & Sleaford Bank.

Records of banks 433

Branches were opened at Newark (1809), Bourne (1810) and Lincoln (1895) and sub-branches were at Heckington and Billinghay. The business was acquired by Lloyds Bank Ltd (est. 1765) in 1912.

L S Pressnell, *Country Banking in the Industrial Revolution* (Oxford, 1956)

Records 1: Lloyds TSB Group plc, Archives, Head Office, 71 Lombard Street, London EC3P 3BS

Customer ledgers (2) 1792–1812; waste books (3) 1802–04; memorandum book 1805–27; profit and loss accounts 1815–21; bank note registers (2) 1816–77; private ledgers (4) 1888–1924; stock exchange loan book 1895–1909; amalgamation papers 1912.

Sleaford: letterbook 1902–03.

Records 2: Lincolnshire Archives, St Rumbold Street, Lincoln LN2 5AB

Partnership papers 1819–1908; customer balances and memoranda 1841; correspondence re customer account 1841; papers re mortgages and lawsuits 1880–1918; amalgamation papers 1912; personal papers of Walter and Francis Fane n.d. [Ref: PSJ 7/26; Fane papers]

J & J W PEASE
Darlington, County Durham

History: The Pease family worked in the worsted trade in the eighteenth century but widened their interests in the nineteenth century to include local railways and the Consett Iron Co. Joseph Pease added banking to these interests in about 1820, trading as Pease & Co, and he remained the sole partner of his banking business until joined by his eldest son in 1870. There may have been family contacts with banks at Whitby and Malton. On his death in 1872 his four other sons joined their brother as partners. The bank's customers were entirely businesses. It had no branches, never issued its own notes and until 1893 was not recorded as a bank in the *Bankers' Almanac*. The bank failed in 1902 when its business was acquired by Barclay & Co Ltd (est. 1896).

M W Kirby, *Men of Business and Politics. The Rise and Fall of the Quaker Pease Dynasty of North East England 1700–1943* (1984); P W Matthews & Anthony W Tuke, *History of Barclays Bank Ltd* (London, 1926); Maberly Phillips, *Banks, Bankers and Banking in Northumberland, Durham and North Yorkshire* (London, 1894)

Records 1: Barclays Bank plc, Group Archives, Dallimore Road, Wythenshawe, Manchester M23 9JA

434   *British banking – a guide to historical records*

Cheques 1901; papers re liquidation 1902–04.

Records 2: Durham County Record Office, County Hall, Durham DH1 5UL

Correspondence of Pease family 1793–1902; notebooks and diaries of John Pease 1817–45; extracts from diaries of Edward Pease 1841–57; papers re failure 1900–06. [Ref: D/HO/C; D/HO/F93, 96–106; D/Pe 3/130–149]

PEASE, HOARE & PEASE
Hull, Humberside

History: This private bank was established in 1754 by Joseph Pease, owner of a linseed crushing business, as Josh. Pease & Son; it was otherwise known as Pease's Old Bank. It was subsequently styled Pease, Knowsley & Wray, as Pease & Liddell and as Pease, Hoare & Pease. It was connected with Machell, Peases & Hoare (est. 1797) of Beverley and with Richardson, Holt & Co (est. 1816) of Whitby. It amalgamated with York Union Banking Co Ltd (est. 1833) in 1894.

P W Matthews & Anthony W Tuke, *History of Barclays Bank Ltd* (London, 1926)

Records 1: Barclays Bank plc, Group Archives, Dallimore Road, Wythenshawe, Manchester M23 9JA

Private account ledgers (3) 1757–66; promissory notes 1761, 1841–64; sales of wheat accounts 1768; stock sold list 1760s; bank notes 1782; cheque 1787; bill of exchange 1788; Pease family investments correspondence 1812–1904; deposit receipt 1838–59; unpaid bills 1851–65.

Records 2: Hull City Record Office, 79 Lowgate, Hull HU1 2AA

Passbooks of Pease family c.1754–1818; correspondence re personal, family and banking matters c.1795–1850; ledger 1809–49; journals of J R Pease 1822–65; partnership papers nineteenth cent. [Ref: DEP 338–43, 897, 1801–4, 1821, 2937, 3002]

PEDDERS & CO
Preston, Lancashire

History: This private bank was formed in 1776 as Atherton, Leak & Co and was subsequently known as Pedders & Co. It was wound up in 1861.

F S Moxon, *A Brief History of Pedders & Co, Preston Old Bank, 1776–1861* (c.1930s)

Records of banks **435**

Records 1: Lancashire Record Office, Bow Lane, Preston PR1 2RE

Cheque book 1851; agreement for winding up 1861; historical papers and notes n.d. [Ref: DDX 103; DDX 842/3, DDP]

Records 2: West Yorkshire Archive Service, Yorkshire Archaeological Society, Claremont, 23 Clarendon Road, Leeds LS2 9NZ

Deed of dissolution of partnership 1827. [Ref: MD 290 bx 9]

PERCIVAL & CO
Northampton, Northamptonshire

History: This private bank was formed by 1797. In 1836 it was reconstructed by John and Samuel Percival as a joint stock bank known as the Northampton Union Bank.

Records: The Royal Bank of Scotland plc, Archive Section, Regent's House, 42 Islington High Street, London N1 8XL

Customer account ledger 1814–17; papers re infringement of Bank of England's monopoly 1836.

PERFECT & CO
Leeds, West Yorkshire

History: This private bank was formed in about 1809 and in 1834 it was acquired by the newly-formed Yorkshire District Banking Co (est. 1834). It was connected with John Seaton, Sons & Foster of Pontefract which was formed in 1801 as Perfect, Seaton & Co.

Records: West Yorkshire Archive Service, Leeds District Archives, Chapeltown Road, Sheepscar, Leeds LS7 3AP

Business and personal papers of the Perfect family 1772–1848; amalgamation papers 1835. [Ref: Acc 1744]

PERTH BANKING CO
Perth, Tayside

History: This copartnery was formed in 1787 to acquire the business of the Perth United [Banking] Co (est. 1766). Its capital was £34,000. The bank was reformed in 1808 and it subsequently prospered. By 1857 its capital stood at £100,000. In 1857 Union Bank of Scotland (est. 1830) purchased the bank for £200,000.

Robert S Rait, *History of the Union Bank of Scotland* (Glasgow, 1930)

436   *British banking – a guide to historical records*

Records 1: Bank of Scotland Archive, Operational Services Division, 12 Bankhead Terrace, Sighthill, Edinburgh EH11 4DY

Sederunt/minute book 1785–1811; progressive ledgers 1768–89; directors' meeting minute book 1786–1832; teller's cash book 1787–88; bill book 1787–88; general ledger 1787–88; inland bills 1787–91; bills of exchange 1787–94; register of bonds 1787–1857; stock journal 1787–1857; bills discounted 1788–92; dividend books 1788–1878; cashier's cash books 1795–1831; stock ledger 1804–57; ledgers 1808–19; contract of co-partnery 1808, 1828; letterbook 1809–11; bankrupt ledger 1811–25; interest receipts 1821–57; minute books 1828–72; letterbook 1829–31; ledger accounts 1829–43; stock transfer minutes 1830–57; interest receipt book 1841–57; investment ledger 1841–57; notes in circulation 1843–67.

Coupar Angus: cash book 1795–1808; cash account ledger 1809–11; **Dunkeld:** ledger 1809–17.

Records 2: Perth & Kinross Council Archive, A K Bell Library, 2–8 York Place, Perth PH2 8EP

Bank note 1798; cash account rules 1790s; counsel's opinion re sequestrated estates of bank agents 1823. [Ref: B59/37/14/3–4, 8]

PERTH UNITED [BANKING] CO
Perth, Tayside

History: This copartnery was formed in 1766 through the merger of six small banking businesses in Perth including the Perth Banking Co (est. 1763), the Tannerie Banking Co (est. 1764) and the Craigie Banking Co (est. 1764). The new business was variously known as the Perth United Banking Co and the Perth United Co. The 1765 Bank Act had put an end to the issue of small notes thus forcing this amalgamation. The bank remained prosperous but was placed in voluntary liquidation in 1787 in compliance with its partnership agreement and was reformed as the Perth Banking Co.

Records: Bank of Scotland Archive, Operational Services Division, 12 Bankhead Terrace, Sighthill, Edinburgh EH11 4DY

Dividend book 1771–90; stock ledger 1766–90; transfer journal 1766–90; general ledger 1766–67.

PETTY & POSTLETHWAITE
Ulverston, Cumbria

History: This private bank was formed as Edmund Petty in about 1804 and by his death in 1816 had 500 accounts. The Pettys were well estab-

Records of banks 437

lished at Ulverston where they were mercers and merchants and had, *inter alia*, shipping, shipbuilding and textile manufacturing interests. From about 1820 the business was known as Petty & Postlethwaite following the admission of William Postlethwaite; it then had district significance serving customers as far afield as Preston, Lancaster and Coniston. In 1863 the bank was acquired by Wakefield, Crewdson & Co (est. 1788) of Kendal.

George Chandler, *Four Centuries of Banking* (London, 1964–68).

Records 1: Barclays Bank plc, Group Archives, Dallimore Road, Wythenshawe, Manchester M23 9JA

Trial balance sheet, Edmund Petty I 1795; private ledger 1810–59; deeds of James Hunter, loan security 1817–40; cash books, includes wine and timber trade, rates etc (9) 1823–73; papers re estate of George Shaw Petty 1828–74; probate papers of James Park including cheques 1820s–1860s; out-letters 1840–66; cash book, George Shaw Petty with Wakefield Crewdson & Co 1864–73; daily cash balances 1864–66.

Records 2: Cumbria Record Office, 140 Duke Street, Barrow-in-Furness LA14 1XW

Waste books and ledgers (7) 1832–61. [Ref: BDX 209]

PETER PEW & CO
Sherborne, Dorset

History: This private bank was established in about 1740 as Pretor & Co and was otherwise known as the Sherborne & Dorsetshire Bank. By 1810 it traded as S Pretor, R Pew & B Chandler and was later known as Peter Pew & Co. It was acquired by National Provincial Bank of England (est. 1833) in 1843.

Records 1: The Royal Bank of Scotland plc, Archive Section, Regent's House, 42 Islington High Street, London N1 8XL

Partner's private cash book 1763–76; partner's private ledger 1793–1824; letterbook 1794–1805.

Records 2: Dorset Record Office, Bridport Road, Dorchester DT1 1RP

Simon Pretor: cash book 1773–76, personal ledger 1793–1824, letterbook 1795–1804. [Ref: MIC/R/12]

PIERSON & SON
Hitchin, Hertfordshire

438   *British banking – a guide to historical records*

History: This private bank was established in 1789 as Wilshere, Pierson, Crabb & Chapman by Joseph Pierson, malster, William Wilshere, attorney with interests in Wilshere & Co (est. 1789), bankers at Hertford, John Crabb, brewer, and Daniel Chapman, gentleman; it was otherwise known as the Hitchin & Hertfordshire Bank. Several partners financed their substantial businesses using the bank's resources. In the nineteenth century, Joseph M Pierson was the most important partner and from 1839 the business was known as Pierson & Son. He also had interests in banks at Biggleswade and Bedford. On his sudden death in 1842, the bank failed but most claimants were subsequently paid in full.

Jack Parker, *Nothing for Nothing for Nobody* (Stevenage, 1986)

Records: Hertfordshire County Record Office, County Hall, Hertford SG13 8DE

Partnership agreement 1789; partner's passbooks (2) 1789–1808; private ledgers (2) 1815–34; account books (3) 1804–24; partner's executors' accounts (3) 1825–36. [Ref: Wilshere family archives 61507–15, 61544, 67367]

PINCKNEY BROS
Salisbury, Wiltshire

History: This private bank was formed in 1811 as Everett & Co but was subsequently known as Hetley, Everett & Co and was renamed Pinckney Bros in about 1859; it was also styled the New Sarum Bank and Salisbury Old Bank. It was acquired by the Wilts & Dorset Banking Co Ltd (est. 1835) in 1897.

Records: Lloyds TSB Group plc, Archives, Head Office, 71 Lombard Street, London EC3P 3BS

Dividend ledgers (7) 1799–1897 [w]; security registers/interest ledgers (4) 1811–42, 1871–97; amalgamation agreement 1896.

PITT, POWELL & FRIPP
Bristol, Avon

History: This private bank was formed in 1808 as Birch, Pitt, Powell, Fripp & Brice. Its partners were leading Bristol businessmen and included two brass founders and a soap manufacturer. In 1812 Edward New joined the partnership which then became known as Birch, Pitt, Powell, Fripp, Brice & New. This was dissolved in 1819 when Samuel Birch, senior partner, died and was reformed as Pitt, Powell, Fripp, Brice & New. By 1826 the partners were Joseph Pitt, Timothy Powell and William Fripp and in that year the bank discontinued business.

Charles H Cave, *A History of Banking in Bristol from 1750 to 1899* (Bristol, 1899)

Records: Bristol Record Office, 'B' Bond Warehouse, Smeaton Road, Bristol BS1 6XN

Partnership agreement 1808. [Ref: 39084(1)]

POCKLINGTON & CO
Newark, Nottinghamshire

History: This private bank was established in about 1797 as Pocklington, Rastell, Oliver & Ray and was otherwise known as the Newark Bank. It was styled Pocklington, Dickinson, Hunter & Co by 1805 when it was issuing its own bank notes. The bank was titled Pocklington, Dickinson & Co from 1806 and Pocklington & Co from 1807. It ceased to trade in 1809.

Records: Nottinghamshire Archives, County House, Castle Meadow Road, Nottingham NG2 1AG

Deed of dissolution of partnership 1799–1800. [Ref: DDSK 191/31–32; CP5/7/128]

POLE, THORNTON, FREE, DOWN & SCOTT
London

History: This private bank was established in 1773 as Marlar, Lascelles, Pell & Down and was based in Lombard Street, City of London. In 1782 it was known as Down & Pell, as Down, Thornton & Free in 1785 and as Down, Thornton, Free & Cornwall in 1794. In 1815 it was known as Pole, Thornton, Free, Down & Scott. In 1825 the bank failed.

Anon, 'Henry Sykes Thornton', *Three Banks Review*, 69 (1966); Anon, 'Letters from a Young Lady [Marianne Thornton]', *Three Banks Review*, 6 (1950); F G Hilton Price, *A Handbook of London Bankers* (London, 1876)

Records: The Royal Bank of Scotland plc, Archive Section, Regent's House, 42 Islington High Street, London N1 8XL

Personal papers of Henry Thornton and his executors including papers re his sugar refinery 1770–1875; country ledger abstracts 1805–12; papers re customer debt 1813–15; customer account balance sheets 1814–17; profit and loss account c.1815; circular re partnership 1815.

POMFRET, BURRA & CO
Ashford, Kent

440   *British banking – a guide to historical records*

History: This private bank was formed in 1791 as Jemmett, Whitfeld & Jemmett. It was styled Jemmett, Curteis & Jemmett from about 1821; Jemmett & Pomfret from about 1836; Jemmett, Pomfret, Burra & Simonds from 1847; and Pomfret, Burra & Co from 1875. It was also known as the Ashford Bank. It was acquired by Lloyds Bank Ltd (est. 1765) in 1902.

Records: Lloyds TSB Group plc, Archives, Head Office, 71 Lombard Street, London EC3P 3BS

Partnership agreements 1833,1848; amalgamation papers 1892.

PRAEDS & CO
London

History: This private bank was formed in Fleet Street, City of London, in 1802 as Praeds, Digby, Box, Babbage & Co. The Praed family, who had been bankers in Cornwall since the seventeenth century and who were principal partners in the Cornish Bank (est. 1771) of Truro, provided the bank's management. Their previous London connection was Biddulph, Cocks, Eliot & Praed (est. 1776) in which they provided partners until 1792 and which acted as the Cornish Bank's London agents until 1786. Praeds' founding partners included John Eliot, later first Earl of St Germains. The bank was styled Praed, Digby, Box, Babbage & Co in 1805; Praed, Digby, Box, Barnard & Newcombe in 1807; Praed, Mackworth & Newcombe in 1810; Praed, Mackworth, Newcombe & Fane in 1818; Praed, Mackworth, Fane & Praed in 1836; and Praed, Fane, Praed & Johnson in 1839. From 1850 the bank was renamed Praeds & Co and it was acquired by Lloyds Bank Ltd (est. 1765) in 1891. The bank's first premises, at 189 Fleet Street, were designed by Sir John Soane.

F G Hilton Price, *A Handbook of London Bankers* (London, 1876)

Records: Lloyds TSB Group plc, Archives, Head Office, 71 Lombard Street, London EC3P 3BS

Partners' ledger 1802–09; stock ledgers (3) c.1806–89 [w]; general ledgers (2) 1845–90; safe custody books (2) 1855–92; signature book c.1879–90; partnership agreement 1888; amalgamation papers 1891.

PRESCOTT'S BANK LTD
London

History: This important private bank was established in 1766 as Prescott, Grote, Culverden & Hollingsworth at Threadneedle Street, City of London. In 1799 the style was Prescott, Grote & Hollingsworth and subsequently it was Prescott, Grote & Prescott (1801); Prescott, Grote,

Records of banks 441

Ames, Baillie & Grote (1838); Prescott, Grote, Ames, Cave & Grote (1839); and Prescott, Grote, Cave & Cave (1848). In 1891 it merged with Dimsdale, Fowler, Barnard & Dimsdales (est. 1760) of Cornhill, London, with Miles, Cave, Baillie & Co (est. 1750) of Bristol, and with Tugwell, Brymer & Co (est. c.1760s) of Bath to become a joint stock bank under the title of Prescott, Dimsdale, Cave, Tugwell & Co Ltd. This bank subsequently acquired Moger, Sons & Jones (est. 1815) of Bath in 1891; Harwood & Co (est. 1808) of Thornbury in 1891; Deane & Co (est. 1787) of Winchester in 1891; Bulpett & Hall (est. 1789) of Winchester in 1892; Hilton, Rigden & Rigden (est. 1796) of Faversham in 1892; Thomas Butcher & Sons (est. 1836) in 1900; and Sanders, Snow & Co (est. 1901) of Exeter in 1902. The bank was renamed Prescott's Bank Ltd in 1903 when there were six branches in London and twenty-five (including agencies) in the provinces. In 1903, when its paid-up capital was £503,000 and its balance sheet total was £6.18 million, it amalgamated with Union of London & Smiths Bank Ltd (est. 1839).

Anon, 'Prescott's Bank', National Provincial Bank Review (1966–68)

Records 1: The Royal Bank of Scotland plc, Archive Section, Regent's House, 42 Islington High Street, London N1 8XL

Customer ledger 1766; partnership agreements (13) 1776–1888; unpaid bills 1778–1893; partners' expenses book 1779–85; papers re bad debts, bankruptcies etc 1787–1888; weekly balance sheets and profit and loss accounts 1780–1864; income and expenditure books of W W Prescott (6) 1799–1863; signature books (8) 1794–1891; partners' passbooks (3) 1801–38; staff salary book 1807–89; fidelity bonds 1809–65; partners' letterbook 1815–36; stock register 1818–31; papers re partners' interests in shipbuilding firms 1825–95; railway company investment papers 1829–96; standing order register 1834–44; partners' minute books (11) 1839–90; directors' private papers: Sir Herbert Barnard 1850–1905, Sir Joseph Cockfield Dimsdale 1892–1901; security register 1852–92; salary lists 1859–1901; bad debts register 1860–1918; statements of final balances 1871; partners' profit distribution sheets 1871–90; half-yearly balance sheets 1871–90; assignment of shares in firm 1872–75; advances registers (3) 1876–1911; staff register 1889–1966; agreement for formation of limited company 1890; articles of association 1890; balance sheets 1890–1903; directors' meeting minute books (2) 1891–1903; agenda books (3) 1891–1903; committee minute books (2) 1891–1904; papers re proposed amalgamations 1891–97; secretary's memorandum book 1891; investment and premises register 1891–1903; letters from branches 1891–1903; central ledger, includes merger details 1891–1902; papers re legal case against Bank of England 1892; law book 1892–1905; profit

442   *British banking – a guide to historical records*

and loss accounts and balance sheets 1900–03; amalgamation papers 1903.

Bath: manager's diaries 1893–1904; **Bristol:** staff salary list 1891; current account book 1892–1905; correspondence re overdrafts 1900; advance register 1901; **London, Cornhill:** security register 1860–82.

Records 2: Hertfordshire County Record Office, County Hall, Hertford SG13 8DE

Letters to Lord Rindlesham from Prescott, Grote & Co 1845–52. [Ref: D/EB/384 F4]

PRESTON BANKING CO LTD
Preston, Lancashire

History: This joint stock bank was formed by Royal charter in 1844, its promoters being largely cotton merchants and manufacturers and corn merchants. Staff were recruited from the local branch of the Manchester & Liverpool District Banking Co (est. 1829). The rapidly expanding local cotton textile industry provided much business and the bank made steady progress. In 1850, when paid-up capital was £100,000 and deposits stood at £300,000, the first branch, at Lancaster, was opened. Two more were added in 1857 at Ormskirk and Southport following the closure of Robert Lawe & Co (est. 1825) of Preston and its branches in those two towns. A branch at Blackburn was established in 1863 and others at Fleetwood, Garstang, Lytham and Blackpool followed in 1864. By the end of this year deposits exceeded £1 million for the first time, but progress was then halted. The bank was damaged severely during the Cotton Famine of the early 1860s when Preston's cotton industry was almost brought to a standstill. With £400,000 locked up in loans to two failed businesses, the bank suspended payments in 1866. It was reconstructed, when paid-up capital was increased to £239,000, and it resumed business five weeks later although the branches at Blackburn and Lancaster never reopened. With confidence restored, it prospered from the 1870s and in 1880 deposits once more exceeded £1 million. In 1883 limited liability was acquired. The number of branches increased; by 1894 there were ten full branches and sixteen sub-branches. In that year the business was acquired by London & Midland Bank Ltd (est. 1836) for the equivalent of £636,000. It then had deposits of £1.8 million and paid-up capital of £200,000 and was the twentieth largest provincial bank.

W F Crick & J E Wadsworth, *A Hundred Years of Joint Stock Banking* (London, 1936)

Records: HSBC Holdings plc, Group Archives, 10 Lower Thames Street, London EC3R 6AE

Provisional committee minutes and report 1844; list of shareholders 1844; directors' meeting minutes (4) 1844–72; annual reports and balance sheets 1844–94; general minute book 1844–60; weekly balance book 1844–65; salary books (2) 1844–66; papers re customers' securities 1840s–93; deed of settlement 1845; royal charter 1845; share transfer registers 1845–94; balance sheets 1845–65; report of shareholders' meeting 1866; applications for advances (6) 1866–67; liquidation papers 1867; customers' balance sheets 1868–69; specimen staff contracts 1871–88; security deposit ledger 1878–94; papers re fraud by manager 1881–86; letterbook 1883–85; investment ledger 1883–84; annual summary of capital and shareholders 1884–92; applications for advances 1884; agreement re Bankers' Guarantee & Trust Fund policies 1894; amalgamation papers 1894.

Fleetwood: security registers (2) 1876–97; **Southport, Lord Street:** general ledgers 1857–76; signature book 1878–85.

PRESTON UNION BANK LTD
Preston, Lancashire

History: This joint stock bank was formed in 1869, as the Preston Adelphi Loan, Discount & Deposit Co Ltd, with a nominal capital of £25,000 which was increased to £50,000 in 1873. Its performance was unremarkable; in 1878, for example, most profits went to write off bad debts. The balance sheet then totalled £57,500, deposits were £22,500 and paid-up capital was £27,500. In 1879 the business was reconstructed as the Union Bank of Preston Ltd and all branches were closed but recovery proved elusive; in 1881 deposits were just £17,000. In 1882 another reconstruction was organised when the bank was reconstituted as the Preston Union Bank Ltd. This involved a major write down in capital but ushered in a period of sustained prosperity. By 1886 paid-up capital was £25,000, rising to £30,000, while the balance sheet totalled £47,000 in 1882 and £131,650 in 1892. In 1894 the business was acquired by the Lancashire & Yorkshire Bank Ltd (est. 1872) for £52,000.

George Chandler, *Four Centuries of Banking* (London, 1964–68)

Records: Barclays Bank plc, Group Archives, Dallimore Road, Wythenshawe, Manchester M23 9JA

Certificates of incorporation 1869–82; letters 1869–76; memorandum and articles of association 1873–82; bills of charges 1873–94; agenda book 1877–94; minutes 1879–1903; report and accounts 1879–93; lists of bad and doubtful debts 1879; resolutions 1879, 1884; annual general meeting

444 *British banking – a guide to historical records*

notices 1882–99; share transfer 1883; share certificates 1883–94; extraordinary general meeting notice 1883; prospectus 1884; dividend warrant 1884; general meeting minutes 1885–94; circular letters re shares 1886–94; cheque 1889; annual meeting report 1893; papers re amalgamation with Lancashire & Yorkshire Bank 1894; affidavit re liquidation 1895–99.

H C PRIESTMAN, GEORGE ROPER & CO
Richmond, North Yorkshire

History: This private bank was formed in 1792 as Sir John Lawson, Bart., Miles Stapleton Esq & Co; it was also known as the Richmond Bank. When Lawson died in 1811, the style became Thomas Stapleton, John Robinson & George Kay and thereafter it operated under several titles until in 1868 it was renamed H C Priestman, George Roper & Co. In 1902 it was acquired by Barclay & Co Ltd (est. 1896).

P W Matthews & Anthony W Tuke, *History of Barclays Bank Ltd* (London, 1926); Maberly Phillips, *Banks, Bankers and Banking in Northumberland, Durham and North Yorkshire* (London, 1894)

Records: Barclays Bank plc, Group Archives, Dallimore Road, Wythenshawe, Manchester M23 9JA

Cheques 1813–1850s; post bills 1822–40.

PRITCHARD, GORDON & CO
Broseley, Shropshire

History: This private bank was formed in 1799 as Vickers, Son & Pritchard and was subsequently known as J G & J Pritchard; Pritchard & Boycott; Pritchard, Nicholas, Potts & Gordon; and Pritchard, Gordon, Potts & Shorting. It was otherwise known as the Broseley & Bridgnorth Bank. In 1799 a branch was established at Bridgnorth. The bank was acquired by Lloyds, Barnetts & Bosanquets Bank Ltd (est. 1765) in 1888.

Records: Lloyds TSB Group plc, Archives, Head Office, 71 Lombard Street, London EC3P 3BS

Memorandum and reference book 1883–1905; amalgamation papers 1888.

PUGH, JONES & CO
Pwllheli, Gwynedd

History: This private bank was established as H & L Pugh & Co in 1848, following the retreat of the North & South Wales Bank (est. 1836) from certain parts of North Wales. It was subsequently known as Pugh, Jones & Co and otherwise as the Pwllheli District Bank or as the Caernarvonshire

Records of banks 445

& District Bank. The founder, Hugh Pugh, was formerly manager of the North & South Wales Bank's branch at Pwllheli which in 1848 was sold to Cassons & Co (est. 1847). The business prospered and by 1891 had established fifteen branches and additional sub-branches, including ones at Caernarvon, Ffestiniog and Bangor. The business was acquired by the National Bank of Wales Ltd (est. 1879) in 1890, when it had deposits of £500,000. Seemingly the acquisition gave the National Bank additional strength but in reality it brought concealed debts of £80,000.

Records 1: HSBC Holdings plc, Group Archives, 10 Lower Thames Street, London EC3R 6AE

Amalgamation agreement 1890–91.

Records 2: Gwynedd Archives Service, County Offices, Caernarfon, Gwynedd LL55 1SH

Promissory note 1874; transfer of life assurance policy 1887. [Ref: XN.W.C./112; XM 3252/44]

PYKE, LAW & CO
Barnstaple, Devon

History: This private bank was established in 1807 as Bury, Pyke & Co and later was known as Pyke, Law & Co; it otherwise traded as the North Devon Bank. It amalgamated with National Provincial Bank of England (est. 1833) in 1836.

Records: The Royal Bank of Scotland plc, Archive Section, Regent's House, 42 Islington High Street, London N1 8XL

Abstracts from ledgers 1813–34; registers of bad and doubtful debts (2) 1816–36; partner's account with London bank 1821–28; papers re account with Exeter General Bank 1823–30; partnership agreements (2) 1826; correspondence with customers 1830–39; letters and statements from London agents 1830–42; memorandum book re advances 1832; letters re partners 1835–40; register of joint notes 1835–36; amalgamation agreement 1835; list of past due bills 1836.

GEORGE QUAYLE & CO
Castletown, Isle of Man

History: This private bank was formed in 1802 by George Quayle and John Taubman, quickly joined by James Kelly and Mark Hyldesley Quayle. Its initial partnership capital was £2,100. It was otherwise known as the Isle of Man Banking Co and operated from George Quayle's residence in Castletown. The bank failed in 1816.

446   *British banking – a guide to historical records*

W S Cowin, 'An Old Castletown Banking House', *Proceedings of the Isle of Man Natural History and Antiquarian Society* (1948); Ernest Quarmby, *Bank Notes and Banking in the Isle of Man* (London, 1994)

Records: Manx Museum and National Trust, Douglas, Isle of Man IM1 3LY

Correspondence re establishment 1802; cash book 1809–14; copy letterbook 1816–25; account book 1828–36. [Ref: Bridge House MS]

RANSOM, BOUVERIE & CO
London

History: This private bank was founded in 1786 at 57 Pall Mall in London's West End by Griffin Ransom, William Morland and Thomas Hammersley; it traded as Ransom, Morland & Hammersley. The family of Lord Kinnaird was closely associated with the bank but their name never appeared in the bank's title. Hammersley left in 1795 to form a bank which was later known as Hammersley, Greenwood & Brooksbank (est. 1796). Some of the bank's partners were also partners in the Dundee New Bank (est. 1802) and in the Glasgow Bank Co (est. 1809). The bank was then known as Ransom, Morland & Co until 1814 and as Morland, Ransom & Co until 1818. The partnership was dissolved in 1818 when its balance sheet total was £623,000. A new firm, Ransom & Co, with 534 accounts, was formed by some of the partners at 34 Pall Mall, later moving to 25 Pall Mall and then moving on to 1 Pall Mall East. Meanwhile the Morland family partners, led by Sir S B Morland, left to form the bank of Morlands, Auriol & Co (est. 1819) which failed in 1832. Ransom & Co flourished, in 1856 amalgamating with Bouverie, Murdoch, Bouverie & James (est. 1813) to form Ransom, Bouverie & Co. Many of its customers were drawn from politics and the arts. The bank amalgamated with Barclay, Bevan, Tritton & Co (est. 1690) in 1888 to form Barclay, Bevan, Tritton, Ransom, Bouverie & Co.

P W Matthews & Anthony W Tuke, *History of Barclays Bank Ltd* (London, 1926); F G Hilton Price, *A Handbook of London Bankers* (London, 1876)

Records 1: Barclays Bank plc, Group Archives, Dallimore Road, Wythenshawe, Manchester M23 9JA

Securities papers 1760–1895; customer account ledgers (18) 1783–1889; passbooks 1784–1878; partnership agreements 1785–1845, 1866–91; cheques and cheque forms 1787–95, 1818–88; correspondence and other papers re customers 1789–1883; deeds as securities 1789–1904; liquidations accounts ledgers 1792–1830; sundries journal 1796–1805; correspond-

Records of banks 447

ence: liquidation accounts 1796–1899, trustees and executors 1805–1908, private accounts 1820–27, Pall Mall property 1864–96; private account ledgers (7) 1798–1878; receipts, bills and cheques 1817–24; dividend authority registers (2) 1818–81; expenses ledger 1818–22; circular re change of name 1818–19; bank note paper 1818–20; letterbook, liquidation account 1819–69; security register 1819–37; memorandum books (3) 1819–91; overdue bills 1820–58; stock book 1822; current account ledger indexes (26) 1823–89; cheque book n.d.; solicitors' bills of charges 1841–54; customer information book 1845–74; statement of accounts book 1848–52; interest received notebook 1857–88; trustee accounts 1864–1909; papers re failure of Overend, Gurney & Co 1866; statement of accounts with Pears, Ellis & Pears 1884–96; partners' signature circular 1888; private account ledger 1888–89; papers re amalgamation 1896.

Records 2: Perth & Kinross Council Archive, A K Bell Library, 2–8 York Place, Perth PH2 8EP

Correspondence and other papers re administration, including amalgamations, and personal papers of Lord Kinnaird 1785–1896

E REED & SONS
Liverpool, Merseyside

History: This private bank was established in 1863 and supplied credit and other financial services to farmers and traders selling in local cattle markets, especially those handling cattle imported from Ireland. Its first branch was opened at Birkenhead in 1911 and subsequent branches were at Salford, Wakefield and Stanley Market, Liverpool. In 1920 the Birkenhead branch was sold and became the Cattle Trade Bank Ltd. The bank was acquired by the Bank of Liverpool & Martins Ltd (est. 1831) for £1,500 in 1925.

Records: Barclays Bank plc, Group Archives, Dallimore Road, Wythenshawe, Manchester M23 9JA

Memorandum and articles of association 1920; certificate of incorporation 1920; annual report 1923; papers re winding up of company 1923; papers re amalgamation with Bank of Liverpool & Martins Ltd 1923–26.

REEVES & PORCH
Glastonbury, Somerset

History: This private bank was formed in 1812 and was otherwise known as the Glastonbury & Shepton Mallet Bank. In 1835 it was acquired by Stuckey's Banking Co (est. 1826).

448   *British banking – a guide to historical records*

P T Saunders, *Stuckey's Bank* (Taunton, 1928)

Records: Somerset Record Office, Obridge Road, Taunton TA2 7PU

Assignment of property for debt 1825–28. [Ref: DD/BR/nw 8]

RICHARDS & CO
Llangollen, Clwyd

History: This private bank was formed in 1854 by Charles Richards (d.1884) and his brother, Watkin (d. c.1900); initially it was known as Llangollen Bank and later as Llangollen Old Bank following the opening of a branch of the North & South Wales Bank (est. 1836) in 1856. It was the last private bank to be formed in North Wales. On the death of the Richards brothers, it was managed by Charles's sons and subsequently by his grandsons. In 1920 it was acquired by the National Provincial & Union Bank of England Ltd (est. 1828).

A Stanley Davies, *The Early Banks of Mid Wales* (Welshpool, 1935)

Records: The Royal Bank of Scotland plc, Archive Section, Regent's House, 42 Islington High Street, London N1 8XL

Balance sheets and profit and loss accounts 1910–19; amalgamation papers 1920.

RIDGE & CO
Chichester, West Sussex

History: This country bank was formed in about 1783 as Griffiths, Chaldecott & Drew. In 1807 it was known as Ridge & Co and in 1841 was acquired by London & County Joint Stock Banking Co (est. 1836).

Records: West Sussex Record Office, County Hall, Chichester PO19 1RN

Passbooks 1809–58; bank notes 1815, 1837, 1841. [Ref: Add. MSS.2233–34, 1005–07, 37, 997]

SIR M RIDLEY BART., CHAS WM BIGGE & CO
Newcastle upon Tyne, Tyne & Wear

History: This private bank was the first bank to be established in Newcastle, being formed in 1755 as Bell, Cookson, Carr & Airey with a capital of £2,000; it was otherwise known as The Old Bank. Subsequently its partners were also drawn from the Saint and Widdrington families and, after trading under a number of names, was known from 1791 as Sir M W Ridley, Cookson, Widdrington, Bell & Co. By 1807 its style was Sir M W Ridley, Bigge, Gibson & Co and in 1832 was known as Sir M W Ridley

Records of banks 449

Bart., Chas. Wm. Bigge & Co. It opened six branches, including one at Durham, and became one of the most important private banks in the North East. In 1839 it was acquired by the Northumberland & Durham District Banking Co (est. 1836) which failed in 1857.

Records 1: Northumberland Record Office, Melton Park, North Gosforth, Newcastle upon Tyne NE3 5QX

Partnership agreements 1756–1836; papers re legal dispute 1804–08; letters to Sir M W Ridley re banking matters 1820s; papers re proposed extension of business to Berwick 1827; statements re assets and liabilities 1836–44; papers re investigation of bank affairs 1836; ledger balances 1836; amalgamation papers 1839; division and final accounts of assets 1868. [Ref: ZR1 34/1–2; ZCE 8/23; ZCK 10]

Records 2: Durham University Library, Archives and Special Collections, 5 The College, Durham DH1 3EQ

Partnership agreements 1756–86. [Ref: Cookson papers]

ROBARTS, CURTIS & CO
London

History: This bank was established at Cornhill, in the City of London, in 1791 as Robarts, Curtis, Were, Hornyold & Berwick. In 1795 it moved to Lombard Street and here it developed to become one of the most prestigious private banks in London. In 1805 it was styled Robarts, Curtis, Robarts & Curtis and by 1818 Sir William Curtis, a Lord Mayor of London in 1795–96 and friend of George IV, was senior partner. The firm was then known as Sir William Curtis, Robarts & Curtis until 1834 when its name was changed to Robarts, Curtis & Co. In 1860 it merged with Lubbock, Forster & Co to form Robarts, Lubbock & Co.

F G Hilton Price, *A Handbook of London Bankers* (London, 1876); Horace G Hutchinson, *Life of Sir John Lubbock, Lord Avebury* (London, 1914)

Records: Coutts & Co, 440 Strand, London WC2R 0QS

Private ledger 1791; signature books, 1805–60; staff book 1810–28; safe deposit books 1835–60; miscellaneous cheques and related papers 1791–1860.

ROBARTS, LUBBOCK & CO
London

History: This leading City of London private bank was formed in 1860 through the merger of Lubbock, Forster & Co (est. 1772) and Robarts,

450   *British banking – a guide to historical records*

Curtis & Co (est. 1791). It was the last private bank to have a seat in the London Clearing House. Its last senior partner was Sir John Lubbock, later 1st Lord Avebury, one of the City's most influential bankers. In 1914, a year after Avebury's death, the firm merged with Coutts & Co (est. 1692). It then had reserves of £500,000 and customer balances of well over £4 million.

Edna Healey, *Coutts & Co 1692–1992. The Portrait of a Private Bank* (London, 1992); William Howarth, *The Banks in the Clearing House* (London, 1907); Horace G Hutchinson, *Life of Sir John Lubbock, Lord Avebury* (London, 1914); P E Smart, 'A Victorian Polymath. Sir John Lubbock', *Journal of the Institute of Bankers*, 100 (1979)

Records: Coutts & Co, 440 Strand, London WC2R 0QS

Signature books 1860–1914; registers of wills and probates 1860–1914; letterbooks; staff books; builders' drawings; cheques and miscellaneous papers; amalgamation papers n.d.

ROBERTS & GREGORY
Newport, Isle of Wight

History: This private bank was established in about 1788 as Henry & John Roberts, Mark Gregory & Co and was later known as Henry & John Roberts & Mark Gregory; it also traded as the Newport Bank. It appears to have failed in 1792 but continued and eventually ceased business in 1838.

Records: Isle of Wight County Record Office, 26 Hillside, Newport, Isle of Wight PO30 2EB

Papers re failure 1790–92. [Ref: M3/4,5,9,23,105,107; FAR/30, 82/51]

ROBIN BROTHERS
Jersey, Channel Islands

History: This private bank was formed in 1808, probably as Janvrin, Durell & Co; it was otherwise known as the Jersey Commercial Bank. It was known as Janvrin, Durell, De Veulle & Co by 1817 and by 1866 as Janvrin, Durell & Co. In 1879 a connection began with the Robin family, owners of the distinguished merchant house of Charles Robin & Co, and at some stage the business became known as Robin Brothers. It was acquired by Parr's Bank Ltd (est. 1865) in 1908.

T E Gregory, *The Westminster Bank Through A Century* (London, 1936)

Records: The Royal Bank of Scotland plc, Archive Section, Regent's House, 42 Islington High Street, London N1 8XL

Records of banks 451

Extracts from partnership agreements 1808–1908; receipts for securities 1888–1908; balance sheets 1896–1907; amalgamation notice 1908.

JAMES & CHARLES ROBINSON & CO
Mansfield, Nottinghamshire

History: This private bank was established in about 1804 as Moore & Co; it was otherwise known as the Mansfield Bank. It was styled Moore & Maltby from 1815, Abney & Maltby from 1816, Maltby & Robinson from 1836, James Robinson from 1839, Robinson & Broadhurst from 1857 and James & Charles Robinson from 1869. In 1871 it was acquired by Samuel Smith & Co (c.1663) of Nottingham and its Chesterfield branch was sold to the Sheffield Banking Co (est. 1831).

J A S L Leighton-Boyce, *Smiths the Bankers 1658–1958* (London, 1958)

Records: The Royal Bank of Scotland plc, Archive Section, Regent's House, 42 Islington High Street, London N1 8XL

Private ledger 1853–67; agreement for sale of business 1870.

ROCHDALE JOINT STOCK BANK LTD
Rochdale, Greater Manchester

History: This small joint stock bank began business in 1861 as the Rochdale Commercial Loan & Discount Co. Its paid-up capital was £5,000 and its business was confined to dealing in bills and other commercial paper. In 1872 it was converted in to a more broadly based bank taking the title Rochdale Joint Stock Bank. Paid-up capital was increased to £12,000 and deposits stood at £44,000 on formation. Two branches, at Castleton and Wardle, were opened. However the bank was seriously damaged by a run following the 1878 City of Glasgow Bank crisis; its paid-up capital was increased to enable its survival. By 1880 this stood at £26,000 when deposits were £44,000. The business struggled on until 1882 when it was acquired by the Oldham Joint Stock Bank (est. 1880) for £5,500.

W F Crick & J E Wadsworth, *A Hundred Years of Joint Stock Banking* (London, 1936)

Records: HSBC Holdings plc, Group Archives, 10 Lower Thames Street, London EC3R 6AE

Prospectus 1858; reports and balance sheets 1861–81; amalgamation papers 1881–82; statement of customer accounts 1882.

ROCKE, EYTON, CAMPBELL & BAYLEY
Shrewsbury, Shropshire

452 British banking – a guide to historical records

History: This private bank was established in 1792 as Eyton, Reynolds & Bishop; it was later known as Rocke, Eyton & Campbell and, from 1830, as Rocke, Eyton, Campbell & Bayley. It also traded as Shrewsbury Old Bank and later as Shrewsbury & Ludlow Bank following the opening of an office at Ludlow (1825). In 1884 it merged with Burton, Lloyd, Lloyd & Salt (est. 1812) to form Eyton, Burton & Co.

Records 1: Lloyds TSB Bank plc, Archives, Head Office, 71 Lombard Street, London EC3P 3BS

Partnership agreement 1866; private correspondence 1883–84.

Records 2: Shropshire Records & Research Centre, Castle Gates, Shrewsbury SY1 2AQ

Partnership agreements 1792–1866. [Ref: 665/477; 665/339; 1135/1]

ROSKELL, ARROWSMITH & CO
Preston, Lancashire

History: This private bank was established in 1825 as Lawe, Roskell, Arrowsmith & Co and was known as Roskell, Arrowsmith & Co from 1833. It failed in about 1868.

Records: Lancashire Record Office, Bow Lane, Preston PR1 2RE

Partnership agreement 1825; ledger abstracts and related correspondence 1834–50; character book 1834–57; legal papers c.1850s; press cuttings re failure 1868. [Ref: DDTs, DX 1923]

N M ROTHSCHILD & SONS LTD
London

History: This City of London merchant bank traced its British origins to the textile business established in Manchester in 1799 by Nathan Mayer Rothschild as a means of extending the merchanting business of his father, Mayer Amschel Rothschild of Frankfurt. Nathan acted as a commission agent, co-ordinating the supply of British textiles to continental markets both for his own account and for the account of his father. This business gradually diversified to trading in other goods and to bill broking and shifted its geographical focus increasingly to London. In 1809 Nathan Mayer moved to New Court, St Swithin's Lane, in the heart of the City. With increasing interests in bullion, specie and government securities, the move towards a wide-ranging merchant banking business was completed in the following years. While commodity trading remained significant to the business throughout the century, N M Rothschild's withdrawal in 1811 from the Manchester firm he had founded marked the end of the first

Records of banks 453

phase of activity in England. A major early transaction was the supply of gold coin to the Duke of Wellington's army fighting in Europe, an achievement that highlighted an important characteristic of Rothschild operations during the nineteenth century. This was close co-operation and speedy communication between the international network of Rothschild family houses which, in the early nineteenth century, were located at Frankfurt, London, Vienna, Paris and Naples. They were bound by interlocking partnerships and much business was undertaken by them on joint account. By the 1820s, N M Rothschild & Sons was a leader in sterling bond issues in London, their major competitors being Barings and their clients including the governments of France, Russia, Prussia, Austria, Portugal and Naples. While continental Europe was, during the first half of the century, their most important territory, significant links developed elsewhere in the world, in particular with the governments of Brazil and Chile, with the United States government and with United States railway companies. In 1847 finance was raised for the British government for the alleviation of famine in Ireland and in the mid-1850s for funding expenditure during the Crimean War. In 1875, £4 million was advanced to enable the government to acquire a controlling interest in the Suez Canal. In the last decades of the century, N M Rothschild & Sons was probably the most important London-based bond-issuer for sovereign clients. During the Boer War, with Morgan Grenfell it managed important debt issues for the British government. Under the leadership of 'Natty', 1st Lord Rothschild, aided by Carl Meyer, substantial interests in South African gold mining companies were acquired. Here Rothschilds supported leading figures such as Rhodes and de Beers and were closely involved with Wernher, Beit & Co. Bond issuing for overseas corporate clients inevitably led to similar transactions for British-based corporate entities including, at the end of the century, the Manchester Ship Canal Co and the two armament manufacturers, Maxim Nordenfeld and Vickers. Bullion dealing continued to be extremely important. The bank was often the major supplier to the Royal Mint of gold for coinage and from 1852 to 1967 operated its own refinery. The firm's position in the bullion world was reinforced when, in 1919, it was chosen by the Bank of England to manage the gold market in the wake of the abandonment of the gold standard, acting as chair of the daily gold price-fixing. Throughout Rothschilds' history private banking has been a significant, if lesser component of its business. In the nineteenth century, the most distinguished private clients were drawn from the Court of Hesse, the Duchy of Baden and the House of Saxe Coburg and included Albert, the Prince Consort. In the years following the First World War, the firm's bond issuing business was largely confined to joint issues with Barings and Schroders and sometimes with Morgan Grenfell, with a shift towards raising finance for corporate clients such as the London under-

454   *British banking – a guide to historical records*

ground companies and F W Woolworth. In the 1980s and 1990s the bank developed a substantial corporate finance business with a particular expertise in privatisation. Bullion dealing and the provision of resource financing in the mining sector built upon longstanding traditions. The business was incorporated with limited liability in 1970 and in 1976 its asset management activities were transferred to Rothschild Asset Management Ltd. It forms part of Rothschilds Continuation Ltd, a worldwide grouping.

Jules Ayer, *A Century of Finance 1804–1904. The London House of Rothschilds* (priv. pub., 1905); S D Chapman, 'N M Rothschild 1777–1836', *Textile History* (1977); Richard Davis, *The English Rothschilds* (London, 1983); Niall Ferguson, *The World's Banker: The History of the House of Rothschild* (London, 1998); Victor Gray & Melanie Aspey (eds.), *The Life and Times of N M Rothschild 1777–1836* (priv. pub., 1998); Georg Heuberger (ed.), *The Rothschilds. Essays on the History of a European Family* (Frankfurt, 1994); Simone Mace, 'The Archives of the London Merchant Bank of N M Rothschild & Sons', *Business Archives*, 64 (1992); Manfred Pohl & Sabine Freitag (eds.), *Handbook on the History of European Banks* (Aldershot, 1994)

Records: N M Rothschild & Sons Ltd, New Court, St Swithin's Lane, London EC4P 4DU

Textile business accounts and correspondence (46) 1800–09; sundry correspondence, extensive, 1802–1918; correspondence from agents, extensive, 1802–1918; accounts current foreign (356) 1806–1914; ledgers, home, foreign and stock (197) 1809–1914; correspondence from banks 1809–1918; correspondence from governments 1809–1918; partnership agreements and correspondence 1810–1909; balance books, Jones Loyd, Masterman (2) 1811–23; cash books (244) 1813–1918; correspondence, Rothschild houses 1814–1918; Rothschild family private business correspondence 1814–1918; copies of house correspondence (450) 1814–1918; bullion invoices and account sales (96) 1816–1918; journals (127) 1817–64; specimen bonds and loan prospectuses 1818–1918; bullion ledgers (31) 1819–1914; accounts current, Rothschilds banks and private accounts (241) 1822–1918; copies of joint business correspondence (22) 1825–26, 1899–1918; accounts current, American general and government (76) 1831–1918; American railways, bullion and commodities accounts (33) 1844–1917; refinery accounts and stock books (33) 1846–1914; accounts current, governments (49) 1850–1918; American journals (2) 1856–74; bullion cash books (31) 1857–1905; accounts current, stock (33) 1870–1918; Bank of England balance books (2) 1873–1914; copies of private correspondence (9) 1877–91, 1907–18; American stock accounts (14) 1888–1918; bullion correspondence 1897–1914.

Records of banks 455

ROYAL BANK OF AUSTRALIA
London and Australia

History: This British registered overseas bank was promoted in 1839 and commenced business in 1842 with a nominal capital of £1 million. It was one of the first British-owned banks to operate in Australia and its chief promoter and manager, Ben Boyd, was an Australian entrepreneur with interests in sheep farming, wool trading, ship owning and whaling, and had established the settlement of Boyd Town. The bank's business, which was largely confined to note issue and the sale of bills on London, was not large and much of its resources were used to finance Boyd's businesses. Boyd was forced out of its management in 1847 and was replaced by his brother, W S Boyd. In 1849 the bank was placed in liquidation when examination of its accounts revealed fraudulent management.

Records 1: Public Record Office, Ruskin Avenue, Kew, Richmond TW9 4DU

Deed of settlement 1840; share application and transfer proforma 1840; shareholders ledger 1840–65; share transfer register 1840–48; debenture book 1840–48; share sale book 1840–48; minute books (3) 1840–50; cash book 1840–49; journal 1840–49; shareholders cash book 1840–48; directors' attendance book 1840–45; deposit notebooks (2) 1840–43; current account ledger 1840–41; letters of credit book 1840–48; drafts on colonies book 1840–48; sundry letters and vouchers 1840 on; deposit ledger 1841–56; dividend books (2) 1841–47; bills receivable book 1841–49; bills payable book 1843–52; passbooks, Union Bank of London (4) 1844–50; general meeting minute book 1845–49; letterbooks (2) 1845–50; cash book 1850–65; liquidator's cash account with Royal Bank of Australia 1850–65; liquidator's ledger 1850–54; liquidator's cash book 1850–65; letters to liquidator etc n.d.; list of creditors 1855.

Australia records (many re Boyd's other business interests):

Adelaide: notebooks n.d.; **Boyd Town:** notebook n.d.; consignment books, London (2) 1840–49; order book for goods 1844–45; saddler's book 1844; ledger 1844–48; store waste book 1847–48; cash book, B Boyd and others, 1847–48; day book, B Boyd and others, 1847–48; ledger, B Boyd & Co and others, 1847–48; invoice and stock book 1847–48; letterbook 1847–48; loose papers and accounts n.d.; **Hobart Town:** notebooks (3) n.d.; journal 1842–48; **Launceston:** notebooks (4) n.d.; Melbourne: notebook n.d.; **Sydney:** notebooks (2) n.d.; journal 1840–43; **Unspecified:** bank ledgers (2) 1840–43; branch account book 1840–47; R Boyd's letters 1840 on; letters from W S Boyd 1840–49; cash books (13) 1840–48; letterbooks (7) 1840–50; general ledgers (3) 1840–50; invoice book 1841–

456   *British banking – a guide to historical records*

43; journals (7) 1841–50; rough journals (2) 1841–45; register of cargo manifests 1841–44; produce received and forwarded book 1841–47; discount bill register 1842–50; letterbook, G H Wray, 1842–45; stock books (2) 1842–50; diaries (9) 1842–50; agenda books (2) 1842–49; general letterbooks 1842–43, 1847; petty cash books (4) 1842–48; voucher books (7) 1843–44; dividend receipt books (4) 1843–47; current account ledger 1843–49; London wool sales book 1843–48; agreement with employees books (2) 1844–45; remarks on flocks and herds 1844–47; 'ledgers' (5) 1843–65; accountant's book 1845–49; journals, B Boyd (3) 1845–48; drafts on Sydney books (2) 1845–48; manifest book 1845–50; Geo Rust's cash book with B Boyd 1845–47; invoice books (2) 1845–46; promissory notebook 1845–46; station stores return books (2) 1846–48; livestock book 1846–47; advance notes 1847; accounts with employees book 1847–48; bonded stores book 1847; 'accounts of ships etc' 1847; cash book, B Boyd, 1848; journal, B Boyd, 1848; ledgers, B Boyd (2) 1848; station returns (7) 1848–50; discount bill diaries (2) 1848; cash book, B Boyd, 1848; letterbook, Eumarella, 1848–50; cash abstract book 1849–50; sheep and cattle returns 1848–50; account of debentures outstanding 1849; register of merchants' rents (3) 1858–60; merchandise shipped books (20) 1860–61; indexes of proprietors (2) n.d.; share applications book n.d.; bills receivable registers n.d. [Ref: J90/1328–1473]

Records 2: The Royal Bank of Scotland plc, Archive Section, Regent's House, 42 Islington High Street, London N1 8XL

Papers re winding up 1841–58.

ROYAL BANK OF LIVERPOOL
Liverpool, Merseyside

History: This joint stock bank was established in 1836 and failed in 1867.

Records: Barclays Bank plc, Group Archives, Dallimore Road, Wythenshawe, Manchester M23 9JA

Deed of settlement 1861; list of shareholders 1867.

THE ROYAL BANK OF SCOTLAND PLC
Edinburgh, Lothian

History: The Royal Bank of Scotland was founded by Royal Charter in 1727; its capital was £111,350. It opened for business in Ship Close, Edinburgh, and was quickly involved in a bank note circulation war with the older Bank of Scotland (est. 1695). It pioneered the 'cash-credit', the forerunner of the overdraft, in 1728. In 1783 a branch was opened in Glasgow which was closely involved with the cotton and sugar trades. By

Records of banks   457

the 1810s it was conducting more business than the Edinburgh head office. Many other branches were acquired following the collapse of the Western Bank of Scotland (est. 1832) in 1857. In 1864 the Dundee Banking Co (est. 1763) was purchased. In 1874 a branch office was opened in London and in 1878 additional branches were acquired following the collapse of the City of Glasgow Bank (est. 1839). Drummonds & Co (est. 1712) of London was acquired in 1924; Williams Deacon's Bank Ltd (est. 1836) of Manchester and London in 1930; and Glyn, Mills & Co (est. 1753) of London, which owned the London banks of Holt & Co (est. 1809) and Child & Co (est. c.1580s), in 1939. Williams Deacon's and Glyn, Mills continued to operate as separate entities and the business became known as the Three Banks Group. In 1969 The Royal Bank of Scotland merged with National Commercial Bank of Scotland, formed in 1959 by the merger of National Bank of Scotland (est. 1825) and Commercial Bank of Scotland (est. 1810) and supplemented in 1966 by the acquisition of the English and Welsh branches of The National Bank (est. 1835). In 1970 the three London clearing bank subsidiaries combined as Williams & Glyn's Bank Ltd. In 1985 the businesses of The Royal Bank of Scotland Ltd and Williams & Glyn's Bank Ltd were merged and the group became The Royal Bank of Scotland plc. It set up a pioneering motor insurance company, Direct Line, in 1985, acquired Citizens Financial Group (est. 1828) of Providence, Rhode Island, United States, in 1988 and Adam & Co (est. 1983), a private banking company based in Edinburgh, in 1992. An independent offshore bank, Royal Bank of Scotland International, was established in 1996 and in 1997 the Royal Bank launched the UK's first on-line banking service over the internet as well as joint financial services ventures with Tesco and Virgin Direct. In 2000 the Royal Bank acquired National Westminster Bank plc.

Anon, *The Royal Bank of Scotland: A History* (priv.pub., 1998); Neil Munro, *The History of the Royal Bank of Scotland 1727–1927* (Edinburgh, 1928); Manfred Pohl & Sabine Freitag, *Handbook on the History of European Banks* (Aldershot, 1994)

Records 1: The Royal Bank of Scotland plc, Archive Section, 36 St Andrew Square, Edinburgh EH2 2YB

Royal charters 1727–1830; royal charter warrant 1727; directors' meeting minutes 1727–1970; account books and diary of John Campbell, bank cashier, 1727–75; bank notes 1727–1999; stock journals 1727–90; management charges books 1727–1969; bank note registers 1728–35, 1894–1966; cash account ledger 1728–29; interest books 1729–51; salary obligations discharge 1731; records of notes struck and cancelled 1742–1953; cheques 1769–1985; bank teller's account statement 1797;

458   *British banking – a guide to historical records*

architectural plans and drawings 1804–1970; directors' sederunt books, with agenda 1816–1967; cashier's letters 1816, 1848; stock ledgers 1817–24; share transfer book 1817; damaged bank note guardbook 1822; engraving of Edinburgh head office 1826; weekly Bank of England returns 1844–78; financial accounting papers 1845–1940; staff establishment books 1845–1900; lists of branches 1846, 1875, 1932–40; salary lists c.1858; branch record books 1855–68; property ledger 1858–62; branch inspection department papers 1858; list of clerks c.1850s; list of agents' bonds outstanding 1861; Edinburgh property register 1863–1928; report and accounts 1864–1999; correspondence re forged bank notes 1865–1918; letter re bank charges 1866; branch establishment book 1869–74; press cuttings 1872–1999; Scottish bank managers' meeting minutes 1872–76; Royal Bank of Scotland Act 1873; papers re Institute of Bankers in Scotland 1875–1969; asset and valuation statements 1875–1940; branch circulars 1875–1904, 1942–77; legal reports: bank directors' liability 1878–79, City of Glasgow Bank failure 1878–82; instructions to agents and accountants 1878, 1911; correspondence re note issue 1881; circular letters of credit 1882, 1944; interbranch receipts 1882; papers re meetings of managers of Scottish banks 1885–90; branch procedure books 1885–1905; correspondence between branch agents and head office 1888–92; agents notebooks c.1880s; share register 1893–1929; directors' fees book 1894–1938; staff magazines: 1895, *Royal Notes* 1950–68, *Countertalk* 1969–83, *Newsletter* 1969–76, *Newsline* 1984–96; balance ledgers 1900–57; branch photographs c.1900–03; cashier's letterbooks 1901–55; staff photographs 1904, 1944–28; heritable property ledgers 1905–68; cashier's and secretary's letters 1908–29; property and rents ledger 1908–25; new branch proposals 1909–37; chief accountant's letterbook 1912–19; officers' guarantee fund cash book 1913–59; field service postcards 1916–18; governor's speeches 1917–39; acquisition papers: Drummonds 1922–24, London Western branch 1928–30, Williams Deacon's Bank 1930, National Commercial Bank of Scotland 1968–69, Williams & Glyn's Bank 1985; war memorial unveiling programme 1923; London branch history notes 1926; capital expenditure ledger 1926–69; golf club papers 1930–69; dividend book 1932–56; cash abstract book 1933–69; air raid precautions papers c.1939; nominee company minute books 1939–86; correspondence from staff on military service 1939–45; wartime circulars 1942–46; chairman's files 1943–69; branch profit and loss statements 1943–66; annual property list 1944–51; pension sheets 1947–52; account of notes and coin circulation 1954–58; correspondents cash book 1955–62; customer journal, *Three Banks Review* 1957–92; advertising literature 1960–99; directors' photographs 1963–91; computer user manuals 1964–69; premises owned and let register 1967–69; corporate identity handbook 1969.

Records of banks 459

Aberdeen: agent's papers 1862–1931; **Alyth:** correspondence from overseas banks 1863–72; correspondence from Dundee Banking Co re transfer of customer accounts 1864–66; **Arbroath:** architectural plans 1858; **Ayton:** correspondence re redecoration 1891–93; **Cumbernauld:** deposit receipt decimal books 1860–1900; deposit receipt ledger 1878–89; opinions book 1882–1900; **Cupar:** cash book 1883–93; **Duns:** opening circular 1856; agent's letterbooks 1856–65; petty cash book 1856–1909; letter re title deeds 1857; programme re new premises construction 1857; **Edinburgh, Dundas Street:** petty cash books 1873–1940; **Edinburgh, Granton:** branch expenses books 1863–1911; opinions book 1878–1900; **Edinburgh, Hunter Square:** agent's private letterbook 1895–99; **Glasgow, Buchanan Street:** general ledgers 1783–1815, 1819–29; day book 1783–84; branch journal 1783–93; staff lists 1828–1900; salary books 1837–1900 [w]; staff books 1847–1900; rates of interest and discount book 1863–1900; register of customer accounts 1875–86; **Greenock, Cathcart Street:** deposit receipt registers 1839–1900; petty cash books 1847–90; **London, Western:** passbooks 1934–1950s; **Tranent:** instruction book, includes inventory and balances 1878.

Records 2: Business Records Centre, Archive Department, University of Glasgow, Glasgow G12 8QQ

Court minutes extracts 1727–1918; balance sheets 1866–1922; computed balance sheets 1817–64; governor's speeches to general meetings 1930–39; extracts from letters of Glasgow joint agent 1801–07. [Ref: Scottish Banking Collection]

Records 3: National Library of Scotland, Department of Manuscripts, George IV Bridge, Edinburgh EH1 1EW

Miscellaneous papers 1696–1813; bonds in favour of bank 1729–81; papers of Lord Milton re administration, relationships with other banks, army payments, bank note circulation etc 1728–65; discharges 1728–74; receipts 1728–1800; passbooks 1728–88, 1867–68; correspondence of officials 1734–1943; officers' voting slips 1734; orders in favour of bank 1737–40; proposals to bank 1741–42; accounts with bank 1745–58; demand by Prince Charles Edward Stuart 1745; obligations 1750–54; bills 1753–67; declaration 1754; report on memorial 1792; note of bills discounted for Earl of Elgin 1835; certificate 1888. [Ref: Numerous, refer to repository]

Records 4: Public Record Office, Ruskin Avenue, Kew, Richmond TW9 4DU

Application by bank for charter n.d. [Ref: T 1/3472]

460   *British banking – a guide to historical records*

Records 5: National Archives of Scotland, HM General Register House, Princes Street, Edinburgh EH1 3YY

Warrants of charter 1727–89; John Clerk: letter re directorship 1727–28, account books 1740–47; papers of Patrick Monzie of Campbell 1750–87; list of proprietors 1751; bonds 1768, 1777; correspondence of William Forbes of Callender with cashier 1785; note on method of giving credit eighteenth cent; papers and passbooks of Menzies of Shian 1843. [Ref: CS96/3484; GD8/3208; GD18/2241; GD190/3/304; GD18/5882; GD171/ 223; GD18/5884; GD306/7]

ROYAL BRITISH BANK
London

History: This joint stock bank was established in 1900 and failed in 1904.

Records: Lloyds TSB Group plc, Archives, Head Office, 71 Lombard Street, London EC3P 3BS

Prospectus 1903.

ROYAL EXCHANGE BANK LTD
London

History: This ill-fated joint stock bank was projected in 1861 as the Metropolitan & Provincial Bank Ltd and was formed a year later (combining with another new promotion, Mercantile Bank Ltd). Paid-up capital was £69,000 and it was the first English bank to acquire limited liability. Branches were opened at Oxford Street, Woolwich and, somewhat oddly, at Macclesfield in response to an invitation from that town's leading manufacturers. By 1864 heavy losses had been made causing a fall in deposits from over £1 million to under £400,000. The 1866 financial crisis compounded these problems and, with £144,000 locked up, the bank closed. As the Metropolitan Bank Ltd, the business was revived in 1867 with a new board and a reconstructed balance sheet. Paid-up capital was reduced from £337,000 to £200,000 and bad debts were written off. The Macclesfield branch was sold to Parr's Banking Co Ltd (est. 1865) in 1867. More bad debts were incurred in 1872 when deposits fell by a third. During the 1878 City of Glasgow Bank crisis, the bank once more collapsed and was again revived, this time as the Royal Exchange Bank Ltd with a paid-up capital of £60,000 and deposits of £100,000. The bank struggled on until 1889 when it was acquired by the Birmingham Banking Co Ltd (est. 1829), the enlarged business being called the Metropolitan & Birmingham Bank Ltd. This strong provincial bank was keen to extend its operations to London and was attracted by the Metropolitan Bank's key asset, its seat in the London Clearing House.

Records of banks **461**

W F Crick & J E Wadsworth, *A Hundred Years of Joint Stock Banking* (London, 1936)

Records 1: HSBC Holdings plc, Group Archives, 10 Lower Thames Street, London EC3R 6AE

Signature books (2) 1862–89; deposit account signature book 1864–92; security books (2) 1883–94; share dividend summary books (6) 1884–89.

Records 2: The Royal Bank of Scotland plc, Archive Section, Regent's House, 42 Islington High Street, London N1 8XL

Notices of opening and amalgamation 1839–41; agreement for amalgamation of Macclesfield branch with Parr's Banking Co Ltd 1867.

A RUFFER & SONS LTD
London

History: This City of London accepting house was formed as A Ruffer & Sons in 1872 by Baron Joseph Ruffer whose family had been merchants at Lyons and Leipzig and had specialised in the silk trade. In London it specialised in finance of the Anglo-French and Belgian wool trade. The firm was in difficulties in the early 1920s when it received Bank of England support. Shortly afterwards the business acquired limited liability and the Bank of England exchanged its loan for a majority equity holding. In the early 1930s substantial losses arising out of the credit collapse in Germany and eastern Europe were avoided but the firm's business was badly damaged by the Second World War. It went into voluntary liquidation in 1941 and its remaining banking business was transferred to Glyn, Mills & Co (est. 1753) in 1946. The company was finally dissolved in 1964.

Records: The Royal Bank of Scotland plc, Archive Section, Regent's House, 42 Islington High Street, London N1 8XL

Security registers (2) 1908–38.

RUFFORDS & WRAGGE
Stourbridge, West Midlands

History: This private bank was established in 1792 and was also known as the Stourbridge Bank. It was associated with Rufford, Bigg & Co (est. 1801) of Bromsgrove. The bank failed in 1851.

Records: Staffordshire Record Office, County Buildings, Eastgate Street, Stafford ST16 2LZ

Papers re salt trade and banking 1838–59. [Ref: D695/1/32/2–3]

462 *British banking – a guide to historical records*

SADDLEWORTH BANKING CO
Saddleworth, Greater Manchester

History: This joint stock bank was formed in 1833 to acquire the business of the private bank of Buckley, Roberts & Co (est. 1806) of Saddleworth. By 1834 branches had been established at Oldham, Ashton-under-Lyne and Dobcross. In 1866 the bank merged with the Manchester & County Bank Ltd (est. 1862).

Records: The Royal Bank of Scotland plc, Archive Section, Regent's House, 42 Islington High Street, London N1 8XL

Deed of settlement 1833; shareholders' journal 1833–36; draft share transfer notices 1834–59; general ledgers (9) 1834–60; list candidates for directorships 1839–63; monthly general ledger abstracts 1842–52; list of shareholders 1865.

Delph: signature book 1862–76; **Dobcross:** customer account ledgers (12) 1806–34; deposit ledger 1824–59; deposit lodgement ledgers (5) 1831–67; day book 1833–34; general ledgers (2) 1834–36; customer progressive ledgers (5) 1834–40; bank note register 1836–57; deposit ledger 1849–74; half-yearly balances 1856–64; title deeds schedule 1868; **Oldham:** customer ledger 1836–38; deposit ledger 1835–39; general ledgers (4) 1836–51.

ST BARBE, DANIELL & CO
Lymington, Hampshire

History: This private bank was formed in about 1788 as C & S St Barbe, its leading partner being Charles St Barbe, a local grocer and salt manufacturer. It was also known as the Lymington Bank. The business was acquired by the Capital & Counties Bank Ltd (est. 1877) in 1896.

Records: Lloyds TSB Group plc, Archives, Head Office, 71 Lombard Street, London EC3P 3BS

Amalgamation papers 1896

ST VINCENT COMMERCIAL BANK
North America

History: This bank applied for a charter in 1838 but appears not to have been established.

Records: Public Record Office, Ruskin Avenue, Kew, Richmond, Surrey TW9 4DU

Papers re application for charter 1838. [Ref: T1/3473]

M SAMUEL & CO LTD
London

History: This City of London merchant bank traced its origins to 1831when Marcus Samuel became established as a trader in oriental shells. By the 1870s the business had developed into an important merchant house dealing in Far Eastern commodities and had strong Japanese links. Following Marcus Samuel's death in 1870, in 1878 his two younger sons, Marcus and Samuel, established Marcus Samuel & Co in London and Samuel Samuel & Co in Japan; these firms soon emerged as leading merchants. In either 1882 or 1883 they acquired their father's business from their elder brother, Joseph. From the mid-1880s the business developed major oil and associated shipping interests and in 1897 formed Shell Transport & Trading Co Ltd of which M Samuel & Co were managers. Alongside this, the firm developed merchant banking functions, for example managing one of the first external bond issues for the Japanese government in the late 1890s. In late 1907 Sir Marcus Samuel retired and in 1920 the business was converted into a private limited company called M Samuel & Co Ltd. In 1960 it became a public company and in 1965 it merged with Philip Hill, Higginson, Erlangers Ltd to form Hill Samuel & Co Ltd which from 1987 was owned by TSB Bank plc and from 1996 by Lloyds TSB Group plc.

Robert Henriques, *Marcus Samuel, First Viscount Bearstead and Founder of the Shell Transport & Trading Co 1853–1927* (London, 1960); Stephen Howarth, *A Century in Oil. The Shell Transport and Trading Co 1897–1997* (London, 1997)

Records: Lloyds TSB Group plc, Group Archives, 71 Lombard Street, London EC3P 3BS

General ledgers 1853–67; partnership agreements 1881–1920; letterbooks 1904–28; papers re oil business 1905–08; agency agreements 1919, 1953; directors' meeting minutes 1920 on; private ledgers (2) 1920–63; analysis of accounts 1920–64; acceptance statistics 1925–28, 1946–55; directors' private office notes 1928–32; papers re issues 1928–35; pension fund papers 1933–65; German standstill debtors 1939; cash book 1939; routine ledgers 1939–64; customer dividend accounts 1956–63.

SAMUEL MONTAGU & CO LTD
London

History: This merchant bank was formed in 1853 by Samuel Montagu (sometime known as Montagu Samuel) and his brother Edwin. Their family had moved to Liverpool from northern Germany in the mid-eighteenth

464   *British banking – a guide to historical records*

century and then moved to London in 1847 when Samuel Montagu (later Lord Swaythling) joined the money changing firm of Adam Spielmann. In 1853, with capital from his father, he and his brother established Samuel & Montagu, a Liverpool banker and bullion merchant, acting as a sleeping partner. Initially the business included bullion and exchange services as well as bill collection and bankers' draft services. Within two decades the firm was an undisputed leader in the silver market. The business was renamed Samuel, Montagu & Co in 1862. In 1868 Montagu established the separate bank of A Keyser, later known as Keyser Ullmann, in order to provide employment opportunities for some of his many sons who, by virtue of their numbers, could not be admitted partners of Montagus. The business became independent of Montagus in 1908. By the 1870s Montagus had established a foreign business, providing credit facilities and issuing bonds, most notably lead-managing a £1million bond issue for the Belgian government in 1896. By this year the firm's capital was over £1 million. It became a member of the Accepting Houses Committee and between the wars emerged as a fully-fledged merchant bank. The firm remained a partnership until 1951 when it registered as a private company in which the Montagu family continued to hold a substantial interest. In 1963, along with its associated banking and insurance broking businesses, it was acquired by Montagu Trust Ltd which became a public company in 1963. In 1967 Midland Bank Ltd acquired a 33 per cent shareholding in Montagu Trust for £7 million and thereby became the first UK clearing bank to acquire a merchant banking interest. Although Samuel Montagu retained complete operational independence, there were joint ventures with the Midland, such as Midland Montagu Industrial Finance Ltd, providers of venture capital. In 1973 the outstanding share capital of Montagu Trust was acquired by Midland Bank. By then Samuel Montagu, with its related companies, was well-established in corporate finance, corporate and project banking, fund management, bullion dealing, insurance broking and overseas banking (through its subsidiary Guyerzeller Bank of Zurich). Aetna Life & Casualty Co took a 40 per cent interest in 1982, but this was reacquired by Midland in 1985 when Aetna acquired the investment management company, Midland Investment Management. After Midland joined the HSBC Group in 1992, Samuel Montagu was transferred to HSBC Investment Banking Group in 1993 and was renamed HSBC Samuel Montagu in 1996.

Anon, *The Samuel Family of Liverpool and London* (London, 1958); Edwin Green, 'Samuel Montagu', *Dictionary of Business Biography* (London, 1985); A R Holmes & Edwin Green, *Midland. 150 Years of Banking Business* (London, 1986)

Records: HSBC Holdings plc, Group Archives, 10 Lower Thames Street, London EC3R 6AE

Records of banks 465

Deeds re investments in East London properties 1810–92; private ledgers 1853–1938; partnership agreements and accounts 1854–1954; letterbook 1890–92; records of various customers 1910–72; correspondence re overseas investments 1914–35; salary register 1920–35; gold stock journals 1935–40; journal of bills payable 1938–73.

SIR SAMUEL SCOTT BART. & CO
London

History: This private bank was established in Cavendish Square, in London's West End, in about 1824. The 1825 balance sheet totalled £209,000. Much of its early business was taken from that of Marsh, Stracey, Fauntleroy & Graham (est. 1792) which failed in 1824. In about 1827 the bank was known as Sir Claude Scott Bart., Dent & Co and in 1847 it was styled Sir Samuel Scott Bart. & Co. In 1894 it amalgamated with Parr's Banking Co & Alliance Bank Ltd (est. 1865).

T E Gregory, *The Westminster Bank Through a Century* (London, 1936); F G Hilton Price, *Handbook of London Bankers* (London, 1876)

Records: The Royal Bank of Scotland plc, Archive Section, Regent's House, 42 Islington High Street, London N1 8XL

Private ledger 1824–32.

GEORGE G SANDEMAN, SONS & CO LTD
London

History: This firm of merchants and merchant bankers was formed in the eighteenth century in the City of London. The firm came to focus on trade in wine with Spain and Portugal. In the 1930s it became close to Sandeman & Sons Ltd (est. c.1760) of Edinburgh and it acquired this firm in 1961.

Records: Guildhall Library, Aldermanbury, London EC2 2EJ

Order book 1792–1809; letterbook 1795–97; cash book 1799–1806; ledger 1800–06; journal 1806–09; waste books (2) 1809–12, 1838–39; merchant banker's ledger 1817–19; investment books (2) 1821–60; trade circulars 1840–42; sherry shipment register 1869–72; inland letterbooks (2) 1885–87. [Ref: MS8642–52]

SANDERS & CO
Exeter, Devon

History: This private bank was established in 1769 as Duntze & Co and was otherwise known as the Exeter Bank. The founding partners were John (later Sir John) Duntze, William Mackworth Praed, Joseph Sanders

466   *British banking – a guide to historical records*

and Daniel Hamilton. Duntze was a leading woollen merchant and MP for Tiverton; his family had come from Bremen in north Germany. By 1810 the only partner still surviving was Joseph Sanders who was then joined in partnership by his two sons. The bank was styled Sanders & Co from 1812. Branches were opened at Exmouth (1896) and at Budleigh Salterton (1897). In 1901 Sanders merged with Milford, Snow & Co (est. 1776) to form Sanders, Snow & Co.

John Ryton, *Banks and Bank Notes of Exeter 1769–1906* (priv. pub., 1983)

Records 1: The Royal Bank of Scotland plc, Archive Section, Regent's House, 42 Islington High Street, London N1 8XL

Partnership agreements 1784–1877; staff surety bonds (2) 1796–1832; banker's licences 1815–1900; probates of partners' wills 1819–40; papers re premises 1835–70; general balance books (3) 1845–1901; private ledgers (3) 1864–1917; papers re partners' indemnity fund 1878–1900; balance sheets 1892–1901; profit and loss accounts 1895–99; amalgamation papers 1901–02.

Records 2: Devon Record Office, Castle Street, Exeter EX4 3PU

Papers 1877–94. [Ref: 1926 B/W/B 1]

SAPTE, MUSPRATT, BANBURY, NIX & CO
London

History: This private bank was established in Lombard Street, City of London, in about 1787 as Vere, Lucadon, Troughton, Lucadon & Smart. Thereafter it traded under many names drawing members from the Baron, Hawkins, Sapte, Muspratt, Nix and Banbury families. By 1856 the firm was known as Sapte, Muspratt, Banbury, Nix & Co and in 1859 it amalgamated with Fullers & Co (est. 1737) to form Fuller, Banbury, Nix & Mathieson which was subsequently known as Fuller, Banbury & Co.

F G Hilton Price, *A Handbook of London Bankers* (London, 1876)

Records: The Royal Bank of Scotland plc, Archive Section, Regent's House, 42 Islington High Street, London N1 8XL

Fidelity bonds 1788–1837; diary of payments 1788–95; accepted bills 1789–1813; correspondence with bankers 1793–1827; correspondence with Loraine, Baker & Co 1797–1820; correspondence re staff securities 1807–28; papers re clerk's fraud 1809–14; papers re liquidation of A Sheath & Son 1814; customer balance books (3) 1815; memorandum books re Christmas gifts to staff (2) 1818–19; correspondence re loans and securities 1826–57; statements of partnership and liquidation accounts 1833–44.

Records of banks 467

SAXTON BROTHERS
Market Drayton, Shropshire

History: This private bank was established in about 1851. It amalgamated with Midland Banking Co Ltd (est. 1836) in 1872.

Records: Barclays Bank plc, Group Archives, Dallimore Road, Wythenshawe, Manchester M23 9JA

Current account ledgers 1874–77.

SCHOLFIELD, CLARKSON & CLOUGH
Howden, Humberside

History: This private bank was formed in 1809 and was otherwise known as the Howden Bank. It had offices at both Howden and Selby. It failed in 1831 when its premises were acquired by the York City & County Banking Co (est. 1830) which appointed a former partner as its local agent.

Records: HSBC Holdings plc, Group Archives, 10 Lower Thames Street, London EC3R 6AE

Private ledger 1830–31.

J HENRY SCHRODER & CO LTD
London

History: This merchant bank traced its origins to Johann Heinrich Schroder (1784–1883), a member of a prosperous German merchant family which had arrived in London from Hamburg in 1802. He was admitted a partner in his brother's firm, but in 1818 established J Henry Schroder & Co followed by the Hamburg house of J H Schroder & Co (Schroder Mahs & Co from 1826) in 1819 and J H Schroder & Co at Liverpool in 1839. Their activities were largely merchanting and trade finance focusing on business with Germany, Russia, the Baltic and Latin America. In 1849 the businesses, by now moderately sized, were reorganised and a new house was formed in Hamburg (wound up in 1883). From then Schroders quickly emerged as one of London's leading trade finance and bond issuing houses, although the Liverpool business retained an important merchanting function, dealing especially in cotton. Notable bond issues were made for Cuban railways, the Confederate States and for Japan, and in making these bond issues a close association was formed with Emile Erlanger & Co. From 1872 until 1876 the firm acted as agents for the worldwide distribution of Peruvian guano. The traditional merchanting business was in sharp decline from the mid-1870s but issuing prospered, the wide range of clients now including Cuban railways; the Chilean nitrate industry; rail-

468   *British banking – a guide to historical records*

ways and municipalities in Brazil and Uruguay; the Imperial Bank of Persia; and business entities in South Africa and New Zealand. A connection with the New York brokerage house of Ladenburg Thalmann & Co was developed in 1885 to facilitate dealings in United States securities and Schroders began to derive revenue from underwriting issues of other London houses from the late 1880s. On the eve of the First World War, Schroders was London's second largest merchant bank, its success based upon a thriving acceptance business largely for United States and German clients and upon issuing for an ever widening group of borrowers: Mexican railways, United States railroad and industrial companies; the State of Sao Paulo for the stabilisation of coffee prices; the City of Valparaiso for waterworks improvements; and newly-emerging governments in eastern Europe, such as Romania. In the 1920s much bond issuing, often on joint account with Barings and Rothschilds, was done for German public and corporate clients as well as for other clients in Europe and Brazil. The first issue undertaken for a British company occured in 1924 and heralded an increasing British business generally. In order to secure business in the United States, J Henry Schroder Banking Corporation (Schrobanco) was formed in 1923 to undertake dollar acceptance finance, foreign exchange dealing and, until 1933, security underwriting. The suspension of German debt repayments in 1931 caused the greatest crisis in Schroders' history and placed a severe break on its domestic activities until the late 1950s. Schrobanco in New York, in contrast, flourished as it participated in dollar-based international banking. In the 1940s and 1950s, the activities of Schroders in London were almost entirely restricted to providing acceptance finance, corporate finance advice and fund management to British companies. In 1954 Schroder Successors Ltd, a private company, was formed to acquire the business, which in 1957 became known as J Henry Schroder & Co Ltd. In 1960 70 per cent of Helbert, Wagg Holdings Ltd which owned Helbert, Wagg & Co Ltd (est. 1848) was acquired, followed by the remaining 30 per cent in 1962, when the business was renamed J Henry Schroder, Wagg & Co Ltd. From the 1960s the new company spread its activities to Europe and the Far East. A majority interest in Schrobanco was sold in 1985. In the 1990s Schroders remained a leading London-based, but internationally spread, merchant bank. In 1995 the business was restyled J Henry Schroder & Co Ltd, by which time it was owned by Schroders plc.

Richard Roberts, *Schroders. Merchants and Bankers* (London, 1992)

Records: J Henry Schroder & Co Ltd, 120 Cheapside, London EC2V 6DS

The archives comprise the business papers of J Henry Schroder & Co and papers of the Schroder family. Pre-1939 records are sparse because

Records of banks 469

of extensive discarding when the firm relocated its offices during the Second World War. No letterbooks have survived although there is some correspondence amongst the family papers. Files exist covering security issues since 1853 though many contain just legal documentation and are therefore of limited interest. A list giving the names of clerks from 1829 to 1914 survives along with other fragmentary personnel papers for the inter-war years. Accounting records, on the other hand, are relatively extensive and formed the basis of Richard Robert's *Schroders. Merchants & Bankers* (1992). Postwar correspondence and other papers are more extensive, particularly files relating to new issues. There are also several runs of committee minutes. The archives are not immediately available and access is limited. Enquiries should be addressed to the company secretary.

SEATON, BROOK & CO
Huddersfield, West Yorkshire

History: This private bank was established in about 1797 by Joseph Brook. It was styled Seaton, Brook & Co from 1806 and it failed in 1810.

W C E Hartley, *Banking in Yorkshire* (Clapham, 1975)

Records: Nottinghamshire Archives, County House, Castle Meadow Road, Nottingham NG2 1AG

Papers re failure 1810–18. [Ref: CP 5/8/85–135]

SECCOMBE, MARSHALL & CAMPION PLC
London

History: This discount house was established in 1922 as Seccombe, Marshall & Campion. It was formed out of the bill business of M W Marshall & Son (est. 1919). Its formation was prompted by the appointment of Lawrence Seccombe, formerly a partner of Marshalls, as the Bank of England's special agent in the discount market. A large part of the firm's business comprised acting for the Bank in the sale or purchase of bills, thereby influencing interest rate levels. In 1947 the firm registered as a private limited company and then registered as a public company in 1956. Its role as Bank agent continued until recent times. In 1985 the firm was acquired by CitiCorp Investment Bank Ltd and in 1989 by CPR-Compagnie Parisienne de Réescompte SA of France.

Gordon Fletcher, 'Lawrence Henry Seccombe', *Dictionary of Business Biography* (London, 1986)

Records: Guildhall Library, Aldermanbury, London EC2P 2EJ

470 **British banking – a guide to historical records**

Journals (21) 1919–22, 1933–86; discount ledgers (2) 1919–24; bill market etc diaries (3) 1922–23, 1925; balance sheets 1923–30, 1936–38, 1941–89; loan ledgers (8) 1929–32, 1947–70 [w]; general ledgers (4) 1934–51, 1959–66; bill ledger 1939–42; Bank of England diaries (131) 1939–85; clearing bank diaries (131) 1939–96; clearing bank cash books (7) 1939–47; excess profit tax papers 1939–46; registers of members (2) 1940–83; Bank of England cash books (4) 1940–47, 1962–77; statements of capital in business 1941–46; articles of partnership 1943; papers re memorandum and articles of association 1943; directors' meeting minutes (5) 1947–85; cash books (34) 1947–63; day books (2) 1947–49, 1986; annual reports 1949–95; stock ledger 1953–67; year end and annual general meeting papers 1954–84; seal registers (15) 1954–86; lists of shareholders 1956–70; public company formation papers 1956; memorandum and articles of association 1956–85; public company formation papers 1956; register of trustees 1966–83; collateral books (20) 1968–76; certificates of deposit diaries (6) 1968–83.

CHARLES SHALES
History: No details of this goldsmith banker are known.

Records: Buckinghamshire Record Office, County Hall, Aylesbury HP20 1UA

Miscellaneous business papers 1710–28; deed of partnership with John Tysoe 1723; probate and will 1734; executors' papers 1734–37. [Ref: D/ LO/8/1/3, 7; D/LO/8/2/1]

SHARPLES, TUKE, LUCAS & SEEBOHM
Hitchin, Hertfordshire

History: This private bank was formed in 1820 as Sharples, Bassett & Co by partners in the Leighton Buzzard bank of Bassett & Grant (est. 1812). The connection with the latter bank ended in 1827 although subsequently its Ampthill and Luton agencies were acquired. In 1827 the business was known as Sharples & Exton, in 1836 as Sharples, Exton & Lucas, in 1851 as Sharples & Lucas, in 1852 as Sharples, Tuke & Lucas and in 1859 as Sharples, Tuke, Lucas & Seebohm. The bank was otherwise known as the Hertfordshire Hitchin Bank. In 1858 a branch was opened at Hertford following the failure of the Unity Joint Stock Mutual Banking Association. A branch briefly existed at Ware in the late 1860s and in the 1870s sub-branches were opened at Stevenage (1873), Hatfield (1877), Hoddesdon (1878) and New Barnet (1885). In 1892 deposits were £750,000 and capital and reserves were £100,000. In 1896 the bank merged with other leading banks to form Barclay & Co Ltd.

Records of banks 471

P W Matthews & Anthony W Tuke, *History of Barclays Bank Ltd* (London, 1926); John Parker, *Nothing for Nothing for Nobody* (Stevenage, 1986)

Records: Barclays Bank plc, Group Archives, Dallimore Road, Wythenshawe, Manchester M23 9JA

Ledgers, cash books and other banking and partners' papers 1675–1896; profit and loss book 1824–49; declaration of confidence 1825; cheques and cheque books 1832–98; private ledgers (3) 1852–96; security registers 1853–84; monthly statements of accounts 1858–83; correspondence re meger Fordham, Gibson & Co and Gibson, Tuke & Gibson 1868–79; customer letter to creditors 1881; branch statistics 1882–94; bank note registers 1882–98; request to open branch 1885; out-letters 1887–94; amalgamation papers re Barclay & Co Ltd 1896.

Ampthill: cheque 1800s.

SHEFFIELD & HALLAMSHIRE BANK LTD
Sheffield, South Yorkshire

History: This joint stock bank was formed in 1836 with a paid-up capital of £124,000. From the outset, it was closely associated with Sheffield's steel and cutlery industries and sought out the accounts of small manufacturers. By 1840 paid-up capital was £75,000 and deposits stood at £122,000; these figures were £183,000 and £404,000 respectively in 1870 and £300,000 and £1.7 million in 1900. Up until the 1880s, as a matter of policy, no branches were opened but by 1913 fourteen existed. Limited liability was acquired in 1889. The business was acquired by London, City & Midland Bank Ltd (est. 1836) in 1913 for the equivalent of £760,000. By then paid-up capital was £300,000 and deposits were £1.875 million.

W F Crick & J E Wadsworth, *A Hundred Years of Joint Stock Banking* (London, 1936); R E Leader, 'The Early Sheffield Banks', *Journal of the Institute of Bankers*, 38 (1917)

Records: HSBC Holdings plc, Group Archives, 10 Lower Thames Street, London EC3R 6AE

Directors' meeting minute books (19) 1836–1913; shareholders' minute books (2) 1836–1913; share transfer registers 1836–1913; deed of settlement 1837; annual reports 1837–1911; declarations of secrecy 1837–99; petition re staff holidays 1846; private minute book re staff 1861–68; proposals for adopting limited liability 1872; staff rules and regulations 1875; managers' minute books (3) 1882–1913; share registers (3) 1893–1912; general ledger 1893–1906; rough directors' meeting minutes (4)

472 *British banking – a guide to historical records*

1894–1913; papers re alterations to articles of association 1897–99; half-yearly returns 1897–1900; dividend books (3) 1898–1913; board agenda books (5) 1901–13; manager's notebook 1909–13; acceptance book 1912–40.

Sheffield, Markets: signature book 1898–1913.

SHEFFIELD & RETFORD BANK
Sheffield, South Yorkshire

History: This joint stock bank was established in 1839 as the Borough of Sheffield Bank. Within two years it established branches at Worksop and Retford, the latter being purchased from the Nottingham & Nottinghamshire Joint Stock Bank (est. 1834). This prompted a name change in 1842 to the Sheffield & Retford Bank. A year later, the last private bank in Sheffield, Rimingtons & Younges (est. 1816), was also acquired. Notwithstanding this, the bank had insufficient resources for the needs of its largest business customers – including many railway companies – while the failure of a Leeds bank, with which it was closely connected, also damaged its prospects. This resulted in 1846 in the sale of the Retford branch to the Sheffield Union Banking Co. A few months later, the remainder of the business ceased trading, many of its best accounts passing to the Sheffield Union Banking Co (est. 1843).

W F Crick & J E Wadsworth, *A Hundred Years of Joint Stock Banking* (London, 1936)

Records: HSBC Holdings plc, Group Archives, 10 Lower Thames Street, London EC3R 6AE

List of shareholders 1839; deed of settlement 1839; directors' meeting minutes 1839–42; schedule of promissory notes and bills of exchange 1840–48; liquidation papers 1849.

SHEFFIELD & ROTHERHAM JOINT STOCK BANKING CO LTD
Sheffield, South Yorkshire

History: This joint stock bank traced its origins to Walkers, Eyre & Stanley, a private bank established in 1792 by a family of local ironfounders. From the outset the bank operated offices in both Sheffield and Rotherham and pursued a prudent and conservative policy, ploughing back profits, investing its capital in government stock and carefully controlling its note issue. The partnership was restyled Walkers & Stanley in 1829; it was otherwise known as the Sheffield & Rotherham Bank. In 1836 it was reorganised as a joint stock bank under the title of the Sheffield &

Records of banks 473

Rotherham Joint Stock Banking Co. In 1837 its first branch was opened at Bakewell. By 1846 paid-up capital reached over £92,500. Thereafter the bank grew rapidly, opening branches at Buxton (1856), Dronfield (1873), Matlock (1877), Baslow (1897), Darley Dale (1893), Park Gate (1899), Higher Buxton (1899), Attercliffe (1902) and Winster (1904), and rebuilding its head offices at Sheffield and Rotherham. In 1880 limited liability was acquired and in 1907 the bank merged with Williams Deacon's Bank Ltd (est. 1836).

Anon, *Sheffield and Rotherham Bank. A Banking Bicentenary 1792–1992* (priv. pub., 1992); Anon, *Williams Deacon's 1771–1970* (Manchester, 1971)

Records: The Royal Bank of Scotland plc, Archive Section, Regent's House, 42 Islington High Street, London N1 8XL

Title deeds, Sheffield 1578–1856; bank notes 1814, 1837, 1899; cash book 1817–53; banker's licences 1817, 1875–1906; staff register and salary book 1818–1900; memorandum re permission to overdraw account 1820; papers re bank history 1820–1966; architectural plans, Sheffield office c.1825–65; bills of exchange 1826–37; private ledgers 1828–1907; partnership agreements 1829–35; articles of agreement re foundation 1836; directors' meeting minute books: 1836–1909, rough 1846–48; annual report and accounts 1836–1907; annual account summaries 1836–1907; annual balance sheets 1836–48; note issue books 1836–1907; deeds of settlement 1837, 1863; general meeting minutes 1837–1906; correspondence from solicitors 1838–53, 1900; old balances register 1841–1907; note circulation books 1845–1907; income tax papers 1846–47, 1902–07; annual accounts working papers 1857–58, 1870–1906; share transfer books 1861–1907; salaries account ledger 1861–1900; correspondence re shares 1862–1900; register of properties 1863–99; indenture for regulation of the bank 1863–81; manager's memorandum books 1863–1907; papers re new Sheffield bank 1865–55; branch premises papers 1865–1907; papers re stoppage of Overend, Gurney & Co 1866; fire insurance policies 1868–86; managers' meeting minute books 1871–1907; banker's bond 1873; branch memorandum book 1874–85; customer correspondence 1879–80; auditor's notes and reports 1880–1906; share transfer certificate book 1880–1900; shareholder circulars 1880–1904; regulations for management of the bank 1881; general meeting proxy forms 1881, 1894; letterbook re shareholders 1881–89; dividend register 1889–95; manager's rough profit and loss accounts 1890–1907; staff and property photograph albums 1890–94; shareholder address books 1890–1905; shareholder annual returns 1890–1906; papers re shares 1893–1907; certificate of registration 1896; share allotment book 1900; cancelled share certificates 1900–01; ledgers, other bank's accounts 1900–01; register of directors 1901–04;

474   *British banking – a guide to historical records*

balance sheet analysis ledger 1902–07; amalgamation papers 1906–07; advisory board minute book 1909–45.

Buxton: staff photographs c.1890s–1900s; **Matlock Bridge:** papers re manager 1891–1900; **Rotherham:** accounts applications 1843–1900; customer ledgers 1792–1800; balance books for customer accounts 1813,1863–64, 1872; customer opinion book 1879–1900; safe custody and securities books 1868–1900; customer stock purchase ledger 1814–1900; **Sheffield:** customer ledgers 1792–1804; deposit receipt books 1853–1900; signature books c.1866–1900; interview book 1899–1900; cheque signatory letterbooks c.1852–89; passbooks 1889–1900; papers and correspondence re securities 1837–1900; register of deeds deposited as safe custody and security c.1860s; schedules of securities with written deposits 1867–1900; safe custody and security books 1869–1900; customer guarantees for accounts and advances 1870–1900; registers of guarantees 1883–1900; copy letterbooks re securities 1888–1900; safe custody registers c.1850–1900; deposit receipt books 1853–1900; securities deposited for safe custody ledger 1894–1900; customer account guarantees 1868–1900; register of customer current accounts 1898–1900; customer stock purchase journals 1849–1900.

SHEFFIELD BANKING CO LTD
Sheffield, South Yorkshire

History: This joint stock bank was formed in 1831 as the Sheffield Banking Co. It opened a branch in Rotherham in 1834 and in Chesterfield in 1861 where it acquired the business of J & C Robinson & Co in 1870. It acquired much of the business of the private bank of Parker, Shore & Blakelock (est. 1774) of Sheffield when it failed in 1843. Paid-up capital was £92,690 in 1838 and grew to £204,650 in 1864, to £333,375 in 1880 and to £404,075 in 1901.The bank acquired limited liability in 1880. By 1886 four branches existed and the number grew to twenty-nine branches by 1918. In 1919 it amalgamated with National Provincial & Union Bank of England Ltd (est. 1833).

Robert Eadon Leader, *The Sheffield Banking Co Ltd. An Historical Sketch 1831–1916* (Sheffield, 1916)

Records: The Royal Bank of Scotland plc, Archive Section, Regent's House, 42 Islington High Street, London N1 8XL

Directors' meeting minute book 1831; general ledger 1831–38; deeds of settlement 1831–80; share receipts 1831–36; shareholder circular 1832; share certificates 1832–57; annual reports and accounts 1833–1918; salary ledgers (3) 1851–1922; historical articles 1853, 1916; bank note

Records of banks 475

printing plates n.d.; register of deeds and investments 1860s–1923; bank note registers 1874–1907; current account commission reduction note 1874; share allotment list 1880; standing order 1888; balance sheet 1906; staff salary and bonus receipts 1916–18; share registers 1918–19; branch premises register 1919; securities forms n.d.; amalgamation papers 1919.

Chesterfield: title deeds 1840–66; passbook 1908–14; **Doncaster:** guardbook of circulars and customer mandates 1917–24; **Gainsborough:** salary register 1919–28; **Rotherham:** minute book 1834–38; article in *The Builder* re premises 1892; **Sheffield:** passbooks 1859–70; photographic plate of banking hall 1916; photograph of early drawing of banking hall in 1847 n.d.; **Sheffield Moor:** passbooks 1915–37; **Swinton:** manager's private memorandum book 1903–34.

SHEFFIELD UNION BANKING CO LTD
Sheffield, South Yorkshire

History: This joint stock bank was established in 1843 with a paid-up capital of £16,000 and took over the Sheffield business of the Yorkshire District Banking Co (est. 1834). It prospered from the late 1840s and in 1846 acquired the Retford branch of the Sheffield & Retford Bank (est. 1839) and, shortly afterwards, much of its remaining business. In 1850 paid-up capital was £41,000 and deposits were £97,000. Early on, its major customer was the engineering firm, Naylor Vickers & Co which, when it temporarily suspended payment in 1857, owed the bank £60,000 at a time when the bank's paid-up capital was only £82,000. Heavy losses were made in 1866 and also in the late 1870s due again to over-exposure to a few major customers. By 1879 six branches existed. By 1880 paid-up capital was £180,000 and deposits were £428,000, the latter rising to £1.3 million in 1900 while paid-up capital remained unaltered. Limited liability was acquired in 1883. In 1901 the bank was acquired by the London, City & Midland Bank Ltd (est. 1836) for the equivalent of £1.472 million. It then had seventeen branches.

W F Crick & J E Wadsworth, *A Hundred Years of Joint Stock Banking* (London, 1936)

Records: HSBC Holdings plc, Group Archives, 10 Lower Thames Street, London EC3R 6AE

Deed of settlement 1843; directors' meeting minute books (6) with indexes (4) 1843–1901; summary of balance sheets 1845–46; list of current account balances 1846; correspondence with London agents 1847–1901; annual reports and balance sheets 1862, 1864–1901; tabulated balance

476   British banking – a guide to historical records

sheets 1862–1900; list of staff, guarantors and amounts of personal bonds 1870s–90s; correspondence re incorporation 1883; list of investments 1884–97; summary history of bank 1891; weekly balance sheets (2) 1893–1901; press cuttings re amalgamation 1899; advisory board minute book 1901–16; circulars re appointment of liquidator 1901, 1917.

SHILSON, COODE & CO
St Austell, Cornwall

History: This private bank was established in 1793 as Coode, Shilson & Co; it was otherwise known as the St Austell Bank. It was styled Shilson, Coode & Co in 1899 and amalgamated with National Provincial & Union Bank of England Ltd (est. 1833) in 1920.

Records: The Royal Bank of Scotland plc, Archive Section, Regent's House, 42 Islington High Street, London N1 8XL

Amalgamation papers 1920.

SHIP BANK
Glasgow, Strathclyde

History: This private bank was established in 1749 as Dunlop, Houston & Co; it was otherwise known as the Ship Bank, a name derived from the motif on its notes. Its original partners were members of wealthy Glasgow merchant families who had made fortunes from the tobacco and West India trades. By 1752 its note circulation was £41,440 and its net profit was £2,160. By 1761, the comparative figures were £82,330 and £12,900. There may have been a lapse in the business, perhaps resulting from the devastating impact of the War of American Independence on Glasgow's tobacco trade. In 1776, however, the bank was reorganised and revived as Moores, Carrick & Co and was known from 1789 as Carrick, Brown & Co when its capital was £12,000. In 1777 its balance sheet totalled £120,350; this rose to £346,640 in 1792 and to £1.028 million in 1821. In 1836 the bank merged with the Glasgow Banking Co (est. 1865) to form the Glasgow & Ship Bank.

J O Leslie, 'Robert Carrick', *Scottish Bankers' Magazine*, 44 (1956); Robert S Rait, *The History of the Union Bank of Scotland* (Glasgow, 1930)

Records 1: Bank of Scotland Archive, Operational Services Division, 12 Bankhead Terrace, Sighthill, Edinburgh EH11 4DY

Daily entry book 1728–1830; interest account ledger 1785–1831; ledgers 1788–1837; bond register 1796–1835; accounts book 1819–28; private ledger 1824–25; deposit receipt register 1824–28.

Records of banks **477**

Records 2: Business Records Centre, Archive Department, University of Glasgow, Glasgow G12 8QQ

Correspondence re routine transactions 1834–37. [Ref: UGD 108]

Records 3: Glasgow City Archives, Mitchell Library, North Street, Glasgow G3 7DN

Cashier's corroboration bond 1750; papers re winding up 1836–60. [Ref: B10/15/6048; T-LX 38–42]

SHROPSHIRE BANKING CO
Shrewsbury, Shropshire

History: This joint stock bank was established in 1836 through the amalgamation of four Shropshire private banks: Horden & Hill (est. 1791) of Newport; Reynolds, Charlton & Co (est. 1805) of Wellington; Darby & Co (est. 1810) of Coalbrookdale; and Biddle, Mountford, Pidcock & Cope (est. 1824) of Shifnal. The bank was closely connected with the local iron and coal industries and its fortunes varied with their performance. The bank also suffered a series of serious internal frauds, but was relatively prosperous when acquired by Lloyds Banking Co Ltd (est. 1765) in 1874.

Records: Lloyds TSB Group plc, Archives, Head Office, 71 Lombard Street, London EC3P 3BS

Deed of settlement 1836; general meeting minute book 1837–73; annual reports 1837–64; list of shareholders c.1871–74; directors' meeting minutes 1871–75; record of customer accounts 1873; amalgamation papers 1874–84.

SHRUBSOLE & CO
Kingston-upon-Thames, Surrey

History: This private bank was established in about 1792 as Knight, Haydon & Shrubsole but had its origins in a drapery business. It was styled Shrubsole & Lambert from 1816 and subsequently as Shrubsole & Co. The business failed in 1825 but continued. It was acquired by Parr's Banking Co & Alliance Bank Ltd (est. 1865) in 1894.

Records: The Royal Bank of Scotland plc, Archive Section, Regent's House, 42 Islington High Street, London N1 8XL

Amalgamation papers 1894.

JOHN SIMONDS, CHARLES SIMONDS & CO
Reading, Berkshire

478   *British banking – a guide to historical records*

History: This private bank was established in King Street, Reading, in 1814 by William Blackall Simonds, his son, Henry, two cousins, John and Charles Simonds and a Mr Nicholson, as Simonds & Nicholson. W B Simonds had formerly been a founding partner in the Reading bank of Micklem, Stephens, Simonds & Harris, formed in 1791. From 1816 the bank traded as Simonds & Co and opened branches in Wokingham (1816) and Henley-on-Thames (1821). From 1839 it was styled John Simonds, Charles Simonds & Co and in 1913 it was acquired by Barclay & Co Ltd (est. 1896). In 1892 its capital equalled £100,000 and its deposits stood at £503,000 rising to £925,000 by 1913. In that year, the bank had twelve branches.

P W Matthews & Anthony W Tuke, *History of Barclays Bank Ltd* (London, 1926)

Records: Barclays Bank plc, Group Archives, Dallimore Road, Wythenshawe, Manchester M23 9JA

Stock memorandum book 1800–57; cash book 1825–36; general balances ledger 1830–33; general ledger 1835–49; mortgage deposit memoranda 1836–37; mortgage, Boulter's Wharf 1838; specifications and bills, new bank premises 1838–39; photographs: branch property 1839, partners and staff 1846–57; balance book, half-yearly extracts (8) 1856–87; general account ledger 1857–97; note and draft books (4) 1865–1908; security register 1860s–80s; banker's licences 1870–71; bank note register 1872–1913; salary books (2) 1874–1914; bills discounted book 1888–1942; letter re stock purchase 1891; balance sheets 1892, 1902–13; branch opening notice, Bracknell 1899; unclaimed balances ledger 1905–17; cheques and cheque forms 1905–12; papers re merger with Barclay & Co Ltd 1913–17.

SIMPSON, CHAPMAN & CO
Whitby, North Yorkshire

History: This private bank traced its origins to Wakefield Simpson, draper and grocer, who was in business on his own account as a banker by 1781. In 1785 he formed a partnership with Abel Chapman, a member of an old-established and wealthy Whitby family. By 1790, the business was known as Simpson, Chapman & Simpson; it also traded as the Whitby Bank and later as the Whitby Old Bank. In 1892 the business was purchased by York Union Banking Co Ltd (est. 1833).

P W Matthews & Anthony W Tuke, *History of Barclays Bank Ltd* (London, 1926); Maberly Phillips, *Banks, Bankers and Banking in Northumberland, Durham and North Yorkshire* (London, 1894)

Records of banks

479

Records: Barclays Bank plc, Group Archives, Dallimore Road, Wythenshawe, Manchester M23 9JA

Drafts 1810s; bank notes 1828–90; passbooks 1877–1929; cheque forms and books 1882–92.

SIMPSON, WHITE & CO
Peterborough, Cambridgeshire

History: This private bank was formed in 1821 and was otherwise known as the Peterborough Bank. In 1849 it was acquired by the Stamford, Spalding & Boston Banking Co

Records: Barclays Bank plc, Group Archives, Dallimore Road, Wythenshawe, Manchester M23 9JA

Bank note 1825.

WILLIAM SKINNER & CO
Stockton, Cleveland

History: This private bank was established in about 1815 as Skinner, Atty & Holt; it was otherwise known as the Stockton & Darlington Commercial Bank. It was subsequently styled William Skinner & Co and was acquired by the National Provincial Bank of England (est. 1833) in 1836.

Records: The Royal Bank of Scotland plc, Archive Section, Regent's House, 42 Islington High Street, London N1 8XL

Legal opinion re amalgamation 1836.

SLOCOCK, MATTHEWS, SOUTHBY & SLOCOCK
Newbury, Berkshire

History: This private bank was formed as Toomer, Bunney, Slocock & King in 1791; its partners were closely connected with the local brewing industry. The business was variously known as Slocock, Bunney & Slocock from about 1817; as Bunney & Slocock from about 1835; and as Bunney, Slocock, Matthews & Slocock from about 1860. The business was in difficulties in the 1890s, apparently as a result of advances made to finance the development of a smokeless fuel; it was sold to the Capital & Counties Bank Ltd (est. 1877) for £24,000 in 1895.

Records 1: Lloyds TSB Group plc, Archives, Head Office, 71 Lombard Street, London EC3P 3BS

Partnership agreements 1820, 1881, 1891; amalgamation agreements 1895.

480   *British banking – a guide to historical records*

Records 2: Berkshire Record Office, Shire Hall, Shinfield Park, Reading RG2 9XD

H Bunney's account [1851–55] 1864. [Ref: D/EX 198 L1]

SAMUEL SMITH, BROS. & CO
Hull, Humberside

History: This private bank was formed in 1784 as Abel Smith & Sons; it was otherwise known as the Customs House Bank and later as the Hull Bank. Its principal partner was Abel Smith II who had been sent to Hull in 1732 as an apprentice to a local merchant. He subsequently became a partner in this firm, which was renamed Wilberforce & Smith; William Wilberforce (1759–1833), the reformer and philanthropist, was also a partner. The bank was the fourth Smith family bank and followed the earlier formations of Samuel Smith & Co (est. c.1688) at Nottingham, Smith, Payne & Smiths (est. 1758) of London and Smith, Ellison & Co (est. 1775) of Lincoln. A later bank was formed at Derby. In 1787 Thomas Thompson was admitted as a partner and in 1791 the firm was renamed Smiths & Thompson. He was to be the principal resident banker at Hull until his death in 1828. In 1812 the balance sheet totalled £634,834. In 1829 the firm was renamed Samuel Smith, Bros. & Co which it remained until 1902. In this year it joined with the other Smith banks in merging with the Union Bank of London Ltd (est. 1839) to form the Union of London & Smiths Bank Ltd.

J A S L Leighton-Boyce, *Smiths the Bankers 1658–1958* (London, 1958); Harry Tucker, *The History of a Banking House* (London, 1903)

Records: The Royal Bank of Scotland plc, Archive Section, Regent's House, 42 Islington High Street, London N1 8XL

General ledgers (8) 1784–1845; partnership agreements (7) 1787–1862; ledger balances 1802–15; D R Smith's letterbooks/dossiers (6) 1866–81; details of general accounts 1870–99; information books (2) 1891–1901.

SAMUEL SMITH & CO
Derby, Derbyshire

History: This private bank traced its origins to Richardson & Co (est. c.1778) which in 1806 was acquired by the Smith family and became their fifth bank following the formation of Samuel Smith & Co (est. c.1688) of Nottingham; Smith, Payne & Smiths (est. 1758) of London; Smith, Ellison & Co (est. 1775) of Lincoln; and Samuel Smith, Bros. & Co (est. 1784) of Hull. The first Smith partners were Samuel Smith and his brothers George and John. In 1809 the balance sheet totalled £102,000 and grew to £265,000

Records of banks

481

by 1825. With Hull, for much of the nineteenth century it was one of the two smallest Smith banks. In 1902 it joined the other family banks in merging with the Union Bank of London Ltd (est. 1839) to form the Union of London & Smiths Bank Ltd.

J A S L Leighton-Boyce, *Smiths the Bankers 1658–1958* (London, 1958); Harry Tucker, *The History of a Banking House* (London, 1903)

Records: The Royal Bank of Scotland plc, Archive Section, Regent's House, 42 Islington High Street, London N1 8XL

General ledger 1806–10; letters to London agent 1806–09; customer list 1816; bank note register 1816–43; private ledgers 1816–1902; petty expenditure book 1817–82; manager's letterbooks (3) 1842–57; note circulation monthly returns book 1844–49; balance sheets 1845–54; information book 1864–72; partner's diaries (3) 1876–1902; loan memorandum book 1876–79; opinion book 1878–84; bad debt accounts 1888–1902; general balance book 1888–1902; partners' letterbooks (3) 1889–1902; bank note 1896; liquidation accounts 1902–03.

SAMUEL SMITH & CO
Nottingham, Nottinghamshire

History: This important private bank traced its origins to Thomas Smith, a mercer and sub-commissioner of excise, who was at work as a banker in 1688 but had probably commenced banking in 1663. His early business resembled that of a goldsmith. The firm was later known as Thomas Smith & Co; as Samuel & Abel Smith from 1727; as Samuel & Abel Smith & Co from 1738; and as Abel Smith & Sons from 1751. From 1751 Abel Smith I was senior partner and on his death in 1758 he was succeeded by his son Abel Smith II when the bank was known as Abel Smith Esq. & Co. He emerged as one of the leading bankers of his time; it was under his leadership that the Smith family established the family-owned banks of Smith, Payne & Smiths (est. 1758) of London; Smith, Ellison & Co (est. 1775) of Lincoln; and Samuel Smith Bros. & Co (est. 1784) of Hull. Another bank was established in 1806 at Derby. All banks were linked to the Nottingham bank but their connections with the London bank became especially close; the London and Nottingham businesses were managed by the same partnership. Abel Smith died in 1788 when the bank was renamed Robert Smith Esq. & Co. Robert Smith was another banker of major importance; he was created Lord Carrington in 1796. On his withdrawal in 1792, the bank was renamed Samuel Smith Esq. & Co and from about 1807 it was known as Samuel Smith & Co. Its balance sheet total increased from £44,728 in 1727, to £139,000 in 1752, to £251,752 in 1792 and to £277,935 in 1808. In 1871 the Mansfield bank of James & Charles

482   British banking – a guide to historical records

Robinson (est. 1804) was acquired followed in 1880 by the Newark bank of Godfrey & Riddell (est. c.1797). From 1873 branches were opened at Basford, Bulwell, Hucknall Huthwaite, Ilkeston, Long Eaton, Pinxton, Shirebrook, Southwell, Sutton in Ashfield and Hucknall Torkard. In 1899 the combined balance sheet of the five family banks was £10.225 million while their combined capital and reserves were £1.2 million of which £200,000 was allocated to Nottingham. In 1902 the five Smith banks merged with the Union Bank of London Ltd (est. 1839) to form the Union of London & Smiths Bank Ltd.

J A S L Leighton-Boyce, *Smiths the Bankers 1658–1958* (London, 1958); Harry Tucker, *The History of a Banking House* (London, 1903)

Records 1: The Royal Bank of Scotland plc, Archive Section, Regent's House, 42 Islington High Street, London N1 8XL

Receivership accounts 1741–58; general ledger 1748–63; Abel Smith's private ledger 1757–74; account with London agent 1756–59; Abel Smith's letterbook 1760–84; interest and discount return books (4) 1774–1878; general balance books (8) 1780–1808; monthly totals of discounts 1783; list of bad and doubtful debts 1799; discounts book 1810–78; overdue debts book 1833–48; salary receipts books (3) 1836–68; private ledgers (5) 1810–82; customer ledger 1814–22; security register 1824–67; debts due and owed book 1833–48; bank notes c.1850–1900; letters re bad debts 1858–60; character book 1859–77; customer information book 1861–79; unclaimed balances 1876–98; partners' household account book 1894–1904.

Ripley: private ledger 1875–1900.

Records 2: Nottinghamshire Record Office, County House, Castle Meadow Road, Nottingham NG2 1AG

Correspondence of Abel Smith family 1733–1839; papers and accounts re A Smith 1788–94; balance sheets with lists of debtors and creditors 1796–98; annual accounts of income in cash, bills and rent 1838–47.

SMITH, ELLISON & CO
Lincoln, Lincolnshire

History: This important private bank was formed as Smith, Ellison & Brown in 1775 by Abel Smith II and was the third Smith family bank formed after Samuel Smith & Co (est. c.1688) of Nottingham and Smith & Payne (est. 1758) of London. Throughout its existence it worked closely with these banks and with later ones formed at Hull and Derby. Its founding partners also included Richard Ellison, a banker who was also a

Records of banks 483

partner in Ellison, Cooke, Childers & Swan (est. 1750) of Doncaster, and John Brown who was formerly agent of a local canal company; he was to be the resident banker at Lincoln. It was Lincoln's first bank. Initial partnership capital was £3,000 but it soon increased to £21,000. The balance sheet totalled £322,294 in 1799 and £728,026 in 1827 and profits grew from £3,384 in 1793, to £9,109 in 1800 and to £19,757 in 1819. The Ellison family withdrew in 1859 and for much of the nineteenth century the bank was managed by Alexander Melville although the Smith family continued to provide partners. Branches or agencies were opened at Brigg, Caistor, Gainsborough, Grantham, Grimsby, Grimsby Docks, Market Rasen, Scunthorpe and Sleaford. It remained a highly important country bank with a note circulation larger than any other. In 1891 its balance sheet totalled £1.5 million. In 1899 the combined capital and reserves of the Smith banks totalled £1.2 million of which £200,000 was contributed by the Lincoln firm. In 1902 it joined with the other Smith banks to merge with the Union Bank of London Ltd (est. 1839) to form the Union of London & Smiths Bank Ltd.

J A S L Leighton-Boyce, *Smiths the Bankers 1658–1958* (London, 1958); Harry Tucker, *The History of a Banking House* (London, 1903)

Records 1: The Royal Bank of Scotland plc, Archive Section, Regent's House, 42 Islington High Street, London N1 8XL

Partnership agreements 1775, 1789; general ledgers (7) 1775–1902; letter re note circulation 1800; declaration of confidence in the bank c.1820s; petition re note issue c.1830s; partners' correspondence and other papers 1830–1900; letters re loan 1835–38; balance sheets 1836–1902; salary books 1839–1910; note re Indiana stock 1847; special accounts schedules 1891–97; numbers of accounts lists 1881–99; order of service for laying cornerstone of new building 1885; correspondence re note issue, country banks and amalgamation 1888–97; premises valuations 1891; letterbooks (3) 1891–1907; managers' terms of service 1894; staff photograph c.1900; amalgamation papers 1901–04; summary of assets 1902; papers re Smith, Melville & Co 1926.

Grimsby: general ledger 1846–57; manager's diaries and interview notes (22) 1878–1920.

Records 2: Lincolnshire Record Office, St Rumbold Street, Lincoln LN2 5AB

Papers re staff and premises 1851–1904. [Ref: SE/32/2]

Records 3: Nottinghamshire Archives, County House, Castle Meadow Road, Nottingham NG2 1AG

484   *British banking – a guide to historical records*

Partnership agreement 1800; list of debtors and creditors 1799–1800.

SMITH, OSBORN & CO
Northampton, Northamptonshire

History: This private bank was formed in 1810 and was otherwise known as the Town & County Bank. It failed in 1825.

Records: Northamptonshire Record Office, Wootton Hall Park, Northampton NN4 8BQ

Papers re failure 1820s; private and business papers of a partner 1820s on. [Ref: O(N) 94–489]

SMITH, PAYNE & SMITHS
London

History: This important and prestigious private bank was formed at Lothbury, City of London, in 1758 as Smith & Payne. It was established by Abel Smith II, senior partner of the leading Nottingham bank of Abel Smith Esq. & Co, and John Payne, a wealthy London mercer and banker. Their articles of partnership covered both the Nottingham and London businesses but Smith managed in Nottingham and Payne managed in London. The London bank was formed to capture the London business of the Nottingham bank's country customers. The London business was renamed Smith, Payne & Smith in 1773, Smith, Payne, Smith & Payne in 1783 and Smith, Payne & Smiths in 1785. From the 1770s Robert Smith, later 1st Lord Carrington, was increasingly important in the firm's management. In 1799 the Payne family finally withdrew and from then on the business was owned and managed by the Smith family. Meanwhile other Smith family banks were opened at Lincoln in 1775 and at Hull in 1784; another firm opened at Derby in 1806. London partnership capital rose from £17,000 in 1764 to almost £50,000 in 1773 and by 1798 the balance sheet totalled £964,000. In 1806 the firm moved from Lothbury to Lombard Street. The balance sheet in 1891 totalled £4.5 million. In 1899 the combined balance sheets of the five family banks was £10.225 million. Their combined capital and reserves then amounted to £1.2 million of which £700,000 was allocated to London and £200,000 each to Nottingham and Lincoln. In 1902 the five Smith banks merged with the Union Bank of London Ltd (est. 1839) to form the Union of London & Smiths Bank Ltd.

J A S L Leighton-Boyce, *Smiths the Bankers 1658–1958* (London, 1958); Harry Tucker, *The History of a Banking House* (London, 1903)

Records 1: The Royal Bank of Scotland plc, Archive Section, Regent's House, 42 Islington High Street, London N1 8XL

Records of banks 485

Miscellaneous papers, letters, deeds, wills 1595–1859; customer list 1762–65; customer and impersonal ledger 1762–64; private ledgers (16) 1776–1854; out clearing book 1777; partners' miscellaneous correspondence 1777–1873; partnership agreements (15) 1782–1857; register of clerks 1783–1918; profit and loss ledgers (13) 1793–1849; order book 1795–1800; balance sheets 1797, 1898; press cutting re government loans 1801–02; correspondence from Robert Smith re executorship 1810–39; private ledger of J H Smith 1829–86; investment ledger of O Smith 1830–63; private diaries of J H Smith 1840–58; investment ledger of J Smith 1856–83; letterbooks (2) 1858–90; salary ledger 1874–94; weekly statistics of note circulation 1884–1904; annual reports 1891–1902; balances books 1891–1902; details of profits 1891–1902; list of bad debts 1892–1901; salary register 1895–1913; balance sheet 1898; private papers of Smith family nineteenth cent; photograph, Lombard Street 1900; amalgamation papers 1902; historical articles and papers c.1903.

Records 2: Nottinghamshire Record Office, County House, Castle Meadow Road, Nottingham NG2 1AG

Partnership agreement 1785; general papers and accounts 1777–1847.

SMITH ST AUBYN & CO LTD
London

History: This City of London discount house was formed in 1891. It registered as a private company in 1932 and as a public company in 1943. In 1986 it merged with King & Shaxson Ltd.

Records: Guildhall Library, Aldermanbury, London EC2P 2EJ

Diaries with notes on business transacted, money market interest rates, press cuttings, etc (66) 1891–1941, 1948–59; ledgers (20) with client (1891–1922) and general accounts 1891–1954; cash books (20) 1891–97, 1937–60; day books (135) 1891–1958; bill balance book 1891–92; trade acceptors ledgers (2) 1927–55; partners' and trustees' accounts ledger 1930–39; private accounts loan book 1931–38; loans ledger 1932–39; 'average rate bills no 1' with details of bill and discount market transactions 1933–56; loans books (4) 1944–52; journals (4) 1946–56 [w]; private accounts interest books 1948–52; rough loan book 1949–52; rough day books (8) 1949, 1955–58; appointment diaries (2) 1954, 1956. [Ref: MS 14894–14909]

SOUTH WALES UNION BANK LTD
Swansea, West Glamorgan

History: This joint stock bank was formed in 1873 as the Swansea Bank Ltd with a paid-up capital of £90,000. Its promoters included several

486   *British banking – a guide to historical records*

businessmen connected with the local tinplate industry from which many of the bank's customers were drawn. Within two years branches were opened at Llanelli and Burry Port. The bank expanded quickly and by 1876 paid-up capital was £201,000 although deposits remained relatively small at only £165,000. A part of the large business of the West of England & South Wales District Bank Ltd (est. 1834) was obtained following that bank's failure in 1878. In 1888 the bank expanded its operations to Cardiff, establishing a branch there in place of a proposed joint stock bank. The business of the proposed bank's promoters was thereby acquired and, also in 1888, the bank was renamed the South Wales Union Bank Ltd. Five new branches were soon opened as the business expanded quickly; in 1891 paid-up capital was £206,000 and deposits reached £841,000. This expansion was checked in the early 1890s when the tinplate industry entered a period of depression. In 1892 the bank amalgamated with the Metropolitan & Birmingham Bank Ltd (est. 1829) which changed its name to the Metropolitan, Birmingham & South Wales Bank Ltd.

W F Crick & J E Wadsworth, *A Hundred Years of Joint Stock Banking* (London, 1936)

Records: HSBC Holdings plc, Group Archives, 10 Lower Thames Street, London EC3R 6AE

Prospectus 1872; directors' meeting minute book 1872–92; shareholders' minute book 1873–92; memoranda of deposit 1873–1905; staff register 1873–91; board committee minute books (3) 1876–85; manager's memorandum book 1876–92; letterbooks (3) 1878–91; board rough minute book 1888–92; amalgamation papers 1892–93.

SPARROW, BROWN, FENN & CO
Sudbury, Suffolk

History: This private bank was established as Addison & Fenn in 1788; it was otherwise known as the Sudbury Bank. It was later known as Fenn & Addison and subsequently was connected with Crowe, Sparrow, Brown & Co (est. 1801) of Bury St Edmunds. The Sudbury business remained distinct and was styled Sparrow, Brown, Fenn & Co. In 1830 the Crowe, Sparrow and Brown families withdrew and their businesses merged with James Oakes & Son (est. 1795) of Bury St Edmunds.

Harold Preston, *Early East Anglian Banks and Bankers* (Thetford, 1994)

Records: Lloyds TSB Group plc, Archives, Head Office, 71 Lombard Street, London EC3P 3BS

Security registers 1820s.

Records of banks

SPARROW, TUFNELL & CO
Chelmsford, Essex

History: This private bank was established in 1805 as Sparrow, Hanbury & Co; it was otherwise known as the Essex & Suffolk Bank. It carried on business under many names including Sparrow, Brown, Hanbury, Saville & Simpson from about 1813; Sparrow, Simpson, Walford, Greenwood & Nottidge, otherwise known as the Essex Bank, from 1825; Sparrow, Simpson, Walford & Greenwood from 1830; Sparrow, Walford, Nottidge, Greenwood & Tufnell from 1838; and Sparrow, Round, Green, Tufnell & Round from about 1851. It acquired Giles & Co (est. 1828) of Rochford in 1853 and was very closely associated with Sparrow, Tufnell & Co (est. 1801) of Braintree. The bank was renamed Sparrow, Tufnell & Co in 1881 and in 1896 amalgamated with other banks to form Barclay & Co Ltd. In that year it had nine branches, viz.: Braintree (c.1808), Halstead (c.1823), Maldon (c.1826), Rochford (1853), Billericay (1857), Ongar (c.1841), Southend (1860), Kelvedon (1891) and Witham (c.1823–26, 1883). Early in the century it also had branches at Coggeshall and Bishop's Stortford.

P W Matthews & Anthony W Tuke, *History of Barclays Bank Ltd* (London, 1926); Harold Preston, *Early East Anglian Banks and Bankers* (Thetford, 1994)

Records 1: Barclays Bank plc, Group Archives, Dallimore Road, Wythenshawe, Manchester M23 9JA

Bill of exchange 1808; partnership agreements 1817, 1823–51; partnership asignments 1824–30; cheques, cheque forms and cheque books 1826–90; private ledgers (3) 1827–66; bank notes 1830–34, 1861–91; banker's ledger 1833–44; partnership meeting minutes 1874–96; balance sheet 1891; amalgamation papers re Barclay & Co Ltd 1890–96.

Billericay: current account ledgers (2) 1817–26; **Braintree:** in-letter indemnity 1802; bank note register 1826–53; draft 1827; **Chelmsford:** current account ledgers 1807–25; banker's accounts ledgers 1833–44; bank note n.d.; statement of accounts 1855–81; private letterbook 1887–90; **Maldon:** current account ledger 1826–29; **Rochford:** profit and loss book 1853–84; journals 1862–65; **Southend:** signature books (2) 1892–1905.

Records 2: Essex Record Office, PO Box 11, County Hall, Chelmsford CM1 1LX

Legal proceeding papers and agency agreement 1823–96; partnership agreements 1825–70; property deeds 1854–1909. [Ref: D/DDw B4/1–19, B8/1–10, T180/1–10]

488   *British banking – a guide to historical records*

SPARROW, TUFNELL & CO
Braintree, Essex

History: This private bank was formed in 1801 as Crowe, Sparrow & Brown and it subsequently traded under several names including Sparrow, Brown, Hanbury & Saville (1807); Sparrow, Simpson, Walford, Greenwood & Nottidge (1825); and Sparrow, Tufnell & Co (c.1881). It was otherwise known as the Braintree Bank (1801), as the Essex & Suffolk Bank (1814) and as the Essex Bank (1825). It was very closely associated with Sparrow, Tufnell & Co (est. 1805) of Chelmsford and sometime had agencies at Great Dunmow and Coggeshall. At some stage it may well have become part of the same firm as Sparrow, Tufnell & Co of Chelmsford. In 1896 it merged with other banks to form Barclay & Co Ltd.

Harold Preston, *Early East Anglian Banks and Bankers* (Thetford, 1994); P W Matthews & Anthony W Tuke, *History of Barclays Bank Ltd* (London, 1926)

Records: Essex Record Office, PO Box 11, County Hall, Chelmsford CM1 1LX

Partnership agreements 1817–23; letters re advance 1826–27. [Ref: D/Do B97, D/DTa B2]

SPOONER, ATTWOOD & CO
London

History: This private bank was established in Fish Street, City of London, in 1801 as Spooner, Attwood & Holmar. The bank moved to Gracechurch Street by 1812 and from about 1845 traded as Spooner, Attwood, Twells & Co. In 1863 it was acquired by Barclay, Bevan, Tritton & Co (est. 1690), the new business being named Barclay, Bevan, Tritton, Twells & Co. There was a family association with the Birmingham private bank of Attwood, Spooner & Co (est. 1791).

F G Hilton Price, *A Handbook of London Bankers* (London, 1876); P W Matthews & Anthony W Tuke, *History of Barclays Bank Ltd* (London, 1926)

Records: Barclays Bank plc, Group Archives, Dallimore Road, Wythenshawe, Manchester M23 9JA

Forged bank note 1806; cheque 1840; country account ledgers (2) 1859–63; death certificate, John Twells 1866.

Records of banks

STAFFORDSHIRE JOINT STOCK BANK LTD
Bilston, later Wolverhampton, later Birmingham, West Midlands

History: This joint stock bank was formed in 1864, its promoters being local corn and iron merchants. It immediately acquired the Bilston private bank of William Jones & Son (est. 1845) for £9,000, the sole surviving partner becoming a director and the manager of the new bank. A few days later the Walsall private bank of H Duignan & Son (est. c.1848) was acquired for £2,250. By 1865 paid-up capital was £130,000 and deposits stood at £410,000; these figures were £175,000 and £685,000 in 1880. The head office was moved to Wolverhampton in 1876 and, a year later, to New Street, Birmingham. In the late 1870s and 1880s a number of large bad debts were incurred which in 1884 almost equalled paid-up capital, but this position was concealed from shareholders. In 1887 the business of the failed private bank of Greenway, Smith & Greenways (est. 1791) of Warwick and Leamington was acquired. In 1889, when deposits exceeded £1 million, the bank was sold to the Birmingham Banking Co Ltd (est. 1829) for £74,375, a price which reflected its precarious position and resulted in substantial losses for shareholders.

W F Crick & J E Wadsworth, *A Hundred Years of Joint Stock Banking* (London, 1936)

Records: HSBC Holdings plc, Group Archives, 10 Lower Thames Street, London EC3R 6AE

Prospectus 1864; half-yearly balance sheets 1874–85; security register 1876–89; general ledger 1884–91; reports on shareholders' meetings 1888–91; investigation committee report 1890; liquidator's reports and passbook 1891; amalgamation papers 1890–91.

Walsall: signature books 1872–89; security register 1877–89; **Willenhall:** signature books 1873–89.

STAMFORD, SPALDING & BOSTON BANKING CO LTD
Stamford, Lincolnshire

History: This joint stock bank was established in 1831 as the Stamford & Spalding Joint Stock Banking Co with a paid-up capital of £15,000. Branches were opened at Stamford, Spalding and Oundle in 1832, each operating independently save in the issue of notes and sharing of profits. The bank proved profitable, in 1834 converted its Boston agency to a branch and in 1836 altered its name to Stamford, Spalding & Boston Banking Co. Branches were opened at Bourne (1835), Peterborough (1836), Oakham (1837), Uppingham (1837) and Grantham (1848). Simpson &

490   British banking – a guide to historical records

White (est. 1821) of Peterborough was acquired in 1849 followed by Bourne, Rhodes & Co (est. 1844) of Alford in about 1861. By 1852 paid-up capital was £40,000 and there were fourteen branches or agencies. Further branches were opened in Leicester (1872) and Northampton (1878). In 1874 limited liability was acquired. The Nottingham Joint Stock Bank Ltd's (est. 1865) business at Grantham was purchased in 1880. In 1882 a branch was opened at Lincoln and also the Stamford, Lincoln and Peterborough business of the Birmingham, Dudley & District Banking Co Ltd (est. 1836) was acquired. In 1888 Eland & Eland (est. 1810) of Thrapston and Kettering was purchased. Branches were opened in Grimsby in 1890 and Louth and Norwich in 1891. Also in 1891 Eaton, Cayley & Co (est. 1800) of Stamford was acquired. By 1898 the bank boasted twenty-two branches and sixteen agencies. It was acquired by Barclay & Co Ltd (est. 1896) in 1911.

P W Matthews & Anthony W Tuke, *History of Barclays Bank Ltd* (London, 1926)

Records 1: Barclays Bank plc, Group Archives, Dallimore Road, Wythenshawe, Manchester M23 9JA

Minute books 1831–33; deed of settlement 1832; reports and accounts 1852–1910; profit and loss accounts 1858; cheques and cheque forms 1865–1909; bank note registers (3) 1868–1908; forms, bond to secure advances 1860s, 1910; articles of association 1870–83; deed of transfer re bank trustees estates 1873; certificate of incorporation 1874; manuscript history n.d., c.1903; terms and conditions of appointment of executors, trustees, includes list of branches 1907; papers re Barclay & Co Ltd merger 1911.

Boston: bank note 1853; **Desborough:** memorandum book 1887–95; **Grimsby:** security register 1890–98; **Louth:** passbook 1892–1901; cheque book 1903; **Market Harborough:** deposit receipts 1896–1912; **Newark:** lease of premises 1900; **Northampton:** general manager's correspondence re staff 1891–1933; **Norwich:** manager's in-letters 1896–1907; **Stamford:** general manager's correspondence re staff 1866–1917; profit and loss returns 1877–1917; customer information form 1896–1912; **Uppingham:** ledgers, current and impersonal accounts (7) 1845–68.

Records 2: Spalding Gentlemen's Society, The Museum, Broad Street, Spalding PE11 1TB

Deed of settlement 1832.

STANDARD BANK OF WEST AFRICA LTD
Liverpool, Merseyside, London and Africa

Records of banks 491

History: The origins of this overseas bank are traced to 1891 when the African Banking Corporation Ltd opened a branch at Lagos, Nigeria, at the behest of the shipowner Sir Alfred Jones of Elder Dempster. It was the first British bank to establish a presence in West Africa. In 1893 the branch was acquired by Elder Dempster which in 1894 incorporated it into the newly-formed Bank of British West Africa Ltd, owned by Jones and his directors, which had its head office at Liverpool. It held the colonial government's account and, more importantly, the monopoly of silver coin imports from the Royal Mint. Branches were opened at Accra (1896) in Gold Coast and Freetown (1898) in Sierra Leone. Soon advances were made to local traders and producers, mostly of rubber and cocoa, against shipment. In 1910 paid-up capital rose from £12,000 to £200,000 with Elder Dempster and Sir Owen Philipps (later Lord Kylsant) being major shareholders. By that year, when the head office was moved to London, fourteen branches and ten agencies had been opened; the numbers grew to thirty-four and twenty-nine respectively by 1916. In 1912 the rival Bank of Nigeria Ltd (est. 1899) was acquired and in the same year, following a reorganisation of the colonial currency, the bank became agents for the newly formed West Africa Currency Board. In 1915 expansion into North Africa occurred and in 1918 and 1920 branches in Egypt were opened (closed 1925). An agency in New York was established in 1916 (closed 1922). The capital base and board were strengthened in 1919 when Lloyds Bank Ltd (est. 1865) and three other major British banks took shareholdings. During the 1920s and early 1930s, as a result of a difficult economic environment, the bank's performance was unremarkable; the number of branches fell from fifty-eight in 1930 to forty in 1938. Most of the Canary Islands and Moroccan branches were closed. In the late 1940s and 1950s, when the old-established European trading companies were withdrawing from West Africa, much of their business of commodity production finance passed to the bank. Also from the late 1940s, long term lending to finance investment in local industry and in public capital infrastructure projects began. Both resulted in the bank's rapid expansion, despite the loss by the early 1960s of business for the government and for the West African Currency Board; by 1963 118 branches were open. In 1957 the bank's name changed to the Bank of West Africa Ltd and then to the Standard Bank of West Africa Ltd in 1966, following merger with Standard Bank Ltd in 1965. In 1969 three separate and locally registered companies, in which local governments and investors took substantial interests, were formed to take over much of the bank's business – namely Standard Bank Nigeria Ltd, Standard Bank Ghana Ltd and Standard Bank Sierra Leone Ltd. By 1974 the Standard Bank of West Africa Ltd operated only two branches, both in the Gambia, and in 1978 these were transferred to Standard Bank Gambia Ltd.

492   *British banking – a guide to historical records*

Richard Fry, *Bankers in West Africa. The Story of the British Bank of West Africa Limited* (London, 1976); A H Milne, *Sir Alfred Lewis Jones KCMG. A Story of Energy and Success* (Liverpool, 1914)

Records 1: Guildhall Library, Aldermanbury, London EC2P 2EJ

Memorandum and articles of association 1894–1971; indexes to directors' meeting minute books (8) c.1894–1911; seal registers (5) 1894–1965; private ledgers (8) 1894–1961; agreements with governments, other banks, government bodies, etc, covering such matters as the opening or acquisition of branches 1894–1961; powers of attorney register 1894–1959; private profit and loss ledgers (5) 1895–1971; guardbook of annual general meeting papers 1895–1905; balance sheet books (3) 1895–1972; photographs of staff, branches, etc (10) 1896–1969; powers of attorney, arranged by branch 1900–57; customer and staff signature books (8) 1900–64 [w]; annual reports 1902–65; investment registers (3) 1902–71; general meeting proceedings 1910–37 [w]; balance books (10) 1908–72; property deeds registers (3) 1909–71; papers re establishment of branches c.1910; papers re establishment of Tenerife branch 1910–20; press cuttings re branch openings etc 1910–14; premises and furniture registers (2) 1910–27; papers re acquisition of Bank of Nigeria 1911–13; general instruction books (4) 1911–76; branch analysis of charges and expenses and annual profit and losses (4) 1911–63; staff social meetings papers 1911–20; branch reports and statistics 1912–65; circular letters from head office 1915–53; discount letters outward bills 1920–30; income tax assessment papers 1920–62; private general ledgers (4) 1921–64; private journals (9) 1921–67; staff committee minute books (5) 1922–65; accounts in liquidation ledger 1922–25; out-letters to and report on Morocco branches 1922; inspector's branch reports 1923–28, 1941; New York liquidation account 1923–25; bad and doubtful accounts book 1923–25; correspondence with Canary Island branches 1924–56; papers re New York agency 1924–63; underwriting register 1925–39; 'statistics registers' re money transfers (12) 1925–67; specimen documents and forms (2) 1926–58; branches outstanding adjustment ledgers (2) 1927–59; reports on Nigerian and Ghanaian premises 1928–29; 'balance sheet general ledgers' (5) 1929–72; directors' 'selective minute' book 1929–59; instructions re bills (2) 1929–44; overseas taxation papers 1929–65; profit and loss data re Nigeria 1931–58; papers re German credit repayments 1933–57; staff passage ticket register 1933–53; 'staff on leave medical examinations' 1933–56; registers of bonds, guarantees and indemnities (19) 1934–68 [w]; officers' provident fund papers 1934–42; 'miscellaneous ledgers foreign currencies' (5) 1934–49, 1957–66; short deposit registers (4) 1935–49; papers re Anglo-Spanish clearing arrangements 1936–65; 'monthly profit and loss totals' 1936–59; papers re closure of Fernando Po branch 1936–40; excess

Records of banks 493

profit tax papers 1936–54; currency accounts ledgers (5) 1937–46, 1949; papers re closure of Canary Islands branches 1937–45; correspondents currency ledgers (3) 1939–55; Canary Islands branches monthly returns 1939–45; 'miscellaneous ledgers' (6) 1940–65; Morocco liquidation account 1940–45; sundry debtors and creditors ledgers (17) 1941–65; papers re Hamburg branch 1937–54; unpublished balance sheets and profit and loss accounts 1943–49; statistics register re branches 1944–63; papers re closure of Casablanca and other Moroccan branches (3) 1945–70; country cheques for clearing journal 1945–67; 'credit register' being letters with banks re credits 1945–63; weekly salary book 1946–51; 'sundry currencies accounts' (4) 1946–55, 1964–65; branches and agencies currency balances 1947–54; analysis of branch charges 1947–62; Hamburg subcommittee minutes 1948–49; Sierra Leone branch transfer statistics 1949–61; London journal 1949–52; Liverpool journals (2) 1949–54; Manchester journal 1950–53; correspondents' currency journals (2) 1950–54; inward bills statistics 1950–64; profit and loss accounts (2) 1952–53; depositors' ledger 1952–66; Chief Accountant's papers re Nigeria and Ghana 1952–63; capital reconstruction papers 1954–55; general ledgers (14) 1954–65; 'bills receivable miscellaneous register' 1956–66; branch analysis of exchange and commission accounts 1956–64; profit and loss journals (5) 1956–68; West African Currency Credit Board account papers 1957–67; general ledgers foreign currencies (8) 1957–71; UK banks ledgers (3) 1957–71; statistics and progress reports from branches 1957–66; advertising scrapbooks (4) 1957–66; premises costs statistics 1957–59; 'miscellaneous ledgers foreign currencies' (4) 1958–71; branch returns 1958–59; impersonal ledgers (6) 1958–65; general ledgers (11) 1960–70; 'sundry debtors and creditors foreign exchange ledgers' (2) 1962–65; foreign currency ledgers (2) 1963–65; branch returns general files 1963–67; profit and loss ledger 1964–65; profit and loss ledgers Nigeria and Ghana (2) 1964–5; company history papers 1973–75.

Canary Islands: 'dormant balances and suspense accounts' 1945–46; **Casablanca:** 'dormant balances and old drafts' 1921–46; **Duala, Cameroons:** security and safe custody register 1922–73; papers re credit facilities 1954–57; general ledger 1969–71; cash books (3) 1972–73; **Lagos, Nigeria:** Church Missionary Society account 1937–39; **Tangier:** list of items and securities held for customers 1960; **Victoria, Cameroons:** bill payable book 1957–74; papers re indemnities 1957–69; general ledgers (2) 1969–73. [Ref: MS 28514–28816]

Records 2: Standard Chartered Bank plc, Head Office, Aldermanbury Square, London EC2V 7SB

Directors' meeting minutes 1894 on; shareholder records 1894 on.

494   *British banking – a guide to historical records*

STANDARD CHARTERED BANK AFRICA PLC
London and Africa

History: This British-based overseas bank was formed in London in 1862 as the Standard Bank of British South Africa Ltd with a nominal capital of £1 million. Its chief office was at Port Elizabeth, the principal port of Cape Colony, and in 1863 it acquired the Bank of Port Elizabeth. The acquisition of local banks became a major means of expansion. In the mid 1860s the Colesberg Bank, the British Kaffrarian Bank, the Fauresmith Bank and Beaufort West Bank were acquired. By 1864, when paid-up capital was £500,000, fifteen branches located across southern Africa were open, although the bank was excluded from the Orange Free State from 1865 until 1900. In 1870 the Standard Bank was larger than all of its local competitors combined and in 1877 it acquired one of the largest of them, the London & South African Bank (est. 1860). In the 1870s and 1880s for the first time the bank became involved with the nascent diamond and gold mining industries; by 1887 £850,000 was advanced to diamond miners making the bank by far the most important bank serving the industry. Early important corporate clients included de Beers, Cecil Rhodes and the Chartered Co. The bank financed the needs of local governments during periodic wars and by the 1880s was assuming the characteristics of a central bank, for example holding government accounts and cash reserves, issuing notes and making bond issues in London. In 1885 the South African head office was moved from Port Elizabeth to Cape Town. In the 1890s expansion into Bechuanaland, Mashonaland and Matabeleland occurred, and the first branch opened in Southern Rhodesia in 1892. In 1901 the first Nyasaland branch opened followed by branches in Northern Rhodesia in 1906. In Hamburg and New York, agencies were opened in 1905 and 1906 and in 1911 expansion occurred into British East Africa and, afterwards, into the Belgian Congo. In 1920 the bank acquired an 11 per cent holding in the Bank of British West Africa Ltd (est. 1894). In 1921 the African Banking Corporation Ltd (est. 1890) was acquired. In 1927 the issue of notes in South Africa and the running of the government's accounts were lost to the newly-formed Reserve Bank and this pattern soon followed in other countries in which the bank operated. After 1945 it expanded especially rapidly, the number of branches and agencies growing from 390 to 900 by 1963. In 1953, recognising the increased need for more local supervision, management boards were established at Johannesburg and Salisbury. The South African head office was moved from Cape Town to Pretoria in the early 1950s. In 1962, in acknowledgment of the spread of activities outside South Africa, the bank was renamed Standard Bank Ltd although, in southern Africa, the old title was retained for a new, locally incorporated company to which the southern African business was transferred. The Bank of West Africa Ltd was ac-

Records of banks **495**

quired in 1965. In 1966 Standard Bank Investment Corporation was formed in South Africa to own the Standard Bank of South Africa Ltd and other local subsidiaries, and part of its equity was sold to local investors. Elsewhere, other groups of branches within political boundaries were transferred to locally registered banks in which Standard Bank's shareholding was reduced from 100 per cent. As a response to the increased 'globalisation' of banking and as a defence measure against takeover, in 1970 Standard merged with The Chartered Bank to form Standard & Chartered Banking Group Ltd, later known as Standard Chartered Bank plc. Subsequently the Standard Bank was renamed Standard Chartered Bank Africa plc to hold the African interests of Standard Chartered. The southern African business became wholly South African owned in 1987.

Anon, *A Story Brought Up To Date* (priv. pub., 1983); G T Amphlett, *History of the Standard Bank of South Africa Ltd 1862–1913* (Glasgow, 1914); J A Henry, *The First Hundred Years of the Standard Bank* (London, 1963)

Records 1: Guildhall Library, Aldermanbury, London EC2P 2EJ

A large quantity of records have been deposited at Guildhall Library which are presently being catalogued.

Records 2: Standard Chartered Bank plc, Head Office, Aldermanbury Square, London EC2V 7SB

Directors' meeting minutes 1862; shareholder records 1862 on.

STEPHENS, BLANDY & CO
Reading, Berkshire

History: This private bank was formed in 1791 as Micklem, Stephens, Simonds & Harris. The founding partners were closely linked with local industry and commerce; John Micklem was a draper, John Stephens and William Simonds were brewers and Robert Harris was a mealman. In 1814 William Simonds withdrew to form a new Reading bank, Simonds & Nicholson, when the bank was renamed Stephens, Harris & Stephens. From 1841 it was restyled Stephens, Blandy & Blandy, following the entry of the Blandy family of brewers and solicitors, and as Stephens, Blandy, Barnett, Butler & Co from 1892. Branches were opened at Maidenhead (1842), Marlow (1869) and Bracknell (1872). In 1899 the business was acquired by Lloyds Bank Ltd (est. 1765).

R S Sayers, *Lloyds Bank in the History of English Banking* (Oxford, 1957)

Records: Lloyds TSB Group plc, Archives, Head Office, 71 Lombard Street, London EC3P 3BS

496   *British banking – a guide to historical records*

Partnership agreements 1791–1892; stock day books (2) 1795–1807; profit and loss books (9) 1797–1887 [w]; stock ledgers (4) 1810–56; bad debt ledger 1814; unclaimed balances book 1814–96; balance sheets 1815–76; cash book 1817–19; customer account balance books (2) 1845–55; amalgamation papers 1899–1902.

Reading, Market Place: security registers (3) 1873–1902; signature books (3) 1875–99.

STEVENSON, SALT & CO
Stafford, Staffordshire

History: John Stevenson, a mercer, formed this bank in about 1737. From about 1777 it was styled Stevenson & Co and later was known as Byrd, Hall & Stevenson, as Stevenson & Webb and as Stevenson, Salt & Co. In 1787 a connected bank was formed in London by William Stevenson which became known as Stevenson, Salt & Sons; in 1867 it amalgamated with Bosanquet & Co. In 1866 the bank, along with its branches at Lichfield (1857), Rugeley (1866) and Eccleshall, was absorbed by Lloyds Banking Co Ltd (est. 1765). One of its senior partners, Thomas Salt, then joined Lloyds and, as Sir Thomas Salt, was chairman from 1886.

Records 1: Lloyds TSB Group plc, Archives, Head Office, 71 Lombard Street, London EC3P 3BS

General ledgers (3) 1777–88.

Records 2: William Salt Library, Eastgate Street, Stafford ST16 2LZ

Partnership agreements 1777–1856; Stevenson and Salt family wills 1777 on; Salt family correspondence re legal and financial matters 1815–57. [Ref: D1716 bdls 1, 3, 5; M597]

STEVENSON, SALT & SONS
London

History: The origins of this private bank are in the London firm of Thomas & John Stevenson, mercers, which was established in 1766 with a capital of £10,000. The Stevenson family were also bankers at Stafford where, in about 1737, they established the private bank which was to become known as Stevenson, Salt & Co. In about 1787 the Stevensons established a bank in Queen Street, City of London, known as William Stevenson. In about 1799 it moved to Lombard Street and from about 1801 it was known as Stevenson & Salt and from about 1838 as Stevenson, Salt & Sons. In 1867 it merged with Bosanquet, Whatman, Harman & Bosanquet (est. 1780) to form Bosanquet, Salt, Whatman, Harman, Salt & Bosanquet.

Records: William Salt Library, Eastgate Street, Stafford ST16 2LZ

Partnership agreements 1766–75. [Ref: 1716 bdl 4]

STILWELL & SONS
London

History: This naval agency was established by James Sykes and John Gathorne at Crutched Friars, City of London, by 1774. After Gathorne died in 1774, Sykes traded alone, moving to Arundel Street, Strand, in 1792 when the Navy Office removed to Somerset House. Subsequently the bank traded as Sykes & Son. In 1813 Thomas Stilwell was taken into partnership and was later joined by his sons and grandsons when the firm became known as Stilwell & Sons. It moved to Great George Street, Westminster, in the 1880s and later to 42 Pall Mall. It amalgamated with Westminster Bank Ltd (est. 1909) in 1923 when its balance sheet totalled £164,620.

T E Gregory, *The Westminster Bank Through A Century* (London, 1936)

Records: The Royal Bank of Scotland plc, Archive Section, Regent's House, 42 Islington High Street, London N1 8XL

Deeds re partners and partners' families 1815–1920; papers re estate of T Stilwell 1846; balance sheet 1922.

London, Haymarket: customer information books (12) 1866–1923.

STOCKTON & DURHAM COUNTY BANK
Stockton, Cleveland

History: This joint stock bank was formed in 1838 with a nominal capital of £150,000. It was a medium-sized bank with a branch at Guisborough; its note issue by 1846 was only £8,290. In this year £90,000 capital was lost through mismanagement and soon afterwards the business was acquired by the National Provincial Bank of England (est. 1833).

Maberly Phillips, *Banks, Banking and Bankers in Northumberland, Durham and North Yorkshire* (London, 1894)

Records: The Royal Bank of Scotland plc, Archive Section, Regent's House, 42 Islington High Street, London N1 8XL

Prospectus 1838; directors' meeting minutes 1838–53; annual general meeting minutes 1838–53; deed of settlement 1839.

STOREY & THOMAS'S BANKING CO
Shaftesbury, Dorset

498   *British banking – a guide to historical records*

History: This private bank was formed in 1816 by William Storey and Edwin Thomas. In 1840 its business was converted into a joint stock bank, Storey & Thomas's Banking Co. It was acquired in 1855 by the Wilts & Dorset Banking Co (est. 1835).

Records: Lloyds TSB Group plc, Archives, Head Office, 71 Lombard Street, London EC3P 3BS

Agreement for purchase of goodwill 1855.

STOURBRIDGE & KIDDERMINSTER BANKING CO
Stourbridge, West Midlands

History: This joint stock bank was formed in 1834 with a paid-up capital of £34,000. Its promoters were local industrialists dissatisfied with the services of private banks and included an iron master, a brick manufacturer, a nail manufacturer, a spade maker and a barrister. The bank's manager was recruited from the Birmingham branch of the Bank of England. The business developed a reputation for conservative management and high profitability. In its first year, branches or agencies were established at Kidderminster, Bromsgrove, Redditch, Shipston on Stour and Chipping Norton. Also in 1834, Tomes, Chattaway & Ford (est. 1810), private bankers at Stratford upon Avon, with an agency at Henley-in-Arden, was acquired. By the late 1840s paid-up capital rose to £100,000, largely the result of capitalisation of profits and reserves, deposits stood at £60,000 and advances amounted to £170,000. Branch expansion occurred in the mid-1860s with branches opening at Worcester and Brierley Hill in 1864; two others opened in 1866. In the mid-1860s annual dividends reached 20 per cent. By 1870 paid-up capital was still £100,000 while deposits rose to £741,000. By 1878 the latter was £1.25 million while paid-up capital was unaltered. In 1880, when the business was acquired by the Birmingham Banking Co Ltd (est. 1829), it had seven branches and three agencies.

W F Crick & J E Wadsworth, *A Hundred Years of Joint Stock Banking* (London, 1936)

Records: HSBC Holdings plc, Group Archives, 10 Lower Thames Street, London EC3R 6AE

Resolutions of inaugural meeting 1834; deed of settlement 1834; directors' meeting minute books (5) 1834–80; general ledgers (9) 1834–77; shareholders' minute books (2) 1835–80; staff surety bonds and apprenticeship indentures 1835–69; weekly balance sheets 1838–62; manager's notebook c.1840–60; monthly balance sheets (7) 1862–71; half-yearly statements 1865–79; manager's interview diary 1867–80; amalgamation agreement 1880.

Records of banks **499**

Chipping Norton: signature book 1838–80; balance statements 1857–65; **Kidderminster:** weekly balance book 1842–45; **Moreton in the Marsh:** balance statements 1857–65; **Shipston on Stour:** balance statements 1857–65; **Stratford on Avon:** letterbook 1843–71; balance statements 1859–60; manager's diary 1860–80.

T & R STRANGE & CO
Swindon, Wiltshire

History: This private bank was formed in 1807 as Strange, Garrett, Strange & Cook and was otherwise known as the Swindon Bank. James Strange, a draper and mercer as well as banker, died in 1826 when his elder brother Thomas, a coal factor and salt merchant, acquired his banking business. Shortly afterwards the bank was renamed T & R Strange & Co, presumably on the withdrawal of Garrett and Cook. A second branch was opened at Highworth when the bank was restyled the Swindon & Highworth Bank. The bank was acquired by the County of Gloucester Banking Co (est. 1836) in 1842.

Records: Lloyds TSB Group plc, Archives, Head Office, 71 Lombard Street, London EC3P 3BS

Amalgamation agreement 1842.

S & G STUCKEY & CO
Langport, Somerset

History: This private bank traced its origins to the merchant firm of Stuckey & Co, established in 1772 by Samuel Stuckey who carried on banking alongside merchanting. In 1800 he was joined in the business by his brother George and subsequently by his nephew Vincent who had formerly been private secretary to Prime Minister William Pitt. From 1806 the banking business was hived off as a separate business called S & G Stuckey & Co; it was otherwise known as the Langport Bank. Branches were opened at Taunton and Wells as well as an agency at Ilminster while interests were also taken in Stuckeys & Woodlands (est. before 1804) of Bridgewater and in Stuckey, Lean, Hart & Maningford (est. 1806) of Bristol. From 1812 Vincent was senior partner. In 1826 Stuckey & Co joined with the other Stuckey family banks and with Ricketts, Thorne & Courtney (est. 1810) of Bristol to form a joint stock bank, Stuckey's Banking Co.

Charles H Cave, *History of Banking in Bristol from 1750 to 1899* (Bristol, 1899); T E Gregory, *The Westminster Bank Through a Century* (London, 1936); Philip T Saunders, *Stuckey's Bank* (Taunton, 1928)

500   *British banking – a guide to historical records*

Records: The Royal Bank of Scotland plc, Archive Section, Regent's House, 42 Islington High Street, London N1 8XL

Correspondence book 1778–1809.

STUCKEY'S BANKING CO LTD
Langport, later Taunton, Somerset

History: This joint stock bank, the second to be formed in the country, was created in 1826 by the amalgamation of three Stuckey family banks – Stuckey, Lean, Hart & Maningford (est. 1806) of Bristol, S & G Stuckey & Co (est. 1772) of Langport and Stuckeys & Woodlands (est. before 1804) of Bridgwater – along with the private Bristol bank of Ricketts, Thorne & Courtney (est. 1810). The banks continued to trade under their separate names until 1828 when all were styled as Stuckey's Banking Co. The early policy of the bank was to expand throughout Somerset and Bristol by acquisition of private banks and by branch and agency openings. It became a major West Country bank under the leadership of Vincent Stuckey. The private banks absorbed were Payne & Co (est. 1810) of Crewkerne in 1829; Sparks & Co (est. 1804) of Crewkerne also in 1829; Waldron, Walters & Co (est. c.1793) of Frome and Trowbridge in 1833; Henry Whitmarsh & Wm. Lambert White (est. 1806) of Yeovil and Wincanton in 1835; Reeves & Porch (est. c.1812) of Glastonbury and Shepton Mallet in 1835; Tufnell, Falkner & Co (est. c.1775) of Bath in 1841; U G & H Messiter (est. c.1801) of Wincanton in 1844; J & H B Batten (est. c.1782) of Yeovil in 1849; M & R Badcock (est. 1777) of Taunton in 1873; Kinglake & Co (est. c.1790) of Taunton in 1838; and Dunsford & Co (est. 1788) of Tiverton in 1883. The latter acquisition marked the beginning of expansion outside Somerset. In about 1831 a London firm, Stuckey, Reynolds & Co, was opened. Walter Bagehot, later to be a distinguished political economist, was secretary of the bank from the 1850s. In 1874 the first published balance sheet showed a paid-up capital of £278,000 and a balance sheet total of £4.29 million. In 1892 limited liability was acquired and in 1908 the head office was moved to Taunton. In 1909 the bank amalgamated with Parr's Bank Ltd (est. 1865). It then had forty-seven branches and twenty-four sub-branches, a paid-up capital of £408,000 and a balance sheet total of £7.52 million.

Charles H Cave, *History of Banking in Bristol from 1750 to 1899* (Bristol, 1899); T E Gregory, *The Westminster Bank Through a Century* (London, 1936); Philip T Saunders, *Stuckey's Bank* (Taunton, 1928)

Records 1: The Royal Bank of Scotland plc, Archive Section, Regent's House, 42 Islington High Street, London N1 8XL

Records of banks 501

Directors' meeting minute books (5) 1827–1909; deed of settlement 1831; accounts of transactions between Bristol and Somerton branch 1838–41; balance sheets 1848–1909; proprietors' minute books (2) 1858–1909; committee minute books (6) 1861–1900; manager's notebook 1876–84; amalgamation agreement 1909.

Clifton, Queen's Road: branch minutes 1874–96; **Yeovil:** security register 1878–85; managers' information books (5) 1879–1925.

Records 2: Somerset Archive and Record Service, Somerset Record Office, Obridge Road, Taunton TA2 7PU

Papers re building of bank 1823; accounts of assets and liabilities c.1830–40. [Ref: DD/FS Bx3; DD/DP Bxs 91–92]

Records 3: Dorset Record Office, Bridport Road, Dorchester DT1 1RP

Yeovil: passbooks of G T Gollop 1848–83. [Ref: D/ASH(A): F18]

SURTEES'S, BURDON & BRANDLING
Newcastle upon Tyne, Tyne & Wear, and Berwick-on-Tweed, Northumberland

History: This private bank was formed as Aubone Surtees & Rowland Burdon in 1768 in Newcastle upon Tyne; it also traded as The Exchange Bank. Both the founding partners were prosperous local merchants. By 1787 the business was known as Surtees, Burdon & Brandling and in 1793 briefly suspended payment. In 1788 an associated bank was set up at Berwick-on-Tweed, known initially as Surtees, Burdon, Wetherby & Co and as Surtees's, Burdon, Brandling & Embleton by the time it failed in 1803. In 1799 Aubone Surtees died when the business was reconstituted as Surtees, Burdon, Surtees's & Brandling. It was known as Surtees's, Burdon & Brandling in 1801. It failed in 1803 and in 1806 its partners were declared bankrupt.

Maberly Phillips, *A History of Banks, Bankers and Banking in Northumberland, Durham and North Yorkshire* (London, 1894)

Records 1: Northumberland Record Office, Melton Park, North Gosforth, Newcastle upon Tyne NE3 5QX

Out-letters 1773–1806. [Ref: 2DE/35/15]

Records 2: Durham County Record Office, County Hall, Durham DH1 5UL

Papers re failure 1806–12. [Ref: D/CG 5/1312, 5/9–12]

502   *British banking – a guide to historical records*

SWALEDALE & WENSLEYDALE BANKING CO LTD
Richmond, North Yorkshire

History: This joint stock bank was formed in 1836 out of the business of the old established bank of Hutton, Other & Co (est. 1805). It began business in 1837 and by 1850 its paid-up capital was £53,000 rising to £63,000 by 1894. Branches were opened at Bedale, Hawes, Leyburn and Marsham. In 1881 limited liability was acquired and in 1899 the bank was acquired by Barclay & Co Ltd (est. 1896).

Maberly Phillips, *Banks, Bankers and Banking in Northumberland, Durham and North Yorkshire* (London, 1894); P W Matthews & Anthony W Tuke, *History of Barclays Bank Ltd* (London, 1926)

Records 1: Barclays Bank plc, Group Archives, Dallimore Road, Wythenshawe, Manchester M23 9JA

Partnership agreements 1802–07, 1835; banker's licences 1810–36, 1857; cheques 1834–73; deeds of settlement 1837; report and accounts 1837–49, 1857–72, 1894; ledger, deposits acquired from Hutton & Co 1837–53; shareholders' registers 1838, 1852; resolutions 1843–51; letters from staff 1845–71; draft 1848; letters 1849–71; lease 1866; bills of exchange 1860s; transfer register 1881–86; shareholder register 1882; cheque form c.1880s; bank note 1898.

Records 2: Durham County Record Office, County Hall, Durham DH1 5UL

Deed of settlement 1837. [Ref: NCB1/D/78]

SWANN, CLOUGH & CO
York, North Yorkshire

History: This private bank was established in 1771 as Willoughby, Raper & Co; it was otherwise known as the York Bank. It was styled Garforth, Raper & Co from 1785, Raper, Swann & Co from 1800, Raper, Swann, Clough, Swan, Bland & Raper from 1820 and Swann, Clough & Co from 1824. It encountered difficulties and was acquired by Beckett & Co (East Riding Bank) (est. 1875) in 1879 when it had branches at Beverley, Malton, Driffield, Pocklington, Pickering and Helmsley.

Records: The Royal Bank of Scotland plc, Archive Section, Regent's House, 42 Islington High Street, London N1 8XL

Opening notice 1771; liquidation report 1879.

JAMES TAYLOR & SONS
Bakewell, Derbyshire

Records of banks **503**

History: This private bank was established in 1846 as an adjunct to the drapery business of James Taylor and his brother-in-law, Robert Johnson. By 1846 the bank was operating separately as James Taylor Esq. It amalgamated with Crompton & Evans' Union Bank Ltd (est. 1877) of Derby in 1879.

Records: The Royal Bank of Scotland plc, Archive Section, Regent's House, 42 Islington High Street, London N1 8XL

Cash account ledger 1797–1809; bill book 1808–13.

THISTLE BANK CO
Glasgow, Strathclyde

History: This private bank was established in 1761 as Maxwell, Ritchie & Co; it was otherwise known as the Thistle Bank. It was the fourth provincial partnership bank to be formed in Scotland, and the third to be based in Glasgow. Virtually all its partners were described as Glasgow tobacco merchants and as landowners, the latter resulting in the firm being known as the 'aristocratic bank'. The original capital was £7,000 and by 1763, when the first balance was struck, note circulation reached £64,000. By 1776 the capital had grown to £11,908. The bank received deposits from at least 1769 and by 1786 these totalled £143,000, rising to £250,000 by 1792. From 1792 the bank's fortunes declined. On amalgamation with the Glasgow Union Banking Co (est. 1830) in 1836, the bank had deposits of £450,000. However, the surplus of assets over liabilities, excluding the amount paid for goodwill, was only £5,000.

Robert S Rait, *The History of the Union Bank of Scotland* (Glasgow, 1930)

Records 1: Bank of Scotland Archive, Operational Services Division, 12 Bankhead Terrace, Sighthill, Edinburgh EH11 4DY

Ledgers 1769–1836; papers re debts due to the company and cash accounts 1786–92; notes of hand 1802–20; transfer ledger 1827–29; private ledger 1827–29; teller's cash book 1835–36.

Records 2: Business Records Centre, Archive Department, University of Glasgow, Glasgow G12 8QQ

Postage accounts 1795–1834; receipts and accounts for expenditure on premises, administration, etc 1795–1836; banker's licences 1813–34. [Ref: UGD 94]

Records 3: Glasgow City Archives, Mitchell Library, North Street, Glasgow G3 7DN

Appointment of cashier 1761. [Ref: B10/15/6748]

504   *British banking – a guide to historical records*

Records 4: National Archives of Scotland, HM General Register House, Princes Street, Edinburgh EH1 3YY

Deposition and assignation 1815. [Ref: GD81/96]

TOMES, CHATTAWAY & FORD
Stratford on Avon, Warwickshire

History: This private bank was formed in 1810 as Oldaker, Tomes & Chattaway and was later known as Tomes, Hobbins & Chattaway and from 1833 as Tomes, Chattaway & Ford. Its first partners included the owner of Stratford Mills, a mercer, a draper, and a partner in the Warwick bankers, Tomes, Russell, Tomes & Russell (est. 1791). By 1813 capital was £9,000. Soon after formation, agencies were opened at Moreton in Marsh and Shipston on Stour. In 1834 the bank, with its agency at Henley-in-Arden, was acquired by the Stourbridge & Kidderminster Banking Co (est. 1834).

Records: HSBC Holdings plc, Group Archives, 10 Lower Thames Street, London EC3R 6AE

Partnership agreements 1813, 1833.

TOMKINS & CO
Abingdon, Oxfordshire

History: This private bank was formed in about 1782 and was otherwise known as the Abingdon Bank. It ceased to trade in 1812.

Records: Berkshire Record Office, Shire Hall, Shinfield Park, Reading RG2 9XD

Papers re J Tomkins 1808–38. [Ref: D/EP 4 B1]

TOMPSON, BARCLAY & IVES
Norwich, Norfolk

History: This private bank was formed in 1792 as Kett, Hatfield & Back and was known as Kett & Back from 1810 and as Tompson, Barclay & Ives from 1820 to 1832 when it was acquired by Gurneys, Birkbeck & Martin of Norwich. It was also known as the Norfolk General Bank.

Harold Preston, *Early East Anglian Banks and Bankers* (Thetford, 1994)

Records: Barclays Bank plc, Group Archives, Dallimore Road, Wythenshawe, Manchester M23 9JA

Cheques 1819–24.

Records of banks 505

TOWN & COUNTY BANK LTD
Aberdeen, Grampian

History: This joint stock bank, the third to be formed in Scotland, was established in 1825 as the Aberdeen Town & County Bank. By 1826 it had a paid-up capital of £112,500 and four branches; by 1837 thirteen branches existed. It acquired a reputation for conservative management and its operations were restricted to the north of Scotland. In 1882 it assumed limited liability when its title changed to Town & County Bank Ltd. However, by the early twentieth century it was falling behind its rivals in terms of size and services offered. In 1908 it merged with its local competitor, the North of Scotland Bank Ltd (est. 1836) to form the North of Scotland & Town & County Bank Ltd, the title being shortened to North of Scotland Bank Ltd in 1923.

Records 1: Clydesdale Bank plc, Head Office, 30 St Vincent Place, Glasgow, G1 2HL

Directors' meeting minute books (13) 1824–1908; sub-committee minute books (2) 1825–85; lists of partners 1828–72; instructions to agents and accountants 1842–73; general meeting minute books (3) 1843–1908; salary books (3) 1878–1908.

Records 2: Business Records Centre, Archive Department, University of Glasgow, Glasgow G12 8QQ

Sederunt book extracts: directors' court 1825–1908, sub-committee 1825–85; balance sheets 1860–1908; annual reports 1876–1908. [Ref: Scottish Banking Collection]

TRAPP, HALFHEAD & CO
Bedford, Bedfordshire

History: This private bank was formed in 1829 as Pierson & Trapp; it was otherwise known as the Bedford & Bedfordshire Bank. It was restyled Trapp, Halfhead & Co in 1849 and was acquired by London & County Banking Co (est. 1836).

Records: Bedfordshire and Luton Archives and Record Service, The Record Office, Cauldwell Street, Bedford MK42 9AP

Partnership agreements 1829–50; Trapp family papers 1832–94. [Ref: X71/270–288]

TROUGHTON, NEWCOMBE & TROUGHTON
Coventry, West Midlands

506   *British banking – a guide to historical records*

History: This private bank was established in about 1782 and failed in 1821.

Records: Warwickshire Record Office, Priory Park, Cape Road, Warwick CV34 4JS

Deeds re bankruptcy of partners 1821. [Ref: CR2582/4/18]

TUBB & CO
Bicester, Oxfordshire

History: This private bank was established in 1793 as Kirby & Co; it was otherwise known as the Bicester & Oxfordshire Bank. From 1815 it was styled Henry M Tubb & George Tubb; from 1863 as George Tubb & William Coleman; from 1873 as George Tubb & Henry Tubb; and from 1885 as Henry Tubb & Co. An association existed with the Oxford private bank of Richard Wooten, Thomas Tubb & Co (est. 1805). The bank was acquired by Barclays Bank Ltd (est. 1896) in 1920.

P W Matthews & Anthony W Tuke, *History of Barclays Bank Ltd* (London, 1926)

Records: Barclays Bank plc, Group Archives, Dallimore Road, Wythenshawe, Manchester M23 9JA

Private account ledgers (5) 1839–1920; current account ledgers, Bicester Savings Bank (2) 1842–71; half-yearly balance extracts 1847–55, 1878–88; partnership agreement 1880; signature book 1887–1919; cheque book and cheque forms 1888–1920s; bank notes 1907–17; banker's licence 1919; agreement re sale to Barclays Bank Ltd 1920.

TUFNELL, FALKNER & CO
Bath, Avon

History: This private bank was established in Bath by 1775 as Atwood, Abrahams, Collett, Salmon & Harris. It was styled Tufnell, Stroud, Collett, Payne & Hope from 1810, Tufnell, Falkner & Falkner from 1812 and subsequently Tufnell, Falkner & Co. It was acquired by Stuckey's Banking Co (est. 1826) in 1841.

A G E Jones, 'The Banks of Bath', *Notes and Queries*, 203 (1958)

Records 1: The Royal Bank of Scotland plc, Archive Section, Regent's House, 42 Islington High Street, London N1 8XL

Papers re bad debts 1822–36; private ledger 1825–34; cash books (2) 1826–44; balance sheets 1826–43; statistics re note circulation and drafts

Records of banks 507

1834–41; papers re note circulation 1841; lists of drafts, notes and debts outstanding 1842; amalgamation papers 1838–41.

Records 2: Somerset Archive and Record Service, Somerset Record Office, Obridge Road, Taunton TA2 7PU

Partnership agreements 1812–25. [Ref: DD/WM 435, 438–441]

TUGWELL, BRYMER, CLUTTERBUCK & CO
Bath, Avon

History: This private bank was established in about the 1760s as an adjunct to the linen drapery business of Robert and William Clement in Wades Passage, Bath. On William Clement's death in the 1780s, the firm became known as John Clement & Son. It was subsequently known as Clement, Tugwell & MacKenzie; as Tugwell, Brymer & Co from 1827; and later as Tugwell, Brymer, Clutterbuck & Co from 1882. It was otherwise known as the Bath Bank and as the Old Bath Bank. In 1891 the bank merged with the private banks of Dimsdale, Fowler, Barnard & Dimsdales (est. 1760) of London; Prescott, Cave, Buxton, Loder & Co (est. 1766) of London; and Miles, Cave, Baillie & Co (est. 1750) of Bristol to form Prescott, Dimsdale, Cave, Tugwell & Co Ltd.

Anon, *'Prescott's Bank'*, National Provincial Bank Review (1966–68); A G E Jones, 'The Banks of Bath', *Notes and Queries*, 203 (1958)

Records: The Royal Bank of Scotland plc, Archive Section, Regent's House, 42 Islington High Street, London N1 8XL

Partnership agreements 1793–1882; property title deeds 1818–79, papers 1880s–1949; cheque form c.1820s; ledger including deposit notes, customer balances and dividends 1847–53; security and safe custody register 1885–1906; customer overdrafts book 1884–89.

TUKE & GIBSON
Saffron Walden, Essex

History: This private bank was formed in 1824 as Gibson, Gibson, Catlin, Gibson & Catlin by the Gibson family of brewers. In 1826 it acquired the business of the failed local bank of Searle & Co (est. 1797). From 1852 the Midgley family were brought into the partnership when the title became Gibson, Gibson, Gibson & Midgley. From 1863 W M Tuke, a tea merchant of London and York, was admitted when the bank was renamed Gibson, Tuke & Gibson. In 1883 it was known as Tuke & Gibson. From 1826 an office existed at Bishop's Stortford and offices also existed at Sawbridgeworth, Stansted and Thaxted. The bank was otherwise known

508   *British banking – a guide to historical records*

as the Saffron Walden & Bishop's Stortford Bank and as the Saffron Walden & North Essex Bank. From 1880 a connection existed with Fordham, Gibson & Co of Royston. In 1896 the business merged with other leading banks to form Barclay & Co Ltd.

P W Matthews & Anthony W Tuke, *History of Barclays Bank Ltd* (London, 1926); Harold Preston, *Early East Anglian Banks and Bankers* (Thetford, 1994)

Records: Barclays Bank plc, Group Archives, Dallimore Road, Wythenshawe, Manchester M23 9JA

Bank note register 1831–71; private ledgers 1867–93; amalgamation papers, Barclay & Co Ltd 1896.

T TURNER
Gloucester, Gloucestershire

History: This private bank was formed as Turner & Morris in about 1793 and failed in 1825. It subsequently resumed as T Turner and in 1834 was acquired by the National Provincial Bank of England (est. 1833). It separated from this bank in 1837 and ceased business in 1855. It was otherwise known as the Gloucester Bank.

Records: Gloucester Library, Local Studies Dept, Brunswick Road, Gloucester GL1 1HT

Resolution of creditors 1827. [Ref: NR 15.2]

TWINING & CO
London

History: The Twining family established their tea purveying business in 1706 and gradually moved into banking. This diversification was formalised in 1824 when a separate bank was established in Strand although initially it concentrated on providing services to the Twining family and their friends. The Twining family also had banking interests at Colchester where as early as 1787 they provided partners in Twining & Mills (est. 1774), later known as Mills, Bawtree, Dawnay, Curzon & Co. Many customers were senior clerics. Initially the bank was located adjacent to Twinings' tea warehouse in Devereux Court, but in 1837 larger premises were acquired at 137 Strand. Lloyds Bank Ltd (est. 1765) acquired the business in 1892.

Stephen H Twining, *The House of Twining 1706–1956* (priv. pub., 1956)

Records: Lloyds TSB Group plc, Archives, Head Office, 71 Lombard Street, London EC3P 3BS

Records of banks **509**

Safe custody registers (5) 1832–92; customer ledger 1834–38; loan ledgers (2) 1851–92 [w]; cash book 1884–87; amalgamation papers 1892.

UNION BANK OF BIRMINGHAM LTD
Birmingham, West Midlands

History: This joint stock bank was formed in 1878 with a paid-up capital of £100,000. By 1880 deposits equalled £300,000 and grew to £400,000 by 1883. In that year a £15,000 fraud by the general manager was uncovered and, fearing a loss of confidence, the business amalgamated with the Birmingham & Midland Bank Ltd (est. 1836), the consideration being the equivalent of £86,000. No branches had been opened and paid-up capital then stood at £108,000.

Records: HSBC Holdings plc, Group Archives, 10 Lower Thames Street, London EC3R 6AE

Share ledger, A–H, 1878–79; staff salary list 1878–83; letterbook 1878–83; share certificate 1879; directors' meeting minute book 1880–81; report and balance sheet 1882; amalgamation papers 1883; share transfer register 1883–84; staff declarations of secrecy 1883.

UNION BANK OF MANCHESTER LTD
Manchester, Greater Manchester

History: This important joint stock bank was founded in 1836 as the Union Bank of Manchester with a nominal capital of £600,000. It opened for business in King Street, moving to Brown Street in 1836 and to York Street in 1846. The bank flourished, opening its first branch, at Knutsford, in 1856 followed by others at Northwich (1862) and Salford (1862). It acquired limited liability in 1862 and in 1863 its paid-up capital was £300,000. By 1873 it had fifteen branches. It acquired the business of J J Fenton & Sons (est. 1819) of Rochdale when it failed in 1878; J Sewell & Nephew (est. 1841) of Manchester in 1888; E W Yates & Co of Liverpool in 1904; Blackburn Bank Ltd in 1906; Downes & Co (est. c.1860s) of Nantwich in 1907; Halifax & District Permanent Banking Co Ltd (est. 1909) in 1917; and East Morley & Bradford District Deposit Bank Ltd (est. 1870) in 1918. In 1898 paid-up capital was increased from £440,000 to £550,000 and was increased again to £625,000 in 1918. It amalgamated with Barclays Bank Ltd (est. 1896) in 1919. In 1925 its paid-up capital was £750,000, its balance sheet totalled over £20.6 million and it had 160 branches. It continued to operate as a separate entity until 1940.

Leo H Grindon, *Manchester Banks and Bankers* (Manchester, 1877); P W Matthews & Anthony W Tuke, *History of Barclays Bank Ltd* (London, 1926)

510   *British banking – a guide to historical records*

Records: Barclays Bank plc, Group Archives, Dallimore Road, Wythenshawe, Manchester M23 9JA

Deed of settlement 1836; registers of shareholders (6) 1836–55, 1918–20; declarations of secrecy 1836–1932; minutes 1836–1939; prospectuses 1836–37; job applications 1836–46; bad debts lists 1837–42; general meeting minutes 1837–1939; letters re premises valuation 1838–48; dividend register 1838–60; special resolutions 1845–1936; bad debts register 1847–48; cheque forms 1858–87; certificate of incorporation 1862; lists of shareholders 1862–95; balance sheets 1863–89, 1913–39; letters re accounts, bills, loans etc 1863–67; registers of customer legal documents (2) 1884–1911; circulars 1897–1904, 1921–39; directors' reports 1898–1938 [w]; photographs: directors 1890s–1940s, staff 1911–16; registers of failures (19) 1900–40; seal books (7) 1902–40; pensions ledger 1903–40; profit and loss abstract 1904; authorised signatories 1905; consultative committee minutes 1905–14; probate books (3) 1906–29; press cuttings 1912–23; list of branches 1913–20; provision accounts 1916–42; staff food allowance scheme 1917; register of directors 1918–38; rules 1918; memorandum and articles of association 1918–26; annual returns 1918–36; share certificate receipt book 1919–36; dividend lists 1920–39; share certificate 1920; inspection department papers 1921–39; branch statistics 1923–36; list of investments 1924–28; salary circulars 1925–27; papers re bank liquidation 1926–43; certificate of registration 1926; advances registers (3) 1929–37; staff statistics 1930–35; board meetings agenda 1931–39; committee meetings agenda 1932–39; advances statistics 1933–37; centenary bonus file 1936; annual returns 1937–39; papers re merger with Barclays Bank Ltd 1937–40; widows' fund rules 1939–40; accounting papers 1939; seal book 1940–80; historical notes 1943.

UNION BANK OF SCOTLAND LTD
Glasgow, Strathclyde

History: This joint stock bank was founded as Glasgow Union Banking Co in 1830 with a nominal capital of £2 million provided largely by merchants and manufacturers in the West of Scotland. The business of the bank grew rapidly between 1833 and 1844 primarily due to amalgamations with the Thistle Bank (est. 1761) of Glasgow in 1836; Sir William Forbes, James Hunter & Co (est. 1723) of Edinburgh in 1843; the Paisley Union Bank Co (est. 1788) in 1833; Hunters & Co (est. 1773) of Ayr in 1843; and the Glasgow & Ship Bank (est. 1837) in 1838. Its title changed to Union Bank of Scotland in 1843 and the balance sheet total increased from £1.2 million in 1836 to over £6 million in 1844. The bank issued bank notes and possessed an authorised issue under the 1845 Bank Act. There were further amalgamations, with the Banking Company in Aber-

Records of banks 511

deen (est. 1767) in 1849 and with the Perth Banking Co (est. 1763) in 1857. From the 1840s the bank developed a policy of lending to the heavy engineering and shipbuilding sectors, deriving its deposits from a rapidly expanding branch network; it had ninety-seven branches by 1857, the largest number of any bank in Scotland. The bank's fortunes were closely tied to the prosperity of Glasgow industry and increasingly it relied upon the investment skills of its London office to smooth out the fluctuations in its performance. In 1882 limited liability was acquired. Between the two wars Norman Hird, the general manager, was the dominant figure in Scottish banking and in 1927 the bank opened a new head office, at 121 St Vincent Street, Glasgow. However, after 1919 the bank was in relative decline compared to its competitors. It was also too small to service the financial requirements of corporate customers after 1945. In 1950 negotiations were opened with Bank of Scotland (est. 1695) with a view to merger and this was achieved in 1955.

Robert S Rait, *The History of the Union Bank of Scotland* (Glasgow, 1930); Norio Tamaki, *The Life Cycle of the Union Bank of Scotland 1830–1954* (Aberdeen, 1983)

Records 1: Bank of Scotland Archive, Operational Services Division, 12 Bankhead Terrace, Sighthill, Edinburgh EH11 4DY

List of partners 1830–41; stock ledgers 1830–90; deposit account ledgers 1830–32; papers re call on shares 1830–39; transfer of stock registers 1830–50; cash balance book 1830–38; private journals 1830–1946; Edinburgh local directors' meeting minutes 1830–1942; private ledgers 1830–1910; bills discounted 1831–1909; partnership ledger 1836–43; cash book 1836–38; abstract quarterly balances 1838–64; private letterbooks 1838–59; minute books 1843–1955; interest receipts 1844–46; claim books 1847–1951; letters from head office to Edinburgh branch 1849–68; secretary's private letterbooks 1852–1914; letterbook 1853–54; heritable properties books: general, head office and Scottish bank circulars, private letterbooks 1853–1957; printed rates of discount and interest 1854–1919; Gilbart prize essay 1854; calculations of interest 1855–83; letters re crisis 1857; abstract annual balances 1857–65; protested bills ledger 1861–1909; general quarterly balances 1862–1954; printed half-yearly statements 1862–1916; abstract of profit and loss accounts Edinburgh and London branches 1863–1900; seal records 1863–1901; abstract profit and loss accounts 1863–1950; register of directors and managers 1863–1915; record of failures and liquidations 1865–81; profit and loss accounts 1865–1910; record of mandates 1873–1923; record of estimated loss on bad debts 1877–1955; London branch profit and loss accounts 1878–79; investment journal 1879–90; accountant's minute book 1879–96; large loans minute book

512 *British banking – a guide to historical records*

1879–1947; deposit money, interest on loans and profit and loss 1884–86; reports on Scottish banks 1884–93; registers of large notes, notes destroyed and notes in circulation 1887–1953; sinking fund book 1889–1926; cashier's notebooks (2) 1890–1921, 1949–50; directors' meeting business letterbooks 1892–1914; journal of securities for advances 1898–1960; agency ledger balances 1899–1928; record of interviews 1912–25; agency ledgers 1914–55; abstract weekly balance books 1914–55; acceptance ledger 1915–29; abstract of general ledgers 1923–55; registers of large depositors 1925–48; board of directors supplementary minute books 1926–53; note circulation returns 1930–55; ledger, general account 1930–50; bank returns 1931–50; registers of advances over £3,000 1935–60; head office deposit book 1936–39; branch balances 1936–40; reserve cash book 1952–62; general ledger 1954.

Aberdeen, George Street: 1878–1943; **Alloa:** 1832–1956; **Alva:** 1895–1955; **Ardrossan:** 1864–1940; **Ayr, High Street:** 1876–1946; **Ayr, Newton:** 1930–42; **Ballater:** c.1883–1912; **Banff & MacDuff:** 1849–1951; **Barrhill:** 1918–52; **Bathgate:** 1848–84; **Bearsden:** 1929–55; **Beith:** 1847–1955; **Blairgowrie (Wellmeadows):** 1865–1934; **Bo'ness:** 1898–c.1955; **Bothwell:** 1927–51; **Braemar:** 1873–1955; **Brechin:** 1892–1955; **Bridge of Weir:** 1945–55; **Broxburn:** 1866–72; **Campbeltown:** 1899–1955; **Carsphairn:** 1928–29; **Castle Douglas:** 1922–50; **Clarkston:** 1921–53; **Clydebank:** 1897–1943; **Coatbridge:** 1851–1947; **Coupar Angus:** 1920–54; **Crieff:** 1907–21; **Cullen & Portknockie:** 1849–1955; **Doune:** 1840–1956; **Dumbarton:** 1929–56; **Dunblane:** 1843–51; **Dunkeld:** 1899–1946; **Dunning:** 1856–1955; **Dunoon:** 1911–50; **Edinburgh (8 branches):** 1854–1955; **Edzell:** 1945–55; **Errol:** 1882–97; **Fairlie:** 1880–1954; **Fochabers:** 1849–1955; **Gatehouse:** 1858–1949; **Girvan:** 1875–1954; **Glasgow (42 branches):** 1844–1955; **Gourock:** 1926–54; **Grangemouth:** 1943–50; **Greenock:** 1907–53; **Hamilton:** 1880–1945; **Helensburgh:** 1920–53; **Hillington:** 1942–47; **Huntly:** c.1887–1951; **Innerleithen:** 1856–82; **Inverary** 1927–54; **Inverurie:** 1874–1955; **Irvine:** 1855–1945; **Johnstone:** 1925–54; **Kilcreggan:** 1937–52; **Kilmarnock:** 1843–1946; **Kirkcaldy:** 1831–50; **Kirkwall:** 1944–47; **Kincardine:** 1832–1907; **Largs:** 1878–1950; **Larkhall:** 1920–50; **Lerwick:** 1838–1955; **Leslie:** 1865–1957; **Linlithgow:** 1923–41; **Lochgelly:** 1856–1955; **Lochgilphead:** 1924–27; **Maybole:** 1923–51; **Millport:** 1907–52; **Moffat:** 1860–1955; **Montrose:** 1856–61; **Motherwell:** 1924–56; **Newport:** 1926–42; **New Pitsligo:** 1852–58; **Newton Mearns:** 1927–52; **Oban:** 1913–48; **Paisley Road Toll:** 1928–42; **Peebles:** 1855–62; **Perth:** 1834–1953; **Pitlochry:** 1853–59; **Port Glasgow:** 1853–1953; **Portsoy:** 1886–1949; **Prestwick:** 1913–55; **Renfrew:** 1923–55; **Rothesay:** 1935–54; **St Andrews:** 1932–

Records of banks

42; **Saltcoats:** 1937–42; **Selkirk:** 1853–60; **Stewarton:** 1916–55; **Stirling:** 1927–48; **Stonehouse:** 1937–52; **Stranraer:** 1837–41; **Strathaven:** 1831–1955; **Tarbet:** 1911–51; **Tarland:** 1857–1953; **Thornhill:** 1836–1955, **Tillicoultry:** c.1854–1955; **Troon:** 1843–1950; **Turriff:** 1881–1955.

Records 2: Business Records Centre, Archive Department, University of Glasgow, Glasgow G12 8QQ

Court minutes extracts 1830–1919; papers re routine transactions 1832–43; papers of general manager 1836–92; letters to general manager 1853, 1876–77, 1910–11; papers re bank note issue 1854–83; papers re Aberdeen district branches 1858–65; balance sheets and related papers 1865–1954; notes re City of Glasgow Bank 1878; papers re advances 1878, 1896; directors' reports 1879, 1918–23; booklet and memoranda re staff funds 1913–20s; trustee and executor terms and conditions 1919; Clydebank agent memorandum 1898; article re centenary 1930. [Ref: UGD 129/1]

UNION OF LONDON & SMITHS BANK LTD
London

History: This joint stock bank was established in Moorgate, City of London, in 1839 as the Union Bank of London with a paid-up capital of £211,500. Branches were opened in Argyle Place (1839), Pall Mall (1840), Charing Cross (1841), Temple Bar (1855), Holborn Circus (1870), Bayswater (1882), Fenchurch Street (1886), Tottenham Court Road (1886), Sloane Street (1888) and Southwark (1892). The head office was moved to Prince's Street in 1844. The bank developed an important foreign business. It acquired Dixon, Brooks & Dixon (est. 1787) of London in 1859, Chasemore, Robinson & Sons (est. 1838) of Croydon in 1891 and the London Commercial & Cripplegate Bank Ltd (est. 1819) in 1900. It was severely damaged by a £250,000 fraud in 1860. Limited liability was acquired in 1882. In 1902 there were twenty-four branches all based in London and its suburbs. In 1902 the bank amalgamated with the large London private bank of Smith, Payne & Smiths (est. 1758) and its country connections: Samuel Smith & Co (est. c.1688) of Nottingham; Smith, Ellison & Co (est. 1775) of Lincoln; Samuel Smith, Bros & Co (est. 1784) of Hull; Samuel Smith & Co (est. 1806) of Derby; and Samuel Smith & Co (est. c.1797) of Newark. The new bank was called the Union of London & Smiths Bank Ltd. Its paid-up capital was £3.55 million in 1904, having grown from £1.2 million in 1864; its balance sheet in 1904 totalled almost £42 million. It had fifty-three branches, many of which were located outside London. In 1903 it acquired Wigan, Mercer, Tasker & Co

514   *British banking – a guide to historical records*

(est. 1821) of Maidstone; London & Yorkshire Bank Ltd (est. 1872); and Prescott's Bank Ltd (est. 1891) which had an important presence in London and the West Country. The bank amalgamated with the National Provincial Bank of England Ltd (est. 1833) to form the National Provincial & Union Bank of England Ltd in 1917.

William Howarth, *Our Leading Banks* (London, 1894); William Howarth, *The Banks in the Clearing House* (London, 1905)

Records: The Royal Bank of Scotland plc, Archive Section, Regent's House, 42 Islington High Street, London N1 8XL

Prospectus 1839; deed of settlement 1839; annual reports 1839–1918; profit and loss books (6) 1839–1920; general ledger 1840–42; investment ledgers (2) 1853–1918; list of proprietors 1858; directors' meeting minute books 1859–1920; staff reports 1870s–1890s; memorandum book 1888–1910s; monthly statements of account 1891–1918; widows' and orphans' fund register of members 1897–1919; amalgamation papers 1902–05; staff Christmas money lists 1902–18; directors' attendance book 1903–19; profit and loss and average balances register 1904–52; press cuttings re Lombard Street office building 1906–07; information book 1908–18; list of staff in forces 1915; amalgamation papers 1918–19.

Bath: security and safe custody register 1880–1906; premises plans c.1880–1949; premises papers including valuation and inventory 1891; manager's interview book 1900–04; mortgage 1904; manager's diary 1910; **Batley:** passbook 1917–29; **Bristol:** law book 1892–1905; loans book 1911–24; **Croydon:** architectural drawings c.1905; **Derby:** manager's diaries 1902–09; **Hucknall:** salary book 1906–35; **Lincoln:** letterbooks (4) 1891–1916; **London, Bedford Row:** branch photographs 1899, 1950; **London, Chancery Lane:** list of promissory notes 1870; **London, Charing Cross:** directors' attendance book 1846–1915; **London, Cornhill:** security registers 1882–1906; customer correspondence 1902–11; security registers 1906–31; book of staff cartoons 1911–20; **London, Holborn Circus:** cheque book 1896; **London, Kensington:** architectural drawing 1897–98; directors' attendence book 1906–19; **London, Prince's Street:** manager's information books (2) 1873–1925; signature book 1883–93; cheque books 1906; **London, Regent Street:** half-yearly profit and loss statements 1841–1929; directors' attendance book 1846–1917; architectural drawings 1915; **London, South Kensington:** architectural drawings 1897–98; **Nottingham:** mandate and standing order guardbook 1898–1906; profit and loss account 1902; security ledgers (4) 1902–21; security journal 1903–09; probate register 1915–20; bond register 1916–20; **Sutton-in-Ashfield:** security register c.1908–19.

UNION PLC
London

History: This publicly quoted City of London discount house was formed in 1885 through the merger of the General Credit & Discount Co of London Ltd (est. 1866) and the United Discount Corporation Ltd (est. 1863). It soon displaced National Discount Co Ltd to become the largest London discount house in terms of both turnover and deposits and remained so until the 1980s. On formation its paid-up capital was £500,000. It acquired the businesses of Harwood, Knight & Allen and Green, Tomkinson & Co in 1891. In 1914 its capital was increased to £2 million and, by degrees, to £7.5 million in 1951 and to £10 million in 1962. Between the wars, as with most discount houses, its business drifted away from foreign bills to concentrate on domestic bills and gilts. Its senior manager in the late 1940s and 1950s was A W Trinder, by far the most influential figure in the discount market at the time. In the 1960s the business set about diversification at a time of unprecedented change in the discount market. A money broking subsidiary, Roberts Union Ltd, was established in 1968 and later renamed Udisco Brokers Ltd; it was sold in 1979. In 1975 Union Discount opened an Edinburgh office, in 1981 diversified into financial futures and established a leasing company in 1983. Following deregulation of the London securities market in the mid 1980s, the Glasgow brokers Aitken Campbell were acquired. In 1988 Winterflood Securities Ltd was established as a specialist market maker in small company stocks; it was sold in the early 1990s. Union Discount Co was renamed Union plc in the early 1990s.

George & Pamela Cleaver, *The Union Discount. A Centenary Album* (London, priv. pub., 1985); Gordon A Fletcher & Peter J Lee, 'Arthur William Trinder', *Dictionary of Business Biography* (London, 1986)

Records: Union plc, 39 Cornhill, London EC3V 3NU

Press cuttings 1867–85, 1930–76; registers of directors (2) 1879 on; amalgamation agreement 1885; balance sheet books (2) 1885 on; directors' meeting minute books (16) 1885 on; general meeting minute book 1885 on; letterbook 1896–1906; investment ledgers (2) 1898–1907; investment commissions (2) 1901 on; stock book 1914–20; commissions on directors' accounts 1914 on; discount ledger re treasury and corporation bills 1915–32; treasury bill and bond tenders averages 1921–38; treasury bill averages 1925–27; treasury bill statistics 1928–46; statement of treasury bills maturing, offered and allotted 1931–41; jubilee celebrations book 1935; bill and loan registers (7) 1938–40, 1944–47, 1960–74, 1983–84; security register 1939–52.

516   *British banking – a guide to historical records*

UNITED COUNTIES BANK LTD
Birmingham, West Midlands

History: This joint stock bank was established in Birmingham in 1836 as the Birmingham Town & District Banking Co with a nominal capital of £500,000. It moved to Colmore Row within weeks of opening. In 1868 paid-up capital was £156,400 and the balance sheet totalled almost £560,000. It acquired the Dudley & West Bromwich Banking Co (est. 1833) in 1874 when it was restyled the Birmingham, Dudley & District Banking Co. It acquired limited liability in 1881 under the title of the Birmingham, Dudley & District Banking Co Ltd when nominal capital was increased to £4 million. In 1881 the Midland Banking Co Ltd (est. 1863) was acquired although its remote branches were soon sold or closed. In 1889 the bank merged with the Wolverhampton & Staffordshire Banking Co Ltd (est. 1832) and was restyled the Birmingham District & Counties Banking Co Ltd. Hughes & Morgan (est. 1855) of Brecon was acquired in 1890 followed by the Midland Counties Bank Ltd (est. 1889) in 1904, the Wakefield & Barnsley Union Bank Ltd (est. 1832) in 1906 and Bradford Old Bank Ltd (est. 1864) in 1907. The bank was renamed United Counties Bank Ltd in 1907 to reflect its broader geographical spread. It amalgamated with Barclay & Co Ltd (est. 1896) in 1916 when its nominal capital was £6.97 million, of which £1.19 million was paid-up, and when its balance sheet totalled £19.34 million.

P W Matthews & Anthony W Tuke, *History of Barclays Bank Ltd* (London, 1926)

Records 1: Barclays Bank plc, Group Archives, Dallimore Road, Wythenshawe, Manchester M23 9JA

Staff register 1823–81; directors' reports 1830–92; deeds of settlement 1836; directors' meeting minute books (4) 1836–84; reports and accounts 1836–1916; private ledgers (2) 1836–75; share certificates 1836; general meeting minute book 1837–1916; share certificates 1837–1906; bank premises registers (3) 1838–1906; balance statement ledgers 1840–66; ledger, liquidation 1843–48; draft balance sheets and other papers 1845–81; correspondence re lending and investment 1850–1910; cheques 1851–74; certificates of incorporation 1858, 1866; protest re unpaid bill 1862; insurance agency book 1862–79; passbook 1864–67; statement of liability 1865; balance sheets 1865–86; due bills, suspense account and debt statements 1865–80; valuation records 1865–66; statement of liability 1865; banker's licence 1866; rules and regulations 1866–74; list of shareholders 1866; losses statements 1866–68; cheques and forms 1866–1917; branch profit and loss figures 1868–1915; salary registers 1869–89; legal opinion 1874; minute books: general meetings (2) 1867–1916, gen-

Records of banks 517

eral purposes 1881, directors' meetings (2) 1905–16, ordinary (3) 1904–17, special (4) 1906–20; private ledgers 1871–98; brokers' loans ledger 1874–1901; certificate of change of name 1874; directors' report 1874; cheques, cheque book and drafts 1874–79; in-letters re commission of London agent and Bank of England 1875–83; differences cash book 1875–88; staff rules 1875, 1884; quarterly statements 1875–88; head office instructions 1876–1904; analyses of half-yearly profit and loss 1877; estates ledger 1879–1908; in-letters re takeover of Leamington Priors & Warwickshire Banking Co 1879; apprenticeship agreements 1870s; incorporation forms and rules 1880–81; statements outstanding balances, overdrafts and advances 1881–82; bad debts ledger 1881–88; notes, assets and liabilities of Midland Banking Co branches 1881; correspondence re takeover of Midland Banking Co 1881–82; certificate of incorporation 1881; mortgage deeds 1881–85; in-letters and deeds, Hereford premises 1881–96; quarterly branch statements 1881–1904; warrants and unclaimed dividends 1881–1906; certificates of incorporation and change of name 1881–91; register bad and doubtful debts 1881–1900; register of shareholders 1881–1906; resolutions and property valuation 1881–1916; salary statement 1882–85; letterbook 1883–85; correspondence with directors and managers 1883; correspondence with Lloyds Bank 1883–85; officers' superannuation fund rules 1884; credit and overdraft statements 1884–86; retirement presentation book 1884; premises valuations 1885–86; security registers 1886–1922; copy letterbook 1887–95; instructions for cashiers 1888–1916; correspondence with Bank of England 1888; circular, merger with Wolverhampton & Staffordshire Banking Co 1889; notes re profits, shares and bad debts c.1889; share allotment register 1889–1907; register of powers of attorney signatures 1889–1903; property agreement 1890; salary registers 1890–94; information cards 1890–93; lists of shareholders 1890, 1903–04; failed account registers (3) 1891–1905; audited half-yearly accounts 1893–1915; in-letters 1895–1902; directors' reports and accounts 1895–1904; licence to keep a carriage 1896; private ledger 1896–1906; rules and regulations 1898; premises valuation 1901; brokers' loans ledgers 1901–16; premises ledger 1901–11; register of directors 1902–15; half-yearly profit statements 1903–25; board and committees attendance book 1903–09; papers re mergers, Wakefield & Barnsley Union Bank, Midland Counties District Bank and Bradford Old Bank 1904–07; branch quarterly statements 1904–16; head office instructions 1904–19; staff salary lists 1905–16; commission ledgers 1905–10; general correspondence 1906–13; letterbooks (2) 1906–19; dividend warrants 1907–16; memorandum and articles of association 1907–08; banker's licence 1907; papers re Bradford Old Bank merger 1907; lease, York premises 1906–07; shareholder registers (8) 1907–17; certificates of registration and change of name 1907; private ledgers (2) 1907–16; special resolutions 1908; sched-

518   *British banking – a guide to historical records*

ule of interest allowed to branches 1908–19; failed accounts registers (3) 1909–16; employment agreement 1913; balance sheet and list of branches 1913; declarations of secrecy 1915; Sheffield staff photographs 1916; papers re merger with Barclay & Co Ltd 1915–16; high court order, appointment of liquidators 1922.

Records 2: Birmingham City Archives, Chamberlain Square, Birmingham B3 3HQ

Deed of settlement 1836; annual reports 1862–66; architectural plans 1876–1903. [Ref: MS 1460.]

UNITED DISCOUNT CORPORATION LTD
London

History: This City of London discount house traced its origins to James Bruce, a stockbroker at work in London in 1825. It subsequently traded as Bruce & Co and emerged as one of London's four big discount houses. In 1857 it suspended payment when its business was eventually incorporated into Discount Corporation Ltd (est. 1863), of which Bruce became a director. Paid-up capital was £200,000. In the wake of the 1866 Overend Gurney crisis, the company was reconstructed as the United Discount Corporation Ltd and in 1885 it amalgamated with General Credit & Discount Co of London Ltd (est. 1866) to form Union Discount Co of London Ltd.

George & Pamela Cleaver, *The Union Discount. A Centenary Album* (priv. pub., 1985)

Records: Union plc, 39 Cornhill, London EC3V 3NU

Circulars 1864–83.

VEASEY, DESBOROUGH & CO
Huntingdon, Cambridgeshire

History: This private bank was established in 1804 as Rust, Sweeting & Veasey; it was otherwise known as the Huntingdon Town & County Bank. It was styled Rust, Sweeting, Veasey & D Veasey jnr from 1817; Rust, Veasey & Veasey from 1819; Rust, Veasey, D Veasey jnr & Charles Veasey from 1825; Veaseys, Desborough & Veasey from 1853; Veasey, Desborough & Veasey from 1855; Veasey, Desborough, Chapman & Henderson from 1857; Veasey, Desborough, Bevan & Tillard from 1865; Veasey, Desborough, Bevan, Tillard & Co from 1872; and subsequently Veasey, Desborough & Co. Early on, an agency existed at St Neots which was converted to a branch in 1844. Another agency opened at St Ives in

Records of banks 519

1853 and became a branch in 1855. In 1896 the bank merged with other banks to form Barclay & Co Ltd.

P W Matthews & Anthony W Tuke, *History of Barclays Bank Ltd* (London, 1926)

Records: Barclays Bank plc, Group Archives, Dallimore Road, Wythenshawe, Manchester M23 9JA

Current account ledgers (3) 1804–21; customer balance books 1808, 1821; private account ledgers (4) 1831–1913; unclaimed balances register 1848–94; partnership agreements 1853–76; partnership papers 1857–95; correspondence: partnership deed 1857–1912, Veasey family affairs 1865, 1874–76, clerk 1907–13; securities for advances 1858–67; counsel's opinion re partnership deeds 1859, 1872; solicitor's bill of charges 1869; indemnities 1871–83; authority and request to Sheffield Banking Co 1876; balance sheet 1895; papers re merger with Barclay & Co Ltd 1896–97.

VINCENT & BARNES
Newbury, Berkshire

History: This private bank was established prior to 1782 as Vincent, Baily & Vincent; it was also known as Newbury Old Bank. It failed in 1816 when it was known as Vincent & Barnes.

Records: Public Record Office, Ruskin Avenue, Kew, Richmond TW9 4DU

Goldsmith book 1788–92; money books 1788–1806; daily cash balance books 1788–1806; memorandum books 1788–1808; partnership agreements and related papers 1788–1815; out-letterbooks 1789–1809; bank note registers 1794–1812; customer ledgers 1800–02; day books 1800–02. [Ref: C171/20, 30–36, 45; J90/321]

VIVIAN, GRYLLS, KENDALL & CO
Helston, Cornwall

History: This private bank was established in 1788 as Glyn & Co. It was known as Grylls & Co from 1814, as Vivian, Borlase & Co from 1835 and as Vivian, Grylls, Kendall & Co from 1838; it was otherwise known as the Union Bank of Cornwall. In 1879 the bank failed when its business was acquired by Bolitho Sons & Co (est. 1807) of Penzance.

Records: Cornwall Record Office, County Hall, Truro TR1 3AY

Banker's licences 1808–47. [Ref: RO 7772–7807]

520 *British banking – a guide to historical records*

VIVIAN, KITSON & CO
Torquay, Devon

History: This private bank was formed in 1833 by a local solicitor, William Kitson, with Edward Vivian and Captain W Vivian. It was also known as the Torquay Bank and had branches at Vaughan Parade, Torquay, and at Higher Union Street, Torre, Torquay (1894). It enjoyed a reputation as the most 'fashionable' bank in this leading seaside resort as well as being important in the local economy. It was acquired by Lloyds Bank Ltd (est. 1765) in 1900.

Records: Lloyds TSB Group plc, Archives, Head Office, 71 Lombard Street, London EC3P 3BS

Signature book 1852–77; amalgamation papers 1899–1912.

VIZARD & CO
Dursley, Gloucestershire

History: This private bank was formed in 1803 by local solicitors and was acquired by the County of Gloucester Banking Co in 1836.

Records: Lloyds TSB Group plc, Archives, Head Office, 71 Lombard Street, London EC3P 3BS

Amalgamation papers 1836–37.

VYE & HARRIS
Ilfracombe, Devon

History: This private bank was established in 1807 as Lee & Lock, and was otherwise known as the Ilfracombe Bank. It was styled Vye & Harris from 1825 and was acquired by the National Provincial Bank of England (est. 1833) in 1836.

Records: The Royal Bank of Scotland plc, Archive Section, Regent's House, 42 Islington High Street, London N1 8XL

Amalgamation papers 1836.

SIR ROBERT VYNER
London

History: Robert Vyner was apprenticed to his uncle, London goldsmith Sir Thomas Vyner (died 1665), from 1646 to 1656. He traded as a goldsmith-banker in Lombard Street from c.1662 and in Coleman Street from 1680. In 1665 he took over his uncle's business. He was elected Lord Mayor of London in 1674 and subsequently knighted. Vyner kept running

Records of banks

cashes. There was a serious run on his bank in 1667. It lost £416,724 with the 'stop' on the Exchequer in 1672 and got into difficulties. Vyner died in 1688.

Records 1: West Yorkshire Archive Service, Leeds District Archives, Chapeltown Road, Sheepscar, Leeds LS7 3AP

Papers re personal and banking transactions 1655–1705.

Records 2: Public Record Office, Ruskin Avenue, Kew, Richmond TW9 4DU

Commission of bankruptcy, Sir Robert Vyner, 1684. [Ref: PRO C107/112]

JOHN WAKEFIELD & SONS
Kendal, Cumbria

History: This private bank was formed in 1788, initially being known as John Wakefield and from 1812 as John Wakefield & Sons. The Wakefields were leading Quaker businessmen who carried on banking functions alongside their merchanting activities prior to forming their bank. A branch was opened at Carlisle which, in 1837, was converted into the Carlisle City & District Banking Co, a joint stock bank. In 1840 the bank merged with its only rival at Kendal, W D Crewdson & Co (est. 1788), to form Wakefield, Crewdson & Co which was otherwise known as the Kendal Bank.

George Chandler, *Four Centuries of Banking* (London, 1964–68)

Records: Barclays Bank plc, Group Archives, Dallimore Road, Wythenshawe, Manchester M23 9JA

Bank notes 1818–34; letter re customer payment 1833; letter re torn bank note 1834.

WAKEFIELD & BARNSLEY UNION BANK LTD
Wakefield, West Yorkshire

History: This joint stock bank was established in 1832 as the Wakefield Banking Co. It was known as the Wakefield & Barnsley Union Banking Co from 1840 following its acquisition of Beckett, Birks & Co (est. 1796) of Barnsley. Its name changed to the Wakefield & Barnsley Union Bank Ltd following its acquisition of limited liability in 1884. In 1906 it amalgamated with the Birmingham District & Counties Banking Co Ltd (est. 1836).

P W Matthews & Anthony W Tuke, *History of Barclays Bank Ltd* (London, 1926)

522   *British banking – a guide to historical records*

Records: Barclays Bank plc, Group Archives, Dallimore Road, Wythenshawe, Manchester M23 9JA

Directors' declarations of secrecy 1832–1905; manager's correspondence 1833–43; directors' meeting minute books (11) 1848–1906; letter to customer re overdraft 1856; cheque books and cheque form, Barnsley 1870–1902; certificates of incorporation 1875–97; share certificates 1887–1905; unpaid dividend statement and receipts 1893; memorandum and articles of association 1897; register of directors 1897–1905; shareholder register 1906.

WAKEFIELD, CREWDSON & CO
Kendal, Cumbria

History: This private bank was formed in 1840 through the amalgamation of the leading Kendal private banks of John Wakefield & Sons (est. 1788) and W D Crewdson & Co (est. 1788), the Wakefields being the dominant partners. Both banks had been formed in 1788 and their partners were drawn from leading and long established families of Quaker businessmen. The merger was a response to growing competition from joint stock banks, the first of which, the Bank of Westmorland, had been formed at Kendal in 1833. In 1863 the Ulverston bank of Petty & Postlethwaite (est. 1804) was acquired followed in 1883 by the Lancaster branch of the Manchester & Salford Bank Ltd (est. 1836) and in 1884 by Grice & Co (est. c.1840) of Bootle. By 1893 branches existed at Ambleside, Barrow, Kirkby Stephen, Lancaster, Ulverston and Windermere while agencies were at Sedbergh, Coniston, Kirkby Lonsdale and probably elsewhere. In this year the bank was acquired by the Bank of Liverpool Ltd (est. 1831).

George Chandler, *Four Centuries of Banking* (London, 1964–68)

Records 1: Barclays Bank plc, Group Archives, Dallimore Road, Wythenshawe, Manchester M23 9JA

Private ledgers (2) 1840–84; letters to partners 1840–85, 1889; guarantees, abstracts of accounts, income tax returns 1840–68; guarantee re John Wakefield & Co and W D Crewdson & Sons 1840–44; loan security registers (5) 1840–92; certificate re bank note issue 1844; customer addresses 1847–61; securities for advances 1849–82; drafts 1853–57; partnership agreements 1854–93; liability for accounts of W D Crewdson & Co 1860; bank notes 1860–82, 1886–91; agreement re merger with Petty & Postlethwaite 1863; lease, Ulverston 1864; securities as bankers 1866–80; customer balance sheets 1867–83; current account ledgers 1868–87; balances with London agents 1869–81; applications for clerkships 1870–92; letters re partnership 1870; in-letters 1871–95; customer ledgers

Records of banks 523

1871–1915; customer account balance book 1875–77; out-letterbooks (2) 1880–95; balance sheets 1883–93; branch statistics 1883–95; note of partners' profit share 1884–92; cheque forms 1890; papers re merger with Bank of Liverpool 1893–95; papers re customer income tax claim 1894–97; memorandum re accounts in abeyance 1895; photographs of partners nineteenth cent.; list of Sedbergh account holders n.d.

Records 2: Cumbria Record Office, County Offices, Kendal LA9 4RQ

J Maude: letter and bill books 1761–1803, cash book 1777–88, letterbook 1794–1801; Crewdson family papers eighteenth to nineteenth cents; account book re loans to S Parrat 1826–27. [Ref: WD/K/181–4; WD/Cr; WDX/314]

JOHN WALTERS & WILLIAM WALTERS
Haverfordwest, Dyfed

History: This private bank was established in 1827 as John & William Walters; both proprietors had been partners in Walters, Voss & Walters (est. 1821) of Swansea. The bank was otherwise known as the Pembrokeshire Bank. A branch was established at Narberth in 1863 while other branches also existed at Milford and Pembroke Dock. It was renamed John Walters & William Walters in about 1870. The bank was acquired by the London & Provincial Bank Ltd (est 1836) in 1872.

Francis West, 'Early Banks in West Wales', *Transactions of the Historical Society of West Wales*, 6 (1916)

Records: Barclays Bank plc, Group Archives, Dallimore Road, Wythenshawe, Manchester M23 9JA

Current account ledgers 1838–56; cheques and drafts 1844, 1864–68; bank notes 1863–70; bill ledgers 1864–72; customer account ledgers 1864–69; liquidation account ledger 1872–78.

S G WARBURG & CO LTD
London

History: This merchant bank traces its origins to the arrival of the German émigré banker, (Sir) Siegmund G Warburg in London in 1934; he had formerly worked as a partner in the Hamburg bank of M M Warburg & Co and had established a Berlin branch for them in 1930. In London he formed a small firm called the New Trading Co Ltd. This grew steadily and after the Second World War developed into a fully-fledged merchant bank. In 1946 it was renamed S G Warburg & Co Ltd. It came to have interests in corporate finance, corporate banking and fund management. It

524   *British banking – a guide to historical records*

developed a reputation for innovation and aggressive business tactics and soon emerged as the City's most successful merchant bank. This was seen no more clearly than in the aggressive stance it took on behalf of its clients in mounting hostile take over bids, in particular during the contested bid for British Aluminium Co Ltd in the late 1950s. Warburgs' emergence as a leading house received substantial impetus in 1957 when it acquired the merchant bank of Seligman Bros (est. 1864) and thereby obtained a seat on the prestigious Accepting Houses Committee. The firm played an innovative role in the development of the eurobond market when in 1963 it launched the first eurobond issue, for Autostrade Italiane. The firm subsequently was owned by a holding company, Mercury Securities Ltd and hived off its asset management activities into Mercury Asset Management Ltd. In 1964 an interest was acquired in the Frankfurt private bank of Hans W Petersen which was renamed S G Warburg & Co. In the 1970s Warburgs international interests grew apace and at the time of 'Big Bang' in the mid-1980s the firm developed into the most successful British-owned investment bank. At this time it acquired the stockbrokers Rowe & Pitman and Mullens and the stockjobbers Arkroyd Smithers. In 1995 Warburgs was acquired by Swiss Bank Corporation (SBC) and became known as SBC Warburg. In 1997 SBC acquired the New York investment bank, Dillon Read & Co Inc which was merged with Warburgs under the title SBC Warburg Dillon Read. Following the merger of SBC with Union Bank of Switzerland in 1998, the title was shortened to Warburg Dillon Read.

Jacque Attali, *A Man of Influence. Sir Siegmund Warburg 1902–1982* (Paris, 1985); Ron Chernow, *The Warburgs. A Family Saga* (London, 1993)

Note: No details are known about the survival or availability of historical records.

WARWICK & LEAMINGTON BANKING CO
Warwick, Warwickshire

History: This bank was established in 1834 through the reorganisation of the private bank of Dawes, Tomes & Russell (est. 1791) into a joint stock bank. Dawes was linked to Tomes, Chattaway & Ford (est. 1810) of Stratford upon Avon which in 1834 formed the Stourbridge & Kidderminster Banking Co. Branches were opened at Leamington Spa and Stratford-on-Avon. The business was acquired by Lloyds Banking Co Ltd (est. 1765) in 1866.

Records 1: Lloyds TSB Group plc, Archives, Head Office, 71 Lombard Street, London EC3P 3BS

Records of banks 525

Deed of settlement 1834; lists of shareholders 1834, 1866; amalgamation agreement 1866.

Records 2: Leamington Spa Library, Avenue Road, Leamington Spa CV31 3PP

Deed of settlement 1834.

Records 3: Warwickshire Record Office, Priory Park, Cape Road, Warwick CV34 4JS

Deed of settlement 1834; assignment of securities 1834. [Ref: CR1097; CR611/506]

WATKINS & CO
Daventry, Northamptonshire

History: This private bank was formed in 1783 as Watkins & Smith, bankers and drapers, by Charles Watkins and John Smith. The business was later styled Watkins & Bricknell, and from 1825 Watkins & Co. It also established an office at Northampton. In 1836 it was converted into a joint stock bank under the title of the Northamptonshire Banking Co.

Records: Northamptonshire Record Office, Wootton Hall Park, Northampton NN4 9BQ

Partnership agreement 1783–85; partner's will 1810; agreement with clerk 1810; miscellaneous papers incl. bank notes, receipts, letters 1794–1835. [Ref: STOP 1–145]

WEBB & CO
Ledbury, Hereford & Worcester

History: This private bank was formed as Hankins & Co in 1790 and was styled Webb & Co from 1815 when Thomas Webb took over the business. It was acquired by the Gloucestershire Banking Co Ltd (est. 1831) in 1883.

Records: Lloyds TSB Group plc, Archives, Head Office, 71 Lombard Street, London EC3P 3BS

Amalgamation papers 1883.

WELLS, HOGGE & LINDSELL
Biggleswade, Bedfordshire

History: This private bank was formed in 1830 through the amalgamation of the private banks of Williamson & Wells (est. 1807) of Baldock and G

526 *British banking – a guide to historical records*

& W Hogge (est. 1810) of Biggleswade; it was also known as the Biggleswade & Baldock Bank. The firm was closely associated with the local brewing industry and the slow decline of this industry precipitated the sale of the bank to Capital & Counties Bank Ltd (est. 1877) in 1893.

Jack Parker, *Nothing for Nobody for Nobody. A History of Hertfordshire Banks and Banking* (Stevenage, 1986)

Records 1: Lloyds TSB Group plc, Archives, Head Office, 71 Lombard Street, London EC3P 3BS

Letterbook 1849–98; general ledger 1862–1908; overdraft book 1877–1907; journals 1895–1908.

Records 2: Bedfordshire and Luton Archives and Record Service, The Records Office, Cauldwell Street, Bedford MK42 9AP

Cheque 1867; papers re appointment as bankers to a firm of attornies 1835. [Ref: AD 1183; LS 225]

WENTWORTH, CHALONER & RISHWORTH
Wakefield, West Yorkshire, & York, North Yorkshire

History: In 1812 two private banks were formed under the same name at Wakefield and York; they were otherwise known as the Wakefield Bank and the York Bank and grew to be of considerable importance. In 1814 the Wakefield Bank acquired the business of the failed local bank of Townsend & Rishworth (est. 1802). There was also a London-based private bank called Wentworth, Chaloner & Rishworth (est. 1813). All three banks failed in 1825.

W C E Hartley, *Banking in Yorkshire* (Clapham, 1975)

Records: Nottinghamshire Archives, County House, Castle Meadow Road, Nottingham NG2 1AG

Papers re failure 1826. [Ref: M 11781–3]

WESTERN BANK OF SCOTLAND
Glasgow, Strathclyde

History: This bank was formed in 1832 with an initial paid-up capital of £210,000. It immediately embarked upon a vigorous lending policy with minimal liquid reserves and by 1834 the bank had consequently run into difficulties. It was supported by a £100,000 loan from the major Edinburgh banks on condition that its lending policy was modified. Western Bank of Scotland also pursued an ambitious policy of branch opening, setting up twenty-three branches in the 1830s and forty-nine in the 1840s; by 1850 it

Records of banks

had seventy-two branches, far more than any other Scottish bank. In 1843 it acquired the business of the failed Greenock Banking Co (est. 1785) followed by Dundee Union Bank (est. 1809) in 1844, Paisley Commercial Bank (est. 1838) in 1845 and Ayrshire Banking Co (est. 1830) also in 1845. In 1847 it was again in difficulty due to excessive lending and was rescued by a £300,000 Bank of England loan. By 1857 Western Bank of Scotland was the second largest bank in Scotland after the Royal Bank of Scotland. It then had a paid-up capital of £1.5 million, £5.3 million deposits, 1,280 shareholders and 101 branches. In this year, during a general financial panic, Western Bank of Scotland collapsed, the victim of bad management and of the failure of three major customers owing almost £1.2 million. The shareholders lost all their paid-up capital of £2 million and had to provide an additional £1.1 million to meet the bank's liabilities.

Anon, *How to Mismanage a Bank. A Review of the Western Bank of Scotland* (Edinburgh, 1859); R H Campbell, 'Edinburgh Bankers and the Western Bank of Scotland', *Scottish Journal of Political Economy*, 2 (1955); S G Checkland, *Scottish Banking. A History 1695–1973* (Glasgow, 1975); I C Macsween, 'The Western Bank of Scotland 1832–1857', *Scottish Bankers' Magazine*, 49 (1957); J Eunson, 'The Western Bank of Scotland 1832 to 9th November 1857', *Scottish Bankers' Magazine*, 75 (1983); S Neave, *The Western Bank Failure and the Scottish Banking System* (Glasgow, 1858)

Records 1: Clydesdale Bank plc, 30 St Vincent Place, Glasgow G1 2HL

Instructions to agents and accountants 1848–56.

Records 2: Business Records Centre, Archives Department, Glasgow University, Glasgow G12 8QQ

Partnership agreements 1832–57; plans and elevation of premises 1845–58; papers re failure 1858–63. [Ref: UGD 84/1–4]

Records 3: National Library of Scotland, Department of Manuscripts, George IV Bridge, Edinburgh EH1 1EW

Letters, accounts and press cuttings 1850–60. [Ref: Adv.MSS 21.1.13–14]

Records 4: The Royal Bank of Scotland plc, Archive Section, 36 St Andrews Square, Edinburgh EH2 2YB

Correspondence with Bank of Scotland 1834–38; correspondence with agents: Greenock 1842, Lockerbie 1858; circular re suspension of payment 1857; list of partners 1858.

Brechin: cheques and receipts 1854–57; **Galashiels:** procedural instructions book 1854.

528 *British banking – a guide to historical records*

Records 5: National Archives of Scotland, HM General Register House, Princes Street, Edinburgh EH1 3YY

Letters re opposition to letters patent 1838. [Ref: GD18/3387]

WESTERN COUNTIES BANK LTD
Liskeard, Cornwall

History: This business traced its origins to the private bank of Clymo, Treffry, Hawke, West & Co, established in 1864. It was closely linked with the Cornish mining industry and it opened branches at Bodmin (1865), Looe (1866), Camelford (1867) and Wadebridge (1879). In 1885 it was reconstructed as a joint stock bank, Western Counties Bank Ltd, and was acquired by the Capital & Counties Bank Ltd (est. 1877) in 1890.

Records: Lloyds TSB Group plc, Archives, Head Office, 71 Lombard Street, London EC3P 3BS

Amalgamation papers 1890.

WESTMINSTER BANK LTD
London

History: This joint stock bank traced its origins to the London & County Bank Ltd (est. 1836) and the London & Westminster Bank Ltd (est. 1834) which in 1909 amalgamated to form the London, County & Westminster Bank Ltd. In 1909 the London & County Bank had seventy metropolitan branches and nearly 200 country branches, mostly south of a line between Bournemouth, Dorset, and Clacton, Essex. The London & Westminster Bank had thirty-seven branches in London and its suburbs. The new bank had paid-up capital of £3.5 million and a balance sheet total of over £80 million. In 1911 it acquired the business of the failed Birkbeck Bank (est. 1851) followed in 1917 by the very much larger Ulster Bank (est. 1836) of Belfast which had 170 branches; the latter continued to operate separately. In 1913 the London, County & Westminster Bank (Paris) Ltd was established; it was known as Westminster Foreign Bank Ltd from 1923 and opened branches in Europe. In 1918, when paid-up capital was £4.12 million, the bank merged with Parr's Bank Ltd (est. 1865) to form the London, County, Westminster & Parr's Bank Ltd. It had 700 branches, paid-up capital of £6.8 million and a balance sheet total of £286 million. The new bank, which was known as Westminster Bank Ltd from 1923, continued to expand through acquisition; its paid-up capital rose from £9 million in 1923 to £40.5 million in 1935. The Nottingham & Nottinghamshire Banking Co Ltd (est. 1834) was acquired in 1919 followed by the banks of Beckett & Co (est. 1774) of Leeds and York in 1921, Stilwell &

Records of banks 529

Sons (est. 1774) of London in 1923 and the Guernsey Commercial Banking Co Ltd (est. 1835) in 1924. By 1939 there were 1,100 branches and the number rose to 1,400 by 1968 when the bank merged with the National Provincial Bank Ltd (est. 1833). It continued to operate as a separate business until 1970 when National Westminster Bank Ltd commenced operations.

T E Gregory, *The Westminster Bank Through a Century* (London, 1936); Fiona Maccoll, *The Key to Our Success. A Brief History of the Natwest Group* (London, 1996); R H Mottram, *The Westminster Bank 1836–1936* (London, 1936); Manfred Pohl & Sabine Freitag, *Handbook on the History of European Banks* (Aldershot, 1994); Richard Reed, *National Westminster Bank. A Short History* (London, 1989);

Records: The Royal Bank of Scotland plc, Archive Section, Regent's House, 42 Islington High Street, London N1 8XL

Bad debt register 1838–1931; staff registers 1868–1970; annual lists of offices 1868–1971; branch architectural drawings c.1860s–1960s; annual reports 1888–1932; head office committee minute book 1896–1914; securities, deeds of appointment and powers of attorney 1897–1969; staff pay award correspondence 1897–1925; premises photographs including agricultural show banks c.1900–69; bank staff magazines 1906–68; hockey club minutes 1907–70; establishment committee: minutes 1907–22, premises reports 1909–11; charitable donation records cards 1909–32; samples of stationery forms 1909–69; memorandum and articles of association 1909–68; directors' meeting minutes 1909–71; register of directors 1909–21; amalgamation papers 1909–27; share register 1909–14; bank officer authorities 1909–39; share certificates 1910–65; annual general meeting reports 1910–69; board daily committee minute books 1910–69; daily committee reports 1910–22; staff pension fund rules 1910–68; staff conditions of service 1910–39, 1951–66; staff appointment requirements 1910, 1919–39; staff declarations of secrecy 1910–28; currency exchange rate books (7) 1910–82; marketing posters 1910–66; Bank of England clearing figure book 1910–28; directors' meeting standing orders 1911–66; chief accountant's statistics 1911–69; manager's guarantee fund rules 1911–66; Yorkshire Penny Bank: correspondence re liability 1912–14, agreement 1916; paying-in books 1912, 1921; sports club papers 1913, 1928–70; new branch recommendation book 1913–30; procedural circulars 1914–45 [w]; instruction manuals 1914–1960s; staff registers 1914–47; lists of staff died, injured and decorated 1914–45; salary book 1914–54; emergency instructions 1914, 1940–63; papers of Walter Leaf, chairman 1915–21; staff letters of appointment 1915–39; correspondence re proposed Spanish branches 1917–21; papers re rates of pay 1918; staff 'victory'

530   *British banking – a guide to historical records*

share registers 1918; certificates of incorporation 1918, 1922–23; advertising guardbooks: 1918–70, competitors 1939–1960s; branch statistics 1918–43; directors' visitor book 1919–70; Cornhill dramatic society minutes 1920–60; New York office papers 1920–46; staff dinner menu cards 1920–53; pensions fund premiums register 1921–63; staff association: booklets, including constitution n.d., correspondence 1921; Westminster Bank Guild: correspondence 1921, lectures 1928–55, leaflets n.d.; code book 1922; authorised signature book, foreign correspondents 1923–36; branch lists 1924–69; branch maps 1924–1960s; general manager's committee minutes 1924–64; bank Christmas cards 1925–68; advertisement artwork and proofs c.1925–1960s; staff photographs 1925–55; swimming club: programmes 1925, 1950, photographs 1930–58; staff association sickness and accident fund rules 1926; insurance fund register 1927–79; press advertising 1927, 1943, 1967–70; coat-of-arms patent 1928; sports club papers 1928–82; bank notes, Isle of Man 1929, 1960; staff employment offer 1920s; drama club: minutes 1920s–1980s, programmes 1895, 1925–67, papers 1953–68, photographs 1926–89; promotional literature 1929–68; legal action papers 1932; arts club minutes 1934–69; directors' red books 1934–n.d.; papers re publication of bank history 1936–37; bank residence inventories 1936; staff statistics 1937; grants to widows register 1938–66; branch mechanisation papers 1939–62; advertising proposals book, Charles Barker & Co 1942; directors' papers 1943; staff manuals 1946–67; advertising account book 1948–66; economic intelligence department papers 1949–60s; staff recruitment booklets 1940s–1969; sub-committee minutes: administration 1951–60, public services 1951–60, city office 1951–64; staff recruitment advertisement guardbook c.1955–65; sailing club papers 1956–62; motor club journal 1958–63; horticultural society card and rules n.d.; head office instruction cards 1960–67; training manuals and lectures 1963–67; shareholder circulars 1964–68; pension fund minute books 1964–69; staff handbooks 1966–67; staff cartoons 1960s.

Alfreton: profit and loss book 1918–38; **Altrincham:** profit and loss statement 1919–38; architectural drawings 1954; **Arundel:** manager's notebook 1900–05; **Ashbourne:** branch alteration estimates 1921; **Aylesbury:** information book 1878–1932; branch minute books (3) 1900–31; **Bakewell:** profit and loss statements 1918–33; **Belper:** manager's staff report 1926–29; **Birkenhead:** staff photographs n.d.; **Birmingham, Colmore Row:** profit and loss statement 1913–37; **Bognor Regis:** architectural drawing 1939; **Bolton:** profit and loss statement books 1918–68; **Bootle:** profit and loss statements 1931–60; **Bradford:** staff photograph 1923; **Brentford:** information books 1885–1936; **Brentwood:** character book 1930s–50s; **Brighton:** branch minute books 1852–1926; customer information books

Records of banks 531

(5) 1886–1932; profit and loss statements 1910–69; manager's private letterbooks 1916–54; loan correspondence 1930; **Brighton, Preston:** passbook 1920–43; **Bristol, Kingswood:** passbook 1918–36; **Bromley:** profit and loss statements 1910–55; letter re history 1932; architectural specification 1967; **Bushey:** contract notes 1918–24; **Buxted:** premises alteration papers 1920–22; **Cambridge:** profit and loss statements 1910–31; **Canterbury:** profit and loss statements 1910–68; branch statistics 1942–65; **Carlisle:** profit and loss book 1918–37; **Chard:** character book 1912–53; **Chesham:** profit and loss statement 1923–35; **Chester:** salary book 1914–54; profit and loss statements 1918–37; **Chislehurst:** profit papers 1964–66; **Cliftonville:** profit and loss books 1910–29; **Cockermouth:** profit and loss book 1910–39; **Coventry:** salary book 1905–38; manager's memorandum book 1906–26; profit and loss book 1918–36; **Cranbook:** staff book 1919–58; **Cranleigh:** profit and loss sheets 1919–69; **Deal:** profit and loss statements 1914–26; branch returns 1961–68; **Dorking:** half-yearly returns 1909–31; conveyance 1929; **Douglas:** property papers 1900–29; profit and loss statements 1918–37; **Eccles:** profit and loss statements 1920–35; **Eltham:** architectural drawings 1921; **Frodsham:** profit and loss statements 1918–38; **Gillingham:** quarterly returns 1899–1916; letterbook 1903–29; **Gloucester:** staff salary book 1920–1940s; profit and loss statements 1931–68; **Godalming:** profit and loss statements 1910–69; **Harrow:** manager's letterbook 1899–1925; head office correspondence re staff 1910–34; profit and loss statements 1929–73; **Harrow, Station Road:** profit and loss statements 1910–69; architectural drawings 1915; **Hertford:** manager's letterbook 1879–1930; **Hinchley Wood:** staff attendance book 1936–39; **Hove, Palmeira:** profit and loss statements 1917–69; statistics book 1940–76; customer interview books (3) 1965–68; **Hythe:** clerical staff return and wartime report 1941; **Ilford:** quarterly and half-yearly returns 1905–54; **Jersey:** paying-in book 1923–25; **Leamington:** branch minute book 1910–30; information book 1910–24; staff list 1911–26; profit and loss statement 1919–29; customer interview memoranda 1966–67; **Leeds, Park Row:** architectural drawings 1922; **Leicester, St Martin's:** profit and loss statements 1918–37; manager's minute book 1921–29; paying-in book 1928; deposit receipt n.d.; **Leighton Buzzard:** quarterly branch returns 1856–1909; profit and loss statements 1910–32; **Lewisham:** architectural drawings 1919; inspector's queries book 1929–41; **Liverpool, Chief Office:** cotton accounts book 1909–69; **Liverpool, Princes Road:** architectural drawings 1957; **Liverpool, Water Street:** profit and loss statements 1919–33; **London, Aldersgate Street:** staff information books (4) 1873–1942; staff letterbooks 1877–1919; **London, Bartholomew Lane:** memorandum book 1904–22; deposit receipts 1922–33; **London, Bloomsbury:** branch minute books (2) 1910–20; passbook 1913–23; procedural instructions 1933–52; **London, Chancery Lane:**

532   *British banking – a guide to historical records*

manager's information books 1908–32; minute books (8) 1911–29; premises papers and photographs n.d.; list of tenancies 1936; architectural drawings 1939, n.d.; **London, Covent Garden:** standing order 1911; staff reunion dinner menus 1932–64; **London, Euston Road:** profit and loss statements 1921–66; **London, Fenchurch Street:** manager's letter n.d.; **London, Finsbury Park:** half-yearly returns 1920; architectural drawings 1936–40; **London, Hammersmith:** profit and loss statements 1910–36; **London, Hampstead:** profit and loss statements 1920–31; **London, Harley Street:** profit and loss statements 1910–27; architectural drawings 1921–23; **London, Havestock Hill:** statement sheet 1938; **London, Highbridge:** safe custody registers 1929–37, 1960s; security register 1930–34; deposit ledger 1930–57; interest book 1937–52; loan ledger 1933–57; cash book 1939; current account ledger 1945–47; impersonal ledger 1950–54; **London, Holborn:** branch minute books (3) 1876–1914; architectural plans 1939; **London, Kennington:** profit and loss statements 1922–68; **London, Kensington:** profit and loss statements 1961–1918; architectural drawings 1930; passbook 1947–55; **London, Kensington Melbury Court:** letter from first customer 1928; **London, Kensington Parr's:** deposit receipt book 1921–32; cheque book 1950; **London, Lambeth North:** profit and loss statements 1910–20; **London, Marylebone Road:** branch minute book (5) 1904–14; **London, Marylebone:** branch minute books (8)1910–27; **London, Mayfair:** architectural drawings 1918–23; **London, Oxford Street:** customer information books 1878–1926; staff book 1910–20; staff register 1911–26; signature books (8) 1830s–1953; profit and loss statements 1921–68; staff book 1834–1940s; **London, Palmers Green:** safe custody register 1939; **London, Park Lane:** architectural drawings 1928; **London, Regent's Park:** profit and loss statements 1910–27; **London, Regent Street:** profit and loss statements 1919–36; **London, South Kensington:** branch minute book 1913–15; **London, Southwark:** bad and doubtful debt returns 1910; **London, St John's Wood:** profit and loss statements 1910–22 [w]; **London, St Martin's le Grand:** architectural drawings 1967; **London, Tavistock Square:** profit and loss returns 1926–64; staff salary book 1933–62; **London, Threadneedle Street:** architectural plans 1920s; **London, Victoria Street:** profit and loss statements 1910–37; inspector's reports 1929–49; **London, West End:** customer correspondence 1891–1916; staff register 1917–47; paying-in book c.1969; **London, West Marylebone:** architectural drawings 1913–15; **London, Westminster Bridge Road:** profit and loss statements 1910–68; architectural drawings 1913; **Longsight:** profit and loss statements 1918–68; **Loughborough:** branch minute book 1928–30; **Manchester, Chief Office:** inspection correspondence 1926; **Matlock:** opening hours notice c.1940; **Middlewich:** architectural drawing 1929; **Milborne Port:** branch minute books 1910–29; memorandum re premises

Records of banks 533

1937; **Millom:** manager's interview book 1960–69; **Newark:** staff photograph 1939; **Newbury:** profit and loss statements 1909–58; **Nottingham, Cattlemarket:** architectural drawings 1954; **Nottingham, Hucknall Road:** profit and loss statements 1930–68; branch statistics 1943–68; **Nottingham, Thurland Street:** staff photographs 1918–39; **Peterborough:** press cutting book re new premises 1933; **Preston:** staff photographs 1936–37; **Pulborough:** opening hours notice 1909; profit and loss statements 1915–63; half-yearly returns 1915–68; branch statistics 1915–70; **Radlett:** profit and loss statements 1915–27; bad debts list 1922–73; inspector's comment record 1929–55; **Redland:** profit and loss statements 1919–69; **Salisbury:** profit and loss statements 1916–30; branch returns 1916–59; **Scarborough:** architectural drawings 1963–64; **Seaford:** correspondence re branch premises and opening 1929; **Sevenoaks:** credit slip book c.1913; **Sherborne:** branch minute book 1916–31; **Sittingbourne:** profit and loss statements 1910–28; **Southend on Sea:** profit and loss statements 1911–28; **Southwark:** deed register 1880s–1910; bad and doubtful debt return 1910; warrant book 1930–55; security books 1952–65; safe custody book 1963–65; **Stratford:** passbook 1911–18; customer interview book 1963; **Sutton:** home safe account passbook n.d.; **Teddington:** branch minute books 1905–30; impersonal ledger 1905–15; branch returns 1923–28; letterbook 1925–27; **Tunbridge Wells:** quarterly returns 1871–1910; **Uckfield:** papers re falling money lodged 1923–30; correspondence re new premises 1925–30; **Uxbridge:** profit and loss statements 1910–19; premises papers 1955–67; **Valencia:** title deed 1920; **Waltham Green:** branch construction estimates 1925; **Walton-on-the-Naze:** profit and loss statements 1922–69; **Wells:** profit and loss books 1920–31; **West Ealing:** architectural drawings 1910; **West Gorton:** profit and loss statements 1919–35; **Westcliffe-on-Sea:** paying-in books 1920–25; **Weston-Super-Mare:** profit and loss statements 1918–30; **Weybridge:** branch property leases and correspondence 1905–20: profit and loss statements 1910–34; **Weymouth:** customer statements 1948–59; **Wigan:** profit and loss statements 1918–33; **Winchmore Hill:** weekly statistics 1929–39; **Winsford:** profit and loss statements 1918–37; **Wolverhampton:** profit and loss statement 1930–68: annual returns 1933; **Yeovil:** letterbooks (8) 1910–30.

WEST OF ENGLAND & SOUTH WALES DISTRICT BANK LTD
Bristol, Avon

History: This joint stock was formed in 1834 as the West of England & South Wales District Bank. Within a year, branches were opened at Barnstaple, Bath, Bridgewater, Exeter, Swansea and Taunton and others followed in Somerset in the 1840s and in South Wales after 1850. The

534 *British banking – a guide to historical records*

bank expanded ambitiously and had sixteen branches by 1860. In the 1860s and 1870s other banks were acquired including Allaway & MacDougall (est. 1807) of Ross on Wye in 1863; Kingsbridge Joint Stock Bank (est. 1841) in 1862; Towgood & Co (est. 1819) of Cardiff in 1855; and Harwood & Harwood (est. 1862) of Clevedon in 1877. Limited liability was acquired in 1878. In this year the bank failed but part of its branch network was reconstituted in 1879 as the Bristol & West of England Bank Ltd. The bank's failure had major financial repercussions in the West of England.

Charles H Cave, *History of Banking in Bristol from 1750 to 1899* (Bristol, 1899)

Records 1: Lloyds TSB Group plc, 71 Lombard Street, London EC3P 3BS

Deed of settlement 1834; directors' meeting minute books (2) 1834–42; committee minute book 1837–39; teller's cash book 1835.

Records 2: Bristol Record Office, 'B' Bond Warehouse, Smeaton Road, Bristol BS1 6XN

Share certificate 1864; account books, correspondence and statements re failure 1878–80. [Ref: 22936(125); 39084(2)]

Records 3: Barclays Bank plc, Group Archives, Dallimore Road, Wythenshawe, Manchester M23 9JA

Cheque form 1867; letter from branch manager 1878.

WEST RIDING UNION BANK LTD
Huddersfield, West Yorkshire

History: This joint stock bank traced its origins to the private bank of Benjamin Wilson (est. 1799) of Mirfield which was later known as Benjamin Wilson & Sons and, from about 1822, as Benjamin Wilson, Sons & Co. It subsequently opened an office at nearby Huddersfield. In 1833 the business was converted into a joint stock bank, the Mirfield & Huddersfield District Banking Co, in which the Wilson family were important shareholders and managers. In 1834 the Mirfield branch was closed but a new branch was opened at Dewsbury. In 1836 the private Dewsbury bank of Hagues & Cook & Wormald (est. 1818), with offices also at Bradford and Wakefield, was acquired; its Bradford office was closed almost immediately. Shortly afterwards the title was changed to West Riding Union Banking Co and nominal capital was increased from £1 million to £2 million; paid-up capital by 1837 was £37,000. In 1841 much of the Dewsbury business of the Yorkshire District Banking Co (est. 1834) was acquired and in 1858 paid-up capital

Records of banks 535

was increased to £100,000, then to £130,000 in 1864, to £200,000 in 1874 and to £320,000 in 1876. It subsequently grew to £474,000 in 1880 and a year later limited liability was acquired. In 1887, as not all of the bank's capital could be profitably employed, it was reduced to £380,000 through the return of surplus capital to shareholders. By the late 1870s only two branches existed, at Dewsbury and Batley, but in the 1880s branch expansion commenced with openings at Cleckheaton, Heckmondwike, Holmfirth, Lindley, Milnsbridge, Moldsgreen and Slaithwaite, although the Lindley and Slaithwaite branches were soon closed. In 1890 another capital reduction exercise was carried out, reducing paid-up capital to £316,000. While deposits rose from £1.25 million in 1883 to £1.9 million in 1901, profits declined and the bank became increasingly unviable. In 1902 this led to amalgamation with the Lancashire & Yorkshire Bank Ltd (est. 1872). There were then nine branches and five sub-branches.

George Chandler, *Four Centuries of Banking* (London, 1964–68)

Records: Barclays Bank plc, Group Archives, Dallimore Road, Wythenshawe, Manchester M23 9JA

Deeds of settlement 1832–36; directors' meeting minute books (8) 1832–1902; applications for clerkships 1832; staff bond 1833–34; branch statistics including profit and loss 1833–77; salary book 1836–1939; deed of accession 1837; private ledgers (3) 1840–1902; list of shareholders 1847; annual reports 1863–1902; declaration of secrecy 1897.

WEST YORKSHIRE BANK LTD
Halifax, West Yorkshire

History: This bank was formed as the Halifax Joint Stock Banking Co in 1829 with a paid-up capital of £17,500; it was one of England's first joint stock banks. Initially it did not open branches, disapproving of them in principle, but between 1873 and 1913 twenty-nine branches and sub-branches were opened including ones at Sowerby Bridge (1873), Huddersfield (1874), Bradford (1883), Leeds (1903), Ilkley (1906) and Keighley (1910). Its paid-up capital increased from £66,000 in 1853, to £200,000 in 1875 and to £300,000 in 1890. In 1875 it acquired limited liability and in 1911 merged with its rival, the Halifax & Huddersfield Union Banking Co Ltd (est. 1836) to form the West Yorkshire Bank Ltd which had a paid-up capital of £400,000. In 1919, when the bank had thirty-four offices, 215 staff, 29,000 accounts and £10 million deposits, it was acquired by Lloyds Bank Ltd (est. 1765).

H Ling Roth, *The Genesis of Banking in Halifax with Side Lights on Country Banking* (Halifax, 1914)

536 *British banking – a guide to historical records*

Records: Lloyds TSB Group plc, Archives, Head Office, 71 Lombard Street, London EC3P 3BS

Chairman's agenda (5) 1910–21; memorandum and articles of association 1911; directors' meeting minute book 1914–20; board committee minute book 1915–22; amalgamation papers 1919–35.

Bradford: memorandum book 1905–13; **Huddersfield:** manager's diaries (3) 1884, 1888, 1912–21; **Leeds:** manager's diaries (2) 1909–19; **Milnsbridge:** manager's diary 1911–49; **Todmorden:** manager's diaries (2) 1898–1935.

THOMAS WHEELER & CO
High Wycombe, Buckinghamshire

History: This private bank was formed in 1812 by Robert Wheeler and his sons, Robert and Thomas; at the same time they purchased a brewery which they managed alongside their bank. Thomas Wheeler took over as senior partner following the death of his father and brother and admitted his son and nephew, Francis and George, to the partnership. Branches were opened in 1889 at Beaconsfield, Amersham and Princes Risborough. The bank was acquired by Capital & Counties Bank Ltd (est. 1877) in 1896.

Records: Lloyds TSB Group plc, Archives, Head Office, 71 Lombard Street, London EC3P 3BS

Amalgamation papers 1896.

WHITCHURCH & ELLESMERE BANKING CO LTD
Whitchurch, Shropshire

History: This joint stock bank was formed in 1840. It was in difficulties in 1878 and in 1880 acquired limited liability. It was acquired by Lloyds Banking Co Ltd (est. 1765) in 1881.

Records: Lloyds TSB Group plc, Archives, Head Office, 71 Lombard Street, London EC3P 3BS

Amalgamation papers 1881.

WHITEHAVEN JOINT STOCK BANK LTD
Whitehaven, Cumbria

History: This joint stock bank was established in 1829 as the Whitehaven Joint Stock Bank. Its paid-up capital was £28,050 and a branch was soon opened at Penrith. Limited liability was acquired in 1888. In 1908 the

Records of banks
537

bank was purchased by Parr's Bank Ltd (est. 1865). It then had branches at Penrith, Maryport, Egremont, Seascale, Cleator Moor, Harrington and Shap. Paid-up capital was £60,150 and deposits were £621,000.

T E Gregory, *The Westminster Bank Through a Century* (London, 1936)

Records: The Royal Bank of Scotland plc, Archive Section, Regent's House, 42 Islington High Street, London N1 8XL

Deeds of settlement 1829–73; papers re transfer of shares 1837–88; statement of money lent and securities 1842; correspondence with customers 1834–1901; annual reports 1846–76; papers re bank investments 1847–1907; balance sheets 1848–60; statement of correspondents' accounts 1848–49; rough board minutes 1857–63; weekly statements of London remittances 1858–59; letters re recruitment of staff 1862–83; general manager's correspondence with his family 1869–83; regulations and provisions 1888; amalgamation papers 1908.

WIGAN, MERCER, TASKER & CO
Maidstone, Kent

History: This private bank was established in 1818 as Wigan, Mercer, Tasker & Co; it was otherwise known as the Kentish Bank. It was acquired by the Union of London & Smiths Bank Ltd (est. 1839) in 1903.

Records: The Royal Bank of Scotland plc, Archive Section, Regent's House, 42 Islington High Street, London N1 8XL

Premises rental agreement 1818; partnership agreement 1821; declaration of confidence 1826; amalgamation papers 1903–05.

WIGNEY & CO
Brighton, East Sussex

History: This private bank was established in 1796 as Wigney & Co and was otherwise known as the Brighthelmston Bank. It failed in 1842.

Records: Barclays Bank plc, Group Archives, Dallimore Road, Wythenshawe, Manchester M23 9JA

Bill of exchange 1826.

WILKINS & CO
Brecon, Powys

History: This private bank was established in 1778 as Wilkins, Jeffreys Wilkins & Williams; it was also known as Brecon Old Bank. Of the four original partners, Walter and Jeffreys Wilkins had worked abroad with the

538   *British banking – a guide to historical records*

East India Co. The firm largely served the local agricultural community and opened branches throughout South Wales, at Merthyr Tydfil (1812), Haverfordwest (1832), Carmarthen (1834), Cardigan (1835), Llanelli (1837), Aberdare (1854), Cardiff (1856) and Dowlais (1875). Wilkins was acquired by Lloyds Bank Ltd (est. 1765) in 1890.

Francis Green, 'Early Banks in West Wales', *Transactions of the Historical Society of West Wales*, 6 (1916); Susan Loram, *John Parry Wilkins and 'The Old Bank'* (priv. pub., 1978); R O Roberts, 'The Operations of The Brecon Old Bank Wilkins & Co 1778–1890', *Business History*, 1 (1958)

Records: Lloyds TSB Group plc, Archives, Head Office, 71 Lombard Street, London EC3P 3BS

Amalgamation papers 1889–1927.

Carmarthen: security register 1834–67.

WILLIAMS & CO
Chester, Cheshire

History: This private bank was formed in 1792 and was otherwise known as Chester Old Bank. Initially it was closely connected with the copper mining industry of Anglesey. Roberts & Co (est. 1792) of Caernarvon was acquired in 1796. The bank expanded by opening offices throughout North Wales where it came to be one of the largest banks. Branches were opened at Caernarvon (1796), Bangor (1823), Llanfairfechan (1884), Port Dinorwic (1886), Llangefni (1889), Wrexham (1889), Connah's Quay (1889), Hawarden (1890), Penmaenmawr (1891) and Amlwch. This business was acquired by Lloyds Bank Ltd (est. 1765) in 1897.

Records 1: Lloyds TSB Group plc, 71 Lombard Street, London EC3P 3BS

Balance sheets 1801, 1807, 1891–96; half-yearly balance sheets 1821–30; staff record book c.1850–95; partnership agreements 1879–81; amalgamation papers 1897–1912.

Chester: memorandum books (6) 1881–99; **Bangor:** memorandum book 1874–94; letterbook 1886–94.

Records 2: City of Chester Archives, Town Hall, Chester CH1 2HJ

Papers re partnership 1817–90; half-yearly balance book 1877–97; profit and loss account book 1885–96; papers and accounts re premises rebuilding 1892–97; amalgamation papers 1895–97; papers re accounts of certain customers late nineteenth cent.

Records of banks 539

Records 3: Gwynedd Archives Service, County Offices, Caernarfon LL55 1SH

Caernarfon: miscellaneous papers 1802–84; letter of credit 1811; passbooks 1829–42, 1887–94; letterbook 1852–72; centenary dinner menu 1892. [Ref: XM 923/202–211; X Vaynol 5049–50, 4916; X Poole 6670]

WILLIAMS & GLYN'S BANK LTD
London

History: This clearing bank was established in 1970 through the merger of three London-based clearing bank subsidiaries of National & Commercial Banking Group Ltd – Glyn, Mills & Co (est. 1753), Williams Deacon's Bank Ltd (est. 1836) and The National Bank Ltd (est. 1835) – which had been formed in 1969 through the merger of The Royal Bank of Scotland Ltd and National Commercial Bank of Scotland Ltd. By 1974 the new bank had 320 branches. Through innovation in advertising and service, for example pioneering free banking for personal customers in credit, it became a major force in English banking, ranking just behind the big four London clearing banks. In 1985 its business was merged fully with that of The Royal Bank of Scotland and thereafter traded as The Royal Bank of Scotland plc, being ultimately owned by The Royal Bank of Scotland Group plc.

Records: The Royal Bank of Scotland plc, Archive Section, Regent's House, 42 Islington High Street, London N1 8XL

Directors' meeting minutes 1969–70; premises ledgers 1969–70; corporate planning papers 1969–70; Williams & Glyns Bank Act 1970; monthly banking statistics 1970; branch photographs 1970–85; papers re student promotions 1970.

WILLIAMS, DEACON & CO
London

History: This private bank was established as Raymond, Vere, Lowe & Fletcher in Cornhill, City of London, in 1771 and subsequently moved to Birchin Lane nearby. The bank operated under many names including Lowe, Vere, Williams & Jennings from 1778; Vere, Williams, Son, Wilkinson & Drury from 1788; Williams, Son & Drury from 1792; Williams, Son, Moffat, Burgess & Lane from 1812; and Williams, Williams, Burgess & Williams from c.1822. In 1825 the bank stopped payment, following the collapse of Pole, Thornton & Co (est. 1773), bankers of City of London, and was reformed with new partners as Williams, Deacon, Labouchere & Co in 1826. It was known as Williams, Deacon, Labouchere,

540   *British banking – a guide to historical records*

Thornton & Co from 1828; Williams, Deacon, Thornton & Co from 1863; and Williams, Deacon & Co from 1882. In 1890 it was taken over by Manchester & Salford Bank Ltd (est. 1836), bankers of Manchester, for which it had acted as London agent since 1836, to form Williams Deacon & Manchester & Salford Bank Ltd. The head office of the merged bank was established in Birchin Lane, City of London, in order to retain Williams, Deacon & Co's membership of the London Clearing House.

Anon, *Williams Deacon's, 1771–1970* (Manchester, 1971)

Records 1: The Royal Bank of Scotland plc, Archive Section, Regent's House, 42 Islington High Street, London N1 8XL

Articles of partnership 1808; solicitors' bills of charges 1816–20, 1868–81; signature books 1824–37, 1848–90; papers re customer advances 1824–57; opinion book 1825–59; quarterly profit and loss accounts 1826–38; information book on country bank accounts 1826–58; London office salary book 1828–90; certificates re incorporation, change of name, etc. 1871–90; private letterbooks 1832–90; staff fidelity bonds and guarantee agreements 1836–90; private ledgers 1840–55, 1877–90; staff books 1853–90; notebook of names 1855; monthly journals 1873–90; staff list c.1880; correspondence re payment of postal orders 1881–90.

Records 2: Department of Manuscripts and Special Collections, Hallward Library, University of Nottingham, University Park, Nottingham NG7 2RD

Private papers of R Lowe, partner c.1771–85. [Ref: Drury Lowe collection]

WILLIAMS DEACON'S BANK LTD
Manchester, Greater Manchester, and London

History: This important joint stock bank was established in 1836, as Manchester & Salford Bank, with paid-up capital of £252,000. Williams, Deacon, Labouchere, Thornton & Co were appointed as the bank's London agents. The bank traded from King Street and moved to a new building in Mosley Street in 1838. No note issue was made but the bank took advantage of special discount facilities offered by the Bank of England's Manchester branch. The first branches were opened at Salford (1862), Southport (1865), Ormskirk (1865), Lancaster (1866), Hulme (1867), St Helens (1868) and Chorley (1868). The bank acquired the private banks of Heywood Brothers & Co (est. 1788) of Manchester in 1874, Hardcastle, Cross & Co (est. 1818) of Bolton in 1878, and Clement Royds & Co (est. 1819) of Rochdale in 1881. In 1881 the business was registered as a

Records of banks

limited liability company, Manchester & Salford Bank Ltd, and by December 1881 had a paid-up capital of £757,480. Branches continued to be opened at the rate of about one each year until 1887 when the pace of expansion quickened and twenty-seven branches were opened in just two years. In 1890 the bank, with forty-seven branches, took over its London agent, the private bank of Williams, Deacon & Co (est. 1771) of City of London, to form Williams Deacon & Manchester & Salford Bank Ltd. The head office transferred to London to retain Williams, Deacon & Co's membership of the London Clearing House, and by the end of 1890 the bank had a paid-up capital of £1 million. In 1901 the name was shortened to Williams Deacon's Bank Ltd. In 1907 it acquired Sheffield & Rotherham Joint Stock Banking Co Ltd (est. 1792) and by late 1907 the bank had 102 branches. After the First World War the bank's policy of expansion was resumed, fifty-two new branches were opened between 1919 and 1922 and a huge programme of branch refurbishment was initiated. However, the bank was badly affected by the recession and in 1930 it was acquired by The Royal Bank of Scotland Ltd (est. 1727) of Edinburgh. However it continued to trade separately with its own Manchester-based head office and board of directors. The principal London office was rebuilt in 1936 and a number of new metropolitan branches were opened in subsequent years, bringing the total number of offices in London to eight by 1939. During the Second World War the bank temporarily closed twenty-nine offices. From the 1950s the directors decided to widen its geographical coverage and new offices were opened in the south, East Anglia and the Midlands. During the 1960s Williams Deacon's Bank was amongst the first of the clearing banks to recognise the potential of offshore financial centres and established a presence in the Channel Islands. A new head office building was opened in Manchester in 1963. In 1970 Williams Deacon's Bank merged with other English banks within the National & Commercial Banking Group Ltd, namely Glyn, Mills & Co Ltd (est. 1753) and The National Bank Ltd (est. 1836), to form Williams & Glyn's Bank Ltd.

Anon, *Williams Deacon's 1771–1970* (Manchester, 1971); Leo H Grindon, *Manchester Banks and Bankers* (Manchester, 1877); William Howarth, *The Banks in the Clearing House* (London, 1905); William Howarth, *Our Leading Banks* (London, 1894)

Records: The Royal Bank of Scotland plc, Archive Section, Regent's House, 42 Islington High Street, London N1 8XL

Deeds of settlement 1836, 1876; provisional committee meeting minute book 1836; managing director's correspondence and papers 1836–38, 1866–69; declaration of secrecy registers 1836–1903; directors' meeting minute

542   *British banking – a guide to historical records*

book: 1836–1970, rough 1836, London directors 1935–70; share journal 1836–1919; private ledgers 1836–75; general ledger 1836–76; staff applications correspondence 1836–38, 1898; balance charts book 1836–1930; common place book 1837–54; banker's licences 1837–77; lists of shareholders 1837, 1881–89; general meetings minute book 1837–1954; annual reports 1837–1969; cash books 1838–43; managing director's out letterbook to other banks 1841–73; papers re bad debts 1848, 1866–69, 1879–86; desk diaries of William Langton 1862, 1864, 1865; doubtful debts memorandum book 1864–1900; particulars of branches books 1865–1970; staff photographs 1866, 1911, 1934–40; architectural drawings 1867–1957; seal order book 1870–98; certificates of incorporation, change of name, etc 1871–1907; general letterbooks 1873–1957; Oliver Heywood's private notebooks 1874–79; circulars to shareholders 1874, 1901, 1926–27; manager's record books c.1874–1925; remembrancers 1874–1954; papers re resignation of Oliver Heywood 1878–1950; merger papers: Hardcastle, Cross & Co 1878–82, Sheffield & Rotherham Bank 1884–1945, other banks, unimplememted 1921–24, The Royal Bank of Scotland 1928–30, Williams & Glyn's Bank c.1970; staff and partners cartoons c.1879–1914; weekly balance book, other banks 1879–85; correspondence from customers 1879–1900; authorised signatures list c.1881; registration of the bank as a limited company 1881; salary sheets 1881–90; papers re agreements re Mosley Street premises 1881, 1923; property ledgers: 1881–1933, sheets 1937–70; share transfers balance book 1882–87; general manager's customer record books 1882–1900; cheque and cheque book 1883–90; correspondence from American banks re Louisiana bond coupons 1883–89; correspondence with the Bank of Liverpool 1886–1900; summary balance table c.1886; letters from shareholders re changes of details 1886; circulars 1888–1970; photographs: branches c.1880s, 1921–70, mobile banks c.1950s; staff books 1890–1900; staff fidelity bonds and guarantees 1890–1900; correspondence with the Bank of England re guarantees 1890–1906; papers re Banker's Guarantee and Trust Fund 1890–1919; monthly balance sheets and statements of account 1890–26; correspondence with branches 1890–1936; general manager's papers, incl copy telegrams c.1890–1924,1945–70; papers re Manchester Exchange Bill 1891–1912; private statistics book re balances 1891–1925; register of stock of John Deacon and Robert Williams 1892–93; annual lists of shareholders 1892–96; branch property correspondence c.1892–1968; pensions ledger 1895–1900; general manager's salary papers 1895–1900; specification for decorating work, St Ann Street branch 1898; balance books: monthly 1898–1958, weekly London office 1911–19; papers re British Wagon Co Ltd 1898–1968; blank letter of credit c.1890s; agreements for engagement of commissioners 1900; papers re half-yearly results: R T Hindley 1918–30, Leslie Fletcher 1968–69, profit and loss summary books c.1900–68;

Records of banks 543

papers re Central Association of Bankers 1903–15; guarantee book 1906–39; papers re administration of staff sport and social clubs 1907–68; list of branches c.1907; head office memoranda files 1907–70; directors' rotation books 1908–69; correspondence with the Public Trustee Office 1910; balance sheets analysis, Manchester banks 1911–15; papers re board of directors 1911–63, 1922–36; authorised signature books 1912–36; papers re emergency legislation 1914–15; tax papers: income tax 1914–18, 1943–62, excess profits tax 1930–49, 1935–46, cheque clearing tax evasion 1942–50; statement re loans, advances, overdrafts and reserves 1916–17; correspondence re setting off balances for the balance sheet 1917; papers re gold standard and gold reserves 1917–25; reserves books 1917–65; papers re new share issue 1918–19; statement of comparison of profit and loss accounts 1921–22; papers re mechanisation and computerisation 1924–70; committee minutes: office administration 1925–27, London office building 1933, Manchester 1966–68, English merger 1969–67; board papers 1925–70; London statistics ledger 1926–41; papers re advertising 1926–67; correspondence and circulars re Exports Credits Guarantee Department c.1927–34; share transfer: registers 1928–69; registers of directors/managers 1929–69; registers of directors' interests c.1929–31; share transfer forms, share certificates and related correspondence c.1920s, 1953–69; annual returns 1930–59; correspondence with The Royal Bank of Scotland 1930–69; register of shareholders 1930–69; papers re rebuilding of the Birchin Lane premises 1932–38; annual information sheets 1932–41; papers re chairman's general meeting speeches 1932–64; out-letterbooks: 1957–70, The Royal Bank of Scotland 1934–69, National & Commercial Banking Group 1969–70; rules of widows' and orphans' fund 1935; Christmas cards 1936–38, 1954–57; directors' remuneration papers 1936–69; weekly balance sheets for the London Foreign Department 1937–38; papers re emergency banking procedures 1938–44; staff wartime passes 1940; correspondence re war damage to properties that were securities for advances 1940; wartime account returns 1940–44; half-yearly balance papers 1940–52; papers re national savings certificates 1940–62; branch guarantees book 1944–58; general instructions books c.1944–70; report on branch profitability 1945–69; papers re branch closures and opening hours 1945–56, 1964–67; property valuations 1953–58; group statistics file re returns on capital 1955–66; papers re visits to foreign banks c.1955–70; papers re Radcliffe Committee on the Working of the Monetary System 1957–60, c.1967; minute book of council of Williams Deacon's Bank Pension Trust Ltd 1958–65; correspondence with Glyn, Mills & Co 1958–69; papers re central intelligence bureau 1959–62; files re New York office 1960–65; profits statistics 1960–67; Manchester committee attendance book 1961–66; papers re inter-bank lending procedures 1962; papers of management consultants 1963–69; papers re Mosley Street premises

544   *British banking – a guide to historical records*

1963–69; annual summaries of branch property expenses 1963–69; correspondence re banker's card terms and conditions 1966; papers re corporate development 1967–69; papers re protected budget accounts 1967–68; balance book 1967–68; papers re re-organisation of trustee department 1967–69; press advertising schedules 1968; papers re re-organisation of overseas department 1968; details of various balances incl branch profit and loss 1968–69; executive director's conference papers 1969–70; minutes of staff terms and conditions working party 1969–70; correspondence with National & Commercial Banking Group 1969–70.

Bolton: manager's notebook 1878–79; ledger re partner's holdings 1878–89; letterbook 1878–80; customer correspondence 1878–80; papers re customer accounts 1878–81; executorship account ledgers and papers 1878–83; papers re release of securities 1878–86; signing authorities books 1878–89; cash book 1878–99; fire assurance registers 1878–1900; signature books 1878–1900; accounts opened books 1878–1900; passbook, Manchester & Liverpool District Bank 1878–79; press cuttings books 1878–1900; papers re building and repair of premises 1879–81; papers re property and income tax 1878–81; balance book re other banks' accounts 1879–85; enquiries books 1879–91; daily remembrancers 1879–1900; insurance agency records 1878–1900; scribbling journals 1880–82; conduct of accounts book 1880–96; power of attorney 1881; monthly return of overdrafts ledger 1884–1900; inventory and valuation 1885; enquiries books 1879–91; passbook 1878–1900; papers re stored cotton cloth 1897–98; **Bolton, Turton:** property agreement 1889, accounts opened book 1889–1900; **Chorley:** branch profit and loss sheets 1870–1900; **London, Birchin Lane:** private ledgers 1890–92; private letterbooks 1890–96; monthly journals 1890–98; signature books 1890–1900; correspondence re payment of postal orders 1890–1915; **London, Pall Mall:** copy inventory, late nineteenth-early twentieth cent.; securities as bankers registers 1892–1900; accounts opened books 1892–1900; probate register c.1894–1900; remembrancers 1895–1900; stock exchange transactions journals 1895–1900; register of allotment letters, banker's receipts, etc. 1896–1900; securities for advances registers 1896–1900; stock book c.1896–1900; bills discounted day book 1896–1900; **Manchester, Chorlton-cum-Hardy:** register of deposited securities 1869–1900; **Manchester, Corn Exchange:** accounts opened book 1889–1900; **Manchester, Longsight:** branch photographs c.1900; records of securities for advances 1894–1900; **Manchester, Mosley Street:** customer interview book 1876–81; manager's opinion book re business customers 1881; sundries safe custody book 1882–97; index book re customer details c.1885–89; cheque book 1893; accounts opened books 1895–1900; **Manchester, St Ann Street:** papers re dissolution of Heywood Brothers & Co and merger with Manchester &

Records of banks

Salford Bank 1874–76; papers re retirements of Benjamin and Thomas Heywood 1874–76; authorities books 1874–1900; notebook containing staff details 1874–1900; summary of business books 1874–1900; stock book 1874–1900; charges account books 1874–1900; probate registers 1874–1900; customer directories 1874–1900; securities for advances book c.1878–92; accounts closed books 1880–98; safe custody ledger 1886–c.1900; securities ledgers 1889–1900; signature book 1896–1900; profit and loss summary book 1899–1900; inventory of securities left for safe custody 1874–84; monthly summary books 1874–87; unpaid bills 1874–5; photographs of Heywood Brothers & Co partners c.1874–1880s; memorial volume re statue of Oliver Heywood c.1894; **Rochdale:** press cuttings book 1881–82; securities for advances register 1881–98; signature book 1881–1900; accounts opened books 1881–1900; daily remembrancers 1881–1900; safe custody book 1882–97; bill ledger 1886–1900; bill book 1894–1900; **St Helens:** architectural drawings 1867; accounts opened book 1868–90; remembrancer 1877–81; drafts issued book 1896–1900; **Walkden:** papers and plans re new branch 1891–94.

P & H WILLIAMS
Wednesbury, West Midlands

History: This private bank was established in 1809 by Samuel Addison, a grocer, in partnership with his sons, Samuel and John, under the title S Addison & Sons. In 1851 the firm was purchased by P & H Williams, wealthy ironmasters, and in 1865 Lloyds Banking Co Ltd (est. 1765) acquired the bank for £15,000.

Records: Lloyds TSB Group plc, Archives, Head Office, 71 Lombard Street, London EC3P 3BS

Amalgamation papers 1865.

WILLIAMS & ROWLAND
Neath, West Glamorgan

History: This bank was established in 1821 by Rees Williams and John Rowlands of Neath. Its customers were drawn from Neath's agricultural and marine industries. The business amalgamated with Eaton, Knight & Stroud (est. 1828) of Swansea to form the Glamorganshire Banking Co in 1836.

Records: Lloyds TSB Group plc, Archives, Head Office, 71 Lombard Street, London EC3P 3BS

Customer ledger 1826–35.

546 *British banking – a guide to historical records*

WILLIAMS & SONS
Dolgellau, Gwynedd

History: This private bank was formed in about 1803 as Thomas & Hugh Jones, drawing many of its customers from the local web, slate quarrying and agricultural industries. From 1819 it was known as Jones & Williams and from 1853 as Williams & Sons; it was otherwise known as the Old Merionethshire Bank. Early on, it opened a branch at Barmouth. The business was acquired by the North & South Wales Bank (est. 1836) in 1873.

W F Crick & J E Wadsworth, *A Hundred Years of Joint Stock Banking* (London, 1936)

Records: HSBC Holdings plc, Group Archives, 10 Lower Thames Street, London EC3R 6AE

List of partners 1873; papers re sale of business 1873.

R & R WILLIAMS, THORNTON, SYKES & CO
Dorchester, Dorset

History: This private bank traced its origins to 1786 when it was established by Robert Albion Cox and Henry Mander. In 1790, on the death of Cox, a new partnership was formed under the title of Williams, Cox & Co. Branches were opened at Swanage (1825), Lyme Regis (1833), Wareham (c.1833), Axminster (1834), Weymouth (1835), Sturminster Newton (1836), Seaton (1868), Bournemouth (1884) and Boscombe (1890). In 1878 the business was renamed R & R Williams, Thornton, Sykes & Co and was also known as Dorsetshire Bank. It was acquired by the Wilts & Dorset Banking Co Ltd (est. 1835) in 1897.

Records 1: Lloyds TSB Group plc, Archives, Head Office, 71 Lombard Street, London EC3P 3BS

Balance sheets 1839–97; private ledgers (2) 1876–97; amalgamation papers 1897.

Records 2: Dorset Record Office, Bridport Road, Dorchester DT1 1RP

Papers of John Brown, including agreement to rent banking room 1832–39. [Ref: D141: B1–2]

WILLIAM WILLIAMS, BROWN & CO
Leeds, West Yorkshire

History: This private bank was formed in 1813 to provide services to the local woollen cloth trade. The bank was initially styled Nicholson, Brown & Co but was known as William Williams, Brown & Co from 1824; it was

Records of banks **547**

otherwise styled Leeds Union Bank. It was connected with the London Bank of Brown, Janson & Co (est. 1813). It was acquired by Lloyds Bank Ltd (est. 1765) in 1900.

Records: Lloyds TSB Group plc, Archives, Head Office, 71 Lombard Street, London EC3P 3BS

Profit and loss ledger 1844–57; indemnities 1852–99; private memorandum books (4) 1872–94; amalgamation papers 1900.

WILLIS, PERCIVAL & CO
London

History: This City of London firm traced its origins to the goldsmith business of Thomas Williams who traded at the sign of The Crown in Lombard Street in 1677. By 1698 Benjamin Tudman, a 'goldsmith and bancker [*sic*] in Linnen' was at the address. In about 1708 he was joined by Stephen Child, formerly of the bankers, Child & Co, when the business was renamed Tudman & Child. Frequent name changes followed as new partners joined: Stephen Child, Thomas Greene & Mathias Eades by 1713; Greene & Eades by 1718; Greene & Tysoe by 1735; Tysoe, Willis & Reade by 1752; Willis & Reade by 1755; Reade, Moorhouse & Co by 1774; Moorhouse, Willis & Reade by 1778; Willis, Wood & Co by 1787; Willis, Wood, Percival & Co by 1792; and finally Willis, Percival & Co by 1814. The bank, *inter alia*, financed international trade, in particular cargoes of sugar from the West Indies in the 1780s. In 1878 the collapse of a large customer, a Greek firm of importers, caused the bank to suspend payment with liabilities of about £500,000. It was acquired by the Hampshire & North Wilts Banking Co Ltd (est. 1834), for the nominal sum of £9,000 and the payment of £238,000 to creditors at the rate of almost 50p in the pound. In making this acquisition, the Hampshire Bank made an unsuccessful attempt to gain access to the London Clearing House.

F G Hilton Price, *A Handbook of London Bankers* (London, 1876); R S Sayers, *Lloyds Bank in the History of English Banking* (Oxford, 1957)

Records: Lloyds TSB Group plc, Archives, Head Office, 71 Lombard Street, London EC3P 3BS

Partnership agreement 1812.

WILLYAMS, WILLYAMS & CO
Truro, Cornwall

History: This private bank was formed in 1759 as Sir William Lemon Bart., Furly, Lubbock, Willyams & Co and was connected to the London

548   *British banking – a guide to historical records*

bank of Sir William Lemon, Buller, Furley, Lubbock & Co (est. 1772, later known as Robarts, Lubbock & Co. It was later known as Bassett & Co; as Rodd, Willyams & Gould from 1797; as Willyams, Willyams & Co from 1809; as Daniell, Willyams, Vivian & John; as Daniell, Willyams, Vivian & Co to 1859; and as Willyams, Willyams & Co from 1859 to 1890. The bank was otherwise known as the Miners' Bank. In 1890 it was acquired by Bolitho, Foster, Coode & Co Ltd (est. 1867) of Penzance.

P W Matthews & Anthony W Tuke, *History of Barclays Bank Ltd* (London, 1926)

Records 1: Barclays Bank plc, Group Archives, Dallimore Road, Wythenshawe, Manchester M23 9JA

Letter 1797; cheque forms and receipts 1843–90.

Records 2: Cornwall County Record Office, County Hall, Truro TR1 3AY

Partnership agreements (3) 1771–78; minute book 1794–1806; accounts 1806–08; correspondence re partnership matters 1808, 1827. [Ref: BU 431; W 78; W 79/1–2; AD 59(3)/2]

WILTS & DORSET BANKING CO LTD
Salisbury, Wiltshire

History: This joint stock bank was formed in 1835 and immediately pursued an aggressive policy of branch opening. As early as 1836, twenty-four branches were open, all within sixty miles of Salisbury. The bank grew steadily and from the 1860s the branch network was extended into Somerset, Hampshire, Gloucestershire and Devon, including places such as Southampton and Bristol. Much expansion was by acquisition of private country banks including Luce & Co (est. 1835) of Malmesbury in 1836; Gundry & Co (est. 1809) of Chippenham in 1837; John West (est. 1800) of Lymington in 1848; Tice & Welch (est. 1837) of Christchurch in 1849; Storey & Thomas (est. 1816) of Shaftesbury in 1855; Ledgard & Sons (est. 1821) of Poole in 1861; William Footner & Sons (est. 1807) of Romsey in 1873; Sealy & Prior (est. 1790) of Bridgewater in 1875; W Hancock & Son (est. 1803) of Wiveliscombe in 1890; Pinckney Brothers (est. 1811) of Salisbury in 1897; and R & R Williams, Thornton, Sykes & Co (est. 1786) of Dorchester in 1897. By 1914 the bank was one of the largest in southern England with 100 branches and over 110,000 accounts. It was acquired by Lloyds Bank Ltd (est. 1765) in 1914.

R S Sayers, *Lloyds Bank in the History of English Banking* (Oxford, 1957)

Records of banks 549

Records 1: Lloyds TSB Group plc, Archives, Head Office, 71 Lombard Street, London EC3P 3BS

Provisional committee minute book 1835; deed of settlement and supplements 1835–65; shareholders' register 1835–53; annual reports 1835–1914; note registers (8) 1835–1914; balance sheets 1841–72 [w]; seal registers (8) 1874–1924; amalgamation papers including letterbooks (7) 1914.

Axminster: salary book 1886–1914; **Bath:** security register 1867–91; signature books (2) c.1867–92; memorandum books (2) 1889–1921; **Bournemouth:** memorandum book 1895–1917; **Bristol:** signature books (6) 1872–1915; salary book 1872–1914; **Cardiff, St Mary Street:** new business and memorandum books (2) 1903–16; **Dorchester:** signature books (2) 1861–98; **Glastonbury:** signature books (2) 1864–98; **Highbridge:** salary book 1905–72; **Lymington:** salary book 1890–1900; head office instructions 1899–1914; **Malmesbury:** signature books (2) 1883–1915; letterbook 1909; **Melksham:** signature books (2) 1868–1917; security register 1877–86; **Mere:** security/bond register c.1836–83; **Pewsey:** head office instructions 1903–14; **Plymouth:** signature book 1892–1900; **Poole:** security register 1861–80; salary book 1885–1938; **Poole, Parkstone:** salary ledger 1895–1951; **Radstock:** head office instructions 1904–14; **Salisbury:** security registers (6) c.1856–1905; advances register 1908–13; **Southampton:** signature books (5) 1875–1917; security registers (2) 1869–90; **Taunton:** security register 1864–75; memorandum book 1886–1906; **Trowbridge:** memorandum book 1895–1911; salary book 1885–1934; **Weymouth:** signature book 1861–85; **Wimborne:** signature books (2) 1861–97; inward correspondence 1862–90 [w]; **Wootton Bassett:** letterbook 1890–1926; **Yeovil:** security register 1869–84.

Records 2: Dorset Record Office, Bridport Road, Dorchester DT1 1RP

Prospectus n.d.; abstract of title, Dorchester premises 1882.

Bridport: passbooks of G T Gollop 1873–84. [Ref: D/ASH(B):X3, E8; D/ASH(A): F19]

WISE, BAKER & BENTALL and WISE, FARNWELL, BAKER & BENTALL
Totnes and Newton Abbott, Devon

History: This private bank was formed in about 1792 as Wise, Farnwell & Bentall and was subsequently known as Wise, Barker & Bentall; it also traded as the Totnes Bank. It was associated with Wise, Farnwell, Baker & Bentall of Newton Abbott, also known as the Newton Bank, which was formed in 1815. Both banks failed in 1841.

550   *British banking – a guide to historical records*

Records: Devon Record Office, Castle Street, Exeter EX4 3PU

Partnership agreements 1792–1807; correspondence 1840–45; papers re failure 1842–49. [Ref: 872 A/PZ 154, 155; 924 B/TC 48; 924 B/B 4/1; 2192 B/B 6,7]

WOLVERHAMPTON & STAFFORDSHIRE BANKING CO LTD
Wolverhampton, West Midlands

History: This joint stock bank was established in 1832. In 1889, when its paid-up capital was £100,000, it amalgamated with the Birmingham, Dudley & District Banking Co Ltd (est. 1836) to form the Birmingham, District & Counties Banking Co Ltd.

Records: Barclays Bank plc, Group Archives, Dallimore Road, Wythenshawe, Manchester M23 9JA

Deed of settlement 1831; bank notes 1870–87; warrants 1889.

WOODALL, HEBDEN & CO
Scarborough, North Yorkshire

History: This private bank was formed in 1788 as Bell, Woodall, Tindall & Taylor; most of its partners were shipowners or merchants and their partnership capital was £2,000. The bank was known as Woodall, Tindall & Taylor from 1791; as Woodall, Tindall, Hebden & Co from 1840; and as Woodall, Hebden & Co from 1863; it also traded as Scarborough Bank and later as Scarborough Old Bank. In 1896 it was one of twenty leading banks that merged to form Barclay & Co Ltd.

P W Matthews & Anthony W Tuke, *History of Barclays Bank Ltd* (London, 1926); Maberly Phillips, *Banks, Bankers and Banking in Northumberland, Durham and North Yorkshire* (London, 1894)

Records: Barclays Bank plc, Group Archives, Dallimore Road, Wythenshawe, Manchester M23 9JA

Current account ledgers 1788–91; waste books 1794–1816; stock journals 1794–1816; bank note registers 1821–1903; schedule of outstanding notes 1821–93; memoranda re bank note indemnities 1866–70; cheque 1874; overdrawn accounts reports 1896; amalgamation papers, Barclay & Co Ltd 1896.

WOODBRIDGE, LACY, HARTLAND, HIBBERT & CO
Uxbridge, Middlesex

History: This private bank was established in 1791 as Norton & Mercer and was carried on alongside the Norton family's milling business; it was

Records of banks 551

otherwise known as Uxbridge Bank and as Uxbridge Old Bank. The bank was acquired by the Hull and Smith families, who were local Quakers, in 1820 when it traded as Hull, Smith & Co. In the 1850s T H Riches, a solicitor, joined the partnership and on his death he was succeeded by another solicitor, Charles Woodbridge. The bank came to be known as Woodbridge, Lacy, Hartland, Hibbert & Co. A sub-branch was opened at Southall in 1879 and in the 1880s and 1890s other branches were opened at Pinner, Northwood, Brentford, Hounslow, Isleworth, Slough, Eton and Windsor. The bank amalgamated with Barclay & Co Ltd in 1900.

P W Matthews & Anthony W Tuke, *History of Barclays Bank Ltd* (London, 1926)

Records 1: Barclays Bank plc, Group Archives, Dallimore Road, Wythenshawe, Manchester M23 9JA

Bank notes 1806–1900; memorandum of deposit of deeds 1878; press cuttings 1881–98; forms of guarantee 1886–89; property papers 1890–1901; alteration of partnership agreement 1894; equitable charges 1896–98; cheque 1898; banker's licence 1898; memorandum re staff salaries 1898; in-letter and photograph, Southall branch construction 1898; advances statement, Windsor branch 1900; papers re takeover by Barclay & Co Ltd 1900–10; premises valuation 1901.

Records 2: London Metropolitan Archive, 40 Northampton Road, London EC1R 0HB

Papers re amalgamation 1900–01. [Ref: Acc 538/2nd dep/1058]

THOMAS WOODCOCK, SONS & ECKERSLEY
Wigan, Greater Manchester

History: This private bank was established in 1792 as Thicknesse & Woodcocks; it was otherwise known as Wigan Old Bank. It was styled Thomas Woodcock, Sons & Eckersley from 1833 and was acquired by Parr's Banking Co Ltd (est. 1865) in 1874 for £80,000.

T E Gregory, *The Westminster Bank Through a Century* (London, 1936)

Records: The Royal Bank of Scotland plc, Archive Section, Regent's House, 42 Islington High Street, London N1 8XL

Customer ledger 1792–98; correspondence with London agents 1800–03; amalgamation agreement 1874.

WOODHEAD & CO
London

552 *British banking – a guide to historical records*

History: This business was established as naval agents in London in c.1804 and was absorbed by Holt & Co (est. 1809) of London in 1915.

Records: The Royal Bank of Scotland plc, Archive Section, Regent's House, 42 Islington High Street, London N1 8XL

Naval precedents book 1781–1801; Admiralty circulars 1860–1905; signature book 1866–1900; bad debts ledger 1871–1900; papers re acquisition by Holt & Co 1914–15.

WOOD, PITT & CO
Tetbury, Gloucestershire

History: This private bank was established in 1792. In 1836 it was reconstructed as a joint stock bank known as the County of Gloucester Bank.

Records: Gloucester Library, Local Studies Dept, Brunswick Road, Gloucester GL1 1HT

Correspondence re Dursley agency 1817–25. [Ref: 8439 RF 115.103]

WOODS & CO
Newcastle upon Tyne, Tyne & Wear

History: This private bank was formed in 1859 as Woods, Parker & Co, a partnership of shipowners and merchants, to acquire the failing Newcastle, Shields & Sunderland Union Joint Stock Bank (est. 1836). The senior partner was William Woods, a merchant, who had been a major shareholder in the joint stock bank and who had worked hard to revive its fortunes. From 1861 the business was known as Woods & Co and it emerged as a major regional bank with numerous branches. By the 1890s it published annual balance sheets; that for 1893 totalled £1.93 million. In 1897 the bank merged with Barclay & Co Ltd (est. 1896).

P W Matthews & Anthony W Tuke, *History of Barclays Bank Ltd* (London, 1926); Maberly Phillips, *Banks, Bankers and Banking in Northumberland, Durham and North Yorkshire* (London, 1894)

Records: Barclays Bank plc, Group Archives, Dallimore Road, Wythenshawe, Manchester M23 9JA

Partners' accounts ledger 1860–1904; monthly balance sheets 1860–70; standing orders letterbooks 1860–91; signature books 1860–1907; passbook, account with Newcastle, Shields & Sunderland Union Joint Stock Banking Co c.1860–75; banker's licences 1861–62; cheques and cheque books 1867–96; Sunderland premises drawing 1874; in-letters and state-

Records of banks   553

ments 1882–1916; staff rules 1880s–90s; private journal 1897–1903; amalgamation papers 1897.

WOOD, WOOD & CO
Cardiff, South Glamorgan

History: This private bank was formed in 1804 and was otherwise known as the Cardiff Bank. It failed in 1823.

Records: Glamorgan Record Office, Glamorgan Building, King Edward VII Avenue, Cathays Park, Cardiff CF1 3NE

Legal and other papers re John Wood c.1785–1845. [Ref: CL MS 3.639, 3.644, 5.135]

WORRALL & GOLD
Bristol, Avon

History: This private bank was formed in 1764 and was otherwise known as the Exchange Bank. It was known as Worrall, Hale & Newnam from 1774, as Worrall & Blatchley from 1785, as Worrall & Oldham from 1809 and as Worrall & Gold in 1818. It ceased business in 1826.

Records: Gloucester Library, Local Studies Dept, Brunswick Road, Gloucester GL1 1HT

Partnership agreement 1764; papers re partnership matters 1764–96; agreement with cashier 1764. [Ref: OF6 3(1–63)]

WORCESTER CITY & COUNTY BANKING CO LTD
Worcester, Hereford & Worcester

History: This joint stock bank was formed in 1840 as Worcester City & County Banking Co at Worcester where banking was dominated by strong private banks. The bank expanded cautiously and by 1857 had only one branch. Limited liability was acquired in 1865. Rapid expansion then followed and by 1889 twenty-four branches were open, all within a thirty mile radius of Worcester. Customers were involved predominantly in agriculture and minor local industries. The Ludlow & Tenbury Banking Co (est. 1840) was absorbed in 1864 followed in 1876 by Parsons & Co (est. 1837) of Presteigne. In 1889 the bank merged with Lloyds Bank Ltd (est. 1765). It then had twenty-four branches.

R S Sayers, *Lloyds Bank in the History of English Banking* (Oxford, 1957)

Records: Lloyds TSB Group plc, Archives, Head Office, 71 Lombard Street, London EC3P 3BS

554   *British banking – a guide to historical records*

General meeting minute book 1866–89; directors' meeting minute book 1879–89; seal register 1883–95; amalgamation papers 1889–95.

Birmingham, Colmore Row: signature book 1872–84; manager's diaries (14) 1876–89; **Bridgenorth:** status enquiry book 1868–89; **Bromsgrove:** security registers (2) 1863–89; **Cheltenham:** signature book 1875–85; **Gloucester:** signature book 1886–89; **Leominster:** memorandum book 1880–85; manager's diaries (3) 1887–89; **Ludlow:** customers' status book c.1875.

THOMAS WORSWICK SONS & CO
Lancaster, Lancashire

History: This private bank was formed in about 1780 as Andrade & Worswick and was subsequently known as Thomas Worswick, Sons & Co. It failed in 1822.

Records: Lancashire Record Office, Bow Lane, Preston PR1 2RE

Papers re failure 1822; valuation of partners' estate 1822. [Ref: DDPa Box 3]

I & I C WRIGHT & CO
Nottingham, Nottinghamshire

History: This private bank was formed in 1760 by the Wright family, merchants that traded with the Baltic countries in commodities such as timber, iron and hemp. The family had extensive connections with Manchester, Stockport, Hull, Sheffield and other industrial centres in the Midlands and North. Initially the bank traded as John & Ichabod Wright and was renamed Ichabod & Ichabod Charles Wright from about 1830. In 1898 the bank was acquired by Capital & Counties Bank Ltd (est. 1877).

Records 1: Lloyds TSB Group plc, Archives, Head Office, 71 Lombard Street, London EC3P 3BS

Private ledgers (3) 1836–97; minute book 1885–90; weekly balance book 1887–92; amalgamation papers 1897–1904.

Records 2: Nottinghamshire Archives, County House, Castle Meadow Road, Nottingham NG2 1AG

Private diaries of I Wright c.1815–62. [Ref: M5586–8]

WULFF, FORBES & CO
Douglas, Isle of Man

Records of banks

History: This private bank was formed in 1826 by John Wulff, a Swede, and Edward Forbes. In 1836 it was converted into a joint stock bank, the Isle of Man Joint Stock Banking Co, due to pressure from the firm's London agents, Williams Deacon's Bank who were concerned about an escalating overdraft. The reconstituted bank ceased business in 1843.

Ernest Quarmby, *Bank Notes and Banking in the Isle of Man* (London, 1994)

Records: Manx National Heritage Library, Douglas, Isle of Man IM1 3LY

Account book 1828–36

WYLDE & CO
Southwell, Nottinghamshire

History: This private bank was established in 1806 and was otherwise known as the Southwell Bank. It ceased business in 1875.

Records: Nottinghamshire Archives, County House, Castle Meadow Road, Nottingham NG2 1AG

Partner's will 1853. [Ref: M3691]

E W YATES & CO
Liverpool, Merseyside

History: This private bank was established by the Samuel family who subsequently formed the merchant bank of Samuel, Montagu & Co (est. 1853). It was acquired by the Union Bank of Manchester Ltd (est. 1836) in 1904 and provided that bank with its first representation in Liverpool.

Records: Barclays Bank plc, Group Archives, Dallimore Road, Wythenshawe, Manchester M23 9JA

Photographs of Edward and Adelaide Yates 1880s; apprenticeship indenture 1890; power of attorney 1899.

YORK CITY & COUNTY BANK LTD
York, North Yorkshire

History: This joint stock bank was formed in 1830 as York City & County Banking Co and became one of England's leading provincial banks. Initially paid-up capital was £22,000 and by the first year end deposits reached £62,000 and the first branch was opened at Malton. In 1832 the business of the failed private bank of Scholfield, Clarkson & Clough (est. 1809) of Howden and Selby was acquired and, at about the same time, agencies were opened at Scarborough and Goole. In 1833 Fletcher, Stubbs & Stott (est.

556   *British banking – a guide to historical records*

c.1813) of Boroughbridge was acquired, followed by the acquisitions of Farrer, Williamson & Co (est. 1801) of Ripon in 1838, Richardson, Holt & Co (est. 1786) of Pickering and Whitby in 1843 and Frankland & Wilkinson (est. 1778) of Whitby in 1845. By the mid-1840s the branch network comprised eight branches and two agencies which had been built up largely through the acquisition of private banks. By 1845 paid-up capital was £100,000 and deposits were £688,000. While expansion of the branch network was modest in the 1850s and 1860s, deposits expanded steadily to reach £1.1 million in 1860. Rapid expansion resumed in the last quarter of the century when the bank extended beyond the agricultural region of North Yorkshire into the iron, steel and engineering districts of North West and North East England, although the wool textile areas of the West Riding were largely avoided. This expansion was initiated by the opening of a branch at Middlesborough in 1871. In 1873 the Thirsk branch of Jonathan Backhouse & Co (est. 1774) of Darlington was acquired. This was followed by the acquisition of the private bankers Harding & Co (est. 1802) of Bridlington and Driffield in 1878 and of the Darlington & District Joint Stock Banking Co (est. 1831) for £70,000 in 1883. However, by far the largest amalgamations were those with Hull Banking Co Ltd (est. 1833) in 1894, Barnsley Banking Co Ltd (est. 1832) in 1896 and Cumberland Union Banking Co Ltd (est. 1829) in 1901. In the 1890s the small Borough of Tynemouth Trading Bank (est. 1885) of North Shields was also acquired and branches were opened at Sheffield and Rotherham. In 1883 limited liability was taken up and subsequently the bank's title was shortened to York City & County Bank Ltd. By 1900 paid-up capital reached £720,000 and deposits stood at over £9 million. In 1909, when the bank had ninety branches and as many sub-branches and agencies, it amalgamated with the London Joint Stock Bank Ltd (est. 1836).

W F Crick & J E Wadsworth, *A Hundred Years of Joint Stock Banking* (London, 1936)

Records: HSBC Holdings plc, Group Archives, 10 Lower Thames Street, London EC3R 6AE

Prospectus 1830; deed of settlement 1830; directors' meeting minute books (42) 1830–1916; general ledgers (2) 1830–74; branch security books (71) 1833–1902; annual reports 1839–1909; branch memorandum book 1841–51; branch reports and balance sheets 1874–1910; annual meeting reports 1883–1900; shareholders' minutes 1894–1909; comparison of profits 1896–1900; quarterly balances 1898–1908; branch managers' instruction book 1902; head office circulars 1908–09.

Bridlington: general ledgers (2) 1879–81; **Carlisle:** signature book 1901–08; **Howden:** memorandum book 1842–70; **Hull:** security register and

Records of banks 557

signature book 1892–1909; **Ripon:** memorandum book 1850–75; **Scarborough:** general ledger 1861–71; **Selby:** cash books (2) 1832–83; **Sheffield:** salary book 1898–1909; staff register 1904–09; **South Shields:** security register 1897–1906; **Wakefield:** general ledger 1863–79; **Workington:** manager's memorandum book 1904–09.

B YORKE & CO
Oundle, Northamptonshire

History: This private bank was established in 1801 as D & J Yorke by Daniel and James Yorke; it was otherwise known as the Oundle & Northants Bank. It was styled B Yorke & Co in 1810 and failed in 1861. It was connected with Daniel Yorke & Co (est. 1801) of Peterborough.

Records: Northamptonshire Record Office, Wootton Hall Park, Northampton NN4 9BQ

Account book with Stephen Eaton 1802–10. [Ref: E&C 16]

YORKSHIRE BANKING CO LTD
Leeds, West Yorkshire

History: This joint stock bank traced its origins to the Yorkshire District Banking Co formed in 1834 largely by railway managers and financiers and by businessmen in the iron trade. Its paid-up capital was £600,000, an unusually large amount. Almost immediately the private bank, Perfect & Co (est. c.1809) of Leeds and Pontefract, was acquired followed in 1835 by the private bank, Dresser & Co (est. 1828) of Thirsk and by the Thirsk business of Britain & Co (est. 1801) of Ripon. Coates, Meek & Carter (est. c.1804) of Knaresborough was acquired in 1835. As the bank's name suggested, its aim was to establish a significant branch network and within three years twenty branches had been opened at places as far apart as Richmond, Sheffield, Halifax and Hull. In 1843, following rumours of poor management, a shareholders' committee investigated the bank's business and uncovered serious mismanagement and heavy losses estimated at £500,000 (£400,000 in Leeds). This prompted a reconstruction of the business under the title of the Yorkshire Banking Co. Paid-up capital was written down by three quarters to £150,000 and a few branches were closed including Sheffield branch which formed the nucleus of the new Sheffield Union Banking Co (est. 1843). The revived bank resumed under a new board and new management and had thirteen branches and twelve agencies. By 1844 deposits had recovered to £600,000 and by 1879 they totalled £1.819 million when paid-up capital was £250,000. The business acquired limited liability in 1880. In 1901 London, City & Midland Bank Ltd (est. 1836) acquired the business for the equivalent of £560,000. It

558 *British banking – a guide to historical records*

then had deposits of £5 million, paid-up capital of £375,000 and twenty-four branches and thirty-eight agencies. It was one of England's largest provincial joint stock banks.

W F Crick & J E Wadsworth, *A Hundred Years of Joint Stock Banking* (London, 1936)

Records 1: HSBC Holdings plc, Group Archives, 10 Lower Thames Street, London EC3R 6AE

Deeds of settlement 1834, 1843, 1865; directors' meeting minute books (20) and indexes (14) 1834–1901; shareholders' minute books (2) 1835–50, 1898–1901; staff secrecy declaration book 1835–98; prospectus 1843; investigation committee notebook 1843; half-yearly reports 1843–1901; profit and loss accounts (2) 1843–1902; half-yearly balances 1843–88; auditors' reports on branches (5) 1844–1901; letterbooks (8) 1878–95; head office circulars 1880–98; half-yearly statements 1880–86; board meeting agenda books (8) 1891–1901; share registers (2) 1892–1901; register of directors 1901; amalgamation papers 1901; liquidator's papers 1901–02.

Beverley: general ledgers (4) 1838–52; **Bradford:** staff book 1880–1901; profit and loss book 1887–1901; **Doncaster:** declarations of secrecy 1835–1914; **Goole:** general ledgers 1838–73; **Guiseley:** letterbook 1899–1912; **Huddersfield:** general ledger 1860–71; **Hull:** profit and loss book 1851–1901; **Leeds:** general ledgers (3) 1866–76; **Pontefract:** deposit receipt ledgers (3) 1843–82; **Ripon:** general ledgers (3) 1843–69; note registers (3) 1843–1901; **Thirsk:** declarations of secrecy 1835–1922; general ledgers (2) 1861–73; **Wetherby:** reference book 1870; **York:** note registers (5) 1843–1901.

Records 2: West Yorkshire Archive Service, Leeds District Archives, Chapeltown Road, Sheepscar, Leeds L57 3AP

Deed of settlement and papers re formation 1834; security registers (2) 1834–51; legal papers re claims on bank 1833–48; securities re loans 1844–1901. [Ref: DB 255; DW 911,916; Brooke, North & Goodwin MSS]

YORKSHIRE BANK PLC
Leeds, West Yorkshire

History: This bank traced its origins to the West Riding of Yorkshire Provident Society & Penny Savings Bank which was established in 1859. This bank was guaranteed by local notables and philanthropists in order to encourage working men to leave their savings on deposit. This ideal remained central to the bank until well into the twentieth century,

Records of banks 559

with customers typically comprising individuals on low incomes and small businesses such as local shops. Strict limits were placed on deposit size. Twenty-four 'evening' branches were opened in 1859, growing to 128 a year later when deposits totalled over £23,000. In 1864 these figures were 184 and £95,000 respectively. The first 'daily' branch – being a conventional bank branch as opposed to evening branches which had no premises and might only open for an hour a week – opened in 1865 at Leeds and others followed before 1878 at Bradford, Halifax and Sheffield. In 1894 there were 955 evening branches and sixteen daily ones. The bank was known as The Yorkshire Penny Savings Bank in 1861 and as The Yorkshire Penny Bank in 1871 when it was limited by guarantee. The Halifax Mechanics Institution Penny Bank was acquired in 1864 and in 1867 lending on mortgaged freehold property began. Cheque books were introduced in 1872 in an attempt to attract small business customers. A school bank scheme was introduced in 1874 and flourished in the twentieth century. Financial difficulties in 1911 resulted in the bank being reorganised and acquired by a consortium of eleven large commercial banks. It was renamed The Yorkshire Penny Bank Ltd, but it continued to maintain its savings bank character. From 1921 overdrafts were allowed and in 1926 an executor and trustee department was opened which, by 1939, had dealt with 15,000 executorships. In 1953 the Midland Bank Ltd sold its shareholding to other bank shareholders. From 1948 a policy of closing the remaining 680 evening branches began; only eighty remained by 1955. The bank was renamed Yorkshire Bank Ltd in 1959, initiating a determined attempt to shed its conservative penny bank image. Lending via loans and overdrafts was promoted in the 1960s and expanded rapidly. Finance and leasing subsidiaries were formed. By process of amalgamation, the shareholder banks diminished to four by the early 1970s – National Westminster, Barclays, Lloyds and Williams & Glyn's. In 1990 the bank was acquired by National Australia Group (UK) Ltd.

Leslie J Broomhead, *The Great Oak: A Study of the Yorkshire Bank* (priv. pub., 1981)

Records 1: Yorkshire Bank plc, 20 Merrion Way, Leeds LS2 8NZ

Provisional committee minutes 1856–59; directors' and general minutes 1858 on; minutes of sub-committees for branches 1859–1912; investment register 1850s–68; balance sheets 1860–62; lists of investments 1863–85; rough minutes 1864–1903; accountant's diary 1864–65; histories of the bank 1872, 1881, 1899; security valuations 1878–1907; press cutting books (14) 1887 on; branch book giving hours of opening per branch 1888–1952; branch statistics (10) 1891–1928; chairman's books (6) 1891–1906; 'schedule of loan repayments to local authorities' (3) c.1894–1912; staff

560   *British banking – a guide to historical records*

instructions 1902; staff magazine (4) 1908–11; registers of members and share transfers 1911 on; annual reports 1911 on; chairman's minutes 1911–14; memorandum and articles of association 1911 on; 'statement of transfers of branches' 1911–14; diaries of company secretary 1912–14; summary of debit ledger accounts 1912 on; staff advances books (5) 1917–1940s; staff sports and recreation club minutes 1921–71; working accounts 1925 on; board papers 1930s on; head office circulars 1930s on; staff rules and notes 1930s–1940s; 'school transfer statistics' being annual returns from schools 1935; 'school banks opened and closed record' 1937–38; evening branches registrations of probates and letters of administration re customer wills 1944–50; published accounts 1966 on; signature book n.d.; branch photographs n.d.

Bridlington: press cuttings book 1911–14; **Hebden Bridge:** account register 1909–25; **Scarborough:** premises specification and bill of quantities 1924.

Records 2: British Bankers' Association, 10 Lombard Street, London EC3V 9EL

Papers re reorganisation 1911–16.

YORK UNION BANKING CO LTD
York, North Yorkshire

History: This joint stock bank was formed in 1833 with a nominal capital of £600,000. Branches were opened at Bridlington, Driffield, Market Weighton, Malton, Pickering, Pocklington, Scarborough and Thirsk. Subbranches were also opened at, *inter alia*, Easingwold, Helmsley and Kirby Moorside. In 1883 limited liability was taken up and in 1892 Simpson, Chapman & Co (est. c.1785), bankers at Whitby, was acquired. In 1894 Pease, Hoare & Pease (est. 1754) of Hull and Machell, Pease & Hoare (est. 1797) of Beverley were also acquired. In 1902 the bank amalgamated with Barclay & Co Ltd (est. 1896).

P W Matthews & Anthony W Tuke, *History of Barclays Bank Ltd* (London, 1926); Maberly Phillips, *Banks, Bankers and Banking in Northumberland, Durham and North Yorkshire* (London, 1894)

Records: Barclays Bank plc, Group Archives, Dallimore Road, Wythenshawe, Manchester M23 9JA

Deeds of settlement 1830; directors' meetings minute books (12) 1833–1902; customer ledger 1833–40; correspondence and other papers 1848–1901; interest schedules 1851–68; memorandum books 1866–81; certificates of incorporation 1874–83; bank note circulation statistics 1878–

Records of banks **561**

96; annual balance sheets 1884–1901; shareholder register 1886–1902; seal register 1888–1911; cheques c.1890s–1900s.

Driffield: bank note registers 1833–86; **Pocklington:** deposit receipt 1800s; **Thirsk:** bank note register 1834–90; **York:** bank note registers 1833–86.

YOUNG & SON
London

History: This private bank was established in 1795 in The Borough, South London, as Weston, Pinhorn, Golding, Mewsome & Weston. It was known as Weston, Pinhorn & Weston from 1817, as Sir John Pinhorn, Weston & Son from 1818, as Weston, Young & Bostock from 1824, as Weston & Young from 1831 and as Young & Son from 1847. The bank was acquired by London & Westminster Bank (est. 1834) in 1847.

F G Hilton Price, *A Handbook of London Bankers* (London, 1876)

Records: The Royal Bank of Scotland plc, Archive Section, Regent's House, 42 Islington High Street, London N1 8XL

Register of bills for collection and acceptance 1798.

Lists of records of associations of banks and bankers

ACCEPTING HOUSES COMMITTEE
London

History: Following the sudden outbreak of war in 1914, this committee was formed by a large group of leading London merchant banks heavily exposed to losses through customers in enemy countries being unable to honour acceptances when they fell due for payment. Its representations to the authorities assisted in the establishment of a moratorium on the settlement of acceptances for enemy account. After the war, the committee continued as a loose-knit body which met irregularly to discuss matters of mutual concern, in particular the Standstill arrangements concluded with Germany and other countries in the early 1930s. On the outbreak of war in 1939, the committee was reorganised into a body of fourteen 'recognised' merchant banks with the remaining members being categorised as 'constituents'. After the war, membership stabilised at seventeen first class houses and no constituents. Membership was by invitation, but an essential qualification was the Bank of England's willingness to take members' bills at the finest discount rate. The committee therefore became the forum and mouthpiece of the City's most respected merchant banks. It had premises and a small secretariat that was shared with the Issuing Houses Association. In 1988 the committee's activities were merged with those of the Issuing Houses Association resulting in the formation of the British Merchant Banking and Securities Houses Association, which was later known as the London Investment Banking Association.

Records: Guildhall Library, Aldermanbury, London EC2P 2EJ

Circulars issued to members and constituents 1914–87; committee minutes 1914–88; annual reports and accounts 1920–80; papers re End of War Treasury Scheme etc 1921; accounts and related papers 1924–80; papers re constitution 1936; papers re future administrative arrangements 1936; meeting notices, agenda and papers 1936–88; general meeting minutes 1939–44; membership files 1939–89; technical sub-committee minutes and papers 1940–74; circulars issued to members 1957–79; standing committee of securities managers' minutes and papers 1970–86; standing

Records of trade organisations 563

committee on personnel matters papers 1971–80; standing committee of accountants papers 1971–80; files re membership, constitution, etc 1972–88; standing committee of computer managers' papers 1973–78; export finance sub-committee papers 1975–82; proposed chief cashiers' committee papers 1976.

Note: A thirty-year closure rule is applied. Permission of the London Investment Banking Association is required for access to more recent material.

ASSOCIATION OF BANKERS OF LONDON AND WESTMINSTER
London

History: This association was established in 1788 to represent the mutual interests of London's City and West End bankers. Its primary concern was the reduction of bank fraud. The association appears to have discontinued its work in about 1792.

Records: Guildhall Library, Aldermanbury, London EC2P 2EJ

Extracts (1788–92) from the proceedings of the association 1792.

ASSOCIATION OF ENGLISH COUNTRY BANKERS
Various locations

History: Although an Association of Country Bankers was at work in the 1790s and subsequent attempts were made to organise country banks in defence of their position and rights, a permanent body to represent the interests of banks was not formed until 1874. Its initial remit was 'to oppose the encroachment of the Scotch banks in England', following the establishment of London offices by several Scottish banks from 1864 and more particularly Clydesdale Bank's opening of three Cumberland branches in 1873. This very specific task was quickly overtaken by the work of observing and commenting upon political and legislative issues of concern to private and joint stock country banks. For example, at the end of the nineteenth century the association endeavoured to obtain agreement on publicity for accounts of private banks. As country banks declined in numbers so did the association's influence and in 1919 it merged with the Central Association of Bankers to form the British Bankers' Association.

Records: The Royal Bank of Scotland plc, Archive Section, Regent's House, 42 Islington High Street, London N1 8XL

Papers of the association's treasurer including committee minute book 1874; papers re subscriptions 1879–81; reports and lists of members 1875–82 [w]; circulars 1888–1910.

564   *British banking – a guide to historical records*

BANKING, INSURANCE AND FINANCE UNION (BIFU)
London

History: The union was established in February 1918 as the Bank Officers' Guild by a group of twenty-six bank clerks in Sheffield to represent managerial and clerical staffs in all banks in England and Wales. Membership reached 25,000 in 1924 and a full-time General Secretary was appointed in the 1930s. The Guild was affiliated to the TUC in 1940. In 1941 Barclays became the first major employer to recognise the Guild and the first non-clerical staff were recruited. In 1946 the Bank Officers' Guild merged with the Scottish Bankers Association (est. 1919) to form the National Union of Bank Employees (NUBE). In 1960 NUBE won pay bargaining rights in a number of banks and in 1968, after industrial action, national negotiations were conceded for the first time in the English banking industry and formal negotiating agreements were subsequently drawn up with the major clearing banks. In 1979 NUBE changed its name to Banking, Insurance and Finance Union (BIFU). New headquarters were opened in Wimbledon in 1981, and moved to Raynes Park in 1987. In 1999 BIFU merged with the unions of NatWest and Barclays Bank to form a new finance industry union, UNIFI.

Records 1: Modern Records Centre, University of Warwick Library, Coventry, Warwickshire CV4 7AL

Executive committee minutes 1919–48; general meetings minutes 1919–66; *The Bank Officer*: journal 1919–69 [w], minutes 1921–46, 1952–64; reports of general meeting proceedings 1919–39, 1965–73; benevolent fund committee minutes 1921–62; president's/policy committee minutes 1921–41, 1947–64; executive committee sub-committee minutes 1922–56; ledgers 1922–50; cash books 1922–53; president's Christmas fund appeal cash book 1924–57; staff provident fund and benevolent fund ledgers 1928–51; finance committee minutes 1931–62, 1966–67; general purposes committee minutes 1936–57; salary books 1941–61; annual delegate meeting minutes 1941–74. [Ref: MSS.56]

Records 2: Glasgow University Archives and Business Records Centre, 13 Thurso Street, Glasgow G11 6PE

Joint Negotiating Council minutes and other papers 1970–72; various committee minutes and other papers 1970–85; subject files re particular banks including Bank of Scotland, The Royal Bank of Scotland and Clydesdale Bank 1972–85; Scottish Area Council papers 1975–85; circulars 1970s–85; staff papers 1970s–80s; Scottish Joint Negotiating Council constitution, minutes and other papers 1981–83. [Ref: UGD 291]

BRITISH BANKERS' ASSOCIATION
London

History: The association was established in 1919 through a merger of the Central Association of Bankers and the Association of English Country Bankers. Its objective was to 'perpetuate the lessons of mutual helpfulness which we learnt in the war', by having just one association responsible for promoting the interests of the banking community. The Central Association had been established in 1895 by representatives of the London Clearing House, the West End banks and the Association of English Country Bankers in order to 'safeguard the interests of bankers as a whole...without in any way interfering with the work of the older societies'. From the start the Central Association was a channel for consultation, information and defence of banks, the importance of their collective action having been underlined by such events as the 1890 Baring Crisis. It was not concerned with the professional interests of bank officials which were cared for by the Institute of Bankers. The Association of English Country Bankers had been formed in 1874 to defend the interests of country banks. In the 1930s the British Bankers' Association was closely involved in preparations for the control of the banking system in the event of war. In the 1950s and 1960s it provided the Bank of England with information on bank lending, thereby establishing one of the first channels for the exchange of information between the Bank and the banking industry. The Association's Foreign Exchange Committee was the banking system's representative body in all discussions with the Bank of England on exchange control and exchange market matters. In 1972 the committee was enlarged to include representatives of all recognised banks operating in Britain. In 1991 the Committee of London & Scottish Bankers was subsumed into the Association.

Records: Guildhall Library, Aldermanbury, London EC2P 2EJ

Index to minutes and circulars 1920–36; annual reports 1920–87; minute books (3) 1924–88; Foreign Exchange Committee: committee minute books (2) 1936–71, attendance book 1936–79, sub-committee minutes (24) 1937–70, circulars 1940–65, balance sheets 1949–70; attendance book 1937–72; balance sheets and accounts 1943–85; Banking Information Service papers 1960s on; files re banking industry and policy, internal administration and procedures, etc twentieth cent.

CHARTERED INSTITUTE OF BANKERS
London

History: The Chartered Institute of Bankers was formed in London in 1879 with the prime but not exclusive functions of promoting the educa-

566   British banking – a guide to historical records

tion of bankers and of establishing professional qualifications. Various provident and guarantee funds for bank clerks had already been established as had the *Bankers' Magazine* in 1844 and the shortlived Banking Institute in 1851. The driving force behind the new institute comprised Richard Martin, of Martin & Co, Lindsey Reid and John Butt; Sir John Lubbock, of Robarts, Lubbock & Co, was the first president. By the end of 1879 membership reached 2,000, premises had been acquired, a full-time secretary recruited, and the first steps taken in the establishment of a library. A journal was published and the Institute, despite representing members rather than their employers, initiated a campaign for legislation to reform banking practice (although by the 1890s the importance for the Institute of this particular function had diminished, especially following the establishment of the Central Association of Bankers in 1895). In 1883 the Bank Clerks' Orphanage Fund was established under management of institute officials and in 1901 the Institute acquired management control of the City of London Sanatorium. The upward trend in membership continued with numbers rising from 3,400 in 1898 to over 10,000 by 1914, the growing acceptance of the Institute's examination certificate as a means of career advancement being a powerful explanation for this. From the 1890s the Institute developed provincial lecture programmes and also permitted its examinations to be taken locally within the UK and overseas. In 1913, in an attempt to involve membership more actively in its affairs, local centres were established, around ten being formed by 1914. In the post-war world the Institute focused as never before on the development of its teaching and examination activities. Closer links were forged with local further education colleges, a number of which were officially recognised and became linked to the increased number of local centres. Membership rose from 10,500 in 1919 to almost 40,000 in 1939, with over 14,000 candidates sitting exams by the latter year. Women were eligible for full membership from 1919. In the 1930s the library was developed as a key institute resource and during the war years the Institute's syllabus and examinations system were completely remodelled. A major feature of the post-war period was the increased financial support of the Institute by the banking community, most obviously manifested by the latter's provision of the Institute's premises in Lombard Street. The library and information resources were expanded and international links were greatly extended, for example through the establishment of a network of overseas centres from 1960 onwards. In the 1970s, for the first time, membership exceeded 100,000, of which 30,000 members were based overseas, and the Institute's regime of examinations and qualifications was substantially overhauled. In 1993 the Institute merged with the Chartered Building Societies Institute.

Records of trade organisations 567

Anon, *The First Fifty Years of the Institute of Bankers 1879–1929* (priv. pub., 1929); Edwin Green, *Debtors to their Profession. A History of the Institute of Bankers 1879–1979* (London, 1979)

Records: Guildhall Library, Aldermanbury, London EC2P 2EJ

Council minutes (50) 1878–1980; public meeting minute books (2) 1879–1969; executive committee minutes 1879–80; prospectuses, acts and other papers re UK banking practices and performance c.1870s–1990s; outletterbook 1895–1906; pension correspondence (11) 1914–64; secretary's office miscellaneous correspondence (10) 1921–79, 1951–56; staff notices 1930–47; index to minutes 1931–40; finance committee correspondence 1935–50; examinations committee papers 1945–53; international banking annual summer school papers 1947–92. [Ref: MS 30850–30862A]

CHARTERED INSTITUTE OF BANKERS IN SCOTLAND
Edinburgh, Lothian

History: In 1874 concern for the lack of facilities for training young bankers prompted the Scottish Bankers' Literary Association (est. 1863) to form a provisional committee, of delegates from each of the banks and from the Association, to discuss the matter. In July 1875 The Institute of Bankers in Scotland was established, upon the recommendation of the committee, 'to improve the qualifications of those engaged in banking and to raise their status and influence'. Funded by subscriptions and donations from the banks it immediately enrolled 178 members and 195 associates, largely from Edinburgh and Glasgow. Members were elected by the provisional committee and were in future to be those who passed examinations or were appointed by virtue of their official positions in the banks. Associates were required to have served for ten years or to have a university degree. The new Institute took premises in Edinburgh and Glasgow and initiated programmes of lectures and examinations. In the provinces local coaching was provided by branch agents and schoolmasters. Membership of the Institute grew steadily but, although from 1890 the banks made payments to staff passing examinations, lack of interest in Institute qualifications limited its influence. Local centres were set up in Aberdeen, Dundee, Greenock, Inverness, Perth, Dumfries and Galashiels, and later in London, Lerwick, Kirkwall, Stirling and Wick. In Edinburgh the Institute occupied various premises until it moved to 62 George Street, which accommodated offices, a library, council room and sports room, in 1908. A quarterly Institute magazine was launched in 1909. In 1919 ladies were allowed to sit institute examinations and from 1922 to qualify as members. By the 1930s the banks made it obligatory for staff to pass the Institute's associate examinations, thereby greatly improving the influence of the Institute.

568   *British banking – a guide to historical records*

Various prize funds had been established from 1911 and the Institute's Educational Trust was launched in 1942. During the Second World War correspondence courses were organised for Scottish bankers who were prisoners of war in Germany. After the war the altered banking environment prompted the restructuring of the examination syllabuses, the publication of a series of study text books and the instigation of independent local centres in Aberdeen, Dundee, Edinburgh, Glasgow, Inverness, London, Ayr/Kilmarnock, Dumfries, Elgin, Fife, Greenock, Oban, Perth and Stirling/Falkirk. In 1955 the Institute secured a grant-of-arms. In 1958 the term member was discarded and students passing final examinations became Associate Members. In 1965 the new grade of Fellow was introduced. Diversification of the range of services and products offered by the banks after 1971 prompted a restructuring of the examination syllabus in 1972. In 1974 the Institute's principal office moved to Rutland Square, Edinburgh, and in 1998 to Drumsheugh Gardens, Edinburgh.

R N Forbes, *The History of The Institute of Bankers in Scotland, 1875–1975* (Edinburgh, 1975)

Records: The Chartered Institute of Bankers in Scotland, 38b Drumsheugh Gardens, Edinburgh EH3 7SW

Press cuttings books: various banks 1848–53, 1879, City of Glasgow Bank failure 1878; *Journal of the Institute of Bankers in Scotland* 1850, 1879–1949; prize essays 1854–73; council minute books 1872–1944 [w]; account books 1874–76, 1971–83; guardbook of minutes, press cuttings, examination papers 1874–90; letterbooks 1875–1940; photographs 1875–1975; annual reports 1875–1976; cash books 1875–96, 1953–54, 1975–84; examination syllabuses, regulations and papers 1876–79, 1929–53, 1973–78; membership admission certificates, bylaws, correspondence, etc 1876–95; letters to bankers 1885; library suggestions book 1908–43; trust fund papers 1927–44; premises papers 1931–32; royal charter papers 1933–91; institute publications 1952–57, 1974; general ledger 1953–68; examination correspondence 1954; pension scheme papers 1955–75; conference papers 1958–75; general purposes, examination, and education committee minutes and reports 1960–90; education policy review 1970; report on role as qualifying association 1972; centenary celebration papers 1975.

Aberdeen district centre: accounts 1979–80; **Edinburgh branch:** papers 1951–52; lectures 1954–55; **Fife local centre:** cash book 1957–80; statement of accounts 1977–78; handbook 1980–81; **Glasgow branch:** lectures 1946, 1952–54; papers 1950–52, 1959–61.

CLEARING BANK UNION

History: The Union was established in 1923 as the Central Council of Bank Staff Associations and subsequently renamed the Council of Bank Staff Associations. As a member of the Banking Staff Council (1968–78) it was represented on the Joint Negotiating Council for Banking. It was renamed the Confederation of Bank Staff Associations in 1977 and in 1980 merged with the staff associations of Barclays, Lloyds and National Westminster banks to form the Clearing Bank Union. The Union was dissolved in 1988, after the clearing banks ended central negotiation for recruitment grades.

Records: Modern Records Centre, University of Warwick Library, Coventry, Warwickshire CV4 7AL

Executive committee and general meeting minutes 1923–79 [w]; accounts 1923–77; constitutions n.d.; circulars 1945–54, 1978–79; membership figures 1949–60; annual conference papers 1980–87; committee minutes: technical and services 1980–87, ad-hoc 1980, management 1981–86, pensions 1981–87; new technology and developments 1982–87; subject files n.d.

Banking Staff Council: minutes 1970–78; annual accounts 1976–78; miscellaneous files n.d.; **Joint Negotiating Council for Banking:** constitution 1968; minutes 1970–87 [w].

[Ref: MSS.283]

COMMITTEE OF LONDON AND SCOTTISH BANKERS
AND
LONDON BANKERS' CLEARING HOUSE
London

History: This committee oversaw the working of the London Clearing House, but it was also important in its own right in representing the views of London 'clearing' bankers. A clearing mechanism through which inter-bank payments were settled was established in the 1770s, when cheques first became a significant means of payment, but use of the clearing house was restricted initially to private banks which administered it. In 1833 the clearing house was established in Lombard Street. In 1854 London joint stock banks were admitted for the first time and in 1858 country banks were admitted. Thus by the end of the 1850s the London Clearing House had gained a major role in money transfer. Between 1840 and 1884 the turnover of cheques handled grew five times to £6 billion. In 1895 Bankers' Clearing House Ltd was established to administer the committee's premises at 10 Lombard Street. The clearing role continued to modern

570 *British banking – a guide to historical records*

times, the Clearing House remaining in Lombard Street. It was transferred to the newly formed Cheque and Credit Clearing Co Ltd, of the Association for Payment Clearing Services, in 1985.

The Committee of London Clearing Bankers, which oversaw the working of the Clearing House from 1821, also came to represent the interests of London private and, later, joint stock banks. The committee grew in influence as the number of banks diminished, especially following the emergence of the so-called 'Big Five' just after the First World War. The need for increased co-operation between bankers and between them and the Bank of England had been demonstrated by the 1890 Baring Crisis. Thus, the Bank of England increasingly referred to the Committee on matters effecting the control and supervision of the banking system. This connection received an element of formality when in 1911 the Governor began to chair a regular quarterly meeting of the Committee on the Bank's premises. The channel thus created enabled the Bank to seek co-operation on a wide range of issues, for example matters relating to the embargo on gold exports after the First World War and on the return to a gold standard in the mid-1920s. After the Second World War, a matter frequently considered was control of bank-lending in support of national economic policy. In 1991 the Committee, which by then had been renamed the Committee of London and Scottish Bankers, was subsumed into the British Bankers' Association.

Records 1: Guildhall Library, Aldermanbury, London EC2P 2EJ

Committee of London Clearing Bankers: minute books (14) 1821–1985; file of material of historical interest 1856–1904; treasury committee minute books (2) 1915–18; attendance book 1949–66; general purposes committee attendance book 1967–69. [Ref: MS32006–13]

Bankers' Clearing House Ltd: agenda book 1895–1937; directors' attendance book 1895–1973; general minute book 1896–1971; premises sub-committee minute book 1896–1905; share transfer register 1901–49; files of papers (18) twentieth cent. [Ref: MS32001–5A, 28–33]

Records 2: The Royal Bank of Scotland plc, Archive Section, Regent's House, 42 Islington High Street, London N1 8XL

Committee of London Clearing Bankers: minutes 1930–60.

COMMITTEE OF REPRESENTATIVES OF JOINT STOCK BANKS
London

History: Unknown

Records of trade organisations 571

Records: Guildhall Library, Aldermanbury, London EC2P 2EJ

Minute books (2) 1853–72, 1893–1900.

COMMITTEE OF SCOTTISH CLEARING BANKERS
Edinburgh, Lothian

History: The Committee developed from meetings of the managers of the Scottish joint stock banks, which took place from at least the late nineteenth century, to consider matters of mutual interest. It was formalised as the Committee of Scottish Banks General Managers and a full-time secretary was appointed in 1959. The Committeee was renamed The Committee of Scottish Clearing Bankers in 1971 to reflect the altered composition of the Committee. The Committee represents Scottish banking in the financial structure of Britain, channelling directions from the Bank of England and Treasury and setting up *ad hoc* committees for the study of particular subjects. It is also a focal point for clearing bank arrangements and the control of the supply and circulation of coin and notes in Scotland.

Records: The Committee of Scottish Clearing Bankers, 38b Drumsheugh Gardens, Edinburgh EH3 7SW

Chief accountants' committee minutes 1933–77; executive committee minutes 1945–66; general circulars 1945–63; automation sub-committee minutes 1957–80; chief executive officer's sub-committee minutes 1958–66; law sub-committee minutes 1960–73; decimalisation sub-committee minutes 1963–70; banking hours working party sub-committee minutes 1964–80.

FEDERATION OF SCOTTISH BANK EMPLOYEES
Edinburgh, Lothian

History: Unknown

Records: The Committee of Scottish Clearing Bankers, 38b Drumsheugh Gardens, Edinburgh EH3 7SW

Executive committee minutes 1944–79; miscellaneous working papers 1959–76; Joint Negotiating Council minutes, incorporating Federation of Scottish Bank Employees/Scottish Staff Bank Council 1970–79; Joint Negotiating Council working papers 1970–79; executive committee working papers 1972–80.

ISSUING HOUSES ASSOCIATION
London

History: This association of merchant banks and other businesses concerned with the issue of securities was formed in 1945 to provide a forum

572 *British banking – a guide to historical records*

for discussion and a vehicle for putting the views of its membership to the government, Bank of England and other authorities. The association was instrumental in the establishment of the Panel on Take Overs & Mergers and its members were required to observe its Code and accept its jurisdiction. Stockbrokers and foreign banks were not eligible for membership. The association worked closely with the Accepting Houses Committee with which it shared premises and a small secretariat. In 1988 its activities were merged with those of the Accepting Houses Committee resulting in the formation of the British Merchant Banking and Securities Houses Association, which was later known as the London Investment Banking Association.

Records: Guildhall Library, Aldermanbury, London EC2P 2EJ

Papers re past members 1945–64; press cuttings 1945–83; executive committee minutes and agenda etc 1945–88; membership files 1945–88; rules 1946–69; annual reports and accounts 1947–88; notes on history and membership c.1970s–80s.

Note: A 30 year closure rule is applied. Permission of the London Investment Banking Association is required for access to more recent material.

LONDON DISCOUNT MARKET ASSOCIATION
London

History: This association represents the interests of the London discount houses. It traces its origins to the London Discount Houses Committee, formed in 1927, and which changed its name to the London Discount Market Association in about 1947.

Records: Bank of England, Threadneedle Street, London EC2R 8AH

Minute books (3) 1927 on.

Guide to minor collections

This section lists collections of archives relating to general banking issues and small collections relating to specific banks. Many record offices hold large collections of individual customers' passbooks, receipts and cheques, bank notes, branch bank title deeds and such material is, for the most part, not included in the following listings.

ENGLAND & WALES

Bedfordshire

Bedfordshire and Luton Archives and Record Service, The Records Office, Cauldwell Street, Bedford MK42 9AP
Williamson, Wells & Prior, bank passbook 1808–22 [X 290/30]

Berkshire

Berkshire Record Office, Shire Hall, Shinfield Park, Reading RG2 9XD
Bond of indemnity re withdrawal from a banking partnership, Dorset 1838 [D/EX 169/20]

County Durham

Durham County Record Office, County Hall, Durham DH1 5UL
Thomas Wright & Co, correspondence with William Salvin 1784–99 [D/Sa/C83]
Easterby, Hall & Co, arrangement with creditors 1811 [D/X 761/1]
Durham Bank, £5 bank note 1815 [D/X 196/5]
Northumberland & District Banking Co, share certificate 1845 [NCB I/X/251]
Thomas Pease, Son & Co, circular re absconder 1849 [D/CG 14/22]

Gloucestershire

Gloucestershire Record Office, Clarence Row, Alvin Street, Gloucester GL1 3DW

574 *British banking – a guide to historical records*

Miscellaneous papers of Pitt, Gardner & Co 1824–39 [D2025]

Gloucester Library, Local Studies Dept, Brunswick Road, Gloucester GL1 1HT
Miscellaneous papers re banking in Gloucestershire collected by Theodore Hannam-Clark for an unpublished book c.1948 [45586]

Hertfordshire

Hertfordshire County Record Office, County Hall, Hertford SG13 8DE
Notice of failure of St Albans Bank (John S Story) 1848 [63671]

Leicestershire

Leicestershire County Record Office, Long Street, Wigston Magna, Leicester LE18 2AH
Copy letterbook, Leicester branch manager to London general manager 1876–88 [Misc 66]
Drafts drawn by Mansfield & Miller, later Miller & Co, Leicester, on Smith, Payne & Smiths, London 1800–16 [Misc 1271]

London

Public Record Office, Ruskin Avenue, Kew, Richmond TW9 4DU
Treasury: The Treasury, notably the Finance Division, dealt with government borrowing and lending, monetary policy, general complexion of the domestic financial scene in the public and private sectors and the balance of payments. Record series containing material re banking include: Finance Division files 1887–1948 (T160); Financial Enquiries Branch (Hawtrey papers) 1859–1947 (T208); currency notes weekly returns 1914–28 (T254); Treasury out-letters 1919–21 (T152); files of Committee of Finance and Industry (Macmillan Committee), set up in 1929 to enquire into banking, finance and credit and to make recommendations to promote the development of trade and commerce, 1929–31 (T200); papers of Committee on the Working of the Monetary System (Radcliffe Committee), set up in 1957 to enquire into and make recommendations on the working of the monetary and credit system, 1957–59 (T159); Report of Committee on Banking Services Law and Practice (Jack Committee), set up in 1987 to review banking services, 1989–90 (T290); and Treasury Solicitor's registered files including papers re Bank Rate Tribunal, 1957–58 (TS58).
Board of Trade, Companies Registration Office: The registration and regulation of joint stock companies was entrusted to the Board of Trade under the Joint Stock Companies Act 1844 (excluding Scottish companies with-

Guide to minor collections 575

out an office in England). Record series containing material re banking include: files of all dissolved companies incorporated 1856–1931 and dissolved pre 1932; of some incorporated 1856–1900 and dissolved 1933–43, and of all public and private non-exempt companies incorporated up to 1970 and dissolved 1948–71. Also samples of exempt private companies, 1855–1970 (BT31); files of all joint stock companies registered under 1844 Act and dissolved pre 1856 Act or those re-registered under the later Act, 1844–c.1860 (BT41); dissolved companies liquidators' accounts, 1890–1932 (BT34); papers re dissolutions and winding up of companies incorporated under legislation other than the Companies Acts, 1883–1937 (BT288).

Board of Inland Revenue: In 1859 the Office of Registration of Bank Returns merged with other offices to form a single Licence Department, from 1877 part of the Office of Controller of Stamps and Shares and subsequently part of the Board of Inland Revenue. Stamp duties, one of the oldest inland revenue taxes, were levied on financial documents, like banker's licences and, until 1971, cheques. The Board of Stamps collected duties and issued stamps. Record series containing material re banking includes, for example, Office of Director of Stamping files re currency notes, 1876–1973 (IR80).

Supreme Court of Judicature: Master Watkin Williams's miscellaneous books re company winding up 1850–1909, Proceedings of the Court of Chancery (J32); Master Chandler's miscellaneous books re liquidation proceedings of the Court of Chancery taken in chambers particularly relating to banking and insurance companies 1847–77 (J45).

Civil Service Pay Research Unit: Registered files re general policy, in-cludes sample files arising from the survey of such private firms as banks, 1956–81 (CSPR2).

Guildhall Library, Aldermanbury, London EC2 2EJ
Account book and letters of John Knight of Whitchurch, Shropshire, re his account with the London banks of Dorset, Johnson, Wilkinson & Berners of Bond Street and Moffatt, Kensingtons & Styan of Lombard Street 1794–1812 [MS5863]
Letters from James, John, Robert and William Adam to Innes & Clerk of London re their credit arrangements 1754–1807 [MS3070]

Archives Department, British Library of Political and Economic Science, London School of Economics, 10 Portugal Street, London WC2A 2HD
Papers of George Arbuthnot, Treasury official, on currency and the Bank of England 1827–78 [Welby SR1017]
Papers of Reginald Earle, Baron Welby, on currency, finance and the Bank of England 1852–93 [Welby SR1017]

576   *British banking – a guide to historical records*

Papers of Alwyn Parker, director of Lloyds Bank, re establishment of British bank consortium re Turkish railways 1920–25 [Coll misc 547]
Minutes and papers of Committee to Review the Functioning of Financial Institutions, 'The Wilson Committee', chaired by Harold Wilson 1977–80 [Financial Institutions]

Oxfordshire

Department of Western Manuscripts, Bodleian Library, Broad Street, Oxford OX1 3BG
Proposal for a general exchange and bank early seventeenth cent. [MS Rawlinson C925]
Typescript of lecture on the failure in 1841 of Daintry, Ryle & Co, Macclesfield 1972 [MS Eng C2714]

Warwickshire

Warwickshire Record Office, Priory Park, Cape Road, Warwick CV34 4JS
Bank notes of Jno Haynes, Richard Bloxham and Jno Morgan, Alcester Bank 1801–02 [CR110]
Bills and bank notes of Smith, Osborn & Co, Northampton Town & County Bank early nineteenth cent. [CR1711/45]

West Yorkshire

West Yorkshire Archive Service, Yorkshire Archaeological Society, Claremont, 23 Clarendon Road, Leeds LS2 9NZ
The Banker's Sure Guide, or Monied Man's Assistant (London, 1782) [DD81/TLE 39/II]

SCOTLAND

Argyll

Argyll & Bute District Council Archives, Kilmory, Lochgilphead PA31 8RT
Letters re proposals to establish branch banks in Campbeltown 1842, 1846 [DR4/3/47]

Dumfriesshire

Dumfries and Galloway Archives, 33 Burns Street, Dumfries DG1 2PS

Guide to minor collections   577

Architectural drawings of branch banks by Walter Newall (1780–1836) – Southern Bank of Scotland, 1838 [GGD 131/F1/7–7B]

Edinburgh

National Archives of Scotland, HM General Register House, Princes Street, Edinburgh EH1 3YY

Board of Trade. Companies Registration Office: These records deal with Scottish-registered joint stock companies following the setting up of the necessary legislation from 1856 onwards. For each company that has been dissolved there is normally held on file copies of the memorandum and articles of association, certificate of company registration, regular returns of directors and shareholders, and date and type of dissolution. These are not, of course, actual company records but returns required by the Registrar of Companies, in modern times located at 'Companies House', to ensure that the company was fulfilling its legal requirements. A card index exists to the names of such dissolved companies in West Register House covering the years 1856 to 1979. The files relate to banks such as Dundee Bank 1863–81 (BT2/141), Glasgow Bank Ltd 1934–49 (BT2/17978), National Bank of Scotland Ltd 1882–1957 (BT2/1108) and Scottish National Banking Co Ltd 1881–88 (BT2/1108).

Records of Criminal Cases: The High Court of Justiciary, Scotland's supreme criminal court, dealt with crimes such as those of uttering forged notes or base coins. An index to its records for the period 1814 to 1900 is available in West Register House. This is an index to the name of the criminal only, not to the type of case. Records can include precognitions (information gathered prior to the crime including witness statements and other evidence), brief minute of trial, and case papers. The first and last are likely to be the most informative. Examples include precognitions on James McDougall, hanged in Edinburgh for uttering forged Bank of Scotland bank notes in 1814 (AD14/14/44), and on John McKana and Joseph Richardson, hanged in Dumfries for uttering forged notes on the Ship Bank of Glasgow in 1823 (AD14/23/1).

Court of Sessions: If a business was involved in litigation, or became sequestrated (bankrupt), evidence of this may be held in the records of the Court of Sessions, Scotland's supreme civil court. The court's records are arranged in a complex manner and there are several different 'offices' within the court's structure. There are, however, various indexes which allow identification of parties: these often name only the pursuer, not the defender, but from 1782 printed and indexed annual minute books record the names of pursuers and defenders. Production in Court of Sessions cases form a separate series, namely CS96, and an index to this for the years c.1760 to c.1840 was produced by the List and Index Society [Spe-

578   *British banking – a guide to historical records*

cial Series, 23, 1987]. Examples of bank-related records contained within this series are: Montrose Banking Co correspondence 1814–31 (CS311/2142); Shetland Bank petition for sequestration 1843 (CS279/1085); Falkirk Union Banking Co sederunt book 1816–18 (CS96/869/1–3) and statement and scheme of division 1821 (CS96/987–8); Paisley Union Banking Co agent's books 1814–16 (CS96/935–7); William Inglis, Edinburgh banker, sederunt book 1828–34 (CS96/841/1–10); Robert Kent, farrier and banker at Kilmarnock, sederunt books 1819–34 (CS96/848, 841/1–10); Robert Allan & Sons, Edinburgh bankers, sederunt books 1839–42 (CS96/551–3); James & Robert Watson, Glasgow bankers books 1832–33 (CS96/450); John Home Scott, Dundee writer and banker, sederunt book 1831–32 (CS96/427); Edinburgh & Glasgow Bank, contract of copartnery 1858 (CS96/46); Merchant Banking Co, Stirling, sederunt books 1805–20, 1826–30 (CS96/2346–50, 2351–60); William Cumming, Edinburgh banker, state 1826–30 (CS96/2379); Bertram, Gardner & Co, bank book 1781–92 (CS96/3200); James Ferguson, banker, sederunt books 1820–22 (CS96/3593–94); Archibald Scott, Langholm banker, 1829–36 (CS96/4654–55); John Tweedie, banker, sederunt books 1831–36 (CS96/4662–66); James Patison, merchant and banker, 1834–38 (CS96/4701); James Miller, banker at Coupar Angus, sederunt books 1835–36 (CS96/4729–30).

Gifts and deposits: These comprise a large part of the holdings of the National Archives of Scotland. Many collections consist of private papers of landed families, of businesses and of individuals. A summary index to collection name is available and about a third of the catalogues are available for on-line searching in the National Archives of Scotland's searchrooms. Such searching will provide many instances of bank names but researchers should be aware that these are often isolated references rather than major collections. Examples of records include a diary of William Ramsay, a director of The Royal Bank of Scotland 1788–1807 (GD193/1/1); letter to Henry Burt, factor at Balgowan, from David Walker of Perth Banking Co 1797 (GD155/622); and an account book of a banker at Madras, India, 1725–31 (GD1/897); correspondence, cheques and drafts of East Lothian Banking Co, n.d. (GD304); and Fife Bank establishment proposal 1799–1800 (GD26/12/28).

Perthshire

Perth & Kinross Council Archive, A K Bell Library, 2–8 York Place, Perth PH2 8EP
Statement re banking companies in Perth detailing dates of foundation, location, etc 1763–67 [B59/37/14/1]
Resolutions of special Perth town council meeting on a proposal to alter the Scottish banking system 1826 [B59/37/14/9]

ISLE OF MAN

The Manx Museum and National Trust, Douglas, Isle of Man IM1 3LY
Holmes' Bank, banker's licence 1845 [MS 1461C]

Index of names

Page numbers in bold indicate main entries for banks and associations of banks and bankers.

Abbott, Robert, 152
Aberdeen Banking Co, **45–6**
Aberdeen Commercial Banking Co, **46**, 396
Aberdeen Town & County Bank, 505
Abergavenny Financial Co Ltd, **46**
Abingdon & Wantage Bank, 306
Abingdon Bank, 504
Abney & Maltby, 451
Accepting Houses Committee, 129, 146, 234, 243, 319, 464, 524, **562–3**, 572
Adam & Co, 457
Adams, Samuel, 46
Adams, Samuel & Co, **46–7**
Adams, Thomas, 46,
Addis, Sir Charles, 282
Addison, John, 545
Addison, Samuel, 545
Addison, S & Sons, 545
Addison & Fenn, 486
Adelphi Bank Ltd, **47**, 311, 369
Aetna Life & Casualty Co, 464
African Banking Corporation Ltd, **47–8**, 491, 494
Agra & Masterman's Bank Ltd, 48, 54
Agra & United Services Bank, 48
Agra Bank Ltd, **48–9**
Agricultural & Commercial Bank of Ireland, 351
Aitken, William *see* Beaverbrook, 1st Lord
Aitken Campbell, 515
Albion Bank Ltd, 353
Alcester Bank, 576

Alcock, J O & G, 191
Alcock, William, 175
Aldenham, Lord, Henry Gibbs, 220
Alexander, A & G W & Co, 49, 126, 181
Alexander, Anne, 49
Alexander, Anne & G W, 49
Alexander, George, W, 49, 50
Alexander, Samuel, 245
Alexander, William, 49
Alexanders, Birkbeck, Barclays & Buxton, 245
Alexanders, C L Discount plc, 50
Alexanders, Cornwell & Spooner, 245
Alexanders, Cunliffe & Co, 50
Alexanders, Riches, Collett & Co, 49
Alexanders & Co,
    Ipswich, 49, 116, 245, 247
    London, 50
Alexanders & Collett, **49**
Alexanders & Maw, 245
Alexanders & Spooner, 245
Alexanders Discount Co Ltd, 50, 181
Alexanders Discount plc, **49–50**
Allahabad Bank, 144, 145
Allahabad Bank Ltd, 425
Allan, Robert & Sons, 578
Allaway & MacDougall, 534
Allday & Co, 302
Allday & Kerrison, 302
Allen, Harvey & Ross, 141
Allen Hellings & Co, 141
Alliance Bank, **50–51**, 74
Alliance Bank Ltd, **51–2**, 353, 429, 430

582 British banking – a guide to historical records

Alliance Bank of London & Liverpool Ltd, 51, 310
Alnwick & County Bank, 189, 416
American Express Co, 23
American First Western Bank & Trust Co, 330
Amyand, Sir George, 190
Amyand, Staples & Mercer, 190
Anderson, Arthur, 418
Andover Bank, 266
Andrade & Worswick, 554
Anglo-African Bank Ltd, 75
Anglo American Trust Co Ltd, 56
Anglo & London-Paris National Bank, 313
Anglo Argentine Bank Ltd, **52**, 55
Anglo-Australian Corporation, 314
Anglo-Austrian Bank, 52
Anglo-Austrian Bank Ltd, **52–3**, 55
Anglo-Brazilian Commercial & Agency Co Ltd, **53**, 342
Anglo-Czecho-Slovakian Bank, 53, 55
Anglo-Egyptian Banking Co Ltd, 54
Anglo-Egyptian Bank Ltd, **53–4**, 87, 89, 158, 398
Anglo-International Bank Ltd, 53, **55**, 125, 233
Anglo-Polish Bank, 125
Anglo-Portuguese Bank, 342
Anglo-Russian Bank, 55
Anglo-South American Bank Ltd, 52, **55–6**, 72, 118, 163, 406
Antrobus, Edmund, 171
ANZ McCaughan Merchant Bank Ltd, 239
ANZ Merchant Bank Ltd, 239
Appleton, Machell & Co, 358
Arbroath Banking Co, **57**, 160
Argyll, 3rd Duke of, Archibald Campbell, 120
Arkroyd Smithers, 524
Arkwright, Toplis & Co, 57
Arkwright & Co, **57**, 386
Armstrong & Co, 325, 326, 329
Asgill, Sir Charles Nightingale & Wickenden, 411
Asgill, Nightingale & Nightingale, 411
Ashburton, 1st Lord, Alexander Baring, 292

Ashby, Thomas & Co, **57–8**, 89
Ashby Senr., Thomas & Sons, 57
Ashford Bank, 440
Ashton, Stalybridge, Hyde & Glossop Bank Ltd, **58**, 429
Association for Payment Clearing Services, 570
Association of Bankers of London and Westminster, **563**
Association of Country Bankers, 563
Association of English Country Bankers, 430, **563**, 565
Atherley, Fall & Atherley, 58, 358
Atherley, Fall & Co, 58
Atherley & Darwin, **58**
Atherton, Leak & Co, 434
Atkins, Honeywood & Fuller, 218
Atkins & Sons, 258
Atkinson, Craig & Co, **58–9**
Atkinson, M, 59
Attwood, Aaron, 59
Attwood, Spooner & Co, **59**, 106, 328, 488
Atwood, Abrahams, Collett, Salmon & Harris, 506
Audley & Fydell, 210
Australia & New Zealand Banking Group, 239, 241
Avebury, 1st Lord, Sir John Lubbock, 358, 450, 566
Aylesbury, Uxbridge & Windsor Union Bank, 367
Aylsham Bank, 166
Aylward, John, **59**
Aynsworth, Thomas, 59
Ayrshire Banking Co, 527

Backhouse, James, 60
Backhouse, James & Jonathan, 60
Backhouse, James & Jonathan & Co, 60
Backhouse, Jonathan, 60
Backhouse, Jonathan & Co, **60**, 84, 88, 419, 556
Backhouse, Thomas, 60
Backwell, Edward, **60–61**, 364
Bacon, Cobbold, Rodwell, Dunningham, Cobbold & Co, 61
Bacon, Cobbold, Tollemache & Co, 62

Index of names

583

Bacon, Cobbold & Co, **61–2**, 138, 175
Badcock, Daniel, 62
Badcock, H, H J & D, 62
Badcock, H J, 62
Badcock, Isaac, 62
Badcock, John, 62
Badcock, M & R, **62**, 500
Bagehot, Walter, 500
Bagge & Bacon, 210
Bailey & Co, 403
Baillie, Ames, Baillie, Cave, Tyndall,
 Palmer & Edwards, 381
Bain, A W & Sons Ltd, 314
Bain, Field, Hitchins & Co, 107
Baker, Hedley & Co, 355
Baker, John, 355
Baker, Samuel, 229
Baker, Shafto, Ormston, Cuthbert &
 Lamb, 355
Bala Banking Co Ltd, **63**, 413
Balfour Williamson & Co Ltd, **63**, 73
Ballantine, John, 285
Banbury Bank, 223, 224
Banbury New Bank, 223
Banca Commerciale Italiana, 88
Banco A Edwards y Cia, 56
Banco Carabassa, 72
Banco de Credito Universal, 117
Banco de Nicaragua, 162
Banc Yr Eidion Ddu, 299
Bankers' Clearing House Ltd, 569, 570
Bankers' Discount Association Ltd,
 225
Bankers' Industrial Development Trust
 Co Ltd, 67, 69
Banking Company in Aberdeen, 510
Banking Institute, 566
Banking, Insurance and Finance Union
 (BIFU), **564**
Bank in Newcastle, 309
Bank of Africa Ltd, **63–4**, 398, 399,
 410
Bank of Asia, **64**
Bank of Birmingham, **64–5**, 370
Bank of Bolton Ltd, **65**, 168
Bank of British West Africa Ltd, 47,
 75, 76, 330, 491, 494
Bank of Calcutta, 368, 369
Bank of Ceylon, 410

Bank of England, 2–3, 4, 5, 10, 53, 55,
 65–70, 72, 76, 77, 101, 105, 128,
 152, 157, 174, 207, 219, 237,
 286, 289, 314, 353, 360, 361,
 369, 390, 394, 453, 461, 469,
 470, 498, 517, 527, 540, 542,
 562, 565, 571, 575
Bank Officers' Guild, 564
Bank of Glasgow, 396
Bank of India, **70–71**
Bank of Ireland, 347, 392, 393,
Bank of Leeds Ltd, **71**, 403
Bank of Liverpool, 89, 361
Bank of Liverpool & Martins Ltd, 141,
 156, 208, 209, 253, 311, 361, 365,
 427, 447
Bank of Liverpool Ltd, 140, 175, 272,
 324, 365, 416, 522, 523, 542
Bank of London, **71**, 163
Bank of London & Brazil Ltd, 117
Bank of London & Montreal Ltd, 73
Bank of London & South America Ltd,
 56, 63, **72–4**, 326, 327, 329, 330,
 342
Bank of Manchester, 50, 160
Bank of Manchester Ltd, **74–5**, 163,
 271
Bank of Mauritius Ltd, **75**, 368, 369
Bank of Mona, 200
Bank of Montreal, 72
Bank of Newfoundland, 159
Bank of New Zealand, 159
Bank of Nigeria Ltd, **75–6**, 491, 492
Bank of Port Elizabeth, 494
Bank of Preston, **76**
Bank of Scotland, 2, **76–80**, 121, 135,
 136, 143, 396, 456, 511, 577
Bank of Stockport, **81**, 168
Bank of Tarapaca & Argentina Ltd, 52,
 55
Bank of Tarapaca & London Ltd, 52, 55
Bank of the Coal Trade, 309
Bank of Wales Ltd, **81**, 348
Bank of Wales plc, 77
Bank of Walsall & South Stafford-
 shire, **81**, 199
Bank of West Africa Ltd, **82**, 491, 494
Bank of Western India, 410
Bank of Westmorland, 522

584   *British banking – a guide to historical records*

Bank of Westmorland Ltd, **82**, 374
Bank of Whitehaven, 263
Bank of Whitehaven Ltd, **82–3**, 191, 192
Bank of Yokohama, 243
Bank West, 77
Banque Anglo Sud Americaine, 56
Banque Arab & Internationale d'Investissement, 237
Banque Franco Américaine, 293
Banque Populaire, 295
Barclay, Bevan, Tritton, Ransom, Bouverie & Co, **83–5**, 88, 254, 446
Barclay, Bevan, Tritton, Twells & Co, 488
Barclay, Bevan, Tritton & Co, 446, 488
Barclay, Bevan & Bening, 83
Barclay, David & Sons, 84
Barclay, H F, 246, 248
Barclay, James, 83
Barclay, Joseph Gurney, 84
Barclay & Co Ltd, 6, 7, 58, 60, 84, 85, 88, 98, 108, 214, 215, 235, 245, 246, 247, 248, 249, 250, 251, 254, 257, 316, 317, 360, 380, 385, 391, 408, 431, 432, 433, 444, 470, 471, 478, 487, 488, 490, 502, 508, 516, 518, 519, 550, 551, 552, 560
Barclay & Tritton, 83
Barclays, Bevan, Tritton, Twells & Co, 83
Barclays, Bevan, Tritton & Co, 83
Barclays, Tritton, Bevan & Co, 83
Barclays Bank (Canada), **85**
Barclays Bank (DCO), 87
Barclays Bank (Dominion, Colonial & Overseas), 54, 85, 87, 90, 158, 279, 398
Barclays Bank (France) Ltd, **86**, 174
Barclays Bank International Ltd, **87**
Barclays Bank Ltd, 6, 54, 85, 86, 87, 88, 89, 121, 122, 158, 174, 203, 244, 330, 350, 355, 362, 398, 506, 509, 510, 559, 569
Barclays Bank (London & International) Ltd, 86

Barclays Bank (Overseas) Ltd, 86
Barclays Bank plc, 87, **88–95**, 564
Barclays Bank SA, 86
Barclays Bank SAI Ltd, **88**
Barclays Canada Ltd, 85
Barclays de Zoete Wedd Ltd, 86, 90
Barclays Export & Finance Co Ltd, 89
Barclays Life Assurance Co Ltd, 89
Barclays Merchant Bank Ltd, 86
Barclays National Bank, 87
Barclays plc, **88–95**
Barclays Trust Co of Canada, 85
Baring, Alexander *see* Ashburton, 1st Lord
Baring, Sir Francis, 290, 291
Baring, Sir Francis & Co, 288
Baring, Jackson, Short & Co, 95
Baring, John, 95
Baring, John & Francis & Co, 95, 288
Baring, Lee, Sellon & Tingcombe, 95
Baring Asset Management Ltd, 289
Baring Brothers & Co, 95, 289, 293, 319, 390
Baring Brothers & Co Ltd, 19, 289, 453, 468
Baring Securities Ltd, 289
Barings, Lee, Sellon & Green, 95
Barings, Short & Collyns, **95**
Barings, Short & Hogg, 95
Barings plc, 289
Barker & Co, 427
Barnard, Barnard & Dimsdale, 190
Barnard, Sir Herbert, 441
Barnard, T & Co, 429
Barnard, Thomas, 95, 96
Barnard, Thomas & Co, **95–6**, 430
Barnett, Hoare, Hill & Barnett, 96
Barnett, Hoare & Co, **96**, 97, 259, 276, 366
Barnetts, Hoares, Hanbury & Lloyd, 96, **97**, 109, 259, 328
Barnsley Bank, 102
Barnsley Banking Co Ltd, **97**, 556
Bartlett, Nelson & Parrott, **98**
Bartlett, Parrott & Co, 98, 131
Bartlett & Nelson, 98
Bassett, Francis *see* De Dunstanville, Lord
Bassett, Son & Harris, 89, **98–9**

Index of names

Bassett & Co, 297, 548
Bassett & Grant, 98, 470
Bate, Thomas, 99
Bate & Robins, **99–100**
Bath Bank, 507
Bath City Bank, 384
Bath Old Bank, 301
Batten, Carne & Carne's Banking Co
Ltd, 107
Batten, J & H B, 500
Baty, J A, 89
Bax, Jones & Co, 274
Beattie, Joseph, 106
Beaufort West Bank, 494
Beaverbrook, 1st Lord, William
Aitken, 158
Beck, James, 172
Beck & Co, **100**, 328
Beck & Prime, 172
Beckett, Birks & Co, 100, **102**, 521
Beckett, Blaydes & Co, 100
Beckett, Calverley & Co, 100
Beckett, Clarke & Co, 102
Beckett, John, 100, 102
Beckett, Joseph, 100, 102
Beckett & Co (Leeds Bank), **100–101**,
102, 111, 164, 528
Beckett & Co (York & East Riding
Bank), 100, **101–2**, 111, 502, 528
Bedford & Bedfordshire Bank, 505
Bedfordshire Bank, 98
Beeching, Thomas, 102
Beeching & Co, **102–3**, 328
Belfast Bank, 375
Belfast Banking Co Ltd, 374
Belfast National Bank of Ireland, 392
Bell, Cookson, Carr & Airey, 448
Bell, Henry, 325
Bell, Woodall, Tindall & Taylor, 550
Bellairs, A W & Son,
Derby, 103
Stamford, **103**
Bellairs, Geo., 103
Benson, Robert & Co, 292, 342
Benson, Robert & Co Ltd, 103
Benson, Robert Lonsdale & Co Ltd,
103–4
Benson, Robert Lonsdale Ltd, 304
Benson & Co, 412

Bentley, William, 104
Bentley & Buxton, **104**
Berkshire Union Banking Co, 344
Berliner Handels-und Frankfurter
Bank, 146
Bernard, Spencer, 202
Bertram, Gardner & Co, 578
Berwick, Joseph, 104, 317
Berwick, Lechmere & Co, **104–5**, 138,
317
Berwick, Lechmere & Isaac, 104
Berwick & Co, 104, 317
Bethnal Green Bank, 142
Bevan, Francis Augustus, 84
Bevan, John, 341
Bevan, Silvanus, 83
Beverley Bank, 358
Bicester & Oxfordshire Bank, 506
Biddle, Mountford, Pidcock & Cope,
477
Biddulph, Cocks, Eliot & Praed, 156,
440
Biddulph, Cocks & Co, 167
Biddulph, Cocks & Ridge, 156, 257
Biddulph, Francis, 156
Bideford Bank, 321
Biggerstaffe, John, 105
Biggerstaffe, William, 105
Biggerstaffe, William & John, **105**
Biggleswade & Baldock Bank, 526
Bignell, Heydon & Watt, 223
Bilston & Staffordshire Bank, 300
Bilston District Banking Co, 170
Birch, Pitt, Powell, Fripp, Brice &
New, 438
Birch, Pitt, Powell, Fripp & Brice,
438
Birch, Samuel, 438
Birkbeck, Henry, 246
Birkbeck, John, 175
Birkbeck, William, 175, 176
Birkbeck, William & John, William
Alcock, John Peart, Jos Smith &
Wm. Lawson, 175
Birkbeck Bank, **105–6**, 528
Birkbeck Building Society, 105
Birmingham, Dudley & District
Banking Co, 199, 372, 373, 490,
516

586   *British banking – a guide to historical records*

Birmingham, Dudley & District Banking Co Ltd, 516, 550
Birmingham & Midland Banking Co, 99, 373, 411
Birmingham & Midland Bank Ltd, 142, 173, 187, 211, 315, 318, 373, 509
Birmingham & Warwickshire Bank, 384
Birmingham Bank, 210
Birmingham Banking Co, 64, 196, 370
Birmingham Banking Co Ltd, 166, 460, 489, 498
Birmingham District & Counties Banking Co Ltd, 46, 114, 379, 380, 516, 521, 550
Birmingham Joint Stock Bank, 59, 328
Birmingham Joint Stock Bank Ltd, **106**
Birmingham Old Bank, 327
Birmingham Town & District Banking Co, 199, 516
Bischoffsheim, H L, 288
Bishop's Waltham & Hampshire Bank, 244
Blackburn Bank Ltd, **106**, 509
Blanchard, Robert, 147
Blanchard & Child, 147
Bland, Barnett & Bland, 96
Bland, Barnett & Co, 96
Bland, Barnett & Hoare, 96
Bland, John, 96
Bland, John & Son, 96
Bland, Randell, Chambers, G Hoar, Smoult & Ashworth, 309
Bland, Thomas Davison, 309
Bland & Barnett, 96
Blount, Sir Edward, 219
Bloxsome & Player, 403
Blurton, Webb & Peel, 133
Boase, C W, 201
Bodenham, Garrett & Son, **107**
Boldero, Carter, Barnston, Snaith & Carter, 107
Boldero, Carter & Co, 107
Boldero, Kendell, Adey & Co, 107
Boldero, Lushington, Boldero & Lushington, **107**

Bolitho, Foster, Coode & Co Ltd, 107, 274, 548
Bolitho, Sons & Co, 107, 108, 519
Bolitho, Williams, Foster, Coode, Grylls & Co Ltd, 89, **107–8**
Bolitho & Co, 107
Bolton, Sir George, 72
Bolton Commercial Bank, 260
Bonn & Co, 267
Booth, Sir Felix, 353
Borough Bank, 140
Borough of St Marylebone Banking Co, **108**
Borough of Sheffield Bank, 472
Borough of Tynemouth Trading Bank, **109**, 556
Bosanquet, Beachcroft, Pitt & Anderdon, 109
Bosanquet, Beachcroft & Reeves, 109, 357
Bosanquet, Pitt, Anderdon & Franks, 109
Bosanquet, Salt, Whatman, Harman, Salt & Bosanquet, 496
Bosanquet, Salt & Co, 97, **109–10**, 328
Bosanquet, Samuel, 109
Bosanquet, Whatman, Harman & Bosanquet, 109, 496
Bosanquet & Co, 496
Bourne, Rhodes & Co, **110**, 490
Bouverie, Murdoch, Bouverie & James, 110, 446
Bouverie, Murdoch & Bouverie, 110
Bouverie, Murdoch & Co, **110**
Bouverie, Norman & Murdoch, 110
Bouverie & Co, 110
Bouverie & Lefevre, 110
Bower, Dewsbury & Co, 110
Bower, Hall & Co, 100, 101, **110–11**
Bower, Hutton & Hall, 110
Bower & Bower, 208
Bowes, Hodgson, Falcon, Key & Co, **111**
Bowles, Beachcroft, Brown, Reeves, Collins & Co, 109
Bowles, Beachcroft & Reeves, 109, 111
Bowles, Ogden, Wyndham & Barrow, **111**

Index of names 587

Bowles, Ogden & Wyndham, 111
Box, Philip, 98
Boyd, Ben, 455, 456
Boyd, W S, 455
Bradford Bank, 314
Bradford Banking Co Ltd, 112, 374
Bradford Commercial Joint Stock
  Banking Co Ltd, 112–13
Bradford District Bank Ltd, 112, 113,
  347, 404
Bradford Old Bank Ltd, 113–15, 516,
  517
Braintree Bank, 488
Brandt, Augustus, 239
Brandt, Emanuel Heinrich, 239
Brandt, Wilhelm, 239
Brandt's, E H Son & Co, 239
Brandt's, Emmanuel Henry Son & Co,
  239
Brandt's, Wm Sons & Co Ltd, 239
Brandts Ltd, 19, 239
Brazilian & Portuguese Bank Ltd, 117
Brecon Old Bank, 537
Brett & Co, 115
Brett & Gilbert, 115
Brickdale, M & J, 115
Brickdale, Matthew & John, 115
Bridges, Cox & Godfrey, 174
Bridges, Marratt & Bridges, 115–16
Bridges & Co, 115, 175
Briggs, Rawdon, 253
Briggs, Rawdon & Sons, 253
Briggs, Rawdon Rawdon Briggs jun.
  & William Briggs, 253
Brighthelmston Bank, 537
Brighton Union Bank, 85, 254
Brightwen, George, 116
Brightwen, Gillett & Co, 116, 225
Brightwen & Co, 116
Bristol & West of England Bank, 328
Bristol & West of England Bank Ltd,
  116–17, 534
Bristol Bank, 380, 381
Bristol Old Bank, 380
Britain & Co, 557
British Bankers' Association, 563, 565,
  570
British Bank of Iran & the Middle
  East, 119

British Bank of London & South
  America Ltd, 118
British Bank of Northern Commerce
  Ltd, 117, 255
British Bank of South America Ltd,
  56, 117–18
British Bank of the Middle East Ltd,
  118–20, 279
British Guiana Bank, 120
British Kaffrarian Bank, 494
British Linen Bank, 77, 120–24, 228
British Linen Co, 45, 120, 121, 426
British Merchant Banking and
  Securities Houses Association,
  562, 572
British Mutual Banking Co Ltd, 124
British Mutual Bank Ltd, 124, 362
British Mutual Bank Nominees Ltd,
  124
British Mutual Investment, Loan &
  Discount Co, 124
British Mutual Investment Co Ltd, 124
British Overseas Bank Ltd, 55, 124–5,
  232, 233, 267, 287
British Overseas Bank Nominees Ltd,
  125
British Trade Corporation, 53, 55, 342,
  399
British Wagon Co Ltd, 542
Broadley, R C Sykes & Co, 110
Brocklehurst, Wm., John & Thos. &
  Co, 191
Bromage, Snead & Co, 126
Bromage, Snead & Snead, 126
Bromage & Co, 126, 328
Brook, Joseph, 469
Brooke, Charles, 157
Brooke, Riches & Collett, 49
Brooks, Joseph, 126
Brooks, William, 181
Brooks & Co, 126, 181, 328
Brooksby & Co, 126–7
Broseley & Bridgenorth Bank, 444
Brothers Swaine & Co, 127, 253, 314
Brown, Alexander, 128
Brown, Alexander & Sons, 128
Brown, Bevan, Moor & Hanbury, 422
Brown, Janson & Co, 127–8, 329, 547
Brown, John, 483

588 *British banking – a guide to historical records*

Brown, Sir William, 128, 361
Brown, William & Co, 128
Brown, William Williams & Co, 328
Brown, Wm & Jas & Co, 128
Brown, Wm & Sons, 369
Brown & Coombs, **127**
Brown Brothers Harriman, 129
Browne, Hall, Lashmar & West, 254
Browne, Hall & West, 254
Browne, James, 254
Brown Shipley & Co, 128, 361
Brown Shipley & Co Ltd, **128–30**
Bruce, David, 170
Bruce, James, 518
Bruce & Co, 518
Bruce-Gardner, Sir Charles, 69
Buckle, Crawshaw Junr. & Proctor, **130**
Buckle, George, William Crawshaw Junr. & James Proctor, 130
Buckley, James, 130
Buckley, Roberts & Co, 130, 462
Buckley, Shaw & Co, **130–31**
Bucks & Oxon Union Bank, 98, 329
Bucks & Oxon Union Bank Ltd, **131**
Buller, John, 357
Bullin, Christopher, 322
Bulpett & Hall, **131–2**, 441
Bunge, Born & Co, 52
Bunge, Edward, 52
Bunney, Bunney & Pepper, 172
Bunney, Slocock, Matthews & Slocock, 479
Bunney & Slocock, 479
Burdekin, Edmond, 75
Burdett-Coutts, Baroness, Angela Burdett, 171
Burdon, Forster, Burrell, Rankin & Kent, **132**
Burlington & Driffield Bank, 261
Burrell, Palfrey, 132
Burt, Frederick & Co, **132–3**, 344
Burt, John & Andrew, **132**
Burton, Lloyd, Lloyd & Salt, **133**, 211, 452
Burton, Uttoxeter & Ashbourne Union Bank, 133
Burton, Uttoxeter & Staffordshire Union Bank, 133

Burton Union Bank, 328
Burton Union Bank Ltd, **133**
Bury, Pyke & Co, 445
Bury & Suffolk Bank, 423
Bury Banking Co, 241, 311
Bury Banking Co Ltd, **133–4**
Butcher, Thomas, 134
Butcher, Thomas & Sons, **134**, 441
Butlin, A & Son, **134–5**, 328
Butlin, Anne, 134
Butt, John, 566
Buxton, Charles, 248
Buxton, S G, 246
Buxton, T F, 246
Byrd, Hall & Stevenson, 496

Cabbell, William B, 228
Caernarvonshire & District Bank, 444
Caithness Banking Co, **135**, 160
Calcutta City Banking Corporation, 241
Caledonian Banking Co, **135–6**
Call, Marten & Co,
London, **136–7**, 270, 360
St Albans, 360
Call (Bart.), Sir W P Arnold & Marten, 137
Cambridge & Cambridgeshire Bank, 215
Cambridge Bank, 391
Campbell, Archibald *see* Argyll, 3rd Duke of
Campbell, Lord Archibald, 171
Campbell, George, 170, 213
Campbell, John,
of Edinburgh, 457
of London, 170, 171
Campbell & Coutts, 170, 213
Cane, Chasemore, Robinson & Sons, 146
Canterbury Bank, 258
Cape of Good Hope Bank, 47
Capital & Counties Bank, 137, 258
Capital & Counties Bank Ltd, 62, 104, **137–9**, 167, 208, 211, 215, 218, 227, 230, 258, 265, 269, 307, 308, 329, 341, 367, 386, 414, 420, 423, 462, 479, 526, 528, 536, 554

Index of names

589

Carden, Sir Robert, 149
Cardiff Bank, 553
Carlisle & Cumberland Banking Co Ltd, **139–40**, 361, 363
Carlisle City & District Banking Co, 521
Carlisle City & District Banking Co Ltd, **140–41**, 374
Carlisle Old Bank, 266
Carrick, Brown & Co, 476
Carrick & Lee, 140
Carrington, 1st Lord, Robert Smith, 481, 484, 485
Carter, J W, 342
Carteret & Co, 258
Cassel, Sir Ernest, 145, 399
Cassons & Co, **141**, 412, 413, 445
Cater, Brightwen & Co Ltd, 116, 182
Cater Allen Holdings plc, 141
Cater Allen Ltd, **141**
Cater Allen plc, 141
Cater & Co Ltd, 116
Cater Ryder plc, 141
Cattle Trade Bank Ltd, **141–2**, 362, 394, 447
Cave, Ames & Cave, 381
Cayley, Edward, 207
Cayley, George, 206
Central Association of Bankers, 543, 563, 565, 566
Central Bank of Liverpool, 412
Central Bank of London Ltd, **142**, 373
Central Bank of Scotland, **142–3**
Central Council of Bank Staff Associations, 569
Channel Islands Bank, 143
Channel Islands Bank Ltd, **143–4**, 374
Chapman, Abel, 478
Chapman, Daniel, 438
Chapman, T & T S, 343
Chapman & Co, 173, 409
Chartered Bank, **144–5**, 203, 295, 425, 495
Chartered Bank of India, Australia & China, 144, 367
Chartered Building Societies Institute, 566
Chartered Institute of Bankers, **565–7**

Chartered Institute of Bankers in Scotland, **567–8**
Chartered Mercantile Bank of India, London & China, 145, 368
Charterhouse Bank Ltd, **145–6**
Charterhouse Industrial Development Co Ltd, 146
Charterhouse Japhet Ltd, 146
Charterhouse Japhet plc, 146
Chasemore, Robinson & Sons, **146**, 513
Chaytor, Bart., Sir Wm. Frankland Wilkinson, Chaytor & Co, 409
Cheese, Edmund, James Davies & James Crummer, 184
Cheltenham & Gloucester Building Society, 330
Cheltenham & Gloucestershire Banking Co, 169
Chepstow Bank, 130
Cheque and Credit Clearing Co Ltd, 570
Chester Bank, 195
Chesterfield & North Derbyshire Banking Co, **146–7**, 177, 178
Chester Old Bank, 538
Chichester Bank, 380
Child, Francis, 147, 148
Child, Robert, 147
Child, Stephen, 547
Child, Stephen Thomas Greene & Mathias Eades, 547
Child & Co, 4, **147–9**, 457, 547
Chippendale, Netherwood & Carr, 175
Chipping Norton Bank, 166
Christie & Cathrow, 46
Christy, Lloyd & Co, 191
Citibank, 368
CitiCorp Investment Bank Ltd, 469
Citizens Financial Group, 457
City Bank Ltd, **149–50**, 373
City of Birmingham Bank Ltd, **150–51**, 374
City of Glasgow Bank, 121, 135, **151**, 167, 205, 207, 451, 457, 458, 460, 513
Clarke, J A, 357
Clarke, John & Josh. Phillips, 152

590 British banking – a guide to historical records

Clarke, Mitchell, Phillips & Smith, **152**
Clarke, Richard Hall, 381
Clarke & Harvey, 141
Clarkes & Roscoe, 322
Clay, Henry, 239
Clay, Henry & Co, 133
Clay, Samuel, 134
Clayton, Robert & Partner, 152
Clayton, Sir Robert, **152–3**
Clayton, William, 152
Clearing Bank Union, **569**
Clement, John & Son, 507
Clement, Robert, 507
Clement, Tugwell & MacKenzie, 507
Clement, William, 507
Clinch, Jno. Wms., Jas. Clinch junr. & Wm.Clinch, 223, 226
Clinch, John, 226
Clinch, John & Co, 226
Clive Discount Co Ltd, 219
Clydesdale & North of Scotland Bank Ltd, 154, 418
Clydesdale Bank, 205, 207, 416, 563
Clydesdale Bank Ltd, 154, 374, 375, 418
Clydesdale Bank plc, **154–5**
Clymo, Treffry, Hawke, West & Co, 528
Coales, Robert, 384
Coates, Meek & Carter, 557
Cobb, Bartlett & Co, 98, 131
Cobb, Francis & Son, 155
Cobb, T R & Son, 98, 131
Cobb & Co, **155**, 328
Cochran, Murdoch & Co, 228
Cocknedge, William, 364
Cocks, Biddulph & Co, **156–7**, 257, 361, 364
Cocks, Sir Charles, 156
Codd & Co, 156
Coggan, Morris & Co, **157**
Colchester Bank 61, 247
Cole, Holroyd & Co, **157**, 403
Cole, John, 157
Colesberg Bank, 494
Collis, William, 99
Colonial Bank, 54, 87, 89, 120, **157–8**, 398

Colonial Bank of New Zealand, **159**
Comber, Benjamin, 385
Commercial Bank, 132
Commercial Banking Co of Aberdeen *see* Aberdeen Commercial Banking Co
Commercial Bank of Alexandria Ltd, 54
Commercial Bank of Greece, 295
Commercial Bank of London, **159–60**, 287, 351
Commercial Bank of Manchester, 160
Commercial Bank of Scotland, 57, 135, 457
Commercial Bank of Scotland Ltd, **160–62**, 396, 400
Commercial Bank of Spanish America Ltd, 56, **162–3**
Committee of London and Scottish Bankers, 565, **569–70**
Committee of London Clearing Bankers, 570
Committee of Representatives of Joint Stock Banks, **570–71**
Committee of Scottish Banks General Managers, 571
Committee of Scottish Clearing Bankers, **571**
Compania Financiera de Londres, 73
Confederation of Bank Staff Associations, 569
Consolidated Bank Ltd, 71, 74, **163–4**, 260, 271, 429
Consolidated Bank of Cornwall, 89, 108
Continental Assets Realisation Trust Ltd, 125
Coode, Shilson & Co, 476
Cook, Thomas Group, 375
Cooke, Ellison & Co, 164
Cooke, Foljambe, Parker & Walker, **164**
Cooke, John & Thos. & Co, 60
Cooke, Sir W B Childers & Co, 164
Cooke, Vernon, Walker, Jackson & Milner, 100, **164–5**
Cooke, Yarborough & Co, 164
Cooke & Co, 164, 316, 356
Coombs, Brown, Coombs & Co, 127

Index of names

591

Coombs, James, 127
Cooper, Purton & Sons, **166**, 371
Co-operative Bank Ltd, 165
Co-operative Bank plc, **165–6**
Co-operative Wholesale Society
(CWS), Loan & Deposit Department, 165
Copeman, George & Thomas, **166**
Copeman, Robert & Edward, 166
Copeman, Robert & George, 166
Copeman & Co, 246
Corgan, Paget & Mathews, **166–7**
Cornish Bank, 156, 440
Cornish Bank Ltd, 138, **167**
Cortes Commercial & Banking Co
Ltd, 162
Cortes, Enrique & Co, 162
Council of Bank Staff Associations,
569
Countrywide Bank Ltd, 77
County Bank Ltd, 90, **167–9**, 191, 192,
404
County of Gloucester Bank, 552
County of Gloucester Banking Co,
169, 229, 328, 499, 520
County of Gloucester Bank Ltd, **169–70**
County of Stafford Bank Ltd, **170**, 403
Cousins, Allen & Co, 211
Coutts, James, 170, 213
Coutts, John, 213
Coutts, John & Co, 213
Coutts, Stephen, Coutts & Co, 213
Coutts, Thomas, 170, 171, 256
Coutts, Thomas & Co, 170, 185
Coutts & Co, 4, 19, 77, **170–72**, 213,
256, 404, 450
Coventry & Warwickshire Banking
Co, **172**, 328
Coventry Union Banking Co, 319, 373
Coventry Union Banking Co Ltd, **172–3**
Cowdray, 1st Lord, W D Pearson, 313
Cox, Charles, 174
Cox, Cobbold & Co, 62, **174–5**
Cox, Cox & Greenwood, 173
Cox, Greenwood & Cox, 173
Cox, Hammersley & Co, 174
Cox, Mair & Cox, 173

Cox, Richard, 173
Cox, Robert Albion, 546
Cox & Co, 86, 89, **173–4**, 270, 303,
329
Cox & Co (France) Ltd, 86
Cox & Cox, 174
Cox & Drummond, 173
Cox & Greenwood, 173
Cox & Knocker, 174
Cox & Mair, 173
Cox & Mills, 422
Cox & Nunn, 174
CPR-Compagnie Parisienne de
Réescompte SA, 469
Crabb, John, 438
Craigie Banking Co, 436
Craven Bank, 175
Craven Bank Ltd, 114, **175–6**, 361, 363
Crawshay, Bailey & Co, 403
Credit Anstalt, 53
Credit Commerce de France, 146
Credit Foncier, 176
Credit Foncier & Mobilier of England
Ltd, 176
Credit Foncier of England Ltd, **176**
Crédit Lyonnais SA, 50
Crédit Mobilier, 176, 293
Crewdson, W D, 177
Crewdson, W D & Co, **177**, 521, 522
Crickitt, Bacon & Co, 61
Crickitt, C A, 61
Crickitt, Round & Crickitt, 251
Crickitt, Round & Green,
Chelmsford, 251
Colchester, 251
Crickitt, Truelove & Kerridge, 61, 251
Crickitt, Wood & Co, 251
Crickitt & Co, 251
Crickitt & Round, 251
Cripplegate Bank Ltd, 352
Cripplegate Savings Bank, 352
Cripps & Co, 229
Crocker Bank, 375
Crompton, Ewbank & Co, **178**
Crompton, Gilbert, 179
Crompton, Gray & Eaton, 178
Crompton, Mortimer & Co, 178
Crompton, Newton, Walker & Co,
177, 178

592 British banking – a guide to historical records

Crompton, Newton & Co, 177, **178**
Crompton, Samuel, 179
Crompton & Evans' Union Bank Ltd,
146, **177–8**, 430, 503
Crossley, Julian, 87
Crowe, Sparrow, Brown & Co, 486
Croxon, Edward, 179
Croxon, Jones & Co, 179, 429, 430
Croxon, Jones & Co (Old Bank) Ltd,
179
Croxon, Longueville, Croxon, Jones &
Co, 179
Cull & Co, 388, 390
Cull & Co Ltd, **179–80**
Culme, Fox & Tingecombe, 208
Cumberland Union Banking Co, 180
Cumberland Union Banking Co Ltd,
180–81, 266, 556
Cumming, William, 578
Cunliffe, Brooks & Co,
Blackburn, 126, 182, 328
London, 126, **181**
Cunliffe, Roger, 181, 182
Cunliffe, Roger & Co, 126
Cunliffe, Roger & Son, 50, 181
Cunliffe, Roger Sons & Co, 181
Cunliffe, Roger Sons & Co Ltd, **181–2**
Cunliffe & Fowler, 401
Cunliffe Brothers, 234
Cunliffes, Brooks, Cunliffe & Co, 182
Currie, B W, 232
Currie, William, 182
Curries & Co, **182–3**, 196, 197, 231,
232
Curteis, E J, Wm. Curteis, Woollet &
Dawes, 183
Curteis, Pomfret & Co, **183**, 328
Curteis, R Pomfret & Co, 183
Curtis, Sir William, 449
Curtis, Sir William Robarts & Curtis,
449
Customs House Bank, 480
Cutcliffe, Ley, Glubb & Willcock,
321
CWS Bank, 165

Daintry, Ryle & Co, 576
Dale, John B, 183
Dale, Miller & Co, 183

Dale, Young, Nelson & Co, 183
Dale, Young & Co, **183–4**, 416
Dalton, William, 284
Daniell, Willyams, Vivian & Co, 548
Daniell, Willyams, Vivian & John, 548
Darby & Co, 477
Darlington & District Joint Stock
Banking Co, 556
Darlington Bank, 60
Davenport, Walker & Co, 343
Davies, Banks & Co, **184**, 371
Davies, Crummer, Cheese & Oliver,
184
Davies, Robert & Co, **184**, 344
Davies & Co, 412
Davison, Alexander, 185
Davison, Noel, Templer, Middleton,
Johnson & Wedgwood, 185
Davison, Noel, Templer, Middleton &
Wedgwood, 171, **185**
Dawes, Tomes & Russell, **185–6**, 524
Day, Day & Day, **186**
Day, Hulkes & Co, 186
Day, Nicholson & Stone, **186**, 348
Day, Starling, 186
Day, Starling & Co, 186
Day, Starling, Starling Day jun.,
Thomas S Day and Henry Day,
186
Day, Starling, Thomas Henry Day &
William Day, 189
Deacon, John, 542
Deane & Co, **186–7**, 441
De Carteret & Co, 258
De Dunstanville, Lord, Francis
Bassett, 167
Dempster, George, 200
Dempster, George & Co, 200
De Nationale Bank der Zuid
Afrikaansche Republic Beperkt,
398
Dendy, Charles, 380
Dendy, Comper, Gruggen, Dendy,
Gruggen & Comper, 380
Dendy, Comper, Gruggen & Comper,
38
Dendy, Halstead & Gruggen, 380
Denison, Heywood, Kennard & Co,
271

Index of names

Denison, Joseph & Co, 271
Dennistoun, James, 228
Derby & Derbyshire Banking Co Ltd, **187**, 429
Derby Bank, 103
Derby Commercial Bank Ltd, **187**, 373
Derby Old Bank, 178
Derbyshire Bank, 57
De Reuter, Julius, 118
De Stein, Edward & Co, 314
Deutsche Bank, 388
Deutsche Morgan Grenfell, 388
De Vismes, Cuthbert, Marsh, Creed & Co, 360
Devizes & Wiltshire Bank, 341
Devon & Cornwall Banking Co, 188, 329
Devon & Cornwall Banking Co Ltd, **188**
Devon County Bank, 157
Devonport Bank, 275
Devonshire Bank, 95
De Zoete & Bevan, 90
Dickinson, Dunsford, Barne & Boase, 203
Dickinson, John Baron, 188
Dickinson, Joseph, 140
Dickinson, Lewis, Besley & Son, 202
Dickinson & Green, **188–9**
Dickson, William, 189
Dickson & Woods, **189**
Dillon Read & Co, 524
Dilworth, Arthington & Birkett, **189**, 311
Dilworth, Hargreaves & Co, 189
Dimsdale, Archer & Byde, 190
Dimsdale, Drewett, Fowler & Barnard, 190
Dimsdale, Drewett, Fowler's & Barnard, 190
Dimsdale, Fowler, Barnard & Dimsdales, **190**, 381, 441, 507
Dimsdale, Fowler & Barnard, 190
Dimsdale, Sir Joseph Cockfield, 441
Dingley, Pearse & Co, **190**, 404
Dingley, Pethybridge & Co, **190**
Dingley & Co, 404
Direct Line, 457
Discount Corporation Ltd, 518

Diss Bank, 212
District Bank Ltd, 7, 168, **191–5**, 404
District Union Banking Co, 191
Dixon, Brooks & Dixon, 513
Dixon, Dalton & Amphlett, **196**, 370
Dixon, Dalton & Co, 196
Dixon, Edward, 196
Dixon, Edward & Son, 196
Dixon, Edward George Dalton & Co, 196
Dixon, Edward Son & Co, 196
Dixon & Chilton, 195
Dixon & Co, **195**, 429, 430
Dixon & Wardell, 195
Dobree, Samuel & Sons, 293
Doncaster Bank, 315
Dore, Smith, Moger & Evans, 384
Dorrien, Magens, Dorrien, Mello & Co, 196
Dorrien, Magens, Mello & Co, 182, 183, **196–7**
Dorrien, Mello & Martin, 196
Dorrien, Rucker, Dorrien & Martin, 196
Dorrien, Rucker & Carleton, 196
Dorset, Johnson, Wilkinson & Berners, 575
Dorset Bank, 217
Dorsetshire Bank, 546
Douglas, Heron & Co, 285
Douglas, Smalley & Co, 412
Dover Old Bank, 383
Down, Thornton, Free & Cornwall, 439
Down, Thornton & Free, 439
Down & Pell, 439
Downes & Co, 509
Drake, James, 304
Draper, W S, 128
Drayton Trust, 375
Dresdner Bank, 304
Dresdner Kleinwort Benson, 304
Dresser & Co, 557
Drewett & Fowler, 190
Drexel, Anthony, 387
Drexel & Co, 387, 389
Drummond, Andrew, 197
Drummond, George, 198
Drummonds & Co, 4, 19, **197–8**, 457, 458

594 **British banking – a guide to historical records**

Dudley & West Bromwich Banking
Co, **198–9**, 516
Duignan, H & Son, 8, **199**, 489
Duignan, Henry, 199
Duignan, William Henry, 199
Dumbell, George, 200
Dumbell, Son & Howard, 199
Dumbell's Banking Co Ltd, **199–200**,
429, 430
Dun, John, 429
Duncombe, Charles, 364
Dundee Bank, 577
Dundee Banking Co, **200–201**, 202,
457, 459
Dundee Commercial Bank, 204
Dundee Commercial Banking Co, 201
Dundee New Bank, **201–2**, 228, 446
Dundee Union Bank, 201, **202**, 527
Dunlop, Houston & Co, 476
Dunsford, Dunsford & Taylor, 203
Dunsford & Barne, 203
Dunsford & Co, **202–3**, 500
Duntze, Sir John, 465, 466
Duntze & Co, 465
Durham Bank, 573

Earle, Reginald *see* Welby, Lord
Easterby, Hall & Co, 573
Eastern Bank Ltd, 145, **203–4**
Eastern Bank of Scotland, 154, **204–5**
East India Co, 144
East London Bank, 142
East Lothian Banking Co, 578
East Morley & Bradford District
Deposit Bank Ltd, **205**, 509
East of England Bank, 186, **205–6**,
348, 412
East Riding Bank, 101, 110, 315, 502
Eaton, Cayley, Eaton & Michelson,
206
Eaton, Cayley, Michelson & Cayley,
206
Eaton, Cayley & Co, **206–7**, 490
Eaton, Cayley & Michelson, 206
Eaton, Hammond & Co, 257
Eaton, Knight & Stroud, 545
Eaton, Richard, 257
Eaton, Stephen, 206, 207
Eaton & Cayley, 206

Eaton & Co, 227
Eaton & Eland, 207
Eaton & Michelson, 206
Edinburgh & Glasgow Bank, 229,
578
Edinburgh & Glasgow Joint Stock
Bank, 154, **207**
Edinburgh & Leith Bank, 207, 229
Edinburgh Linen Co-partnery, 120
Edwards, Gerard Noel, 185
Edwards, Smith, Templer, Middleton,
Johnson & Wedgwood, 185
Eland, George, 207
Eland & Eland, **207–8**, 490
Eland & Elands, 207
Eland & Yorke, 207
Elder Dempster, 491
Elford, Sir Wm. Tingecombe & Co,
208
Eliot, John *see* St Germains, 1st Earl
of
Eliot, Pearce & Co, 138, **208**
Eliot, Pearce & Eliot, 208
Eliot, William & Edward Pearce, 208
Ellison, Cooke, Childers & Swan, 164,
483
Ellison, Richard, 482
Elton, Baillie, Ames, Baillie, Cave,
Tyndall, Palmer & Edwards, 381
Elton, Edwards, Baillie, Tyndall &
Skinner, 381
Elton, Edye, Edwards & Skinner, 381
Elton, Isaac, 380
Emmerson, Hodgson & Emmerson,
343
English & Jersey Union Bank, 258
English Bank of Rio de Janeiro Ltd,
72, 117
English Joint Stock Bank Ltd, 263
Equitable Bank Ltd, **208–9**, 362, 363
Erlanger, Emile, 209
Erlanger, Emile & Cie, 209
Erlanger, Emile & Co, 209, 467
Erlangers Ltd, **209**, 273
Esdaile, Hammet & Esdaile, 209
Esdaile, Sir James Esdaile, Grenfell,
Thomas & Co, **209–10**, 232
Esdaile, Sir James Esdaile, Hammett,
Esdaile & Hammett, 209

Index of names

Esdaile, Sir James Esdaile, Smith, Wright, Hammett & Co, 209
Essex & Suffolk Bank, 487, 488
Essex Bank, 487, 488
Evance, Stephen *see* Evans, Sir Stephen
Evans, Charles, 417
Evans, Sir Stephen, **210**
Evans, W & S & Co, 177, 178
Everards & Blencowe, 210
Everards & Co, **210–11**, 249
Everett, Ravenhill & Co, 420
Everett & Co, 438
Exchange & Discount Bank Ltd, **211**, 373
Exchange Bank,
Bristol, 553
Newcastle upon Tyne, 501
Exeter Bank, 465
Exeter City Bank, 381
Exeter General Bank, 445
Eyles, Patrick & Co, 266
Eyton, Burton & Co, 133, 138, **211–12**, 452
Eyton, Reynolds & Bishop, 452

Fakenham Bank, 248
Falkirk Union Banking Co, 578
Fane, Sarah Sophia, 147
Farley, Lavender & Co, **212**
Farley, Turner & Jones, 212
Farrer, Gaspard, 319
Farrer, Williamson & Co, 556
Farrow's Bank Ltd, **212**
Fauntleroy, Henry, 360
Fauresmith Bank, 494
Faversham Commercial Bank, 274
Fector & Minet, 383, 403
Federation of Scottish Bank Employees, **571**
Fellows, John, 263
Fellows & Hart, 263
Fenn & Addison, 486
Fenton, J J & Sons, 509
Ferguson, James, 578
Fife Bank, 122, 578
Finch, John, 196
Fincham, French & Simpson, 212
Fincham & Simpson, **212–13**, 348

First Direct, 375
Firth, Thomas, 213
Firth, Thomas & Son, **213**, 429, 430
Fisher, James, 307
Fisher & Son, 391
Fishers, Simmonds & Mammatt, 319
Fletcher, Leslie, 542
Fletcher, Stubbs & Stott, 555
Fletcher, William, 431
Fletcher & Parsons, 431
Flood, Flood & Lott, 213
Flood, Lott & Lott, 213
Flood & Lott, **213**
Foljambe, H S, 164
Foljambe's Bank, 164
Footner, William & Sons, 548
Forbes, Edward, 555
Forbes, William, 214
Forbes, Sir William, 213, 214
Forbes, William James Hunter & Co, 285
Forbes, Sir William James Hunter & Co, **213–14**, 510
Fordham, Flower & Fordham, 214
Fordham, Gibson & Co, 89, **214–15**, 471, 508
Fordham, John & Co, 214
Forster, Charles & Sons, 370
Forster, Edward, 357
Forster, Lubbock, Bosanquet & Co, 357
Forster, Lubbocks, Forster & Clarke, 357
Forster & Co, 138
Foster, Burrell, Rankin & Anderson, 132
Foster, Francis, 132
Foster, Lubbock & Co, 109
Foster & Baldwin, 300
Foster & Co, **215**
Foster & Foster, 215
Fowle, Robert, 215
Fowle, Thomas, **215–16**
Fox, Fowler & Co, **216–17**, 329
Fox, George & Co, 188
Fox, Steele, Seymour & Gunner, 244
Fox, Thomas, 216
Fox & Co, 216
Fox Bros, Fowler & Co, 216, 226

596 British banking – a guide to historical records

Frankland & Wilkinson, 556
Fraser, William, 359
Freame, Barclay & Freame, 84
Freame, John, 83
Freame, Joseph, 83
Freame, Smith & Bening, 83
Freame & Barclay, 83
Freame & Gould, 83, 84
Freshfields, 69–70
Fripp, William, 438
Fruhling & Goschen, 293
Fryer, Andrews & Co, **217**, 403
Fryer, R & W F, **217**, 328
Fryer, Richard, 217
Fryer, William, Edwin Andrews, John
Fryer & W R Fryer, 217
Fuller, Banbury, Nix & Co, **217–18**,
429, 430
Fuller, Banbury, Nix & Mathieson,
218, 466
Fuller, Banbury & Co, 466
Fuller, Blake & Halford, 218
Fuller, Halford & Vaughan, 218
Fuller, Richard George Fuller & Co,
218
Fuller, Richard Sons & Vaughan, 218
Fuller, Son, Halford & Vaughan, 218
Fuller & Cope, 218
Fullers & Co, 218, 466
Furley, Lubbock, Bosanquet & Co,
357

Gales, Dixon & Massey, 298
Galton & James, 370
Garfit, Claypon & Co, 137, **218**
Garforth, Raper & Co, 502
Gathorne, John, 497
Gee, Wise & Gee, 323
General Credit & Discount Co of
London Ltd, **219**, 515, 518
General Credit & Finance Co, 219
General Credit & Finance Co of
London Ltd, 54
Gerrard, W D, 219
Gerrard & Co, 219
Gerrard & King Ltd, **219–20**
Gerrard & Middleton, 219
Gerrard & National Discount Co Ltd,
219, 401

Gerrard & National Ltd, 220
Gerrard & Reid, 219
Gerrard & Reid Ltd, 401
Gibbins & Lovell, 370
Gibbons, John, 179
Gibbons, Joseph, 370
Gibbs, Anthony Son & Branscombe,
220
Gibbs, Antony, 220
Gibbs, Antony & Son, 220
Gibbs, Antony & Sons Ltd, **220–22**
Gibbs, Casson & Co, 220
Gibbs, Henry *see* Aldenham, Lord
Gibson, Joseph William Gibson,
Warwick Pearson & Edward
Wilson, 222
Gibson, Gibson, Catlin, Gibson &
Catlin, 507
Gibson, Gibson, Gibson & Midgley,
507
Gibson, Tuke & Gibson, 89, 471, 507
Gibson & Wilson, **222–3**, 312
Gilbert & Co, 266
Giles, James, 223
Giles & Co, **223**, 487
Gill, Morshead & Co, 216, **226**
Gill, Rundle & Co, 226
Gill & Rundle, 226
Gillett, Alfred, 225
Gillett, Charles, 224
Gillett, George, 225
Gillett, J A, 224
Gillett, J C & A & Co, 223
Gillett, Joseph, 224
Gillett, Martha, 224
Gillett, Tawney & Gillett, 223
Gillett, William, 116, 225
Gillett & Co, 89, **223–4**, 226
Gillett & Tawney, 223
Gillett Brothers & Co, 116, 225
Gillett Brothers Discount Co Ltd, 223,
224–6, 299
Gilletts & Clinch, 223, **226**
Gipps, George, 258
Gipps, Henry, 258
Gipps, Simmons & Gipps, 257
Glamorganshire Banking Co, 545
Glamorganshire Banking Co Ltd, 138,
227

Index of names

Glasgow & Ship Bank, **227**, 228, 396, 476, 510
Glasgow Arms Bank, **228**
Glasgow Bank, 202
Glasgow Bank Co, **228-9**, 446
Glasgow Banking Co, 227, 476
Glasgow Bank Ltd, 577
Glasgow Joint Stock Bank, 207, **229**
Glasgow Union Banking Co, 214, 227, 426, 503, 510
Glastonbury & Shepton Mallet Bank, 447
Glegg &Vere, 411
Glencross, Hodge & Norman, 275
Gloucester Bank, 508
Gloucester County & City Bank, 169, 229
Gloucestershire Bank, 263
Gloucestershire Banking Co, 137, 263
Gloucestershire Banking Co Ltd, 229, 525
Glyn, George, 52
Glyn, G G, 232
Glyn, Hallifax, Mills & Co, 230
Glyn, Mills, Currie & Co, 182, 231
Glyn, Mills, Currie, Holt & Co, 231
Glyn, Mills, Hallifax & Co, 230
Glyn, Mills, Hallifax, Glyn & Co, 230
Glyn, Mills & Co, 52, 55, 125, 147, 149, 182, 183, **230-33**, 277, 278, 309, 342, 457, 461, 539, 541, 543
Glyn, Mills & Mitton, 230
Glyn, Mills Finance Co, 231
Glyn, P C, 232
Glyn, Richard, 230
Glyn & Co, 519
Glyn & Hallifax, 230
Godalming Bank, 367
Godfray, Charles, 144
Godfrey, Hutton & Godfrey, 233
Godfrey & Hutton, 233
Godfrey & Riddell, **233**, 482
Godwin, Minchin, Carter & Goldson, 233
Godwin, Minchin & Carter, 234
Godwin, Minchin & Co, **233-4**
Golding, William, 254
Goodacre & Buzzard, 152
Goodall, Gulson & Co, 172

Goodchild, Jackson, Goodchild Junr. & Heurtley, 297
Goodchild, Jackson, Goodchild Junr., Jackson & Jones, 297
Goodricke & Holyoake, 372
Goschens & Cunliffe, **234**, 243
Gosling, Bennett & Gosling, 235
Gosling, Clive & Gosling, 235
Gosling, Sir Francis, 234
Gosling, Sir Francis Gosling & Clive, 235
Gosling, Robert & Francis, 235
Gosling, Robert, Francis & William, 235
Gosling & Bennett, 234
Gosling & Clive, 235
Goslings & Sharpe, 89, **234-5**
Gotch, John C & Sons, **235-6**
Gould, J, 83
Grahamstoun Banking Co, **236**
Granet, Sir Guy, 273
Grant, Albert, 176
Grant, Gillman & Long, 236
Grant & Gillman, 358
Grant & Maddison's Union Banking Co Ltd, **236**, 329, 358
Grantham Bank, 302
Gray Dawes Bank Ltd, **236-7**
Gray, A, 237
Green, Edward, 188
Green, John, 188
Green, Joseph, 157
Green, Thomas, 188
Green, Tomkinson & Co, 515
Green & Vittery, 188
Greene & Eades, 547
Greene & Tysoe, 547
Greenly, Harris, Thomas, Meredith & Co, 184
Greenock Banking Co, **237-8**, 527
Greenock Union Bank, 154
Greenway, Smith & Greenways, **238**, 489
Greenwood, Cox & Co, 174
Greenwood & Cox, 173
Gregson, James, 239
Gregson, John, 239
Gregson, Parke & Clay, **238-9**
Gregson, William, 238

598   *British banking – a guide to historical records*

Gregson, William Sons, Parke & Clay, 238

Gregson, William Sons, Parke & Morland, 238

Grenfell, Edward, 387

Gresham, Sir Thomas, 364

Grice & Co, 522

Grieveson Grant, 304

Griffiths, Chaldecott, Drew & Godwin, 233

Griffiths, Chaldecott & Drew, 234, 448

Grindlay, Christian & Matthews, 240

Grindlay & Co, 240

Grindlay & Co Ltd, 241

Grindlay Brandts Ltd, **239–40**

Grindlays Bank Ltd, 239, 241

Grindlays Bank plc, 239, **240–41**

Gruggen, Dendy, Halstead & Gruggen, 380

Gruggen & Comper, 380

Grundy, Edward, 241

Grundy, John, 241

Grundys & Wood, 134, **241–2**

Grylls & Co, 519

Guernsey Banking Co, 242

Guernsey Banking Co Ltd, **242**, 404

Guernsey Commercial Banking Co Ltd, **242**, 529

Guinness, Arthur, 242

Guinness, Mahon & Co, 234, 242, 243, 355

Guinness, Richard, 243

Guinness, Robert R, 242

Guinness & Mahon, 242, 243

Guinness & Mahon (Ireland) Ltd, 243

Guinness & Mahon Ltd, 243

Guinness Mahon & Co Ltd, 129, **242–3**

Guinness Mahon Holdings Ltd, 243

Guinness Mahon Holdings plc, 243

Guinness Peat Group Ltd, 243

Gundry & Co, **244**, 548

Gunner & Co, **244**

Gunner & Sons, 89, 244

Gurney, John, 246, 424

Gurney, Joseph John, 247

Gurney, Henry, 246

Gurney, Richard H, 247

Gurney, Samuel, 424

Gurney, Birkbeck, Barclay & Buxton, Norwich, 84

Wisbech, 88

Gurney, Birkbeck & Taylor, King's Lynn, 248

Gurney & Co, Great Yarmouth, 247

Gurneys, Alexanders, Birkbeck, Barclay, Buxton & Kerrison, Ipswich, 88, **244–6**

Gurneys, Alexanders, Birkbeck, Barclay & Buxton, Ipswich, 244

Gurneys, Birkbeck & Cresswell, 210

Gurneys, Birkbeck & Martin, 246, 504

Gurneys, Birkbeck & Taylor, King's Lynn, 249

Wisbech, 248

Gurneys, Birkbeck, Barclay, Buxton & Cresswell, King's Lynn, 88, 249, 298

Gurneys, Birkbeck, Barclay, Buxton & Orde, Halesworth, **249–50**

Gurneys, Birkbeck, Barclay, Buxtons & Orde, Great Yarmouth, 88, **250–51**

Halesworth, 88

Gurneys, Birkbeck, Barclay, Orde & Buxtons, Halesworth, 250

Gurneys, Birkbeck, Barclay & Buxton, Fakenham, 88, **248**

Norwich, 88, 264, 284

Wisbech, **248–9**

Gurneys, Birkbeck, Brightwen & Orde, Great Yarmouth, 250

Halesworth, 250

Gurneys, Birkbeck, Taylor & Peckover, Fakenham, 248

Wisbech, 248, 249

Gurneys, Birkbecks, Barclay & Buxton, Norwich, **246–8**

Gurneys, Birkbecks & Co, Norwich, 166

Gurneys, Round, Green, Hoare & Co, Colchester, 89, **251**, 383

Gurneys, Turner, Brightwen & Lloyds, Halesworth, 250

Gurneys & Birkbeck,

Index of names

599

Fakenham, 248
Norwich, 246
Gurneys, Turner & Brightwen,
Great Yarmouth, 250
Halesworth, 250
Gurneys & Birkbecks,
Fakenham, 248
Norwich, 246
Gurneys & Turner, Great Yarmouth,
249, 250
Guthrie, James, **251–2**
Guyerzeller Bank, 464

Hack, Dendy & Co, 380
Hack, James, 380
Hadleigh Bank, 115
Hagues & Cook & Wormald, 534
Hainsworth, Holden, Swaine &
Pollard, 127, 314
Hainsworth, Swaine & Pollard, 127
Haldimand, A F, 390
Haldimand, A F & Sons, 390
Hale, Matthew, 380
Hales, William, 210
Halesworth & Suffolk Bank, 250
Halford, Baldock & Co, 343
Halifax & District Permanent Banking
Co Ltd, **252**, 509
Halifax & Huddersfield Union
Banking Co, 253, 323
Halifax & Huddersfield Union
Banking Co Ltd, **252–3**, 535
Halifax Bank, 253
Halifax Commercial Bank, 127
Halifax Commercial Banking Co, 253
Halifax Commercial Banking Co Ltd,
253–4, 361
Halifax Equitable Bank Ltd, 208
Halifax Equitable Building Society, 208
Halifax Joint Stock Banking Co, 535
Halifax Joint Stock Banking Co Ltd,
252
Halifax Mechanics Institution Penny
Bank, 559
Halifax New Bank, 253
Hall, Bevan, West & Bevans, 84, **254**
Hall, Bevan, West & Hall, 254
Hall, J W R, 229
Hall, Lloyd & Bevan, 254

Hall, Nathaniel, 254
Hall, Oakden & Co, 254
Hall, West & Borrer, 254
Hall, West & Co, 254
Hall & Jenkins, **254**
Hall & Morgan, 254
Hall & West, 254
Hallett & Co, 156
Hallifax, Glyn, Mills & Mitton, 230
Hallifax, Mills, Glyn, Mills & Mitton,
230
Hallifax, Mills, Glyn & Mitton, 230
Hallifax, Thomas, 230
Halstead, Woodbridge, Gruggen &
Gauntlett, 380
Hambro, Baron, Calmer Joahim,
Hambro, 255
Hambro Countrywide, 255
Hambro Life, 255
Hambro, Calmer Joahim, 254
Hambro, Calmer Joahim see Hambro,
Baron
Hambro, C J & Son, 117, 255
Hambro, Everard, 255, 256
Hambro, Joseph, 255
Hambros Bank Ltd, 255
Hambros Bank of Northern Commerce
Ltd, 117, 255
Hambros Ltd, 255
Hambros plc, **254–6**
Hamilton, Daniel, 466
Hamilton, Hugh, 285
Hammersley, Greenwood &
Brooksbank, 171, **256–7**, 446
Hammersley, Hugh, 256
Hammersley, Thomas, 256, 270, 446
Hammond & Co,
Canterbury, 138, **257–8**
Newmarket, 89, 206, **257**
Hammond, Plumptre, Furley, Hilton &
Furley, 258
Hammond, Plumptre, Furley, Hilton &
McMaster, 258
Hammond, Plumptre, Hilton & Furley,
258
Hammond, Plumptre, Hilton,
McMaster & Furley, 258
Hampshire & North Wilts Banking Co,
137, 258

600   *British banking – a guide to historical records*

Hampshire & North Wilts Banking Co
Ltd, 547
Hampshire Banking Co, 137, **258**, 266,
420
Hampson, Austin & Griffiths, **259**
Hanbury, Taylor & Lloyd, 96, 259
Hanbury, Taylor, Lloyd & Bowman,
259
Hanbury & Lloyd, 96, 97, **259–60**
Hancock, W & Son, 548
HandelsBank NatWest, 171
Handley, Peacock & Handley, 432
Handley, Peacock, Handley &
Peacock, 432
Hankey, Hall, Hankey & Alers, 260
Hankey, Sir Henry & Sons, 260
Hankey, Sir Joseph & Co, 260
Hankey, Samuel, 260
Hankeys & Co, 163, **260**
Hankins & Co, 525
Harben, Thomas, 385
Hardcastle, Cross & Co, **260–61**, 540,
542
Hardcastle, Cross, Ormrod, Barlow &
Rushton, 260
Harding, Mortlock & Co, 261
Harding, Smith & Stansfeld, 261
Harding, Smith, Faber & Foster, 261
Harding & Co, **261**, 556
Hardy, John, 262
Hardy, Newcome & Walkington, 262
Hardy, Walkington & Hardy, 262
Hardy & Co, **262**, 320
Harrimans, 129
Harris, Bulteel & Co, **262**
Harris, Charles, 113
Harris, Charles, Henry & Alfred, 114
Harris, Cheese, Davies & Crummer,
184
Harris, H, A & W M, 114
Harris, Joseph, 132
Harris, Robert, 495
Harris & Co, 114, 403
Harrison & Co, 114
Hart, Fellows & Co, **263**, 328
Hart, Francis, 263
Hart Son & Co (London) Ltd, 264
Hart Son & Co Ltd, **264**
Hart Son & Ichenhausen, 264

Hartland & Co, 229
Hartland, Nathaniel, 229, 263
Hartland, Prior, Proctor & Easthorpe,
263
Hartley & Co, 82, **263**
Hartsinck, Hutchinson & Playfair,
263–4
Harvey, Robert, 264
Harvey, Sir Robert, 264
Harvey & Hudsons, 264, 302
Harveys & Hudsons, 246, **264–5**, 307
Harwich Bank, 174
Harwood & Co, **265**, 441
Harwood & Harwood, 534
Harwood, Knight & Allen, 515
Hatton, William, 300
Hawks, Grey, Priestman & Co, 183
Haydon, Smallpiece & Co, 137, **265**
Haydon, William, 265
Haydon's, Messrs, 265
Hayes, Leatham & Co, 316
Haynes, Jno, Richard Bloxham and
Jno Morgan, 576
Haythorne, Joseph & George Wright,
416
Head, Charles & Co, 180
Head, George, 265
Head, J M & Co, **266**
Head, Joseph Monkhouse & Co, 180,
266
Head & Co, **265**
Heath & Co, 258, **266**, 293
Hector, Lacy & Co, **266–7**, 343
Hedges, Wells & Co, **267**, 329
Helbert, Wagg & Campbell, 267
Helbert, Wagg & Co, 267
Helbert, Wagg & Co Ltd, **267–8**, 468
Helbert, Wagg & Russell, 267
Helbert, Wagg Holdings Ltd, 268, 468
Helston Banking Co, **268**
Henderson Crosthwaite, 243
Henley, Clarke, Wheadon & Hallett,
268
Henty & Co, 137, **269**
Henty, Hopkins & Henty, 269
Henty, Upperton & Olliver, 269
Hereford City & County Bank, 107
Herefordshire Banking Co, 81, **269**
Herne, Joseph, 210

Index of names

601

Herries, Cochrane & Co, 269
Herries, Farquhar & Co, 137, **269–70**, 328, 360
Herries, Robert, 23, 213, 269
Herries, Sir Robert & Co, 270
Hertford & Ware Bank, 46
Hertfordshire Hitchin Bank, 470
Hetley, Everett & Co, 438
Heydon, Watt & Heydon, 223
Heydon & Watt, 223
Heygate, James, 427
Heygate, William, 427
Heywood, Arthur,
    of Arthur Heywood, Sons & Co, 270, 272
    of Heywood Brothers & Co, 271
Heywood, Arthur Sons & Co, 270, **272**, 301, 361
Heywood, Benjamin, 270, 272, 545
Heywood, Benjamin & Co, 270, 272
Heywood Bart., Benjamin & Co, 271
Heywood, Benjamin Arthur, 270
Heywood, Benjamin Sons & Co, 270
Heywood, Charles, 271
Heywood, Edward, 271
Heywood, Kennard & Co, 74, 75, 163, **271–2**
Heywood, Nathaniel, 270
Heywood, Oliver, 271, 542, 545
Heywood, Richard, 270
Heywood, Thomas, 270, 545
Heywood Brothers & Co, **270–71**, 540, 544, 545
Hill & Son, **273**, 329
Hill, Bate & Robins, 99
Hill, Bates & Robins, 373
Hill, Charles, 273
Hill, George, 273
Hill, John, 273
Hill, Philip, 273
Hill, Philip Higginson & Co Ltd, 209, **273–4**
Hill, Philip Higginson, Erlangers Ltd, 209, 273, 463
Hill, Waldron & Co, 99
Hill Samuel & Co Ltd, 209, 273, 463
Hills, Osborne & Co, 386
Hilton, Rigden & Rigden, **274**, 441
Hindley, R T, 542

Hingston & Prideaux, 188
Hird, Norman, 511
Hitchin & Hertfordshire Bank, 438
Hoare, Barnett, Hoare & Co, 96
Hoare, Benjamin, 274
Hoare, C & Co, 4, 19, **274–5**
Hoare, Charles & Co, 274
Hoare, Henry, 274, 275
Hoare, Henry & Benjamin, 274
Hoare, Henry & Co, 274
Hoare, Henry Hugh & Co, 274
Hoare, Hill & Barnett, 96
Hoare, John Gurney, 251
Hoare, Richard & Partners, 274
Hoare, Richard Hoare, 274
Hoare, Sir Richard, 274
Hoare, Sir Richard & Partners, 274
Hoare, Robert Gurney, 274
Hoare, Samuel, 96
Hodge & Co, 107, **275–6**
Hodges, Frank, 69
Hodgkin, Barnett, Pease, Spence & Co, **276**, 329
Hodgkin & Co, 309
Hodgson, Isaac, 427
Hogg, John, 381
Hogge, G & W, 526
Hohler & Co, 225
Holden, Edward, 373
Holmes' Bank, 579
Holroyd, George, 157
Holt, King & Co, 302
Holt, King & Newcome, 262
Holt, Vesey, 277
Holt & Co, 231, **277–8**, 457, 552
Honeywood, Fuller & Cope, 218
Honeywood & Fuller, 218
Hongkong & Shanghai Banking Corporation, 7, 12, 144, 203, 221, 368, 369
Hongkong & Shanghai Banking Corporation Ltd, 119, **278–83**, 375
Hongkong Bank of Canada, 279
Honiton Bank, 213
Hope, Samuel & Co, 323
Hope & Co, 269, 289
Hopkins, Drewett & Co, 343
Horden & Hill, 477

602 British banking – a guide to historical records

Horman, Anthoine, Ahier, Le Gros & Co, 143
Hornden, C H, 199
Hornden, Molineux & Co, 199
Hornden & Molineux, 199
Hoskins & Co, 432
Hove Banking Co Ltd, 344
How, Lott & Lathy, 213
Howden Bank, 467
HSBC, 7, 12, 375
HSBC Group, 464
HSBC Holdings plc, 279, 375
HSBC Investment Banking Group, 464
HSBC Samuel Montagu, 464
Huddersfield Banking Co, 283
Huddersfield Banking Co Ltd, **283–4**, 374
Huddleston, Cooper, Greene & Co, 284
Huddleston, Greene & Co, 284
Huddleston & Co, 284
Hudson, James, 264
Hudson & Hatfield, 264
Hughes, Locke, Oliver & Co, 341
Hughes & Morgan, 516
Hulke & Son, 403
Hull, East Riding & North Lincolnshire Banking Co, 284
Hull, Smith & Co, 551
Hull Bank, 480
Hull Banking Co, 284, 323
Hull Banking Co Ltd, **284–5**, 556
Hunt, Trim & Co, 301
Hunter, Colonel William, 285
Hunter, James, 285
Hunter, Robert, 285
Hunter-Blair, Sir James, 213, 285
Hunters & Co, **285–6**, 303, 510
Huntingdon Town & County Bank, 518
Hurley, Molineux, Whitfield & Dicker, 385
Hurley & Co, 188
Husband & Co, 403
Huth, Frederick, 286
Huth, Frederick & Co, 5, 125, **286–7**, 293
Huth & Co, 286
Huth Coffee Sales Ltd, 287

Huth Produce Sales Ltd, 287
Hutton, Other & Co, 502

Ilfracombe Bank, 520
Imperial Bank Ltd, **287–8**, 353
Imperial Bank of Canada, 85
Imperial Bank of Iran, 119
Imperial Bank of Persia, 118, 203, 468
Imperial Ottoman Bank, 399
Inchcape & Co Ltd, 236, 237
ING Baring Holdings Ltd, **288–92**
ING Group, 290
Inglis, William, 578
Ingram, Francis & William & Co, **292**
Ingram, Kennet & Ingram, 292
Innes & Clerk, 575
Institute of Bankers, 565
Institute of Bankers in Scotland, 458, 567
International Bank for Reconstruction and Development, 67
International Bank of Hamburg & London Ltd, 292
International Bank of London Ltd, **292**
International Financial Society, 52, 234, **292–3**
International Westminster Bank Ltd, **293–4**
Investec, 243
Ionian Bank, 145, 294
Ionian Bank Ltd, **294–6**
Ionian Securities Ltd, 295
Ionian State Bank, 294
Irano British Bank, 145
Irish Permanent Building Society, 243
Isaac, Baldwin & Shapland, 104
Isaac, Elias, 104
Isle of Man Banking Co, 445
Isle of Man Bank Ltd, 404
Isle of Man Joint Stock Banking Co, **296–7**, 555
Isle of Thanet Bank, 155
Isle of Wight Joint Stock Banking Co, **297**, 403
Issuing Houses Association, 562, **571–2**

Jackson, Goodchild & Co, 297

Index of names

Jackson, Jackson, Goodchild, Jackson & Jones, **297**
Jackson, James, 315, 316
Jackson, Sir Thomas, 278
Jackson, William,
  of Rochford, 223
  of Stamford, 206
Jackson & Johnson, 206
James, Paul, 370
James, William, 180
Janvrin, Durell, De Veulle & Co, 450
Janvrin, Durell & Co, 450
Japhet, S, 145
Japhet, Saemy, 145, 146
Jarvis, Sir Lewis, 298
Jarvis & Jarvis, 249, **297–8**
Jeffreys & Hill, 343
Jemmett, Curteis & Jemmett, 440
Jemmett, Pomfret, Burra & Simonds, 440
Jemmett, Whitfeld & Jemmett, 440
Jemmett & Pomfret, 440
Jenkins, David, 167
Jenner & Co, **298**, 328
Jennings, Francis, 298
Jennings, F W, **298**, 429
Jersey, 8th Earl of, George Henry Robert Child-Villiers, 147
Jersey Commercial Bank, 450
Jersey Joint Stock Bank, 258
Jersey Old Bank, 144
Jessel, Toynbee & Co, 298
Jessel, Toynbee & Gillett plc, 50, 225, **298–9**
Jessel Toynbee plc, 225
Johnson, Eaton & Eland, 206
Johnson, Robert, 503
Johnson, William, 206
Johnson, William & Stephen Eaton, 206, 207
Joint Stock Banking Co of Pontefract, Wakefield & Goole, 318
Jones, Barkers, Jones & Co, 356
Jones, Daniel Barker, Loyd & Co, 300
Jones, David, 299
Jones, David & Co, **299**, 329
Jones, Evans & Co, 299
Jones, Fox & Co, 356
Jones, John, 356

Jones, John & Co, 300, 356
Jones, Joseph, 300, 356
Jones, Joseph & Co, 300, 356
Jones, Joseph & Daniel & Co, 300
Jones, Loyd, Hulme & Co, 300
Jones, Loyd & Co, **300–301**, 351, 356
Jones, Samuel & William, Loyds & Co, 356
Jones, Sir Alfred, 491
Jones, Son & Foster, 300
Jones, Thomas & Hugh, 546
Jones, W & D & Co, 299
Jones, William, 300
Jones, William & Son, **300**, 489
Jones, Wright & Co, 274
Jones & Blewitt, **299**, 386
Jones & Davis, **300**, 386
Jones & Williams, 546
Joplin, Thomas, 403

Kaffrarian Colonial Bank, 47
Keep & Co, 235
Kellow & Pritchard, **301–2**
Kelly, James, 445
Kelynge, Greenway & Co, 238
Kendal Bank, 177, 521
Kensingtons, Styan & Adams, **302**
Kensingtons & Co, 302
Kent, Richard, 364
Kent, Robert, 578
Kentish Bank, 537
Kerfoot, Walter, 429
Kerridge, J, 61
Kerrison, Sir Roger, 302
Kerrison & Kerrison, 302
Kerrison & Sons, **302**
Kett, Hatfield & Back, 504
Kett & Back, 504
Kewney & King, **302–3**
Keyser, A, 464
Keyser Ullmann, 464
Keyser Ullmann Ltd, 146
Kidd, William, 57
Kilmarnock Banking Co, 285, **303**
Kindersley, 1st Lord, Robert Kindersley, 313
Kindersley, Robert see Kindersley, 1st Lord
King, Henry, 303

604 **British banking – a guide to historical records**

King, Henry S & Co, 174, **303**, 329
King, Richard, 385
King & Shaxson Ltd, 220, 485
Kinglake & Co, 500
Kingsbridge Joint Stock Bank, 534
Kington & Radnorshire Bank, 184
Kinnaird, Lord, 446, 447
Kinnersley & Sons, **303–4**
Kinnersley, T, 303
Kinnersley, Thomas & Sons, 303, 403
Kirby, Samuel, 425
Kirby & Co, 506
Kirkland, William, 277
Kirkpatrick, James, 297
Kissin, Lord, 243,
Kitson, William, 520
Kleinwort, Alexander, 304
Kleinwort Benson Ltd, 19, 103, **304–6**
Kleinwort Sons & Co Ltd, 103, 304
Knapp, Henry & John Tomkins, **306–7**
Knapp, Son & Co, 131
Knaresborough & Claro Banking Co,
    307
Knaresborough & Claro Banking Co
    Ltd, **307**, 404
Knight, Haydon & Shrubsole, 477
Knight, James & Sons, **307**
Knight, Jenner & Co, 137, 307
Knox, Thomas, 380
Konig Brothers, 286
Koppel, Frank A, 72
Kylsant, Lord, Sir Owen Philipps, 491

Lacon, Edmund, 307
Lacons, Fisher & Co, 307
Lacons, Youell & Co, 307
Lacons, Youell & Kemp, 138, **307–8**
La Coste & Co, 58
Lacy, Benjamin W, 308
Lacy, Hartland, Woodbridge & Co,
    308, 374
Lacy, Son & Hartland, 308
Lacy & Son, 308
Ladbroke, Felix, 309
Ladbroke, Kingscote & Gillman, 309
Ladbroke, Sir Robert, 309
Ladbroke, Sir Robert Son, Rawlinson
    & Porker, 309
Ladbroke & Co, 231, **309**

Ladbrokes & Gillman, 309
Ladenburg Thalmann & Co, 468
Lambton, Ralph John, 309
Lambton, Williamson, Randell,
    Chambers & Smoult, 309
Lambton & Co, **309–10**, 329
Lambton Banking Co, 309
Lancashire & Yorkshire Bank Ltd, 47,
    51, 134, 310–11, 362, 363, 370,
    443, 444, 535
Lancaster Banking Co, 222
Lancaster Banking Co Ltd, 191, 192,
    311–13
Langport Bank, 499
Langton, William, 271, 542
Large, J & J, **313**
Lashmar, Richard, 254
Lawe, Robert & Co, 442
Lawe, Roskell, Arrowsmith & Co, 452
Lawrie & Son, 277
Lawson, Sir John Bart., Miles
    Stapleton Esq & Co, 444
Lawson, William, 175
Laycock, Samuel, 112
Lazard, Alexandre, 313
Lazard, Lazare, 313
Lazard, Simon, 313
Lazard Brothers & Co, 313
Lazard Brothers & Co Ltd, **313–14**
Lazard Frères, 313
Le Blanc, Charles, 284
Le Neveu, Sorel & Co, 258
Leach, Pollard & Hardcastle, **314**
Leaf, Walter, 529
Leamington Bank, 314
Leamington Priors & Warwickshire
    Banking Co, 517
Leamington Priors & Warwickshire
    Banking Co Ltd, **315**, 373
Leatham, Jackson & Co,
    Doncaster, 315
    Pontefract, 316
Leatham, John, 315, 316
Leatham, Tew, Trueman & Co,
    Doncaster, 315
    Pontefract, 316
Leatham, Tew & Co,
    Doncaster, 164, **315–16**
    Pontefract, 89, **316–17**

Index of names

Leaver, Assheton, 105
Lechmere, Anthony, 104, 317
Lechmere, Isaac, Martin & Cherry, **317**
Lechmere & Co, 104
Ledgard, Geo. Welch & Sons, 318
Ledgard & Sons, **317–18**, 548
Lee, Higginson & Co, 273
Lee & Lock, 520
Leeds & County Bank Ltd, **318**, 373
Leeds & West Riding Joint Stock Banking Co, **318**
Leeds Bank, 100
Leeds Joint Stock Bank Ltd, 347
Leeds Union Bank, 547
Leek Bank, 298
Lefevre, H S & Co, 125, **319**
Leicester & Leicestershire Bank, 152
Leicester & Warwickshire Banking Co, **319**
Leicester Bank,
  Bellairs, Geo., 103
  Bentley & Buxton, 104
Leicestershire Banking Co, 173, 319, 372
Leicestershire Banking Co Ltd, 262, **319–21**, 374
Leith Banking Co, 140
Lemon, Sir William, 357
Lemon, Sir William Buller, Furley, Lubbock & Co, 357, 548
Lemon, Sir William Furley, Lubbock & Co, 357
Lemon Bart., Sir William Furly, Lubbock, Willyams & Co, 547
Leslie & Grindlay, 240
Levy, Calmer Joachim *see* Hambro, Calmer Joachim
Lewes Bank, 385
Lewes New Bank, 385
Lewes Old Bank, 385
Lewis, William & Thomas Salt, **321**
Lewis & Peat Ltd, 243
Lewis's Bank Ltd, **321**, 330, 362
Ley & Co, **321–2**, 403
Leyland, Thomas, 322
Leyland & Bullin, 322
Leyland & Bullins, **322**, 413
Lichfield, Rugeley & Tamworth Banking Co, 403

Lincoln & Lindsey Banking Co Ltd, **322–3**, 374
Lister, Moorson & Co, 316
Little & Woodcock, 370
Liverpool Bank, 238
Liverpool Borough Bank, **323–4**
Liverpool Commercial Bank, 324
Liverpool Commercial Banking Co Ltd, **324**
Liverpool Union Bank, 328
Liverpool Union Bank Ltd, **324–5**
Liverpool United Trades Bank, **325**
Llandovery & Llandeilo Bank, 299
Llangollen Bank, 448
Llangollen Old Bank, 448
Lloyd, Elton, Miller, Tyndall, Knox & Hale, 381
Lloyd, George Butler, 133
Lloyd, Harford, 380
Lloyd, Howard, 216
Lloyd, Sampson, 328
Lloyd, Sampson S, 52
Lloyd, Thomas, 105
Lloyds, Barnetts & Bosanquets Bank Ltd, 97, 106, 109, 328, 444
Lloyds & Bolsa International, 326, 327, 330
Lloyds & Bolsa International Bank Ltd, 73
Lloyds & Co, 328, 384
Lloyds & National Provincial (Foreign) Bank Ltd, 325
Lloyds Bank (BLSA) Ltd, 73
Lloyds Bank California, 330
Lloyds Bank (Europe), 73, **325–7**, 329, 330
Lloyds Bank (Foreign), 326
Lloyds Bank (France) & National Provincial Bank (France) Ltd, 325
Lloyds Bank (France) Ltd, 325, 327, 329, 404
Lloyds Banking Co Ltd, 52, 97, 100, 106, 109, 135, 172, 217, 328, 384, 477, 496, 517, 524, 536, 545
Lloyds Bank International, 326, **327**
Lloyds Bank International Ltd, 73
Lloyds Bank Ltd, 7, 72, 73, 102, 109, 126, 128, 131, 133, 137, 155, 161, 169, 174, 181, 183, 188,

606   *British banking – a guide to historical records*

216, 236, 259, 262, 263, 265, 267, 270, 273, 276, 298, 299, 310, 321, 325, 327, 328, 329, 330, 343, 366, 396, 425, 433, 440, 491, 495, 508, 520, 535, 538, 547, 548, 553, 559, 569, 576

Lloyds Bank plc, 73, **327–41**

Lloyds TSB Group plc, 7, 330, 463

Lock, Hulme & Co, 81

Locke, Tugwell & Meek, 137, **341–2**

Lockhart, James & James, 342

Lockharts, Maxtone, Wallis & Paterson, **342**

Lockharts & Maxtone, 342

London, Buenos Aires & River Plate Bank Ltd, 72

London, City & Midland Bank Ltd, 112, 150, 320, 323, 353, 371, 373, 413, 422, 424, 471, 475, 557

London, County, Westminster & Parr's Bank Ltd, 100, 101, 421, 430, 528

London, County, Westminster & Parr's Foreign Bank Ltd, 293

London, County & Westminster Bank Ltd, 105, 293, 344, 351, 430, 528

London, County & Westminster Bank (Paris) Ltd, 293, 528

London, Provincial & South Western Bank Ltd, 86, 89, 348, 350, **355**

London & Argentine Bank Ltd, 52

London & Brazilian Bank Ltd, 53, 72, 329, **342–3**

London & County Banking Co, 343, 505

London & County Banking Co Ltd, 132, **343–7**, 351, 422

London & County Bank Ltd, 528

London & County Joint Stock Banking Co, 184, 267, 448

London & Dublin Bank, **347**, 393, 394

London & Hanseatic Bank Ltd, 355

London & Lancashire Bank Ltd, 369

London & Liverpool Bank of Commerce Ltd, 125

London & Middlesex Bank, 185, 351

London & Midland Bank Ltd, 82, 140, 142, 144, 149, 283, 308, 359, 373, 420, 442

London & Northern Bank Ltd, 113, **347**

London & Northern Joint Stock Bank Ltd, 372

London & Provincial Bank Ltd, 86, 212, 347–8, 350, 355, 417, 523

London & River Plate Bank Ltd, 53, 72, 329, 343

London & South African Bank, 349, 494

London & South Western Bank Ltd, 86, 174, 348, **349–50**, 355

London & Westminster Bank, 160, 288, 301, 314, 344, 351, 561

London & Westminster Bank Ltd, **351–2**, 528

London & Yorkshire Bank Ltd, **352**, 514

London Bank of Central America Ltd, 162

London Bank of Mexico & South America Ltd, 56

London Bankers' Clearing House, **569–70**

London Clearing House, 7, 109, 137, 361, 365, 373, 393, 429, 460, 565, 569, 540, 541, 547, 570

London Commercial & Cripplegate Bank Ltd, **352–3**, 513

London Commercial Bank, 349

London Discount Co, 116

London Discount Houses Committee, 572

London Discount Market Association, **572**

London Exchange Banking Co, 269

London Investment Banking Association, 562, 572

London Joint, City & Midland Bank Ltd, 154, 353, 374

London Joint Stock Bank, 51

London Joint Stock Bank Ltd, 288, **353–4**, 374

London Merchant Bank Ltd, 243, **354–5**

London Merchant Securities Ltd, 355

Long & Haldimand, 390

Lonrho Ltd, 63

Lonsdale Bank, 222

Index of names 607

Lonsdale Investment Trust Ltd, 103
Loraine, Sir C Baker, Pearson, Maude, Loraine & Co, 356
Loraine Bt., Sir Charles Baker, Pearson, Maude, Loraine & Co, 355–6
Loraine Bt., Sir Wm. Baker, Pearson, Maude & Co, 355
Loughborough Bank, 372
Lovatt, Thomas, 179
Loveband & Co, 356, 403
Lowe, R, 540
Lowe, Vere, Williams & Jennings, 539
Loyd, Entwisle & Co, 191, 356–7
Loyd, Samuel Jones see Overstone, Lord
Lubbock, J W, 357
Lubbock, Forster & Co, 449
Lubbock, Sir John see Avebury, 1st Lord
Lubbock, Sir John, Lubbock, Forster & Clarke, 357
Lubbock, Sir John, William Forster, Clarke & Co, 357
Lubbock, Sir John, William Forster & Co, 357
Luce & Co, 548
Ludlow & Tenbury Banking Co, 358, 553
Lumsden, James, 154
Lusk, Sir Andrew, 287
Luton Bank, 259
Lymington Bank, 462
Lynn Bank, 210
Lynn Regis & Lincolnshire Bank, 249
Lynn Regis & Norfolk Bank, 298
Lyon, Thomas, 429

Macardy, Joseph, 191
Mcgrigor Bart., Sir Charles E & Co, 366
Machell, Pease & Hoare, 560
Machell, Peases & Hoare, 358, 434
Mackie, Davidson & Gladstone, 140
Mackinnon, Mackenzie & Co, 236
Mackinnon, Sir William, 236
McLean, David, 279, 282
McLean, James & Co, 81
MacLeay, Alexander, 135

MacLeay, John, 135
MacLeay, Kenneth, 135
MacLeay, William, 135
Maddison, Atherley & Co, 236, 358
Maddison, Atherley, Hankinson & Darwin, 58
Maddison & Co, 58
Maddison & Pearce, 358
Magens, John Dorrien, 196
Malcolm, W R, 171
Maltby & Robinson, 451
Manchester & County Bank Ltd, 65, 81, 167, 462
Manchester & Liverpool District Banking Co, 191, 301, 356, 357, 442
Manchester & Liverpool District Banking Co Ltd, 83, 312
Manchester & Salford Bank, 260, 261, 271, 540, 545
Manchester & Salford Bank Ltd, 153, 522, 540, 541
Manchester Joint Stock Bank Ltd, 359, 374
Mander, Henry, 546
Manningtree & Colchester Bank, 422
Manningtree & Mistley Bank, 115
Mansell, M D, 98
Mansfield Bank, 451
Manx Bank Ltd, 359–60, 369
Mare & Eaton, 417
Margate Bank, 155
Margesson, Henty, Henty & Hopkins, 269
Marine Midland, 279
Marjoribanks, Edward, 171
Marlar, Lascelles, Pell & Down, 439
Marnie, James, 57
Marsh, Sibbald, Stracey & Fauntleroy, 360
Marsh, Stracey, Fauntleroy & Graham, 360, 465
Marshall, Harding & Hiern, 216
Marshall, M W & Son, 469
Marten, Part & Co, 89, 360
Martin, James, 365
Martin, John, 364, 365
Martin, John Biddulph, 365
Martin, Joseph, 365

608 British banking – a guide to historical records

Martin, Richard, 364, 566
Martin, Sir Richard, 364
Martin, Richard Biddulph, 364, 365
Martin, Simon, 246
Martin, Thomas, 364
Martin & Hartwright, 390
Martin's Bank Ltd, 361, 363, **364–6**
Martins Bank Ltd, 7, 89, 124, 321, 330, **361–3**
Mason, Currie, James & Yallowley, 182
Mason, John, 182
Massey & Jarvis, 298
Masterman, Peters, Mildred, Birkbeck & Co, 48
Matheson & Co, 125
Matthews & Co, 81
Matthias, James, 59
Maude, Joseph, 177
Maude, Wilson & Crewdson, 177
Maude, Wilson & Smith, 177
Mauritius Commercial Bank Ltd, **366**
Maxwell, Ritchie & Co, 503
May, Wyborn, White & Mercer, **366**
Mediterranean Bank, **367**
Medley, Son & Co, **367**
Meek, Mousley & Co, 133
Meinertzhagen, Daniel, 286
Mellersh, John, 367
Mellersh, Moline & Weale, 367
Mellersh & Co, 137, **367**
Mello, John Arnold, 196
Mellon, Harriot, 171
Mellon Bank & Trust Co, 73
Mellor, Mr, 263
Melly, Prevost & Co, 390
Melly & Co, 390
Melville, Alexander, 483
Mercantile Bank Ltd, 279, **367–9**, 460
Mercantile Bank of Bombay, 367
Mercantile Bank of India, London & China, 367
Mercantile Bank of India Ltd, 75, 368
Mercantile Bank of Lancashire Ltd, 311, 359, **369–70**
Mercantile Credit Co Ltd, 362
Mercantile House Holdings plc, 50
Mercer, George, 190
Merchant Banking Co, 578

Mercury Asset Management Ltd, 524
Mercury Securities Ltd, 524
Meredith & Co, 184
Merriman, E B, 137
Messiter, U G & H, 500
Metropolitan, Birmingham & South Wales Bank Ltd, 371, 400, 486
Metropolitan & Birmingham Bank Ltd, 371, 460, 486
Metropolitan & Provincial Bank Ltd, 460
Metropolitan Bank, **370**, 430
Metropolitan Bank Ltd, 460
Metropolitan Bank (of England & Wales) Ltd, 184, **370–72**, 374
Meyer, Carl, 453
Micklem, John, 495
Micklem, Stephens, Simonds & Harris, 478, 495
Middleton, Cradock & Co, **372**
Middleton, George, 120, 170
Middleton & Co, 320
Midland Bank Finance Corporation, 374, 375
Midland Banking Co Ltd, 269, **372–3**, 467, 516, 517
Midland Bank Ltd, 7, 12, 99, 374, 418, 464, 559
Midland Bank plc, 279, **373–9**
Midland Counties Bank Ltd, 516
Midland Counties District Bank, 517
Midland Counties District Bank Ltd, **379–80**
Midland Investment Management, 464
Midland Montagu Industrial Finance Ltd, 464
Milbanke, Woodbridge & Co, 89
Milbanke, Woodbridge, Gruggen & Gauntlett, **380**
Miles, Cave, Baillie & Co, 190, **380–81**, 441, 507
Miles, Miles, Harford, Miles & Miles, 381
Milford, Hogg, Nation & Co, 381
Milford, John, 381
Milford, Samuel, 381
Milford, Snow & Co, **381–2**, 466
Milford & Clarke, 381
Miller, James, 578

Index of names

Miller, Tyndall, Elton, Gillam & Edye, 381
Miller, William, 380
Miller & Co, 319
Million Bank, 382–3
Milloy, Thomas, 105
Mills, A H, 232
Mills, Bawtree & Co, 383
Mills, Bawtree, Dawnay, Curzon & Co, 383, 508
Mills, Bawtree, Errington, Bawtree & Grimwade, 383
Mills, John, 310, 383
Mills, J R & J, 383
Mills, Nunn, Bawtree & Nunn, 383
Mills, Nunn & Co, 422
Mills, William, 230
Milton, Lord, 120
Miners' Bank, 357, 548
Minet, Fector & Co, 383–4
Minors, Thomas, 107
Minors & Boldero, 107
Minster Trust Ltd, 219, 220
Mirfield & Huddersfield District Banking Co, 534
Moffatt, Kensington & Boler, 302
Moffatt, Kensingtons & Styan, 302, 575
Moger, Sons & Jones, 384, 441
Moger & Sons, 384
Moilliet, Jean Louis, 384
Moilliet, J L & Sons, 328, 384
Moilliet, Smith, Pearson & Moilliet, 384
Moilliet & Sons, 64
Molesworth, Sir John, 167
Molesworth, Sir John & Son, 167
Moline, Robert, 367
Molineux, Hurley, Whitfield & Dicker, 385
Molineux, Joseph, 385
Molineux, Whitfield, Dicker & Co, 385
Molineux, Whitfield, Dicker & Molineux, 385
Molineux, Whitfield & Co, 385
Molineux, Whitfield & Whitfield, 385
Molineux & Co, 89, 385
Monmouth Bank, 126

Monmouthshire & Glamorganshire Banking Co, 299, 300, 386
Montagu, Edwin, 463
Montagu, Samuel, see Swaythling, Lord
Montagu Trust Ltd, 464
Montgomeryshire Old Bank, 100
Montolieu, Brooksbank, Greenwood & Drewe, 256
Montrose Banking Co, 578
Moore, Harrison & Co, 263
Moore, Maltby & Robinson, 386
Moore, Maltby, Evans & Middlemore, 386
Moore, Thomas, 386
Moore, William, 403
Moore & Co, 451
Moore & Maltby, 451
Moore & Robinson's Nottinghamshire Banking Co, 386
Moore & Robinson's Nottinghamshire Banking Co Ltd, 57, 138, 386
Moores, Carrick & Co, 476
Moorhouse, Willis & Reade, 547
Morgan, Drexel & Co, 387
Morgan Grenfell & Co, 387, 453
Morgan Grenfell & Co Ltd, 180, 388
Morgan Grenfell Group, 386–90
Morgan Grenfell Group plc, 388
Morgan Grenfell Holdings Ltd, 388
Morgan, J P & Co, 387, 388, 389
Morgan, J Pierpont, 387
Morgan, J S & Co, 387
Morgan, Junius S, 387
Morice, Humphrey, 70
Morland, Ransom & Co, 446
Morland, Sir Scrope Bernard, 257, 446
Morland, William, 446
Morlands, Auriol & Co, 446
Morris, Clayton & Co, 152
Morris, David & Sons, 403
Morris, John, 152
Morris, John & Partner, 152
Morris, Prevost & Co, 390–91
Mortlock, John, 391
Mortlock, John & Co Ltd, 89, 391–2
Mortlock, John & Sons, 391
Moss, Dales & Rogers, 419
Moule & Co, 420

610   *British banking – a guide to historical records*

Mounts Bay Bank, 107
Mowbray, Hollingsworth & Co, 60
Moxon & Percival, 415
Mullens, 524
Murray, Thomas Lamie, 393

Nantwich & South Cheshire Joint
   Stock Bank, 191
Natal Bank, 392
Natal Bank Ltd, **392**, 398
Nation, William, 381
National & Commercial Banking
   Group Ltd, 539, 541, 543, 544
National & Grindlays Bank, 329
National & Grindlays Bank Ltd, 241
National Australia Bank Ltd, 154
National Australia Group (UK) Ltd,
   559
National Bank Ltd, 347, **392–5**, 400,
   457, 539, 541
National Bank of Egypt, 174, 329
National Bank of India Ltd, 241
National Bank of Ireland, 392, 393, 395
National Bank of Liverpool Ltd, 51,
   310, 394, **395**, 429, 430
National Bank of New Zealand, 329,
   330
National Bank of Scotland, 46, 359
National Bank of Scotland Ltd, 161,
   396–8, 400, 457, 577
National Bank of South Africa, 54, 87,
   89
National Bank of South Africa Ltd, 64,
   158, 392, **398–9**
National Bank of the Orange River
   Colony Ltd, 398
National Bank of Turkey, **399**
National Bank of Wales, 371
National Bank of Wales Ltd, **399–400**,
   445
National Commercial and Schroders
   Ltd, 400
National Commercial Bank of
   Scotland Ltd, 161, 393, 396, **400–**
   401, 457, 458, 539
National Discount Co Ltd, 50, 219,
   401–3, 515
National Overseas & Grindlays Bank
   Ltd, 241

National Provincial and Rothschild, 406
National Provincial & Union Bank of
   England Ltd, 105, 113, 171, 190,
   404, 415, 448, 474, 476, 514
National Provincial Bank Ltd, 7, 168,
   191, 193, 241, 242, 325, 326,
   327, **403–8**, 425, 529
National Provincial Bank of England,
   71, 157, 217, 297, 303, 321, 356,
   383, 403, 437, 445, 479, 497,
   508, 520
National Provincial Bank of England
   Ltd, 170, 307, 417, 514
National Union of Bank Employees
   (NUBE), 564
National Westminster Bank Ltd, 7,
   168, 404, 559, 569
National Westminster Bank plc, 171,
   293, 457, 529, 564
National Westminster Bank SA, 293
NatWest International Trust Holdings
   Ltd, 171
Naval & Commercial Bank, 275
Naval Bank, 262
Needham Market Bank, 245
Nelthorpe, Henry, 210
Nevile, Reid & Co, 89, **408–9**
Newark & Sleaford Bank, 432
Newark Bank, 439
Newark upon Trent Bank, 252
Newbury Old Bank, 519
Newcastle & Staffs Bank, 303
Newcastle Commercial Joint Stock
   Bank, 276, **409**
Newcastle, Shields & Sunderland
   Union Joint Stock Bank, 189,
   276, **409–10**, 419, 552
Newcastle, Sunderland, Durham &
   North & South Shields District
   Banking Co, 419
Newcome, Frank, 262
New, Edward, 438
New London & Brazilian Bank Ltd,
   342
Newmarket Bank, 257
New Oriental Bank Corporation, 75,
   118
New Oriental Bank Corporation Ltd,
   410

Index of names

611

Newport Bank, 450
New Sarum Bank, 438
Newton Bank, 549
New Trading Co Ltd, 523
Nicholls, Baker & Crane, 373, **411**
Nicholson, Brown & Co, 128, 546
Nicholson, Janson & Co, 127
Nicholson, Mr, 478
Nicholson & Co, 188
Nightingale, John, William & George, 411
Nightingale, William & George, **411**
Noel, Gerard, 185
Norfolk & Norwich Joint Stock Banking Co, 205, **411–12**
Norfolk General Bank, 504
Norman, Montagu, 67, 128
North, John, 55
Northampton Town & County Bank, 576
Northampton Union Bank, 415, 435
Northamptonshire Banking Co, 319, 525
Northamptonshire Banking Co Ltd, 137, **414–15**
Northamptonshire Central Banking Co, 414
Northamptonshire Union Bank, 254
Northamptonshire Union Bank Ltd, 404, **415**
North & South Wales Bank, 63, 141, 184, 444, 445, 448, 546
North & South Wales Bank Ltd, 322, 374, **412–14**
North British Bank, 204
North Central Wagon & Finance Co Ltd, 404
North Devon Bank, 445
North Eastern Banking Co Ltd, 183, 189, 361, 363, **415–16**
Northern & Central Bank of England, 50, 74, **416–17**, 421
Northern Bank Ltd, 375
Northern Counties Bank, 167
North Kent Bank Ltd, 348, **417**
North of England Union & Joint Stock Banking Co, **417**, 419
North of Scotland & Town & County Bank Ltd, 418, 505

North of Scotland Bank, 135, 151
North of Scotland Bank Ltd, 154, 374, **417–18**, 505
Northumberland & District Banking Co, 573
Northumberland & Durham District Bank, 183
Northumberland & Durham District Banking Co, 60, 189, 416, **418–19**, 449
North Western Bank Ltd, 374, **419–20**
North Wilts & Hampshire Banking Co, 420
North Wilts Banking Co, 137, 258, **420**
Norton & Mercer, 550
Norwich & Norfolk Bank, 246
Norwich & Swaffham Bank, 186
Norwich Bank, 247, 302
Norwich Crown & Suffolk & Norfolk Bank, 264
Norwich Crown Bank, 264
Nottingham & District Bank Ltd, 379
Nottingham & Nottinghamshire Banking Co, 323, 421
Nottingham & Nottinghamshire Banking Co Ltd, **420–21**, 528
Nottingham & Nottinghamshire Joint Stock Bank, 421, 472
Nottingham & Notts Bank, 263
Nottingham Joint Stock Bank Ltd, 374, **421–2**, 490
Nunn, Mills & Co, 422
Nunn, Nunn & Nunn, 422
Nunn & Co, 344
Nunn & Webster, **422**
NWS Bank plc, 77

Oakes & Co, 212
Oakes, Bevan & Co, 422
Oakes, Bevan & Hanbury, 422
Oakes, Bevan, Moor & Bevan, 422
Oakes, Bevan, Moor & Hanbury, 422
Oakes, Bevan, Tollemache & Co, 138, **422–3**
Oakes, Fincham, Bevan, Moor & Simpson, 212
Oakes, Fincham & Co, 212
Oakes, James, 423

612 British banking – a guide to historical records

Oakes, James & Son,
  Bury St Edmunds, 422, 486
  Stowmarket, 422
Oldaker, Tomes & Chattaway, 504
Old Bank,
  Newcastle under Lyme, 303
  Newcastle upon Tyne, 448
Old Bath Bank, 507
Oldham Joint Stock Bank Ltd, 374,
  423–4, 451
Old Merionethshire Bank, 546
Oriental Bank, 410
Oriental Bank Corporation, 48, 63, 75,
  410
Oswestry Old Bank, 179
Ottoman Bank, 52, 53
Oundle & Northants Bank, 557
Overend, John, 424
Overend Gurney & Co, 84, 246, 247,
  424
Overend Gurney & Co Ltd, 245, 251,
  316, 401, 424–5, 447, 473
Overstone, Lord, Samuel Jones Loyd,
  300
Oxford Old Bank, 431

Paget, Joseph, 425
Paget, Thomas, 425, 427
Paget, William, 425
Pagets & Co, 328
Pagets & Kirby, 425–6
Paisley Banking Co, 121, 426
Paisley Commercial Bank, 527
Paisley Union Bank Co, 426, 510,
  578
Paisley Union Banking Co, 426
Palatine Bank Ltd, 361, 427
Palmer & Greene, 427
P&O Banking Corporation Ltd, 144,
  425
P&O Steam Navigation Co, 425
Panmure, Earl of, 120
Pardoe & Nichols, 411
Pares, John, 427
Pares, Thomas, 427, 428
Pares & Heygate, 425, 427
Pares' Leicestershire Banking Co, 428
Pares' Leicestershire Banking Co Ltd,
  427–8, 429

Parke, Thomas, 238
Parker, Alwyn, 576
Parker, Shore & Blakelock, 428, 474
Parker, Shore & Co, 301, 428–9
Parr, Joseph, 429
Parr, Lyon & Co, 429
Parr, Lyon & Greenall, 429
Parr & Co, 429
Parrott, G & Co, 98
Parr's Banking Co & Alliance Bank
  Ltd, 51, 163, 179, 429, 465, 477
Parr's Banking Co Ltd, 195, 213, 218,
  298, 395, 429, 460, 461, 551
Parr's Bank Ltd, 58, 163, 177, 187,
  200, 428, 429–31, 450, 500, 528
Parsons, Herbert, 431, 432
Parsons, Thomson, Parsons & Co, 89,
  431
Parsons, Thomson & Co, 431–2
Parsons & Co, 553
Patison, James, 578
Payne, Hope & Co, 432
Payne, John, 484
Payne & Co, 432, 500
Peabody, George, 386
Peabody, George & Co, 293, 387
Peabody, Riggs & Co, 387
Peacock, Handley & Co, 432
Peacock, Handley & Kirton, 432
Peacock, Willson & Co, 329, 432–3
Pearson, W D see Cowdray, 1st Lord
Pearsons, 314
Peart, John, 175
Pease, Hoare & Pease, 358, 434, 560
Pease, J & J W, 89, 433–4
Pease, John W, 276
Pease, Joseph,
  of Darlington, 433
  of Hull, 434
Pease, Josh. & Son, 434
Pease, J W Beaumont see Wardington,
  Lord
Pease, Knowsley & Wray, 434
Pease, Thomas Son & Co, 573
Pease & Liddell, 434
Pease & Co, 433
Pease's Old Bank, 434
Peckover, Edmund, 113, 114
Peckover, Harris & Co, 113

Index of names

Peckover, Harris & Harris, 114
Peckover, Jonathan, 248
Peckover, Joseph, 248
Peckover, May, 114
Pedders & Co, **434–5**
Pember & Boyle, 388
Pembrokeshire Bank, 523
Percival, J & Son, 415
Percival, John, 415, 435
Percival, Peter, 210
Percival, Samuel, 415, 435
Percival & Co, **435**
Perfect, Seaton & Co, 435
Perfect & Co, **435**, 557
Perham, Phelps & Co, 432
Perring, Philip, 157
Persian Bank Mining Rights Corp, 120
Perth Banking Co, **435–6**, 511, 578
Perth Union Banking Co, 396
Perth United Banking Co, 435, **436**
Perth United Co, 436
Peterborough Bank, 479
Petersen, Hans W, 524
Petersfield & Hampshire Bank, 266
Petty, Edmund, 436
Petty & Postlethwaite, **436–7**, 522
Pew, Peter & Co, 403, **437**
Pewte, James, 215
Philipps, Sir Owen *see* Kylsant, Lord
Pictet, G & Co, 390
Pierson, Joseph, 438
Pierson, Joseph M, 438
Pierson & Son, **437–8**
Pierson & Trapp, 505
Pinchin & Denny, 388
Pinckney, Henry, 234
Pinckney Brothers, **438**, 548
Pinhorn, Sir John Weston & Son, 561
Pitt, Bowley, Croome & Wood, 169
Pitt, Gardner & Co, 574
Pitt, Joseph, 438
Pitt, Powell, Fripp, Brice & New, 438
Pitt, Powell & Fripp, **438–9**
Platt, John, 130
Playfair, William, 264
Plymouth & Devonport Banking Co, 188
Plymouth Bank, 208

Pocklington, Dickinson, Hunter & Co, 439
Pocklington, Dickinson & Co, 439
Pocklington, Joseph, 308
Pocklington, Lacy & Son, 308
Pocklington, Rastell, Oliver & Ray, 439
Pocklington & Co, **439**
Pocklington & Lacy, 308
Pole, Thornton, Free, Down & Scott, **439**
Pole, Thornton & Co, 46, 539
Pomfret, Burra & Co, 329, **439–40**
Pontefract Bank, 316
Portsmouth, Portsea & Hampshire Bank, 234
Postlethwaite, William, 437
Post Office Savings Bank, 283
Powell, Timothy, 438
Praed, Digby, Box, Babbage & Co, 440
Praed, Digby, Box, Barnard & Newcombe, 440
Praed, Fane, Praed & Johnson, 440
Praed, Mackworth, Fane & Praed, 440
Praed, Mackworth, Newcombe & Fane, 440
Praed, Mackworth & Newcombe, 440
Praed, William Mackworth, 465
Praed & Co, 167
Praeds, Digby, Box, Babbage & Co, 440
Praeds & Co, 167, 328, **440**
Prescott, Cave, Buxton, Loder & Co, 190, 381, 507
Prescott, Dimsdale, Cave, Tugwell & Co Ltd, 132, 134, 187, 190, 265, 274, 381, 384, 441, 507
Prescott, Grote, Ames, Baillie & Grote, 441
Prescott, Grote, Ames, Cave & Grote, 441
Prescott, Grote, Cave & Cave, 441
Prescott, Grote, Culverden & Hollingsworth, 440
Prescott, Grote & Hollingsworth, 440
Prescott, Grote & Prescott, 440
Prescott's Bank Ltd, **440–42**, 514
Preston Adelphi Loan, Discount & Deposit Co Ltd, 443

614 *British banking – a guide to historical records*

Preston Banking Co Ltd, 374, **442–3**
Preston Union Bank Ltd, 311, **443–4**
Pretor, S, R Pew & B Chandler, 437
Pretor, Simon, 437
Pretor & Co, 437
Prevost, A L, 390
Prevost, Morris & Co, 390
Priaulx Le Marchant & Co, 242
Prideaux & Bentall, 188
Priestman, H C George Roper & Co,
   444
Priestman, Roper & Co, 89
Pritchard, Gordon & Co, 328, **444**
Pritchard, Gordon, Potts & Shorting,
   444
Pritchard, J G & J, 444
Pritchard, Nicholas, Potts & Gordon,
   444
Pritchard & Boycott, 444
Prout & Stapleton, 188
Provincial Banking Corporation Ltd,
   81, 186, 205, 348
Provincial Bank of Ireland, 392
Prudential Assurance Co, 125
Pugh, H & L & Co, 444
Pugh, Hugh, 445
Pugh, Jones & Co, 400, **444–5**
Pung, Clement, 364
Pute, James *see* Pewte, James
Pwllheli District Bank, 444
Pybus, Call, Marten & Hale, 137
Pybus, Hyde, Dorset & Cockell, 136
Pyke, Law & Co, 403, **445**
Pym, R R, 171

Quayle, George, 445
Quayle, George & Co, **445–6**
Quayle, Mark Hyldesley, 445

Rae, George, 412
Raggett, Seymour & Co, 258
Raikes, Currie & Co, 110
Raikes, Robert & Co, 110
Ralli, A A, 288
Ralli, P C, 288
Ralph, Yates & Parslaw, 265
Ramsay, William, 578
Ramsays, Bonars & Co, 154
Ramsbottom & Baverstock, 408

Rankin, Robert, 132
Ransom, Griffin, 446
Ransom, Bouverie & Co, 84, 85, 110,
   446–7
Ransom, Morland & Co,
   Dundee, 201
   London, 201, 228, 446
Ransom, Morland & Hammersley,
   256, 446
Ransom & Co, 110, 446
Raper, Swann, Clough, Swan, Bland &
   Raper, 502
Raper, Swann & Co, 502
Rawlinson, Abraham, 248
Rawson, Christopher, 252, 324
Rawson, John, 252, 253
Rawson, John, William & Christopher,
   153
Rawson, John, William & Christopher
   & Co, 253
Rawson, John, William Rawson,
   Charles Rawson & Co, 252
Rawson, John, William Rawson, John
   Rhodes & Rawdon Briggs, 127
Rawson, John, William Rawson &
   Christopher Rawson, 252
Rawson, Thomas, 153
Rawson, William, 252, 253
Raymond, Vere, Lowe & Fletcher, 539
Rayne, Lord, 355
Read, Richard, 341
Reade, Moorhouse & Co, 547
Reed, E & Sons, 141, **447**
Reeves & Porch, **447–8**, 500
Reid, Lindsey, 566
Reynolds, Charlton & Co, 477
Rhodes, Briggs & Garlick, 253
Rhodes, John, 253
Richards, Charles, 448
Richards, Michael, 264
Richards, Watkin, 448
Richards & Co, 404
Richardson, Holt & Co, 434, 556
Richardson, Overend & Co, 424
Richardson, Thomas, 424
Richardson & Co, **448**, 480
Riches, Collett & Co, 49
Riches, T H, 551
Richmond Bank, 444

Index of names

Ricketts, Enthoven & Co, 107
Ricketts, Thorne & Courtney, 499, 500
Rickford & Son, 98
Rickman, John, 49
Ridge & Co, 343, **448**
Ridley, Bigge & Co, 419
Ridley, Sir M W, 449
Ridley, Sir M W Bart., Chas. Wm.
  Bigge & Co, **448–9**
Ridley, Sir M W Bigge, Gibson & Co,
  448
Ridley, Sir M W Cookson,
  Widdrington, Bell & Co, 448
Rimingtons & Younges, 472
Ringwood & Poole Bank, 318
Robarts, Curtis, Robarts & Curtis, 449
Robarts, Curtis & Co, 49, 104, 357,
  449
Robarts, Curtis, Were, Hornyold &
  Berwick, 449
Robarts, Lubbock & Co, 171, 357,
  449–50, 548, 566
Roberts, Baker & Crane, 411
Roberts, Henry & John & Mark
  Gregory, 450
Roberts, Henry & John Mark Gregory
  & Co, 450
Roberts, John, 130
Roberts, Skey & Kendrick, 411
Roberts & Co, 538
Roberts & Gregory, **450**
Roberts Union Ltd, 515
Robertson, Fraser & Co, 359
Robin, Charles & Co, 450
Robin Brothers, 429, **450–51**
Robins, Foster, Coode & Bolitho, 107,
  108
Robins, William, 99
Robinson, Frederick, 386
Robinson, James, 451
Robinson, James & Charles, 451, 481
Robinson, James & Charles & Co, **451**
Robinson, J & C & Co, 474
Robinson, Parsons & Co, 431
Robinson, Thomas, 431
Robinson & Broadhurst, 451
Rochdale Commercial Loan &
  Discount Co, 451
Rochdale Joint Stock Bank, 451

Rochdale Joint Stock Bank Ltd, 423,
  451
Rochdale Old Bank, 153
Rochester, Chatham & Stroud Bank,
  186
Rocke, Eyton, Campbell & Bayley,
  133, 211, **451–2**
Rocke, Eyton & Campbell, 452
Rodd, Willyams & Gould, 548
Roebuck, Benjamin, 428
Roskell, Arrowsmith & Co, **452**
Rothschild, Mayer Amschel, 452
Rothschild, Nathan Mayer, 452
Rothschild, N M & Sons, 267, 453
Rothschild, N M & Sons Ltd, 19,
  452–4
Rothschild, 1st Lord, 453
Rothschild Asset Management Ltd,
  454
Rothschilds, 289, 293, 468
Rothschilds Continuation Ltd, 454
Rotton & Co, 403
Round, Green, Green & Pattison, 251
Round, Green & Co, 251
Rowe & Pitman, 524
Rowlands, John, 545
Rowton, Rordkin & Marshall, 195
Royal Bank, 403
Royal Bank of Australia, 207, **455–6**
Royal Bank of Liverpool, **456**
Royal Bank of London & Westminster,
  351
Royal Bank of Scotland, 76, 121, 146,
  147, 149, 197, 198, 201, 228,
  231, 233, 277, 400, 426, 456,
  527, 542, 543
Royal Bank of Scotland Group plc,
  539
Royal Bank of Scotland International,
  457
Royal Bank of Scotland plc, **456–60**,
  539
Royal British Bank, **460**
Royal Exchange Bank Ltd, 371, **460–
  61**
Royal Trust Co, 85
Royds, Clement, 153, 253
Royds, Clement & Co, **153–4**, 540
Royds, Clement Molyneux, 153, 154

616 British banking – a guide to historical records

Royds, Smith & Co, 153
Royds, William Edward, 153
Royston Bank, 214
Ruffer, A & Sons, 461
Ruffer, A & Sons Ltd, **461**
Ruffer, Baron Joseph, 461
Rufford, Bigg & Co, 461
Ruffords & Wragge, **461**
Russell, Brooke, Green, Cole, Perring & Co, 157
Russell, Brooke & Co, 157
Russell, Robert, 157
Russell & Skey, 229
Rust, Sweeting, Veasey & D Veasey jnr., 518
Rust, Sweeting & Veasey, 518
Rust, Veasey, D Veasey jnr & Charles Veasey, 518
Rust, Veasey & Veasey, 518
Rye Bank, 183

Saddleworth Banking Co, 131, 168, **462**
Sadleir, Hilgrove, Lowder & Durell, 58
Sadleir, John, 409
Saffron Walden & Bishop's Stortford Bank, 508
Saffron Walden & North Essex Bank, 508
St Albans Bank, 574
St Austell Bank, 476
St Barbe, C & S, 462
St Barbe, Charles, 462
St Barbe, Daniell & Co, 137, **462**
St Germains, 1st Earl of, John Eliot, 440
St Vincent Commercial Bank, **462**
Salisbury & Shaftesbury Bank, 111
Salisbury Old Bank, 438
Salop Bank, 133
Salop Old Bank, 211
Salt, Sir Thomas, 496
Samuel, Joseph, 463
Samuel, M & Co, 463
Samuel, M & Co Ltd, 273, **463**
Samuel, Marcus, 463
Samuel, Sir Marcus, 463
Samuel, Marcus & Co, 463

Samuel, Montagu *see* Swaythling, Lord
Samuel, Montagu & Co, 464, 555
Samuel, Samuel, 463
Samuel & Montagu, 464
Samuel Montagu & Co Ltd, 264, 375, **463–5**
Samuel Samuel & Co, 463
Sandeman, George G Sons & Co Ltd, 465
Sandeman & Sons Ltd, 465
Sandeman Reid, 219
Sanders, Joseph, 465, 466
Sanders, Snow & Co, 382, 441, 466
Sanders & Co, 382, **465–6**
Sanderson, Joseph, 140
Sandgate & Shorncliffe Bank, 298
Sankey, R & Co, 412
Sapte, Muspratt, Banbury, Nix & Co, **466**
Sapte, Muspratt, Banbury & Co, 218
Sassoon, E D & Co, 203
Saxton Brothers, 372, **467**
SBC Warburg, 524
SBC Warburg Dillon Read, 524
Scarborough Bank, 550
Scarborough Old Bank, 550
Scarsdale & High Peak Bank, 178
Scholfield, Clarkson & Clough, **467**, 555
Scholefield, Joshua, 353
Scholvin, C & Co, 239
Schrobanco, 468
Schroder, J H & Co, 467
Schroder, J Henry & Co, 209, 273, 467
Schroder, J Henry & Co Ltd, 268, **467–9**
Schroder, J Henry Banking Corporation, 468
Schroder, J Henry Wagg & Co Ltd, 268, 400, 468
Schroder, Johann Heinrich, 467
Schroder Mahs & Co, 467
Schroders Ltd, 268, 453
Schroders plc, 468
Schroder Successors Ltd, 468
Scott, Archibald, 578
Scott, Burton, Pemberton, Lloyd & Coupland, 133
Scott, J B, 427

Index of names

Scott, John Home, 578
Scott Bart., Sir Claude Dent & Co, 465
Scott Bart., Sir Samuel & Co, 429, 430, **465**
Scottish Bankers' Association, 564
Scottish Bankers' Literary Association, 567
Scottish Midland Guarantee Trust Ltd, 161
Scottish Motor Traction Ltd, 161
Scottish National Banking Co Ltd, 577
Sealy & Prior, 548
Searle & Co, 507
Seaton, Brook & Co, **469**
Seaton, John Sons & Foster, 435
Seccombe, Lawrence, 469
Seccombe, Marshall & Campion, 469
Seccombe, Marshall & Campion plc, **469–70**
Second Consolidated Trust Ltd, 293
Securities Management Ltd, 67
Securities Management Trust Ltd, 69
Seligman Bros, 524
Sewell, J & Nephew, 509
Sewell & Nephew, 359
Seymour & Gunner, 244
Shales, Charles, **470**
Sharpe & Sons, 273
Sharples, Bassett & Co, 98, 470
Sharples, Exton & Lucas, 470
Sharples, Tuke & Lucas, 470
Sharples, Tuke, Lucas & Seebohm, 89, **470–71**
Sharples & Exton, 470
Sharples & Lucas, 470
Shaw, Robert, 130
Sheffield, Rimingtons & Younges, 472
Sheffield & Hallamshire Bank Ltd, **471–2**
Sheffield & Hallamshire Banking Co Ltd, 374
Sheffield & Retford Bank, **472**, 475
Sheffield & Rotherham Bank, 472, 542
Sheffield & Rotherham Joint Stock Banking Co, 472
Sheffield & Rotherham Joint Stock Banking Co Ltd, **472–4**, 541
Sheffield Bank, 428

Sheffield Banking Co, 451, 474
Sheffield Banking Co Ltd, 404, **474–5**
Sheffield Old Bank, 429
Sheffield Union Banking Co, 429, 472, 557
Sheffield Union Banking Co Ltd, 374, **475–6**
Shell Transport & Trading Co Ltd, 463
Sheppard, John, 179
Sherborne & Dorsetshire Bank, 437
Shetland Bank, 578
Shilson, Coode & Co, 404, **476**
Ship Bank, 227, 228, 577, **476–7**
Shipley, William, 128
Shore, John, 428
Shrewsbury & Ludlow Bank, 452
Shrewsbury & Welshpool Old Bank, 100
Shrewsbury Old Bank, 452
Shropshire Banking Co, 328, **477**
Shrubsole & Co, 429, **477**
Shrubsole & Lambert, 477
Sikes, Sir Charles, 283
Simmons, James, 257
Simonds, Charles, 478
Simonds, Henry, 478
Simonds, John, 478
Simonds, John Charles Simonds & Co, **477–8**
Simonds, Simonds & Co, 59
Simonds, William, 495
Simonds, William Blackall, 478
Simonds & Co, 478
Simonds & Nicholson, 478, 495
Simpson, Chapman & Co, **478–9**, 560
Simpson, Chapman & Simpson, 478
Simpson, Wakefield, 478
Simpson, White & Co, **479**
Simpson & White, 490
Skey, Samuel Son & Co, 411
Skey, William, 411
Skinner, Atty & Holt, 479
Skinner, William & Co, 403, **479**
Sleaford Bank, 432
Slocock, Bunney & Slocock, 479
Slocock, Matthews, Southby & Slocock, 137, **479–80**
Smallpiece, William Haydon, 265
Smith, Abel I, 481

618 British banking – a guide to historical records

Smith, Abel II, 480, 481, 482, 484
Smith, Abel & Sons, 480, 481
Smith, Abel Esqre. & Co, 481, 484
Smith, Bevan & Bening, 83
Smith, E C Marten & Co, 360
Smith, Ellison & Brown, 482
Smith, Ellison & Co, 480, 481, **482–4**, 513
Smith, George, 480
Smith, George & Son, 318
Smith, John, 480, 525
Smith, Jos., 175
Smith, Moger & Evans, 384
Smith, Osborn & Co, **484**, 576
Smith, Payne & Smiths, 480, 481, **484–5**, 513, 574
Smiths, Payne & Smith, 77, 484
Smith, Payne, Smith & Payne, 484
Smith, Richard, 364
Smith, Robert Esqre. & Co, 481
Smith, Robert *see* Carrington, 1st Lord
Smith, Samuel, 480
Smith, Samuel & Abel, 481
Smith, Samuel & Abel & Co, 481
Smith, Samuel & Co,
    Derby, **480–81**, 513
    Newark, 513
    Nottingham, 233, 451, 480, **481–2**, 513
Smith, Samuel Bros. & Co, **480**, 481, 513
Smith, Samuel Esq. & Co, 481
Smith, Thomas, 481
Smith, Thomas & Co, 481
Smith, Wright & Co, 209
Smith, Wright & Gray, 49, 216
Smith & Payne, 259, 482, 484
Smith Elder & Co, 303
Smith St Aubyn & Co Ltd, **485**
Smiths & Thompson, 480
Société Générale, 219, 255
Southern Bank of Scotland, 207, 577
Southern District Banking Co, 258
South Hants Joint Stock Bank, 348
Southport & West Lancashire Banking Co Ltd, 191
South Wales Union Bank Ltd, 371, **485–6**

Southwell Bank, 555
Sparkes & Co, 188
Sparks & Co, 500
Sparrow, Brown, Fenn & Co, **486**
Sparrow, Brown, Hanbury, Saville & Simpson, 487
Sparrow, Brown, Hanbury & Saville, 488
Sparrow, Hanbury & Co, 487
Sparrow, Round, Green, Tufnell & Round, 487
Sparrow, Simpson, Walford, Greenwood & Nottidge,
Sparrow, Simpson, Walford & Greenwood,
    Braintree, 488
    Chelmsford, 487
Sparrow, Tufnell & Co,
    Braintree, 89, 487, **488**
    Chelmsford, 89, 223, **487**, 488
Sparrow, Walford, Nottidge, Greenwood & Tufnell, 487
Spence, Robert, 276
Spielmann, Adam, 464
Spiers, Murdoch & Co, 228
Spinks, Elmes, 364
Spooner, Attwood, Twells & Co, 83, 488
Spooner, Attwood & Co, **488**
Spooner, Attwood & Holmar, 488
Spooner, Isaac, 59
Squire, Edmund, 284
Stable Bank, 411
Staffordshire Joint Stock Bank, 199, 238
Staffordshire Joint Stock Bank Ltd, 300, 371, **489**
Staines Bank, 57
Stamford & Rutland Bank, 206
Stamford & Spalding Joint Stock Banking Co, 489
Stamford Bank, 103
Stamford, Spalding & Boston Banking Co, 110, 479, 489
Stamford, Spalding & Boston Banking Co Ltd, 89, 206, 207, **489–90**
Standard & Chartered Banking Group Ltd, 495
Standard Bank Gambia Ltd, 491

Index of names

Standard Bank Ghana Ltd, 491
Standard Bank Investment Corporation, 495
Standard Bank Ltd, 145, 491, 494
Standard Bank Nigeria Ltd, 491
Standard Bank of British South Africa Ltd, 349, 494
Standard Bank of South Africa, 279
Standard Bank of South Africa Ltd, 47, 495
Standard Bank of West Africa Ltd, **490–93**
Standard Bank Sierra Leone Ltd, 491
Standard Chartered Bank Africa plc, **494–5**
Standard Chartered Banking Group Ltd, 145
Standard Chartered Bank Ltd, 375
Standard Chartered Bank plc, 12, 495
Standard Chartered plc, 145
Staples, Baron, Dimsdale, Son & Co, 190
Staples, Roger, 190
Stapleton, Thomas, John Robinson & George Kay, 444
Stephen, John, 214
Stephens, Blandy, Barnett, Butler & Co, 495
Stephens, Blandy & Blandy, 495
Stephens, Blandy & Co, 328, **495–6**
Stephens, Harris & Stephens, 495
Stephens, John, 495
Stern, D, 288
Stern Brothers, 293
Stevens, James, 307
Stevens & Co, 307
Stevenson, John, 496
Stevenson, Salt & Co, 109, 328, **496**
Stevenson, Salt & Sons, 109, **496–7**
Stevenson, Thomas & John, 496
Stevenson, William, 109, 496
Stevenson & Co, 307, 496
Stevenson & Salt, 109, 496
Stevenson & Webb, 496
Stilwell, Thomas, 497
Stilwell & Sons, **497**, 528
Stockholms Enskilda Bank, 117
Stockton & Darlington Commercial Bank, 479

Stockton & Durham County Bank, 403, **497**
Stokes, Humphrey, 96
Stone, Andrew, 364
Stone, George, 364
Stone & Co, 364
Storey, William, 498
Storey & Thomas, 548
Storey & Thomas's Banking Co, **497–8**
Story, John S, 574
Stourbridge & Kidderminster Banking Co, 371, **498–9**, 504, 524
Stourbridge Bank, 461
Stourbridge Old Bank, 99
Stoveld, J & Co, 343
Strange, Garrett, Strange & Cook, 499
Strange, James, 499
Strange, T & R, 169
Strange, T & R & Co, **499**
Strange, Thomas, 499
Stuckey, George, 499
Stuckey, Lean, Hart & Maningford, 499, 500
Stuckey, Reynolds & Co, 500
Stuckey, Samuel, 499
Stuckey, S & G & Co, **499–500**
Stuckey, Vincent, 499, 500
Stuckey & Co, 499
Stuckeys & Woodlands, 499, 500
Stuckey's Banking Co, 62, 432, 447, 499, 500, 506
Stuckey's Banking Co Ltd, 203, 429, **500–501**
Sudbury Bank, 486
Surrey, Kent & Sussex Banking Co, 343
Surtees, Aubone, 501
Surtees, Aubone & Rowland Burdon, 501
Surtees, Burdon, Surtees's & Brandling, 501
Surtees, Burdon, Wetherby & Co, 501
Surtees, Burdon & Co, 132
Surtees's, Burdon, Brandling & Embleton, 501
Surtees's, Burdon & Brandling, **501**
Sutton, James, 341
Sutton, Leech, Bevan & Read, 341

620 British banking – a guide to historical records

Swaledale & Wensleydale Banking Co
Ltd, 89, **502**
Swann, Clough & Co, 101, **502**
Swansea Bank Ltd, 485
Swaythling, Lord, Samuel Montagu,
463, 464
Swindon & Highworth Bank, 499
Swindon Bank, 499
Swiss Bank Corporation, 524
Sykes, Sir Christopher & Co, 110
Sykes, Creyke & Co, 110
Sykes, James, 497
Sykes & Son, 497

Tallack & Co, 219
Tannerie Banking Co, 436
Taubman, John, 445
Taunton Bank,
M & R Badcock, 62
M & J Brickdale, 115
Taunton Old Bank, 115
Tavistock Bank, 226
Tawney, A R, 224
Tawney, Charles, 223
Tawney, R & C, 223
Tawney, R C, 224
Tawney, Richard, 223
Taylor, J & Sons, 177
Taylor, James, 503
Taylor, James Esq., 503
Taylor, James & Sons, **502–3**
Taylor, John, 327
Taylor, Lloyd, Hanbury & Bowman,
259
Taylor, Lloyd, Hanbury & Co, 259
Taylor, Lloyd & Bowman, 259
Taylor & Dyson, 264
Taylor & Lloyds, 259, 327
Tempest, Robert, 274
Templer, George, 185
Tennent, Andrew, 229
Tew, Thomas William, 315, 316
Tewkesbury Old Bank, 317
Thicknesse & Woodcocks, 551
Thistle Bank, 45, 228, 503, 510
Thistle Bank Co, **503–4**
Thomas, Edwin, 498
Thompson, Thomas, 480
Thornbury Old Bank, 265

Thrapston & Kettering Bank, 207
Thrapston Bank, 206
Three Banks Group, 457
Three Towns Banking Co Ltd, 188
Tice & Welch, 548
Tipperary Bank, 409
Tiverton & Devonshire Bank, 203
Tiverton Bank, 203
Tomes, Chattaway & Ford, 498, **504**,
524
Tomes, Hobbins & Chattaway, 504
Tomes, Russell, Tomes & Russell, 504
Tomkins & Co, **504**
Tompson, Barclay & Ives, **504**
Toomer, Bunney, Slocock & King, 479
Toplis, John, 57
Torquay Bank, 520
Torrington Bank, 356
Totnes Bank, 549
Towgood & Co, 386, 534
Town & County Bank, 484
Town & County Bank Ltd, 418, **505**
Town & County of Poole Bank, 318
Townsend & Rishworth, 526
Transinternational Life, 304
Trapp, Halfhead & Co, 344, **505**
Trim & Toomer, 301
Trinder, A W, 515
Tring, Aylesbury & Chesham Bank,
134
Trinkaus & Burkhardt, 375
Tritton, Sir Ernest, 116
Tritton, J H, 83
Trotter, Coutts, 171
Troughton, Newcombe & Troughton,
505–6
Truelove, William, 61
Trueman, Edward, 315, 316
TSB Bank plc, 463
TSB Group, 7, 330
Tubb, George & Henry Tubb, 506
Tubb, George & William Coleman, 506
Tubb, Henry & Co, 89, 506
Tubb, Henry M & George Tubb, 506
Tubb & Co, **506**
Tudman, Benjamin, 547
Tudman & Child, 547
Tufnell, Falkner & Co, 500, **506–7**
Tufnell, Falkner & Falkner, 506

Index of names   621

Tugwell, Brymer, Clutterbuck & Co, 190, **507**
Tugwell, Brymer & Co, 381, 441, 507
Tufnell, Stroud, Collett, Payne & Hope, 506
Tuke, W M, 507
Tuke & Gibson, **507–8**
Turner, Hardy & Newcome, 262
Turner, James, 250
Turner, T, **508**
Turner & Morris, 508
Tweedie, John, 578
Tweedy, Williams & Co, 167
Twining & Co, 328, **508–9**
Twining & Mills, 383, 508
Tyndall, Elton, Edye, Edwards, Edye & Skinner, 381
Tyndall, Elton, Gillam & Edye, 381
Tyndall, Lloyd, Elton, Miller, Knox & Hale, 380
Tyndall, Siphorus, 380
Tyne Bank, 355
Tysoe, John, 470
Tysoe, Willis & Reade, 547

Udisco Brokers Ltd, 515
Ulster Bank, 528
UNIFI, 564
Union Bank of Birmingham, 373
Union Bank of Birmingham Ltd, **509**
Union Bank of Cornwall, 519
Union Bank of Croydon, 146
Union Bank of London, 370, 513
Union Bank of London Ltd, 146, 352, 480, 481, 482, 483, 484
Union Bank of Manchester, 509
Union Bank of Manchester Ltd, 89, 106, 205, 252, 430, **509–10**, 555
Union Bank of Preston Ltd, 443
Union Bank of Scotland, 45, 135, 214, 285, 435, 510
Union Bank of Scotland Ltd, 77, 125, **510–13**
Union Bank of Switzerland, 524
Union Discount Co of London Ltd, 50, 219, 401, 515, 518
Union of London & Smiths Bank Ltd, 352, 404, 441, 480, 481, 482, 483, 484, **513–14**, 537

Union plc, **515**
United Counties Bank Ltd, 89, 114, **516–18**
United Discount Corporation Ltd, 219, 515, **518**
Unity Joint Stock Bank, 360
Unity Joint Stock Mutual Banking Association, 470
Uxbridge Bank, 551
Uxbridge Old Bank, 551

Vaile, Allen & Co, 141
Vaile & Carew, 141
Vaile & Co, 141
Vallance & Payne, 344
Vanner, James, 150
Veasey, Desborough, Bevan, Tillard & Co, 518
Veasey, Desborough, Bevan & Tillard, 518
Veasey, Desborough, Chapman & Henderson, 518
Veasey, Desborough & Co, 89, **518–19**
Veasey, Desborough & Veasey, 518
Veaseys, Desborough & Veasey, 518
Vere, Glyn & Hallifax, 230
Vere, Joseph, 230
Vere, Lucadon, Troughton, Lucadon & Smart, 466
Vere, Williams, Son, Wilkinson & Drury, 539
Vere & Asgill, 411
Vickers, Son & Pritchard, 444
Vincent, Baily & Vincent, 519
Vincent & Barnes, **519**
Vivian, Borlase & Co, 519
Vivian, Captain W, 520
Vivian, Edward, 520
Vivian, Grylls, Kendall & Co, 107, **519**
Vivian, Kitson & Co, 328, **520**
Vizard & Co, 169, **520**
Vye & Harris, 403, **520**
Vyner, Sir Robert, **520–21**
Vyner, Thomas, 61
Vyner, Sir Thomas, 520

Wakefield, Crewdson & Co, 177, 361, 363, 437, 521, **522–3**

622   *British banking – a guide to historical records*

Wakefield, John, 521
Wakefield, John & Sons, 177, 189, **521**, 522
Wakefield & Barnsley Union Bank, 517
Wakefield & Barnsley Union Banking Co, 102, 521
Wakefield & Barnsley Union Bank Ltd, 516, **521–2**
Wakefield & Co, 140
Wakefield Bank, 292, 526
Wakefield Banking Co, 102, 521
Wakeman, Farley & Turner, 104
Waldron, Walters & Co, 500
Wales Bank, 413
Walkers, Eyre & Stanley, 472
Walkers & Stanley, 472
Wall, Samuel, 104
Wallenberg, Knut, 117
Wallers & Co, 186
Wallingford Bank, 267
Walters, J & W, 348
Walters, John & William, 523
Walters, John & William Walters, **523**
Walters, Voss & Walters, 227, 523
Warburg, M M & Co, 523
Warburg, S G & Co, 524
Warburg, S G & Co Ltd, **523–4**
Warburg, Sir Siegmund G, 523
Warburg Dillon Read, 524
Ward, Brown & Co, 420
Wardell, D, 195
Wardington, Lord, J W Beaumont Pease, 276
Ware Bank,
 Samuel Adams & Co, 46
 Dickinson & Green, 188
Warrington Bank, 429
Warschauer, Robert & Co, 145
Warwick & Leamington Banking Co, 186, 328, **524–5**
Warwick & Warwickshire Bank, 238
Warwick Old Bank, 186
Watkins, Charles, 525
Watkins & Bricknell, 525
Watkins & Co, 414, **525**
Watkins & Smith, 525
Watson, James & Robert, 578
Watts, Wyatt & Co, 169

Watts & Co, 137
Weale, James, 367
Webb, Thomas, 525
Webb & Co, 229, **525**
Wedd, Durlacher, Mordaunt & Co, 90
Wedgwood, John, 185
Welby, Lord, Reginald Earle, 575
Welby, Godfrey & Lawrence, 233
Welch, Geo. Ledgard & Sons, 318
Wells, Allnatt, Wells & Wells, 267
Wells, Hogge & Lindsell, 137, **525–6**
Wentworth, Chaloner & Co, 112
Wentworth, Chaloner & Rishworth, **526**
West of England & South Wales District Bank, 533
West of England & South Wales District Bank Ltd, 116, 167, 216, 486, **533–4**
West Riding Bank, 316
West Riding of Yorkshire Provident Society and Penny Savings Bank, 558
West Riding Union Banking Co, 534
West Riding Union Bank Ltd, 311, **534–5**
West Yorkshire Bank Ltd, 252, 329, **535–6**
West, John, 548
West, Thomas, 254
Western Bank of London, 344
Western Bank of Scotland, 121, 202, 207, 237, 457, **526–8**
Western Counties Bank Ltd, 137, **528**
Western District Banking Co, 188
Western Province Bank, 47
Westminster Bank Ltd, 7, 242, 404, 425, 497, 528–33
Westminster Foreign Bank Ltd, 293, 528
Weston, Pinhorn, Golding, Mewsome & Weston, 561
Weston, Pinhorn & Weston, 561
Weston, Young & Bostock, 561
Weston & Young, 561
Weymouth Old Bank, 208
Wheeler, Francis, 536
Wheeler, George, 536
Wheeler, Robert, 536

Index of names

623

Wheeler, Thomas, 536
Wheeler, Thomas & Co, 138, **536**
Wheeler, William, 147
Whitaker, K H, 219
Whitby Bank, 478
Whitby Old Bank, 478
Whitchurch & Ellesmere Banking Co
   Ltd, 328, **536**
Whitehaven Joint Stock Bank, 536
Whitehaven Joint Stock Bank Ltd,
   429, **536–7**
Whitehead, Greenway, Lowe &
   Gillett, 238
Whitehead, Weston & Co, 238
Whitfield, Comber, Molineux & King,
   385
Whitfield, Francis, 385
Whitfield, Molineux, Whitfield &
   Molineux, 385
Whitfield, Molineux & Whitfield, 385
Whitfield & Molineux, 385
Whitmarsh, Henry & Wm. Lambert
   White, 500
Wickenden, Moffatt, Kensington &
   Boler, 302, 411
Wickham & Co, 258
Wigan, Mercer, Tasker & Co, 513, **537**
Wigan Old Bank, 551
Wigney & Co, **537**
Wilberforce, William, 480
Wilberforce & Smith, 480
Wilkins, Jeffreys, 537
Wilkins, Jeffreys Wilkins & Williams,
   537
Wilkins, Walter, 537
Wilkins & Co, 328, **537–8**
Williams & Co, 328, **538–9**
Williams & Glyn's Bank Ltd, 231,
   457, 458, **539**, 541, 542, 559
Williams & Rowland, 227, **545**
Williams & Son, 413
Williams & Sons, **546**
Williams Brown, Janson, Barr & Co,
   128
Williams, Cox & Co, 546
Williams, Deacon, Labouchère,
   Thornton & Co, 539, 540
Williams, Deacon, Labouchère & Co,
   539

Williams, Deacon, Thornton & Co,
   540
Williams, Deacon & Co, 408, **539–40**,
   541
Williams Deacon & Manchester &
   Salford Bank Ltd, 540, 541
Williams Deacon's Bank Ltd, 125,
   231, 296, 457, 458, 473, 539,
   540–45, 555
Williams, P & H, 328, **545**
Williams, R & R Thornton, Sykes &
   Co, **546**, 548
Williams, Rees, 545
Williams, Robert, 542
Williams, Son, Moffat, Burgess &
   Lane, 539
Williams, Son & Drury, 539
Williams, Thomas, 547
Williams, William Brown & Co,
   546–7
Williams, Williams, Burgess &
   Williams, 539
Williams, Williams & Grylls, 107
Williamson, Wells & Prior, 573
Williamson & Wells, 525
Willis, Percival & Co, 137, 148, **547**
Willis, Wood, Percival & Co, 547
Willis, Wood & Co, 547
Willis & Reade, 547
Willoughby, Raper & Co, 502
Willyams, James, 537
Willyams, Treffry & Co, 107
Willyams, Willyams & Co, 107, **547–8**
Wilmshurst & Co, 343
Wilshere, Pierson, Crabb & Chapman,
   438
Wilshere, William, 438
Wilshere & Co, 438
Wilson, Beckett, Calverley & Lodge,
   100
Wilson, Benjamin, 534
Wilson, Benjamin & Sons, 534
Wilson, Benjamin Sons & Co, 534
Wilson, Crewdson & Co, 177
Wilson, Crewdsons, Bateman & Co,
   177
Wilson, Dalrymple & Co, 133
Wilson & Sons, 177
Wilts & Dorset Banking Co, 318, 498

624   *British banking – a guide to historical records*

Wilts & Dorset Banking Co Ltd, 329,
438, 546, **548–9**
Wimborne, Poole & Blandford Bank,
217
Winchester, Alresford & Alton Bank,
131
Winchester Bank, 131
Windsor Bank, 408
Windsor & Eton Bank, 127
Winterflood Securities Ltd, 515
Wirksworth Bank, 57
Wisbech & Lincolnshire Bank, 248
Wise, Barker & Bentall, **549–50**
Wise, Farnwell, Baker & Bentall, **549–
50**
Wise, Farnwell & Bentall, 549
Witney Bank, 226
Wolff, Sir Henry, 219
Wolverhampton & Staffordshire
Banking Co Ltd, 516, 517, **550**
Wood, Abraham, 241
Wood, James, 229
Wood, Pitt & Co, 169, **552**
Wood, Wood & Co, **553**
Woodall, Hebden & Co, 89, **550**
Woodall, Tindall, Hebden & Co, 550
Woodall, Tindall & Taylor, 550
Woodbridge, Charles, 551
Woodbridge, H W, 308
Woodbridge, Lacy, Hartland, Hibbert
& Co, 89, 308, **550–51**
Woodbridge Bank, 49
Woodcock, Thomas Sons & Eckersley,
429, 430, **551**
Woodhead & Co, 277, 278, **551–2**
Woods, Parker & Co, 409, 552
Woods, William, 189, 409, 552
Woods & Co, 89, 189, **552–3**
Woodstock Bank, 126
Wooten, Richard, Thomas Tubb & Co,
506
Wooten, Tubb & Co, 89
Worcester Bank, 212
Worcester City & County Banking Co,
328, 358, 553
Worcester City & County Banking Co
Ltd, **553–4**
Worcester Commercial Bank, 47
Worcester Old Bank, 104

Workington Bank, 111
Worlledge, Huddleston & Cooper, 284
Worlledge, J & Co, 284
Worlledge, John, 284
Worlledge & Cooper, 284
Worrall, Hale & Newnam, 553
Worrall & Blatchley, 553
Worrall & Gold, **553**
Worrall & Oldham, 553
Worswick, Thomas Sons & Co, 312,
554
Worthing & Sussex Bank, 269
Wotton, Thomas, 215
Wright, I & I C & Co, 138, **554**
Wright, John, 294
Wright, John & Co, 294
Wright, John & Ichabod, 554
Wright, Thomas & Co, 573
Wright & Co, 353
Wright & Hilton, 274
Wrigley, John, 130
Wulff, Forbes & Co, 296, **554–5**
Wulff, John, 555
Wylde & Co, **555**

Yarborough & Co, 164
Yarmouth, Norfolk & Suffolk Bank, 307
Yarmouth & Suffolk Bank, 250
Yates, E W & Co, 509, **555**
York & East Riding Bank, 101
York Bank, 502, 526
York City & County Banking Co, 261,
467, 555
York City & County Bank Ltd, 97,
109, 180, 285, 353, **555–7**
York Union Banking Co Ltd, 89, 358,
434, 478, **560–61**
Yorke, B & Co, **557**
Yorke, D & J, 557
Yorke, Daniel, 557
Yorke, Daniel & Co, 557
Yorke, James, 557
Yorkshire Banking Co, 557
Yorkshire Banking Co Ltd, 374, **557–8**
Yorkshire Bank Ltd, 559
Yorkshire Bank plc, **558–60**
Yorkshire District Banking Co, 435,
475, 534, 557
Yorkshire Penny Bank, 559

Index of names

Yorkshire Penny Bank Ltd, 529, 559
Yorkshire Penny Savings Bank, 559
Young & Son, **561**
Yule, Andrew & Co Ltd, 387

Yule, George & Co, 387

Zachary, Long & Haldimand, 390
Zaharoff, Sir Basil, 146

Index of places

Page numbers shown in bold indicate the geographical locations of banks or branches of banks for which details of records and/or histories are provided. All other page numbers refer to places mentioned generally in the text.

Aberavon, Dyfed, 227
Aberdare, Mid Glamorgan, **331**, **399**, 400, 418, 538
Aberdeen, Grampian **45**, **46**, **78**, **122**, 135, **162**, 396, **417**, **459**, **505**, 510, **512**, **513**, 567, **568**
Aberfeldy, Tayside, **78**
Aberfoyle, Central, **79**
Abergavenny, Gwent, **46**, 230, 386, 403
Aberystwyth, Dyfed, 412, **414**
Abingdon, Oxfordshire, 223, **306**, **345** **345**, **504**
Accra, Ghana, 491
Accrington, Lancashire, **90**, **168**
Acle, Norfolk, 307
Adelaide, Australia, **455**
Adlington, Lancashire, **193**
Africa, **47**, **53**, **63**, 64, **75**, 76, **82**, 87, 89, **120**, 158, **159**, 243, 279, **349**, **366**, **368**, **392**, **398**, 399, **410**, 453, 468, **490**, 491, **492**, **493**, **494**, 495
Agra, India, 48
Airdrie, Strathclyde, **79**, **122**, **397**
Alcester, Warwickshire, **576**
Aldeburgh, Suffolk, 250
Alderley Edge, Cheshire, **193**
Aldershot, Hampshire, **331**, **345**
Alexandra, Strathclyde, **79**, **122**
Alexandria, Egypt, 54, 174, 295, 296
Alford, Lincolnshire, **90**, **110**, **138**, **218**, 322, **331**, 490
Alfreton, Derbyshire, 177, **530**

Alloa, Central, **79**, 426, **512**
Alnwick, Northumberland, **90**, 132, **189**, **276**, **331**, 416, 417, 419
Alresford, Hampshire, 131, **138**, **331**
Alston, Cumbria, 139, 140
Alton,
  Derbyshire, 179
  Hampshire, 131, **331**
Altrincham, Greater Manchester, **181**, **331**, **530**
Alva, Central, **79**, **512**
Alyth, Tayside, 201, **459**
Amble, Northumberland, 416
Ambleside, Cumbria, 82, **90**, 522
Amersham, Berkshire, **331**, 536
Amiens, France, 86
Amlwch, Gwynedd, 538
Ammanford, Dyfed, 227, 299, **331**
Amoy, China, **280**
Ampthill, Bedfordshire, 98, 470
Amsterdam, Netherlands, 269, 289
Ancoats, Greater Manchester, 47
Andover, Hampshire, **138**, 258, **266**, **331**
Anglesey, Gwynedd, 538
Annan, Dumfries & Galloway, **79**, **122**, **124**, **162**
Antigua, Antigua & Barbuda, **159**
Antofagasta, Chile, **74**
Antwerp, Belgium, 293, **294**, 314, **326**
Appleby, Cumbria, 139
Arbroath, Tayside, 46, **57**, **122**, 200, 201, **459**
Archangel, Russia, 239

Index of places

Ardgay, Highland 79, 136
Ardrossan, Strathclyde, 79, 512
Arequipa, Peru, 222
Argentina, 52, 55, 56, 72, 73, 74, 117, 118, 239, 289, 290, 342, 343, 387, 389
Arundel, West Sussex, 269, 331, 343, 345, 530
Ashbourne, Derbyshire, 133, 530
Ashburton, Devon, 188, 332
Ashby de la Zouch, Leicestershire, 319, 320, 332, 428
Ashford, Kent, 329, 332, 345, 439, 440
Ashington, Northumberland, 332
Ashton under Lyne, Greater Manchester, 58, 168, 193, 429, 462
Asia, 48, 53, 54, 67, 70, 75, 77, 87, 89, 118, 119, 120, 144, 145, 159, 174, 185, 203, 221, 239, 240, 241, 243, 256, 278, 279, 280, 281, 282, 283, 289, 290, 295, 296, 303, 306, 329, 353, 355, 359, 367, 368, 369, 374, 376, 387, 388, 398, 410, 425, 430, 453, 463, 467, 468, 491, 493, 494, 578
Aspatria, Cumbria, 83
Astley, Greater Manchester, 90
Asuncion, Paraguay, 74
Athens, Greece, 295, 296
Atherstone, Warwickshire, 173, 319, 320, 332
Atherton, Greater Manchester, 90
Attercliffe, Sheffield, South Yorkshire, 473
Attleborough, Warwickshire, 90
Attleburgh, Norfolk, 246
Auchterarder, Tayside, 79, 143
Auchtermuchty, Fife, 79
Australasia, 48, 77, 144, 151, 159, 207, 220, 221, 222, 267, 290, 314, 352, 353, 367, 410, 424, 455, 468
Australia, 77, 144, 207, 220, 221, 222, 267, 290, 314, 352, 353, 367, 410, 455
Austria, 52, 53, 55, 289, 290, 355, 453
Aviemore, Highland, 122
Avoch, Highland, 79, 136

Avon, 66, 104, 116, 165, 187, 190, 216, 220, 222, 229, 265, 301, 313, 321, 328, 330, 333, 338, 341, 348, 349, 377, 380, 381, 384, 406, 417, 438, 441, 442, 499, 500, 501, 506, 507, 514, 531, 533, 534, 548, 549, 553
Axminster, Devon, 332, 546, 549
Aylesbury, Buckinghamshire, 98, 131, 134, 343, 345, 367, 530
Aylsham, Norfolk, 90, 166, 246
Ayr, Strathclyde, 79, 122, 285, 510, 512, 568
Ayrshire see Strathclyde
Ayton,
  Borders, 459
  North Yorkshire, 60

Bacup, Lancashire, 167, 168, 193, 311
Baden, Duchy of, Germany, 453
Bahia, Brazil, 72, 73, 74, 342
Bahia Blanca, Argentina, 72
Bahrain, 119, 203
Bakewell, Derbyshire, 177, 473, 502, 530
Bala, Gwynedd, 63
Baldock, Hertfordshire, 332, 525
Balfron, Central, 122
Ballater, Grampian, 79, 512
Baltimore, United States of America, 128, 387
Bamford, Oxfordshire, 224
Bampton, Devon, 62
Banbury, Oxfordshire, 89, 90, 98, 131, 193, 223, 224, 225, 226, 315, 332
Banff, Grampian, 45, 79
Banff & MacDuff, Grampian, 512
Bangkok, Thailand, 144, 368
Bangor, Gwynedd, 406, 417, 445, 538
Bannockburn, Highland, 80
Banstead, Surrey, 90
Barcelona, Spain, 269, 293, 294
Bargoed, Mid Glamorgan, 332
Barmouth, Gwynedd, 414, 546
Barnard Castle, County Durham, 60
Barnoldswick, Lancashire, 175
Barnsley, South Yorkshire, 90, 97, 102, 377, 516, 517, 521, 522, 556
Barnstaple, Devon, 216, 403, 445, 533

628   *British banking – a guide to historical records*

Barranquilla, Colombia, 56, 74
Barrhead, Strathclyde, 79
Barrhill, Strathclyde, **512**
Barrow in Furness, Cumbria, 180, **193**,
    312, 416, 522
Barry Docks, South Glamorgan, 169
Barton, Humberside, 284, **285**, 323
Basford, Nottinghamshire, 482
Basingstoke, Hampshire, **138**, 258,
    332
Baslow, Derbyshire, 473
Batavia, Indonesia, 144
Bath, Avon, 187, 190, 301, 313, 349,
    381, **384**, **406**, 441, **442**, 500,
    506, **507**, 514, 533, **549**
Bathgate, Lothian, 79, **122**, **512**
Batley, West Yorkshire, 283, **284**, **514**,
    535
Battle, East Sussex, 385
Beaconsfield, Buckinghamshire, **332**,
    536
Bearsden, Strathclyde, 79, **122**, **512**
Beauly, Highland, **79**
Beaumaris, Gwynedd, **406**
Beccles, Suffolk, 250, 307, **332**
Bechuanaland *see* Botswana
Bedale, North Yorkshire, 502
Bedford, Bedfordshire, **95**, **98**, **332**,
    344, 429, **431**, 438, **505**
Bedfordshire, 89, **91**, **93**, **95**, **98**, **99**,
    137, **138**, **259**, **332**, **335**, **338**,
    344, **346**, **347**, 429, **431**, 438,
    470, **505**, **525**, 526, **531**, **573**
Bedworth, Warwickshire, 320
Beith, Strathclyde, **512**
Belfast, Northern Ireland, 374, 375,
    392, 528
Belgian Congo *see* Zaire
Belgium, 289, 290, 293, **294**, 314, 325,
    326, 327, 398, 461, 464
Bellingham, Northumberland, **276**,
    332
Bellshill, Strathclyde, 79
Belper, Derbyshire, 187, 372, **530**
Berbice, Guyana, **159**
Berkshire, 89, **91**, **94**, **127**, 137, **139**,
    169, 171, **267**, 328, 329, **331**,
    334, **336**, **338**, **339**, **340**, 343,
    346, 367, **407**, **408**, **477**, 478,

    479, **495**, **504**, **519**, 551, **533**,
    573
Berlin, Germany, 523
Berwick on Tweed, Northumberland,
    409, 417, 426, 449, **501**
Beverley, Humberside, 101, **102**, **110**,
    284, **358**, 434, 502, 560, **558**
Bewdley, Hereford & Worcester, 373,
    377, **411**
Bexhill on Sea, East Sussex, 102
Biarritz, France, **326**
Bicester, Oxfordshire, 89, **90**, **506**
Bideford, Devon, 216, **321**, **322**, 403
Biggleswade, Bedfordshire, 137, **138**,
    332, 438, **525**, 526
Bilbao, Spain, 293, **294**
Billericay, Essex, **487**
Billinghay, Lincolnshire, 433
Bilston, West Midlands, **90**, **170**, **300**,
    489
Bingley, West Yorkshire, 113, 175
Birchington on Sea, Kent, 155
Birkenhead, Merseyside, 51, **90**, 141,
    273, 325, **332**, 361, **377**, 395,
    413, 447, **530**
Birmingham, West Midlands, **59**, **64**,
    66, 97, **106**, 109, **150**, 196, 199,
    210, 211, 259, 315, 318, **321**, **327**,
    328, 329, **334**, **345**, 348, **370**,
    372, **373**, 374, 376, 380, **384**,
    400, 403, **406**, 421, 460, 486,
    488, **489**, 490, 498, **509**, **516**,
    521, 550, **554**
Aston, **332**
Bartholomew Road, 384
Bourneville, **332**
Bristol Street, **332**
Coleshill, **332**
Colmore Row, **332**, **384**, 516, **530**
Corporation Street, **332**
Cradleigh Heath, **332**
Dale End, 327
Deritend, **332**
Edgbaston, **332**
Erdington, **332**, 377
Gravelly Hill, **332**
Great Hampton Street, 106, **332**
Halesowen, **332**
Handsworth, **332**, **377**

Index of places

Harborne, 332
Highgate, 332
Holyhead Road, 332
King's Heath, 332
King's Norton, 332
Ladywood, 332
Long Acre, 332
Moseley, 332
New Street, 106, 332, 377, 489
Oldbury, 328, 332
Old Square, 333
Selly Oak, 333
Shirley, 333
Smallbrook Queensway, 333
Small Heath, 333, 377
Sparkbrook, 333
Sparkhill, 333
Stirchley, 333
Summerfield, 333
Temple Row, 106, 333, 377
Waterloo Street, 377
Birtley, Tyne & Wear, 333
Bishop Auckland, County Durham, 60
Bishop's Stortford, Hertfordshire, 90, 138, 215, 391, 392, 487, 507
Bishop's Waltham, Hampshire, 89, 90, 244
Bishopton, Strathclyde, 122
Blackburn, Lancashire, 106, 126, 167, 168, 181, 182, 311, 328, 333, 442, 509
Blackford, Tayside, 79, 143
Blackhill, Tyne & Wear, 333
Blackpool, Lancashire, 312, 442
Blackwaterfoot, Strathclyde, 79
Blaenavon, Gwent, 99, 141, 333
Blairgowrie, Tayside, 79, 512
Blandford, Dorset, 217, 333
Blaydon on Tyne, Tyne & Wear, 276, 333
Bloxwich, West Midlands, 333
Blyth, Northumberland, 333, 417
Bodmin, Cornwall, 188, 528
Bognor Regis, West Sussex, 530
Bogota, Colombia, 56, 74, 163
Bolivia, 220
Bolton, Greater Manchester, 65, 168, 260, 261, 530, 540
Corporation Street, 260

Market Street, 260
Turton, 544
Water Street, 260
Bombay, India, 48, 144, 174, 240, 303, 367, 369, 410
Bonar Bridge, Highland, 79, 136
Bo'ness, Central, 79, 122, 512
Bonnyrigg, Lothian, 79
Bootle, Merseyside, 47, 90, 361, 395, 522, 530
Bordeaux, France, 86, 293, 326
Borders, 78, 79, 80, 122, 123, 162, 459, 512, 513, 527, 567
Boroughbridge, North Yorkshire, 556
Boston, Lincolnshire, 137, 138, 206, 207, 218, 323, 333, 403, 479, 490
Boston, United States of America, 389
Botesdale, Suffolk, 246, 264
Bothwell, Strathclyde, 79, 512
Botswana, 494
Bourne, Lincolnshire, 433, 489
Bournemouth, Dorset, 208, 546, 549
Boscombe, 208, 333, 377, 546
Malmesbury Park, 333
Old Christchurch Road, 377
Westbourne, 333
West Southbourne, 333
Bourton on the Water, Gloucestershire, 169
Bowdon, Greater Manchester, 311
Bowness, Cumbria, 82, 193
Boyd Town, Australia, 455
Brackley, Northamptonshire, 98, 223, 333
Bracknell, Berkshire, 478, 495
Bradford, West Yorkshire, 90, 101, 112, 113, 114, 175, 205, 211, 252, 253, 314, 347, 374, 377, 404, 405, 406, 509, 516, 517, 530, 534, 535, 536, 558
Bradford on Avon, Wiltshire, 420
Braemar, Grampian, 79, 512
Braintree, Essex, 89, 487, 488
Brampton, Cumbria, 140, 180, 181, 266
Brandon, Suffolk, 246, 423
Brazil, 53, 56, 72, 73, 74, 117, 118, 290, 329, 342, 343, 453, 468
Brechin, Tayside, 79, 80, 122, 200, 201, 426, 512, 527

630   British banking – a guide to historical records

Brecon, Powys, 328, **333**, 403, 516,
   537
Bremen, Germany, 466
Brentwood, Essex, **345, 530**
Bridgend, Mid Glamorgan, 81, **333,
   406**
Bridge of Weir, Strathclyde, **512**
Bridgewater, Somerset, 216, **217, 333,**
   499, 500, **533**, 548
Bridgnorth, Shropshire, **166**, 328, 371,
   444, **554**
Bridlington, Humberside, 102, **261,
   556, 560**
Bridlington Quay, Humberside, 261
Bridport, Dorset, **244**
Brierfield, Lancashire, **90, 168, 193**
Brierley Hill, West Midlands, 498
Brigg, Humberside, 284, 322, **323,
   333**, 483
Brighouse, West Yorkshire, 252
Brighton, East Sussex, 84, **90, 138,
   254, 259, 333**, 343, **345**, 385,
   530, 531, 537
Bristol, Avon, 66, **116**, 165, 190, 220,
   222, 229, 321, 328, 330, 348,
   349, **380, 406**, 417, **438**, 441,
   442, 499, 500, 501, 507, **514**,
   533, 548, **549, 553**
   Baldwin Street, **377**
   Cheltenham Road, **333**
   Clare Street, **333**
   Clifton Street, **333**
   Corn Street, **333, 406**
   Kingswood, **333, 531**
   Merchant Street, **333**
   Redland, **333, 406, 533**
   St George, **333**
   Temple Gate, **333**
   Whiteladies, **333**
British Guiana *see* Guyana
Briton Ferry, West Glamorgan, 81, 227
Brixham, Devon, 188
Broadford, Highland, **79, 136**
Broadstairs, Kent, 155, **334**
Brodick, Strathclyde, **79**
Bromsgrove, Hereford & Worcester,
   334, 461, 498, **554**
Bromyard, Hereford & Worcester, 104
Brosley, Shropshire, **334**, 444

Broughty, Tayside, 201
Broxburn, Lothian, **122, 512**
Brownhill, Strathclyde, 285
Brussels, Belgium, 293, **294**, 314, **326**
Brynamman, Dyfed, 299
Buchlyvie, Central, **79**
Buckie, Grampian, **79, 136**
Buckingham, Buckinghamshire, **98,
   131, 334**
Buckinghamshire, **91, 93, 94, 98, 99,
   131**, 134, **138, 139**, 329, **332,
   334, 335, 340**, 343, **345, 346,**
   367, 495, **530, 531, 533, 536**
Buckley, Clwyd, **334**
Budleigh Salterton, Devon, **343**, 466
Buenos Aires, Argentina, 52, 56, 72,
   73, 74, 117, 342, **343**
Builth Wells, Powys, **90, 334**
Bulwell, Nottinghamshire, 482
Bungay, Suffolk, **90**, 250, 412
Buntingford, Hertfordshire, 214
Burford, Oxfordshire, 169
Burgess Hill, West Sussex, 254
Burghead, Grampian, **79, 123**
Burma, 144, 174
Burnley, Lancashire, **90**, 168, 175, 311
Burnside, Cumbria, **122**
Burry Port, Dyfed, 486
Burslem, Staffordshire, 191, **193, 334**
Burton on Trent, Staffordshire, **133,**
   320, 328, **334**
Bury, Greater Manchester, **90, 91**, 133,
   193, 241, 311
Bury St Edmunds, Suffolk, **138**, 211,
   246, **284, 422**, 423, 486
Bushey, Hertfordshire, **531**
Buxted, East Sussex, **531**
Buxton, Derbyshire, **168**, 473, **474**
Byfield, Northamptonshire, 224

Cadishead, Greater Manchester, 47
Cadiz, Spain, 220
Caernarvon. Gwynedd, **414, 445, 538**
Caerphilly, Mid Glamorgan, **334, 408**
Cairo, Egypt, 54, 174
Caistor, Lincolnshire, 483
Caithness, Highland, **135**
Calcutta, India, 144, 174, 239, 240,
   241, 303, 368, **369**

Index of places 631

California, United States of America, 63, 330
Callander, Central, **79**, 460
Callington, Cornwall, **334**
Calne, Wiltshire, 420
Calstock, Cornwall, 226
Camborne, Cornwall, **334**
Cambridge, Cambridgeshire, 89, **91**, 214, **215**, **334**, **345**, **391**, **479**, 490, **531**
Cambridgeshire, 88, 89, **91**, **94**, 114, **138**, 206, 214, **215**, **248**, **249**, 257, 308, 320, **334**, **335**, **336**, **339**, **341**, **345**, 372, **391**, **392**, 403, **407**, 423, **479**, 489, **518**, **531**, **532**, **533**
Camelford, Cornwall, 528
Camelon, Central, **79**
Cameroons, **493**
Campbeltown, Strathclyde, **79**, **512**, **576**
Canada, **85**, **86**, 197, 231, 267, 279, 289, 290, 353, 361, 389
Canary Islands, Spain, 491, **492**, **493**
Cannes, France, **326**
Cannock, Staffordshire, **193**, **334**
Cannock Chase, Staffordshire, 217
Canterbury, Kent, 138, **257**, 258, 343, **345**, **531**
Canton, China, 48
Cape Colony, South Africa, 494
Cape of Good Hope, South Africa, 63, 349
Cape Town, South Africa, 63, 349, 494
Caracas, Venezuela, 163
Cardiff, South Glamorgan, 81, **91**, 169, **334**, **377**, 386, **399**, 400, 486, 534, 538, **549**, **553**
Cardigan, Dyfed, 412, 538
Carlisle, Cumbria, **91**, **139**, **140**, 154, **180**, **181**, **266**, **334**, 361, 363, 374, **377**, 426, 521, **531**, **556**
Carluke, Strathclyde, **122**
Carmarthen, Dyfed, **334**, 348, 403, 538
Carnoustie, Tayside, **79**, **155**
Carrick on Shannon, Ireland, 347
Carsphairn, Dumfries & Galloway, 512
Cartagena, Colombia, 56

Casablanca, Morocco, **493**
Castle Douglas, Dumfries & Galloway, **79**, **122**, **397**, **512**
Castleford, West Yorkshire, 316, 317
Castleton, Greater Manchester, 423, 451
Castletown, Isle of Man, 200, 359, **431**, **445**
Caterham Valley, Surrey, **334**
Caversham, Berkshire, **91**, **334**
Central, **78**, **79**, **80**, **122**, **123**, **143**, **236**, 426, 460, **512**, **513**, 567, 568, **578**
Central America see Latin America
Cephalonia, Greece, 295
Ceylon see Sri Lanka
Chadderton, Greater Manchester, **168**, **193**
Channel Islands, **91**, 119, **138**, **143**, **242**, 258, **259**, **335**, 374, **378**, 404, 406, 429, **450**, 529, **531**, 541
Chard, Somerset, **268**, 349, **431**, **531**
Charlbury, Oxfordshire, 223
Charleston, United States of America, 361, 362
Chatham, Kent, 186, 343, **345**, 348, **377**
Chatteris, Cambridgeshire, 248
Cheadle, Greater Manchester, **193**
Cheetham Hill, Greater Manchester, **194**
Chefoo, China, **280**
Chelford, Cheshire, **193**
Chelmsford, Essex, 89, **91**, 223, 252, **345**, **487**, 488
Cheltenham, Gloucestershire, **169**, 229, 263, 330, **334**, **554**
Chepstow, Gwent, 126, **130**, **299**, 386
Chertsey, Surrey, 58
Chesham, Buckinghamshire, 131, 134, **531**
Cheshire, 47, **52**, **91**, **93**, **94**, **168**, 181, 191, **193**, **194**, **195**, **213**, 311, 325, 328, 417, **429**, 430, **431**, 460, 461, 509, **531**, **532**, **533**, **538**, 540, **576**
Chester, Cheshire, **193**, **195**, 325, 328, 429, **431**, **531**, **538**
Chester le Street, County Durham, **334**, 416

632 *British banking – a guide to historical records*

Chesterfield, Derbyshire, **146**, 177, **334**, 451, 474, **475**
Chichester, West Sussex, 89, **91**, **138**, 234, **259**, **334**, 343, **345**, **380**, **448**
Chile, 55, 56, 63, 72, **74**, 220, **222**, 286, 289, 290, 387, 453, 467
China, 48, 144, 145, **278**, 279, **280**, **281**, **282**, **283**, 289, 367, 368, **369**, **388**, 410, 425, 430
Chippenham, Wiltshire, **138**, 548
Chipping Norton, Oxfordshire, **166**, 223, **371**, 498, **499**
Chorley, Lancashire, **168**, **193**, 312, 540, **544**
Chorleywood, Hertfordshire, **406**
Christchurch, Dorset, **138**, 548
Chumleigh, Devon, **406**
Chungking, China, **280**
Cirencester, Gloucestershire, **138**, **169**, 229, **334**
Clacton, Essex, 383
Clare, Suffolk, 245, 423
Clarkston, Strathclyde, **122**, **512**
Clay Cross, Derbyshire, 146
Clayton, West Yorkshire, 113
Cleator Moor, Cumbria, 180, 537
Cleckheaton, West Yorkshire, **284**, 535
Clevedon, Avon, 534
Cleveland, 60, 88, **93**, **338**, **340**, 403, 416, **479**, **497**, 556
Cliftonville, Kent, **531**
Clitheroe, Lancashire, 175, 417
Clwyd, 63, **334**, **335**, **339**, **341**, **378**, **379**, 404, **407**, 412, 413, **414**, **431**, **448**, 538
Clydach, West Glamorgan, 227
Clydebank, Strathclyde, **122**, **512**, 513
Coalbrookdale, Shropshire, 477
Coalville, Leicestershire, 133, 320
Coatbridge, Strathclyde, **79**, **122**, **512**
Cockermouth, Cumbria, 139, 140, 180, **531**
Coggeshall, Essex, 487, 488
Colchester, Essex, 61, 89, **91**, 115, 116, 247, **251**, **383**, 422, 508
Coldstream, Borders, **79**, **122**
Coleford, Essex, 230
Coleshill, Warwickshire, **173**, **377**
Colne, Lancashire, **168**, 175

Cologne, Germany, 86
Colombia, 56, 72, **74**, 162, 163
Colombo, Sri Lanka, 144
Concepcion, Chile, **222**
Coniston, Cumbria, 437, 522
Connah's Quay, Clwyd, 538
Consett, County Durham, **334**, 416
Constantinople *see* Istanbul
Conway, Gwynedd, **406**
Copenhagen, Denmark, 254, 255
Coquimbo, Chile, 56
Cordoba, Argentina, 72
Corfu, Greece, 294, 296
Cornwall, 89, **94**, **107**, **108**, 138, 156, 167, **188**, **190**, 216, 226, 262, **268**, 329, **334**, **335**, **336**, **339**, 349, 357, 404, 440, **476**, **519**, **528**, **547**, 548
Corsham, Wiltshire, 420
Corunna, Spain, 286
Corwen, Clywd, 63
Cotteridge, West Midlands, **334**
Coupar Angus, Tayside, **79**, **143**, **436**, **512**, **578**
Coventry, West Midlands, **172**, **193**, 319, 328, **334**, 370, 373, **377**, **431**, **505**, **531**
Cowbridge, South Glamorgan, 81, **91**
Crail, Fife, **162**
Cranbrook, Kent, **91**, **334**, 343, **531**
Cranleigh, Surrey, **531**
Crawley, West Sussex, 269, **334**
Crediton, Devon, 216
Crete, Greece, 296
Crewe, Cheshire, **91**, **193**
Crewkerne, Somerset, **334**, 349, **432**, 500
Crich, Derbyshire, 187
Cricklade, Wiltshire, 169
Crieff, Tayside, **79**, **122**, **143**, **512**
Cromarty, Highland, **79**, **136**
Cromer, Norfolk, **138**, 246, **308**, 307, **334**
Cross Hills, North Yorkshire, 113, 175
Cuba, 234, 290, 304, 467
Cuckfield, West Sussex, 254
Cullen, Grampian, **79**, **512**
Cullompton, Devon, 188, **334**
Cumberland *see* Cumbria

Index of places

Cumbernauld, Strathclyde, **122, 459**
Cumbria, **58, 82, 83, 90, 91, 93, 94,**
  111, 122, 139, 140, 154, 175,
  177, **180, 181,** 189, 191, 192,
  193, 194, 195, 222, 223, 263,
  266, 312, 334, 336, 339, 341,
  354, 361, 363, 374, **377, 378,**
  379, 407, 416, 426, 429, **436,**
  437, 521, 522, 523, **531, 532,**
  533, 536, 556, 557, 563
Cupar, Fife, **79, 122, 162, 459**
Curitiba, Brazil, 72
Cwmgorse, Dyfed, 299
Cyprus, 54, 145, 295, 296
Czechoslovakia, 53, 55

Dakar, Senegal, **159**
Dalkeith, Lothian, **162**
Dalmuir, Strathclyde, **122**
Dalry, Strathclyde, **122**
Dalton in Furness, Cumbria, **377**
Darlaston Green, West Midlands, **334,**
  377
Darley Dale, Derbyshire, 473
Darlington, County Durham, **60,** 84,
  88, 89, **334,** 419, **433,** 479, 556
Dartford, Kent, **334, 345,** 365
Dartmouth, Devon, 188, 262, 403,
  406
Darwen, Lancashire, 168, 181, **334**
Datchet, Berkshire, **407,** 408
Daventry, Northamptonshire, **138, 254,**
  334, 414, 415, 525
Dawlish, Devon, **377**
Deal, Kent, **334, 366,** 403, **531**
Debenham, Suffolk, 62, 245, 423
Deddington, Oxfordshire, 224
Delhi, India, 241, 303
Delph, Greater Manchester, **168, 193,**
  462
Demerara, Guyana, **159**
Denbigh, Clwyd, 412
Denholme, West Yorkshire, 175
Denmark, 254, 255, **256**
Denny, Central, **79**
Derby, Derbyshire, 103, 133, **177, 178,**
  187, 334, 373, 429, 430, **431,**
  480, 481, 482, 483, 513, **514**
Derby Road, Ipswich, 62

Derbyshire **57, 58,** 103, 133, **139,**
  146, 168, 177, 178, 187,191,
  193, 334, 340, 372, 373, **386,**
  407, 421, 429, 430, **431,** 451,
  473, **474, 475, 480,** 481, 482,
  483, **502,** 513, **514, 530, 532**
Dereham, Norfolk, 246, 411
Desborough, Northamptonshire, **490**
Devizes, Wiltshire, 137, **341, 342, 377,**
  420
Devon, 62, 66, 91, **95,** 99, 107, **108,**
  137, **157, 188, 190, 202, 208,**
  213, 216, **217,** 220, **226, 262,**
  275, 288, **321, 322,** 328, 329,
  332, 334, 335, 336, 338, 339,
  340, 349, **356, 377, 381,** 403,
  404, **406, 407,** 441, **445, 465,**
  466, **520,** 533, 534, 546, 548, **549**
Devonport, Devon, 107, **108,** 188, 262,
  275, 403
Dewsbury, West Yorkshire, 113, 253,
  283, **284,** 311, **377,** 534
Didcot, Oxfordshire, 224
Didsbury, Greater Manchester, **91**
Dingwall, Highland, **79, 136,** 398
Diss, Norfolk, **212,** 246, 264, 348
Dobcross, Greater Manchester, **168,**
  462
Dolgellau, Gwynedd, 63, **406,** 413,
  414, 546
Dominica, Lesser Antilles, **159**
Doncaster, South Yorkshire, **101, 164,**
  315, 316, **334, 475,** 483, **558**
Dorchester, Dorset, 208, **334, 546,**
  548, **549**
Dorking, Surrey, **345, 531**
Dornoch, Dumfries & Galloway, **79,**
  136
Dorset, **94, 111, 138, 139,** 188, **208,**
  217, 244, 329, **333, 334, 335,**
  337, 339, 340, 341, 377, 379,
  403, **407, 431, 437, 438, 497,**
  533, 546, 548, 549, 573
Douglas, Isle of Man, **199, 296,** 325,
  359, 360, 531, 554
Doune, Central, **79, 512**
Dover, Kent, **334, 383,** 403
Dovercourt, Essex, 62, **138, 334**
Dowlais, Mid Glamorgan, **334,** 538

634   *British banking – a guide to historical records*

Downham Market, Norfolk, 249
Driffield, Humberside, 101, **102**, 187,
   261, 502, 556, 560, **561**
Droitwich, Hereford & Worcester, **334**
Dronfield, Derbyshire, 473
Drumnadrochit, Highland, 136
Duala, Cameroons, **493**
Dubai, United Arab Emirates, 119
Dublin, Ireland, 242, 243, **347**, 393,
   394, 400
Dudley, West Midlands, **91, 196, 198,**
   199, **334**, 370, 372, 373, 490,
   516, 550
Dukinfield, Greater Manchester, 193
Dulverton, Somerset, 216
Dumbarton, Strathclyde, **79, 122, 512**
Dumfries, Dumfries & Galloway, 567,
   568, **577**
Dumfries & Galloway 78, **79, 80,** 121,
   122, 123, 124, 136, 269, **397,**
   426, **512, 513,** 527, 567, 568,
   577, 578
Dunblane, Central, **79, 512**
Dundalk, Ireland, 347
Dundee, Tayside, **79,** 154, **162, 200,**
   201, 202, 204, 228, 426, 446,
   457, 527, 567, 568, **577, 578**
Dunedin, New Zealand, 159
Dunfermline, Fife, **79, 122**
Dunkeld, Tayside, **79, 143, 436, 512**
Dunnichen, Tayside, 200
Dunning, Tayside, **79, 512**
Dunoon, Strathclyde, **122, 512**
Duns, Borders, **122, 459**
Dunstable, Bedfordshire, 98, **335, 347**
Dunstone, Devon, 62
Durban, South Africa, 349, 392
Durham, City of, County Durham, **60,**
   88, **335,** 403, 417, 419, 449, **573**
Durham, County of, **60,** 84, 88, 89, **94,**
   276, 334, 335, 339, 340, 403,
   416, 417, **418,** 419, **433,** 449,
   479, 556, **573**
Dursley, Gloucestershire, **169, 520,**
   552
Dyfed, 81, 91, 227, **299,** 329, **331,**
   334, 336, 339, 348, 403, **407,**
   412, **414,** 486, **523,** 538
Dysart, Fife, **79**

Easingwold, North Yorkshire, 560
Eastbourne, East Sussex, **335,** 348,
   385
East Dereham, Norfolk, 307
East Grinstead, West Sussex, **91, 132,**
   265, 385
East Harling, Norfolk, 212, 246
East Kilbride, Strathclyde, **122**
East Morley, West Yorkshire, **205,** 509
East Oxford, Oxfordshire, 223
East Sussex, 84, 89, **90, 91, 138, 183,**
   254, 258, 259, 328, **333, 335,**
   338, 339, 343, 344, **345, 346,**
   348, **385, 530, 531, 533, 537**
Eastwood, Nottinghamshire, 421
Ebbw Vale, Gwent, **335**
Eccles, Greater Manchester, **531**
Eccleshall, Staffordshire, 496
Ecuador, 163, **222**
Edenbridge, Kent, 265, **335**
Edinburgh, Lothian 76, **120, 122,** 154,
   160, 162, 197, 200, 201, 204,
   205, **213,** 214, 285, **396, 400,**
   418, **456,** 457, 465, 510, 511, **512,**
   515, 526, 541, **567, 571, 578**
   Drumsheugh Gardens, 568
   Dundas Street, **459**
   Granton Street, **459**
   Hunter Square, **459**
   Leith, **79,** 140, 207, 229, **397**
   Palmerston Place, **397**
   Rutland Square, 568
   St Andrew Square, 396
   Ship Close, 456
Edzell, Tayside, **79, 512**
Egremont, Cumbria, 180, **377,** 537
Egypt, **53,** 54, 87, 89, 174, 295, 296,
   303, 329, 398, 453, 491
Elgin, Grampian, **79, 122, 136,** 568
Elland, West Yorkshire, 252, 311
Ellesmere, Shropshire, 328, **335**
Elstree, Hertfordshire, 360
Ely, Cambridgeshire, **138,** 215, **335,**
   391, 392
Epsom, Surrey, **335**
Errol, Tayside, **512**
Eskbank, Lothian, **79**
Eskdale, Cumbria, 193
Esher, Surrey, **91**

Index of places 635

Essex, 61, 62, 66, 89, **91, 94, 115,** 116, **138, 174,** 175, 215, 216, **223,** 246, 247, **251,** 273, **334, 335, 339, 341,** 344, **345, 346, 383, 392, 422, 487, 488, 507,** 508, **530, 533**
Estonia, 125
Eton, Berkshire, 127, 171, 551
Europe (excluding UK), **52,** 53, 54, **55,** 56, 59, 67, 72, 73, 86, **88, 117, 220, 124,** 125, 130, 144, 146, 163, 174, 209, 220, 221, 234, 239, 240, 242, 243, 254, 255, 256, 267, 268, 269, 273, 279, 286, 287, 289, 290, **292, 293, 294,** 295, **296,** 304, 306, 313, 314, **325, 326, 327,** 329, **339,** 342, **347,** 353, **354,** 355, 374, 375, 377, 384, 387, 390, **392,** 393, **394,** 395, 398, **399,** 400, 404, 409, 403, 447, 452, 453, 461, 463, 464, 465, 466, 467, 468, 491, **492, 493,** 523, 524, 528, **529,** 547, 555, 562
Evesham, Hereford & Worcester, 229, 230, 263, **335,** 417
Exeter, Devon, **95, 157, 188,** 220, 288, **381,** 403, 441, 445, **465,** 533
Exmouth, Devon, 466
Exton Park, Leicestershire, 185
Eye, Suffolk, 212, 250, 348, **378,** 423
Eynsham, Oxfordshire, 224

Fairford, Gloucestershire, 169
Fairlie, Strathclyde, **512**
Fakenham, Norfolk, 88, 114, 246, **248,** 307, 412
Falkirk, Central, 79, **122,** 236, 568, **578**
Falkland, Fife, **122**
Falmouth, Cornwall, 107, 167
Fareham, Hampshire, **138**
Faringdon, Oxfordshire, 169, **335**
Farnborough, Hampshire, 277, 278
Farnham, Surrey, 137, **307, 346**
Farnworth, Greater Manchester, **65, 168**
Faversham, Kent, **274, 335,** 441
Felixstowe, Suffolk, 62, 245

Felling, Tyne & Wear, **335**
Feltwell, Norfolk, 423
Fenny Stratford, Buckinghamshire, 98
Fenton, Staffordshire, **193, 335**
Fernando Po, Ghana, **492**
Ferndown, Dorset, **335**
Ffestiniog, Gwynedd, 141, **378,** 412, **414,** 445
Fife, **78, 80, 122, 123,** 228, **459, 512, 568, 578**
Filial Porto, Brazil, **343**
Finland, 255
Fleetwood, Lancashire, **312,** 442, **443**
Fochabers, Grampian, 79, **512**
Foleshill, West Midlands, **335**
Folkestone, Kent, **335**
Foochow, China, **280**
Forfar, Tayside, 57, **79, 122,** 200, 201
Forres, Grampian, 79, **122, 136**
Fort Augustus, Highland, **79, 136**
Fortrose, Highland, **79, 136**
Fort William, Highland, **79, 122,** 136
Foulsham, Norfolk, 308
Fowey, Cornwall, **335**
Framlingham, Suffolk, 250, 412
France, 56, 59, 72, **73, 86,** 163, 174, 209, 289, 290, 293, **294,** 306, 313, 314, 325, **326, 327,** 329, **339,** 387, 399, 404, 453, 461, 528
Frankfurt, Germany, 209, 452, 453, 524
Fraserburgh, Grampian, **79**
Freetown, Sierra Leone, 491
Frodsham, Cheshire, **531**
Frome, Somerset, **335,** 500

Gainsborough, Lincolnshire, 284, 322, 323, **406, 475,** 483
Gairloch, Highland, 136
Galashiels, Borders, 79, **122, 527,** 567
Galston, Strathclyde, **123**
Gambia, 491
Garmouth, Grampian, **79, 136**
Garstang, Lancashire, 442
Gatehouse of Fleet, Dumfries & Galloway, **79, 512**
Gateshead, Tyne & Wear, **335**
Geneva, Switzerland, **326,** 390
Genoa, Italy, 88

636   *British banking – a guide to historical records*

Germany, 55, 56, 67, 86, 125, 130, 144, 209, 234, 239, 240, 267, 268, 286, 287, 290, 292, 304, 325, 326, 353, 355, 375, 377, 398, 399, 452, 453, 461, 463, 466, 467, 468, 492, **493**, 523, 524, 562

Ghana, 158, 491, **492, 493**

Gibraltar, 54, 220

Giggleswick, North Yorkshire, 175

Gillingham,
    Dorset, **335**
    Kent, **346, 531**

Girvan, Strathclyde, **123, 512**

Gisburn, Lancashire, 175

Glasgow, Strathclyde, 76, 77, **79**, 121, **123, 151, 154,** 161, **162,** 201, 202, **207,** 214, **227, 228, 229,** 321, **396,** 418, 426, 446, 456, **459,** 460, **476, 503, 510,** 511, **512,** 515, **526,** 567, **568, 577, 578**

Glastonbury, Somerset, **335, 447,** 500, **549**

Glenlivet, Grampian, **79, 136**

Glenrothes, Fife, **79, 122**

Glenurquhart, Highland, **79, 136**

Glossop, Derbyshire, **58,** 429

Gloucester, Gloucestershire, 66, **169, 229, 230,** 328, 330 **335,** 403, 405, **508, 531**

Gloucestershire, 66, **105,** 107, 137, **138, 139, 169, 229, 230, 263, 317,** 328, 330, **334, 335, 338, 340,** 366, 403, 405, **407, 499,** 504, **508, 520, 531, 544,** 548, **552, 554, 573,** 574

Godalming, Surrey, 137, **346, 367, 531**

Gold Coast *see* Ghana

Golspie, Highland, **123**

Goole, Humberside, **102,** 284, 316, **317,** 318, 555, **558**

Gorebridge, Lothian, **79**

Gorleston on Sea, Norfolk, 308

Gosport, Hampshire, 236, **335**

Gourock, Strathclyde, **123, 512**

Grahamston, Falkirk, Central, **79, 236**

Grahamstoun *see* Grahamston

Grahamstown, South Africa, 349

Grampian, **45, 46, 78, 79, 80, 122, 123, 135, 136, 162,** 396, **417,** 418, **459, 505,** 510, **512, 513,** 567, **568**

Grangemouth, Central, **79, 512**

Grange over Sands, Cumbria, **193**

Grangetown, South Glamorgan, **91**

Grantham, Lincolnshire, **262, 302, 320, 335,** 417, 483, 490

Grantown on Spey, Highland, **79, 136**

Grasmere, Cumbria, **91**

Grassington, North Yorkshire, 175

Gravesend, Kent, **335**

Grays, Essex, **91**

Great Berkhamsted, Hertfordshire, 134

Great Bridge, West Midlands, **335**

Great Crosby, Merseyside, **91**

Great Dunmow, Essex, 488

Greater Manchester, 47, **50,** 51, **58, 65,** 66, **74, 81,** 89, **90, 91, 93, 94,** 118, **130,** 133, 134, 144, **153, 160, 163, 165, 167, 168, 169, 181, 191, 193, 194, 195,** 205, **241,** 253, **260,** 261, **270,** 271, 272, 283, 286, 300, 301, **310,** 311, 312, 321, **331, 338, 339, 356,** 357, **359,** 361, 362, **369,** 374, **379,** 390, **399,** 400, **407, 416,** 417, **423, 427,** 429, 430, **431,** 442, 452, 457, **462,** 493, **509,** 522, **530, 531, 532, 533, 540, 541,** 542, **544, 545, 551,** 554, 555

Great Missenden, Buckinghamshire, 131

Great Yarmouth, Norfolk, 88, 138, 246, 247, 249, **250, 307, 308, 335**

Greece, 221, 255, 256, **294,** 295, 296, 547

Greenock, Strathclyde, **79,** 123, **237, 459, 512,** 527, 567, 568

Grimsby, Humberside, 284, **285,** 323, **335,** 490

Grimsby Docks, Humberside, 483

Guatemala, 163

Guayaquil, Ecuador, **222**

Guernsey, Channel Islands, **91, 138, 242, 335,** 404, 529

Index of places

Guiana, 120
Guildford, Surrey, 137, **138, 265, 335,**
 346
Guisborough, Cleveland, 497
Guiseley, West Yorkshire, **558**
Gullane, Lothian, 79
Gulmarg, India, 174
Gunnislake, Cornwall, 226
Guyana, 120, 157, 159
Gwent, **46,** 81, 99, **126, 130,** 141, 169,
 299, 300, 328, **333, 335, 338,**
 339, 340, 379, 386, 403
Gwynedd, **63, 141, 339, 378, 379,** 400,
 406, 407, 408, 412, 413, **414,**
 417, **444,** 445, **538, 546**

Haddington, Lothian, **79, 123**
Hadleigh,
 Essex, **115,** 116, 175, 383
 Suffolk, 245, **335**
Hailsham, East Sussex, 385
Halesworth, Suffolk, 88, **91,** 246, **249,**
 250, 307
Halifax, West Yorkshire, 113, **127,**
 153, **208, 252,** 290, 324, 361,
 362, 509 **535,** 557
Halkirk, Highland, **79, 136**
Halstead, Essex, **346,** 487
Haltwhistle, Cumbria, 140
Hamburg, Germany, 56, 144, 234, 239,
 286, 292, 304, 467, **493,** 494, 523
Hamilton, Strathclyde, **79, 123, 512**
Hampshire, **58,** 66, 89, **90, 94, 131,**
 137, 138, 139, 194, 208, 217,
 233, 234, **236, 244, 258, 259,**
 266, 277, 278, **301, 317,** 318,
 329, **331, 332, 333, 335, 338,**
 339, 340, 341, 345, 348, 349,
 353, **358, 407, 408,** 420, 441,
 462, 547, 548, **549**
Hankow, China, 144, **280**
Hanley, Staffordshire, **91,** 191, **193,**
 321, **335**
Harare, Zimbabwe, 494
Harbin, China, **281**
Harlech, Gwynedd, 141
Harleston, Norfolk, 250
Harpenden, Hertfordshire, 360
Harrington, Cumbria, 180, 537

Harrogate, North Yorkshire, **101,** 114
Harwich, Essex, 62, 115, **138, 174, 335**
Haslemere, Surrey, **335**
Haslingden, Lancashire, **193,** 311
Hastings, Kent, 102, **335, 346**
Hatfield, Hertfordshire, 470
Hatherton, Staffordshire, 217
Havant, Hampshire, **335**
Haverfordwest, Dyfed, 81, **91,** 348,
 523, 538
Haverhill, Suffolk, 423
Hawarden, Clwyd, **335, 538**
Hawes, North Yorkshire, 502
Hawick, Borders, **79, 123, 162**
Hawkshead, Cumbria, **91**
Haworth, West Yorkshire, 175
Haydon Bridge, Northumberland, 139
Hayfield, Derbyshire, **168, 193**
Hayle, Cornwall, 107
Hay on Wye, Powys, 81
Haywards Heath, West Sussex, **91,**
 254, **335**
Heathfield, East Sussex, 385
Heaviley, Stockport, **195**
Hebburn, Tyne & Wear, **335**
Hebden Bridge, West Yorkshire, **560**
Heckington, Lincolnshire, 433
Heckmondwike, West Yorkshire, 283,
 284, 535
Hednesford, Staffordshire, **335**
Helensburgh, Strathclyde, **79, 123, 512**
Helmsdale, Highland, **123**
Helmsley, North Yorkshire, 101, 502,
 560
Helston, Cornwall, 107, **108, 268,** 349,
 519
Hemel Hempstead, Hertfordshire, 131,
 335
Henley, Oxfordshire, **91,** 478
Henley in Arden, Warwickshire, 498,
 504
Hereford, Hereford & Worcester, 81,
 104, **107, 138,** 230, **269,** 328,
 517
Hereford & Worcester, 81, **104, 105,**
 107, 138, 139, 156, **184, 212,**
 229, **230,** 263, **269, 334, 335,**
 336, 338, 339, 340, 341, 358,
 366, 371, 373, **377, 407, 411,**

638   *British banking – a guide to historical records*

412, 417, 461, 498, **499**, 504,
517, 524, 525, 534, **553, 554**
Herefordshire *see* Hereford & Worcester
Herne Bay, Kent, **346**
Hersham, Surrey, **91**
Hertford, Hertfordshire, 46, **346**, 438,
470, **531**
Hertfordshire, 46, 89, **90, 91, 93, 94**,
98, 131, **134, 138, 188, 214, 215**,
332, **335, 339, 340, 341, 346**,
360, 391, 392, 406, 437, 438,
470, 507, 508, 525, **531, 533, 574**
Hesse, Germany, 453
Heswall, Merseyside, 325, **335**
Hexham, Northumberland, 180, **276**,
335, 417
Heyford, Oxfordshire, 223
Heywood, Greater Manchester, 134
Higham, Suffolk, 246
Highbridge, Somerset, **335, 549**
Higher Buxton, Derbyshire, 473
Highland, 45, **78, 79, 80, 122, 123**,
135, 136, 160, 398, **512, 513**,
567, 568
High Wycombe, Buckinghamshire, **91**,
138, 335, 536
Highworth, Wiltshire, 169, 499
Hillington, Strathclyde, **512**
Hinchley Wood, Surrey, **531**
Hinckley, Leicestershire, **319, 320**, 428
Hitchin, Hertfordshire, 89, 98, **346**,
437, 438, **470**
Hobart Town, Australia, **455**
Hoddesdon, Hertfordshire, 470
Holbeach, Lincolnshire, 248, **249, 335**
Holborn Hill, Cumbria, 180
Hollingworth, Greater Manchester,
168
Hollinwood, Greater Manchester, **168**
Holmfirth, West Yorkshire, 535
Holsworthy, Devon, **91**, 216, 226, **335**
Holt, Norfolk, **91**, 246, 248, 308
Holywell, Clwyd, 412
Hong Kong, 119, 144, **278, 279**, 281,
282, 367, 368, 410
Honiton, Devon, **213**, 216, 349
Hopeman, Grampian, **79**, 136
Horbury, West Yorkshire, **91**

Horley, Surrey, 265, **335**
Horncastle, Lincolnshire, 218, 322
Houghton le Spring, Tyne & Wear, 416
Hove, East Sussex, 254, 344, **531**
Howden, Humberside, 284, **378, 467**,
555, **556**
Hoylake, Merseyside, **91**
Hucknall, Nottinghamshire, **422**, 482,
514
Huddersfield, West Yorkshire, 113,
252, 283, 324, 374, **378, 469**,
534, 535, **536, 558**
Hull, Humberside, 66, **91**, 101, 110,
211, 253, **284**, 323, **336, 354**, 358,
378, 406, 434, 480, 481, 482,
484, 513, 554, **556**, 557, **558**, 560
Hulme, Cheshire, 540
Humberside, 66, **91**, 101, **102, 110**,
187, 211, **253, 261, 284, 285**,
316, **317**, 318, 321, **323, 333**,
335, 336, 339, 354, 358, 378,
379, 406, 434, 467, 480, 481,
482, 483, 484, 490, 502, 513,
554, 555, **556**, 557, **558, 560**,
561
Hungary, 255
Hungerford, Berkshire, **336**
Hunslett, West Yorkshire, **101**
Hunstanton, Norfolk, 246
Huntingdon, Cambridgeshire, 89, **91**,
336, 518
Huntly, Grampian, **79, 123**
Huthwaite, Nottinghamshire, 482
Hyde, Greater Manchester, 47, **58, 91**,
429
Hythe, Kent, **346, 531**

Ilfracombe, Devon, 216, 403, **520**
Ilkeston, Derbyshire, **407**, 421, 482
Ilkley, West Yorkshire, 175
Ilminister, Somerset, 499
India, 48, 67, **70**, 144, 145, 174, 185,
203, 239, 240, 241, 278, 290,
303, 329, 353, **359**, 367, 368,
387, **388**, 398, 410, 425, **578**
Indiana, United States of America,
483
Indonesia, 144
Innerleithen, Borders, **123**

Index of places

Inverness, Highland, 79, **123, 135,**
   136, 567, 568
Inverurie, Grampian, **79, 512**
Ionian Islands, Greece, 294
Ipswich, Suffolk, 49, **61, 62,** 89, **91,**
   116, **138,** 175, **244,** 245, 246, 251,
   336, **407**
Iquique, Chile, 55, 56, **222**
Iquitos, Peru, 163
Iran, 118, **119, 120,** 203, 468
Ireland, 242, 243, **347,** 374, **392,** 393,
   394, 395, 400, 409, 447, 453
Irlam, Greater Manchester 91
Ironbridge, Shropshire, 336
Irthlingborough, Northamptonshire, **378**
Irvine, Strathclyde, 121, **123,** 285,
   426, **512**
Isle of Lewis, Scotland, 396
Isle of Man, **199,** 200, **296,** 325, **359,**
   360, 404, 430, **431, 445,** 530,
   531, 554, 555, **579**
Isle of Wight, 258, **297,** 403, **450**
Israel, 54
Istanbul, Turkey, 295, 296, 399
Italy, 59, **88,** 255, 256, 290, 295, 390,
   453
Ivory Coast, 76
Ivybridge, Devon, 262

Jamaica, 158, **159,** 222
Japan, 144, 221, 243, 278, 280, 289,
   388, 410, 430, 463, 467
Jarrow, Tyne & Wear, 183, **336,** 416
Jedburgh, Borders, **79, 123**
Jersey, Channel Islands, **91,** 119, **143,**
   258, **259, 378,** 429, **450, 531**
Jerusalem, Israel, 54
Johannesburg, South Africa, 494
Johnstone, Strathclyde, **123, 512**
Jordan, **159**

Karachi, Pakistan, 144, 174
Keighley, West Yorkshire, 175, 535
Kells, Ireland, 347
Kelso, Borders, **79, 123**
Kelvedon, Essex, 383, 487
Kendal, Cumbria, **82, 91,** 140, 175,
   177, 189, **336,** 361, 416, 437,
   521, 522

Kenilworth, Warwickshire, 315
Kent, **91, 94, 102,** 138, **139, 155,**
   183, **194, 257,** 258, 265, **274,**
   298, 328, **332, 334, 335, 338,**
   339, 340, 341, 343, 344, **345,**
   346, 347, 348, 365, **366, 377,**
   383, 385, **403, 439, 440, 441,**
   514, **531, 533, 537**
Keswick, Cumbria, 139, **193, 378**
Kettering, Northamptonshire, **138,**
   207, **235, 320, 336,** 414, **415,** 490
Kidderminster, Hereford & Worcester,
   104, 212, **336,** 371, **498, 499,**
   504, 524
Kilcreggan, Strathclyde, **512**
Killearn, Central, **123**
Killin, Central, **79, 143**
Kilmarnock, Strathclyde, **79, 123, 285,**
   303, **512,** 568, **578**
Kincardine, Highland, 45, **79, 512**
Kinghorn, Fife, **79, 123**
Kingsbridge, Devon, 188, 262, **336,**
   534
King's Lynn, Norfolk, 88, **138,** 175,
   210, 246, 248, **249, 297,** 298,
   307, **336,** 412
Kingston, Jamaica, 158
Kingston upon Thames, Surrey, **431,**
   477, 429
Kington, Hereford & Worcester, **184,**
   371, 412
Kingussie, Highland, **79, 123, 136**
Kinross, Tayside, **123**
Kirkbride, Cumbria, **194**
Kirkby Lonsdale, Cumbria, **194, 222,**
   223, 312, 522
Kirby Moorside, North Yorkshire, 560
Kirkby Stephen, Cumbria, 82, 522
Kirkcaldy, Fife, **79, 123,** 200, 228, **512**
Kirkconnel, Dumfries & Galloway,
   123
Kirkcudbright, Dumfries & Galloway,
   79, 426
Kirkham, Lancashire, 312
Kirkoswald, Cumbria, 180
Kirkwall, Orkney, **79, 123, 512,** 567
Kirriemuir, Tayside, **79, 123**
Knaresborough, North Yorkshire, 114,
   307, 354, 404, 557

640   *British banking – a guide to historical records*

Knighton, Powys, **184, 336, 414**
Knutsford, Cheshire, **194**, 509
Kobe, Japan, 144
Kula Trengganu, India, **369**
Kuwait, 119
Kyle of Lochalsh, Highland, **79**, 136

Lagos, Nigeria, 47, **491, 493**
Lahore, India, 48, 241
Lairg, Highland, **79, 136**
Lakenheath, Suffolk, 423
Lamlash, Strathclyde, 79
Lampeter, Dyfed, 299, 329, **336**
Lanark, Strathclyde, **123**
Lancashire, **76, 90, 93, 94, 106**, 126,
     167, **168**, 175, **181**, 182, **189**,
     191, 192, **193, 194, 195**, 208,
     222, **311, 312**, 313, 328, **333**,
     334, 359, 362, 363, **369**, 370,
     374, 417, **434**, 437, **442, 443**,
     452, 509, 522, **533**, 535, 540,
     544, 554
Lancaster, Lancashire, **189**, 191, 192,
     194, 222, **311, 312**, 437, 442, 522,
     540, **554**
Langholm, Dumfries & Galloway,
     123, 578
Langley, Berkshire, **336**
Langport, Somerset, 216, **499, 500**
Largs, Strathclyde, **123, 512**
Larkhall, Strathclyde, **512**
Latin America, **52, 53, 55**, 56, **63, 72**,
     73, **74**, 103, **117, 118, 120**, 158,
     159, 162, 163, **220, 222**, 239,
     240, 256, 286, 287, 289, 290,
     327, 329, **342, 343**, 387, **388**,
     389, 453, 462, 467, 468
Latvia, 239, 355
Lauder, Borders, **79**
Launceston,
     Australia, **455**
     Cornwall, **190**, 216, 226, 404
Lavenham, Suffolk, 245
Leamington Priors, Warwickshire,
     315, 373, 517
Leamington Spa, Warwickshire, 238,
     314, 328, **336, 371**, 489, **524**,
     531
Leatherhead, Surrey, **138, 336**

Lechlade, Gloucestershire, 169
Ledbury, Hereford & Worcester, 156,
     229, 407, 525
Leeds, West Yorkshire, 66, **71, 91,**
     100, 101, 102, 111, 127, 164,
     211, 252, 253, **318**, 321, 329,
     336, 347, 372, 373, **378**, 403,
     407, 435, 472, 528, **531**, 535,
     536, 546, 547, **557, 558**
Leek, Staffordshire, **298**, 429
Le Havre, France, 86, 325, **326**
Leicester, Leicestershire, 66, **91**, 103,
     104, 152, 206, 319, 320, 321,
     328, **336, 378, 425, 427**, 428,
     431, 490, **531, 574**
Leicestershire, 66, **91, 93, 94**, 103,
     104, 133, **152**, 185, **206**, 262,
     319, 320, 321, 328, **332, 336**,
     338, 372, 374, **378, 379, 421**,
     425, 427, 428, 429, **431**, 489,
     490, **531, 532, 574**
Leigh, Greater Manchester, **91**, 163
Leighton Buzzard, Bedfordshire, 89,
     91, 98, 99, 346, 470, **531**
Leipzig, Germany, 461
Leominster, Hereford & Worcester,
     336, 554
Lerwick, Shetland, **79, 162, 397, 512**,
     567
Leslie, Fife, **79, 512**
Lesmahagow, Strathclyde, **123**
Lesser Antilles, **159, 462**
Letchworth, Hertfordshire, **91**
Le Touquet, France, **326**
Leven, Fife, **123**
Levenshulme, Greater Manchester,
     194
Lewes, East Sussex, 89, **91**, 343, **385**
Leyburn, North Yorkshire, 502
Lichfield, Staffordshire, **336**, 403, **407**,
     427, 496
Lille, France, **326**
Lima, Peru, 220, **222**, 286, 287
Lincoln, Lincolnshire, 218, 284, **285**,
     322, 323, 374, 433, 480, 481,
     482, 483, 484, 490, 513, **514**
Lincolnshire, 89, 90, **103, 110**, 137,
     138, 139, 206, 207, **218**, 248,
     249, 262, 284, **285**, 302, **320**,

Index of places   641

322, 323, 329, 331, 333, 335,
340, 372, 374, 379, 403, 406,
414, 415, 417, 432, 433, 475,
479, 480, 481, 482, 483, 484,
489, 490, 513, 514
Lindley, West Yorkshire, 535
Lindsey, Lincolnshire, 374
Linlithgow, Lothian, 123, 512
Lisbon, Portugal, 220
Liskeard, Cornwall, 107, 188, 336,
528
Litchurch, Derbyshire, 187
Littleborough, Greater Manchester, 194
Littlehampton, West Sussex, 269, 336
Littleport, Cambridgeshire, 215, 336,
391
Liverpool, Merseyside, 47, 51, 63, 66,
89, 103, 125, 128, 129, 141,
145, 191, 208, 209, 220, 222,
238, 270, 272, 273, 286, 288,
290, 301, 310, 311, 312, 321,
322, 323, 328, 329, 336, 348,
356, 357, 361, 362, 365, 366,
378, 390, 395, 407, 412, 413,
414, 416, 419, 420, 427, 429,
430, 442, 447, 456, 463, 464,
467, 490, 491, 493, 509, 522,
523, 531, 542, 544, 555
Castle Street, 91, 378, 414
Church Street, 336, 361
Clubmoor, 91
Cotton Exchange, 378, 420
Dale Street, 420
Moss Street, 361
North Docks, 378, 414
Old Hall Street, 378
Princes Road, 531
Smithdown Road, 94, 361
Stanley Market, 447
Toxteth, 361
Victoria Street, 92, 336
Walton, 361, 378
Water Street, 92, 194, 531
Llandeilo, Dyfed, 299
Llandovery, Dyfed, 299
Llandridod Wells, Powys, 336
Llandudno, Gwynedd, 407
Llanebrie, Dyfed, 299
Llanelli, Dyfed, 336, 486, 538

Llanfairfechan, Gwynedd, 538
Llanfyllin, Powys, 414
Llangefni, Gwynedd, 408, 538
Llangollen, Clwyd, 378, 404, 414, 448
Llanidloes, Powys, 414
Llanrwst, Gwynedd, 378, 414
Llanybyther, Dyfed, 299
Loanhead, Lothian, 123
Loch Carron, Highland, 136
Lochgelly, Fife, 79, 512
Lochgilphead, Strathclyde, 512
Loch Maddy, Western Isles, 79, 136
Lockerbie, Dumfries & Galloway, 79,
527
Loddon, Norfolk, 246
London, 47, 48, 49, 51, 52, 53, 55,
59, 60, 61, 63, 65, 66, 70, 71,
72, 75, 77, 82, 83, 84, 85, 89,
94, 96, 97, 103, 104, 105, 107,
108, 109, 110, 112, 116, 117,
118, 120, 121, 123, 124, 126,
127, 128, 130, 131, 132, 136,
137, 138, 139, 141, 142, 144,
145, 147, 149, 152, 154, 156,
157, 158, 159, 160, 162, 163,
165, 167, 170, 171, 173, 174,
176, 179, 181, 182, 183, 184,
185, 190, 191, 192, 194, 196,
197, 200, 201, 203, 209, 210,
212, 213, 215, 216, 217, 218,
219, 220, 221, 223, 224, 228,
230, 231, 234, 236, 239, 240,
242, 243, 246, 254, 255, 256,
258, 259, 260, 263, 264, 267,
269, 270, 271, 273, 274, 275,
276, 277, 278, 279, 280, 286,
287, 288, 292, 293, 294, 296,
297, 298, 300, 301, 302, 303,
304, 308, 309, 310, 313, 314,
319, 321, 325, 328, 329, 327–
41, 342, 343, 344, 347, 348,
349, 350, 351, 352, 353, 354,
355, 356, 357, 358, 360, 361,
362, 364, 365, 366, 367, 370,
373, 374, 381, 382, 384, 386,
390, 392, 393, 394, 396, 397,
399, 400, 401, 403, 404, 408,
410, 411, 417, 424, 425, 427,
429, 431, 439, 440, 442, 445,

642 *British banking – a guide to historical records*

446, 449, 452, 455, 457, 459,
460, 461, 463, 465, 466, 467,
469, 480, 481, 482, 484, 485,
488, 490, 491, 494, 496, 497,
500, 507, 508, 511, 513, 515,
518, 520, 522, 523, 526, 528,
529, 530, 533, 539, 540, 541,
542, 543, 544, 547, 548, 551,
556, 561, 562, 563, 564, 565,
569 570, 571, 572, 574, 575,
576
Abchurch Lane, 128
Addiscombe, 90
Aldersgate, 346, 378
Aldersgate Street, 92, 531
Aldgate, 150
Angel Court, 378
Argyle Place, 513
Arundel Street, 497
Austin Friars, 152
Baker Street, 395
Balham, 92, 336
Barbican, 378
Barnet, 346
Bartholomew Lane, 431, 53
Battersea, 52, 92
Bayswater, 395, 513
Bedford Row, 514
Belgrave Road, 336
Belgravia, 390
Bermondsey, 92, 308, 378
Bethnal Green, 142
Bexley, 365
Bexleyheath, 90, 364, 365
Blackfriars, 142
Blackheath, 336
Birchin Lane, 209, 230, 231, 539,
540, 543, 544
Bishopsgate, 92, 403
Bloomsbury, 92, 352, 531
Bond Street, 92, 575
Borough, 346, 561
Bow, 92
Brentford, 90, 308, 345, 530, 551
Bromley, 149, 334, 365, 377, 406,
531
Brompton Square, 351; Bush Hill
Park, 90
Butler Place, 336

Camberwell, 92, 336
Cambridge Circus, 150, 378
Camden Town, 336, 349, 395
Cannon Street, 92
Cavendish Square, 92, 108, 465
Chancery Lane, 353, 354, 378, 514,
531
Change Alley, 183, 231
Charing Cross, 71, 163, 197, 277,
431, 513, 514
Cheapside, 61, 274
Chelsea, 92
Chislehurst, 364, 365, 531
Chiswick, 378
Clerkenwell, 142
Coleman Street, 353, 520
Cornhill, 109, 132, 142, 152, 182,
183, 190, 194, 264, 303, 309,
344, 378, 441, 442, 449, 514,
530, 539
Covent Garden, 138, 336, 353, 378,
532
Craven Street, 110
Crayford, 365
Cricklewood, 336
Croydon, 146, 149, 343, 345, 513,
514
Crutched Friars, 497
Deptford, 273, 308, 336, 345
Devereux Court, 508
Ealing, 94
Ealing Broadway, 378
Earl's Court, 92
East Dulwich, 336
East Sheen, 92
Edgware, 336
Edgware Road, 336, 348, 378
Electra House, 378
Elephant & Castle, 346
Eltham, 92, 364, 365, 531
Enfield, 336
Erith, 91
Euston Road, 532
Exchange Alley, 109
Fenchurch Street, 93, 163, 260, 271,
336, 349, 378, 513, 532
Finchley Road, 336, 407
Finsbury, 92
Finsbury Circus, 336

Index of places 643

Finsbury Park, **336, 532**
Fish Street, **488**
Fishergate, **194**
Fleet Street, **92**, 215, 234, 274, 440
Fore Street, **378**
Fulham, **92**
Golden Square, **378**
Golders Green, **336**
Goswell Road, **378**
Gracechurch Street, **378**, 488
Great George Street, 497
Great Portland Street, **336**
Greenwich, **337, 346**, 417
Grosvenor Gardens, **395**
Hackney, **93, 346, 407**
Hammersmith, **346, 532**
Hampstead, **93, 337**, 351, **532**
Hampton, **91**
Hanover Square, **346**
Hanwell, **91**
Harley Street, **532**
Harringay, **337**
Harrow, **346, 531**
Haverstock Hill, **532**
Haymarket, 110, **326**
Hendon, **337**
Hendon Central, **337**
Herne Hill, **337**
Highbridge, **532**
High Street Kensington, 337, 351
Holborn, **150, 346, 532**
Holborn Circus, 351, **378**, 513, **514**
Holborn Viaduct, **378**
Hounslow, 551
Ilford, **346, 531**
Isleworth, 551
Islington, 273, 308, **337**, 351, 353, **395, 407**
Kennington, **93, 532**
Kensington, **337, 346**, 351, **407, 514, 532**
Kew, **93**
Kilburn, **93**
Kings Cross, **139, 337, 395**
Kingsland, **9**
King's Road, **93**
Kingsland Road, 348
Kingston Hill, **93**
Kingsway, **337, 354**, 365

Knightsbridge, **337**
Lambeth, 351, **354, 378**
Lambeth North, **532**
Lampton Hall, 232, 277, 278
Leadenhall Street, **354**
Leicester Square, **337**
Lewisham, **337**, 348, **531**
Leytonstone, **93**
Limehouse, **346, 354, 378**
Lombard Street, 61, 83, **93**, 96, 97, 109, 126, 137, **162**, 163, 171, 181, 209, 210, 218, 230, 231, 232, 259, 271, 302, 309, 328, 343, 345, **346**, 349, 357, 364, 365, **407**, 411, 425, **431**, 439, 449, 466, 484, 485, 496, **514**, 520, 547, 568, **575**
Lordship Lane, Tottenham, **379**
Lothbury, 160, 301, 348, 351, **352, 354**, 484
Lower Edmonton, **354**
Lowndes Street, 275
Ludgate Circus, **93, 139**
Ludgate Hill, **337**
Marylebone, **346**, 351, **352, 532**
Marylebone Road, **532**
Mayfair, **378, 532**
Merton, **93**
Mile End, 142, **337**
Millbank, 231
Mincing Lane, **337, 378**
Minories, **346**
Moorgate, **337, 378**, 513
Mottingham, 365
New Barnet, **93**, 470
New Bond Street, 136, **378**
Newgate Street, 142
Newington Causeway, **337**
Newnham, **338**
New Oxford Street, **337, 346**
Nicholas Lane, 397.
Northwood, 551
Notting Hill Gate, 378, 395
Old Bond Street, 137, **150**, 270, **337, 378**
Old Broad Street, 392, 393
Old Jewry, 152
Old Kent Road, **354, 378**
Old Street, **150, 337**

644   *British banking – a guide to historical records*

Orpington, 365
Osterley Park, 231, 233, 277, 278
Oxford Street, **139**, 185, 460, **532**
Paddington, **150, 337**, 353, **407**
Pall Mall, 84, **93, 130**, 174, 185,
    256, 303, 342, 351, 353, **354**,
    370, **379**, 446, 447, 497
Palmers Green, **93, 532**
Park Lane, 275, **337, 532**
Peckham, **337**
Peckham High Street, **379**
Peckham Rye, **337**
Piccadilly, **139, 194, 337, 407**
Pimlico, 394
Pinner, 551
Poplar, **93**
Poultry, 348
Prince's Street, 353, **354, 407**, 513,
    514
Queen Street, 496
Regent's Park, **532**
Regent Street, 349, **379, 407, 514**,
    532
Richmond, **94, 346**, 348
Ruislip, **194**
St James's Square, 351
St James's Street, 124, 270, 277, **337**
St John's Wood, **532**
St Martin's le Grand, **532**
St Mary Axe, 271, **346, 354, 407**
St Mary Cray, 364, 365
St Paul's Churchyard, 156
St Swithin's Lane, 452
Shaftesbury Avenue, 142
Shoreditch, 142, 184, **337**, 344, **346**
Sidcup, **94**, 364, 365
Smithfield, 273, 308, 353
Southall, 308, **379**, 551
Southfields, Wimbledon, **379**
South Kensington, **346, 514, 532**
Southwark, 51, 142, 343, 351, **352**,
    353, 513, **532**
Spitalfields, **93, 337**
Stock Exchange, **93**
Stoke Newington, 348
Strand, 170, 171, **395**, 508
Stratford, **337, 533**
Stratford Place, 185
Streatham, **52, 93, 337**

Swiss Cottage, **337**
Tavistock Square, **532**
Teddington, **346, 431, 533**
Temple Bar, 351, **352**
Threadneedle Street, 66, 71, 127,
    149, 150, 163, 440, **532**
Throgmorton Street, 351
Tooting, **93**
Tooting Broadway, **337**
Tottenham, **93**, 142, **337, 379**
Tottenham Court Road, **150, 337**,
    351, **407**, 513
Tulse Hill, **93**
Twickenham, **340**, 348
Upper Thames Street, 297
Upper Tooting, **337**
Uxbridge, 308, **340, 346**, 367, **533**,
    550, 551
Victoria Street, **532**
Waltham Abbey, **288**
Wanstead, **93**
Wealdstone, 131
West Dulwich, **337**
West Ealing, **379, 533**
West End, **532**
West Kensington, **337**
West Marylebone, **532**
West Smithfield, 105, **337, 407**
Westbourne Grove, 351, **379**
Westminster, **288**, 351, **352**, 528
Westminster Bridge Road, **532**
Westminster House, **337**
Whitechapel, 142, **337**, 351
Whitehall, **93**, 156
Whitehall Place, 277
Willesden Green, **379**
Wimbledon, **93, 379**, 564
Wood Green, **337, 379**
Woolwich, **139, 337**, 343, 348, 460
Long Eaton, Derbyshire, 187, 421, 482
Longfleet, Dorset, **337**
Long Melford, Suffolk, 245
Longton, Staffordshire, **337**
Longtown, Cumbria, 139
Lorraine, France, 313
Lossiemouth, Grampian, 79
Lothian, **76, 78, 79, 80, 120, 122, 123**,
    154, **155, 160, 162**, 197, 200,
    201, 204, 205, **207, 213**, 214,

Index of places

229, 285, **396**, **397**, **400**, 418, **456**, **457**, **459**, 465, 510, **511**, **512**, 515, 526, 541, **567**, **568**, **571**, **578**
Loughborough, Leicestershire, **93**, **372**, 421, 425, 428, **532**
Loughborough Junction, Leicestershire, **379**
Louisiana, United States of America, 289, 542
Louth, Lincolnshire, **218**, 284, 322, **323**, **379**, **490**
Lower Saxony, Germany, 286
Lowestoft, Suffolk, 250, 307
Ludlow, Shropshire, **338**, **358**, **407**, 452, 553, **554**
Luton, Bedfordshire, **93**, **259**, **338**, **347**, 470
Lutterworth, Leicestershire, 152, 428
Lydney, Gloucestershire, 230, **338**
Lye, West Midlands, **379**
Lyme Regis, Dorset, **244**, 546
Lymington, Hampshire, 137, **338**, **462**, 548, **549**
Lymm, Cheshire, **93**, 311
Lyndhurst, Hampshire, 236
Lynton, Devon, 216, **338**
Lyons, France, 86, 293, 461
Lytham, Lancashire, **312**, 442

Macclesfield, Cheshire, 47, **52**, 191, 430, 460, 461, **576**
Macduff, Grampian, 79
Machynlleth, Powys, **379**
Madras, India, 48, 144, **578**
Madrid, Spain, 220, 293, **294**, 314
Maidenhead, Berkshire, 495
Maidstone, Kent, **338**, 343, **346**, 514, **537**
Malaga, Spain, 59
Malawi, 398, 494
Malaysia, 144
Maldon, Essex, 346, 487
Mallaig, Highland, **79**, **136**
Malmesbury, Wiltshire, **139**, 548, **549**
Malta, 54
Malton, North Yorkshire, 101, **102**, 110, 316, 433, 502, 555, 560
Malvern, Hereford & Worcester, 104, **105**, **139**, **338**

Malvern Link, Hereford & Worcester, 104, **338**
Manaos, Brazil, 72
Manchester, Greater Manchester, 47, **50**, 51, 66, **74**, 89, 118, 144, **160**, **163**, **165**, **167**, **181**, **191**, 205, 260, 261, **270**, 271, 272, 286, 300, 301 **310**, 312, 321, **338**, **356**, 357, **359**, 361, 362, **369**, 374, 390, **399**, 400, **407**, **416**, 417, **427**, 430, **431**, 442, 452, 457, **493**, **509**, 522, **532**, **540**, 541, 542, **543**, 554, 555
  Brown Street, 509
  Chester Road, **379**
  Chorlton cum Hardy, **544**
  Corn Exchange, **544**
  Deansgate, 163, 260, **379**
  Exchange Street, 270
  Fallowfield, **193**
  King Street, **93**, 167, **194**, **379**, 509, 540
  Longsight, 163, **532**
  Market Place, **338**
  Mosley Street, 540, 542, **543**, **544**
  New Cross, 311
  Norfolk Street, **93**, 191
  Old Trafford, **93**
  Portland Street, **194**
  Rusholme, 357
  St Ann Street, 270, 271, 542, **544–5**
  Spring Gardens, 191
  York Street, **93**, 167, 509
Manchuria, China, 430
Manila, Philippines, 103
Manningtree, Essex, **115**, 116, 175, 245, 344, **346**, **422**
Mansfield, Nottinghamshire, 177, **338**, 421, **422**, **451**, 481
March, Cambridgeshire, 248, **407**
Margate, Kent, **155**, 328, **338**
Market Bosworth, Leicestershire, 320
Market Drayton, Shropshire, **194**, 372, **467**
Market Harborough, Leicestershire, 319, **338**, **490**
Market Hill, Barnsley, South Yorkshire, **377**

646   *British banking – a guide to historical records*

Market Rasen, Lincolnshire, 284, 322, 483
Market Weighton, Humberside, 284, 560
Marlborough, Wiltshire, 420
Marlow, Buckinghamshire, **139**, 495
Marple, Greater Manchester, **168**
Marseilles, France, 86, 293
Marsham, North Yorkshire, 502
Marshfield, Avon, 104
Maryport, Cumbria, 140, 180, **194**, 537
Mashonaland, 494
Matabeleland, 494
Matlock, Derbyshire, 187, 473
Matlock Bridge, Derbyshire, 187, **474, 532**
Mauritius, **75, 366**, 368, 398, 410
Maybole, Strathclyde, 285, **512**
Melbourne,
   Australia, 48, **222**
   Derbyshire, 187
Melksham, Wiltshire, **139, 338, 420, 549**
Melrose, Borders, **123**
Melton Mowbray, Leicestershire, 152, 320, **338**, 425, 428
Mendoza, Argentina, 72, 73
Mere, Wiltshire, **338, 549**
Merseyside, **47, 51**, 63, 66, 89, **90, 91, 93**, 94, 103, 125, **128**, 129, **141**, 145, 191, **194**, 208, 209, **220, 222, 238**, 270, **272**, 273, 286, **288**, 290, 301, 310, 312, **321, 322, 323, 324, 325**, 328, 329, **332, 335, 336**, 348, 356, 357, **361**, 362, 365, 366, **377, 378, 379**, 390, **395, 407, 412**, 413, **414**, 416, **419, 420**, 427, 430, 442, **443, 447, 456**, 463, 464, 467, **490**, 491, **493**, 509, 522, 523, **530, 531**, 540, 542, 544, **545, 555**
Merthyr Tydfil, Mid Glamorgan, 538
Methil, Fife, **123**
Methwold, Norfolk, 246
Mexico, 56, 103, 163, 222, 289, 290, 468
Middlesborough, Cleveland, **93, 338**, 416, 556

Middlesex, **57, 157**, 351, **550**
Middlewich, Cheshire, **532**
Mid Glamorgan, 81, **90, 94**, 99, 227, **331, 332, 333, 334, 339, 399, 406, 408**, 538
Midsomer Norton, Avon, **338**
Milborne Port, Somerset, **532**
Mildenhall, Suffolk, 284, **338, 423**
Miles Platting, Greater Manchester, **93**
Milford, Powys, 523
Millom, Cumbria, **93, 533**
Millport, Strathclyde, **512**
Milngavie, Strathclyde, 79
Milnsbridge, West Yorkshire, **338**, 535, **536**
Minehead, Somerset, 216
Mirfield, West Yorkshire, 534
Modbury, Devon, 262, **338**
Moffat, Dumfries & Galloway, **79**, **123, 512**
Mold, Clwyd, **407**, 412, **414**
Moldsgreen, West Yorkshire, 535
Monkwearmouth, Tyne & Wear, **338**
Monmouth, Gwent, **126**, 230, **300**, 328, **338**, 386
Monte Carlo, 86, **326**
Montevideo, Uruguay, 52, 56, 72, 73, 74, 117, **118**, 342
Montpellier, Cheltenham, **334**
Montreal, Canada, 85, **86**, 361
Montrose, Tayside, **79, 123, 512**
Moray Firth, Highland, 135
Morecambe, Lancashire, **93**
Moreton in the Marsh, Gloucestershire, 230, **499, 504**
Morley, West Yorkshire, **338, 379**
Morocco, 47, 491, **492, 493**
Morpeth, Northumberland, **276, 338**, 417
Morriston, West Glamorgan, 227
Morwellham, Devon, 226
Motherwell, Strathclyde, **79, 123, 512**
Moukden, China, **281**
Mozambique, 64, 398
Muir of Ord, Highland, 136
Mullingar, Ireland, 347
Muree, India, 174
Musselburgh, Lothian, **123**
Mutley, Devon, 262

Index of places

Nablus, Jordan, 159
Nailsworth, Gloucestershire, 338
Nairn, Highland, 79, 123, 136
Nanking, China, 281
Nantes, France, 293
Nantwich, Cheshire, 191, 194, 417, 509
Naples, Italy, 453
Narberth, Dyfed, 523
Natal, South Africa, 63, 64, 349, 392
Neath, West Glamorgan, 81, 227, 371, 545
Needham Market, Suffolk, 93, 245
Nelson, Lancashire, 175, 311
Nessgate, York, North Yorkshire, 379
Netherfield, East Sussex, 338
Netherlands, 240, 269, 289, 290, 306, 398
Newark, Nottinghamshire, 126, 233, 251, 338, 421, 432, 433, 439, 482, 490, 513, 533
Newbiggin by the Sea, Northumberland, 338
New Brighton, Merseyside, 93
Newbury, Berkshire, 137, 139, 338, 346, 479, 519, 533
Newcastle under Lyme, Staffordshire, 303, 338
Newcastle upon Tyne, Tyne & Wear, 66, 89, 93, 132, 165, 183, 189, 276, 309, 329, 355–6, 403, 409, 415, 417, 418, 419, 448, 501, 552
  Byker and Heaton, 338
  Cattle Market, 416
  Collingwood Street, 276
  Elswick Road, 310, 338
  Grey Street, 338, 416
  Osbourne, 338;
  Pilgrim Street, 416
  Quayside, 310, 338, 416
  Westgate Road, 276, 338
Newcastleton, Borders, 123
New Cumnock, Strathclyde, 79
Newent, Gloucestershire, 230
New Granada, 290
Newhaven, East Sussex, 385
Newmarket, Suffolk, 89, 93, 206, 215, 246, 257, 308, 338

Newnham, Gloucestershire, 229
New Orleans, United States of America, 313
New Pitsligo, Grampian, 80, 512
Newport,
  Fife, 512
  Gwent, 81, 169, 299, 338, 386, 403
  Isle of Wight, 297, 450
  Shropshire, 338, 477
Newport Pagnell, Buckinghamshire, 93, 98, 99
New Swindon, Wiltshire, 169, 420
Newton Abbott, Devon, 188, 262, 549
Newton Mearns, Strathclyde, 512
Newtonmore, Highland, 123
Newton Stewart, Dumfries & Galloway, 123, 426
Newtown St Boswells, Borders, 123
New York City, United States of America, 47, 56, 72, 103, 128, 129, 130, 144, 158, 163, 222, 279, 286, 296, 305, 313, 314, 387, 388, 389, 468, 491, 492, 494, 530, 543
New York State, United States of America, 361
New Zealand, 77, 151, 159, 424, 468
Nicaragua, 163
Nice, France, 293, 294, 326
Nicosia, Cyprus, 296
Nigeria 47, 75, 76, 158, 491, 492, 493
Norfolk, 60, 66, 84, 88, 90, 91, 94, 96, 114, 138, 139, 163, 166, 175, 186, 205, 210, 212, 245, 246, 247, 248, 249, 250, 264, 284, 297, 298, 302, 307, 308, 334, 335, 336, 340, 348, 407, 411, 412, 423, 424, 504
Normanton, West Yorkshire, 317
Northallerton, North Yorkshire, 60
North America, 47, 63, 72, 77, 85, 86, 103, 128, 129, 130, 144, 146, 151, 158, 163, 174, 197, 222, 231, 255, 267, 273, 278, 279, 282, 286, 289, 290, 291, 296, 305, 306, 313, 314, 353, 361, 362, 375, 386, 387, 388, 389, 453, 457, 468, 483, 491, 492, 494, 530, 542, 543 85, 157, 222,

648   *British banking – a guide to historical records*

240, 255, 361, 362, 386, 387,
388, 389, 462
Northampton, Northamptonshire, 93,
139, 320, 414, 415, 435, 484,
490, 525, 576
Northamptonshire, 93, 98, 137, 138,
139, 206, 207, 223, 235, 254,
319, 320, 333, 334, 336, 339,
378, 379, 404, 414, 415, 435,
484, 489, 490, 525, 557, 576
North Berwick, Lothian, 123
Northern Ireland, 374, 375, 392, 528
Northern Rhodesia *see* Zambia
North Shields, Tyne & Wear, 109, 276,
310, 338, 409, 417, 419, 552, 556
Northumberland, 90, 123, 132, 139,
180, 189, 219, 276, 331, 332,
333, 335, 338, 339, 409, 416,
417, 418, 419, 426, 449, 501,
573, 574
North Walsham, Norfolk, 246, 307
Northwich, Cheshire, 93, 213, 429,
431, 509
North Yorkshire, 60, 84, 89, 94, 101,
102, 110, 113, 114, 175, 178, 194,
307, 316, 339, 340, 353, 354,
361, 379, 404, 407, 433, 434,
444, 467, 478, 502, 507, 526,
528, 533, 550, 555, 556, 557,
558, 560, 561
Norwich, Norfolk, 60, 66, 84, 88, 94,
96, 114, 163, 166, 186, 205, 245,
246, 247, 249, 264, 284, 302,
307, 308, 348, 407, 411, 424, 504
Nottingham, Nottinghamshire, 138,
139, 263, 323, 328, 374, 379,
386, 407, 420, 421, 451, 472,
480, 481, 482, 484, 490, 513,
514, 528, 554
   Alfreton Road, 338
   Bridlesmith Gate, 263
   Cattle Market, 533
   Hucknall Road, 533
   Hucknall Torkard, 482
   Pelham Street, 421
   Thurland Street, 533
Nottinghamshire, 101, 126, 138, 139,
164, 177, 233, 251, 263, 284,
323, 328, 338, 374, 379, 386,

407, 420, 421, 422, 439, 451,
472, 475, 480, 481, 482, 484,
490, 513, 514, 528, 533, 554, 555
Nuneaton, Warwickshire, 320, 338
Nyasaland *see* Malawi

Oakengates, Shropshire, 339
Oakham, Leicestershire, 152, 206,
320, 489
Oban, Strathclyde, 80, 123, 426, 512,
568
Odiham, Hampshire, 258
Okehampton, Devon, 190, 216, 404
Oldham, Greater Manchester, 168,
191, 194, 339, 374, 423, 427,
451, 462
Old Hill, West Midlands, 339
Ollerton, Nottinghamshire, 164
Olney, Buckinghamshire, 98
Ongar, Essex, 487
Oporto, Portugal, 117
Orange Free State, South Africa, 64,
494
Orkney Islands, 400, 512, 567
Ormskirk, Lancashire, 442, 540
Orton, Cumbria, 82
Osaka, Japan, 430
Ossett, West Yorkshire, 94
Oswestry, Shropshire, 179, 414, 429
Otley, West Yorkshire, 94, 175, 177,
372
Ottawa, Canada, 267
Ottery St Mary, Devon, 349
Oundle, Northamptonshire, 489, 557
Oxford, Oxfordshire, 89, 94 147, 149,
223, 339, 343, 345, 346, 431, 506
Oxfordshire, 89, 90, 91, 94, 98, 126,
131, 147, 149, 166, 169, 193,
223, 224, 225, 226, 267, 306,
315, 329, 332, 335, 339, 340,
343, 345, 346, 371, 431, 478,
498, 499, 504, 506, 576
Oxted, Surrey, 265, 339

Padiham, Lancashire, 175, 194
Paignton, Devon, 262
Paisley, Strathclyde, 80, 123, 426, 510,
527, 578
Paisley Road Toll, Strathclyde, 512

Index of places

Pakistan, 144, 174
Palestine, 54
Palmeira, Hove, East Sussex, **531**
Para, Brazil, 72, **73**, **74**, 117, 118, **343**
Paraguay, 72, **74**
Paris, France, 56, 72, **73**, 86, 163, 209, 293, **294**, 313, 314, 325, **326**, **327**, 329, 387, 453, 528
Parsontown, Ireland, 347
Partick, Strathclyde, **80**
Pateley Bridge, North Yorkshire, 114
Patras, Greece, 295
Patricroft, Greater Manchester, 163
Pau, France, **326**
Paysandu, Argentina, 72, **73**
Peebles, Borders, **80**, **123**, **162**, **512**
Peel, Isle of Man, 359
Peking, China, **281**
Pelotas, Brazil, **74**, **343**
Pembroke, Dyfed, 81
Pembroke Dock, Dyfed, 81, 523
Penang, Malaysia, 144
Penarth, South Glamorgan, **94**
Pendleton, Greater Manchester, 163, 311
Penmaenmawr, Gwynedd, 538
Penrith, Cumbria, **58**, 139, 180, **339**, **407**, 426, 536, 537
Penryn, Cornwall, 167
Penybont, Powys, **184**
Penzance, Cornwall, 89, **94**, **107**, 349, 519
Pernambuco, Brazil *see* Recife do Pernambuco
Persia *see* Iran
Perth,
  Australia, 77
  Tayside, **80**, **123**, **142**, 143, 396, **435**, **436**, 511, **512**, 567, 568, **578**
Peru, 163, 220, **222**, 286, 287, 290, 467
Peshawar, India, 241
Peterborough, Cambridgeshire, 206, 320, **339**, 372, **479**, 489, 490, **533**, 557
Petersfield, Hampshire, **266**, 343
Petrograd *see* St Petersburg
Petworth, West Sussex, 343, 346
Pewsey, Wiltshire, **94**, **339**, 420, **549**

Philadelphia, United States of America, 128, 387, **389**
Philippines, 103
Pickering, North Yorkshire, 101, 502, 556, 560
Pietermaritzburg, South Africa, 392
Pinmore, Strathclyde, 285
Pinxton, Derbyshire, 482
Pisagua, Chile, 55
Pitlochry, Tayside, **80**, **143**, **512**
Pittenweem, Fife, **397**
Plymouth, Devon, 66, 99, **188**, **208**, **262**, 275, **339**, 349, **549**
Plymouth Dock, Devon *see* Devonport
Pocklington, Humberside, 101, 502, 560, **561**
Poland, 125, 355
Polmont, Central, **80**, **123**
Pontefract, West Yorkshire, 89, 253, 316, **317**, 318, **379**, 435, 557, **558**
Ponteland, Northumberland, **339**
Pontypool, Gwent, **299**, **339**
Pontypridd, Mid Glamorgan, 227
Poole, Dorset, 217, 318, **339**, **379**, 548, **549**
Portardawe, West Glamorgan, 227
Portarddulais, West Glamorgan, 227
Port Dinorwic, Gwynedd, 538
Port Elizabeth, South Africa, 63, 349, 494
Port Erin, Isle of Man, 359
Port Glasgow, Strathclyde, **80**, **123**, **512**
Porthmadog, Gwynedd, **141**, 412, **414**
Portland, Dorset, 208, **339**
Port Louis, Mauritius, 75
Portmadoc, Gwynedd, 413, **414**
Porto Alegre, Brazil, **74**
Portobello, Lothian, **155**
Portree, Highland, 135, 136
Port Said, Egypt, 303
Port St Mary, Isle of Man, **431**
Portsea, Hampshire, 234
Portsmouth, Hampshire, 66, 94, **233**, 234, 236, 258, **339**, 353, 358, **408**
Portsoy, Grampian, **80**
Portswood, Southampton, Hampshire, **139**, **340**

650   *British banking – a guide to historical records*

Port Talbot, West Glamorgan, **339**
Portugal, 53, 117, 220, 289, 290, 342, 453, 465
Portuguese East Africa *see* Mozambique
Port William, Dumfries & Galloway, **123**
Powys, 81, **90, 184**, 328, **333, 334, 336, 339, 341, 379**, 403, 412, **414**, 516, 523, **537, 553**
Presteigne, Powys, **339, 553**
Preston, Lancashire 76, **94**, 167, **194**, 311, **312**, 374, 437, **434, 442, 443, 452, 533**
Prestwick, Strathclyde, **123, 512**
Pretoria, South Africa, 494
Princes Risborough, Buckinghamshire, 536
Providence, Rhode Island, United States of America, 457
Prussia, 255, 453
Puerto Cabello, Venezeula, 163
Pulborough, West Sussex, **533**
Punta Arenas, Chile, 56
Pwllheli, Gwynedd, 141, **339**, 400, 412, **414, 444**, 445

Radcliffe, Greater Manchester, 134, 163, **311**
Radlett, Hertfordshire, 360, **533**
Radstock, Avon, **549**
Ramsbottom, Greater Manchester, 134, **194**
Ramsey, Isle of Man, 200, 359, **431**
Ramsgate, Kent, **139, 258, 339**
Rangoon, Burma, 144, 174
Rawalpindi, India, 174
Raynes Park, Surrey, 564
Reading, Berkshire, 89, **94**, 328, **339, 477, 478, 495**
Recife do Pernambuco, Brazil, 72, **74**, 117, 342, **343**
Redditch, Hereford & Worcester, **139, 230, 339**, 498
Redhill, Surrey, **139**
Redruth, Cornwall, 107, 167, **188, 339**, 349
Reeth, North Yorkshire, 60
Renfrew, Strathclyde, **123, 512**

Retford, Nottinghamshire, **101, 164**, 284, 421, 475
Rhayader, Powys, **184**
Rhode Island, United States of America, 457
Rhodesia *see* Zimbabwe
Rhyl, Clwyd, **379**, 413, **414**
Rhymney, Mid Glamorgan, 99, **339**
Richmond, North Yorkshire, 60, 89, **94, 339, 444, 502**, 557
Rickmansworth, Hertfordshire, **339**
Riga, Latvia, 239
Ringwood, Hampshire, 217, **317**, 318
Rio de Janeiro, Brazil, 72, **73, 74**, 117, **118**, 342, **343**
Rio Grande do Sul, Brazil, **74**, 342, **343**
Ripley, Derbyshire, 421
Ripon, North Yorkshire, **102**, 114, 556, **557, 558**
Roath, South Glamorgan, 169
Rochdale, Greater Manchester, **153, 194**, 253, 311, 423, 427, **451**, 509, 540, **545**
Rochester, Kent, 348
Rochford, Essex, **223, 487**
Romania, 53, 55, 255, 468
Rome, Italy, 88
Romford, Essex, 273, **339**
Romsey, Hampshire, 548
Rosario, Argentina, 72, **73, 74, 343**
Roslin, Lothian, **123**
Ross on Wye, Hereford & Worcester, 229, 534
Rothbury, Northumberland, **276, 339**
Rotherham, South Yorkshire, 472, **474, 475**, 541, 542, 556
Rothes, Grampian, **80, 136**
Rothesay, Strathclyde, **80, 123, 512**
Rotterdam, Netherlands, **472**
Roubaix, France, **326**
Rouen, France, 86
Royston, Hertfordshire, 89, **214**, 215, **339**, 391, **392**, 508
Rugby, Warwickshire, **134**, 328, **339, 379, 407**
Rugeley, Staffordshire, **194, 339**, 403, 496
Runcorn, Cheshire, 429

Index of places

Rushden, Northamptonshire, 339
Russia, 77, 239, 240, 256, **282**, 289,
    290, 306, 355, 374, 376, 453, 467
Rutherglen, Strathclyde, **123**
Ruthin, Clwyd, **379**, **414**
Rye, East Sussex, **183**, 328, **339**

Sacriston, County Durham, 339
Saddleworth, Greater Manchester, **130**,
    283, **462**
Saffron Walden, Essex, 89, **94**, 215,
    392, **507**
Saigon, Vietnam, 144
St Albans, Hertfordshire, 89, **346**, **360**,
    574
St Andrews, Fife, **80**, **512**
St Austell, Cornwall, 107, **108**, 188,
    404, **476**
St Clears, Dyfed, **339**
St Helena, South Atlantic Ocean, 398
St Helens, Merseyside, 429, 540, **545**
St Ives,
    Cambridgeshire, 94, 215, 339, 518
    Cornwall, 107
St Jean de Luz, France, 326
St Just, Cornwall, 107
St Kitts, Lesser Antilles, **159**
St Leonards on Sea, East Sussex, **339**,
    346
St Lucia, Lesser Antilles, **159**
St Marlo, France, 59
St Neots, Cambridgeshire, 215, **339**,
    518
St Petersburg, Russia, 239, 240, 374,
    376
St Vincent, Lesser Antilles, **462**
Salcombe, Devon, **339**
Sale, Greater Manchester, 181, **339**
Salford, Greater Manchester, 163, 165,
    260, 261, 271, 447, 509, 522,
    540, 541, 545
Salisbury,
    Rhodesia *see* Harare, Zimbabwe
    Wiltshire, **111**, **139**, 329, 420, **438**,
    533, **548**, **549**
Salonika, Greece, 295
Saltaire, West Yorkshire, 205
Saltash, Cornwall, 262
Saltcoats, Strathclyde, **80**, **513**

Saltley, West Midlands, **407**
Salto, Uruguay, **74**
Sandgate, Kent, **298**, 328, **339**
Sandwich, Kent, **339**, 343, **346**
Sandyford, Staffordshire, **80**
San Francisco, United States of
    America, 163, 313
Sanquhar, Dumfries & Galloway, **123**
San Salvador, 163
Santiago, Chile, 55, 56, 72, **74**, **222**
Santos, Brazil, 72, **74**, 117, 118
Sao Paulo, Brazil, 72, **74**, 117, **118**,
    343, 468
Sardinia, Italy, 255, 256
Sawbridgeworth, Hertfordshire, 507
Saxmundham, Suffolk, **250**, 307
Scarborough, North Yorkshire, 89,
    102, 316, **407**, **533**, **550**, 555,
    557, **560**
Schleswig Holstein, Germany, 255
Scone, Tayside, **80**
Scotland **45**, **46**, **57**, **58**, **76**, 77, **78**, **79**,
    80, **120**, **121**, **122**, **123**, **124**, **135**,
    136, **142**, **143**, **151**, **154**, **155**,
    160, 161, **162**, 197, **200**, **201**,
    202, **204**, 205, **207**, **213**, 214,
    227, **228**, **229**, 236, **237**, 269,
    285, **303**, 321, 374, 393, **396**,
    397, 398, 400, **417**, 418, **426**,
    435, **436**, 446, **456**, 457, **459**,
    460, 465, **476**, **503**, **505**, **510**,
    511, **512**, **513**, 515, **526**, 527,
    541, **567**, **568**, **576**, **571**, **577**,
    578
Scunthorpe, Humberside, **102**, **339**,
    379, 483
Seaford, East Sussex, 385, **533**
Seaham, County Durham, **94**
Seascale, Cumbria, 537
Seaton, Devon, 546
Sedbergh, Cumbria, 82, 523
Selby, North Yorkshire, 467, 555, **557**
Selkirk, Borders, **123**, **513**
Serbia, 430
Settle, North Yorkshire, 94, 114, **175**,
    194
Sevenoaks, Kent, 194, 343, 533
Seychelles, 75
Shaftesbury, Dorset, 111, **497**, 548

652   *British banking – a guide to historical records*

Shanghai, China, 144, **278**, 282, 367, 368, **369**
Shap, Cumbria, 537
Shaw, Greater Manchester, 427
Shawlands, Strathclyde, 80
Sheffield, South Yorkshire, 252, 339, **354, 379**, 407, 374, 404, **428, 429, 451, 471, 472**, 473, **474, 475**, 518, 519, 541, 542, 554, 556, **557**, 564
Sheffield Moor, South Yorkshire, **475**
Shepshed, Leicestershire, **421**
Shepton Mallet, Somerset, 339, 447, 500
Sherborne, Dorset, 403, **407, 431, 437, 533**
Sheringham, Norfolk, **139**, 308
Shetland, **512**, 567, **578**
Shian, Strathclyde, 460
Shifnal, Shropshire, **339**, 477
Shipley, West Yorkshire, **94**, 113
Shipston on Stour, Warwickshire, 238, **339**, 498, **499**, 504
Shirebrook, Derbyshire, 482
Shoreham, West Sussex, 254
Shorncliffe, Kent, 298
Shotley, Suffolk, **339**
Shotley Bridge, County Durham, **276**
Shotton, Clwyd, **339**
Shotts, Strathclyde, **123**
Shrewsbury, Shropshire, **100, 133**, 138, **194, 211, 339, 451**, 452, 477
Shropshire, **100, 133**, 138, **166, 179**, 191, **194, 211**, 328, **334, 335, 336, 338, 339, 341, 358**, 371, 372, **407, 414**, 429, **444, 451**, 452, **467, 477, 536, 554**, 553, **575**
Shudehill, Greater Manchester, 311
Siam *see* Thailand
Sidmouth, Devon, 349
Sierra Leone, 158, 491, **493**
Silsden, West Yorkshire, 113
Simla, India, 241, 303
Singapore, 144, 410
Sittingbourne, Kent, 344, 365, **533**
Skegness, Lincolnshire, 218
Skipton, North Yorkshire, **175**, 361
Slaithwaite, West Yorkshire, 535
Slamannan, Central, **80**

Sleaford, Lincolnshire, 322, 329, **340, 432**, 483
Slough, Berkshire, 551
Slough Trading Estate, Slough, Berkshire, **340**
Smethwick, West Midlands, **94, 333**
Smithfield, Cambridgeshire, 249
Snaith, Humberside, 317
Soham, Cambridgeshire, 257, 423
Solihull, West Midlands, **333**
Somerset, **62, 115, 216, 217, 268, 333, 334, 335, 339, 341**, 349, **431, 432, 447, 499, 500, 531, 532, 533**, 548, **549**
Somerton, Somerset, **431**, 501
South Africa, 63, 64, 87, 89, **159**, 243, 279, **349, 392, 398**, 399, 410, 453, 468, 494, 495
Southam, Warwickshire, 315, **340**
South America *see* Latin America
Southampton, Hampshire, **58, 137, 139, 194, 236, 258, 259, 301**, 329, **340**, 349, **358, 407**, 548, **549**
Southborough, Kent, 102
South Brent, Devon, 262
South Cave, Humberside, 284
Southend, Essex, **94, 487, 533**
Southern Rhodesia *see* Zimbabwe
South Glamorgan, 81, **91, 94**, 169, **334, 377, 387, 399**, 486, 534, 538, **549, 553**
South Molton, Devon, 216
Southport, Merseyside, **94**, 191, **379**, 442, **443**, 540
Southsea, Hampshire, **340**
South Shields, Tyne & Wear, 60, **183, 276, 340**, 409, 416, 417, 419, 552, **557**
Southwell, Nottinghamshire, 421, 482, **555**
Southwold, Suffolk, 250, 307
South Yorkshire, **90, 97, 101, 102, 164**, 252, 311, **315, 316, 334, 339, 354**, 374, **377, 379**, 404, **407, 428**, 429, 451, **471, 472**, 473, **474, 475**, 483, 517, **518**, 519, 521, 522, 541, 542, 554, 556, **557, 558**, 564

Index of places

Sowerby Bridge, West Yorkshire, **94**, 252, 253, 311, 535
Spain, 56, 59, 125, 146, 220, 269, 286, 287, 289, 290, 293, **294**, 314, 390, 465, 491, **492, 493, 529**
Spalding, Lincolnshire, 89, 206, 207, 217, **340**, 479
Spennymoor, County Durham, **340**, 416
Spilsby, Lincolnshire, **139**, **218, 323**
Sri Lanka, 144, 410, 425
Srinagar, India, 174
Stafford, Staffordshire, 109, **194**, 328, **340**, 404, **496**
Staffordshire, **80, 91**, 109, **115, 133**, 191, **193, 194, 195**, 199, 217, 238, **298**, 300, **303**, 320, 321, 328, **334, 336, 335, 337, 338, 339, 340**, 371, 403, 404, **407, 427, 429, 489, 496**, 516, **550**
Staindrop, County Durham, 60
Staines, Surrey, **57**, 89, **157**
Stalbridge, Dorset, **407**
Stalybridge, Greater Manchester, **58**, **195**, 429
Stamford, Lincolnshire, 89, **103, 139**, **206**, 207, **340**, 414, **415**, 479, **489, 490**
Stanley, County Durham, **340**
Stanstead, Essex, 507
Steeple Aston, Oxfordshire, 223
Stevenage, Hertfordshire, 470
Stevenston, Strathclyde, **80, 123**
Stewarton, Strathclyde, **123, 513**
Steyning, West Sussex, 269
Stirling, Central, **80, 123, 513**, 567, **568, 578**
Stockport, Greater Manchester, **81, 94**, **168**, 191, **195**, 554
Stockton on Tees, Cleveland, 60, 88, **340**, 403, **479, 497**
Stoke on Trent, Staffordshire, **195**, **340**
Stone, Staffordshire, **115**, **195, 340**, 403
Stonehaven, Grampian, **80**
Stonehouse, Strathclyde, **512, 513**
Stony Stratford, Buckinghamshire, 98, **340**

Stornoway, Western Isles, **80, 123**, **135, 136**
Storrington, West Sussex, **340**
Stourbridge, West Midlands, **99**, 371, 373, **379, 461, 498**, 504, 524
Stourport on Severn, Hereford & Worcester, **340**
Stowmarket, Suffolk, 422, **423**
Stow on the Wold, Gloucestershire, 229
Straits Settlements, 425
Stranraer, Dumfries & Galloway, 121, **123, 426, 513**
Stratford on Avon, Warwickshire, 238, **340, 498, 499, 504**, 524
Strathaven, Strathclyde, **80, 513**
Strathclyde, 76, 77, **78, 79, 80**, 121, **122, 123, 151, 154**, 161, **162**, 201, 202, **207**, 214, **227, 228, 229, 237, 285, 303**, 321, **396, 397, 418, 426**, 446, 456, 460, **476, 459, 503, 510**, 511, **512, 513**, 515, **526**, 527, 567, **568, 576, 577, 578**
Stroud,
Gloucestershire, 169, 229, **230, 340**
Kent, 186
Sturminster Newton, Dorset, 546
Sudbury, Suffolk, **94, 139, 245, 423**, **486**
Suez Canal, Egypt, 453
Suffolk **49, 61, 62**, 88, 89, **90, 91, 93, 94**, 116, **138, 139**, 175, 206, 212, 215, **244, 245**, 246, **249, 250**, 251, **257**, 264, **284**, 307, **332, 335, 336, 338, 339, 341**, 348, **378, 407**, 412, **422, 423, 486**, 487, 488
Summertown, Oxfordshire, 223
Sunbury on Thames, Surrey, **94**
Sunderland, Tyne & Wear, 60, 189, **276, 297, 310, 340**, 409, 416, 417, 419, 552
Surrey, 58, 59, 89, **90, 91, 94**, 137, **138, 139, 157**, 185, 258, **265**, 307, **334, 335, 336, 339, 341**, 343, **345, 346, 367**, 429, 431, **477, 531, 533**, 564
Sutton, Surrey, 348, **533**

654 British banking – a guide to historical records

Sutton Bridge, Lincolnshire, 248
Sutton Coldfield, West Midlands, 340, 407
Sutton in Ashfield, Nottinghamshire, 482, 514
Swadlincote, Derbyshire, 133, 320, 340
Swaffham, Norfolk, 186, 249
Swaledale, North Yorkshire, 89, 502
Swanage, Dorset, 546
Swanley, Kent, 365
Swansea, West Glamorgan, 66, 81, 94, 227, 407, 485, 523, 533, 545
Sweden, 146, 273, 555
Swindon, Wiltshire, 169, 420, 499
Swinton, South Yorkshire, 311, 475
Switzerland, 325, 326, 384, 390, 464
Sydney, Australia, 48, 455

Tacna, Peru, 222
Tadcaster, North Yorkshire, 102, 114
Tain, Highland, 80, 123
Tamworth, Staffordshire, 340, 407
Tangier, Morocco 47, 493
Tarapaca, Chile, 55, 222
Tarbet, Highland, 80, 513
Tarland, Grampian, 46, 80, 513
Taunton, Somerset, 62, 115, 216, 217, 499, 500, 533, 549
Tavistock, Devon, 188, 216, 217, 226, 340, 407
Tayside, 46, 57, 78, 79, 80, 122, 123, 142, 143, 154, 155, 162, 200, 201, 202, 204, 228, 396, 426, 435, 436, 446, 457, 459, 511, 512, 527, 567, 568, 577, 578
Tehran, Iran, 118, 119, 120
Teignmouth, Devon, 137
Tenbury Wells, Hereford & Worcester, 104, 340, 553
Tenby, Dyfed, 81, 407
Tenerife, Canary Islands, Spain, 492
Tenterden, Kent, 183, 340
Tetbury, Gloucestershire, 169, 552
Tewkesbury, Gloucestershire, 104, 105, 139, 229, 263, 317, 340
Thailand, 144, 280, 368
Thame, Oxfordshire, 340
Thaxted, Essex, 507
Thetford, Norfolk, 94, 246, 423, 340

Thirsk, North Yorkshire, 60, 340, 556, 557, 558, 561
Thornaby on Tees, Cleveland, 340
Thornbury, Avon, 265, 441
Thornhill, Dumfries & Galloway, 123, 513
Thrapston, Northamptonshire, 206, 207, 490
Thurso, Highland, 80, 123, 136
Thurston, Strathclyde, 285
Tientsin, China, 144, 282
Tillicoultry, Central, 80, 123, 513
Tipperary, Ireland, 409
Tiverton, Devon, 202, 340, 466, 500
Toddington, Bedfordshire, 98
Todmorden, West Yorkshire, 311, 340, 536
Tokyo, Japan, 430
Tomintoul, Grampian, 136
Tonbridge, Kent, 102, 328, 343
Toronto, Canada, 85, 86
Torquay, Devon, 188, 328, 340, 520
Torre, Devon, 520
Torrington, Devon, 216, 356, 403
Totnes, Devon, 188, 407, 549
Tottington, Greater Manchester, 134
Towcester, Northamptonshire, 415
Tranent, Lothian, 459
Transvaal, South Africa, 392, 398
Trawsfynydd, Gwynedd, 379
Tredegar, Gwent, 340, 379
Tregaron, Dyfed, 299
Treherbert, Mid Glamorgan, 94
Trieste, Italy, 295
Tring, Hertfordshire, 134
Troon, Strathclyde, 80, 123, 513
Trowbridge, Wiltshire, 340, 500, 549
Truro, Cornwall, 107, 156, 167, 188, 440, 547
Tsingtao, China, 282
Tucuman, Argentina, 72
Tunbridge Wells, Kent, 94, 102, 340, 343, 346, 385, 533
Tunstall, Staffordshire, 195
Turkey, 290, 295, 296, 399
Turriff, Grampian, 80, 123, 513
Tutbury, Staffordshire, 133, 340
Tyldesley, Greater Manchester, 94, 163, 169

Index of places

Tyne & Wear, 60, 66, 89, **93, 109, 132,**
165, 183, 189, **276, 297, 309,**
310, 329, **333, 335, 336, 338,**
340, 355, 356, 409, 415, 416,
417, 418, 419, **448, 501, 552,**
556, 557

Uckfield, East Sussex, 385, **533**
Uddingston, Strathclyde, **80, 123**
Ullapool, Highland, **80, 136**
Ulster *see* Northern Ireland
Ulverston, Cumbria, **94, 195, 312, 436,**
437, 522
United Arab Emirates, 119
United States of America, 47, 63, 72,
77, 103, 128, 129, 130, 144, 146,
151, 158, 163, 174, 197, **222,**
255, 273, 278, 279, **282,** 286,
289, 291, 296, 305, 306, 313,
314, 353, 361, 362, 375, 386,
387, **388, 389,** 453, 457, 468,
483, 491, **492,** 494, 530, 542, **543**
Uphall, Lothian, **123, 162**
Uppermill, Greater Manchester, **169**
Uppingham, Leicestershire, **94,** 152,
206, 320, 489, **490**
Upton upon Severn, Hereford &
Worcester, 104
Uruguay, 52, 56, 72, **73, 74,** 117, **118,**
290, 342, 468
Usk, Gwent, 81
Uttoxeter, Staffordshire, 133, **340**

Valencia, Spain, 293, **294**
Valparaiso, Chile, 55, 56, 72, **74,** 220,
222, 286, 468
Vancouver, Canada, 85, **86**
Venezuela, 163
Venice, Italy, 295
Victoria,
Australia, 352
Cameroons, **493**
Vienna, Austria, 52, 53, 453
Vietnam, 144
Vitoria, Brazil, 72, **74**
Vladivostock, Russia, **282**

Wadebridge, Cornwall, 528
Wainfleet, Lincolnshire, 218

Wakefield, West Yorkshire, 89, **195,**
283, **292, 316, 317,** 447, 516,
517, **521, 526,** 534, **557**
Wales, **46, 63,** 66, **81, 90, 91, 94,** 99,
126, 130, 141, 169, 179, **184,**
191, **227, 299, 300,** 328, 329,
230, **331, 332, 333, 334, 335,**
336, 338, 339, 340, 341, 348,
355, **370, 371, 377, 378, 379,**
386, 387, **393, 399,** 400, 403,
404, **406, 407, 408,** 412, **414,**
431, 444, 445, **448,** 457, **485,**
486, 516, **523, 533,** 534, **537,**
538, 545, 546, 549, 553, 564
Walkden, Greater Manchester, **169,**
545
Walkerburn, Borders, **80**
Wallasey, Merseyside, **414**
Wallingford, Berkshire, **94, 267,** 329,
346
Wallsend, Tyne & Wear, **338**
Walsall, West Midlands, **81, 94, 199,**
340, 370, 403, **489**
Waltham Green, Essex, **533**
Walton le Dale, Lancashire, **195**
Walton on Thames, Surrey, **94**
Walton on the Nase, Essex, 383, **533**
Wantage, Oxfordshire, 306
Wardle, Greater Manchester, 423, 451
Ware, Hertfordshire, **46, 188,** 470
Wareham, Dorset, **340, 546**
Warminster, Wiltshire, 420
Warrington, Cheshire, **195, 429**
Warsaw, Poland, 125
Warwick, Warwickshire, **185, 238,**
315, 328, **340,** 489, 504, **524**
Warwickshire, **90, 134, 173, 185, 238,**
314, 315, 319, 320, 328, **332,**
336, 338, 339, 340, 371, 373,
377, 379, 384, **407,** 489, 498,
499, 504, 517, **524, 531, 576**
Washington, Tyne & Wear, **340**
Waterfoot, Lancashire, 311
Waterloo, Merseyside, 395
Watford, Hertfordshire, **94,** 131, **340,**
346
Watford Junction, Hertfordshire, **341**
Watlington, Oxfordshire, 131
Wavertree, Merseyside, **94,** 361

656 British banking – a guide to historical records

Wednesbury, West Midlands, 328, **341**, **373**, **379**, **545**
Wellingborough, Northamptonshire, **139**, **320**, **379**, 414, **415**
Wellington,
  Shropshire, **341**, 477
  Somerset, **216**, 329
Wells, Somerset, **432**, 499, **533**
Welshpool, Powys, **341**, **379**, **414**
Wenlock, Shropshire, 166
Wensleydale, North Yorkshire, 89, **502**
West Bromwich, West Midlands, 94, **198**, **341**, 516
Westbury, Wiltshire, **341**
Westcliff on Sea, Essex, **341**, **533**
Western Isles, **80**, **123**, 135, 136
Wester Ross, Highland, 135
Westgate on Sea, Kent, 155, **341**
West Glamorgan, 66, **81**, **94**, 227, **339**, **340**, **341**, **371**, **407**, **485**, 523, **533**, **545**
West Gorton, Greater Manchester, **533**
West Hartlepool, Cleveland, 416
West Houghton, Greater Manchester, **169**
West Indies *see* Latin America
West Linton, Borders, **80**
West Malvern, Hereford & Worcester, 104
West Midlands, **59**, **64**, 66, **81**, **90**, **91**, **94**, 97, **99**, **106**, 109, **150**, **170**, **172**, **193**, **196**, **198**, **199**, 210, 211, **217**, 259, **300**, 315, 318, 319, **321**, **327**, 328, 329, **332**, **333**, **334**, **335**, **339**, **340**, **341**, **345**, 348, **370**, 371, **372**, **373**, 374, 376, **377**, **379**, 381, **384**, **384**, 400, 403, **406**, **407**, 421, **431**, 460, 486, 488, **489**, 490, **498**, **505**, **509**, **516**, 521, 524, **530**, **531**, **533**, **545**, **550**, 554
Westmorland *see* Cumbria
Weston super Mare, Avon, 216, **341**, **533**
West Sussex, 89, **91**, **132**, **138**, 234, 254, 258, **259**, **265**, **269**, **331**, **334**, **335**, **336**, **340**, **341**, 343, **345**, **346**, **347**, **380**, 385, **448**, **530**, **533**

West Worthing, West Sussex, **341**
West Yorkshire, 71, 89, **91**, **94**, **100**, **101**, **102**, 111, **112**, **113**, 114, 127, 153, 164, 175, 177, **193**, **205**, **208**, **211**, **252**, **253**, **283**, **284**, **292**, **307**, 311, **314**, **316**, **317**, **318**, 321, 324, 329, **336**, **338**, **340**, 347, 361, 362, 372, 373, **374**, **377**, **378**, **379**, **384**, 403, 404, 405, **406**, **407**, **435**, 447, **469**, 472, 509, 516, 517, **521**, **526**, 528, **534**, **535**, **536**, **546**, 547, **557**, **558**, **560**, **576**
Wetherby, West Yorkshire, **558**
Weybridge, Surrey, **346**, **533**
Weymouth, Dorset, **94**, 138, **139**, **208**, **341**, **533**, 546, **549**
Whitby, North Yorkshire, 433, 434, **478**, 556, 560
Whitchurch, Shropshire, 328, **536**, 575
Whitefield, Greater Manchester, 134
Whitehaven, Cumbria, **82**, 154, 191, **195**, 263, 266, **341**, **407**, 429, **536**
Whitstable, Kent, **258**, **341**
Whittlesey, Cambridgeshire, 248
Wibsey, West Yorkshire, 113
Wick, Highland, **80**, **135**, 160, 567
Wickham Market, Suffolk, 245
Wicklow, Ireland, 347
Wigan, Greater Manchester, **169**, **195**, 429, **551**, **533**
Wigton, Cumbria, 180, **341**, 426
Wigtown, Dumfries & Galloway, **123**
Willenhall, West Midlands, **341**, **372**, **379**, **489**
Williton, Somerset, 62
Wilmslow, Cheshire, **195**
Wiltshire, **94**, 111, 137, **138**, **139**, 169, 258, **313**, 329, **334**, **338**, **339**, **340**, **341**, **341**, **342**, **377**, **420**, **438**, 498, **499**, **500**, **533**, 546, 547, **548**, **549**
Wimborne, Dorset, **217**, 403, **549**
Wincanton, Somerset, 500
Winchcombe, Gloucestershire, 169
Winchester, Hampshire, **131**, **139**, 258, **341**, 441
Winchmore Hill, Buckinghamshire, **94**, **533**

Index of places 657

Windermere, Cumbria, **195, 312**, 522
Windsor, Berkshire, **127, 346**, 367, **408**, 551
Winsford, Cheshire, 213, **533**
Winslow, Buckinghamshire, 98
Winster, Derbyshire, 473
Wirksworth, Derbyshire, **57, 139**, 177, **386**
Wirral, Merseyside, 413
Wisbech, Cambridgeshire, 88, **94**, 114, 215, 246, **248**, 308, **341**, 403
Wishaw, Strathclyde, **80, 123**
Witham, Essex, 383, 487
Witney, Oxfordshire, 223, **226**
Wiveliscombe, Somerset, 548
Woburn, Bedfordshire, 98
Woburn Sands, Buckinghamshire, 98
Woking, Surrey, **94, 139, 341**
Wokingham, Berkshire, **94**, 478
Wolverhampton, West Midlands, **170**, 199, **217, 341**, 372, **407, 489**, 516, 517, **533, 550**
Wolverton, Buckinghamshire, 98, 131
Woodbridge, Suffolk, **49**, 62, **94, 139, 245**, 250, 251, **341, 407**
Woodstock, Oxfordshire, **126**, 223, 224
Wooler, Northumberland, **123**, 417
Woolton, Merseyside, 361
Wooton under Edge, Gloucestershire, 403, **407**
Wootton Bassett, Wiltshire, **313**, 420, **549**
Worcester, Hereford & Worcester, **104**,

105, 138, **139, 212**, 317, 328, **341**, 358, 498, **553**
Worcestershire *see* Hereford & Worcester
Workington, Cumbria, **83, 111**, 140, 154, **180**, 266, **341, 354, 379, 557**
Worksop, Nottinghamshire, **101**, 164, 472
Worthing, West Sussex, 138, **269, 341**
Wotton,
  Norfolk, 246
  Gloucestershire, 169
Wrexham, Clwyd, **341, 407, 414, 431**, 538
Wrotham, Kent, **347**
Wymondham, Norfolk, 246

Yarm, Cleveland, 60
Yealmpton, Devon, 262
Yeovil, Somerset, **341, 431**, 500, **533, 549**
Ynysybwl, Mid Glamorgan, **94**
Yokohama, Japan, 243, 430
York, North Yorkshire, **94, 101, 102, 178**, 285, **379**, 353, 358, 434, 467, 478, **502**, 507, **517, 526, 528, 555**, 556, **558, 560, 561**
Yoxford, Suffolk, 250

Zaire, 494
Zambia, 398, 494
Zante, Greece, 294
Zimbabwe, 494
Zurich, Switzerland, 326, 464

Index of types of bank and association

army agent, 86, 173, 197, 239, 277, 366

bankers' association, 562, 563, 565, 569, 570, 571, 572

central bank, 65

discount house, 49, 116, 141, 181, 219, 224, 298, 401, 424, 469, 485, 515, 518

goldsmith banker, 60, 83, 96, 107, 147, 152, 170, 197, 210, 215, 234, 260, 274, 309, 364, 411, 470, 481, 519, 520

joint stock bank,
Channel Islands, 143, 242
England, 47, 50, 51, 58, 64, 65, 71, 74, 76, 81, 82, 88, 97, 105, 106, 108, 109, 112, 113, 116, 124, 131, 133, 137, 139, 140, 141, 142, 146, 149, 150, 159, 160, 163, 165, 167, 169, 170, 172, 175, 177, 180, 187, 188, 191, 198, 204, 205, 208, 211, 212, 229, 236, 252, 253, 258, 268, 269, 283, 284, 287, 297, 307, 310, 311, 314, 315, 318, 319, 321, 322, 323, 324, 325, 327, 343, 347, 349, 351, 352, 353, 355, 358, 359, 361, 364, 369, 370, 372, 373, 379, 382, 391, 395, 403, 409, 411, 414, 415, 416, 417, 418, 419, 420, 421, 423, 427, 429, 440, 442, 443, 451, 456, 460, 462, 471, 472, 474, 475, 477, 489, 497, 498,

500, 502, 505, 509, 513, 516, 521, 524, 528, 533, 534, 535, 536, 539, 540, 548, 550, 553, 555, 557, 558, 560, 573, 574;
Isle of Man, 199, 296, 359
Scotland, 45, 46, 57, 76, 120, 135, 142, 151, 154, 160, 200, 202, 204, 207, 227, 228, 229, 237, 396, 400, 417, 426, 435, 436, 456, 476, 503, 505, 510, 526, 577, 578
Wales, 46, 63, 81, 184, 227, 386, 399, 412, 485, 533

merchant bank, 63, 103, 128, 145, 176, 179, 209, 220, 234, 236, 242, 254, 264, 267, 273, 286, 288, 292, 304, 313, 319, 386, 452, 461, 463, 465, 467, 523

navy agent, 277, 497

overseas bank, 47, 48, 52, 53, 55, 63, 64, 70, 72, 75, 82, 85, 86, 87, 88, 117, 118, 120, 124, 144, 157, 159, 162, 203, 239, 240, 278, 292, 293, 294, 325, 327, 342, 347, 349, 354, 366, 367, 390, 392, 398, 399, 410, 425, 455, 462, 490, 494

private bank,
Channel Islands, 143, 242, 450
England, 46, 49, 57, 58, 59, 60, 61, 62, 64, 95, 98, 99, 101, 102, 103, 104, 107, 110, 111, 115, 126, 127, 130, 131, 132, 133, 134, 152, 153, 155, 157, 164, 166, 174, 177, 178, 179, 181,

Index of types of bank and association 659

183, 185, 186, 188, 189, 190,
195, 196, 199, 202, 206, 207,
208, 210, 211, 212, 213, 214,
215, 216, 217, 218, 222, 223,
226, 233, 235, 238, 241, 244,
246, 248, 249, 250, 252, 254,
257, 259, 260, 261, 262, 263,
264, 265, 266, 267, 268, 269,
270, 272, 274, 275, 276, 284,
292, 297, 298, 300, 301, 302,
303, 306, 307, 309, 313, 314,
315, 316, 317, 319, 321, 322,
341, 355, 356, 358, 360, 366,
367, 372, 380, 381, 383, 384,
385, 386, 391, 408, 411, 422,
425, 427, 428, 431, 432, 433,
434, 435, 436, 437, 438, 439,
444, 445, 447, 448, 450, 451,
452, 461, 462, 465, 467, 469,
470, 476, 477, 478, 479, 480,
481, 482, 484, 486, 487, 488,
495, 496, 499, 501, 502, 504,
505, 506, 507, 508, 518, 519,
520, 521, 522, 523, 525, 526,
536, 537, 538, 545, 546, 549,
550, 551, 552, 553, 554, 555,
557, 573, 574, 576

Isle of Man, 199, 445, 554, 579

London, 59, 83, 96, 97, 105, 107,
109, 110, 126, 127, 132, 136,
146, 147, 156, 170, 173, 182,
184, 185, 190, 196, 197, 209,
217, 230, 234, 256, 259, 260,
263, 269, 271, 273, 274, 277,
300, 302, 303, 308, 309, 342,
357, 360, 364, 366, 390, 411,
439, 440, 446, 449, 465, 466,
488, 496, 497, 508, 539, 547,
551, 561, 575

Scotland, 135, 201, 213, 228, 285,
303, 577, 578;

Wales, 126, 130, 141, 299, 300, 444,
537, 545, 546, 553

staff association, 564, 565, 567, 569,
571

Index of archive repositories

Alexanders Discount plc, 50, 226, 299
Angus District Council, Local Studies
  Library, 80
Argyll and Bute District Council
  Archives, 155, 576
Australian & New Zealand Banking
  Group Ltd, Group Archives, 241

Bank of England, 68–70, 572
Bank of Scotland, Archive, 42, 45, 77–
  80, 121–3, 136, 143, 214, 227,
  228, 285–6, 303, 426, 436, 476,
  503, 511–13
Barclays Bank, Group Archives, 42,
  46, 47, 49, 54, 58, 64, 81, 84, 85–
  6, 87 88, 90–94, 99, 102, 106,
  108, 110, 114, 124, 127, 134, 140,
  142, 156, 158–9, 166, 175–6,
  177, 184, 186, 189, 199, 205–6,
  208, 209, 211, 213, 214–15, 223,
  224, 226, 235, 241–2, 244, 245–
  6, 247–8, 249, 250–51, 252, 253,
  253–4, 257, 264–5, 269, 272,
  276, 284, 292, 298, 302, 308, 311,
  314, 316–17, 321, 323, 324, 342,
  348–9, 350, 355, 358, 359–60,
  362–3, 365–6, 370, 372–3, 379–
  80, 383, 385, 391, 392, 398–9,
  408, 410, 412, 416, 417, 419,
  427, 432, 433–4, 437, 443–4,
  446–7, 456, 467, 471, 478, 479,
  487, 488, 490, 502, 504, 506,
  508, 510, 516–18, 519, 521, 522–
  3, 534, 535, 537, 548, 550, 551,
  552–3, 555, 560–61
Baring Archive, ING Baring Holdings
  Ltd, 42, 49, 53, 71, 95, 290–91,
  319, 324, 325, 390–91, 399, 403,
  410

Bedfordshire and Luton Archives and
  Record Service, 96, 99, 139, 259,
  347, 415, 505, 526, 573
Berkshire Record Office, 126, 267,
  292, 306–7, 408, 480, 504, 573
Birmingham Central Library, 341
Birmingham City Archives, 65, 372,
  518
Bloomsbury Science Library, Univer-
  sity College London, 56, 73–4,
  118, 163, 287, 343
Bodleian Library, Department of
  Western Manuscripts, 70, 106,
  576
Bristol Record Office, 350, 381, 439,
  534
British Bankers' Association, 560
British Library of Political and
  Economic Science, London
  School of Economics, 153, 240,
  295–6, 301, 575–6
Brynmor Jones Library, University of
  Hull, 111, 272, 293, 379
Buckinghamshire Record Office, 98,
  153, 202, 257, 367, 470

Calderdale District Archives,
  Calderdale Central Library,
  252–3
Cater Allen Ltd, 141
Cambridge County Record Office,
  391–2
Cambridge University Library,
  Department of Manuscripts and
  University Archives, 59, 366
Centre for Kentish Studies, 51, 103,
  155, 357–8, 363
Centre for Middle East Studies, St
  Antony's College, 120

Index of archive repositories 661

Chartered Institute of Bankers in Scotland, 568
City of Chester Archives, 538
City of Westminster Archives Centre, 108, 185
Clydesdale Bank plc, 151, 154–5, 205, 207, 229, 418, 505, 527
Committee of Scottish Clearing Bankers, 571
Co-operative Bank plc, 165–166
Cornwall Record Office, 108, 268, 519, 548
Coutts & Co, 42, 171–2, 185, 257, 357, 449, 450
Cumbria Record Office, 82, 111, 263, 297, 313, 437, 523

Derby Local Studies Library, 428
Devon Record Office, 95, 176, 213, 382, 466, 550
Dorset Record Office, 217, 244, 437, 501, 546, 549
Dudley Archives & Local History Service, 196
Duke of Norfolk's Archives, Arundel Castle, 59
Dumfries and Galloway Archives, 123–4, 576–7
Dundee Central Library Local Studies Department, 201
Durham County Record Office, 60, 184, 189, 354, 410, 425, 501, 502
Durham University Library, Archives and Special Collections, 60, 297, 356, 449

Essex Record Office, 115, 116, 251, 383, 487, 488

Gerrard Group plc, 220, 402–3
Glamorgan Record Office, 408, 553
Glasgow City Archives, 151, 228, 236, 477, 503
Gloucester Library, Local Studies Department, 169–70, 229, 230, 508, 552, 553, 574
Gloucestershire Record Office, 170, 313, 381, 573–4

Guernsey Island, States of, Archives Service, see States of Guernsey Island Archives Service
Guildhall Library, London, 48, 76, 82, 103, 107, 116, 117, 129–30, 145, 153, 180, 182, 198, 203–4, 221–2, 225, 234, 237, 256, 264, 287, 304–6, 349, 388–90, 399, 401–2, 465, 469–70, 485, 492–3, 495, 562–3, 565, 567, 570, 571, 572, 575
Guinness Mahon & Co Ltd, 243
Gwent Record Office, 130, 300, 386
Gwynedd Archives Service, 445, 539

Hampshire Record Office, 198, 244
Hereford Record Office, The Old Barracks, 157
Hertfordshire County Record Office, 47, 145, 189, 382, 438, 442, 574
Hoare, C & Co, 275
HSBC Holdings, Group Archives, 42, 52, 63, 64, 75, 82, 97–8, 99, 109, 112, 119–20, 140–41, 142, 144, 150, 166, 173, 180–81, 184, 187, 199, 211, 238, 261, 262, 264, 266, 279–82, 283–4, 285, 288, 300, 308, 315, 318, 320, 322, 323, 354, 359, 368–9, 371–2, 375–9, 400, 411, 413–14, 420, 422, 424, 429, 443, 445, 451, 461, 464–5, 467, 471–2, 475–6, 486, 489, 498–9, 504, 509, 546, 556–7, 558
Hull City Record Office, 434

Isle of Wight County Record Office, 450

John Rylands University Library, University of Manchester, 153

Lancashire Record Office, 76, 239, 325, 435, 452, 554
Lancaster District Library, Local History Department, 189, 313
Leamington Spa Library, 238, 314, 315, 525

662 British banking – a guide to historical records

Leicestershire County Record Office, 104, 152, 160, 185, 212, 320–21, 425, 428, 574

Lewisham Local Studies & Archives, 291

Lincolnshire Archives, 384, 433, 483

Liverpool Libraries and Information Services, Record Office and Local History Department, 130, 408

Lloyds TSB Group, Archives, 42, 52, 53, 56, 57, 58, 59, 62, 63, 73, 96, 97, 98, 100, 102, 104–5, 106, 110, 116–17, 118, 126, 128, 131, 133, 135, 137, 138, 155, 167, 169, 172, 174, 175, 181, 183, 186, 188, 196, 208, 209, 211, 215, 216, 217, 218, 226, 227, 229, 230, 236, 252, 258, 259, 260, 262, 263, 265, 266, 267, 269, 270, 273–4, 276, 298, 299, 303, 307, 308, 310, 318, 321, 325, 326, 327, 330–41, 342, 343, 358, 366, 367, 384, 386, 397, 415, 420, 423, 425–6, 433, 438, 440, 444, 452, 460, 462, 463, 477, 479, 486, 495–6, 498, 499, 508–9, 520, 524–5, 526, 528, 534, 536, 538, 545, 546, 547, 549, 553–4

London Merchant Securities plc, 355

London Metropolitan Archive, 157, 257, 347, 408, 551

Manx Museum and National Trust, 200, 446, 579

Manx National Heritage Library, 297, 555

Modern Records Centre, University of Warwick, 94–5, 363, 564, 569

National Archives of Canada, 233, 292

National Archives of Scotland, 80, 124, 228–9, 286, 398, 460, 504, 528, 577–8

National Library of Scotland, Department of Manuscripts, 80, 123, 292, 459, 527

Norfolk Record Office, 211

Northamptonshire Record Office, 206, 235, 415, 484, 525, 557

Northumberland Record Office, 132, 233, 356, 409, 419, 449, 501

Nottinghamshire Archives, 127, 233, 252, 302–3, 439, 469, 482, 483–4, 485, 526, 554, 555

Oxfordshire Archives, 166–7, 224

Perth and Kinross Council Archive, A K Bell Library, 143, 202, 205, 436, 447, 578

Portsmouth City Record Office, 234, 408

Public Record Office, 53, 64, 70, 71, 107, 108, 120, 125, 159, 210, 212, 216, 282–3, 299, 300, 319, 363, 366, 367, 382, 410, 417, 455–6, 459, 462, 519, 521, 574–5

Rothschild, N M & Sons, Archive, 43, 454

Royal Bank of Scotland, Archive, 43, 46, 51, 55, 57, 58, 61, 62, 65, 70, 71, 74, 81, 83, 95, 100–101, 105,111, 113, 125, 131, 132, 133, 134, 135, 146, 147, 148–9, 153–4, 157, 160, 161–2, 164, 165, 168–9, 170, 177–8, 179, 182–3, 184, 187, 190, 191–5, 196–8, 200, 201, 202, 203, 208, 210, 213, 217, 218, 223, 231–3, 237–8, 241, 242, 254, 260, 261, 265, 267, 271, 272, 274, 277–8, 292, 293–4, 297, 298, 301, 303, 307, 309, 312, 316, 321–2, 327, 344–7, 351–2, 353, 356, 357, 370, 381, 382, 384, 393–5, 396–7, 401, 404–7, 408, 411, 415, 417, 418, 421, 422, 425, 428, 430–31, 432, 435, 437, 439, 441–2, 445, 448, 450–51, 456, 457–9, 461, 462, 465, 466, 473–5, 476, 477, 479, 480, 481, 482, 483, 484–5, 497, 500, 500–501, 502, 503, 506–7, 514, 520, 527, 529–33, 537, 539, 540, 541–5, 551, 552, 561, 563, 570

Index of archive repositories

School of Oriental & African Studies, Library, 282
Schroder, J Henry & Co Ltd, 268, 468–9
Shropshire Records and Research Centre, 179, 212, 452
Somerset Record Office, 62, 115, 268, 432, 448, 501, 507
Southampton City Archives Office, 159, 302
Spalding Gentlemen's Society, 218, 490
Staffordshire Record Office, 196, 304, 427, 461
Standard Chartered Bank plc, 48, 145, 204, 493, 495
States of Guernsey Island Archives Service, 341
Suffolk Record Office, 423
Surrey Record Office,
Guildford Muniment Room, 152–3
Kingston upon Thames, 309

Union plc, 219, 515, 518
University College London,
Bloomsbury Science Library *see* Bloomsbury Science Library, University College London
University of Glasgow Archives, Business Records Centre, 80, 123, 143, 151, 155, 162, 202, 227, 228, 397, 418, 459, 477, 503, 505, 513, 527, 564

University of Hull, Brynmor Jones Library *see* Brynmor Jones Library, University of Hull
University of London Library, 71, 360
University of Manchester, John Rylands University Library *see* John Rylands University Library, University of Manchester
University of Nottingham, Hallward Library, Department of Manuscripts and Special Collections, 103, 240, 540

Walsall Local History Centre, 81, 199
Warrington Local Studies Library, 431
Warwickshire Record Office, 172, 173, 238, 314, 315, 506, 525, 576
West Sussex Record Office, 132, 139, 260, 266, 448
West Yorkshire Archive Service,
Bradford District Archives, 112, 113, 114–15, 284
Leeds District Archives, 176, 318, 435, 521, 558
Yorkshire Archaeological Society, 149, 176, 435, 576
William Salt Library, Stafford, 115, 321, 496, 497
Wiltshire and Swindon Record Office, 111
Worcester Record Office, St Helen's branch, 100, 212, 230, 317, 366

Yorkshire Bank plc, 559–60